AMERICAN STATE GOVERNORS, 1776-1976

VOLUME II

(Biographical Data: Alabama - Montana)

by

Joseph E. Kallenbach

*Professor Emeritus of Political Science,
University of Michigan*

and

Jessamine S. Kallenbach

*Associate Professor,
Library Humanities Division,
Eastern Michigan University,*

1981
OCEANA PUBLICATIONS, INC.
Dobbs Ferry, New York

Library of Congress Cataloging in Publication Data   (Revised)

Kallenbach, Joseph Ernest, 1903-
    American State Governors, 1776-1976.

        CONTENTS: v. 1. Electoral and personal data.—v. 2. Bio-
graphical data, Alabama-Montana.
        1. Governors—United States—History. 2. Governors—
United States—Biography. I. Kallenbach, Jessamine S.,
1915-   joint author. II. Title.
JK2447.K35   353.9'131'0922   76-51519
ISBN 0-379-00665-0

FOREWORD

The brief biographical sketches presented in this Volume of the series, <u>American State Governors, 1776-1976</u>, cover the nearly 1100 individuals who occupied the office of Alabama through Montana over the 200-year period. A final Volume of the series, currently in preparation, will present similar data on the Governors of Nebraska through Wyoming. We have followed the principle of including sketches of all occupants of the office of Governor whenever the office has had to be filled because of a permanent vacancy. Occasionally the powers and duties of the office of Governor have devolved temporarily upon other officers in the line of succession by reason of absence from the State, illness, or some other temporary incapacitation of the regular incumbent. Succeeding officers in those circumstances have not been included in the biographical sketches. In some of the older States, through operation of succession rules, legislative officers became "Acting Governors" for short periods of time in the interval between the end of the regular incumbent's tenure and the installation of a regularly-chosen successor. Data on such temporary occupants are included, if available. The unusual circumstances arising from the Civil War in the 1860s have been dealt with by inclusion of the names of both the pro-Union and the pro-Confederate incumbents in those States wherein there were two persons claiming to be the legitimate occupants of the office of Governor during the course of the conflict.

An Index containing the names of all individuals mentioned in this Volume as occupying the office of Governor is included. The Index notes reference also to all the pertinent matter in Volume I of this series concerning the States and Governors dealt with in this Volume. A similar Index will be included in Volume III with reference to the States and their Governors covered therein.

Sources from which the information presented in this Volume has been drawn include, in addition to those cited in connection with the data of Volume I, <u>Who's Who in America</u>, 1897 to date, and <u>Who Was Who in America</u>, 1963 to date, both published by Marquis Who's Who, Inc., Chicago, Ill.; <u>Current Biography</u>, 1940 to date, published by the H.H.Wilson Co., New York; <u>The Biographical Dictionary of the American Congress, 1774-1971</u>, and the <u>United States Congressional Directory</u>, issued bi-annually since 1876, both published by the United States Government Printing Office, Washington, D.C.; the <u>National Cyclopedia of American Biography</u>, 1891 to date, published by James T. White and Co., Clifton, N.J.; and the files of the <u>New York Times</u>, 1851 to

date. Materials found in State manuals, registers, direct-
ories and almanacs, State historical works and journals,
and individual biographical studies have also been drawn
upon. A complete listing of all published works and other
sources from which the information for all three Volumes of
this reference work has been derived will be included in
Volume III.

The writers wish to acknowledge indebtedness to Prof.
Emeritus Samuel R. Solomon, of Eastern Michigan University,
for encouragement and assistance in carrying forward this
undertaking. Data presented in his compilations, The Governors of the States, 1900-1974, and The Governors of the
American States, Commonwealths and Territories, 1900-1980,
both published by the Council of State Governments, Lexington, Ky., were useful in connection with some of the more
recent Governors. The compilation of data found in Roy R.
Glashan, American Governors and Gubernatorial Elections,
1775-1978, published by Meckler Books, Westport, Conn., was
also helpful as a source regarding some individuals. We
also wish to express our appreciation to Miss Shannon
Anderson and Mrs. Judy Leppala for their efficient services
in putting the material for this Volume into final form for
printing. For any inaccuracies in the data presented, of
which there are undoubtedly a number in a work of this nature, the authors, of course, assume responsibility.

J.E.K.
J.S.K.
Ann Arbor, Michigan
November, 1980

TABLE OF CONTENTS

VOLUME II

(Biographical: Alabama Through Montana)

Foreword. iii
Table of Abbreviations. vii
Biographical Sketches of Governors
     Alabama. 1
     Alaska 29
     Arizona. 32
     Arkansas 39
     California 62
     Colorado 89
     Connecticut. 107
     Delaware 143
     Florida. 169
     Georgia. 191
     Hawaii 231
     Idaho. 233
     Illinois 246
     Indiana. 269
     Iowa 295
     Kansas 316
     Kentucky 339
     Louisiana. 370
     Maine. 397
     Maryland 431
     Massachusetts. 468
     Michigan 508
     Minnesota. 537
     Mississippi. 557
     Missouri 585
     Montana. 612
Index 621

TABLE OF ABBREVIATIONS

A

A.A.: Associate of Arts

A.A.U.P.: American Association of University Professors

A.B.: Bachelor of Arts

Acad. (or acad.): academy

acctg.: accounting

A.C.L.U.: American Civil Liberties Union

A.D.A.: Americans for Democratic Action

Admin. (or admin.): administration, or administrative, as appropriate

Adminr. (or adminr.): administrator

Adjt. (or adjt.): adjutant

A.E.F.: American Expeditionary Forces

A.F.L.: American Federation of Labor

Agri. (or agri.): agriculture, or agricultural, as appropriate

AHEPA: American Hellenic Educational Programs Association

Ala.: Alabama

Alas.: Alaska

A.M.: Master of Arts

Amdt.(s) (or amdt.(s)): amendment(s)

Amer.: America, or American, as appropriate

AMVETS: American Veterans of World War II

Anc. and Hon. Art. Co.: Ancient and Honorable Artillery Company

Anti-Fed.: Anti-Federalist (party)

A.O.U.W.: Ancient Order of United Workers

apptd.: appointed

apptmt.: appointment

Arb. (or arb.): arbitration, or arbitrator, as appropriate

Ariz.: Arizona

Ark.: Arkansas

Assoc. (or assoc.): association, associate, or associated, as appropriate

A.T. and S.F. R.R.: Atchison, Topeka and Santa Fe Railroad

Atl.: Atlantic

Attd. (or attd.): attended

Atty. (or atty.): attorney

Atty. Gen.: Attorney General

Aud. (or aud.): auditor

Aud. Gen.: Auditor General

Aux.: Auxiliary

B

b.: born

B.A.: Bachelor of Arts

B. and O. R.R.: Baltimore and Ohio Railroad

Bd.(s)(or bd.(s)): board(s)

Benj.: Benjamin

B.L.: Bachelor of Literature

Bldg.(s) (or bldg.(s)): building(s)

B.P.O.E.: Benevolent and Protective Order of Elks

Brig. Gen. (or brig. gen.): brigadier general

B.R.T.: Brotherhood of Railroad Trainmen

B.S.: Bachelor of Science

Bur. (or bur.): buried

bus.: business

Bus. Admin. (or bus. admin.): Business Administration (degree)

C

Calif.: California

Calif. Pac. R.R.: California and Pacific Railroad

cand.(s): candidate(s)

C. and A. R.R.: Chicago and Alton Railroad

C. and O. R.R.: Chesapeake and Ohio Railroad

Capt. (or capt.): captain

C.B.I.: China, Burma, India

C.B. and Q. R.R.: Chicago, Burlington and Quincy Railroad

CC: Chamber of Commerce

Cem. (or cem.): cemetery

Cent. (or cent.): central, or center, as appropriate

Cent. Pac. R.R.: Central Pacific Railroad

ch.: chairman

Chem. (or chem.): chemistry, or chemical, as appropriate

cir.: circuit

Civitan: Civitan International

C.L.U.: Certified Life Underwriter

Co. (or co.): county, or company, as appropriate

co-ch.: co-chairman

Col. (or col.): colonel

Coll.(s) (or coll.(s)): college(s)

Colo.: Colorado

Commdr. (or commdr.): commander

Commdr.-in-ch. (or commdr.-in-ch.): commander-in-chief

Commn. (or commn.): commission

Commnr. (or commnr.): commissioner(s)

Commt.(s) (or commt.(s)): committee(s)

Conf. (or conf.): conference

Confed.: Confederate, Confederacy, or Confederation, as appropriate

Cong.: Congress

Congr. (or congr.): congressional

Conn.: Connecticut

Const. (or const.): constitution

constl.: constitutional

Contl.: continental

Conv.(s) (or conv.(s)): convention(s)

Coop. (or coop.): cooperative

Corp.(s) (or corp.(s)): corporation(s), or corporate, as appropriate

C.R.I. and Pac. R.R.: Chicago, Rock Island and Pacific Railroad

C.S.A.: Confederate States of America

Ct.(s) (or ct.(s)): court(s)

C.V.A.: Confederate Veterans of America

D

d.: daughter, or daughters, as appropriate

D.: died

D.A.R.: Daughters of the American Revolution

D.A.V.: Disabled American Veterans

Dec.: December

Dec. of Indep.: Declaration of Independence

D.C.: District of Columbia

D.D.S.: Doctor of Dental Surgery

D. Ed.: Doctor of Education

Del.: Delaware

Dem.: Democrat or Democratic (party)

Dept. (or dept.): department

deptl.: departmental

Devel. (or devel.): development

D.F.C.: Distinguished Flying Cross

D.F.L.: Democrat-Farmer-Labor (party)

Dir.(s) (or dir.(s)): director(s)

Dist. (or dist.): district

Div. (or div.): division

D.S.C.: Distinguished Service
    Cross

D.S.M.: Distinguished Service
    Medal

E

Eagles: Fraternal Order of
    Eagles

Econ. (or econ.): economics,
    economy, or economic, as
    appropriate

Ed.(s) (or ed.(s)): editor,
    edition, or editorial,
    as appropriate

Educ. (or educ.): education,
    or educated, as appro-
    priate

educl.: educational

El. (or el.): elected

Elks: Benevolent and Protec-
    tive Order of Elks

Engr. (or engr.): engineer,
    or engineering, as appro-
    priate

E.S.B.: Economic Stabiliza-
    tion Board

Exec. (or exec.): executive

Exch.: Exchange

Expo.: Exposition

F

Farm.-Lab.: Farmer-Labor
    (party)

FBI: Federal Bureau of Inves-
    tigation

Feb.: February

Fed.: Federal, Federalist
    (party), or Federation,
    as appropriate

Fla.: Florida

Fla. So. R.R.: Florida South-
    ern Railroad

Found.(s) (or found.(s)):
    foundation(s)

Ft.: Fort

G

Ga.: Georgia

G.A.R.: Grand Army of the
    Republic

G.C.A.: Association of Gen-
    eral Contractors of
    America

Gen.(s) (or gen.(s)):
    general(s)

Gov.(s): Governor(s) (State)

Govt.(s) (or govt.(s)):
    government(s)

govtl.: governmental

grad.: graduate, graduated,
    or graduating, as appro-
    priate

H

Haw.: Hawaii

H.E.W.: Health, Education and
    Welfare, Dept. of

Hon. (or hon.); the Honorable,
    or honorary, as appropri-
    ate

Hosp.(s) (or hosp.(s)):
    hospital(s)

House: House of Representa-
    tives

H.S. (or h.s.): high school

H.U.D.: Housing and Urban
    Development, Dept. of

I

Ida.: Idaho

Ill.: Illinois

Ill. Cent. R.R.: Illinois
    Central Railroad

I.L.O.: International Labor
    Organization

Ind.: Indiana

Indep.: Independence, or
    Independent (party)

indus.: industry, or indus-
    trial, as appropriate

I.O.O.F.: International Order
    of Odd Fellows

Ins. (or ins.): insurance

Inst.: Institute

Inter-govtl.(or inter-govtl.):
    inter-governmental

I.T.B.: Inter-urban Transit
  Board

J

Jan.: January
JCC: Junior Chamber of Com-
  merce
Jeff. Rep.: Jeffersonian
  Republican (party)
j.g.: junior grade
Jr.: Junior
Jt.: Joint
jud.: judicial
J.W.V.: Jewish War Veterans

K

Kans.: Kansas
K.C.: Knights of Columbus
K.G.C.: Knights of the Gold-
  en Circle
Kiwanis: Kiwanis Interna-
  tional
KKK: Ku Klux Klan
K.M.: Knights of Malta
K.P.: Knights of Pythias
K.T.: Knights Templar
Ky.: Kentucky

L

La.: Louisiana
L. and N. R.R.: Louisville
  and Nashville Railroad
L.D.S.: Latter Day Saints
Lions: Lions International
  Association
Lib. Rep.: Liberal Republi-
  can (party)
Lieut. (or lieut.): lieuten-
  ant
Lieut. Gen. (or lieut. gen.):
  lieutenant general
Lieut. Gov.: Lieutenant
  Governor (State)
lieut., j.g.: Lieutenant,
  junior grade

M

m.: married
M.A.: Master of Arts
Mar.: March
Masons: Free and Accepted Or-
  der of Masons
Mass.: Massachusetts
mbr.(s): member(s)
mbrshp.: membership
Md.: Maryland
M.D.: Doctor of Medicine
Me.: Maine
Me. Cent. R.R.: Maine Central
  Railroad
Mech.: Mechanics or Mechanical
Med. (or med.): medicine, or
  medical, as appropriate
merc.: mercantile
mfg.: manufacture, or manu-
  facturing, as appropriate
mfr.(s): manufacturer(s)
mgmt.: management
mgr.: manager
Mich.: Michigan
Mil. (or mil.): military
Minn.: Minnesota
Miss.: Mississippi
Mo.: Missouri
Mont.: Montana
Moose: Loyal Order of Moose
Mun. (or mun.): municipal
M.W.A.: Modern Woodmen of
  America

N

N.A.A.C.P.: National Associa-
  tion for Advancement of
  Colored People
Natl. (or natl.): national
NATO: North Atlantic Treaty
  Organization
NBC: National Broadcasting
  Company
N.C.: North Carolina
N.C.C.J.: National Conference
  of Christians and Jews
N.D.: North Dakota
Nebr.: Nebraska

Nev.: Nevada
N.H.: New Hampshire
N.J.: New Jersey
N.M.: New Mexico
No.: North or Northern, as
    appropriate
nom.: nomination, or nominat-
    ed, as appropriate
Nov.: November
N.R.A. (or NRA): National
    Recovery Administration
N.R.O.A.: National Reserve
    Officers Association
NROTC: National Reserve Of-
    ficers Training Corps
N.S.: Nova Scotia
N.S.G.W.: Native Sons of the
    Golden West
N.W.: Northwest or Northwest-
    ern
N.W. Va. R.R.: Northwest
    Virginia Railroad
N.Y.: New York

O

O.A.M.: Order of American
    Machinists
O.C.S. (or OCS): Officers
    Candidate School
Oct.: October
O.E.S.: Order of the Eastern
    Star
Okla.: Oklahoma
Ont.: Ontario
O.P.A.: Office of Price Ad-
    ministration
O.P.S.: Office of Price Sta-
    bilization
O.R.C.: Order of Railroad
    Conductors
Org.(s) (or org.(s)): organ-
    ization, organize(d), or
    organizational, as ap-
    propriate
Ore.: Oregon
O.T.C. (or OTC): Officers
    Training Corps

Owls: Interantional Order of
    Owls
O.W.W.: Military Order of
    World Wars

P

Pa.: Pennsylvania
Pac.: Pacific
Pharm. (or pharm.): pharmacy
Ph. B.: Bachelor of Philoso-
    phy
Ph. D.: Doctor of Philosophy
Poly.: Polytechnical or Poly-
    technic
Pop.: Populist (or Peoples)
    (party)
prep.: preparatory
Pres. (or pres.): president
    or presidential, as ap-
    propriate
Prof. (or prof.): professor
    or professional, as ap-
    propriate
Prog.: Progressive (party)
Proh.: Prohibition (party)
pros. atty.: prosecuting
    attorney
Pub. (or pub.): public
publ.: publisher, or publish-
    ed, as appropriate
P.W.A.: Public Works Admin-
    istration
pvt.: private

Q

q.v.: quod vide (which see)

R

R.E.A.: Rural Electrification
    Administration
re-apptd.: re-appointed
Reel. (or reel.): reelected
Re-nom. (or re-nom.): re-
    nominated, or re-nomina-
    tion, as appropriate
Rep.: Republican (party)
Repr. (or repr.): represen-
    tative

reorg.: reorganization, or
    reorganize(d), as appro-
    priate
Re-sub. Dem.: Re-submission
    Democrat (party)
Rev. Reverend
Rev. War: American Revolu-
    tionary War
R.I.: Rhode Island
R.O.A.: Reserve Officers
    Association
Robt.: Robert
Rotary: Rotary International
ROTC (or R.O.T.C.): Reserve
    Officers Training Corps
R.R.: railroad
Rts.: rights
Ry. (or ry.): railway

S

s.: son, or sons, as appro-
    priate
S.A.R.: Sons of the American
    Revolution
S.C.: South Carolina
Sci. (or sci.): science, or
    scientific, as appropri-
    ate
S.C.V.: Sons of Confederate
    Veterans
S.C.W.: Society of Colonial
    Wars
S.D.: South Dakota
Sect. (or sect.): secretary
Sect.-Treas.(or sect.-treas.):
    secretary-treasurer
Sem. (or sem.): seminary
Sen.: senator
sgt.: sergeant
Shriner: Ancient Arabic Order
    of Nobles of the Mystic
    Shrine (Masons)
So.: South, or Southern, as
    appropriate
Soc.: Society, or Socialist
    (party), as appropriate
So. Pac. R.R.: Southern
    Pacific Railroad

S.O.V.: Sons of Veterans
S.P.C.A.: Society for the
    Prevention of Cruelty to
    Animals
spec.: special
Sr.: Senior
Surg. Gen.: Surgeon General
Supt. (or supt.): superinten-
    dent

T

T.C.L.: Tall Cedars of
    Lebanon
Tech. (or tech.): technical
Tel. (or tel.): telephone or
    telegraph
temp.: temporary
Tenn.: Tennessee
Terr. (or terr.): territory,
    or territorial, as appro-
    priate
Tex.: Texas
Transp. (or transp.): trans-
    portation
Treas. (or treas.): treasury,
    or treasurer, as appro-
    priate
Twp.: township
TV: television
TVA: Tennessee Valley Author-
    ity

U

U.C.L.A.: University of
    California at Los Angeles
U.C.T.: United Commercial
    Travelers
U.C.V.A.: United Confederate
    Veterans of America
UN: United Nations
unconstl.: unconstitutional
UNESCO: United Nations Educa-
    tional, Scientific and
    Cultural Organization
Univ.(s) (or univ.(s)): uni-
    versity (universities)
Un. Pac. R.R.: Union Pacific
    Railroad

UNRRA: United Nations Relief and Rehabilitation Administration

U.R.C.: Union of Railway Clerks

U.S.: United States of America

USAFR: United States Air Force Reserve

USAR: United States Army Reserve

USCC: United States Chamber of Commerce

USCGR: United States Coast Guard Reserve

USJCC: United States Junior Chamber of Commerce

USMCR: United States Marine Corps Reserve

USNR: United States Naval Reserve

U.S.W.V.: United Spanish War Veterans

USO (or U.S.O.): United Services Organization

V

Va.: Virginia

Vets.: Veterans

V.F.W.: Veterans of Foreign Wars

W

Wash.: Washington

Wisc.: Wisconsin

Wm.: William

Woodmen: Modern Woodmen of America, or Woodmen of the World

W.O.W.: Woodmen of the World

W.P.A. (or WPA): Works Progress Administration

W.P.B.: War Production Board

W. Va.: West Virginia

Wyo.: Wyoming

Y

YMCA: Young Men's Christian Association

AMERICAN STATE GOVERNORS

BIBB, WILLIAM WYATT (1819-1820). b. Oct. 1, 1781 in
Prince Edward Co., Va. Eldest s. of Wm. and Sally (Wyatt) B.
Father had been a mbr. of Va. legislature and was a capt. in
the Contl. Army during the Rev. War. Family moved to Egbert
Co., Ga. After father's death in 1786 his widow reared the
family of eight children, all of whom became persons of distinction. Attd. Wm. and Mary Coll. and the Univ. of Pa.,
from which he was grad. as a physician in 1801. Established
practice at Petersburg, Ga. Mbr. of Ga. legislature, 1803-
1807. El. to U.S. House from Ga. to fill a vacancy, assuming his seat Jan. 26, 1807. Reel. for next three terms.
Unsuccessful cand. for Speaker. Resigned seat Nov. 6, 1813
to take seat in U.S. Senate to fill vacancy occasioned by
resignation of Sen. Wm. H. Crawford. Resigned Senate seat
in Nov., 1816 after failing to win reel. for a full term.
In Sept., 1817 was apptd. by Pres. Monroe as Gov. of the recently created Terr. of Ala., and was serving in that office
when the Ala. statehood bill was passed by Cong. in 1819.
El. as the State's first Gov. in Sept., 1819. Assumed office provisionally on Nov. 9 and officially in Dec., 1819
when statehood became effective. D. July 9, 1820 at Ft.
Jackson, Ala. from injuries after being thrown from his
horse, which bolted during a thunderstorm. Succeeded by his
brother, Thomas, who had become Pres. of Ala. Senate (q.v.).
m. to Mary Freeman, of Wilkes Co., Ga. Two children. Bur.
at Coosada, near Montgomery, Ala.

BIBB, THOMAS (1820-1821). b. in 1784 in Prince Edward
Co., Va. One of eight children of Wm. and Sally (Wyatt) B.,
who were left to be reared by the mother when the father
died in 1786. Was a younger brother of Wm. Wyatt B., the
first Gov. of Ala. (q.v.). Received classical educ. and became a planter and merchant. Removed to Miss. Terr. in 1811,
settling in area that became a part of Ala. Terr. in 1817
upon admission of Miss. to statehood. Mbr. of conv. that
drafted first const. for the State of Ala. in 1819. Mbr. of
first Ala. Senate and was el. as its presiding officer. After death of his brother Wm., the State's first Gov., in
1820 succeeded to the office of Gov. for the remainder of
the term. Returned to private life after tenure as Gov. In
1829 was el. to a seat in Ala. House. m. to Pamela Thompson
of Madison Co., Ala. Father of eleven children, of whom
three died in infancy. D. Sept. 20, 1839 at Belle Mina,
Ala. Bur. at Huntsville, Ala.

PICKENS, ISRAEL (1821-1825). b. Jan. 31, 1780 near
Concord, Mecklenburg (later Caburrus) Co., N.C. s. of
Samuel and Jane (Carrigan) P. Father was a gentleman of
Huguenot descent who had served as a Contl. Army capt.

during the Rev. War. Attd. pvt. schools and Washington
(later Washington and Jefferson) Coll., in Pa., from which
he was grad. in 1802. Excelled in scientific studies, and
while a student invented an improved type of lunar dial.
Read law, admitted to bar and began practice in Morgantown,
N.C. Served in N.C. Senate, 1808-1810. El. as Jeff. Rep.
to U.S. House, and served from the 12th through the 14th
Congresses (1811-1817). Was a strong supporter of Pres.
Madison's policies and of the War of 1812. In 1817 was
apptd. register of U.S. land office at St. Stephens, in the
part of Miss. Terr. that later became a part of Ala. Terr.
Mbr. of Ala. constl. conv. of 1819. El. Gov. of Ala. in
1821 and was reel. in 1823. Admin. largely concerned with
completion of org. of state and local govt., and with numerous controversies over land title matters regarding which he
had much first-hand knowledge as prior register of lands.
Was official host to Marquis de Lafayette when he visited
Ala. on his tour of U.S. Declined apptmt. to a U.S. dist.
ct. judgeship by Pres. J.Q. Adams; but in April, 1826 accepted apptmt. to the U.S. Senate to fill a vacancy caused
by the death of Sen. Henry Chambers, whom he had defeated in
his two contests for Gov. Declined to be a cand. for continuance in the Senate seat later in 1826 for reasons of
health. m. to Martha Orella Lenoir on June 9, 1814. One d.;
two s. Presbyterian. D. at Matanzas, Cuba on April 24,
1827. Bur. in family cem. near Greensboro, Ala.

MURPHY, JOHN (1825-1829). b. in 1786 in Robeson Co.,
N.C. s. of Neil and ----- (Downing) M. Father was of Scotch
ancestry. Family moved to Columbia, S.C. during early youth
where he received early educ. Worked as a teacher to earn
money to attend coll. Grad. in 1808 from S.C. Coll. (now
Univ. of S.C.). Studied law and was admitted to bar. Served
as clerk as S.C. Senate, 1810-1817. Trustee of S.C. Coll.,
1809-1818. Moved to Monroe Co. in Ala. Terr. in 1818 where
he engaged in planting. Influential mbr. of Ala. constl.
conv. of 1819. Mbr. of first Ala. House and of the Ala.
Senate in 1822. El. Gov. in 1825 and was reel. in 1827.
Had no organized opposition either time. Took active role
in establishment of the Univ. of Ala. at Tuscaloosa; also in
measures to improve navigation on rivers of Ala. Unsuccessful cand. of Union (Jackson Dem.) party for seat in U.S.
House in 1830 but was successful in 1832 election for that
office. Served only one term. Defeated for U.S. House seat
in 1838 by a former classmate at S.C. Coll., Judge James
Dellet. Retired to plantation near Gosport, in Clarke Co.
m. first to Sarah Hails, of S.C. After her death, m. to a
widow ----- (Darrington) Carter, of Clarke Co., Ala. Two

children. Presbyterian. Mbr., Masons. D. at his home
Sept. 21, 1841. Bur. in family cem. on his plantation near
Gosport.

MOORE, GABRIEL (1829-1831). b. in 1785 in Stokes Co.,
N.C. Facts as to parentage unknown. After grad. from the
Univ. of N.C. in 1810 moved to Huntsville, Ala. (then in
Miss. Terr.). El. to Miss. Terr. legislature in 1811. Became first Speaker of Ala. Terr. legislature in 1817 when
the area that later became the State of Ala. was detached
from Miss. following admission of the latter to statehood.
Mbr. of Ala. constl. conv. of 1819. El. to Ala. Senate and
while serving as Pres. of that body in 1821 was el. to U.S.
House to fill a vacancy, and for succeeding three terms.
Resigned to accept office of Gov. in 1829, to which he had
been el. Resigned as Gov. to take seat in U.S. Senate in
1831. Because of his opposition to confirmation of Pres.
Jackson's nominee, Martin Van Buren, as Minister to Great
Britain, the Ala. legislature in 1832 demanded that he resign, but he refused to do so. Was not reel. at end of his
Senate term. In 1837 was unsuccessful as cand. for a seat
in U.S. House. During term as Gov., work proceeded on improvement of navigation on Tennessee River by canal and railroad to by-pass Muscle Shoals; and a treaty with Choctaw
Indians was concluded involving surrender of land in Ala.
and Miss. to U.S. m. to a Miss Collier, whom he soon afterward divorced. Fought a duel with her brother, whom he
wounded. Moved to Tex. in 1843. D. at Caddo, Tex., June 9,
1845. Bur. there.

MOORE, SAMUEL B. (1831). b. in 1789 in Franklin Co.,
Tenn. (then a part of N.C.). Received limited educ. there.
Moved to Jackson Co., Ala., where he became a planter. El.
to Ala. House for several terms, and in 1828 to the Ala.
Senate. Was chosen Pres. of Senate, and while serving in
that capacity succeeded to the office of Gov. in March, 1831
when Gov. Gabriel Moore resigned to take U.S. Senate seat.
Completed Moore's term, which had only several months to
run. The State Univ. of Ala. was opened in April, 1831,
soon after he assumed office as Gov. El. to Ala. Senate
again in 1833 and was chosen again as its presiding officer
in 1835. Became a judge in Pickens Co. in 1835 and served
in that capacity until 1841. Never married. D. at Carrollton, Ala., Nov. 7, 1846. Bur. there.

GAYLE, JOHN (1831-1835). b. Sept. 11, 1792 in Sumter
Dist., S.C. s. of Matthew and Mary (Reese) G. Father was
a planter who had served under Gen. Pickens in Rev. War.
Educ. at Newberry Acad. and S.C. Coll. (later the Univ. of

S.C.), from which he was grad. Settled in Claiborne, Monroe
Co., Ala. (then a part of Miss. Terr.), where he studied law
and was admitted to bar in 1813. Mbr. of first Ala. Terr.
legislature in 1817. Apptd. as solicitor for his jud. dist.,
and served until his election to the Ala. House in 1822.
Mbr. of Ala. Supreme Ct., 1823 to 1828, when he resigned.
Mbr. of Ala. House in 1829 and was chosen Speaker, defeating
former Gov. Thomas Bibb for the office. El. Gov. as a Jeff.
Rep. (Dem.) in 1831 and again in 1833. In 1832 nullification crisis supported Pres. Jackson's pro-Union stand.
Later became mbr. of the Whig party. Unsuccessful cand. for
U.S. Senate seat against Wm. R. King in 1841. El. to U.S.
House in 1846, serving for only one term. Apptd. U.S. dist.
ct. judge by Pres. Taylor in March, 1849, and continued to
serve in that post until his death ten years later. m. in
1819 to Sarah Ann Haynsworth, of Claiborne, Ala. Two s.;
four d. After her death, m. in 1839 to Clarissa Stedman
Peck, of Greensboro, Ala. Three s.; one d. During admin.
as Gov., the Ala. ct. system was reorg.; the first cotton
cloth factory in Ala. was founded in 1832; a treaty with the
Creek Indians was concluded under which they ceded their
lands to the U.S.; and the first railroad line in Ala. from
Tuscumbia to Decatur was completed. Presbyterian. Was an
advocate of prohibition. D. at Mobile, Ala. July 28, 1849.
Bur. in Magnolia Cem. there.

CLAY, CLEMENT COMER (1835-1837). b. Dec. 17, 1789 in
Halifax Co., Va. Father, who was of English ancestry, was a
planter who had served in the Contl. Army during Rev. War.
Family moved to a plantation near Knoxville, Tenn., where
son received early educ. Grad. from East Tenn. Univ. in
1807. Studied law with Hugh L. White, later a U.S. Senator
from Tenn., and was admitted to bar in 1809. In 1811 moved
to Huntsville, Ala. (then Miss. Terr.), where he established
law practice. Volunteered and served as regimental adjt.
during Creek War, 1813. Mbr. of Ala. Terr. legislature,
1817-1819 and of the Ala. constl. conv. in 1819. Chosen as
one of four cir. ct. judges in 1819 and became Chief Justice
in 1820 at age 30. Resigned in 1823 to take up pvt. law
practice. El. to Ala. House in 1827 and was chosen Speaker
El. to U.S. House in 1828 and continued to serve therein
until 1835. Nom. and el. Gov. in 1835 as a Jackson Dem.
During admin., a treaty was signed with the Cherokee Indians
and he later assisted in their removal from Ala. to west of
the Miss. River. Resigned as Gov. in June, 1837 after being
chosen to fill a vacancy in U.S. Senate. Served therein
until Nov., 1841, when he resigned because of wife's illness.
In 1842-1843 assisted in compiling digest of Ala. laws.
Served briefly on Ala. Supreme Ct. in 1843 as an appointee

to fill a vacancy. Apptd. as spec. commnr. in 1846 to terminate affairs of State Bank. Resumed law practice with two of his sons. Was an ardent supporter of secession movement in 1861. Extensive holdings of lands and slaves were seized by Fed. troops during course of Civil War, and he was placed under arrest temporarily at end of the war. m. to Susanna Claiborne Withers, of Dinwiddie Co., Va. Three s., one of whom became a U.S. Sen. and also a mbr. of the Senate of the So. Confed. D. Sept. 9, 1866 at Huntsville, Ala. Bur. in Maple Hill Cem. there.

McVAY, HUGH (1837). b. in 1788 in Greenville Co., S.C. Moved to Lauderdale Co., Ala. where he became a planter. El. to Ala. legislature, becoming Pres. of Senate. In 1837 while serving in that capacity succeeded to the office of Gov. following the resignation of Gov. C.C. Clay. Served from June to Nov. of that year, completing the term for which Clay had been el. D. May 9, 1851.

BAGBY, ARTHUR PENDLETON (1837-1841). b. in 1794 in Louisa Co., Va. Antecedents were mbrs. of old, aristocratic families. Received classical educ. Moved to Claiborne, in Ala. Terr., where he studied law and was admitted to bar in 1819. Mbr. of Ala. House in 1821 and continued to serve a number of terms thereafter, being chosen Speaker in 1822 and again in 1836. Mbr. of Ala. Senate in 1825. During early political career was an Adams Rep., but switched party affiliation to Jackson Dem. as a result of his views on U.S. Bank and the nullification crisis of 1832. El. Gov. in 1837 and again in 1839. Major concerns as Gov. were completion of removal of Cherokee Indians to the West; measures to relieve financial distress following the panic of 1837; and measures to combat yellow fever outbreak in Mobile in 1839 and the severe drought conditions of that year. Apptd. in 1841 to fill vacancy in U.S. Senate seat following resignation of Sen. Clay. Served there until June, 1848, when he resigned to accept post of Minister to Russia. Tenure in that post ended in May, 1849 after Gen. Taylor became Pres. of U.S. Retired to law practice in Ala. Mbr. of Ala. law codification commn. in 1852. m. to Emily Steele, of Ga. After her death, m. to Anne Elizabeth Connell, of Darlington, S.C. Father of six d. and three s. Baptist. D. of yellow fever Sept. 21, 1858 at Mobile, to which place he had moved in 1856. Bur. in Magnolia Cem. there.

FITZPATRICK, BENJAMIN (1841-1845). b. June 30, 1802 in Greene Co., Ga. Father, who was of Irish descent, had been a mbr. of Ga. legislature. Mother was ----- (Phillips) F., of Clark Co. Left an orphan at age 7, the son was cared for by

older mbrs. of his family. Moved with an older brother to
Ala. (then Miss. Terr.) in 1815 or 1816 to help manage land
belonging to family on Ala. River, north of Montgomery. Received limited educ. Worked as sheriff's deputy, clerk in
trading house, and studied law. After admission to bar began practice in Montgomery. Served as solicitor in his jud.
dist. from 1822 to 1829, when he retired from law to engage
in planting. Chosen as pres. elector on Dem. party ticket
in 1840. El. Gov. as Dem. in 1841 and was reel. in 1843
without opposition. Admin. much concerned with banking reform legislation. Near end of term in 1845, voters of state
approved removal of the State capital from Tuscaloosa to
Montgomery. In Nov., 1848 was apptd. to U.S. Senate seat as
a States Rts. Dem. to fill vacancy. Served until a regular
successor was chosen in Nov., 1849. Apptd. again to U.S.
Senate seat in Jan., 1853 to fill a vacancy. Mbr. of U.S.
Senate again in 1855, and served until Jan., 1861, when he
withdrew, along with other mbrs. of the Ala. delegation to
U.S. Cong., following the adoption of an ordinance of secession by Ala. conv. Pres. pro tem of the U.S. Senate from
Dec., 1857 until he left that body in 1861. In 1860 was nom.
for the office of Vice Pres. of U.S. on the Douglas (Dem.)
ticket, but declined. Although opposed to secession, he
nevertheless supported the Southern cause through relief
work during the Civil War. Was a mbr. and ch. of the post-
war Ala. constl. conv. of 1865. Was subsequently disfranchised during Reconstruction era, but continued to maintain an active interest in politics. m. for first time in
1827 to Sarah Terry Elmore, of Ala. After her death in 1837,
m. in 1845 to Aurelia Rachel (Blassingame) Blaine, of Perry
Co. Father of six s. and one d. D. Nov. 21, 1869 at
Wetumpka, Ala. Bur. in Oakwood Cem., Montgomery.

MARTIN, JOSHUA LANIER (1845-1847). b. Dec. 5, 1789 in
Blount Co., Tenn. s. of Warner and Martha (Bailey) M. Father, who was of Huguenot ancestry, was a farmer. Received
academic educ. and became a school teacher. Also began
study of law. Moved to Ala. in 1819 and continued study of
law with a brother at Russellville. Admitted to bar and began practice at Athens, Ala. Mbr. of Ala. legislature for
several terms beginning in 1822. Solicitor for his jud.
dist. from 1827 to 1834, when he became a cir. ct. judge.
El. in 1834 to the U.S. House as a Dem. Retired voluntarily
from seat after two terms. Became mbr. of chancery ct.,
Middle Ala. Div., and served until 1841. In 1845 was chosen
Gov. as an Indep. Dem. in opposition to the regular Dem.
party nominee over issues growing out of liquidation of the
State Bank. During admin., a spec. commn. was set up to
deal with matters connected with liquidation of the Bank.

Was a strong supporter of U.S. war with Mexico and assisted
in raising troops. Returned to law practice in 1847. El.
to Ala. House in 1853. Had distinction of never having lost
an election in which he was a contender. m. first to Mary
Gillam Mason, of Va. After her death, m. to her sister,
Sarah Ann. Father of five s. and two d. A son, John Mason
M., became a mbr. of U.S. House from Ala. in 1885. D. at
Tuscaloosa, Ala. Nov. 2, 1856. Bur. in Evergreen Cem. there.

CHAPMAN, REUBEN (1847-1849). b. July 15, 1799 at Bowling Green, Va. s. of Col. Reuben and Anne (Reynolds) C.
Father, who was of Scotch descent, was a man of considerable
means who had served in the Rev. War. Received academic
educ. in Va. In 1824 went to Ala., where he studied law in
office of his brother, Samuel, at Huntsville. Admitted to
bar in 1825 and began practice in Somerville, Ala. El. to
Ala. Senate in 1832, where he served until election to U.S.
House in 1835. Served in that body for six terms, 1835-1847.
Was not a cand. for reel., having been nom. and el. Gov. as
a Dem. without having solicited nom. for the office. Refused nom. for second term in 1849 when he failed to obtain
a two-thirds majority vote in the state conv. Admin. concerned largely with continuing problems arising out of liquidation of the Ala. State Bank. Retired from politics
temporarily to manage estate; but was el. to a seat in Ala.
House in 1855. Delegate to Dem. natl. convs. in 1856 and
1860 (Baltimore). During the Civil War, represented the
Confed. govt. as a foreign envoy, 1862-1865. Lost home and
much of property at hands of Union troops during the war,
and was imprisoned for a short time at its conclusion. m. to
Felicia Pickett, of Limestone Co., Ala., who was originally
from Va. Four d.; two s. Mbr., Protestant Episcopal church.
D. at Huntsville May 16, 1882. Bur. in Maple Hill Cem.
there.

COLLIER, HENRY WATKINS (1849-1853). b. Jan. 17, 1801
in Lunenburg Co., Va. s. of James and Elizabeth (Bouldin)
C. Antecedents had resided in Va. for several generations
and had had prominent roles in Va. mil. and political affairs. While he was still a child the family moved to Abbeville Dist., in S.C., where he received classical schooling.
Moved to Madison Co., Ala. Terr., in 1818. Studied law in
Nashville, Tenn. Admitted to bar in 1822 and began practice
at Huntsville, later moving to Tuscaloosa, where he resided
thereafter. El. to Ala. legislature in 1823. Became dist.
ct. judge in 1827 and served until 1836, when he was apptd.
to the Ala. Supreme Ct. Served as Chief Justice of that
body for twelve years. Nom. and el. Gov. in 1849 as Dem.
and was reel. in 1851. Admin. characterized by his support

for many schemes for internal improvements and promotion of
philanthropic programs, including prison reforms and plans
for a hosp. for the insane, as advocated by Dorothy Dix. Offered seat in U.S. Senate at end of second term, but declined for reasons of health. Served as first pres. of Ala.
Historical Soc. m. to Mary Ann Battle, of Nash Co., N.C.
Three d.; one s. Active in Methodist Episcopal church affairs. D. at Bailey Springs, Ala., Aug. 28 (8?), 1855. Bur.
at Tuscaloosa, Ala.

WINSTON, JOHN ANTHONY (1853-1857). b. Sept. 4, 1812 in
Madison Co., Ala. s. of Wm. and Mary Bacon (Cooper) W.
Attd. La Grange Coll., in Ala. and Nashville Univ. Became
a planter in Sumter Co., Ala. in 1835. Org. a cotton commn.
bus. at Mobile in 1844, which continued to function until
his death. El. to Ala. House in 1840 and in 1845 to the Ala.
Senate, where he was the presiding officer for two sessions.
In 1846 raised a company of volunteers for service in the
Mexican War, becoming its col.; but the unit eventually disbanded without seeing battle service. Delegate to 1848 Dem.
natl. conv. and to the So. States (Nashville) conv. in 1849.
Strong advocate of States Rts. with regard to the slavery
issue. Mbr. of Ala. Senate again in 1851, and was a Dem.
elector-at-large for Pierce ticket in 1852 pres. election.
Nom. and el. Gov. in 1853 as a Dem., becoming the first
native-born citizen of the State to hold that office. Reel.
in 1855. Legislation creating a state pub. school system
was passed in 1854. Came to be known as the "veto Gov." because of his many vetoes of bills for internal improvements,
which he refused to approve so long as the State was in debt.
Delegate to Dem. natl. conv. in Charleston in 1860, where he
was a supporter of Sen. Douglas for the nom. for Pres. of
the U.S. Joined in the State's war effort after Civil War
began. Served in the Confed. Army for about one year, seeing much active service during the Peninsular campaign in
1862. Retired from active mil. service thereafter because
of poor health, but continued to support war effort. Mbr.
of Ala. constl. convs. of 1865 and 1867. Apptd. to seat in
U.S. Senate in 1865, but was refused seat by the Senate on
grounds of his refusal to take oath of allegiance to U.S. at
end of the Civil War. Delegate to the Dem. natl. conv. in
1868. m. first to Mary Agnes Jones. After her death was m.
for a second time. One d. D. at Mobile Dec. 21, 1871.
Bur. there.

MOORE, ANDREW BARRY (1857-1861). b. March 7, 1807 in
Spartanburg Dist., S.C. Father was a planter who had participated actively in state and local political affairs. Received classical educ. in S.C. In 1826 went to Perry Co.,

Ala., where he was a school teacher for two years. Studied
law and was admitted to bar in 1833. Served as justice of
the peace for eight years. In 1839 was el. to the Ala.
House, where he served for four terms. Dem. pres. elector
in 1848. Became cir. ct. judge in 1852, serving until 1857
when he was nom. and el. Gov. as a Dem. without formal opposition. Was reel. in 1859. Major event of his admin. was
the adoption of an ordinance of secession in Jan., 1861 by a
spec. conv. assembled by the legislature with his cooperation after the results of the 1860 pres. election were made
known. Made energetic efforts to prosecute the ensuing war
on behalf of the State. Fed. forts were seized by his orders and 60,000 troops were raised and equipped. After completion of second term, served as spec. aide to his successor in the office of Gov. in connection with admin. of war
program. Arrested and imprisoned for a short time at the
end of the Civil War. Was in poor health when released. m.
in 1837 to Mary Goree, of Marion, Ala. Two d.; one s. D.
at Marion, April 5, 1873. Bur. there.

SHORTER, JOHN GILL (1861-1863). b. April 23, 1818 at
Monticello, Ga. s. of Reuben C. and Mary (Gill) S. Father,
who was a native of Va. and was a physician and planter, had
moved to Ga. at the time of his marriage. In 1837 the family
moved to Eufala, in Barbour Co., Ala. Educ. at Franklin
Coll., in Athens. Studied law and was admitted to the bar
in 1838. Apptd. in 1842 solicitor for his jud. dist. El.
to Ala. Senate in 1845, and in 1851 to the Ala. House. Resigned seat in 1852 to accept apptmt. to a cir. ct. judgeship, in which capacity he was serving when the Civil War
began. Was a strong advocate of secession. Chosen as one
of Ala.'s delegates to the Provisional Confed. Cong. in
1861. Was serving in that capacity when he was el. Gov. in
1861. During the course of his term, gave vigorous aid to
the war programs of the Confed. govt. generally, including
the proposal to conscript troops. Discontents arising from
the invasion of the northern area of the State by Union
troops, the capture of Mobile by Union naval forces, the
mil. draft, and other war hardships led to his defeat for
reel. in 1863. Retired to law practice at Eufala, and took
no active part in politics thereafter. m. to Mary Battle.
One d. survived infancy. Baptist. D. at Eufala May 29,
1872. Bur. there.

WATTS, THOMAS HILL (1863-1865). b. Jan. 3, 1819 near
Greenville, Butler (then a part of Conecuh) Co., Ala. Terr.
s. of John Hughes and Prudence (Hill) W. Family was of
English and Welsh descent. Grad. from the Univ. of Va. in
1840, having chosen to receive a coll. educ. rather than an

interest in his father's estate. Admitted to bar in 1841
and began practice at Greenville. Became a mbr. of the Whig
party. Campaigned for Whig pres. ticket in 1840, and was on
Whig pres. elector slate in 1848. El. to Ala. House in 1842
and 1844. In 1845 moved to Montgomery, Ala., and was el. to
the Ala. House again from that area in 1849 and 1853. Widely
regarded as an authority on constl. matters. Unsuccessful
cand. of Amer. (Know Nothing) party for U.S. House in 1856.
Supported the Constl. Union party ticket in pres. campaign
of 1860. Was a pro-Union man, but went along nevertheless
with his State in secession after Lincoln's election as
Pres. of U.S. Mbr. of Ala. conv. in 1861 that adopted secession ordinance. Assisted in organizing an Ala. regiment
and was chosen its col. when war began. Was opposition cand.
against Shorter in 1861 gubernatorial election, but did not
campaign for the office and was defeated. Apptd. to the
post of Atty. Gen. of the Confed. govt. in April, 1862. Was
serving in that office when he was el. Gov. in 1863. Defeated incumbent Gov. Shorter by 3 to 1 margin, carrying
every county in the State but one. As Gov., resisted actions of C.S.A. government in matters he maintained were
of exclusive concern to the State. Surrendered
authorities at end of the war, and was imprisoned for a
short time. Lost most of his extensive property holdings
during the war and became bankrupt, but continued nevertheless to try to pay off debtors until his death. Served one
term as mbr. of Ala. House, 1880-1881. Pres. of Ala. Bar
Assoc., 1889-1890. Baptist. m. first in 1842 to Eliza
Brown Allen, who died in 1873. Four s.; seven d. m. in
1875 to Ellen C. (Noyes) Jackson, widow of a former law
partner. D. Sept. 16, 1892 at Montgomery, Ala. Bur. there.

PATTON, ROBERT MILLER (1865-1868). b. July 10, 1809 at
Russell, Va. s. of Wm. and Martha (Hays) P. Family was of
Scotch and Irish descent. Father was a planter and merchant.
Moved to Huntsville, Ala. (then Miss. Terr.) in 1813. Father, who was founder of one of the first cotton mills in
Ala., became quite wealthy. Attd. Green Acad., in Huntsville. Assisted in mgmt. of family bus. interests at
Florence. El. as a Whig to Ala. legislature in 1832 from a
strong Dem. dist. Continued to serve therein most of the
time from 1837 onward to the beginning of the Civil War, becoming Pres. of the Senate on several occasions. When Civil
War began was owner of some 4,000 acres of land and more
than 300 slaves. Delegate to Dem. natl. conv. at Charleston
in 1860. Mbr. of Ala. conv. called to consider question of
secession, which he opposed. After war began, nevertheless
supported the Southern cause in connection with raising
funds for the war effort. Three sons served in the Confed.

Army, two of whom were killed in action. Lost much property
during war. Mbr. of conv. assembled in 1865 to revise the
Ala. const. Chosen Gov. under the revised const. in Nov.,
1865. Recognized as such as Pres. Johnson, but after U.S.
Cong. assumed control over natl. policy toward former Confed.
States, was permitted to continue in office only under close
Fed. supervision. Admin. concerned largely with relieving
economic distress brought about by the war. Removed from
office in June, 1868 by Fed. mil. authorities after a revised const. was put into effect. Concerned himself thereafter with bus. and philanthropic affairs. Assisted in replacing bldgs. on Univ. of Ala. campus that had been destroyed during the war. Became trustee of several institutions of higher learning, including the Univ. of Ala. and
the Univ. of Mo. m. in 1832 to Jane Locke Brahan. Seven s.;
two d. Very active in Presbyterian church affairs, serving
as elder in church at Florence for 54 years. D. at Sweet
Water, Ala. Feb. 28, 1885. Bur. at Huntsville.

PARSONS, LOUIS ELIPHALET (1865). b. April 27, 1817 at
Lisle, Broome Co., N.Y. s. of Erastus and Jennette (Hepburn)
P. Family was distantly related to that of the eminent
theologian, Jonathan Edwards, of New England. Studied law
in law offices in N.Y. and Pa. Moved to Talledega, Ala. in
1841, where he began practice. Mbr. of Whig party, and was
a pres. elector cand. on the Fillmore (Amer. party) ticket
in 1856 pres. election. El. to Ala. House in 1859. Switched
party affiliation to Dem., and was a delegate to Dem. natl.
conv. at Baltimore in 1860. Pro-Union in views at outbreak
of Civil War. Mbr. of Ala. legislature in 1863. Opposed
militia draft by the State as means of supporting Confed.
cause, maintaining prosecution of the war was a responsibility of the central Confed. govt. After collapse of Confed.
govt., was apptd. by Pres. Andrew Johnson as Provisional
Gov. of Ala. Served until a state constl. conv. was assembled which revised the const., abolished slavery, and
repudiated the ordinance of secession. Chosen by the newly
el. legislature to be one of the two U.S. Senators of Ala.,
but the Senate refused to seat him. A supporter of Pres.
Johnson's policies, he was apptd. U.S. dist. atty. for No.
Ala. in 1866. Prosecuted offenders against the reformed
govtl. regime with vigor, at some personal risk to himself.
El. to Ala. House in 1872, and was subsequently chosen
Speaker. m. to Jane Chrisman, of Ky. Four s.; three d.
Presbyterian. Mason. D. at Talledega, Ala. June 8, 1895.

SMITH, WILLIAM HUGH (1868-1870). b. April 9 (26?),
1826, in Fayette Co., Ga. s. of Jeptha V. and Nancy (Dick-
son) S. Father was a planter. Studied law, was admitted to

bar in 1850 and began practice in Ga. Mbr. of Ga. legislature, 1855-1859. Cand. for pres. elector on Dem. (Douglas)
ticket in 1860 pres. election. Although father was a Dem.
and a slave-owner, he and his sons were strongly pro-Union
in political views. During course of the Civil War, left Ga.
to support Union cause, along with three of his brothers,
who served in the Union Army. At end of the war was apptd.
to a cir. ct. judgeship in Ala. by Gov. Parsons. Later was
made chief of voter registration bureau in Ala. El. Gov. as
Rep. under the revised const. of 1867 in Feb., 1868 and assumed office in the following July. Admin. was unpopular
with a large part of former pro-Southern White element because of lavish grants and expenditures by the legislature
for internal improvements and other purposes. However,
under his admin. a bill became law under which political
disabilities of a considerable part of the former pro-
Southern element were relaxed. Defeated in attempt to win
reel. in 1870. Refused to vacate office when his term was
scheduled to end, maintaining there was fraud in connection
with ascertainment of result, which was close. Eventually
was forced to vacate office following a cir. ct. order. Became a cir. ct. judge in 1874. Later was apptd. to post of
U.S. dist. atty. in Ala. by Pres. Arthur. m. to Lucy
Wortham, of Randolph Co., Ala. Five d.; three s. D. at
Birmingham Jan. 1, 1899. Bur. there.

LINDSAY, ROBERT BURNS (1870-1872). b. July 4, 1824 at
Lochmaben, Dumfrieshire, Scotland. s. of John and Elizabeth
(McKnight) L. Educ. at Univ. of St. Andrews, where he distinguished himself as a scholar. Came to N.C. in 1844 to
visit brother and decided to remain in this country. Became
teacher in an acad. for young men; also studied law. In
1849 moved to Tuscumbia, Ala., where he established practice.
El. as Dem. to Ala. House in 1853 and to the Ala. Senate in
1859. Apptd. to Bd. of Visitors of West Point Mil. Acad.
Nom. as pres. elector by Dem. state conv. in 1860. After
party split he refused to support Breckinridge, but ran as
a Douglas elector in that election. Opposed secession, but
supported Ala. in Civil War, serving in a cavalry unit. El.
to Ala. Senate in 1865 under the revised const. of that
year. Nom. and el. Gov. in 1870 as cand. of the Conservative (Dem.) faction. Assumed office only after intervention
by a cir. ct., which held he had been duly el. to the office.
Admin. characterized by financial difficulties and by political unrest growing out of U.S. govt.'s policies, and
the rise of KKK. Refused to be cand. for second term. Two
months after leaving office became partially paralyzed, but
continued to practice law despite disability. Had high
reputation as linguist, scholar and teacher. m. in 1854 to

Sarah Miller Winston, sister of Gov. Winston of Ala. (q.v.).
Father of nine children. Presbyterian. Mbr., I.O.O.F. D.
at Tuscumbia, Ala. Feb. 13, 1902. Bur. there.

LEWIS, DAVID PETER (1872-1874). b. in 1820(?) in
Charlotte Co., Va. s. of Peter C. and Mary Smith (Buster)
L. Family moved to Huntsville, Ala. during his youth. Received educ. there. Studied law. After admission to bar
moved to nearby Lawrence Co. and established practice there.
Mbr. of Ala. conv. called to consider question of secession
in 1861, in which he opposed secession. Went along with his
State, however, and was el. as an Ala. Repr. to the Provisional Confed. Cong. in 1861. Resigned seat after serving a
short time, and was apptd. to a cir. ct. judgeship by Gov.
Shorter in 1863. After serving in that office a short time,
he went over to the Union side, and remained at Nashville,
Tenn. until the end of the Civil War. Returned to Huntsville in 1865 and resumed law practice. El. Gov. as Rep. in
1872. Result of the election was disputed by a substantial
part of the legislature, but his faction was supported by
Fed. authorities and he was declared el. Admin. was beset
with financial difficulties arising out of the war and U.S.
govt.'s policies. Defeated by Dem. cand. in try for reel.
in 1874. Retired to law practice at Huntsville. Never
married. D. at Huntsville July 3, 1884. Bur. in Maple Hill
Cem. there.

HOUSTON, GEORGE SMITH (1874-1878). b. Jan. 17, 1811
near Franklin, Tenn. s. of David and Hannah (Reagan) H.
Parents were mbrs. of a respected but poor family. While he
was still a youth, family moved to Lauderdale Co., Ala.,
where he received a common school educ. Began study of law
in Harrodsburg, Ky. Admitted to bar in 1831 and began practice in Lauderdale Co. El. to Ala. legislature in 1832.
Became solicitor for his jud. dist. in 1834. In 1840 was
el. to U.S. House as a Dem. and continued to serve therein
for next three terms. Declined to seek reel. in 1848, but
was nom. and el. again in 1850 and for four succeeding terms
as a Union Dem. Became influential mbr., serving as ch. of
the Judiciary Commt. and later as ch. of Ways and Means
Commt. Also was a mbr. of a spec. commt. set up to deal
with question of secession crisis. Supported Sen. Douglas
in 1860 pres. election and opposed secession movement in
Ala., but after Ala. seceded, withdrew from House along with
other mbrs. of Ala. delegation. After war began went along
with State's action, and sons served in Confed. Army. At
end of the war was chosen to U.S. Senate in 1865, but was
refused seat by Senate. Delegate to Union party ("Loyalist")
conv. in 1866. Defeated in contest for Senate seat in 1866

by former Gov. Winston (q.v.). El. Gov. in 1874 as a Dem.,
defeating incumbent Gov. Lewis, and was reel. in 1876.
Admin. notable for conservative fiscal policies followed.
Reduced pub. debt; secured adoption of policy of making the
state penitentiary self-supporting by leasing out prisoners
for labor; and obtained restoration of Ala. to full participation in the Union. El. to seat in U.S. Senate at end of
term as Gov. Served during spec. session of 1879, but did
not return thereafter because of poor health. m. first in
1835 to Mary Bealy, of Athens, Ala. Eight children. After
her death, m. in 1861 to Ellen Irvine. Two children. D.
Dec. 21, 1879 at Athens, Ala. Bur. there.

COBB, RUFUS WILLS (1878-1882). b. Feb. 25, 1829 at
Ashville, Ala. s. of John W. and Catherine Peak (Stevens)
C. Father was a native of Va. Grad. from the Univ. of
Tenn. in 1850. Studied law and was admitted to bar in 1855.
Began practice in Shelby Co., Ala. Upon outbreak of Civil
War entered mil. service as capt. of a Confed. infantry unit;
later was in the cavalry. After the war, resumed practice
at Marion, in Perry Co. In 1868 moved to Columbiana and
later to Helena, in Shelby Co., where he practiced law and
also engaged in various bus. activities. El. to Ala. Senate
in 1872, and became Pres. of Senate in 1876. Nom. and el.
Gov. as Dem. in 1878 without formal opposition. Reel. in
1880 over Greenback party opponent. During admin., completed retirement of state debt and adopted further reforms
in penitentiary labor system. After leaving office engaged
in bus. activities concerned with mining, iron mfg., planting, and served as atty. for various railroad interests. In
1888 became probate judge of Shelby Co. Later established
residence in Birmingham. Baptist. Prominent mbr. of Masonic order. m. first in 1850 to Margaret McCluny, of Knoxville, Tenn. One s.; one d. m. second time in 1866 to
Frances Fell, a native of Md. One s.; one d. D. at Birmingham Nov. 26, 1913.

O'NEAL, EDWARD ASBURY (1882-1886). b. Sept. 20, 1818
in Madison Co., Ala. s. of Edward and Rebecca (Wheat) O'N.
Father, who was of Irish and French Huguenot descent and was
a native of Va., died when son was four years old. Educ. at
home and at La Grange Coll., from which he was grad. in 1836
with highest honors. Studied law and was admitted to bar in
1840. Set up practice at Florence, Ala. El. solicitor for
his jud. dist. in 1841. Unsuccessful cand. for U.S. House
in 1848. Was a strong advocate of States Rts., and supported secession in 1861. Became capt. in Confed. Army following outbreak of Civil War. Rose to rank of col. in 1862
and to brig. gen. in 1864. Saw much action in Va. campaigns,

including Battles of Seven Pines, Chancellorsville and
Gettysburg. Severely wounded on one occasion. After the
war returned to law practice in Ala. Mbr. of Ala. constl.
conv. in 1875, where he was influential as ch. of commt. on
educl. matters. Dem. elector on Hancock ticket in 1880 pres.
election. Nom. and el. Gov. as Dem. in 1882 over Rep.-
Greenback opponent. Reel. without opposition in 1884. During admin., normal schools were established; a State Dept.
of Agri. created; and the office of examiner of accounts for
prisons established in order to improve system of mgmt. of
prison labor. m. in 1838 to Olivia Moore, of Huntsville,
Ala. Father of nine children, one of whom, Emmett, became
Gov. of Ala. (q.v.). Methodist. Mason. D. at Florence,
Ala. Nov. 7, 1890. Bur. there.

SEAY, THOMAS (1886-1890). b. Nov. 20, 1846 in Green
(now Hale) Co., Ala. s. of Reuben and Ann (McGee) S. Parents were natives of Ga. who had settled in Ala. after their
marriage. Began schooling at home on father's plantation.
Continued studies in Greensboro after family moved there
when he was 12 years old. Entered So. Univ., but schooling
was interrupted by Civil War. Enlisted as pvt. in Confed.
regiment at age 16 in 1863. Saw much active service and was
twice made prisoner. After war, reentered So. Univ., from
which he received an A.M. degree in 1867. Read law in law
office, and after admission to bar in 1869 became partner of
his mentor, Judge A.A. Coleman. Unsuccessful cand. for Ala.
Senate in 1874, but was el. in second try for the office in
1876. Served in Ala. Senate for ten years and was its presiding officer in several sessions. Delegate to Dem. natl.
conv. in 1880. Ch. of Dem. state conv. in 1884. Nom. and
el. Gov. as Dem. in 1886 and again in 1888. During admin.,
urged constl. revision and making suffrage right dependent
on educl. attainment (literacy). m. first in 1875 to -----
Shaw, of Greene Co., Ala., who died four years later. One
s.; two d. Unsuccessful as cand. for U.S. Senate seat in
1890. D. at Greensboro March 30, 1896. Bur. there.

JONES, THOMAS GOODE (1890-1894). b. Nov. 26, 1844 at
Mason, Ga. s. of Samuel G. and Martha (Ward) J. Father and
mother were natives of Va. The antecedents of both were
prominent in mil. and political affairs of Va. as a colony
and as a State. Educ. by pvt. tutors and later at schools
in Montgomery, Ala., to which place his family had moved in
1850. Entered Va. Mil. Inst. in 1859, where he studied
under Thomas ("Stonewall") Jackson. Joined Confed. Army in
1862 and served with distinction under Gen. Jackson in Va.
campaigns. Later became commdr., as col., of Ala. Home
Guard troops under the direct control of Gov. Watts. After

the war, finding planting unprofitable, studied law. In
1868 became ed. of a Dem. newspaper at Montgomery, the Daily
Picayune. Orator at 1874 Confed. Memorial Day ceremonies,
and was voted a medal by Confed. Veterans. Mbr. of Montgomery city council, 1875-1884. From 1870 to 1880 was official
reporter of Ala. Supreme Ct. Drew up a code of ethics that
was adopted by Ala. Bar Assoc. El. to Ala. House in 1884.
Was reel. and became Speaker. Nom. and el. Gov. as Dem. in
1890 and was reel. in 1892. Favored sound money system;
prison reform; and opposed secret societies and caucuses in
party politics. In 1894 took vigorous action to quell disorders growing out of labor unrest in mining indus. In 1896
presided over Dem. state conv. that opposed Free Silver
platform, and served as delegate to the Gold Standard Dem.
natl. conv. in Indianapolis prior to the 1896 pres. election.
Served as ch. of relief commt. formed to deal with victims
of yellow fever outbreak. Pres. of Ala. State Bar Assoc. in
1901. Appt. U.S. dist. ct. judge for No. Ala. by Pres.
Theodore Roosevelt in 1901. Author of articles on historical
topics. Memorial orator at Pres. Grant's Tomb in 1902.
Episcopalian. Mbr., K.P.; Elks. m. in 1866 to Georgena
Bird, of Montgomery, Ala. Six s.; seven d. D. April 28,
1914 at Montgomery. Bur. there.

     OATES, WILLIAM CALVIN (1894-1896). b. Nov. 30, 1835 at
Oates Cross Roads, Pike (now Bullock) Co., Ala. s. of Wm.
and Sally (Sellers) O. Father was a planter. Educ. at
Lawrenceville Acad. Left home at age 16 and led a roving
life in Southwest for a time as a laborer and ranch hand.
Became a teacher in Henry Co., 1851-1853. Studied law in
law office at Eufala and was admitted to the bar in 1858.
Practiced at Abbeville, Ala. until 1861. Ed. of a weekly
Dem. newspaper in 1860. Entered Confed. Army in 1861 as a
capt., having raised a company of volunteers. Rose to rank
of col., participating in numerous battles, including Gettysburg. Wounded several times, one wound resulting in loss of
right arm. After the war returned to law practice and bus.
interests at Abbeville. Delegate to Dem. natl. conv. in
1868. Mbr. of Ala. House in 1870-1872. Unsuccessful cand.
for Dem. nom. for Gov. in 1872. Delegate to Ala. constl.
conv. in 1875, in which he served as ch. of commt. on jud.
matters. El. to U.S. House in 1880 as Dem. and served
therein for seven terms. While in Cong., advocated laws restricting alien ownership of land; restrictions of immigration; incorporation of Nicaragua Canal Co.; appropriations
for improvements of waterways; revision of silver purchase
laws to permit increased coinage of silver. Resigned House
seat in 1894 after being nom. and el. as a "sound money"
Dem. over the Pop. party cand., who had the support of the

Free Silver Dem. faction. Unsuccessful in contest for U.S. Senate seat in 1897, losing to cand. favored by Free Silver faction. Volunteered services to U.S. during Spanish-Amer. War. Commanded a volunteer unit as brig. gen., but was not involved in battle action. Mbr. of Ala. constl. conv. in 1901, where he was ch. of commt. on the legislative branch. Unsuccessfully opposed changes in suffrage laws designed to discriminate further against Negro voting. m. in 1882 to Sallie Toney. One s. D. Sept. 9, 1910 at Montgomery. Bur. in Oakwood Cem. there.

JOHNSTON, JOSEPH FORNEY (1896-1900). b. March 23, 1843 near Lowesville, Lincoln Co., N.C. Father was a planter of Scotch-Irish ancestry. Received common school educ. Moved to Ala. at age 17. Was a student at a mil. acad. in Talledega when Civil War began. Enlisted as pvt. in Confed. Army and rose to rank of capt. Wounded four times. After war, studied law in office of Gen. W.H. Forney in Jacksonville. Admitted to bar in 1866 and established practice in Selma. Became involved in banking, mining and iron mfg. enterprises in that area. In 1884 moved to Birmingham. Mbr. of Ala. Dem. exec. commt. for several years. After having sought Dem. nom. for Gov. unsuccessfully on two occasions was nom. and el. in 1896, defeating Pop. opponent. Reel. in 1898. Governorship was first elective pub. office held by him. Notable for his frankness and candor. Declared that he "coveted" the office of Gov.; and that he sought it solely because he wanted it, and not because anyone had urged him to run or that he was seeking it out of a sense of pub. duty. Admin. as Gov. characterized by economy in pub. finance, efforts to improve admin. efficiency, and a sense of accountability to pub. Sought Dem. nom. for Gov. unsuccessfully in 1902. In 1907 was el. to U.S. Senate to fill unexpired portion of term of Sen. Pettus. Was reel. for regular term in 1909. m. in 1869 to Theresa Virginia Hooper. Three s. D. Aug. 8, 1913 in Washington, D.C. while still a mbr. of U.S. Senate. Bur. at Birmingham in Elmwood Cem.

SAMFORD, WILLIAM JAMES (1900-1901). b. Sept. 16, 1844 at Greenville, Ga. s. of Wm. Flewellyn and Susan Lewis (Dowdell) S. Father was a prof. of belles lettres at Emory Coll. and a writer on political subjects. Educ. in a pvt. school in Auburn, Ala. After working as typesetter on a newspaper for a year, entered East Ala. Coll. at Auburn. Later enrolled at the Univ. of Ga. Left coll. in 1862 at age 17 to enlist in Confed. Army as a pvt. Rose to rank of lieut. Saw action in Ky. and Tenn. campaigns. Was taken prisoner, and while being held, continued studies under a former teacher who was a fellow prisoner. Released in 1864

and returned to regiment until the close of the war. Engaged in cotton planting and studied law. Admitted to bar
in 1867 and began practice at Opelika. Mbr. of bd. of aldermen of Ala. City, 1872-1873. Mbr. of exec. commt. of Dem.
state commt. in 1874. Delegate to the Ala. constl. conv. of
1875. Alternate pres. elector for the Tilden ticket in 1876
pres. election. El. to U.S. House in 1878, but did not seek
reel. Mbr. of Ala. House in 1882. Later was el. to Ala.
Senate, of which he was chosen presiding officer. Nom. and
el. Gov. as Dem. in 1900. Was unable to assume office at
beginning of the term because of illness. Functions of the
office were assumed by Wm. Jelks, the presiding officer of
the Senate, for the first month of the term. m. in 1865 to
Carolyn Elizabeth Drake. Seven s.; three d. Very active in
Methodist Episcopal church, serving as part-time minister of
"exhorter," steward, lecturer, and delegate to church con-
ferences. Engaged extensively in writing and lecturing on
historical, patriotic and literary subjects. Trustee of the
Univ. of Ala. in 1896. Mbr., Masons; K.P.; Amer. Legion of
Honor; Ala. Historical Soc. D. at Tuscaloosa June 11, 1901,
after serving about six months of term as Gov. Bur. at
Opelika.

JELKS, WILLIAM DORSEY (1901-1907). b. Nov. 25, 1855 at
Warrior Stand in Russell (now Macon) Co., Ala. s. of Joseph
W.D. and Jane Goodrum (Frazer) J. Father was killed in ac-
tion in 1862 during Civil War. Family moved to Union
Springs, Ala. Attd. Mercer Univ., from which he received an
M.A. degree in 1876. Acquired interest in a local newspaper.
Later moved to Eufala, Ala., where he became owner and publ.
of the Eufala Times. Became widely known in Ala. through
his newspaper writings. Mbr. of Union Springs city council
at age 22. Mbr. of Eufala school bd. In 1898 was el. to
Ala. Senate. As presiding officer of that body in 1900 at
beginning of Gov. Samford's term, immediately became acting
Gov. for about a month because of Samford's illness. Succeeded to office of Gov. in June, 1901 upon death of Gov.
Samford. As Pres. of Senate, had been influential in bringing about the holding of the constl. conv. of 1901. Became
first Gov. el. for a four-year term under the new const. of
1902, defeating former Gov. Johnston for the Dem. nom. for
the office. From April 25, 1904 to March 5, 1905, surrendered powers of the office to Lieut. Gov. Cunningham during
a period of absence from the State because of ill health.
As Gov., favored reduction of State debt; increased financial support for pub. schools and higher educl. system;
adoption of direct primary system; reform of system of contracting out convict labor; and closer regulation of railroad rates. Delegate to Dem. natl. conv. in 1912 where he

gave speech nominating Woodrow Wilson for Pres. of U.S. Mbr.
of Dem. natl. commt. Advocated, unsuccessfully, abolition
of the "unit rule" for voting by Ala. delegation at the Dem.
natl. conv. After leaving office org. and became pres. of a
life ins. firm in Birmingham. m. in 1883 to Alice Keith
Shorter, neice of Gov. Shorter of Ala. (q.v.). One d. D.
Dec. 13, 1931.

COMER, BRAXTON BRAGG (1907-1911). b. Nov. 7, 1848 at
Spring Hill, Barbour Co., Ala. s. of John Fletcher and
Catherine (Drewry) C. Father was a prosperous planter and
mill owner. Studied with pvt. tutor. Enrolled at the Univ.
of Ala. in 1864, but withdrew in 1865 after some of the
campus bldgs. were burned by Union troops. Entered the
Univ. of Ga., but withdrew shortly afterward because of poor
health. Entered Emory and Henry Coll., in Va., in 1868.
Received an A.M. degree from there in 1869, having distinguished himself as a student in natural sciences. After returning home engaged in bus. enterprises in cotton raising,
milling, banking and merchandising. Mbr. of Barbour Co. ct.,
1874-1880. Moved to Anniston, Ala. in 1885, and in 1890 to
Birmingham, Ala. Became pres. of City Natl. Bank at Birmingham, and engaged in other bus. enterprises there. Pres. of
Ala. R.R. Commn. in 1905. Won Dem. nom. for Gov. in 1906,
becoming the first cand. for Gov. to be nom. by direct primary, and was el. Gov. Called spec. session of the legislature to act upon platform pledges, involving closer regulation of corp. enterprises, more aid to educ., and tax reforms. Was an advocate of prohibition. After completion of
term resumed bus. interests. Apptd. to U.S. Senate in March,
1920 to fill vacancy caused by death of Sen. Bankhead. Refused to be a cand. for continuation in the office. m. to
Eva Jane Harris in 1872. Five s.; four d. Methodist. Mbr.,
Masons. Hon. degree from So. Univ. D. at Birmingham Aug.
15, 1927. Bur. in Elmwood Cem. there.

O'NEAL, EMMET(T) (1911-1915). b. Sept. 23, 1853 at
Florence, Ala. s. of Gov. Edward and Olivia (Moore) O'N. of
Ala. (q.v.). Attd. pub. schools in Florence; Florence Wes-
leyan Univ.; the Univ. of Miss., 1870-1871; and the Univ. of
Ala., from which he was grad. in 1873. Studied law in father's office and was admitted to bar in 1875. Practiced at
Florence with father until latter became Gov. Served as
Dem. pres. elector in 1884, 1892 and 1908. Served from 1893
to 1897 as U.S. dist. atty. by apptmt. from Pres. Cleveland.
Delegate to Ala. constl. conv. in 1901, where he was ch. of
commt. on local legislation and a mbr. of commt. on rules
and suffrage. Favored educl. and tax-paying qualifications
for voters. Delegate to Dem. natl. conv. in 1904 and again

in 1912, serving as ch. of the Ala. delegation in latter
year. Opposed state-wide prohibition, favoring local option
plan instead. Pres. of Ala. Bar Assoc. in 1909, and mbr. of
Amer. Bar Assoc. Council, 1911. Nom. and el. Gov. as Dem.
in 1910. At 1911 Govs.' Conf., engaged in a notable debate
with Gov. Woodrow Wilson, of N.J. (q.v.), on the popular
initiative, referendum and recall, which he opposed. Was a
strong advocate of States Rts. During admin., a rural library system was founded; a bd. of trustees for the State's
normal schools established; a local option liquor law
adopted; an intermediate State Ct. of Appeals and a Highway
Commn. established; mine safety and child labor laws were
strengthened; a commn. form of city govt. authorized; and
improved sanitation laws for hotels and restaurants enacted.
Defeated as cand. for the Dem. nom. for a U.S. Senate seat
in 1920 against incumbent Sen. Heflin. Presbyterian. Mbr.,
K.P.; Elks. m. in 1887 to Lizzie Kirkman. Two d.; one s.
D. Sept. 7, 1922.

     HENDERSON, CHARLES (1915-1919). b. April 26, 1860 at
Henderson, Pike Co., Ala. s. of Jeremiah A. and Mildred
(Hill) H. Educ. in pub. schools at Troy, Ala. Entered
Howard Coll. at Marion, Ala., but soon withdrew because of
death of father. Engaged in merc. bus. in Troy. Mayor of
Troy, 1885-1891 and 1901-1907. Apptd. inspector gen. on
staff of Gov. Samford, and as aide de camp to Gov. Jelks.
Extended bus. interests into local banking, utilities, chemical, oil and ins. enterprises, becoming quite wealthy.
Helped found Troy State Normal Coll. and became a mbr. of
its governing bd. Influential in establishment of graded
pub. school system in Troy. El. to Ala. R.R. Commn. in 1906,
becoming its pres. in 1908, and serving until 1915. Nom.
and el. Gov. as Dem. in 1914. Became a "war governor" following entry of U.S. into World War I. Major actions during
admin. were those connected with U.S. mil. and econ. war
measures; a temporary depression in cotton prices; reforms
in the tax system and fiscal admin.; elimination of deficits;
and jud. local govtl. and penal system reforms. An Illit-
eracy Commn. was established and a compulsory school attendance law was enacted. After leaving office resumed bus.
activities. Episcopalian. Mbr., Masons (K.T.). Served on
governing bd. of Ala. Poly. Inst. Hon. degree from the
Univ. of Ala. m. in 1888 to Laura Parker Montgomery. D.
Jan. 7, 1937 at Troy.

     KILBY, THOMAS ERBY (1919-1923). b. July 9, 1865 at
Lebanon, Tenn. s. of Peyton P. and Sarah Ann (Marchant) K.
Family, which was of English and Welsh descent, formerly
lived in N.C. Attd. pub. schools in Atlanta, Ga., to which

place his family had removed in his youth. First employment
was as bus. agent for Ga. and Pac. R.R. at Anniston, Ala.
In 1899 went into bus. for himself by founding the Kilby Car
and Foundry Co. at Anniston. Later became pres. of Kilby
Frog and Switch Co. in Birmingham, and pres. of Anniston City
Bank in 1905. Mbr. of city council of Anniston, 1898-1900,
and of Anniston school bd., 1900-1905. Mayor of Anniston,
1905-1909. Energetic as mayor in promoting city govtl. reforms, going to Europe in 1910 to study local govtl. systems
there. Mbr. of Ala. Senate, 1911-1915, where he became influential advocate of budget reform, and prohibition. El.
Lieut. Gov. in 1914. As such, saw need for reforms in legislative org. and procedures. Nom. for Gov. in 1918 in Dem.
primary over strong opposition, emphasizing prohibition issue, and was el. Was successful as Gov. in getting budget
system reforms adopted; tax revision; creation of a State
Bd. of Educ.; highway improvements through a bond issue; enactment of a workmen's compensation law; abolition of convict lease system; and ratification of 19th Amdt. to the
U.S. Const. Episcopalian. Mbr., Masons (Shriner); K.P.
Hon. degree from Univ. of Ala. m. in 1894 to Mary Elizabeth
Clark. Two s.; one d. D. Oct. 22, 1943, at Anniston.

BRANDON, WILLIAM WOODWARD (1923-1927). b. June 5, 1868
at Talledega, Ala. s. of the Rev. Frank T.J. and Caroline
(Woodward) B. Attd. Cedar Bluff Inst. and the Tuscaloosa,
Ala. pub. schools. Left school to go to work at age 13.
Later attd. the Univ. of Ala., from which he received a law
degree in 1892. Began practice in Tuscaloosa. City clerk
of Tuscaloosa in 1891 and was later apptd. justice of the
peace. In 1892 became publ. of a mil. journal, the Citizen
Soldier. Mbr. of Ala. House, 1894-1899. Volunteered for
service in Spanish-Amer. War, reaching the rank of major by
the end of war. Apptd. Adjt. Gen. on Gov.'s staff in 1899
and served as such in Ala. State Guard until 1906. During
tenure, reorg. the Guard, and was made brig. gen. Reading
clerk for Ala. constl. conv. in 1901. State Aud. in 1906.
In 1911 was el. probate judge of Tuscaloosa Co., serving
until 1923. Defeated as cand. for Dem. nom. for Gov. in
1918, but was nom. and el. Gov. as Dem. in 1922 on a platform advocating reduction in taxes; decreased expenditures
for Gov.'s staff; strict enforcement of prohibition laws;
decentralization of govtl. powers; providing more support
for institutions for the relief of handicapped and unfortu-
nate. Favored devel. of Muscle Shoals dam project under
plans advanced by Henry Ford. Opposed KKK during latter
part of career, but was sympathetic to its aims in earlier
stages of his career. Achieved natl. attention as ch. of
Ala. delegation at the 1924 Dem. natl. conv. by announcing

at the beginning of each roll call, for over 100 ballots,
the undeviating support of the Ala. delegation for Sen. Un-
derwood as its choice for the Dem. nom. for Pres. of U.S.
Came to be known as "the little man with the big voice," and
was offered lucrative radio announcer jobs, which he refused.
At end of term, served again as probate judge of Tuscaloosa
Co. Delegate at 1932 Dem. natl. conv. Methodist. Mbr.,
Masons (Shriner); K.P.; I.O.O.F.; Elks; Kiwanis; Sigma Alpha
Epsilon. Pres. of U.S. Good Roads Assoc. m. in 1900 to a
widow, Mrs. Elizabeth (Andrews) Nabors. D. Dec. 7, 1934 at
Tuscaloosa. Bur. in Tuscaloosa Memorial Cem.

　　　GRAVES, D(AVID) BIBB (1927-1931; 1935-1939). b. April
1, 1873 at Hope Hull, Montgomery Co., Ala. s. of David and
Martha (Bibb) G. Mother was related to the first two Govs.
of Ala., Wm. Wyatt Bibb and Thomas Bibb (q.v.). Father died
when son was an infant. Brought up by grandfather, and
later by an uncle who resided in Tex. Attd. pub. schools in
Tex., and the Univ. of Ala., from which he was grad. in 1893.
Capt. of cadet corps while there. Studied law at the Univ.
of Tex., 1893-1894 and later at Yale Univ., from which he
received a law degree in 1896. Became capt., later a major,
in Ala. State Guard. Mbr. of Ala. House, 1898-1901. City
atty. for Montgomery, 1901-1902. Apptd. Adjt. Gen. of Ala.
State Guard by Gov. Comer in 1907. Ch. of Ala. Dem. exec.
commt., 1914-1918. Became col. of Ala. cavalry unit that
was called into U.S. service in 1916 for duty on Tex.-Mexico
border. At the beginning of World War I commanded an Ala.
field artillery unit with A.E.F. in France. Following the
war was instrumental in organizing the Ala. Legion of Honor
and served temporarily as its ch. Defeated as cand. for
Dem. nom. for Gov. in 1922, but was nom. and el. Gov. as a
Dem. in 1926. During admin., succeeded in efforts to expand
state aid for rural schools; a state sales tax was adopted;
took strong stand to protect Ala. interests in connection
with U.S. devel. of Muscle Shoals dam project; opposed Gov.
Al Smith's candidacy for the U.S. presidency in 1928. Was
prohibited by Ala. const. from seeking immediate reel. in
1930, but was nom. and el. to a second term in 1934, becoming the first Ala. Gov. to serve two four-year terms. During second term, gave active support to Pres. Roosevelt's
programs of econ. reform and recovery, including the TVA
project. Very successful in obtaining U.S. funds for pub.
works projects. A state local option liquor law was enacted
over his veto. Mbr., Christian (Disciples) church, and of
the governing bd. of Jones Coll. m. to a first cousin,
Dixie Bibb, in 1900. No children. He apptd. her to a U.S.
Senate seat vacancy in 1937, and she held the post until it

was filled by election. D. March 14, 1942 at Sarasota, Fla.
while recuperating from surgery.

MILLER, BENJAMIN MEEK (1931-1935). b. March 13, 1864
at Oak Hill, Wilcox Co., Ala. s. of the Rev. Dr. John and
Sarah (Pressly) M. Father was a minister of the Associate
Reform Presbyterian church. Educ. at pub. schools at Oak
Hill and Camden, Ala. Grad. from Erskine Coll., in S.C., in
1884 with class honors. Attd. the Univ. of Ala., from which
he received a law degree in 1888. Admitted to bar and began
practice in Camden. Mbr. of Ala. House, 1888-1889. In 1904,
was el. cir. ct. judge of his dist., and continued in that
office for two terms. During third term was apptd. to Ala.
Supreme Ct. After six years of service thereon, retired to
law practice at Camden. Nom. and el. Gov. as Dem. in 1930.
Strongly opposed the KKK during campaign. During admin.,
laws on income tax and pub. financial mgmt. were enacted.
The widely-noted Scottsboro trials occurred during his term.
Supported strict enforcement of prohibition laws, yet favored
light sentences for offenders. Granted 5,223 paroles and
383 pardons during tenure as Gov. At end of term retired to
Camden to law practice and mgmt. of plantation. Presbyterian. Mbr., Kappa Alpha; professional legal orgs. m. in
1892 to Margaret Duggan, who died while he was Gov. One s.;
one d. D. at Selma, Ala. Feb. 6, 1944.

GRAVES, D(AVID) BIBB (1935-1939). See above, 1927-1931.

DIXON, FRANK MURRAY (1939-1943). b. July 25, 1892 at
Oakland, Calif. s. of Frank and Laura (Murray) D. Was a
nephew of Thomas D., author of the widely-read novel, "The
Clansman" concerning the Reconstruction era in the South.
Attd. Phillips-Exeter Acad., 1906-1909; Columbia Univ.; and
the Univ. of Va., from which he received a law degree in
1911. Admitted to Ala. bar in 1917 and began practice at
Birmingham. During World War I, served in the French Army
for a time. Later served with U.S. Army in a coast artillery unit as second lieut. Was seriously wounded resulting
in amputation of a leg. Deptl. commdr., Amer. Legion, 1926-
1927. Defeated for Dem. nom. for Gov. in 1934. Nom. and
el. Gov. as Dem. in 1938. As Gov., was concerned with problems arising from U.S. entry into World War II. During
admin., a State civil service system was created and a Bd.
of Pardons and Paroles, designed to limit Gov.'s authority
over granting of clemency, was established. Was unsympa-
thetic toward various aspects of Pres. F.D. Roosevelt's New
Deal programs, particularly WPA projects, because of their
impact on labor and segregation practices. Retained political influence in Dem. party after leaving office and his

return to law practice. Had leading role in 1948 revolt
against Pres. Truman's leadership of Dem. party, and supported Gov. Thurmond's candidacy for Pres. of U.S. as the
States Rts. Dem. party nominee in that year. In 1960, as an
unpledged Dem. pres. elector, voted for Sen. Byrd, of Va.,
for Pres. of U.S., rather than the regular Dem. party nominee, Sen. Kennedy. Ch. of So. Govs.' Conf., 1941-1942.
Baptist. Recipient of Croix de guerre, with palm. Mbr.,
Masons; French Legion of Honor; Amer. Legion; D.A.V.; Kiwanis; various professional legal orgs. and collegiate fraternal bodies. Hon. degrees from Birmingham So. Coll. and
the Univ. of Ala. m. to Juliet Jolly Perry in 1920. One
s.; one d. D. at Birmingham Oct. 11, 1965. Bur. at Oak Hill
Cem. there.

SPARKS, CHAUNCEY M. (1943-1947). b. Oct. 8, 1884 in
Barbour Co., Ala. s. of George Washington and Sarah E.
(Castellow) S. Father and mother were natives of Ga., where
father had engaged in farming and teaching. Educ. at pub.
schools in Quitman Co., Ga. and at Mercer Univ., at Marion,
Ga., from which he received a law degree in 1910. Began
practice at Eufala, Ala. in 1910. Apptd. to local judgeship
by Gov. O'Neal in 1911, and served until 1916. Was a second
lieut. in Ala. Natl. Guard, 1912-1915. Sect. of Ala. Dem.
exec. commt., 1914-1918. Mbr. of Ala. House, 1919-1923 and
1931-1939. Nom. and el. Gov. as Dem. in 1942. During admin., a State Marketing Bd., a Dept. of Vets. Affairs, and a
Labor Dept. were established; a retirement plan for State
employees adopted; approval given for Ala. to participate in
a regional higher educl. system; pub. health programs extended; and increased aid to pub. educ. provided. Advocated
segregation and separate devel. of races except in bus. and
labor relations. Defeated as cand. for Dem. nom. for second
term as Gov. in 1950. Baptist. Mbr., Phi Beta Kappa; Kiwanis. Hon. degree from Howard Coll., 1943. Never married.
D. at Eufala, Nov. 6, 1968.

FOLSOM, JAMES ELISHA (1947-1951; 1955-1959). b. Oct. 9,
1808 near Elba, Coffee Co., Ala. s. of Joshua and Eulala
Cornelia (Dunnevant) F. Father owned and operated a small
farm. As a youth, worked as a farm laborer. Came to be
known as "Big Jim" as he reached manhood because of his size
(6'8" in height, weight 245 lbs.). Participated in sports.
Educ. at Elba pub. schools. Attd. the Univ. of Ala. and
Howard Coll. one year each. Was forced to leave coll. for
financial reasons. Joined merchant marine in 1931. Worked
for Ala. Relief Admin., 1933-1936. Engaged in oil and ins.
business at Cullman, Ala. from 1937 onward. Entered a volunteer officers training program in 1943, and served until

discharged 20 months later. Entered merchant marine again
for one year. Unsuccessful cand. for U.S. House in 1936 and
1938, and for Dem. nom. for Gov. in 1942. Delegate to Dem.
natl. conv. in 1944. Supported re-nom. of F.D. Roosevelt
for President of U.S. and also the nom. of Henry Wallace for
Vice Pres. against the wishes of a majority of the Ala. delegation. Nom. in run-off primary as Dem. cand. for Gov. in
1946 after an extensive "stumping" campaign. Advocated
minimum wage for teachers; old age pensions; better roads;
repeal of poll tax requirement for voting; constl. revision;
and aid to small farmers and businesses. Admin. sparked by
controversy over selection of mbrs. of governing bd. for Ala.
Poly. Inst.; by proposed amdt. to const. by which legislature could assemble itself without a call by the Gov.; and
by his feuds with press. Unsuccessfully opposed adoption of
(Boswell) amdt. to the state const. designed to impose additional barriers to Negro voting. The provision, which was
adopted, was later held void by the U.S. Supreme Ct. Favored
greatly increased aid for segregated Negro schools; opposed
KKK activities; banned flogging in jails. Cand. for Dem.
nom. for Pres. in 1948, but failed to attract much support.
Nom. and el. Gov. for second term in 1954. Was defeated in
attempts to win Dem. nom. for third term as Gov. in 1966 and
again in 1974. m. in 1936 to Sarah Carnley, who died in
1944. Two d. m. in 1948 to Jannelle Moore. Two s.; two d.

PERSONS, (SETH) GORDON (1951-1955). b. Feb. 5, 1902 at
Montgomery, Ala. s. of Frank Stanford and Kate (-----) P.
Educ. at Starke Univ. School in Montgomery and at Ala. Poly.
Inst., at Auburn. Employed by Ala. Farm Bureau Cotton Assoc., 1922-1923. Engaged in a variety of bus. enterprises
at Montgomery, including an auto tire shop, a radio service,
and a broadcasting station. Served as ch. and gen. mgr. of
Ala. Rural Electrification Authority, 1935-1939. Org. and
directed the Gordon Persons Co., a constr. and engr. enterprise, 1939-1942. From 1941 to 1943 was chief radio consultant to U.S. Office of War Information. Became mbr. of
Ala. Pub. Service Commn. in 1943, and continued service
thereon until 1951, acting as pres. the last four years.
Nom. and el. Gov. as Dem. in 1950, defeating former Gov.
Sparks in Dem. primary. Admin. high-lighted by efforts at
prison reform and energetic efforts to combat crime follow-
the murder of his party's cand. for Atty. Gen., who had
pledged a war on the criminal elements of the State. Made
use of Natl. Guard to "clean up" Phenix City on Ala.-Ga.
border near Ft. Benning Ga., which had become notorious as
a center of lawlessness. Abolished corporal punishment in
prisons. Ill health prevented his return to politics after

serving as Gov. m. in 1928 to Alice McKeither. One s.;
one d. D. at Montgomery May 29, 1965.

FOLSOM, JAMES ELISHA (1955-1959). See above, 1947-1951.

PATTERSON, JOHN MALCOLM (1959-1963). b. Sept. 27, 1921
near Goldsville, Ala. s. of Albert Love and Agnes Louis
(Benson) P. Father was a school teacher and lawyer. Educ.
at pub. schools in Rockford, Opelika, Alexander City, and
Phenix City. At beginning of World War II enlisted as a pvt.
in U.S. Army. Rose to rank of major by the end of the war.
Grad. from the Univ. of Ala. in 1949 with a law degree. Admitted to bar and began practice with father in Phenix City.
Served in judge advocate section in criminal cases for U.S.
Army in Germany for a time. Was on active duty with U.S.
Army during the Korean conflict. Discharged in 1953 with
rank of lieut. col., and continued thereafter to be a mbr.
of USAR. Father was murdered in 1954 shortly after having
been nom. for office of State Atty. Gen., having given a
pledge to clean up vice and crime conditions in Phenix City.
Was nom. as his replacement as the Dem. cand. for the office,
and was el. As Atty. Gen., with support of Gov. Persons,
carried on vigorous prosecution program against criminal element there. Was named Outstanding Man of the Year by USJCC.
Was leading cand. in Dem. party primary for Gov. in May,
1958. Won nom. in run-off against (later Gov.) George Wallace, and was el. Inaugurated at age 37, he became the
youngest Gov. Ala. has had. During admin., extensive bond
issues were authorized for constr. of roads and school bldgs.;
new laws were passed to regulate small loan bus.; and broadened pub. welfare programs adopted. A strong advocate of
racial segregation, he came into conflict with Fed. authorities on a number of fronts. Secured a ct. injunction, later
overthrown by U.S. Supreme Ct., against activities of
N.A.A.C.P. in Ala. Also was unsuccessful in challenges to
authority of Fed. govt. to investigate allegations of dis-
crimination against Negroes in admin. of voter registration
laws and in effort to punish protesters against maintenance
of segregation practices in pub. facilities. Unsuccessful
as cand. for Dem. nom. for Gov. in 1966. Methodist. Mbr.,
Amer. Legion; V.F.W.; W.O.W.; Eagles; Lions; various fraternal and professional legal orgs. m. in 1947 to Mary Jo
McGowin. One s.; one d.

WALLACE, GEORGE CORLEY, Jr. (1963-1967; 1971-1979).
b. Aug. 25, 1919 at Clio, Barbour Co., Ala. s. of George C.
and Mozella (Smith) W. Father was a farmer of modest means.
Attd. pub. schools in Clio and the Univ. of Ala., from which
he received a law degree in 1942. Began practice in Tusca-

loosa, but within a few months entered U.S. Air Force as a
pvt. Saw much action in Pac. theater during World War II.
Apptd. to staff of Ala. Atty. Gen. by Gov. Sparks in 1946.
Mbr. of Ala. House, 1947-1951. El. cir. ct. judge in 1952.
Unsuccessful as cand. for Dem. nom. for Gov. in 1958. In
1962 was again a cand. for the office and was nom. and el.
on a strong pro-segregation platform. During admin., unsuccessfully resisted efforts of U.S. authorities to desegregate schools, higher educl. institutions, and pub. facilities. Became identified nationally as advocate of resistance to Fed. jud. encroachment on state authority and as
defender of segregationist practices. Unsuccessful as cand.
for Dem. nom. for Pres. of U.S. in 1964. As Gov., advocated
govtl. involvement in matters of interest to laboring class,
farmers and small businessmen. Sponsored system of state
trade and vocational schools. Unsuccessful in effort during
first term to obtain a constl. amdt. permitting a Gov. to be
el. to a second successive term. Helped obtain the Dem.
party nom. for Gov. by his wife, Lurleen, in 1966, and she
was el. Gov. In 1968 was nom. by the Amer. Indep. (States
Rts.) party for Pres. of U.S. Failed to win election, but
received some 10,000,000 popular votes (13.6 per cent) and
46 electoral votes in the ensuing contest. Won Dem. nom.
for a second term as Gov. in 1970 and was el., his major opposition coming from a cand. supported by the natl. org. of
the Dem. party. Announced as a cand. for the Dem. party
nom. for Pres. of U.S. in 1972. While campaigning for delegate support in Laurel, Md. in June of that year was shot
and seriously wounded by a would-be assassin. Injury left
him partially paralyzed and confined to a wheelchair; but he
later resumed his official duties and the effort to secure
the Dem. presidential nom. Was a major contender against
the ultimate nominee, Sen. McGovern, when the conv. met. A
state constl. amdt. having been approved in 1968 making an
incumbent Gov. eligible for one successive term, he was
again successful in winning nom. and el. to the office of
Gov. in 1974. He thus became the first person to be el. in
Ala. as Gov. for three four-year terms, as well as for a
successive four-year term. Was again an announced cand. for
the Dem. nom. for Pres. of U.S. in 1976 but failed to
achieve much popular and delegate support. m. in 1943 to
Lurleen Burns, who became Gov. of Ala. (q.v.). One s.;
three d. After her death in 1968, m. to Cornelia (Ellis)
Snively, a niece of former Gov. James Folsom. Marriage
ended in divorce in 1978. Mbr., Masons (Shriner; O.E.S.);
Amer. Legion; V.F.W.; Moose; Elks; Civitan; professional
legal orgs. Methodist.

WALLACE, LURLEEN BURNS (1967-1968). b. Sept. 19, 1926
at Foster, Tuscaloosa Co., Ala. d. of Henry Morgan and
Janie E. (Burroughs) Burns. Educ. in pub. schools of Tuscaloosa Co. and Tuscaloosa Bus. Coll. At age 16 went to work
as clerk in a variety store, and later worked in office of
Boy Scouts org. In 1943 was m. to George C. Wallace, Jr.,
who became Gov. of Ala. in 1963 (q.v.). As the end of her
husband's first term as Gov. approached in 1966 she was put
forward as a cand. for the Dem. nom. to succeed him as Gov.,
since he was ineligible to succeed himself. Won nom. by
majority vote in first primary, defeating two former Govs.
(Patterson and Folsom) and others. Easily defeated her Rep.
opponent in the gen. election, who had support of strong
anti-Wallace Dem. faction. She thereby became the third
woman to have been el. Gov. in the U.S. As Gov., insisted
on not permitting consumption of alcoholic beverages in the
executive mansion, and maintained an "open door" policy of
easy accessibility to the public. Displayed initiative in
promoting programs for the ill and handicapped. Mbr., Women
for Constl. Govt.; O.E.S.; D.A.V.; Amer. Legion Aux.; Natl.
Rehabilitation Assoc. Methodist. Underwent surgery for
cancer in July, 1967. D. while still in office May 7, 1968
after having served some 16 months of term. One s.; three d.
Bur. in Greenwood Cem., Montgomery.

BREWER, ALBERT PRESTON (1968-1971). b. Oct. 26, 1928
at Bethel Springs, Tenn. s. of Daniel Austin and Clara Alberta (Yarber) B. Educ. at Bethel Springs and Decatur Co.
pub. schools. Attd. the Univ. of Ala., from which he received an A.B. degree in 1950 and a law degree in 1952.
Admitted to bar and established practice at Decatur, Ala.
Ch. of Decatur Planning Commn, 1956-1963, being named Out-
standing Young Man of the Year at Decatur in 1963 and by the
Ala. JCC. Mbr. of Ala. House, 1954-1966, serving as Speaker,
1963-1966. El. Lieut. Gov. in 1966 as Dem. Upon death of
Gov. Lurleen Wallace in 1968, succeeded to the office of
Gov. and completed her term. Sought Dem. party nom. for
Gov. in 1970, but was defeated in primary by former Gov.
George Wallace. Baptist. Mbr., Phi Alpha Delta; Delta
Sigma Phi; professional legal orgs. m. in 1950 to Martha
Helen Farmer, of Chattanooga, Tenn. Two d.

WALLACE GEORGE CORLEY, Jr. (1971-1979). See above,
1963-1967.

EGAN, WILLIAM ALLEN (1959-1966; 1970-1974). b. Oct. 8, 1914 at Valdez, Alas. Terr. Father, who was a gold miner, was killed in a snowslide when son was 10 years old. Attd. Valdez schools. Worked in a cannery and as a truck driver. Acquired interest in a gen. store at Valdez. Mbr. of Valdez city council. El. to Alas. Terr. legislature in 1941, where he immediately became an active supporter of Alas. statehood. During World War II served in U.S. Air Force. Again el. to Alas. Terr. legislature in 1947. As Speaker of the House, 1951-1955, continued to be a leader in statehood movement. Became presiding officer of conv. called to draft a const. for the proposed State of Alas. in 1956. After popular approval of the draft const. in April, 1956, was chosen as one of two "U.S. Senators" on a provisional basis in that year. Went to Washington, D.C., where he engaged in lobbying for Alas. statehood bill until its enactment in 1958. Nom. and el. first Gov. of Alas. as a Dem. in 1958. Took oath of office on Jan. 3, 1959 when statehood became effective, but was unable to assume full powers of office for several months because of illness and resulting surgery. During his absence, Hugh J. Wade, Sect. of State, acted as Gov. Reel. in 1962. Defeated in gen. election as Dem. nominee for Gov. in 1966, but was nom. and el. for a third term in 1970. Defeated again for Gov. in 1974. He was thus the Dem. nominee for the office in each of the first five gubernatorial elections in Alas. During admin., backed measures to promote Alas. indus. Initiated action in 1962 to protect fisheries in off-shore waters against encroachment by Japanese. Vice ch. in 1961 and ch. in 1962 of Western Govs.' Conf. Roman Catholic. Mbr., Pioneers of Alas.; Eagles; V.F.W.; Amer. Legion; Moose; Elks. m. to Neva McKittrick, of Wilson, Kans. Two children.

HICKEL, WALTER JOSEPH (1966-1969). b. Aug. 18, 1919 in Ellinwood, Kans. s. of Robert A. and Anna (Zecha) H. Father, who was a tenant farmer, was of German descent. Attd. pub. schools in Claflin, Kans. Left home at age 19 and went to Calif., where he worked as a carpenter. Desired to go to Australia, but because of delay in obtaining passport decided to go to Alas. instead. Arrived there penniless. Worked at various jobs, including restaurant employee, bartender, and railroad and constr. worker. Went into bus. for himself as a builder and developer at Anchorage. Rep. natl. committeeman for Alas., 1954-1964. Nom. and el. Gov. as Rep. in 1966, defeating incumbent Gov. Egan. During admin., advocated extensive reorg. of state govt.; measures to develop natural resources; opening up Northern Alas. for mining and oil exploration; improvements in transp. system. Co-ch. of Western States regional org. for Nixon for Pres.

of U.S., 1968. Apptd. Sect. of the Interior by Pres. Nixon
in 1969. Resigned as Gov. in Jan., 1969 to assume that post
after a controversy in the Senate over his confirmation because of his views on permitting utilization of natural resources by pvt. enterprise. Resigned Cabinet post in Nov.,
1970 because of differences with Pres. Nixon over conservation measures to be taken in connection with oil resource
devel. Defeated for Rep. nom. for Gov. in 1974 primary by
Jay Hammond in an extremely close contest. Lost again to
Hammond in the 1978 Rep. gubernatorial primary in which the
major issue was the policy to be pursued in opening up U.S.
govt.-owned lands to pvt. devel. Sought unsuccessfully
through cts. to have the primary election voided and another
one held. Hammond had won the nom. by less that 100 votes
in the original primary. Defeated for Rep. nom. for Gov.
again by Hammond in 1978. Continued in bus. operations
thereafter. Roman Catholic. Mbr., Elks; various clubs.
m. in 1941 to Janice Cannon. One s. After her death in
1943, m. to Ermalee Strutz. Five s.

MILLER, KEITH (1969-1970). b. Mar. 1, 1925 in Seattle,
Wash. s. of Hopkins Keith and Margaret (Harvey) M. Attd.
pub. schools in Seattle and the Univ. of Wash., from which
he was grad. in 1952 with a degree in bus. admin. Served in
U.S. Air Force, 1943-1945. From 1949 to 1953 was employed
by the Olympia Holly Farms in Wash. Set up and worked in a
bill collecting service, 1954-1957 at Seattle. In 1959
moved to Alas., where he homesteaded property at Talkeetna
while engaged in life ins. bus. El. to Alas. legislature in
1962, serving until 1965. Delegate to Rep. natl. conv. in
1964. El. Sect. of State as a Rep. in 1966 on ticket with
Gov. Hickel. After Hickel's resignation in 1969, became
Gov. for remainder of Hickel's term. Defeated as Rep. nominee for election to a full term as Gov. in 1970 by former
Gov. Egan. Was also defeated in attempt to win Rep. nom.
for Gov., 1974. m. to Diana Mary Doyle, a resident of Wash.,
in 1953. Mbr., Amer. Legion; Lions; Elks; Moose.

EGAN, WILLIAM ALLEN (1970-1974). See above, 1959-1966.

HAMMOND, JAY STERNER (1975----). b. July 21, 1922 in
Troy, N.Y. s. of Morris S. and Edna Brown (Sterner) H.
Attd. local pub. schools and Pa. State Univ. from 1940-1942.
Left coll. to enlist in U.S. Marine Corps. Served as
fighter pilot during World War II, holding rank of capt. at
time of discharge. Moved to Alas. in 1946 and entered the
Univ. of Alas., from which he received a degree in biologi-
cal sci. in 1948. Later studied at Alas. Methodist Univ.,
from which he received a law degree in 1975. Worked as a

bush pilot and agent for U.S. Fish and Wild Life Service, 1949-1956. Homesteaded land at Lake Clark, 1956-1974, and established a hunting lodge there. Built own home at Naknek, Alas. Worked as a commercial fisherman, guide and air taxi operator. El. in 1960 to Alas. House as an Indep., continuing to serve therein until 1966. Affiliated with Rep. party. El. to Alas. Senate in 1967, serving until 1972. Pres. of Alas. Senate, 1971-1972. Did not seek reel. to Senate, but was nom. and el. Gov. as Rep. in 1974. Won Rep. nom. in a very close contest with former Gov. Hickel, with whom he had differences in views on natural resources devel., and defeated former Gov. Egan in the gen. election by a margin of less than 300 votes following a recount. Won nom. again from former Gov. Hickel in an extremely close contest, and was reel. in 1978. m. to Bella W. Gardiner. Two children.

HUNT, GEORGE WYLIE PAUL (1912-1917; 1917-1919; 1923-1929; 1931-1933). b. Nov. 1, 1859 at Huntsville, Mo. s. of George Washington and Sarah Elizabeth (Yates) H. Grandfather was a native of N.C. who had emigrated to Mo. and had settled in Randolph Co. Educ. at pub. and pvt. schools. As a young man went to Colo. Terr. as a prospector. Settled in Gila Co., Ariz. Terr., where he engaged in a variety of jobs, including work as a waiter, ranch hand and prospector. Acquired interest in merc. firm in Globe. Became its pres. in 1900 and also became pres. of Old Dominion Bank there. Treas. of Gila Co., 1894-1898. Mbr. of Ariz. Terr. legislature, 1893-1894 and of Terr. Senate, 1897-1898 and 1905-1909. Served as pres. of Senate during latter period. Delegate to Dem. natl. conv. in 1900. Very active supporter of statehood for Ariz. Mbr. and pres. of Ariz. constl. conv. of 1910. Nom. and el. first Gov. of Ariz. as Dem. in 1911. Re-el. in 1914, and was Dem. nominee for succeeding term in 1916. Opponent was declared el. in a close contest and assumed the office at the beginning of the term in 1917. H. challenged the announced result of the election in Ariz. cts. and was eventually declared to have won the 1916 election. Assumed the office late in 1917 and served the last half of the term. In 1920-1921 served as U.S. Minister to Siam. Nom. and el. Gov. again for three terms, 1923-1929. Defeated as Dem. nominee for Gov. in 1928. Nom. and el. for seventh term in 1930, but failed in effort to win re-nom. in 1932. Was the Dem. nominee for Gov. in eight of first ten elections in Ariz. As Gov., was an advocate of numerous progressive causes, including prison reform; regulatory labor legislation; the direct initiative, referendum and recall. Unsuccessful opponent of capital punishment, becoming pres. of Anti-Capital Punishment Soc. of Amer. in 1914. Generous in use of exec. clemency power. Favored legislation against alien land-holding. Opposed Colo. River Interstate Compact on grounds it failed to protect adequately the interests of Ariz. citizens. m. in 1904 to Helen Duett Ellison, of Ellison, Ariz. One d. Mbr., S.A.R.; Masons; I.O.O.F. D. at Phoenix, Ariz. Dec. 24, 1934.

CAMPBELL, THOMAS EDWARD (1917; 1919-1923). b. Jan. 18, 1878 at Prescott, Ariz. Terr. s. of Daniel and Eliza (O'Flynn) C. Father, a native of Pa., was in U.S. Army service, and had been sent to Ariz. in 1867 with the Wheeler expedition, and had settled there. Attd. Prescott schools and St. Mary's Coll., in Oakland, Calif. Mbr. of Ariz. Terr. legislature in 1900. Apptd. postmaster at Jerome in 1902. Became ch. of Yavapai Co. Rep. commt. in 1906. El. assessor of Yavapai Co. in 1907, serving in that office until 1915. Defeated as Rep. nominee for U.S. House in 1912. El. State

Tax Commnr. in 1914. As Rep. nominee for Gov. in 1916 was
declared el. by the canvassing bd. and took over the office
in Jan., 1917. The election result as announced was challenged in the Ariz. cts. by his opponent, former Gov. Hunt,
and the latter was eventually declared the winner. Relinquished the office of Gov. in Dec., 1917. Nom. and el. Gov.
as Rep. in 1918 and again in 1920. Defeated as Rep. nominee
for the succeeding term in 1922. During admin., child welfare and soldier's land settlement commns. were established;
also agencies for licensing nurses, engineers, architects
and land surveyors. State budgeting system was established.
Became pres. of League of Southwest while Gov., and was also
ch. of Commt. of Western Govs. on Colo. River devel. projects. After leaving office was ch. of a U.S. fact-finding
commn. on reclamation projects in 1925. Mbr. of Rep. natl.
commt.; counsel for Natl. Highways Assoc.; and U.S. Commnr.
Gen., 1927-1930, for the Intl. Exposition at Seville, Spain.
Ch. of U.S. Civil Service Commn., 1930-1933. Defeated as
Rep. nominee for Gov. in 1936. Mbr., various clubs. Roman
Catholic. m. to Eleanor Gayle Allen, of Jerome, Ariz. in
1900. Two s. D. March 1, 1944 at Phoenix, Ariz.

HUNT, GEORGE WYLIE PAUL (1917-1919). See above, 1912-
1917.

CAMPBELL, THOMAS EDWARD (1919-1923). See above, 1917.

HUNT, GEORGE WYLIE PAUL (1923-1929). See above, 1912-
1917.

PHILLIPS, JOHN C. (1929-1931). b. Nov. 13, 1870 near
Vermont, Ill. s. of Wm. Henry and Elizabeth (Wood) P. Fa-
ther, who was of Welsh ancestry, had served with the Union
Army in the Civil War. Attd. Hedding Coll., at Abingdon,
Ill., 1889-1893. Studied law in law office and with Sprague
Correspondence School. Admitted to bar in 1896 and set up
practice in Vermont, Ill. In 1898 moved to Phoenix, Ariz.
Terr., where he worked as a common laborer for a time before
establishing a law practice. Served as probate judge, 1903-
1912 and as superior ct. judge, 1912-1916, in Maricopa Co.
Mbr. of Ariz. House, 1917-1922 and of Ariz Senate, 1923-1924.
Nom. and el. Gov. as Rep. in 1928. As Gov., opposed constr.
of Boulder Dam on terms prescribed by Swing-Johnson Act of
1928 on grounds that Ariz. interests in waters of the Colo.
River were inadequately protected. Continued to oppose
constr. of the dam under the Colo. River Interstate Compact
after the U.S. Supreme Ct. had upheld its validity. Advocate of strict economy in govt., and came to be known as
"Honest John." Took steps to protect fossil remains on

Indian reservation lands. Defeated for reel. in 1930 by former Gov. Hunt, whom he had defeated in 1928. Engaged in law practice in Phoenix with son as partner. m. in 1895 to Minnie Rexroat, of McComb, Ill. One s.; two d. Methodist. D. June 25, 1943 near Flagstaff while on a fishing outing.

HUNT, GEORGE WYLIE PAUL (1931-1933). See above, 1912-1917.

MOEUR, BENJAMIN BAKER (1933-1937). b. Dec. 22, 1869 at Decherd, Tex. s. of John Baptist and Esther Kelly (Knight) M. Was of French ancestry on mother's side. Father was a physician and surgeon who had served as such with the Confed. Army during Civil War. Attd. schools in Hondo, Tex. Studied med. at Indus. Univ. of Ark., graduating as an M.D. in 1896. Later did post-grad. work at Rush Med. Coll., in Chicago. Established practice in 1896 in Tempe, Ariz. Terr. Practice involved much travel by horse and buggy over wide area. Generous in providing services without charge to widows, ministers, families of former soldiers, etc. Physician at Ariz. State Coll. at Tempe, and for 12 years served as sect. of its Bd. of Trustees. Mbr. of Ariz. constl. conv. in 1910. Nom. and el. Gov. as Dem. in 1932 and was reel. in 1934. Admin. concerned particularly with relieving distress arising from the depression of the 1930s. Was active in seeking U.S. funds to help unemployed and needy. Reduced property taxes and secured adoption of alternative sources of revenue. Aggressive in supporting claims of Ariz. to water and power rights in constr. of Parker Dam. Used Natl. Guard troops to protect State's interests by stopping constr. work for a time. m. in 1896 to Honor Glint Anderson. Two s.; two d. Mbr., Masons; K.P.; I.O.O.F.; W.O.W.; Spanish-Amer. Alliance; professional med. orgs. D. at Tempe March 16, 1937 shortly after end of tenure as Gov.

STANFORD, RAWGHLIE CLEMENT (1937-1939). b. Aug. 2, 1879 at Buffalo Gap, Tex. s. of Monroe Agee and Margaret (Gamble) S. Attd. schools in Buffalo Gap and Tempe, Ariz., Normal for two years. From 1899 to 1901 served with U.S. Army in the Philippines. Following discharge, having attained the rank of sgt., became a rancher in Ariz. Began study of law in law office in 1904. Admitted to bar in 1907 and established practice in Phoenix. El. judge of superior ct. in Maricopa Co. in 1915 and served for seven years. Mbr. of school bd. for Union H.S., 1920-1936. Ch. of Dem. state commt., 1928-1929. Nom. and el. Gov. as Dem. in 1936, defeating former Gov. Campbell in gen. election. Was not a cand. for second term. Ch. of Ariz. State Council of Defense, 1941-1942. Became mbr. of Ariz. Supreme Ct. in 1942,

serving as its Chief Justice, 1944-1953. Presbyterian.
Mbr., Masons; I.O.O.F.; Elks; U.S.W.V. m. Ruth Butler in
1906. Two s.; five d., two of whom died in infancy. D. at
Phoenix Dec. 15, 1963.

JONES, ROBERT TAYLOR (1939-1941). b. Feb. 8, 1884 at
Rutledge, Tenn. s. of Samuel and Sarah (Legg) J. After obtaining training in field of civil engr., moved to Ariz.
Terr., where he engaged in road constr. and other types of
engr. work. Also became proprietor of a drug store enterprise at Phoenix. Engaged in political activity, and was
el. to the Ariz. Senate. Nom. and el. Gov. as Dem. in 1938,
serving for only one term. m. to Elon Armstrong. One s.;
one d. Mbr., Masons; Elks. D. at Phoenix June 11, 1958.

OSBORN, SIDNEY PRESTON (1941-1948). b. May 17, 1884 in
Phoenix, Ariz. Terr. s. of Neri Ficklin and Marilla (Murray)
O. Father was a pub. accountant. Attd. Phoenix pub.
schools, graduating from high school as an honor student.
During youth served as page in Ariz. Terr. legislature. Be-
came sect. to Col. Wilson. Delegate to Cong., 1903-1905.
Worked as a reporter, later as circulation mgr., of Arizona
Democrat beginning in 1905. Mbr. of Ariz. constl. conv. in
1910, being the youngest mbr. of that body. Ariz. Sect. of
State in 1913-1919. Acquired a cotton ranch at Higley, Ariz.
In 1925 became owner of a weekly newspaper in Phoenix, Dun-
bar's Weekly, and served as its ed. and publ. until 1940.
Ch. of Dem. state commt., 1932. Apptd. U.S. Collector of
Internal Revenue for Ariz. dist. in 1933. Nom. and el. Gov.
as Dem. in 1940 and was reel. for three succeeding terms.
During admin., completed agreement with U.S. Dept. of the
Interior concerning water and power rights of Ariz. in connection with Colo. River projects. Launched aggressive campaign to combat crime in Phoenix. Advocate of various progressive measures, including aid for Jewish survivors of
World War II. Methodist. m. in 1912 to Marjorie Grant, who
died in 1918. One d. m. in 1925 to Gladys Smiley. During
fourth term became partially disabled from a muscular disorder that left him unable to walk or speak, but he continued nevertheless to perform functions of his office daily
until his death. D. May 25, 1948 while still in office.

GARVEY, DAN(IEL) E. (1948-1951). b. June 19, 1886 at
Vicksburg, Miss. s. of Andrew F. and Johanne (Horrigan) G.
Attd. local schools and St. Aloysius Coll., in Vicksburg,
1901-1903. Became an accountant for Ill. Cent. R.R. in 1903.
In 1909 removed to Ariz. Terr., where he continued to work
as an accountant for various railroad companies at Tucson,
Globe, Phoenix, and Guadalajara, Mexico. Mbr. of Tucson

city council, 1930. Tucson city treas., 1938, and treas. of
Pima Co., 1935. Became Asst. Sect. of State of Ariz. in
1939. El. Sect. of State in 1942 as a Dem. and was reel. for
three succeeding terms. Was serving in that office when Gov.
Osborn died in 1948, and he moved to the office of Gov. by
succession. Completed Osborn's term, and was nom. and el.
for a regular term in 1948. Defeated in Dem. primary for re-
nom. for the office of Gov. in 1950, losing to Mrs. Anna
Frohmiller, who had served as Ariz. State Aud. for some 24
years. Returned to bus. activities in Tucson. Mbr., W.O.W.;
K.C. Roman Catholic. m. in 1912 to Thirza Jeannette Vail.
One s.; one d. D. Feb. 5, 1974 at age 87.

PYLE, (J.) HOWARD (1951-1955). b. Mar. 25, 1906 at
Sheridan, Wyo. s. of the Rev. Thomas Miller and Marie (Anderson) P. As a child removed with the family to Waco, Tex.,
where his father studied for the ministry at Baylor Univ.
As a youth, engaged in a variety of jobs and aspired to become a professional singer and entertainer. Established
residence in Tempe, Ariz., where he worked as a real estate
salesman and in advertising and promotional activities. Became program dir. at Radio Station KTAR. Co-founder and
producer of Grand Canyon Easter Sunrise Service. Radio reporter at 1945 San Francisco World Security Conf. War correspondent for Pac. area for Ariz. Broadcasting Co., NBC.
Was solicited to run as Rep. cand. for Gov. in 1950. Did so
and won, and was reel. in 1952. Ch. of Western Govs.' Conf.
At end of second term was apptd. by Pres. Eisenhower to his
exec. staff in a pub. relations capacity. Mbr. and ch. of
President's Commt. on Highway Safety, 1959-1960. Subsequently was active in various promotional and fund-raising
enterprises for charitable orgs. Baptist. Trustee, Redlands Univ. Mbr., Rotary. Hon. degrees from Redlands Univ.;
Ariz. State Univ.; Chapman Coll.; Bradley Univ.; and Lebanon
Coll. m. in 1930 to Lucile Hanna. Two d.

McFARLAND, ERNEST WILLIAM (1955-1959). b. Oct. 9, 1894
at Earlsboro, Okla. Terr. s. of Wm. Thomas and Kesiah
(Smith) McF. Attd. pub. schools at Earlsboro and Seminole,
Okla. and East Cent. State Teachers Coll., at Ada; and the
Univ. of Okla., from which he received an A.B. degree in
1917. Seaman in U.S. Navy during World War I. After the
war, worked briefly for a bank in Phoenix, Ariz., then entered Stanford Univ., from which he received a law degree in
1921. Admitted to bar in 1920 and began practice at Casa
Grande, Ariz. Asst. Atty. Gen. of Ariz., 1923-1924. Moved
to Florence, Ariz. in 1925. Co. atty., Pinal Co., 1925-1930.
Judge of superior ct., Pinal Co., 1936-1941. El. as Dem. to
U.S. Senate in 1940 and continued to serve therein until

defeated for reel. in 1952 by Barry Goldwater. Was Senate
majority party (Dem.) leader during last two years in Senate.
Nom. and el. Gov. as Dem. in 1954 and was reel. in 1956.
Unsuccessful as Dem. nominee for U.S. Senate seat in 1958,
losing again to Barry Goldwater. Ch. of Ariz. delegation to
Dem. natl. conv. in 1964. Mbr., Ariz. Supreme Ct., 1965-
1971, serving as Chief Justice in 1968. Mbr., Natl. Commn.
on Causes and Prevention of Violence, 1968-1969. Pres. of
Ariz. TV Co., 1955; dir., Fed. Home Loan Bank of San Francisco, 1963. Methodist. Mbr., Amer. Legion; Masons
(Shriner); Jesters; K.P.; Elks; I.O.O.F.; professional legal
orgs. m. to Eva Eveland. One d.

FANNIN, PAUL JONES (1959-1965). b. Jan. 29, 1907 at
Ashland, Ky. s. of Thomas Newton and Katherine (Davis) F.
Father was a farmer who moved to Ariz. Terr. in 1907. Attd.
the Univ. of Ariz. and Stanford Univ., from which he was
grad. in 1930. Went into bus. at Phoenix. Became vice pres.
of a gas and equipment firm at Phoenix in 1932 and pres. in
1956. Became head also of another service and supply firm
in Safford, Ariz. in 1945. Pres. of Maricopa Co. Better Bus.
Bureau, 1948-1949. Pres., Phoenix CC. Nom. and el. Gov. as
Rep. in 1958 and was reel. in 1960 and 1962. During admin.,
was ch. of Western Govs.' Conf.; mbr. of the exec. commt. of
the Council of State Govts.; mbr. of Natl. Civil Defense Advisory Council and of the Pub. Land Review Commt. Nom. and
el. to U.S. Senate in 1964 and was reel. in 1970. Mbr.,
U.S.-Mexican Interparliamentary Conf. Delegate to I.L.O.,
1966. Was not a cand. for reel. to the Senate in 1976.
Methodist. Mbr., Elks; Moose; Rotary; Kappa Sigma; Natl.
Council of Boy Scouts of Amer. m. in 1934 to Elma Addington.
Three s.; one d.

GODDARD, SAM(UEL) PEARSON, Jr. (1965-1967). b. Aug. 8,
1919 at Clayton, Mo. s. of Samuel Pearson and Florence
Hilton (Denham) G. Attd. Clayton pub. schools and Harvard
Univ., from which he was grad. with an A.B. degree in 1941.
Served in U.S. Air Force, 1941-1946, holding rank of major
at the end of World War II. Continued to serve in USAFR,
with rank of col. Entered Univ. of Ariz. and received a law
degree in 1949. Admitted to bar and began practice in Tuc-
son. Very active in United Fund and related community ac-
tivities. Ch. of Tucson Youth Study Commn. Pres. of Tucson
United Fund, 1960-1962, and pres., Western Conf. of United
Funds, 1961-1963. Mbr., White House Conf. on Children and
Youth; Tucson Hosp. Coordinating Commt., 1964; organizer of
Tucson Civic Chorus; mbr., Tucson Festival Soc. and of
Tucson Watercolor Guild. Vice pres., United Community Funds
and Councils of Amer. Mbr., bd. of dir. of Ariz. Acad.,

1963-1964. Ch., Ariz. Dem. state commt., 1960-1962. Defeated as Dem. nominee for Gov. in 1962; but was nom. again
and el. to that office in 1964. Dem. nominee again in 1966
and 1968, but was defeated both times in gen. election.
Mbr., V.F.W.; Air Force Assoc.; R.O.A.; Moose; Amer. Legion;
Phi Alpha Theta; Rotary; pres., Harvard So. Ariz. Club.,
1957-1958. m. in 1944 to Julia Hatch. Three s.

WILLIAMS, JOHN RICHARD ("JACK") (1967-1975). b. Oct.
29, 1909 at Los Angeles, Calif. s. of James Maurice and
Laura (La Cossit) W. Attd. Phoenix Jr. Coll., after which
he went into bus. there. Became owner of Radio Station KOY,
and pres., KOY Investment Co. Vice pres., Phoenix CC in
1946. Pres., Phoenix Housing Authority, 1944-1947. Mbr. of
city council in Phoenix, 1953-1954 and mayor, 1956-1960.
Nom. and el. Gov. as Rep. in 1966. Reel. in 1968 and 1970,
becoming by the latter election the first person to be
chosen to a four-year term to that office. Did not seek
reel. in 1974. Episcopalian. m. in 1942 to Vera May.
Two s.; one d.

CASTRO, RAUL HECTOR (1975-1977). b. June 12, 1916 at
Cananea, Sonora, Mexico. s. of Francisco D. and Rosario
(Acosta) C. Emigrated to U.S. when 10 years old. Attd.
Ariz. State Univ., from which he was grad. in 1939. Mbr.,
Ariz. Natl. Guard, 1935-1939. Became U.S. citizen in 1939.
Served as clerk for U.S. Dept. of State in Mexico, 1941-
1946. Instructor in Spanish at the Univ. of Ariz., 1946-
1949 while also studying law. Received law degree from the
Univ. of Ariz. in 1949. Engaged in law practice at Tucson,
1949-1951. Deputy co. atty. of Pima Co., 1951-1954. Co.
atty., 1954-1958. Judge of superior ct., 1958-1964 and
juvenile ct. judge, 1961-1964. Apptd. U.S. Ambassador to
El Salvador by Pres. Johnson in 1964, and served there until
1968. U.S. Ambassador to Bolivia, 1968-1969. Engaged in
intl. law practice at Tucson, 1969-1974. Dem. nominee for
Gov. in 1970, but was defeated in gen. election. Nom. again
in 1974 and was el. Resigned office of Gov. in Oct., 1977
to become U.S. Ambassador to Argentina. Operator of Castro
Pony Farm, 1954-1964. Pres., Pima Co. Tuberculosis and
Health Assoc. and of Tucson Youth Bd. Mbr., Ariz. Horse-
men's Assoc.; bd. of dir. of Tucson Red Cross chapter;
N.C.C.J.; Amer. Foreign Service Assoc.; Amer. Judicature
Soc. and other professional legal orgs. Decorations or
awards for outstanding pub. service from the govt. of El
Salvador, D.A.R., Univ. of Ariz. Outstanding Naturalized
Citizen Award from Pima Co. Bar Assoc. Roman Catholic.
Hon. degrees from No. Ariz. Univ. and Ariz. State Univ. m.
in 1954 to Patricia M. Norris. Two d.

CONWAY, JAMES SEVIER (1836-1840). b. Dec. 9, 1798 near
Greenville, Tenn. s. of Thomas and Ann (Rector) C. Father,
who was a native of Va., traced ancestral line back to time
of Edward I of England to occupants of Castle Conway, in
Wales. Mother was related to the Sevier family, which had
an important role in the early history of the State of Tenn.
A younger brother, Elias N., was later a Gov. of Ark. (q.v.);
and an older brother, Henry, was the Ark. Terr. Delegate to
Cong. from 1823-1827. The Conways, along with a cousin, Ambrose H. Sevier, Ark. Terr. Delegate to Cong. from 1827-1836
and U.S. Sen. from 1836 to 1848, were members of a group of
relatives (Conways, Rectors, Seviers, Harrisons and Johnsons)
known as "The Family," who dominated Ark. Dem. party politics
during the early statehood period. James C. was educ. in
Tenn. Became a surveyor and worked with his brother Henry
in the area of Mo. Terr. which, in 1819, became Ark. Terr.
With brother, helped to lay out the town site of Little Rock.
Apptd. surveyor gen. of Ark. Terr. in 1823, becoming responsible for survey of Ark.'s western boundary between the Ark.
and Red Rivers. El. as first Gov. of the State of Ark. in
1836. Admin. characterized by financial difficulties arising from land speculations and bank failures. At end of
admin. retired to cotton plantation on Red River. m. to a
Miss Bradley, of Tenn. Several children. D. March 3, 1855
at Walnut Hills, Lafayette Co., Ark.

YELL, ARCHIBALD (1840-1844). Facts regarding time and
place of birth are uncertain. b. in N.C.(?) or Jefferson
Co. Tenn.(?) in 1797(?) or Aug., 1799(?). Family background
obscure. Spent early youth near Shelbyville, Bedford Co.,
Tenn. Enlisted in volunteer company for Creek War in 1811.
Also participated in War of 1812, and fought at the Battle
of New Orleans in a Tenn. unit under Gen. Andrew Jackson.
Later served as lieut. under Jackson in the Seminole War in
Florida. Returned to Fayetteville, Tenn. Studied law, admitted to Tenn. bar, and practiced law there. Mbr. of Tenn.
legislature in 1827. Apptd. receiver of U.S. moneys in Ark.
Terr. in 1831. Returned to Tenn. after a short time. Offered post of Terr. Gov. of Florida by Pres. Jackson but declined, preferring a position as a terr. ct. judge in Ark.,
which was also offered to him by Jackson. Moved to Fayetteville, Ark. El. to U.S. House as a Van Buren Dem. in 1836
after admission of Ark. to statehood, and was continued in
that office for a regular term, serving until 1839. Nom.
and el. Gov. of Ark. as a Dem. in 1840. Resigned that office in April, 1844, when he was again el. to the U.S. House.
Resigned House seat on July 1, 1846 to org. a regiment of
volunteers, of which he became col., to participate in the
War with Mexico. Killed in action at the Battle of Buena

Vista, Feb. 22, 1847. Body later interred at Fayetteville,
Ark. m. in 1821 to Mary Scott, of Bedford Co., Tenn., who
died one year later after giving birth to twin daughters.
m. in 1827 to Ann Jordan Moore, of Danville, Tenn. Three d.;
one s. She died in 1835. m. in 1836 to Mary Ficklin, a
widow, of Lawrence Co., Ark., who died in 1838. Was a close
personal friend of James K. Polk, Gov. of Tenn. and later
Pres. of U.S. (q.v.). Mbr., Masons.

ADAMS, SAMUEL (1844). b. June 5, 1805 in Halifax Co.,
N.C. Ancestors had formerly been residents of Md. and Va.
Moved with parents in 1810 to Humphreys Co., Tenn. Grew up
under rugged pioneer conditions, receiving rudimentary educ.
In 1835 moved to Western Ark. to area that later became
Johnson Co. El. to Ark. Senate in 1840 and served two terms,
becoming Pres. of Senate in second term. Succeeded to office of Gov. in April, 1844 when Gov. Yell resigned, and
completed Yell's term. In 1846 was el. State Treas. of Ark.
m. to Rebecca May, of Tenn., who died in 1840 leaving six
young children to his care. D. Feb. 27, 1850 at Little Rock.

DREW, THOMAS STEVENSON (1844-1849). b. Aug. 25, 1802
in Wilson Co., Tenn. s. of Newton D., a native of Va., who
had moved to Tenn. to engage in farming. Educ. in country
schools. In 1818 settled in Ark., where he became an itinerant merchant and school teacher for several years. Served
as clerk of Clark Co., 1823-1825. Later moved to Lawrence
Co. m. to a d. of a prosperous pioneer planter, thus acquiring a plantation with slaves. Mbr. of Ark. constl.
conv. of 1836. In 1844 was nom. and el. Gov. as Dem. after
Elias N. Conway (q.v.) had refused to run for the office.
Reel. in 1848; but after serving part of second term resigned in Jan., 1849, citing inadequate salary as reason.
Admin. beset with financial difficulties arising from policies pursued in connection with Ark. Real Estate Bank affairs. After resignation went to Calif., where he engaged
unsuccessfully in gold mining ventures. Moved to Lipan,
Hood Co., Tex., where he died and was bur. in 1879.

BYRD, RICHARD (1849). b. in 1805 in an area of Miss.
Terr. that later became a part of the State of Ala. As a
young man moved to Ark., where he engaged in planting near
Pine Bluff, in Jefferson Co. El. to Ark. Senate, and became Pres of that body. Unsuccessful cand. for the office
of Gov. in 1844, running as an Indep. As Pres. of Senate
succeeded to the office of Gov. upon resignation of Gov.
Drew in Jan., 1849. Acted as Gov. for some three months
pending the holding of a spec. el. to choose a successor for
the remainder of Drew's term. D. June 1, 1854.

ROANE, JOHN SELDEN (1849-1852). b. Jan. 8, 1817 in
Wilson Co., Tenn. Father was a planter in comfortable circumstances. Attd. Cumberland Coll., in Princeton, Ky.
Studied law and was admitted to bar. In 1837 moved to Pine
Bluff, Ark., where he established law practice. El. pros.
atty. for his jud. dist. in 1840 and to the Ark. House in
1842. In 1843 moved to Van Buren, in Western Ark. El. to
Ark. House again from Crawford Co. in 1844, and became
Speaker. During Mexican War served as lieut. col. in regiment commanded by former Gov. Yell, and became col. upon
latter's death at the Battle of Buena Vista. Returned to
law practice at Pine Bluff. El. Gov. as Dem. by very narrow
margin in spec. el. in April, 1849 to complete Gov. Drew's
term. Upon outbreak of Civil War assisted in raising troops
for South and entered Confed. Army, with rank of brig. gen.
Saw active service in Southwestern theater of war. Retired
to home at Pine Bluff after war ended. m. in 1855 to Mary
K. Smith, daughter of Gen. Nat Smith, of Tulip, Ark. D. at
Pine Bluff, April 17, 1867. Bur. in Oakland Cem., Little
Rock.

CONWAY, ELIAS NEWTON (1852-1860). b. May 17, 1812 at
family homestead near Greeneville, Greene Co., Tenn. s. of
Thomas and Ann (Rector) C. Was a younger brother of James
Sevier C., first Gov. of Ark. (q.v.). Moved with parents to
Boone Co., Mo. at age of six, where he received a liberal
educ. In 1833 moved to Ark. Terr., where he joined his two
older brothers, James and Henry, who had become prominent in
the bus. and politics of Ark. Terr. Engaged in surveying in
northwestern area of Ark. Apptd. first Aud. Gen. of Ark.
when state govt. was set up in 1836, and served in that capacity for 14 years. While in that office, advanced idea of
a homestead system as means of disposing of pub. lands, a
system that was eventually adopted by U.S. govt. Nom. for
Gov. of Ark. by Dem. state conv. in 1844, but declined. At
his suggestion Thomas Drew (q.v.) was nom. instead. Nom.
and el. Gov. as Dem. in 1852 and again in 1856. As Gov.,
opposed influence of State Real Estate Bank; secured establishment of a chancery ct.; encouragement given to internal
improvements and railroad constr.; and a geological survey
of State was initiated. Left State in sound financial condition. After tenure as Gov. engaged in mgmt. of his large
land holdings. Never married. D. at Little Rock Feb. 28,
1892. Bur. at Mt. Holly Cem. there.

RECTOR, HENRY MASSEY (1860-1862). b. May 1, 1816 at
Fountain's Ferry, near Louisville, Ky. s. of Elias and
Fanny B. (Thruston) R., being the only one of seven children
to survive to adulthood. Father, who was related to the

Conway family that was prominent in early Ark. politics, had
earlier resided in St. Louis, Mo., where he had become prominent in city affairs and had acquired real estate holdings
in Ark. Terr. Educ. mostly by his mother, attending school
in Louisville, for only one year. At age 19 moved to Ark.
to take over mgmt. of lands left him by father. Worked as
teller for State Real Estate Bank and later engaged in planting. Served as U.S. marshal by apptmt. from Pres. Tyler in
1842-1843. Mbr. of Ark. Senate, 1848-1852. Later served as
U.S. surveyor gen. of Ark. In 1854 began law practice in
Little Rock, having in the meantime studied law in a law office. In 1855 was el. to the Ark. House, and in 1859 to a
seat on the Ark. Supreme Ct. Unsuccessfully sought Dem.
nom. for Gov. in 1860. He thereupon broke with "The Family"
faction and successfully opposed its regular Dem. party
nominee, Richard H. Johnson, as an Indep. Dem. and was el.
that year in a close and bitter el. After outbreak of Civil
War, refused to respond to Pres. Lincoln's call for volunteers to suppress rebellion. Seized U.S. arsenals in Little
Rock and Ft. Smith. After the state conv. adopted an ordinance of secession, cooperated with the secessionist movement. In the revision of the state const. effected by a
state conv. after Ark. became a member of the C.S.A., no
provision was made for continuance in office of current
state officials. Accordingly, a spec. el. was held in Oct.,
1862, at which R. was defeated for continuance in office.
He resigned immediately after the el. results became known.
Served as a mbr. of the state conv. that drafted a revised
state const. in 1874. m. in 1838 to Jane Elizabeth Field,
who died in 1857. Four s.; three d. m. in 1860 to Ernestine Flora Linde. One d. D. Aug. 12, 1899 at Little Rock.

FLETCHER, THOMAS (1862). b. April 8, 1819 in Lawrence
(now Randolph) Co., Ark. Self-educ. Removed to Pulaski Co.,
Ark., where he engaged in planting. El. sheriff, acquiring
during his tenure the sobriquet of "Honest Tom" for his
honest and fearless discharge of the duties of his office.
El. to Ark. Senate, in which he was serving as its Pres. when
Gov. Rector resigned in Nov., 1862. Acted as Gov. briefly
pending installation of the new Gov. chosen in the spec.
Oct., 1862 el. Later served as U.S. marshal by apptmt.
from Pres. Cleveland. D. at Little Rock, Feb. 21, 1900.

FLANAGIN, HARRIS (1862-1865). b. Nov. 3, 1817 at
Roadstown, N.J. s. of James and Mary F. Family was of
Irish descent. Attd. pub. schools in Roadstown. As youth,
went to Ill., where he studied law in law office. Moved to
Greenville, Clark Co., Ark. in 1837, where he began practice
of law. In 1842 moved to Arkadelphia, and in that same year

was el. to Ark. legislature. On outbreak of Civil War entered Confed. Army as capt., later becoming col. of regiment
of mounted rifles. El. Gov. as Dem. in spec. el. in Oct.,
1862, defeating incumbent Gov. Rector, whose tenure had been
held by the Ark. Supreme Ct. to have been cut short by failure of the revised const. of 1861 to include a provision for
continuance in office of current personnel. Continued in
office under Confed. auspices in that part of State not under
Union control until end of Civil War. Resumed law practice
at Arkadelphia. Mbr. of state constl. conv. of 1874, in
which he was a prominent figure. m. in 1851 to Martha E.
Nash. Two s.; one d. D. Oct. 23, 1874 at Arkadelphia. Bur.
in Rose Hill Cem. there.

MURPHY, ISAAC (1864-1868). b. Oct. 16, 1802 near
Pittsburgh, Pa. s. of Hugh and Jane (Williams) M. Father
was a paper manufacturer, who moved to Montgomery Co., Tenn.
in 1819. Son received basic academic educ. and became a
school teacher. In 1834 he moved to Fayetteville, Ark., and
later to Huntsville, in Madison Co., where he continued in
school teaching. Also studied law, and was admitted to Ark.
bar in 1835. Engaged as civil engr. and in land survey work
in northwestern and eastern areas of Ark. Mbr. of Ark.
legislature, 1848-1849. In 1849 went to Calif. with the
McCulloch expedition, one of the first emigrant trains to go
west after discovery of gold in Calif. Engaged in gold mining ventures there, without much success. Returned to Ark.
in 1854 where he resumed school teaching in a pvt. school
for girls operated by him in collaboration with a d. Mbr.
of Ark. Senate, 1856-1860. Was a mbr. of the state conv.
called in 1861 to consider question of secession. Was the
only mbr. to cast vote against adoption of ordinance of
secession after the conv. finally took that step following
the outbreak of fighting in the Civil War. Joined Union
forces in Mo. in 1862, serving as staff officer with Gen.
Curtis. Took part in capture of Little Rock by Union forces
in 1863. Apptd. Provisional Gov. in Jan., 1864 by the pro-
Union conv. set up to revise the state const. El. Gov. for
a four-year term under Union auspices in a spec. el. conducted in March, 1864 in areas of State under Fed. control.
After term as Gov. expired, retired to law practice in Huntsville. m. in 1830 to Angelina A. Lockhart, of Tenn. Five
children. D. at Huntsville, Sept. 8, 1882. Bur. there.

CLAYTON, POWELL (1868-1871). b. Aug. 7, 1833 at Bethel,
Pa. s. of John and Ann (Clark) C. Educ. in pub. schools
there; at Partridge Mil. Acad., in Bristol, Pa.; and in
Wilmington, Del. Became a civil engr. Moved to Leavenworth,
Kan. in 1855, where he became the city's civil engr. Upon

outbreak of Civil War raised a company of volunteers for the
Union, of which he became capt. Later was col. of cavalry
unit. Promoted to brig. gen. in 1864. Participated in a
number of campaigns in Southwestern theater of the war. Following the war, settled at Pine Bluff, Ark., where he became
a planter. Took prominent role in Ark. Rep. party affairs.
Served as Rep. natl. committeeman from Ark. for many years
and was delegate to Rep. natl. convs. in 1872 and 1896. Nom.
and el. Gov. without formal opposition in 1868. During his
admin., articles of impeachment were voted against him by the
Ark. House, but he was not brought to trial on the charges by
the Ark. Senate. Resigned office of Gov. in 1871 to take
seat in U.S. Senate, where he served one term. As a mbr. of
Senate was active, but unsuccessful, supporter of legislation to require all bus. corps. operating through interstate
commerce to be incorporated under natl. law. Returned to
bus. interests in Pine Bluff in 1877. In 1882 moved to
Eureka Springs, Ark., where he supervised constr. of Eureka
Springs R.R., of which he later became pres. and gen. mgr.
Also engaged in other bus. enterprises there. Apptd. Minister (later Ambassador) to Mexico by Pres. McKinley in 1897,
serving until 1905. As Ambassador participated in settlement
of claims of Catholic Church of Calif. against Mexico through
a proceeding before the intl. tribunal at The Hague, the
first case in which the U.S. appeared as a litigant before
that body. Retired to Washington, D.C. in 1905. m. in 1865
to Adeline McGraw. Three d.; one s. D. at Washington, D.C.
Aug. 25, 1914. Bur. in Arlington Natl. Cem.

HADLEY, OZRA A. (1871-1873). b. June 30, 1826 at Cherry
Creek, Chautauqua Co., N.Y. At age 29 moved to Minn., where
he engaged in farming until 1859. Aud. of Colfax Co., Minn.
in 1859. Served in that office until 1865, when he moved to
Little Rock, Ark., and set up a gen. store bus. there. El.
to Ark. Senate as a Rep. in 1869, and became Pres. pro tem
of that body. Became acting Gov. in 1871 when Gov. Clayton
resigned, the Lieut. Gov. having resigned previously. Completed Clayton's term. In 1873 was apptd. register of U.S.
land office in Little Rock; and in 1878 became the U.S. postmaster there. In 1882 moved to Watrous, Terr. of N.M., where
he had acquired extensive land holdings. Engaged in cattle
ranching. D. there July 18, 1915.

BAXTER, ELISHA (1873-1874). b. Sept. 1, 1827 in Rutherford, N.C. s. of Wm. and Catherine (Lee) B. Father was a
thrifty farmer of some wealth. Was one of 17 children.
Educ. in common schools. Engaged in farming and bus. activities in N.C. In 1852 moved to Batesville, Ark., where
he started a gen. merc. bus., which soon failed. Worked for

a printing house. Read law in a law office, and was admitted
to bar in 1856. El. to Ark. legislature as a Whig in 1854
and 1858. Defeated for office of pros. atty. of his dist.
in 1860. Although a slave owner, was opposed to secession.
Upon outbreak of Civil War sought to maintain a neutral stand,
which made him unpopular. Took refuge behind Union lines in
1862. Captured by Confed. forces in Mo. in 1863 and was imprisoned for a time by Ark. civil authorities on charge of
treason. Escaped and fled behind Union lines again and
helped raise a regiment for Union cause. Placed in command
of garrison at his home town of Batesville until 1864. Under
revised pro-Union const. of 1864 was apptd. Chief Justice of
Ark. Supreme Ct. El. to U.S. Senate but was refused seat by
that body. In 1868 became registrar in bankruptcy for U.S.
and by apptmt. from Gov. Clayton, a cir. ct. judge. Held
both offices for four years. In 1872 gubernatorial el. was
the nominee of a Rep. faction, popularly known as the "Min-
strels," for Gov. Ensuing contest with Brooks, the cand. of
an opposing ("Brindletails") Rep. faction, was bitter. Baxter
was declared el. and assumed office, but his opponent sought
to oust him by mil. force, claiming fraud in the el. Baxter
was eventually recognized as the lawful Gov. by the Fed.
govt. only after a struggle of several months, known as the
"Brooks-Baxter War," ensued in which some lives were lost.
His term of office was shortened to two years by adoption of
a new state const. in 1874 setting up a new term and el.
schedule. Declined the Dem. party nom. for Gov. in 1874.
Was unsuccessful as a cand. for a U.S. Senate seat in 1878.
m. in 1849 to Harriet Patton. Six children. D. at Batesville May 31, 1899. Bur. there.

GARLAND, AUGUSTUS HILL (1874-1877). b. June 11, 1832
in Tipton Co., Tenn. s. of Rufus and Barbara (Hill) G.
Attd. St. Mary's Coll., Lebanon, Ky. and St. Joseph's Coll.,
Bardstown, Ky., from which he was grad. in 1849. Studied law
and was admitted to bar in 1853. Practiced law in Washington, Ark. until 1856, when he moved to Little Rock, continuing in practice of law. Cand. for pres. elector on Bell-
Everett (Constl. Union party) ticket in 1860 el. Mbr. of
state constl. conv. to consider question of secession in
1861. Originally opposed to secession, changed stand later
after hostilities began. Mbr. of Confed. Provisional Cong.
in 1861. Later became a mbr. of C.S.A. Cong., first as a
mbr. of House and later as Senator. Served until end of
Civil War. Pardoned by Pres. Andrew Johnson and sought to
resume law practice before U.S. cts. Being unable to take
the "ironclad oath" of loyalty to Union prescribed by act of
Cong. as a condition for engaging in that activity, he contested the validity of the act before the U.S. Supreme Ct.

In one of its notable decisions in the post-Civil War era
the Ct. held the act unconstl. El. to a seat in U.S. Senate
from Ark. in 1866, but was denied seat. Became acting Ark.
Sect. of State in 1874, and in that year was el. Gov. as a
Dem. under the 1874 state const. El. to U.S. Senate in 1877,
and was reel. in 1883. In 1885 was apptd. U.S. Atty. Gen.
by Pres. Cleveland, and served until 1889. Retired to law
practice thereafter. Delegate to Dem. natl. conv. in 1892.
m. in 1853 to Virginia Sanders, of Washington, Ark. D. in
Washington, D.C. Jan. 26, 1899. Bur. in Mt. Holly Cem.,
Little Rock.

    MILLER, WILLIAM R. (1877-1881). b. Nov. 27, 1823 in
Independence Co., Ark. s. of John and Clara (Moore) M.
Father was one of the early pioneer settlers in Terr. of
Ark. and had achieved a degree of social and economic prominence in the community. Educ. in common schools. El. clerk
of Independence Co. in 1848 and was reel. for three terms.
Apptd. to fill vacancy in office of State Aud. by Gov. Conway in 1854. In 1855-1856 served as accountant for State
Real Estate Bank. El. to office of State Aud. in 1856. 'Continued to serve by reel. in that capacity until adoption of
1864 state const., under which he became ineligible because
of his collaboration with secessionist movement. Became
State Aud. again under 1874 state const. Nom. and el. Gov.
as Dem. in 1876 and again in 1878, becoming the first native
of Ark. to hold that office. Admin. characterized by beginning of economic recovery from effects of Civil War and
by his firmness in dealing with opponents of restoration to
political power of former pro-Southern elements in population. m. in 1849 to Susan E. Bevens. Five d. and two s.,
only four of whom survived infancy. D. Nov. 27, 1887 at
Little Rock while again serving as State Aud. Bur. at Mt.
Holly Cem., Little Rock.

    CHURCHILL, THOMAS JAMES (1881-1883). b. Mar. 10, 1824
at Louisville, Ky. s. of Col. Samuel and Abby (Oldham) C.
Father's ancestors had been early colonists in Va., where
the family had achieved distinction. Attd. St. Mary's Coll.
in Lebanon, Ky., grad. in 1844. Read law at Transylvania
Coll. Did not choose to pursue law as a career, choosing instead to become a planter in Ark. In 1846 enlisted in a
cavalry unit that fought in U.S.-Mexican War. In 1856 was
apptd. postmaster at Little Rock. Upon outbreak of Civil
War joined the Confed. Army as col. of a cavalry regiment.
Later was promoted to brig. gen. and in 1864 to major gen.
Participated in various campaigns in Mo., Ark., Ky., Tenn.
and La. At the Battle of Arkansas Post, in 1863, was taken
prisoner with his entire command. Later was exchanged. At

the end of the war returned to Little Rock. In 1866 was
chosen Lieut. Gov. under the 1864 state const., but he was
not allowed to take office because of his Civil War activities. During the "Brooks-Baxter War" disturbance of the
early 1870s, was placed in command of state troops by Gov.
Baxter to resist efforts of his opponent to take over control
of the state govt. El. State Treas. in 1874 and was reel.
for two terms. Nom. and el. Gov. as Dem. in 1880 over a
Greenback party opponent. Retired to pvt. life after one
term. Episcopalian. m. in 1849 to Anna Maria Sevier, d. of
Sen. Ambrose H. Sevier. Two s.; four d. D. on estate near
Little Rock, Mar. 10, 1905.

BERRY, JAMES HENDERSON (1883-1885). b. May 15, 1841
near Bellefont, Jackson Co., Ala. s. of James M. and Isabella (Orr) B. Father's family originally resided in Va.,
but had moved to Tenn., where father was born. Family
moved to Carrollton, Ark. in 1848, where the father engaged
in farming and merc. bus. Son assisted in these activities
while attending school. Enlisted as a lieut. in Confed.
Army soon after Civil War began. Suffered wound resulting
in loss of a leg at Corinth, Miss., in 1862. Returned home
and engaged in school teaching at Ozark, Ark. Also studied
law. After admission to bar began practice in Berryville,
Ark. El. to Ark. legislature in 1866 from Carroll Co.
Moved to Bentonville, Ark. in 1869 and was again el. to the
legislature in 1872 and 1874. In 1878 was el. to a cir. ct.
judgeship. While serving in that post was nom. and el. Gov.
as a Dem. in 1882. Declined to run for reel. in 1884, preferring instead to compete for a U.S. Senate seat. Was unsuccessful in that effort after a protracted contest in the
legislature; but was successful a short time later in winning
el. to a U.S. Senate seat to fill a vacancy occasioned by
resignation of former Gov. Garland. Served continuously for
22 years in that body. Defeated for reel. in 1906. Retired
thereafter to his home in Bentonville. His only pub. service thereafter was as a mbr. of a commn. for marking the
graves of former Confed. dead. m. in 1865 to Lizzie Quaile.
D. at Bentonville Jan. 20, 1913. Bur. in Knights of Pythias
Cem. there.

HUGHES, SIMON P. (1885-1889). b. Aug. 14, 1830 at
Carthage, Tenn. s. of Simon P. and Mary (Hubbard) H. Father, who originally resided in Va., died in 1844, after
which the son moved to Ark. He soon returned to Tenn.,
where he attd. Sylvan Acad. and later, for a time, Clinton
Coll., in Sumner Co. Worked as manual laborer to meet living expenses while at school. Became a pub. school teacher
for two years. In 1849 moved to Clarendon, Monroe Co.,

Ark., where he became a farmer. El. sheriff of Monroe Co. in 1854. Studied law and was admitted to bar in 1857. Was opposed to secession, but nevertheless entered Confed. Army in 1862 as a capt., later becoming lieut. col. Deprived of command by a troop reorg., he enlisted as a pvt. in Gen. Morgan's cavalry unit, and served therein until the end of the Civil War. Resumed law practice. El. to Ark. legislature in 1866, but was disqualified because of Civil War activities. Mbr. of state const. conv. of 1874, and after adoption of the new const. in that year was el. Ark. Atty. Gen., serving until 1877. Unsuccessful cand. for Dem. nom. for Gov. in 1878; but in 1884 was nom. and el. to that office as a Dem. Reel. in 1886. Defeated in attempt to win nom. for a third term in 1888. The next year became a mbr. of Ark. Supreme Ct. Served thereon until he retired in 1904. As Gov., was active in promoting interests of farmers. Mbr. and Grand Master of Ark. Grange. Pres. of Ark. State Fair Assoc. m. in 1857 to Ann Eliza Blakemore. Nine children. D. June 19, 1906.

EAGLE, JAMES PHILIP (1889-1893). b. Aug. 10, 1837 in Maury Co., Tenn. s. of James and Charity (Swaim) E. Family had formerly resided in Pa. and then in N.C. In 1839 father moved with the family to Pulaski Co., Ark., where he engaged in farming. Son received rudimentary educ. in schools there. Upon outbreak of Civil War he enlisted in an Ark. Confed. regiment. Transferred to a cavalry unit in which he became a lieut., and was later promoted to major and to lieut. col. Saw extensive fighting during the war, and was wounded and became a prisoner of war for several months. Returned to home at end of the war to find the family plantation in ruins. Restored it to a productive enterprise, and eventually became owner of several thousand acres. Resumed educ. at age 30. Became an ordained Baptist minister, choosing to serve in localities too poor to pay minister a salary. Pres. of Ark. Baptist Conv. for 15 years. Also pres. of So. Baptist Conv. on three occasions. Entered politics in 1872 when he accepted unsolicited nom. for a seat in the Ark. legislature, and was el. Mbr. of state constl. conv. of 1874. El. again to the legislature from Lonoke Co. in 1876 and 1884, serving as House Speaker in latter term. Nom. and el. Gov. as Dem. in 1888 and was reel. in 1890. Retired to farming and ministerial activities thereafter. m. in 1882 to Mary Kavanaugh Oldham. D. Dec. 20, 1904. Bur. at Mt. Holly Cem., Little Rock.

FISHBACK, WILLIAM MEADE (1893-1895). b. Nov. 5, 1831 at Jeffersonton, Culpeper Co., Va. s. of Frederick and Sophia (Yates) F. Family originally resided in Md., and

were propertied and well-educ. Attd. Univ. of Va., from
which he was grad. in 1855. Studied law in Richmond, Va.,
and was admitted to Va. bar in 1858. Engaged in teaching
while completing law study. Moved to Greenwood, Ark. in
1860, and in 1862 to Fort Smith, Ark., where he practiced
law. Mbr. of conv. that adopted ordinance of secession in
1861. Was a Unionist, but opposed coercion of Southern secessionists. After Civil War hostilities began in his area,
moved behind Union lines. After occupation of Little Rock
by Union forces in 1863 founded a newspaper there, the Un-
conditional Unionist. Raised a cavalry unit for Union cause,
but it was never mustered into active service. Participated
in formation of a revised const. for Ark. in 1864, which was
sometimes referred to later as the "Fishback Constitution"
because of his influence in shaping it. Insisted on retain-
ing in it a clause restricting suffrage to White race.
Chosen to U.S. Senate seat in 1864 by pro-Union legislature,
but was refused seat by the Senate. Apptd. U.S. Treas.
agent for Ark. in 1865. Affiliated with Dem. party from
1867 onward. Mbr. of state constl. conv. of 1874. Served
in Ark. legislature in 1877-1881 and 1885-1886. Influential
in passage of legislation forbidding redemption of state
bonds issued during Reconstruction on ground they were the
product of fraud. Unsuccessful cand. for Dem. nom. for Gov.
in 1888. Pres. elector-at-large on Dem. ticket in 1888.
Nom. and el. Gov. as Dem. in 1892. During admin., sponsored
idea of assembling all So. State Govs. at Richmond, Va. to
present a united front on natl. issues affecting South. Presided over the meeting, which was a forerunner of later
annual U.S. and regional meetings of Govs. Author of a
history of Reconstruction era in the South. m. to Adelaide
Miller. Three s.; two d. D. Feb. 9, 1903 at Fort Smith,
Ark.

CLARKE, JAMES PAUL (1895-1897). b. Aug. 18, 1854 at
Yazoo City, Miss. s. of Walter and Ellen (White) C. Father
was a civil engr. and architect. Both parents died when son
was seven years old. Attd. schools in Miss. and Tutwilder's
Acad., in Green Brier, Ala. Received a law degree from the
Univ. of Va. in 1878. Admitted to bar and began practice of
law at Helena, Ark. in 1879. Was very successful in law
profession. Mbr. of Ark. House, 1886-1888 and of Ark.
Senate, 1888-1892, becoming the presiding officer of that
body in last term. El. Atty. Gen. of Ark. in 1892. Declined nom. for second term in 1894, preferring to become a
cand. for Dem. nom. for Gov., which he won after a spirited
conv. struggle. El. Gov. that year over strong Rep. and
Pop. opposition. Advocate of strong law enforcement and
protection of State's land interests in long-standing dispute

with U.S. govt. That dispute was settled during admin.
After term expired, resumed law practice in Little Rock.
El. as Dem. to U.S. Senate in 1902 and continued in that
office for next two terms. Pres. pro tem of U.S. Senate,
1913-1916. Mbr. of Dem. natl. commt. from Ark. m. to
Sallie Moore in 1883. One s.; two d. D. Oct. 1, 1916 while
still a mbr. of U.S. Senate. Bur. in Oakland Cem., Little
Rock.

JONES, DAN(IEL) WEBSTER (1897-1901). b. Dec. 15, 1839
in Bowie Co., Tex. s. of Isaac Newton and Elizabeth Wilson
(Littlejohn) J. Father was a physician who had originally
resided in N.C. Attd. schools in Washington, Ark. Studied
law there in law office. Upon outbreak of Civil War enlisted in an Ark. Confed. company, rising to rank of col. by
end of war. Admitted to bar in 1865 and soon achieved a
wide reputation as an able criminal lawyer. Apptd. to fill
vacancy in office of pros. atty. in his dist. in 1866 and
was later el. to a regular term. Pres. elector on Dem.
ticket in 1876 and 1880. El. Atty. Gen. of Ark. in 1884 and
was reel. in 1886. Mbr. of Ark. House from Pulaski Co. in
1891-1893. Nom. and el. Gov. as Dem. in 1896. Reel. in
1898. Returned to law practice after serving as Gov. El.
to Ark. House again in 1915. m. in 1864 to Margaret Hadly.
Three s.; two d. Episcopalian. D. at Little Rock, Dec. 25,
1918.

DAVIS, JEFF(ERSON) (1901-1907). b. May 6, 1862 near
Richmond, Little River Co., Ark. s. of Lewis W. and Mary D.
Family later moved to Dover, Pope Co., Ark. Attd. schools
in Russellville, Ark. Studied law in law office, being admitted to bar at age 19. Later received a law degree from
Vanderbilt Univ. in 1884. Began practice in Russellville.
Served as pros. atty. for his dist., 1892-1896. Atty. Gen.
of Ark., 1898-1900. Nom. and el. Gov. as Dem. in 1900. Was
reel. in 1902 and 1904, thereby becoming the first Ark. Gov.
to serve three consecutive terms. As Gov., was noted for
vigorous enforcement of anti-trust laws. Delegate-at-large
to Dem. natl. conv. in 1904. In 1907 was el. to U.S. Senate,
where he served until his death at Little Rock on Jan. 3,
1913 shortly before end of his first term. m. to Ina
McKenzie in 1882, who preceded him in death. m. in 1911 to
Leila Carter of Ozark, Ark. Bur. at Mt. Holly Cem., Little
Rock.

LITTLE, JOHN SEBASTIAN (1907). b. Mar. 15, 1853 at
Jenny Lind, Ark. s. of Jessie and Mary Elizabeth (Tatum) L.
Attd. Cane Hill Coll., in Ark. Studied law, was admitted to
bar and began practice at Greenwood, Ark. in 1874. Served

four terms as pros. atty. of his dist., 1877-1885. Mbr. of
Ark. House, 1885-1886. Served as cir. ct. judge, 1887-1890.
El. in Dec., 1894 to U.S. House to fill an unexpired term
and was reel. for six succeeding terms. Resigned seat Jan.
14, 1907 after having been nom. and el. Gov. as a Dem. After
holding office of Gov. about one week suffered a physical and
nervous breakdown. Surrendered powers of office temporarily
to his successor, and then resigned about one month later
because of impaired health. Mbr., Masons; professional legal
orgs. Methodist. m. in 1877 to Elizabeth Jane Erwin. Five
children. D. at Little Rock Oct. 29, 1916. Bur. in City
Cem., Greenwood, Ark.

MOORE, JOHN I. (1907). b. Feb. 7, 1856 near Oxford,
Miss. Studied law. Moved to Helena, Ark., where he was el.
cir. ct. judge of his dist. Later was el. to Ark. Senate
and became Pres. of that body. While serving in that capacity succeeded to powers of office of Gov. in Jan., 1907 when
Gov. Little became incapacitated. Later became Gov. when
Gov. Little resigned after having been in office about one
month. Served approximately three months until end of
legislative session at which he had been chosen Pres. of
Senate. D. Mar. 18, 1937.

PINDALL, XENOPHON OVERTON (1907-1909). b. Aug. 21,
1893 near Middle Grove, Mo. s. of Libbeus Aaron and Nora
(Snell) P. Family originally resided in Md. Attd. Mo. Mil.
Acad.; Central Coll., at Fayette, Mo.; and the Univ. of Ark.,
from which he was grad. in 1896 with a law degree. Established practice with a cousin in Ark. City, Ark. Served as
deputy pros. atty. for a short time. Mbr. of Ark. House,
1903-1905. Defeated in Dem. state conv. for nom. for Atty.
Gen. in 1906, although favored in popular primary vote that
year. El. to Ark. Senate, and was chosen Pres. of that body
in May, 1907. This had the effect of elevating him to the
office of Gov., which had been vacated by Gov. Little.
Served as Gov. until Jan. 11, 1909, when his successor in
the office of Pres. of the Senate was chosen. Took up practice of law in Little Rock thereafter. Mbr., Masons; Kappa
Sigma; professional legal orgs. Christian (Disciples)
church. m. in 1902 to Mae Ruth Quilling, from whom he was
divorced in 1913. No children. D. Jan. 2, 1935.

MARTIN, JESSE M. (1909). b. Mar. 1, 1877 near London,
Pope Co., Ark. Studied law and established practice at
Russellville, Ark. El. to Ark. Senate. After being chosen
Pres. of that body in Jan., 1909, assumed post of Gov. for
last four days of Gov. Little's term pending installation
of newly el. Gov. D. Jan. 22, 1915.

DONAGHEY, GEORGE W. (1909-1913). b. July 1, 1856 at
Oakland, Union Parish, La. s. of Columbus and Elizabeth
(Ingram) D. Father was a farmer. Supported self at various
jobs while attending the Univ. of Ark. Established residence in Little Rock, engaging in various occupations, including cabinet making, hardware bus., constr. work, railway
contracting, and banking. Became politically active and was
nom. and el. Gov. as Dem. in 1908. Reel. in 1910. Admin.
marked by educl. reforms; completion of new state Capitol
bldg; establishment of juvenile ct. system; adoption of initiative and referendum. Opposed practice of contracting
out state prisoners for labor. Lenient in granting pardons
to prisoners, for which he was strongly criticized in some
quarters. After service as Gov. engaged in banking, constr.
work and merc. bus. in Little Rock. Pres. of Ark. Bd. of
Control of State Eleemosynary Institutions, 1922-1926. m.
in 1883 to Louvenia Wallace. Mbr., Masons. Methodist. D.
Dec. 15, 1937 at Little Rock.

ROBINSON, JOSEPH TAYLOR ("JOE") (1913). b. Aug. 16,
1872 near Lonoke, Ark. s. of James and Matilda Jane (Swaim)
R. Attd. the Univ. of Ark. and the Univ. of Va. Studied
law, and was admitted to bar in 1895. Began practice at
Lonoke. Became a mbr. of Ark. House in 1895, where he
sponsored legislation creating a State R.R. Commn. Delegate
to Dem. natl. conv. and pres. elector on Bryan-Stevenson
ticket in 1900. El. to U.S. House in 1902 and continued in
that post for four succeeding terms. As mbr. of the House,
sponsored a child labor bill, anti-trust law reforms, and
reduction of tariff. Resigned House seat in 1913 after having been nom. and el. Gov. as a Dem. Outlined a program involving state tax and financial reform, state banking law
revision, anti-corrupt practices legislation, and a local
option liquor regulation system. Resigned office of Gov.
after serving less than two months, having been el. in the
meantime to a U.S. Senate seat following the death of former
Gov. and Sen. Jeff Davis. He thus within a period of two
months held three important offices--U.S. Repr., Gov. of
Ark., and U.S. Senator. Retained seat in U.S. Senate until
his death. Became Dem. floor leader in the Senate in 1933.
Nom. for Vice Pres. of U.S. on Dem. ticket with Gov. Alfred
E. Smith, of N.Y. in 1928. Delegate to Dem. natl. convs.,
1920-1936, and was permanent ch. in that body in 1920, 1928,
and 1936. m. in 1896 to Ewilda Gertrude Miller. D. July 14,
1937. State funeral held in U.S. Senate chamber. Bur. at
Roselawn Memorial Park, near Little Rock.

OLDHAM, WILLIAM K. (1913). b. May 29, 1865 at Richmond,
Ky. Acquired land near Lonoke, Ark., and engaged in farming.

El. to Ark. Senate and was Pres. of that body when Gov.
Robinson resigned in Mar., 1913. Became Gov. by succession
until his own term as a mbr. of the Senate expired three days
later. In subsequent litigation the Ark. Supreme Ct. ruled
that his tenure as Acting Gov. terminated when he ceased to
be Pres. of the Senate, and that his successor in the office
of Pres. of the Senate should be regarded as having succeeded
to the office of Gov. immediately upon being chosen to the
office of Pres. of the Senate. D. May 6, 1938.

FUTRELL (FUTTRELL?), J(UNIUS) MARION (1913; 1933-1937).
b. Aug. 14, 1870 in Greene Co., Ark. s. of Jeptha and Ar-
minia F. Attd. the Univ. of Ark., 1892-1893. Became a
school teacher and also engaged in farming. Cir. ct. clerk
of Greene Co. Studied law and was admitted to bar in 1913.
Mbr. of Ark. House, 1897-1899. Mbr. of Ark. Senate, 1913-
1917. Was chosen Pres. of Senate for the next session at
conclusion of the first session in Mar., 1913, and as such,
became Acting Gov. for some five months until a successor
was chosen at a spec. el. to complete Gov. Robinson's term.
Became a cir. ct. judge in 1922, and a chancery ct. judge,
1923-1933. Nom. and el. Gov. as a Dem. in 1932 and was reel.
in 1934. After tenure as Gov. engaged in legal practice.
m. in 1893 to Tera Ann Smith. Four d.; two s. D. June 20,
1955 at Paragould, Ark.

HAYS, GEORGE WASHINGTON (1913-1917). b. Sept. 23, 1863
at Camden, Ark. s. of Thomas and Parthena Jane (Ross) H.
Studied law at Washington and Lee Univ. Admitted to bar and
began practice of law in Camden. Became co. and probate
judge of Ouachita Co., 1900-1904. Cir. ct. judge of his
dist., 1906-1913. Nom. and el. Gov. as Dem. in a spec. el.
in 1913 to choose a successor to complete the term of Gov.
Robinson, who had resigned. Nom. and el. for a full term in
1914. As Gov., signed a bill establishing state-wide prohibition. After serving as Gov. resumed law practice. m.
in 1905 to Ida Virginia Yarbrough. Two s. D. at Little
Rock Sept. 15, 1927.

BROUGH, CHARLES HILLMAN (1917-1921). b. July 9, 1876
at Clinton, Miss. Father was a banker who had also engaged
in mining for a time in Utah. Attd. Miss. Coll., from which
he was grad. in 1893; Johns Hopkins Univ., from which he received a Ph.D. degree in 1898; and the Univ. of Miss., from
which he received a law degree in 1902. From 1898 to 1901
was prof. of history and econ. at Miss. Coll. Prof. of
history, econ. and philosophy at Hilman Coll., Clinton,
Miss., 1903-1904; and prof. of econ. and sociology at the
Univ. of Ark., 1904-1916. Achieved state-wide reputation

through lectures on political and other matters. Nom. and el. Gov. as Dem. in 1916 and was reel. in 1918. During admin., used U.S. troops to quell racial riots in Phillips Co.; inaugurated a state highway system; extended state aid for educ.; successfully urged ratification of women's suffrage and natl. prohibition amdts. to U.S. Const. After tenure as Gov. became a chautauqua lecturer in 1925, and in 1925-1928 was dir. of Ark. Pub. Information Bureau. m. in 1908 to Anne Wade Roark. No children. Mbr., Amer. Econ. Assoc.; Amer. Political Sci. Assoc.; Ark. State Teachers Assoc., of which he was pres. in 1913; pres. of So. Sociological Cong., 1916-1918; mbr., Amer. Historical Assoc.; Longfellow Soc.; U.S. Good Roads Assoc.; Beta Theta Pi; Tau Kappa Alpha; Masons (Shriner); K.P.; Woodmen; Maccabees; Lions; Kiwanis; Rotary; various social clubs. Baptist. D. at Washington, D.C., Dec. 26, 1935.

McRAE, THOMAS CHIPMAN (1921-1925). b. Dec. 21, 1851 at Mount Holly, Ark. s. of Duncan L. and Mary Ann (Chipman) McR. Family originally resided in N.C. Attd. pvt. schools at Shady Grove and Mount Holly, Ark.; the Masonic Acad., at Falcon, Ark.; Soule's Bus. Coll., New Orleans; and Washington and Lee Univ., from which he received a law degree in 1872. Admitted to bar in 1873 and established practice in Rosston, Ark. Moved later to Prescott, Ark., where he practiced law and also engaged in banking. Co. commnr., Nevada Co., 1874; city recorder and city atty., Prescott, 1879; pres. elector on Hancock-English ticket in 1880 pres. el. El. to U.S. House in 1884, in which he continued to serve until 1903. In Cong., identified himself prominently with pub. lands and free silver issues. Ch. of Nevada Co. Dem. commt., 1880; delegate to Dem. natl. conv. in 1884; ch., Ark. Dem. conv. in 1902, and in 1926 was made a life mbr. of that body. Mbr. of Dem. natl. commt., 1896-1900. Mbr. of Ark. constl. conv. in 1918 and of Ark. Bd. of Charities, 1909-1913. Nom. and el. Gov. as Dem. in 1920 and again in 1922. Pres. of Ark. Bankers' Assoc., 1909-1910 and of the Ark. Bar Assoc., 1917-1918. After tenure as Gov. engaged in law and bus. activities at Prescott. Mbr., Masons (K.T.); I.O.O.F.; K.P.; W.O.W. Active in Presbyterian church, serving as mbr. of Council of Reformed Churches of Amer. m. in 1874 to Amelia Ann White. Five d.; two s. D. June 2, 1929 at Prescott. Bur. in De Ann Cem. there.

TERRAL, THOMAS JEFFERSON (1925-1927). b. Dec. 21, 1884 in Union Parish, La. s. of George W. and Celia T. Father was a merchant and planter. Attd. schools in La. and Miss.; the Univ. of Ky.; and the Univ. of Ark., from which he received a law degree in 1910. Admitted to bar and established

practice at Little Rock. In 1911 became asst. sect. and
from 1913-1915, sect. of Ark. Senate. Also served as deputy
for Ark. Supt. of Pub. Instruction. Sect. of State for Ark.,
1917-1921. In 1924 was nom. and el. Gov. as Dem. During
admin., established a gasoline tax for support of highway
system; urged reform of state admin. system; promoted ratification of U.S. child labor amdt.; advocated changes in
state initiative system and limitations on state legislature's power to control local govt.; favored strong prohibition law enforcement; an increase in number of State Supreme
Ct. judges; and creation of a State Bd. of Corrections and
Charities. Failed to win re-nom. for second term as Gov. in
1926. Also was unsuccessful in attempts to win Dem. nom.
for Gov. in 1928, 1932 and 1936. Mbr., professional legal
orgs.; Masons; M.W.A. Baptist. m. in 1914 to Eula -----,
a widow. No children, but had a foster d. D. at Little
Rock Mar. 9, 1946.

MARTINEAU, JOHN ELLIS (1927-1928). b. Dec. 2, 1873 in
Clay Co., Mo. s. of Gregory and Sarah Hettie (Lamb) M.
Antecedents were of French origin, who had formerly resided
in Canada. Parents moved to Ark. when he was four years old.
Attd. schools at Lonoke, Ark. and the Univ. of Ark., from
which he was grad. with a law degree in 1898. Established
law practice in Little Rock, where he soon attracted attention for ability. Served in Ark. legislature, 1903-1905.
From 1907 to 1926 was Ark. chancery ct. judge. Nom. and el.
Gov. as Dem. in 1926, being the only one of several candidates to oppose the KKK and defeating the incumbent Gov.,
T.J. Terral, among other, for the party's nom. Advocated a
moderate program of prohibition law enforcement, emphasizing
effort to apprehend and convict major law-breakers rather
than the minor ones. Worked closely with U.S. Sect. of
Commerce Herbert Hoover in relieving distress from 1927
Miss. River floods. Resigned as Gov. in 1928 to accept
apptmt. as U.S. dist. ct. judge in Eastern Ark. by Pres.
Coolidge. As such, attracted natl. attention while on spec.
duty in New York City by ordering padlocking of "speak-easy"
saloons; also for conducting a case involving anti-peonage
law prosecution against the city marshal of Earle, Ark. m.
in 1907 to Anne Holcombe Mitchell, who died in 1914. m. in
1919 to Mabel Erwin Thomas. Both wives had been widows. No
children. Mbr., Masons; K.P.; Phi Beta Kappa; various professional legal orgs. and social clubs. Mbr., Methodist
Episcopal, South Church. D. at Little Rock, Mar. 6, 1937.

PARNELL, HARVEY (1928-1933). b. Feb. 28, 1880 at New
Edinburgh, Cleveland Co., Ark. s. of Wm. R. and Mary (Martin) P. Attd. h.s. at Warren, Ark. Worked in hardware

store, later establishing his own bus. as a hardware dealer
in Dermott, Ark. Acquired land and also engaged in farming.
Mbr. of Ark. House, 1919-1921. Mbr. of Ark. Senate, 1923-
1925. El. Lieut. Gov. as Dem. in 1926 and succeeded to office in Mar., 1928 when Gov. Martineau resigned. Completed
term for which Martineau was el. and was nom. and el. to
regular terms in 1928 and 1930. During admin., approved law
against teaching of evolution in state-supported schools; a
state income tax law; advocated revision of state laws governing the teaching of med. sci.; and farm credit relief.
Vetoed bill for legalization of racing. In 1931, apptd.
Mrs. Hattie Caraway to a seat in U.S. Senate occasioned by
the death of her husband, she thereby becoming the first
woman to serve in the U.S. Senate from Ark. After tenure as
Gov. became an appraiser for U.S. Reconstr. Finance Admin.
Mbr., Masons (Shriner); K.P.; W.O.W. Mbr., Methodist Episcopal, South church. Expert hunter and marksman. m. in
1903 to Mabel Winston. Two d. D. at Little Rock, Jan. 16,
1936.

FUTRELL, J(UNIUS) MARION (1933-1937). See above, 1913.

BAILEY, CARL EDWARD (1937-1941). b. Oct. 8, 1894 at
Bernie, Mo. s. of Wm. Edward and Margaret Elmyra (McCorkle)
B. Attd. school at Campbell, Mo. and Chillicothe, Mo., Bus.
Coll. Worked at various occupations, including laborer,
farmer, school teacher, bookkeeper, accountant. Became
asst. sect. to Ark. Cotton Growers Assoc. in 1923. Studied
law and was admitted to bar in Ark. Practiced law at Little
Rock; deputy pros. atty., 1927-1931; pros. atty., 1931-1935.
El. Atty. Gen. of Ark. in 1934, serving until 1937. Nom.
and el. Gov. as Dem. in 1936, and again in 1938. Unsuccessful in attempt to win U.S. Senate seat to fill vacancy occasioned by Sen. Robinson's death in 1937, although he had
strong support from the natl. Dem. admin. at the spec. el.
During admin., a state civil service system was created; a
new highway financing program was adopted; and the state
admin. system was reorganized extensively. Unsuccessful in
attempt to win nom. for a third successive term as Gov. in
1940. After tenure as Gov., resumed practice of law at
Little Rock. Mbr., Masons; professional legal orgs. Christian (Disciples) church. m. in 1915 to Margaret Bristol,
from whom he was divorced in 1942. Five s.; one d. m. in
1943 to Marjorie Compton. D. Oct. 23, 1948 at Little Rock.

ADKINS, HOMER MARTIN (1941-1945). b. Oct. 15, 1890 at
Jacksonville, Ark. s. of Ulysses and Lorena (Wood) A.
Attd. local schools and Draughon's Bus. Coll., Springfield,
Mo., 1907-1919. Studied pharmacy at coll., 1910-1911. Be-

came a registered pharmacist at Little Rock, Ark., where he
was employed, 1911-1916. Also worked as a salesman of pharmaceutical products. Served as capt. in U.S. Army Med.
Corps, 1917-1919. Resumed bus. interests in Little Rock
after discharge. El. sheriff and collector of taxes for
Pulaski Co. in 1922, serving in that office until 1926. Proprietor of ins. firm in Little Rock, 1926-1933. Apptd. U.S.
Internal Revenue Collector for Ark. in 1933, serving in that
capacity until 1940. Nom. and el. Gov. as Dem. in 1940 and
was reel. in 1942. Campaigned on platform of reform and
strict law enforcement. As Gov. during World War II, gave
full support to U.S. war effort. Unsuccessful cand. for Dem.
nom. for U.S. Senate seat in 1944. Mbr., Amer. Legion;
W.O.W.; Masons; Elks. Methodist. m. in 1921 to Estelle
Elise Smith. D. Feb. 26, 1964.

LANEY, BEN(JAMIN TRAVIS) (1945-1949). b. Nov. 25, 1896
near Smackover, Ouachita Co., Ark. s. of Benj. Travis and
Martha Phoebe (Saxon) L. Father was a farmer. Attd. Hendrix
Coll., Conway, Ark., 1915-1916. Entered U.S. Navy as apprentice seaman in 1917, serving until 1919. Was a radioman
when discharged. Attd. Ark. State Teachers' Coll., Conway,
Ark., from which he was grad. in 1921; and the Univ. of Utah
for a short time. Became a school teacher. Later engaged
in various bus. activities, including banking. Acquired
land and became a farmer. In 1927 established his residence
at Camden, Ark., where he became vice pres. of a motor financing agency. Very active in civic and community affairs.
Mayor of Camden, 1935-1937. Nom. and el. Gov. as Dem. in
1944 and again in 1946. Returned to bus. interests after
tenure as Gov. Unsuccessful cand. for Dem. nom. for Gov. in
1950. Very active in Methodist church affairs, including
teaching of Bible class for 14 years. Mbr., Rotary. m. in
1926 to Lucile Kirtley. Three s. D. at Magnolia, Ark.
Jan. 21, 1977.

McMATH, SIDNEY SANDERS (1949-1953). b. June 14, 1912
at Magnolia, Ark. s. of Hal Pearce and Nettie (Sanders) McM.
Father was a barber. Attd. pub. schools in Hot Springs.
Worked at various jobs while attending Henderson State
Teachers Coll. at Arkadelphia. Received a law degree from
the Univ. of Ark. in 1936. After grad., received a commn. in
U.S. Marine Corps as ROTC trainee, and served one year on active duty. Established law practice in Hot Springs. Called
to active mil. duty as a reserve officer in 1940 and saw active service in So. Pac. during World War II. Promoted to
lieut. col. and was invalided back to U.S. in 1944. Assisted
in Marine Corps training activities thereafter until end of
the war. After discharge from mil. service, returned to Hot

Springs, where he helped organize a "clean-up" drive against
the mayor of Hot Springs and others. El. to office of pros.
atty. in 1946 and led moves against gambling interests in
Hot Springs area. Nom. and el. Gov. as Dem. in 1948 and was
reel. in 1950. Opposed States Rts. ("Dixiecrat") element of
Dem. party in 1948 pres. campaign, and helped carry Ark. for
Pres. Truman by the highest percentage of any State in 1948
el. In 1952 sought nom. for third term. Received a plurality in the first primary, but lost in the ensuing "run-off"
primary. Defeated again as cand. for Dem. nom. for Gov. in
1962. As Gov., was active supporter of increased highway
funding; improvements in state educl. system; broadened pub.
welfare system; promotion of electric power cooperatives.
Mbr., V.F.W.; Amer. Legion; AMVETS; Masons; Elks; Kiwanis;
Lions; Sigma Alpha Epsilon. Methodist. m. in 1937 to Elaine
Broughton, who died in 1942. One d. m. in 1944 to Anne
Phillips. Two s.

CHERRY, FRANCIS ADAMS (1953-1955). b. Sept. 8, 1908 at
Forth Worth, Tex. Youngest of five children of Scott and
Clarabell (Taylor) C. Father was a railroad conductor.
Attd. pub. schools in El Reno and Enid, Okla. and Okla. Agri.
and Mech. Coll., 1926-1930. Worked at various jobs while
attending the Univ. of Ark., from which he received a law
degree in 1936, and was chosen pres. of senior class. Established law practice at Little Rock. In 1937-1942 was a
mbr. of a law firm at Jonesboro, Ark. Served as U.S. ct.
commnr., 1939-1942; referee for U.S. Workmen's Compensation
Commn., 1940-1942; chancellor and probate judge, 1942-1945.
Served as lieut., j.g., in U.S. Navy in World War II. After
war service, returned to chancery ct. bench. Nom. and el.
Gov. as Dem. in 1952, defeating incumbent Gov. McMath in
run-off Dem. primary. Refused to take a "hard line" position against U.S. Supreme Ct.'s school desegregation ruling
in 1954. As Gov., program included reform of fiscal code;
reorg. of State Highway Dept.; revision of property tax
system; attraction of new industries to Ark.; and diversification of agri. indust. Defeated for Dem. nom. for succeeding term in 1954, losing to O.E. Faubus after having obtained the highest vote in the first primary. Apptd. in
1955 by Pres. Eisenhower to the U.S. Subversive Activities
Control Bd. Became ch. of that body in 1963 by apptmt. from
Pres. Kennedy. m. in 1933 to Margaret Frierson, who was
"Campus Queen" at the Univ. of Ark. One d.; two s. Mbr.,
Amer. Legion; U.C.T.; Masons; Elks; Eagles; Delta Theta Pi;
Kappa Alpha; Lions. Presbyterian. D. July 15, 1965 in
Washington, D.C. Bur. in Jonesboro, Ark.

FAUBUS, ORVAL EUGENE ("GENE") (1955-1967). b. Jan. 7,
1910 at Combs, Ark. s. of John Samuel and Addie (Joslin) F.
Attd. rural schools, grad. from h.s. at Huntsville, Ark.
Taught in rural schools while still attending h.s. An expert
in hunting and woods craft, he worked as a forester, 1934-
1936. Cir. ct. clerk and recorder, Madison Co., 1939-1942.
Served in U.S. Army during World War II, rising to rank of
major. Acting postmaster at Huntsville, 1946, and postmaster, 1953-1954. Became publ. of a local newspaper.
Apptd. State Highway Commnr. in 1947. Sought and won Dem.
nom. for Gov. in run-off primary against incumbent Gov.
Cherry in 1954, and was el. Reel. for five succeeding terms,
becoming the first Ark. Gov. to be el. to more than three
terms. Admin. highlighted by his refusal to use force in
1956 to carry out a Fed. ct. order for integration of Little
Rock schools, resulting in mil. intervention by Pres. Eisenhower to carry out the ct. order. Urged reorg. of state financial admin. and changes in manner of dealing with welfare
recipients who worked. Sought to attract outside indus. to
Ark., appointing a Rep., Winthrop Rockefeller, later Gov. of
Ark. (q.v.), as ch. of a State Indus. Devel. Commn. Commdr.
of Rural Boy Scouts, 1924-1938. Mbr., Lions; Elks; S.C.V.;
Amer. Legion; V.F.W. Pres., Madison Co. CC, 1953-1954.
Ch., So. Govs.' Conf., 1963. Baptist. Received plurality
in first primary contest for Dem. nom. for Gov. in 1970, but
lost in run-off to Dale Bumpers. Also lost in attempt to
win Dem. nom. for Gov. in 1974. m. in 1931 to Alta Haskins.
One s. Marriage ended in divorce in 1969.

ROCKEFELLER, WINTHROP (1967-1971). b. May 1, 1912 in
New York City. s. of John D., Jr. and Abby Greene (Aldrich)
R. Was a brother of Nelson R., Gov. of N.Y. (q.v.). A
nephew, John D.R., IV became Gov. of W. Va. in 1977. Attd.
Loomis School; Lincoln H.S. of Columbia Univ. Teachers'
Coll.; and Yale Univ., leaving latter without receiving a
degree in 1934. Became trainee in Humble Oil and Refining
Co., working in oil fields as a laborer. Studied finance at
Chase Natl. Bank in N.Y. Exec. vice pres. of N.Y. Fund in
1939; dir. of exec. bd. of Natl. Urban League, 1940; indus.
relations consultant for Rockefeller Center, N.Y. Entered
U.S. Army as pvt. in 1941 and attd. O.C.S. Saw service in
So. Pac. area during World War II. Suffered serious injury
from burns in 1945 and was invalided home. Held rank of
lieut. col. when discharged in 1946. Engaged in various
family oil and low-cost housing enterprises, 1946-1953. In
1953 purchased 900 acres of land near Morrilton, Ark., and
established a stock farm ("Winrock") as demonstration farm
project. Established model integrated school at Morrilton,
which his step-children attd. Ch. of Ark. Indus. Devel.

Commn. in 1955. Nom. as Rep. cand. for Gov. in 1964, but
was defeated in gen. el. Nom. again in 1966 and was el.,
becoming the first Rep. to occupy the office of Gov. since
Reconstruction era. Made reorg. and modernization of state
govt. a major objective during admin. A revised const.,
which he strongly supported, was rejected in 1970 by the
voters. Reel. Gov. in 1968, but was defeated in the 1970
gen. el. for a third term. Continued to be active in various bus. and philanthropic interests sponsored by his family
after leaving office. m. in 1948 to Mrs. Barbara ("Bobo")
Sears, d. of a coal miner. One s. Marriage ended in divorce in 1954. m. in 1956 to Mrs. Jeannett Edris, of Seattle,
Wash. Marriage again ended in divorce. Two step-children by
second wife. Baptist. Recipient of five hon. degrees. D.
at Palm Springs, Calif., Feb. 22, 1973. Bur. at Morrilton,
Ark.

BUMPERS, DALE L. (1971-1975). b. Sept. 12, 1925 at
Charleston, Franklin Co., Ark. s. of Wm. Rufus and Lottie
(Jones) B. Attd. local pub. schools. Enlisted as pvt. in
U.S. Marine Corps in 1943 and served in Pac. theater of
World War II. Held rank of sgt. when discharged in 1946.
Grad. from the Univ. of Ark. in 1948. Attd. Northwestern
Univ., from which he received a law degree in 1951. Began
law practice in Charleston. City atty., Charleston, 1952-
1970. Became owner and operator of furniture bus., 1951-
1956. Acquired and operated a nearby farm, specializing in
breeding of Angus cattle. Active in numerous community orgs.
and enterprises. Won Dem. party nom. for Gov. in 1970, defeating former Gov. Faubus in run-off primary and incumbent
Gov. Rockefeller in gen. el. Reel. in 1972. Won Dem. nom.
for U.S. Senate seat in 1974, defeating incumbent Sen. Wm.
Fulbright for the nom., and was el. Resigned office of Gov.
shortly before term expired in order to take U.S. Senate
seat. m. to Betty Flanagan, of Franklin Co. Two s.; one d.
Methodist.

RILEY, ROBERT C. ("BOB") (1975). b. Sept. 18, 1924 at
Little Rock, Ark. Following grad. from h.s., enlisted in
U.S. Marine Corps, and served from 1941 to 1945 during World
War II. Engaged in action in Pac. theater of the war. After release from mil. service, attd. the Univ. of Ark., from
which he was grad. in 1950. Mbr. of Ark. House, 1946-1951.
Received an M.A. degree from the Univ. of Ark. in 1951 and a
D.Ed. degree in 1957. Engaged in teaching, and became a
mbr. of the faculty at Ouachita Baptist Univ., in Arkadelphia, Ark. in 1957. Head of div. of social studies there in
1960. Pres. of Ark. Political Sci. Assoc. Delegate to Dem.
natl. conv. in 1968. Consultant for Ark. anti-poverty and

educl. assistance for blind students programs. Nom. and el.
Lieut. Gov. as Dem. in 1970 and was reel. in 1972. Succeeded to office of Gov. for approximately two weeks in Jan.,
1975 following resignation of Gov. Bumpers, who had been el.
to the U.S. Senate. Unsuccessful in effort to win Dem. nom.
for Gov. in 1974. m. to Claudia M. Zimmerman in 1956.
One d.

PRYOR, DAVID HAMPTON (1975-1979). b. Aug. 29, 1934 at
Camden, Ark. s. of Edgar and Susan (Newton) P. Attd. pub.
schools in Camden; Henderson State Teachers Coll.; and the
Univ. of Ark., from which he was grad. in 1957 with a degree
in political sci. Established a newspaper, the Ouachita
Citizen, at Camden in 1957, which he continued to publish
for the next four years. Attd. the Univ. of Ark., from
which he received a law degree in 1964. Admitted to bar and
began practice in Camden. El. to the Ark. House in 1960,
and continued in office for next two terms. El. in 1966 to
U.S. House to fill a vacancy, and was reel. in 1968 and 1970.
Defeated for Dem. nom. for U.S. Senate seat in 1972. Nom.
and el. Gov. as Dem. in 1974, defeating former Gov. Faubus
and Lieut. Gov. Riley for the nom. Nom. and el. to U.S.
Senate seat in 1978. m. in 1957 to Barbara Lumsford.
Three s.

BURNETT, PETER HARDEMAN (1849-1851). b. Nov. 15, 1807
at Nashville, Tenn. s. of George and Dorothy (Hardeman) B.
Parents originally lived in Va. Father was a carpenter. At
age of 10 moved with parents to Howard Co., Mo., and later
to Clay Co., where he received common school educ. In 1826
returned to Tenn., where he worked for a time as a store
clerk and engaged in a merc. bus. of his own, which failed.
Returned to Clay Co., Mo. where he established a merc. bus.,
which again failed. Studied law and was admitted to Mo. bar
in 1833. Became ed. and publ. of a weekly newspaper, the
Far West, at Liberty, Mo. Represented several Mormon leaders,
including Joseph Smith, as counsel in a trial in 1839 which
was attd. by much tension because of the feeling against de-
fendants. Later, served as pros. atty. of Clay Co., 1840-
1842, during period when continued local disturbances arising from presence of Mormons in the area required him to act
on behalf of anti-Mormon complainants. In 1842-1843 moved
to Ore. country by wagon train with wife and family of six
children, hoping to settle on extensive land claim there.
Engaged in farming and the practice of law. Was very active
in movement to organize a provisional govt. there pending
settlement of question of U.S. claim to Ore. country. Became a judge in Ore. Terr. govt. when it was finally set up
in 1846. In 1848 moved to Calif., where he engaged in mining and acted as agent for the Sutter family mining interests at New Helvetia. Became a leader in movement in 1849
to org. a provisional state govt. in Calif. Advocated a
clause prohibiting entry of free Negroes as well as an anti-
slavery provision in the provisional const., as he had in
Ore. also. El. Gov. of Calif. on a provisional basis as a
Dem. after const. was drafted and put into effect in 1849.
Served until Jan., 1851, when he resigned before news of admission of Calif. to statehood had been received. Major
problems dealt with were provision for a revenue system for
the new govt.; protection against Indians in some areas; and
maintenance of pub. order. Resumed law practice. Served as
mbr. of Calif. Supreme Ct., 1857-1858. Founded and became
pres. of Pac. Coast Bank at San Francisco, 1863-1880. Had
become wealthy when he retired in 1880. Author of several
works on political and religious topics, including The Path
Which Led a Protestant Lawyer to the Catholic Church; The
American Theory of Government; Recollections and Opinions of
an Old Pioneer; and Reasons Why We Should Believe in God.
Originally a mbr. of Christian (Disciples) church, was converted to Roman Catholicism while residing in Ore. m. in
1828 to Harriet W. Rogers, of Tenn. Three s.; three d. D.
at San Francisco May 17, 1895.

McDOUGAL, JOHN (1851-1852). b. in 1818 in Ross Co.,

Ohio. While still a small child moved with parents to Indianapolis, Ind., where he attd. common schools. Volunteered for service during Black Hawk War in 1832 at age 14.
Apptd. supt. of Ind. prison at Jeffersonville in 1841.
Served as capt. of volunteer company in the War with Mexico,
1846-1847. Left for Calif. with family by way of Panama in
1848. Settled at Sacramento in 1849, where an older brother
had become a merchant. Learned of discovery of gold in
Calif. while en route. Engaged in mining for a short time,
but with little success. Became proprietor of a merc. bus.
at Sacramento. Mbr. of conv. that drew up a provisional
const. for the proposed State of Calif. in 1849, and was el.
provisional Lieut. Gov. under that plan of govt. Succeeded
to office of Gov. in Jan., 1851 when Gov. Burnett resigned,
and completed the term of Gov. Burnett. During admin.,
legislation was adopted by the legislature, which had convened at San Jose, providing for its meeting at Vallejo with
purpose of making that the capital of Calif., a plan later
abandoned in favor of making Sacramento the capital. Steps
were taken to complete the org. of govt. and ground-work
laid for establishment of a pub. school system. Admin.
marked by formation of first San Francisco Vigilante Commt.,
an assoc. of bus. men and others who during the summer of
1851 took into their own hands the apprehension and punishment of wrong-doers against the lives and property of the
city's inhabitants. Some of those apprehended were executed;
others were banished from the city by the Vigilantes. McD.
lost popularity by taking a stand against the Vigilantes,
who challenged his authority by re-taking into custody two
persons accused of serious crimes and executing them. Described as a man of "intemperate habits," which impaired his
ability to function effectively as Gov. Somewhat eccentric
in dress and manners. Unsuccessful cand. for reel. in 1851.
After tenure as Gov., continued to play a role in state
politics. Judgment became impaired in later years of life
because of excessive drinking. Challenged a newspaper ed.
to a duel because of alleged defamatory remarks about his
performance as Gov. Wounded his opponent slightly in the
ensuing encounter. Another duel in which he was about to
engage was stopped by govtl. authorities. Sought to commit
suicide late in life, believing he was afflicted with an incurable malady. m. to ----- of Indianapolis, Ind. D. at
San Francisco March 30, 1866.

    BIGLER, JOHN (1852-1856). b. Jan. 8, 1805 near Car-
lisle, Pa. s. of Jacob and Susan (Dock) B., a family of
German origin. Was the older brother of Wm. B., who became
Gov. of Pa. (q.v.). Received common school educ. Entered
Dickinson Coll., but withdrew when family moved to area near

Pittsburgh. Learned printer's trade. Became ed. of <u>Centre</u>
<u>County Democrat</u>, at Bellefonte, Pa., 1827-1832. Studied law,
and was admitted to bar and began practice there. In 1846
moved with wife and small child to Mt. Sterling, Ill., and
in 1849 to Calif. after learning of discovery of gold there.
Engaged in a variety of occupations for a time in and around
Sacramento. El. to first Calif. Assembly in 1849, serving
as Speaker of that body on two occasions. Nom. and el. Gov.
as Dem. in 1851, assuming office in Jan., 1852 a few days
before his brother Wm. assumed the office of Gov. in Pa.
Reel. by very close vote in 1853, but was defeated in try
for a third term in 1855 by the Amer. party cand. Both the
1851 and 1853 elections were contested, but he was declared
the winner by the legislature each time after it had investigated the manner in which the vote had been taken and
counted in certain areas. Admin. marked by problems arising
from rapid flow of immigrants, including Chinese, into Calif;
state financial difficulties; and corruption among officials.
Favored steps to encourage White immigration, but advocated
restrictions on Oriental immigrants. Establishment of U.S.
Mint and Navy Yard at San Francisco occurred during his
admin., as well as the beginning of the Pac. Coast survey.
Sacramento was designated as the State's capital. Following
tenure as Gov., served from 1857 to 1861 as U.S. Minister to
Chile by apptmt. from Pres. Buchanan. Defeated as Dem. nominee for U.S. House seat in 1863. Delegate to Dem. natl.
convs. in 1864 and 1868. Nom. by Pres. Johnson for post of
U.S. internal revenue collector for Sacramento dist., but
the Senate refused to confirm the apptmt. In 1868 established a newspaper in Sacramento, the <u>State Capital Reporter</u>.
m. and was the father of one d. D. at Sacramento Nov. 29,
1871.

JOHNSON, J(AMES?) NEELY (NEELEY?) (1856-1858). b. Aug.
2, 1825 in Gibson Co., Ind. Father was a soldier and prominent Ind. politician. Moved to Evansville as a young man,
and later to Iowa. Began study of law and was admitted to
Iowa bar in 1846. In 1849 went overland to Calif. after
learning of discovery of gold there. Settled in Sacramento,
where he engaged in various occupations before beginning law
practice. El. city atty. for Sacramento in 1850, and later
served as pros. atty. for his dist. Served as col. on the
staff of Gov. McDougal and participated in the so-called
Mariposa War against Indians which resulted in the discovery
and exploration of the Yosemite Valley. Mbr. of Calif. Assembly in 1853. Originally a Whig, affiliated with the Amer.
(Know Nothing) party when it was organized in Calif. in 1854,
and he was nom. as its cand. and el. Gov. in 1855, defeating
incumbent Gov. Bigler. Advocated economy in govt. and re-

duction of pub. debt. Pressed claims of the State for reimbursement from the Fed. govt. for expenditures in connection with expeditions against Indians. Admin. marked by a
resurgence of the Vigilante movement in San Francisco. It
assumed the powers of a de facto govt. in the city and State,
with some 8,000 men organized into para-military units at
its disposal. It seized a prominent local political figure,
an ed. who was being held in jail on a charge of killing a
rival ed., and executed him forthwith. During its resurgence, the Vigilantes effected four executions, deported 25
individuals from the State, and induced the departure of an
estimated 800 other "undesirables." Resistance was offered
against its demands and actions by the Gov., which cost him
much loss of popularity. As Civil War and disunion threatened, J. took a strong stand for the preservation of the
Union. Although advocating sparing use of the veto, he
vetoed 14 bills on constl. grounds. After tenure as Gov.,
engaged in a mining venture, but suffered serious losses.
Moved to Carson City, Nevada Terr., in 1860 and resumed practice of law there. Became a mbr. of the Nevada constl.
convs. in 1863 and 1864, and after the State of Nevada was
created, became a mbr. of the Nevada Supreme Ct. in 1867.
In 1871 was apptd. by Pres. Grant as mbr. of the Bd. of Examiners for West Point Mil. Acad. Moved to Salt Lake City,
Utah, in 1872, where he practiced law. m. in 1852 to Mary
Zabriskie, of Sacramento. Two children. D. Aug. 31, 1872
at Salt Lake City. Bur. at Camp Douglas Cem. there.

WELLER, JOHN B. (1858-1860). b. Feb. 22, 1812 at
Montgomery, Hamilton Co., Ohio. Parents, who were natives
of N.Y., had moved to Ohio in 1810. Attd. local schools and
Miami Univ., 1825-1829. Studied law, was admitted to bar in
1832, and began practice in Hamilton, Ohio. Pros. atty.,
Butler Co., 1833-1836. Mbr. of Bd. of Trustees of Miami
Univ., 1836-1846. El. to U.S. House from Ohio in 1838 and
served for two succeeding terms. Did not seek reel. in 1844.
Assisted in raising a volunteer regiment for U.S.-Mexican
War in 1846 and served as lieut. col., later as col., 1846-
1847. Nom. as Dem. party cand. for Gov. of Ohio in 1848.
Lost by very close margin after a recount of votes. Apptd.
by Pres. Taylor to a joint commn. to establish boundary between U.S. and Mexico in 1849. Resigned that post in 1850
and settled in San Francisco, where he engaged in law practice. El. to U.S. Senate as a Union Dem. in 1852, but
failed to be reel. in 1857. Delegate to Dem. natl. conv. in
1852, where he received the vote of the Calif. delegation
for Pres. of U.S., and of the Calif. and Ohio delegations
for Vice Pres. of U.S. Nom. and el. Gov. as Dem. in 1857.
Admin. highlighted by bitter feud in Dem. party between

factions led by U.S. Senators Gwin and Broderick, respectively. Sen. Broderick, who opposed the pro-slavery policies
of natl. Dem. party, was killed in a duel by David S. Terry,
a former mbr. of Calif. Supreme Ct., in Sept., 1859. The
party feud gave rise to much tension. Six southern counties
of the State voted to withdraw from Calif. and form a new
State. Legislature passed a resolution giving its consent,
which the Gov. approved; but the U.S. Cong. failed to take
any action on the matter. Gov. found it necessary to use
force to take over control of state prison at San Quentin
because of poor mgmt. Also had to use militia forces against
certain Indian tribes, and to quell an anti-Chinese riot in
Shasta Co. Was not considered for re-nom. for Gov. in 1860.
Apptd. by Pres. Buchanan to post of Minister to Mexico in
Nov., 1860, a post he held until he was replaced at the beginning of Pres. Lincoln's admin. in 1861. Supported John
C. Breckenridge for Pres. of U.S. in 1860 pres. election.
As Civil War began, became definitely sympathetic with Southern cause. Engaged in farming on his ranch during Civil War.
Defeated as Dem. cand. for U.S. House in 1863. Delegate to
Dem. natl. conv. in 1864. In 1867 moved to New Orleans, La.,
where he practiced law until his death. Married four times.
First wife was ----- Ryan, of Hamilton, Ohio; second wife
was ----- Bryan, d. of State Aud. of Ohio (one s.); third
wife, whom he m. in 1845, was Susan McDowell Taylor, of Va.,
d. of a U.S. Congressman and niece of Sen. Thomas H. Benton,
of Mo.; fourth wife, whom he m. in 1854, was Lizzie Brockle-
bank Stanton, a widow. One s. D. of smallpox at New Orleans Aug. 17, 1875. Bur. in Lone Mountain Cem., San
Francisco.

LATHAM, MILTON SLOCUM (1860). b. May 23, 1827 in
Columbus, Ohio. s. of Bela and Juliana (Sterrit) L. Grad.
from Jefferson Coll., in Pa., in 1845. Settled in Russell
Co., Ala. Taught school while studying law. Admitted to
Ala. bar in 1848, and became ct. clerk. Moved to Calif.
shortly thereafter, where he became ct. clerk and practiced
law in Sacramento, 1848-1850. Dist. atty. for Sacramento
and El Dorado Counties, 1851. El. to U.S. House as Dem. in
1852. Did not seek reel. Apptd. collector of the port of
San Francisco by Pres. Pierce in 1855, serving until 1857.
Nom. and el. Gov. as a Lecompton Dem. in 1859. Served as
Gov. only a few days. Resigned to take seat in U.S. Senate,
having been el. to fill vacancy caused by death of Sen.
Broderick. Served remainder of Broderick's term, until
March, 1863. Attitude on Civil War wavered. Supported the
candidacy of John C. Breckenridge for Pres. of U.S. in 1860
pres. election. Spoke for Union cause in early stages of
the war, but later became quite critical of Pres. Lincoln's

policies. After retirement from the Senate, travelled in
Europe for two years and then engaged in bus. and law practice at San Francisco. Became mgr. of San Francisco office
of the London and San Francisco Bank, 1865-1878. Also acquired interest in Calif. Pac. R.R., and steamship lines.
Became quite wealthy, but lost much of fortune in subsequent
bus. ventures. Moved to New York City in 1879, where he became pres. of N.Y. Mining and Stock Exch., 1880-1882. m. in
1853 to Sophie Birdsall, who died in 1867. m. in 1870 to
Mary McMullen. One child. D. March 4, 1882 in New York
City. Bur. in Lone Mountain Cem., San Francisco.

DOWNEY, JOHN GATELY (1860-1862). b. June 24, 1827 in
County Roscommon, Ireland. s. of Dennis and Bridget (Gately)
D. Father was a stock farmer. Son emigrated to Md. in 1842,
where he attd. school. Apprenticed as a pharmacist in Washington, D.C. Worked for a drug and stationery firm in
Vicksburg, Miss. Became proprietor of his own pharmacy bus.
in Cincinnati, Ohio in 1846. Went to Calif. during the 1849
"Gold Rush." After brief experience as miner, worked for a
wholesale drug firm in San Francisco, and later opened own
firm with a partner in Los Angeles in 1850. Became a U.S.
citizen in 1851. Bus. prospered and he accumulated a substantial sum of money within a few years, which he invested
in real estate. Also engaged in stock raising. Eventually
acquired some 75,000 acres of land around site of present
city of Downey, which he developed as town site. Became active in politics in 1850s, serving two terms on Los Angeles
city council. Nom. and el. Lieut Gov. as Lecompton Dem. in
1859. Succeeded to office of Gov. shortly after beginning
of Gov. Latham's term and completed Latham's term. As Civil
War neared, expressed views sympathetic to the pro-slavery
wing of the Dem. party. Supported Sen. Douglas for Pres. of
U.S. in 1860 pres. election. After outbreak of conflict,
considered it his duty to cooperate with Lincoln admin. in
raising volunteer units for the Union cause, but advocated
use of troops only for defensive purposes. Favored move to
create a separate State by southern counties to Calif.
Vetoed bill to place devel. of San Francisco water-front in
hands of a pvt. corp. Defeated for nom. of Union Dem. party
for regular term in 1861. Devoted attention thereafter
mainly to real estate devel. and other bus. activities.
Union Dem. cand. for Gov. in 1863, but lost in the gen.
election. Delegate to the Union Dem. party natl. conv. in
1864. Declined nom. for U.S. House as Dem. in 1864. Also
declined to become cand. of the Workingmen's party for Gov.
in 1879. Along with others, donated land for site of the
Univ. of So. Calif. in 1870, and was a mbr. of its first
governing bd. Founder and vice pres. of the Historical

Soc. of So. Calif. m. first in 1852 to Maria Guirado, of
Los Angeles, who was killed in a railroad accident in 1883.
m. in 1888 to Rose V. Kelley, who died in 1892. No children.
D. at Los Angeles March 1, 1894.

STANFORD, (AMASA) LELAND (1862-1863). b. March 9, 1824
at Watervliet, N.Y. s. of Josiah and Elizabeth (Phillips) S.
Father was a prosperous farmer who also engaged in construction of pub. works, including railroads. Received academic
educ. Studied law, admitted to bar, and entered law firm in
Albany in 1845. In 1848 moved to Port Washington, Wisc.,
where he practiced law. After he lost his library and other
property by fire there in 1852, moved to Cold Springs, Calif.
and later to Michigan Bluff, Calif. Joined three of his
brothers who were already established in bus. at latter
place. In 1855 started merc. bus. of his own in Sacramento,
which prospered. Formerly a Whig, became active in the newly-formed Rep. party. Defeated as Rep. nominee for Gov. in
1859. Chosen as delegate to Rep. natl. conv. in 1860, but
did not attend. Nom. and el. Gov. as Rep. in 1861. Cooperated with U.S. govt. in prosecution of Civil War. Favored use of pub. funds for railroad constr. Signed measure
establishing Calif. State Normal Coll. (now San Jose State).
In 1863 became pres. of newly-organized Cent. Pac. R.R.
After Civil War devoted attention to building Pac. end of
transcontinental railroad, which was completed in 1869. Became involved in other bus. enterprises, including a steamship line. Organized So. Pac. R.R., of which he was pres.
from 1885-1890. It became a powerful factor in Calif.
politics for several decades. El. to U.S. Senate as Rep. in
1884 and was reel. in 1890. m. in 1850 to Jane Elizabeth
Lathrop, of Albany, N.Y. One s., Leland S., Jr., who died
in Italy at the age of 16. Founded Leland Hanford Univ.,
at Palo Alto, Calif., contributing land and endowment, as a
memorial to his son. D. at Palo Alto June 21, 1893 while
still a mbr. of U.S. Senate. Bur. in family mausoleum on
grounds of Stanford Univ.

LOW, FREDERICK FERDINAND (1863-1867). b. June 30,
1828 at Frankfort (now Winterport), Me. Father was a farmer
of modest means. Attd. pub. schools there and Hampden Acad.
Trained as apprentice in merc. firm in Boston for five years.
In 1849 went to Calif. by ship via Panama. Engaged in mining for a short time with moderate success, and then became
involved in merc. bus. in San Francisco. Was one of the incorporators of the Calif. Steam Navigation Co. in 1854.
Later engaged in banking at Marysville, Calif. El. to U.S.
House as a Rep. in 1861 as one of three House mbrs. from
Calif. Was at first refused seat by the House on the ground

that the State was entitled to only two seats, but was eventually seated under the terms of a spec. act permitting Calif. to have a third congressman. Did not seek reel. In 1863 was apptd. by Pres. Lincoln to the post of U.S. revenue collector at the port of San Francisco. Later that year was nom. and el. as Union (Rep.) cand. for Gov., defeating former Gov. Downey. As Gov., gave strong support to Union cause. Advocated economy in govt. Used veto freely, particularly against local and spec. legislation. Favored establishment of a State Univ. by a merger with the Coll. of Calif., a step that was taken in 1868. Recommended ratification of 14th Amdt. to U.S. Const. Opposed further immigration by Chinese, but advocated fair treatment of those already in U.S. Following the assassination of Pres. Lincoln, serious riots occurred in San Francisco directed against certain anti-Lincoln newspapers, which necessitated placing the city under martial law for a time. Declined renom. for a second term. In 1869 was apptd. by Pres. Grant Minister to China, a post in which he served until 1874. As such, negotiated several treaties directed toward improving trade relations with China. Retired to devote attention to bus. interests in banking, lumbering, and the sugar-cane indus. in Hawaii. m. in 1850 to Mollie Creed, of San Francisco. One d. D. at San Francisco July 21, 1894. Bur. in Laurel Hill Cem. there.

HAIGHT, HENRY HUNTLEY (1867-1871). b. May 20, 1825 at Rochester, N.Y. s. of Fletcher M. and Elizabeth S. (McLachlan) H. Father was a lawyer who later became a U.S. dist. judge in Mo. Attd. Rochester Collegiate Inst., and Yale, from which he was grad. in 1844 with high honors. Joined father in Mo. Studied law and was admitted to bar at St. Louis in 1846. Practiced there until 1849, when he went to Calif. Father also moved to Calif. in 1854, where he again became a U.S. dist. ct. judge in 1861. Son rapidly gained recognition in Calif. as an able lawyer. Became active in newly-formed Rep. party, serving as ch. of its state commt. in 1859-1860. Opposed secession, but became a supporter of Gen. McClellan in the 1864 pres. election because of the abolitionist trend in the Rep. party. In post-Civil War period was a supporter of Pres. Johnson's reconstruction policies. Having become disillusioned with the Rep. party, changed affiliation to the Dem. party. Became the Dem. cand. for Gov. in 1867 and was el. As Gov., opposed railroad interests, which he felt had become too dominant in Calif. politics. Opposed granting of subsidies for railroad constr. and the granting of pay increases to mbrs. of the legislature. Opposed ratification of the proposed 14th and 15th Amdts. to the U.S. Const. Opposed enfranchisement of

Chinese as well as mbrs. of the Black race. Supported legislation which sought to regulate admission of Oriental
laboring people into Calif. independently of the policies of
the natl. govt. in that regard, a position that was later
held invalid by the U.S. Supreme Ct. Favored legislation
setting the eight-hour day standard for some industries.
Nom. for the succeeding term, but was defeated in the gen.
election of 1871. Retired thereafter to law practice. El.
as delegate to the state constl. conv. in 1878, but died before it met. m. in 1855 to Anna E. Bissell, of St. Louis,
Mo. Five children. Presbyterian. D. at San Francisco
Sept. 2, 1878. Bur. in Oakland.

BOOTH, NEWTON (1871-1875). b. Dec. 30, 1825 at Salem,
Ind. s. of Beebe and Hannah (Pitts) B. Parents were Quakers. Father was a native of Conn.; mother of N.C. Grad. in
1846 from Asbury (now De Pauw) Univ. with an A.B. degree and
with an A.M. degree in 1850. Worked in a merc. firm for two
years. Studied law at Terre Haute and was admitted to bar
in 1849. Moved to Calif. in 1850. Engaged in wholesale
grocery bus. at Sacramento until 1856, when he returned to
Terre Haute. Practiced law there for two years and travelled
in Europe until 1860, when he returned to Sacramento. Resumed merc. bus. activities and practiced law there. Originally a Dem., he affiliated with Rep. party in 1860 and in
1862 was el. to the Calif. Senate. Nom. and el. Gov. in
1871, defeating incumbent Gov. Haight. As Gov., advocated
legislation against monopolies and favored abolition of subsidies to railroads and closer regulation of corps. Reduced
state debt; favored restriction of immigration of Chinese,
but was willing to let policy thereon be set by the natl.
govt. The Univ. of Calif. at Berkeley began operations during his tenure as Gov. El. to the U.S. Senate as an anti-
monopolist ("Dolly Varden") party mbr. in Nov., 1873, but
did not take seat therein until late in Feb., 1875. An attempt was made unsuccessfully in the interval by the legislature to amend the Calif. const. to make a Gov. ineligible
to any other office during the term to which he was el.; but
such a clause was introduced into the Calif. const. in 1879.
Resigned as Gov. on Feb. 21, 1875 to take Senate seat. Did
not seek reel. at end of term. Resumed bus. activities in
Sacramento. Remained a bachelor until late in life. m. in
1892 to Mrs. J.T. Glover, widow of a bus. assoc. No children. Was an uncle of Booth Tarkington, the Amer. novelist.
D. at Sacramento July 14, 1892. Bur. in City Cem. there.

PACHECO, ROMUALDO (1875). b. Oct. 31, 1831 at Santa
Barbara, Calif. s. of Romualdo and Ramona (Carillo) P.
Father, who was an officer in the Mexican mil. service, was

killed in a skirmish while protecting the life of the Mexican Gov. of the Province. Mother, who was a resident of San
Diego and a famous beauty, later married a Scottish sea
capt. Educ. by pvt. tutors. Attd. school run by mission-
aries in Hawaii until 1843, where he was an apprentice seaman for a time and studied navigation. Returned to Calif.
and worked on stepfather's ships in Calif. coastal trade and
also helped in mgmt. of ranch owned by his mother. Became
active in politics. El. to Calif. Assembly in 1853 and to
the Senate in 1857. Served as co. judge, 1855-1859. Again
a mbr. of Calif. Senate in 1861. Switched party affiliation
from Dem. to Rep. following outbreak of Civil War. El.
State Treas. in 1863, but was defeated for reel. in 1867.
Mbr. of Calif. legislature again, 1869-1871. Nom. and el.
Lieut. Gov. as a Rep. in 1871, and succeeded to the office
of Gov. in 1875 when Gov. Booth resigned. Completed term
for which Booth was el., becoming thereby the first native-
born Californian to occupy the office of Gov. Failed to win
Rep. nom. for either the office of Gov. or Lieut. Gov., but
ran unsuccessfully as the cand. of the People's ("Dolly
Varden") party for Lieut. Gov. and received more votes than
the regular Rep. cand. for that office. El. by margin of
one vote in 1876 to U.S. House as a Rep. in 1876 and assumed seat, but was eventually unseated by the House in 1878
following a contest initiated by his opponent. El. to the
U.S. House again in 1879 and 1881. Was not a cand. for continuation in seat in 1883. Apptd. U.S. Minister to Cent.
Amer. States by Pres. Harrison, serving from 1890 to 1893.
Retired to pursue bus. interests at Oakland, Calif. m. in
1863 to Mary Catherine McIntire, of Danville, Ky. She was
the author of a number of successful plays and a novel.
One d.; one s. D. Jan. 23, 1899 at Oakland. Bur. in
Mountain View Cem. there.

    IRWIN, WILLIAM (1875-1880). b. in 1827 in Butler Co.,
Ohio. Attd. local schools and Carey's Acad., near Cincinnati. Grad. from Marietta Coll. in 1848. Became a school
teacher in Port Gibson, Miss. for a year. Returned to
Marietta Coll., where he acted as a tutor and studied law
for two years. Emigrated to Calif. in 1852 and then went on
to Ore., where he joined an uncle in the lumbering bus. for
a time. Returned to Calif. in 1854, and engaged in a variety of occupations for several years, including prospect-
ing, operating a livery stable and stage coach line, and
lumbering. Settled finally in Siskiyou Co. El. to the
Calif. Assembly in 1861 and was reel. in 1863. Became ed.
of a local Dem. newspaper in Yreka in 1865. El. to the
Calif. Senate in 1869 and continued in that office until
1875. Was acting Pres. of Senate and warden of San Quentin

penitentiary during time Lieut. Gov. Pacheco was serving in
office of Gov. Nom. and el. Gov. as Dem. in 1875, winning
by a narrow plurality in a three-man contest involving candidates of the Dem., Rep. and People's Indep. ("Dolly
Varden") parties. There was a great deal of political
change and unrest during tenure. Popular agitation against
Chinese immigrant labor was strong. A radical "Workingman's
League" third party took form under the leadership of an
Irish labor leader, Dennis Kearney, featuring opposition to
monopolies, the wealthy element, and Chinese immigrants.
Kearney was arrested and jailed for incitement to riot on
several occasions. An advisory referendum was taken in 1879
on the question of exclusion of Chinese laborers, which resulted in approval of a policy of exclusion by practically
a unanimous vote. I., as Gov., favored the holding of a
constl. conv., and one was held in 1879. He unsuccessfully
opposed adoption of the document it drafted. Approval of
the new const. had the effect of extending his term of office about one year by reason of a change in the term and
election schedule. After tenure as Gov., served from 1883
until time of his death as ch. of the Bd. of Harbor Commnrs.
at San Francisco. m. in 1865 to Amelia Elizabeth Cassidy,
of Fort James, Calif. One d. D. at San Francisco Mar. 15,
1886.

PERKINS, GEORGE (1880-1883). b. Aug. 23, 1839 at
Kennebunkport, Me. s. of Clement and Lucinda (Fairfield) P.
Father was a farmer. Received a rudimentary educ. at neigh-
borhood schools. At age 12 ran away from home to go to sea
as a cabin boy. After several voyages to European ports returned home at age 14 and obtained further schooling, but
soon resumed sea life as a cabin boy. After several more
voyages to Europe, shipped on a vessel bound for Calif. by
way of Cape Horn. Arrived at San Francisco at age 16 in
1855 and decided to remain there. Engaged in various occupations, including mining, teamstering, clerk, lumbering,
whaling and merc. bus. Became proprietor of a gen. store at
Oroville. Later expanded bus. interests into banking and
sheep ranching. Affiliated with Rep. party, and was a mbr.
of its state commt. in 1867. El. to Calif. Senate in 1869
and was reel. for succeeding term. As a mbr., sponsored
measure extending state financial support to the Univ. of
Calif. at Berkeley for the first time. Relocated in San
Francisco, where he became a stockholder in a steamship enterprise, which expanded and prospered. Also became involved in a whaling bus., banking, and railroads. Served as
pres. of San Francisco Merchants Exch.; dir. of Calif. Acad.
of Sci.; mbr. of San Francisco CC; pres. of San Francisco
Art Assoc. Nom. and el. Gov. in 1879 as a Rep. Advocated

policies generally in opposition to those that brought about
adoption of the new const. in 1879, which he opposed; but
used recently granted item veto power over appropriations
freely.   As Gov., advocated restrictions on hydraulic mining
to preserve agri. lands.   After one term, resumed bus. activities.   In 1893 was apptd. to U.S. Senate to fill a vacancy.   Continued in that office until 1915.   As a Senator,
showed spec. interest in maritime affairs and advocated a
strong Pac. Navy.   m. in 1864 to Ruth A. Parker.   Three s.;
four d.   D. at Oakland Feb. 26, 1923.   Bur. in Mountain View
Cem. there.

STONEMAN, GEORGE (1883-1887).   b. Aug. 8, 1822 at
Busti, N.Y.   s. of George and Catherine (Cheney) S.   Attd.
Jamestown Acad. and West Point Mil. Acad., from which he was
grad. with high honors in 1846.   Entered U.S. mil. service as
cavalry officer and served in war with Mexico.   After the
war, was stationed at posts in the West.   Remained in that
area on mil. duty until 1856, when he was transferred to a
post in Tex.   Refused to surrender to Confed. authorities
when Civil War began.   Seized a steamer and made way, with
his command, to N.Y.   Was given a major's commn. and served
on Gen. McClellan's staff.   During the Peninsular campaign
was a brig. gen. in charge of cavalry operations.   Later
served in Western theater of action under Gen. Grant and
Gen. Sherman.   Was captured during the Atlanta campaign in
1864, and was confined for a time at Andersonville prison in
Ga.   After being exchanged resumed U.S. mil. career.   Served
in the West until 1871, when he retired from the Army.   Established residence in Los Angeles, where he acquired a
fruit ranch.   Apptd. by Gov. Irwin to the post of State R.R.
Commnr. in 1876 and in 1879 was el. to that position after
it was made elective.   Opposed influence of railroad companies in politics.   Nom. and el. Gov. as Dem. in 1882,
serving for one term.   During admin., practiced economy in
govt., reducing taxes to the lowest ratio in the State's
history.   Was not a cand. for re-nom. in 1886.   Lost home by
fire during his tenure as Gov.   Retired to his ranch thereafter.   Later moved to Buffalo, N.Y. to reside with a sister.
By spec. act of Cong. was re-instated in the Army in 1891
with the rank of col. to afford him the advantages of mil
retirement privileges then in effect. ˙ m. in 1865 to Mary
Oliver Hardesty, of Baltimore, Md.   Four children.   D. at
Buffalo, N.Y. Sept. 5, 1894.   Bur. in Lakewood Cem.,
Chautauqua Lake, N.Y.

BARTLETT, WASHINGTON (1887).   b. Feb. 29, 1824 at
Savannah (Augusta?), Ga.   s. of Cosam E. and Sarah E.B.
Family was originally from New England.   Father was an ed.

and publ. of a newspaper. Educ. in schools in Savannah and
at Tallahassee, Fla., to which place his family had moved in
1837. Learned printer's trade. Went to Calif. in 1849 and
engaged in printing work at San Francisco. Printed first
book published in Calif., a guide to gold mining regions.
Founded a newspaper with a partner, the San Francisco Daily
Journal of Commerce, in 1850. After its office was destroyed by fire the next year, went into partnership with
brother as publ. of the Daily Evening News in 1853, which
became the True Californian in 1857. Newspaper eventually
failed, leaving him with a debt which he paid off in the
course of the next ten years. Advocated passage of Compromise of 1850, which included admission of Calif. to statehood. Participated in the Vigilante movement of 1856. El.
clerk of San Francisco Co. in 1859 as a cand. of the People's
party, an arm of the Vigilante movement, and was reel. for
three terms. Studied law and was admitted to bar in 1863.
Practiced law with a brother in San Francisco until 1867.
Served as San Francisco Harbor Commnr., 1870-1872. Mbr. of
Calif. Senate, 1873-1877. Affiliated with Dem. party in
1875. El. mayor of San Francisco in 1882 and continued for
succeeding term. Maintained order in the face of threats of
labor violence, and kept the city out of financial difficulties. Nom. and el. Gov. as Dem. in 1886, defeating his
Rep. opponent by a narrow margin in an election in which
most Dem. candidates lost. Generous in support of worthy
charitable and other social uplift causes, never allowing
his personal fortune to rise above $100,000. Lived very
frugally. Never married. Mbr., I.O.O.F. D. at Oakland at
the home of a sister Sept. 12, 1887, some seven months after
inauguration as Gov. Bur. in Mountain View Cem. there.

WATERMAN, ROBERT WHITNEY (1887-1891). b. Dec. 15, 1826
at Fairfield, N.Y. s. of John D. and Mary Graves (Waldo) W.
Father was a merchant, who died soon after son was born.
Brought up by older brothers, who had moved to Ill. Educ.
in Sycamore, Ill. schools. Worked as clerk in a store until
1846. Went into merc. bus. on his own at Belvidere, Ill.
Apptd. to postmastership at Geneva, Ill. in 1850, but soon
left for Calif. to prospect for gold on the Feather River.
Remained there two years. Returned to Ill., where he resumed bus. activities at Wilmington. Became publ. of a
weekly newspaper there, the Independent, from 1852 to 1860.
Was one of the founders of the Rep. party in Ill., and was
an active supporter of Lincoln in his campaigns for the
Senate in 1858 and the presidency of U.S. in 1860. In 1873
moved to Calif. again, settling first at Redwood City, later
moving to San Bernardino Co. With a partner, discovered and
developed silver mine in Calico dist. Expanded mining

operations. Acquired extensive land holdings and mine properties. Became founder of the town of Waterman Junction,
which was later re-named Barstow, and participated in the
org. of San Diego, Guyanaca and Eastern R.R. in So. Calif.
Nom. and el. Lieut. Gov. as Rep. in 1886, although a Dem.
(Bartlett) was chosen Gov. at same time   Also had the endorsement of the Amer. party in the election. Succeeded to
the office of Gov. upon death of Gov. Bartlett and completed
Bartlett's term. Did not make extensive changes in admin.
personnel at once, despite the change in party control of
the office of Gov. Recommended changes in system of financial admin. procedures. Opposed lingering movement for
separation of southern counties to form a new State. State
Normal at Chico was opened during admin. Was not considered
for nom. for full term in 1890 by Rep. conv. m. to Jane
Gardner, of Belvidere, Ill. in 1847. Two children. D.
April 12, 1891 at his home in San Diego shortly after leaving office.

MARKHAM, HENRY HARRISON (1891-1895). b. Nov. 16, 1840
at Wilmington, N.Y. s. of Nathan B. and Susan (McLeod) M.
Educ. in pub. and pvt. schools, including Wheeler's Acad.,
in Vt. Worked on the family farm until 1862. Moved to
Manitowoc, Wisc. in that year, and became a school teacher
there. Enlisted in U.S. Army in 1863 as a pvt., and served
during the remainder of the Civil War. Participated in
Sherman's march to the sea in 1864, and received a serious
wound in 1865, from which he never fully recovered. Studied
law, admitted to Wisc. bar in 1867, and practiced law in
Milwaukee until 1878. Moved to Pasadena, Calif. in 1879 for
reasons of health. Engaged in law practice and eventually
became involved in various bus. enterprises there in the
fields of gold and silver mining, furniture mfg., banking
and oil. In 1884 was el. as Rep. to the U.S. House. Declined to seek reel. in 1886. Nom. as Rep. cand. for Gov.
in 1890, defeating a cand. favored by the natl. org. of the
party for the nom., and was el. after an exciting campaign.
Was the first Rep. from So. Calif. to be chosen Gov. Opposed trusts and lavish expenditures by govt. Favored legislation restricting Chinese immigration and the adoption of
the Australian ballot system. Advocated arb. of labor disputes, on which legislation was passed that proved to be
largely ineffectual. Second half of term accompanied by
economic distress and severe drought conditions. Labor unrest, particularly in the railroad indus., required use of
militia forces to maintain order. Declined to seek reel.
in 1894. Mbr., Bd. of Mgrs. of Natl. Home for Disabled
Volunteer Soldiers from 1889 until death, except for the

period he was Gov. m. in 1876 to Mary Adams Dana. Five d.
D. at Pasadena Oct. 9, 1923. Bur. in Mountain View Cem.

BUDD, JAMES HERBERT (1895-1899). b. May 18, 1851 at
Janesville, Wisc. s. of Joseph H. and Lucinda (Ash) B.
Parents were natives of N.Y. Father was a lawyer. Moved
with parents to Calif. in 1858, the family eventually settling in Stockton in 1861. Attd. pub. schools there; Brayton
Coll., in Oakland; and the Univ. of Calif., Berkeley, from
which he was grad. in 1873 as a mbr. of its first class.
Studied law in father's office, admitted to bar in 1874 and
began practice in Stockton. Becoming interested in politics
at an early age, was a mbr. of the Dem. state commt. while
still in college. Deputy dist. atty., 1873-1874. Served in
Calif. State Guard as lieut., later as major. Lieut. col.
on Gov. Booth's staff, 1873-1874. Refused nom. for seat in
Calif. Assembly in 1876, but was nom. and el. to U.S. House
in 1882 in a dist. normally Rep. Did not seek second term.
Became police and fire commnr. at Stockton in 1889, and was
ch. of Dem. co. and city commts. Mbr. of Stockton city
charter commn. and also a trustee of Stockton Library for
six years. Nom. and el. Gov. as Dem. in 1894 by a narrow
plurality over Rep. and Pop. party candidates. Advanced
strong criticism of involvement of So. Pac. R.R. in Calif.
politics during campaign. Recommended reform of system of
admin. of state institutions as well as changes in local
govt.; but the legislature, controlled by the opposition
parties, was reluctant to respond favorably. San Diego
State Normal Coll. began operations during tenure. Apptd. a
mbr. of his party to the office of Lieut. Gov. when the office became vacant some ten months after his term began, an
action subsequently upheld by the Calif. cts. as being within his authority. Retired after one term to resume law
practice. Became a mbr. of Univ. of Calif. Bd. of Regents
in 1900. m. in 1873 to Inez A. Merrill, a widow. D. at
Stockton July 30, 1908. Bur. in Rural Cem. there.

GAGE, HENRY TIFFT (1899-1903). b. Nov. 25, 1852 near
Geneva, N.Y. s. of Dewitt C. and Catherine (Glover) G.
Father was a lawyer. Parents moved to East Saginaw, Mich.
when son was quite young. Attd. pub. schools; also studied
with pvt. tutors. Studied law in father's office and was
admitted to Mich. bar in 1873. Moved to Calif. in 1874 and
established residence eventually in Los Angeles in 1877,
where he practiced law. Prospered in his profession, having
many large corps. as clients, including the So. Pac. R.R.
Engaged in local and state politics as mbr. of Rep. party.
City atty. for Los Angeles in 1881. Delegate to Rep. natl.
conv. in 1888. Nom. and el. Gov. as Rep. and Union party

cand. in 1898, having had the support of the So. Pac. R.R.
interests.   Campaign featured heavily issues arising from
the Spanish-Amer. War and its aftermath.   During admin., intervened successfully to bring about settlement of a team-
sters and dockworkers strike that was endangering pub. order
and threatening to bring bus. activity in San Francisco to a
standstill.   Was one of first instances of a Gov.'s serving
successfully as a mediator to avert serious disruptions
arising from labor-mgmt. disputes.   Failed to win re-nom.
for the office of Gov. in the Rep. conv. in 1902 because of
factional disputes in the party.   Resumed law practice and
bus. activities.   Apptd. U.S. Minister to Portugal by Pres.
Taft in 1909, serving until 1911.   m. in 1890 to Frances V.
Rains, a mbr. of a distinguished landed So. Calif. family of
Spanish ancestry.   Five children.   The family residence, on
a large livestock and fruit ranch at Downey, was a show-
place for many years.   D. at Downey Aug. 28, 1924.

PARDEE, GEORGE COOPER (1903-1907).   b. July 25, 1857 at
San Francisco, Calif.   s. of Enoch Homer and Mary Elizabeth
(Pardee) P.   Family was of French Huguenot extraction.
Father had gone to Calif., where he worked as a mechanic,
later becoming an oculist and aurist.   Father was active in
politics, having served as mayor of Oakland and as a mbr. of
Calif. Senate.   Attd. pub. schools in San Francisco and Oakland.   Grad. from the Univ. of Calif., Berkeley, in 1879,
and received an A.M. degree from there in 1881.   Attd.
Cooper Med. Coll. for two years.   Received an M.D. degree
from the Univ. of Leipzig, Germany, in 1885.   Entered practice at Oakland with father in 1885, specializing in diseases of the eye and ear.   Mbr., Oakland Bd. of Health,
1889-1891; city councilman, 1891-1893; mayor, 1893-1895.
Nom. as the "anti-machine" cand. and el. Gov. as Rep. in
1902, becoming the first native-born Californian to be el.
directly to the office.   Result of election was close, and
was contested in the cts.; but his election by a plurality
of some 2,000 votes was allowed to stand.   Sought to maintain an "open door" policy so as to receive benefit of advice or complaints from all.   During admin., the city of
San Francisco experienced the disastrous earthquake and fire
of 1906, requiring the setting in motion of various relief
and re-building programs.   Called a spec. session of the
legislature for that purpose.   Recommended revision of state
revenue system as well as introducing an exec. budget system.
Promoted land conservations programs, becoming vice pres. of
the Natl. Irrigation Cong. in 1904.   Failed to win re-nom.
for Gov. in 1906.   Delegate to Rep. natl. convs. in 1900,
1904, 1912, and 1924.   Joined in the Prog. party movement in
1912, and was a delegate to its natl. conv. that year which

nom. Theodore Roosevelt for Pres. of U.S. Mbr., Astronom-
ical Soc. of Pac.; S.A.R.; Bd. of Regents, Univ. of Calif.,
1899-1903; Natl. Conservation Commn., 1907-1911; ch., Con-
servation Commt. of Calif., 1911-1915; ch., Calif. Forestry
Commn., 1919-1923, and mbr., 1928-1930; pres., East Bay Mun.
Utilities Dist., 1924; mbr., Oakland Port Commn., 1927; ch.,
Calif. Jt. Fed.-State Water Resources Commn., 1930. Mbr.,
Masons; various social clubs and professional med. orgs.
Hon. degree in 1932 from the Univ. of Calif. m. in 1887 to
Helen N. Penniman, of Oakland. Four d. D. at Oakland Sept.
1, 1941.

GILLETT, JAMES NORRIS (1907-1911). b. Sept. 20, 1860
at Viroqua, Wisc. s. of Cyrus Foss and Sarah Jane (Norris)
G. Family was originally from New England. Attd. schools
at Sparta, Wisc., to which place his family had moved in
1865. Studied law, admitted to bar in 1881 and practiced in
Sparta for two years. In 1883, moved to Bozeman, Mont. and
then to Seattle, Wash., where he worked for a lumber firm
and also practiced law. Moved to Eureka, Calif. in 1884,
where he was again employed in the lumbering bus. and also
practiced law. City atty. for Eureka, 1889-1895. Mbr. of
Calif. Senate, 1897-1899. El. to U.S. House as Rep., serving from 1903 to 1906. Resigned House seat in 1906 after
having been nom. and el. Gov. as Rep. Won nom. contest
against incumbent Gov. Pardee. During admin., the banking
and ins. code was revised; a railroad rate bill passed; a
pure food law enacted; and a highway program advanced. A
direct primary system for partisan nominations for pub. office was adopted by the voters in 1908. At request of Pres.
Roosevelt, assisted in defeat of a bill providing for segregated schools for Oriental children. Called a spec. session
of the legislature to deal with banking problems arising from
the financial panic of 1907. Was not a cand. for reel. in
1910. Retired to law practice after tenure as Gov. Mbr.,
Amer. Astronomical Soc.; various clubs and professional
legal orgs. m. in 1886 to Adelaide M. Pratt, who died in
1896. Two d.; one s. m. in 1898 to Elizabeth Erzgraber.
One s. D. at Berkeley, Calif. April 21, 1937.

JOHNSON, HIRAM WARREN (1911-1917). b. Sept. 2, 1866 at
Sacramento, Calif. s. of Grove Laurence and Annie (de Mont-
fredy) J. Father, who was a lawyer, had moved from N.Y. to
Calif. in 1863 and had been a mbr. of U.S. House from Calif.
Attd. schools in Sacramento and the Univ. of Calif., Berkeley, which he left in junior year to get married. Studied
law in father's office while also working as a ct. reporter.
Admitted to bar in 1888 and practiced law in Sacramento with
father and brother. Broke with father as political differ-

ences developed.   In 1902 moved to San Francisco, where he
continued in law practice and also served as mbr. of the
staff of the dist. atty.   Came to wide pub. notice for vigorous prosecution of criminal elements, including Abe Ruef,
the Rep. "boss" in San Francisco.   Nom. by Rep. party at the
primary for Gov. in 1910 on a "reform" platform.   Ensuing
campaign was very bitter, with pub. service corps., So. Pac.
R.R. interests, the party "machine," and his father in opposition, but he won election.   Successfully sponsored a series
of sweeping reform amdts. to the state const. and other regulatory legislation while Gov.   Used "ripper" bills to remove uncooperative officials from office.   Urged admin. reforms designed to strengthen Gov.'s control over policy
formulation and admin.   Was a strong supporter of Theodore
Roosevelt for the Rep. nom. for Pres. of U.S. in the 1912
Rep. conv., and later accepted the nom. for Vice Pres. of
U.S. on the Prog. party ticket with Roosevelt.   Reel. Gov.
in 1914 as a Prog., defeating Rep. and Dem. party opponents.
Sponsored legislation permitting a cand. to file for nom. at
a primary by a party or parties other than his own, with a
proviso that he must win his own party's nom. to appear on
the gen. election ballot as a nominee of one or more par-·
ties.   Signed bill restricting Japanese land ownership, despite strong objections of Pres. Wilson.   Resigned as Gov.
in Mar., 1917, having been el. to a seat in U.S. Senate.
Continued to hold a seat in the Senate until his death.   Unsuccessful cand. for Rep. nom. for Pres. of U.S. in 1920 and
1924.   Also received some delegate support in 1928 conv.
Was one of the leaders of bi-partisan group in the Senate to
refuse consent to ratification of the Versailles Treaty in
1919-1920, unless reservations were added to it.   Continued
to oppose U.S. involvement in the League of Nations thereafter.   Mbr., N.S.G.W.; Masons (K.T.); professional legal
orgs.   m. in 1886 to Minnie L. McNeal, of San Francisco.
Two s.   D. at Bethesda, Md. Aug. 6, 1945.   Bur. at Cyprus
Lawn Cem., San Francisco.

STEPHENS, WILLIAM DENNISON (1917-1923).   b. Dec. 26,
1859 at Eaton, Ohio.   s. of Martin F. and Alvira (Leibee) S.
Attd. pub. schools in Eaton.   Became a rural school teacher.
Studied law, but was not admitted to the bar until after removal to Calif. later.   Became an employee of railroad engr.
firm and engaged in railroad constr. work in various places
in Midwest and South, 1880-1887.   Moved to Los Angeles in
1887.   Became salesman for a wholesale grocery firm there.
Went into grocery bus. with a partner, 1902-1909.   Vice pres.
of Amer. Natl. Bank at Los Angeles, 1909.   Mbr. of Los Angeles school bd., 1906.   Dir. and pres., Los Angeles CC,
1907.   Mayor of Los Angeles for a short time after Mayor

Harper resigned in face of recall movement. Pres. of Bd. of
Water Commnrs. of Los Angeles, 1910. El. to U.S. House in
1910 and continued in office for two more terms, being reel.
in 1914 as Prog. party nominee. Resigned seat in July, 1916
to accept apptmt. as Lieut. Gov. from Gov. Johnson to fill a
vacancy in that office, and was later el. to the office.
Succeeded to office of Gov. when Gov. Johnson resigned in
Mar., 1917 to take seat in U.S. Senate. Completed Johnson's
term and was el. to a regular term as nominee of Rep., Prog.
and Proh. parties in 1918. Labor unrest during World War I
led to strikes, bombings and other violence, and the Gov.'s
mansion was bombed. Thomas J. Mooney, a labor leader, was
convicted of involvement in a bombing attempt in the San
Francisco "Preparedness Day" parade on the same day S. had
assumed the office of Lieut. Gov. After he became Gov.,
commuted Mooney's sentence of death to life imprisonment,
after intercession had been made by Pres. Wilson. A more
restrictive alien land law directed against Japanese was
adopted by popular referendum in 1920, despite Pres. Wilson's
plea for its rejection. During admin., extensive revamping
of the state admin. system was achieved; taxes on pub. utilities increased; measures adopted to secure better prohibition law enforcement. Was defeated in effort to obtain re-
nom. for another term as Gov. in 1922. Won the Proh. party
nom., but lost the Rep. party nom., which eliminated him as
a cand. in the gen. election. Retired to bus. interests and
law practice. m. to Flora Rawson, of Los Angeles, in 1891.
One d. Mbr., Masons (Shriner, K.T.); Phi Delta Phi; various
social clubs. Hon. degree from the Univ. of So. Calif. in
1921. Methodist. D. April 24, 1944 at Los Angeles. Bur.
in Rosedale Cem. there.

      RICHARDSON, FRIEND WILLIAM (1923-1927). b. at a Quaker
settlement near Ann Arbor, Mich. in Dec., 1865. s. of Wm.
and Rhoda (Dye) R. Descendant of several generations of
Quakers, one of his grandfathers having been an Amer. soldier
during the Rev. War. Had the name "Friend" legalized as a
proper name because in accordance with Quaker custom, that
term was usually employed by associates addressing him during his youth. Family moved to San Bernardino, Calif. when
he was a small child. Attd. pub. schools there. Attd. San
Bernardino Coll. and Sturges Coll. Served as deputy co.
clerk in San Bernardino Co. for four years while studying
law, but did not seek admission to bar until later while
serving as Gov. Became ed. for the San Bernardino Times-
Index, serving from 1895-1901. Moved to Berkeley, Calif. in
1901, where he was the owner and publ. of the Berkeley
Gazette for the next 20 years. Pres. of Calif. Press Assoc.
for 39 years, beginning in 1902. State Printer, 1912-1915.

El. State Treas. in 1914 after having been nom. by both the
Rep. and Prog. parties, and was reel. in 1918. Nom. and el.
as the Rep. cand. for Gov. in 1922, defeating incumbent Gov.
Stephens for the Rep. nom. During admin., favored reduction
of govtl. expenditures and achieved a treas. surplus; favored strict enforcement of laws, including prohibition.
Used veto power extensively. Defeated for Rep. nom. in 1926.
After term as Gov. was State Bldg. and Loan Commnr., 1932-
1934; also served as State Supt. of Banking, 1934-1939.
Publ. of Alameda Times, 1931-1932. Mbr., Masons (Shriner,
K.T., O.E.S.); I.O.O.F.; Elks; M.W.A.; Moose; Rotary; Kiwanis; various clubs. Mbr., Soc. of Friends (Quaker) church.
m. in 1891 to Augusta Felder, of San Bernardino. One s.;
two d. D. Sept. 6, 1943 at Berkeley.

YOUNG, CLEMENT CALHOUN (1927-1931). b. April 28, 1869
at Lisbon, N.H. s. of Isaac E. and Mary R. (Calhoun) Y.
Family moved to Calif. when son was still a child. Attd.
high school at San Jose and Santa Rosa. Grad. from Univ. of
Calif., Berkeley, in 1892. Became a high school teacher of
English at Santa Rosa. From 1893 to 1906 was a teacher and
head of English dept. at Lowell H.S. in San Francisco. Co-
author of a text-book volume on English poetry. Became associated with a suburban bldg. and loan firm in Berkeley and
San Francisco following the 1906 earthquake and fire, continuing in that bus. until 1944. El. to Calif. Assembly in
1908 and was reel. for four succeeding terms. Served as
Speaker, 1913-1919. Identified with Prog. wing of the Rep.
party in 1912. Delegate to Rep. natl. conv. in 1912 and was
a Rep. pres. elector in 1920 election. Nom. and el. Lieut.
Gov. in 1918 and was reel. in 1922, having returned to Rep.
party. Nom. and el. Gov. as Rep. in 1926, defeating incumbent Gov. Richardson in the Rep. primary. As Gov., pursued
policies and programs associated with the more liberal element of Rep. party. Launched a long-range pub. works constr.
program. Set up a Gov.'s Council in 1927, made up of officials of his choice from his admin. Supported enforcement
of prohibition. Favored Colo. River Compact for devel. of
water power. Defeated for re-nom. in 1930. Was also unsuccessful cand. for Rep. nom. for Gov. in 1934. Mbr., Phi
Beta Kappa; Phi Delta Theta; Bd. of Regents of the Univ. of
Calif., 1913-1920. Congregationalist. m. to Lyla Jeannette
Vincent, of San Francisco in 1902. Two d. D. at Berkeley
Dec. 25, 1947.

ROLPH, JAMES, Jr. (1931-1934). b. Aug. 23, 1869 at
San Francisco, Calif. s. of James and Margaret (Nichol) R.
Father had emigrated from London, England to Calif. Attd.
pub. schools in San Francisco and Trinity Acad. there.

Worked as newsboy, cash boy, office boy during vacations.
Became cashier of a shipping and commn. firm. Went into
that bus. on his own in 1898. Later expanded interests into
banking, ins., and ship-building, becoming quite wealthy.
Lost heavily in ship-building program for U.S. govt. during
World War I. Various enterprises were reorg. into one after
the war, the James Rolph Co. Became mayor of San Francisco
in 1911, and continued in that office until 1930. Vice pres.
of Panama Pac. Exposition in 1915. Sought both the Rep. and
Dem. party noms. for Gov. in 1918. Won the Dem. party nom.,
but failed to win that of the Rep. party. Under the State's
cross-filing system then in effect, had to relinquish the
Dem. party nom. Ran nevertheless in the ensuing election as
an Indep. without a party designation, but lost. Nom. as
Rep. cand. for Gov. in 1930, defeating incumbent Gov. Young
for the nom. Was el. by 3-1 margin over his Dem. opponent.
During admin., in Dec., 1933 a mob seized and lynched two
kidnappers at San Jose. R. received both praise and criticism for failure to use mil. force to prevent the lynching.
Secured passage of measure to impose limitations on oil company operations, but it was defeated in a popular referendum.
Criticized the manner in which the system of prohibition was
being carried out, and eventually advocated repeal of the
18th Amdt. Championed a vast water conservation project for
the Sacramento River basin. Onset of the depression of the
1930s curtailed projected pub. works programs, placed state
finances in a precarious condition, and led to adoption of a
gen. sales tax, which was unpopular. Known as "Sunny Jim"
because of his geniality and exuberant personality. Mbr.,
Masons; Elks; I.O.O.F.; N.S.G.W.; Pres. of Merchants Exch.
and of Shipowners Assoc. of Pac. Coast. m. in 1900 to Annie
Marshall Reid, of San Francisco. Two d.; one s. Episcopalian. D. June 2, 1934 at Linforth Ranch, near Santa Clara,
Calif. while still in office, after having previously decided not to seek reel. because of poor health.

MERRIAM, FRANK FINLEY (1934-1939). b. Dec. 22, 1865
near Hopkinton, Iowa. s. of Henry Clay and Anne Elizabeth
(Finley) M. Father, who was in the lumbering bus., had held
a number of local political offices. Grad. in 1888 from
Lenox Coll., in Hopkinton. Was a teacher in Hopkinton
school system for three years, and later, school principal
at Harper, Iowa and school supt. at Postville, Iowa. Mbr.
of Iowa House, 1895-1899. Iowa State Aud., 1899-1903. From
1893 to 1898 was owner and publ. of the Hopkinton Leader, a
weekly newspaper. In 1904 moved to Muskogee, Okla., where
he became owner and publ. of the Muskogee Evening Times. In
1910 moved to Long Beach, Calif., where he was associated
with the Long Beach Telegram for one year and with the Long

Beach Press from 1912 to 1924. Pres. of Citizens Bank of
Long Beach, 1924-1926. El. to Calif. Assembly in 1916 and
continued in that office for four succeeding terms. Served
as Speaker, 1923-1927. Unsuccessful as cand. for Rep. nom.
for Lieut. Gov. in 1926, but was nom. and el. to that office
in 1930. Succeeded to office of Gov. when Gov. Rolph died
in 1934. Completed Rolph's term and was nom. and el. for a
regular term in 1934. Defeated Upton Sinclair for the office in a nationally-noted contest because of support by
Sinclair, formerly a Socialist, of the "End Poverty in California" plan, an extensive econ. reform program. During
admin., the Oakland Bay Bridge was completed and the State's
highway constr. program expanded and carried on vigorously.
Labor disturbances arising from longshoremen's and agri.
workers strikes were a continual problem. Sponsored measures, including tax revisions, designed to allay econ. distress arising from the depression of the 1930s. Usec veto
power quite freely. Expressed favorable views toward the
Townsend Plan for dealing with plight of the indigent aged.
Was opposed to much of the natl. admin.'s New Deal program
at the outset, but later cooperated freely in measures designed to relieve the plight of the unemployed, the aged, as
well as home owners. Nom. for a succeeding term in 1938,
but was defeated in the gen. election. Mbr., Bd. of Regents
of the Univ. of Calif. for 12 years; ch. of Advisory Pardon
Bd. for four years; mbr. of Calif. Toll Bridge Authority for
eight years. Active in Boy Scout movement, Red Cross, and
Calif. CC. Mbr., S.A.R.; S.O.V.; Masons; Calif. Publishers
and Press Assoc.; Lincoln club. Active in Sunday School
work and Men's Brotherhood of his (Presbyterian) church.
m. in 1889 to Nancy Elnora Hitchcock. One s. m. in 1903 to
Mrs. Mary Bronson-Day, who died in 1931. m. in 1936 to Mrs.
Jessie (Stewart) Lipsey. D. at Long Beach April 25, 1955.

   OLSON, CULBERT LEVY (1939-1943). b. Nov. 7, 1876 at
Fillmore, Utah Terr. s. of Daniel and Delilah (King) O.
Mother was active in women's suffrage movement and was the
first woman to be el. to pub. office in Utah when she was
chosen co. treas. and recorder of Millard Co. Attd. Brigham
Young Univ., 1890-1891 and 1893-1895; Columbian Law School
(now George Washington Univ.), in Washington, D.C., 1897-
1899 and 1900-1901, from which he received a law degree in
in 1901; and the Univ. of Mich., 1899-1900. Worked as a
telegraph operator, 1891; as a reporter and ed. for Ogdem,
Utah, Standard, 1895-1897 and as a Washington correspondent,
1897-1899 while serving on the staff of his cousin, U.S.
Repr. Wm. H. King. Admitted to Utah bar and practiced law
in Salt Lake City, 1901-1920. Also engaged in mining, banking and real estate bus. during that time. Mbr. of Utah

Senate, 1916-1920. Moved to Los Angeles, Calif. in 1920,
where he practiced law. Delegate to Dem. natl. conv. from
Utah in 1920 and from Calif. in 1940, 1944 and 1948. Supported candidacy of Sen. Robt. La Follette as the Prog.
party nominee for Pres. of U.S. in 1924 pres. election. El.
to Calif. Senate as Dem. in 1934. Apptd. asst. to U.S. Atty.
Gen. in 1936 in connection with suits against oil companies,
serving until 1937. Ch. of Calif. Dem. commt. in 1934. Nom.
and el. Gov. as Dem. in 1938, defeating incumbent Gov. Merriam. Dem. nominee for reel. in 1942, but lost in the gen.
election to Earl Warren. Was the first Dem. to hold the office of Gov. since the 1890s. During admin., advocated measures favored generally by union labor interests, and was an
enthusiastic supporter of the New Deal. Granted pardon to
Thomas Mooney, who had been convicted of conspiracy for
murder growing out of Preparedness Day bombings in 1917.
After tenure as Gov. engaged in law practice. Served on
Dem. natl. commt. for a time. Travelled in Europe and the
Near East, and engaged in lecturing and writing. m. in 1905
to Kate Jeremy. Three s. Mbr., Phi Delta Phi. D. at rest
home in Los Angeles April 13, 1962. Bur. in Forest Lawn
Cem., Glendale.

    WARREN, EARL (1943-1953). b. Mar. 19, 1891 at Los
Angeles, Calif. s. of Methias H. and Chrystal (Hernlund) W.
Grandfather emigrated to U.S. from Norway, and had settled
in Iowa. Father was a railroad repairman. Attd. schools in
Bakersfield, Calif. and the Univ. of Calif., Berkeley, from
which he received a B.L. degree in 1912 and a law degree in
1914. Admitted to the bar and joined an Oakland, Calif. law
firm in 1914 after brief employment by an oil firm in San
Francisco. Enlisted as pvt. at beginning of World War I,
and rose to rank of first lieut. by the end of the war.
Later was a capt. in USAR. Clerk of Calif. Assembly Judiciary Commt. in 1919 and was also deputy city atty. of Oakland. Deputy dist. atty. for Alameda Co., 1920-1925 and
dist. atty., 1925-1939. Nom. and el. Calif. Atty. Gen. in
1938, having been nom. by Rep., Dem. and Prog. parties.
Treas., Interstate Commn. on Crime, 1938. Pres., Natl. Assoc. of Attys. Gen., 1940-1941. Delegate to Rep. natl.
convs., 1928, 1932. Ch., Rep. state commt., 1934-1936.
Mbr., Rep. natl. commt., 1936-1938. Nom. and el. Gov. as
Rep. in 1942, defeating incumbent Gov. Olson in the gen.
election. Reel. in 1946, having been nom. by both the Rep.
and Dem. parties. Reel. for third term in 1950 as a Rep.,
defeating the Dem. nominee, James Roosevelt, and becoming
the first Gov. of Calif. el. for third consecutive term.
Temp. ch. and keynote speaker at Rep. natl. conv. in 1944.
Major contender for Rep. nom. for Pres. of U.S. in 1948.

Accepted nom. for Vice Pres. of U.S. in that year on ticket
with Gov. Dewey, of N.Y. (q.v.), but lost in close contest
with Dem. opposition. As Gov., achieved recognition for
vigorous action in field of criminal law enforcement; created
a greatly expanded office staff; supported natl. admin.'s
war effort during World War II, including detainment program
for Japanese-Amers. on West Coast suspected of possible disloyalty; advocated legislation to eliminate corruption in
politics; gave support to merit system; and displayed concern regarding problems arising from rapid industrialization
of Calif. and its rise in importance as an agri. State. Resigned office of Gov. in Oct., 1953 to accept apptmt. as
Chief Justice of U.S. Supreme Ct., a post he held until 1969.
Tenure as Chief Justice notable for numerous landmark decisions in the areas of civil rights and expansion of jud.
control over pub. policy. Ch. of a commn. that investigated
circumstances of the assassination of Pres. John F. Kennedy
in 1963. Mbr., Masons; professional legal orgs.; numerous
clubs. Recipient of over twenty hon. collegiate degrees and
spec. recognition awards from eight foreign govts., including Great Britain, France, Sweden, Italy, the Netherlands,
and Luxemburg. m. in 1925 to Nina (Palmquist) Meyers.
Three s.; three d. D. July 9, 1974 in Washington, D.C.
Bur. in Arlington Natl. Cem.

KNIGHT, GOODWIN JESS (1953-1959). b. Dec. 9, 1896 at
Provo, Utah. s. of Jesse J. and Lillie Jane (Milner) K.
Father was a lawyer and mining engr. who moved family to Los
Angeles when son was eight years old. Worked in lead and
zinc mines in Nev. Later was employed as a reporter for the
Los Angeles News. Attd. Stanford Univ. for a time, but left
in 1918 to serve in U.S. Navy during World War I. Re-entered
Stanford Univ., from which he received a degree in 1919. As
a student was prominent in debating, athletics, student orgs.
Attd. Cornell Univ. as a univ. scholar in 1919-1920. Active
worker in Sen. Hiram Johnson's campaigns for Pres. of U.S.
in 1920 and for the U.S. Senate. Admitted to Calif. bar in
1921 and began practice in Los Angeles. Acquired real estate and mining interests, which proved very profitable.
Keynote speaker at Calif. Rep. conv. in 1934. Apptd. by
Gov. Merriam to vacant superior ct. judgeship, and was continued in that post for regular terms in 1936 and 1942.
Nom. and el. Lieut. Gov. as a Rep. in 1946, and was reel. in
1950, having been made the nominee of both the Rep. and Dem.
parties in latter election. Succeeded to the office of Gov.
in Oct., 1933 after Gov. Warren resigned to become Chief
Justice of U.S. Supreme Ct. Positions on some local issues
were more conservative than those of Gov. Warren. Took vigorous action to combat smog problem in cities, particularly

in Los Angeles area. Successful as Rep. nominee for full
term in 1954. Made question of securing larger royalties
for State from off-shore oil leases a major issue. Was dis-
suaded from becoming a cand. for re-nom. for Gov. in 1958.
Became instead the Rep. nominee for the U.S. Senate seat being vacated by Sen. Knowland, who sought the office of Gov.
as the Rep. nominee. Was defeated in the gen. el. Became
active thereafter in bus. affairs, and as a radio commentator. Stated intention to seek the Rep. nom. for Gov. in
1962, but did not follow through because of illness. Mbr.,
Amer. Legion; V.F.W.; Masons (Shriner); Eagles; I.O.O.F.;
K.P.; Elks; various clubs and fraternal orgs. Episcopalian.
m. in 1925 to Arvilla Pearl Cooley. Two d. After her death
in 1952, m. in 1954 to Virginia Carlson, widow of a World
War II Air Force bomber pilot. D. May 22, 1970 at Inglewood,
Calif.

     BROWN, EDMUND GERALD, Sr. ("PAT") (1959-1967). b.
April 21, 1905 at San Francisco, Calif. s. of Edward J.
and Ida (Schuckman) B. Father had emigrated to Calif. in
the "Gold Rush" era. Father was a Catholic, but mother was
a Protestant. Attd. Catholic parochial schools for a time,
but later attd. pub. schools. Acquired nickname of "Pat"
from his school mates because of his fondness for reciting
lines from Patrick Henry's orations. Worked in his father's
store and amusement parlor. Studied law in night school and
received a law degree from San Francisco Law School, a branch
of the Univ. of Calif., in 1927. Admitted to bar and practiced in San Francisco. Unsuccessful as Rep. cand. for
Calif. Assembly in 1928. Changed affiliation to Dem. party
in 1934 and was unsuccessful as Dem. cand. for dist. atty.
of San Francisco in 1939. Mbr., Calif. Code Commn. in 1942,
and of the Golden Gate Bridge and Highway Commn. Delegate
to Dem. natl. conv. in 1940. Ch. of Dem. speakers bureau in
Pres. Roosevelt's campaigns in 1940 and 1944. Nom. and el.
as Dem. dist. atty. for San Francisco in 1942, serving 1943-
1950. Unsuccessful cand. for Atty. Gen. of Calif. in 1946,
but was nom. and el. to that office as Dem. in 1950. Reel.
in 1954, having been nom. by both the Rep. and Dem. parties
for the office. As Atty. Gen., conducted investigations of
liquor and narcotics law enforcement, racial frictions, and
juvenile delinquency. Nom. and el. Gov. as a Dem. in 1958,
defeating Sen. Knowland, the Rep. nominee, in the gen. el.
Reel. in 1962, defeating former Vice Pres. Richard M. Nixon
in the gen. el. During admin., advocated measures to attract new indus.; enactment of a fair employment practices
act; new and expanded higher educl. programs; reform of
labor unions; water resources devel.; opposed "right to work"
law that labor unions also strongly opposed in 1958 election.

Favored abolition of the death penalty in state law enforcement. Carried out an extensive program of admin. reorg.
Was the Dem. nominee for a third term in 1966, but was defeated in the gen. el. by Ronald Reagan. Retired to law
practice and lecturing at the Univ. of Calif. at Los Angeles.
Mbr., professional legal orgs., serving as pres. of Amer. Bar
Assoc. for one term; Elks; N.S.G.W.; numerous clubs. m. in
1930 to Bernice Layne, of San Francisco. Three d.; one s.,
Edmund, Jr. ("Jerry"), who became a Gov. of Calif. (q.v.).

REAGAN, RONALD WILSON (1967-1975). b. Feb. 6, 1911 at
Tampico, Ill. s. of John Edward and Nelle (Wilson) R. Father was a shoe salesman, of Irish descent and a Roman Catholic. Mother was devoted to theater. Family settled in
Dixon, Ill., where son attd. school. Entered Eureka Coll.
in 1928, majoring in econ. and sociology. Active in drama-
tics and sports, and was chosen pres. of student body.
Helped to org. strike by students to protest economy measures of school admin. Worked at part-time jobs while in
college. Received an A.B. degree in 1932 and became a radio
sports announcer at a Davenport, Iowa station. Also wrote a
sports column for a local newspaper. After a screen test
for Warner Brothers studios in 1937, began successful career
as a motion picture actor. Entered U.S. Army in 1942. Held
rank of capt. at time of discharge in 1945. Became involved
in promotion of liberal causes as mbr. of A.D.A. Was a cooperative witness during early 1950s before the House Un-
Amer. Activities Commt. in its investigation of Communist
infiltration into the moving picture indus., particularly
the Screen Actors Guild, of which he had served as pres.
from 1947 to 1952. Became thereafter increasingly conservative in his views on pub. issues. In 1952 and 1956 pres.
campaigns participated in Dems. for Eisenhower orgs. Became
involved in television work as host and news commentator;
also engaged in pub. relations work for Gen. Electric Co.
Acquired a ranch, which he operated as a hobby. Entered
primary campaign of 1966 for Rep. nom. for Gov. Was nom.,
and defeated incumbent Gov. Brown in the gen. el. by a wide
margin. Reel. Gov. in 1970. Admin. characterized by successful efforts to put govt. of state on a sounder financial
basis by tax reforms and controls on expenditure programs.
Major contender for the Rep. nom. for Pres. of U.S. in 1968
and again in 1976, narrowly losing nom. contest in latter
year to incumbent Pres. Ford. Successful contender for the
Rep. nom. for Pres. in 1980. Mbr., Christian (Disciples)
church. Ch., Natl. Govs.' Assoc. in 1969. Mbr., Advisory
Commt. on Intergovtl. Relations, 1970. Mbr., Bd. of Trustees of Eureka Coll. Recipient of awards from N.C.C.J.;
Amer. Red Cross; Freedoms Found.; Amer. Legion; Natl. Safety

Council; Amer. Newspaper Guild. Mbr., Tau Kappa Epsilon;
Amer. Fed. of Radio and TV Artists. m. in 1940 to Jane Wy-
man, a motion picture and stage actress. One d. and one
adopted s. Marriage ended in divorce in 1948. m. in 1952
to Nancy Davis, also an actress. One d.; one s.

BROWN, EDMUND GERALD, Jr. ("JERRY") (1975----). b.
April 7, 1938 at San Francisco. s. of Gov. Edmund G.B., Sr.
(q.v.) and Bernice (Layne) B. Attd. local pub. and parochial schools as a youth. Enrolled at Santa Clara Univ. in
1955, but discontinued work there in 1956 to enter the
Jesuits Sacred Heart Sem., at Los Gatos, to prepare for en-
trance into Catholic priesthood. After four years, withdrew
from that training program and entered the Univ. of Calif.,
Berkeley, from which he received an A.B. degree in 1961.
Attd. Yale, from which he received a law degree in 1964.
Worked in civil rights movement in Miss. during the summer
of 1962. Served as law clerk for a mbr. of Calif. Supreme
Ct., 1965. Spent some time in Latin Amer. travelling and
studying Spanish language. Returned to Los Angeles in 1966
and joined a law firm. Participated in anti-Vietnam War
movement in 1967-1968. Active supporter of Sen. Eugene
McCarthy's attempt to win Dem. nom. for pres. of U.S. in
1968. El. to Bd. of Trustees of Los Angeles Community Coll.
in 1969. Nom. and el. Calif. Sect. of State in 1970. Nom.
and el. Gov. in 1974 as a Dem. and was reel. in 1978. In
first contest for nom. for Gov., was a strong supporter of
an initiative proposal to limit campaign expenditures, a
measure that was adopted at that time. As Gov., became a
supporter of liberal programs for benefit of disadvantaged
and for protection of the environment, but also took a
strong stand against excessive govtl. expenditures and for
strict law enforcement, which conservatives favored. Made
apptmts. to offices which offended some powerful elements of
his own party. Became an announced cand. for Dem. nom. for
Pres. of U.S. in 1976. Made a strong showing of popular
support in late state primaries, but failed to win nom. Unmarried. Regarded as something of an eccentric personality.
Refused to occupy the Gov.'s mansion during tenure, preferring to live in a small apartment instead. Contender for
Dem. nom. for Pres. of U.S. again in 1980, but withdrew after failing to win substantial support.

ROUTT, JOHN LONG (1876-1879; 1891-1893). b. April 25, 1826 at Eddyville, Ky. s. of John and ---- (Haggard) R. Both his father and grandfather were soldiers during the War of 1812. Father was a farmer who died when s. was still an infant. Mother moved to Bloomington, Ill. with family in 1836. Received common school educ. Apprenticed to a builder and machinist until 1851, when he went into real estate bus. on his own. Sheriff of McLean Co., 1860-1862. Raised a company of volunteers for Union in Civil War. Commissioned as capt. and saw service during Arkansas and Vicksburg campaigns, rising to rank of col. After Civil War returned to Bloomington. Treas. of McLean Co. for two terms, 1865-1869; also resumed bus. activities. Apptd. U.S. marshal for dist. of So. Ill., 1869-1871. Second Asst. Postmaster Gen. of U.S., 1871-1875. Apptd. in 1875 Gov. of Terr. of Colo. by Pres. Grant, who was personally acquainted with him through a contact made during the course of the siege of Vicksburg. Supported movement to secure statehood for Colo. Nom. by Rep. party and el. first Gov. of the State of Colo. in 1876. During admin., org. of first State govt. carried out and U.S. land grants for the State secured to help it operate on sound financial basis. Declined to seek second term as Gov. Became involved in various mining enterprises. Mayor of Denver, 1883-1885. Mbr. of bd. set up to supervise bldg. of new State Capitol in Denver. Nom. and el. Gov. again in 1890. m. in 1845 to Hester Woodson, of Ill., who died in 1872. m. in 1875 to Eliza Franklin. One d. D. at Denver, Aug. 13, 1907.

PITKIN, FREDERICK WALTER (1879-1883). b. Aug. 31, 1837 at Manchester, Conn. s. of Eli and Hannah (Torrey) P. Father belonged to a prominent family. Descendant of William P., colonial Gov. of Conn., 1766-1769. Grad. with honors from Wesleyan Univ., Middletown, Conn. in 1858 and from Albany Law School in 1859. Admitted to bar. Moved to Milwaukee, Wisc., where he became a member of a law firm. Withdrew in 1872 because of poor health; travelled in Europe, then in Fla., and eventually settled in Colo. in 1874. Outdoor life he followed there caused health to improve. Engaged in mining bus. Nom. and el. Gov. as Rep. in 1878, and was reel. in 1880. An uprising of Ute Indian tribe at White River was quelled during admin. Tribe was removed to lands farther West. Labor disturbances at mining camps were a continual problem. Unsuccessful cand. for U.S. Senate seat in 1882. Resumed practice of law and mining interests. m. in 1862 to Fidelia M. James. D. at Pueblo, Dec. 18, 1886.

GRANT, JAMES BENTON (1883-1885). b. Jan. 1, 1848 in
Russell Co., Ala. s. of Thomas McDonough and Mary (Benton)
G. Father was a physician and planter. Schooling was in-
terrupted by Civil War. After working for a time on
father's plantation entered Confed. Army at age of 16.
After Civil War, the family's plantation having been
destroyed, worked for a time as a laborer. In 1871 moved to
Iowa, where an uncle assisted him in obtaining further educ.
Attd. Iowa Agri. Coll. (now Iowa State Univ.), at Ames.
Studied civil engr. at Cornell Univ., Ithaca, N.Y., and then
studied mineralogy for two years at the School of Mines,
Freiburg, Germany. Returned to the U.S. by way of
Australia and New Zealand, where he observed mining operations for several months. After arrival at San Francisco,
went to Gilpin Co., Colo., where he acquired and operated a
mine. In 1877 obtained interests in other mines at Clear
Creek and Leadville. Established a smelting plant in latter
place. Became vice pres. of Denver Natl. Bank. Nom. and
el. Gov. as Dem. in 1882. Did not seek reel. Gave attention thereafter to bus. interests. m. in 1881 to Mary
Matteson Goodell. D. at Excelsior Springs, Mo., Nov. 1,
1911.

EATON, BENJAMIN HARRISON (1885-1887). b. Dec. 15,
(25?), 1833 in Coshocton Co., Ohio. s. of Levi and Hannah
E. Father was a farmer of Quaker ancestry. Entered West
Bedford Acad. at age 16. After grad. there in 1852 engaged
in teaching. In 1854 moved to Louisa Co., Iowa, where he
engaged in farming and teaching. In 1859 went to Colo.,
where he worked as a prospector and miner for three years.
Went to New Mexico in 1862, and engaged in farming and
ranching there for two years. Returned to Colo. in 1864,
and acquired lands near Greeley. Developed land through
irrigation, and became operator of a large-scale farming
enterprise. Also owned and operated a gristmill and warehouse bus. Town of Eaton founded as center of his bus. and
farming operations. Became justice of the peace, mbr. of
local school bd. and mbr. of the Penitentiary Commn. of
Colo. Terr. Mbr. of Colo. legislature in 1872. Nom. and
el. Gov. as a Rep. in 1884. m. in 1856 to Delilah Wolfe,
who died in 1857. One s. m. in 1864 to Rebecca Jane Hill.
Two children. D. at Eaton, Colo., Oct. 29, 1904.

ADAMS, ALVA (1887-1889; 1897-1899; 1905). b. May 14,
1850 at Blue Mound, Iowa Co., Wisc. s. of John and Eliza
(Blanchard) A. Was an older brother of Wm. Herbert A.,
also a Gov. of Colo. (q.v.) and an uncle of Alva Blanchard
A., a U.S. Sen. from Colo. in 1923-1924 and 1933-1941.

Father was a farmer who had moved from Ky. to Wisc., and
had served in Wisc. Senate. Father moved to Colo. with family in 1871, seeking a better climate for health reasons.
Established his home at Pueblo, and later moved to Denver,
where son worked for a time as laborer for a railroad.
Moved to Colorado Springs, where he went into lumber and
hardware bus. Set up branches at Pueblo and Alamosa in
partnership with brother Wm. Mbr. of first State legislature of Colo. in 1876. Nom. for Gov. as Dem. in 1884, but
was defeated in gen. election. Nom. again in 1886 and was
el. Nom. and el. for another term in 1896, winning in a
three-way race with nominees of Rep. and Natl. Silver
parties. Was nom. and declared el. as Dem. cand. for Gov.
again in 1904; but after a contest initiated by his opponent,
the incumbent Gov., he agreed to vacate the office of Gov.
in March, 1905. Defeated as Dem. cand. for Gov. in 1906.
Apptd. U.S. Commnr. Gen. to Australia, New Zealand, Java,
Siam, Cochin China and China in 1915 to obtain the cooperation of those countries in connection with the Pan-American
Expo. in San Francisco. Mbr. of Dem. natl. commt. in 1908
and for some time thereafter. Mbr., Masons. D. at Battle
Creek, Mich., Nov. 1, 1922.

COOPER, JOB ADAMS (1889-1891). b. Nov. 6, 1843 near
Greenville, Ill. Charles C., his father, was a farmer and
mechanic in comfortable circumstances who had emigrated to
Amer. in 1820 and had resided for short times in N.J. and
Ohio before settling in Ill. Attd. schools at Greenville;
and Knox Coll., at Galesburg, from which he was grad. with
high honors in 1865 and with an M.A. degree in 1868. Served
in Union Army with an Ill. regiment during later stages of
Civil War. Studied law; was admitted to Ill. bar and began
practice at Greenville. El. clerk of cir. ct. and recorder
in Bond Co. in 1868. Moved to Denver, Colo. in 1872, and
engaged in practice of law there. In 1876 became assoc.
with German Natl. Bank there as vice pres. and cashier.
During next twelve years became widely known in bus.
community. Nom. and el. Gov. as a Rep. in 1888. After one
term resumed bus. interests in field of banking. Also engaged in bldg. and mining enterprises. Mbr., Masons. m.
in 1867 to Jennie Barnes. Three d.; one s. D. at Denver,
Jan. 20, 1899.

ROUTT, JOHN LONG (1891-1893). See above, 1876-1879.

WAITE, DAVID HANSEN (1893-1895). b. April 9, 1825 at
Jamestown, N.Y. s. of Joseph and Olive (Davis) W. Father
was a lawyer who had settled in Western N.Y. in 1815.

Educ. in local schools and Jamestown Acad. Studied law in father's office, but did not engage in practice immediately. In 1850 moved to Fond du Lac, Wisc. and the following year to Princeton, Wisc., where he engaged in merc. bus. until 1857. El. to Wisc. legislature as Rep. in 1856. In 1857 moved to St. Louis, Mo., and later to Houston, Mo., where he became a h.s. teacher in 1859-1860. Forced to leave that area after Civil War began because of his strong pro-Union views. Returned to Jamestown, N.Y., where he was admitted to bar. Also became ed. and part owner of the Chautauqua Democrat, the Rep. party organ in that area. Later also acquired the Jamestown Journal. In 1876 moved to Larned, Kans., where he engaged in ranching and practiced law until 1879. El. to Kans. legislature in that year as a Rep., but soon after moved to Leadville, Colo., where he engaged in law practice. In 1881 moved to Aspen, Colo., where he engaged in law practice. Also became ed. of a reform-oriented newspaper, the Union Era. Supt. of schools of Pitkin Co. in 1891. Delegate to conf. at St. Louis, Mo. that resulted in formation of Natl. Peoples (Populist) party. Nom. and el. Gov. as cand. of the Pop. and Free Silver wing of Dem. party in 1892. During admin., reform measures he espoused involving supplanting of existing government in Denver necessitated resort to use of militia forces. Labor unrest among miners also was a problem. Bus. interests of State became generally aligned against him. Defeated in attempt to win a second term as cand. of Pop. party. Ran as the nominee of the "Middle of the Road" faction of the Pop. party for Gov. in 1896, but received little support. m. in 1851 to Frances E. Russell. Three children. After first wife's death, m. in 1855 to a widow, Mrs. Celia Maltby, a cousin of his first wife. One s. D. at Aspen, Nov. 27, 1901.

McINTIRE, ALBERT WASHINGTON (1895-1897). b. Jan. 15, 1853 at Pittsburgh, Pa. s. of Joseph Philips and Isabelle A. (Wells) McI. Father was of Scotch-Irish descent, whose family line included individuals active in politics and mil. service. Attd. Newell's Inst. in Pittsburgh. Grad. from Yale Coll. in 1873 and received a law degree from Yale in 1875. Admitted to bar and began practice in Pittsburgh. In 1876 moved to Denver, Colo., where he practiced law. In 1880 moved to San Luis Valley, in Conejos Co., where he engaged in ranching and practiced law. El. co. judge of Conejos Co. as nominee of both the Rep. and Dem. parties, serving from 1883 to 1886. Declined to seek second term. Apptd. cir. ct. judge by Gov. Routt in 1891. Nom. by acclamation as Rep. cand. for Gov. in 1894, and was el. defeating incumbent Gov. Waite. Did not seek reel. Resumed

activities as rancher. Also engaged in gold mining ventures.
m. in 1873 to Florence Johnson, of New York City. After her
death, married Ida Noyes Beaver, an M.D. D., Jan. 30, 1935.

ADAMS, ALVA (1897-1899). See above, 1887-1889.

THOMAS, CHARLES SPALDING (1899-1901). b. Dec. 6, 1849
at Darien, Ga. s. of Wm. S. and Caroline B. (Wheeler) T.
Moved with parents to Mich. while still a youth. Attd. the
Univ. of Mich., graduating with a law degree in 1871. Went
to Denver, Colo. Terr., where he began practice of law.
City atty. of Denver, 1875-1876. In 1879 moved to Leadville,
where he practiced law until 1884, when he returned to
Denver. Continued in law practice there as mbr. of prominent law firm. Became active in Dem. politics. Defeated as
Dem. nominee for the U.S. House in 1884. Delegate to Dem.
natl. convs. in 1880, 1896, 1900, 1904 and 1908. Mbr. of
Dem. natl. commt., 1884-1896. Unsuccessful as Dem. nominee
for U.S. Senate seat in 1888. Nom. and el. Gov. in 1898 as
Dem., having also the endorsement of the Pop. party. Unsuccessful cand. for U.S. Senate seat in 1900. Served as
temp. ch. and keynote speaker of Dem. natl. conv. of 1900.
In 1913 was el. as a Dem. to fill vacancy in U.S. Senate
seat, and was reel. in 1914 for a full term. Defeated for
reel. in 1920 as an Indep., having failed to win Dem. nom.
to continue in office. Spec. counsel for Korean Commn. in
Washington seeking recognition of independence of Korea
following World War I. Served as spec. asst. to U.S. Dept.
of Justice in 1923-1924. m. in 1873 to Emma Fletcher, of
Kalamazoo, Mich. Two d.; three s. Hon. degree from the
Univ. of Mich. D. June 24, 1934, in Denver. Ashes interred
in Fairmont Cem. there.

ORMAN, JAMES BRADLEY (1901-1903). b. Nov. 4, 1849 at
Muscatine, Iowa. s. of John and Sarah Josephine (Bradley)
O. Father was a farmer. Attd. local pub. schools in Iowa
and also in Chicago, Ill. Worked on father's farm until
1866, when he and a brother went to Denver, Colo. Set up a
freighting bus. there, and later engaged in work as a contractor with Kans. Pac. R.R. Extended bus. interests into
railroad constr. work. Moved to Pueblo and made that the
center for his operations in real estate devel., constr.
work and irrigation projects. Mbr. of Pueblo city council.
Mbr. of Colo. House, 1881-1883 and of Colo. Senate, 1883-
1885. Unsuccessful as Dem. cand. for U.S. Senate seat in
1883. Mayor of Pueblo in 1887. Delegate to Dem. natl.
conv. in 1892. Advocate of free coinage of silver. Nom.
and el. Gov. in 1900 as Dem., with endorsement of Pop.

party. Resumed bus. activities thereafter. Mbr., Masons.
m. to Nellie Martin in 1877. D. July 21, 1919.

PEABODY, JAMES HAMILTON (1903-1905). b. Aug. 21, 1852
at Topsham, Vt. s. of Calvin and Susan P. Father was a
farmer of Puritan ancestry whose forebears had resided in
Salem, Mass. Educ. in local pub. schools. Became a teacher
at age of 16 to assist in meeting schooling expenses. Prepared to work as a bookkeeper. In 1871 went to Pueblo,
Colo., where he clerked in a dry goods store. Later was employed in Denver for a time. Became proprietor of merc.
bus. at Canyon City. In 1885 became vice pres. of First
Natl. Bank there. In that same year was el. to office of
co. clerk, serving for four years. Also served on the city
council and held other local city and school offices in
Canyon City. Nom. and el. Gov. as Rep. in 1902. During
admin. serious strike occurred in Cripple Creek mining area,
requiring use of militia forces to maintain order. Nom. for
a succeeding term in 1904. His opponent, former Gov. Alva
Adams, was declared el. and assumed office; but Peabody
challenged the results before the legislature, charging
fraud in the casting and counting of some votes. After some
two months of investigation, which disclosed that there had
been fraud involving the vote for both the major candidates,
an agreement was reached that Peabody should be installed
in office, but that he should resign immediately thereafter
to permit the newly el. Lieut. Gov., Jesse McDonald, to
succeed to the office. Peabody accordingly served only one
day, March 17, 1905, of a second term, and then resigned.
m. to Frances L. Clelland in 1878. Held high offices in
Masonic order, and was a K.T. D. Nov. 23, 1917.

ADAMS, ALVA (1905). See above, 1887-1889.

McDONALD, JESSE FULLER (1905-1907). b. June 20, 1858
at Ashtabula, Ohio. s. of Lyman Mixer and Carolyn (Bond)
McD. When he was seven years old, family moved to
Springfield, Pa. Attd. pub. schools there and worked on
farm in summers. At age of 21 moved to Leadville, Colo.,
where he worked for a civil and mining engr. firm.
Acquired property and became operator of a mining enter-
prise. Became vice pres. of American Natl. Bank in
Leadville. Mayor of Leadville for three terms, 1899-1903.
Mbr. of Colo. Senate, 1903-1905, serving during latter part
of that time as presiding officer of Senate. Nom. and el.
Lieut. Gov. as Rep. on ticket with Gov. Peabody in 1904.
Assumed office of Gov. when Peabody resigned following out-
come of a disputed election. Completed the term for which

Peabody was el. Rep. nominee for Gov. in 1908, but lost in
the gen. election. Ch. of Rep. state commt., 1910-1914;
also in 1931-1934. m. in 1900 to Flora Collins. After her
death in 1918, m. to Mrs. Madeleine Harrington, a widow, in
1924. Mbr., Masons. Active in Colo. Mining Assoc., serving
as its pres. for a time. Also headed Colo. chapter of
American Mining Cong. Mbr., Amer. Inst. of Mining and
Metallurgical Engrs. Hon. degree from Colo. School of Mines.
D. Feb. 25, 1942.

BUCHTEL, HENRY AUGUSTUS (1907-1909). b. Sept. 30, 1847
near Akron, Ohio. s. of Dr. Jonathan and Eliza (Newcomer)
B. Father, who was of German descent, was a physician and
had originally resided in Pa. Family moved to South Bend,
Ind., when son was an infant. Educ. in pvt. schools and at
Asbury (now De Pauw) Univ. Left college after one year to
enter wholesale drug and grocery bus. Soon turned to
religion as major interest and returned to Asbury Univ. to
study for the ministry. Received an A.B. degree there in
1872 and an A.M. degree in 1875. Served for a brief time
as missionary in Bulgaria. Pastor of Methodist Episcopal
church in Zionsville, Ind. From 1876 to 1891 held a pas-
torate in Denver, Colo. Later served as pastor for
churches in N.Y. and N.J. Recalled in 1899 to Denver to become Chancellor of Denver Univ. Was successful as adminr.
in that position and achieved state-wide notice. Nom. and
el. Gov. as Rep. in 1906. Inaugural ceremony was held in
Trinity Church where he had formerly served as pastor. m.
in 1873 to Mary Stevenson, of Greencastle, Ind. Two s.;
two d. Hon. degrees from Asbury Univ. in 1884 and 1900.
D. at Denver, Oct. 22, 1924.

SHAFROTH, JOHN FRANKLIN (1909-1913). b. June 8, 1854
at Fayette, Mo. Father, who was of Swiss descent, and
mother, who was of German descent, had emigrated to Mo.
while they were young. Educ. at local schools. Attd. the
Univ. of Mich., from which he was grad. in 1875. Studied
law, and was admitted to bar in 1876. Began practice in
Fayette. Moved to Denver, Colo. in 1879 and continued law
practice there. City atty. for Denver, 1887-1891. El. to
U.S. House in 1894 as a Silver Rep. Reel. for next four
terms as a Silver Rep., with Dem. endorsement. Resigned
seat in Feb., 1904, declaring his belief that his opponent,
who had unsuccessfully contested his election in 1902,
should have been seated. Defeated as Dem. nominee for
Congressman-at-large in the ensuing 1904 election. Returned
to law practice in Denver. Nom. and el. Gov. as Dem. in
1908, defeating former Gov. McDonald. Reel. in 1910.

As Gov., advocated successfully a number of reform measures,
including the direct primary and the popular initiative and
referendum. Nom. and el. to U.S. Senate in 1912 as Dem.
Failed to win reel. in 1918. Served as ch. of U.S. War
Minerals Relief Commn., 1919-1921. m. in 1881 to Virginia
Morrison. Four children. D. at Denver, Feb. 20, 1922.
Bur. in Fairmont Cem. there.

   AMMONS, ELIAS MILTON (1913-1915). b. July 28, 1860 on
a farm near Franklin, in Macon Co., N.C. s. of Jehu R. and
Margaret C. (Brindle) A. Family's antecedents had been
among the first White settlers in N.C. Father was a farmer
and a Baptist minister. When son was 10, family moved to
Colo., where father engaged in ranching in Jefferson Co.
As a youth worked in a woolen factory, as a street lamp-
lighter, and as a teamster. Attd. pub. school in Denver.
Became correspondent for the Denver Tribune. Was also employed as a wild game hunter. Had poor eyesight because of
early illness, and it was further impaired by a hunting
accident. Became city ed. of Denver Times, but was forced
to abandon journalism in 1885 because of poor eyesight. Became a farmer and rancher. Apptd. clerk of dist. ct. of
Douglas Co. in 1890. Mbr. of Colo. House, 1890-1894,
serving as Speaker during second term. Mbr. of Colo. Senate,
1898-1902. Unsuccessful as Dem. cand. for Lieut. Gov. in
1904 and 1906; but was nom. and el. Gov. as Dem. in 1912.
During admin., the tax system was revised; new banking code
enacted; highway dept. reorganized; ins. code revised.
Serious labor disturbances in mining indus. necessitated
use of militia to preserve order, with U.S. troops being
called in eventually. Move to impeach him was made in
Colo. House, but was not successful. After term as Gov. de-
voted attention to ranching and livestock improvement.
Helped to org. first Denver livestock show in 1905, which
grew into a major annual event. Mbr. of governing bd. of
Colo. Agri. Coll. (now Colo. State Univ.), 1909. Pres. of
Farmers Life Ins. Co.; dir. and gen. mgr. of Middle Park
Land and Livestock Co.; pres., Natl. Western Stock Show
Assoc. and of the Grand Co. Fair Assoc. Mbr., Natl. Grange;
Farmers Union; Sons of Colo. Vice pres., State Bd. of Agri.
m. in 1889 to Elizabeth Fleming, of Denver. A son, Teller
A., became Gov. of Colo. (q.v.). D. at Denver, May 20,
1925.

   CARLSON, GEORGE ALFRED (1915-1917). b. Oct. 23, 1876
at Alta, Iowa. s. of Charles A. and Louisa Piternilla
(Gustafson) C. Father had emigrated from Sweden to Amer.
in 1872, settling first in Pa., where he worked as a coal

miner, before moving on to Iowa, where he continued to work
as a miner. Family later moved to Colo. Attd. Colo. Agri.
Coll. (now Colo. State Univ.); Colo. Normal (now Colo. State
Teachers Coll.); and the Univ. of Colo., from which he received an A.B. degree in 1902 and a law degree in 1904. Admitted to bar and practiced law for a time at Lewiston,
Idaho, but returned to Ft. Collins, Colo. in 1905 and
practiced law there. Served as deputy dist. atty. for two
years, and from 1908 to 1915 was dist. atty. in his jud.
dist. Nom. and el. Gov. as Rep. in 1914. During admin., a
state prohibition law was enacted; legislation was passed
establishing a workmen's compensation system; and an indus.
relations commn. created. Order was restored following
serious miners' strikes during the previous admin. Nom. in
1916 for succeeding term, but was defeated in the ensuing
gen. election. m. in 1906 to Rosa Lillian Alps, of
Loveland, Colo. Five children. After her death in 1922, m.
a second time. Mbr., Masons; Phi Beta Kappa; Sigma Nu;
various social clubs and professional legal orgs. Presbyterian. D. Dec. 6, 1926.

GUNTER, JULIUS CALDEEN (1917-1919). b. Oct. 31, 1858
at Fayetteville, Ark. s. of Thomas Montague and Marcella
(Jackson) G. Father was a lawyer who had been a col. in the
Confed. Army during the Civil War and had later served five
terms as a mbr. of U.S. House. Attd. the Univ. of Va. for
a time, but withdrew for reasons of health to go to Colo.
Studied law, was admitted to bar in 1881, and began practice
in Trinidad, Colo. Handled a number of important cases involving irrigation and land devel. matters. Served as cir.
ct. judge of his dist., 1889-1895. Apptd. judge of first
Colo. Ct. of Appeals in 1901, serving until 1905, when he
was apptd. to the Colo. Supreme Ct. After two years resumed
law practice in Denver. Nom. and el. Gov. as Dem. in 1916,
defeating incumbent Gov. Carlson. As Gov., was active in
assisting U.S. in raising troops and promoting U.S. war
effort during World War I. Defeated in Dem. primary for
nom. for succeeding term in 1918. Returned to law practice.
Declined offer of apptmt. to Colo. Supreme Ct. in 1925. m.
in 1884 to Bettie Brown, of Trinidad, Colo. Pres. of Colo.
Bar Assoc. Mbr., Masons; S.A.R.; Phi Gamma Delta. Mbr. of
the governing bd. of Clayton Coll., 1911-1917; pres. of
governing bd. of Tillston Acad., 1886-1889; mbr., Bd. of
Regents of the Univ. of Colo., 1913-1915. Protestant
Episcopal church. D. at Denver, Oct. 26, 1940.

SHOUP, OLIVER HENRY (1919-1923). b. Dec. 13, 1869 at
Boggs Corner, in Champaign Co., Ill. s. of Wm. R. and Delia

J. (Ferris) S. Father was a farmer, teacher and soldier.
Family moved to Colo. when son was 13 years old. Attd. pub.
schools, and Colo. Coll., 1886-1889. Employed after grad.
there by the Colorado Springs Company. From 1895 to 1912
was assoc. with Verner Z. Reed as his pvt. sect. and mgr. of
his bus. enterprises in mining, banking, oil, land reclama-
tion and irrigation projects in various areas of the West.
Eventually became a bus. partner of Reed. Pres. of Midwest
Oil Co. in 1911, of which he was one of founders, and of the
Midwest Refining Co. in 1914. Vice pres. of Colorado
Savings Bank of Colorado Springs and of the Grand Valley
Natl. Bank, Grand Junction. Active during World War I in
civilian duties connected with U.S. war effort. Mbr. of
Colorado Springs school bd., 1917-1919. Won Rep. nom. for
Gov. in 1918 primary, defeating the cand. endorsed by the
party's state conv., and was el. Reel. in 1920. During
admin., strikes in mining indus. were a serious problem.
Use of state militia was required in connection with a
strike by transp. workers. State admin. reorg. was under-
taken. Admin. characterized generally by attempt to apply
bus. methods in govt. and to maintain law and order. Refused to be a cand. for a third term in 1922. Was the Rep.
nominee for Gov. again in 1926, but was defeated in the gen.
election. m. in 1891 to Unetta Small. Three s.; one d.
After her death, m. in 1930 to Mary Alice Hackett. Mbr.,
Colo. Coll. Bd. of Trustees, 1917-1931; K.P.; Elks; various
social and bus. clubs. Active in Presbyterian church
affairs, and participated in the founding of Presbyterian
Hosp., in Denver. D. at Santa Monica, Calif., Sept. 30,
1940.

SWEET, WILLIAM ELLERY (1923-1925). b. Jan. 27, 1869 in
Chicago, Ill. s. of Channing and Emeroy L. (Stevens) S.
Parents were natives of Canada who had emigrated to U.S.
but whose antecedents were originally from New England.
Grad. from Swarthmore Coll. in 1890. Worked as apprentice
in a Chicago bus. firm until 1894, when he established his
own investment banking bus. in Denver, Colo. The enterprise
flourished and he retired from active mgmt. in 1920. In
1922 was nom. and el. Gov. as Dem. During admin., a law
encouraging marketing cooperatives was enacted and the state
ranger system was abolished. Nom. again for Gov. in 1924,
but was defeated in the gen. election. Was a vigorous
supporter of natl. prohibition. Refused to support Gov. Al
Smith, the Dem. nominee for Pres. of U.S., in 1928 pres.
election. Strongly supported U.S. entry into the League of
Nations; and was also a supporter of Pres. F. D. Roosevelt's
New Deal programs. Educl. dir. for NRA in 1933. Defeated

as Dem. nominee for U.S. Senate seat in 1926. Very active
in YMCA movement, serving as pres. of YMCA Intl. Conv. in
1920, and also as mbr. of its Natl. Council for some time.
Mbr., Phi Beta Kappa; Phi Kappa Psi; S.A.R., of which he was
pres. of Colo. chapter. Active in Congregational church,
serving as moderator of its Gen. Council, 1940-1942. Hon.
degree from Swarthmore in 1936. m. in 1892 to Joyeuse L.
Fullerton, of Philadelphia. Three s.; one d. D. at Denver,
May 9, 1942.

MORLEY, CLARENCE JOSEPH (1925-1927). b. Feb. 9, 1869
at Dyersville, Dubuque Co., Iowa. s. of John and Mary Dyer
(Plaister) M. Father was a railroad agent. Attd. pub.
schools in Dyersville and Cedar Falls, Iowa. Became a ct.
reporter. Employed in that capacity in Iowa and later in
Denver, Colo. Studied law and was admitted to Colo. bar
in 1897. Received law degree from the Univ. of Denver in
1899. Practiced law in Denver, 1897-1904, specializing in
corp. and probate cases. Pub. adminr. for Denver, 1901-1908;
mbr., Colo. Bd. of Pardons, 1915-1918; dist. ct. judge,
1919-1924. Nom. and el. Gov. as Rep. in 1924, defeating incumbent Gov. Sweet. Admin. emphasized economy in govt. A
major controversy occurred in connection with his removal
of the Warden of the State Penitentiary. Mbr., Masons;
professional legal orgs. Methodist. m. in 1893 to Maud M.
Thompson, of Cedar Falls, Iowa. Two s.; two d. D. Nov. 15,
1948.

ADAMS, WILLIAM HERBERT ("BILLY") (1927-1933). b. Feb.
15, 1862 at Blue Mound, Wisc. s. of John and Eliza
(Blanchard) A. Was a younger brother of Alva Adams, also a
Gov. of Colo. (q.v.). A nephew, Alva Blanchard A., was a
U.S. Sen. from Colo. in 1923-1924 and 1933-1941. Father was
a farmer who had moved from Ky. to Wisc. and had served in
Wisc. Senate. Attd. pub. schools in Black Earth, Wisc., and
at Pueblo, Colo., to which place the family had moved in
1871. Worked as a cowboy, teamster and farm hand on Colo.
ranches. Entered hardware bus. with older brother at
Alamosa, Colo. Sold interest in 1887 after having acquired
a cattle ranch near Alamosa in 1883. Served as co. commnr.
of Conejos Co., 1883-1884 and as mayor of Alamosa, 1884-
1885. Mbr. of Colo. House for one term, 1887-1888. El. to
Colo. Senate in 1888 and continued to serve therein for 38
years by reel. until 1927. Pres. pro tem of Senate in six
of the legislative terms from 1901 to 1919. As a legislator
had leading role in expansion of system of higher educ. in
Colo. Adams State Teachers Coll. was named in his honor.
Also was a supporter of labor reform legislation, including

minimum wage, eight-hour day, and workmen's compensation
laws; a cattle indus. code; and water rights laws for the
protection of farmers. Active in opposing Ku Klux Klan in
1920s. Nom. and el. Gov. as Dem. in 1926, defeating former
Gov. Shoup in gen. election. Reel. for two succeeding terms,
becoming the first Gov. to serve three full two-year terms.
m. in 1891 to Emma Ottoway. The marriage ended in divorce.
m. in 1916 to Hattie Mullins, who died in 1918. Congregationalist. D. at Alamosa, Feb. 4, 1954.

JOHNSON, ED(WIN) CARL (1933-1937; 1955-1957). b. Jan.
1, 1884 at Scandia, Kans. s. of Nels and Anna Belle (Lund)
J. Father had emigrated to U.S. from Sweden in 1871 and
had engaged in farming and cattle raising. Son grew up on
cattle ranch near Elsie, in Western Nebr., to which place
his family had moved. Attd. local schools. Worked as
laborer and telegrapher-train dispatcher, 1901-1909. Homesteaded land in Colo. in 1910, to which place he had moved
for health reasons. Engaged in ranching until 1920. Mgr.
of Farmers Cooperative Assoc. at Craig, Colo., 1920-1931.
Also engaged in produce bus. Served four terms in Colo.
House, 1923-1931. Lieut. Gov., 1931-1933. Nom. and el.
Gov. as Dem. in 1932 and was reel. in 1934. During admin.,
assembled the legislature in spec. session on five occasions
to deal with problems arising from the depression of the
1930s. Resigned as Gov. a few days before end of second
term to take seat in U.S. Senate, to which he had been el.
in 1936. Reel. to Senate in 1942 and 1948, but did not seek
fourth term in 1954, preferring to run for office of Gov.
Nom. and el. Gov. again in 1954. Was not a cand. for reel.
in 1956. As Gov., advocated policies generally in line with
New Deal domestic programs. As a U.S. Sen. was involved in
a number of controversies. Opposed Pres. Roosevelt's ct.
reform proposals; also opposed Roosevelt's being nominee for
third and fourth terms as Pres. of U.S. Generally was an
isolationist on foreign policy matters, but supported
World War II effort and U.S. entry into the UN. Was charged
with having improperly revealed mil. secret of U.S. devel.
of hydrogen bomb in 1949. Served as pres. of Western Baseball League for a time after service as Gov. Mbr., Upper
Colorado River Basin Commn. and the Colorado Commn. on the
Aged. Mbr., Masons; Elks; Red Men; M.W.A. Lutheran. m.
in 1907 to Fern Claire Armitage, of Kearney, Nebr. Two d.
(one adopted). D. at Denver, May 30, 1970.

TALBOT, RAY H. (1937). b. Aug. 19, 1896 at Chicago,
Ill. Obtained training as an electrical engr. and established residence in Pueblo, Colo., where he engaged in work

in the electrical engr. field. El. Lieut. Gov. as Dem. in
1932 and was reel. in 1934. Assumed office of Gov. for a
period of less than two weeks in 1937 at the end of second
term of Gov. Ed Johnson, following latter's resignation to
take seat in U.S. Senate. D. Jan. 31, 1955.

AMMONS, TELLER (1937-1939). b. Dec. 3, 1896 (1895?) at
Denver, Colo. s. of Elias M. and Elizabeth (Flemming) A.
Father was a Gov. of Colo. (q.v.). Attd. Univ. of Denver,
but left before grad. to serve with an infantry div. of the
A.E.F. in World War I. Returned to complete studies at the
Univ. of Denver, 1919-1921. Received law degree from
Westminster Law School in 1929. Admitted to bar in Colo.
and began practice in Denver. El. to Colo. Senate in 1930,
and continued in that office for two terms. Atty. for the
City and Co. of Denver, 1935-1936. Nom. and el. Gov. as
Dem. in 1936, becoming the first native Coloradoan to be el.
to that office. Nom. for succeeding term, but was defeated
in gen. election in 1938. Entered U.S. Army again following
outbreak of World War II, and attained rank of lieut. col.
by end of the war. Served as trial judge and advocate in
Provost Marshal's dept. in mil. govt. of Guam, 1944-1945.
Resumed law practice in Denver thereafter. Mbr., Amer.
Legion; V.F.W.; Elks; various social fraternities and clubs
and professional legal orgs. m. in 1933 to Esther Davis,
of Denver. D. Jan. 16, 1972.

CARR, RALPH L. (1939-1943). b. Dec. 11, 1887 at Ronta,
Custer Co., Colo. s. of Wm. Frank and Mattie (Kimberlin) C.
Father, who was of Scotch descent, was a miner. Attd. pub.
schools in Cripple Creek, Colo. and the Univ. of Colo., from
which he received an A.B. degree in 1910 and a law degree
in 1912. Served as newspaper correspondent while in
college. Began practice of law in Victor, Colo. In 1912-
1913 served as mgr. and ed. of the Victor Daily Record.
Moved to Trinidad, Colo. in 1915, where he practiced law
and was ed. of the Trinidad Picketwire. Later practiced
law at Antonito and at Denver. Co. atty. for Conejos Co.,
1922-1929. Asst. Atty. Gen. of Colo., 1927-1929. U.S.
dist. atty. for Colo., 1929-1933. Legal adviser to Colo.
Interstate River Commn. on Rio Grande pact, 1928-1929,
1934-1935, and 1937-1938. Nom. and el. Gov. as Rep. in
1938 and was reel. in 1940. During tenure, state admin.
reorg. plan was enacted designed to strengthen position of
Gov. as head of admin. Left state treas. with a surplus.
Defeated as Rep. nominee for U.S. Senate seat in 1942. Resumed practice of law in Denver. Won Rep. nom. for Gov. in
1950 and was campaigning for election to another term when

he died of complications arising from diabetes, with which
he had long been afflicted. Mbr., Masons; various fraternal
and professional legal orgs.; USCC, of which he served as
dir. for a time; Bd. of Regents, Univ. of Colo. Christian
Scientist. m. in 1913 to Gretchen Fowler, of Colorado
Springs. One s.; one d. D. at Denver, Sept. 27, 1950.

VIVIAN, JOHN CHARLES (1943-1947). b. June 30, 1887 at
Golden, Colo. s. of John Frederick and Emma Addie (Higgins)
V. Attd. pub. schools at Golden; the Univ. of Colo, 1905-
1911; and the Univ. of Denver, from which he received a law
degree in 1913. While at the Univ. of Colo. served as
correspondent for Denver newspapers. In 1911-1912 was state
ed. of Denver Times. Active in Rep. party affairs during
college career and afterward. Deputy ch. of Natl. Rep.
Coll. League, 1908-1912; ch. of Charles Evans Hughes Coll.
Clubs, 1916; Colo. ch. of Natl. Coolidge Clubs, 1924; state
ch. of Rep. Service League, 1928-1936. In 1913-1914 was
spec. counsel for the atty. of Denver and Denver Co. Began
pvt. practice of law in Denver in 1914, specializing in
corp. law. U.S. food adminr. for Jefferson Co., 1917-1918.
In 1918 enlisted in U.S. Marine Corps. After leaving service in 1919, became capt. in Judge Advocate dept. of USMCR,
1923-1943. Co. atty., Jefferson Co., 1922-1932. Spec.
asst. to Colo. Atty. Gen., 1925-1929. Nom. and el. Lieut.
Gov. in 1938 and was reel. in 1940. Nom. and el. Gov. as
Rep. in 1942 and was reel. in 1944. As Gov., increased
state aid to schools; effected compacts with neighboring
States on water use; left treas. with increased surplus.
Nominee of Rep. party for U.S. Senate seat in 1948, but was
defeated in gen. election. Mbr., Amer. Legion, serving as
Commdr. of Colo. chapter; Sigma Nu; Phi Alpha Delta.
Episcopalian. m. in 1925 to Maude Charlotte Kleyn, of
Holland, Mich. D. Feb. 10, 1964.

KNOUS, WILLIAM LEE (1947-1950). b. Feb 2, 1889 at
Ouray, Colo. s. of John Franklin and Julia (Bain) K. Attd.
the Univ. of Colo., from which he received a law degree in
1911. Admitted to bar and joined a law firm in Montrose,
Colo. City atty. for Ouray, 1911-1916 and deputy dist.
atty. for Ouray Co., 1913-1918. Established residence at
Montrose in 1917. City commnr. of Montrose, 1926-1928 and
mayor, 1928-1930. El. to Colo. House in 1928 and to the
Colo. Senate in 1930, where he served by reel. until 1937.
Majority (Dem.) floor leader, 1932-1936 and Pres. pro tem
of Senate during last term. Became a mbr. of Colo.
Supreme Ct. in 1937, and was made Chief Justice in 1946.
Mbr. of 9th U.S. Regional War Labor Bd. during World War II.

In that capacity served as ch. of spec. panel to deal with
disputes in the sugar indus., and as a mbr. of panels dealing with cases arising in Montgomery Ward and Co., the meat-
packing indus., and daily newspapers. Nom. and el. Gov. as
Dem. in 1946 and was reel. in 1948. Resigned as Gov. in
April, 1950 to accept apptmt. as U.S. dist. ct. judge for
Colo. Served in that office until death. Mbr., exec.
commt. of Natl. Govs.' Conf., 1947-1949. Pres., Western
Colo. Bar Assoc., 1932-1934 and of Montrose CC, 1924-1928.
Mbr., Masons; Elks; Rotary; various social clubs and fraternities. Episcopalian. Hon. degrees from Colorado Coll. and
Univ. of Denver. m. in 1915 to Elsie Marie Grabow. Three
s., one of whom became Lieut. Gov. of Colo. in 1959 and was
defeated as the Dem. nominee for Gov. in 1966. D. Dec. 12,
1959.

JOHNSON, WALTER WARREN (1950-1951). b. April 16, 1904
at Pueblo, Colo. Attd. local schools. Began work in 1924
with the Colo. Fuel and Iron Co. as a sales repr. in Texas
and Okla. Went into ins. bus. for himself in Pueblo in
1930. Mbr. of Colo. Senate, 1941-1949. Nom. and el. Lieut.
Gov. as Dem. in 1948. Succeeded to office of Gov. in
April, 1950 when Gov. Knous resigned to accept post of U.S.
dist. ct. judge. Completed term for which Knous was
elected. Was the Dem. nominee for election to a regular
term as Gov. in 1950, but was defeated in gen. election.
Married. One s.; one d.

THORNTON, DAN(IEL I. J.) (1951-1955). b. Jan. 31, 1911
in Hall Co., Tex. s. of Clay C. and Ida (Fife) T. Father
was a share cropper farmer, who moved to a large ranch near
Slaton, Tex. in 1920. Attd. Posey community school and h.s.
at Lubbock, Tex. Active in youth in 4-H Club work. Pres.
of 4-H Clubs of Tex. in 1927. Attd. Texas Tech. Coll.,
and U.C.L.A., from which he was grad. in 1933. Worked at
various jobs while in college and for several years thereafter. In 1937 purchased a cattle ranch in Ariz., where
he specialized in breeding high grade Hereford cattle.
Transferred operations to a ranch in Gunnison, Colo. in
1941. Very successful in ranching and cattle breeding, conducting a sale of prize stock on one occasion totalling
approximately one million dollars. El. to Colo. Senate in
1948. In 1950, when the Rep. cand. for Gov., R. L. Carr,
died during the campaign, was named by Rep. state commt. as
a replacement cand., and was el. Reel. in 1952. As Gov.,
was successful in obtaining passage of legislation to control Bangs disease in cattle; a revised workmen's compensation law; and a fair employment act for govt. employees.

Very active supporter of Gen. Eisenhower for Rep. nom. for
Pres. of U.S. in 1952. Mbr. of exec. commt. of Natl. Govs.'
Conf., in 1952 and ch. of that org. in 1953. Defeated as
Rep. nominee for U.S. Senate seat in 1956. m. in 1934 to
Jessie Willock, whom he met while a student at U.C.L.A.
Mbr. of President's Commn. on Intergovtl. Relations in 1953.
Hon. degree from Texas Tech. Coll. Returned to ranching
and bus. interests after tenure as Gov. D. Jan. 19, 1976.

JOHNSON, ED(WIN) CARL (1955-1957). See above, 1933-
1937.

McNICHOLS, STEPHEN L. R. ("STEVE") (1957-1963). b.
Mar. 7, 1914 at Denver, Colo. s. of Wm. H. and Catherine
Frances (Warner) McN. Father was very active in state and
local Dem. politics and served as Denver City Aud. for 34
years. Attd. Regis Coll., from which he was grad. in 1936;
and Catholic Univ., in Washington, D.C., from which he received a law degree in 1939. Admitted to bar and became
field agent for the FBI in 1939. Returned to Denver in
1940 and began practice of law there. Deputy dist. atty. in
Denver, 1940-1941. Spec. asst. to Atty. Gen. of U.S., 1941-
1942. Enlisted in Navy OTC in 1942. Commissioned, and saw
much service in amphibious operations in both the Atl. and
Pac. theaters of World War II. Wrote manual on ship to
shore movements. Awarded Bronze Star. Left service in 1946
with rank of lieut. commdr. Spec. asst. to U.S. Atty. Gen.,
1946-1948. Resumed law practice in Denver in 1948,
specializing in mining law. El. to Colo. Senate in 1948 and
continued in that office until 1955. Nom. and el. Lieut.
Gov. in 1954 as Dem. During 1955 acted for a time as Gov.
during illness of Gov. Johnson. Nom. and el. Gov. as Dem.
in 1956, and was reel. in 1958, becoming the State's first
four-year term Gov. Nom. for another term in 1962, but
lost in the gen. election. As Gov., was active in promotion
of programs to improve conditions of migrant workers;
preservation of natural resources and the environment; increased Fed. aid to educ.; and expansion of Social Security
programs. Mbr., Natl. Dem. Advisory Council, 1958; Amer.
Legion; V.F.W.; Elks; Eagles; Moose; K.C.; Rotary; various
social clubs and professional legal orgs. Defeated as Dem.
nominee for U.S. Senate seat in 1968. m. in 1942 to
Marjory Roberta Hart. Three s.; two d.

LOVE, JOHN ARTHUR (1963-1973). b. Nov. 29, 1916 near
Gibson City, Ill. At age of 4 moved with parents to
Colorado Springs, Colo. Attd. Cheyenne Mt. School and the
Univ. of Denver, from which he was grad. in 1938, and

obtained a law degree in 1941. Admitted to bar, but soon
afterward enlisted in U.S. Navy aviation cadet program. Received wings and became a flying officer in 1942. Saw
active service with "Black Cat" squadron in Pac. theater
during World War II. Received two D.F.C. decorations and
Air Medal with clusters before leaving service in 1945 with
rank of commdr. Resumed law practice in Colorado Springs.
Pres. of Colorado Springs CC in 1954. Active in securing
location of U.S. Air Force Acad. near Colorado Springs that
year. Pres. of El Paso Co. Young Reps. and mbr. of Rep.
state commt. in 1960. Nom. and el. Gov. as Rep. in 1962,
defeating incumbent Gov. McNichols. Reel. in 1966 and 1970.
Resigned office in July, 1973 to become Dir. of U.S. Energy
Policy Office under Pres. Nixon. Served in that post until
1974. Widely mentioned as possible nominee for Vice Pres.
of U.S. on Rep. ticket in 1968. Engaged in bus. and
professional interests in Denver after 1974. Mbr., Amer.
Legion; R.O.A.; Kiwanis; Omicron Delta Kappa; Sigma Phi
Epsilon. Congregationalist. Hon. degrees from Univ. of
Denver and Colorado Coll. m. in 1942 to Ann Daniels, of
Colorado Springs. Two s.; one d.

VANDERHOOF, JOHN D. (1973-1975). b. May 27, 1922 at
Rocky Ford, Colo. Family moved to a ranch near Fort
Collins, Colo. during son's youth. Attd. pub. schools
there and Glendale Coll., from which he was grad. with A.A.
degree in 1942. Entered U.S. Navy as officer trainee and
in 1943 became a bomber pilot. Saw service in Pac. theater
of World War II. Recipient of D.F.C. and Purple Heart.
After war service settled in Glenwood Springs, Colo., where
he became the proprietor of a sports goods bus. in 1946.
Pres. of Glenwood Indus. Bank in 1953 and of the Bank of
Glenwood in 1963. El. to Colo. House in 1950, continuing
to serve by reel. until 1970. House Speaker, 1963-1964 and
1967-1970. Nom. and el. Lieut. Gov. in 1970 as a Rep.
Succeeded to office of Gov. July 16, 1973 following the
resignation of Gov. Love, and completed Love's term. Nom.
as Rep. cand. for regular term as Gov. in 1974, but was
defeated in gen. election. Married twice. Two children by
first marriage. m. second time in 1973 to Merrie Lynn
Junkin. Two stepchildren.

LAMM, RICHARD DOUGLAS (1975-----). b. Aug. 3, 1935 at
Madison, Wisc. s. of Arnold E. and Mary (Townsend) L.
Attd. the Univ. of Wisc., from which he received a degree
in bus. admin. in 1957. Served as a lieut. in U.S. Army,
1957-1958. Worked as an accountant in Salt Lake City, Utah
in 1958. Entered the Univ. of Calif., Berkeley, from which

he was grad. with a law degree in 1961. Employed by
Ernst and Ernst, in Denver, Colo., 1961-1962. Admitted
to Colo. bar in 1962. Atty. for Colo. Anti-Discrimination
Commn., 1962-1963. Engaged in law practice at Denver, 1963-
1974. Assoc. prof. of law at Univ. of Denver, 1969. Became
active in local Dem. politics, serving as pres. of Denver
Young Dems. in 1963 and vice pres. of Colo. Young Dems.,
1964. Mbr. of Colo. House, 1966-1974, serving as asst.
minority (Dem.) leader. Nom. and el. Gov. as Dem. in 1974,
defeating incumbent Gov. Vanderhoof. Stressed issues
related to environmental protection and conservation during
campaign and during admin. as Gov. Reel. in 1978. m. to
Dorothy Vennard in 1963. One s.; one d.

TRUMBULL, JONATHAN (I) (1776-1784). b. Oct. 12, 1710 at Lebanon, Conn. s. of Joseph and Hannah (Higley) T. Entered Harvard at age 13, completing studies there in 1727. Studied for ministry under his local pastor at Lebanon. Served as pastor at Colchester, Conn. until 1731, when he discontinued ministerial work to assist father in merc. bus. Studied law in the meantime, and established a school at Lebanon in 1743. El. mbr. of the colonial Assembly in 1733 and became Speaker in 1739. In 1740 he became a mbr. of the Gov.'s Council, in which office he continued to serve for 22 years. Lieut. col. in a volunteer regiment in 1739, but saw no active service in ensuing war with France. Became a co. ct. judge and later a mbr. of the superior ct. of the Colony, serving as chief judge of the latter, 1766-1769. As mbr. of Gov.'s Council refused to take oath to carry out the unpopular Stamp Act. El. Deputy Gov. in 1767, and served in that office until 1769, when he succeeded to the office of Gov. of the Colony. Continued in that office by annual election until outbreak of the Rev. War. Championed cause of opposition to British policies, and after Dec. of Independence was adopted, continued in the office of State Gov. Reel. each year from 1776 to 1784. During Rev. War became a close friend of Gen. Washington, who addressed him as "Brother Jonathan" in frequent communications. Energetically supported the Amer. cause by raising troops and supplies. Declined further service in post of Gov. after election in 1783 because of old age and infirmities. His final state document was a paper urging the granting of sufficient powers to the natl. govt. to enable it to function effectively, as advocated by Washington, Madison and others. Hon. degrees from Yale and the Univ. of Edinburgh. m. in 1735 to Faith Robinson, a descendant of John and Priscilla Alden, of Plymouth. Four s.; two d. One of his sons, Jonathan (II), became Gov. of Conn. (q.v.), as did also a grandson, Joseph (q.v.). Another son, John, became famous as an early American painter. D. at Lebanon Aug. 17, 1785.

GRISWOLD, MATTHEW (1784-1786). b. March 25, 1714 at Lyme, Conn. s. of John and Hannah (Lee) G. Father belonged to a wealthy, landed family. Educ. at home. Studied law and admitted to bar in 1743. El. to colonial Assembly in 1751, and in 1759 became a mbr. of Gov.'s Council. In 1765, as a mbr. of the Council, refused to take oath to enforce the Stamp Act. Apptd. superior ct. judge in 1766, and became its chief judge in 1769, serving in that capacity for the next 15 years. Capt. of Lyme militia band in 1739, and became its major in 1766. Head of Conn. Council of Safety in 1775. El. Deputy Gov. in 1771 and continued in

that office until 1784, when he was el. Gov. Reel. in 1785.
As Gov., favored granting power to tax imports to the Cong.
of the U.S. Following tenure as Gov. was presiding officer
of Conn. conv. that ratified the U.S. Const. Spent remaining days in retirement, engaging in farming and writing.
Hon. degree from Yale in 1779. Mbr. of Soc. for Propagation
of Gospel in New England. m. in 1743 to Ursula Walcott,
mbr. of a distinguished Conn. family. Four d.; three s.
His youngest son, Roger, later became Gov. of Conn. (q.v.).
D. April 28, 1799 at Lyme (now Old Lyme).

HUNTINGTON, SAMUEL (1786-1796). b. July 3, 1731 at
Windham, Conn., s. of Nathaniel H., a farmer and clothier.
Educ. in local schools and at home while assisting on
father's farm and learning cooper's trade. Borrowed law
books and studied law. Admitted to bar in 1758 and practiced at Windham. Later moved to Norwich, where he became
prominent as an atty. Mbr. of colonial Assembly in 1764.
In 1765 was appointed Royal Atty. for the Colony, a post he
held until 1774. Became a superior ct. judge in 1774, and
its chief judge in 1784. As mbr. of Gov's Council in 1775,
espoused cause of those resisting British colonial policies.
Apptd. delegate from Conn. to the Contl. Cong. in 1775, and
continued to serve in that body from time to time until
July, 1781. Was a signer of the Dec. of Indep. Pres. of
Contl. Cong., 1779-1781. Chosen Deputy Gov. in 1785. Was
reel. to that post in 1786; but when no cand. received a
popular majority as successor to the retiring Gov., he was
el. to the office of Gov. by the Gen. Assembly. Continued
in that office by annual popular el. for the next nine years
until his death. A supporter of the new Const. of the U.S.,
became a Fed. after party alignments began to form in 1790s.
Hon. degrees from Yale and Dartmouth. m. Martha Devotion
of Scotland, Conn. No children; but adopted and brought up
a s. and a d. of his brother, Joseph. The adopted s. and
nephew, Samuel H., became a Gov. of Ohio (q.v.). D. while
still in office at Norwich on Jan. 5, 1796.

WOLCOTT, OLIVER, Sr. (1796-1797). b. Dec. 1, 1726, at
Windsor, Conn. Youngest s. of Roger and Sarah (Drake) W.
Father was colonial Gov. of Conn. from 1750 to 1754. Attd.
Yale, from which he was grad. in 1747. Capt. of militia in
1747, serving on Canadian border against French. Held rank
of major when he left mil. service in 1748. Studied med.
with an older brother and with other physicians. Established residence at Litchfield, Conn. Served as co. sheriff
there for 14 years; also acted as judge of common pleas and
probate ct. In 1774, presided over meeting called to

protest Boston Port Bill. Mbr. of Gov.'s Council in 1774.
Continued to serve in that post until 1786. Apptd. col. of
militia regiment in 1774, later becoming a brig. gen. Was
commdr. of brigade at the surrender of Gen. Burgoyne at
Saratoga in 1777. Mbr. of Contl. Cong., 1775-1778, and was
a signer of the Dec. of Indep. Mbr. of Cong. of U.S., 1780-
1784. During Rev. War assisted in keeping Iroquois Indians
neutral in northern part of country. Served as spec.
commnr. in mediating disputes between Pa. and Conn. over
Western lands, and between N.Y. and Vt. in connection with
boundaries. Spec. commnr. for negotiation of treaties with
Wyandotte Indians in the Ohio country, 1784-1785. El.
Deputy Gov. in 1786 and continued to serve in that post by
annual election for the next nine years. When Gov.
Huntington died in 1786, succeeded to office of Gov. El to
that office for a regular term in that year, but died during
course of term. Pres. elector on Adams ticket in 1796.
m. in 1755 to Laura (Loraine?) Collins. Three s.; two d.
One of his sons, Oliver, Jr., became Gov. of Conn. (q.v.).
D. Dec. 1, 1797 at Litchfield. Bur. in East Cem. there.

TRUMBULL, JONATHAN (II) (1797-1809). b. March 26, 1740
at Lebanon, Conn. s. of Jonathan and Faith (Robinson) T.
Father was the first State Gov. of Conn. (q.v.). A nephew
Joseph T., was also a Gov. of Conn. (q.v.). Grad. with
honors from Harvard in 1759. Represented town of Lebanon in
Conn. colonial Assembly a number of terms. Upon outbreak of
Rev. War became paymaster of Northern Dept. of Contl. Army,
1775-1778. In 1780 became sect. and aide to Gen. Washington
serving in that capacity until end of war. El. to Conn.
Assembly, serving as Speaker on two occasions. El. to U.S.
House in first Cong. under the U.S. Const. Reel. for two
terms, serving as Speaker during second term. El. to U.S.
Senate in 1795 to fill a vacancy. Resigned in June, 1796,
to take office of Deputy Gov., to which he had been el.
Reel. to that office in 1797 and became Gov. in Dec. of that
year when Gov. Wolcott died. Reel. by popular majorities
annually thereafter, serving until his death in 1809. Also
held office of chief judge of Supreme Ct. of Errors while
serving as Gov. As Gov., became identified with programs
and policies of Fed. party. m. in 1767 to Eunice Backus.
One s.; four d. D. at Lebanon Aug. 7, 1809. Bur. in Old
Cem. there.

TREADWELL, JOHN (1809-1811) b. Nov. 23, 1745 at
Farmington, Conn. s. of Ephraim and Mary T. Father was a
well-to-do mechanic and mfr. Family observed strict Puritan principles. Grad. from Yale in 1767. Studied law, but

did not take bar examination. Nevertheless, engaged in some
forms of legal practice at Farmington. Engaged in merc. and
mfg. bus. he inherited from father. El. to Conn. Assembly
in 1776 and continued to serve therein until 1783, with
exception of one year. Became mbr. of Gov.'s Council in
1783, serving in that capacity until 1798. Also served as
clerk of probate ct., 1777-1784; judge of probate in 1789;
and was judge of common pleas ct. and of the co. ct. Mbr.
of the Cong. of U.S., 1785-1786. Mbr. of state conv. that
ratified U.S. Const. in 1788. El. Deputy Gov. in 1798, and
continued to serve in that office by annual election until
August, 1809, when he succeeded to office of Gov. upon death
of Gov. Trumbull. Reel. in 1810 by vote of the Gen.
Assembly, but failed to win reel. in 1811. Delegate to the
Hartford Conv. in 1814 that opposed continuation of war with
Great Britain. Mbr. of state constl. conv. in 1818. Aided
in negotiations between Conn. and Ohio over sale of Western
Reserve lands in 1795. As Gov., was advocate of system of
common pub. schools. Served on Bd. of Mgrs. of school funds
1800-1810. Mbr. of Yale Corp., 1790-1809. First pres. of
Amer. Bd. of Commnrs. for Foreign Missions. Active in Con-
gregational church affairs. Writer of essays on religious
subjects. Hon. degree from Yale in 1800. m. to ----------
Pomeroy, of Northhampton. One child. D. at Farmington,
August 18, 1823. Bur. in Old Cem. there.

GRISWOLD, ROGER (1811-1812). b. May 21, 1762 at Lyme,
Conn. Youngest s. of Matthew and Ursula (Wolcott) G.
Father was second Gov. of Conn. (q.v.), and his mother was
a d. of Roger Wolcott, a colonial Gov. of Conn. His uncle,
Oliver Wolcott, Sr. (q.v.) and a cousin, Oliver Wolcott, Jr.
(q.v.) were also Govs. of Conn. Grad. from Yale in 1780,
where he distinguished himself as a scholar. Studied law
with father and was admitted to bar in 1783. Practiced law
for a time at Lyme, and later at Norwich, Conn. Returned to
Lyme in 1784. El. to U.S. House as a Fed. in 1794, and
continued in office for five succeeding terms. Became involved in bitter feud and controversy concerning Matthew
Lyon, a U.S. Repr. from Vt., who was tried and convicted of
violation of the 1798 Sedition Act. Offered post of Sect.
of War by Pres. Adams in 1801, but declined. Resigned seat
in Cong. in 1807 to accept position on Conn. Supreme Ct. of
Errors. Pres. elector on Fed. ticket in 1808. El. Deputy
Gov. as a Fed. in 1809. Defeated as cand. for Gov. in 1810;
but was successful in 1811, defeating incumbent Gov.
Treadwell. Reel. in 1812. Died before end of term. Was
strongly opposed to U.S. entry into war with Great Britain
in 1812, and refused to cooperate with U.S. govt. in raising

troops for war. Hon. degrees from Yale in 1810 and Harvard
in 1811. m. in 1788 to Fannie Rogers. Seven s.; three d.
D. at Lyme (now Old Lyme) Oct. 25, 1812. Bur. in Griswold
family cem. there.

SMITH, JOHN COTTON (1812-1817). b. Feb. 12, 1765 at
Sharon, Conn. s. of the Rev. Cotton Mather and Temperance
Gale (Worthington) S. Ancestral line included a number of
outstanding Congregational ministers. Entered Yale at age
of 14, and was grad. with honors in 1783. Studied law.
Admitted to bar in 1787 and began practice at Sharon. El.
to Conn. Assembly in 1793. Mbr. of that body in 1796 to
1800, serving as Speaker in last term. El. to U.S. House
in 1800, continuing for two succeeding terms. Retired for
a time to law practice, farming and writing. El. to the
Assembly in 1808, where he served as Speaker. Became
superior ct. judge in 1809. El. Deputy Gov. in 1809, and
was reel. for next two terms. Acted as Gov. from time to
time during 1810 and 1811 because of illness of Gov.
Griswold, and succeeded to the office in 1812 upon Gov.
Griswold's death. Reel. in the succeeding four annual elections; but was defeated in 1817. A strong Fed. in principle
he opposed movement to revise the State's const. Withdrew
thereafter from pub. life to manage estate and to engage in
writing. Mbr. of various historical societies. Pres. of
the Litchfield Co. Missionary Soc. and of the Temperance
Soc. First pres. of Conn. branch of the Amer. Bible Soc.,
and mbr., 1831-1845. Mbr. of Bd. of Commnrs. for Foreign
Missions, 1826-1841. Hon. degree from Yale in 1814. m. to
Margaret Evertson. One s. D. at Sharon, Dec. 7, 1845.
Bur. in Hillside Cem. there.

WOLCOTT, OLIVER, Jr. (1817-1827). b. Jan. 11, 1760 at
Litchfield, Conn. s. of Gov. Oliver Wolcott, Sr. (q.v.) and
Laura (Loraine?) (Collins) W. Grandson of Roger W.,
colonial Gov. of Conn., and a cousin of Gov. Roger Griswold
(q.v.). Very precocious as youth. Entered Yale at age of
13, but at urging of parents, deferred studies for a year.
Left college in 1776 temporarily to serve in Conn. militia
forces. Grad. from Yale in 1778. Became aide to father in
mil. service in 1779. Studied law at Litchfield under
Judge Tapping Reeves, and was admitted to bar in 1781. Employed at Hartford in financial dept. of State of Conn.
Completed studies for M.A. degree at Yale. In 1784 was a
mbr. of commn. to adjust claims of Conn. with U.S. govt.
Became head of U.S. office of comptroller of accounts in
1788. When new Treas. Dept. was organized he became Aud. of
U.S. Treas. and comptroller of accounts in 1791. Offered

post of pres. of first Bank of U.S., but declined. Became
U.S. Sect. of Treas. in 1795 as successor to Alexander
Hamilton in that office. Continued to serve until 1800 when
he resigned after he felt he had not been fully exonerated
of charges of peculation following an investigation by his
opponents in Cong. Apptd. to newly-created post on U.S.
cir. ct. by Pres. Adams, but lost position in 1802 when
Cong. repealed the 1801 Judges Act. Moved to New York City
where he engaged in bus. Aided in founding Bank of N.Y. in
1812 and served as its pres. for two years. In 1815 moved
back to Litchfield, where he engaged in woolen mfg. bus.
with brother. Gave support to "Toleration" movement to
discontinue taxation of religious denominations other than
the state-recognized Congregational church. Nom. for Gov.
by the party formed on this issue in 1816, but failed to win.
Nom. again in 1817 and was el., defeating incumbent Gov.
John Cotton Smith. Achieved objective of repeal of the
religious denomination tax, and also espoused cause of reform of Conn. const. Was successful in the latter objective
in 1818 in alliance with most elements of the Jeff. Rep.
party. Reel. Gov. each year until 1827, when he was defeated for reel. as Gov. Retired thereafter to New York City.
Hon. degrees from Yale; Coll. of N.J. (Princeton); and
Brown Univ. m. in 1785 to Elizabeth Stoughton, of Windsor,
Conn. Two s.; one d. D. in New York on June 1, 1833.
Bur. at Litchfield.

TOMLINSON, GIDEON (1827-1831). b. Dec. 31, 1780 at
Oronoque (Stratford), Conn. s. of Jabez H. and Rebecca
(Lewis) T. Father was a man of importance in the community.
Grad. from Yale in 1802. Became tutor in a well-to-do
family in Virginia. Studied law. Returned to Conn. and began law practice in Greenfield Hill (Fairfield), Conn. in
1807. In 1817 became clerk of Conn. Assembly, and after
election to that body served as its Speaker in 1818. Became
identified with movement to obtain revision of Conn. const.,
and was a delegate to 1818 constl. conv. El. to U.S. House
in 1818, continuing in that office for three succeeding
terms. El. Gov. in 1827 as Jeff. Rep., defeating incumbent
Gov. Oliver Wolcott, Jr. Reel. annually for next three
terms. Resigned shortly before end of fourth term in 1831
to take seat in U.S. Senate, in which he served one term.
Became first pres. of Housatonic R.R. Nominee of Whig party
for Gov. in 1836, but was defeated in gen. election by incumbent Gov. Edwards. Trustee of Trinity Coll. m. to
Sarah Bradley of Greenfield Hill. Two s. D. Oct. 8, 1854
at Greenfield Hill (Fairfield). Bur. in Old Congregational
Cem. there.

PETERS, JOHN SAMUEL (1831-1833). b. Sept. 21, 1772 at
Hebron, Conn. s. of Bemslee and Annis (Shipman) P. Family
were British Loyalists at outbreak of Rev. War. Father went
to England in 1777, but later returned to Canada. Son
worked on farm and acquired common school educ. At age of
18 became a school teacher. Studied med. with a relative at
Marbletown, N.Y., while continuing to teach school during
winters. Also studied with other physicians, completing
studies in Philadelphia in 1796. Engaged in med. practice
at Hebron. Served as town clerk at Hebron for 20 years.
El. to Conn. Assembly, and later to the Conn. Senate. El.
Lieut. Gov. in 1827 and continued in that office until 1831.
Succeeded to office of Gov. in Mar., 1831 when Gov.
Tomlinson resigned. El. for a regular term as a Natl. Rep.
in that year and was reel. in 1832. In the 1833 election
he received a plurality of the popular vote for Gov., but
his Jackson Dem. opponent was chosen Gov. by the Gen.
Assembly. Retired to med. practice. Fellow of Conn. Med.
Soc. Never married. D. at Hebron March 30, 1858.

EDWARDS, HENRY WAGGAMAN (1833-1834; 1835-1838). b. Oct.
--, 1779 at New Haven, Conn. s. of Pierrepont and Frances
(Ogden) E. Grandson of Jonathan E., noted writer on
religious and philosophical subjects. Father, who was a
well-known lawyer, had served in the Contl. Cong. and as a
U.S. dist. judge. Attd. Coll. of New Jersey (Princeton),
grad. in 1797. Studied law at Judge Tapping Reeves' law
school in Litchfield, Conn. Began practice in New Haven.
El. to U.S. House in 1818 and 1820. Apptd. to U.S. Senate
to fill a vacancy in 1823 and was later el. to complete term,
serving until 1827. Mbr. of Conn. Senate, 1827-1829 and of
Conn. Assembly in 1830, serving as Speaker in latter body.
El. Gov. as Jackson Dem. by Gen. Assembly in 1833, defeating
incumbent Gov. Peters. Defeated for succeeding term in
1834, although he received a popular plurality. El. Gov.
again by popular majorities in 1835, 1836 and 1837. Resumed
law practice thereafter. During admin., railroad constr.
began to flourish in Conn. Successfully advocated a geological and minerals survey of State. Hon. degree from Yale
in 1833. m. to Lydia Miller. One d.; four s., one of whom,
Pierrepont, became famous as a lawyer and judge in N.Y.
D. at New Haven July 22, 1847. Bur. in Grove Street Cem.
there.

FOOTE, SAMUEL AUGUSTUS (1834-1835) b. Nov. 8, 1780 at
Cheshire, Conn. s. of John F., a Congregational minister.
Mother was a descendant of Jonathan Law, a colonial Gov. of
Conn. Very precocious as a youth. Entered Yale at age 13.

Grad. in 1797. Studied law under Judge Tapping Reeves, at
Litchfield, but did not continue for long in that profession
because of poor health. Entered bus. with brother in West
Indian trade at New Haven in 1803. Venture fared badly in
1813 because of War of 1812. Abandoned it and returned to
Cheshire to assist father on farm. El. to Conn. Assembly as
an anti-Fed. in 1817. El. to U.S. House in 1818, serving
one term. Again a mbr. of Conn. Assembly, 1821-1823.
Chosen to U.S. House seat in 1822, serving one term. Mbr.
of Conn. Assembly 1825-1827, serving in that body as Speaker
in 1825 and 1826. El. to U.S. Senate in 1827, but failed to
win reel. in 1833. Sponsored measure in Senate relating to
limitation of sale of U.S. pub. lands that provided the
occasion for the famous debate between Senators Hayne and
Webster on the nature of the Fed. Union. El. to U.S. House
for the third time in 1833. Resigned seat in 1834 after
having been el. Gov. by the Gen. Assembly as the Whig cand.
Defeated for reel. in 1835 by former Gov. Edwards. Pres.
elector on Whig ticket in 1844. Hon. degree from Yale.
m. to Eudocia Hull of Wallingford, Conn. Six s., one of
whom, Andrew H., achieved distinction as an admiral in U.S.
Navy during Civil War. D. at Cheshire, Sept. 15, 1846.
Bur. in Hillside Cem. there.

EDWARDS, HENRY WAGGAMAN (1835-1838). See above, 1833-
1834.

ELLSWORTH, WILLIAM WOLCOTT (1838-1842). b. Nov. 10,
1791 at Windsor, Conn. s. of Oliver and Abigail (Wolcott)
E. Father was a mbr. of the U.S. Constl. Conv. of 1787 and
was later Chief Justice of the U.S. Supreme Ct. Mother belonged to the distinguished Wolcott family which had supplied a colonial Gov. and two State Govs. of Conn. Attd.
Yale, from which he was grad. in 1810. Studied law in
Judge Tapping Reeves' law school at Litchfield and in a law
office in Hartford. Admitted to bar in 1813 and began practice at Hartford. Apptd. prof. of law at Trinity Coll. in
1827, a post he held until death. El. to U.S. House as
Natl. Rep. (Whig) in 1828. Continued in that office for
succeeding terms until he resigned in 1834. Supported Pres.
Jackson's actions in the S.C. nullification crisis of 1832.
Active in promotion of copyright law reform and investigation of U.S. Bank. El. Gov. in 1838 as a Whig. Continued
in office for three succeeding terms, but was defeated for
reel. in 1842. During admin., recommended investigation of
pub. school system. In 1847 became a superior ct. judge
and was also a mbr. of the Supreme Ct. of Errors. Continued
to serve as a judge until retirement at the age of 70.

Twice refused to become a cand. for U.S. Senate. Active
in movements to found institutions for handicapped. Hon.
degree from the Univ. of N.Y. m. in 1813 to Emily Webster,
d. of Noah Webster, the famous lexicographer. Two s.; four
d. Active in Congregational church affairs, serving as deacon in his local church for 47 years. D. Jan. 15, 1868, at
Hartford. Bur. in Old North Cem. there.

CLEVELAND, CHAUNCEY FITCH (1842-1844). b. Feb. 16,
1799 at Hampton, Conn. s. of Silas and Lois (Sharpe) C.
Educ. in pub. schools. Began teaching at age of 15, continuing therein for five years. Studied law in the meantime,
admitted to bar in 1819 and began practice in Hampton. Became pros. atty. for Windham Co. El. to Conn. Assembly as
Jackson Dem. in 1826, 1827, 1829, 1832, 1835 and 1836,
serving as Speaker during last three terms. Became State
Banking Commnr. in 1837. Moved to Norwich, Conn. in 1841.
Nom. and el. Gov. as a Dem. in 1842 by action of the Gen.
Assembly, defeating incumbent Gov. Ellsworth. Reel. in
1843, but was defeated for reel. in 1844. Mbr. of U.S.
House, 1849-1853. His strong opposition to slavery alien-
ated elements of his constituency, but obtained for him the
support of Free Soil party. Later joined the Rep. party,
serving as delegate to its natl. convs. in 1856 and 1860.
Pres. elector on Rep. ticket in 1860. Served as delegate to
the unsuccessful "Peace Congress" of 1861, which sought to
avert Civil War conflict. El. as Rep. to Conn. Assembly in
1863 and served as Speaker. Retired thereafter to farming
and law practice. Hon. degree from Trinity Coll. m. in
1821 to Diantha Hovey. One s.; one d. After first wife's
death in 1867, m. in 1869 to Helen Cornelia Litchfield. A
nephew Edward Spicer C., was the unsuccessful Dem. cand. for
Gov. of Conn. in 1886. D. at Hampton, June 6, 1887. Bur.
in South Cem. there.

BALDWIN, ROGER SHERMAN (1844-1846). b. Jan. 4, 1793 at
New Haven, Conn. s. of Simeon and Rebecca (Sherman) B.
Father had been a mbr. of U.S. Cong. and a judge of the
Conn. Supreme Ct. of Errors, and was a descendant of one of
the original settlers in Conn. Mother was a d. of Roger
Sherman, a signer of the Dec. of Indep. and an influential
mbr. of the Constl. Conv. of 1787. Attd. Yale, graduating
with high honors in 1811. Studied law in father's office
and with Judge Tapping Reeves, of Litchfield. Admitted to
bar in 1814. Practiced at New Haven. Supported Prudence
Crandall in her attempt to establish a school for Negro
children at New Haven. Achieved prominence as one of the
attys., along with former Pres. J.Q. Adams, who successfully

defended the fugitive slaves from a slave ship, the <u>Amistad</u>, who had seized the ship and brought it to New London in an effort to win their freedom. Mbr. of New Haven city council in 1826 and of the city's bd. of aldermen in 1829. Mbr. of Conn. Senate, 1837-1838 and of Conn. Assembly, 1840-1841. Defeated as Whig cand. for Gov. in 1843, but was successful in contest for that office in 1844 and 1845. Veto of Washington Bridge bill on grounds of its unconstitutionality was a cause of controversy during admin., but his position was subsequently upheld by cts. Apptd. to fill vacancy in U.S. Senate seat in 1847 and served remainder of term. As a mbr. of Senate, opposed the measures making up the Compromise of 1850 on grounds they gave too many concessions to slavery interests. Failed to win reel. to Senate. Served as pres. elector on Rep. ticket in 1860. Mbr. of the futile "Peace Congress" in Washington in 1861 that sought to avert Civil War. Hon. degrees from Yale and Trinity Coll. m. in 1820 to Emily Perkins. Nine children. One of his sons, Simeon C., became a Gov. of Conn. (q.v.). D. at New Haven, Feb. 19, 1863. Buried in Grove Street Cem. there.

TOUCEY, ISAAC (1846-1847). b. Nov. 5, 1796 at Newtown, Conn. Was a descendant of the Rev. Thomas T., the first Congregational minister of the town. Educ. by pvt. tutors. Studied law, admitted to bar in 1818 and began practice at Hartford. Soon acquired wide reputation as able lawyer. City atty. for Hartford, 1822-1835. El. as Dem. to U.S. House in 1834. Continued in office for succeeding term, but was defeated for third term. Pros. atty. for Hartford Co., 1842-1844. Nom. for Gov. as Dem. in 1845 against incumbent Gov. Baldwin, but was defeated in ensuing el. Nom. again in 1846 and was el. by action of the Gen. Assembly. Defeated for reel. in 1847. Apptd. Atty. Gen. of U.S. by Pres. Polk in June, 1848, serving until the end of Polk's term as Pres. in March, 1849. El. to Conn. Senate in 1850. Mbr. of Conn. Assembly in 1852. El. to U.S. Senate, serving from 1852 to 1857. Declined to run again for that office. Apptd. U.S. Sect. of the Navy by Pres. Buchanan, serving from 1857 to 1861. Retired to law practice thereafter. Was considered to be friendly to Southern cause during Civil War. m. in 1827 to Catherine Nichols. Episcopalian. During lifetime made extensive donations to Trinity Coll. D. at Hartford, July 30, 1869.

BISSELL, CLARK (1847-1849). b. Sept. 7, 1782 at Lebanon, Conn. s. of Joseph W. and Betty (Clark) B. Ances- tors were among first settlers at Plymouth Colony in 1626. During youth worked on father's farm and engaged in

teaching while studying to qualify for admission to Yale.
Grad. from Yale with honors in 1806. Engaged for a time as
tutor for a Md. family, and later was a tutor at Saugatuck
(Westport), Conn. Studied law there and at Fairfield. Admitted to bar in 1809. Established practice at Norwalk.
Mbr. of Conn. Assembly in 1829. Apptd. superior ct. judge
and later was a mbr. of the Supreme Ct. of Errors, serving
in that capacity for ten years. Mbr. of Conn. Senate, 1842-
1843. In 1847 became Kent Prof. of Law at Yale, from which
he received an hon. degree that same year. Nom. as Whig
cand. for Gov. in 1846. Received a popular plurality, but
his Dem. opponent was chosen Gov. by the Gen. Assembly.
Nom. again for Gov. in 1847 and was el. Continued in office
for second term. After service as Gov., resumed teaching
post at Yale, in which he continued until 1855. Mbr. of
Conn. Assembly in 1850. m. in 1811 to Sally Sherwood, of
Saugatuck. Four s.; two d. D. at Norwalk, Sept. 15, 1857.

TRUMBULL, JOSEPH (1849-1850). b. Dec. 7, 1782 at
Lebanon, Conn. s. of David and Sarah (Backus) T. Was a
grandson of Jonathan Trumbull (I) and nephew of Jonathan
Trumbull (II), both Govs. of Conn. (q.v.). Grad. from Yale
in 1801. Studied law, went to Ohio, and was admitted to
bar in Ohio in 1802. Returned to Conn. in 1803, where he
was admitted to Conn. bar at Windham, and began law practice
in Hartford. Became pres. of Hartford Bank in 1828, in
which capacity he continued to serve until 1839. Later became pres. of Providence, Hartford and Fishkill R.R. Co.
Mbr. of Conn. Assembly in 1832. El. to U.S. House as a
Whig in 1834 to fill a vacancy and completed term. Chosen
for succeeding terms in 1838 and 1840. Was a strong advocate of internal improvements and aid to educ. while a mbr.
of Cong. Mbr. of Conn. Assembly again in 1848. Nom. and
el. Gov. as a Whig in 1849 by Gen. Assembly after a very
close race against Dem. and Free Soil party opponents. El.
to Conn. Assembly again in 1851. Active in support of
institutions for handicapped and orphans. Hon. degree from
Yale in 1849. m. in 1820 to Harriet Champion. One s.; one
d. After death of first wife, m. to Eliza Storrs. One d.
D. at Hartford, August 4, 1861. Bur. in Old North Cem.
there.

SEYMOUR, THOMAS HART (1850-1853). b. Sept. 29, 1807
at Hartford, Conn. s. of Major Henry S. and Jane (Ellery)
S. Educ. in Hartford schools and at Capt. Partridge's Mil.
Inst., Middletown, Conn. Studied law and was admitted to
bar in 1833. Became commanding officer of Governor's foot
guards. Ed. of the _Jeffersonian_, a Dem. newspaper in

Hartford, 1837-1838. Judge of probate for his dist., 1836-1838. El. to U.S. House as Dem. in 1842. Did not seek second term. Major of New England regiment following outbreak of Mexican War. Distinguished self with U.S. troops in capture of Mexico City. Left active service with rank of col. Unsuccessful as Dem. nominee for Gov. in 1849; but in 1850 was nom. again and was el. Reel. for next three terms. Pres. elector on Pierce ticket in 1852. Resigned post of Gov. during last term to take post of Minister to Russia, to which he was apptd. by Pres. Pierce. After four years of service in that position, travelled in Europe for another year before returning to Hartford. During Civil War became leader and spokesman of Conn. "Peace" Democrats. Because he was suspected of being a Southern sympathizer, the Conn. Council voted to remove his portrait from the Council's chamber in 1862; but it was eventually restored to its place. Defeated as Dem. cand. for Gov. in 1860 and 1863 against incumbent Gov. Buckingham. At the 1864 Dem. natl. conv. he received 38 votes on the first ballot as cand. for nom. for Pres. of U.S. Mbr., Masons and was Eminent Commdr. of Washington Commandery at Hartford. D. at Hartford, Sept. 3, 1868. Bur. in Cedar Hill Cem. there.

POND, CHARLES HOBBY (1853-1854). b. April 26, 1781 at Milford, Conn. s. of Capt. and Martha (Miles) P. Entered Yale at age 17, grad. in 1802. Noted for muscular strength and wit as a student. Studied law and was admitted to bar in 1804, but did not practice law. Because of poor health, went to sea. Eventually regained health and rose to rank of ship capt. Took up residence in Milford and in 1819 was apptd. judge of co. ct. Sheriff of New Haven Co. in 1820, and continued in that office for 15 years. Judge of co. ct., 1836-1837. El. Lieut. Gov. as Dem. in 1850. Unsuccessful cand. for a seat in Conn. Assembly in 1851; but was el. Lieut. Gov. again as Dem. in 1852 and 1853. Succeeded to office of Gov. when Gov. Seymour resigned in 1853 and completed Seymour's term. Retired from pub. life thereafter. D. April 28, 1861.

DUTTON, HENRY (1854-1855). b. Feb. 12, 1796 at Plymouth, Conn. s. of Thomas D., a farmer of limited means. Ancestral line included one of the founders of the first church at New Haven and a grandfather who had been a capt. in the Contl. Army during the Rev. War. Was obliged to assist father on the family farm near Northfield, Conn., to which place his family moved during his youth, until age 20. Attd. local schools and prepared for college while working as farm laborer and teacher. Entered Yale in 1814. Grad.

with highest honors in 1818. Studied law while teaching at
Fairfield Acad. Tutor at Yale, 1821-1823. Admitted to bar
in 1823 and began practice at Newtown, Conn. Later moved to
Bridgeport, where he soon became well-known as an able
lawyer and built up a lucrative practice. Served as mbr. of
Conn. Assembly two terms while residing at Newtown, and
again for two terms while at Bridgeport. In 1847 became
Kent Prof. of Law at Yale. Mbr. of a commn. in 1847 to revise Conn. statutes. Performed a similar function in 1854
and again in 1866. Held position of State's atty. in
Fairfield Co. for one year, and also served as co. judge for
one year. Mbr. of Conn. Senate in 1849. In 1853 was
defeated as Whig cand. for Gov. Again was nom. as Whig cand
for Gov. in 1854, and though failing to receive a plurality
of the popular vote, was el. Gov. by the Gen. Assembly. Defeated as cand. of the Whig and Free Soil parties for Gov.
in 1855. Became a superior ct. judge, and in 1861 a mbr. of
Conn. Supreme Ct. of Errors. Served until he reached
retirement age in 1866. Engaged in teaching and practice of
law thereafter. m. to Elizabeth Joy, of Boston. Three d.;
one s. D. at New Haven, April 26, 1869.

MINOR, WILLIAM THOMAS (1855-1857). b. Oct. 3, 1815 at
Stamford, Conn. s. of Simon H. and Catherine (Lockwood) M.
Father was a prominent lawyer and judge. Entered Yale at
age 15, graduating in 1834. Studied law in father's office
while also engaged in teaching. Admitted to bar in 1841.
Mbr. of Conn. Assembly for seven of the twelve years from
1841 to 1852. Judge of probate of his dist. in 1847. Mbr.
of Conn. Senate in 1854. Nom. for Gov. by the Amer. and
Temperance parties in 1855, and was el. by action of the
Gen. Assembly. Finished second in the popular vote for Gov.
in 1856, but was reel. by the Gen. Assembly. Retired to law
practice. Strong supporter of Union cause when Civil War
began. Delegate to Rep. natl. conv. in 1864. Apptd. U.S.
Consul Gen. at Havana by Pres. Lincoln in that year. Action
in obtaining surrender of a Confederate privateer to U.S. by
Cuban authorities was a notable achievement while there.
Resigned office when Andrew Johnson became Pres. of U.S.
El. superior ct. judge in 1868, serving in that office until
1873. Defeated as Rep. cand. for seat in U.S. Senate in
1873 and again in 1874. One of commnrs. that settled
boundary dispute between N.Y. and Conn. in 1879. Hon.
degree from Wesleyan Univ. in 1855. m. in 1849 to Mary
Leeds. Five children. D. at Stamford, Oct. 13, 1889, and
was buried there.

HOLLEY, ALEXANDER HAMILTON (1857-1858). b. Aug. 12,

1804 at Lakeville, in the town of Salisbury, Conn. s. of
John Milton and Sally (Porter) H. Father was a merchant
and manufacturer of iron products. Prepared for college at
schools in Sheffield, Mass., Ellsworth, Conn., and Hudson,
N.Y. Because of poor health did not enter college, as
planned. Worked in father's bus. and became its head when
his father died in 1836. Incorporated the bus. in 1854, becoming its pres. Also acquired interests in banking and
railroads, and became wealthy. A strong advocate of Whig
party principles, he was a delegate to that party's natl.
conv. in 1844. Nom. and el. Lieut. Gov. in 1854. Joined
Rep. party when it was formed in mid-1850s. Nom. and el.
Gov. as Rep. in 1857. Retired to devote attention to bus.
interests after one term. Strong advocate of Union cause
during Civil War. Was an opponent of slavery, and supported
temperance movement. Participated in founding of school for
feeble-minded. Congregationalist. m. Jane Lyman in 1831.
One s. After her death in 1832, m. to Marcia Coffing in
1835. Five s.; one d. After second wife's death in 1854,
m. to Sarah Coit Day in 1856. D. at Lakeville, Conn.,
Oct. 2, 1887. Buried there.

BUCKINGHAM, WILLIAM ALFRED (1858-1866). b. May 28,
1804 at Lebanon, Conn. s. of Samuel and Joanna (Matson) B.
Father was a prosperous farmer who also owned a shad fishery
bus. A family ancestor had been among the original
settlers at Saybrook, Conn., and had participated in the
founding of Yale Coll. Attd. local schools and Bacon Acad.
at Colchester, where he prepared for work as a land surveyor. After engaging briefly in that line of work, returned to Lebanon to assist father on family farm. Also
engaged in teaching for a time. In 1822 became clerk in
uncle's store at Norwich. Later went into merc. bus. for
himself. Expanded bus. into carpet mfg. field and in 1848
became a partner in a rubber shoe mfg. firm, both of which
prospered. Mayor of Norwich in 1849-1850 and 1856-1857.
Joined newly formed Rep. party in 1850s, serving as pres.
elector for that party in 1856. Nom. as Rep. cand. for
Gov. in 1858 and was el. Reel. for seven succeeding terms.
Became close friend of Abraham Lincoln, who campaigned on
his behalf in 1860 election, which Buckingham won by a
close margin against former Gov. Seymour. As "war Gov." he
effectively supported Union cause, becoming in May, 1861,
the first Gov. to supply fully effective and equipped regiment in response to Lincoln's call for troops. Retired
from office at end of eighth term in 1866. El. to seat in
U.S. Senate in 1869, serving therein until his death.
Active in affairs of Congregational church, serving as

moderator of its first Natl. Council in 1865. Benefactor
of several missionary orgs. Left bequest to Yale for an
endowed chair in its Divinity School. m. to Eliza Ripley.
Two children. D. Feb. 5, 1875, shortly before end of first
term in U.S. Senate. Bur. in Yantic Cem. at Norwich.

HAWLEY, JOSEPH ROSWELL (1866-1867). b. Oct. 31, 1826
at Stewartsville, N.C. s. of the Rev. Francis and Mary
(McLeod) H. Father, who was a minister of the Baptist
church, was a native of Stratford, Conn. Family was of
Scotch-Irish descent. After his birth, family returned to
Conn., where the father became widely known for his abolitionist views. Family moved later to Cazenovia, N.Y. while
son was still a youth. Attd. Hamilton Coll. in N.Y.
Returned to Hartford, where he studied law and was admitted
to bar in 1850. Practiced law for six years. Became ed.
of an abolitionist journal, the Charter Oak, in 1852. It
merged with the Hartford Evening Press in 1857, a Rep. newspaper; and in 1867 that newspaper merged with the Hartford
Courant, with Hawley acting as part-owner and ed. Delegate
to Free Soil party natl. conv. in 1852. Chaired a meeting
at Hartford in Feb., 1856, which resulted in formation of
Rep. party in Conn. Active in campaigns of Gen. Fremont in
1856 and of Lincoln in 1860. At outbreak of Civil War org.
and was capt. of first company of volunteers from Conn. for
Union army. Pursued army career during entire course of the
Civil War, seeing much active service in engagements in Va.,
the Carolinas, and Fla. Left service with rank of major
gen. Nom. and el. Gov. as Rep. in 1866 in very close election, but lost campaign for reel. the next year against the
same opponent, James English. Ch. of Rep. natl. conv. in
1868, and pres. elector that year. El. to U.S. House in
1872 to fill a vacancy. Was subsequently el. for a full
term, but was defeated for reel. in 1874. In 1873-1876 was
ch. of commn. to plan U.S. Centennial Exhibition of 1876.
Delegate to Rep. natl. convs. in 1872, 1876 and 1880. El.
again to U.S. House in 1878. El. to U.S. Senate in 1881 and
was continued in office for next three terms. Achieved
prominence as party leader there. Received 15 votes for
nom. for Pres. of U.S. in the 1884 Rep. natl. conv. m. in
1855 to Harriet Foote. No children. After her death, m. in
1887 to Edith A. Hornor, of Philadelphia. Two d. Hon. degrees from Hamilton Coll., Yale, and Trinity Coll. D. in
Washington, D.C., March 17, 1905, shortly after end of fourth
term in U.S. Senate. Bur. in Cedar Hill Cem., Hartford.

ENGLISH, JAMES EDWARD (1867-1869; 1870-1871). b. Mar.
13, 1812 at New Haven, Conn. s. of James and Nancy

(Griswold) E. Father was a mbr. of a well-known Conn. family. Grandfather had lost his life in a British invasion of Conn. during Rev. War. Father was engaged in West India trade as a ship capt. Mother was a mbr. of the Griswold family from which two Conn. Govs. had come. Son was "bound out" to work on a neighboring farm as youth. Attd. local schools. Apprenticed to a master carpenter to learn trade. Acquired bldg. skills quickly and went into bus. for himself at an early age. Extended activities into lumber, banking and mfg. of clocks and rubber footware. Latter bus. expanded into Goodyear Rubber Shoe Co., which prospered. Became active in mun. affairs, serving a mbr. of city council of New Haven and on its bd. of selectmen, 1847-1861. Mbr. of Conn. Assembly in 1855 and of Conn. Senate, 1856-1858. Defeated as Dem. cand. for Lieut. Gov. in 1860. El. to U.S. House later that year and again in 1862. Declined to run for a third term, although Pres. Lincoln urged Rep. support for him because of his strong advocacy of Union cause during Civil War. Delegate to Union party natl. conv. at Philadelphia in 1866. Defeated as Dem. cand. for Gov. in 1866, but was el. to that office in 1867 and 1868. Defeated for succeeding term in 1869 by very narrow margin, but was nom. and el. Gov. again in 1870, defeating incumbent Gov. Jewell. Lost again in 1871 to former Gov. Jewell by margin of approximately 100 votes. As Gov., successfully advocated expansion of free pub. school system. Mbr. of Conn. Assembly in 1872. Defeated for U.S. House seat in 1872. Apptd. by Gov. to fill vacant U.S. Senate seat in 1875, but failed in attempt to continue in the office by election the next year. Defeated as Dem. nom. for Gov. in 1880. Pres. elector cand. on Dem. ticket in 1868, 1876 and 1884. Received 19 votes in 1868 Dem. natl. conv. for nom. for Pres. of U.S. Made generous gifts during lifetime for pub. purposes, including gifts to Yale. m. in 1835 to Caroline Augusta Fowler. Four children. D. at New Haven, March 2, 1890. Bur. in Evergreen Cem. there.

JEWELL, MARSHALL (1869-1870; 1871-1873). b. Oct. 20, 1825 at Winchester, N.H. s. of Pliny and Emily (Alexander) J. Father, who was in tanning bus., was a prominent Whig. Received common school educ. and was apprenticed in father's bus. to learn tanner's trade. Decided not to follow that trade. Went to Boston where he studied electricity and learned telegraphy. Employed for a time as a telegrapher in Rochester, N.Y., and later in Akron, Ohio. In 1848 was put in charge of constr. of telegraph line between Louisville, Ky. and New Orleans, La. Returned to Hartford in 1849 to join father in tanning and belting mfg. bus.

that his father had established there in 1845. Became part
owner of Hartford _Evening Post_. Acquired other bus.
interests in telegraph and mfg. fields. Helped org. Rep.
party in Conn. in 1850s. Defeated as cand. of that party
for Conn. Senate. Defeated as cand. of Rep. party for Gov.
in 1868, but was nom. again in 1869 for that office. El. by
some 400 votes, defeating incumbent Gov. English to whom he
had lost in 1868. Nom. for succeeding term in 1870 but lost
to former Gov. English by narrow margin. Nom. again for
Gov. against English in 1871 and was el. by plurality of
about 100 votes. Reel. in 1872. During admin., state
militia system was reorg. Apptd. Minister to Russia by
Pres. Grant in 1873. Served in that office until 1874, when
he was apptd. U.S. Postmaster Gen. by Pres. Grant. As such,
initiated first fast mail train service between New York and
Chicago. Became embroiled in controversy arising from the
"Whiskey Ring" and "Star Route" scandals in Grant's admin.,
and was forced to resign in 1876. Opposed movement to nom.
Grant for a third term as Pres. of U.S. in 1880, having
ceased to be a supporter of Grant earlier. Became ch. of
Rep. natl. commt. in 1880 and held the post until 1883. m.
in 1852 to Esther Dickinson, of Newburgh, N.Y. Two children. D. at Hartford, Feb. 10, 1883.

ENGLISH, JAMES EDWARD (1870-1871). See above, 1867-
1869.

JEWELL, MARSHALL (1871-1873). See above, 1869-1870.

INGERSOLL, CHARLES ROBERTS (1873-1877). b. Sept 16,
1821 at New Haven, Conn. s. of Ralph Isaacs and Margaret
Eleanor (Van den Heuvel) I. Grandfather had been a Lieut.
Gov. of Conn. Father had served in Conn. legislature, the
U.S. House, as Atty. Gen. of Conn., and as U.S. Minister to
Russia. Educ. at Hopkins Grammar School in New Haven and at
Yale, from which he was grad. in 1842. Travelled abroad for
two years, after which he studied law at Yale. Admitted to
bar in 1845 and joined father's law firm. Mbr. of Conn.
Assembly 1856-1858. Delegate to Dem. natl. conv. in 1864.
Mbr. of Conn. Assembly again from 1866 to 1871. Nom. and
el. Gov. as Dem. in 1873. Reel. for next three terms. Declined to be cand. for fifth term. Pres. elector on Dem.
ticket in 1876. After service as Gov., retired to practice
of law and bus. interests. Involved as an atty. in a number
of important cases before U.S. Supreme Ct. Was one of the
incorporators of Conn. Savings Bank in New Haven. Hon. degree from Yale in 1874. m. in 1847 to Virginia Gregory.
One s.; three d. D. at New Haven, Jan. 25, 1903.

HUBBARD, RICHARD DUDLEY (1877-1879). b. Sept. 7, 1818
at Berlin, Conn. s. of Lemuel and Elizabeth (Dudley) H.
Family had limited means, and he was orphaned while still a
youth. Determined to obtain educ., he attd. Yale while
supporting himself by working in a variety of jobs. Grad.
from Yale in 1839. Studied law and admitted to bar in 1842.
Established practice in Hartford. Mbr. of Conn. Assembly
in 1842 and 1855-1858. Pros. atty. for Hartford Co. in
1846, and continued to hold that position, with exception of
two years, until 1868. During Civil War was a supporter of
Union cause. Nom. and el. to U.S. House in 1866 as Dem.
Declined to run for second term. Defeated as Dem. cand. for
Gov. in 1872. Was nom. again for that office in 1876 and
was el., becoming the first Conn. Gov. to be chosen for a
two-year term. Nom. for succeeding term in 1878, but lost
in the gen. election. During admin., successfully sponsored
bill to define more liberally and insure property rights of
married women. Retired to law practice after tenure as Gov.
m. in 1845 to Juliana Morgan. Three s.; three d. D. at
Hartford, Feb. 28, 1884. Bur. in Cedar Hill Cem. there.

ANDREWS, CHARLES BARTLETT (1879-1881). b. Nov. 4, 1836
at North Sunderland, Mass. s. of the Rev. Erastus and
Elmira (Bartlett) A. Father was a Baptist minister who had
moved to Mass. from Hartford, Conn. soon after his marriage.
Family had only limited means, and the son obtained a
college educ. largely by own efforts. Grad. from Amherst
Coll. in 1858. Studied law in law office at Sherman, Conn.
while supporting himself by teaching. Admitted to bar in
1861. Established practice in Litchfield in partnership
with John Hubbard. Upon the latter's having been el. to
Cong., took over the partner's large law practice there.
Mbr. of Conn. Senate 1868-1870. El. to Conn. Assembly as
Rep. in 1878, where he achieved distinction as leader of his
party. Nom. as Rep. cand. for Gov. in 1878 and was el.
through action of Gen. Assembly, defeating incumbent Gov.
Richard Hubbard. During admin., succeeded in reaching
agreement with N.Y. in defining N.Y.-Conn. boundary and in
obtaining revision of civil practice code of procedure. Did
not seek second term. Apptd. superior ct. judge in 1882 and
was made Chief Justice of the ct. in 1889. Retired from
office in 1901. Mbr. of commn. in 1886 to adjust Conn.-R.I.
boundary. Mbr. of Bd. of Educ. for Blind in 1893, and of
the State Bd. of Pardons in 1894. Was presiding officer of
Conn. constl. conv. of 1902. Bus. involvements included
his being pres. of Litchfield Mutual Fire Ins. Co. and
Litchfield Natl. Bank. Hon. degrees from Amherst, Conn.
Wesleyan and Yale. m. in 1866 to Mary J. Carter, who died

the following year. m. in 1870 to Sarah M. Wilson, of Bethlehem, Conn. One s. D. Sept. 12, 1902, at Litchfield, Conn.

BIGELOW, HOBART B. (1881-1883). b. May 16, 1834 at North Haven, Conn. s. of Levi L. and Belinda (Pierpont) B. Father was a mbr. of a prominent Mass. family. Mother was a descendant of James Pierpont, a New Haven minister who was one of the founders of Yale Coll. Family moved to South Egremont (Great Barrington), Mass. when son was 10 years old. Educ. at a local acad. Engaged in farm work for a time. Apprenticed at age 17 to a mfr. at Guilford to learn machinist's trade. Company failed and he then went to New Haven, Conn. to complete apprenticeship. Acquired an interest in a machine shop and foundry there. Org. and became head of Bigelow Mfg. Co. at New Haven. Served as mbr. of the city council in New Haven, 1863-1864; as alderman, 1864-1865; as supervisor, 1871-1874; and as fire commnr., 1874-1876. Mbr. of Conn. Assembly in 1875. Mayor of New Haven, 1879-1881. Nom. and el. Gov. as a Rep. in 1880. Did not seek second term. Devoted attention thereafter to bus. interests. m. in 1857 to Eleanor Lewis. Two s. D. at New Haven, Oct. 12, 1891.

WALLER, THOMAS MACDONALD (1883-1885). b. in 1839 (1840?) in New York City. s. of Thomas Christopher and Mary (Macdonald) Armstrong. Parents had emigrated to Amer. from Ireland. Became an orphan while still a young boy. Earned living as newsboy. Later became a cabin boy and cook's mate and made several sea voyages out of New York. In 1849 attracted notice of Robt. K. Waller, a resident of New London, Conn., when the two met on a wharf in New York. Waller was struck by the boy's intelligence and manner and offered to give him a home. The offer was accepted, the boy assuming the name of his benefactor. Educ. in New London schools. Studied law and was admitted to bar in 1861. Enlisted as a pvt. in Conn. regiment that year, but had to leave mil. service after a short time because of an eye disease. Returned to New London and engaged in law practice, in which he was quite successful. Mbr. of Conn. Assembly from New London in 1867, 1868, 1872 and 1876, serving as Speaker during last term. El. Sect. of State in 1870. Mayor of New London in 1873 and atty. for New London Co., 1875-1883. Nom. and el. Gov. as Dem. in 1882. Nom. for second term. Received a plurality of popular votes, but his Rep. opponent was chosen by Gen. Assembly. Widely recognized for his oratory and wit. Gave nominating speech for Grover Cleveland at Dem. natl. conv. in 1884. Apptd. U.S.

Consul Gen. at London, England by Pres. Cleveland in 1885,
serving until 1889. Resumed law practice at New London.
Mbr. of Conn. constl. conv. in 1902. Served as commnr. for
Conn. at Chicago World's Fair in 1893. Hon. degree from
Yale. m. to Charlotte Bishop, of New London. Five s.;
one d. D. at New London, Jan. 25, 1924.

HARRISON, HENRY BALDWIN (1885-1887). b. Sept. 11, 1821
at New Haven, Conn. s. of Ammi and Polly (Barney) H. Attd.
Lancastrian Acad. in New Haven, where he also served as
teaching asst. while continuing studies at Yale. Grad. from
Yale in 1846 with highest honors in class. Studied law, was
admitted to bar in 1848 and began practice at New Haven.
El. as Whig to Conn. Senate in 1854. Was a strong opponent
of slavery. Authored "personal liberty" bill to assist
fugitive slaves. Became mbr. of Free Soil party. Later
assisted in formation of Rep. party in Conn. Defeated as
Rep. cand. for Lieut. Gov. in 1856. Mbr. of Conn. Assembly
in 1865 and again in 1873. Defeated as Rep. cand. for Gov.
in 1874 against incumbent Gov. Ingersoll. Received several
hundred votes for Gov. as Greenback party cand. in 1880.
El. again to Conn. Assembly in 1883, serving as its
Speaker. Nom. and el. Gov. as Rep. in 1884, although his
opponent, incumbent Gov. Waller, received a popular plurality. As legislator, favored granting suffrage to Negroes.
During admin. as Gov., a State Bureau of Labor Statistics
was created and a compulsory school attendance law passed.
Mbr. of Yale Corp., 1872-1875. Hon. degree from Yale in
1885. Episcopalian. m. to Mary Elizabeth Osborne. No
children. D. at New Haven, Oct. 29, 1901. Bur. there.

LOUNSBURY, PHINEAS CHAPMAN (1887-1889). b. Jan. 10,
1841 at Ridgefield, Conn. s. of Nathan and Delia A.
(Scofield) L. Father was a farmer and shoemaker, and was a
descendant of one of the early Conn. families. An older
brother, George, later also became Gov. of Conn. (q.v.).
Attd. local pub. and pvt. schools while assisting father on
farm. In 1858 went to New York City, where he worked as a
clerk in a shoe store, later becoming a travelling salesman. Returned to New Haven at age of 21 and began shoe mfg.
bus. with his brother, George. Plant was moved to South
Norwalk in 1869. Enlisted in a Conn. regiment in 1861 at
beginning of Civil War, but was discharged because of illness after a short period of service. Became active in
Rep. politics. Mbr. of Conn. Assembly in 1874, where he
championed cause of local option liquor license act.
Served as Rep. pres. elector in 1880. Sought Rep. nom. for
Gov. in 1882 and again in 1884, but failed to win both

times. Was nom. in 1886 and was el. by Gen. Assembly, although he failed to obtain a popular plurality. During
admin., a measure was enacted providing for long-term incar-
ceration of repeat offenders. After tenure as Gov., gave
attention to bus. interests in banking, mfg., and ins.
fields. Trustee of Wesleyan Univ., from which he received
an hon. degree in 1887. Mbr., Masons. Methodist. m. in
1867 to Jane Wright. D. June 22, 1925 at Ridgefield, Conn.

BULKELEY, MORGAN GARDNER (1889–1893). b. Dec. 26, 1837
at East Haddam, Conn. s. of Eliphalet Adams and Lydia S.
(Morgan) B. Father, who was a mbr. of an old and prominent
New England family, was a lawyer. Father had helped to
form Rep. party in Conn., and had served as Speaker of Conn.
Assembly. Attd. pub. schools in Hartford. Began work as
errand boy in uncle's merc. bus. in Brooklyn, N.Y. in 1852
and in a few years became a partner in the enterprise. Enlisted in a New York regiment at beginning of Civil War and
saw much active service in Va. campaigns under Gen.
McClellan. After death of his father in 1872, moved to
Hartford. Founded U.S. Bank there, of which he was pres.
until 1879. Became pres. of Aetna Life Ins. Co. and also
became involved in a number of other bus. enterprises. Mbr.
of city council of Hartford in 1874, and of its bd. of
aldermen, 1880–1888. Nom. as Rep. cand. for Gov. in 1888,
and was el. by Gen. Assembly when neither of two leading
candidates received a popular vote majority. Was not a
cand. for succeeding term in 1890; but when the two
branches of the Gen. Assembly were unable to agree on a
joint meeting to canvass and declare the result in the close
gubernatorial election of 1890, he held over as Gov. for the
next two years. El. to a seat in U.S. Senate in 1905.
Served only one term, being defeated for reel. Mbr., S.A.R.;
G.A.R., serving as commdr. of Conn. dept. thereof in 1903.
Became pres. of Natl. Baseball League in 1876. Hon. degrees
from Yale and Trinity Coll. m. in 1885 to Fannie Briggs
Houghton. Two s.; one d. D. at Hartford, Nov. 6, 1922.
Bur. in Cedar Hill Cem. there.

MORRIS, LUZON BURRITT (1893–1895). b. April 16, 1827
at Newtown, Conn. s. of Eli Gould and Lydia (Bennett) M.
Attd. local schools. At age 17 began work as a blacksmith
and tool-maker to earn funds to continue educ. Entered
Yale in 1850, continuing to work in vacation periods, but
had to withdraw during senior year because of lack of funds.
Eventually received degree in 1858. Obtained employment in
Seymour, Conn., where he began study of law. Completed law
studies at Yale. Was admitted to bar in 1856 and began

practice at Seymour. Mbr. of Conn. Assembly, 1855-1856.
Moved to New Haven in 1857, and was el. judge of probate
there, serving from 1857-1863. Mbr. of New Haven school
bd. in 1861, continuing to serve in that capacity for a number of years. Mbr. of Conn. Assembly in 1870, 1876, 1880
and 1881. Mbr. of Conn. Senate in 1874, serving as Pres.
pro tem of that body. Mbr. of commn. to adjust N.Y. and
Conn. boundary in 1879-1880. Mbr. and ch. of commn. to revise Conn. probate laws in 1884. Nom. as Dem. cand. for
Gov. in 1890. Received plurality of popular vote, but because the two branches failed to agree on convening to canvass votes and make the result official, there was no final
election, and the incumbent Gov. (Bulkeley) continued in the
office of Gov. for the full term. Nom. again for Gov. in
1892, and was el. by popular majority. Did not run for
second term. Pres. of Conn. Savings Bank and dir. of N.Y.,
New Haven and Hartford R.R. m. in 1856 to Eugenia Tuttle.
Six children. D. at New Haven, Aug. 22, 1895, shortly after
tenure as Gov. ended.

COFFIN, O(WEN) VINCENT (1895-1897). b. June 20, 1836
in Mansfield, N.Y. s. of Alexander H. and Jane (Vincent) C.
Father, who was a farmer, was a descendant of Tristam
Coffin who had emigrated from Devonshire, England in 1642
to Mass., and had a prominent role in the early history of
Nantucket Island. Attd. dist. schools; Cortland Acad., and
Charlottesville, N.Y. Sem. Became a school teacher at age
16. Later became a salesman in a New York City merc.
establishment, eventually becoming a partner in the enterprise. In 1864 moved to Middletown, Conn., where he served
as exec. officer of Farmers and Mechanics Bank. Ill health
forced his retirement temporarily; but he recovered and returned to active participation in a number of bus. firms,
including an ins. co., which he headed. Mayor of Middletown
1872-1873. Mbr. of Conn. Senate, 1886-1890. Nom. and el.
Gov. as a Rep. by popular majority in 1894. Retired after
one term to devote attention to varied bus. interests.
Active in YMCA movement. Pres. of Middlesex Co. Agri. Soc.
in 1875. Hon. degree from Wesleyan Univ. in 1896. m. in
1858 to Ellen Elizabeth Coe, of Middletown. Congregationalist. D. at Middletown, Jan. 3, 1921.

COOKE, LORRIN ALANSON (1897-1899). b. April 6, 1831 at
New Marlboro, Mass. s. of Levi and Amelia (Todd) C. One of
his ancestors was the first settler in New Marlboro. Great-
grandfather was a soldier in the Contl. Army during the Rev.
War, and grandfather served in U.S. Army in War of 1812.
Family moved to Norfolk, Conn. when he was a youth. Attd.
common schools and Norfolk Acad. Became a school teacher.

Mbr. of Conn. Assembly in 1856. In 1869 moved to Riverton, Conn. and became mgr. of Eagle Scythe Co. there. Mbr. of Conn. Senate 1882-1884, serving as pres. pro tem during last term. Served as postmaster in Riverton in early 1880s. El. Lieut. Gov. in 1884. Delegate to Rep. natl. conv. in 1892. Nom. and el. Gov. as Rep. in 1896 by a large popular majority. Held no pub. office thereafter. Active in affairs of Congregational church, serving as moderator of its Natl. Council in 1886. m. in 1858 to Matilda E. Webster. After her death in 1868, m. to Josephine E. Ward in 1870. Two s.; one d. D. at Winstead, Conn., Aug. 12, 1902.

LOUNSBURY, GEORGE EDWARD (1899-1901). b. May 7, 1838 at Pound Ridge, N.Y. s. of Nathan and Delia A. (Scofield) L. A younger brother, Phineas, was also a Gov. of Conn. (q.v.). Father was a shoemaker and farmer and was a descendant of one of the early settlers of Conn. who came there from England in 1651. While he was still an infant, family moved to Ridgefield, Conn. Attd. local schools. Became a teacher at age 17, continuing to work on family farm during vacations. Entered Yale at age 20, grad. in 1863 with high honors. Although his parents were mbrs. of the Methodist church, he became an Episcopalian and studied for the ministry at Berkeley Divinity School in Middletown, Conn., from which he was grad. in 1866. Held parish posts for two years, but difficulties with throat led to his abandoning the ministry. Went into shoe mfg. bus. with brother Phineas at New Haven. Bus. was moved to Norwalk in 1869, and it prospered. El. to Conn. Senate in 1894. Reel. to Senate in 1896. Nom. and el. Gov. as Rep. by large majority in 1898. Admin. characterized by economy in govt. Used veto freely. After one term retired to farm. Noted for many acts of charity to needy individuals. m. in 1894 to Frances Josephine Potwin, of Amherst, Mass. D. Aug. 16, 1904 at Farmington, Conn.

McLEAN, GEORGE PAYNE (1901-1903). b. Oct. 7, 1857 at Simsbury, Conn. s. of Dudley B. and Mary (Payne) McLean. Both parents were members of old and distinguished Conn. families. Attd. local schools and h.s. at Hartford, where he was ed. of school paper. Became a reporter on the Hartford Evening Post for two years. Studied law and was admitted to bar in 1881. Began practice in Hartford. Mbr. of Conn. Assembly in 1883. As ch. of Commt. on State Prisons, secured passage of legislation changing procedure for acting on prisoners' petitions for pardons by establishment of a Bd. of Pardons. Became clerk of that body in 1884, a position he held until 1901. Mbr. of commn. to revise Conn. statutes, 1885. El. to Conn. Senate in 1886.

Rep. cand. for Sect. of State in 1890, but no election result was declared because of deadlock in legislature. Apptd.
U.S. dist. atty. by Pres. Harrison in 1892, serving until
1896. During that period also served as counsel for the
State Comptroller and State Treas., successfully defending
them in an important suit brought by Yale Univ. to prevent
the State from diverting U.S. funds to Storrs Agri. Coll.
(now the Univ. of Conn.). Nom. and el. Gov. as Rep. in
1900. During admin., supported movement for assembling
conv. to revise Conn. const. Did not seek second term as
Gov. El. to U.S. Senate seat in 1911, and was continued in
office for two succeeding terms. Declined to be cand. for
reel. in 1928. Hon. degrees from Yale Univ. and Trinity
Coll. m. in 1907 to Juliette Goodrich. D. June 6, 1932.
Bur. in Simsbury Cem.

CHAMBERLAIN, ABIRAM (1903-1905). b. Oct. 7, 1837 at
Colebrook River, Conn. s. of Abiram and Sophronia Ruth
(Burt) C. Both father and mother were descendants of early
colonial Mass. families. Father was a civil engr. and
farmer. Attd. local schools and Williston Sem., Easthampton,
Mass., specializing in civil engr. Family moved to New
Britain, Conn. and he joined his father there as a civil
engr. for a time. Worked in a factory as a rule-maker, but
soon changed endeavors to that of a banking employee in New
Britain. At age 30 became cashier of Home Natl. Bank in
Meriden, Conn., where he made his home thereafter. Extended
bus. interests into fields of railroads, hotel operations,
and mfg. enterprises. Mbr. of Conn. Assembly in 1877. Nom.
and el. State Comptroller in 1900. Nom. and el. Gov. as a
Rep. in 1902. As Gov., found it necessary to use militia
forces to maintain order during a transit workers strike in
Waterbury. Did not seek second term. m. in 1872 to
Charlotte E. Roberts. Two s. Hon. degree from Wesleyan
Univ. D. at Meriden, May 15, 1911.

ROBERTS, HENRY (1905-1907). b. Jan. 22, 1853 in
Brooklyn, (Conn.?). s. of George and Elvira (Evans) R.
Father had been a businessman at Hartford, Conn. prior to
son's birth. Both parents were of Welsh ancestry and their
forebears included persons who had participated in inter-
colonial wars with France and in the Rev. War. Spent youth
living on a farm with parents at South Windsor, Conn. Attd.
local schools there and at Hartford. Entered Yale, from
which he was grad. in 1877. Continued in study of law there
and at Columbia Univ., but never practiced law. Entered the
office of the Hartford Woven Wire and Mattress Co. in 1878.
Became sect. of the firm in 1884, and its pres. in 1886.

Later extended bus. interests into various banking and pub.
utility enterprises in Hartford area. Mbr. of bd. of aldermen of Hartford in 1897; the Conn. Assembly, 1899-1901; and
the Conn. Senate, 1901-1903. El. Lieut. Gov. in 1902. Nom.
and el. Gov. as Rep. in 1904. Did not seek second term.
Trustee of Slater Indus. School at Winston, N.C. Mbr.,
S.A.R.; Conn. Soc. of Colonial Wars; various social and bus.
clubs. Congregationalist. m. in 1881 to Carrie E. Smith,
of Bridgeport, Conn. Two s. D. May 1, 1929.

     WOODRUFF, ROLLIN SIMMONS (1907-1909). b. July 14, 1854
at Rochester, N.Y. s. of the Rev. Jeremiah and Clorise
(Clarisse?) (Thompson) W. When son was 11 years old the
family moved to Lansing, Iowa. After father died there,
family returned to Rochester, and then in 1870 moved to
Meriden, Conn. Later moved to New Haven, Conn. Educ. in
pub. schools. Became errand boy in hardware store at an
early age, and later worked in various merc. establishments.
In 1876 became associated with C.S. Mersick and Co., a
wholesale iron and steel firm in New Haven. Became a mbr.
of the firm and later, in 1889, its pres. Also engaged in
banking and other bus. operations, becoming pres. of Conn.
Computing Machine Co. of New Haven. Pres. of New Haven CC,
1905-1907. Mbr. and Pres. pro tem of Conn. Senate, 1903-
1905. Lieut. Gov., 1905-1907. Nom. and el. Gov. as a Rep.
in 1906. Did not seek second term. Trustee of Wesleyan
Univ., from which he received an hon. degree. Trustee of
Norwich State Hosp. and of Grace Hosp. Mbr., Union League.
m. in 1880 to Kaorneo E. Perkins, of New Haven. Three
children. D. June 30, 1925.

     LILLEY, GEORGE LEAVENS (1909). b. April 3, 1859 at
Oxford, Mass. s. of John and Caroline (Adams) L. Attd.
Oxford pub. schools and Worcester Tech. Inst. At age 18 began work as salesman for a wholesale meat distribution
firm. Moved to Waterbury, Conn. in 1881. Engaged in merc.
and real estate bus. there. Mbr. of Conn. Assembly, 1901-
1903. Served on Rep. state commt. El. to U.S. House in
1902 and continued in that office for two succeeding terms.
As mbr. of House Naval Affairs Commt., initiated charges of
favoritism in the awarding of contracts for the constr. of
submarine boats, but the charges were not substantiated
after an investigation. Did not seek reel. to Cong. in
1908, but was nom. and el. Gov. as a Rep. in that year.
Seat in U.S. House, which he did not resign immediately, was
declared vacant by the House in Jan., 1909. Supported program of anti-monopoly legislation, regulation of lobbyists,
and the establishment of a pub. service commn. Mbr., Elks;

Forresters; various clubs and bus. orgs. m. in 1884 to
Anna Steele. Three s. D. April 21, 1909, at Hartford, after
being in office for only about three months. Bur. in
Riverside Cem., at Waterbury.

WEEKS, FRANK BENTLEY (1909-1911). b. Jan. 20, 1854 in
Brooklyn, N.Y. s. of Daniel L. and Frances M. (Edwards) W.
Attd. pub. schools and a mil. acad. Grad. from Eastman Bus.
Coll., at Poughkeepsie, N.Y. in 1872. In 1874 became asst.
to supt. of Conn. Hosp. for the Insane. In 1880 went into
grain and milling enterprise with a partner in Middletown,
Conn., continuing in that bus. until 1895. Later became
involved in banking and ins. bus. Founder and first pres.
of Middletown Bd. of Trade. Conn. repr. to Cotton States
Intl. Exposition at Atlanta, Ga. Mbr., Middletown city
council, 1881-1883. Rep. pres. elector in 1904. Nom. and
el. Lieut. Gov. as a Rep. in 1908. When Gov. Lilley died
in April, 1909, succeeded to the office of Gov. and completed Lilley's term. Delegate to Rep. natl. convs. in
1912 and 1916. Trustee of Wesleyan Univ. Trustee of Conn.
Hosp. for the Insane for more than 30 years, and also served
as pres. of its governing bd. Commnr. from Conn. for the
Sesquicentennial Expo. in Philadelphia in 1926. Charter
mbr. of Middlesex Historical Soc. Mbr., Soc. of Colonial
Wars; New England Soc. of N.Y. Hon. degree from Wesleyan
Univ. Congregationalist. m. in 1875 to Helen Louise
Hubbard. D. at Middletown, Oct. 2, 1935.

BALDWIN, SIMEON EBEN (1911-1915). b. Feb 5, 1840 at
New Haven, Conn. s. of Roger S. and Emily (Perkins) B.
Father, who was a U.S. Sen. and Gov. of Conn. (q.v.), was
a direct descendant of Roger Sherman, the distinguished
Conn. statesman of the era of the Amer. Rev. War. Grad.
from Yale in 1861. Received law degree from Harvard in
1863. Admitted to bar in Conn. and practiced widely there
for 30 years. Instructor in law at Yale Univ., 1869 and
prof. of law there from 1872 until his retirement in 1919.
Also lectured at Andover Theological Sem., Univ. of Md. and
Harvard Univ. Proposed graduate program in law at Yale in
1875. Served on commns. to revise educl. code in Conn. in
1872; on gen. law revision in 1873; and on legal procedures
in 1878. Mbr. of commn. to propose tax law reforms in 1885.
Apptd. to Supreme Ct. of Errors in 1893 and became its
Chief Justice in 1907. After retirement from his jud. post,
was nom. and el. Gov. as Dem. in 1910 at age of 70. Reel.
in 1912. Unsuccessful as Dem. cand. for U.S. Senate in
1914. Was one of the founders of Amer. Bar Assoc. and
served as its pres. in 1890. Pres. of Amer. Social Sci.

Assoc. in 1897 and of New Haven Colonial Historical Soc.,
1884-1896. Pres. of Intl. Law Assoc., 1899-1901 and of the
Amer. Political Sci. Assoc. in 1909. Mbr. of Amer. Historical Assoc. and of various other academic and professional
legal orgs. Hon. degrees from Yale, Harvard, Columbia and
Conn. Wesleyan. Published extensively on legal and political matters. m. in 1865 to Susan Winchester, of Boston.
Two d.; one s. Congregationalist. D. at New Haven, Jan. 30,
1927.

HOLCOMB, MARCUS HENSEY (1915-1921). b. Nov. 24, 1844
at New Hartford, Conn. s. of Carlos and Adah Lavinia
(Bushness) H. Both parents were descendants of old Conn.
families. Attd. pvt. school in New Hartford, and Wesleyan
Sem., at Wilbraham, Mass. Poor health prevented his attending college. Became a teacher and also studied law in law
office. Admitted to bar in 1871. Began practice in
Southington, Conn. Moved to Hartford in 1893, where he continued law practice. Affiliated with Dem. party until 1888
when he left that party because of its stand on tariff issue.
Judge of probate, 1873-1910, and also judge of borough ct.,
1905-1909. Treas. of Hartford Co., 1893-1908. Mbr. of Conn.
Senate, 1893-1894. Mbr. of Conn. constl. conv. in 1902.
Mbr. of Conn. Assembly, 1905-1906, serving as its Speaker.
State Police Commnr., 1903. Atty. Gen. of Conn., 1906. Became superior ct. judge by apptmt. from Gov. Weeks, serving
until 1914 when he reached retirement age. Nom. and el.
Gov. as Rep. in 1914 at age of 70. Continued for two
succeeding terms, becoming the first Conn. Gov. to be el. to
the office for three successive two-year terms. Supported
U.S. war effort as Gov. by appropriate measures during
World War I. During admin., legislature refused to ratify
18th Amdt. to U.S. Const., but did ratify the 19th Amdt., an
action which he opposed. Resumed law practice after tenure
as Gov. Pres. of Southington Savings Bank, and mbr. of bds.
of dir. of other banking and bus. concerns. Mbr., Masons;
K.P.; Elks; Natl. Grange. Baptist. Hon. degree from
Trinity Coll. m. to Sarah Carpenter Bennet. No children.
D. March 5, 1932, at Southington, Conn.

LAKE, EVERETT JOHN (1921-1923). b. Feb. 8, 1871 at
Woodstock, Conn. s. of Thomas A. and Martha A. (Cockings)
L. Father was active in Rep. politics, having served in the
Conn. Assembly and Senate and other govtl. posts. Attd.
h.s. in Stromsburg, Nebr.; Worcester Polytechnic Inst., from
which he received a degree in 1890; and Harvard Univ., from
which he received an A.B. degree in 1892. Prominent in
athletics while a student, being named to an All-American

football team in 1891. Employed by Hartford Lumber Co. in
1892. Advanced to pres. of the co. in 1900, in which
position he continued to serve until 1939. El. to Conn.
Assembly in 1902 and to Conn. Senate in 1904. Lieut. Gov.,
1907-1909. During World War I served on the staff of the
YMCA overseas. Nom. and el. Gov. as Rep. in 1920. Did not
seek second term in 1922. Mbr., bds. of dir. of Hartford
Natl. Bank and Trust Co. and of the Hartford-Aetna Natl.
Bank. Trustee of Worcester Polytechnic Inst. Mbr., Masons;
K.P.; Forresters; Delta Kappa Epsilon. Congregationalist.
Hon. degrees from Wesleyan Univ. and Trinity Coll. m. in
1895 to Eva Louise Sykes, of Rockville, Conn. One s.; one
d. After first wife's death, m. to Barbara Grace Lincoln
in 1940. D. at Hartford, Sept. 16, 1948.

TEMPLETON, CHARLES AUGUSTUS (1923-1925). b. Mar. 3,
1871 at Sharon, Conn. s. of Theodore and Ella Phoebe
(Middlebrooke) T. Father was a farmer. Attd. local
schools at Winstead, Plymouth, and the Episcopal School at
Plainville, Conn. Worked while a student as errand boy,
machinist, store clerk, postoffice employee, and cook. Became bookkeeper in hardware store at Waterbury in 1888 and
later acquired partnership interest in the firm. Became
involved in other bus. enterprises in Waterbury, including
the field of banking. Pres. of bd. of aldermen at
Waterbury. El. to Conn. Senate in 1918. Lieut. Gov. in
1920. Nom. and el. Gov. as Rep. in 1922. Admin. marked by
controversy within his party over issues growing out of
natl. and state politics. Served one term. Major interest
was promotion of conservation measures in Conn. Mbr. of
State League of Sportsmen; Rotary; Masons; Red Men; Conn.
Humane Soc.; YMCA; Waterbury CC; and various clubs. Became dir. of Natl. Wildlife Restoration project in 1938.
Trustee, Ste. Marguerite's School for Girls, 1920-1948.
Episcopalian. m. in 1897 to Martha Amelia Castle. Three d.
D. at Waterbury, Aug. 15, 1955.

BINGHAM, HIRAM (1925). b. Nov. 19, 1875 in Honolulu,
Oahu, in Hawaii. s. of Hiram and Minerva Clarissa
(Brewster) B. Father was a missionary in Gilbert Islands.
Attd. schools in Hawaii, 1882-1892; Phillips-Andover Acad.;
and Yale Univ., from which he was grad. in 1898. Supt. of
Palama Chapel Mission school in Honolulu and also was employed briefly as chemist by Amer. Sugar Co. Attd. the
Univ. of Calif., Berkeley, 1899-1900, receiving M.A. degree in history and political sci. Attd. Harvard Univ. and
served as teaching asst., 1901-1905. Received Ph.D. degree
in 1905. Preceptor in history at Princeton, 1905-1906.

Embarked on career as explorer and lecturer. In 1906-1907
explored in Venezuela and Columbia. Lecturer and prof. at
Yale, 1907-1917, in field of So. Amer. history and geography.
Also lectured at other universities. Delegate to first
Pan-Amer. Sci. Cong. at Santiago, Chile, in 1908. Led geographical and exploration trips in So. Amer. from time to
time. Served in U.S. Signal Corps during World War I, and
continued in U.S. mil. service in various spec. service
capacities for some time thereafter, achieving rank of lieut.
col. Delegate to the Rep. natl. convs.,1916-1936. Served as
Rep. pres. elector in 1916. Lieut. Gov., 1923-1925. Nom.
and el. Gov. as Rep. in 1924. Before being inaugurated was
chosen to a vacant seat in U.S. Senate. Was inaugurated as
Gov. in Jan., 1925, but resigned after one day in office to
take Senate seat. Continued to serve in Senate until 1933.
Defeated for reel. in 1932. In the Senate, was opponent of
U.S. mbrship. in League of Nations, but favored joining
World Court system. Served as ch. of U.S. Civil Service
Loyalty Bd., 1951-1953. Author of numerous publications on
historical, political and geographical topics. Mbr.,
Masons; Natl. Grange; numerous professional academic orgs.
Hon. degree from Univ. of Cuzco. m. in 1900 to Alfreda
Mitchell, of New London, Conn. Seven s. D. at Washington,
D.C., June 6, 1956. Bur. in Arlington Natl. Cem.

TRUMBULL, JOHN HARPER (1925-1931). b. March 4, 1873
at Ashford, Conn. s. of Hugh and Mary Ann (Harper) T.
Parents had emigrated to Amer. from Ireland. Attd. local
schools. As one of seven children, assisted in work on
small family farm as a youth. In 1899 began work with a
firm engaged in mfg. of electrical equipment. Org. his own
mfg. enterprise in Plainville, Conn. in 1900, the Trumbull
Electrical Mfg. Co. Served as its pres., 1900-1945. Also
extended bus. interests into fields of banking, utilities
and other areas. Mbr. of Conn. Senate, 1921-1925. Nom.
and el. Lieut. Gov. as Rep. in 1924, and when Gov. Bingham
resigned shortly after inauguration in 1925, succeeded to
office of Gov. and completed Bingham's term. El. for
regular terms in 1926 and 1928. Defeated as Rep. nominee
for Gov. in 1932. Mbr. of Conn. Natl. Guard for five years,
holding rank of capt. Col. on staff of Gov. Templeton.
Became interested in aviation in later years, and learned
to pilot his own plane at age 51. Came to be known as the
"Flying Gov." during course of his admin. because of his
use of a plane to travel about the State. Vice ch., Aero-
space Commn. of Conn. Mbr., Natl. Electrical Mfg. Assoc.,
serving as its pres. on one occasion; Conn. Historical Soc.;
Conn. Humane Soc.; Masons; I.O.O.F.; Red Men; bus.,

recreational and social clubs. Congregationalist. m. in
1903 to Maud Usher. Two d., one of whom became the wife of
John Coolidge, son of Calvin Coolidge, former Pres. of the
U.S. and Gov. of Mass. (q.v.). D. May 21, 1961, at
Hartford, Conn.

CROSS, WILBUR LUCIUS (1931-1939). b. April 10, 1862
at Mansfield, Conn. s. of Samuel and Harriet Maria
(Gurley) C. Father was a farmer and miller, and was a
descendant of old Conn. family. Worked at various jobs
while attending local h.s. and Yale Univ., from which he received an A.B. degree in 1885. Became a teacher while continuing grad. studies in English literature at Yale. Received Ph.D. degree there in 1889. Taught English literature at Shadyside Acad., Pittsburgh, 1889-1894. Returned to
Yale as instructor in 1894, and also taught at Sheffield
Sci. School. Ch. of English Dept. at Yale, 1902-1921. Dean
of the Graduate School there, 1916-1930. Apptd. Sterling
Prof. of English in 1921. Acting Provost at Yale, 1922-
1923. Published extensively on Eighteenth Century English
authors, becoming widely recognized as authority on Laurence
Sterne. Published autobiography, A Connecticut Yankee, in
1943. Ed. of Yale Review, 1911-1940. Following retirement
at Yale, was nom. and el. Gov. as Dem. in 1930 at age of 68.
Reel. in 1932, 1934 and 1936, becoming first Conn. Gov. to
be el. to four two-year terms. As Gov., favored repeal of
18th Amdt.; passage of laws against child labor and for
improvement of working standards for women; state admin.
reorg.; a balanced budget. Opposed sit-down strikes. Defeated for fifth term in 1938 by a narrow margin. Also defeated as Dem. nominee for U.S. Senate seat in 1946. Mbr.
of numerous learned societies. Chancellor of Acad. of Arts
and Letters; pres., Natl. Inst. of Arts and Letters;
Chevalier of Legion of Honor; Trustee, Conn. Coll. for
Women. Numerous hon. degrees. m. in 1889 to Helen Baldwin
Avery, of Willimantic, Conn. Two s.; two d. D. Oct. 5,
1948 at New Haven.

BALDWIN, RAYMOND EARL (1939-1941; 1943-1946). b. Aug.
31, 1893 at Rye, N.Y. s. of Lucien Earl and Sarah Emily
(Tyler) B. Family moved to Middletown, Conn. early in his
youth. Attd. pub. schools there and Conn. Wesleyan Univ.,
from which he was grad. in 1916. Entered Yale Univ. Law
School, but withdrew in 1917 to enlist in U.S. Navy. Attd.
U.S. Naval Acad., and was commissioned as a lieut., j.g., in
1918. Served on destroyer escort duty during World War I.
Travelled in Europe after the war ended, then returned to
re-enter Yale Law School. Grad. in 1921 and was admitted

to bar. Employed in law office in New York City. Moved to
New Haven in 1922, and to Bridgeport in 1924, where he continued to practice law. Pub. pros. of Stratford Co., 1927,
and judge of town ct., 1931-1933. Mbr. of Conn. Assembly,
1931-1933 where he served as majority (Rep.) party leader.
Continued in law practice and the ins. bus., 1933-1938.
Nom. and el. Gov. as Rep. in 1938, defeating incumbent Gov.
Cross. Was the Rep. nominee for Gov. again in 1940, but
lost in the gen. election. Was successful as the Rep. cand.
for Gov. in 1942 and again in 1944. As Gov. during World
War II, incurred hostility of org. labor by use of Natl.
Guard to preserve order during a strike at Yale and Towne
Mfg. Co. in Stamford. Set up a labor-mgmt. advisory council
to aid in post-war adjustment and recovery period. El. to
fill vacant seat in U.S. Senate in 1946, and resigned office
of Gov. in Dec., 1946. Served in Senate until Dec., 1949,
when he resigned to accept seat on Conn. Supreme Ct. Mbr.,
Delta Tau Delta; professional legal orgs. Episcopalian.
m. in 1922 to Edith Lindholm, of Middletown, Conn. Three s.

HURLEY, ROBERT AUGUSTUS (1941-1943). b. Aug. 25, 1895
at Bridgeport, Conn. s. of Robt. Emmett and Sabina (O'Hara)
H. Father was engaged in constr. bus. Attd. Cheshire
Acad., 1914-1915 and Lehigh Univ., 1915-1917, working while
continuing engr. studies. During World War I served in U.S.
Navy as a radio electrician. Joined father in constr. work
in 1919. Formed own bus. firm in Bridgeport with a partner
in 1921. Became dir. of W.P.A. for Fairfield Co. in 1935.
Spec. repr. of U.S. govt. to coordinate relief activities
following Hartford flood in 1936. State W.P.A. Adminr.,
1936-1937. State Commnr. of Pub. Works, 1937-1940. During
tenure, supervised constr. of $25 million program of
institutional bldgs. Nom. and el. Gov. as Dem. in 1940, defeating incumbent Gov. Baldwin. Defeated as Dem. cand. for
Gov. again against Baldwin in 1942 and 1944. As Gov., obtained a no-strike pledge from labor and indus. Formed War
Industries Commn. to channel war orders to local firms.
Mbr. of U.S. Surplus Property Bd., 1944-1945. Exec. dir. of
Council of Lingerie Assoc. and Mfrs., 1946. Formed consult-
ing engr. firm in West Hartford, from which he retired in
1958. m. in 1925 to Evelyn L. Hedberg. Two d.; one s. Was
the first Roman Catholic Gov. of Conn. D. at West Hartford,
Conn., May 3, 1968.

BALDWIN, RAYMOND EARL (1943-1946). See above, 1939-
1941.

SNOW, (CHARLES) WILBERT (1946-1947). b. April 6, 1884

at White Head Island, St. George, Me. s. of Forrest Alwin
and Katherine (Quinn) S. Attd. pub. schools at Thomaston,
Me. and Bowdoin Coll., from which he was grad. in 1907. Received an M.A. degree from Columbia Univ. in 1910. Became
a school teacher in Alaska, 1911-1912. Instructor in English at New York Univ., 1912, and later served as faculty
mbr. at Bowdoin Coll., Williams Coll., Univ. of Utah, Reed
Coll. and the Univ. of Ind. Served with U.S. Army, 1917-
1919. Became asst. prof. of English literature at Wesleyan
Univ. in 1921, later becoming prof. Pres., Conn. Assoc. of
Bds. of Educ. in 1940. Nom. and el. Lieut. Gov. as Dem. in
1944. Succeeded to office of Gov. in Dec., 1946, when Gov.
Raymond Baldwin resigned to take U.S. Senate seat, and completed last two weeks of Baldwin's term. Nominee of Dem.
party for Gov. in 1946, but was defeated in the gen.
election. Author of several volumes of poetry, and was a
close acquaintance of Robert Frost, Carl Van Doren, and
other contemporary literary figures. Fellow of Yale Corp.
Mbr., Modern Languages Assoc.; Phi Beta Kappa; Beta Theta
Phi. Hon. degrees from Bowdoin, Wesleyan Univ., Marietta
Coll. m. in 1922 to Jeanette Simmons. Five s. D. at
Spruce Island, Me., Sept. 29, 1977.

McCONAUGHY, JAMES LUKENS (1947-1948). b. Oct. 21,
1887 in New York City. s. of James and Eleanor (Underhill)
McC. Father was a clergyman, author and YMCA sect. Attd.
Mt. Hermon, Mass. prep. school, where his father was head of
the English Bible dept. Received an A.B. degree from Yale,
1909; an M.A. degree from Bowdoin Coll., 1911, and from
Dartmouth, 1915; and a Ph.D. degree from Columbia Univ.,
1915. Prof. of Educ. and English, Bowdoin Coll., 1909-1913
and also dir. of admissions there, 1915-1918. Pres. of
Knox Coll., Galesburg, Ill., 1918-1925. Pres. of Wesleyan
Univ., Middletown Conn., 1925-1943. School expanded consid-
erably in enrollment and programs while pres. Lieut. Gov.
of Conn., 1937-1941. Mbr. of Gov's. Highway Safety Commn.,
1933; also served as ch. of Conn. Labor Arb. Commn. Pres.
of United China Relief, 1942. Resigned as pres. of
Wesleyan Univ. in 1943 to work as civilian deputy to the
head of U.S. Office of Strategic Services, 1943-1946. Ch.
of Naval Advisory Commt. by apptmt. from Sect. of Navy
Forrestal, in 1946. Nom. and el. Gov. as Rep. in 1946.
Mbr. of numerous clubs and professional academic orgs. Hon.
degrees from eight institutions of higher learning, as well
as honors from several foreign govts. Phi Beta Kappa.
Mbr., bd. of dir. of Conn. Power Co. Congregationalist.
m. in 1913 to Elizabeth Townsend Rogers. Two s.; one d. D.
March 7, 1948, at Hartford, during second year of term as

Gov.

SHANNON, JAMES COUGHLIN (1948-1949). b. July 21, 1896
at Bridgeport, Conn. s. of Henry E. and Ellen (Coughlin) S.
Attd. Georgetown Univ. in Washington, D.C., graduating with
an A.B. degree in 1918. Received a law degree from Yale in
1921. Mbr. of U.S. Air Corps, 1918. Admitted to bar in
1921, and began practice in Bridgeport. Nom. and el. Lieut.
Gov. as Rep. in 1946. Succeeded to office of Gov. in March,
1948, following death of Gov. McConaughy, and completed
McConaughey's term. Nom. as Rep. cand. for full term in
1948, but was defeated in gen. election in a very close contest. Defeated as cand. for Rep. nom. for Gov. in 1950.
Judge of superior ct., 1953-1965, and mbr. of Conn. Supreme
Ct., 1965-1966. Served thereafter as a trial referee,
residing in Bridgeport. Mbr., Amer. Legion; K.C.; K.M.;
Kiwanis; professional legal orgs. Roman Catholic. m. in
1925 to Helen McMurray. Two s.; one d. D. March 6, 1980,
at Fairfield, Conn.

BOWLES, CHESTER (1949-1951). b. April 5, 1901 at
Springfield, Mass. s. of Charles Allen and Nellie (Harris)
B. Father was a descendant of old Mass. family and was the
owner of a paper mill supply firm. Attd. Choate School,
Wallingford, Conn.; Yale Univ., from which he received a B.S.
degree in 1924; and Sheffield Sci. School. Employed on ed.
staff of Springfield Daily Republican, a family-owned newspaper, 1924-1925. Mbr. of New York City advertising firm,
1925-1929. Founded own advertising and market research bus.
with Wm. S. Benton in 1929, which prospered. Retired from
active mgmt. of firm in 1941. Originally a Rep., he affiliated with Dem. party during the 1930s. Conn. State Adminr.
for Rationing, 1941-1942, and head of Conn. O.P.A., 1942-
1943. Deputy to U.S. O.P.A. Adminr., and later Adminr.,
1943-1946. Dir. of U.S. E.S.B., 1946. Resigned because of
failure of Cong. to enact what he considered to be an
effective price control law in 1946. Defeated for Dem. nom.
for Gov. in 1946; but won nom. in 1948, and was el. in
close contest with incumbent Gov. Shannon. Promoted legislation in fields of housing and welfare. Apptd. former
partner, Wm. S. Benton, to vacant U.S. Senate seat. Nom. in
1950 for second term, but lost in gen. election. Delegate
to Dem. natl. convs. in 1940, 1948, 1956 and 1960, being
ch. of the resolutions commt. of the conv. in 1960. U.S.
delegate to first UNESCO conf. in 1946. Mbr. of Amer. Natl.
Commns. for UNESCO, 1946-1947. Spec. consultant to UN
Sect.-Gen. in 1947. U.S. Ambassador to India and Nepal,
1951-1953. Mbr. of U.S. House, 1959-1961. U.S. Under-Sect.

of State, 1961-1963. U.S. Ambassador to India again, 1963-
1969. Mbr. of bds. of dir. of various foundations. Lecturer and author of books on natl. and intl. affairs. Hon. degrees from numerous colleges and universities and recipient
of awards and decorations from several foreign govts. m. in
1925 to Julia Mayo Fisk, from whom he was divorced in 1933.
One s.; one d. m. in 1934 to Dorothy Stebbins. One s.;
two d.

LODGE, JOHN DAVIS (1951-1955). b. Oct. 20, 1903 in
Washington, D.C. s. of George Cabot and Mathelda Elizabeth
Frelinghuysen (Davis) L. Grandson of Sen. Henry Cabot
Lodge (I) of Mass., and brother of Sen. Henry Cabot Lodge
(II) of Mass. Attd. Evans School, Mesa, Ariz. and Middlesex
School, Concord, Mass. Received an A.B. degree from Harvard
in 1925. In 1925-1926 studied at Ecole de Droit in Paris,
France. Grad. from Harvard Law School in 1929. Admitted to
bar in 1932. Employed as counsel by U.S. motion picture
indus., 1932-1940, and by New York theater concerns, 1940-
1942. From 1942 to 1946 served in U.S. Navy as liaison
officer in European theater during World War II.
Continued as capt. in USNR thereafter. Mbr. of U.S. House
from Conn., 1947-1951. In 1950, was nom. as Rep. cand. for
Gov. and defeated incumbent Gov. Bowles in the gen. election,
becoming the first Conn. Gov. to be el. for a four-year
term. Nom. for second term in 1954, but was defeated in the
gen. election in a close contest. As Gov., espoused legislation implementing the revised const. adopted during his
admin. Mbr. of exec. commt. of Natl. Govs.' Conf., 1951-
1952, and ch. of New England Govs.' Conf., 1953-1955. U.S.
repr. on spec. mission to Puerto Rico, Panama and Costa Rica
in 1953. U.S. Ambassador to Spain, 1955-1961. Mbr., Amer.
Legion; V.F.W.; R.O.A.; Natl. Order of Polish Legion;
AMVETS; various clubs. Natl. pres. of Junior Achievement,
1963-1964. Hon. degrees from Hobart Coll.; Wm Smith Coll.;
Fairfield Univ.; Trinity Coll.; Middlebury Coll.; Worcester
Poly. Inst. Decorations and awards from govts. of France,
Italy, Spain and Poland. m. in 1929 to Francesca
Braggiotti. Two d.

RIBICOFF, ABRAHAM J. (1955-1961). b. April 9, 1910 at
New Britain, Conn. s. of Samuel and Rose (Sable) R.
Parents had emigrated to this country from Poland in 1908.
Father was a factory worker. Attd. local pub. schools and
enrolled at New York Univ. in 1928. Moved to Chicago in
1929, where he had employment, and enrolled at the Univ. of
Chicago. Received law degree there in 1933, graduating with
honors. Admitted to bar and began practice at Hartford,

Conn. Hearing officer under Conn. Fair Employment Practices
Act, 1937. Mbr. of Conn. Assembly, 1938-1942. Judge of
mun. ct. in Hartford, 1941-1943; 1945-1947. Ch. of Conn.
Assoc. of Mun. Ct. Judges, 1941-1942. Mbr., arb. panel for
motion picture indus., 1941. Ch. of Conn. Commn. for study
of alcoholism and crime, 1943. Mbr., Hartford Charter
Revision Commn., 1945-1947, and of its Inter-racial
Relations Commn., 1947-1949. Mbr. of U.S. House, 1949-1953.
Supported policies of Truman admin. generally while in
House. Unsuccessful cand. for U.S. Senate as Dem. in 1952.
Nom. and el. Gov. as Dem. in 1954, defeating incumbent Gov.
Lodge by narrow margin. Reel. in 1958. During admin., pro-
moted legislative reforms, traffic safety measures, flood
relief and rehabilitation programs, welfare and institution-
al reforms, and reorg. of state and co. govt. Resigned
office of Gov. in Jan., 1961 to become U.S. Sect. of the
Dept. of H.E.W. As head of that Dept., successfully advocated passage of a revised Natl. Defense Educ. Act. Resigned that post in June, 1962 to become cand. for seat in U.S.
Senate, to which he was el. Continued to serve in the
Senate through 1970s. Hon. degrees from some twenty colleges and universities. Jewish. m. in 1931 to Ruth Siegel,
of Hartford. One s.; one d.

    DEMPSEY, JOHN NOEL (1961-1971). b. Jan. 3, 1915 at
Cahir, County Tipperary, Ireland. s. of Edward Patrick and
Ellen (Luby) D. Father, who was employed in the textile
mfg. bus., emigrated to Putnam, Conn. in 1925. Became an
Amer. citizen when father was naturalized in 1931. Attd.
Putnam schools and Providence Coll., 1934-1935. Worked in
Putnam woolen mills. Later became personnel mgr. for Amer.
Glassite Co. Went into bus. as partner in an auto agency.
Mbr., Putnam city council, 1936-1942. Mgr. of Putnam Water
Dept., 1940-1946. Alderman, 1946-1948. Served as local
exec. sect. for Congresswoman Chase Going Woodhouse, 1945-
1950. Mayor of Putnam, 1947-1961. Mbr. of Conn. Devel.
Commn., 1942-1947. Mbr., Conn. Assembly, 1949-1955, serving
as minority (Dem.) leader in 1953-1955. Exec. sect. to
Gov. Ribicoff, 1955-1958. El. Lieut. Gov. as Dem. in 1958.
Succeeded to office of Gov. in Jan., 1961 when Gov. Ribicoff
resigned. Completed Ribicoff's term and was nom. and el.
to regular terms in 1962 and 1966. During admin., major
concerns were flood relief and rehabilitation; tax revision;
initiation of job restoration program; establishment of
nuclear research center; highway constr. program; extension
of aid to educ. and to mentally ill; and emergency relief
for N.Y., New Haven and Hartford R.R. Ch. of New England
Govs.' Conf., 1963-1965. After tenure as Gov., served as

consultant for So. New England Tel. Co. Mbr., Forresters;
Elks; Rotary; Eagles; K.C. Roman Catholic. m. in 1940 to
Mary Madalene Frey, of Barrington, R.I. Two s.; one d.
Hon. degrees from Providence Coll. and St. Anselm's Coll.
Various pub. service awards.

MESKILL, THOMAS JOSEPH (1971-1975). b. Jan. 30, 1928
at New Britain, Conn. s. of Thomas J. M., who was active in
Rep. party affairs in New Britain. Attd. local pub. schools
and St. Thomas Sem., at Bloomfield, Conn. Entered Trinity
Coll., from which he was grad. in 1950. Also attd. New York
Univ. Law School in 1955. Received law degree from Univ. of
Conn. in 1956. Ed. of Univ. of Conn. Law Review while a
student there. Mbr. of U.S. Air Force, 1950-1953, seeing
service in Alaska and holding rank of lieut. at time of discharge. Began law practice in New Britain in 1956. Asst.
corp. counsel, 1960-1962. Mayor of New Britain, 1962-1964.
Mbr. of Conn. constl. conv. in 1965. New Britain corp.
counsel, 1965-1966. Mbr. U.S. House, 1967-1971, but was not
a cand. for reel. in 1970. Nom. and el. Gov. as Rep. in
1970. Mbr., K.C.; Elks; Amer. Legion; professional legal
orgs. Pres. of New Britain Council of Social Agencies and
of New Britain JCC, from which he received an award for
distinguished pub. service. Roman Catholic. m. to Mary T.
Grady. Three s.; two d. Returned ᴄo law practice after
tenure as Gov. Apptd. to U.S. Cir. Ct. of Appeals in 1975
by Pres. Ford.

GRASSO, ELLA (TAMBUSSI) (1975-----). b. May 10, 1919
at Windsor Locks, Conn. d. of James and Maria Oliva
Tambussi. Attd. Mt. Holyoke Coll., 1936-1942, graduating
magna cum laude with an A.B. degree in 1940 and with an M.A.
degree in 1942. Asst. dir. of research for U.S. War Manpower Commn. for Conn. during World War II. Mbr. of Conn.
House, 1953-1957, serving as Dem. floor leader in 1955.
Delegate to Conn. Dem. conv. in 1956 and was ch. of its resolutions commt. Sect. of State for Conn., 1959-1971. Delegate to Dem. natl. convs. in 1960, 1964 and 1968, and to
Dem. mid-term conf., 1974. Co-ch. of resolutions commt. at
1964 and 1968 natl. convs. Delegate to Conn. constl. conv.
in 1965. Mbr. of U.S. House, 1971-1975. Nom. and el. Gov.
as Dem. in 1974, becoming the first woman to hold that
office in Conn. Reel. in 1978. Very active in numerous
orgs. concerned with human welfare and health. Mbr., Bd. of
Trustees of Conn. Coll. Recipient of service awards and
citations from numerous orgs. Hon. degrees from Mt. Holyoke
Coll.; Sacred Heart Univ. Phi Beta Kappa. Roman Catholic.
m. in 1942 to Dr. Thomas A. Grasso. One s.; one d.

McKINLEY (McKINLY?), JOHN (1777). b. Feb. 24, 1721 in Northern Ireland. Became a physician there. Emigrated to Amer. in 1743, establishing a med. practice at Wilmington, Del. Active in local militia affairs, serving as a lieut., 1747-1748; as a major in 1756; later a col.; and in 1775 a brig. gen. Sheriff of New Castle Co., 1759-1776. Mbr. of Del. colonial Assembly, 1771. Participated in protest movement against British policies, serving as ch. of the Del. Commt. of Correspondence in 1773. El. to the Assembly under the first Del. const. and became Speaker of that body. Apptd. Pres. of the Council of Safety in Nov., 1776, and soon afterward was chosen as the first Pres. (Gov.) of Del., assuming office in Feb., 1777. In Sept. of that year on the day following the Battle of Brandywine was captured with his command by British forces. Taken as a prisoner to Philadelphia and later to N.Y. In the summer of 1778 was released on parole in exchange for colonial Gov. Franklin, of N.J., who had been made prisoner by Amer. forces. Returned to Wilmington in Sept., 1778. Did not participate in politics thereafter. Practiced med. and became founder of the Del. Med. Soc. m. to Jane Richardson circa 1761. Presbyterian. D. Aug. 31, 1796 at Wilmington. Bur. in First Presbyterian Church Cem. there.

McKEAN, THOMAS (1777). b. Mar. 19, 1734 in New London Twp., Chester Co., Pa. s. of Wm. and Letitia (Finney) McK. Parents were of Irish origin. Father was a farmer and tavern keeper. Family moved to New Castle, Del., where son attd. school and was also privately tutored. Studied law and was admitted to Del. bar in 1755. Became register of probate for Sussex Co. in 1756, and clerk of the Del. colonial Assembly in 1757. Studied law at Middle Temple, London, in 1758. Held various local admin. offices after return to Del. Mbr. of Del. colonial Assembly, 1762-1776, and of the Del. Assembly, 1776-1777, serving as Speaker in 1772 and in 1776-1777. Delegate to the Stamp Act Cong. in 1765. Delegate from Del. to the Contl. Cong., 1774-1776. Signed the Dec. of Indep. Mbr. of conv. that framed first const. for Del. in 1776. Served as Pres. (Gov.) of Del. for several weeks immediately after the capture of Pres. McKinly by the British in 1777, succeeding to the office by reason of being Speaker of the Assembly, the office of Speaker of the Council being temporarily vacant. Established residence in Pa. from 1777 onward. Became a mbr. and then Chief Justice of the Pa. Supreme Ct. soon after going to Pa. in 1777, and Gov. of Pa., 1799-1808. m. in 1763 to Mary Borden, of Bordentown, N.J. After her death in 1773, m. to Sarah Armitage, of New Castle, Del., in 1774. Eleven

children. Hon degrees from Princeton, Dartmouth, and the
Univ. of Pa. D. at Philadelphia, June 24, 1817. Bur. in
Laurel Hill Cem. there. (See also Pa., 1799-1808).

READ, GEORGE (1777-1778). b. Sept. 18, 1733 near North
East, Cecil Co., Md. s. of Col. John and Mary (Howell) R.
Received classical educ. Studied law in Philadelphia and
was admitted to the bar in Pa. in 1753. Established practice at New Castle, Del., in 1754. Atty. Gen. for Del.,
1763-1764. Mbr. of Del. Assembly, 1765-1776. Delegate
from Del. to the Contl. Cong., 1774-1777. Signed Dec. of
Indep. after some delay, inasmuch as he continued to maintain hope of reconciliation with Great Britain for some time
after that document was formulated. Presided at conv. that
framed the first const. for Del. in 1776. Chosen Speaker
of the Council (Senate) under that plan of govt. in 1777.
Succeeded to the office of Pres. (Gov.) of Del. after capture of Pres. McKinly by the British in 1777, and served
for some five months until a new Pres. was chosen. Mbr. of
Del. legislature, 1779-1780. Apptd. judge of U.S. Admiralty
Ct. by Cong. in 1782. Commnr. for resolution of boundary
dispute between N.Y. and Mass. in 1784-1785. Delegate to
Annapolis Conv. in 1786, and to the U.S. Constl. Conv. in
1787. Signer of U.S. Const. Mbr. of first U.S. Senate in
1789, serving until 1793, when he resigned to become Chief
Justice of Del. Supreme Ct., in which capacity he served
until death. Correspondence and biography were published
in 1870. m. in 1763 to Gertrude (Ross) Till, of New Castle.
One d.; four s. Mbr. of Church of England, later the
American Episcopal church. D. at New Castle, Sept. 21,
1798. Bur. in Emmanuel Church Cem. there.

RODNEY, CAESAR (1778-1781). b. Oct. 7, 1728 near
Dover, Del. Family was of English origin. Inherited considerable property in land. Received classical educ.
Studied law and also engaged in agri. pursuits. Sheriff of
Kent Co., 1755-1758, and capt. of militia, 1756. Served as
justice of the peace and as a judge in minor cts. in Kent
Co. In 1759 was in charge of preparation of paper money
for the colonial govt., and in 1769, supt. of loans. Mbr.
of Del. colonial Assembly, 1762-1769. Served as delegate
to Stamp Act Cong. in 1765; and in 1766 and again in 1769,
helped prepare remonstrances to King George III relative to
colonial tax policies of British govt. As Speaker of the
Assembly in 1769, sought to bring to an end importation of
slaves. Mbr. of Del. Commt. of Correspondence in 1773-1774,
and of the Council of Safety in 1776. Mbr. of Del. Supreme
Ct., 1769-1777. Delegate to the Contl. Cong. in 1774-1776

and 1777-1778. Signed Dec. of Indep., hastening to
Philadelphia from his home to become a signer to counteract
reluctance of his colleague, George Read, to sign the document. Became a col., later a brig. gen., and ultimately a
major gen. of Del. militia during course of Rev. War. Very
active in raising troops for Amer. cause. Apptd. Pres. of
Del. in March, 1778. Declined second term, but was apptd.
delegate to Cong. of U.S. in 1782 and 1783. Was unable to
assume active role therein because of illness. A brother,
Thomas, was also a mbr. of Cong., as was a nephew, Caesar
A. Rodney. D. at his home near Dover, June 29 (26?), 1784.
Bur. on his farm, "Byfield", there. Body later re-interred
in Episcopal Cem. in Dover.

DICKINSON, JOHN (1781-1782). b. Nov. 8, 1732 near
Trappe, Talbot Co., Md. s. of Samuel and Mary (Cadwalader)
D. In 1740 family moved to a place near Dover, Del., where
father became a co. judge. Educ. by pvt. tutor. At age 18
began study of law in office in Philadelphia. Continued
study at Middle Temple, in London, 1753-1756. Returned to
Philadelphia, was admitted to the bar and began practice
there. Quickly attained reputation as able lawyer and as a
scholar in field of British constl. law and history. Mbr.
of Del. colonial Assembly in 1760. Mbr. of Pa. colonial
Assembly, 1762-1764, where he became involved in controversy
with Franklin and Galloway over proposal to establish provincial form of govt. for Pa. Unsuccessfully espoused
cause of Penn family as proprietors, which caused him to
lose popularity for a time. Attd. Stamp Act Cong. in 1765
as Pa. delegate. Afterward published tracts advocating
united front by colonies and cessation of trade with Great
Britain as means of opposing British taxation policies.
Ch. of Pa. Commt. of Correspondence in 1773. Delegate from
Pa. to Contl. Cong., 1774-1776, where he played important
role in drafting a petition to King George III, protesting
British trade and other colonial policies. Delegate from
Del. to Contl. Cong. in 1776-1777, and again in 1779. Was
not an advocate of armed resistance to British at beginning
of Rev. War. Refused to sign Dec. of Indep., continuing to
advocate reconciliation for some time afterward; nevertheless assisted in recruitment of Pa. militia to carry on
resistance to British. In Nov., 1781, was apptd. Pres. of
Del. After serving in that office for approximately a year,
resigned when he was apptd. Pres. of the Exec. Council
(Gov.) of Pa. After tenure in that office from 1782 to
1785, was chosen as a delegate from Del. to U.S. Constl.
Conv. in 1787. Signed the completed document, the adoption
of which he advocated in a series of pamphlets authored

under the psuedonym of "Fabius". Later became an Anti-Fed.
in politics. Hon. degree from Coll. of N.J. (Princeton).
A wealthy man, he made contributions to that institution,
and to Dickinson Coll., in Pa., as well as to other schools.
Founder of an org. for improvement of conditions in prisons.
Although a slave owner, advocated abolition of slavery by
law. m. in 1770 to Mary Norris. D. at Wilmington, Del.,
Feb. 14, 1808. Bur. in Friends Cem. there. (See also Pa.,
1782-1785).

COOK, JOHN (1782-1783). b. in 1780 near Smyrna, Kent
Co., Del. Became a planter there. Also practiced law. El.
to Del. Council (Senate) during the course of Rev. War. As
the presiding officer thereof and ex officio Vice Pres.,
succeeded to the office of Pres. (Gov.) in 1782, following
the resignation of Pres. Dickinson. Served as Pres. for
approximately three months until Nicholas Van Dyke was el.
Pres. and assumed the office. A d., Sarah, became the wife
of Gov. John Clarke of Del. (q.v.). D. Oct. 27, 1789 at
Smyrna, Del.

VAN DYKE, NICHOLAS (1783-1786). b. Sept. 25, 1738 in
New Castle, Del. s. of Nicholas and Lytie (Dirks) Van D.
Descendant of a Dutch burger of Amsterdam, Holland, who
emigrated to Amer. in 1652. In early 1700s his father
moved to St. George's Hundred, in Del., where he had purchased large land holdings. Son studied law in
Philadelphia. Admitted to bar there in 1765. Later returned to New Castle, where he began law practice. Went along
with protest movement against British colonial policies,
but was a moderate in opposition. Served on Del. Commt. of
Correspondence in 1773. Served on commt. for relief of
people of Boston in 1774. Mbr., Del. Council of Safety in
1776 and was a delegate to conv. that drafted the first
const. for Del. Admiralty ct. judge in 1777. El. to Del.
Council (Senate) and became Speaker of that body in 1779.
Held commn. as major in militia during Rev. War, but saw
no combat service. Delegate to the Contl. Cong., 1777-1782.
Chosen Pres. of Del. by the legislature in 1783, serving
until Oct., 1786. During admin., measures to aid commerce
and finances were chief concerns. Advocated making Northwest Territories common property of all the States. Returned to service on the Govs.' Council in 1786 after tenure as
Pres., and became its Speaker, serving until his death. m.
first to Elizabeth Nixon. After her death, m. to Charlotte
Standley. A son, Nicholas, was a U.S. Repr. from Del.,
1807-1811, and a U.S. Sen., 1817-1826. D. at his home in
St. George's Hundred, Feb. 19, 1789. Bur. in Emmanuel

Church Cem. in New Castle.

COLLINS, THOMAS (1786-1789). b. in 1732 in England.
Emigrated to Amer., and eventually acquired an extensive
tract of land in Kent Co., near Smyrna, Del. Became sheriff
of Kent Co. in 1767. Served in Del. colonial Assembly and
as judge of the ct. of common pleas. Joined in protest
movement against British policies as Rev. War neared. Mbr.
of Del. Commt. of Safety in 1776, and was a delegate to
conv. that drafted first const. for Del. in that year. Became a mbr. of Govs.' Council (Senate) under the first
const. of Del. Active in mil. service during the Rev. War.
As brig. gen. of militia, helped org. and maintain a brigade at his own expense. Participated in battles in N.J.
in 1777 and 1778 under Gen. Washington's command. Chosen
Pres. of Del. by the Del. legislature in Oct., 1786. During admin., legislation was passed creating the Bank of
North America and prohibiting the exportation of slaves.
D. at Duck Creek, Kent Co., Mar. 29, 1789, several months
before end of term. Bur. in family burying ground on his
plantation there.

DAVIS, JEHU (1789). b. in Kent Co., Del. Became a
planter there. El. to the Del. Assembly, of which he became Speaker. When Pres. Collins died in March, 1789,
succeeded to the office of Pres., the office of Speaker of
the Council (Senate) having become vacant by reason of the
death of Nicholas Van Dyke shortly before the death of
Collins. Immediately called a spec. session of the two
branches of the legislature for the purpose of electing a
Pres. As soon as it effected a choice, the newly-chosen
Pres., Joshua Clayton, assumed the office, Davis having acted as Pres. for approximately two months. D. May 11, 1802,
at his home in Mispillion Hundred, Kent Co.

CLAYTON, JOSHUA (1789-1796). b. July 20, 1744, at
Bohemia Manor, the family estate near Mount Pleasant, Del.,
close to the Del.-Md. border. s. of John and Grace C.
Father had come to Amer. with Wm. Penn's family. Studied
med. in Philadelphia and established med. practice in
Middletown, Del. Helped to org. a Md. regiment at outbreak
of Rev. War. Later joined the Contl. Army and became a
mbr. of Gen. Washington's staff. Participated in the
Battle of Brandywine. Mbr. of Del. Assembly, 1785. State
Treas., 1786, and was a judge of Del. Ct. of Appeals. After the death of Pres. Collins in 1789 was chosen Pres. to
complete Collins' term, and was continued in office thereafter for a regular term. Following adoption of a revised

const. for Del. in 1792, was el. Gov. by popular vote. Be-
came the first chief exec. of Del. to be el. by direct pop-
ular vote and to bear the title of Gov.   In 1798 was chosen
to fill a vacant seat in U.S. Senate. Died of yellow fever
during the course of that year. m. in 1776 to Mrs. Rachel
McCleary, adopted d. of Richard Bassett, later a Gov. of
Del. (q.v.).   Three s., one of whom, Thomas, became a U.S.
Repr. and a U.S. Sen. from Del. and also served as Chief
Justice of the Del. Supreme Ct. Was the uncle of John M.
Clayton, a U.S. Repr. and Sen. from Del., as well as U.S.
Sect. of State, 1849-1850. D. Aug. 11, 1798. Bur. in
Bethel Church Cem., Cecil Co., Md.

BEDFORD, GUNNING (1796-1797). b. April 7, 1742 at
Philadelphia, Pa. s. of Wm. B., owner of a considerable
estate in lands in Pa. Cousin of Gunning Bedford, Jr., a
signer of U.S. Const. Established residence in New Castle,
Del. Commissioned as lieut., later as major and as lieut.
col., in the Contl. Army during the course of the Rev. War.
Wounded at the Battle of White Plains. Became quartermaster gen. in the Contl. Army, remaining in mil. service
until 1779. Studied law and was admitted to bar in 1779.
Prothonotary of New Castle Co. Mbr. of Del. Assembly, 1784-
1786. Apptd. delegate to the Cong. of U.S. in 1783, but
did not attend. Mbr. of Govs.' Council, 1783, 1790. Register of wills, New Castle Co., 1788, and justice of the
peace, 1789. Mbr. of Del. conv. that ratified the U.S.
Const. in 1787. Was a pres. elector in the first pres.
election in 1788. El. Gov. in 1795. During admin., foundation was laid for a pub. school system, and the Bank of
Del. was established. m. in 1796 to Mary Read, sister of
Pres. George Read of Del. (q.v.). D. Sept. 30, 1797 at
New Castle before completion of term as Gov.

ROGERS, DANIEL (1797-1799). b. Jan. 3, 1754 in
Accomack Co., Va. Became a farmer and businessman in Sussex
Co., Del. after achieving adulthood. El. to Del. Senate
and became Speaker of that body. Succeeded to office of
Gov. in Sept., 1797, upon the death of incumbent Gov.
Bedford and served the remainder of Bedford's term. D. Feb.
2, 1802.

BASSETT, RICHARD (1799-1801). b. April 2, 1745 on
father's plantation in Kent Co., Md. s. of Michael and
Judith (Thompson) B. Family was of Norman-English descent.
Father was a prosperous planter. Was orphaned at an early
age and was brought up by relatives. Studied law and was
admitted to bar. Established practice at Dover, Del. and

quickly achieved prominence as a lawyer. Mbr., Del.
Commt. of Safety in 1776. Became capt. of a light horse
company in 1777 and participated in a number of engagements
during Rev. War under Gen. Washington's command. Delegate
to Annapolis Conv. in 1786, and to U.S. Constl. Conv. of
1787, and was a signer of U.S. Const. Also served as mbr.
of Del. ratification conv. in 1787, and of the convs. that
drafted the first Del. const. and the revised const. of
1792. Mbr. of Del. Council (Senate), 1782-1792. Chosen as
one of the first two U.S. Senators from Del. in 1789, serving for four years. As a Sen., had a prominent role in
helping to establish permanent U.S. capital at Washington,
D.C. From 1793 to 1799 was chief judge of the ct. of common pleas. Pres. elector on Adams ticket in 1796. El. Gov.
as a Fed. in 1798. Resigned office after approximately two
years to accept apptmt. by Pres. Adams to newly created U.S.
cir. ct. judgeship post in 1801, but the position was abolished by Cong. the following year. m. to Ann Ennalls. After her death, m. to ----Bruff. Three d. Two of his grand-
sons, James A. Bayard and Richard H. Bayard, became U.S.
Senators from Del., as did also a great-grandson, Thomas F.
Bayard. Was the father-in-law of Joshua Clayton, first Gov.
of Del. (q.v.). Acquired considerable wealth, becoming the
owner of three homes. Converted to Methodism by Whitfield,
the evangelist. D. on his estate at Bohemian Manor, Cecil
Co., Md., on Aug. 15, 1815. Bur. in Wilmington and
Brandywine Cem. in Wilmington, Del.

SYKES, JAMES (1801-1802). b. March 27, 1761 near
Dover, Del. Father, James S., was prominent in Del. politics, having served in the Contl. Cong., as a mbr. of the
Govs.' Council, and as a mbr. of the Del. constl. conv. of
1776. Attd. schools in Wilmington and Dover. Studied med.
under Joshua Clayton, who later became the first Gov. of
Del. (q.v.), as well as under several other physicians.
Established med. practice in Cambridge, Md., where he remained for four years, and then returned to Dover, where he
continued to practice med. El. to Del. Council (Senate)
over a fifteen-year period, serving as Speaker during latter
part of tenure. Affiliated with Fed. party after party
alignments began to take form. As Speaker of Del. Senate,
succeeded to office of Gov. in March, 1801, when Gov.
Bassett resigned. Served as Gov. for approximately ten
months until a new Gov. was el. and installed in office. In
1814 moved to New York, where he remained for six years.
Returned to Dover in 1820. m. to Elizabeth Goldsborough,
of Cambridge, Md. D. at Dover, Oct. 18, 1822.

HALL, DAVID (1802-1805). b. Jan. 4, 1752 at Lewes,
Del. Received a classical educ. Studied law and was admitted to bar in 1773. Mbr. of Del. Commt. of Safety, 1776.
Enlisted as pvt. in a volunteer company soon after outbreak
of the Rev. War. Rose to rank of col. in 1777, and participated in engagements in N.Y., N.J. and Pa. Was seriously
wounded at the Battle of Germantown in 1777. Resumed practice of law after end of mil. service. Defeated as the
Jeff. Rep. cand. for Gov. in 1798, but was that party's
nominee again in 1801 and was el. in a very close election.
After tenure as Gov. became a mbr. of Del. Supreme Ct. m.
to Catherine Tingley, of N.Y. One s. D. at Lewes, Sept.
18, 1817.

MITCHELL, NATHANIEL (NATHANAEL?) (1805-1808). b. in
1753 near Laurel, Sussex Co., Del. s. of James and Margaret
(Dogworthy) M. Followed agri. pursuits on family estate.
Became an adj. in Col. Dogworthy's battalion at the beginning of the Rev. War. Served in other units later and participated in a number of engagements during the war. Served
as brig. major and inspector under Gen. Muhlenberg in later
stages of the conflict. Was captured by the British, but
was released on parole in 1781. Delegate from Del. in the
Cong. of the U.S., 1786-1788. Prothonotary of Sussex Co.,
1788-1805. Pres. elector on the Fed. ticket in 1800 pres.
election. Defeated as the Fed. cand. for Gov. in 1801,
losing by a very narrow margin to his Jeff. Rep. opponent;
but was nom. again and el. Gov. in 1804 by a plurality of
341 votes. After tenure as Gov., served as mbr. of the Del.
Assembly, 1808-1810, and as a mbr. of the Del. Senate, 1810-
1812. m. to Hannah Morris. One s. D. at Laurel, Feb. 21,
1814. Bur. in Broad Creek Episcopal Church Cem. there.

TRUITT, GEORGE (1808-1811). b. in 1756 near Felton,
Kent Co., Del. Lived most of life on family estate there,
on place known as "Burberry's Berry". El. to Del. Assembly
for four terms and to the Del. Council (Senate) for one
term. Mbr. of Del. conv. that ratified U.S. Const. in 1787.
Nom. as Fed. and el. Gov. in 1807 by margin of approximately
250 votes. m. to ----Hodgson. One d. D. on family estate,
Oct. 8, 1818.

HAZLETT (HASLET?), JOSEPH (1811-1814; 1823). b. in
1769 (?) in Kent Co., Del. Only s. of John H., who was a
physician of Irish ancestry. Father had served in the Del.
Assembly and had joined Amer. forces when Rev. War began.
Father was killed at the Battle of Princeton in 1777, and
shortly thereafter the son's mother died. s. became a ward

of Chief Justice (later Chancellor) Killen, of Del. Was
raised and received schooling in Cedar Creek Hundred, in
Sussex Co. Followed agri. pursuits there. Defeated as
Jeff. Rep. nominee for Gov. in 1804 and again in 1807,
losing to his Fed. opponent by narrow margins on both occasions. Was the Jeff. Rep. nominee again in 1810 and was el.
by margin of 67 votes. During admin., was successful in
efforts to repel British incursions into Del. during War of
1812. Became Jeff. Rep. nominee for Gov. again in 1822 and
was el. by a plurality of only 22 votes over his Fed. opponent. D. June 23, 1823, at Wilmington, after serving only
about six months of second term.

RODNEY, DANIEL (1814-1817). b. Sept. 10, 1764 at
Lewes, Del. s. of John and Ruth (Hunn) R. A younger brother, Caleb, was also a Gov. of Del. later by succession
(q.v.). Great-grandfather had emigrated to Amer. with Wm.
Penn in 1682. Father was a prominent person in the community. Received no formal educ., but studied on his own.
Entered upon merc. pursuits and became master of a coasting
vessel, later expanding his shipping operations. His ships
were captured by the British on two occasions. Served as
common pleas ct. judge, 1793-1805. Pres. elector on the
Pinckney-King (Fed.) ticket in the 1808 pres. election.
Defeated as the Fed. cand. for Gov. by very narrow margin
in 1810, but was nom. again and el. in 1813. Chosen in
1822 to fill a vacancy in U.S. House, serving during the
1822-1823 session. In 1826 was apptd. to seat in U.S. Senate to fill a vacancy, serving for some two months until el.
of a successor. m. in 1788 to Sarah Fisher. Five s.; two
d. D. at Lewes, Sept. 2, 1846. Bur. in St. Peter's Church
Cem. there.

CLARK(E), JOHN (1817-1820). b. Feb. 1, 1761 at Smyrna,
Del. s. of Capt. Wm. Clark, who had been a soldier in Rev.
War. Grandfather was of Irish origin. Father was a man of
some wealth, but had lost a considerable part of estate in
meeting a fellow soldier's debts. Son inherited and resided
on remaining part of estate, engaging in farming. Col. of
militia during War of 1812. Also was a justice of the
peace. Nom. and el. Gov. as a Fed. in 1816. In the 1819
election, his el. successor died before he could be inaugurated. C. accordingly held office for a short time after
next term began, then resigned to permit the newly-chosen
Speaker of the Senate, Jacob Stout, to assume the office.
Active in promotion of Clay's "American System", he organized the Society for Promotion of American Manufactures in
Del. m. in 1784 to Sarah Cook, a d. of Pres. John Cook, of

Del. (q.v.).   D. at Smyrna, Aug. 14, 1821.   Bur. in
Presbyterian Cem. near there.

STOUT, JACOB (1820-1821).   b. in 1764 near Leipsic,
Kent Co., Del.   Engaged in farming.   El. to Del. Senate and
was chosen Speaker of that body after 1819 election.   As
such, he succeeded to the office of Gov., when the Gov.-
elect, Henry Molleston, died before he could be inaugurated,
and the out-going Gov. resigned.   Acted as Gov. for approximately a year until a new Gov., John Collins, was chosen
in the regular manner and was inducted into office.   D. in
1855.

COLLINS, JOHN (1821-1822).   b. in 1775 near Laurel,
Sussex Co., Del.   s. of Capt. John Collins, an owner of an
extensive landed estate, with slaves.   Estate included a
mill, which became property of son on his father's death in
1804.   Set up a charcoal forge bus. on estate in 1812.   Nom.
and el. Gov. as a Jeff. Rep. in 1820 for a regular term
following death of the Gov.-elect chosen the preceding year.
D. April 15, 1822, at Wilmington, before end of term, having
served as Gov. slightly more than one year.

RODNEY, CALEB (1822-1823).   b. April 19, 1767 at Lewes,
Sussex Co., Del.   s. of John and Ruth (Hunn) R.   Was a
younger brother of Gov. Daniel Rodney of Del. (q.v.).   Became a mbr. of the Del. Senate, and as Speaker of that
body, succeeded to the office of Gov. in April, 1822,
following the death of Gov. John Collins.   Acted as Gov.
for approximately nine months until a regularly el. suces-
sor was chosen and installed in office.   Was a mbr. of the
Fed. party.   D. April 29, 1840.

HAZLETT (HASLET?), JOSEPH (1823).   See above, 1811-
1814.

THOMAS, CHARLES (1823-1824).   b. June 23, 1790 in New
Castle Co., Del.   Studied law and entered into practice
there.   El. to Del. Senate, and as Speaker of that body,
succeeded to the office of Gov. in June, 1823, following
the death of Gov. Joseph Hazlett.   Served in that capacity
for approximately six months until a duly el. successor
assumed the office.   Was a Jeff. Rep. in politics.   D. Feb.
8, 1848.

PAYNTER, SAMUEL (1824-1827).   b. in 1768 at Paynter's
Drawbridge, near Lewes, Del.   s. of Samuel and Elizabeth
(Stockley) P.   Father was a prominent member of community,

having served in the Del. Assembly, as a judge, and as a
col. in the Del. militia. Son continued in family merc.
and farming enterprises. Extended operations into field of
banking for some bus. associates. Active as a mbr. of Fed.
party. Held various local offices. Nom. and el. Gov. as
a Fed. in 1823. Resumed bus. interests after tenure as
Gov. El. to Del. Assembly in 1844. m. to Elizabeth
Rowland, Two s.; two d. D. at Lewes, Oct. 2, 1845.

POLK, CHARLES (1827-1830; 1836-1837). b. Nov. 15,
1788 near Bridgeville, Sussex Co., Del. s. of Charles and
Mary (Manlove) P. Family was of Irish origin. Received
classical educ. Studied law, but did not practice. Acquired large tract of land near Milford, in Kent Co., where
he resided thereafter. A natural orator, he entered politics at an early age. El. to Del. Assembly from Sussex Co.,
in 1814, and became Speaker of that body. In 1817 was el.
to Assembly again from Kent Co., and in 1824 to Del. Senate.
Mbr. of levy ct. of Kent Co., 1819. Nom. and el. Gov. as
a Fed. in 1826, defeating his Jeff. Rep. opponent by about
100 votes. Served as pres. of Del. constl. conv. in 1831.
El. to Del. Senate again in 1834, and as Speaker of that
body succeeded to office of Gov. in July, 1836, when Gov.
Bennett died. Completed last six months of Bennett's term.
Register of wills for Kent Co., 1843-1848. Apptd. U.S.
collector for port of Wilmington by Pres. Polk, serving
from 1849 to 1853. Apptd. commnr.-judge of Supreme Ct. of
Del. in 1857. Declined apptmt. as Chancellor and also his
party's nom. for U.S. Senate. m. to Mary Powell. Nine
children. D. Oct. 27, 1857, on estate near Milford.

HAZZARD, DAVID (1830-1833). b. May 18, 1781 at
Broadkiln Neck, near Milton, Sussex Co., Del. s. of John
and Mary Purnell (Houston) H. Family antecedents originally resided in Va., but became established in Del. after
1700. Father served as a major in the Contl. Army during
the Rev. War. Son entered U.S. mil. service as an ensign
in the War of 1812. Studied law. Engaged in family bus.
and in politics thereafter. Defeated as Jeff. Rep. cand.
for Gov. in 1823 and again in 1826. Was nom. for a third
time in 1829 and was el. by a margin of 167 votes over his
opponent, a Jackson Dem. During admin., a constl. conv.
was held which resulted in a change in the term of the Gov.
to four years. Apptd. to the Del. Supreme Ct. in 1844,
serving until 1847. Mbr. of Del. constl. conv. of 1852.
m. in 1804 to Elizabeth Collins. Several children. D.
July 8, 1864.

BENNETT, CALEB (1833-1836). b. Nov. 11, 1758 in
Chester Co., Pa. s. of Joseph B. One of his grandmothers
was a sister of Daniel Boone. Family, who were Quakers,
moved to Wilmington, Del. in 1761 where father engaged in
shipping bus. as the owner of a vessel engaged in East India
trade. At age 17 son entered Contl. Army in Rev. War as a
sgt. Rose to rank of lieut. Took part in Battles of
Brandywine and Germantown and was wounded. Was with Amer.
troops at Valley Forge and was present at surrender of Gen.
Cornwallis at Yorktown. Served as major of militia during
War of 1812. Continued in father's bus. activities. From
1807 to 1832 was treas. of New Castle Co. Nom. for Gov. as
Jackson Dem. in 1832 and was el. by a plurality of 57 over
his Natl. Rep. opponent. He thereby became the first Del.
Gov. to be el. for a four-year term. Legislature was controlled by opposing party during his admin., and it insisted on petitioning Cong. in 1834 for restoration of U.S.
govt. deposits with the United States Bank, a policy he
opposed. D. July 11, 1836, while still in office.

POLK, CHARLES (1836-1837). See above, 1827-1830.

COMEGYS, CORNELIUS PARSONS (1837-1841). b. Jan. 15,
1780 in Kent Co., Md. s. of Cornelius and Hannah (Parsons)
C. Father had served in a Md. regiment during Rev. War,
and was a descendant of a Dutch family that emigrated to
Md. from Holland in 1666. Son was first employed by a
Baltimore merchant. Moved to Del., and eventually settled
on a farm belonging to his second wife, at Cherbourg, Del.
Commissioned as a major in Del. militia in 1808, and in
1814 became a lieut. col. Mbr. of Del. Assembly, 1812-1816,
serving as Speaker. From 1820 to 1833 was State Treas.
Served as cashier of Farmers' Bank at Dover, 1819-1829.
Nom. and el. Gov. as a Whig in 1836. First wife, whom he
married in 1801, was Ann Blackiston. After her death, m.
in 1804 to Ruhamah Marvin, of Cherbourg. Seven s.; five d.
A son, Joseph, became a U.S. Sen. from Del. and also served
on the Del. Supreme Ct. as Chief Justice. D. at Dover,
Jan. 27, 1851.

COOPER, WILLIAM B. (1841-1845). b. Dec. 16, 1771 near
Laurel, Sussex Co., Del. Studied law and engaged in law
practice. Also engaged in farming. Became a mbr. of the
Del. Supreme Ct. in 1817. Nom. and el. Gov. as a Whig in
1840, and served one term. Acquired reputation as a brilliant conversationalist. During admin., legislation was
passed permitting suspension of specie payments by state-
chartered banks. Legislature addressed a memorial to Cong.

urging U.S. govt. to issue $200,000,000 in stock for form-
ing companies for an internal improvements program. One of
his sons, who favored the South during the Civil War, fled
to the South and enlisted in the Confed. Army. D. April
27, 1849.

STOCKTON, THOMAS (1845-1846). b. April 1, 1781 at New
Castle, Del. s. of John and Ann (Griffith) S. Father had
been in U.S. mil. service. Attd. Coll. of N.J. (Princeton).
Settled in New Castle where he was apptd. prothonotary of
New Castle Co. in 1810. Resigned in 1812 to become capt.
of a volunteer company in War of 1812. Saw action at Fort
George on Canadian border in 1813. Promoted to major for
gallantry in action. Remained in U.S. mil. service until
1825, when he returned to New Castle. Register in chancery
for New Castle Co., 1832-1835. Nom. and el. Gov. as a Whig
in 1844, defeating his Dem. opponent by margin of 45 votes.
During admin., the Del. legislature opposed admission of
Texas as a State. m. in 1804 to Fidelia Rogerson Johns.
Six children. D. while still in office, March 1, 1846.

MAULL, JOSEPH (1846). b. Sept. 6, 1781 at Pilottown,
near Lewes, Del. Studied med. and established med. practice
at Milton, Del. El. as a Whig to Del. Senate, and was
chosen Speaker of that body. Succeeded to office of Gov.
in Mar., 1846, following death of Gov. Stockton. Acted as
Gov. for some two months until his own death on April 30 of
the same year.

TEMPLE, WILLIAM (1846-1847). b. Feb 28, 1814 in Queen
Anne Co., Md. Received a liberal educ. Established home
at Smyrna, Del., where he engaged in merc. bus. El. as a
Whig to Del. Assembly in 1844, and became Speaker of that
body. Upon the death of Acting Gov. Maull, succeeded to
office of Gov. on May 1, 1846. Served until Jan., 1847,
when a newly-elected successor assumed office of Gov. Mbr.
of Del. Senate, 1848-1852. Was el. to a seat in U.S. House
in 1862 as a Dem., but died before taking seat. D. at
Smyrna, May 28, 1863. Bur. in Episcopal Cem. there.

THARP, WILLIAM (1847-1851). b. Nov. 27, 1803 near
Farmington, Del. s. of James and Eunice (Fleming) T.
Descendant of English family that had emigrated to Del. in
colonial times. Became a farmer and land owner. El. to
Del. Assembly for several terms. Defeated as cand. for Del.
Senate. Nom. as Dem. cand. for Gov. in 1844, but lost to
Whig opponent by 45 votes. Nom. again in 1846 and was el.
by a plurality of 236 votes. During admin., a long-standing

dispute between U.S. govt. and Del. over ownership of Pea
Patch Island in the Del. River was resolved in favor of U.S.
A grandson, Wm. T. Watson, was Acting Gov. of Del. for
nearly two years (q.v.).   D. at Milford, Del., Jan. 1, 1865.

ROSS, WILLIAM (HENRY) HARRISON (1851-1855).   b. June
2, 1814 at Laurel, Sussex Co., Del.   s. of Caleb R. and
Letitia (Lofland) R.   Attd. Laurel schools and an acad. in
Pa.   Read widely on his own.   In 1836 travelled with father
in Great Britain and Ireland.   In 1837 went into bus. in
Adams Co., Ill, but soon afterward returned to Laurel.   In
1845 established himself in bus. in Seaford, Del., where he
continued to reside thereafter.   Also engaged in fruit farming.   Nom. and el. Gov. as Dem. in 1850 by a plurality of
23 votes over his Whig opponent.   Delegate to Dem. natl.
convs. in 1844, 1848, 1856 and 1860.   Held no other pub.
office after tenure as Gov.   m. to Elizabeth E. Hall.   Ten
children, of whom seven were living when he died.   D. at
Philadelphia, June 29, 1887.

CAUSEY, PETER FOSTER (1855-1859).   b. Jan. 11, 1801
near Bridgeville, Sussex Co., Del.   s. of Peter Taylor and
Tamzey (Eaton) C.   Family, which was of Welsh origin, had
emigrated to Del. around 1780.   Attd. local schools.   Went
into merc. and mfg. bus. with father.   Later became pres.
of Junction and Breakwater R.R.   Mbr. of Del. Assembly in
1832 and of Del. Senate in 1833.   Delegate to Whig party
natl. convs. preceding 1840 and 1844 pres. elections.   Served as aide to Gov. Stockton in 1846.   Nom. as Whig cand.
for Gov. in 1846 and in 1850, but lost on each occasion by
very narrow margin.   Nom. for third time for Gov. in 1854
by the Amer. and Whig parties and was el.   During admin.,
much controversy was occasioned by his veto of an amdt.
proposed by the legislature abolishing all life tenure pub.
offices in Del.   The veto was upheld.   m. in 1825 to Maria
Williams.   Two s.   While he was serving as Gov. of Del. a
nephew, Trusten Polk, was chosen Gov. of Mo. (q.v.).   D.
Feb. 15, 1871, at Stockton, Del.

BURTON, WILLIAM (1859-1863).   b. Oct. 16, 1789 near
Milford, Kent Co., Del.   s. of John and Mary (Vaughn) B.
Brought up on father's farm and attd. local schools.   Studied med. at the Univ. of Pa., and established med. practice
first at Lewes, Del. and later at Milford, where he soon
had a wide practice.   El. sheriff of Kent Co. in 1830.   Nom.
as Dem. cand. for Gov. in 1854, but was defeated by his
Whig-Amer. party opponent, Peter Causey, a close neighbor
in his community.   Nom. again as Dem. cand. for Gov. in

1858 and was el. by a plurality of about 200 votes. As the
Civil War approached he sought, as the Gov. of a slave
State, to avert armed conflict. Supported use of armed
forces in Union cause after the war began, however. m.
first to Mrs. Eliza Wolcott. No children. After her death
m. in 1830 to Ann C. Hill. One d. D. at Milford, August 5,
1866.

CANNON, WILLIAM (1863-1865). b. March 15, 1809 near
Bridgeville, Sussex Co., Del. s. of Josiah and Nancy
(Bowlin) C. Received common school educ. Established merc.
bus. and became active in politics. Mbr. of Del. Assembly
in 1845-1849. Became State Treas. in 1851. Served as delegate to the "Peace Congress" in 1861 that sought to avert
Civil War conflict. Nom. and el. Gov. as Rep. (Union)
party cand. in 1862, defeating Dem. party opponent by 111
votes. As Gov., defended use of troops to preserve order
at elections and the arrest of citizens who were deemed
disloyal to U.S. Actions gave rise to movement in the
Assembly to vote impeachment charges against him, but the
attempt failed. Cooperated with Lincoln admin. in encouragement of Negroes to enlist in Union Army, by which action
they could gain freedom from slavery. State legislature
failed to cooperate with Lincoln's plan to bring about
gradual emancipation, however. Took steps in 1864 to prevent movement of Confed. troops through Del., and placed
the State under martial law in July, 1864, to achieve that
objective. m. to Margaret N. B. Laws. D. at Bridgeville,
March 1, 1865, while still in office.

SAULSBURY, GOVE (1865-1871). b. May 29, 1815 at
Mispillion Hundred, Kent Co., Del. s. of Wm. Mecham and
Margaret (Smith) S. Father had served as sheriff of Kent
Co., and two younger brothers, Eli and Willard, became U.S.
Senators from Del. Attd. local schools and Delaware Coll.
Taught school for a time, then studied med. at the Univ. of
Pa., from which he received an M.D. degree in 1842. Estab-
lished med. practice in Dover, Del. El. to Del. Senate as
Dem. in 1862, and was reel. in 1864, becoming Speaker of
that body. As such, succeeded to office of Gov. in March,
1865, following death of Gov. Cannon. Nom. and el. for
four-year term in 1866. Opposed ratification of 14th and
15th Amdts. to U.S. Const., maintaining they were submitted
by fraud and coercion, and denounced actions of U.S. Cong.
and President in seeking to control So. state elections.
Served as delegate to Dem. natl. party convs. in 1856, 1876,
and 1880. Active in affairs of Methodist church, and
helped found Wilmington Acad. for that church. Served as

pres. of its governing bd. and also was on Bd. of Trustees
of Delaware Coll. m. in 1848 to Rosina Jane Smith. Three
s.; two d. D. at Dover, July 31, 1881.

PONDER, JAMES (1871-1875). b. Oct. 31, 1819 at Milton,
Sussex Co., Del. s. of John and Hettie (Milby) P. Forebears, of English descent, had resided in Va. originally.
Father, who was prominent in local govt. and politics,
owned extensive tracts of land and also engaged in ship-
building and shipping enterprises. Attd. pvt. schools in
Lewes and Georgetown, Del. At age 20 went into bus. with
father. Became involved in various enterprises in fields
of shipping, real estate and railroads. Pres. of Farmers'
Bank of Georgetown. El. to Del. Assembly, 1856, and to Del.
Senate in 1864, becoming Speaker of latter body in 1867.
Nom. and el. Gov. as a Dem. in 1870. Held no pub. offices
after tenure as Gov. m. in 1851 to Sally Waples. Two s.;
one d. D. at Milton, Nov. 5, 1897.

COCHRAN, JOHN P. (1875-1879). b. Feb. 7, 1809 in
Appoquinink Hundred, New Castle Co., Del. Family was of
Scotch-Irish origin. Father had resided originally in Md.
Brought up on father's farm, on which he continued to live
most of life, adding lands to estate. Became one of the
State's most extensive land owners. Active in politics for
most of life, but refused major pub. office until el. Gov.
From 1838 to 1846 was mbr. of New Castle Co. levy ct. Nom.
and el. Gov. as Dem. in 1874. During admin., a State Bd.
of Educ. was established and the office of State Supt. of
Schools created. Also a very liberal gen. incorporation
law was enacted. D. at home in New Castle, near Middletown,
Dec. 27, 1898.

HALL, JOHN WOOD (1879-1883). b. Jan. 1, 1817 at
Frederica, Kent Co., Del. s. of John and Henrietta (Bowman)
H. Father, who was a descendant of an early Del. colonial
family, was a merchant and had served as a soldier in War
of 1812. Began work as a clerk at age 16. Bought cabinet
shop and extended bus. interests into lumber, grain and
shipping. Eventually became a ship-builder and a landed
proprietor. Also was on bd. of dir. of Farmers' Bank of
Dover. In earlier years was a mbr. of Whig party, but later
changed affiliation to Dem. party. Mbr. of Del. Senate in
1866. Delegate to Dem. natl. conv. in 1876. Nom. for Gov.
by acclamation at Dem. state conv. in 1878 and was el. After tenure as Gov. retired to give attention to bus. affairs
but in 1890 was again el. to Del. Senate. m. in 1842 to
Caroline Warren. Four children. D. at Frederica, Jan. 23,

1892.

STOCKLEY, CHARLES CLARK (1883-1887). b. Nov. 6, 1819
at Georgetown, Sussex Co., Del. s. of Jehu and Hannah
Rodney (Kollock) S. Father's ancestors had emigrated from
England to Va. in 1780, later moving to Del. Mother was
descendant of one of the original proprietors of Del., and
her family had been active in mil. and political affairs of
colonial Del. Attd. Georgetown Acad. Entered bus. at
Millsboro, Del. and extended interests into fields of shipping, railroads and banking. Treas. of Sussex Co. in 1852,
and sheriff in 1856. El. to Del. Senate in 1872, becoming
Speaker of that body in 1875. Nom. and el. Gov. as Dem. in
1882. After tenure as Gov. returned to bus. interests.
Apptd. register of wills and probate judge of Sussex Co. in
1891. m. in 1857 to Ellen Wright Anderson. One d. D. at
Millsboro, April 20, 1901.

BIGGS, BENJAMIN THOMAS (1887-1891). b. Oct. 1, 1821
near Summit Bridge, New Castle Co., Del. s. of John B., a
farmer. Attd. Pennington Sem., in N.J., and Wesleyan Univ.,
Middletown, Conn. Taught school while obtaining educ.
Entered farming and horticultural bus. in 1847, in which he
was quite successful. Later was pres. and dir. of Kent and
Queen Anne R.R., which he built. Commissioned as major
during War with Mexico, but saw no active service. Noted
for speaking ability. Mbr. of Del. constl. conv. of 1852.
Originally was a Whig, but changed party affiliation to Dem.
in 1854. Unsuccessful as Dem. cand. for U.S. House in 1860.
Nom. and el. to that office in 1868 and was reel. in 1870.
Did not seek third term in 1872. Came to be known as the
"Delaware Plowboy" while in Cong. because of his espousal
of programs designed to assist agri. interests. Delegate
to Dem. natl. party conv. in 1872. Moved to Middletown,
Del. in 1877. Nom. and el. Gov. as a Dem. in 1886. During
admin., legislation was enacted permitting vote on calling
a state constl. conv. m. in 1853 to Mary Scott Beekman.
Two s.; one d. D. at Middletown, Dec. 25, 1893. Bur. in
Bethel Cem., near Chesapeake City, Md.

REYNOLDS, ROBERT JOHN (1891-1895). b. March 17, 1838
at Smyrna, Kent Co., Del. s. of Robert W. and Sally R.
Descendant of old Del. family. Father was prominent in
Del. politics, having served as sheriff and register of
wills of Kent Co., and also was an unsuccessful cand. for
the Dem. nom. for Gov. in 1862, which he lost by a narrow
margin in the Dem. state conv. Family moved to South
Murderkill Hundred, where son attd. local schools. He also

attd. school in Herkimer Co., N.Y. In 1861 settled on a
farm near Petersburg, Del., where he engaged successfully
in farming and horticulture. Mbr. of Del. Assembly in
1869. State Treas., 1879-1883. Active in Dem. party affairs, serving as ch. of state party commt. in 1882 and
1884 elections. Nom. and el. Gov. as Dem. in 1890. During
admin., opposed the Lodge "Force Bill" being considered in
Cong. and favored adoption of Australian ballot system.
Boundary question between Del. and Pa. was resolved. Delegate to Dem. natl. conv. in 1892. Represented Del. at
Columbian Expo. in 1893. m. in 1862 to Lovenia Riggs. One
s. D. June 10, 1909.

MARVIL, JOSHUA HOPKINS (1895). b. Sept. 2, 1825 at
Laurel, Sussex Co., Del. Father died when son was 9 years
old. Worked on family farm until he was of age, while
attending local schools. Spent one year at sea. Began
work in ship-building yard, soon becoming a foreman. Established his own shop for making farm implements in 1853,
which prospered. In 1870 invented and patented a machine
for mfg. of berry and peach baskets. Bus. grew into large
indus. Held no pub. office until nom. and el. Gov. as Rep.
in 1894. m. in 1849 to Sarah Ann Sirman. Three s. D. at
Dover, April 8, 1895, having served only about three months
of term as Gov.

WATSON, WILLIAM T. (1895-1897). b. June 22, 1849 at
Milford, Del. Through his mother he was a grandson of Gov.
Wm. Tharp, of Del. (q.v.). Engaged in bus. activities at
Milford. El. to Del. Senate as a Dem., and became Speaker
of that body. As such, succeeded to office of Gov. upon
death of Gov. Marvil in April, 1895. Served nearly two
years as Gov. until a successor was el. at the next gen.
election and installed in office. D. April 14, 1917.

TUNNELL, EBE WALTER (1897-1901). b. Dec. 31, 1844 at
Blackwater, Sussex Co., Del. s. of Nathaniel and Maria
(Walter) T. Attd. local schools and pvt. schools in
Milford and Lewes, Del. Entered merc. bus. at Blackwater
in 1862, continuing therein until 1898. Mbr. of Del.
Assembly, 1871. Moved to Lewes in 1872, where he established a drug and hardware bus. in which he continued to be active until 1903. Clerk of ct. of Sussex Co., 1884-1889.
Nom. for Gov. as Dem. in 1894 but was defeated in gen. election. Nom. again in 1896 and was el. by plurality of
approximately 4,500 against divided Rep. opposition. After
tenure as Gov., engaged in railroad and banking enterprises.
Pres. of Bd. of Commnrs. of Seaside Resort at Rehoboth

Beach. Presbyterian. Unmarried. D. at Lewes, Dec. 13, 1917.

HUNN, JOHN (1901-1905). b. June 23, 1847 near Odessa, New Castle Co., Del. s. of John and Annie E. (Jenkins) H. Descendant of an old Del. family. Father was a farmer who was an opponent of slavery and participated actively in assisting fugitive slaves to flee to the North. Attd. Friends School at Camden, and Bordentown Inst., in N.J. Entered Union army in 1861. Returned to Del. after Civil War. In 1876 set up a grain, lumber and fruit marketing bus. at Wyoming, Del. Became dir. of First Natl. Bank of Dover. Refused political office until 1900, when he was nom. by both factions of the Rep. party for Gov. and was el. by a substantial margin. m. in 1874 to Sarah Cowgill Emerson, of Camden. One d. D. at Wyoming, Sept. 1, 1926.

LEA, PRESTON (1905-1909). b. Nov. 12, 1841 at Wilmington, Del. s. of Wm. and Jane Scott (Lovett) L. Father, who was a merchant and miller, was descendant of a Quaker ancestor who had emigrated to Del. with Wm. Penn. Son was educ. at Lawrenceville, N.J. At age 18 joined father in bus. and eventually became head of firm. Expanded bus. interests into fields of banking, ins., and railroads. Pres. of Union Natl. Bank in 1888; vice pres. of Farmers Mutual Ins. Co.; pres. of Equitable Guarantee Bank; and pres. of the Wilmington City Ry. Co. Nom. and el. Gov. as a Rep. in 1904. m. in 1870 to Adelaide Moore, who died in 1888. m. in 1897 to Eliza Naudain Corbit. Four d. Mbr. of Union League and Art clubs of Philadelphia and various other clubs. D. at Wilmington, Dec. 4, 1916.

PENNEWILL, SIMEON SELBY (1909-1913). b. July 23, 1867 at Greenwood, Del. s. of Simeon and Anna (Curry) P. Attd. local pub. schools and Wilmington Acad. Went into bus. at Dover, Del., becoming pres. of Delaware Apple Co. Mbr. of Del. Senate, 1899-1907. Nom. and el. Gov. as a Rep. in 1908. After tenure as Gov., served as pres. of Del. Bd. of Educ., and Bd. of Immigration. Mbr., State Bd. of Agri. m. in 1920 to Elizabeth Haisley. m. in 1929 to Lydia Wright Elder. Presbyterian. D. at Dover, Sept. 9, 1935.

MILLER, CHARLES R. (1913-1917). b. Sept. 30, 1857 near West Chester, Pa. s. of Robt. H. and Margaretta (Black) M. Attd. Westtown Friends School; Swarthmore Coll., from which he was grad. in 1881; and the Univ. of Pa., from which he received a law degree in 1884. Began legal practice in Wilmington, Del. and soon became involved in a

number of bus. enterprises in fields of mfg., railways, and
mining, gas and electric utilities, and waterpower. Retired from active bus. mgmt. in 1911, but continued to
serve on bds. of dir. of a number of corps. El. to Del.
Senate in 1910. Nom. and el. Gov. as a Rep. in 1912, the
only Rep. to be elected in state-wide election that year.
During admin., legislation was enacted furthering establishment of a Women's Coll. at Del. Coll.; for improvement of
road system; revising election laws; providing more aid for
schools; and for encouragement of sci. farming. Mbr. of
exec. commt. of Rep. Natl. Commt. and of the exec. commt.
of the Amer. Bankers Assoc. Trustee of Del. Coll. Pres.
of Del. Hosp.; State Bd. of Charities; and of Del. Bldg.
and Loan Assoc. Hon. degree from Del. Coll. Mbr., Union
League and various clubs. Episcopalian. m. in 1884 to
Abigail M. Woodnutt, of Richmond, Ind. Two s.; one d.
D. at Berlin, N.J., Sept. 18, 1927.

TOWNSEND, JOHN GILLIS, Jr. (1917-1921). b. May 31,
1871 at Bishop Station, near Selbyville, Md. Father was a
farmer and mechanic of modest means. Attd. local schools.
Worked as telegrapher for Pa. R.R. for a time, after which
he went into timber and sawmill bus. for himself. Moved to
Selbyville in 1895. Acquired extensive land-holdings in
Md. and Del., and extended interests into horticultural and
banking activities. Founded Baltimore Trust Co. of
Selbyville. Having acquired some 20,000 acres of land, engaged in developing, producing and marketing fruit products
on a large scale, becoming known as the "Strawberry King"
in 1920s. Became a multi-millionaire. Mbr. of Del. Assembly, 1901-1903. Col. on staffs of Govs. Lea, Pennewill,
and Miller. Nom. and el. Gov. as a Rep. in 1916, being the
only Rep. to be elected in state-wide vote in that year.
As Gov., sponsored workmen's compensation legislation; laws
for protection of women workers and for a vocational educ.
system; and for state income and inheritance taxes. Supported ratification of 19th Amdt. to U.S. Const. Delegate
to all Rep. natl. convs. from 1904 to 1960, except for 1920.
Ch. of Del. Rep. state commt. in 1936. El. to U.S. Senate
in 1928. Reel. in 1934, but was defeated for third term in
1940. Ch. of Rep. Senate campaign commt., 1936. Influential mbr. of Senate Banking and Currency Commt. while in
Senate. Mbr. of Rushmore Natl. Monument Commn., 1939. Alternate delegate from U.S. to first UN Assembly in London
in 1946. Mbr., Bd. of Trustees of Del. Coll.; Goucher
Coll., and American Univ. m. in 1890 to Jennie L. Collins.
Wife preceded him in death in 1914. Three s. D. at
Philadelphia, April 10, 1964.

DENNEU, WILLIAM DuHAMEL (1921-1925). b. March 31, 1873
at Dover, Del. s. of Wm. and Anna (DuHamel) D. Attd.
Wesleyan Collegiate Inst. at Dover. Employed as clerk in
Kent Co. Mutual Fire Ins. Co., of which his father was an
officer. From 1905 to 1925 was associated with Hartford
Fire Ins. Co. in various capacities and became a partner in
Dover Ins. Agency. Dir. of Farmers' Bank of Dover, 1916.
Mbr. of Del. Assembly, 1905-1907, serving as Speaker. From
1907 to 1913 was sect. to U.S. Sen. Richardson of Del.
Served in U.S. Army during World War I as first lieut. and
continued in USAR thereafter until 1939. Nom. and el. Gov.
as Rep. in 1920. During admin., a State Highway Dept. was
created by consolidation; school laws were revised; improved
budget system was adopted; a Child Welfare Commn. estab-
lished; and a State Health and Welfare Commn. set up in
1924. Mbr. of Del. Rep. state commt. in 1920 and ch., 1926-
1928. Delegate to Rep. natl. convs. in 1908, 1924 and 1928.
Acting Sect. of State for Del., 1931. Custodian of State
House, 1933. State Motor Vehicle Commnr., 1940. State
Librarian, 1941-1948. Active in Boy Scouts movement and in
Christ Episcopal church. Mbr., Amer. Legion; S.A.R.;
I.O.O.F.; various clubs. m. in 1917 to Alice Godwin, of
Reisterstown, Md. Two d. D. at Elsmere, Del., Nov. 22,
1953.

ROBINSON, ROBERT PYLE (1925-1929). b. March 28, 1869
near Wilmington, Del. s. of Robt. Lewis and Frances Ellen
(Delaplaine) R. Attd. local schools and Rigby Acad., at
Wilmington. Began work as messenger with Cent. Natl. Bank,
of Wilmington. Rose through various positions, becoming
pres. in 1916 and continued therein until death. Active in
state and local politics, but held no pub. office until
nom. and el. Gov. as Rep. in 1924. During admin., recommended constr. of state office bldg. and enlargement of
state police force, on which the legislature cooperated.
A life-time hobby was maintenance and operation of family
farm, "Robinhurst", which had been acquired from Penn family by his great-great-grandfather. Master of Del. Grange,
1922-1936. Treas. of Natl. Grange, 1923. Active in Hanover
Presbyterian church, of Wilmington, of which he was a
trustee and treas. m. in 1904 to Margaret Fouraker, of
Clayton, Del. One s.; one d. D. at the family estate,
"Robinhurst", March 4, 1939.

BUCK, C(LAYTON) DOUGLAS (1929-1937). b. March 21, 1890
on family estate, "Buena Vista", at New Castle Co., Del.
s. of Francis Nickson and Margaret (Douglass) B. Father was

a banker. Family line included a number of distinguished
pub. officials of Del., including Sen. John M. Clayton, of
whom he was a great-grandnephew. Attd. Friends School in
Wilmington, and Wilmington Mil. Acad. Studied engr. at the
Univ. of Pa., 1911-1913. Withdrew to begin work with Del.
State Highway Dept. Became asst. engr. of that Dept. in
1920, and chief engr., 1922-1929. Planned constr. of the
Du Pont Highway from Wilmington to Selbyville. Served for
ten months in U.S. Army during World War I. Pres. of Assoc.
of State Highway Officials of No. Atl. States in 1928. Nom.
and el. Gov. as Rep. in 1928. Reel. in 1932, becoming the
first Del. Gov. to be el. for second four-year term. Mbr.,
Rep. natl. commt., 1929-1937. During admin., a number of
measures were advanced, including old age pension system
and authorization of sterilization of mental defectives and
habitual criminals. When legislature disagreed on program
of state aid for unemployed and indigent after the depression of the 1930s became acute, set up a temp. relief system by exec. order. Pres. of Equitable Trust Co. (now Bank
of Del.), 1931-1941. El. to U.S. Senate in 1942, but was
defeated for reel. in 1948. Returned to banking bus. Mbr.,
State Tax Commn., 1953-1957. Hon. degree from the Univ. of
Del. Episcopalian. m. in 1921 to Alice Du Pont Wilson.
One s.; one d. D. at Buena Vista estate, Jan. 27, 1965.
Bur. in Immanuel Episcopal Church Cem. at New Castle.

McMULLEN, RICHARD CANN (1937-1941). b. Jan. 2, 1868
at Glasgow, Del. s. of James and Sarah Louise (Bouldon)
McM. Grandfather had emigrated to Amer. from Ireland.
Father was a farmer. Attd. local schools. After his
father died began work as farm hand to earn money to obtain
further educ. Completed bus. course in 1888 at Goldey
Coll., in Wilmington. Began work as timekeeper for leather
mfg. firm in Wilmington. Rose to foreman, and became partner in a leather mfg. firm of his own in 1917. Bus. expanded, with branches in several cities in N.J. and Pa. Merged
with Allied Kid Co. in 1929, of which he became vice pres.
and mbr. of bd. of dir. Also became a dir. of Indus. Trust
Co. of Wilmington. Mbr., Wilmington city council for two
years and served for two years as Wilmington Pub. Utilities
Commnr. Nom. and el. Gov. in 1936, the first Dem. to be
elected to the office in 40 years. Advocate of a balanced
budget. After tenure as Gov., acquired several farms and
maintained a herd of registered cattle. Mbr., Del. Society;
S.A.R.; I.O.O.F.; Red Men; A.O.U.W.; Masons; Kiwanis;
various clubs. Recipient of Emblem of North Star from
Sweden. Methodist. m. to Florence Hutchinson, of Delaware
City. Two d.; one s. D. at Wilmington, Feb. 18, 1944.

BACON, WALTER W.   (1941-1949).   b. Jan. 20, 1879 at
New Castle, Del. s. of John G. and Margaret L. (Foster) B.
Worked as a newsboy while attending local schools. After
grad. from h.s. worked as a timekeeper in the Delaware Iron
Works at New Castle, 1897-1899. Later was employed in
various capacities by the U.S. Steel and the E.L. Du Pont
de Nemours Cos. at Chester, Pa. and at Philadelphia, 1903-
1918. Associated in an exec. capacity with Gen. Motors
Corp. at Flint, Mich., 1918-1930. Retired from position as
sect. of the Buick Div. of Gen. Motors in 1931. Returned
to Wilmington, Del. El. mayor of Wilmington in 1935 and
was reel. in 1937 and 1939. Nom. and el. Gov. as a Rep. in
1940 and was continued in office for succeeding term in
1944. As Gov., gave effective support to U.S. war effort
during World War II. m. in 1906 to Mabel H. McDaniel.
Mbr., Masons; various social clubs. D. March 18, 1962, in
Wilmington.

CARVEL, ELBERT NOSTRAND (1949-1953; 1961-1965). b.
Feb. 9, 1910 at Shelter Island Heights, N.Y. s. of Arnold
Wrightson and Elizabeth (Nostrand) C. Father was a businessman. Family moved to Baltimore, Md. when son was a
youth. Attd. pub. schools there. Received degree in engr.
from Baltimore Poly. Inst., and in 1931 a law degree from
the Univ. of Baltimore. Also studied accountancy at John
Hopkins Univ. Sales engr. for a Baltimore utility company,
1931-1936. In 1936 moved to Laurel, Del., where he became
associated with Valliant Fertilizer Co., of which he became
pres. in 1945. Engaged in banking, grain, radio broadcasting and fertilizer mfg. fields, as well as farming. As
mbr. of Fed. grand jury investigating election practices in
Del. in 1941-1942, became interested in politics. Nom. and
el. Lieut. Gov. in 1944. Pres., Del. Bd. of Pardons, 1945-
1949. Nom. and el. Gov. as Dem. in 1948. Mbr. of exec.
commt. of Natl. Govs.' Conf., 1950-1951. Defeated for reel.
in 1952. Unsuccessful as Dem. cand. for U.S. Senate in
1958. Nom. and el. Gov. again in 1960. As Gov., supported
veterans bonus plan; additional school aid; withholding
system in state income tax admin.; improved workmen's compensation law; creation of state devel. agency; highway
improvements. Mbr. of exec. commt. of Natl. Govs.' Conf.,
1962-1963, and vice ch., So. Govs.' Conf., 1964. Unsuccessful as Dem. cand. for U.S. Senate in 1964. Ch., Del.
Dem. state commt., 1946-1947 and 1954-1957. Delegate to
Dem. natl. convs. in 1948 through 1960. Trustee of Univ.
of Del.; mbr., Natl. Fertilizer Assoc. Mbr., Masons; Elks;
Eagles; Lions; Del. Historical Soc. Received honor award

from govt. of the Netherlands.   Active in affairs of
Episcopal church.   m. in 1932 to Ann Hall Valliant, of
Centreville, Md.   Three d.; one s.

BOGGS, J(AMES) CALEB (1953-1960).   b. May 15, 1909 at
Cheswold, Del.   s. of Edgar J. and Lettie (Vaughn) B.   Attd.
rural pub. schools; the Univ. of Va.; and the Univ. of Del.,
from which he was grad. in 1931.   Received law degree from
Georgetown Univ. in 1937.   Admitted to bar and began practice in Dover.   Served in U.S. Army during World War II,
from 1941 to 1946, holding rank of col. when discharged.
Continued in USAR thereafter with rank of brig. gen.   War
decorations included Legion of Merit; Bronze Star with Oak
Leaf Cluster; Croix de guerre with palm.   Became deputy
judge of family ct. in New Castle Co., 1946.   El. to U.S.
House in 1946 and continued in office for succeeding two
terms.   Had a generally conservative voting record in opposition to measures of the Truman admin.   Nom. and el. Gov.
as Rep. in 1952, defeating incumbent Gov. Carvel.   As Gov.,
signed into law an alien registration act.   Reel. for second term in 1956.   Ch. of Natl. Govs.' Conf., 1959.   Pres.,
Council of State Govts., 1960.   Resigned as Gov. in Dec.,
1960, shortly before end of second term after having been
el. to the U.S. Senate.   Served in Senate for two terms,
being defeated for reel. in 1972.   Trustee of Legal Aid
Soc. of Del.   Mbr., Amer. Legion; V.F.W.; Kiwanis.
Methodist.   m. in 1931 to Elizabeth Muir.   One s.; one d.

BUCKSON, DAVID PENROSE (1960-1961).   b. July 25, 1920
at Townsend, Del.   s. of Leon J. and Margaret (Hutchison)
B.   Attd. local schools; the Univ. of Del., from which he
was grad. in 1941; and the Dickinson School of Law, from
which he received a degree in 1948.   Entered U.S. Army as
second lieut. in 1941.   Served in Southwest Pac. area, 1942-
1945.   Held rank of major when discharged.   Established law
practice at Smyrna, Del. in 1948.   Ch., Kent Co. Rep. exec.
commt., 1956.   Nom. and el. Lieut. Gov. as Rep. in 1956.
Succeeded to office of Gov. in Dec., 1960, following resignation of Gov. Boggs.   Completed term for which Boggs had
been elected, which had only a short time to run.   Atty.
Gen. of Del., 1963-1971.   Defeated as Rep. cand. for Gov.
in 1964.   Mbr., Am. Judicature Soc.; Rotary; Amer. Legion;
V.F.W.; Del. Vets. Assoc.; Union Lodge 5, Del. Consistory,
Nur Temple; Sigma Nu; Del. Assoc. of Chiefs of Police; Natl.
Sojourners, Inc.   Methodist.   m. in 1963 to Patricia
Maloney.   Four s.; one d.

CARVEL, ELBERT NOSTRAND (1961-1965).   See above, 1949-

1953.

TERRY, CHARLES LAYMEN, Jr. (1965-1969). b. Sept. 17,
1900 at Camden, Del. s. of Charles L. and Elizabeth (Maxon)
T. Attd. Swarthmore Coll., where he was an active participant in intercollegiate sports. Attd. Washington and Lee
Univ., from which he received a law degree in 1923. Admitted to bar in 1924 and established practice at Dover, Del.
Mbr., Del. legislature, 1933-1934. Del. Sect. of State,
1937-1938. Became a mbr. of Del. Supreme Ct. in 1938. Nom.
and el. Gov. as a Dem. in 1964. Defeated for reel. in 1968.
Mbr., Phi Sigma Kappa; professional legal orgs.; various
social clubs. Episcopalian. m. in 1924 to Jessica Irby.
One s. D. Jan. 6, 1970.

PETERSON, RUSSELL WILBUR (1969-1973). b. Oct. 3, 1916
at Portage, Wisc. s. of John Anton and Emma Marie (Anthony)
P. Attd. the Univ. of Wisc., from which he received a B.S.
degree in 1938 and a Ph.D. degree in chemistry in 1942.
Employed by E. I. Du Pont de Nemours Co. in research and as
supervisor of textile fibers dept., 1946-1951. Technical
supt., Seaford, Del. and Kinston, N.C. plant, 1953-1954.
Research dir., Wilmington, Del., 1954. Later became merchandising mgr. of the company. Ch., finance commt., Del.
Rep. state commt., 1965-1968. Nom. and el. Gov. as Rep.
in 1968. Defeated for reel. in 1972. Apptd. in Nov.,
1973, as ch. of President's Council on Environmental
Quality. Resigned this position in Sept., 1976, to become
head of a citizens' org., New Directions. Author of numer-
ous articles in technical journals. As Gov., was ch. of
Educ. Commt. and mbr. of Commt. on Nuclear Energy and Space
Technology of the So. Govs.' Conf. Mbr. of Committee on
Law Enforcement, Justice and Public Safety of the Natl.
Govs.' Conf. Vice pres., Natl. Mun. League, 1970-1971.
Ch., Del. River Basin Commn., 1971-1972. Mbr., Phi Beta
Kappa; Sigma Xi; Phi Eta Sigma; Phi Lambda Upsilon. Recip-
ient of N.C.C.J. Award, 1966. Unitarian. m. in 1937 to
Eva Lillian Turner. Two s.; two d.

TRIBBETT, SHERMAN WILLARD (1973-1977). b. Nov. 9, 1922
at Denton, Md. s. of Sherman L. and Minnie (Thawley) T.
Attd. Beacom Coll., from which he was grad. with an A.A.
degree in 1941. Served in U.S. Navy, 1942-1945. Employed
as bank teller, 1941-1942 in Wilmington, Del. Went into
supply bus. at Odessa, Del. as owner, 1947-1975. Dir. of
Farmers' Mutual Ins. Co.; ch. of advisory bd., Farmers Bank
and Del. Savings and Loan Assoc. Mbr. of Del. Assembly,
1957-1965, 1970-1972. Served as Speaker, 1958-1965, and as

minority (Dem.) leader, 1970–1972. Lieut. Gov., 1965–1969.
Nom. and el. Gov. as Dem. in 1972. Defeated as Dem. nomi-
nee for succeeding term in 1976. Recipient of Legislative
Conservation Award, 1965. Mbr., V.F.W.; Amer. Legion;
Masons; Moose; Rotary. Methodist. m. in 1943 to Jeanne
Cleaver Webb. Two s.; one d.

MOSELEY, WILLIAM DUNN (1845-1849). b. Feb. 1, 1795 on family homestead, "Moseley Hall," near Lagrange, Lenoir Co., N.C. s. of Matthew and Elizabeth Herring (Dunn) M. Descendant of an English colonist who came to Va. in 1649. Father was a planter. Attd. a local acad. Worked on family farm and taught school to earn money to attend Univ. of N.C., from which he was grad. in 1818. Won highest honors as freshman there and became a tutor in senior year. Studied law at Wilmington, N.C. Admitted to bar and began practice there. Mbr. of N.C. Senate, 1829-1836, serving as Pres. of that body in 1832-1836. Nom. by Dem. party for Gov. of N.C. in 1834, but lost el. in the legislature by three votes. In 1835 acquired a plantation near Lake Miccosoukee in Jefferson Co., Fla. Terr., and moved there in 1839. Mbr. of Terr. legislature and became a mbr. of the Terr. Council. El. to Fla. Senate in 1844. In May, 1845 was el. as Dem. to office of State Gov., defeating R.K. Call, the last Terr. Gov. of Fla. Admin. concerned largely with measures to implement the State's const. and govt. thereunder. Retired to plantation after leaving office. In 1851 moved to Palatka, Fla. Mbr. of Fla. House from Putnam Co. in 1855. m. in 1822 to Susan Hill, of Wilmington, N.C. Six children. D. at Palatka, Jan. 4, 1863.

BROWN, THOMAS (1849-1853). b. Oct. 24, 1785 in Westmoreland Co., Va. s. of Wm. and Margaret (Templeton) B. Descendant of an early Va. settler. Attd. school in Alexandria with brother. Served in U.S. Army during War of 1812. Became chief clerk at Richmond, Va. post office. Mbr. of Va. legislature in 1817. In 1828 moved to Tallahassee, Fla. Terr., where he had acquired plantation. As owner of slaves, was known for his good treatment of them. After a crop failure because of a freeze, went into hotel bus. at Tallahassee. Aud. of Fla. Terr., 1834. Mbr. of Terr. Legislative Council in 1838 and mbr. of conv. in 1838-1839 that framed first state const. of Fla. Mbr. of first legislature of Fla. in 1845, after statehood was achieved. Nom. and el. Gov. as a Whig in 1848. Was a Unionist in views. During admin., promoted internal improvements, including study of feasibility of draining Everglades. Active as a Mason, being a compiler of a book on the Order. m. in 1809 to Elizabeth Simpson, of Westmoreland Co., Va. Seven children. D. at Tallahassee Aug. 24, 1867.

BROOME, JAMES E. (1853-1857). b. Dec. 15, 1808 at Hamburg, Aiken Co., S.C. s. of John and Jeanette (Witherspoon) B. Father, who was a native of England, had emigrated to Amer. in 1785. In 1837 son moved to Tallahassee, Fla. Terr., where he engaged in merc. bus. for several years. In

1843 was apptd. probate judge for Leon Co., in which post he
served until 1848. As such, administered oath of office to
the first Gov. of the State, Wm. Moseley, in 1845. Nom. and
el. Gov. as Dem. in 1852 in a very close el. His opposition
to tariff and his being a strong supporter of States' Rts.
were major issues in campaign. During admin., used veto
freely and was sustained in all instances, including his veto
of a bill to abolish existing Fla. Supreme Ct. Retired to
plantation and to wholesale merc. bus. Supported secession
movement in 1860-1861 and was el. to Fla. Senate as supporter
of Confed. cause in 1861. Following Civil War moved to N.Y.
City. Married five times. Three children. D. at De Land,
Fla., Nov. 23, 1883, while visiting there.

PERRY, MADISON S. (1857-1861). b. in 1814 in Lancaster
Co., S.C. Acquired large plantation in Alachua Co., Fla.
where he established his residence. El. to Fla. House in
1849, and in 1850 to Fla. Senate. Nom. and el. Gov. as Dem.
in 1856. During admin., helped to settle long-standing
boundary dispute with Ga. Encouraged railroad bldg. and
econ. devel. of the State. Anticipating secession and possible war, urged reestablishment of militia system in 1858;
and in 1860 advised the legislature that el. of Lincoln as
Pres. of U.S. made secession inevitable. Cooperated with
secessionists in the State to bring about adoption of ordinance of secession. Became col. of Fla. Confed. regiment
during Civil War until illness compelled his retirement from
service. D. in March, 1865 at his plantation in Alachua Co.

MILTON, JOHN (1861-1865). b. April 20, 1807 near Louisville, Jefferson Co., Ga. s. of Gen. Homer Virgil and Elizabeth (Robinson) M. Ancestor on father's side had emigrated
from England to N.C. in 1730, and was a direct descendant of
the brother of the famous English poet. Grandfather had
been a prominent leader in Ga. during the Rev. War. Attd.
Louisville Acad., in Ga. Studied law and began practice in
Louisville. Moved to Columbus, Ga. Defeated as cand. for
seat in U.S. House, 1832. Practiced law in Mobile, Ala. In
1835-1837 served as capt. of volunteer company during Seminole War in Fla. Practiced law at Marion, Ala. and New
Orleans, La. In 1846 acquired farm near Marianna, Jackson
Co., Fla., which became his residence thereafter. Became
active in Fla. politics, and was noted for his fiery oratory.
Pres. elector for Dem. party in 1848. Mbr. of Fla. legislature in 1849. Nom. and el. Gov. as Dem. in 1860. As Gov.,
directed seizure of U.S. arsenals, forts and navy yards by
Confed. forces and assisted Southern cause by raising troops
and furnishing supplies. Mbr. of Soc. of Cincinnati. m. in
1826 to Susan Amanda Cobb, of Athens, Ga. One s., two d.

m. in 1840 to Caroline Howze, of Marion, Ala.   Two s., seven
d.   As State was being taken over completely by Union forces,
on April 1, 1865 took his own life at his home, "Sylvania,"
near Marianna, Fla.

MARVIN, WILLIAM (1865).   b. April 14, 1808 at Fairfield,
Herkimer Co., N.Y.   s. of Selden and Charlotte (Pratt) M.
Descendent of an English colonist who emigrated to Conn. in
1638.   Father was a farmer in Tompkins Co., N.Y.   Attd. local
schools and Homer Acad.   Began teaching school at age 15.
Studied law and was admitted to N.Y. bar in 1833.   Estab-
lished practice in Phelps, N.Y.   Apptd. U.S. atty. for Key
West dist. in Fla. Terr. by Pres. Jackson in 1835.   Became
U.S. dist. ct. judge there in 1839.   Served two terms on
Fla. Terr. Council before admission of Fla. to statehood.
Delegate to conv. that drafted first Fla. const. in 1838-
1839.   Became a Fla. dist. ct. judge, serving in that capacity until 1863 when he resigned office because of poor
health.   Apptd. Provisional Gov. of Fla. by Pres. Andrew
Johnson in 1865 to carry forward Reconstruction in Fla.
after Civil War.   After adoption of a revised const. for the
State in that year that abolished slavery, was el. to U.S.
Senate, but was refused seat by the Senate because Fla. still
denied suffrage to Negroes.   Refused to be cand. for any office thereafter.   Established residence in Skaneateles, N.Y.,
where he engaged in writing.   Published work on Laws of Wreck
and Salvage.   m. in 1846 to Harriet Newell, of Cooperstown,
N.Y.   One d.   After her death, m. to Mrs. Elizabeth Riddle
Jewell, of Skaneateles.   D. July 9, 1902.

ALLISON, ABRAHAM (ABRAM?) KURKINDOLL (KYRKENDAL?)
(1865).   b. Dec. 10, 1810 in Jones Co., Ga.   s. of Capt.
James and Sarah (Fannin) A.   Established merc. bus. at Columbus, Ga., later moving to Henry Co., Ala.   Moved to
Apalachicola, in Franklin Co., Fla.   Mayor of Apalachicola
for a time.   Apptd. judge of Franklin Co. ct.   Later served
as clerk of U.S. dist. ct.   Mbr. of Fla. Terr. legislature.
In 1835-1837 served as capt. of Franklin Rifles company during Seminole War.   Moved to Quincy, in Gadsden Co., Fla. in
1839, from where he was again el. to the Terr. legislature.
Mbr. of Fla. House, 1845, 1847 and 1852, serving as Speaker
in last term.   Mbr. of Fla. Senate, 1862-1865, becoming the
presiding officer thereof.   Supported Southern cause during
Civil War.   Upon death of Gov. Milton in April, 1865, assumed office of Gov.; but he was not recognized as such by
Union authorities.   Taken prisoner by them on May 29, 1865,
and was confined at Ft. Pulaski for about six months before
being released.   In 1872 he was tried and convicted of

intimidating Negroes at Quincy, and was fined and imprisoned
for a time in Tallahassee. D. at Quincy July 8, 1893.

WALKER, DAVID SHELBY (1865-1868). b. May 2, 1815 near
Russellville, Ky. s. of David and Mary (May?) (Barbour) W.
Family line included a number of distinguished individuals,
his father having served as a mbr. of U.S. House. Attd. pvt.
schools in Ky. and Tenn. Studied law with older brother.
Established residence in Leon Co., Fla. Terr., in 1837. Influential in movement to establish state govt. in Fla. Mayor
of Tallahassee, 1842-1852. Mbr. of first Fla. Senate in 1845
and of Fla. House, 1848-1849. From 1849 to 1854 was Register
of Pub. Lands, and ex officio State Supt. of Pub. Instruction. Defeated in close el. in 1856 as Amer. party cand. for
Gov. Judge of Fla. Supreme Ct., 1858-1865. El. Gov. under
revised const. of 1865 as Conservative (Union) cand. During
tenure as Gov. his admin. of affairs was supervised closely
by U.S. mil. authorities. Resigned in July, 1868 after refusing to take "iron clad" oath of loyalty as required by
Fed. legislation, although he had not been an active supporter of secessionist cause. Practiced law, 1868-1876.
Apptd. dist. ct. judge by Gov. Drew in 1879 and held that
position until death. Trustee of Fla. Agri. Coll. and of
So. Fla. Sem. Influential in establishment of pub. school
system in Tallahassee and of a pub. library there, for which
he contributed a bldg. in 1883. Episcopalian. m. in 1847
to Philoclea Alston. Six children. m. in 1875 to Elizabeth
Duncan. D. at Tallahassee July 20, 1891.

REED, HARRISON (1868-1873). b. Aug. 26, 1813 at Little-
ton, Mass. s. of Seth H. and Rhoda (Finney) R. Father became a hotel operator at Castleton, Vt., and son received
schooling there. At age 16 he was apprenticed to learn
printing trade in office of a local newspaper. After three
years of employment his health failed. Entered merc. bus.
in Troy, N.Y. In 1836 went to Milwaukee, Wisc., where he
opened merc. bus. which soon failed in financial panic of
1837. Settled on farm at Summit, Wisc., along with father
and brother. Engaged as ed. and publ. of Milwaukee Sentinel,
which became the first Whig newspaper in the area. When
Wisc. Terr. was organized, moved to Madison, Wisc., where he
became ed. of Madison Enquirer. In 1843 moved to Winnebago
Co., Wisc. Engaged in milling bus. and laid out town of
Neenah there. Ch. of first bd. of commnrs. for Winnebago
Co. Served as Whig mbr. of Wisc. constl. conv. in 1848.
Nom. as pres. elector on Whig ticket in el. of 1848. Established newspaper at Neenah; later moved again to Madison
where he was associated with the State Journal, the official
organ of new state govt. In 1861 went to Washington, D.C.,

where he was employed by Treas. Dept. as mbr. of bd. of tax
commnrs. for the Fla. dist. Resigned that post in 1865 and
moved to Fernandina, Fla., where he acted as spec. agent for
the U.S. Post Office in Ala. and Fla. El. Gov. as Rep. in
1868 under revised state const. of that year. Admin. was
troubled by factionalism in Rep. party. Successfully resisted effort of Lieut. Gov. Gleason to take over as Gov. in
Nov., 1868 after impeachment charges against Reed were voted
in House. Supreme Ct. of Fla. ousted Gleason on ground he
lacked constl. qualifications for office and held the impeachment procedures were irregular. Again was impeached in
Feb., 1872. Surrendered official powers temporarily to
Lieut. Gov. Day, but the impeachment trial was never completed by Senate. Resumed office of Gov. in May, 1872 and
the charges were eventually dropped. Retired to farm in St.
Johns River, in Fla. Became ed. of a journal, the Semi-
Tropical. Served as U.S. postmaster at Tallahassee, 1889-
1893. m. in 1869 to Chloe Merrick, of Syracuse, N.Y., who
was active in movement to establish schools for ex-slaves.
D. at Jacksonville, March 25, 1899.

HART, OSSIAN BINGLEY (1873-1874). b. Jan. 17, 1821 at
Jacksonville, Fla. Terr. s. of Isaiah D. and Nancy (Nelson)
H. Antecedents, who were English, had resided originally in
Va. and Ga. Father was an influential plantation owner in
community. At age 16 son was sent to Washington, D.C. to
complete educ. Studied law, was admitted to bar and practiced at Jacksonville. Moved to Ft. Pierce in 1843 where he
had obtained a land grant. Served in first state legislature of Fla. as Whig mbr. from that area in 1845. In 1846
moved to Key West, and in 1856 to Tampa, where he engaged in
law practice. As Civil War approached he took a stand
against secession, which made him unpopular. His political
views resulted in his being persecuted during course of the
war. Returned to Jacksonville after the war ended and participated in efforts to set up locally-controlled state govt.
acceptable to U.S. authorities. Apptd. to Fla. Supreme Ct.
in 1868. Nom. as Rep. cand. for U.S. House in 1870. Was
declared el., but result was contested and his Dem. opponent
was seated. Nom. and el. Gov. as Rep. in 1872, becoming the
first native-born citizen of Fla. to hold the office of Gov.
Admin. concerned with putting the State's finances in order.
m. in 1843 to Catherine Smith Campbell, of Newark, N.J. D.
of pneumonia at Jacksonville March 18, 1874 while still in
office.

STEARNS, MARCELLUS LOVEJOY (1874-1877). b. April 29,
1829 at Lovell, Me. s. of Caleb and Eliza W. (Russell) S.
Father was a merchant and farmer. Attd. Waterville Acad.

(later Coburn Classical Inst.), in Me., and in 1859 enrolled at Waterville (now Colby) Coll. Taught school during vacations. Left college in junior year to enlist in a Me. volunteer regiment upon outbreak of Civil War. Rose to rank of second lieut. in 1863. Wounded at Battle of Winchester, losing an arm. Became an officer in the reserves, and while stationed at Portland, Me., studied law. In 1868 was stationed at Quincy, Fla., while still a reserve officer. Assisted in registering Negro voters in area to participate in 1868 election. Mbr. of Fla. constl. conv. in that year. El. to Fla. House under the 1868 const. and continued to serve until 1872. Speaker of House in 1869. In that year accepted post of U.S. Surveyor Gen. of Fla., serving until 1873. In the 1872 election, was nom. and el. Lieut. Gov. as Rep. Succeeded to office of Gov. in March, 1874, following death of Gov. Hart, and completed Hart's term. Nom. for a full term in 1876. Was declared to have been el. by State Bd. of Canvassers, but the result was challenged by his Dem. opponent, George Drew. The latter was eventually declared el. by the State Supreme Ct., and was installed in office. Apptd. U.S. commnr. to inspect pub. works in Fla. in 1877. In 1886 travelled in Europe, after which he established his home in Atlantic, Iowa, where he engaged in banking. m. in 1878 to Ellen Austin Walker, of Bridgewater, Mass. D. at Palantine Bridge, N.Y., Dec. 8, 1891. Bur. at Lovell, Me.

DREW, GEORGE FRANKLIN (1877-1881). b. Aug. 6, 1827 at Alton, N.H. s. of John and Charlotte (Davis) D. Descended from an old colonial family. Attd. local schools and Gilmanton Acad. At an early age was apprenticed to shops in Lynn and Lowell, Mass., to learn machinist's trade. In 1846 went to Cohoes, N.Y., where he worked for a year. Moved to Columbus, Ga., where he opened a machine shop. In 1854 went into sawmill bus. there. Transferred operations to Ellaville, in Madison Co., Fla. Also operated in Lee Co., Fla. Built bus. into a large enterprise, shipping lumber to many points in U.S. and abroad. As Civil War came on maintained his loyalty to the Union. His views led to his imprisonment by Confed. authorities at Savannah for some 22 months and to confiscation of his properties. After the war ended, assisted in movement to restore locally-controlled govt. and in resistance against "carpetbagger" element. Became ch. of Bd. of Commnrs. of Madison Co. in 1870. Nom. for Gov. by Dem. party in 1876. Campaign against incumbent Gov. Stearns was very bitter. Stearns was declared el. by State Bd. of Canvassers, but Drew carried the issue of whether certain ballots should be counted to the State

Supreme Ct., which ruled in his favor so as to give him a
plurality, and he was installed in office. During admin.,
attention was given to reduction of taxes and financial reform and to restoration of White rule in State. After
leaving office resumed sawmill bus. at Ellaville for a time.
In 1883 disposed of that bus. and moved to Jacksonville,
where he formed a wholesale hardware co. m. in 1845 to
Amelia Dicken (Dickens?), of Columbus, Ga. Two s.; two d.
D. Sept. 26, 1900, only two hours after his wife had also
passed away.

BLOXHAM, WILLIAM DUNNINGTON (1881-1885; 1897-1091). b.
July 9, 1835 near Tallahassee, Leon Co., Fla. Terr. s. of
Wm. and Martha (Williams) B. Family was of English descent.
Father, who was a Va. planter, had moved to Leon Co. in 1825
when the area was inhabited mainly by Indians. At age 13,
was sent to prep. school in Va. Afterward attd. William and
Mary Coll., from which he was grad. in 1853. Continued to
study law there. Health failed and he returned to Fla.,
where he engaged in planting. Became interested in politics.
El. to Fla. legislature in 1861. In 1862 organized a company of volunteers, of which he became capt., to serve in
Confed. cause during Civil War. A popular speaker, after
the war he became one of the leaders of the resurgent Dem.
party and an opponent of Reconstruction. Served as Dem.
pres. elector in 1868. Lieut. Gov. in 1870. Nom. for Gov.
as Dem. in 1872, but was defeated in the gen. election.
Mbr. of Dem. state commt. in 1876 election, and was el. to
office of Sect. of State, serving until 1880. Nom. and el.
Gov. as Dem. in 1880. During admin., sale of large tracts
of state-owned land brought State out of debt and led to
extensive railroad constr. Offered position of Minister to
Bolivia by Pres. Cleveland in 1885, but he declined.
Accepted apptmt. to office of U.S. Surveyor Gen. for Fla.,
which post he held until 1889. Apptd. to vacancy in office
of State Comptroller in 1890, and later was el. to the post,
holding it until 1896. Nom. and el. Gov. as Dem. again in
1896, becoming the first Gov. to be el. to two non-consecu-
tive terms. Financial problems resulting from crop failures
because of freezes and destructive storms were matters of
major concern during second admin. m. in 1856 to Mary C.
Davis (David?), of Lynchburg, Va. After her death, m. in
1907 to Mrs. G. Moss Nowell. D. at Tallahassee, Fla.,
March 15, 1911.

PERRY, EDWARD AYLESWORTH (1885-1889). b. March 15,
1831 at Richmond, Mass. s. of Asa and Philura (Aylesworth)
P. Descended from an old Mass. family. Educ. at Lee Acad.

in Richmond and at Yale. Taught school for a short time in
Ala. Moved to Pensacola, Fla. Studied law and was admitted
to bar in 1853. Upon outbreak of Civil War enlisted in
Confed. Army. Rose through the ranks to capt., col. in
1862, and later, brig. gen. Saw much mil. action in Fla.
and Va. Participated in Battles of Fredericksburg and
Spotsylvania. Was wounded, and also suffered from serious
case of typhoid fever. Returned to Pensacola after war, and
resumed practice of law there. Held no pub. office until
nom. and el. Gov. as Dem. in 1884. During admin., a revised
const. was drafted and adopted, and a State Bd. of Educ. established. m. in 1859 to Wathen Hebert Taylor, of Greenville, Ala. One s.; four d. D. at Pensacola Oct. 15, 1889,
less than a year after completing term as Gov.

FLEMING, FRANCIS PHILIP (1889-1893). b. Sept. 28, 1841
at Panama Park, Duval Co., Fla. Terr. s. of Col. Lewis and
Margaret (Seton) F. Mbr. of one of older and widely respected Fla. families, with an estate in St. Johns River
area. Educ. by pvt. tutors. Engaged in bus. until outbreak
of Civil War. Enlisted in Fla. Confed. regiment, rising to
rank of first lieut. Saw much action in Fla., Va., Tenn.,
and Ga. during course of the war. Later studied law, was
admitted to bar in 1868, and began practice in Jacksonville.
Rose to prominence in profession and in Dem. politics. Nom.
and el. Gov. as Dem. in 1888, receiving the nom. in state
conv. after prolonged struggle requiring 40 ballots. During
admin., a State Bd. of Health was created by action of the
legislature called into spec. session in midst of yellow
fever outbreak. Former partner in his law firm had died of
the disease the year before. m. in 1871 to Floride Lydia
Pearson. D. Dec. 20, 1908, at Jacksonville.

MITCHELL, HENRY LAWRENCE (LAURENS?) (1893-1897). b.
Sept. 3, 1831 near Birmingham, Ala. s. of Thomas and
Elizabeth (Starns) M. Attd. common schools in Ala. and an
acad. at Jacksonville, Fla. At age 15 began study of law in
office of Judge James Gettis, at Tampa. Admitted to bar in
1849 and became partner with Judge Gettis. Apptd. State's
atty. for his jud. cir. At the beginning of Civil War, enlisted in Confed. Army. Served as capt. throughout war.
El. to Fla. legislature in absentia in 1864. El. again in
1873 and 1875. In 1875 was apptd. to a cir. ct. judgeship.
Became mbr. of State Supreme Ct. in 1888. Nom. and el. Gov.
as Dem. in 1892. During admin., industrialization of Fla.
advanced rapidly. Took strong stand against prize fighting,
and when the Corbett-Mitchell fight was staged within the
State, had the participants arrested and convicted for

violation of the State's law. State financial system was
revised; pub. educ. promoted; and a State R.R. Commn. established. After leaving the office of Gov., served as clerk
of cir. ct. for four years and later as treas. of
Hillsborough Co. D. at Tampa, Oct. 14, 1903.

BLOXHAM, WILLIAM DUNNINGTON (1897-1901). See above,
1881-1885.

JENNINGS, WILLIAM SHERMAN (1901-1905). b. March 24,
1863 near Walnut Hill, Ill. s. of Josephus W. and Amanda
(Couch) J. Father was a successful farmer and fruit grower.
Educ. in pub. schools in Marion Co., Ill. and at So. Ill.
Normal (now Univ.) at Carbondale, from which he was grad. in
1883. Studied law at Union Coll. of Law, in Chicago, and in
law office of his brother, who was State's atty. in Marion
Co. Moved to Fla. in 1885. Admitted to bar and began
practice at Brooksville. In 1887 was apptd. cir. ct.
commnr., and in 1888 became a cir. ct. judge in Hernando
Co., serving until 1893. Mbr. of Fla. House, 1893-1895,
serving as Speaker. Col. in Fla. militia in 1889. Pres.
elector on Dem. ticket in 1896 when his cousin, Wm. Jennings
Bryan, was the Dem. cand. for Pres. of U.S. Pres. of
Brooksville town council for eight years and mbr. of its bd.
of aldermen for nine years. Ch. of Fla. Dem. conv. in 1898.
Nom. and el. Gov. as Dem. in 1900. During admin., a direct
primary law was adopted; Indian wars claims against U.S.
govt. were collected; State Capitol bldg. remodeled; sale of
pub. lands of the State restricted; and tax law modifica-
tions enacted. After tenure as Gov., moved to Jacksonville,
where he became involved in studies and plans for drainage
of swamp lands. Vice pres. and gen. counsel for Fla. Bank
and Trust Co. Associated with other firms connected with
land devel. Gen. counsel for Intl. Improvement Fund and
State Bd. of Drainage Commnrs. Ch. of State Tax Commn.,
1911-1912. Mbr. of Intl. Commn. for Advancement of Peace
under a treaty between U.S. and Paraguay in 1915. Baptist.
Hon. degree from John B. Stetson Univ. m. in 1890 to
Corrine Jordan, who died five months after marriage. m. in
1891 to May Mann. One s. D. Feb. 28, 1920.

BROWARD, NAPOLEON BONAPARTE (1905-1909). b. April 19,
1857 near Jacksonville, Duval Co., Fla. s. of Napoleon
Bonaparte and Mary Dorcas (Parsons) B. Descendant of a
Huguenot family that had migrated to S.C. before Rev. War.
Great-grandfather was a soldier in Contl. Army during Rev.
War and later had settled in Spanish Fla., where he obtained
a substantial land grant in 1816. Obtained a rudimentary

educ. in a rural school, which he attd. only two terms.
Family plantation was ravaged during Civil War. Was
orphaned at age 12. Worked at various jobs in lumber camps,
orange groves and on river boats. Became pilot on vessels
operating along coast, later becoming capt. of a river boat
operating on St. Johns River. In 1882 acquired interest in
shipping bus. at New Berlin, operating freight and passenger
steamer. Also engaged in woodyard bus. at Jacksonville.
Was apptd. sheriff of Duval Co. in 1888, and moved vigorously against local gambling interests. Defeated for election
to the office in 1889. Was apptd. sheriff again when his
successful Rep. opponent was disqualified on a technicality.
El. sheriff again in 1892, but was removed from office by
the Gov. on grounds of over-zealousness in attempting to
protect elections from fraud in violation of govtl. regulations. El. sheriff again in 1896. Became involved in
assisting Cuban rebels by running shipments of arms in 1895,
his boat, the "Three Friends" being seized by U.S. authorities on two occasions. Served as mbr. of Jacksonville city
council. Mbr. of Fla. legislature and of the State Bd. of
Health, 1901-1904. Active in political movements directed
against railroad and land co. interests. Advocate of
drainage projects in South Fla. area. Identified with
liberal reform wing of Dem. party. Nom. and el. Gov. as
Dem. in 1904. During admin., sponsored Everglades drainage
program; a Bd. of Control was established to oversee state
admin.; a new food and drug law enacted; a compulsory school
attendance law passed; and the seven state institutions of
higher learning were consolidated into four, with the Univ.
of Fla. being located at Gainesville, and Fla. State Coll.
for Women (now Fla. State Univ.) being located at
Tallahassee. Delegate to Dem. natl. conv. in 1908. Defeated as cand. for Dem. nom. for U.S. Senate in 1908, but won
the Dem. nom. for that office in 1910. D. at Jacksonville
on Oct. 1 of that year before the final election was conducted. m. in 1883 to Caroline Georgia Kemps, d. of a bus.
assoc.,who died during that year. m. in 1887 to Annie
Isabel Douglas, of Jacksonville. Nine children. Mbr.,
K.P.; Macabees. Presbyterian.

   GILCHRIST, ALBERT WALLER (1909-1913). b. Jan. 15, 1858
at Greenwood, S.C. s. of Gen. Wm. E. and Rhoda Elizabeth
(Waller) G. Descendant of Scottish family that had emigrated to S.C. in 1750. Ancestral line included the grandfathers of George Washington and James Madison and others
who were distinguished in pub. and mil. affairs in S.C.
Educ. at Caroline Mil. Inst., at Charlotte, N.C. and at West
Point Mil. Acad. Worked as clerk in gen. store in Quincy,

Fla. for a time.   Later was employed as a civil engr. by a
railroad co. in 1882 and by Fla. So. R.R. Co. in 1885. Went
into real estate bus. in 1887, later becoming owner of an
orange grove. Brig. gen. in Fla. militia. Mbr. of Bd. of
Visitors of West Point Mil. Acad., 1896. In 1898 resigned
commn. to enter U.S. Army as a pvt. Served in Cuba during
Spanish-Amer. War and was a capt. when mustered out in 1899.
Mbr. of Fla. House, 1893-1895, serving as Speaker. Again a
mbr., 1903-1905, again serving as Speaker. Nom. and el.
Gov. as Dem. in 1908. During admin., legislation was enacted for regulation of dental and osteopathic professions; a
State Tuberculosis Sanitarium created; control of live stock
diseases and products established; election reforms adopted.
Engaged in producing oranges on his estate after tenure as
Gov. Defeated as cand. for Dem. nom. for U.S. Senate in
1922. Mbr., Masons. D. May 16, 1926 at Punta Gorda, Fla.

TRAMMELL, PARK (N.) (1913-1917). b. April 9, 1876 in
Macon Co., Ala. s. of John W. and Ida E. (Park) T. In 1877
family moved to Polk Co., Fla., where father served as co.
treas., mbr. of the Fla. legislature, and as Supt. of State
Hosp. for the Insane. Attd. local schools. Worked on farm,
in newspaper office as a printer, and as a clerk and bookkeeper in local stores. In 1894 was employed at Tampa as
marine clerk for U.S. Customs Service. During Spanish-Amer.
War was employed by U.S. Quarter-master Corps. Studied law
at Vanderbilt Univ. and Cumberland Univ., receiving a law
degree from latter in 1899. Admitted to bar and established
practice at Lakeland, Fla. Also engaged in fruit growing
and was ed. of a local newspaper. Mayor of Lakeland, 1899-
1903. Mbr. of Fla. House, 1903-1905, and of the Fla.
Senate, 1905-1908, serving as Pres. of Senate. Atty. Gen.
of Fla., 1909-1913. Nom. and el. Gov. as Dem. in 1912.
During admin., legislation was passed for regulation of campaign expenditures, and for creation of a State Tax Commn.
with equalization powers. Favored improved rural and vocational schools; free pub. libraries; restriction of sale of
pub. lands to pvt. owners; and regulation of commn. merchants to protect fruit growers. Nom. and el. to U.S.
Senate as a Dem. in 1916. Continued to serve therein until
his death. Baptist. m. in 1900 to Virginia Darby, of
Lakeland. D. May 8, 1936, in Washington, D.C. Bur. in
Roselawn Cem., in Lakeland.

CATTS, SIDNEY JOHNSTON (1917-1921). b. July 31, 1863
near Pleasant Hill, Ala. s. of Capt. Samuel W. and Adeline
(Smyly) C. Descendant of a Dutch family that had emigrated
to Pa. originally. Attd. Ala. Poly. Inst., at Auburn, and

Howard Coll., at Marion, Ala.   Received law degree from
Cumberland Univ. in 1882.   Practiced law in Dallas Co., Ala.
and managed mother's plantation for three years.   Entered
Baptist ministry in 1885.   Ordained and held pastorates in
Dallas Co. and Lowndes Co. and at Tuskegee and Fort Deposit,
in Ala.   Resigned from ministry in 1904.   Unsuccessful as
cand. for U.S. House from Ala. in 1904.   Moved to Fla.,
where he farmed and engaged in merc. and ins. bus.   Also
preached in rural churches, becoming pastor of a Baptist
church at De Funiak Springs in 1911.   Defeated by close margin following a re-count, in attempt to win Dem. nom. for
Gov. in 1916.   Nevertheless ran as an Indep. Dem., with support of Prohibition party, and was el.   Press, liquor
interests, and Catholic hierarchy opposed him during campaign.   Admin. filled with controversy.   Advocated strict
economy in govt., lower taxes, sanctions to compel ct.
officials to perform duties; and strict prohibition law
enforcement.   Created a "Friends of Convicts" position in
connection with prison admin. to assist in counseling and
rehabilitation efforts.   After leaving office was indicted
on peonage charges and was tried thereon in a U.S. dist. ct.
and on corruption charges in a state ct., but was acquitted
in both trials.   Unsuccessful cand. for Dem. nom. for U.S.
Senate seat in 1920.   Was also defeated for Dem. nom. for
Gov. in 1924 in a run-off primary, and again in 1928.   Mbr.,
Masons; Woodmen; Jr. Order of Amer. Mechanics; K.P.; Guard-
ians of Liberty; various farm orgs.   m. in 1886 to Alice
May Campbell, of Montgomery, Ala.   Six children.   D. March
9, 1936 at De Funiak Springs.

HARDEE, CARY AUGUSTUS (1921-1925).   b. Nov. 13, 1876
near Perry, Taylor Co., Fla.   s. of James B. and Amanda
(Johnson) H.   Family was originally from Ga., and he spent
early youth in that State.   Worked on farm at Perry.   Taught
school until 1900, studying law in the meantime.   Admitted
to bar in 1898.   Began practice at Live Oak, Fla.   Helped to
org. First Natl. Bank there and became its pres. in 1907.
Also was an officer of banks at Branford and Mayo, Fla.
From 1905 to 1913 was State's atty. for his jud. dist.   Mbr.
of Fla. House, 1915-1917, serving as Speaker.   Nom. and el.
Gov. as Dem. in 1920.   During admin., constl. amdts. were
adopted prohibiting state income and inheritance taxes and
reapportioning legislature.   Law was enacted prohibiting
leasing of convict labor to pvt. contractors.   After tenure
as Gov., gave attention to banking interests.   Served as co.
tax collector for many years.   Mbr., Masons; K.P.; Elks;
Woodmen.   Trustee of Fla. Historical Soc., and possessor of
large pvt. library.   Baptist.   m. in 1900 to Maud Randle,

of Madison, Fla. One d. D. Nov. 21, 1957. Bur. at Oak
Ridge Cem. in Madison, Fla.

MARTIN, JOHN WELBORN (1925-1929). b. June 21, 1884 at
Plainfield, Fla. s. of John Marshall and Willie (Owens) M.
Antecedents had emigrated from England to Va., later moving
to S.C. Family possessed land and was one of prestige in
the community. Attd. local schools. Worked on father's
farm, and engaged in truck farming for himself. Studied law
at night, and was admitted to bar in 1914. Established
practice in Jacksonville. Mayor of Jacksonville, 1917-1924.
Nom. and el. Gov. as Dem. in 1924, defeating former Gov.
Catts in Dem. run-off primary. During first year of term
the Fla. "land boom" of early 1920s reached its height, to
be followed by rapid collapse in last two years of his term,
with consequent numerous bus. and bank failures. Also
serious hurricanes occurred that damaged crops and orchards
extensively. During admin., an Everglades reclamation project was revitalized and re-funded; highway constr. carried
forward; and free textbook system and direct financial aid
to pub. school system originated. Retired to law practice
at Jacksonville after tenure as Gov. Defeated for Dem. nom.
for U.S. Senate seat in 1928 by Sen. and former Gov. Park
Trammell. Also lost in run-off primary for Dem. nom. for
Gov. in 1932. Trustee of Fla. East Coast Ry. Co., beginning
in 1942. Mbr., Masons (Shriner); I.O.O.F.; Moose. Baptist.
m. in 1907 to Lottie Wilt Pepper, of Lake City, Fla. D.
Feb. 22, 1958.

CARLETON, DOYLE ELAM (1929-1933). b. July 6, 1887 at
Wauchula, Fla. s. of Albert and Martha (McEwen) C. Father
was a banker and orange grower. Received an A.B. degree
from Stetson Univ. in 1909 and also from the Univ. of
Chicago in 1910. Studied law at the Univ. of Chicago and
Columbia, receiving a law degree in 1912. Began law practice in Tampa. Mbr. of Fla. Senate, 1917-1919, where he was
active in promoting highway constr. program. Nom. and el.
Gov. as Dem. in 1928, defeating former Gov. Catts for Dem.
nom. in a run-off primary. Difficulties arising from
collapse of land boom, hurricanes, invasion of Mediterranean
fruit fly, and onset of the depression of the 1930s resulted
in his calling two emergency sessions of the legislature.
During admin., new banking legislation was passed; gasoline
tax adopted; federal aid secured to combat fruit fly; and a
plan formulated by which U.S. govt. took over admin. of
Everglades reclamation work. Defeated as cand. for Dem.
nom. for U.S. Senate in 1936. Retired to law practice.
Acted as spec. counsel for State of Fla. in 1947 in

connection with establishment of pub. ownership of Ringling
Museum at Sarasota. Pres. of Fla. CC, 1951–1952. Hon.
degrees from Stetson Univ. and the Univ. of Fla. Mbr.,
Masons; K.P.; Elks; Moose; Kiwanis. Baptist. m. in 1912
to Nell Ray, of Tampa. Two d.; one s., Doyle E., Jr., who
was defeated as Dem. cand. for Dem. nom. for Gov. in 1960.
D. Oct. 25, 1972.

SHOLTZ, DAVID (1933–1937). b. Oct. 6, 1891 at
Brooklyn, N.Y. s. of Michael and Annie (Bloon) S. Father
was a Polish immigrant who became a very prosperous and
successful bus. man after settling in N.Y. Attd. pub.
schools in Brooklyn, and Yale Univ., from which he received
an A.B. degree in 1914. Went to Fla. in 1915. Studied law
and was admitted to bar there. Began practice in Daytona,
where his father had an interest in a utility enterprise.
Mbr. of Fla. House, 1917–1919. Resigned as State Food
Commnr. to enlist in U.S. Navy in 1918, becoming an ensign.
Continued as lieut. commdr. in USNR after World War I.
State's atty. for 7th jud. dist., 1919–1921. Judge of
Daytona mun. ct., 1921. Nom. in run-off primary against
former Gov. Martin and el. Gov. as Dem. in 1932. As Gov.,
promoted admin. reforms; provided financial aid to schools
by a liquor tax; sought devel. of tourist trade by wealthy
while discouraging in-migration by indigents; cooperated
with U.S. govt. in connection with welfare and pub. works
programs. Sought to remove Mayor Irene Armstrong, of
Daytona, but ouster order was resisted and eventually
dropped by his successor. Defeated in attempt to win Dem.
nom. for U.S. Senate seat in 1938. m. in 1919 to Agatha M.
Roberts, of Key West. m. for second time in 1925 to Alice
Mae Agee, of Norfolk, Va. Two d.; one s. Mbr., Amer.
Legion; O.W.W., of which he was Natl. Commndr. in 1944;
Masons (Shriner); Elks; Rotary; various bus. and profession-
al orgs. and social clubs. Pres. of Daytona CC and Fla. CC.
Hon. degree from Stetson Univ. D. at Miami, March 21, 1953.

CONE, FREDERICK PRESTON (1937–1941). b. Sept. 28, 1871
at Benton, Fla. s. of Wm. Henry and Sarah Emily (Branch) C.
Father, who had been a Fla. state senator, traced ancestry
to a Scottish colonist who had emigrated to Conn. in 1650.
Attd. local pub. schools; Jasper Normal Inst.; and Fla.
State Agri. Coll. Became a school teacher while also
studying law. Admitted to bar in 1892 and began practice in
Lake City, Fla. In 1940 org. the Columbus Co. Bank at
Lake City, which he continued to serve as pres. until his
death. Mayor of Lake City, 1902–1907. Mbr. of Fla. Senate,
1907–1913, serving as Pres. of that body in his last term.

Did not seek pub. office again until 1936 when he was nom.
for Gov. in a run-off primary and was el. During admin.,
an unemployment compensation law was enacted; the poll tax
requirement for voting was abolished; and a State Dept. of
Pub. Safety and a State Highway Patrol established. Cooperated with Fed. agencies in promotion of New Deal objectives. Delegate to Dem. natl. convs. in 1912, 1924 and
1932. Defeated as cand. for Dem. nom. for U.S. Senate in
1940. Mbr., Masons; Elks; Rotary; various bus. and professional legal orgs. and social clubs. Baptist. m. in
1901 to Ruby Scarborough, of Lake City. One d. m. for second time in 1929 to Mildred Thompson, of Macclenny, Fla.
D. at Lake City, July 28, 1948.

   HOLLAND, SPESSARD LINDSEY (1941-1945). b. July 10,
1892 at Bartow, Fla. s. of Benj. Franklin and Fannie
Virginia (Spessard) H. Attd. local pub. schools; Emory
Univ., from which he was grad. magna cum laude in 1912; and
the Univ. of Fla., from which he received a law degree in
1916. Taught school at Warrenton, Ga., 1912-1914. Was
outstanding in athletics and was chosen pres. of student
body while in college. Began law practice at Bartow, Fla.
Enlisted as lieut. in coast artillery unit of U.S. Army in
1918. Transferred to Air Force and served overseas in
World War I. Brig. judge advocate and asst. adjt. Volunteered as air observer and saw combat service, becoming
recipient of D.S.C. Held rank of capt. at time of discharge.
Pros. atty. for Polk Co., 1919. Co. judge, 1921-1929. Mbr.
of Fla. Senate, 1933-1940. Active in revision of school
code and in adoption of workmen's compensation law and an
old age pension plan. Nom. and el. Gov. as Dem. in 1940,
winning nom. in run-off primary. During admin., cooperated
with U.S. govt. in war measures; revised tax structure;
Everglades Natl. Park was established; Everglades drainage
dist. bonds refunded; and a Fish and Game Commn. was established. Apptd. to vacant seat in U.S. Senate in Sept.,
1946, after having won Dem. nom. for a regular term, and
was subsequently el. Continued in office for three
succeeding terms. Did not seek reel. in 1970. As mbr. of
U.S. Senate was active in promotion of farm legislation;
conservation measures; the Tidelands Act; a U.S. constl.
amdt. (24th) prohibiting taxpaying requirement for voting;
and the U.S. Interstate Highway system. Mbr., Amer.
Legion; 40 and 8; V.F.W.; R.O.A.; Masons; Kiwanis; Phi Beta
Kappa. Pres. of Univ. of Fla. Alumni Assoc. Trustee, Fla.
So. Coll., 1932-1935 and of Emory Univ., 1945-1946. Hon.
degrees from a number of institutions of higher learning.
Methodist. m. to Mary Agnes Groover, of Lakeland, Fla.

Two s.; two d.   D. Nov. 6, 1971.

CALDWELL, MILLARD FILLMORE, Jr. (1945-1949).   b. Feb.
6, 1897 at Beverly, near Knoxville, Tenn.   s. of Millard
Fillmore and Martha Jane (Clapp) C.   Antecedents, who were
Scottish, had emigrated to Pa. in 1727, and later had
resided in Va.   Father was an atty., cotton planter, author
and newspaper ed.   Attd. local pub. schools; Carson-Newman
Coll., 1913-1914; and the Univ. of Miss., from which he
withdrew in 1918 to enlist in U.S. Army as a pvt.   Served
until end of World War I.   Rose to rank of second lieut.
before discharge.   Attd. the Univ. of Va., 1919-1922, where
he studied law.   Admitted to Tenn. bar in 1922.   Operated
cotton plantation in Miss. until 1924, when he moved to
Milton, Fla.   Practiced law there until 1933.   Pros. atty.
for Santa Rosa Co., 1926-1932.   Mbr. of Fla. House, 1929-
1931.   El. to U.S. House in 1932 and continued to serve
therein until 1941.   Delegate to Interparliamentary Conf.
in 1938 and 1939.   Did not seek reel. to House seat in 1940.
Retired to plantation near Tallahassee and practiced law,
1941-1944.   Nom. and el. Gov. as Dem. in 1944.   As Gov.,
was successful in inducing outstanding persons to serve in
his admin.; revised tax and school aid structure; promoted
devel. of Capitol Center.   Ch. of Natl. Govs.' Conf., 1946-
1947 and pres. of Council of State Govts., 1947.   Delegate
to Dem. natl. convs. on three occasions.   Ch. of Bd. of
Control for So. Regional Educ., 1948-1951.   Head of Fed.
Civil Defense Admin., 1950-1952.   Ch., Fla. Commn. on
Constl. Govt., 1957-1965.   Assoc. Justice of Fla. Supreme
Ct., 1962-1966 and Chief Justice, 1966-1969.   Retired to
engage in bus. and professional interests in Tallahassee.
Mbr., Masons; Huguenot Soc.; S.A.R.; various fraternal and
professional legal orgs.   Hon. degrees from Fla. So. Coll.;
Rollins Coll.; and Fla. State Univ.   m. in 1925 to Mary
Rebecca Harwood, of Saluda, Va.   Two d.; one s.

WARREN, FULLER (1949-1953).   b. Oct. 3, 1905 at
Blountstown, Fla.   s. of Charles Ryan and Grace (Fuller) W.
Father, who was of Irish descent, was a lawyer.   Attd. pub.
schools in Calhoun and Walton counties.   Worked at a
variety of jobs as a youth and young man, including farm-
hand, delivery boy, mill hand, newsboy, clerk, seaman,
salesman, and auctioneer.   Inherited money from an uncle
which enabled him to attend college.   Attd. Thomas Indus.
Inst., 1922 and the Univ. of Fla., 1922-1927.   Formed
ambition to become Gov. at an early age.   El. to Fla.
legislature from Calhoun Co. in 1926 at age 21, becoming
the youngest mbr. ever to serve in that body up to that

time.   Received law degree from Cumberland Univ. in 1928
and began practice of law at Jacksonville in 1929.   Delegate
to Dem. natl. conv. in 1928.   Mbr. of city council of
Jacksonville, 1931-1937.   Mbr. of Fla. House from Duval Co.,
1939-1941.   Defeated as cand. for city commnr. of
Jacksonville and in Dem. primary for Gov. in 1940.   In 1943
entered U.S. Navy and saw service as gunnery officer.   Resumed law practice after naval service in 1945.   Nom. and
el. Gov. as Dem. in 1948, winning nom. in run-off against
Dan McCarty, his successor as Gov.   Sponsored legislation
penalizing gambling agents who failed to pay taxes revealing
their occupation; laws to exclude cattle from highways;
reforestation program; expansion of turnpike system;
assistance to citrus industry; and promotion of tourist industry.   Favored an anti-Ku Klux Klan bill which the
legislature refused to pass.   Gained natl. attention during
tenure by refusal to respond to subpoena to testify before
U.S. Sen. Kefauver's Crime Investigation Commt. on matters
concerning org. crime and its relation to govt.   Resumed
practice of law after tenure as Gov.   Defeated as cand. for
Dem. nom. for Gov. in 1956.   Mbr., Amer. Legion; V.F.W.;
AMVETS; Elks; Masons; Theta Chi.   Baptist.   Author of two
books on oratory and politics, and was a newspaper columnist,
1940-1948.   m. three times.   Third wife was Barbara Jeanne
Manning.   D. Sept. 23, 1973.

   McCARTY, DAN(IEL THOMAS) (1953).   b. Jan. 18, 1912 at
Fort Pierce, Fla.   s. of Daniel T. and Frances (Florence?)
Lardner (Moore) McC.   Father was a pineapple and orange
grower.   Attd. local pub. schools and the Univ. of Fla.,
from which he received a B.S. degree in 1934.   Worked in
groves and packing houses.   Org. the Indian River Citrus
Assoc., a cooperative packing and marketing firm.   Served
as its treas. until 1945, and thereafter as pres. until
1949, when he sold his interest.   From 1939 to 1953 was also
pres. of Circle M. Ranch, Inc., a family-owned corp. in
St. Lucie Co., Fla.   Active in devel. of improved breeds of
cattle.   Involved in other bus. enterprises at Fort Pierce.
Mbr. of Fla. House, 1937-1943, serving as Speaker during
last term.   As col. in ROTC reserves, was called into
active service in 1941 at beginning of World War II.   Served
overseas in Africa and Europe.   Was with Seventh Army on
D-day in France.   Recipient of Legion of Merit, Croix de
guerre, Bronze Star and Purple Heart decorations.   Defeated
as cand. for Dem. nom. for Gov. in 1948, losing in a run-
off primary.   Nom. and el. Gov. as Dem. in 1952.   Advocated
advancement of bldg. program at state institutions; setting
up of a system of centralized purchasing; opposed

exploitation of Everglades Park by oil firms. Mbr., Amer.
Legion; V.F.W.; Masons (O.E.S.); I.O.O.F.; Elks; Moose;
Rotary; various social clubs. Episcopalian. Active in
numerous community, school and welfare orgs. m. in 1940 to
Olie Lela Brown, of Fort Pierce. Two s.; one d. Suffered
heart attack about two months after inauguration as Gov.
D. at Tallahassee, Sept. 28, 1953 while still in office.
Bur. in family plot at Fort Pierce, Fla.

JOHNS, CHARLEY (EUGENE) (1953-1955). b. Feb. 27, 1905
at Starke, Fla. s. of Everett E. and Annie Elizabeth
(Pettit) J. Father was killed while on duty as a deputy
sheriff in Nassau Co. Worked at various occupations, including railroad conductor, ins. salesman, ice bus. Attd.
the Univ. of Fla. Mbr. of Fla. House, 1935-1937 and of Fla.
Senate, 1938-1965. Was Pres. of Senate in 1953 when Gov.
McCarty died in office. Succeeded to office of Gov. in
Sept., 1953 and served until Jan., 1955, when a regularly
chosen successor assumed office. Defeated as cand. for Dem.
nom. for Gov. in a run-off primary in 1954, although he
received a plurality in the first primary. Returned to Fla.
Senate thereafter. As Gov., promoted highway constr. program and abolition of tolls on the Overseas Highway. Engaged in ins. bus. at Starke. Pres. of County State Bank
at Starke, from 1957 onward. Mbr., O.R.C.; B.R.T.; Elks;
Masons (Shriner); various bus. orgs. Baptist. m. in 1927
to Thelma Brinson. One s.; one d.

COLLINS, T(HOMAS) LEROY (1955-1961). b. Mar. 10, 1909
at Tallahassee, Fla. s. of Marvin H. and Mattie (Brandon)
C. Father operated a grocery bus. Attd. pub. schools;
Eastman School of Bus., at Poughkeepsie, N.Y., 1928-1929;
and Cumberland Univ., from which he received a law degree
in 1931. Worked at various jobs while attending college.
Established law practice at Tallahassee. In 1934 at age 25
was el. to Fla. House and continued in office for the next
two terms. El. to Fla. Senate in 1940, continuing therein
for 12 years except for period of 1944-1945 when he served
in U.S. Navy. Was lieut. when discharged from the Navy.
Achieved reputation in Senate as good debater and effective
legislator. Nom. and el. Gov. as Dem. in 1954 to fill last
two years of Gov. McCarty's term, defeating incumbent Gov.
Johns in Dem. run-off primary. Reel. for full term in 1956,
having received a popular majority in first Dem. primary in
which former Gov. Warren was a contestant. Promoted holding of conv. to revise the state const.; legislative
reapportionment; creating of a State Devel. Commn; and encouragement of diversification of indus., including devel.

of nuclear energy. Ch. of So. Govs.' Conf. in 1957 and of
Natl. Govs. Conf., 1958. Led delegation of Amer. Govs. to
Russia on a good-will tour in 1959. Ch. of So. Regional Bd.
of Educ., 1955-1957. Permanent ch. of commt. on Goals for
Higher Educ. in South, 1961-1962; Dir. of Community
Relations Service, U.S. Dept. of Commerce, 1964-1965; Under-
Sect., Dept. of Commerce, 1965-1966; pres., Natl. Assoc. of
Broadcasters, 1961-1964. Defeated as Dem. nominee for U.S.
Senate in 1968. Mbr., I.O.O.F.; Masons; Elks; various clubs
and professional orgs. Trustee of Randolph-Macon Coll.
Episcopalian. Hon. degrees from numerous So. colleges and
universities. m. in 1932 to Mary Call Darby, of
Tallahassee, a direct descendant of R. K. Call, the last
Terr. Gov. of Fla. Two s.; two d.

   BRYANT, C(ECIL) FARRIS (1961-1965). b. July 26, 1914
at Ocala, Fla. s. of Charles Cecil and Lila Margaret
(Farris) B. Father was an accountant. Attd. local pub.
schools; Emory Univ., 1931-1932; the Univ. of Fla., from
which he received a law degree in 1938. Worked for two
years in State Comptroller's office. Began law practice at
Ocala in 1940. Became interested in politics through his
uncle, who was Speaker of Fla. House. Mbr. of Fla. House,
1942-1943. Resigned to enter U.S. Navy in 1943, serving as
lieut. on anti-submarine vessels. Saw action in Atlantic,
Mediterranean and Pac. areas. Continued in USNR as lieut.
after World War II. Mbr. of Fla. House, 1946-1956, being
chosen Speaker in 1953. Recipient of various citations and
awards for outstanding legislative service. Defeated as
cand. for Dem. nom. for Gov. in 1956; but won nom. for that
office in a run-off primary in 1960 and was el. Advocated
legislative re-apportionment; constl. revision; revision of
tax system for pub. utilities; and a welfare lien law. Was
opposed to integration rulings of U.S. Supreme Ct., and
sought to resist them. Delegate to Dem. natl. convs. in
1952, 1960, 1964 and 1968, serving as ch. of Fla. delegations in 1952 and 1960. Refused to endorse the Dem. party's
cand. for Pres. of U.S. in 1960 as well as the Dem. party
platform. Dir. of U.S. Office of Emergency Planning, 1966-
1967. Defeated in run-off primary for Dem. nom. for U.S.
Senate seat in 1970. Ch. of bd. of dir. of Voyagers Life
Ins. Co., 1965 and of Eagles Life Ins. Co., 1967. Pres. of
Natl. Life Ins. Co. of Fla., 1968. Mbr., Masons (Shriner);
Elks; Amer. Legion; V.F.W.; Rotary; Navy League; various
fraternities and professional legal orgs. Hon. degrees
from four colleges and universities. Methodist. Co-author,
Government and Politics in Florida. m. in 1940 to Julia
Burnett, of Madison, Fla. Three d.

BURNS, (WILLIAM) HAYDON (1965-1967).   b. March 17, 1912
at Louisville, Ky.   During youth moved with parents to
Jacksonville, Fla., where he attd. pub. schools.   Attd.
Babson Bus. Coll., in Mass. for a time, but did not graduate.
Engaged in bus. consultant and pub. relations work in Jacksonville.   El. mayor of that city in 1949, serving in office
until 1965.   In 1964 was confronted by street demonstrations
against continuance of segregation practices in places of
pub. accommodation.   Supported police in taking strong stand
against demonstrators, giving rise to litigation concerning
actions taken.   Unsuccessful as cand. for Dem. nom. for Gov.
in 1960.   Was again a cand. in 1964, and won nom. in run-off
primary against Mayor Robt. High, of Miami.   In his primary
campaign, expressed opposition to the pending U.S. Civil
Rights bill, while his opponent endorsed it.   Was el. for a
two-year term in Nov. under a spec. arrangement designed to
cause gubernatorial elections to occur thereafter in non-
pres. election years.   Pursued a moderate course during term
on matters of race relations, appointing a number of Black
citizens to govtl. posts.   Sought re-nom. in 1966 for a
four-year term, but lost in Dem. run-off primary to Mayor
High, although being the recipient of a plurality in the
first primary.   Resumed bus. activities thereafter.

KIRK, CLAUDE ROY, Jr. (1967-1971).   b. Jan. 7, 1926 at
San Bernardino, Calif.   s. of Claude R., Sr. and Sarah
Myrtle (McClure) K.   Both parents were employed as railroad
clerks.   Family moved to suburban Chicago area when son was
a youth, where he attd. pub. schools.   Family moved later to
Montgomery, Ala., where father was employed as a salesman.
Enlisted in U.S. Marine Corps during World War II, serving
with an artillery unit.   Held commn. as lieut. when discharged.   Attd. Emory Univ. and later, Duke Univ., from
which he was grad.   Received law degree from the Univ. of
Ala. in 1949.   Employed as ins. salesman and as instructor
in ju jitsu for Ala. Highway Patrol during period of law
school study.   Recalled to U.S. mil. duty, 1950-1952, during
Korean War.   Awarded Air Medal of Marine Corps.   Engaged as
salesman of ins. and bldg. supplies.   In 1956 formed Amer.
Heritage Life Ins. Co., in Jacksonville, and later, an investment firm, both of which prospered.   During 1960 pres.
campaign switched party affiliation from Dem. to Rep.   Defeated as Rep. cand. for U.S. Senate seat in 1964.   Nom. as
Rep. cand. for Gov. in 1966.   Campaigned against ultra-
liberal element and desegregationists.   Was el., becoming
the first Rep. Gov. of Fla. since the 1870s.   Admin. was
characterized by controversies with the legislature, which

was dominated by opposition party. Much of the press and
some other executives in high office in state govt. also
were generally hostile. During admin., a reapportionment
plan for legislature was required by ct. order to be set up.
In a spec. election in March, 1967, Rep. party candidates,
aided by campaign efforts by Gov., made extensive gains,
giving the State the foundation for a two-party system. Refused invitation of Gov. Wallace, of Ala., to attend a conf.
of Govs. to map plan for resistance against integration of
schools and pub. facilities. Delegate to Rep. natl. conv.
in 1968, where he was prominently mentioned as possible
nominee for Vice Pres. of U.S. Nom. for Gov. again in 1970,
but was defeated in gen. election. m. three times. First
wife, Sarah Stokes, whom he married in 1947 and from whom he
was divorced in 1950, was mother of two d. Second wife,
whom he married in 1951, was mother of twin sons. His
marriage to her so soon after divorce led to his being
temporarily ex-communicated by his church (Episcopal).
Divorced second wife in 1966, and in 1967 m. to Erika
Mattfeld, a divorcee of German birth. Hon. degree from
Rollins College.

   ASKEW, REUBIN O'DONOVAN (1971-1979). b. Sept. 11,
1928 at Muskogee, Okla. Youngest of six children of Leo
Goldberg and Alberta (O'Donovan) A. Father was an
itinerant carpenter who abandoned family shortly after
youngest son's birth. Mother moved with family to Pensacola,
Fla. in 1937, where she provided support for them by working as a waitress, seamstress, and hotel maid. Children
assisted with odd jobs as soon as they were old enough to
help. Attd. local schools. Served with U.S. Army, 1946-
1948. Attd. Fla. State Univ., graduating with a law degree
in 1956. Had formed a dislike for segregation practices
through experiences in the Army and as a college student.
Ed. of Fla. Law Review during last year of attendance at
Fla. State Univ. Began law practice at Pensacola, becoming
asst. solicitor for Escambia Co., 1956-1958. Mbr. of Fla.
House, 1959-1963 and of Fla. Senate, 1963-1971. Became
Pres. pro tem of Senate. Resisted efforts to close pub.
schools as protest action against court-ordered desegregation. Nom. and el. Gov. as Dem. in 1970, defeating incumbent Gov. Kirk. Reel. in 1974. Campaigned on foot in many
areas of State, furthering image of a man close to the people. Pursued a moderately liberal course as Gov. on issues
of the day. Called legislature into spec. session at
beginning of first term to submit a constl. amdt. permitting
adoption of a 5 per cent profits tax, which was submitted,
approved, and implemented. Advanced integration of state

pub. employment; secured adoption of penal and jud. reforms;
made advancements in state planning; and promoted bond
issue for environmental improvements. Keynote speaker at
1972 Dem. natl. conv. Apptd. by Pres. Carter as Spec. Repr.
for U.S. Trade Negotiations in Aug., 1979. Mbr., Masons;
Rotary; Amer. Legion; professional legal orgs. Presbyterian. m. to Donna Lou Harper in 1956. Two children.

BULLOCH, ARCHIBALD (1776-1777). b. circa 1730 at
Charleston, S.C. s. of James and Jean (Strobo) B. Received
classical educ. locally. Studied law and was admitted to
bar. Served as lieut. in S.C. militia regiment in 1757.
Moved to Savannah, Ga. in 1762 (?). Had an active role in
early resistance to British policies leading up to the Rev.
War. Mbr. of Ga. Provincial Assembly, serving as its
Speaker in 1772. Pres. of Ga. Provincial Cong. in 1775 and
1776, which ousted colonial Gov. Wright, and which became
the de facto govt. of the Province in early stages of Rev.
War. Delegate to Contl. Cong. in 1775 and 1776. Signed
Dec. of Indep. Led a company which cleared Tybee Island of
British control. El. as first Pres. and Commdr.-in-Chief
of Ga. under the temp. plan of govt. of 1776, serving in
that capacity from June 20, 1776 to Feb. 22, 1777. m. in
1764 to Mary de Veaux. Father of Wm. Bulloch, who became
a mbr. of U.S. Senate from Ga. in 1813, and was the great-
great-grandfather of Theodore Roosevelt, Gov. of N.Y. and
Pres. of U.S. (q.v.). D. at Savannah, Ga., on Feb. 22,
1777, when a permanent const. for the State was about to be
put into operation. Bur. in Colonial Cem. there.

GWINNETT, BUTTON (1777). b. in 1732 (1735?) in Down
Heatherly, Gloucestershire, England. s. of Samuel and Anne
(Emes) G. Received a classical educ. and went into merc.
pursuits at Bristol, England. Moved to Charleston, S.C. in
1760s and in 1765 settled in Savannah, Ga., where he engaged in trading. Mbr. of Ga. Provincial Assembly, 1769.
In 1770 acquired a plantation on St. Catherine Island, and
engaged in planting. Mbr. of Ga. Provincial Cong., 1776-
1777, serving as Speaker. Delegate from Ga. to the Contl.
Cong. in 1776 and 1777, and was a signer of the Dec. of
Indep. Became Acting Pres. and Commdr.-in-Chief of Ga.
following death of Pres. Bullock in Feb., 1777. Served in
that capacity for approximately two months pending adoption
and implementation of first permanent const. for Ga. Defeated as cand. for the office of Gov. under the const. of
1777, when it was in process of being implemented. Engaged
in a duel near Savannah with Gen. McIntosh over political
differences on May 16, 1777, and died three days later from
wounds received in the duel. m. in 1757 to Ann Bourne.
Bur. (probably) in Old Colonial Cem. (later known as
Colonial Park) there.

TREUTLEN (TREUTLIN?), JOHN (ADAM) (1777-1778). b. in
1726 (?) in Austria. Emigrated to Ga. after reaching manhood and engaged in agri. pursuits in St. Matthews Parish.
Supported resistance movement against British policies.

Mbr. of Ga. Provincial Cong. in early 1775 from Parish of
St. Andrews in Savannah area. El. as first Gov. of Ga.
when a permanent const. went into effect in 1777, defeating
Button Gwinnett for the office. Served until Jan., 1778.
D. in 1782. Circumstances of death uncertain, but believed
to have been killed in an ambush by Tory guerillas near
Orangeburg, S.C.

HOUSTON (HOUSTOUN?), JOHN (1778-1779; 1784-1785). b.
Aug. 31, 1744 at Waynesboro, Ga. s. of Sir Patrick Houston,
bart., who had come to Ga. with Gen. Oglethorpe in 1733 and
had served the Colony as register of grants and receiver of
quit rents. Received liberal educ. Studied law and began
practice in Savannah. Helped org. the "Sons of Liberty" to
oppose British policies in 1774, calling and presiding over
its first meeting. Mbr. of Ga. Provincial Cong. in 1775
that ousted Provincial Gov. Wright. Delegate to Contl.
Cong. in 1775-1777. Would have been a signer of the Dec.
of Indep., but had been called home to oppose local opponents of independence at the time of adoption and signing.
Mbr. of Ga. Exec. Council in 1777 under first Ga. const.
El. Gov. in Jan., 1778. During that year helped lead unsuccessful expedition against British in Fla. Savannah was
captured by the British in Dec., 1778, resulting in the
granting of extraordinary powers to the Gov. by the legislature. Delegate to the Contl. Cong. from Ga. in 1779.
Chosen Gov. again by the Assembly in 1784. During admin.,
was dissenting mbr. of commn. set up to adjust boundary
dispute with S.C. Chief Justice of Ga., 1786, and superior
ct. judge from Chatham Co., 1792. Unsuccessful cand. for
Gov. again in 1787. Mayor of Savannah, 1789-1790. D. at
his home, "White Bluff", near Savannah, July 20, 1796.

WEREAT, JOHN (1779-1780). b. in 1730 (?) in England.
Emigrated to Ga. in early manhood and became an early advocate of resistance to British colonial policies. Mbr. of
Ga. Provincial Cong. in 1775, and served as presiding
officer of that body in 1776. British occupation of
Savannah in Dec., 1778, prevented the Assembly from meeting
to choose a successor to Gov. Houston in Jan., 1779. The
capital of the State was transferred temporarily to Augusta,
where some mbrs. of the Exec. Council met. They assumed to
exercise authority on a de facto basis in the absence of a
duly elected Gov. Presiding officers of the group in the
early part of 1779 were Wm. Glasscock and Seth J. Cuthbert.
When W. was chosen as presiding officer of this group in
Aug., 1779, he laid claim to the office of Gov. by right of
succession in the absence of a duly el. Gov. His authority

to do so was challenged, however, by other elements of the
Council and the Assembly, who charged the Wereat faction
with being sympathetic with the Tory (British Loyalist) element in the State and of contemplating restoration of
British rule. Continued to maintain his claim to the
office of Gov., however, while denying the charges against
his faction, until a new Assembly met and chose a Gov. in
1780. Became chief judge of superior cts. in 1781. In
1782, aided distressed families in the region west of
Augusta with food and supplies out of his own wealth.
Served as commnr. to negotiate with Fla. authorities in
1783, and again in 1788, over border disturbances. Pres.
of Ga. conv. that ratified U.S. Const. in 1788. D. at his
home in Bryan Co., Jan. 27, 1799.

WALTON, GEORGE (1779-1780; 1789). b. _circa_ 1741
(1750?) near Farmville, Cumberland Co., Va. s. of Robt.
and Sally (Mary?) (Hughes) W. Received a common school
educ. Apprenticed to learn carpenter trade, but continued
studies on his own initiative at night. Moved to Savannah,
Ga. in 1769. Studied law, was admitted to the bar in 1774,
and began practice in Savannah. Was active in resistance
movement against British colonial policies. Sect. of the
Ga. Provincial Cong. in 1775. Mbr. of Ga. Council of
Safety, serving as pres. of that body in Dec., 1775. Delegate to Contl. Cong., 1776-1778; 1780-1781; 1787-1788.
Signed the Dec. of Indep. While serving as col. of a Ga.
regiment was wounded and captured in 1778 at the siege of
Savannah. Was exchanged in Sept., 1779, and soon afterward
he was designated Gov. by a faction of the Assembly opposed
to the claim of J. Wereat to the office, after the full
Assembly had been unable to meet and elect a Gov. in Jan.,
1779. When a new Assembly met in 1780 it chose Richard
Howley, a mbr. of Walton's faction, as Gov. Became chief
judge of Ga. superior cts. in his dist., 1783-1786. Served
as U.S. commnr. to deal with Cherokee Indian tribes in Pa.
in 1777 and in Tenn. in 1783. Commnr. for settlement of
Ga.-S.C. boundary in 1786. Apptd. as delegate to U.S.
Constl. Conv. of 1787, but did not attend sessions. Mbr.,
Ga. constl. conv. of 1789. Pres. elector in first pres.
election under the U.S. Const. Chosen Gov. again in 1789,
serving most of the year. Became a superior ct. judge in
1790, and in 1793, chief judge of the superior cts. of his
dist. Apptd. to vacancy in U.S. Senate in Nov., 1795,
serving until a successor was chosen in Feb., 1796. Later
served two terms as mbr. of Ga. legislature. From 1799 until his death, again served as a judge. Trustee of
Richmond Acad. and of the Univ. of Ga. m. in 1775 to

Dorothy Camber. Two children. D. at his home, "Meadow
Garden", near Augusta, Feb. 2, 1804. Bur. in Rosney Cem.
there, but was re-interred in 1848 near monument at the
courthouse in Augusta.

HOWLEY, RICHARD (1780). b. in 1740 (?) in Liberty Co.,
Ga. Received a liberal academic educ. Studied law and was
admitted to bar. Engaged in law practice and also engaged
in rice growing on plantation in St. John's Parish. Mbr.
of Ga. Assembly in 1779-1783. Chosen Gov. in Jan., 1780.
Much of State was under British control at the time and he,
along with other State officials, was forced to flee,
narrowly escaping capture by British on one occasion.
Apptd. as delegate to Contl. Cong. in Feb., 1780, and continued in that office during 1781. During 1780 while serving in Contl. Cong. he returned to the State for only brief
periods, and the exercise of exec. control was assumed by
the Council Pres. and other mbrs. of the Exec. Council,
from time to time. Active in Contl. Cong. in seeking aid
for Ga. in combatting British. Returned to Sunbury, Ga. in
1782, where he resumed law practice. Chief judge of Ga.
superior cts. from Oct., 1782 to Jan., 1783. Moved to
Savannah, where he died in Dec., 1784.

HEARD, STEPHEN (1780). Believed to have been born
circa 1740 in Va. (possibly Ireland). s. of John H., who
was a native of Ireland. Came with father to Ga. during
course of the last colonial war with France, in which he
had participated as a soldier. Settled in Wilkes Co. circa
1773. After Rev. War began, entered the armed forces of
State under Col. Clarke, participating in engagements in
Western Ga. In Feb., 1780, after Gov. Howley left Ga. to
attend Cont. Cong., conditions in the State were chaotic
because of occupation of much of the State by British
forces and because of factional strife among supporters of
the Rev. cause. During Howley's absences for most of 1780
and from Jan. to August, 1781, there having been no new
Gov. chosen at the beginning of 1781, exec. authority was
exercised nominally by various mbrs. of the Exec. Council.
From Feb. to Aug., 1780, H., as Pres. of the Council, served in this capacity. Other mbrs. of the Council who, as
presiding officers thereof, acted in a similar ex officio
capacity for brief periods in 1780, were George Wells and
Humphrey Wells, and in 1781, Myrick Davies. H. resumed
farming after the end of the war. Served as co. judge. m.
first to a Miss Germany, who died of exposure caused by
flight from enemy forces. m. later to Elizabeth Darden.
One s. D. at his home in Wilkes Co., Nov. 15, 1815.

BROWNSON, NATHAN (1781-1782). b. May 14, 1742 at
Woodbury, Conn. Grad. from Yale in 1761. Studied med.,
and practiced med. at Woodbury for short time. In 1764
moved to Liberty Co., Ga., where he became the first physician to practice med. in that vicinity. During the Rev.
War served as surgeon in a Ga. brigade. Mbr. of Ga. Provincial Cong. in 1775. Delegate from Ga. to Contl. Cong.
in 1776-1778 and in 1783. Mbr. of Ga. Assembly in 1781,
serving as Speaker. In August, 1781, was chosen Gov. for
the remainder of term, no election of a Gov. having been
made in Jan. of that year. Mbr. of Ga. Assembly in 1788,
again serving as Speaker. Delegate to Ga. conv. that ratified U.S. Const. in 1788, and mbr. of Ga. constl. conv. of
1789. Mbr. of Ga. Senate, 1789-1791, serving as Pres. of
that body. D. Nov. 6, 1796, at his plantation near
Riceboro, Ga. Bur. in Old Midway Cem. there.

MARTIN, JOHN (1782-1783). b. in 1730 in R.I. In 1761
became port naval officer at Sunbury, Ga. Became a supporter of Rev. War in 1775 as a mbr. of Provincial Cong. from
Savannah, and was apptd. to the Council of Safety. Served
during the Rev. War as capt. of an artillery company. Was
later promoted to lieut. col. in a Ga. brigade. Mbr. of
the Ga. Assembly from Chatham Co., and in Jan., 1782, was
chosen Gov. During admin., Savannah was freed from British
occupation. While in office found it necessary to appeal
to the legislature for relief for his family, who were destitute. His appeal was successful. Advocated a policy of
reconciliation with Loyalist element at the end of the war.
Mbr. of bd. of commnrs. apptd. to negotiate treaty with the
Cherokee Indians in 1783. Treas. of Ga. in 1783. D. Jan.
(?), 1786.

HALL, LYMAN (1783-1784). b. April 12, 1724 in
Wallingford, Conn. s. of John and Mary (Street) H. Grad.
from Yale in 1747. Studied theology and was a minister for
two years in Conn. parishes. Decided to leave ministry,
studied med., and began med. practice in Wallingford.
Moved to Dorchester, S.C. in 1752, and a few years later to
Sunbury, in Liberty Co., Ga., where he practiced med. and
was also a rice planter. Mbr. of Provincial Cong. in 1774
and 1775, and became an opponent of British colonial policies. In 1775 was apptd. as a delegate to the Contl. Cong.
from St. John's Parish. Continued to serve in the Contl.
Cong. until 1778. Also was a mbr. of Cong. in 1780. Used
influence to obtain additional representation from Ga. to
the Cong. Signed the Dec. of Indep. In 1778 was forced to

flee with family from Ga. by British forces, and his property was confiscated. Resided in the North until 1782,
when he returned to Savannah, Ga. and resumed med. practice.
Chosen Gov. in Jan., 1783 by the legislature. After one
year in office served as judge in a lower ct. in Chatham
Co. Was an early advocate of using funds from pub. land
sales for pub. educ. purposes. Moved to Burke Co., where
he continued to reside until his death. m. first to
Abigail Burr in 1752. Second wife was Mary Osborn. One s.
D. Oct. 19, 1790. Bur. on his plantation near Shell Bluff,
in Burke Co. Body re-interred in 1848 near his monument in
courthouse yard in Augusta, Ga.

HOUSTON (HOUSTOUN?), JOHN (1784-1785). See above,
1778-1779.

ELBERT, SAMUEL (1785-1786). b. in 1740 (1743?) in
Prince William Parish, S.C. Became an orphan early in life.
As a young man moved to Savannah, Ga., where he engaged in
merc. pursuits. Capt. of militia company in 1774. In 1775
was a mbr. of Ga. Council of Safety. Became a lieut. col.
and later, col. in Contl. Army. Commdr. of an expeditionary force against British in East Florida in 1777. Participated in a number of engagements and was captured by the
British in Mar., 1779, at Briar Creek, S.C. Was later exchanged, and served as brig. gen. under Gen. Washington in
closing years of the Rev. War. Chosen Gov. of Ga. in 1785
by the legislature. After one-year term as Gov. continued
to serve in militia forces of the State, with rank of major
gen. Sheriff of Chatham Co. m. to Elizabeth Rae. Six
children. Mbr. and vice pres. of Ga. chapter of Soc. of
Cincinnati. Grand Master of Masonic Order in Ga. D. at
Savannah, Nov. 1, 1788.

TELFAIR, EDWARD (1786-1787; 1789-1793). b. in 1735 at
"Town Head", Kirkendbright, Scotland. Attd. grammar school
there. Came to Amer. as agent of a commercial house circa
1758. Resided for a time in Va., then in Halifax, N.C.
Established a branch of his bus. at Savannah, Ga. in 1766.
Engaged in commercial activities there; also set up a sawmill and acquired land in Burke Co. and engaged in agri.
pursuits. Mbr. of "Sons of Liberty" in 1774, and was
active as mbr. of commt. that sought to raise funds for
those suffering from the effects of Boston Port Bill. Was
one of the leaders in armed resistance to colonial Gov.
Wright, and participated in seizure of British magazine in
Savannah harbor in 1775. Mbr. of Ga. Council of Safety in
1775-1776. Delegate to Provincial Cong. that drew up a

temp. plan of govt. for Ga. in 1776. Delegate to the Contl.
Cong. in 1778-1782, 1784-1785 and 1788-1789, but did not
take seat in 1784 and 1788. In 1783 served as one of the
commnrs. to negotiate treaty with Cherokee Indians; also
served as agent of Ga. for determination of northern boundary of the State. Prospered in bus. and as planter after
the end of Rev. War. Chosen Gov. in 1786, serving for a
year. Chosen Gov. again in 1789 and continued in office
for succeeding two-year term. Mbr. of Ga. conv. that ratified U.S. Const. in 1788. As Gov., in May, 1791, entertained Pres. Washington at his home in Savannah during the
course of Washington's tour of the So. States. m. in 1774
to Sally Gibbons. Six children. D. at Savannah, Sept. 17,
1807. Bur. in Bonaventure Cem. there. His d. gave his
family mansion, "The Grove", to the city for an art museum
after his death. A son, Thomas, became a mbr. of the U.S.
House from Ga. in 1813-1817.

MATHEWS, GEORGE (1787-1788; 1793-1795). b. Aug. 30,
(Sept. 10?), 1739 in Augusta Co., Va. Father, John M., who
was a native of Ireland, had emigrated to Va. two years before son was born. Served as capt. in volunteer company in
1757 during the French and Indian War. Continued in mil.
service of Va. thereafter and fought in battle against
Indians at Point Pleasant, in Western Va., in 1774. Served
under Gen. Washington during early part of Rev. War. Participated in the Battles of Brandywine and Germantown. Was
wounded and captured in a later engagement. Exchanged in
Dec., 1781 and later served as col. of a regiment under
Gen. Greene in the Carolinas. Acquired plantation at
Goose Pond on the Broad River in Oglethorpe Co., Ga. in
1785. Chosen Gov. of Ga. in 1787. El. to U.S. House in
1788, serving as mbr. of First Cong. under the U.S. Const.,
1789-1791. Chosen Gov. again in 1793 for a two-year term.
During admin., the Yazoo Lands Act for disposal of pub.
lands in Western Ga. became law. The Act later became the
basis for charges of extensive frauds, and in consequence
his pub. career was adversely affected. His nom. by Pres.
John Adams to become Gov. of the newly-formed Terr. of
Miss. had to be withdrawn from the Senate. In 1811, as a
brig. gen., led an expedition into West Fla., and was em-
powered as a commnr. to negotiate a treaty for its acquisition from Spain. He did so, but Pres. Madison disavowed
the treaty. Married three times. m. first to a Miss Woods.
Second wife was a widow, Mrs. Reed. Third wife was a widow,
Mrs. Flowers. Six children. D. at Augusta, Aug. 30, 1812.
Bur. in St. Paul's churchyard there.

HANDLEY, GEORGE (1788-1789). b. Feb. 9, 1752 in
Sheffield, Yorkshire, England. s. of Thomas Handley. Emigrated to Savannah, Ga. in May, 1775. Became a supporter
of the Amer. Rev. cause, and became a capt., later a lieut.
col., in the Contl. Army in 1776. Participated in a number
of engagements in Ga. and S.C. during the course of the
Rev. War. Was captured and held prisoner for a time at
Charleston, S.C. After his release, was el. sheriff of
Richmond Co., where he had established his residence. Mbr.
of Ga. Assembly from Richmond Co. In 1785-1786 served as a
commnr. to the proposed State of Franklin to deal with matters of mutual concern of Ga. and the proposed State.
Apptd. Inspector Gen. of Ga. militia in 1787. Chosen Gov.
of Ga. in 1788 after James Jackson (q.v.) had been chosen,
but had declined the office. Apptd. by Pres. Washington in
1789 as collector of U.S. revenues at the port of Brunswick,
Ga., a position he held until his death. m. to Sarah Howe,
a niece of Gov. Elbert, of Ga. (q.v.). D. at Rae Hall, the
home of a friend, Sept. 17, 1793.

WALTON, GEORGE (1789). See above, 1779-1780.

TELFAIR, EDWARD (1789-1793). See above, 1786-1787.

MATHEWS, GEORGE (1793-1795). See above, 1787-1788.

IRWIN, JARED (1796-1798; 1806-1809). b. in 1750
(1751?) in Mecklenburg Co., N.C. In his early manhood settled on plantation in Burke Co., Ga. During Rev. War
served in Ga. militia forces, seeing action on frontier in
Western Ga. against Creek Indians. In 1788 moved to a
plantation in Washington Co., Ga. Mbr. of state constl.
conv. in 1789 and was el. to lower House of legislature the
next year. Mbr. of constl. conv. in 1795. Chosen Gov. in
1796. During admin., the Yazoo Lands Act was rescinded and
state lands sold under it recovered. Pres. of state conv.
in 1798 that revised state const. Served in militia as
brig. gen. El. to Ga. Senate and as Pres. of that body
succeeded to office of Gov. in Sept., 1806 when Gov.
Milledge resigned. Was then chosen Gov. for the succeeding
regular term. Later served as mbr. of Ga. Senate, acting
as presiding officer of that body. D. at his plantation,
"Union Hill", in Washington Co. on March 1, 1818.

JACKSON, JAMES (1798-1801). b. Sept. 21, 1757 in
Moreton-Hampstead, Devonshire, England. s. of James and
Mary (Webber) J. Emigrated to Savannah, Ga. in 1772, hav-
ing earlier formed a friendship in England with John Wereat,

later a claimant of office of Gov. of Ga. (q.v.). Studied
law at Savannah. Joined Amer. mil. forces in 1775, rising
to rank of col. during the Rev. War. Later held rank of
brig. gen. Was wounded in action. Served as ct. clerk,
1776-1777. Mbr. of conv. that framed first permanent const.
for Ga. in 1777. In 1778 was charged with entertaining
Loyalist sympathies and, along with some friends, came near
to being executed as a spy by Amer. forces. Fought several
duels growing out of these charges. Commanded Amer. forces
that accepted surrender of Savannah from the British in
1782. Was presented a house by the Ga. Assembly for services during the Rev. War. Chosen Gov. in 1788, but declined the office, citing his youth and inexperience as
reason (he was 30 years old at the time). Pres. elector in
the first pres. election under the U.S. Const. El. to seat
in U.S. House in 1788, serving in the First Cong. under the
Const. Defeated for succeeding term in 1790 in a heated
contest with Gen. Anthony Wayne, an election that was later
voided by the House by margin of one vote in 1792. Mbr. of
U.S. Senate, 1793-1795. Resigned seat in Senate to return
to Ga. legislature to participate in struggle for rescind-
ing the Yazoo Lands Act, in which effort he was successful.
Pres. elector for Jefferson and Clinton in 1796. Chosen
Gov. of Ga. in 1798 and continued in office by reel. until
1801, when he resigned after having been el. to U.S. Senate
again. m. to Mary Charlotte Young. Five children. Mbr.
of Masonic order, serving as Grand Master in Ga., 1786-
1789. Hon. mbr. of Soc. of Cincinnati. D. in Washington,
March 19, 1806, while still a mbr. of U.S. Senate. Bur. in
Congressional Cem. there. A son, Jabez, and a grandson,
James, became mbrs. of U.S. House from Ga. in 1835 and
1857, respectively.

EMANUEL, DAVID (1801). b. in 1744 (1742?). Place of
birth unknown. Circa 1768 established residence on plantation in Burke Co., Ga. Active in political movements that
culminated in Rev. War. During the course of the war was
captured by enemy forces and sentenced to be executed along
with two friends, but managed to escape. After the war
ended was el. to Ga. legislature. Mbr. of spec. commt.
thereof that investigated and exposed Yazoo Lands Act
frauds in 1796. Was serving as Pres. of Ga. Senate when
Gov. Jackson resigned in March, 1801. Succeeded to the
office of Gov. until a successor was el. later that year.
D. at his plantation in Burke Co. in 1810 (1808?).

TATTNALL, JOSEPH (1801-1802). b. in 1764 (1765?) at
"Bonaventure", the family plantation near Savannah, Ga.

Received early educ. at Nassau, in the Bahama Islands.
Both his father and grandfather were Loyalist in sympathies
when the Rev. War began. Was taken by father to England
soon after the war began. Family estates were confiscated
by the pro-Rev. War govt. in Ga. Attd. Eaton Coll. in
England for a time. At age 18 ran away from home in
England and returned to Ga., where he joined Amer. forces
under Gen. Wayne in 1782. Some of his father's lands were
returned to him after the Rev. War ended in recognition of
his services. Was a capt. in Ga. militia, and in 1793 was
col. of regiment engaged in Indian wars on Ga. frontier.
Became a brig. gen. of Ga. militia in 1801. Mbr. of Ga.
legislature, 1795-1796. Apptd. to U.S. Senate to fill vacancy caused by resignation of James Jackson, and served
from 1796 to 1799. Chosen Gov. in 1801 to fill vacancy
caused by resignation of Gov. James Jackson. Served only
about one year before resigning because of poor health.
Established residence at Nassau, in the Bahamas, where he
died on June 6, 1803. Bur. at Bonaventure Cem., Savannah.

MILLEDGE, JOHN (1802-1806). b. in 1757 at Savannah,
Ga. s. of Capt. John and ---- (Robe) M. Father had emigrated to Ga. with Gen. Oglethorpe and had been an important
personage and pub. official in the Province. Received
classical educ. by tutors. Studied law, and began practice
in Savannah. Apptd. King's Atty. at age 18. Participated as
a soldier in early stages of Rev. War. Assisted in seizure
of the powder magazine in Savannah in 1775, the powder
seized later being used to supply Amer. forces at the Battle
of Bunker Hill. Also was present at the arrest leading to
expulsion of the colonial Gov., James Wright. During course
of the Rev. War was nearly hanged as a spy, along with James
Jackson, when taken prisoner by pro-Revolutionary troops.
Took part in a number of engagements in Ga. as mbr. of Amer.
mil. forces. Apptd. Atty. Gen. of Ga. in 1780 at age of 23.
Mbr. of Ga. Assembly in 1782. Mbr. of U.S. House in 1792-
1793; 1795-1799; and 1801-1802. Helped to expose Yazoo Land
Act frauds in 1796, and was one of Ga. commnrs. who negotiated agreement with U.S. in 1802 by which Yazoo lands were
sold by Ga. to U.S. govt. Resigned House seat after being
chosen Gov. in 1802 to complete Gov. Tattnall's term and was
continued in office by reel. until 1806, when he resigned to
take seat in U.S. Senate. Served there until 1809. Was
Pres. pro tem of the Senate when he resigned seat that year
to retire to his plantation near Augusta. Was a close
friend of Thomas Jefferson. Donor of 700 acres of land to
Ga. to help establish the Univ. of Ga. An endowed chair in
Ancient Languages was later established at the Univ. in his

honor. m. first to Martha Galpin. Second wife was Ann
Lamar. Four children. D. at his plantation near Augusta,
Feb. 9, 1818. Bur. in Summerville Cem.

IRWIN, JARED (1806-1809). See above, 1796-1798.

MITCHEL(L), DAVID BRYDIE (BRADIE?) (1809-1813; 1815-
1817). b. Oct. 22, 1766 at Muthill, in Perthshire, Scotland.
In 1783 moved to Ga. to take possession of property willed
to him by his uncle, Dr. David Bradie, who had been taken
prisoner by British forces during the Rev. War and had died
on a prison ship. Studied law under a former colonial Gov.
of Ga., Wm. Stephens. Became clerk of commn. to revise
criminal code of Ga. Solicitor Gen. of Ga. in 1795. Mbr.
of Ga. legislature in 1796, where he assisted in exposure
of Yazoo Lands Act frauds. Major gen. of Ga. militia in
1804. Chosen Gov. in 1809. Chosen Gov. again in 1815.
Supported program of internal improvements and promoted pub.
educl. system. Signed into effect an act prohibiting dueling. Resigned during last year of term to serve as U.S.
commnr. to negotiate a treaty with the Creek Indians. A
treaty was concluded in 1818 under which 1,500,000 acres of
land were ceded to Ga. by the Indians. The Indian agency
post he was directing was terminated in 1821 after charges,
which Pres. Monroe upheld, were made that he was engaged in
smuggling slaves into the area. D. at Milledgeville, Ga.,
April 22, 1837.

EARLY, PETER (1813-1815). b. June 20, 1773 in Madison
Co., Va. s. of Joel Early. Attd. Lexington Acad. and
Coll. of N.J. (Princeton), from which he was grad. in 1792.
Studied law at Philadelphia. Settled in Wilkes Co., Ga. in
1796 and began law practice there. In 1801 moved to Greene
Co. Achieved reputation as brilliant lawyer. El. in 1803
as Jeff. Rep. to U.S. House, and continued to serve therein
until 1807. In 1804 was one of House mgrs. in the impeachment trials of Judge Pickering and of U.S. Supreme Ct.
Justice Samuel Chase. Judge of superior ct. in Ga., 1807-
1813. Chosen Gov. by the legislature in 1813. His diver-
sion of funds to assist U.S. mil. operations in War of 1812
and his veto of a popular proposed debtor law caused him
to fail to be continued in office in 1815. Mbr. of Ga.
Senate, 1815-1817. Was opposed to continuance of African
slave trade. m. in 1793 to Anne Smith. D. at his home
near Greensboro, Ga., Aug. 15, 1817. Bur. near plantation
mansion, but body was later re-interred in City Cem., at
Greensboro.

MITCHELL, DAVID BRYDIE (1815-1817). See above, 1809-1811.

RABUN, WILLIAM (1817-1819). b. April 8, 1771 in Halifax Co., N.C. Father moved with family to Wilkes Co., Ga. in 1785. Later family moved to Hancock Co., Ga. Son received a limited educ., but read widely on his own initiative. El. to lower House of Ga. legislature, and later was a mbr. of Ga. Senate. Was Pres. of Ga. Senate when Gov. Mitchell resigned in March, 1817, and as such succeeded to office of Gov. Completed Mitchell's term and was continued in office for regular term by election. During admin., engaged in bitter exchange with Gen. Andrew Jackson over the destruction of an Indian village on Fla.-Ga. frontier by one of Jackson's subordinates. D. Oct. 24, 1819, some two weeks before expiration of regular term as Gov.

TALBOT(T), MATHEW (MATTHEW?) (1819). b. in 1767 in Va. Early in life moved to a plantation near Washington, in Wilkes Co., Ga. Later moved to Oglethorpe Co. Mbr. of Ga. Assembly from Wilkes Co. a number of terms. Mbr. of Ga. constl. conv. in 1798 from Oglethorpe Co. Mbr. of Ga. Senate, 1808-1823, serving as Pres. of that body, 1818-1823. As Pres. of Senate, succeeded to office of Gov. in Oct., 1819 when Gov. Rabun died. Served last two weeks of Rabun's term. Unsuccessful cand. of Clark faction of Jeff. Rep. party for Gov. in 1823 against George Troup. Nominee of the Clark faction for Gov. again in 1827, but died before the election occurred. D. in Wilkes Co., Sept. 17, 1827.

CLARK(E), JOHN (1819-1823). b. Feb. 28, 1766 in Edgecomb Co., N.C. s. of Gen. Elijah Clark, who achieved distinction as an Amer. officer during the Rev. War. Attd. school in Wake Co., N.C. and at age 16 joined the Contl. Army as a lieut. Participated in engagement at Augusta, Ga. At end of the war, settled on a plantation in Wilkes Co., Ga. on lands received as bounty for mil. services. Retained connection with armed services, in which he attained rank of brig. gen., and later major gen. In 1812 commanded Amer. forces assigned to protect Ga. coast and the southern area of U.S. against the British. Pres. elector in 1816 election. Chosen Gov. in 1819 and was reel. in exciting contest with George Troup in 1821. The cand. backed by Clark to succeed himself as Gov. (Mathew Talbot) was defeated by Troup in 1823, who had become the leader of the States Rts. faction of the Jeff. Rep. party in opposition to Clark. In the 1825 gubernatorial election, the first to be conducted under the direct popular vote system, Troup defeated Clark

by a plurality of some 700 votes out of a total of over
40,000.   In 1827 moved to Florida Terr. after having been
apptd. U.S. Indian affairs agent there by Pres. J. Q. Adams.
m. to Nancy Williamson in 1787.   A son, Edward, succeeded
to the office of Gov. of Tex. in 1861 (q.v.).   D. Oct. 12,
1832, at St. Andrews Bay, Fla. Terr., from yellow fever.

TROUP, GEORGE MICHAEL (McINTOSH?) (1823-1827).   b.
Sept. 8, 1780 at McIntosh's Bluff, on the Tombigbee River,
in what is now Ala., but was then a part of Ga.   s. of
George and Catherine (McIntosh) T.   Father, who was of
English descent, was a merchant and planter.   Mother was a
mbr. of a distinguished early Ga. family of Scottish descent.   Received early schooling by tutors.   Attd. Erasmus
Hall, in Flatbush, N.Y. and the Coll. of N.J. (now
Princeton), from which he was grad. in 1797.   Studied law
and began practice in Savannah in 1799.   Mbr. of Ga. legislature, 1803-1805.   Unsuccessful cand. for U.S. House in
1804, but was el. to that body in 1806, continuing to serve
therein until 1815.   Supported U.S. measures that led eventually to the War of 1812.   Did not seek reel. in 1814, but
retired to plantation in Laurens Co.   El. to U.S. Senate in
1816, serving from March, 1817 to Sept., 1818, when he resigned.   Unsuccessful cand. for Gov. in 1819 and 1821, but
was el. to that office in 1823.   Won el. in 1825 in first
use of direct popular election system in Ga., defeating
former Gov. Clark.   Became leader of a faction of the Jeff.
Rep. party favoring States Rts. in opposition to the Clark
faction which held to views later associated with Whig
party.   Favored state program of internal improvements.   As
Gov., insisted that the State had paramount authority in
Indian lands within State as opposed to U.S. under treaties.
Conflict on this point led ultimately to the ruling by U.S.
Supreme Ct. under Chief Justice Marshall in the Cherokee
Indians case, which upheld natl. authority.   El. again to
U.S. Senate in 1828, serving from March, 1829 to Nov., 1833,
when he resigned.   In the Senate was a staunch defender of
States Rts.   Opposed re-chartering of U.S. Bank.   At
Milledgeville, Ga. conv., favored approval of nullification
action by S.C. in 1832.   Retired to private life in 1833 to
devote attention to mgmt. of plantation.   Favored annexa-
tion of Texas.   Delegate to So. States conv. in 1850, where
he opposed Compromise of 1850.   Nom. for Pres. of U.S. by
So. Rights party of Ala. in 1852, but electors pledged to
him were on the ballot in only Ga. and Ala., and he made no
campaign for the office.   m. in 1803 to Ann St. C.
McCormick, who died in 1804.   m. in 1808 to Ann Carter, of
Va.   Six children.   D. April 26, 1856 in Montgomery Co.,

Ga.   Bur. at "Rosemont", his plantation there.

FORSYTH, JOHN (1827-1829).   b. Oct. 22, 1780 at
Fredericksburg, Va.   s. of Robt. and Fannie (Johnson) F.
Father, who was born in England, had been a Rev. War soldier.   Family moved to Ga. in 1784.   Educ. at Princeton,
graduating from there in 1799.   Studied law, admitted to
bar in 1802, and began practice at Augusta, Ga.   Atty. Gen.
of Ga., 1808-1812.   Mbr. of U.S. House from 1813 to Nov. 23,
1818, when he was apptd. to fill a vacant seat in U.S.
Senate.   Served therein for some three months, resigning to
accept apptmt. from Pres. Monroe as U.S. Minister to Spain.
Served in that capacity until March, 1823, during which
time he assisted in negotiation of treaty with Spain by
which Florida was ceded to U.S.   El. to U.S. House again in
1822 while still in Spain and was reel. in 1824.   El. Gov.
as Jackson (Troup) Dem. in 1827.   Reapptd. to U.S. Senate
in 1829 to fill out an unexpired term.   Served until June,
1834, when he resigned after having been apptd. U.S. Sect.
of State by Pres. Jackson.   Continued to serve in that
office through Pres. Van Buren's admin.   Delegate to anti-
tariff conv. at Milledgeville, Ga. in 1832, where he opposed
nullification action of S.C.   Supported Clay's compromise
plan for resolution of Ga.-U.S. dispute concerning jurisdiction over Indian lands; and Pres. Jackson's removal of
U.S. deposits from U.S. Bank.   m. to Clara Meigs.   Several
children.   D. at Washington, D.C., Oct. 21, 1841.   Bur. in
Congressional Cem. there.

GILMER, GEORGE ROCKINGHAM (1829-1831; 1837-1839).   b.
April 11, 1790 near Lexington, in Wilkes (now Oglethorpe)
Co., Ga.   s. of Thomas Meriwether and Elizabeth (Lewis) G.
Family, of Scottish origin, had emigrated to Va. in 1731.
Parents later settled in Ga. in 1784.   Educ. at Wilson's
School, in Abbeville, S.C., and Dr. Waddell's Georgia Acad.
Was fluent in languages, serving as tutor for younger
brothers.   Did not attend college because of poor health.
Studied law and was admitted to bar.   Served in U.S. Army
as lieut. during War of 1812, and the Creek War.   Returned
to law practice in Oglethorpe Co. in 1818.   Mbr. of Ga.
lower House, 1818-1821.   Mbr. of U.S. House in 1821-1823,
and again in 1827-1829.   In the 1828 election he was declared el., but the election was voided for technical reasons, and he refused to run in the ensuing spec. election.
El. Gov. in 1829 with the support of the States Rts. (Troup)
faction of the Jeff. Rep. party.   During admin., the issue
of State jurisdiction over Indian lands in the State became
complicated, and he took the position that the Indians

should be removed from the State. Defeated for reel. as
Gov. in 1831. El. to U.S. House in 1832. Opposed nullification movement in S.C. Served as States Rts. Whig pres.
elector for White-Tyler ticket in 1836 pres. election. El.
Gov. again as States Rts. Whig in 1837, defeating incumbent
Gov. Schley. Pres. elector for Harrison-Tyler (Whig) party
in 1840. Trustee for Univ. of Ga. from 1836 to 1857, and
left bequests to that institution. Developed interest in
minerals and antiquities in Oglethorpe Co. Published a
book on early history of State, The Georgians, in 1855.
Pres. of Agri. Assoc. of Slave-holding States in 1854. m.
in 1822 to Eliza Frances Grattan. No children. D. at
Lexington, Ga., Nov. 16, 1859. Bur. in Presbyterian Cem.
there.

LUMPKIN, WILSON (1831-1835). b. Jan. 14, 1783 near
Dan River, Pittsylvania Co., Va. s. of John and Lucy
(Hopson) L. Father moved with family to Point Peter, and
later to Lexington, Ga. Received common school educ. As-
sisted father at age 14 as ct. clerk while studying law.
Attd. Univ. of Ga. and was admitted to bar in 1804. Began
practice in Athens, Ga. Later practiced for a time at
Madison, Ala. and Monroe, Ala. Mbr. of Ga. legislature,
1805-1815 and 1819-1821. Mbr. of U.S. House, 1815-1817.
In 1823 was apptd. by Pres. Monroe as commnr. to settle
Ga.-Fla. boundary question. Mbr. of U.S. House again, serving 1827-1831. El. Gov. as cand. of Unionist faction of
Jeff. Rep. party, defeating incumbent Gov. Gilmer. Reel. in
1833. Apptd. commnr. to Cherokee Indian tribe by Pres.
Jackson in 1835. Apptd. to U.S. Senate to fill a vacancy
in 1837, serving until March, 1841. Mbr. of Bd. of Pub.
Works created by Ga. legislature to survey and devel. plans
for system of internal improvements, including railroads.
Delegate to So. Commercial Conv. at Montgomery, Ala. in
1858. Trustee of Univ. of Ga. m. in 1800 to Elizabeth
Walker. m. for second time to Annis Hopkins in 1821.
Twelve children. D. at Athens, Ga., Dec. 28, 1870. Bur. at
Oconee Cem. in Athens.

SCHLEY, WILLIAM (1835-1837). b. Dec. 15, 1786 at
Frederick, Md. Moved with family as a child to Ga., where
he attd. academies in Louisville and Augusta. Studied law,
was admitted to the bar in 1812, and practiced law at
Augusta until 1825. Judge of superior ct., 1825-1828. Mbr.
of Ga. legislature, 1830-1832. El. to U.S. House as a Dem.
in 1832 and was continued in office for succeeding term.
Resigned seat in July, 1835, to seek office of Gov., having
been nom. as cand. of Union Dem. party, and was el. During

admin., advocated encouragement of railroad constr. and
conduct of geological survey of the State. War against
Creek Indians began, in which he conducted mil. operations
in person for a time. Advocate of strict constr. of U.S.
Const. so far as States Rts. were concerned. Defeated for
reel. as Gov. in 1837 by former Gov. Gilmer. Published a
digest, English Statutes in Force in Georgia, in 1826.
Pres. of Ga. Med. Coll., at Augusta. D. at Augusta, Nov.
20, 1858. Bur. in family cem. at Richmond Hill, near
Augusta.

GILMER, GEORGE ROCKINGHAM (1837-1839). See above,
1829-1831.

McDONALD, CHARLES JAMES (1839-1843). b. July 9, 1793
at Charleston, S.C. s. of Charles and Mary Glas (Burn) McD.
Moved as a child with parents to Hancock Co., Ga. Educ. at
a pvt. acad. and at S.C. Coll., at Columbia, from which he
was grad. in 1816. Studied law and was admitted to bar in
1817. El. solicitor of his jud. dist. in 1822, and in 1825
became a superior ct. judge. Mbr. of lower House of the
legislature in 1830, and of Ga. Senate in 1834. Nom. and
el. Gov. as a Union Dem. in 1839. State's finances were a
difficult problem as a consequence of the financial panic
of 1837. Took steps, against strong opposition in the
legislature, to revise tax system and restore the State's
credit. Reel. Gov. in 1841. Nom. for Gov. again as States
Rts. Whig in 1851, but lost in the gen. election. Delegate
to Nashville So. States conv. in 1850. El. to Ga. Supreme
Ct. in 1857. Was a strict constructionist in views on U.S.
Const. m. in 1819 to Ann Franklin. m. for second time to
a widow, Mrs. Ruffin. Five children. D. Dec. 16, 1860, at
Marietta, Ga.

CRAWFORD, GEORGE WASHINGTON (1843-1847). b. Dec. 22,
1798 in Columbia Co., Ga. s. of Peter C., an early settler
and prominent citizen of the area. Grad. from Princeton in
1820. Studied law in office of U.S. Repr. Richard Wilde.
Admitted to bar and began practice in Augusta in 1822.
Atty. Gen. of Ga., 1827-1831. Mbr. of Ga. legislature,
1837-1842 except for one year. El. to U.S. House in 1843
to complete an unexpired term. Nom. and el. Gov. as a Whig
in 1843, and was reel. in 1845. During admin., pledged his
personal fortune to back State's financial operations.
Cooperated with U.S. govt. in raising troops for the U.S.-
Mexican War. Apptd. U.S. Sect. of War by Pres. Taylor in
1849. Resigned following Taylor's death in July, 1850.
Delegate to So. Commercial Conv. at Montgomery, Ala. in 1858

Mbr. and presiding officer of conv. that voted for secession
by Ga. in 1861. Supported So. cause during Civil War. After the war ended, resided in Europe for a time, but eventually returned to his estate in Richmond Co. D. July 22,
1872 at his home, "Bel Air", near Augusta. Bur. in
Summerville Cem.

TOWNS, GEORGE WASHINGTON BONAPARTE (1847-1851). b.
May 4, 1801 in Wilkes Co., Ga. s. of John Hardwick and
Margaret (George) T. Father was a native of Va., who had
served with Amer. forces during Rev. War. When he was a
boy was injured in a fall from a horse, which left him a
semi-invalid for a number of years. As a consequence, he
did not receive a formal educ., but studied at home. Became a merchant. Studied law in Ala., admitted to bar in
1824 and practiced at Montgomery. Also was ed. of a local
political newspaper for a time before returning to Ga. in
1826. Began law practice at Talbotton, in Talbot Co. Acquired a good practice and became wealthy. Mbr. of lower
House of the legislature, 1829-1830, and of the Ga. Senate,
1832-1834. El. to U.S. House as a Union Dem. in 1835,
serving until Sept., 1836, when he resigned. El. to U.S.
House again in 1836. Served one term but was not a cand.
for second term in 1838. El. to U.S. House again in 1848
to fill a vacancy, but was defeated for a regular term later that year. Nom. and el. Gov. as a Union Dem. in 1847
and was reel. in 1849. During admin., called a conv. in
Ga. to consider question of actions by Cong., relative to
the slavery issue. After tenure as Gov., resumed law practice. m. first to a Miss Campbell. m. for second time to
Mary Jones. Seven children. D. at Macon, Ga., July 15,
1854.

COBB, HOWELL (1851-1853). b. Sept. 7, 1815 at Cherry
Hill, Jefferson Co., Ga. s. of John and Sarah (Rootes) C.
Family moved to Athens, Ga. when he was a child. Father
was a native of N.C. who had served as a col. with Amer.
mil. forces. An uncle of the same name was a mbr. of U.S.
House from 1807 to 1812. Mother was a native of Va. Grad.
in 1834 from Franklin Coll., at Athens, Ga. Studied law,
was admitted to bar in 1836 and began practice in Augusta.
Served as Dem. party pres. elector in 1836. Solicitor gen.
of his jud. dist., 1837-1841. El. to U.S. House in 1842,
and continued in office for three succeeding terms. Was
leader of Dem. party in House in 1848. Chosen Speaker of
the House in 1849 after a long contest with former Speaker
Winthrop, of Mass., a Whig. Refused to sign Southern
Manifesto of 1849 protesting Fed. encroachment on States

Rts. Nom. and el. Gov. as a Union Dem. (Constl. Union)
party nominee in 1851, defeating former Gov. McDonald. Returned to U.S. House in 1854, where he became a leading
spokesman for Southern slavery interests. Advocated extension of slavery into new States, but also defended the
Union. Supported the Compromise of 1850. Apptd. U.S. Sect.
of Treas. by Pres. Buchanan in 1857, serving until 1860.
After 1860 election result became known, supported secession
movement. Served as permanent ch. of conv. at Montgomery,
Ala., in Feb., 1861, that set up a provisional govt. for the
C.S.A. Prominently mentioned for the post of provisional
Pres. of the C.S.A. Served in the Confed. Army as a brig.
gen., later as a major gen., during the ensuing war. Op-
posed Reconstruction policies of Fed. govt. in post-Civil
War era. m. in 1834 to Mary Ann Lamar. D. at New York
City, Oct. 9, 1868. Bur. in Oconee Cem. in Athens, Ga.

JOHNSON, HERSCHEL VESPASIAN (1853-1857). b. Sept. 18,
1812 near Farmer's Bridge, in Burke Co., Ga. s. of Moses
and Nancy (Palmer) J. Attd. pvt. schools; Monaghan Acad.,
at Warrenton; and Franklin Coll., from which he was grad.
in 1834. Studied law while in college, admitted to bar,
and began practice in Augusta in 1834. In 1839 moved to a
plantation, "Shady Grove", near Louisville, in Jefferson
Co., Ga., where he built up a good law practice. Refused
nom. for U.S. House seat in 1841, but accepted such a nom.
in 1843, and was defeated. Moved to Milledgeville in 1844.
Pres. elector on Polk-Dallas ticket in 1844 pres. election.
Presented as cand. for nom. for Gov. in 1845, but withdrew
name. Apptd. to vacancy in U.S. Senate by Gov. Towns,
serving from Feb., 1848 to March, 1849. Superior ct. judge,
1849-1853. Delegate to Dem. natl. convs. in 1848, 1852 and
1856. Pres. elector on Dem. ticket in 1852. Nom. and el.
Gov. in 1853 as Union Dem. and was reel. in 1855. Nominee
for Vice Pres. of U.S. on Dem. ticket with Sen. Douglas in
1860 pres. election. Was a strong So. Rts. advocate and a
signer of So. States "Address" on questions of natl. policy
in 1849, but he acquiesced in Compromise of 1850. Was not
an advocate of secession at Ga. conv. in 1861, feeling victory by South was impossible. Accepted election to Confed.
Senate, however, serving from 1862 to 1865. Pres. of Ga.
conv. assembled in 1865 that rescinded secession ordinance,
abolished slavery and repudiated Ga. Civil War debt.
Chosen U.S. Senator in 1866 under the new state govt., but
was refused seat. Resumed practice of law at Louisville,
Ga. Became superior ct. judge in 1873, a position he held
until death. m. to Mrs. Anna (Polk) Walker, a niece of
Gov. James K. Polk, of Tenn. (q.v.). D. in Jefferson Co.,

Aug. 16, 1880. Bur. in Old Louisville Cem.

BROWN, JOSEPH EMERSON (1857-1865). b. April 15, 1821
in Pickens Dist., S.C. Moved with family to Union Co., Ga.
while still a youth. Left home in 1840 to make his own way.
Attd. Calhoun Acad. in S.C., borrowing money to meet expenses. Returned to Ga. and became a teacher at Canton.
Studied law, and was admitted to bar at Augusta in 1845.
Attd. Yale Law School in 1846. Returned to practice law at
Canton. El. to Ga. Senate in 1849. Pres. elector on Dem.
ticket in 1852. Became a superior ct. judge in 1855. Nom.
and el. Gov. as Dem. in 1857, and was reel. in 1859, defeating the Amer.-Whig party cand. on each occasion. Supported
secessionist movement in 1860-1861. Reel. Gov. in 1861 and
in 1863. As Gov., cooperated with Confed. govt. Had a
close relationship with Pres. Jefferson Davis, but opposed
his policy of conscription to raise troops for Confederate
forces. Removed from office by Fed. authorities at end of
Civil War, and was imprisoned for a time in Washington, D.C.
Urged South to accept Reconstruction program. Supported
Gen. Grant for Pres. of U.S. in 1868. Unsuccessful as Rep.
cand. for U.S. Senate seat in 1868. Apptd. Chief Justice
of Ga. Supreme Ct. in 1868, but resigned in 1870 to become
pres. of Western and Atlanta R.R. Apptd. to U.S. Senate
seat in 1880 to fill a vacancy and continued in office as
Dem. until 1891, when he retired. Left numerous bequests
for pub. uses after death. m. to Elizabeth Grisham. A son,
Joseph M., was later a Gov. of Ga. (q.v.). D. Nov. 30,
1894, at Atlanta. Bur. in Oakland Cem. there.

JOHNSON, JAMES (1865). b. Feb. 12, 1811 in Robeson
Co., N.C. s. of Peter and Sarah (McNeil) J. Family was of
Scottish descent. Attd. Univ. of Ga., graduating with
highest honors in 1832. Taught school while studying law,
admitted to bar in 1835, and began practice at Columbus,
Ga. Pros. atty. for Muscogee Co. In 1855 was el. as
Unionist cand. to U.S. House. Espoused cause of So. Rts.
element, but was defeated for reel. in 1856. Affiliated
with Amer. (Know-Nothing) party in 1857, serving as delegate
to its state conv. in 1858. Did not take active role in
secessionist movement. Apptd. Provisional Gov. of Ga. by
Pres. Andrew Johnson in June, 1865, following ousting of
Gov. Brown. Served until Dec., 1865, when a reconstructed
govt. was placed in power. Unsuccessful cand. for U.S.
Senate seat in 1866. Pres. elector on Rep. ticket in 1868
and 1872 elections. Apptd. U.S. collector of customs at
Savannah in 1866, serving until 1869. In 1870 became a
judge of superior ct., serving until he resigned in 1875.

Practiced law for a time thereafter. m. in 1834 to Ann
Harris, of Jones Co. D. Nov. 20, 1891, at his plantation
in Chattahoochie Co. Bur. in Linwood Cem., Columbus, Ga.

JENKINS, CHARLES JONES (1865-1868). b. Jan. 6, 1805
on father's plantation, "Grimball Hill", in Beaufort Dist.,
S.C. s. of Charles Jones J. In 1816 family moved to
Jefferson Co., Ga. Received early educ. at pvt. schools in
S.C. and Ga. Attd. Franklin Coll., at Athens, Ga., and
Union Coll., in Schnectady, N.Y. Studied law, admitted to
bar in 1827, and began practice in Sandersville, Ga. In
1829 moved to Augusta. Mbr. of lower House of legislature
in 1830. Atty. Gen. of Ga. in 1831 and solicitor gen. of
his jud. dist. Resigned to run unsuccessfully for a seat
in legislature, but was el. in a later try, serving from
1836 to 1841, when he was defeated for reel. El. again in
1843, serving for eight years. Was House Speaker in 1840,
1843 and 1845. Mbr. of conv. that drew up the "Georgia
Platform" in 1850. Declined offer of post of Sect. of
Interior from Pres. Fillmore in 1850. Nominee for Vice
Pres. of U.S. on the Daniel Webster (Whig) ticket in 1852.
Unsuccessful as Constl. Union party cand. for Gov. in 1853.
El. to Ga. Senate in 1856. Apptd. to Ga. Supreme Ct. in
1860. Mbr. of conv. assembled in 1865 to revise state
const. El. Gov. in Nov., 1865, under the revised const.
and assumed office; but after 1867, functioned under close
supervision of U.S. mil. authorities. In Jan., 1868 was
removed from office by Gen. Meade for refusing to sign
warrant for release of funds for holding another conv. to
further revise the state const. in pursuance of Cong. policies. Left Ga., taking with him the State seal, some of the
State's funds, and exec. documents. Went to Washington,
D.C., later to Baltimore, Md. and still later to Halifax,
N.S. Resisted efforts of Ga. govt. to compel return and
release of State properties in his possession, but eventually returned them voluntarily to Gov. Smith in 1872. Pres.,
Bd. of Trustees of Univ. of Ga.; pres., Merchants and
Planters Bank of Augusta, and of an Augusta cotton factory.
Presided over state const. conv. in 1877. m. twice. Hon.
degree from Union Coll. D. at his home near Augusta, June
14, 1883.

RUGER, THOMAS HOWARD (1868). b. April 2, 1833 at Lima,
N.Y. Grad. from West Point Mil. Acad. in 1854. Served in
Army Engr. Corps at New Orleans. Resigned from Army in
April, 1855. Studied law and practiced at Janesville,
Wisc. until June, 1861, when he returned to U.S. mil. ser-
vice as lieut. col. of a volunteer Wisc. regiment. Rose to

rank of brig. gen. in 1862. Served in campaigns in Va.,
participating in numerous engagements, including Gettysburg.
Assisted in quelling anti-draft riots in New York City in
1863. Served later in Tenn. area, and was under Gen.
Sherman's command in 1864-1865. Mustered out in 1866 with
rank of col. in regular army. Returned to regular army
service as brig. gen. in 1867, and was assigned as Mil. Gov.
of Ga. by Gen. Meade in Jan., 1868, following removal of
Gov. Jenkins. Acted in that capacity until July, 1868, when
a new govt. was set up under the revised const. Served as
head of a bd. of mil. officers apptd. in 1871 to investigate
eligibility of a number of mbrs. of the Ga. legislature,
five of whom were found to be ineligible for seats, and were
disqualified. Supt. of U.S. Mil. Acad. at West Point, 1871-
1876. Assigned to mil. service in Dept. of South, 1876-
1878. Later served in Depts. of Mo. and of the Dakotas.
Promoted to major gen. in 1895. Retired from the Army in
1897. D. June 3, 1907.

   BULLOCK, RUFUS BROWN (1868-1871). b. March 28, 1834
at Bethlehem, Albany Co., N.Y. Grad. at age 16 from
Albion Acad. Studied telegraphy and became expert at trade.
Worked for Adams Express Co., and helped to construct telegraph lines from New York City to South. Established residence in Augusta. As Civil War approached opposed secession
but went along with South in its cause. Served as an asst.
quartermaster, with the rank of lieut. col. Surrendered
with Lee's army at Appomattox, was paroled, and went back
to Augusta. Engaged in various bus. enterprises there.
Pres. of Macon and Augusta R.R. in 1867, and org. First
Natl. Bank at Augusta. Urged South to accept Reconstruction. Mbr. of state conv. that revised Ga. const. in 1868.
Nom. and el. Gov. as Rep. in that year for four-year term.
Resigned in Oct., 1871, because he felt his govt. had in-
sufficient popular support. Retired from politics. Established his residence in Atlanta, and engaged in various
bus. activities, including operation of cotton mills and
serving on bd. of dir. of Un. Pac. R.R. Vice pres. of
Piedmont Expo., and pres. of local CC. Trustee of Atlanta
Univ. Active in church affairs. D. April 24, (27?), 1907.

   CONLEY, BENJAMIN (1871-1872). b. Mar. 1, 1815 at
Newark, N.J. Received a common school educ. At age 15 went
to Augusta, Ga., where he engaged in merc. pursuits. Mbr.
of Augusta city council, 1845-1857 and mayor, 1857-1858.
Affiliated with Whig party. During Civil War operated a
plantation near Montgomery, Ala. Returned to Augusta at
end of the war and resumed bus. activities. Supported Cong.

Reconstruction policies. Mbr. of city council of Augusta
by apptmt. by Fed. authorities in 1867. Delegate to conv.
in 1868 that revised state const. El. to Ga. Senate as
Rep. and was chosen Pres. of that body in Jan., 1869. Presiding officer at Rep. state conv. in 1869. When Gov.
Bullock resigned in Oct., 1871, assumed office of Gov. as
successor. A controversy ensued over whether he, as past
Pres. of Senate, or the newly chosen presiding officer of
that body should hold powers of governorship. It was resolved by the ordering of a spec. election for the following Dec., at which a successor to serve the remainder of
Bullock's term would be elected, with C. acting as Gov. until the election. The Speaker of the House, James Smith,
was el. Gov. at that time and assumed office in Jan., 1872.
Apptd. U.S. postmaster at Atlanta. Became pres. of Macon
and Atlanta R.R. in 1868. m. in 1842 to Sarah A. Semmes,
of Washington, Ga. Originally a Presbyterian, he affiliated
with the Protestant Episcopal church after his marriage.
Mbr., I.O.O.F. D. Jan. 10, 1886.

SMITH, JAMES MILTON (1872-1877). b. Oct. 24, 1823 in
Twiggs Co., Ga. Attd. Culloden Acad. in Monroe Co., Ga.
Studied law, admitted to bar and began practice in Columbus,
Ga. Defeated for U.S. House in 1855. Entered Confed. Army
in 1861 as a major and was promoted to col. in 1862. Participated in a number of major battles in Va. in 1861-1863
and was wounded. El. to Confed. Cong. in 1863 from Ga.,
and continued to serve therein until end of Civil War. Resumed practice of law at Columbus. El. to Ga. House and
was chosen Speaker. El. Gov. at spec. election in Dec.,
1871, to serve last year of Gov. Bullock's term. Reel. for
full term in 1872 as nominee of Dem. and Lib. Rep. faction.
During admin., a State Dept. of Agri. and a Geological
Survey agency were created. Unsuccessful cand. for U.S.
Senate in 1877. Apptd. mbr. of newly created State R.R.
Commn. in 1879, later becoming ch. of that body. Served
thereon until 1885. Became a superior ct. judge in 1888, a
position he held until death. Married twice. No children.
D. Nov. 25, 1890.

COLQUITT, ALFRED HOLT (1877-1882). b. Nov. 20, 1824 in
Monroe, Walton Co., Ga. s. of Walter T. and Nancy (Lane) C.
Father was prominent in Ga. govt. and politics, having serv-
ed as a mbr. of the Ga. legislature, the U.S. House, and the
U.S. Senate. Grad. from Princeton in 1844. Studied law,
was admitted to the bar in 1846, and began practice in
Monroe. Served as staff officer with rank of major during
the War with Mexico. Mbr. of U.S. House, 1853-1855. Did

not seek reel. in 1854. Mbr. of Ga. legislature in 1859.
Pres. elector on the Breckenridge-Lane Dem. ticket in 1860
pres. election. Mbr. of conv. in 1861 that adopted ordinance of secession. Served in Confed. Army throughout the
Civil War, rising from rank of capt. to major gen. Presided at Dem. state conv. in 1872. Nom. and el. Gov. as
Dem. for four-year term in 1876 and was reel. for a two-
year term in 1880 after a change in the term had been approved by a constl. revision. Dem. party became dominant
in Ga. politics during his admin. with the ending of Reconstruction programs. El. to U.S. Senate in 1883, in which
he continued to serve until his death. Pres. of Intl.
Sunday School Conv. in 1878. m. in 1848 to Dorothy Tarver.
After her death, m. to Sarah Tarver. D. March 26, 1894, in
Washington, D.C. Bur. in Rose Hill Cem., Macon Ga.

STEPHENS, ALEXANDER HAMILTON (1882-1883). b. Feb. 11,
1812 near Crawfordsville, Ga. s. of Andrew and Margaret
(Grier) S. Grandfather had emigrated to Pa. in 1746, and
after the Rev. War had settled in Ga. Became an orphan at
age 15, but an uncle took over responsibility of his upbringing. Attd. acad. at Washington, Ga. and Franklin Coll.
in Athens, Ga. on a scholarship from the Presbyterian Educl.
Soc. Grad. with highest honors in 1832. Taught school for
à time to repay loan incurred for educ. Studied law for
two months, admitted to bar in 1834, and soon had a successful practice at Crawfordsville. Acquired an estate nearby,
"Liberty Hill". Mbr. of Ga. legislature, 1836-1841, where
he opposed idea of nullification. Mbr. of Ga. Senate, 1842.
El. to fill vacancy in U.S. House seat in 1843, and continued in that office thereafter until 1859. As mbr. of the
U.S. House, opposed dispatching of U.S. troops to Rio Grande
River by Pres. Polk in 1846; opposed the Wilmot Proviso of
1847; and supported the Compromise of 1850 measures. Was
not a cand. for reel. in 1858. His farewell speech in the
U.S. House was widely noted for its eloquence. Mentioned
widely as possible compromise cand. for the Dem. nom. for
Pres. of U.S. in 1860, as dis-union threat became strong.
Was nom. as pres. elector for the Douglas-Johnson ticket in
that election. Delegate to the Ga. conv. of 1861, in which
he voted against secession, although maintaining a State
had a right to secede. Mbr. of conv. in Montgomery, Ala.
that drafted const. for the So. Confed. El. Vice Pres. of
C.S.A. govt. After the Civil War ended, was arrested and
imprisoned for several months in Boston, being granted a
parole by Pres. Johnson in Oct., 1865. Chosen to U.S.
Senate in 1866, but was refused seat by the Senate. Unsuccessful as cand. for U.S. Senate in 1868. Became

proprietor of an Atlanta newspaper, the <u>Southern</u> <u>Daily</u> <u>Sun</u>,
in 1871. Opposed fusion of Dem. party with Lib. Rep. party
in 1872. Again defeated for U.S. Senate seat in 1872, but
was el. to U.S. House in 1873 to fill a vacancy, and was
continued in that office until Nov., 1882, when he resigned
after being el. Gov. as a Dem. in that year. Generally regarded as one of the leading statesmen of Ga. Wrote extensively on constl. and political topics. Famous for his
oratory. Always frail in health, he died at Atlanta on
March 4, 1883 after holding the office of Gov. for only a
few months. Bur. on estate near Crawfordsville.

BOYNTON, JAMES STODDARD (1883). b. May 7, 1833 in
Henry Co., Ga. Was of English-French ancestry. Received
academic educ. in local schools. Studied law and passed
bar after only seven weeks of study. Began practice in
Monticello, Ga. Moved to Jackson, Ga. in 1858. El. ordi-
nary of Butts Co. in 1860. At beginning of Civil War entered Confed. Army as pvt. Was wounded, and was cited for
heroic conduct on several occasions. Rose to rank of col.
of Ga. regiment by end of war. Resumed law practice at
Griffin, 1869-1872. Mbr. of Ga. Senate in 1880, becoming
Pres. of that body. When Gov. Stephens died in March, 1883,
succeeded to office of Gov. until a successor was chosen
later that year to serve remainder of term. In Jan., 1886,
was apptd. superior ct. judge, and continued in that office
by election for two terms. m. first to Fannie Layal, of
Monticello. Two s. m. in 1883 to Susie T. Harris. D. Dec.
22, 1902.

McDANIEL, HENRY DICKERSON (1883-1886). b. Sept. 4,
1836 at Monroe, Ga. s. of Ira Oliver and Rebecca (Walker)
McD. Father was one of the pioneer merchants of Atlanta.
Grad. in 1856 from Mercer Univ. with highest honors. Studied law, admitted to bar and began practice in Monroe.
Youngest mbr. of Ga. conv. in 1861 that declared for secession. Opposed secession, but later signed the ordinance.
Entered Confed. Army as lieut. in 1861, rising to rank of
major. Participated in engagements in Pa. and Md., and was
wounded and taken prisoner. Confined at Johnson's Island
in Ohio until released at end of Civil War. Resumed law
practice in Monroe. Mbr. of state constl. conv. in 1865.
El. to Ga. House in 1872 and to Ga. Senate in 1874, 1878
and 1880. Declined to run for another term in 1882; but in
1883 was nom. and el. Gov. as Dem. in a spec. election to
fill out term of Gov. Stephens. Reel. in 1884. After tenure as Gov. resumed law practice in Monroe. Trustee of
Univ. of Ga., 1884, serving as pres. of the Bd. in 1889.

Trustee of So. Theological Sem. at Louisville, Ky., 1883-1890. Hon. degree from Univ. of Ga. in 1907. Baptist. m. in 1865 to Hester C. Felker, of Monroe. One s.; one d. D. at Monroe, July 25, 1926.

GORDON, JOHN BROWN (1886-1890). b. Feb. 6, 1832 in Upson Co., Ga. Family was prominent in community affairs. Attd. pvt. schools and the Univ. of Ga., from which he was grad. with highest honors in 1852. Studied law, admitted to bar in 1853 and began practice in Atlanta with brother-in-law, who later became Chief Justice of Ga. Supreme Ct. Assisted father in coal mining enterprises in Ga. and Tenn. for some years. In 1861 at outbreak of Civil War, org. a volunteer company, known as the "Raccoon Roughs", for Confed. service, becoming its capt. Rose to rank of lieut. gen. by end of war, serving as corps commdr. with Gen. Lee in final Va. campaign. Participated in numerous major battles. Wounded on five occasions, on one of which his life was saved by his wife, who was accompanying him. At end of Civil War resumed law practice in Atlanta. Delegate to Natl. Union party conv. at Philadelphia in 1866. Delegate to Dem. natl. party convs. in 1868 and 1872. Pres. elector on Dem. ticket in 1868 and 1872. Defeated as Dem. cand. for Gov. in 1868. Testified before a commt. of Cong. investigating the KKK in 1871, and defended So. views regarding it. El. to U.S. Senate in 1873 and was reel. in 1879. Resigned in 1880 to become associated with bldg. of Ga. Pac. R.R. Nom. and el. Gov. as Dem. in 1886 and again in 1888. El. to U.S. Senate again in 1891. Conservative views on finance policies antagonized Farmers Alliance and its successor, the Peoples (Populist) party, while in Cong. Did not seek reel. for succeeding term. Devoted time thereafter to writing, lecturing and agri. pursuits. Author of book, Reminiscences of the Civil War. Natl. Commdr.-inch. of U.C.V.A. for a number of years. m. to Fannie Haralson, d. of a Ga. Congressman in the 1840s. D. Jan. 9, 1904, at Miami, Fla. Bur. in Oakland Cem., Atlanta.

NORTHEN, WILLIAM JONATHAN (1890-1894). b. July 9, 1835 in Jones Co., Ga. Family, which was of Scottish descent, had moved from N.C. to Ga. about 1800. Grad. from Mercer Univ. in 1853. Taught school from 1854 to 1858, becoming dir. of Mt. Zion Acad. in 1858. Upon outbreak of Civil War, enlisted in Confed. service as a pvt. in a Ga. company commanded by his father, who was 70 years of age. After war service, returned to home near Sparta, in Hancock Co., and resumed teaching until 1874. Ill health caused him to retire from teaching. Gave attention to farming activities

at his place near Sparta. Mbr. of state Dem. conv. in
1867. Mbr. of lower House of Ga. legislature in 1877, and
again in 1880. Mbr. of Ga. Senate in 1884, where he served
as ch. of commt. on educ. Active in farmers orgs. Vice
pres. of State Agri. Soc. and later pres., 1886-1888. Pres.
of Young Farmers Club of So. States. Nom. and el. Gov. as
a Dem. in 1890 and reel. in 1892. Trustee of Mercer Univ.
and pres. of Bd. of Trustees of Washington Inst. Baptist.
m. in 1860 to Mattie M. Neel. D. March 25, 1913.

ATKINSON, WILLIAM YATES (1894-1898). b. Nov. 11, 1854
at Oakland, Ga. s. of John P. and Theodora P. (Ellis) A.
Father was a native of Va. who had moved to Ga., where he
became a planter. Spent boyhood on father's farm. Acquired
college educ. by his own efforts, since his father died when
s. was still quite young. Grad. from the Univ. of Ga. in
1877. Studied law and established practice at Newnan, in
Coweta Co., Ga. Mbr. of Ga. House, 1886-1892, serving as
Speaker during last term. Nom. and el. Gov. as Dem. in 1894
and again in 1896. An advocate of free coinage of silver,
he defeated the Pop. party cand. as his major opponent in
each election. Trustee of Univ. of Ga. Pres. of Bd. of
Trustees for Ga. Normal and Indus. Coll. for Girls. m. in
1880 to Susie C. Milton, a grand-daughter of Gov. John
Milton, of Fla. (q.v.). D. at Newnan, Aug. 8, 1899.

CANDLER, ALLEN DANIEL (1898-1902). b. Nov. 4, 1834 at
Homer, in Banks Co., Ga. s. of Daniel G. and Nancy C.
(Matthews) C. Family antecedents had emigrated from England
to Amer. before the Rev. War, eventually settling in Ga.
Attd. local schools and Mercer Univ., from which he was
grad. in 1859. Founded h.s. at Clayton, Ga., becoming its
dir. Studied law but did not practice. Enlisted in Confed.
Army as a pvt. in 1861. Rose to rank of col. by 1865. Received an A.M. degree from Mercer Univ. in 1866 and returned
to teaching. Pres. of Monroe Female Coll., 1865-1866. Also engaged in farming while teaching, 1867-1869. Pres. of
Bailey Inst., 1870-1871. Mbr. of Ga. House, 1873-1877, and
of Ga. Senate, 1877-1879. Acquired interests in mfg. and
other businesses, serving as pres. of a railroad company,
1877-1892. Mbr. of U.S. House, 1883-1891. Did not seek
reel. in 1890. Ga. Sect. of State, 1894-1898. Resigned to
become cand. for Gov. Nom. and el. Gov. as Dem. in 1898
and again in 1900, defeating a Pop. party cand. on each
occasion. In 1903 became State Historian. Hon. degree from
Mercer Univ. in 1908. m. in 1864 to Eugenia Williams. D.
Oct. 26, 1910, at Atlanta. Bur. in Alta Vista Cem.,
Gainesville, Ga.

TERRELL, JOSEPH MERIWETHER (1902-1907). b. June 6, 1861 at Greenville, Meriwether Co., Ga. s. of Joel Edward Green and Sarah Rebecca (Anthony) T. Father was a leading physician in Western Ga. Managed father's plantation while also studying law, 1876-1881. Admitted to bar in 1883, and began practice at Greenville. Became mbr. of Ga. House in 1884, serving two terms. Mbr. of Ga. Senate in 1890. Atty. Gen. of Ga., 1892-1902, resigning to become cand. for Gov. Nom. and el. Gov. as a Dem. in 1902 and again in 1904. Regular term extended by some eight months by change in time of legislative sessions. As Gov., sponsored a franchise tax as a voter qualification; an amdt. to the state const. limiting tax rate; and improvements in rural school system. m. in 1886 to Jessie Lee Spivey. D. Nov. 17, 1912.

SMITH, HOKE (1907-1909; 1911). b. Sept. 2, 1855 at Newton, N.C. s. of H. H. Smith, a distinguished educator who was a native of N.H. and who had become a mbr. of the faculty at the Univ. of N.C. Mother was Mary Brent Hoke, of Lincolnston, N.C., whose family line included a number of jurists and others prominent in pub. life in Va. and N.C. Studied for the most part with father. In 1872 went to Atlanta, Ga., where he studied law. Also taught school at Waynesboro, Ga. Admitted to bar in 1873 and began practice in Atlanta. Soon achieved reputation as able lawyer. Ch. of Fulton Co. Dem. commt. at age 21. In 1877 canvassed Northwest Ga. in support of proposal to establish capital at Atlanta. Pres. of Young Men's Library Assoc., 1881-1883. In 1887 org. and became pres. of company which published the Atlanta Evening Journal. Served as its ed. for a time. Acquired extensive real estate holdings. Delegate to Dem. natl. conv. in 1892, where he supported nom. of former Pres. Cleveland. Was strongly opposed to a high protective tariff. Apptd. U.S. Sect. of Interior by Cleveland in 1893. Resigned in Sept., 1896, to resume law practice and bus. interests. Pres. of Atlanta school bd., 1896-1907. Nom. and el. Gov. in 1906, defeating a cand. for the nom. favored by Gov. Terrell. Became rival of Joseph M. Brown, the leader of an opposing faction of the Dem. party in Ga. for over a decade thereafter. Removed Brown from the State R.R. Commn. because of differences over rate regulation and other policies. Defeated in 1908 Dem. primary for re-nom. as Gov. by Brown, who was el.; but successfully opposed Brown for the Dem. nom. for Gov. in 1910, and was el. Chosen to fill vacancy in U.S. Senate seat in 1911 shortly after beginning of term, and resigned as Gov. in Nov. of that year to assume Senate seat. Continued in U.S. Senate until 1921, having

lost primary contest for re-nom. in 1920. As a Senator,
opposed Pres. Wilson on issue of U.S. entry into the League
of Nations. Retired thereafter to law practice in Atlanta
and Washington, D.C. Served as counsel for the govt. of
Chile during 1920s. Mbr. of bd. of dir. of Peabody Fund;
dir. of Fulton Natl. Bank, which he helped to org., and of
Piedmont Hotel Co., of Atlanta. Mbr., Masons (Shriner);
Elks. m. to Birdie Cobb, a d. of Gen. T. R. R. Cobb. Four
children. After her death, m. to Maxie Crawford, of
Cordele, Ga., who had been his sect. for a number of years.
D. Nov. 27, 1931, at Atlanta. Bur. in Oakland Cem. there.

BROWN, JOSEPH MACKEY (1909-1911; 1912-1913). b. Dec.
28, 1851 at Canton, Ga. s. of Gov. Joseph E. and Elizabeth
(Grisham) B. (q.v.). Descended from an Irish colonist who
had come to N.C. in 1745. Grad. from Oglethorpe Univ. in
1872 with highest honors. Studied law for a time in
brother's law office and later attd. Harvard Law School.
Admitted to bar in 1873, but soon gave up practice of law
because of failing eyesight. Studied for a time at a bus.
coll. in Atlanta. Employed as clerk by the Western and
Atlantic R.R. in Atlanta. Rose to position of traffic mgr.
for the company by 1889. In 1904 was apptd. by Gov. Terrell
to Ga. R.R. Commn. Served until 1907 when he was removed
by Gov. Hoke Smith because of a disagreement over rate regulation and other policies. Entered 1908 Dem. primary
against Gov. Hoke Smith and, though conducting no speech-
making campaign, won the nom. for Gov. and was el. The same
two were opponents in the 1910 Dem. primary contest, and on
that occasion Smith won and was el. After Smith resigned as
Gov. the following year to become a U.S. Sen., B. was el.
Gov. again in 1912 in a spec. election to complete Smith's
term. After tenure as Gov. devoted self to bus. interests.
Vice pres. of First Natl. Bank of Marietta. Interested in
history and archeology. Author of several works on the
Civil War. m. in 1889 to Cora Annie McCord, of Augusta.
Two s.; one d. D. at Marietta, March 3, 1932. Bur. in
Oakland Cem., Atlanta.

SMITH, HOKE (1911). See above, 1907-1909.

SLATON, JOHN MARSHALL (1911-1912; 1913-1915). b. Dec.
25 (26?), 1866 in Meriwether Co., Ga. s. of Wm. Franklin
and Nancy Jane (Martin) S. Father was a distinguished educator who had served during the Civil War as a major in an
Ala. regiment of the Confed. Army. Attd. rural schools.
Entered the Univ. of Ga. at age 16, and worked while attending college. Grad. with an M.A. degree in 1886 with highest

honors. Studied law, was admitted to the bar and began
practice in Atlanta in 1887. Mbr. of Ga. House, 1896-1909,
and of Ga. Senate, 1909-1913. Served in two sessions as
House Speaker and in two sessions as Pres. of Senate. As
Pres. of Senate, cast the deciding vote for ratification of
the Federal Income Tax (16th) Amdt. Was presiding over the
House in 1906 when an acrimonious debate was conducted on
the issue of prohibition. Succeeded to the office of Gov.
in Nov., 1911, following resignation of Gov. Hoke Smith,
serving for some two months pending election of a successor
to complete Smith's term. Was nom. and el. Gov. as a Dem.
in 1912. After tenure as Gov. was ch. of Ga. Bd. of Law
Examiners for a number of years. Defeated as cand. for Dem.
nom. for U.S. Senate seat in 1930. Mbr., Phi Beta Kappa,
serving as pres. of Ga. chapter. Recipient of Legion
d'Honneur award from French govt. Hon. degrees from the
Univ. of Ga. and Oglethorpe Univ. m. in 1898 to Sarah
Frances Grant, of Atlanta. D. Jan. 11, 1955, at Atlanta.
Bur. in Oakdale Cem. there.

BROWN, JOSEPH MACKEY (1912-1913). See above, 1909-
1911.

SLATON, JOHN MARSHALL (1913-1915). See above, 1911-
1912.

HARRIS, NATHANIEL EDWIN ("NATE") (1915-1917). b. Jan.
21, 1846 near Jonesboro, Tenn. s. of Alexander Nelson and
Edna (Hayes) H. Ancestral line went back to an English
colonist who came to Jamestown, Va. in 1611. Was attending
Martin Acad., in Tenn., when Civil War began. Entered
Confed. Army and was an officer in a Va. cavalry unit at end
of war. Received an A.B. degree from Univ. of Ga. in 1870.
Studied law at Sparta, Ga. and admitted to bar. Moved to
Macon, Ga. in 1873 where he became partner in a law firm.
City atty. of Macon, 1874-1882. Mbr. of Ga. House, 1882-
1885, and of Ga. Senate, 1894-1895. Judge of superior ct.,
1912-1915. Resigned to seek office of Gov. Nom. and el.
Gov. as Dem. in 1914. Soon after he assumed office, a prisoner, Leo Frank, who had been convicted of murder in a trial
attracting wide attention because of attendant anti-Semitic
overtones, and whose death sentence had been commuted to
life imprisonment by Gov. Slaton, was taken from prison by
a mob at Marietta, and lynched. Gov. was unsuccessful in
efforts to thwart mob action, for which he was criticized
in many quarters. Admin. also marked by bitter struggle
between prohibition and anti-prohibition forces in legislature, necessitating the calling of a spec. session to enact

appropriation bills. Pension Commnr. of Ga., 1924-1925.
Pres. elector on Dem. ticket in 1924. Compiler of digests
of Ga. Reports in 1876 and 1882; also published his autobiography in 1925. Trustee of Univ. of Ga. and of
Wesleyan Coll. Hon. degrees from Univ. of Ga. and Emory
Univ. Pres. of Macon Bar Assoc. Methodist Episcopal
church. m. in 1873 to Fannie Burke. Seven children. m. in
1899 to Hattie Jobe, of Elizabeth, Ga. D. Sept. 21, 1929 at
Hampton, Tenn.

  DORSEY, HUGH MANSON (1917-1921). b. July 10, 1871 at
Fayetteville, Ga. s. of Rufus Thomas and Sarah Matilda
(Bennett) D. Grad. from the Univ. of Ga. in 1893. Studied
law at the Univ. of Va. for a year. Admitted to bar and
began practice in Atlanta with father's law firm. Became
active in pub. affairs, serving on Atlanta Water Bd. and on
Bd. of Trustees of Grady Hosp. Lieut. col. on staff of Gov.
Atkinson. Apptd. solicitor of Atlanta jud. cir. in 1910,
and continued in that office until 1916. Was in charge of
prosecution in widely noted Leo Frank murder trial, in which
he secured a conviction. Resigned in 1916 to run for Gov.
Nom. and el. Gov. in 1917 and again in 1919. Strongly denounced the lynching of Frank, which occurred during the
admin. of Gov. N. E. Harris (q.v.). In 1921 wrote and published a pamphlet, The Negro in Georgia, which called for
improvement in condition of Negro population of the State.
Became a controversial figure as a result. Unsuccessful
cand. for Dem. nom. for Senate seat in 1920. Resumed law
practice in father's firm in 1921. Judge of city ct. of
Atlanta, 1926-1935. Superior ct. judge, 1935-1948. Mbr.,
Masons; I.O.O.F.; various fraternal orgs. and driving clubs.
Methodist. m. in 1911 to Mary Adair Wilkinson, of Valdosta,
Ga. Two s. D. June 11, 1948.

  HARDWICK, THOMAS WILLIAM (1921-1923). b. Dec. 9, 1872
at Thomasville, Ga. s. of Robt. Wm. and Zemulda Schley
(Matthews) H. Antecedents had been English colonists who
had moved to Ga. after Rev. War. Attd. Mercer Univ., grad.
in 1892. Studied law at Lumpkin Law School, in Athens, Ga.
Admitted to bar in 1893 and began practice in Sandersville,
Ga. Became active in politics at early age. Pros. atty. of
Washington Co., 1895-1897. Mbr. of Ga. House, 1898-1899,
1901-1902. Capt. in Ga. state troops, 1900-1901. Mbr. of
U.S. House, 1903-1914. Apptd. to fill vacant seat in U.S.
Senate and was el. to fill out term in 1914. As a Senator,
opposed some measures backed by Pres. Wilson, including the
Selective Service Act of 1917, and a child labor bill.
Pres. Wilson intervened in Dem. primary against him in 1918

and he was defeated for re-nom. for Senate seat. Nom. and
el. Gov. in 1920 as Dem. in reaction against Pres. Wilson
and his policies. During admin., the KKK was revived, with
headquarters in Atlanta. While not opposed to its aims, he
opposed their use of masks. Defeated in 1922 in spec. primary for Dem. nom. for U.S. Senate seat. Also was defeated
in 1922 for Dem. nom. for Gov. by Clifford Walker, the cand.
he had defeated in 1920 primary. Spec. asst. to U.S. Atty.
Gen., 1923-1924, in connection with investigation of World
War I. financial transactions. Defeated again for Dem. nom.
for U.S. Senate seat in 1924. Resumed law practice in
Sandersville. Publ. of a local newspaper, the Dublin
Courier Herald. Defeated for Dem. nom. for Gov. in 1932 by
Eugene Talmadge. m. in 1894 to Maude Elizabeth Perkins, of
Washington Co., Ga. One d. D. Jan. 31, 1944, in
Sandersville. Bur. in Old City Cem. there.

WALKER, CLIFFORD MITCHELL (1923-1927). b. July 4, 1877
at Monroe, Ga. s. of Billington Sanders and Alice
(Mitchell) W. Father was a lawyer, banker and businessman.
Attd. Ga. Mil. Inst. and the Univ. of Ga., from which he was
grad. in 1897. Studied law, admitted to bar in 1897, and
began practice in Monroe. Mayor of Monroe, 1905-1907. Solicitor gen. for his jud. cir., 1909-1913. Atty. Gen. of
Ga., 1914-1919. Unsuccessful cand. for Dem. nom. for Gov.
in 1920, but won nom. for that office in 1922 Dem. primary
against incumbent Gov. Hardwick and was el. Reel. in 1924.
During admin., the state tax system was revised; pub.
schools and state highway system improved; and a State Bd.
of Forestry created. After tenure as Gov. retired to law
practice in Atlanta. Pres. of Woodrow Wilson Coll. of Law,
and later, gen. counsel for the Ga. Bureau of Unemployment
Compensation. Mbr. of Bds. of Trustees of the Univ. of Ga.,
Mercer Univ. and Shorter Coll. Phi Beta Kappa. Baptist.
m. in 1902 to Rosa Carter Mathewson, of Westminster, S.C.
Three s. D. Nov. 9, 1954. Bur. in Walker family cem., in
Monroe.

HARDMAN, LAMARTINE GRIFFIN (1927-1931). b. April 14,
1856 near Commerce, Ga. s. of the Rev. Wm. B. J. and Susan
Elizabeth (Colquitt) H. Father was a Baptist minister.
Grad. from the Univ. of Ga. Med. Coll. in 1877. Received
further med. training in hospitals in New York City; London,
England; and Philadelphia. Established med. practice at
Commerce in 1885, where he, in association with brother,
const. a modern hosp. facility. Also became involved in
bus. enterprises in fields of cotton cloth mfg., milling,
drug merchandising, and sci. farming. Mbr. of Ga. House,

1900-1907, and of Ga. Senate, 1907. As mbr. of legislature
advocated legislation for improvements in agri.; establishment of technical schools; survey of lands by govt. to improve drainage for pub. health benefits; creation of State
Bd. of Health; and prohibition. During World War I served
as mbr. of State Fuel Admin. Cand. for Dem. nom. for Gov.
in 1926 on a "businessman's platform". Won nom. in run-off
primary despite opposition of KKK, and was el. Won nom.
again in 1928 and was el. for succeeding term. Signed measure to "preserve racial integrity of Ga." by requiring
registration by race and restricting issuance of marriage
licenses for mixed marriages. Although a "dry", supported
Gov. Alfred E. Smith for Pres. of U.S. in 1928. Trustee of
So. Baptist Theological Sem. at Louisville, Ky.; of Shorter
Coll.; and of State Coll. of Agri. and Mech. Arts, to which
he donated a bldg. Dir. of Ga. Experiment Station, at
Griffin. Was a leading Baptist layman. Mbr. of various
professional med. orgs. m. in 1907 to Emma Wiley Griffin,
of Valdosta, Ga. One s.; three d. D. at Atlanta, Feb. 18,
1937.

RUSSELL, RICHARD BREVARD, Jr. (1931-1933). b. Nov. 2,
1897 at Winder, Ga. Fourth of 13 children of Richard B.,Sr.
and Ina (Dillard) R. Father was a lawyer who served as
Chief Justice of Ga. Supreme Ct. Attd. dist. agri. and
mech. school at Powder Springs, Ga.; Gordon Inst., from
which he was grad. in 1915; and the Univ. of Ga., from which
he received a law degree in 1918. Admitted to bar and began practice in Winder. In 1918-1921 was an apprentice seaman in USNR. Mbr. of Ga. House, 1921-1931, serving as
Speaker pro tem in 1923-1927 and Speaker, 1927-1931. Unsuccessful cand. for Dem. nom. for U.S. Senate in 1926.
Nom. and el. Gov. as Dem. in 1930. During admin., promoted
admin. reorg. of state govt.; all state institutions of
higher learning were placed into one system; office of Atty.
Gen. given supervisory authority over all legal work of
state govt. El. to vacant U.S. Senate seat in 1932, and continued in that office until death in 1971. Became one of
the major figures in the Senate, and was one of the leaders
of the "Southern Bloc" there. Ch. of Senate Armed Services
Commt., 1951-1969. Pres. pro tem of Senate, 1969-1971. Ch.
of commt. that investigated Pres. Truman's removal of Gen.
McArthur as commdr. of U.S. forces in Korea in 1952. Warned
against U.S. mil. involvement in Southeast Asia in 1954, but
supported U.S. there after mil. action began. Major contender for Dem. nom. for Pres. of U.S. in 1952. Also received some delegate support in 1948, 1956 and 1960 convs.
Mbr., Bd. of Visitors of U.S. Naval Acad., 1934-1951; of

U.S. Mil Acad., 1948-1951; and of U.S. Air Force Acad. from
1957 onward. Hon. degree from Mercer Univ. George
Washington Award of Amer. Good Govt. Soc., 1958. R.O.A.
Award, 1959. Mbr., Masons; I.O.O.F.; Amer. Legion; Kiwanis;
various clubs and professional legal orgs. Methodist.
Never married. D. Jan. 21, 1971.

TALMADGE, EUGENE (1933-1937; 1941-1943). b. Sept. 23,
1884 at Forsyth, Ga. s. of Thomas Romalgus and Carrie
(Roberts) T. Ancestral line traced back to an English colonist who emigrated to Mass. in 1631. Father was a farmer,
mill mgr., and banker. Attd. local schools and the Univ.
of Ga., from which he received a law degree in 1907. Admitted to bar and began practice in Atlanta. In 1909 moved
to Montgomery Co., where he practiced until 1912; and then
moved to McRae, Telfair Co., where he engaged in law practice and farming. Solicitor for McRae, 1918-1920. Co.
atty. for Telfair Co., 1920-1923. State Commnr. of Agri.,
1927-1933. Instrumental in obtaining new legislation providing for testing of fertilizers, dairy products, animal
feeds and drugs. Nom. and el. Gov. as Dem. in 1932, defeating former Gov. Hardwick in primary. Reel. in 1934. As
Gov., used martial law powers to oust ch. of State Highway
Commn. when that officer refused to discharge mbrs. of engr.
staff T. claimed to be incompetent. Action eventually sustained by Ga. cts., but resulted in temp. withholding of
highway funds by U.S. govt. Removal of mbrs. of State Pub.
Service Commn. also resulted in controversy. Defeated as
cand. for Dem. nom. for U.S. Senate seat in 1936 and again
in 1938. Nom. and el. Gov. again in 1940. During admin.,
sought and eventually secured dismissal of two highly placed
admin. officials in State Univ. system over differences of
views on segregation policies. Action caused temp. denial
of accreditation of Ga. institutions of higher learning by
So. Assoc. of Colleges and Universities, on grounds of
political interference. Unsuccessful in Dem. primary for
re-nom. in 1942. Won Dem. party's nom. for Gov. in 1946 by
virtue of "county unit" vote majority, although he failed to
win a plurality of the popular vote, a system of nom. subsequently held unconstl. by the U.S. Supreme Ct. Was el. in
ensuing gen. election, but died before being installed in
office. Mbr., Masons; I.O.O.F.; Woodmen; various clubs and
fraternal orgs. Baptist. m. in 1909 to Mattie Thurmond
(Peterson). Two d.; one s., Herman E., who later became a
Gov. of Ga. (q.v.). D. at Atlanta, Dec. 21, 1946.

RIVERS, EURITH DICKINSON (1937-1941). b. Dec. 1, 1895
at Center Point, Ark. s. of Dr. James Matthew and Millie

Annie (Wilkerson) R.   Attd. Young Harris Coll., in Northwestern Ga., from which he was grad. in 1914.   Taught
school at Climax and Cairo, Ga. while studying law by correspondence.   Received law degree from Atlanta Law School in
1916.   Began practice in Cairo.   Co. atty., Grady Co., in
1916 and also city atty. for Cairo.   In 1920 moved to
Lakeland, in Lanier Co., where he served as co. atty., and
city atty.   Mbr. of Ga. House, 1925-1926, serving as Speaker.   Mbr. of Ga. Senate, 1927-1928, serving as Pres.
pro tem.   Unsuccessful as cand. for Dem. nom. for Gov. in
1928 and 1930.   Nom. and el. Gov. as Dem. in 1936, campaigning as an opponent of major policy positions of his
predecessor, Eugene Talmadge, and as a supporter of Pres.
Roosevelt's New Deal programs.   Nom. and el. again in 1938.
During admin., sought improvements in educl. system, welfare programs, and prison mgmt. system.   While in office,
Gov. Hurley's (Mass.) refusal of his request for return of
an escapee from a Ga. prison on grounds of inhumane treatment of prisoners in Ga. brought natl. attention of an un-
favorable kind to the State.   On one occasion employed
Natl. Guard troops to oust a mbr. of the Ga. Highway Commn.
who refused to vacate his office after R. had removed him
and a ct. order had been obtained ordering the officer's
re-instatement.   After tenure as Gov. had expired, charges
were brought against him alleging mis-appropriation of pub.
funds and the granting of pardons for "pecuniary gain".
The charges, which he attributed to the hostility of former
Gov. Talmadge, were eventually dropped.   Dir., Farmers and
Merchants Bank of Lakeland.   Pres., Suncoast Broadcasting
Corp., of Miami.   Trustee, Young Harris Coll. and of Ga.
Chapter, Natl. Found. for Infantile Paralysis.   Mbr.,
Masons; Elks; I.O.O.F.; Eagles; K.P.; Woodmen; various pro-
fessional legal orgs.   Baptist.   Hon. degree from Atlanta
Law School.   m. in 1914 to Mattie Lucille Lashley.   One s.;
one d.   D. June 11, 1967, at Atlanta, Ga.

TALMADGE, EUGENE (1941-1943).   See above, 1933-1937.

ARNALL, ELLIS GIBBS (1943-1947).   b. March 20, 1907 at
Newnan, Ga.   s. of Joseph Gibbs and Bessie (Ellis) A.
Father was a grocer.   Attd. Mercer Univ., 1924-1925 and the
Univ. of the South, from which he was grad. in 1928.   Received law degree from the Univ. of Ga. in 1931, and began
practice in Newnan.   Mbr. of Ga. House, 1933-1937.   Served
as Speaker, 1933-1935.   Asst. Atty. Gen. of Ga., 1937, and
became Atty. Gen. in 1939 at age 31.   Reel. Atty. Gen. in
1940.   In 1942 won Dem. nom. for Gov., defeating incumbent
Gov. Eugene Talmadge in a primary campaign attracting natl.

attention, and was el. Became the first four-year term
Gov. of Ga. During admin., championed various reforms.
State schools of higher learning regained accreditation;
powers of the governorship were curtailed; state debt was
liquidated; prison reforms instituted, including abolition
of "chain gangs"; a reformed Dept. of Corrections established. A revised const. was adopted in 1945. In 1944 he
personally argued successfully an anti-discrimination rate
suit before the U.S. Supreme Ct., in a case against Pa. R.R.
and 19 other railroad companies. Held over in office of
Gov. for a short time at end of term because of an unre-
solved election dispute concerning his successor, then resigned to permit the newly-chosen Lieut. Gov. (Thompson) to
claim the office. Received plurality in regular Dem. primary for Gov. in 1966, but was defeated in run-off primary.
Defeated as Indep. cand. for the office in the ensuing gen.
election. Recipient of Thomas Jefferson Award of So. Conf.
of Human Welfare in 1946. Pres., Ga. JCC in 1940. Hon.
degree from Piedmont Coll. Mbr., Masons; Elks; Woodmen;
Eagles; Lions; Kiwanis; Phi Beta Kappa. Baptist. m. in
1935 to Mildred DeLaney Slomons. One s.; one d.

TALMADGE, HERMAN EUGENE (1947; 1948-1955). b. Aug. 9,
1913 near McRae, in Telfair Co., Ga. s. of Eugene and
Mattie Thurmond (Peterson) T. Father was a Gov. of Ga.
(q.v.). Attd. local pub. schools at McRae and Atlanta; and
the Univ. of Ga., from which he received a law degree in
1936. Admitted to bar and practiced with his father at
Atlanta until 1941. Entered U.S. Navy as ensign trainee at
Northwestern Univ., 1942. In 1943-1945 saw service in So.
Pac. area during World War II, participating in a number of
engagements. Discharged in 1945 with rank of lieut. commdr.
Returned to law practice in Atlanta. Also became mgr. of
two farms owned by family. In 1946 gubernatorial election,
in which his father was the Dem. nominee, received several
hundred write-in votes for Gov. After his father died as
the Gov.-elect before inauguration, the Ga. legislature,
contending it had authority to choose a Gov. from among the
remaining living gen. election contestants, el. him as Gov.
Took the oath and occupied the office of Gov. for approximately nine weeks until the Ga. Supreme Ct. ruled against
his claim and directed that a spec. mid-term election be
held to choose a successor for the remainder of his
father's term, with the Lieut. Gov. to act as Gov. in the
meantime. Won the Dem. party nom. and was el. at the spec.
election in 1948. Assumed the office of Gov. as soon as
the final election result was announced. Was nom. for a
regular term in 1950 by a very narrow margin, despite a

provision in the Ga. const. prohibiting an immediately
successive term. In 1956 was nom. and el. to U.S. Senate
seat, and continued therein by reel. thereafter. As a Sen.,
played an important role in opposing Fed. civil rights
legislation and jud. decisions relating thereto. Also was
prominent in efforts to enact legislation designed to curb
the powers of U.S. cts., and as ch. of Senate Commt. on
Agri., of measures to promote farming indus. Was subjected
to an investigation by Senate Ethics Commt. on charges of
conversion of election campaign funds to his personal use,
and was "denounced" by vote of the Senate for his role in
the matter in 1979. Mbr., Masons; Eagles; Amer. Legion;
S.C.V.; V.F.W.; Navy League; Amer. Farm Bureau; various
clubs and professional legal orgs. Baptist. Hon. degree
from Atlanta Law School. m. in 1941 to Leila Elizabeth
Shingler, of Ashburn, Ga. Two s. Marriage ended in
divorce.

THOMPSON, MELVIN ERNEST (1947-1948). b. May 1, 1903
at Millen, Jenkins Co., Ga. s. of Henry J. and Eva Inez
(Edenfield) T. Attd. Emory Univ., from which he received
an A.B. degree in 1926; the Univ. of Ga., from which he
received an M.A. degree in 1935; also did post-grad. study
at Emory Univ.; the Univ. of Ala., and Peabody Coll. Principal and teacher at Emanuel Co. Inst., 1926. Supt. of pub.
schools at Hawkinsville, Ga., 1933-1937. Asst. State Supt.
of Schools, 1937-1943. Exec. sect. to Gov. Arnall, 1943-
1945. State Revenue Commnr., 1945. El. Lieut. Gov. as Dem.
in 1946. When the Gov.-elect, Eugene Talmadge, died before
he could be inaugurated, T., after taking the oath as Lieut.
Gov., assumed the office of Gov. by right of succession on
Jan. 18, 1947. Was physically ousted from office by
officers acting under orders of a rival claimant to the
office, Herman Talmadge. Later the Ga. Supreme Ct. ruled
that T., as Lieut. Gov., should occupy the office of Gov.
by right of succession until election of a successor at
mid-term for the remaining part of the term. Re-assumed the
office of Gov. in March, 1947. Lost by a narrow margin
Dem. nom. for Gov. at a spec. primary conducted in 1948.
Having previously been obliged by law to resign the office
of Lieut. Gov. as a condition for becoming a cand. for Gov.
at the spec. primary, he surrendered the office of Gov. to
his successful opponent, H. Talmadge, in Nov., 1948. Defeated as cand. for the Dem. nom. for Gov. in 1950, again
losing to H. Talmadge by a very close margin. Also was defeated for the Dem. nom. for Gov. in 1954 and for the U.S.
Senate in 1956. Mbr., Masons; Woodmen; Elks; various professional educl. orgs. Baptist. Author, with Dr. M. Pound,

of <u>Georgia Citizenship</u> in 1939, and ed. of various pamphlets
and aids to teachers, 1939-1943. m. in 1927 to Anne Newton.
One s.

TALMADGE, HERMAN EUGENE (1948-1955). See above, 1947.

GRIFFIN, S(AMUEL) MARVIN (1955-1959). b. Sept. 4,
1907 at Bainbridge, Ga. s. of Ernest Howard and Josephine
(Baker) G. Father was a newspaper publ. who had served in
Ga. legislature. Attd. local pub. schools and the Citadel,
in S.C., from which he was grad. in 1929. Served for a time
as instructor in mil. sci. at Randolph-Macon Acad. in Front
Royal, Va. When father died in 1933, took over as ed. and
publ. of family weekly newspaper, the Bainbridge <u>Post-
Searchlight</u>. Mbr. of Ga. legislature, 1935-1936. In 1940
became exec. sect. to Gov. Rivers. Resigned in Oct., 1940,
to enlist as a pvt. in Ga. Natl. Guard, soon achieving rank
of capt. Called into natl. service, receiving command of
an anti-aircraft battalion in So. Pac. in 1942. Rose to
rank of lieut. col. in New Guinea campaign during World War
II. Returned to U.S. in 1944 to become Adjt. Gen. of Ga.,
serving until 1947. Lost as cand. for Dem. nom. for Lieut.
Gov. in 1946; but in 1948 spec. election was nom. and el.
to that office. Reel. for full term as Lieut. Gov. in 1950.
Nom. and el. Gov. as Dem. in 1954. As Gov., sought to
attract indus. to State. Also took active role in opposing
U.S. govtl. efforts to desegregate pub. schools. Supported
move of Ga. legislature to adopt an intervention resolution
denying validity of U.S. Supreme Ct.'s desegregation case
rulings of 1954. Took leading role in org. of Ga. State
Rts. Councils to resist desegregation. Gave support to
plan to give pub. aid to pvt. schools. Defeated for Dem.
nom. for Gov. in 1962. Mbr., Masons; Lions; Amer. Legion;
V.F.W.; Moose; Eagles; Woodmen; Elks; various clubs and
fraternities. Presbyterian. m. in 1931 to Mary Elizabeth
Smith, of Winchester, Va. One s.; one d.

VANDIVER, S(AMUEL) ERNEST, Jr. (1959-1963). b. July 3,
1918 at Canon, Ga. s. of Samuel Ernest and Vanna (Bowers)
V. Attd. pub. schools at Lavonia, Ga.; Darlington Prep.
school, at Rome, Ga.; and the Univ. of Ga., from which he
was grad. with an A.B. degree in 1940 and a law degree in
1942. Served as a bomber pilot in U.S. Air Force during
World War II. Mayor of Lavonia, 1945. In 1946 began practice of law in Winder, Ga. Assisted in campaign of Eugene
Talmadge for Gov. in 1946, and was campaign mgr. for Herman
Talmadge for Gov. in 1948. In Sept., 1948, became Adj. Gen.
of State's mil. forces, with rank of brig. gen. Also was

dir. of Ga. Selective Service system. Dir. of Civil Defense
in 1951. Named as one of five Outstanding Young Men by Ga.
JCC. In 1954 was el. Lieut. Gov. Nom. and el. Gov. as Dem.
in 1958. During admin., created state budget office; improved state purchasing system; expanded support for educ.,
med. services, highways, agri.; and launched an extensive
pub. works program. Ch. of Commts. on Indus. Devel. and on
the Natl. Guard of So. Govs.' Conf. and mbr. of the Civil
Defense Council of the Natl. Govs.' Conf. Defeated as cand.
for the Dem. nom. for U.S. Senate seat in 1972 in both the
regular primary and a spec. primary. Baptist. m. in 1947
to Sybil Elizabeth Russell, of Winder, Ga. One s.; two d.

SANDERS, CARL EDWARD (1963-1967). b. Nov. 15, 1925 at
Augusta, Ga. s. of Carl T. and Roberta (Jones) S. Attd.
local pub. schools. Served as a bomber pilot in U.S. Air
Force in latter stages of World War II. Attd. the Univ. of
Ga., from which he received a law degree in 1947. Began
law practice in Augusta in 1948. Mbr. of Ga. House, 1954-
1956, and of Ga. Senate, 1959-1962. Served as Pres. pro tem
of Senate, 1960-1962. Nom. and el. Gov. as Dem. in 1962.
Returned to law practice after tenure as Gov. Defeated for
Dem. nom. for Gov. in 1970 by James E. Carter. Mbr. of
various community service orgs., including the exec. council
of Ga.-S.C. Boy Scouts, and vice pres. of bd. of YMCA, and
of Amer. Red Cross. Mbr., Masons; Elks; Moose; Amer.
Legion; several fraternities. Named as one of five outstanding Young Men of Ga. in 1959 by Ga. JCC. Baptist. m.
in 1947 to Betty Bird Foy. One s.; one d.

MADDOX, LESTER GARFIELD (1967-1971). b. Sept. 30, 1915
at Atlanta, Ga. One of seven children of Dean Garfield and
Flonnie (Castlebury) M. Father was a steel plant worker
who became unemployed during depression of 1930s, leaving
family in very poor circumstances. Dropped out of h.s. in
junior year, but later finished h.s. program by correspondence. Worked at a variety of jobs. Tried poultry farming
unsuccessfully. Started small food grill bus. in Atlanta
in 1944 which expanded into a prosperous restaurant enterprise. Became involved in local politics as defender of
States Rts. and opponent of U.S. govt.'s interference with
pvt. enterprise. Unsuccessful cand. for mayor of Atlanta
in 1957 and 1961, and for Dem. nom. for Lieut. Gov. in 1962.
Uncompromising stand against desegregation of his bus. after
passage of U.S. Civil Rights Act of 1964 caused him to become symbol of anti-desegregation struggle in Atlanta and
the State. Supported Sen. Goldwater for Pres. of U.S. in
1964. In 1965 was tried and acquitted on charge of

displaying pistol to intimidate Negroes seeking to desegregate his place of bus. Disposed of his restaurant rather
than submit to ct. orders regarding how it should be operated. Entered Dem. primary race for Gov. in 1966 and won nom.
in run-off against former Gov. Arnall. In the ensuing gen.
election in which Arnall ran as an Indep. (Dem.), the Rep.
cand. received a plurality of the popular vote, but not a
majority, thus requiring the outcome to be determined by
joint vote of the two branches of the legislature. M. was
el. after cts. upheld validity of that method of resolving
the issue under a provision of the state const. that had
never before been successfully employed since its adoption
in 1824. This resulted in the submission and adoption of
an amdt. to the state const. during his admin. providing
for a run-off popular election in this kind of contingency
in the future. Admin. proved to be relatively moderate,
with no major clashes with U.S. authority over desegregation
policies. Refused to give his support to the third party
candidacy of Gov. Wallace of Ala. for the U.S. presidency
in 1968. Being debarred by the state const. from seeking
immediate reel., he was nom. and el. to the office of
Lieut. Gov. in 1970. Defeated for Dem. nom. for Gov. in a
run-off primary contest in 1974, although he received a
plurality of popular votes in the first primary. In 1976,
accepted the nom. of the Amer. Indep. party for Pres. of
U.S., and received some 170,000 popular votes in the nation.
Mbr., Masons (Shriner); O.A.M.; Moose; various bus. orgs.
Baptist. m. in 1936 to Hattie Virginia Cox, of Birmingham,
Ala. Two s.; two d.

    CARTER, JAMES EARL ("JIMMY"), Jr. (1971-1975). b. Oct.
1, 1924 at Plains, Ga. s. of James Earl and Lillian (Gordy)
C. First mbr. of ancestral line bearing the family name
came to Va. in 1635 as an indentured servant. Great-great-
grandfather moved from Va. to vicinity of Plains in 1850s.
Father was a prosperous farmer and operator of a peanut
processing bus. Attd. Ga. Southwest Coll., 1941-1942; Ga.
Inst. of Tech., 1942-1943; and U.S. Naval Acad., from which
he was grad. in 1947. Later did post-grad. study in nuclear
physics at Union Coll. Served as U.S. naval officer until
1954, resigning commn. as lieut., j.g., in that year. Returned to Plains where he assisted in operation of family
farming and peanut processing bus. Ch. of Sumter Co.
school bd., 1955-1962. Ch. of the bd. of Americus and
Sumter Co. Hosp. Authority and of Sumter Redevelopment Corp.
Mbr. of West Cent. Ga. Area Planning and Devel. Commn.
Mbr. of Ga. Senate, 1963-1967. Defeated as cand. for Dem.
nom. for Gov. in 1966. Nom. for Gov. in Dem. run-off

primary in 1970, defeating former Gov. Sanders, and was el.
During admin., promoted reorg. of state admin. services;
sought diversification of indus. of State. After leaving
office in 1975, launched effort to win Dem. nom. for Pres.
of U.S., which proved successful. El. Pres. of U.S. in
1976, defeating incumbent Pres. Gerald Ford by a narrow
margin. Nom. for second term as Pres. in 1980. Mbr.,
Lions. Baptist. Author of Why Not the Best? in 1975, in
which he outlined his political philosophy. m. in 1946 to
Rosalynn Smith, of Sumter Co., Ga. Three s.; one d.

BUSBEE, GEORGE DEKLE (1975------). b. Aug. 7, 1927 at
Vienna, Ga. s. of Perry G. and Nell (Dekle) B. Served in
U.S. Navy during World War II. Attd. Duke Univ. and the
Univ. of Ga., from which he was grad. with a bus. admin.
degree in 1949, and a law degree in 1952. Admitted to bar
and engaged in practice at Albany, Ga., 1952-1974. Mbr. of
Ga. House, 1957-1974, serving as Dem. floor leader there
during 1967-1974. Nom. and el. Gov. as Dem. in 1974. Defeated former Gov. Maddox in Dem. run-off primary for the
nom., although latter had received a plurality of the
popular vote in the first primary. Reel. in 1978. Ch.,
So. Growth Policies Bd. Ch. of Commt. on Transp., Commerce
and Technology of Natl. Govs.' Assoc. Recipient, Margaret
Sanger Planned Parenthood Award. Mbr., Phi Delta Theta;
various professional legal orgs. Baptist. m. in 1949 to
Mary Elizabeth Talbot. One d.; three s.

QUINN, WILLIAM FRANCIS (1959-1962). b. July 13, 1919
at Rochester, N.Y. s. of Charles Alvin and Elizabeth
(Dorrity) Q. Family moved to St. Louis, Mo. when son was
four years old. Attd. St. Louis Univ., graduating summa cum
laude in 1940. Entered Harvard Univ. to study law, but
withdrew in 1942 to enter U.S. Navy. Received commendation
for engagement in action at Okinawa. Returned to Harvard,
and received law degree in 1947. Became mbr. of law firm in
Honolulu, Terr. of Haw., continuing therein until 1957. Was
a strong advocate of statehood for Haw. In July, 1957, was
apptd. Gov. of Terr. of Haw. by Pres. Eisenhower. As Terr.
Gov., continued to work for statehood. Successful in bringing to an end by mediation in June, 1958, a 126-day old
strike by maritime workers that had seriously impaired
economy of the Terr. Upon passage of Hawaiian Statehood Act
by Congress in 1959 was nom. and el. first Gov. of the State
as a Rep. in July of that year. During admin., state govt.
was org. under the new const. Defeated as Rep. cand. for
succeeding term in 1962. Resumed law practice. Defeated as
Rep. nominee for U.S. Senate in 1976. Exec. vice pres. of
Dole Co., 1964-1965, and pres. from 1965 onward. Dir. of
Bishop Trust Co. Mbr. of Bd. of Regents, Chaminade Coll.
Mbr., various bus. and professional legal orgs. Trustee,
Nutrition Found. Roman Catholic. m. in 1912 to Nancy Ellen
Witbeck. Five s.; two d.

BURNS, JOHN ANTHONY (1962-1974). b. March 30, 1909 at
Ft. Assinneboine, Mont. s. of Harry J. and Anna Florida
(Scolly) B. Father was a U.S. Army sgt. Attd. pub. schools
in Honolulu, where his father was stationed at the time, and
also at Atchison, Kans. Attd. the Univ. of Haw. Mbr. of
Honolulu police dept., serving as chief of espionage bureau,
1941-1943. Defended loyalty of Japanese-Amer. citizens to
U.S. during World War II. Served one year in U.S. Army. In
1945 entered retail store bus., later becoming pres. and
mgr. of a real estate firm at Kailua. One of organizers of
Dem. party in Haw. Ch. of Oahu Dem. commt., 1948-1952, and
ch. of Haw. Dem. commt., 1952-1956. Delegate to Dem. natl.
convs., 1952 through 1968. From 1956 to 1959 was Terr.
Delegate to U.S. Cong. from Haw. Was a strong advocate of
statehood for both Alas. and Haw. Defeated as Dem. cand.
for Gov. in 1959 in first election after statehood was
achieved, but was nom. again and el. in 1962, defeating incumbent Gov. Quinn. Reel. in 1966 and 1970. Became
incapacitated by illness during last 14 months of third term
and relinquished powers of office to Lieut. Gov. Ariyoshi
during that time, but did not resign office. Pres. of Haw.
chapter, Natl. Soc. for Crippled Children and Adults. Mbr.,

Civitan; Lions; various clubs. Hon. degrees from Univ. of
Haw.; St. Benedict's Coll.; Gonzaga Univ.; Chaminade Coll.
Roman Catholic. m. in 1931 to Beatrice Majors Van Fleet.
Two s.; one d. Wife was stricken by disabling attack of
polio during course of marriage. D. April 5, 1975, at
Honolulu a few months after completion of term as Gov. Bur.
in Natl. Memorial Cem. of the Pac., on Oahu.

ARIYOSHI, GEORGE RYOICHI (1974------). b. March 12,
1926 at Honolulu, Terr. of Haw. s. of Ryozo and Mitsue
(Yoshikawa) A. Attd. local pub. schools; the Univ. of Haw.;
Mich. State Univ., from which he was grad.; and the Univ. of
Mich., from which he received a law degree. Served in U.S.
Army as a pvt., 1945-1946. Mbr. of Haw. Terr. House, 1954-
1958, and of Haw. Terr. Senate, 1958-1959. El. to Haw.
Senate after statehood was achieved, continuing to serve
therein until 1970. Served as majority (Dem.) leader in
1965-1966 and 1969-1970. Also engaged in practice of law in
Honolulu, 1952-1970. Mbr. of constl. conv. of 1968. El.
Lieut. Gov. as Dem. in 1970. Was Acting Gov. during last
14 months of Gov. Burns' final term because of latter's ill-
ness. Nom. and el. Gov. as Dem. in 1974 and was reel. in
1978. Was first person of Japanese ancestry to become an
Amer. State Gov. Mbr., bd. of dir. of First Natl. Bank of
Haw., 1962-1970; of Honolulu Gas Co., 1964-1970; and of
Hawaiian Ins. Guaranty Co., 1966-1970. Pres., Hawaiian
Club, Univ. of Mich. Mbr., various professional legal orgs.
Protestant. m. in 1953 to Jean Miya Hayashi. Two s.; one d

SHOUP, GEORGE LAIRD (1890). b. June 15, 1836 at
Kittanning, Pa. Family was of German descent. Attd. pub.
schools at Freeport and Slate Lick, Pa. In 1852 family
moved to Ill., where he engaged in farming and stock-raising
near Galesburg. In 1859 went to Colo., where he engaged in
mining and merc. bus. When Civil War began, org. a volunteer Union cavalry unit which engaged in scouting and Indian
fighting in the West during the war. Rose from rank of second lieut. to col. Mbr. of Colo. constl. conv. in 1864.
Engaged in merc. bus. in Virginia City, Mont. for a time,
and in 1866 at Salmon City, Ida. Also engaged in mining and
stock-raising. Held local offices, including co. treas. and
supt. of schools. Mbr. of Ida. Terr. legislature in 1874
and of the Terr. Council, 1878. Delegate to Rep. natl. conv.
in 1880 and mbr. of Rep. natl. commt., 1880-1884 and 1888-
1890. U.S. commnr. for Ida. at the World's Cotton Centennial Expo. at New Orleans, 1884-1885. Apptd. Gov. of Ida.
Terr. by Pres. Benj. Harrison in 1889. Supported admission
of Ida. as a State, and was el. as the first Gov. of the
State of Ida. as a Rep. in 1890. Resigned within two weeks
after assuming office, having been el. to the U.S. Senate by
the legislature. Continued to serve therein until 1901. Defeated for second full term in 1901. m. in 1868 to Lena
Darnutzer. Six children. D. at Boise, Dec. 24, 1904. Bur.
in Masonic Cem. there.

WILLEY, NORMAN BUSHNELL (1890-1893). b. Mar. 25, 1838
at Guilford, N.Y. s. of Hiram and Caroline (Church) W.
Descended from an English colonist who emigrated to Mass. in
1640. Spent childhood on father's farm. Attd. local
schools and an acad. at Franklin, N.Y. In 1858 went to
Calif., where he engaged in mining until 1864. In that year
moved to Warren, Ida. Terr. Held various local offices.
Mbr. of Terr. legislature, 1872-1873 and 1878-1879, serving
as presiding officer in latter term. As mbr. of legislature,
opposed Mormon influence in the Terr. In 1890 was nom. and
el. Lieut. Gov. as a Rep. in first election after Ida. became a State. Succeeded to office of Gov. very shortly after assuming office of Lieut. Gov. because of resignation of
Gov. Shoup to take U.S. Senate seat. Served until end of
Shoup's term. Admin. concerned mainly with setting up state
and local govt. in the newly created State. After tenure as
Gov., returned to Calif., where he engaged in various mining
enterprises. Never married. D. Nov. 20, 1931, at the age
of 93.

McCONNELL, WILLIAM JOHN (1893-1897). b. Sept. 18, 1839
at Commerce, Mich. s. of James and Nancy (Coulter) McC.

Parents had emigrated from No. Ireland to Amer. Attd. local
schools. In 1860 went to Calif., where he engaged in mining
for a time. Taught school in Ore. in 1862-1863. Moved to
Ida. Terr. in 1863 after gold mining began at Boise. Engaged in farming for a time, and was a U.S. deputy marshal.
Returned to Ore. where he engaged in cattle ranching, banking and merc. bus. until 1886. Mbr. of Ore. Senate in 1882,
serving as Pres. of that body. Delegate to Rep. natl. conv.
in 1884. Moved to Moscow, Ida. Terr., in 1886 and became
active in local politics. Was an advocate of statehood for
Ida. Mbr. of Ida. constl. conv. in 1889-1890. El. to partial term as one of Idaho's first two U.S. Senators in 1890.
Nom. and el. Gov. as Rep. in 1892. Reel. in 1894. After
tenure as Gov. served as Indian reservation inspector by
apptmt. from Pres. McKinley, 1897-1901. Inspector in U.S.
Immigration Service, stationed in Moscow, Ida. from 1909 until death. m. in 1866 to Louisa Brown, of Ore. Five
children. D. Mar. 30, 1925, at Moscow. Bur. in Moscow Cem.

STEUNENBERG, FRANK (1897-1901). b. Aug. 8, 1861 at
Keokuk, Iowa. Parents emigrated to Amer. from Holland, and
later established their residence at Knoxville, Iowa. Attd.
Knoxville schools and Iowa State Coll. (now Univ.), at Ames.
Learned printing trade at an early age, and was employed by
a number of daily newspapers in the area. Acquired a newspaper, the Knoxville Express, which he published with a
partner for two years. In 1887 moved to Caldwell, Idaho
Terr., where in partnership with a brother became publ. of
Caldwell Tribune. Became influential in Idaho politics.
Mbr. of town council at Caldwell. Mbr. of Idaho constl.
conv. of 1889, and of the first Ida. legislature. El. Gov.
in 1896 as nominee of Dem. and Pop. parties and the Silver
Rep. faction. Reel. in 1898 as Dem. and Silver Rep.
nominee. During admin., serious labor troubles in the Couer
d'Alene mining dist. resulted in disturbances necessitating
resort to martial law and his calling for assistance of Fed.
troops. Subsequent trials and convictions of some of the
labor leaders on riot and other serious charges caused much
controversy. Unsuccessful as cand. for Rep. nom. for U.S.
Senate seat in 1900. m. in 1885 to Belle Keppel, of Keokuk,
Iowa. Four children. Was murdered at his home by use of a
bomb on Dec. 30, 1905. The resultant investigation, trial
and conviction of some leaders of the Western Miners Union,
believed to have been responsible for his death, was a matter attracting natl. attention during the admin. of Gov.
Gooding, (q.v.).

HUNT, FRANK WILLIAMS (1901-1903). b. Dec. 16, 1861 at

Newport, Ky. s. of Thomas B. and Eugenia A. (Montmolin) H.
Father was a capt. in Union Army during the Civil War.
Attd. local common schools. As a young man moved to
Gibbonsville, Ida. Terr. in 1888, where he engaged in mining
and various bus. enterprises. Mbr. of Ida. Senate, 1893-
1894. Served as a volunteer in the Spanish-Amer. War, entering service as a lieut. Participated in several engagements in the Philippine Islands. Rose to rank of capt., and
was decorated for bravery. Nom. and el. Gov. as Dem. in
1900. As Gov., advocated measures to improve agri. and
commerce, and sought to attract Eastern capital for devel.
of the State's resources. Sought U.S. govt.'s aid for
irrigation projects. Defeated for reel. in 1902. m. in
1896 to Ruth Maynard, of Boise. D. Nov. 25, 1906.

MORRISON, JOHN TRACY (1903-1905). b. Dec. 25, 1860 in
Jefferson Co., Pa. s. of John and Sophia Elizabeth (Tracy)
M. Attd. the Univ. of Wooster, from which he received an
A.B. degree in 1887 and an A.M. degree in 1890. Entered
Cornell Univ., from which he received a law degree in 1890.
Moved to Caldwell, Ida., and engaged in law practice. Became active in Rep. party affairs, serving as sect. of Rep.
state commt. in 1896 and ch., 1897-1900. Unsuccessful cand.
for seat in U.S. House in 1896 and 1900. Nom. and el. Gov.
as Rep. in 1902, defeating incumbent Gov. Hunt. Active in
affairs of Presbyterian church, serving as a commnr. to its
Natl. Gen. Assembly in 1892 and again in 1897. m. in 1886
to Grace Darling Mackey, of Jamestown, N.Y. D. Dec. 20,
1915.

GOODING, FRANK ROBERT (1905-1909). b. Sept. 16, 1859
at Tiverton, Devonshire, England. s. of John and Elizabeth
(Wyatt) G. Emigrated with parents to Paw Paw, Mich. in
1867. Attd. pub. schools there. In 1874 went to the
Sacramento Valley in Calif., where he engaged in farming and
mining for several years. In 1881 moved to Ketchum, in Ida.
Terr., where he worked as mail carrier and engaged in fire-
wood and charcoal bus. In 1888 homesteaded a claim and engaged in farming and stock-raising. Expanded land holdings
and became operator of largest sheep ranch in Ida. Town of
Gooding grew up as center of farming and stock-raising enterprises. Became active in Rep. party politics, serving
as ch. of Rep. state commt. in 1902. Mbr. of Ida. Senate,
1901-1905, serving as Pres. pro tem in last term. Nom. and
el. Gov. as Rep. in 1904, and again in 1906. During admin.,
the murder of former Gov. Stuenenberg (q.v.) was the occasion for trial and conviction of several prominent labor
union officials deemed responsible for the murder, which

attracted natl. attention. Served as State Fuel Admin. during World War I. Unsuccessful cand. for U.S. Senate seat in
a special election in 1918; but was apptd. to fill a vacancy
in that body in 1920 and subsequently el. Continued to
serve in the Senate until his death. As Sen., was prominently identified with the "Farm Bloc"; supported attempts
at closer regulation of railroad rates; and was a strong advocate of strict prohibition enforcement. Mbr., Masons.
Episcopalian. m. in 1879 to Amanda J. Thomas. Two d.; one
s. D. at Gooding, Ida., June 24, 1928.

BRADY, JAMES HENRY (1909-1911). b. June 21, 1862 in
Indiana Co., Pa. s. of John and Catherine (Lee) B. Family
ancestral line included a number of distinguished soldiers.
Father, who was a farmer, moved to Johnson Co., Kans. in
1865. Attd. pub. schools there and Leavenworth Normal, at
Leavenworth, Kans. Taught school for a time. Studied law.
Ed. of a weekly newspaper at Enterprise, Kans. for two
years. Went into real estate bus. at Abilene, Kans. Operated in various Western locations, eventually settling in
Pocatello, Ida. in 1895. Became actively identified with
bldg. of irrigation projects and devel. of water power
resources in Snake River Valley. Pres. and main owner of
Ida. Consolidated Power Co. at American Falls; also head of
James H. Brady Investment Co. Vice pres., Natl. Irrigation
Cong., 1896-1898 and 1904-1906, and mbr. of its exec.
commt., 1900-1904. Delegate to Rep. natl. convs. in 1900
and 1908, serving as ch. of Ida. delegation in latter year.
Ch. of Rep. state commt., 1904-1908. Nom. and el. Gov. as
Rep. in 1908. As Gov., supported direct primary system;
local option prohibition law; mining safety and employer
liability legislation; state care for homeless children;
and indeterminate sentencing for persons convicted of felo-
nies. Unsuccessful as Rep. cand. for reel. in 1910.
Apptd. to U.S. Senate to fill vacancy in 1913 and continued
in that office until his death. Mbr., Masons; I.O.O.F.;
Elks; W.O.W.; Eagles; numerous clubs and bus. assoc. Congregationalist. Two s. D. Jan. 13, 1918. Ashes interred
at Mountain View Cem., in Pocatello, Ida.

HAWLEY, JAMES HENRY (1911-1913). b. Jan. 17, 1847 at
Dubuque, Iowa. s. of Thomas and Annie (Carr) H. Anteced-
ents came to Amer. from England, settling originally in
Brooklyn, N.Y. in 1811. Attd. Dubuque pub. schools. Went
to Calif. in 1861, moving the next year to Ida. Terr. En-
gaged in mining. Also enrolled at City Coll., in
San Francisco and studied law in law office. El. to lower
House of Ida. Terr. legislature in 1870, and to Ida. Terr.

Council in 1874. Admitted to bar in 1871. Soon acquired
extensive criminal practice. Dist. atty. in Ida., 1879-
1883, and from 1884 to 1887 was U.S. dist. atty. for the
Terr. Participated as one of pros. attys., along with Wm.
E. Borah, in trials growing out of Couer d'Alene disturbances. Acquired extensive civil practice in connection with
mining, irrigation and water power interests. Mayor of
Boise, 1904-1905. Nom. and el. Gov. as Dem. in 1910, defeating incumbent Gov. Brady in very close election. Defeated for reel. in 1912. Unsuccessful cand. for U.S.
Senate seat in 1914. Continued in law practice at Boise
thereafter. m. in 1875 to Mary E. Bullock, of Quartzburg,
Ida. Four s.; three d. D. Aug. 3, 1929.

HAINES, JOHN MICHINER (1913-1915). b. Jan. 1, 1863 in
Jasper Co., Iowa. s. of Isaac L. and Eliza (Bushong) H.
Spent boyhood on father's farm. Entered Penn Coll., at
Oskaloosa, Iowa, at age 17, but was forced to withdraw because of poor health at end of junior year. Went to Friend,
Nebr., where he was a bank employee for two years. Moved
to Richfield, Kans., in 1885 and engaged in real estate bus.
there. Moved to Boise, Ida., in 1890, continuing in real
estate bus. there with former partners. Enterprise proved
successful. Mayor of Boise, 1907. Nom. and el. Gov. as
Rep. in 1912, despite split in party growing out of Prog.
party movement. Defeated for reel. in 1914. m. in 1883 to
Mary Symonds, of Jasper Co., Iowa, d. of a Quaker minister.
Mbr. of Quaker (Friends) church. D. June 4, 1917.

ALEXANDER, MOSES (1915-1919). b. Nov. 13, 1853 at
Obrigheim, Rheinpfalz, Bavaria. s. of Nathan and Eva
(Frankel) A. Emigrated to New York City with parents. Became an orphan at age 14. Moved to Chillicothe, Mo. in
1868, where he worked in a merc. establishment. Became
partner in firm in 1873. Mbr. of city council of
Chillicothe, 1886 and mayor, 1887. In 1891 moved to Boise,
Ida., where he continued in merc. bus. Expanded bus. operations with branches in Ore. and other cities of Ida. Also
launched real estate and irrigation enterprises. Mayor of
Boise, 1897-1898 and 1901-1902. Unsuccessful as Dem.
nominee for Gov. in 1908, but was successful as Dem.
nominee for that office in 1914, defeating incumbent Gov.
Haines. Reel. in close vote in 1916, winning by less than
600 votes out of a total of almost 135,000. During admin.,
reduced taxes; supported prohibition; a workmen's compensation law was enacted; highway constr. program launched. Cooperated in World War I measures of U.S. govt. Delegate to
Dem. natl. convs. in 1920, 1924 and 1928. Dem. nominee for

Gov. again in 1922, but finished third in three-man race
against Rep. and Prog. party candidates. Was the first
Jewish Gov. of Ida. m. in 1876 to Hedwig Keastner, of
St. Catherine, Mo. Three d.; one s. D. at Boise, Jan. 4,
1932.

DAVIS, DAVID WILLIAM (1919-1923). b. April 23, 1873 at
Cardiff, Wales. s. of John Wynn and Frances (Lewis) D. In
1875 came to Amer. with parents, who settled in Southeastern
Iowa. Started work in coal mine at age of 12. At age 15,
became a clerk in mine company store at Dawson, Iowa. At
age 21, became mgr. of a farm cooperative store at Rippey,
Iowa, and in 1899 cashier of a bank there. In 1905 moved to
Dayton, Wash., and soon afterward to American Falls, Ida.
Org. a bank there, of which he became pres. Also acquired
interest in a newspaper, the American Falls Press. Delegate
to Rep. natl. conv. in 1912. Mbr. of Ida. Senate, 1913-1914.
Unsuccessful as Rep. nominee for Gov. in 1916, losing to
incumbent Gov. Alexander by 572 votes out of a total of some
135,000. Ch. of War Loan Committee for Ida. during World
War I. Nom. and el. Gov. in 1918. Reel. in 1920. During
admin., a nine-mbr. Bd. of Commnrs. was created to supervise
all civil admin. functions of the State; road-building expanded by a bond issue; a budget and taxation bureau created;
and the State Supreme Ct. was reorg. and given enlarged
functions. Apptd. as spec. asst. to U.S. Sect. of Interior
in 1923, and soon afterward became U.S. Commnr. of Reclamation. In 1924-1926, served as finance dir. of U.S. Reclamation Bureau and dir. of crop production loans in U.S. Dept.
of Agri. After govtl. service, engaged in farming and
stock-raising. Trustee of Gooding Coll. Pres. of Ida.
Bankers Assoc. Mbr., Masons. Methodist. m. in 1894 to
Florence O. Gilleland, of Rippey, Iowa, who died in 1903.
m. in 1905 to Nellie Johnson, of Rippey. Two s.; one d. D.
at Lincoln, Ida., Aug. 5, 1959.

MOORE, CHARLES CALVIN (1923-1927). b. Feb. 26, 1866
in Holt Co., Mo. s. of Socrates and Eliza (McCune) M.
Father was a farmer who had moved to Mo. from Pa. Attd.
h.s. in Mound City, Mo. Student at Warrensburg, Mo. Normal
(now Cent. Mo. State Univ.). From 1886 to 1895 taught
school and farmed in Holt Co. and Atchison Co., Mo. Deputy
assessor for one year, and co. aud. and recorder, 1895-1899.
Moved in 1899 to St. Anthony, Ida., where he had acquired
land. Taught school at St. Anthony and engaged in drug
store bus. there. In 1903, went into real estate bus.
while continuing to operate own farm. Formed a real estate
devel. co. with partner in 1906, and laid out townsite of

Ashton, Ida. Mbr. of pub. school bd. at St. Anthony. Org.
and became pres. of St. Anthony Bank and Trust Co. Mbr.,
Ida. House, 1903-1907. U.S. postmaster at St. Anthony,
1908-1913. El. Lieut. Gov. in 1918. In 1922, was nom. and
el. Gov. as a Rep., and again in 1924. During admin., took
steps to alleviate economic distress arising from farm depression of 1920s. Taxes and appropriations reduced; measures for protection of state forests adopted; pardoning and
reprieve powers used freely. U.S. Commnr. of Gen. Land
Office, 1929-1933. Mbr., Masons; Elks; I.O.O.F.; W.O.W.;
Christian (Disciples) church. m. to Minnie McCoy, of Holt
Co., Mo., who died in 1909. Four children. m. in 1915 to
Clara E. Wallen, of Adams, Ore. D. March 19, 1958. Bur.
at Mt. Olivet Cem., in Salt Lake City, Utah.

   BALDRIDGE, H. CLARENCE (1927-1931). b. Nov. 24, 1868
at Carlock, Ill. s. of John and Caroline (Wright) B. Family line traced back to a colonist who came to Baltimore,
Md. in 1637 from Ireland. Attd. local schools and entered
Ill. Wesleyan Coll. in 1890. Left college in 1893 to engage in teaching and farming. In 1896 org. a grain dealing
firm at Carlock, Ill. Sold bus. in 1904 and moved to Parma,
Ida., where he set up a gen. merc. bus. Sold that bus. in
1909 and opened an implement and hardware store. Expanded
the firm, with son as partner, into points in Ore. Mbr.,
Ida. House, 1911-1913 and of Ida. Senate, 1913-1915. Founded First Natl. Bank of Parma, becoming its pres. El. Lieut.
Gov. in 1922 and was reel. in 1924. Nom. and el. Gov. as
Rep. in 1926, and again in 1928. As Gov., opposed indis-
criminate expansion of pub. bldg. programs; instituted gasoline tax for highway constr.; educl. programs extended;
water power devel. and water rights placed under closer
govtl. control. Defeated in 1942 as Rep. nominee for U.S.
House seat. Trustee of Coll. of Idaho, at Caldwell. Mbr.,
Masons; Elks; Phi Gamma Delta. Presbyterian. m. in 1893
to Cora McCreight, of Hudson, Ill. Two children. D. June
7, 1947 at Parma.

   ROSS, C(HARLES) BEN(JAMIN) (1931-1937). b. Dec. 27,
1876 at Parma, Ida. Terr. s. of John M. and Jeannette
(Hadley) R. Father was a stockman, miner and freighter.
Attd. local pub. schools and bus. coll. at Boise, Ida. and
Portland, Ore. Became interested in reclamation of arid
lands by irrigation, crop diversification, and improvement
of farm life generally. Vice pres. of Riverside Irrigation
Dist., 1906-1915. Ch. of Bd. of Commnrs. of Canyon Co. un-
til 1921. Pres. of Ida. Farm Bureau, 1921. Mayor of
Pocatello, Ida., 1922-1930. Unsuccessful as Dem. nominee

for Gov. in 1928; but was nom. again and el. in 1930. Reel.
in 1932 and 1934. Became the first native-born Idahoan to
hold office of Gov. During admin., tax system was revised;
primary law and initiative, referendum and recall systems
revised. Opposed liberalization of divorce law, but his
veto of a revisory act was overridden by the legislature.
Unsuccessful as Dem. nominee for U.S. Senate seat in 1936.
Nominee of Dem. party for Gov. again in 1938, but was defeated in gen. election. Mbr., I.O.O.F.; Elks; Eagles:
Kiwanis; Rotary. Congregationalist. m. in 1900 to Edna
Reavis, of Washington Co., Ida. Three adopted children. D.
at Boise, March 31, 1946.

CLARK, BARZILLA WORTH (1937-1939). b. Dec. 22, 1881 at
Hadley, Ind. s. of Joseph Addison and Eunice (Hadley) C.
When he was four years old the family moved to Eagle Rock,
Ida., where father, as a civil engr., planned and surveyed
first irrigation systems using Snake River waters, and was
the first mayor of Idaho Falls. Attd. grade school in
Idaho Falls and h.s. in Terre Haute, Ind. Entered Rose
Poly. Inst., but withdrew in 1900 because of poor health.
Began farming, stock-raising, and mining in Ida. As farmer,
introduced production of sugar beets. Licensed as civil
engr. in 1905. Involved thereafter in a number of reservoir
and power devel. projects in Ida. Mbr. of city council of
Idaho Falls, 1908-1912, and mayor, 1913-1915 and 1926-1936.
Nom. and el. Gov. as Dem. in 1936. As Gov. emphasized importance of devel. of hydro-electric power resources; advocated pub. ownership of utilities; and sponsored legislation
regulating lumbering bus. Early history of Ida. was a
hobby. Published Bonneville County in the Making in 1941.
Methodist. m. in 1905 to Ethel Salome Peck. Three d.;
one s. A brother, Chase A., later became Gov. of Ida.
(q.v.); and a nephew, D. Worth Clark, was a U.S. Repr. and
Sen. from Ida. D. at Idaho Falls, Sept. 21, 1943.

BOTTOLFSEN, CLARENCE ALFRED (1939-1941; 1943-1945).
b. Oct. 10, 1891 at Superior, Wisc. s. of Andrew C. and
Mary (Carlson) B. Grandfather emigrated to Amer. from
Norway in 1862, settling in Wisc. after the Civil War. In
1902 family moved to Fessenden, N.D. Attd. pub. school in
Fessenden and Natl. Bus. Coll. in Minneapolis, Minn. In
1905 became printer's helper at the Wells County News, in
Fessenden. In 1910 moved to Arco, Ida., where he became
mgr. of Arco Advertiser, and in 1912 the owner and pub. of
that newspaper until he sold it in 1947. Also was ed. of
the Blackfoot, Ida., Daily Bulletin, 1934-1938. From 1934
to 1947 was parliamentarian for the Natl. Educl. Assoc.

Pres. of Ida. Editorial Assoc. in 1929. Mbr. of Ida. House,
1921-1925 and 1929-1933. Clerk of the House, 1925-1929.
Floor leader of Rep. party in House, 1929-1931 and Speaker,
1931-1933. Ch. of Ida. Rep. state commt., 1936-1938. Nom.
and el. Gov. as Rep. in 1938. Defeated as Rep. cand. for
second term in 1940, but was nom. again and el. in 1942.
Defeated as Rep. nominee for U.S. Senate in 1944. As Gov.,
placed State on a sound financial basis, and assisted in
org. of Northwestern Devel. League, composed of five Northwestern States. Served in training cadre during World War
II at Ft. Lewis, Washington. Mbr., Masons; Elks; 40 and 8;
Amer. Legion; Ida. Historical Assoc. Author of booklet in
1926, Little Bits of Lost History. m. in 1912 to Elizabeth
Hanna, of Arco, Ida. D. July 18, 1964. Bur. in Hillcrest
Cem. there.

CLARK, CHASE ADDISON (1941-1943). b. Aug. 21, 1883 at
Hadley, Ind. s. of Joseph Addison and Eunice (Hadley) C.
Soon after his birth the family moved to Eagle Rock, Ida.,
where father engaged in civil engr. work. Attd. pub.
schools in Idaho Falls. Held clerical, mining and farm work
jobs for a time. Attd. Univ. of Mich. Law School, 1903-
1904. Admitted to bar in 1904 and began practice in Idaho
Falls. Became mayor of Idaho Falls. Defeated as Dem.
nominee for U.S. Senate seat in 1928. Nom. and el. Gov. as
Dem. in 1940, defeating incumbent Gov. Bottolfsen. Nom. for
succeeding term in 1942 but was defeated by Bottolfsen in
the gen. election by about 400 votes. Apptd. U.S. dist. ct.
judge by Pres. Roosevelt in 1943, serving in that post until
retirement in May, 1964. m. in 1906 to Jean Burnett. One
s.; one d., who became the wife of Frank Church, later a
U.S. Sen. from Ida. Was a brother of Barzilla Clark, Gov.
of Ida. (q.v.), and was the uncle of D. Worth Clark, a U.S.
Repr. and Sen. from Ida. D. Dec. 30, 1966. Bur. in Idaho
Falls.

BOTTOLFSEN, CLARENCE ALFRED (1943-1945). See above,
1939-1941.

GOSSETT, CHARLES CLINTON (1945). b. Sept. 2, 1888 in
Pricetown, Ohio. s. of Wyatt Henry and Maggie (Finnegan) G.
Attd. local pub. schools. Moved to Cunningham, Washington,
in 1907 and in 1910 to Ontaria, Ore. In 1922 moved again
to Nampa, Ida., where he engaged in farming, livestock
raising, and feed bus. Mbr. of Ida. House, 1933-1937 from
Canyon Co. El. Lieut. Gov. in 1936, serving until 1939.
El. again to office of Lieut. Gov. in 1940. Nom. and el.
Gov. as Dem. in 1944. In Nov. 1945, resigned office and was

immediately thereafter apptd. by his successor to fill a
vacancy in a U.S. Senate seat. Served therein until Jan.,
1947. Defeated in 1946 primary election for nom. as Dem.
cand. to continue in Senate post. Resumed bus. and ranching
interests, residing in Boise. Mbr., Masons; Elks; Eagles;
Natl. Grange. Christian (Disciples) church. m. in 1916 to
Clara Louise Fleming. Three s. D. Sept. 20, 1974.

WILLIAMS, ARNOLD (1945-1947). b. May 21, 1898 at
Fillmore, Utah. s. of Wm. and Annie Mariah (Rutherford) W.
Attd. pub. schools in Fillmore and Hennington Bus. Coll.,
in Salt Lake City. Mbr. of A.E.F. during World War I. In
1920 moved to Ida., where he became involved in a cleaning
bus. at Roxbury, with which he continued to be assoc. until
1945. In that year acquired an auto dealership bus. at
St. Anthony, Ida. Co. commnr. of Madison Co., 1933-1937.
Mbr. of Ida. House, 1937-1941, serving as majority (Dem.)
floor leader during last term. El. Lieut. Gov. as a Dem.
in 1944. Succeeded to office of Gov. when Gov. Gossett
resigned in Nov., 1945. He immediately apptd. Gossett to a
vacancy in a U.S. Senate seat occasioned by the death of the
incumbent. Completed Gossett's term. Defeated as Dem.
nominee for a regular term in 1946. As Gov., called a spec.
session of the legislature to enact a teachers' retirement
act; also sponsored legislation creating a commn. to supervise operations of all state elementary institutions. Mbr.,
Amer. Legion; Rotary. Mormon church. m. to Luella
Huskinson in 1919. One s.; one d. D. May 25, 1970.

ROBINS, CHARLES ARMINGTON (1947-1951). b. Dec. 8, 1884
at Defiance, Iowa. s. of Charles Macalester and Rebecca
Jane (Burke) R. Attd. William Jewell Coll., Liberty, Mo.,
from which he was grad. in 1907. Entered the Univ. of
Chicago Med. School and received an M.D. degree in 1917.
From 1919 to 1946 engaged in med. practice at St. Marie's,
Ida., where he managed St. Marie's Hosp., 1939-1946 and was
dist. surgeon for the C.M. and St. P.R.R. Mbr., Ida Senate,
1939-1947, serving as Pres. pro tem in 1943-1944. Nom. and
el. Gov. as Rep. in 1946, becoming the State's first four-
year term Gov. Recipient of award for post history from
Amer. Legion. Mbr., Masons (O.E.S.); Elks; Eagles; Kiwanis;
Phi Gamma Delta; various fraternal and professional med.
orgs. m. in 1939 to Patricia Simpson. Three d. D. Sept.
20, 1970.

JORDAN, LEONARD BECK ("LEN") (1951-1955). b. May 15,
1899 at Mt. Pleasant, Utah. s. of Leonard Eugene and
Irene (Beck) J. Attd. pub. schools at Enterprise, Ore.;

Utah State Coll., 1917-1918; and the Univ. of Ore., from
which he was grad. with a degree in bus. admin. in 1923.
Entered U.S. Army as pvt. in 1918 during World War I.   Held
rank of second lieut. when discharged.   Engaged in farming
and livestock bus. in Ida.   Became owner and mgr. of Jordan
Motor Co., Inc., at Grangeville, Ida., in 1949.   Mbr., Ida.
legislature, 1947-1949.   Nom. and el. Gov. as Rep. in 1950.
Ch. of U.S.-Canadian Intl. Jt. Commn. by apptmt. from Pres.
Eisenhower, 1955-1958.   Mbr., U.S. Devel. Advisory Bd.,
1958-1959.   Apptd. to vacant seat in U.S. Senate in August,
1962 and continued in that office until 1973.   Did not seek
reel. in 1972.   Delegate to Rep. natl. conv. in 1968.   Mbr.,
Masons (Shriner); Amer. Legion; Rotary; Phi Beta Kappa;
Alpha Tau Omega.   m. in 1924 to Grace Edgington.   Two s.;
one d.

SMYLIE, ROBERT EBEN (1955-1967).   b. Oct. 3, 1914 at
Marcus, Iowa.   s. of Lorne F. and Ida Mae (Stevens) S.
Father was a school teacher.   Attd. pub. schools in Cresco,
Iowa; the Coll. of Idaho, from which he was grad. in 1938;
and George Washington Univ., Washington, D.C., from which he
received a law degree in 1942.   Worked as law clerk with a
Washington, D.C. law firm, 1940-1942.   Mbr., U.S. Coast
Guard, 1942-1946, continuing thereafter as lieut. in USCGR
until 1954.   Decorated for service during World War II.   Admitted to bar in 1942 and practiced law in Washington D.C.
until 1946.   Moved to Ida. where he continued in law practice at Boise and Caldwell.   Ch. of Young Rep. Club of Ada
Co., 1947.   Apptd. asst. Atty. Gen. of Ida. in 1947, and became acting Atty. Gen. in Nov. of that year when the incumbent died.   El. to that office in 1948, and again in 1950.
As Atty. Gen., opposed U.S. constr. of hydro-electric dam at
Hell's Canyon, on the Snake River, favoring instead constr.
of three smaller dams by privately-owned utilities.   Nom.
and el. Gov. as Rep. in 1954.   Hell's Canyon project continued to be a matter of major concern during admin., with
decision eventually being made in favor of permitting Idaho
Power Co. to construct three smaller dams, an outcome he
favored.   Reel. for second term in 1958 and for a third term
in 1962, the state constl. restriction against reel. of an
incumbent to a succeding term having been abolished in 1956.
Defeated as cand. for Rep. nom. for a fourth term in 1966.
Defeated as a cand. for the Rep. nom. for a U.S. Senate seat
in 1972.   Co-sponsor of Western Govs.' Conf. in Nov., 1955,
at which mining and other indus. problems of the States in
the Northwest were major topics of discussion.   Co-ch.,
Fed.-State Relations Commt. of the Natl. Govs'. Conf.   Mbr.,
U.S. Advisory Commn. on Intergovtl. Relations.   Mbr.,

Masons; Elks; Moose: V.F.W.; Amer. Legion; Phi Alpha Theta.
Methodist Episcopal church. Hon. degree from George
Washington Univ. Author of journal articles on political
and legal topics. m. in 1943 to Lucille Caroline Irwin.
Two s. Continued in law practice at Boise after tenure as
Gov.

SAMUELSON, DON(ALD) WILLIAM (1967-1971). b. July 27,
1913 at Woodhull, Ill. s. of Fred W. and Nellie (Johnson)
S. Attd. Knox Coll., at Galesburg, Ill. Served in U.S.
Navy during World War II, and remained in the USNR after
discharge in 1946. Established residence in Boise, Ida.,
where he engaged in bus. Mbr. of Ida. Senate, 1960-1966.
Nom. and el. Gov. as Rep. in 1966, defeating former Gov.
Smylie for the Rep. party's nom. Nom. for second term in
1970 but lost in the gen. election to Cecil Andrus, whom he
had defeated in 1966 election. Delegate to Rep. natl. conv.
in 1968. Mbr., Amer. Legion; Elks; Kiwanis; various social
clubs. Methodist. m. in 1936 to Ruby A. Mayo. One s.;
one d.

ANDRUS, CECIL DALE (1971-1977). b. Aug. 25, 1931 at
Hood River, Ore. s. of Hal S. and Dorothy (John) A. Grew
up on a farm in logging country. As a young man worked in
lumber camps and sawmills in Northern Ore. Attd. Ore. State
Univ., 1948-1949. Served in U.S. Navy during the Korean
War, 1951-1955, and received service medal. Established
home in Orefina, Ida. and engaged in lumbering work after
mil. service. Moved to Lewiston, Ida. in 1967, where he became involved in ins. bus., eventually becoming an exec.
officer with the Paul Revere Life Ins. Co. El. to Ida. Senate in 1960, continuing therein until 1971 except for the
1967-1969 period. Defeated for Dem. nom. for Gov. in 1966;
but when the Dem. nominee died before the gen. election, was
named as replacement nominee by the Ida. Dem. state commt.
Defeated in gen. election. In the legislature, identified
himself with measures to improve state educl. system; conservation of natural resources; improvement of pub. social
services; and devel. of agri. Won Dem. nom. for Gov. in
1970 and was el., defeating incumbent Gov. Samuelson.
Stressed issue of preserving wilderness areas against open
pit mining operations, particularly in the Castle Rock
region, and urged restricted approach to devel. of projected
dam sites for power and irrigation purposes. Reel. in 1974.
During admin., a land use act was passed; revision of state
income tax system effected; and additional aid for educ. secured while maintaining a balanced budget. Resigned office
of Gov. in Jan., 1977 to accept apptmt. as U.S. Sect. of the

Interior from Pres. Carter. Mbr., Amer. Legion; V.F.W.;
Elks; Masons. Named by Ida. post of V.F.W. as Man of the
Year, and by the League of Conservation Voters and Ida. Wild
Life Fed. as Conservationist of the Year. Mbr., exec.
commt. of the Natl. Govs.' Assoc. in 1976, and ch. of Fed.
of Rocky Mountain States, 1971-1972. Lutheran. m. in 1949
to Carol Mae May. Three d.

BOND, SHADRACH (1818–1822).   b. Nov. 24, 1773 at Fredericktown, Md.   s. of Nicholas B., a planter. Ancestors had
resided in Md. for over a century. Grew up on father's plantation, receiving only an elementary educ. In 1794 moved to
the Northwest Terr., where he lived with an uncle on a farm
in what was then known as the "Amer. Bottom" area. Mbr. of
the Ind. Terr. legislature, 1805–1808. Delegate from Ill.
Terr. to U.S. Cong. in 1812–1814. As Delegate, helped to
secure for constituents recognition of their right of pre-
emption in lands on which they had settled. Apptd. by Pres.
Madison as U.S. receiver of pub. moneys for Ill. Terr. Resided at Kaskaskia, the capital of the Terr., from 1814 onward. In Sept., 1818 was chosen Gov. of the proposed State
of Ill. on a provisional basis, and assumed the office of
Gov. de jure in Dec. of that year after the act admitting
Ill. to statehood became effective. Affiliated with the
Jeff. Rep. party. During admin., directed the org. of the
first state govt., with its capital at Vandalia. Urged
constr. of a canal connecting Lake Mich. with the Miss.
River system, an objective eventually achieved in 1840s.
Following tenure as Gov. held post of registrar of U.S. land
office until death. D. at Kaskaskia April 12, 1832. Survived by his wife, three d., and two s. At the time of his
death was the owner of nine slaves which he had purchased
with an understanding that each would be emancipated after
service for a stipulated number of years. Bur. in Evergreen
Cem., Chester, Ill.

COLES, EDWARD (1822–1826).   b. Dec. 15, 1786 in Albe-
marle Co., Va.   s. of Col. John and Rebecca (Tucker) C.
Attd. Hampden–Sydney Coll. and later, William and Mary Coll.
Poor health caused him to withdraw before graduating.   Inherited plantation with slaves in 1808, but was opposed to
institution of slavery. Was a close friend of Pres. Madison,
for whom he was a pvt. sect., 1809–1815. Also was a close
friend of Thomas Jefferson, to whom he wrote in 1814 seeking
support for plan to end slavery in Va. Left Va. to take up
residence in Ill. Terr. in 1815 because he wished to live in
free terr. Settled on lands near Edwardsville. Sent as
spec. emissary by Pres. Madison to St. Petersburg, Russia to
conduct negotiations with the Czar. Mbr. of conv. that
drafted first state const. for Ill. Influential in securing
inclusion of an anti-slavery clause in the const. Apptd.
registrar of U.S. land office at Edwardsville by Pres. Monroe
in 1819. Emancipated his own slaves when he came to Ill.,
giving each family a tract of 160 acres of land. El. Gov.
in 1822 in four-man contest. Advocated sound currency system and the devel. of Lake Mich. to Miss. waterway. Much
controversy ensued during admin. over whether Ill. was

obliged under the Northwest Ordinance to prohibit slavery.
Pro-slavery elements were successful in bringing about a
conv. in 1824 to consider question of modifying anti-slavery
clause in the state const., an effort which C. as Gov. opposed. Pro-slavery element were defeated when the conv. assembled. Meanwhile, C. was brought to trial for failure to
comply with a state law requiring that an owner of slaves
must give bond for any slave he freed to insure the ex-slave
would not become a pub. charge. Was found guilty and fined
$2,000 in a lower court, but the decision was reversed by
the Ill. Supreme Ct. in 1826. After retiring from office,
farmed for a time; but after 1833 travelled in Eastern U.S.
Eventually settled in Philadelphia. m. in 1833 to Sally
Logan Roberts, of that city. Two children. D. at Philadelphia July 7, 1868.

EDWARDS, NINIAN (1826-1830). b. Mar. 17, 1775 on family
plantation, "Mt. Pleasant," in Montgomery Co., Md. s. of
Benj. and Margaret (Beall) E. Father, who was a native of
Va., was a prosperous planter and merchant who had been active in Va. and Md. politics and had served briefly as ambr.
of U.S. House from Md. Received classical educ. Attd.
Dickinson Coll., from which he was grad. in 1792. Later
studied both law and med. Moved with father's family to
Bardstown, Ky. in 1795. Mbr. of Ky. legislature in 1796 before he was 21 years old, and was reel. in 1797. Admitted to
Ky. bar in 1798 and practiced at Russellville. Ct. clerk,
1803 and cir. ct. judge, 1804. Mbr. of Ky. Ct. of Appeals in
1806, becoming Chief Justice in 1808. Apptd. first Gov. of
Terr. of Ill. by Pres. Madison in 1809, serving in that office until Ill. was admitted to statehood in 1818. Was one
of three commnrs. apptd. in 1816 to negotiate treaty with
Indians in area. El. as one of the first two U.S. Senators
from Ill., serving until March, 1824 when he resigned after
having been apptd. U.S. Minister to Mexico. Was recalled
while en route to Mexico to answer charges brought against
him by U.S. Sect. of Treas. Crawford regarding alleged failure to account for U.S. funds in his custody. Resigned ministerial post and returned to Ill., where he engaged in law
practice and bus. for a time at Belleville. Nom. and el.
Gov. as Natl. Rep. in 1826. m. in 1802 to Elvira Lane, of
Montgomery Co., Md. Three s., two d. D. at Belleville
July 20, 1833. Bur. there; but in 1855 body was re-interred
in Oak Ridge Cem. in Springfield.

REYNOLDS, JOHN (1830-1834). b. Feb. 26, 1788 near
Philadelphia, Pa. s. of Robt. and Margaret (Moore) R. A
younger brother, Thomas, became Gov. of Mo. (q.v.). Father
had emigrated from Ireland to Amer. in 1785. Family moved

in 1788 to Tenn., and in 1800 to Kaskaskia, Ill. (then a part of Ind. Terr.). Still later the family moved to Collinsville, Ill. Received limited classical schooling. Studied surveying for a time. Entered Coll. of Tenn. at Knoxville in 1809, where he continued in studies for two years. Studied law, admitted to bar in 1812, and began practice at Cahokia, Ill. Also operated a gen. store. Served as scout for Amer. forces during War of 1812. In 1818 became a cir. ct. judge and then was a mbr. of the Ill. Supreme Ct. Unsuccessful cand. for U.S. Senate seat in 1823. Supported unsuccessful efforts of pro-slavery element in Ill. to secure repeal of anti-slavery clause of Ill. const. in 1824. Mbr. of Ill. legislature, 1827-1829. Nom. and el. Gov. as Natl. Rep. in 1830. Major event during admin. was the Black Hawk War of 1831-1832, during which as Gov. he took field command of militia forces for a time. Resigned office of Gov. in 1834 near the end of term to take seat in U.S. House, to which he had been chosen in a spec. el. to fill a vacancy. El. for succeeding full term but was defeated for reel. in 1836. El. again to House seat in 1838 and 1840. As mbr. of Cong., opposed nullificationbut was sympathetic toward So. slavery interests generally. Mbr. of Ill. House, 1846-1850 and 1852-1854, serving as Speaker in latter period. Became ed. of a Belleville newspaper, Star of Egypt, in 1856. Delegate to Dem. natl. conv. at Charleston in 1860. After Civil War began was sympathetic to So. cause, but did not participate actively in conflict. Author of various books and pamphlets, including Pioneer History of Illinois, published in 1848. m. twice. No children. D. at Belleville May 8, 1865. Bur. in Walnut Hill Cem. there.

EWING, WILLIAM LEE DAVIDSON (1834). b. Aug. 8, 1795 near Paris, Logan Co., Ky. s. of the Rev. Finis and Peggy (Davidson) E. Antecedents were Scotch-Irish colonists who had emigrated to Va. before the Rev. War. Father was one of the founders of the Cumberland Presbyterian church. Studied law and was admitted to bar. About 1818 moved to Shawneetown, Ill. Apptd. U.S. receiver of pub. moneys at Vandalia, Ill. Clerk of Ill. House, 1826-1828 and mbr. of that body in 1830. Served as col., later as brig. gen. of militia forces during Black Hawk War, 1831-1832. Mbr. of Ill. Senate, 1832. Became presiding officer of that body after Lieut. Gov. Zadoc resigned in March, 1833. When Gov. Reynolds resigned in Nov., 1834, acted as Gov. for the last two weeks of Reynolds' term. Apptd. to vacancy in U.S. Senate seat as a Jackson Dem. in 1835, serving until 1837. Mbr. of Ill. House, 1838-1840, serving as Speaker. Clerk of House, 1842. Chosen State Aud. in 1843, in which post he served

until his death. m. to ----- Berry. D. at Vandalia Mar. 25,
1846. Bur. in Oak Ridge Cem. at Springfield.

DUNCAN, JOSEPH (1834-1838). b. Feb. 22, 1794 at Paris,
Ky. Father, who was of Scottish ancestry, had resided originally in Va. Educ. in Ky. Joined U.S. Army during War of
1812, rising to rank of first lieut. by end of war. Established residence in Ill. in 1818 at Kaskaskia, where he engaged in farming. Justice of the peace, 1821-1823. Mbr. of
Ill. Senate, 1824-1826. Mbr. of U.S. House, 1827-1834. Established residence at Jacksonville, Ill. in 1829. Became a
brig. gen. of Ill. militia in 1822, and commanded Ill. militia during the Black Hawk War in 1832-1832. Was voted a
medal for gallantry by U.S. Cong. in 1835 for his services
during War of 1812. Resigned seat in Cong. in 1834 after
having been el. Gov. of Ill. as the Anti-Jackson party cand.
As Gov., advocated continuation of work for a Lake Mich. to
Miss. canal, and the establishment of a state pub. school system. The killing of the abolitionist newspaper ed., Elijah
P. Lovejoy, at Alton, Ill. in Nov., 1837 was an event causing much pub. controversy during admin. Nom. as Whig cand.
for Gov. in 1842 but lost in the gen. el. Opposed slavery
and was an advocate of temperance. Active in Presbyterian
church affairs. Donated land and money to Ill. Coll., at
Jacksonville. m. in 1828 to Elizabeth Caldwell Smith, of
New York City. Ten children, of whom only three lived to
adulthood. D. at Jacksonville Jan. 15, 1844. Bur. in
Diamond Grove Cem. there.

CARLIN, THOMAS (1838-1842). b. July 18, 1789 in
Fayette Co., Ky. s. of Thomas C., who was of Irish descent.
Largely self-educ., after reaching maturity. In 1800 the
family moved to Mo., which was then a part of French Louisi-
ana. After his father died in 1812, moved to Madison Co.,
in Ill. Terr. Served as a ranger in volunteer company during War of 1812. Acquired lands in Western Ill. Donated
lands upon which Carrollton, later the co. seat of Greene
Co., was founded. Served as first sheriff of Greene Co.
Served two terms in Ill. Senate and later was a mbr. of Ill.
House. Commanded battalion of militia forces during Black
Hawk War in 1832. Apptd. U.S. receiver of pub. moneys by
Pres. Jackson in 1834. Nom. and el. Gov. as Jackson Dem. in
1838. As Gov., advocated program of internal improvements,
including canal constr. Settlement of the Mormons at Nauvoo
in the western part of the State, and in the last year of his
term, a gen. depression and a number of bank failures gave
rise to much discontent and financial stringency. Retired
to his farm at Carrollton. El. to the Ill. legislature for

a partial term in 1849 to fill a vacancy. m. in 1814 to
Rebecca Hewitt. Seven children. D. at Carrollton Feb. 14,
1852.

FORD, THOMAS (1842-1846). b. Dec. 5, 1800 at Uniontown,
Pa. s. of Robt. and Elizabeth Logue (Forquer) F. Family was
of English and Irish origin. Father died in 1802, leaving
widow and family of eight children in poor circumstances.
Mother, with children, moved to Mo. (then Louisiana Province) expecting to receive free land. Upon arrival at St.
Louis found U.S. had acquired Louisiana Terr., and the land
would have to be purchased. Rented farm near St. Louis for
a time. Son studied at home; later attd. Transylvania Univ.,
at Lexington, Ky. for one year. Studied law and was admitted to bar in 1823. Assisted in editing a St. Louis newspaper in 1824 that supported Jackson for U.S. Pres. Joined
brother in law practice at Edwardsville, Ill. in 1825. In
1826 moved to Galena, Ill., and in 1829 to Quincy, Ill.,
continuing to practice law. Apptd. State's atty. for his
jud. cir. by Gov. Edwards in 1829 and continued in that office by Gov. Reynolds in 1831. Became State's atty. in
newly created cir. in 1835, and later became judge of that
cir. El. to Ill. Supreme Ct. in 1840. Nom. and el. Gov. as
Dem. in 1842, having been made the party nominee after the
regular nominee died. Defeated former Gov. Duncan in the
gen. el. During admin., opposed repudiation of state debt,
which the legislature favored, and cooperated with U.S.
govt. in raising troops for war with Mexico. Difficulties
arising from settlement of Mormons at Nauvoo came to a crisis
resulting in fighting in which Joseph Smith and his brother,
Hyrum, were killed. Mormons were forced to leave the State.
Continued to carry on program of internal improvements.
Left office a bankrupt man, and lived in straightened circumstances thereafter. Resumed law practice at Peoria, Ill.
Author of a History of Illinois, published in 1854. m. in
1828 to Frances Hambaugh, of Edwardsville. Two s., three d.
D. at Peoria Nov. 3, 1850.

FRENCH, AUGUSTUS C. (1846-1853). b. Aug. 2, 1808 at
Hill, N.H. Father died during son's childhood. When his
mother died soon after, became responsible at age 19 for
care of four younger brothers and a sister. Attd. dist.
school. Entered Dartmouth Coll., but was forced to withdraw
before grad. because of lack of funds and family responsi-
bilities. Studied law at home and was admitted to bar. In
1823 moved to Albion, Ill. Established residence in Paris,
Ill. in 1825, where he practiced law. Mbr. of Ill. legislature in 1837, serving for two terms. Apptd. U.S. receiver
of pub. moneys at Palestine, Ill. Served as pres. elector

on Polk-Dallas ticket in 1844. Nom. and el. Gov. as Dem. in
1846. During admin., the remaining mbrs. of Mormon settlement left the State; the Ill.-Lake Mich. canal project was
completed; and the second railroad to be built in the State
began operations. Gave strong support in raising troops
during war with Mexico. In 1848 by reason of a change in
the election and term schedule effected by revision of the
State's const., an election was held at which he was nom. and
el. for a four-year term beginning in Jan., 1849. Following
tenure as Gov. resumed law practice; also served as prof. of
law at McKendree Coll. Mbr. of constl. conv. assembled in
1862. D. at Lebanon, Ill. Sept. 4, 1864.

MATTESON, JOEL ALDRICH (1853-1857). b. Aug. 8, 1808 at
Watertown, N.Y. s. of Elnathan and Eunice (Aldrich) M.
Father had emigrated from England to U.S. and was owner of a
large farm at Watertown. Son worked on farm while attending
local schools. Opened a store in Prescott, Canada but soon
returned to Watertown. Taught school for two terms at
Brownsville, N.Y. Worked as foreman during constr. of first
railroad in S.C. In 1833 moved to Ill., settling near Joliet,
where he farmed until 1836. Sold farm and went into bus. in
Joliet in 1838. Acquired contracts in connection with
constr. of Ill.-Lake Mich. canal project in that year. Mbr.
of Ill. Senate, 1842-1848. Nom. and el. Gov. as Dem. in
1852. During admin., there was great activity in railroad
building in the State and a beginning made in establishing
state-wide system of free pub. educ. Defeated as Dem. cand.
for seat in U.S. Senate. After tenure as Gov. became pres.
of the C. and A. R.R. Also acquired interest in banks in
Joliet, Quincy, Peoria, and Shawneetown. m. in 1831 to
Mary Fish. Three s., four d. D. in Chicago Jan. 31, 1873.

BISSELL, WILLIAM HENRY (HARRISON?) (1857-1860). b.
April 25, 1811 at Hartwick, N.Y. s. of Luther and Hannah B.
Attd. dist. schools. Continued studies by himself at home
while teaching in local schools. Studied at Cooperstown,
N.Y. Acad. Attd. Jefferson Med. Coll., in Philadelphia,
grad. in 1835. After practicing med. for two years at
Painted Post, N.Y., moved to Waterloo, in Monroe Co., Ill.
in 1837. Taught school there until 1840. Mbr. of Ill.
legislature, 1840-1842. Friends persuaded him to remain in
politics, and he attd. Transylvania Univ., in Ky., to study
law. Admitted to bar in 1843, and opened law office at
Belleville. State's atty. for his jud. dist. in 1844.
Served as col. of regiment of volunteers during Mexican War,
1846-1847. El. to U.S. House as an Indep. Dem. in 1848 and
continued in office for next two terms. A strong opponent
of slavery, he became spokesman in Cong. for the anti-slavery

elements of his party in opposition to pro-slavery So. Dems.
Did not compete for House seat in 1854, but was nom. and el.
Gov. as cand. of the newly-formed Rep. party in 1856. Legislature failed to support him on most major issues. m. in
1840 to Emily S. James, of Waterloo, Ill., who died in 1846.
In 1852, m. to Elizabeth Kintsing Kane, of Kaskaskia. Two d.
by first wife. D. at Springfield on Mar. 18, 1860 while
still in office. Bur. in Oak Ridge Cem. there.

WOOD, JOHN (1860-1861). b. Dec. 20, 1798 at Moravia,
N.Y. s. of Daniel and Catherine (Crouse) W. Father was a
surgeon who had served with Amer. forces as a capt. during
Rev. War and had received lands in N.Y. in payment for
services. Son left home in 1818 intending to settle in Tenn.
or Ala., but settled in Western Ill. instead. Worked on farm
in Pike Co. for two years. In 1822 bought land and built
first cabin on tract in what later became town of Quincy,
Ill. Became prominent as community leader, assisting in
org. of Adams Co. Served as town trustee of Quincy, 1834-
1840; also as alderman for a number of years and mayor for
seven terms. Was a strong opponent of slavery, but also was
critical of abolitionists. El. to Ill. Senate as a Whig in
1850, serving until 1854. Nom. and el. Lieut. Gov. as Rep.
in 1856. Succeeded to office of Gov. in Mar., 1860 when
Gov. Bissell died, and completed Bissell's term. Apptd. by
Gov. Yates as one of five delegates from Ill. to the "Peace
Congress" in Washington, D.C. in 1861. Served as quartermaster for Ill. troops during the war. Col. of Ill. regiment in 1862, and was in command of a brigade at Memphis,
Tenn. at end of war. m. in 1826 to Anne M. Streeter, of
Salem, N.Y., who died in 1863. Eight children. m. in 1865
to Mrs. Mary A. Holms, widow of a minister. D. June 11,
1880 at Quincy.

YATES, RICHARD, Sr. (1861-1865). b. Jan. 18, 1815 at
Warsaw, Ky. s. of Henry and Millicent (Yates) Y., who were
cousins. Family traced ancestry to an English colonist who
had come to Va. before Rev. War. Family related to that of
Chief Justice Marshall. Moved with parents from Ky. to
Springfield, Ill. in 1831, later settling at New Berlin, Ill.
Received common school educ. in Ky. Attd. Miami Univ., in
Ohio, and Georgetown Coll., in Ky. Also attd. Ill. Coll.,
at Jacksonville, becoming one of two mbrs. of its first grad.
class in 1835. Studied law in office at Jacksonville and at
Transylvania Univ., in Ky. Admitted to bar in 1837 and began practice at Jacksonville, soon acquiring wide reputation
as an able lawyer. El. to Ill. legislature as a Whig in
1842. Continued to serve therein until 1850, when he was
el. to U.S. House. Served from 1851-1855. Opposed exten-

sion of slavery and the Compromise of 1850. Defeated for
reel. in 1854. Became one of founders of Rep. party in Ill.
in that year. Continued law practice; also promoted interests of Tonica and Petersburg R.R., of which he became
pres. Active in Fremont campaign for Pres. of U.S. in 1856
and in Lincoln's attempt to win U.S. Senate seat in 1858.
Delegate to Rep. natl. conv. in 1860 and also in 1868. Nom.
and el. Gov. as Rep. in 1860. During admin., took active
role in promoting Union cause and supporting Lincoln's war
measures. Favored emancipation of slaves and the enlistment
of Negroes in U.S. armed forces. Compelled adjournment of
Ill. legislature for a time in 1862 to prevent its adoption
of various anti-war proposals. El. to U.S. Senate at end of
term, serving until 1871. Supported Reconstruction measures; a homestead law; and constr. of transcontinental railway. Was not a cand. for second term. m. in 1838 to Catherine Geers. One d., two s., one of whom, Richard, Jr.,
later became a Gov. of Ill. (q.v.). D. suddenly at St.
Louis, Mo., Nov. 27, 1873 while returning from a journey to
Ark. Bur. in Diamond Grove Cem., Jacksonville.

OGLESBY, RICHARD JAMES (1865-1869; 1873; 1885-1889).
b. July 25, 1824 at Floydsburg, Ky. s. of Jacob and Isabel
(Walton) O. Parents were natives of Va., who had moved to
Ky. They died when son was 8 years old, and his upbringing
was assumed by an uncle, who moved to Decatur, Ill. in 1835.
Attd. local schools. Engaged in a variety of occupations
for a time, including carpentry. Studied law in lawyer's
office in Springfield. Admitted to bar in 1845. Upon outbreak of war with Mexico, joined an Ill. regiment of volunteers and served as lieut. until end of war. Resumed law
practice and attd. a law school in Louisville, Ky. for one
year. In 1849 went to Calif. to seek gold. Returned to Ill.
in 1851. Resumed law practice in Decatur. In 1856-1857
travelled in Europe and North Africa. Defeated as Rep. nominee for seat in U.S. House in 1858. El. to Ill. Senate in
1860, but resigned seat after first session to become col.
of Ill. regiment raised in response to Lincoln's call for
troops. Rose to rank of brig. gen. in 1862. Seriously
wounded at Corinth, Miss. and was believed to be dying, but
recovered after several months. During his convalescence,
spoke before Ill. Senate, sharply criticizing Dem. mbrs. who
were seeking to pass anti-war resolutions. Promoted to major
gen. and was assigned to ct. martial duty. Nom. and el. Gov.
as Rep. in 1864. During admin., a State Bd. of Tax Equalization was created and an Indus. Coll. (later Univ. of Ill.)
was founded at Champaign. Was prevented by state const.
from seeking immediate reel.; but in 1872 was nom. and el.
again to office of Gov. Resigned shortly after term began,

having been chosen to U.S. Senate seat by the legislature. Served one term there, declining to seek another term. Nom. and el. Gov. again in 1884, becoming the only person to have been el. to the office on three different occasions. Major event of last term was the Haymarket Riot in 1886 growing out of labor troubles in Chicago, which resulted in the trial, conviction and confinement in prison of a number of prominent labor leaders on conspiracy charges. After completion of term retired to his farmstead, "Oglehurst," near Elkhart, Ill. m. in 1874 to Emma Gillett, of Elkhart Park. Seven children. D. at his home April 24, 1899. Bur. in Elkhart Cem.

PALMER, JOHN McAULEY (1869-1873). b. Sept. 13, 1817 at Eagle Creek, Scott Co., Ky. s. of Louis D. and Ann Hanaford (Tutt) P. Descendant of an English colonist who emigrated to Va. in 1621. Family moved from Ky. to Paddock's Prairie, Ill. in 1831 because of feelings against slavery. Attd. common schools in Ky. and Ill. Entered Alton (now Shurtleff) Coll. in 1834, but withdrew before grad. because of lack of funds. Taught school, 1836-1838, and studied law. Admitted to bar in 1839 and began practice in Carlinville. Probate judge of Macoupin Co., 1843-1847. Delegate to state constl. conv. in 1847. Co. judge, 1849-1852. Mbr. of Ill. Senate, 1852-1854, resigning seat because his opposition to Kansas-Nebraska Act displeased constituents. Reel. to Ill. Senate as an Indep. in 1855. Resigned in 1856. Participated in org. of Rep. party in Ill., serving as presiding officer of first Rep. state conv. in 1856 and as a delegate to Rep. natl. conv. in that year. Pres. elector on Rep. ticket in 1860. One of five delegates sent to represent Ill. at the 1861 "Peace Congress" in Washington, D.C. Raised an Ill. regiment upon outbreak of Civil War, becoming its col. Participated in engagements in West. Promoted to brig. gen. in 1862 and to major gen. later. Was in command of Ky. Dept. of Union Army at end of Civil War. Returned to law practice in Carlinville. Moved to Springfield in 1867. Nom. and el. Gov. as Rep. in 1868. During admin., took measures to relieve victims of Chicago Fire. Took active part in Lib. Rep. movement in 1872 pres. campaign, becoming a supporter of Greeley for Pres. of U.S. against Grant. Supported Gov. Tilden, the Dem. nominee for Pres. of U.S., in 1876 election. Practiced law in Springfield, 1873-1890. Delegate to Dem. natl. conv. in 1884. Unsuccessful as Dem. party nominee for Gov. in 1888, losing gen. el. contest by narrow margin. El. to U.S. Senate as Dem. in 1890. Was not a cand. for reel. in 1896, having broken with Dem. party on free silver issue after nom. of Bryan for Pres. of U.S. in that year. Accepted nom. for Pres. of U.S. by the Gold Standard faction of Dem. party

in 1896, but won no electoral votes. Wrote memoirs, which
were published posthumously in 1901. Mbr., Masons; G.A.R.
m. in 1842 to Melinda Ann Neely, of Ky. After her death,
m. in 1888 to a widow, Mrs. Hannah L. Kendall. D. Sept. 25,
1900 at Springfield. Bur. in Carlinville City Cem.

OGLESBY, RICHARD JAMES (1873). See above, 1865-1869.

BEVERIDGE, JOHN LOURIE (1873-1877). b. July 6, 1824 at
Greenwich, N.Y. Descended from a Scottish colonist who had
emigrated to N.Y. in 1770. Father was a farmer who moved to
Ill. in 1842, settling at Somonauk, in De Kalb Co. Attd.
Rock River Acad. at Mt. Morris. After grad. in 1845 went to
Tenn., where he taught school in Wilson and Overton counties
while also studying law. Admitted to bar in Tenn. Returned
to Ill. in 1851 where he practiced law at Sycamore. In 1854
enlisted with an Ill. cavalry unit. Rose to rank of col.
Participated in major campaigns and engagements of Army of
the Potomac in the East, 1861-1863. Held rank of brig. gen.
at end of war. Returned to Evanston. El. sheriff of Cook
Co. in 1866. Mbr. of Ill. Senate, 1871. Resigned office in
Nov., 1871 after having been el. to a seat in U.S. House in
that year to fill a vacancy. Resigned House seat in Jan.,
1873, having been el. Lieut. Gov. as a Rep. in Nov., 1872.
Held office of Lieut. Gov. for only about one week, succeeding to office of Gov. in Jan., 1873 following resignation of
Gov. Oglesby. Completed Oglesby's term as Gov. Resumed law
practice in Evanston and Chicago. Apptd. as U.S. Treas. officer at Chicago, serving until 1885. Moved to Hollywood,
Calif., in 1895. m. in 1848 to Helen M. Judson. One s., one
d. D. May 3, 1910 in Hollywood. Bur. in Rose Hill Cem.,
Chicago.

CULLOM, SHELBY MOORE (1877-1883). b. Nov. 22, 1829 at
Monticello, Ky. s. of Richard Northcraft and Elizabeth
(Coffey) C. Father was a farmer who moved to Tazewell Co.,
in Ill., the year after son was born, and had been a mbr. of
Ill. legislature for several terms. Two brothers of his
father, Alvan C. and Wm. C., were mbrs. of U.S. House from
Tenn. After receiving a good academic educ., went to Springfield, Ill. in 1853 where he began study of law. Admitted
to bar in 1855 and was el. city atty. of Springfield that
same year. Pres. elector cand. on Fillmore (Amer. party)
ticket in 1856 pres. campaign. El. to Ill. House in 1856
and 1860, and was chosen Speaker in 1861. Joined Rep. party
after Civil War began. El. to U.S. House as a Rep. in 1864
and continued in office until 1871, being defeated for reel.
in 1870. As ch. of House Commt. on Territories, backed effort
to suppress polygamy in Utah. Delegate to Rep. natl. conv.

in 1868. Engaged in banking and law practice at Springfield
for several years. El. to Ill. House in 1872 and 1874, serving as Speaker in 1873 session. Nom. and el. Gov. as a Rep.
in 1876. Reel. in 1880. Resigned office in Feb., 1883
after having been el. to U.S. Senate. Continued in that office until 1913, serving as Rep. floor leader in 1910-1913.
A report of a spec. study commt. which he headed in the 1880s
on problem of railroad rate regulation provided the basis for
creation of the U.S. Interstate Commerce Commn. in 1887. Was
one of the commnrs. who drafted a plan for org. of govt. of
Hawaii after its annexation in 1898. Delegate to Rep. natl.
convs. in 1872, 1884 and 1892. Regent of Smithsonian Inst.,
1885-1913. Ch. of Lincoln Memorial Commn., 1913-1914. Published an autobiography, Fifty Years of Public Service, in
1912. m. in 1855 to Hannah Fisher. Two d. After her death
m. to her sister, Julia. D. Jan. 28, 1914 at Washington,
D.C. Bur. in Oak Ridge Cem., Springfield.

HAMILTON, JOHN MARSHALL (1883-1885). b. May 28, 1847
at Ridgewood, Union Co., Ohio. s. of Samuel and Nancy
(McMorris) H. Family was originally from Va. Moved to
Wenona, Ill. in 1854 where father engaged in farming. Son
enlisted in Ill. regiment in 1864. Participated in engagements in Ky. and Tenn. against Confed. guerilla units. After the war, taught school for one term and in 1866 entered
Ohio Wesleyan Univ., from which he was grad. with honors in
1868. Tutor in acad. at Henry, Ill. in 1868-1869, and prof.
of languages at Wesleyan Coll. at Bloomington, Ill. in 1870.
Studied law while teaching. Admitted to bar and began practice in Bloomington in 1870. Mbr. of Ill. Senate, 1876-1880.
Initiated legislation creating appellate court system for
State. Also was influential in creation of State Bd. of
Health and in militia reorg. Nom. and el. Lieut. Gov. as
Rep. in 1880. Succeeded to office of Gov. in Feb., 1883
when Gov. Cullom resigned, and completed Cullom's term. Re-
sumed law practice at Bloomington thereafter. Later moved
to Chicago. m. in 1870 to Helen W. Williams. D. in Chicago
Sept. 23, 1905.

OGLESBY, RICHARD JAMES (1885-1889). See above, 1865-
1869.

FIFER, JOSEPH WILSON (1889-1893). b. Oct. 28, 1840 at
Staunton, Va. s. of John and Mary (Wilson) F. In 1857 the
family moved to McLean Co., Ill. where father built a log
cabin and engaged in farming, and later in a brick mfg. enterprise. Attd. local schools while assisting on the farm
and in brick-making. In 1861 enlisted in Union Army as a
pvt. Participated in Vicksburg campaign, 1862-1863 and was

seriously wounded at Jackson, Miss. Continued in military
service as a pvt. for some time thereafter, After release
from mil. service entered Ill. Wesleyan Univ. at Bloomington,
earning money while attending coll. to finance his own and a
younger brother's educ. Was grad. in 1868 and studied law
in office in Bloomington. Admitted to bar in 1870. Served
as city counsel for Bloomington, 1871. State's atty. for
his jud. dist., 1872-1879, acquiring reputation as vigorous
prosecutor of criminal offenders. Mbr. of Ill. Senate, 1880-
1884. Retired to law practice for several years. Nom. and
el. Gov. as Rep. in 1888, defeating former Gov. Palmer by a
narrow margin. During the campaign came to be referred to
as "Private Joe," since he won the Rep. nom. in competition
with three former Civil War gens., one col., one major, and
one capt., and the Dem. opponent he defeated had also been a
major gen. Nom. for a second term in 1892 but was defeated
in gen. el. As Gov., successfully advocated adoption of
Australian ballot system. After tenure as Gov. continued in
law practice. Was placed in nom. for Vice Pres. of U.S. at
the Rep. natl. conv. in 1896, but failed to win nom. Mbr.,
U.S. Interstate Commerce Commn., 1899-1906. Hon. degree
from Ill. Wesleyan Univ. m. in 1870 to Gertrude Lewis. One
s., one d. D. Aug. 6, 1938 at Bloomington, Ill., at age of
97. Bur. in Park Hill Cem. there.

ALTGELD, JOHN PETER (1893-1897). b. Dec. 30, 1847 in
Niedersfelters, Nassau, Germany. Emigrated to Amer. in 1848
to Richland Co., Ohio with parents, who settled on a farm.
Attd. local pub. schools. In 1864 enlisted in Union Army at
age 16. After the Civil War, taught school for a time in
Ohio. In 1869 started out for the West, travelling by foot.
Stopped in Northwestern Mo. Taught school while studying
law there. Admitted to bar in 1872. Served as city atty.
of Savannah, Mo. El. pros. atty. of Andrew Co., Mo. in 1874.
Resigned the following year and went to Chicago. Practiced
law, soon acquiring a large clientele. Unsuccessful cand.
for seat in U.S. House in 1884. El. to post of superior ct.
judge in 1886, later becoming chief judge of that ct. Resigned in 1891. Nom. and el. Gov. as Dem. in 1892 in exciting contest, defeating incumbent Gov. Fifer. Became thereby
the first person of foreign birth and the first resident of
Chicago to hold office of Gov. in Ill. His pardoning on
grounds of alleged illegality of their convictions of three
anarchists who had been imprisoned on charges growing out of
the Haymarket Riots of 1886 aroused much controversy, as did
his unwillingness to use mil. force to maintain order in
connection with a wide-spread railroad strike in Chicago in
1894. Pres. Cleveland intervened with U.S. mil. forces, despite the Governor's failure to request aid. Delegate to

Dem. natl. conv. in 1896, where he was one of the strong advocates of free silver plank in party platform. Nom. for
reel. as Gov. in 1896. Was denied support of Gold Standard
Dem. faction, but was endorsed by the Pop. party as its cand.
also. Lost in gen. el. Resumed law practice. Defeated as
Indep. cand. for mayor of Chicago in 1899. Author of numerous articles, pamphlets and speeches on political topics.
m. in 1877 to Emma Ford, of Washington, Ohio. D. Mar. 12,
1902, in Joliet, Ill.

TANNER, JOHN RILEY (1897-1901). b. April 4, 1844 near
Booneville, Warrick Co., Ind. s. of John and Eliza (Downs)
T. Family lived in a log cabin on a small farm. Following
outbreak of Civil War the father and all five of his sons
enlisted in Union Army. Father died while being held as a
mil. prisoner and two of the brothers died of wounds during
the course of the war. J. and his two remaining brothers
served until the end of the war, after which he purchased a
small farm near Flora, in Clay Co., Ill. Engaged in farming
and various local bus. enterprises. El. to Ill. Senate in
1880. Apptd. U.S. marshal for So. Dist. of Ill. by Pres.
Arthur in 1884. El. to office of State Treas. in 1886.
Later was apptd. to Ill. R.R. and Warehouse Commn. Resigned
that post in 1891 when he was apptd. asst. U.S. Treas. at
Chicago by Pres. Harrison. Removed from office by Pres.
Cleveland in 1893 for partisan reasons. Ch. of Rep. state
commt. in 1894. Nom. and el. Gov. as Rep. in 1896, defeating incumbent Gov. Altgeld. During admin., a widespread
coal miners' strike and financial embarrassment of the State
as a result of the financial panic of 1893 were major concerns. Cooperated with U.S. govt. in raising troops for
Spanish-Amer. War. m. in 1866 to Lauretta Ingraham, of Clay
Co., Ill. Two children. After her death in 1887, m. to
Cora Edith English, of Springfield in 1896. D. at Springfield May 23, 1901 shortly after leaving office of Gov.

YATES, RICHARD, Jr. (1901-1905). b. Dec. 12, 1860 at
Jacksonville, Ill. s. of Gov. Richard, Sr. and Catherine
(Geers) Y. (q.v.). Attd. pub. schools in Jacksonville and
Ill. Women's Coll., 1870-1874. Grad. from Ill. Coll. at
Jacksonville in 1880 and received an A.M. degree there in
1883. From 1878 to 1883 served as part-time ed. of local
newspapers. Won state oratorical contest in Champaign in
1879 and represented Ill. at final contest at Oberlin Univ.
in 1880, finishing second. Studied law at the Univ. of
Mich., grad. in 1884. Admitted to Ill. bar. City atty. of
Jacksonville, 1887-1891. Served in Ill. Natl. Guard, 1885-
1890. Co. judge in Morgan Co., 1894-1897. Became active in
Rep. politics at early age. Nom. for U.S. Repr.-at-large in

1892 but was defeated in gen. el. Apptd. U.S. collector of
internal revenue for Ill. by Pres. McKinley, serving 1897-
1900. Nom. and el. Gov. as Rep. in 1900, becoming the first
native-born inhabitant of the State to be el. to that office.
Mbr. of Ill. Pub. Utilities Commn., 1914-1916. Asst. Atty.
Gen. for Ill., 1917-1918. El. to U.S. House in 1918, and
served continuously thereafter, except for part of one term,
until 1933, when he was defeated for reel. Failed to win
re-nom. for U.S. House seat in 1928, but later was el. to
fill a vacancy in that post. Active in affairs of Methodist
church. Hon. degree from Ill. Coll. m. in 1888 to Helen
Wadsworth, of Jacksonville. Two d. Wrote memoirs in later
years. D. April 11, 1936 at Springfield. Bur. in Diamond
Grove Cem. in Jacksonville.

DENEEN, CHARLES SAMUEL (1905-1913). b. May 4, 1863 at
Edwardsville, Ill. s. of Samuel H. and Mary F. (Ashley) D.
Father was a coll. prof. Educ. in pub. schools at Lebanon,
Ill. to which place family had moved during his youth. Grad.
from McKendree Coll. in 1882 and from Union Coll. of Law
(later Northwestern Univ.), in Chicago, in 1885. Supported
himself while attending coll. by teaching school. Admitted
to bar in 1886. Practiced law in Chicago, 1890-1904. El.
to Ill. legislature in 1892. Atty. for Chicago Sanitary
Dist., 1895-1896. State's atty. for Cook Co., 1896-1904.
Nom. and el. Gov. as Rep. in 1904 by a large majority and
was reel. in 1908. During admin., a direct primary law and
state civil service law were enacted; a mun. ct. system for
Chicago created; a state highway commn. and a state geological commn. established; forest preserve districts set up;
a state dental bd. established; railway safety and indus.
workers' protective legislation passed; and action taken to
provide homes for destitute children. Resumed law practice
after leaving office. El. to U.S. Senate in 1924. Was
apptd. to the post in Feb., 1925 shortly before beginning of
regular term following death of incumbent Senator McCormick.
Defeated for re-nom. for the office in 1930. Hon. degree
from Union Coll. of Law. m. in 1891 to Bina Day Maloney, of
Mt. Carroll, Ill. One s., three d. D. Feb. 5, 1940 in
Chicago. Bur. in Oak Woods Cem.

DUNNE, EDWARD FITZSIMMONS (1913-1917). b. Oct. 12,
1853 at Waterville, Conn. s. of P.N. and Delia M. (Lawler)
D. Educ. in Peoria, Ill. pub. schools. Attd. Trinity Coll.
of the Univ. of Dublin for three years, but was not a grad.,
having to withdraw because of lack of funds. Studied law at
Union Coll. of Law (now Northwestern Univ.) in Chicago, grad.
in 1877. Admitted to bar and practiced law in Chicago,
1877-1892. El. to cir. ct. judgeship of Cook Co. in 1892,

and continued to serve there until his resignation in 1905.
Mayor of Chicago, 1905-1907. Defeated for reel. in 1907.
Vice pres., Natl. Civic Fed., 1905, and pres. of League of
Amer. Municipalities, 1906. Advocate of pub. ownership of
street railway system. Pres. elector on Dem. ticket in 1900.
Resumed law practice, 1907-1913. Nom. and el. Gov. as Dem.
in 1912, defeating incumbent Gov. Deneen and a Prog. party
cand. for the office. Inauguration delayed for some three
weeks because of delay in org. of the Ill. House, which pre-
vented announcement of the popular vote results officially.
Was Dem. nominee again in 1916, but was defeated in the gen.
el. Mbr. of commt. representing Irish societies at the
Paris Peace Conf. in 1919 to urge self-determination for
Ireland. Ch. of Natl. Unity Council. Mbr., U.S. Commn.
for Century of Progress Expo. in Chicago, 1934-1935. Author
of a history of Illinois. Roman Catholic. m. in 1881 to
Elizabeth J. Kelly, of Chicago. Seven s., five d. D. in
Chicago May 24, 1937.

LOWDEN, FRANK ORREN (1917-1921). b. Jan. 26, 1861 at
Sunrise City, Minn. s. of Lorenzo Orren and Nancy Elizabeth
(Breg) L. Father was a farmer and blacksmith who had settled
in Minn. in 1850s. Family moved to Point Pleasant, Iowa, in
1868 where he attd. pub. schools while working on father's
farm. At age 15 began to teach school while studying for
coll. Attd. the State Univ. of Iowa, grad. as valedictorian
of class in 1885. Taught school for two years, then began
study of law in Chicago. Grad. from Union Coll. of Law
(later Northwestern Univ.) in 1887 as valedictorian of class.
Admitted to bar and practiced law in Chicago, 1887-1906.
Lieut. col. in Ill. Natl. Guard, 1893-1903. Prof. of law at
Northwestern Univ. in 1899. Delegate to Rep. natl. convs.
in 1900 and 1904. Mbr. of Rep. natl. commt., 1904-1912,
serving on its exec. commt. in 1904 and 1908 pres. campaigns.
Unsuccessful cand. for Rep. nom. for Gov. in 1904. El. to
U.S. House in 1906 to fill vacancy and was reel. in 1908.
Did not seek reel. in 1910. Acquired farm at Oregon, Ill.,
where he became widely known as breeder of high grade livestock. Nom. and el. Gov. as Rep. in 1916. During admin.,
supported war effort during World War I. Sponsored measures
for admin. reorg. to promote economy and efficiency and set
up exec. budget system. Was a major contender for Rep. nom.
for Pres. of U.S. in 1920 natl. conv., but failed to win
when conv. became deadlocked among three major contenders.
Contender again for Rep. nom. for Pres. in 1924 natl. conv.,
receiving support of over 300 delegates. Received nom. for
Vice Pres. of U.S. but declined it. Also received some delegate support for nom. for Pres. of U.S. at 1928 Rep. natl.
conv. Acquired many bus. interests during career in fields

of banking, mfg., and railroads. Trustee, Thomas Orchestra
Assoc.; St. Luke's Hosp.; Chicago Relief and Aid Soc.; Car-
negie Endowment for Intl. Peace; Inst. for Pub. Admin.; Pub.
Admin. Clearing House. Pres., Holstein-Friesian Assoc. of
Amer. Dir. of Intl. Livestock Exhibition; Farm Found.;
Pullman Free School of Manual Training; Foreign Bondholders
Protective Council, Inc. Hon. degrees from twelve colleges
and universities. m. in 1896 to Florence Pullman. One s.,
three d. D. Mar. 20, 1943 at Tucson, Ariz., where he had
gone because of health. Bur. in Graceland Cem., Chicago.

SMALL, LEN(NINGTON) (1921-1929). b. June 16, 1862 at
Kankakee, Ill. s. of Abram Lennington and Colesta (Currier)
S. Father was a physician. Reared on family farm and attd.
local pub. schools. Studied at Ill. Normal Coll., at Bloomington, for a time; also attd. a local bus. coll. Engaged
in teaching to acquire funds to buy farm near Kankakee and
enlarged holdings from time to time later. Became interested
in promotion of improved farm methods. Helped establish annual farm fair at Kankakee and also served as sect. of Ill.
State Fair at Springfield. El. co. supervisor of Kankakee
Co. in 1895. Clerk of cir. ct., 1896 and later was el. to
Ill. Senate. Apptd. to Bd. of Trustees of Kankakee State
Hosp. in 1897, serving eight years as pres. of bd. El.
State Treas. in 1904, serving one term. Apptd. Asst. U.S.
Treas. in charge of Ill. office by Pres. Taft, serving from
1910 to 1913. El. State Treas. again in 1916, serving one
term. Nom. and el. Gov. as Rep. in 1920. Indicted on
charge of misusing interest on state funds while in the office of State Treas. Acquitted of charge, but settled civil
suit by payment of a large sum of money. El. Gov. in 1924
for second term. During admin., advocated economy in govt.;
constr. of a system of paved state roads begun. Lived at
home in Kankakee rather than in Gov.'s mansion at Springfield during much of term. Unsuccessful cand. for Rep. nom.
for Gov. in 1928. Became party nominee for the office again
in 1932, but was defeated in gen. el. Owner and publ. of
newspaper in Kankakee. Pres. of First Trust and Savings
Bank of Kankakee. m. in 1883 to Ida Moore, of Kankakee.
Two s., one d. D. May 17, 1936 at Kankakee.

EMMERSON, LOUIS LINCOLN (1929-1933). b. Dec. 27, 1863
at Albion, Ill. s. of Jene and Fannie (Suardet) E. Attd.
local pub. schools. In 1883 established a gen. merc. bus.
at Mt. Vernon, Ill., which prospered. In 1901 org. and became pres. of Third Natl. Bank at Mt. Vernon. Ch. of Rep.
party commt. of Jefferson Co. for 12 years, and also was ch.
of his party's cong. dist. commt. Mbr. and ch. of Rep. state
commt. Mbr., State Bd. of Tax Equalization, 1905-1908; and

from 1908 to 1913, of the Bd. of Commnrs. for So. Ill. penitentiary. Unsuccessful cand. for Rep. nom. for State Treas.
in 1912. Ill. Sect. of State, 1917-1929. Nom. and el. Gov.
as Rep. in 1928, defeating incumbent Gov. Small for the party
nom. During admin., highway constr. program was carried forward and the Great Lakes to Gulf Waterway system was completed. Econ. distress caused by the depression of the 1930s
required major attention in latter years of term, necessitating his calling the legislature into a series of spec. sessions and the enactment of revisions in tax system. Was not
a cand. for another term. Mbr., Masons; Union League. Hon.
degrees from Ill. Coll. and Milliken Coll. m. in 1887 to
Anna Mathews, of Graysville, Ill. Two d. D. Feb. 4, 1941
at Mt. Vernon.

HORNER, HENRY (1933-1940). b. Nov. 31, 1879 in Chicago,
Ill. s. of Solomon A. and Dilah (Horner) Levy. His father
was born in Bavaria, Germany, and his mother was a mbr. of
an Amer. Jewish family engaged in the wholesale grocery bus.
When son was four years old his parents separated, and he
adopted thereafter his mother's family name as his own.
Attd. local pub. schools and South Side Acad. Received law
degree from the Chicago-Kent Law School in 1896 and began
practice in Chicago. El. judge of probate for Cook Co. in
1914 and reel. for four successive terms, resigning in 1933.
As probate judge acquired recognition for rapid disposal of
cases, handling as many as 46,000 in one year. Devised a
rapid and efficient system of handling estates of World War I
veterans without cost to parties involved. Campaigned for
better care for the insane and for arb. of labor disputes.
Nom. and el. Gov. as Dem. in 1932, defeating former Gov.
Small in the gen. el. During admin., cooperated with U.S.
govt. in adoption of measures to relieve economic distress
resulting from depression of 1930s. Backed tax and mortgage
relief measures. Nom. and el. Gov. for second term in 1936,
winning re-nom. over opposition of the Kelly-Nash Dem. org.
in Chicago. During second admin., became ill with heart
disorder and relinquished powers of office for several months
in 1938-1939 to the Lieut. Gov. while recuperating in Fla.
Upon his return, reassumed powers of office; but was stricken
again in mid-1940. The Lieut. Gov. sought unsuccessfully for
a period of some three weeks to assume powers of office on
the ground the Gov. was incapacitated, but was compelled to
desist when other state exec. officers refused to recognize
his right to do so. Was a collector of materials on Lincoln,
bequeathing some 6,000 volumes to the State Historical Soc.
at his death. Hon. degrees from several colleges and universities. Recipient of Rosenthal Civic Award in 1927;
Grand Officer of the Order of the Crown of Italy. Mbr.,

Chicago Geographical Soc.; Ill. State Historical Soc.; Art
Inst. of Chicago; Lincoln Center Assoc.; Chicago Boy Scouts
Council; Masons; professional legal orgs.; numerous clubs.
Jewish. Never married. D. at Winnetka, Ill., Oct. 6, 1940
while still in office. Bur. in Mt. Mayriv Cem.

STELLE, JOHN HENRY (1940-1941). b. Aug. 10, 1891 at
McLeansboro, Ill. s. of Thompson Beverly and Laura (Blades)
S. Attd. local pub. schools and Western Mil. Acad., at
Alton, Ill. Studied law at Washington Univ., in St. Louis,
Mo., 1914-1915. Admitted to bar and began practice at
McLeansboro. Enlisted in U.S. Army in 1917. Served with
A.E.F. in France and was wounded and gassed. Held rank of
capt. when discharged in 1919. Obtained interest in creamery
bus. at McLeansboro; also acquired interests in other enter-
prises, including structural materials, coal mining, and
aeronautical mfg. Also acquired large dairy farm. Pres. of
Cahokia Race Track. Participated actively in Dem. politics,
serving as dir. of org. for Dem. state cent. commt. in 1932.
Asst. State Treas., 1931-1932. Asst. State Aud., 1933-1934.
State Treas., 1934-1936. Nom. and el. Lieut. Gov. as Dem.
in 1936. Acted as Gov. from Nov., 1938 to June, 1939 during
absence of Gov. Horner because of latter's illness. Sought
unsuccessfully to become Acting Gov. again for a time in
1940 during recurrence of illness of Gov. Horner, resulting
in a controversy for several weeks as to his authority to do
so. Succeeded to office of Gov. in Oct., 1940 following
Horner's death, and completed the term. Defeated in effort
to obtain Dem. nom. for Gov. in that year, being opposed by
the Kelly-Nash Dem. org. in Chicago. Helped form Dem.
Service Men's Org. in 1926. Active in affairs of the Amer.
Legion, serving as ch. of its natl. commt. on legislation in
1944 and was its Natl. Commndr. in 1945. Instrumental in
securing passage of U.S. "G.I. Bill of Rights" legislation.
Mbr., Masons; I.O.O.F.; M.W.A.; Elks; K.P.; Lions; various
social clubs. Methodist. m. in 1912 to Wilma Wiseheart, of
Shawneetown, Ill. Two s. D. at St. Louis, Mo. July 5, 1962.
Bur. in McLeansboro Cem.

GREEN, DWIGHT HERBERT (1941-1949). b. Jan. 9, 1897 at
Ligonier, Ind. s. of Harry and Minnie (Gerber) G. Ancestors had emigrated from Bavaria, Germany to Amer. in 1853,
settling first in Ohio and moving to Ligonier in 1862.
Father was a banker and businessman. Attd. Wabash Coll.,
1915-1917. Served as second lieut. in Signal Corps of U.S.
Army, 1917-1919, stationed at Mather Field, Calif. Attd.
Stanford Univ. in 1919 and later the Univ. of Chicago, from
which he received a law degree in 1922. Worked as newspaper
reporter and law clerk while attending coll. Practiced law

in Chicago, 1922-1926. Apptd. spec. atty. for U.S. Bureau
of Internal Revenue in 1926. Specialized in tax fraud cases,
securing convictions of a number of prominent officials and
of the notorious gangster, Al Capone. Became U.S. dist.
atty. for No. Ill. in 1932, serving until 1935. Resumed pvt.
law practice. Nom. and el. Gov. as Rep. in 1940 and again
in 1944. During admin., cooperated fully with U.S. govt. in
war effort; secured legislation requiring teaching of U.S.
history and govt. courses in pub. institutions; Chicago Port
Authority created; pub. ownership of Chicago elevated railway authorized; pub. housing and slum clearance legislation
passed; and conservation of water resources promoted. Resumed law practice and bus. interests after tenure in office.
Pres. of Midwest Post-war Planning Conf. of Council of State
Govts. in 1943. Participated in Mackinac Conf. of Rep. party
in 1943, where he urged U.S. participation in post-war intl.
orgs. Helped shape Rep. party platform in 1944 pres. campaign. Temp. ch. and keynote speaker at Rep. natl. conv. in
1948. Delegate to Rep. natl. convs. in 1952 and 1956. Active in promotion of numerous fund-raising drives for orgs.
in med. care and research fields. From 1953 onward was ch.
of bd. of Elmwood State Bank. Trustee of Wabash Coll. Hon.
degrees from eight colleges and universities. Mbr., Amer.
Legion; 40 and 8; O.W.W.; Masons; various fraternities and
clubs. Episcopalian. m. in 1936 to Mabel Victoria Kingston,
of New York City. Two d. D. in Chicago Feb. 20, 1958.

STEVENSON, ADLAI EWING II (1949-1953). b. Feb. 5, 1900
at Los Angeles, Calif. s. of Lewis Green and Helen Louise
(Davis) S. Descendant of an Irish immigrant who came to Pa.
in 1748, and later moved to N.C. Paternal grandfather had
served as Vice Pres. of U.S. during Cleveland's second term
and was defeated as the Dem. cand. for Gov. of Ill. in 1908.
Father was an agriculturalist who had served as Ill. Sect.
of State. Grad. from Princeton in 1922. Travelled abroad
for a time, then worked for a Bloomington, Ill. newspaper.
Studied law at Northwestern Univ., grad. in 1926. Joined a
Chicago law firm. Spec. counsel for U.S. Agri. Adjustment
Admin. in Washington, D.C., 1933-1934. Resumed law practice
in Chicago. Also managed family farm at Libertyville, Ill.
Asst. to U.S. Sect. of Navy, 1941-1944. Headed U.S. mission
to Italy in 1943 to study civilian supply needs. Apptd.
asst. to U.S. Sect. of State in 1945. Adviser to U.S. delegation to San Francisco Conf. in 1945. Chief of U.S. Prep.
Commn. for UN at London. U.S. delegate to first UN Assembly
in N.Y., 1946-1947. Nom. and el. Gov. of Ill. as Dem. in
1948. During admin., legislation was passed expanding state-
supported educl. programs; commn. on reorg. of state govt.
created. Nom. as Dem. cand. for Pres. of U.S. in 1952, but

failed to be el. Resumed law practice in Chicago and N.Y.
Nom. again for Pres. of U.S. at Dem. natl. conv. in 1956,
but again was defeated in gen. el. by Pres. Eisenhower.
Asst. to U.S. Sect. of State in 1957. Apptd. by Pres.
Kennedy chief of U.S. delegation to UN in 1961, with rank of
Ambassador. Continued to serve in that capacity until his
death. Affiliated with Ill. Childrens' Home and Aid Soc.;
Immigrants Protective League; Hull House; ch. of Council of
Foreign Relations; ch. of Woodrow Wilson Found.; and ch. of
Eleanor Roosevelt Memorial Found. Author of books and ar-
ticles on political topics. Recipient of numerous awards
and hon. degrees from U.S. and foreign institutions. Uni-
tarian. m. in 1928 to Ellen Borden, from whom he was later
divorced. Three s., one of whom, Adlai III, became a U.S.
Senator from Ill. D. in London, England, July 14, 1965.
Bur. at Bloomington, Ill.

STRATTON, WILLIAM GRANT (1953-1961). b. Feb. 26, 1914
in Ingleside, Ill. s. of Wm. J. and Zula (Van Wormer) S.
Father had served as Ill. Sect. of State, 1922-1923. Attd.
local pub. schools and the Univ. of Ariz., from which he
was grad. in 1934. Engaged in farming and bus. activities
at Morris, Ill. Nom. and el. to U.S. House as Repr.-at-
large in 1940. Was not a cand. for reel. in 1942, but was
nom. and el. Ill. State Treas. in that year. Served until
1945 when he resigned and enlisted as a lieut., j.g., in the
U.S. Navy. Served in the Pac. area until 1946. Nom. and el.
to U.S. House again in 1946. Was not a cand. for reel. in
1948, but was nom. and el. State Treas. in 1950. Nom. and
el. Gov. as a Rep. in 1952 and again in 1956. Nom. for a
third term in 1960 but was defeated in gen. el. Delegate to
Rep. natl. convs. in 1952, 1956 and 1960, serving as ch. of
the Ill. delegation in 1956 and 1960. During admin. as Gov.,
was ch. of Natl. Govs.' Conf. in 1957 and ch. of its Interstate Oil Compact Commt. in 1955. Pres. of Council of State
Govts., 1958. Mbr. of Lincoln Sesquicentennial Commn., 1958
and of the Fed. Advisory Commn. on Intergovtl. Relations,
1959. Operator of farm at Cantrall, Ill., specializing in
breeding of Black Angus cattle. Was indicted by a Fed. grand
jury in April, 1964 on charge of income tax evasion in connection with campaign funds received in 1957-1960 and allegedly converted to his personal use. Was subsequently acquitted of criminal charges after a trial in 1965, but was
later assessed additional income tax liability by action of
U.S. Tax Ct. Mbr., Masons (Shriner); Amer. Legion; AMVETS;
Rotary; V.F.W. Methodist. Trustee of Robt. Morris Coll.
Recipient of hon. degrees from the Univ. of Ariz. and several
Ill. colleges and universities. m. first to Marion Munyon,

of Lynn Haven, Fla. Two d. After first marriage ended in
divorce in 1949, m. in 1950 to Shirley Breckinridge. One d.

KERNER, OTTO (1961-1968). b. Aug. 8, 1908 in Chicago,
Ill. s. of Otto and Rose Barbara (Chmelek) K. Father was
a lawyer and judge. Attd. local pub. schools in Oak Park,
Ill.; Brown Univ., from which he was grad. in 1930; and
Northwestern Univ., from which he received a law degree in
1934. During 1930-1931 was a student at Trinity Coll. of
Cambridge Univ., in England. Admitted to bar in Chicago and
practiced law there. Enlisted as a pvt. in Ill. Natl. Guard
in 1934. Advanced to rank of capt. by 1941. Was on active
duty with U.S. Army in No. Africa and Sicily, 1942-1943; and
after attending Field Artillery School in Okla. in 1943, saw
service in the Philippines and Japan, 1945-1946. Held rank
of lieut. col. at time of discharge. Recipient of Bronz
Star for war service. Apptd. U.S. dist. atty. for No. Ill.
in 1947 by Pres. Truman, serving until 1954. El. judge of
dist. ct. in Cook Co. in 1954 and was reel. in 1958. Resigned in 1960 after being nom. as Dem. cand. for Gov. El.
to that office, defeating incumbent Gov. Stratton. Reel. in
1964. In 1967-1968 served as ch. of Pres. Johnson's Spec.
Advisory Commn. on Civil Disorders, which issued a widely-
noted report on racial and civil rights problems in U.S. Resigned office of Gov. in May, 1968 to accept apptmt. as mbr.
on the U.S. Cir. Ct. of Appeals. Was indicted in Dec., 1971
by a U.S. grand jury on charges of tax evasion, fraud and
conspiracy growing out of his actions, along with those of
his former State Revenue Dir., in connection with issuance
of race track licenses and other regulatory matters during
his admin. as Gov. Resigned his U.S. jud. post in 1973
after he was found guilty of the charges and was sentenced
to a three-year prison term. Released from prison in March,
1975, having become afflicted with an incurable illness.
Vice Pres. of Chicago Council of Boy Scouts. Trustee of
Brown Univ.; dir. of John Howard Assoc. and of the Adult
Educ. Council of Greater Chicago. Mbr., Masons; Moose; various clubs, professional legal orgs., and fraternities.
Hon. degrees from seven colleges and universities. m. to
Helena Cermak, of Chicago. One s., one d. D. at Chicago
May 8, 1976. Bur. in Arlington Natl. Cem. in Va.

SHAPIRO, SAMUEL HARVEY (1968-1969). b. April 25, 1907
in Esthonia. Family emigrated to Amer. Attd. St. Viator's
Coll. and the Univ. of Ill., from which he was grad. with a
law degree in 1929. Began practice at Kankakee, Ill., and
became active in Dem. party, serving as sect.-treas. of
Young Dem. org. of Ill. City atty., Kankakee, 1933. State's
atty. for Kankakee Co., 1936. Served in U.S. Navy anti-

submarine warfare unit during World War II. Mbr. of Ill.
House, 1946-1960. Served as ch. of Gov.'s Advisory Council
on Mental Retardation and as mbr. of Intergovtl. Commn. Was
also a mbr. of the Ill. Legislative Council. Nom. and el.
Lieut. Gov. as Dem. in 1960 and was reel. in 1964. Ch. of
Ill. Mental Health Commn., 1961. Ch. of Natl. Conf. of Lieut.
Govs., 1962. Succeeded to office of Gov. when Gov. Kerner
resigned in March, 1968 and completed Kerner's term. Ch. of
rules commt., Dem. natl. conv. in 1968. Nom. as Dem. cand.
for Gov. for regular term in 1968, but was defeated in the
gen. el. Mbr., Decalogue Soc. of Lawyers; Natl. Civil Rights
Cong.; Amer. Legion; AMVETS; B'nai B'rith; Anti-defamation
League; Amer. Fed. of Musicians; Moose; Elks; various social
clubs and professional legal orgs. Jewish. m. in 1939 to
Gertrude Adelman.

OGILVIE, RICHARD BUELL (1969-1973). b. Feb. 22, 1923
at Kansas City, Mo. At age 7 moved with parents to Evanston,
Ill. Later resided at Rockville Center and then at Port
Chester, N.Y., where he finished pub. school educ. Entered
Yale Univ., but withdrew in 1942 to enlist in U.S. Army.
Served as tank commdr. in France during World War II. Was
wounded and received discharge in 1945. Grad. from Yale in
1947 and attd. Chicago-Kent Coll. of Law, receiving law degree in 1949. Began law practice in Chicago. Served as
asst. U.S. dist. atty. in 1954-1955. During 1958-1961, took
leading role in campaign against org. crime as spec. asst. to
U.S. Atty. Gen. El. sheriff of Cook Co., 1962. Pres. of
Cook Co. Bd. of Commnrs., 1966, where he achieved reputation
for improving admin. and employing high standards of merit
for apptmts. Nom. and el. Gov. as Rep. in 1968. As Gov.,
sponsored adoption of first state income tax law as part of
a gen. revision of tax system; improved law enforcement;
modernized welfare system; increased aid for educ. and
revenue-sharing with cities. Nom. in 1972 for succeeding
term but was defeated in gen. el. Engaged in legal practice
and bus. activities in Chicago after tenure as Gov. m. to
Dorothy Shruen. One d.

WALKER, DAN(IEL) (1973-1977). b. Aug. 6, 1922 in Washington, D.C. s. of Lewis W. and Virginia (Lynch) W. Family
moved to San Diego, Calif. during his youth, where he attd.
local pub. schools. Enlisted in U.S. Navy in 1939 and in
1940 became a cadet at U.S. Naval Acad., from which he was
grad. and commissioned as a junior officer in 1945. Served
in U.S. Navy until 1947. Also served for a time on active
duty in 1951, having been a USNR officer in the meantime.
Attd. Northwestern Univ., from which he received a law degree in 1950, grad. second in class. Admitted to Ill. bar.

Served as law clerk to Chief Justice Vinson of the U.S.
Supreme Ct. in 1950.   Commnr. of U.S. Ct. of Mil. Appeals,
1951-1952.   Admin. sect. to Gov. Adlai Stevenson, of Ill.,
1952.   Became a practicing atty. in Chicago, 1953-1971.
Served as gen. counsel and vice pres. of Montgomery Ward and
Co. and of Marcor, Inc.   Mbr. of Chicago Crime Commn., 1957-
1971, serving as its pres. for two terms.   Dir. of Chicago
team of Natl. Commn. on Causes and Prevention of Violence
(the Kerner Commn.), 1967-1969, and assisted in preparation
of its report, Rights in Conflict, in 1968.   Campaign mgr.
for Adlai Stevenson III for U.S. Senate seat in 1970.   Nom.
and el. Gov. as Dem. in 1972, defeating incumbent Gov.
Ogilvie in a close el.   Won nom. without the support of Mayor
Daley, of Chicago, with whom he was at odds during his admin.
as Gov.   Campaigned for office of Gov. by a walking tour of
the State covering over 1,100 miles.   Defeated for re-nom.
in 1976 by a cand. backed by Mayor Daley.   Recipient of
Northwestern Univ. Alumni Merit Award; Roger Baldwin Award;
Civic Award of Chicago Newspaper Guild; hon. degree from
Carroll Coll.   Mbr., professional legal orgs. and various
social clubs.   Author of Military Law in 1955.   m. in 1947
to Roberta Dowse.   Four d., three s.

JENNINGS, JONATHAN (1816-1822). b. in 1784 in
Hunterton Co., N.J. s. of Jacob and Mary (Kennedy) J.
Father, who was a Presbyterian minister, moved with family
to Dunlap's Creek, in Fayette Co., Pa. in 1790. Son attd.
pvt. school at Canonsburg, Pa. Moved to Jeffersonville,
Ind. Terr., in 1806. Studied law and was admitted to bar.
Became involved in local politics as mbr. of Jeff. Rep. party. Asst. clerk of Ind. Terr. legislature. Moved to
Vincennes in 1807 and in 1808 to Charleston, Ind. Engaged
in newspaper work along with law practice. Terr. Delegate
to Cong. in 1809. Election, in which the issue was retention or repeal of the provision in the Northwest Ordinance
forbidding slavery in the Northwest Terr. area, was extremely close. His victory by 26 votes an an advocate of retention of the anti-slavery provision settled question of
Indiana's eventually becoming a free State. Continued in
office as Terr. Delegate until admission of Ind. to statehood in 1816. Presided over conv. that framed first const.
of Ind. El. as first Gov. in that year, assuming office
provisionally in Nov., 1816, one month before the statehood
act became effective. Reel. in 1819. During admin.,
Indianapolis was designated as capital in 1820. Served as
U.S. commnr. by apptmt. by Pres. Monroe to negotiate treaty
with Indians in the area in 1818. Resigned as Gov. in
Sept., 1822, to take seat in U.S. House, having been el. to
fill a vacancy. Served until Mar. 4, 1831, being defeated
for reel. in 1830. Retired to farm near Jacksonville.
Served as one of three commnrs. in 1832 to negotiate treaty
with Indian tribes in No. Ind. and So. Mich. m. in 1811 to
Ann Hay. m. in 1827 to Clarissa Barber. No children. D.
near Charleston, Ind., July 26, 1834. Bur. in Charleston
Cem.

BOON(E), RATLIFF (1822). b. Jan. 18, 1781 in
Franklin Co., N.C. While still a child, family moved to
Warren Co., Ky., where he attd. common schools. Learned
the gunsmith's trade at a shop in Danville. In 1809 moved
to Boon(e)ville, in Ind. Terr. Engaged in farming and local
bus. enterprise. Treas. of Warrick Co. in 1813 when the
co. was first org. Mbr. of first legislature of Ind. in
1816. El. to Ind. Senate in 1818, and in 1819 to office of
Lieut. Gov. as Jeff. Rep. Succeeded to office of Gov. in
Sept., 1822 when Gov. Jennings resigned, and completed last
three months of Jennings' term. Reel. Lieut. Gov. in 1822.
Resigned office in 1824 to become successful cand. for seat
in U.S. House. Defeated for reel. in 1826, but was el.
again in 1828. Continued in that office until 1839. Defeated for U.S. Senate seat in 1836 as a Jackson Dem. cand.

In 1839 moved to Pike Co., Mo., where he soon became involved in politics. Engaged in sharp controversy with Sen.
Wm. H. Benton over issues concerning natl. banking, currency and other policies. m. to Deliah Anderson, of Ky. D.
at Louisiana, Mo., Nov. 20, 1844. Bur. in Riverview Cem.
there.

HENDRICKS, WILLIAM (1822-1825). b. Nov. 12, 1782 in
Ligonier Valley, Westmoreland Co., Pa. s. of Abraham and
Ann (Jamieson) H. Descendant of a Huguenot family that had
emigrated to N.J. in 1683, and which later established residence in Pa. Father had served in Pa. legislature. Attd.
local schools and Washington and Jefferson Coll., from
which he was grad. in 1810. Moved to Cincinnati, Ohio,
where he taught school for two years while studying law.
Located at Madison, Ind. Terr. in 1814, where he practiced
law and also engaged in printing bus. Mbr. of Ind. Terr.
legislature in 1814. Became sect. of the Gen. Assembly,
later Speaker. Mbr. of conv. that drafted first const. for
the State in 1816, serving as sect. of that body. El. in
1816 as first mbr. of U.S. House from Ind. and continued in
office for succeeding three terms. Resigned in 1822 to become cand. for Gov., and was el. without opposition.
During admin., capital was moved from Corydon to
Indianapolis. Resigned office in Feb., 1825, to take seat
in U.S. Senate, where he became a supporter of Andrew
Jackson. Continued to serve in Senate until 1837 when he
was defeated for reel. Retired to Madison where he engaged
in law practice and as publ. of an influential weekly newspaper, the Western Eagle. Trustee of Ind. Univ., 1829-
1840. Hon. degree from Washington and Jefferson Coll. m.
to Ann Parker Paul, of Madison, Ind. in 1816. Two s., both
of whom lost their lives as soldiers during the Civil War.
A nephew, Thomas A. Hendricks, was later a Gov. of Ind.,
U.S. Repr., U.S. Sen., and Vice Pres. of U.S. (q.v.). D.
at Madison, Ind., March 16, 1850. Bur. in Fairmont Cem.
there.

RAY, JAMES BROWN (1825-1831). b. Feb. 19, 1794 in
Jefferson Co., Ky. Received common school educ. there.
Moved to Cincinnati, Ohio where he studied law and was ad-
mitted to the bar in 1816. Established practice at
Brookville, Ind., where he soon became prominent as a law-
yer and political leader. El. to Ind. Senate in 1822, and
in 1824 was chosen Pres. pro tem of that body. When Gov.
Hendricks resigned in Feb., 1825, succeeded to office of
Gov., the office of Lieut. Gov. being vacant at the time.
Completed Hendricks' term and was el. to a regular term as

Gov. in that same year as a Clay Rep. El. for second term
in 1828. During admin., which was a period of gen. prosperity, the system of pub. schools was strengthened; the
Univ. of Ind. was org. with its seat at Bloomington; and
a program of internal improvements was launched. Served as
mbr. of U.S. commn. to negotiate treaty with Pottawattomie
and Miami Indian tribes in 1826, which caused controversy
and loss of popularity because of contention that he was
forbidden by Ind. const. from holding any office under U.S.
while serving in office of Gov. Retired to law practice
in Indianapolis after term expired. Defeated as cand. to
fill vacant seat in U.S. House in 1837. Became very eccentric in later years of life. m. in 1818 to Mary Riddle, of
Cincinnati. After her death, m. in 1825 to Mrs. Esther
Booker, of Centreville, Ind. D. Aug. 4, 1848, at
Cincinnati, Ohio.

   NOBLE, NOAH (1831-1837). b. Jan. 15, 1794 near
Berryville, Va. s. of Thomas and Elizabeth Claire
(Sedgwick) N. Descendant of a Scottish colonist who came
to Amer. in 1738. Grew up in Campbell Co., Va. In 1816
moved to Brookville, Ind. to join his brother, James, who
became one of the first two U.S. Senators from Ind. in that
year. Engaged in bus. there. El. sheriff of Franklin Co.
in 1820 and was reel. in 1822. Mbr. of Ind. legislature in
1824. Apptd. by Pres. Adams in 1826 receiver of pub.
moneys for Indianapolis dist. Removed from that office by
Pres. Jackson in 1829 for political reasons. One of
commnrs. to locate road from Ohio River to Lake Michigan in
1830. Nom. and el. Gov. as Natl. Rep. (Whig) cand. in
1831. Reel. in 1834. During admin., internal improvements
program was promoted; pub. educ. system expanded; State
Capitol bldg. built. After tenure as Gov. became mbr. of
Ind. Bd. of Internal Improvements and in 1841, Ind. Fund
Commnr. Unsuccessful cand. for U.S. Senate seat in 1836
and again in 1838, after prolonged struggle in the legislature. m. in 1819 to Katherine Van Swearingen, of
Berryville, Va. D. Feb. 8, 1844 at home near Indianapolis.

   WALLACE, DAVID (1837-1840). b. April 4, 1799 near
Lewiston Pa. s. of Andrew and Eleanor (Jones) W. Attd.
local schools there and also in Ohio, where family resided
for a short time. Father moved with family to Brookville,
Ind. in 1817. Attd. U.S. Mil. Acad., grad. in 1821. Remained at the Acad. as an instructor in mathematics for
two years. Resigned from mil. service in 1822. Studied
law in office of Sen. James Noble in Brookville and was
admitted to bar in 1824. Formed partnership with Noble and

soon acquired lucrative practice. Mbr. of Ind. legislature, 1828-1830. Moved to Covington, Ind. in 1830, continuing in law practice there. El. Lieut. Gov. in 1831 and again in 1834. Nom. and el. Gov. as a Whig in 1837. As Gov., continued to promote internal improvements programs and pub. educ. system. Financial stringency in latter part of term necessitated rigid economies. During admin., a treaty was formed with Miami Indians under which they agreed to move west of Mississippi River within three years. Was first Gov. of Ind. to proclaim Thanksgiving Day and first to reside in the Gov.'s mansion. El. to U.S. House in 1840, where he cast tie-breaking vote in commt. to grant $30,000. to S. F. B. Morse, leading to constr. of first telegraph line in country. Defeated for reel. to Cong. in 1842. Resumed law practice. Mbr. of state constl. conv. in 1850. El. as Marion Co. prosecutor and in 1856 to Marion Co. ct. of common pleas, on which he served until death. m. to Esther Test, _circa_ 1824. After her death, m. in 1836 to Zerelda G. Sanders, of Indianapolis. Seven children. Was the father of Lewis ("Lew") W., who was a Union Army gen. during the Civil War, Terr. Gov. of N.M. in 1878-1881, and author of a number of well-known novels, including Ben Hur. D. Sept. 4, 1859. Bur. in Crown Hill Cem., Indianapolis.

BIGGER, SAMUEL (1840-1843). b. March 29, 1802 in Warren Co., Ohio. s. of Col. John B., who had served as mbr. of Ohio legislature. Grad. from Athens Univ. in Ohio. Studied law at Lebanon, Ohio. In 1829 moved to Liberty, Ind., and later to Rushville, Ind., where he practiced law. Mbr. of Ind. legislature, 1834-1836. Cir. ct. judge for his dist., 1836-1840. Nom. and el. Gov. as a Whig in 1840. Defeated for second term in 1843. During admin., a complete revision of Ind. statutes was effected. After tenure as Gov., established residence at Ft. Wayne, Ind., where he practiced law until his death. m. in 1830 to Ellen Williamson, of Liberty, Ind. D. Sept. 9, 1846, at Ft. Wayne, Ind.

WHITCOMB, JAMES (1843-1848). b. Dec. 1, 1795 at Windsor, Vt. s. of John and Lydia (Parmenter) W. Family moved to a farm near Cincinnati, Ohio, soon after son was born. An avid reader as a youth, was largely self-educ. Entered Transylvania Univ., in Ky. and grad. in 1819. Supported self by teaching and other work during vacations while attending college. Studied law and was admitted to Ky. bar in 1822. Practiced in Fayette Co., Ky. In 1824 moved to Bloomington, Ind., continuing to practice law. Pros. atty. for Monroe Co. cir., 1826. Mbr. of Ind. Senate,

1830-1836, where he achieved reputation as orator and as critic of state internal improvements program. Apptd. U.S. land office commnr. by Pres. Jackson in 1836, continuing in that office until 1841. Resumed law practice at Terre Haute. Nom. and el. Gov. as Dem. in 1843, defeating incumbent Gov. Bigger in close contest. Reel. in 1846. During admin., was confronted by a gen. depression, necessitating state financial reforms; refunded state debt; established institutions for insane, deaf, dumb and blind. Resigned in 1848 to take seat in U.S. Senate beginning in Mar., 1849. Published Facts for the People in 1843, which was a criticism of the protective tariff system. Vice pres., Amer. Bible Soc. in 1852. m. in 1846 to Mrs. Martha Ann Hurst. A d., Martha, was married in 1868 to Claude Matthews, later a Gov. of Ind. (q.v.). D. in New York City, Oct. 4, 1852, while still a mbr. of U.S. Senate. Bur. in Crown Hill Cem., Indianapolis.

DUNNING, PARIS CHIPMAN (1848-1849). b. Mar. 15, 1806 in Guilford Co., N.C. s. of James and Rachel (North) D. Both parents had been born in England. Attd. local school and an acad. Grad. from Greensboro Univ. in 1823 before 17th birthday. After father's death, mother moved with family to Ky., and then to Bloomington, Ind. Taught school and studied med. in Louisville, Ky. Practiced med. at Rockport and at Rushville, Ind., for a time. Studied law. Admitted to Ind. bar in 1833. Mbr. of Ind. House for three terms and of Ind. Senate, serving from 1833 to 1846. Nom. and el. Lieut. Gov. as a Dem. in 1846. When Gov. Whitcomb resigned in Dec., 1848, succeeded to office of Gov. and completed Whitcomb's term. Resumed law practice at Bloomington. Delegate to Dem. natl. convs. at Charleston, S.C. and Baltimore, Md. in 1860, serving as mbr. of platform commt. Was a supporter of Sen. Douglas for Pres. of U.S. in 1860 campaign. Mbr. of Ind. Senate in 1863, becoming presiding officer therein. Declined to run for U.S. House seat in 1864. Noted for oratorical ability. m. in 1826 to Sarah Alexander. After her death, m. in 1865 to Mrs. Allen D. Ashford. D. May 9, 1884, at Bloomington, Ind.

WRIGHT, JOSEPH ALBERT (1849-1857). b. April 17, 1810 in Washington, Pa. s. of John and Rachel (Seaman) W. Family moved to Bloomington, Ind. during his youth. Father died in 1823, after which son became self-supporting. Attd. local schools and the Univ. of Ind. for two years. Supported self while attending college by working as a janitor and doing odd jobs. Studied law, admitted to bar in 1829 and began practice at Rockville, Ind. Mbr. of Ind.

House in 1833. Pros. atty. for his jud. cir., 1836-1838
and mbr. of Ind. Senate, 1839-1840. El. to U.S. House as
a Dem. in 1842 but was defeated for reel. in 1844. Nom.
and el. Gov. as Dem. in 1849 and was reel. for first four-
year term in 1852 under the revised const. During admin.,
a revised state const. was put into effect; internal improvements program assigned to pvt. corps. and completed;
state financial difficulties resolved; townships given control of pub. schools; cause of temperance advanced; and
state laws were codified. Gov. and legislature were in conflict over legislation for revision of banking system. His
vetoes on the subject of banking code revision and charter-
ing of a state bank were overridden. Apptd. U.S. Minister
to Prussia by Pres. Buchanan in 1857, serving until 1861.
Upon outbreak of Civil War, broke with his party and became
a supporter of Pres. Lincoln's policies. Apptd. to seat in
U.S. Senate by the legislature in Feb., 1862, as replacement for Sen. Bright, who had been expelled by the Senate
for pro-Southern views. Served approximately one year.
Apptd. by Pres. Lincoln as U.S. commnr. to Hamburg Expo. in
Germany in 1863. Apptd. by Pres. Johnson as U.S. Minister
to Prussia in 1865, serving in that office until his death.
During tenure as Minister was instrumental in bringing
about introduction of new varieties of farm crops to U.S.
A younger brother, George Grover W., was a U.S. Sen. from
Iowa, 1871-1877. m. in 1831 to Louisa Cook, of Park Co.,
Ind. D. in Berlin, Germany, May 11, 1867. Bur. in N. Y.
City.

WILLARD, ASHBEL PARSONS (1857-1860). b. Oct. 31, 1820
at Vernon, N.Y. s. of Col. Erastus and Sarah (Parsons) W.
Attd. Oneida Liberal Inst. and Hamilton Coll., from which
he was grad. in 1842 with highest honors. Studied law.
Moved to Marshall, Mich., where he practiced law for a
short time. Made trip by horseback to Tex., returning by
way of Ky., where he taught school for a short time. During the 1844 pres. campaign he toured the Midwest, speaking
in support of Polk's candidacy. His oratorical abilities
made such a favorable impression upon the people of New
Albany, Ind., they induced him to settle there, where he
opened a law office. Mbr. of New Albany city council in
1849. El. to Ind. legislature in 1850, where he quickly
became a party leader and won acclaim as an orator. Nom.
and el. Gov. as Dem. in 1856, becoming the youngest man to
have held the office up to that time. Admin. marked by
sharp conflicts over issues concerning slavery. Legislature failed to pass necessary appropriations acts, and Gov.
was forced to borrow funds from pvt. sources to pay

interest on state debt and keep govt. solvent. When his
health began to fail went to Minn. in a vain effort to re-
gain it, dying there before end of term. m. in 1847 to
Caroline Cook, of Haddam, Conn. D. in Minn., Oct. 4, 1860.

HAMMOND, ABRAM ADAMS (1860-1861). b. Mar. 21, 1814 at
Brattleboro, Vt. s. of Nathaniel and Betty (Ball) H. When
son was six years old the family moved to Brookville, Ind.
Attd. pub. schools there. Studied law, was admitted to
bar and began practice of law at Greenfield, Ind. in 1835.
Continued in law practice at Columbus, Ind. in 1840; at
Indianapolis in 1846; at Cincinnati, Ohio in 1847; and
again in Indianapolis in 1849. El. judge of newly-created
ct. of common pleas in Marion Co. in 1850, but soon resigned. Went to San Francisco, Calif. in 1852 and practiced
law there until 1855, when he returned to Terre Haute, Ind.
Nom. and el. Lieut. Gov. as Dem. in 1856. Succeeded to
office of Gov. in Oct., 1860, when Gov. Willard died, and
completed last three months of Willard's term. m. to Mary
B. Amsden, of Oxford, Ohio. D. Aug. 27, 1874, at Denver,
Colo. after he had gone there for health reasons.

LANE, HENRY SMITH (1861). b. Feb. 24, 1811 near
Sharpsburg, Ky. s. of Col. James Harding L., who had
fought in Indian wars as a militia officer. Educ. in local
schools and by tutors. Studied law and admitted to Ky. bar
in 1832. In 1834 moved to Crawfordsville, Ind., where he
practiced law. Mbr. of Ind. Senate, 1837 and of Ind.
House, 1838-1839. El. to fill vacancy in U.S. House seat
in 1840, continuing to serve therein until 1843. Left politics for a time. Served as lieut., later as lieut. col.
in a volunteer regiment during U.S.-Mexican War. In 1854
entered banking bus. at Crawfordsville with father-in-law.
In 1856 took an active role in formation of Rep. party in
Ind., and served as ch. of natl. party conv. at
Philadelphia that year. Nominee of Rep. and Amer. parties
for U.S. Senate seat in 1857, but the seat was awarded to
his opponent, Jesse Bright, by the Senate after the result
was contested. Delegate to Rep. natl. conv. in Chicago in
1860, where he played an important role in the nom. of
Lincoln for Pres. of U.S. Nom. and el. Gov. as a Rep. in
1860. Resigned a few days after taking office, having been
el. to a U.S. Senate seat, which he held for one term.
Apptd. by Pres. Grant as a commnr. to Indian tribes in
1869, serving until 1871. Mbr. of U.S. commn. on improvement of navigation on Mississippi River in 1872. Delegate
to Rep. natl. convs. in 1868 and 1872. m. to Pamela B.
Jamieson, of Ky., who died in 1842. m. in 1845 to Joanna

Elston, of Crawfordsville, Ind. D. June 18, 1881, at
Crawfordsville. Bur. in Oak Hill Cem. there.

MORTON, OLIVER HAZARD PERRY (THROCK) (1861-1867). b.
Aug. 4, 1823 at Old Saulsbury, Wayne Co., Ind. s. of James
Throck and Sarah (Miller) M. Descendant of John
Throckmorton, who had emigrated to R.I. in 1631. His father had dropped "Throck" from family name as result of
dispute with mother. Attd. a pvt. school in Springfield,
Ohio and Wayne Co. Sem. Served apprenticeship for hatter's
trade with older brother. Entered Miami Univ., at Oxford,
Ohio, in 1843, grad. in 1845. Studied law; was admitted to
bar in 1847 and began practice at Centreville, Ind. Apptd.
cir. ct. judge in 1852, serving six months pending election
of successor. Campaigned as an anti-slavery Dem. for
Franklin Pierce for Pres. of U.S. in 1852. Refused to go
along with party in support of Kans.-Nebr. Bill in 1854 and
was expelled from state Dem. conv. at Indianapolis in that
year. Helped org. an opposition party, the Peoples party,
in 1856 and was defeated as that party's nominee for Gov.
in that year. Attd. Free Soil party natl. conv. at
Pittsburgh and affiliated later with newly formed Rep. party. Nom. and el. Lieut. Gov. as Rep. in 1860. When Gov.
Lane resigned soon after assuming office in 1861 to take
U.S. Senate seat, succeeded to office of Gov. Completed
Lane's term and was el. to succeeding term in 1864 as Union
(Rep.) party cand. Became the first native-born Indianian
to be el. to the office. Admin. filled with considerable
turmoil. Gave vigorous support to Pres. Lincoln's policies,
beginning the raising of troops to suppress secession movement even before Lincoln's call was issued. Dem. party secured control of legislature in 1862 and sought to obstruct
support of Union cause. Rep. mbrs. withdrew, preventing
assembling of quorum, and as Gov. he proceeded to carry on
admin. without legislative support through appropriations,
borrowing funds from pvt. sources. Opposition by anti-war
and pro-Southern orgs. in State during course of war was a
continual problem. Several unsuccessful attempts were made
to assassinate him during his tenure. In Oct., 1865, he
suffered a stroke which left his lower body paralyzed.
Went to France, where he was treated by French med. special-
ists for four months. Recovered partially, but was never
able thereafter to walk, and could stand only with the aid
of two canes. Resigned office of Gov. in Jan. 1867, after
having been el. to U.S. Senate. Became an important figure
there, favoring course of rigorous Reconstruction policies
in South. Favored elimination of U.S. paper currency system at first, but changed attitude on this issue after 1873.

Served as mbr. of spec. Electoral Commn. in 1877 set up to
resolve issues in connection with pres. election dispute of
1876. Proposed a constl. amdt. providing for direct popular election of Pres. Had significant support for nom.
for Pres. of U.S. in 1876 Rep. natl. conv., but eventually
used influence to bestow nom. on Gov. Hayes, of Ohio (q.v.).
m. in 1845 to Lucinda Burbank, of Springdale, Ohio. Five
children. His health gave way on a trip to Oregon as mbr.
of a Senate commt. to investigate a contested senatorial
election. D. Nov. 1, 1877, in Indianapolis. Bur. in Crown
Hill Cem. there.

BAKER, CONRAD (1867-1873). b. Feb. 12, 1817 on a farm
in Franklin Co., Pa. s. of Conrad and Mary (Winter) B.
Grandfather had emigrated from Holland to Pa. Attd.
Pennsylvania Coll., at Gettysburg, but withdrew before grad.
Studied law in office of firm headed by Thaddeus Stevens,
later an important figure in U.S. House during the Reconstruction era. Admitted to bar in 1839 and began practice
in Gettysburg. In 1841 moved to Evansville, Ind., where he
continued to practice law. Became judge of common pleas
ct. in 1852, serving for 18 months before resigning. Unsuccessful as cand. of newly formed Peoples party for Lieut.
Gov. in 1856. Following outbreak of Civil War, was commissioned as col. of Ind. volunteer troops; later became asst.
Provost Marshal Gen. for Indiana. In 1864 was nom. and el.
Lieut. Gov. as Union (Rep.) party cand. Acted as Gov. for
several months after Gov. Morton was stricken with disabling illness in 1865. Succeeded to office of Gov. in
Jan., 1867, when Gov. Morton resigned to assume U.S. Senate
seat. El. for a regular term in 1868 in very close contest
with Dem. opponent. During admin., the 14th and 15th Amdts.
to the U.S. Const. were approved by the legislature. In
the aftermath of the war, lawlessness became a serious
problem in the State for a time. The first train robbery
in U.S. occurred at Seymour, Ind. in May, 1868. After tenure as Gov., resumed law practice at Indianapolis, where he
achieved distinction as an able equity lawyer. m. in 1838
to Matilda E. Sommers, of Baltimore, Md. Five s.; two d.
After her death in 1855, m. in 1868 to Charlotte F. Chute,
of Madison, Ind. Two s.; four d. D. at Indianapolis,
April 28, 1885. Bur. at Evansville, Ind.

HENDRICKS, THOMAS ANDREWS (1873-1877). b. Sept. 7,
1819 on a farm near Zanesville, Ohio. s. of John H. and
Jane (Thomson) H. Family resided originally in Pa. An
uncle, Wm Hendricks, was a Gov. of Ind. (q.v.). Father
moved family to Madison Co., Ind. and shortly afterward, in

1832, to Shelby Co., Ind. Father was a founder of the
Presbyterian church in Ind. Attd. a local church school
and Hanover Coll., from which he was grad. in 1841. Studied law in office of mother's brother in Chambersburg, Pa.
Admitted to bar in 1843 and began practice in Shelbyville,
Ind., soon becoming involved in politics. El. to Ind.
legislature in 1848 and in 1849 to Ind. Senate. Declined
to run for reel. in 1850, but was delegate to Ind. constl.
conv. in that year. El. to U.S. House as a Dem. in 1850
and again in 1852, but was defeated for another term in
1854. Returned to law practice at Shelbyville. Apptd. U.S.
land office commnr. by Pres. Pierce in 1855, serving until
1859. Defeated as Dem. nominee for Gov. in 1860. Resumed
law practice until 1862, when he was el. to U.S. Senate.
Supported Union effort in Civil War, but opposed Reconstruction program originated by Cong., including the post-Civil
War Amdts. to U.S. Const. Nom. for Gov. in 1868 as Dem.,
but was defeated in gen. election by some 900 votes, losing
to incumbent Gov. Baker. After term in U.S. Senate, resumed law practice in a firm that became very successful.
Nom. and el. Gov. as Dem. in 1872 in an election in which
liquor regulation was a major issue. Ch. of Dem. state
conv. in 1874. At Dem. natl. conv. in 1876, gave nominating
speech for Gov. Tilden, of N.Y., who became the party nominee for Pres. of U.S. Nom. to run for Vice Pres. on
Tilden ticket, but the Dem. party candidates were held to
have lost in the disputed electoral vote count following
the popular voting. Delegate to Dem. natl. conv. in 1884,
where he was placed in nom. for Pres. of U.S. Withdrew
name from consideration for nom. as Pres., but accepted
nom. for Vice Pres. on ticket with Cleveland, and was el.
m. to Eliza C. Morgan. One child. Active in the affairs
of St. Paul's Episcopal church. D. Nov. 25, 1885, in
Indianapolis after serving only some eight months as Vice
Pres. of U.S. Bur. in Crown Hill Cem., Indianapolis.

WILLIAMS, JAMES DOUGLAS (1877-1880). b. Jan. 16, 1808
in what is now Pickaway Co., Ohio. Father, George W., was
a farmer. In 1818 parents moved to a farm near Wheatland,
Ind. After father's death in 1825, became responsible for
care of mother and upbringing of younger brothers and sisters. Received little formal schooling and was largely
self-educ. Became leader in his community while following
agri. pursuits. El. to Ind. House in 1843, 1847, 1851,
1856 and 1868 and to the Ind. Senate in 1858, 1862 and 1870,
continuing in latter body until 1874. Became influential
in legislature. Helped to create and served on the Ind.
Bd. of Agri. for 16 years. Delegate to Dem. natl. conv. in

1872, where he was a supporter of Horace Greeley for nom. for Pres. of U.S. Defeated as Dem. nominee for U.S. Senate seat in 1873. El. to U.S. House in 1874. Resigned seat in Dec., 1876, after having been nom. and el. Gov. as a Dem. Defeated Benj. Harrison, later Pres. of U.S., for the office of Gov. in that election. As Gov., promoted interests of agri.; supported pub. school system expansion. Dubbed "Blue Jeans Williams" by his political opponents for his rustic manners and background, he nevertheless had support of the rural population, despite his narrow and unsophisticated views on some questions of pub. policy. m. in 1831 to Nancy Huffman, who died in 1880. Seven children. D. later in the same year, Nov. 25, 1880, at Indianapolis while still in office of Gov. Bur. in Walnut Grove Cem., near Monroe City, Ind.

GRAY, ISAAC PUSEY (1880-1881; 1885-1889). b. Oct. 18, 1828 at Downington, Pa. s. of John and Hannah (Worthington) G. Descended from Quaker ancestor who had come to Pa. with Wm. Penn. Parents moved with family to Urbana, Ohio in 1836, and in 1842 to New Madison, Ohio. Attd. common schools, but also did much reading on his own. In 1846 became clerk in a dry goods store, later becoming its proprietor. In 1855 moved to Union City, Ind., where he continued in bus. endeavors while also studying law. Upon outbreak of Civil War became col. of an Ind. cavalry regiment, but poor health compelled retirement from active service. Continued to serve in militia forces and was involved in efforts to resist raid by Gen. Morgan in late stages of the war. Practiced law at Union City after Civil War. Rep. cand. for U.S. House, but lost in close election. Mbr. of Ind. Senate, 1868-1872, where he became Pres. pro tem. As such was instrumental in obtaining approval of Ind. Senate for ratification of 15th Amdt. to U.S. Const. As presiding officer of Ind. Senate, ordered doors of chamber to be locked to preserve quorum and also to keep out some Dem. opponents who were seeking to prevent vote by lack of quorum. Delegate to Lib. Rep. natl. conv. in 1872, where he supported nom. of Greeley for Pres. of U.S. Became mbr. of natl. commt. of Lib. Rep. party. Declined nom. for Atty. Gen. of Ind. in 1874, but was nom. and el. Lieut. Gov. as Dem. in 1876. Succeeded to office of Gov. when Gov. Williams died in 1880, and completed Williams' term. Defeated as Dem. nominee for U.S. Senate seat in 1881. Nom. and el. Gov. as Dem. in 1884. Was chosen as Dem. nominee for U.S. Senate seat in 1887, but withdrew because the Rep. Pres. pro tem would succeed to the office of Gov. if he resigned. Resumed law practice after tenure as Gov.

Apptd. U.S. Minister to Mexico by Pres. Cleveland in 1893.
m. to Eliza Jaqua, of Yankeetown, Ind. in 1850. Two s.
D. in Mexico City, Feb. 14, 1895, while serving as U.S.
Minister.

PORTER, ALBERT GALLATIN (1881-1885). b. April 20,
1824 at Lawrenceburg, Ind. s. of Thomas and Myra (Tousey)
P. Father was a native of Pa. who operated a ferryboat on
the Ohio River. Assisted in father's bus. as a youth.
Attd. prep. dept. of Hanover Coll., then entered Asbury
Univ. (now De Pauw Univ.) at Greencastle, Ind., from which
he was grad. in 1843. Established residence in
Indianapolis in 1844, where he worked in office of State
Aud. Studied law, admitted to bar in 1845, and began practice in Indianapolis. City atty. for Indianapolis, 1851-
1853. Apptd. reporter for Ind. Supreme Ct. in 1853, continuing to serve in that office by el. until 1857. Mbr.,
Indianapolis city council, 1857-1859. Broke with Dem. party over repeal of Mo. Compromise by Kans.-Nebr. Bill in
1854 and joined Rep. party. El. to U.S. House in 1858 and
again in 1860. Did not seek another term in 1862, and resumed law practice. Cand. for pres. elector on Hayes ticket in 1876. Apptd. first Comptroller of U.S. Treas. by
Pres. Hayes in 1878, resigning in 1880. Nom. and el. Gov.
as Rep. in 1880. Had support from labor because of his
serving as defense counsel for railroad workers who had
been prosecuted for riot growing out of railway strike in
1877. As Gov., encountered much opposition from legislature because of apptmts. he made. Initiated reclamation
of swamp lands in northwestern section of State; established State Bureau of Statistics and State Health Dept.; state
hosp. constr. program was begun. Retired after one term
to law practice and to do historical research. Author of
unfinished History of Indiana and of five volume series on
decisions of Ind. Supreme Ct. Delegate to 1888 Rep. natl.
conv. at which his law partner, Benj. Harrison, was nom.
for Pres. of U.S. Apptd. U.S. Minister to Italy in 1889,
serving until 1892. m. in 1846 to Minerva Virginia Brown,
of Indianapolis. m. for second time in 1881 to Cornelia
Stone, of Jamestown, N.Y. Five children. D. May 3, 1897,
at Indianapolis. Bur. in Crown Hill Cem. there.

GRAY, ISAAC PUSEY (1885-1889). See above, 1880-1881.

HOVEY, ALVIN PETERSON (1889-1891). b. Sept 6, 1821 at
Mt. Vernon, Posey Co., Ind. s. of Abiel and Frances
(Peterson) H. Parents, who were originally from New
England, had moved to Ind. and became pioneer settlers in

Posey Co. Became an orphan when he was a child. Educ. in common schools and by tutors. Worked as laborer and brick-layer in constr. bus. while also studying law at night in law office. Also taught school for one year. Admitted to bar in 1842. Volunteered for service in War with Mexico, serving as a first lieut. Delegate to state constl. conv. in 1850-1851. Cir. ct. judge, 1851-1854. Ch. of Ind. Dem. conv. in 1855. Apptd. to Ind. Supreme Ct. in 1854 while only 32 years of age. In 1856 was apptd. U.S. dist. atty. by Pres. Pierce. Because of his support of Sen. Douglas, was removed from office by Pres. Buchanan in 1858. Upon outbreak of Civil War, org. and became col. of volunteer Ind. regiment. Saw action early in war in Mo., Ky. and Tenn. Participated in Gen. Grant's campaigns in the West in 1862-1863, culminating in the capture of Vicksburg. Al-so served in early stages of Chattanooga campaign under Gen. Sherman. Rose to rank of brig. gen. in 1863, and to major gen. in 1864. Placed in command of Arkansas Dept. in 1863 and in 1864 of the Ind. Dept. of the Union Army. En-countered much opposition from pro-Southern guerillas in latter post. Arrested, tried and sentenced to hang under military law five mbrs. of "Sons of Liberty", a pro-South-ern group, in 1864; but their sentences were commuted to life imprisonment by Pres. Lincoln. Resigned commn. at end of war. Apptd. U.S. Minister to Peru, with support from Gen. Grant, by Pres. Johnson in 1865, serving until 1870. Declined to become cand. for Gov. in 1872. El. to U.S. House as Rep. in 1886. Resigned in Jan., 1889 before end of term, having been nom. and el. Gov. as Rep. in 1888. During admin., state control over school textbooks was es-tablished, and the Australian ballot system was adopted. Became pres. of Service Pensions Assoc. in 1888, an org. seeking pensions for Civil War veterans. m. first to Mary James, in 1844. After her death, m. in 1863 to Rosa Smith, a d. of Gen. Caleb Smith. D. Nov. 23, 1891 in Indianapolis, while still serving as Gov. Bur. in Bellefontaine Cem.

CHASE, IRA JOY (1891-1893). b. Dec. 7, 1834 at Clarkson, N.Y. s. of Benj. and Lorinda (Mix) C. Antece-dents had emigrated to Amer. before Rev. War. Parents moved to Medina, N.Y. soon after he was born, where they resided for 12 years. They then moved to Milan, Ohio. Was tutored by a Presbyterian minister there for three years, then returned to Medina where he attd. a local acad. In 1855 moved to Ill., near Barrington, where he taught school. In 1861 enlisted in Ill. infantry regiment, but was dis-charged in 1862 because of poor health. Entered hardware bus., but it soon failed. Studied for ministry and held

pastorates in Pa., Ill., and at Danville, Ind. In 1886
was made chaplain of Ind. Dept. of G.A.R. and in 1887,
deptl. commdr. Nom. and el. Lieut. Gov. as a Rep. in 1888.
Succeeded to office of Gov. in Nov., 1891 following death
of Gov. Hovey, and completed Hovey's term. Nom. for succeeding regular term in 1892, but lost in gen. election.
Retired thereafter to ministerial duties and lecturing. m.
in 1859 to Rhoda Jane Castle, of Barrington, Ill. D. at
Lubec, Me., May 11, 1895. Bur. at Indianapolis.

MATTHEWS, CLAUDE (1893-1897). b. Dec. 14, 1845 at
Bethel, Ky. s. of Thomas A. and Eliza Ann (Fletcher) M.
At age 13 moved with family to Maysville, Ky., where he
attd. prep. school. Attd. Centre Coll. at Danville, Ky.,
graduating in 1867. Engaged in grain and livestock raising
near Clinton, Ind. Specialized in improvement of breeds,
and was leader in formation of first livestock breeders
assoc. in U.S., the Natl. Assoc. of Breeders of Shorthorn
Cattle of U.S. and Canada. Mbr. of Ind. legislature in
1876, but resumed farming after one term. Defeated as cand.
for U.S. Senate in 1882. El. Ind. Sect. of State in 1890,
receiving the support of the Farmers Alliance as well as
Dem. party. Nom. and el. Gov. as Dem. in 1892. Admin. was
beset with difficulties following financial panic of 1893.
Was required to use state militia forces to maintain order
during course of the Pullman railroad strike in 1894. To
provide pay for militia had to rely on personal credit.
Incurred hostility of corp. interests set up to conduct
races, prize fights, etc., which he opposed. An advocate
of free coinage of silver, his name was presented as a cand.
for Dem. nom. for Pres. of U.S. at the Dem. natl. conv. in
1896, which eventually nom. Wm. J. Bryan. m. in 1868 to
Martha Whitcomb, d. of former Gov. James Whitcomb (q.v.).
D. at Indianapolis, Aug. 28, 1898.

MOUNT, JAMES ATWELL (1897-1901). b. March 23, 1843 on
a farm in Montgomery Co., Ind. s. of Atwell and Lucinda
(Fulenwider) M. Parents were natives of Va. and Ky. who
had moved to Ind. as pioneers. Received limited educ. in
local schools during winters while working on father's farm,
but was an energetic and enthusiastic student and continued
studies on his own. Enlisted in volunteer regiment in
Wilder's Brigade in 1862 and saw action at Battle of
Chickamauga and under Gen. Sherman in subsequent campaigns
in Tenn. and Ga. In one engagement insisted on fighting
although suffering from an attack of measles. Following
the Civil War, studied at Presbyterian Acad. in Lebanon,
Ind., but withdrew after one year because of lack of funds.

Leased farm near Shannondale, Ind., and after nine years,
purchased it. Prospered, and by 1895 was owner of 500 acres
clear of debt. Nom. for Ind. Senate as Rep. in 1888
against his wishes, and was el. in a dist. normally held by
Dem. Nom. for seat in U.S. House in 1890, but lost in gen.
election. Continued political activities as speaker and
party leader. Nom. as Rep. cand. for Gov. in 1896 from
among a field of 12, and was el., defeating cand. backed by
Dem. and Pop. parties. Advocate of gold standard. During
admin., the state prison system was reformed; child labor
legislation enacted; office of State Labor Commnr. set up;
legislation passed restricting monopolistic practices;
examinations prescribed for entering med. profession; and a
compulsory educ. law passed. Active in affairs of
Presbyterian church. m. in 1867 to Kate Boyd, of Lebanon,
Ind. Two d.; one s. D. at Indianapolis, Jan. 16, 1901,
only two days after leaving office.

DURBIN, WINFIELD TAYLOR (1901-1905). b. May 4, 1847
at Lawrenceburg, Ind. s. of Wm. Sappington and Eliza Ann
(Sparks) D. Descendant of pioneer family that had resided
in Md. and Ky. Parents moved to New Philadelphia, Ind.,
when he was a child. Educ. in common schools. In 1862 at
age 15, enlisted in Union Army with five brothers and
served for remainder of the Civil War. Taught school in
Washington and Jackson counties; also took courses at a
commercial coll. in St. Louis, Mo. Employed by a dry goods
firm in Indianapolis. Acquired interest in a number of mfg.
and banking enterprises there and at Anderson, Ind. Involved in devel. of electric motors and electric railways.
Became active in Rep. party affairs, serving as delegate to
state and natl. convs. Mbr. of Rep. natl. commt., 1892-
1900, and was in charge of Western campaign headquarters at
Chicago in 1896 pres. campaign. Served as col. of volunteer regiment in Spanish-Amer. War. Nom. and el. Gov. as
Rep. in 1900. As Gov., advocated economy in govtl. expenditures; reduced taxes; retired state debt. In 1903 employed state militia to protect prisoners in custody following race riot at Evansville. Retired to bus. interests after tenure as Gov. Mbr., G.A.R.; Loyal Legion; Masons.
Methodist. m. in 1875 to Bertha McCullogh, of Anderson.
One s.; one d. D. at Anderson, Dec. 18, 1928.

HANLY, J(AMES) FRANK(LIN) (1905-1909). b. April 4,
1863 near St. Joseph, Ill. s. of Elijah and Jane Anne
Eliza (Calton) H. Father, who was of Scotch-Irish ancestry,
was a cooper. Largely self-educ. by reading at home.
Worked at various jobs, including farm laborer, to obtain

funds to attend dist. school. At age 16 went to
Williamsport, Ind., where he taught in country schools from
1881 to 1889, teaching in winters and working vacations.
Attd. Eastern Ill. Normal (now Eastern Ill. Univ.), at
Charleston, for short terms in 1879-1881. Became interest-
ed in politics, participating in campaigns as speaker.
Studied law, admitted to bar in 1889, and began practice in
Williamsport. Mbr. of Ind. Senate, 1890. El. to U.S.
House in 1894, but was defeated for re-nom. in 1896 follow-
ing rearrangement of dist. boundaries. Moved to Lafayette,
Ind., where he resumed law practice. Unsuccessful cand.
for U.S. Senate in 1899. Nom. and el. Gov. in 1904 as Rep.
As Gov., insisted on strict enforcement of laws and high
standards of integrity of govt. officials; supported legislation tightening state control over pvt. banking; State
R.R. Commn. established; local option liquor law passed.
Resumed law practice after tenure as Gov. An advocate of
prohibition, became widely known as lecturer on liquor
issue after leaving office. Org. Enquirer Publishing Co.
of Indianapolis and became ed. of a newspaper, the
Indianapolis Commercial. In 1916 election was unsuccessful
as the cand. of Proh. party for Pres. of U.S., receiving
some 226,000 popular votes. m. in 1881 to Eva Simmer, of
Williamsport. Five children. D. Aug. 1, 1920, as result of
an auto accident near Dennison, Ohio. Bur. in Hillside
Cem., near Williamsport.

MARSHALL, THOMAS RILEY (1909-1913). b. Mar. 14, 1854
in North Manchester, Ind. s. of Daniel Miller and Martha
Ann (Patterson) M. Attd. Wabash Coll., graduating with an
A.B. degree in 1873 and an M.A. degree in 1876. Studied
law in law office, admitted to bar in 1875, and began practice in Columbia City, Ind. Law firm with which he was
assoc. became very prominent. Unsuccessful cand. for co.
pros. atty. in 1880, his only attempt to gain pub. office
prior to becoming Gov. Ch. of Dem. party cong. dist.
commt., 1896-1898. Nom. as compromise cand. and el. Gov.
as Dem. in 1908, even though State voted for Rep. cand. for
Pres. of U.S. that year. During admin., a stronger child
labor law was passed; employers' liability law enacted;
pure food law adopted; reforms in elections procedures effected; and railroad and corp. tax laws revised. Placed in
nom. as favorite son for Dem. nom. for Pres. of U.S. at Dem.
natl. conv. in 1912. Nom. for Vice Pres. on ticket with
Woodrow Wilson, and was el. Reel. Vice Pres. in 1916. Advocate of representative democracy; local self-govt.;
States Rts. Opposed Natl. Proh. Amdt. Name entered in Ind.
pres. primary for Dem. party nom. for Pres. of U.S. in 1920

and 1924.   Engaged in law practice and lecturing after
leaving vice presidency.   Noted for his dry humor.   Mbr.,
Masons; Phi Gamma Delta; Phi Beta Kappa.   Hon. degrees from
seven colleges and universities.   m. in 1895 to Lois Irene
Kimsey, of Angola, Ind.   D. June 1, 1925, in Washington,
D.C.

RALSTON, SAMUEL MOFFET (1913-1917).   b. Dec. 1, 1857
on a farm near Cumberland, Ohio.   s. of John and Sarah
(Scott) R.   Parents were from Va. and Pa.   In 1865 moved
with parents to Owen Co., Ind., where father had purchased
a large stockfarm.   As result of financial depression in
1873 father lost this property and moved to Fontanet, Ind.
Attd. local pub. schools.   Taught in country schools for
seven winters while attending normal school in summers.
Attd. No. Ind. Normal at Valparaiso and Cent. Ind. Normal
at Danville, grad. from latter in 1884.   Studied law, admitted to bar in 1886, and established practice at Lebanon,
Ind.   Soon acquired wide reputation as able lawyer.   Was on
Dem. ticket as cand. for pres. elector in 1888 and 1892.
Mbr. and pres. of Lebanon school bd., 1908-1911.   Nom. and
el. Gov. as Dem. in 1912, winning by large plurality
against the Rep. and Prog. party nominees.   During admin.,
legislation was passed creating a Pub. Utility Commn.; laws
for indus. and vocational educ. schools enacted; and a
graduated inheritance tax system adopted.   Resumed law
practice for a time after term as Gov.   In 1922 was el. to
U.S. Senate as a Dem.   m. in 1881 to Mary Josephine Backaus,
who died the following year.   m. in 1889 to Jennie Craven
(Cravens?), of Hendricks Co., Ind.   Two s.; one d.   Mbr.,
Masons; K.P.   Presbyterian.   D. Oct. 14, 1925, while serving first term in U.S. Senate.   Bur. in Oak Hill Cem.,
Lebanon.

GOODRICH, JAMES PUTNAM (1917-1921).   b. Feb. 18, 1864
in Winchester, Ind.   s. of John B. and Elizabeth Putnam
(Edger) G.   Descendant of English settler who emigrated to
Va. in colonial times.   Father was a lawyer.   Attd.
Winchester schools and was preparing to enter U.S. Naval
Acad. when physical injury caused him to be disqualified.
Attd. De Pauw Univ., grad. in 1885.   Studied law and ad-
mitted to bar in 1886.   Practiced law with uncle in
Winchester.   In 1910 became mbr. of law firm in
Indianapolis.   Withdrew from law practice in 1914 to devote
attention to various bus. interests he had acquired in
fields of banking, farming, oil refining, railroads, utilities, grain elevators and bonding houses.   Held posts of
pres., vice pres., or mbr. of bds. of dir. in a number of

corps. Served as ch. of Randolph Co. Rep. commt. for a
number of years. Ch. of Rep. state commt. for nine years,
beginning in 1901. Natl. Rep. commt. mbr., 1915-1916.
Nom. and el. Gov. as Rep. in 1916, this being the first political office to which he was el. As Gov., during World
War I, cooperated with U.S. govt. in war measures, particularly in programs to increase food supplies. Promoted
economy and efficiency in state admin. Introduced plan in
1919 to control pub. expenditures of local govts. Launched
program in 1919 in collaboration with Amer. Legion for
constr. of elaborate memorial in Indianapolis to honor war
veterans. Resumed bus. activities after tenure as Gov.,
but continued also to be involved in Rep. party affairs as
delegate to natl. convs. Mbr. and spec. investigator for
Amer. Relief Admin., making several trips to Russia. Close
assoc. of Herbert Hoover in war relief work. In 1923 was
apptd. to Indiana Deep Waterways Commn., and in 1924 became
a mbr. of St. Lawrence Waterways Commn. by apptmt. from
Pres. Coolidge. Donor of numerous gifts to young people to
attend college or other educl. institutions. Trustee of
Wabash Coll. in 1904 and of Presbyterian Theological Coll.,
1919-1940. Donor of park to city of Winchester. Mbr.,
Masons; S.A.R.; K.P.; Rotary; various professional and bus.
orgs. and social clubs. Active in affairs of Presbyterian
church. Hon. degrees from Wabash Coll., Notre Dame Univ.,
Hanover Coll. m. in 1888 to Cora Frist, of Lynn, Ind. One
s. D. at Winchester, Aug. 15, 1940.

   McCRAY, WARREN TERRY (1921-1924). b. Feb. 4, 1865 on
a farm in Newton Co., Ind. s. of Greenberry Ward and
Martha Jane (Galey) McC. Descendant of a colonist who emigrated from Scotland to Del. in early 1700s. Parents moved
to Kentland, Ind. in 1870. Attd. local pub. schools. At
age 15 began working as clerk in a bank in Ky. After six
years, founded a grocery bus. which he sold in 1890 to
build a grain elevator. Developed into a corp. enterprise
of which he was vice pres. In 1897 became a founder of
Natl. Grain Dealers Assoc., becoming its first pres. In
1913 returned to banking field, becoming successor of his
father as pres. of Discount and Deposit Bank in Kentland.
Also went into farming and stock-raising, acquiring a 3,200
acre farm, "Orchard Lake Stock Farm", where he specialized
in breeding of pure-bred Hereford cattle. Helped org.
Amer. Hereford Cattle Breeders Assoc. Served as Trustee of
No. Ind. State Hosp. for Insane at Logansport, 1900-1917,
and of Ind. State Bd. of Agri., 1912-1918, of which he was
pres., 1915-1917. Mbr., Bd. of Trustees of Purdue Univ.,
1917-1918. Ch. of Ind. Food Conservation Commn. and mbr.

of U.S. Livestock Advisory Commn. during World War I.   Ch.
of Corn Belt Advisory Commn., 1922.   Defeated as cand. for
Rep. nom. for Gov. in 1916; but was nom. and el. Gov. as
Rep. in 1920.   As Gov., supported tax on gasoline to finance road constr.; inaugurated modern highway system; vetoed a farmer cooperative measure because it contained no
limits on indebtedness; placed Bd. of Agri. under closer
legislative control; improved State Fair grounds; and introduced exec. budget system.   During course of term was indicted by a U.S. grand jury on mail fraud charges growing
out of his efforts to prevent loss of personal fortune
following sharp decline in farm commodity prices in early
1920s.   Was convicted on the charges, which did not concern
his acts as Gov., in April, 1924, and sentenced to prison.
Immediately resigned office of Gov.   Was paroled in 1927
and pardoned by Pres. Hoover in 1930.   With financial help
from friends began to recoup his losses and eventually regained possession of his farm.   Regained natl. reputation
among stock breeders before his death.   Presbyterian.   m.
in 1892 to Ella Maria Ade.   Two d.; one s.   D. at Kentland,
Dec. 19, 1938.

BRANCH, EMMET FOREST (1924-1925).   b. May 16, 1874 at
Martinsville, Ind.   s. of Elliott F. and Alice (Parks) B.
Attd. the Univ. of Ind., grad. in 1896.   Won distinction in
athletics (baseball) while a student.   Studied law in
office of an uncle, who was a judge.   Admitted to bar in
1899 and began practice in Martinsville.   Volunteered for
service in Spanish-Amer. War, holding rank of first lieut.
when discharged.   Continued in State Guard service, attaining rank of major in 1905.   Accompanied Natl. Guard units
as lieut. col. to Mexican border under Gen. Pershing in
1916.   Served as col. of Ind. infantry unit during World
War I, commanding a brigade at end of war.   El. to Ind.
House in 1902 and again for two succeeding terms.   Became
Speaker of the House.   Regarded as an authority on parlia-
mentary procedure.   Continued to be active in Rep. party
affairs after leaving legislative service.   Nom. and el.
Lieut. Gov. as a Rep. in 1920.   Succeeded to office of Gov.
when Gov. McCray resigned in April, 1924, and completed
McCray's term.   Ch. of Rep. state conv. in 1924 and dele-
gate to Rep. natl. conv. that year.   Resumed law practice,
and also maintained an interest in farming, being the owner
of a large farm in Morgan Co.   Pres. of Branch Grain and
Seed Co.   m. in 1905 to Katherine Bain.   One s.   D. at
Martinsville, Feb. 23, 1932.

JACKSON, ED(WARD) F. (1925-1929).   b. Dec. 27, 1873

near Kokomo, Ind. s. of Presley Howard and Elizabeth
(Howell) J. Received little formal educ., but studied at
home. At age 18 began study of law in office of a judge
at Tipton, Ind. Admitted to bar in 1898 and began practice
at New Castle, Ind. Soon afterward moved to Kennard, in
Henry Co. El. pros. atty. of Henry Co. in 1898 and reel.
in 1900. Apptd. to judgeship vacancy in Henry Co. cir. ct.
in 1907 and continued in office by election the next year.
Nom. for office of Ind. Sect. of State in 1914, but was defeated. Re-nom. in 1916 and was el. Resigned in 1917 to
enlist in U.S. Army at beginning of World War I. Commissioned as capt., rising to rank of major by end of war.
Apptd. to office of Sect. of State to fill vacancy in 1918,
and el. to the office in 1920. Nom. and el. Gov. as Rep.
in 1924 in a bitter campaign in which allegations of his
membership in the K.K.K. and his previous record in pub.
office were major issues. During admin., a state income
tax was adopted; assessment procedures were revised to
assist farmers; a stringent prohibition law was enacted;
criminal code revised; state highway system expanded; and a
2,000-acre state park on the Lake Michigan shore created.
In Feb., 1928, he was indicted on bribery conspiracy
charges in connection with his actions as Sect. of State in
1923 in seeking to obtain a friend's appointment to pub.
office, but the charges were eventually dismissed under the
statute of limitations. Retired to law practice at end of
term. Mbr., Disciples (Christian) church. m. in 1897 to
Rosa Wilkinson, of Henry Co. Two d. m. for second time to
Mrs. Lida (Beaty) Pierce, of Osawatomie, Kans., in 1920.
D. Nov. 20, 1954. Bur. in Green Hills Cem., Orleans, Ind.

LESLIE, HARRY GUYER (1929-1933). b. April 6, 1878 at
Lafayette, Ind. s. of Daniel and Mary (Burkhardt) L. Grad.
from Purdue Univ. in 1905 and received law degree from the
Univ. of Ind. in 1907. Admitted to bar and practiced law
in West Lafayette for seven years. El. treas. of
Tippecanoe Co. in 1912, serving until 1917. Engaged in
farming and also was dir. and vice pres. of Battle Ground
State Bank. El. to Ind. legislature in 1922, continuing
to serve until 1927, becoming House Speaker during last
term. In 1924 was employed as div. chief of U.S. Income
Tax Bureau. Nom. and el. Gov. as Rep. in 1928. Admin.
covered period of onset of depression of 1930s, creating
financial distress. Sponsored measures to aid depression
victims, including reduction of income tax. After tenure
in office, org. and became pres. of Standard Life Ins. Co.
of Indianapolis. Mbr., Masons; I.O.O.F.; Kiwanis; various
fraternities and professional legal orgs. Hon. degree from

Purdue Univ., at which he continued to maintain an interest
in athletic programs. Methodist. m. in 1910 to Martha
Morgan, of Battle Ground, Ind. Three s. D. Dec. 10, 1937,
at Miami Beach, Fla.

McNUTT, PAUL VORIES (1933-1937). b. July 19, 1891 at
Franklin, Ind. s. of Crittenden and Ruth (Neely) McN.
Father was a lawyer and a judge. Grad. from the Univ. of
Ind. in 1913 and received law degree from Harvard Univ. in
1916. Admitted to bar and practiced law at Martinsville,
Ind. as father's partner. Instructor in law at the Univ.
of Ind. in 1917, but resigned during year to enter U.S.
Army as capt. Served as instructor of command officers
and enlisted men. Rose to rank of lieut. col. by end of
World War I, continuing to serve thereafter as an officer
in USAR. Returned to Ind. Univ. Law School as a prof. in
1919. Became dean of the law faculty in 1925, continuing
in that capacity until 1933. Active in Amer. Legion and
N.R.O.A. Served as Natl. Commdr. of Amer. Legion in 1928,
and vice pres. of N.R.O.A. in 1927. Mbr., Advisory Council
of U.S. Veterans Bureau. Ch. of sub-commt. of Corporations
Survey Commn. by apptmt. of Gov. in 1927. Nom. and el.
Gov. as Dem. in 1932. During admin., a revised income tax
law was passed to relieve precarious financial condition
of the State; and a novel state admin. reform measure,
later repealed, was adopted, designed to strengthen Gov.'s
control of indep. agencies and depts. of govt. Exerted
strong control over work of legislature. Mbr., exec.
commt. of Natl. Govs.' Conf., 1933-1936 and ch., 1934-1936.
Pres., Council of State Govts., 1936-1937. Mbr. of Advisory Bd. of W.P.A. Apptd. U.S. High Commnr. to Philippine
Islands in 1937, serving until 1939. Apptd. Dir. of U.S.
Fed. Security Admin. in 1939, serving until 1941. Widely
mentioned as possible Dem. nominee for Pres. of U.S. as
1940 Dem. natl. conv. neared, but withdrew from contention
when Pres. F. D. Roosevelt announced willingness to run for
a third term. Refused to permit his name to be presented
to the conv. as cand. for nom. for Vice Pres. of U.S. at
that conv., although he had wide support. Ch., U.S. War
Manpower Commn., 1942-1945. Mbr., U.S. W.P.B. and of
E.S.B. during course of World War II. Apptd. High Commnr.
and then as first U.S. Ambassador to Philippine Islands in
1945, serving until 1947. Became mbr. of prestigious law
firms in Washington, D.C. and New York City. Ch. of bd. of
Philadelphia-Amer. Life Ins. Co. in 1948, and mbr. of bds.
of dir. of other ins. companies. Mbr., Masons; Elks;
Rotary; Kiwanis; A.A.U.P.; Amer. Legion; Amer. Peace Soc.;
Phi Beta Kappa; various professional legal orgs. and social

clubs. Recipient of U.S. Medal of Merit and of awards of
distinction from govts. of Poland and France. Hon. degrees
from eight colleges and universities. Methodist. m. in
1918 to Kathleen Timolat, of San Antonio, Texas. One d.
D. in New York City, March 24, 1955.

TOWNSEND, M(AURICE) CLIFFORD (1937-1941). b. Aug. 11,
1884 in Blackford Co., Ind. s. of David and Lydia Ann
(Glancy) T. Father was a farmer. Attd. Marion, Ind. Normal, 1902-1907, and Marion Bus. Coll. in 1908. Worked on
family farm during vacations. Began to teach school in
1907 at Hartford City, Ind. Supt. of schools in Blackford
Co., 1909-1919. Farmed in Grant Co., 1919-1925. Supt. of
schools at Marion, Ind., 1925-1929. El. to Ind. legislature in 1922. Defeated as Dem. cand. for U.S. House in
1928. Dir. of org. for Ind. Farm Bureau, 1928-1932. Nom.
and el. Lieut. Gov. as a Dem. in 1932 and as Gov. in 1936.
During admin., used Natl. Guard forces to maintain order
and bring to an end a strike in steel indus. that had shut
down major plants in Ind. for a month. Called spec.
session of legislature in 1938 to authorize program of pub.
works to relieve unemployment. Dir. of Food Production for
U.S. Food Admin., 1941-1943, and ch. of Jt. Bd. of Fed.
Crop Ins. Corp. and Adminr. of Agri. Conservation and Adjustment Admin. Assumed post in pub. relations dept. of
Cent. Soya Co., of Ft. Wayne, in 1943. Resigned in 1946.
Defeated as the Dem. nominee that year for U.S. Senate.
Hon. degree from Marion Coll. Methodist. m. in 1910 to
Nora Adele Harris, of Marion. Two d.; two s. D. Nov. 11,
1954 in Hartford City, Ind.

SCHRICKER,HENRY FREDERICK (1941-1945; 1949-1953). b.
Aug. 30, 1883 at North Judson, Ind. s. of Christopher and
Magdalena (Meyer) S. Both parents were natives of Bavaria,
Germany. Father first settled in N.J. after emigrating to
Amer. in 1860s, and he had worked for a railroad, in a
flour mill, and farmed, before he moved to North Judson in
1893 and opened a gen. store there. Attd. local schools.
After one year in h.s., attd. bus. coll. in South Bend,
Ind., in 1900-1901, while also working in father's store.
Became deputy to clerk of cir. ct. Unsuccessful cand. for
office of clerk in 1906. Studied law in law office, admitted to bar in 1907, and began practice in Knox, Ind.
Cashier of bank at Hamlet, Ind. in 1908. Purchased a newspaper, the Starke County Democrat, becoming its ed. and
publ. in 1909 and continued therein until 1919, when he
sold it. Mbr. of Ind. State Guard, 1915-1916. Mbr. of bd.
of dir. of Farmers Bank and Trust Co., and later its

cashier. Mbr. of Knox school bd. for nine years. Sect. of
Knox Bldg. and Loan and Savings Assoc. for 16 years. Mbr.
of Ind. Senate, 1933-1937. Nom. and el. Lieut. Gov. as
Dem. in 1936. As such, also served as mbr. of various
commns. overseeing admin. depts. in fields of farming and
educ. Nom. and el. Gov. as Dem. in 1940. Defeated as Dem.
nominee for U.S. Senate seat in 1944. Resumed banking activities as vice pres. of Fletcher Trust Co. of
Indianapolis in 1945. Nom. again as Dem. cand. for Gov. in
1948 without solicitation on his part and was el., becoming
the only Gov. of Ind. to be el. for a second term under the
constl. provision prohibiting an immediately successive
term. As Gov., espoused "moderate" Dem. policies, including balanced budget; social security programs only in cases
of extreme necessity; compulsory arb. of labor disputes;
and a non-compulsory type of fair employment practices law.
Defeated as Dem. nominee for U.S. Senate seat in 1952. Was
an admirer of Thomas Jefferson's philosophy of govt.
Lutheran. m. in 1914 to Maude L. Brown. Two s.; one d.
D. Dec. 28, 1966.

GATES, RALPH FESLER (1945-1949). b. Feb. 24, 1893 at
Columbia City, Ind. s. of Benton and Alice (Fesler) G.
Father was a lawyer. Attd. local pub. schools and the
Univ. of Mich., from which he received an A.B. degree in
1915 and a law degree in 1917. Admitted to bar in 1916.
As an ensign in USNR was called to active duty from 1917 to
1919 during World War I. In 1919 joined father's law firm.
After his father's death, formed law firm with three broth-
ers in Columbia City. Became a mbr. of bds. of dir. of two
banks. El. dist. atty. of Whitley Co. in 1922, serving until 1926. Also was city atty. for South Whitley and city
atty. of Columbia City for a number of years. Ch. of
Twelfth Dist. Rep. commt., 1926-1928 and of the Fourth Dist.
Rep. commt., 1934-1940. Ch. of Rep. state commt., 1941.
In 1944 was nom. and el. Gov. as Rep. During admin., won
popularity with org. labor by appointing a union man as
State Labor Commnr., but lost favor in that quarter when he
employed troops to preserve order in connection with a
strike by an electrical workers' union. Introduced practice of holding govtl. "service clinics" at which admin.
procedures were carried on before pub. in various population centers of the State. In 1946 was a signer of state-
ment by 26 Govs. at the Natl. Govs.' Conf. condemning U.S.
deficit spending and urging U.S. and state revenue sources
be kept separate and distinct. Mbr., Amer. Legion; V.F.W.;
Masons; Elks; Moose; Rotary; various bus. and professional
orgs. Presbyterian. m. in 1919 to Helene Edwards. One s.;

one d.   Retired to bus. activities at Columbia City after
tenure as Gov.   D. July 28, 1978, at Columbia City.

SCHRICKER, HENRY FREDERICK (1949-1953).   See above,
1941-1945.

CRAIG, GEORGE NORTH (1953-1957).   b. Aug. 6, 1909 at
Brazil, Ind.   s. of Bernard Clyde and Clo (Branson) C.
Attd. local schools and Culver Mil. Acad.   Enrolled at the
Univ. of Ariz., 1928-1929, and later at the Univ. of Ind.,
from which he received a law degree in 1932.   Admitted to
bar and began practice with a law firm in Indianapolis.
Served in U.S. Army, 1942-1946, rising from rank of first
lieut. to col.   Recipient of Bronze Star, Croix de guerre,
Freedom Found. Award.   Mbr., French Legion of Honor.   Nom.
and el. Gov. as Rep. in 1952.   During admin., charges were
brought against the State Highway Dept. for alleged misuse
and embezzlement of pub. funds, causing internal dissention
in admin.   Resumed law practice after tenure as Gov.   Mbr.,
Amer. Legion, serving as its Natl. Commdr., 1949-1950;
Masons; Delta Chi (pres.); Delta Theta Phi (pres.); Amer.
Judicature Soc.; Inst. for Psychiatric Research; Fellow of
Amer. Intl. Acad.; various professional legal orgs. and
social clubs.   Methodist.   m. in 1931 to Kathryn Heiliger.
One s.; one d.

HANDLEY, HAROLD WILLIS (1957-1961).   b. Nov. 27, 1909
at La Porte, Ind.   s. of Harold Lowell and Lottie Margaret
(Brookhill) H.   Father was a furniture mfr.   Attd. local
schools and the Univ. of Ind., from which he was grad. in
1932.   Employed as salesman by a furniture firm.   Vice pres.
of Darling Motion Picture Sales Co., 1949-1953 and also
sales repr. for a Hollywood, Calif. film production firm.
El. to Ind. Senate in 1940, but resigned in 1941 to enter
U.S. Army as a second lieut. in World War II.   Rose to rank
of lieut. col. by end of the war.   Returned to bus. activities after the war.   El. to Ind. Senate in 1948, continuing in office until 1953.   Nom. and el. Gov. as Rep. in
1956.   Campaign marked by bitterness over revelations of
bribery and embezzlement in State Highway Dept. he had
helped to uncover during admin. of Gov. Craig.   As Gov.,
advocated home rule; restriction of distribution and sale
of obscene literature; resistance to extension of U.S.
govt.'s power over state and local govts. through financial
aid programs; revision of tax system.   His refusal to veto
a right to work bill passed by the legislature aroused much
criticism and caused demonstrations by org. labor groups.
Rep. nominee for U.S. Senate in 1958, but was defeated in

gen. election. Mbr., Masons (Shriner, K.T.); Amer. Legion;
Eagles; Moose; Elks; Lions. Presbyterian. Hon. degrees
from five Ind. universities and colleges. m. in 1944 to
Barbara Jean Winterble. One s.; one d. D. at Rawlins,
Wyo., Aug. 30, 1972 while vacationing there.

WELSH, MATTHEW EMPSON (1961-1965). b. Sept. 15, 1912
in Detroit, Mich. s. of Matthew W. and Inez (Empson) W.
Father was a banker. Attd. pub. schools in Brownstown and
at Vincennes, Ind., to which area family had moved during
his youth. Grad. from the Univ. of Pa. in 1934. Attd. the
Univ. of Ind., 1935-1936, and the Univ. of Chicago, 1937,
from which he received a law degree. Admitted to bar and
began practice in Vincennes. El. to Ind. legislature in
1940 and reel. in 1942. Resigned in 1943 to enter U.S.
Navy as a commissioned officer. Returned to law practice
at Vincennes at end of World War II. Ch., Dem. dist.
commt. in 1948. U.S. dist. atty. for So. Ind., 1950-1952.
Mbr. of Ind. Senate, 1955-1960, serving as Dem. floor leader during the last three years of term. Nom. and el. Gov.
as Dem. in 1960. Mbr., exec. commt., Natl. Govs.' Conf. and
ch., Interstate Oil Compact commt. of that body, 1963.
Mbr. of Dem. natl. commt., 1964-1965. Mbr. of bd. of dir.,
Security Bank and Trust Co.; sect. of Universal Scientific
Co.; dir., Kennedy Memorial Home; co-ch., Ind. Constl.
Revision Commn., 1967; ch., U.S.-Canadian Jt. Intl. Commn.,
1966-1970. Nominee of Dem. party for Gov. again in 1972,
but was defeated in gen. election. Mbr., Amer. Legion;
Elks; Delta Kappa Epsilon; Kiwanis; various clubs and professional legal orgs. m. in 1937 to Mary Virginia Homann,
of Washington, Ind. Two d.

BRANIGIN, ROGER DOUGLAS (1965-1969). b. July 26, 1902
at Franklin, Ind. s. of Elba L. and Zula Francis B. Attd.
Franklin Coll., from which he was grad. in 1923, and
Harvard Univ., from which he received a law degree in 1926.
Served as gen. counsel for the Fed. Land Bank, Louisville,
Ky., 1930-1938. Also was gen. counsel for the U.S. Farm
Credit Admin. at Louisville, 1933-1938. Moved to Lafayette,
Ind., and began law practice there in 1938. Ch.,
Tippecanoe Co. Dem. commt. in 1938. Commissioned as capt.
in the Judge Advocate Gen. Dept. of U.S. Army in 1942.
Chief of legal div., Transport Corps, 1944-1946. Held rank
of lieut. col. when World War II ended. Recipient of
Legion of Merit and Army Commendation Awards. Returned to
bus. and legal practice interests at Lafayette. Dir.,
Lafayette Life Ins. Co.; Lafayette Natl. Bank; Dennison
Electric Co.; Gen. Telephone Co. of Ind.; Peerless Wire

Goods Co.; Natl. Homes Corp.; Erie and Lackawanna R.R. Ch.,
Ind. Conservation Commn., 1948-1950. Nom. and el. Gov. as
Dem. in 1964. After term as Gov., returned to bus. interests. Mbr., Amer. Legion; Elks; Masons (Shriner); numerous
bus. and professional legal orgs., social clubs and fraternities. Baptist. Noted for his wit and forthrightness.
m. in 1929 to Josephine Mardis. Two s. Hon. degrees from
four colleges and universities. D. Nov. 19, 1975, at
Lafayette, Ind.

WHITCOMB, EDGAR D. (1969-1973). b. Nov. 6, 1917 at
Hayden, Ind. s. of John Wm. and Louise (Doud) W. Attd.
the Univ. of Ind., 1936-1939. Entered U.S. mil. service as
cadet in Army Air Corps in 1940. During World War II saw
service in Air Transport Command and in Asiatic theater.
Held rank of major when released in 1946. Became col. in
USAFR in 1965. Recipient of Air Medal and unit citation.
Grad. with law degree from the Univ. of Ind. in 1950. Engaged in law practice in Seymour, Ind. Mbr., Ind. Senate,
1951-1954. Asst. U.S. dist. atty., 1955-1956. Ch., Great
Lakes Commn., 1965-1966. El. Sect. of State of Ind., serving from 1966 to 1969. Nom. and el. Gov. as Rep. in 1968,
and served one term. Defeated for Rep. nom. for U.S.
Senate seat in 1976. Mbr., Amer. Legion; V.F.W. Methodist.
Author of Escape from Corregidor, published in 1958. m. in
1951 to Patricia Louis Dolfuss. Four d.; one s.

BOWEN, OTIS RAY (1973-----). b. Feb. 26, 1918 at
Rochester, Ind. s. of Vernie and Pearl (Wright) B. Attd.
the Univ. of Ind., receiving an A.B. degree in 1939, and
an M.D. degree in 1942. Intern at Memorial Hosp., South
Bend, 1942-1943. Served as capt., U.S. Army Med. Corps, in
Pac. theater during World War II, 1943-1946. Began gen.
med. practice at Bremen, Ind. in 1946, serving on staffs of
hospitals in Bremen, South Bend and Mishawaka. Co. coroner
of Marshall Co., 1956. Mbr., Ind. House, 1956-1958, 1960-
1972. Served as minority (Rep.) leader in 1965-1966 and as
Speaker, 1967-1972. Ch., Ind. Legislative Council, 1967-
1968. Nom. and el. Gov. as Rep. in 1972, defeating former
Gov. Welsh in the gen. election. Reel. in 1976, a constl.
amdt. permitting a second successive term having been adopted in 1972. Mbr., U.S. Advisory Commn. on Intergovtl. Relations, 1976. Mbr., President's Commn. on Fed. Paperwork,
1975. Mbr., V.F.W.; Amer. Farm Bureau; Kiwanis; various
fraternities and professional med. orgs. Author of articles
in med. journals. Active in promotion of recreational
activities. Lutheran. m. in 1938 to Elizabeth A. Steinman.
Three s.; one d.

BRIGGS, ANSEL (1846-1850). b. Feb. 3, 1806 in Vt. s. of Benj. Ingley and Electa B. Attd. local schools and Norwich Co. Acad. for three years. In 1830 moved with family to Cambridge, Guernsey Co., Ohio, where he engaged in merc. bus. Sheriff of Guernsey Co. for two terms. In 1836 moved to Davenport, in what was then Wisc. Terr., where he obtained a contract for a U.S. mail route. Also became deputy treas. of Jackson Co. Mbr. of Iowa Terr. legislature, 1842. Upon Iowa's achieving statehood was nom. and el. first Gov. of the State as an Equal Rts. Dem. in close contest with Whig opponent. During admin., first state govt. was org. and a number of new counties created; boundary dispute with Mo., which threatened to give rise to violence, was settled; pub. and normal school system established, which he helped finance with personal funds. Became associated in 1854 with a land co. operating in Western Iowa and Eastern Nebr. Terr. Also acquired extensive land interests elsewhere. Helped establish first Masonic lodge in Iowa at Bellefontaine. From 1860 to 1865 engaged with son in overland freighting bus. to Colo. and Montana areas from Iowa. Established residence in Council Bluffs, Iowa in 1876 and after 1879 resided in Omaha, Nebr. m. in 1830 to Nancy Dunlap. Eight children. After her death, m. a widow, Mrs. Frances Carpenter, in 1849. D. May 5, 1881 in Omaha, Nebr.

HEMPSTEAD, STEPHEN (1850-1854). b. Oct. 1, 1812 at New London, Conn. s. of Joseph and Celinda (Hutchinson) H. Descendant of Welsh colonist who was a mbr. of one of the families that founded New London in 1645. Son moved with family in 1828 to St. Louis, Mo. Worked as a clerk at Galena, Ill. for a time. Served as militia officer in 1832 during Black Hawk War. Studied at Illinois Coll., in Jacksonville, for two years. Read law in an uncle's office. Admitted to bar in 1836. Began practice at Dubuque, Iowa, which was then a part of Wisc. Terr. When Iowa was org. as a separate Terr. in 1838, was el. to Terr. Council, later becoming its pres. Continued to serve thereon until Iowa was admitted to statehood. Mbr. of commn. set up to codify Iowa laws in 1848. Nom. and el. Gov. as Dem. in 1850. After serving four years was el. co. judge of Dubuque Co. in 1855. Continued to serve in that capacity until 1869, when the position was abolished. Aud. of Dubuque Co., 1869-1873. Retired from that office because of impaired health. Later served as justice of the peace. m. in 1837 to Lavinia Moore Lackland, in Baltimore, Md. Three s.; three d. D. at Dubuque, Feb. 16, 1883.

GRIMES, JAMES WILSON (1854-1858). b. Oct. 20, 1816 at

Deering, N.H. s. of John and Elizabeth (Wilson) G. Descendant of Scotch-Irish ancestor who came to N.H. in 1719.
Father was a thrifty farmer. Attd. Hampton Acad. and
Dartmouth Coll., from which he was grad. in 1836. Read law
in office at Peterboro, N.H. Moved to Burlington, Iowa,
then a part of Wisc. Terr., in 1836 where he began a successful law practice. Sect. of commn. to negotiate treaty
with Indians under which they sold lands along Mo. River to
U.S. Mbr. of Iowa Terr. legislature in 1838 and 1845. El.
to Iowa legislature in 1852. Nom. and el. Gov. in 1854 as
cand. of Whig and Free Soil parties. Later assisted in formation of Rep. party in Iowa. As Gov., opposed repeal of
Mo. Compromise provision regarding slavery in U.S. territories; capital of State was moved from Iowa City to Des
Moines. Called spec. session of Gen. Assembly in 1856 to
act on matter of land grants from U.S. to encourage railroad
constr. During admin., a constl. conv. was held in 1857
that resulted in alteration of term and election schedule of
Gov. His term was shortened by approximately one year as a
result. El. as a Rep. to U.S. Senate in 1858, continuing to
serve therein until 1869 when he resigned for health reasons. Mbr. of "Peace Congress" in Washington, D.C. in 1861
that sought to avert Civil War. Instrumental in obtaining
order from U.S. Sect. of War in 1861 setting free escaped
slaves held in Washington jail, this being the first emancipation action resulting from Civil War. In Cong., became
an authority on U.S. naval matters. Opposed a high protective tariff, and criticized Pres. Lincoln's enlargement of
regular army without prior approval of Cong. Voted for
acquittal of Pres. Johnson at his impeachment trial. Founder of free library in Burlington, Iowa and of endowed pro-
fessorship at Iowa (now Grinnell) Coll. Also established
scholarships at Iowa Coll. and Dartmouth Coll., from each of
which he received an hon. degree. m. in 1846 to Elizabeth
Sarah Neeley. D. Feb. 7, 1892, in Burlington, Iowa. Bur.
in Aspen Grove Cem. there.

LOWE, RALPH PHILLIPS (1858-1860). b. Nov. 27, 1805 in
Warren Co., Ohio. s. of Jacob Derrick and Martha (Per-Lee)
L. Descendant of a settler who emigrated from Holland to
N.J. Attd. local schools and Miami Univ., at Oxford, Ohio.
Went to Ashville, Ala., where he engaged in teaching for a
time. Studied law, admitted to bar and began practice with
brother at Dayton, Ohio. In 1840 moved to Bloomington (now
Muscatine), Iowa Terr., where he practiced law and farmed.
Mbr. of first Iowa constl. conv. in 1845. After statehood
was achieved became a dist. atty. and later, a dist. judge.
Nom. and el. Gov. as Rep. in 1857 under revised provision

setting up two-year term. After tenure as Gov., was el. to
Iowa Supreme Ct. Became involved in prosecution of claim
by State of Iowa for reimbursement for lands granted to en-
listees to induce them to join Union Army during Civil War.
Resigned post on Iowa Supreme Ct. to prosecute the claim as
a U.S. dist. atty. in Washington, D.C. Eventually lost suit
when U.S. Supreme Ct. ruled against his contentions and
Cong. refused to act in the matter. m. in 1837 to Phoebe
Carleton, of Cincinnati, Ohio. D. in Washington, D.C.,
Dec. 22, 1883.

KIRKWOOD, SAMUEL JORDAN (1860-1864; 1876-1877). b.
Dec. 20, 1813 in Harford Co., Md. Attd. local schools and
McLeod's Acad. in Washington, D.C. At age 14 began work as
druggist's clerk, and later engaged in teaching in Pa. In
1835 moved to Richland Co., Ohio. Studied law, admitted to
bar in 1843 and began practice at Mansfield, Ohio. Served
two terms as pros. atty. of Richland Co., 1845-1849. Mbr.
of Ohio state constl. conv. in 1850-1851. In 1855 moved to
Coralville, Johnson Co., Iowa, where he engaged in farming
and milling bus. Had active role in formation of Rep. party
in Iowa in 1856. Mbr. Iowa Senate, 1856-1859. Nom. and el.
Gov. as Rep. in 1859 and was reel. in 1861. Gave strong
support to Union cause during Civil War. Apptd. by Pres.
Lincoln and confirmed to post of Minister to Denmark in
1863, but declined office. El. to U.S. Senate in Jan.,
1866 to fill vacancy, serving for approximately one year.
Returned to law practice and bus. activities in Iowa City in
1867. Pres. of Iowa and Southwestern R.R. Nom. and el.
Gov. again as Rep. in 1875, becoming first person to be el.
to the office for third term. Resigned in 1877 after ser-
ving approximately one year to take seat in U.S. Senate.
Continued to serve there until Mar., 1881 when he resigned
to accept apptmt. as U.S. Sect. of the Interior under Pres.
Garfield. Was replaced the following year by Pres. Arthur.
Resumed law practice in Iowa City. Pres. of Iowa City Natl.
Bank. Defeated as cand. for U.S. House in 1886. D. at
Iowa City, Sept. 1, 1894. Bur. in Oakland Cem. there.

STONE, WILLIAM MILO (1864-1868). b. Oct. 14, 1827 in
Jefferson Co., N.Y. s. of Truman and Lovinia (North) S.
Received limited educ. At age 16 began work as driver on
Ohio Canal, at Coshocton, Ohio. From 1844 to 1850 worked
as a chair maker. Continued studies by reading on his own.
Studied law and was admitted to bar in 1851, becoming law
partner of his law teacher, at Coshocton. In 1854 moved to
Knoxville, Iowa, where he became ed. of the Knoxville
Journal in 1855. Mbr. of conv. that formed Rep. party in

Iowa in 1856. El. cir. ct. judge in 1857. Delegate to Rep.
natl. conv. in 1860, where he supported nom. of Lincoln for
Pres. of U.S. Upon outbreak of Civil War, enlisted as pvt.
in Union Army. Soon rose to rank of capt. and then major
in an Iowa regiment. Wounded and taken prisoner in 1861.
After release was promoted to col., later to brig. gen.
Participated in campaigns leading up to capture of Vicksburg
in 1863. Nom. and el. Gov. as Rep. in 1863 and was reel. in
1865. As Gov., gave strong support to Pres. Lincoln in
prosecution of Civil War. Was present at Ford's Theater and
witnessed Lincoln's assassination in 1865, later serving as
hon. pall bearer at his funeral. After tenure as Gov. resumed law practice. Mbr. of Iowa legislature in 1877. In
1880 became interested in mining ventures in Ariz. and later
in Colo. Moved to Pueblo, Colo. in 1883. Returned to Des
Moines, Iowa in 1885, where he practiced law. Pres. elector
on Rep. ticket in 1888. Apptd. U.S. Commnr. of Gen. Land
Office by Pres. Harrison in 1889, serving until 1893. Moved
to Okla. Terr. in that year, where he engaged in farming and
law practice at Oklahoma City until his death. m. in 1856
to Caroline Mathews. One s. D. at Oklahoma City, July 13,
1893.

MERRILL, SAMUEL (1868-1872). b. Aug. 7, 1822 in
Turner, Oxford Co., Me. s. of Abel and Abigail Hill
(Buxton) M. Descendant of an English colonist who emigrated
to Salisbury, Mass. in 1636. Brought up on father's farm,
receiving rudimentary educ. in local schools. Became school
teacher at age 17, in which occupation he continued to engage for a number of years. In 1847 moved to Tamworth,
N.H., where he became a merchant. Served in N.H. legislature. In 1856 moved to McGregor, Iowa, where he was a merchant and banker. Also served in Iowa legislature. Upon
outbreak of Civil War enlisted in an Iowa regiment, of
which he became col. Served under Gen. Grant in Mo. in
1861. Was wounded severely and resigned commn. after recovery. Subsequently donated Civil War pension to a Des
Moines hosp. for benefit of U.S. soldiers. In 1867 was
nom. and el. Gov. as a Rep. Reel. in 1869. As Gov.,
opposed use of U.S. notes in payment of interest and principal on U.S. bonds. During admin., a constl. amdt. was
adopted abolishing racial restrictions on suffrage; constr.
of new Capitol bldg. begun; educ. and prison reforms adopted. After tenure as Gov. returned to bus. interests. In
1889 moved to Calif. m. in 1844 to Catherine Thomas, of
Standish, Me. After her death in 1845, m. to Elizabeth D.
Hill, of Buxton, Me. in 1851. After her death in 1888, m.
in 1895 to a widow, Mrs. Mary S. Greenwood, of Mass. D. in

Los Angeles, Calif., Aug. 31, 1899.

CARPENTER, CYRUS CLAY (1872-1876). b. Nov. 24, 1829
near Harford, Pa. s. of Asahel and Amanda (Thayer) C. Related through his mother to Gen. Sylvanus Thayer, who was a
founder of West Point Mil. Acad. and of the School of Civil
Engr. at Dartmouth Coll. Became an orphan at age 12. Attd.
local schools and Harford Acad., from which he was grad. in
1853. Moved to Licking Co., Ohio, where he taught school
for a term. In 1854 moved to Des Moines, Iowa, and later to
Ft. Dodge, Iowa, where he became a teacher in the first pub.
school there. Also engaged in land survey work and opened
office as land agent. Studied law, but never practiced.
Co. surveyor of Webster Co., 1856-1858. Mbr. of Iowa House,
1858-1860. Following outbreak of Civil War enlisted as a
pvt. in an Iowa regiment in 1862. Became capt., later a
col. in charge of commissary functions. Served as register
of Iowa land office, 1866-1868. Nom. and el. Gov. as Rep.
in 1871, and was reel. in 1873. Supported expansion of
higher educ. program, including establishment of agri. experiment stations; advocated state regulation of railroad
rates, securing adoption of one of the first "Granger laws"
on this point. Apptd. Second Comptroller of U.S. Treas. in
1876, serving until 1877. One of the mbrs. of first Iowa
R.R. Commn., 1878. Mbr., U.S. House, 1879-1883. Declined
to run for third term. Mbr. of Iowa House, 1884-1886. U.S.
postmaster at Ft. Dodge, 1889-1893. Also engaged in farming
and real estate bus. m. in 1864 to Susan C. Burkholder, of
Ft. Dodge. D. at Ft. Dodge, May 29, 1898. Bur. in Oakdale
Cem. there.

KIRKWOOD, SAMUEL JORDAN (1876-1877). See above, 1860-
1864.

NEWBOLD, JOSHUA G. (1877-1878). b. May 12, 1830 in
Cookstown, Fayette Co., Pa. Family was of English descent,
and were Quakers. Educ. in local schools and engaged in
teaching. In 1854 moved to Hillsboro, Henry Co., Iowa,
where he became a farmer and a merchant. Enlisted in Iowa
volunteer regiment in 1862 and served until end of Civil
War. Held rank of capt. when he left service. Saw active
service in Ark., the Chattanooga campaign, and in Gen.
Sherman's march to Savannah. Mbr. of Iowa House, 1869-1875,
becoming Speaker pro tem during last term. Nom. and el.
Lieut. Gov. in 1875 as a Rep. Succeeded to office of Gov.
in Feb., 1877 after Gov. Kirkwood resigned to go to U.S.
Senate, and completed Kirkwood's term. Moved to Mt.
Pleasant, Iowa in 1878, where he engaged in bus. activities.

Mayor of Mt. Pleasant in 1901. D. there June 10, 1903.

GEAR, JOHN HENRY (1878-1882). b. April 7, 1825 at
Ithaca, N.Y. s. of Ezekiel and Harriet (Cook) G. Father
was an Episcopal minister who served as a missionary to
Indian tribes. Family, which was of Scottish descent, moved
in 1836 to Galena, Ill. and in 1838 to Ft. Snelling, in Iowa
Terr. Attd. local schools and was also tutored by father.
In 1843 established residence in Burlington, Iowa, where he
became a salesman and later, a merchant. Had active role in
formation of Rep. party in Iowa in 1856. Mayor of
Burlington in 1863. Mbr. of Iowa House, 1871-1877, serving
as Speaker during last four years. Nom. and el. Gov. as
Rep. in 1877 and was reel. in 1879. During admin., a State
Bd. of Health was established and the issue of natl. currency policy resulted in the rise of the Greenback party to
prominence in state politics for a time. Signed measure revising the "Granger law" of 1874, changing the focus of
regulatory action from the legislature to a commn. El. to
U.S. House in 1886. Reel. in 1888, but was defeated for
third successive term in 1890. Delegate to Rep. natl.
convs. in 1892 and 1896. Apptd. Asst. Sect. of U.S. Treas.
by Pres. Harrison in 1892, serving until Mar., 1893. El. to
U.S. House again in 1892. El. to U.S. Senate in 1895. m.
in 1852 to Harriet Foote, of Middlebury, Vt. Four children.
D. in Washington, D.C., July 14, 1900, while still a mbr. of
U.S. Senate, after having been reel. for the succeeding
term. Bur. in Aspen Grove Cem., in Burlington, Iowa.

SHERMAN, BUREN ROBINSON (1882-1886). b. May 28, 1836
in Phelps, N.Y. s. of Phineas L. and Eveline (Robinson). S.
Father was a mfr. of axes. Moved with family to Iowa in
1855, where he engaged in farming. Attd. local schools in
N.Y. and Elmira Acad., from which he was grad. in 1853.
Moved with family to Vinton, Iowa in 1855. Studied law and
was admitted to the bar in 1859, beginning practice at
Vinton. At outset of Civil War, enlisted in an Iowa regiment as a pvt., and rose to the rank of capt. Wounded at
Battle of Shiloh in 1862 and was again wounded in 1863. Resigned commn. near end of the war. Judge of Benton Co. ct.,
1865-1867. Clerk of cir. ct., 1869-1874. El. State Aud.
in 1874 and continued in office for two succeeding terms.
Nom. and el. Gov. as Rep. in 1881, and was reel. for next
term in 1883. As Gov., favored enactment of a prohibitory
law against sale of alcoholic beverages; creation of a Dept.
of Agri.; a compulsory school attendance law; and creation
of a single bd. of control over all state welfare institutions. A state prohibition amdt. was approved by popular

vote of the people in 1882, but it was held invalid on technical grounds by the State Supreme Ct. Prominent in activities of Masonic order, holding Royal Arch, K.T., and
Scottish Rite degrees. Hon. degree from State Univ. of
Iowa. m. in 1862 to Lena Kendall, of Vinton, Iowa. D. Nov.
11, 1904, at Vinton.

LARRABEE, WILLIAM (1886-1890). b. Jan. 20, 1832 at
Ledyard, Conn. s. of Capt. Adam and Hannah Gallup (Lester)
L. Father was a West Point Mil. Acad. grad. and pursued a
career in U.S. mil. service. Attd. local schools. In 1853
moved to Iowa, where he taught school for a time in Hardin
Co. Engaged in farming later, and extended interests into
milling, banking and mfg. of farm machinery. Invented a new
type of grain separator which was widely used in farming
indus. Active in formation of Rep. party in Iowa in 1850s.
Mbr. of Iowa Senate for 18 years beginning in 1867. As mbr.
of Senate took leading role in passage of legislation creating a State R.R. Commn. and in mgmt. of state fiscal
affairs. Nom. and el. Gov. as a Rep. in 1885 and was reel.
in 1887. Refused to be a cand. for third term. Apptd. ch.
of State Bd. of Control of State Institutions in 1898, serving until 1900. Travelled in Europe and Palestine. Author
of The Railroad Question in 1893. Delegate from Iowa to
St. Louis Expo. in 1904. m. in 1861 to Ann Appelman, of
Clermont, Iowa. Six children. D. Nov. 16, 1912.

BOISE, HORACE (1890-1894). b. Dec. 7, 1827 near
Aurora, N.Y. s. of Eber and Hattie (Henshaw) B. Brought up
on father's farm, attending local schools in winters. In
1844 went to Wisc. Terr., where he worked as a farm laborer
there and in Ill. in summers. Saved money and returned to
N.Y. in winters to further educ. Studied law in N.Y. and
was admitted to bar in 1849. Began practice in Buffalo,
N.Y. In early years identified with Whig party; later
joined Rep. party when it was formed in 1850s. Mbr. of N.Y.
legislature in 1858. Defeated by two votes in race for
dist. atty. in Erie Co. in 1864. Retired from politics for
a time. Moved to Waterloo, Iowa in 1867, where he practiced
law and also engaged in farming. Became involved in politics again as a result of prohibition issue. Because of
tariff and prohibition issues, switched affiliation to the
Dem. party. In 1884 supported Grover Cleveland for Pres. of
U.S. Nom. and el. Gov. as Dem. in 1889 in a campaign
featuring prohibition issue through his advocacy of local
option and his attack on existing laws prohibiting liquor
traffic. Also favored adoption of Australian ballot system.
Became first Dem. to hold office of Gov. since before the

Civil War. Reel. in 1891. Offered post of Sect. of Agri.
by Pres. Cleveland, but declined it. Nom. for a third term
in 1893 but lost in gen. election. Resumed law practice at
Waterloo. Placed in nom. for Pres. of U.S. at Dem. natl.
conv. in 1896. Received 86 votes for the nom. which eventually was won by Wm. J. Bryan on fifth ballot. Defeated as
Dem. cand. for U.S. House in 1902. Spent much of his time
thereafter in Calif., returning to Iowa in summers. m. in
early life while residing in New York. Two s.; one d. D.
April 4, 1923, at Long Beach, Calif. Bur. at Waterloo, Iowa

JACKSON, FRANK DARR (1894-1896). b. Jan. 26, 1854 at
Arcade, N.Y. s. of Hiram W. and Marian (Jenks) J. Father
and mother served Union cause during Civil War, his mother
working as a nurse. After the war ended, family moved to
Jesup, Iowa in 1867, where he attd. common schools. Entered
Iowa State Agri. Coll. in 1870 and after three years, the
Univ. of Iowa, from which he received a law degree in 1874.
Admitted to bar in 1875 and began practice at Independence,
Iowa. In 1880 moved to Greene, Iowa, where he continued in
law practice. Became sect. of Iowa Senate in 1882, continuing in that office until 1884. El. Sect. of State, and continued to hold that office until 1889. Formed a life ins.
co. at Des Moines, becoming its pres. Nom. and el. Gov. in
1893 as a Rep., defeating incumbent Gov. Boise. Was
sympathetic toward plight of labor following the financial
panic of 1893, but insisted on maintenance of law and order.
Was not a cand. for second term in 1897. Retired from politics to devote attention to bus. and legal professional
interests. m. in 1877 to Anne F. Brock, of Council Bluffs,
Iowa. Four s. D. Nov. 16, 1938.

DRAKE, FRANCIS MARION (1896-1898). b. Dec. 20, 1830 at
Rushville, Ill. s. of John Adams and Harriet Jane (O'Neal)
D. Parents were natives of N.C. In 1837 family moved to
Ft. Madison, Iowa (then Wisc. Terr.), where son received a
common school educ. In 1846 family moved again to Davis
Co., Iowa where father engaged in gen. merc. bus. Town of
Drakeville grew up around his store. Worked in father's
bus. until 1852. At age 22 successfully led an ox-team wagon train of six wagons from Omaha, Nebr. to Calif. Encountered a band of about 300 hostile Pawnee Indians on the way.
They were routed in a fight in which he killed their leader.
In 1854 led another wagon train with a large herd of cattle
to Calif. On the return trip by sea his ship was wrecked
off the coast of Mexico, and some 800 passengers lost their
lives. He escaped with a few others to land, and they
seized a rowboat from a band of looters who were intent on

plundering the wrecked vessel. He and his companions were
eventually picked up and brought to an Amer. port after en-
during severe privations. Engaged in work as father's partner until 1858, when he moved to Unionville, Iowa, where he
went into bus. for himself. Enlisted as pvt. in Union Army
upon outbreak of Civil War, and soon rose to rank of major.
Saw action with Iowa troops in Northwest Mo. Became lieut.
col., then col. in 1862. Participated in engagements in
Ark. Was wounded and was thought to have been killed; but
was taken prisoner on battlefield and life was saved. Recovered from wounds after six months of critical illness.
After being exchanged, was promoted to brig. gen. and served
until end of the war. Returned to Iowa, where he studied
law, establishing practice at Centerville, Iowa. Helped org.
Albia and Centerville R.R. and became its pres. Was also
pres. of banks at Centerville and Albia. Made extensive
gifts to Iowa (Grinnell) Coll., Iowa Wesleyan Coll. and to
Drake Univ., which was named in his honor. Served on Drake
Univ. Bd. of Trustees. Nom. and el. Gov. as Rep. in 1895.
Served only one term, retiring to give attention to bus.
affairs. Mbr., I.O.O.F.; Masons. Christian (Disciples)
church. m. in 1855 to Mary Jane Lord, a native of Nova
Scotia, who had moved to Bloomfield, Iowa. Two s.; four d.
D. Nov. 20, 1903, at Centerville, Iowa.

SHAW, LESLIE MORTIER (1898-1902). b. Nov. 2, 1848 at
Morristown, Vt. s. of Boardman Osias and Louisa Warren
(Spaulding) S. Descendant of an English colonist who came
to Cambridge, Mass. in 1636. Family moved to Stowe, Vt. in
1852, where he received early educ. Attd. Peoples Acad.,
at Morrisville, Vt. Engaged in school teaching for a time.
In 1869 went to Mt. Vernon, Iowa, to visit relatives and decided to remain there. Grad. from Cornell Coll., at Mt.
Vernon, in 1874 working while attending college. Received
law degree from Iowa Coll. of Law in 1876. Began practice
in Denison, Iowa, and soon became a community leader. Contributed to Denison Acad. and Normal School, becoming pres.
of its governing bd. Also served on Denison school bd. and
on the governing bd. of Cornell Coll. Pres. of banks in
Denison, Manilla, and Charter Oak, Iowa. Took active role
in pres. campaign of 1896 as speaker, favoring gold standard, and helped carry Iowa for McKinley ticket. Nom. and
el. Gov. as Rep. in 1897 and was reel. in 1899. In 1898
presided at Intl. Monetary Conf. at Indianapolis. Refused
to run for third term as Gov. in 1901. Apptd. U.S. Sect.
of Treas. by Pres. Roosevelt in 1902, serving until 1907.
Became pres. of Carnegie Trust Co. in New York City in 1908.
Was an announced cand. for Rep. nom. for Pres. of U.S. in

1908, but withdrew before the natl. conv. in favor of Wm. H.
Taft. Pres. of First Mortgage and Guaranty Trust Co. of
Philadelphia, 1909-1913, and mbr. of bds. of dir. of other
bus. corps. Wrote and published extensively on econ. and
political subjects. Works included Current Issues, in 1908;
Vanishing Landmarks and The Trend Toward Bolshevism, in
1919. Hon. degrees from Simpson, Cornell, Iowa Wesleyan,
and Dickinson Colleges. Active in Methodist church affairs.
m. in 1876 to Alice Crawshaw. Two d.; one s. D. Mar. 28,
1932, at Washington, D.C. Bur. at Denison, Iowa.

CUMMINS, ALBERT BAIRD (1902-1908). b. Feb. 15, 1850
near Carmichael, Pa. s. of Thomas L. and Sarah Baird
(Flenniken) C. Family was of Scotch-Irish descent. Attd.
local pub. schools and Waynesburg Coll., from which he was
grad. in 1869. Moved to Elkader, Iowa, where he became a
clerk in Clayton Co. recorder's office, and later was employed for a time as a carpenter, his father's trade.
Worked as a railway clerk and express mgr., and was a deputy
surveyor of Allen Co., Ind. in 1871. Worked as a railroad
constr. engr. in Midwest area. Studied law in Chicago, admitted to Ill. bar and began practice in Chicago. Moved
law practice to Des Moines, Iowa in 1878. Acquired wide
clientele, specializing in field of patent law. Won considerable notice by successfully representing clients'
claims against the so-called "barbed wire trust". Mbr., bd.
of dir. of Des Moines Union R.R. and of Northern and Western
R.R. Mbr. of Iowa legislature, 1888-1890. Delegate to Rep.
natl. conv. in 1880 and to natl. and state Rep. convs.
thereafter until death. Mbr. of Rep. natl. commt., 1896-
1900. Temp. ch. of Iowa Rep. conv. in 1892 and pres. elect-
or on Harrison ticket that year. Defeated as cand. for Rep.
nom. for U.S. Senate in 1894 and again in 1900. Nom. and
el. Gov. as Rep. in 1901. Reel. in 1903 for a term extended
to three years because of change in term and election
schedule effected in 1904. Reel. Gov. in 1906, becoming the
first Gov. of Iowa to be el. to three successive terms.
Was identified with progressive policies, including closer
regulation of railways and opposition to high protective
tariff. During admin., a State Highway Commn. was established; a direct primary law was enacted; a pure food law
passed; and legislation providing for mun. govtl. reform
embodying the commn. plan of govt. (the "Des Moines Plan")
was adopted. Defeated as cand. for U.S. Senate seat in
1908, but later that year was nom. by the primary system as
Rep. cand. and was el. to fill a vacancy in Senate. Resigned as Gov. before end of term to take Senate seat. Continued in Senate by reel. until his death in 1926, shortly

after having been defeated for re-nom. for that office.   In
1912 pres. campaign announced his support of Theodore
Roosevelt for the Rep. nom. for Pres. of U.S., but refused
to join in the Prog. party movement subsequently.   Cand.
for nom. for Pres. of the U.S. at the Rep. natl. conv. in
1916, receiving 85 votes on each of the first two ballots
before nom. was won by Charles E. Hughes.   As U.S. Senator,
served as Pres. pro tem, 1919-1925.   Sponsor of legislation
in 1920 under which railroads were restored to pvt. mgmt.
under closer natl. regulation following World War I.   Hon.
degrees from Waynesburg and Cornell Colleges.   m. in 1874
to Ida Lucette Gallery.   One d.   D. at Des Moines, July 30,
1926.   Bur. in Woodlawn Cem there.

GARST, WARREN (1908-1909).   b. Dec. 4, 1850 at Dayton,
Ohio.   s. of Michael and Maria Louisa (Morrison) G.   Attd.
pub. schools at Dayton.   In 1869 went to Boone, Iowa, where
he was employed as a railroad brakeman.   Later joined his
father and brother, who had moved to Iowa, in bus. enterprises at Coon Rapids.   Engaged in farming and banking
there.   Org. bank in Coon Rapids in 1902 which became Iowa
State Savings bank in 1915.   El. to Iowa Senate in 1893 and
continued in office for two succeeding terms.   Nom. and el.
Lieut. Gov. as Rep. in 1906.   Succeeded to office of Gov.
in Nov., 1908, when Gov. Cummins resigned.   Completed
Cummins' term, which had about two months to run.   Retired
to bus. activities thereafter.   Later served as the first
State Indus. Commnr. by apptmt. from Gov. Clarke after a
workmen's compensation law was enacted.   m. in 1878 to
Lizzie P. Johnson, of Champaign, Ill., who died in 1881.
One d.   m. in 1889 to Clara Clarke, of Boone, Iowa.   One s.;
one d.   D. at Des Moines, Oct. 5, 1924.

CARROLL, BERYL FRANKLIN (1909-1913).   b. Mar. 15, 1860
in Davis Co., Iowa.   s. of Willis and Christina (Wright) C.
Descendant of an Irish immigrant who came to Amer. during
18th century.   Attd. So. Iowa Normal and Sci. Inst. at
Bloomfield, Iowa, and Northwest Mo. State Normal at
Kirksville, Mo., from which he was grad. in 1884.   Taught
in country and graded schools in Iowa and Mo., 1884-1889.
Engaged in livestock bus. at Bloomfield, 1889-1891.   Owner
and ed. of a newspaper, the Davis County Republican, 1891-
1913.   Pres. elector on Rep. ticket in 1892.   Unsuccessful
cand. for Iowa legislature in 1893.   Mbr. of Iowa Senate,
1895-1898.   U.S. postmaster at Bloomfield, 1898-1902.   El.
Iowa State Aud. in 1903, continuing in office by reel. until
1909.   Nom. and el. Gov. as Rep. in 1908 and again in 1910.
Was the first native-born Iowan to occupy the office of

Gov. During admin., a Dept. of Commerce was established.
After tenure as Gov., engaged in investment and real estate
bus. in Des Moines. Active in Methodist Episcopal church.
Hon. degree from Simpson Coll. Author of Evolution: An
Unproven Theory, in 1926. m. in 1886 to Jennie Dodson, of
Kirksville, Mo. One s.; one d. D. Dec. 16, 1939.

CLARKE, GEORGE W. (1913-1917). b. Oct. 24, 1852 in
Shelby Co., Ind. s. of John and Eliza (Akers) C. In 1856
family moved to Davis Co., Iowa. Son worked on family farm
while attending local schools. Engaged in teaching while
continuing studies. Attd. Oskaloosa Coll., and the State
Univ. of Iowa, from which he received a law degree in 1878.
Admitted to bar and began practice at Adel, Iowa. El. to
Iowa legislature in 1899 and continued to serve therein until 1907. House Speaker, 1904-1907. Nom. and el. Lieut.
Gov. in 1908 and was reel. in 1910. Nom. and el. Gov. as
Rep. in 1912 by narrow margin over Dem. and Prog. party
opponents. As Gov., recommended enactment of a workmen's
compensation law; legislation for closer regulation of pub.
utilities; improvements in roads, schools, pensions, health,
and ct. systems; a "blue sky" law; and legislation on arb.
of labor disputes. Served as dean of law college at Drake
Univ., 1917-1918. Practiced law in Des Moines, 1918-1921.
Hon. degree from Drake Univ. m. in 1878 to Arletta Greene,
of Adel, Iowa. Two s.; two d. D. Nov. 28, 1936.

HARDING, WILLIAM LLOYD (1917-1921). b. Oct. 3, 1877 at
Sibley, Iowa. s. of Orlando Boardman and Emalyn (Moyer) H.
Father, who was a farmer, had moved from Pa. to Iowa. Attd.
rural schools; Morningside Coll. in Sioux City, for four
years; and the Univ. of S.D., from which he was grad. with
a law degree in 1905. Began practice in Sioux City, soon
acquiring wide recognition as able lawyer. Mbr. of Iowa
legislature, 1907-1913. El. Lieut. Gov. in 1912 and again
in 1914. Nom. and el. Gov. as Rep. in 1916 and was reel.
in 1918. During admin., cooperated with U.S. in prosecution
of World War I programs and policies; consolidated rural
school system established; state park system inaugurated
with purchase of sites of historical and sci. value. With
cooperation of U.S. Sect. of Interior, assembled first Natl.
Conf. on Parks. After tenure as Gov., resumed law practice
in Sioux City. Mbr., Council of States of Great Lakes; St.
Lawrence Tide Water Assoc.; Masons. Methodist. m. in 1907
to Carrie M. Lamoreau, of Meriden, Iowa. One d. D. Dec.
17, 1934.

KENDALL, NATHAN EDWARD ("NATE") (1921-1925). b. Mar.

17, 1868 on a farm near Greenville, Iowa. s. of Elijah L.
and Lucinda (Stephens) K. Family was of Irish descent.
Attd. rural schools. Studied law in office at Chariton,
Iowa. Admitted to bar and began practice in Albia, Iowa.
City atty. of Albia, 1890-1892. Co. atty. of Monroe Co.,
1893-1897. Mbr. of Iowa House, 1899-1909, serving as
Speaker, 1907-1909. El. to U.S. House in 1908 and also for
succeeding term. Did not seek reel. in 1912. Del. to Rep.
natl. conv. in 1916, where he delivered nom. speech for Sen.
Cummins. Resumed law practice at Albia. Moved to Des
Moines in 1921. Finished second in Rep. primary for nom.
for Gov. in 1920, but received nom. at hands of the state
party conv., no cand. having received a plurality of at
least 35 per cent in the primary, and was el. Reel. in
1922. During admin., launched admin. reorg. program; expanded state highway system and state park system; legislation enacted regulating securities brokers; children's aid
programs expanded. For approximately two months, Aug. to
Oct., 1923, surrendered authority of office of Gov. to
Lieut. Gov. Hammill while absent from the State recovering
from a serious illness. Continued to reside at Des Moines
after tenure as Gov. Mbr., Masons; Rotary; various social
and professional legal orgs. m. in 1896 to Belle Wooden,
of Centerville, Iowa, who died in 1926. m. in 1928 to Mrs.
Mabel Mildred (Fry) Brownell, of Naples, Italy. D. at Des
Moines, Nov. 4, 1936. Ashes interred on lawn of his former
home in Albia, Iowa.

HAMMILL, JOHN (1925-1931). b. Oct. 14, 1875 at Linden,
Wisc. s. of George and Mary (Brewer) H. Father, who had
been a miner in Colo., settled on a farm in Iowa. Attd.
rural schools and the Univ. of Iowa, from which he received
a law degree in 1897. Began practice in Britt, Iowa. Co.
atty. of Hancock Co., 1903-1907. Mbr. of Iowa Senate, 1909-
1913. El. Lieut. Gov. in 1920 and again in 1922. During
Aug.-Oct., 1923, acted as Gov. for two months during absence of Gov. Kendall because of latter's illness. Nom. and
el. Gov. as Rep. in 1924 and for next two terms. During
admin., gave major attention to strengthening state control
over banking and to expansion of state highway system. Bond
issue for latter purpose was overthrown, however, by Iowa
Supreme Ct. After tenure as Gov. returned to law practice
and to farming on an extensive scale. Became involved in
breeding blooded livestock. Served as school bd. mbr. for
nine years. Mbr. of Better Iowa Schools Commn. Served on
natl. commn. to study prisons and prison labor problems.
Advocate of relief measures for farmers. Exec. head of
Hancock Co. Red Cross and ch. of Liberty Loan drive during

World War I. Hon. degree from Iowa Wesleyan. Mbr., Iowa
Historical Assoc.; Masons (O.E.S.); professional legal orgs.
Methodist. m. in 1899 to Fannie Richards, of Garner, Iowa.
No children. D. April 5, 1936, in Minneapolis, Minn.

TURNER, DAN(IEL WEBSTER) (1931-1933). b. Mar. 17, 1877
at Corning, Iowa. s. of Austin Bates and Almira (Baker) T.
Attd. Corning Acad. Began farming near Corning in 1894.
Served with Iowa infantry regiment in Philippine Islands,
1898-1899. Mbr. of Iowa Senate, 1903-1909. Delegate to
Rep. natl. convs. in 1928, 1932 and 1936. Nom. and el. Gov.
as Rep. in 1930. During admin., the worsening of farm depression was a continuing problem, necessitating curtailment
of expenditures for various state programs. Was forced to
employ Natl. Guard units to assist in enforcement of law
requiring testing of cattle for tuberculosis. Farm mortgage
foreclosures resulted in local disorders. Defeated for
succeeding term in 1932. Was again defeated as the Rep.
nominee for Gov. in 1934. Was one of founders of Natl.
Farmers Org. in 1955. m. in 1900 to Alice Sample. One d.;
two s. D. April 15, 1969 at Corning, at age of 92.

HERRING, CLYDE LAVERNE (1933-1937). b. May 3, 1879 at
Jackson, Mich. s. of James Gwynn and Stella Mae (Addison)
H. Grandfather had emigrated from Wales to Mich. in 1852.
Father was a farmer. Attd. local pub. schools. Employed
as a clerk in jewelry store in Detroit, in 1897. Served
with U.S. Army during Spanish-Amer. War. After discharge
moved to Spinney, Colo., where he engaged in ranching from
1902 to 1906. Postmaster there by apptmt. of Pres. Theodore
Roosevelt, 1906-1908. Operated farm at Massena, Iowa for a
short time. Went into auto bus. as Ford Motor Co. agent at
Atlantic, Iowa. In 1910 moved agency to Des Moines, serving
as Ford distributor for dist., consisting of Iowa and Eastern Nebr. Expanded operations into fields of farm implements, Curtis airplanes, and wholesale oil distribution.
Fuel Adminr. for Polk Co., Iowa and participant in Liberty
Loan drives during World War I. Also served with Iowa Natl.
Guard unit on Mexican border. Defeated as Dem. party nominee for Gov. in 1920. Also defeated as Dem. nominee for
U.S. Senate in 1922. Mbr., Dem. natl. commt., 1924-1928.
Nom. and el. Gov. as Dem. in 1932 and again in 1934, becoming first Dem. in 40 years to hold office of Gov. Admin.
beset by depression in farm indus. Strikes by farmers and
resistance to farm foreclosures led to his issuing proclamation 11 days after assuming office forbidding foreclosure
sales, pending enactment of mortgage moratorium law by legislature. Also issued proclamation of bank holiday,

anticipating similar action by Pres. Roosevelt nationally.
Reorg. state finances; inaugurated state liquor monopoly
system after repeal of 18th Amdt., which became model for
other states.   Inaugurated state old age assistance program
and cooperated with U.S. govtl. programs for refinancing
home, bus. and farm indebtedness.   El. to U.S. Senate in
1936, taking office after term as Gov. expired.   Supported
U.S. defense effort as a Sen. Delegate to Dem. natl. conv.
in 1940. Defeated for second term in Senate in 1942. Resumed auto agency bus. in Des Moines. Apptd. senior deputy
adminr. for O.P.A. in 1943. Congregationalist. m. to Emma
Pearl Spinney. Three s. A son, Clyde E., was defeated as
the Dem. nominee for Gov. in 1954. D. Sept. 15, 1945, in
Washington, D.C. Bur. in Glendale Cem., Des Moines.

KRASHEL, NELSON GEORGE (1937-1939).   b. Oct. 27, 1889
in Macon, Ill.   s. of Fred K. and Nancy Jane (Poe) K.
Father was a farmer and stock breeder who had emigrated to
Amer. from Germany.   Attd. pub. schools at Macon and
Decatur, Ill.   Engaged in livestock auctioneering.   Moved to
Harlan, Iowa in 1910, where he continued to work as auctioneer.   Conducted sales in 26 States over the next 25 years,
making sales totalling over $50 million.   Also engaged in
farming in Iowa.   Lieut. Gov., 1933-1937.   Nom. and el. Gov.
as Dem. in 1936 in a very close contest.   During admin.,
intervened in strike at the Maytag Co. plant in Newton,
Iowa, employing Natl. Guard to oust strikers when they occupied factory.   Resisted intervention in the affair by
Natl. Labor Relations Bd. by declaring state of martial law.
His veto of a farm-to-market road bill passed by the legislature also occasioned controversy.   Defeated for second
term in 1938 by same opponent he had defeated in 1936,
losing by some 60,000 votes.   Defeated again as Dem. cand.
for Gov. in 1942 gen. election.   Apptd. gen. agent for U.S.
Farm Credit Admin. in Omaha, Nebr. in 1943, serving until
1949.   Also continued activities in farming and auctioneering.   Successfully supported Sen. Gillette in 1944 for re-
nom. as Dem. cand. for U.S. Senate against Harry Hopkins,
who had backing of Dem. natl. admin.   Mbr., Masons; Kiwanis;
various clubs.   Methodist.   m. in 1913 to Agnes Johnson, of
Harlan, Iowa.   Three s.   D. at Harlan, March 15, 1957.

WILSON, GEORGE ALLISON (1939-1943).   b. April 1, 1884
at Menlo, Iowa.   s. of James Henderson and Martha Green
(Varley) W.   Grandfather had emigrated to N.Y. from Scotland.
Father was a farmer and local pub. official.   Attd. pub.
schools at Menlo; Grinnell Coll., 1900-1903; and the Univ.
of Iowa, from which he received a law degree in 1907.   Began

practice in Des Moines. Was active in politics at early
age, having served as page in Iowa Senate in 1898 while
still a school boy. Asst. sect., Iowa Senate, 1906-1909 and
sect., 1911. Asst. pros. atty. of Polk Co., 1912; pros.
atty., 1915-1916. Apptd. and later el. dist. ct. judge,
1917. Resigned office in 1921 to engage in law practice.
Mbr. of Iowa Senate, 1925-1935. Defeated as Rep. nominee
for Gov. in 1936, but was nom. and el. to that office in
1938, defeating incumbent Gov. Krashel to whom he had lost
by a narrow margin in 1936. Reel. in 1940. As Gov., his
removal of three mbrs. of the Bd. of Control over State Institutions in 1939 because of bad conditions and misbehavior
of certain inmates aroused much controversy. State Bd. of
Assessments was abolished and a new Bd. of Tax Review
created, which also caused controversy. Nom. and el. to
U.S. Senate in 1942, but was defeated for second term in
1948. Retired thereafter to law practice in Des Moines.
Mbr., Masons; Elks; Moose; various professional legal orgs.
Methodist. m. in 1921 to Mildred Elizabeth Zehner, of Des
Moines. Three s.; one d. D. at Des Moines, Sept. 8, 1953.
Bur. in Glendale Cem. there.

HICKENLOOPER, BOURKE BLAKEMORE (1943-1945). b. July
21, 1896 at Blockton, Iowa. s. of Nathan and Margaret A.
(Blakemore) H. Father was of Dutch ancestry. Attd. local
pub. schools and Iowa State Coll. until April, 1917, when
he enrolled in O.T.C. at Ft. Snelling, Minn. Commissioned
as second lieut. and served overseas in 1918 during World
War I. After discharge in 1919, re-enrolled at Iowa State
Coll., from which he was grad. in June, 1919. Received law
degree from the Univ. of Iowa in 1922 and began practice at
Cedar Rapids, Iowa. Mbr. of Iowa legislature, 1934-1937.
Lieut. Gov., 1939-1943. Nom. and el. Gov. as Rep. in 1942.
El. to U.S. Senate in 1944. Continued to serve therein un-
til Jan., 1969, when he retired from politics. As a mbr. of
Senate was co-ch. of Jt. Commt. on Atomic Energy, and as
such was one of major contributors in drafting of the Atomic
Energy Act of 1954 providing for the devel. and use of
atomic energy technical knowledge for peaceful uses. Ch. of
Rep. Senate Policy Commt. in 1962. Delegate to Rep. natl.
conv. in 1968. Hon. degrees from Parsons, Loras and Elmira
Colleges and from Upper Iowa Univ. Mbr., Masons; Amer.
Legion; V.F.W.; I.O.O.F.; Elks; various fraternal and professional legal orgs. m. in 1927 to Verna E. Bensch. One
s.; one d. D. Sept. 4, 1971, at Shelter Island, N.Y.

BLUE, ROBERT DONALD (1945-1949). b. Sept. 24, 1898 at
Eagle Grove, Iowa. s. of Donald and Myrtle Emily (Newell)

B.   Attd. local pub. schools, where he was active in sports
and pub. speaking.   Attd. Capital City Commercial Coll. at
Des Moines, for one year, and Iowa State Coll., 1918-1919.
Enrolled in O.T.C. and served at Ft. Dodge, Iowa in 1919-
1920.   Entered Drake Univ., from which he received a law degree in 1922, graduating with honors.   Began practice of law
at Eagle Grove.   Pros. atty. of Wright Co., 1925-1931.   Also
city atty. of Eagle Grove during part of that time.   Delegate to Rep. natl. conv. in 1932.   Mbr. of Iowa House, 1935-
1943.   Rep. floor leader in House, 1937-1941 and Speaker,
1941-1943.   Nom. and el. Lieut. Gov. as Rep. in 1942 and as
Gov. in 1944.   Reel. Gov. in 1946, but was defeated for re-
nom. for third term in 1948.   During admin., issues related
to reconversion after end of World War II were of major concern, along with housing shortage and ending of price controls.   Sponsored county assessor law; comprehensive devel.
of Mo. Valley Waterways system by Army Corps of Engineers;
soil conservation measures.   Signing of bill banning closed
shop labor contracts caused him to incur hostility of org.
labor.   Instrumental in assembling first Midwestern Govs.'
Conf., of which he was ch. in 1948.   Mbr., Masons (Shriner);
Amer. Legion; Moose; Isak Walton League; various professional legal orgs.   Methodist.   Hon. degrees from Drake Univ.
and Upper Iowa Univ.   m. in 1926 to Cathlene Beale, of Tama,
Iowa.   One s.; one d.

     BEARDSLEY, WILLIAM S.   (1949-1954).   b. May 13, 1901 at
Beacon, Mahaska Co., Iowa.   s. of Wm. and Carrie (Shane) B.
Father was a pharmacist.   Attd. local schools at Birmingham,
Iowa, and Bowen Inst. of Pharm. and Chem., at Brunswick, Mo.
After grad. there in 1922 established pharmacy and drug
store bus. at New Virginia, Iowa.   Mbr. of Iowa Senate,
1933-1941, serving as Rep. floor leader.   Purchased 900-acre
farm near New Virginia in 1938 and engaged in livestock
raising thereafter.   El. to Iowa legislature in 1946.   Disagreed with Gov. Blue on a number of issues, including his
signing of right to work bill opposed by labor unions.   Defeated Gov. Blue for Rep. nom. for Gov. in 1948 primary
election with support from farmer and labor elements, and
was el.   Continued for next two terms as Gov.   As Gov., supported balanced budget; opposed natl. administration's
Brannan plan of subsidies for supporting farm incomes.
Joined with five other Rep. Govs. in 1950 in endorsing declaration of "progressive" Rep. party principles advanced by
Gov. Duff of Pa.   Mbr., Masons; I.O.O.F.; Rotary; Lions.
Methodist.   m. in 1919 to Charlotte E. Manning, of
Birmingham, Iowa.   Three s.; two d.   D. in auto accident,
Nov. 21, 1954, shortly before end of third term.   Bur. in

New Virginia Cem.

ELTHON, LEO (1954-1955). b. June 9, 1898 near Fertile,
Worth Co., Iowa. As young man engaged in teaching rural
schools and also farmed. Later was proprietor of limestone
quarry bus. Mbr. of Iowa Senate, 1933-1953. Nom. and el.
Lieut. Gov. as a Rep. in 1952. Succeeded to office of Gov.
on Nov. 21, 1954, and completed term of Gov. Beardsley, who
died in an auto accident. Resumed office of Lieut. Gov.,
to which he had been reel. in Nov., 1954, and served in that
office during 1955-1957. Mbr. of Iowa Senate in 1960, serving from 1961 to 1965. D. April 16, 1967.

HOEGH, LEO ARTHUR (1955-1957). b. Mar. 30, 1908 in
Audubon Co., Iowa. s. of Wm. and Annie K. (Johnson) H.
Attd. the Univ. of Iowa, receiving an A.B. degree in 1929
and a law degree in 1932. Practiced law at Chariton, Iowa,
1932-1966. Mbr. of Iowa legislature, 1937-1942. City atty.
of Chariton, 1941-1942. Entered U.S. Army in 1942 as first
lieut., and served until 1946. Held rank of lieut. col.
when released. Continued to serve in USAR, attaining rank
of col. in 1959. Ch., Iowa Rep. finance commt., 1948-1950,
and ch., Iowa Rep. state commt., 1950-1953. Mbr., Iowa for
Eisenhower commt., 1951-1952. Atty. Gen. of Iowa, 1953-
1955. Nom. and el. Gov. as a Rep. in 1954, but was defeated as Rep. nominee in 1956 for second term. At end of term
was apptd. by Pres. Eisenhower to Dir. of U.S. Office of
Civilian Defense Mobilization, serving from 1957 to 1961.
Dir., Iowa Fund, Inc., 1961-1966. Dir. and gen. counsel,
Soy-pro, Inc. Moved to Colorado Springs, Colo. in 1966.
Dir. of Bank of Manitou and of other bus. corps. Mbr. of
Legion of Honor and recipient of Croix de guerre and Bronze
Medal. Mbr., Amer. Legion; AMVETS; V.F.W.; Rotary; various
fraternal and professional legal orgs. Methodist. m. in
1936 to Mary Louise Foster. Two d.

LOVELESS, HERSCHEL CELIEL (1957-1961). b. May 5, 1911
at Hedrick, Iowa. s. of David Helm and Ethel (Beaver) L.
Attd. local schools. Employed in railroad constr. and
maintenance work, 1927-1939. Turbine operator for John
Morrell Co., Ottumwa, Iowa, 1939-1943. Foreman of bridge
constr. crews for railroad until 1949. Supt. of streets,
Ottumwa, 1947. Mayor of Ottumwa for two terms, 1949-1953.
Mbr., legislative commt., Iowa League of Municipalities,
1951. Became owner-mgr. of Gen. Mun. Equipment Co., 1953.
Delegate to Dem. natl. convs., 1952, 1956, 1960 and 1964;
ch. of Iowa delegation, 1960. Defeated as Dem. nominee for
Gov. in 1952. Nom. again and el. Gov. as Dem. in 1956 and

reel. in 1958. Mbr., exec. council, Natl. Govs.' Conf. Ch.
of its Continuing Research Commt. on Taxes and of Mo. Basin
Inter-agency Commn., 1959. Ch., Natl. Advisory Commn. on
Agri. of Dem. natl. commt., 1959-1960. Ch., Farmers for
Kennedy and Johnson, 1960. Defeated as Dem. nominee for
U.S. Senate seat in 1960. Mbr., U.S. Renegotiation Bd.,
1961-1969. Vice pres., Chromalloy of Amer. Corp., 1969.
Mbr. of exec. council of Boy Scouts of Amer. and dir. of So.
Iowa Boy Scouts Council. Mbr., Lions; Elks; Eagles; U.R.C.
Methodist. m. in 1922 to Amelia R. Howard, of Ottumwa.
One s.; one d.

ERBE, NORMAN ARTHUR (1961-1963). b. Oct. 25, 1919 at
Boone, Iowa. s. of Otto Louis and Louise Julia (Festner) E.
Grandfather had emigrated from Germany to Mo. in early
1900s, later moving to Iowa. Father was a clergyman. Attd.
pub. schools at Boone. Entered U.S. Army at beginning of
World War II and was a company commdr., 1941-1942. Transferred to Air Force as combat pilot. In 1943-1945 served
on a number of combat missions over Germany. Held rank of
capt. when discharged. Continued to serve in Iowa Natl.
Guard, transferring to Judge Advocate Gen. dept. in 1960.
Received A.B. degree from the Univ. of Iowa in 1946 and a
law degree in 1947. Practiced law at Boone, 1947-1958.
Ch., Boone Co. Rep. commt., 1952-1957. Co. atty., 1952.
Asst. Atty. Gen. of Iowa, 1955-1957, being assigned to Highway Commn. affairs. Atty. Gen. of Iowa, 1957-1961. Nom.
and el. Gov. as Rep. in 1960. Re-nom. in 1962, but was de-
feated in gen. election. During admin., aid to educ. was
increased. After tenure as Gov. served as regional repr.
for U.S. Sect. of Transp., stationed in Seattle, Wash.
Exec. dir., Natl. Paraplegia Found. Ch. of Eastern Boone
Co. Amer. Red Cross, 1949-1950. Recipient of D.S.C. and
U.S. Air Medal with four clusters. Author of Iowa Highway,
Road and Street Laws in 1956 and Iowa Drainage Laws in 1957.
Hon. degree, Parsons Coll. Mbr., Amer. Legion; V.F.W.;
AMVETS; Lions; Lutheran Laymen's League; various fraternal
and professional legal orgs. Lutheran. m. in 1942 to
Jacqueline de Elda Doran, of Boone, Iowa. Three children.

HUGHES, HAROLD EVERETT (1963-1969). b. Feb. 10, 1922
near Ida Grove, Iowa. s. of Louis C. and Etta E. (Kelly) H.
Parents were natives of Ky. Father had been a farmer but
later became a constr. foreman and then a proprietor of
greenhouse and florist bus. Attd. local pub. schools,
where he was an outstanding student, participating in athletics, debate and music. Attd. Univ. of Iowa, 1940-1941.
Worked with Des Moines Parks dept. until drafted into U.S.

Army in 1942. Served as pvt., seeing action in Tunisia,
Sicily and Italy. Released in July, 1945 with med. discharge, having contracted malaria. Army experience led to
heavy indulgence in liquor. Became abstainer in 1952 and
later joined Alcoholics Anonymous, breaking drinking habit.
Took correspondence courses at So. Methodist Univ. for two
years to prepare for ministry, but abandoned this goal while
continuing to serve as lay speaker in Methodist churches.
Employed in various occupations, 1946-1958, eventually becoming field repr. of Iowa Motor Trucking Assoc. and later
an operator of his own trucking bus. Also started an ins.
agency and a real estate enterprise. El. to State Commerce
Commn. as a Dem. in 1958, having recently changed his party
affiliation from Rep. to Dem. Served on various U.S. Interstate Commerce Commn. jt. bds. and as mbr. of commt. on
pub. safety and educ. of Natl. Assoc. of R.R. Utility
Commns., 1959-1962. Defeated as cand. for Dem. nom. for
Gov. in 1960. Nom. and el. Gov. as Dem. in 1962, defeating
incumbent Gov. Erbe in gen. election. Reel. in 1964 and
1966. As Gov., advocated revision of state liquor laws to
make them more enforceable; favored mun. home rule. Delegate to Dem. natl. convs. in 1964 and 1968. Mbr., exec.
commt. of Natl. Govs.' Conf., 1966-1968. Mbr. of Advisory
Council, U.S. Office of Econ. Opportunity, 1966-1968.
Trustee, States Urban Action Center, 1967-1968. Ch. of ad
hoc commt. on selection of pres. nominee, and vice ch.,
spec. Dem. party commt. on party structure and delegate selection, 1969. Mbr., Iowa State Commn. on Alcoholism, 1957-
1961, and of Natl. Commn. on Marihuana and Drug Abuse, 1971.
El. to U.S. Senate as Dem. in 1968 and resigned office of
Gov. shortly before end of third term. Became asst. majority whip in Senate. Did not seek reel. in 1974. Mbr.,
Amer. Legion; Masons (Shriner); K.P. Methodist. Hon. degrees from nine colleges and universities. m. in 1941 to
Eva Mae Mercer. Three d.

    FULTON, ROBERT DAVID (1969). b. May 13, 1929 at
Waterloo, Iowa. s. of Lester Charles and Fern (Ryan) F.
Attd. pub. schools in Waterloo; the State Coll. of Iowa,
Cedar Falls, from which he was grad. in 1952; and the Univ.
of Iowa, from which he received a law degree in 1958.
Served for two years in U.S. Air Force, 1953-1955, holding
rank of corporal at time of discharge. Began law practice
at Waterloo in 1958. Mbr. of Iowa House, 1959-1961 and of
Iowa Senate, 1963-1965. El. Lieut. Gov. as Dem. in 1964 and
was reel. in 1966. Succeeded to office of Gov. early in
Jan., 1969 and completed last two weeks of Gov. Hughes'
term after Hughes resigned to enter U.S. Senate. Delegate

to Dem. natl. conv. and mbr. of Dem. natl. commt., 1968.
Defeated as Dem. nominee for Gov. in 1970. Mbr., Black
Hawk Co. Legal Aid Soc., 1959-1961; Amer. Legion; AMVETS;
professional legal and bus. orgs. m. in 1955 to Rachel
Breault. Two s.; two d.

RAY, ROBERT D. (1969-----). b. Sept. 26, 1928 at Des
Moines, Iowa. s. of Clark A. and Mildred (Dolph) R. Attd.
local pub. schools and Drake Univ., from which he received
a degree in bus. admin. in 1952 and in law in 1954. Served
in U.S. Army, 1946-1948. Began practice of law in Des
Moines. Ch. of Iowa Rep. commt., 1963; of Midwest Rep.
Chairmen, 1965; and of Natl. State Rep. Chairmen, 1967.
Nom. and el. Gov. as Rep. in 1968. Continued in office in
1970, 1972, 1974 and 1978, becoming the first Iowa Gov. to
be el. to five consecutive terms. Mbr. of exec. commt. of
Natl. Govs.' Conf., 1969. Prominent in natl. Rep. party
affairs, being strongly considered for the Rep. nom. for
Vice Pres. of U.S. in 1976. Recipient of Natl. Service
Award, Future Farmers of Amer., 1970. State ch., March of
Dimes; mbr., bd. of dir., Family Service. Hon. degrees
from Central (Iowa) and Iowa Wesleyan Colleges. Distinguished Alumni Award, Drake Univ. Mbr., legal professional
orgs. Active in Christian (Disciples) church. m. in 1951
to Billie Lee Hornberger. Three d.

ROBINSON, CHARLES LAWRENCE (1861-1863). b. July 18, 1818 at Hardwick, Mass. s. of Jonathan and Hulda (Woodward) R. Attd. local schools and Hadley Acad. Enrolled at Amherst Coll., but withdrew before grad. because of poor health and eye trouble. Studied med. at Woodstock, Vt. and Fitchburg, Mass., grad. with honors. Practiced med. at Belchertown, Springfield, and Fitchburg, Mass. As a physician joined overland train bound for Calif. in 1849, but decided to remain in Lawrence, Kans., where he had stopped for rest while on journey. Later went on to Sacramento, Calif., where he followed various occupations for two years. Became involved in struggles between settlers and land speculators there, and was imprisoned for a time on a prison ship. While confined, was el. to Calif. legislature where he championed cause of settlers and anti-slavery, and supported John C. Fremont for seat in U.S. Senate. Returned to Fitchburg, Mass. in 1852, where he became ed. of Fitchburg News. When Kans. and Nebr. were organized as territories in 1854, returned to Lawrence, Kans., as agent of New England Aid Soc. that was seeking to make Kans. Terr. a free State. Became a leader of Kans. "Free State" volunteers and took part in so-called "Wakarusa War". Served as delegate to constl. conv. at Topeka in 1856 which sought admission of Kans. as a free State, and was el. Gov. on a provisional basis under the Topeka const. Was arrested by Terr. Govt. authorities, indicted and imprisoned for four months during 1856. Eventually was acquitted of charges of treason and usurpation. El. Gov. on a provisional basis under the Wyandotte const. in 1859 and after admission of Kans. as a State, assumed office in Feb., 1861. A year later, along with two other state officials, was impeached on charges of mishandling state funds from a bond issue, but was acquitted in trial before Senate. Mbr. of Kans. House in 1863 and of the Kans. Senate in 1864. Acquired farm near Lawrence where he spent later years. Defeated in 1882 as Greenback-Labor party cand. for Gov. and defeated again in 1890 as cand. of Resub.-Dem. (anti-prohibition) party. Defeated for U.S. Senate in 1886. Supt. of Haskell Inst., a school for Indians at Lawrence, 1887-1889. Regent of Univ. of Kans. for twelve years. Received hon. degree from it and bequeathed lands to it. Author of The Kansas Conflict in 1892. m. in 1843 to Sarah Adams, of Mass. Two children, both of whom died in infancy. After first wife's death, m. in 1851 to Sarah Tappan Doolittle Lawrence, an author and literary figure. D. at Lawrence, Aug. 17, 1894.

CARNEY, THOMAS (1863-1865). b. Aug. 20, 1827 in Delaware Co., Ohio. s. of James Carney, a farmer. Father

died when son was four years old. Spent early youth on the
family farm and worked as a clerk in a gen. store at
Columbus. In 1852 went to Cincinnati, where he subsequently
became a partner in a merc. bus. Left bus. in 1857 because
of poor health. Acquired a farm in Ill., but soon sold it
and went to Leavenworth, Kans., where he engaged in a wholesale dry goods bus. Helped org. and became pres. of First
Natl. Bank of Leavenworth in 1863. Bus. ventures proved
profitable and he became wealthy. Took active interest in
Kans. politics immediately after arrival in Kans. Nom. and
el. Gov. as Rep. in 1862. During admin., condition of
State's finances was a critical problem because of disturbances arising from guerilla warfare. Took steps to establish State's credit on its bond issues, employing his own
means in part to do so. Made contributions out of his own
funds to assist victims of Quantrill's raid on Lawrence in
1863, and gave $5,000 to assist in getting the Univ. of
Kans. under way at Lawrence. Legislation was passed providing for establishment of Kans. State Agri. Coll. (now Kans.
State Univ.) at Manhattan during admin. El. to U.S. Senate
seat in Feb., 1864 for a term beginning in Mar., 1865, but
it was ultimately concluded that the election was pre-mature,
and he made no effort to take seat. Helped Union cause by
raising troops during Civil War. Was not a cand. for reel.
in 1864. Resumed bus. activities in Leavenworth after term
as Gov. ended. m. in 1851 to Rebecca Ann Canady, of Kenton,
Ohio. Four s. D. July 28, 1889.

CRAWFORD, SAMUEL JOHNSON (1865-1868). b. April 10,
1835 near Bedford, in Lawrence Co., Ind. s. of Wm. and
Jane (Morrow) C. Father was a farmer. Both father and
mother were natives of N.C. who had left there in 1815 because of dislike of slavery. Attd. rural schools and
Bedford Acad. Studied law, and was admitted to bar in 1851.
In 1857 attd. law school at Cincinnati Coll., grad. in 1858.
Moved to Garnett, Kans. in 1859 and began law practice
there. Mbr. of first Kans. legislature, which met in 1861.
Became cand. for Gov. in that year and was el. without opposition, but the election was voided by the Kans. Supreme Ct.
which held that the next election of Gov. should not occur
until 1862 because of delay in getting new govt. established
under the 1859 const. El. to Kans. legislature in 1862, but
resigned seat and raised a volunteer company, of which he
became capt. Participated on Union side in a number of border skirmishes in Mo. and Kans. Continued in mil. service
until near the end of Civil War, rising to rank of brig.
gen. Resigned commn. after having been nom. and el. Gov. in
1864 as a Rep. Reel. in 1866. Resigned office of Gov. in

1868 shortly before end of term after having been defeated
in effort to win seat in U.S. House. Assumed command of a
regiment of troops engaged in warfare in western Kans.
against Indians for several months. Resumed farming and
practice of law at Emporia, Kans. in 1869, later moving to
Topeka. Defeated as cand. for U.S. Senate seat in 1871.
Supported the Lib. Rep.-Dem. pres. campaign effort in 1872.
Defeated as Greenback-Dem. cand. for U.S. House in 1876 and
also in 1878. Became repr. in Washington, D.C. of Kans.
interests in effort to secure return of pub. lands from U.S.
and railroads to the State. Served in that capacity from
1877 to 1891, and was successful in obtaining restoration to
State of lands valued at $1,200,000. Supported Bryan for
Pres. of U.S. in 1900 election, being opposed to U.S. expan-
sionist policies following Spanish-Amer. War. Subsequently
returned to Rep. party affiliation. Acquired farm near
Baxter Springs, Kans. where he resided during later years.
Author of Kansas in the Sixties in 1911. m. in 1866 to
Isabel M. Chase. One s.; one d., Florence, who became the
wife of Gov. and Sen. Arthur Capper of Kans. (q.v.). D.
Oct. 21, 1913 at Topeka, Kans.

GREEN, NEHEMIAH (1868-1869). b. Mar. 8, 1837 at
Grassy Point, in Hardin Co., Ohio. With two older brothers
in 1855 went to Palmyra (now Baldwin), Kans., where he became an active participant in the Free State movement. Returned to Ohio in 1856 to enter Ohio Wesleyan Univ., from
which he was grad. In 1860 became a minister in the
Methodist church. Enlisted as a lieut. in an Ohio volunteer
regiment in 1862. Resigned commn. after several months for
reasons of health, but re-enlisted later, serving as a sgt.
until mustered out in 1864. Returned to Kans. and became
pastor of a Methodist church at Manhattan, Kans. In 1866
was el. Lieut. Gov. as a Rep. Succeeded to office of Gov.
in Nov., 1868 when Gov. Crawford resigned, and completed
last two months of Crawford's term. Mbr. of Bd. of Regents
of Kans. Agri. Coll. (now Kansas State Univ.), 1873-1874.
Mbr. of Kans. House in 1881-1882, serving as Speaker pro tem.
D. Jan. 12, 1890, at Manhattan, Kans.

HARVEY, JAMES MADISON (1869-1873). b. Sept. 21, 1833
near Salt Sulphur Springs in Monroe Co., Va. (now W. Va.).
s. of Thomas and Margaret (Walker) H. Family later moved to
Ind., then to Ill., where he attd. pub. schools. Studied
surveying and engaged in surveying and engr. work in Iowa
for several years. In 1859 moved to Riley Co., Kans., where
he acquired a farm. Supported Union cause, and on outbreak
of Civil War enlisted in a volunteer company, becoming its

KANSAS 319

capt. Was in U.S. mil. service until 1864. El. to Kans.
House in 1864 and in 1866 to Kans. Senate. Nom. and el.
Gov. as Rep. in 1868. Reel. in 1870. During admin., the
found. was laid for a pub. school system in the State.
Bldg. of the Union Pacific R.R. across the State resulted in
rapid expansion of population and indus., including farming.
Kans. State Bd. of Agri. was established to foster farming.
El. to fill a vacancy in U.S. Senate seat in 1874, serving
until March, 1877. Engaged thereafter in govt. surveying
work in N.M., Utah, Nev. and Okla. Returned later to farming in Geary Co., Kans. Resided at Norfolk, Va. for several
years because of poor health. m. in 1854 to Charlotte R.
Cutter, of Adams Co., Ill. Six children. D. April 15, 1894
at home near Junction City, Kans. Bur. in Highland Cem.
there.

OSBORN, THOMAS ANDREW (1873-1877). b. Oct. 26, 1836 at
Meadville, Pa. s. of Carpenter and Elizabeth (Morris) O.
Attd. local pub. schools and Allegheny Coll., at Meadville.
Worked as apprentice printer while attending college. Began study of law in Meadville in 1856. In 1857 moved to
Pontiac, Mich., where he was admitted to bar. Later that
year moved to Lawrence, Kans., where he was employed in
printing dept. of a newspaper, the Herald of Freedom. In
1858 moved to Elwood, Kans., where he practiced law. Affiliated with Rep. party and supported efforts to obtain admission of Kans. to statehood as a free State. El. to Kans.
Senate in 1859, and though he was the youngest mbr. of that
body, was chosen Pres. pro tem in 1862. El. Lieut. Gov.
later that year. In 1864 was apptd. U.S. marshal for Kans.
by Pres. Lincoln. Served in that capacity until 1867, when
he was removed because of opposition to Pres. Johnson's
policies. Practiced law in Leavenworth, Kans. El. Gov. as
Rep. in 1872 and was reel. in 1874. During admin., legislation was passed prohibiting lotteries; creating a State Bd.
of Educ.; establishing a State Hosp. for the Insane; and
providing for biennial rather than annual sessions of the
legislature. Assisted in raising funds for the relief of
farmers ruined by grasshopper plague in 1874-1875. Unsuccessful as cand. for U.S. Senate in 1877. At end of second
term was apptd. Minister to Chile by Pres. Hayes. Served in
that office until 1881, when he was transferred to U.S.
mission in Brazil. Presided at conf. in 1880 that resolved
war between Chile, Bolivia and Peru. Returned to Topeka,
Kans. in 1886. Became involved as mbr. of bds. of dir. of
several railroad companies, including the A.T. and S.F.R.R.
El. to Kans. Senate in 1888. Recipient of Grand Cross of
Order of the Rose from govt. of Brazil. m. in 1870 to

Julia Delahay. One s. D. at Meadville, Pa., Feb. 4, 1898.

ANTHONY, GEORGE TOBEY (1877-1879). b. June 9, 1824 at
Mayfield, N.Y. s. of Benj. and Anna (Knox) A. Parents were
Quakers. Attd. local schools, working on farm during summers. Served apprenticeship for tin and coppersmith trade
at Union Springs, N.Y. and engaged in that occupation for
five years. Moved to Medina, N.Y. in 1850 where he engaged
in hardware and tinning and farm implement bus. Later moved
to N.Y. City, where he was a commn. salesman. In 1862 assisted in raising troops for Union Army, and was commissioned as capt. Served in Washington, D.C. and Va. theater of
the Civil War, rising to rank of major gen. In Nov., 1865,
moved to Leavenworth, Kans., where he became ed. of a newspaper, the Daily Bulletin and later, the Daily Conservative.
Later became owner and publ. of the Kansas Farmer. Apptd.
asst. to U.S. revenue collector in Kans. and later, head of
the Kans. dist. office. Served as pres. of Kans. Bd. of
Agri. for three years. Also was pres. of Kans. Bd. of Mgrs.
for U.S. Centennial observance at Philadelphia in 1876.
Nom. and el. Gov. as Rep. in 1876. During admin., a fisheries commn. was established, and the State normal school
system was reorg. Was the first Kans. Gov. to deliver
messages to the legislature in person. After term as Gov.
was employed for a number of years by the A.T. and S.F.R.R.
Co. in constr. of line through N.M. Mbr. of Kans. House in
1885. El. to Kans. Bd. of R.R. Commnrs. in 1889, serving
until 1893. Nom. for U.S. House in 1892 but was defeated
in gen. election. Apptd. Kans. Supt. of Ins. in 1895. m.
in 1852 to Rosa Lyon, of Medina, N.Y. One s. D. Aug. 5,
1896, at Topeka.

St. JOHN, JOHN PIERCE (1879-1883). b. Feb. 25, 1833
at Brookville, Ind. S. of Samuel and Sophia (Snell?) St. J.
Family was of Huguenot ancestry. Family moved to Olney,
Ill. when he was 15 years of age. Worked as youth on
father's farm and as a store clerk. Self-educ. for the most
part. In 1853 at age 20 crossed plains by wagon train to
Calif. Worked at various occupations, including mining,
while there. Also saw service in Indian wars in Calif. and
Ore., and was twice wounded. Travelled to So. Amer.,
Mexico, Cent. Amer., and Hawaii. Studied law, and in 1859
moved to Charleston, Ill., where he finished law study and
was admitted to bar in 1861. Was indicted and tried under
an old Ill. law on charge of harboring a colored person.
Affiliated with Rep. party in Ill. when it was formed in
1850s. Helped raise a volunteer company for Union service
in Civil War, and became its capt. Participated in

engagements in Ill., Va., and in campaigns in the
Mississippi Valley. Was lieut. col. when discharged at the
end of the war. Returned to law practice at Charleston.
Later moved to Independence, Mo., and in 1869 to Olathe,
Kans. Acquired wide reputation as lawyer and able political
speaker. Mbr. of Kans. Senate, 1873-1874. Nom. and el.
Gov. as Rep. in 1878 and was reel. in 1880. Nom. for third
term in 1882, but lost in the gen. election. As Gov.,
successfully advocated submission of a prohibition amdt. to
the voters, which they approved; favored providing assistance to Negro immigrants who had come to Kans. in considerable numbers. Accepted nom. of Proh. party for Pres. of
U.S. in 1884. Ticket received only scattered popular support in ensuing election. Advocated free trade; U.S. govtl.
regulation of railways; free coinage of silver; direct
election of Pres. and U.S. Senators; and women's suffrage.
In 1900 pres. election supported Wm. J. Bryan, the Dem.
party's cand. Made speaking tour of Kans. in 1912 as advocate of women's suffrage, and in 1914 toured U.S. as a
speaker for prohibition movement. Delivered some 4,500
speeches for prohibition during his lifetime. Escaped
assassination attempts on two occasions. m. in 1860 to
Susan J. Parker, of Charleston, Ill. D. Aug. 31, 1916, at
Olathe, Kans.

GLICK, GEORGE WASHINGTON (1883-1885). b. July 4, 1827
at Greencastle, Ohio. s. of Isaac and Mary V. (Sanders) G.
Descendant of German immigrant who came to Pa. in 1754.
Father, a farmer, was active in Ohio politics. Reared on
farm. Attd. school at Sandusky, Ohio, and Central Coll.,
in Ohio, for a time. Enlisted in Ohio regiment as volunteer during war with Mexico, but saw no combat service.
Studied law and was admitted to bar in 1850. Established
practice at Fremont, Ohio. Apptd. judge advocate gen. of
an Ohio guard div. by Gov. Chase in 1858. Nom. for a seat
in U.S. House in 1858, but declined to run. Lost contest
for the Ohio Senate in that year. Moved to Atchison, Kans.
in 1859, where he became mbr. of a law firm. Mbr. of Kans.
legislature, 1862-1868. In 1864 enlisted in a Kans. volunteer regiment, and participated in minor engagements on
Mo.-Kans. border during Civil War. From 1867 to 1874 was
an atty. for the Un. Pac. R.R. Nominee of Dem. party for
Gov. in 1868, but was defeated in gen. election. Retired
from law practice in 1874 and engaged in farming and livestock raising in Atchison Co. until 1903, becoming well-
known as breeder of Shorthorn cattle. Mbr. of Kans. Senate
in 1872 and of Kans. House in 1874, 1876 and 1882, serving
as Speaker pro tem in 1877 although the body was controlled

by the opposition party. Nom. and el. Gov. as Dem. in 1882,
defeating incumbent Gov. St. John and becoming the first
Dem. to hold that office. During admin., a State R.R.
Commn. was established, but the legislature failed to carry
out his recommendation for modification of prohibition law.
Nom. for succeeding term but was defeated in gen. election.
Apptd. U.S. pension agent for Kans. by Pres. Cleveland in
1885 and again in 1893. Mbr. of Kans. Bd. of Agri. for 32
years and was U.S. postmaster at Atchison for 12 years.
Delegate to Dem. natl. convs. in 1856, 1868, 1884 and 1892.
Author of numerous articles on agri. topics. Commr. for
Kans. at Chicago Expo. in 1892-1893 and at St. Louis Expo.
in 1903-1904. Mbr., Masons (K.T.); Kans. Historical Soc.
m. in 1857 to Elizabeth Ryder, of Massillon, Ohio. Two
children. D. April 13, 1911.

MARTIN, JOHN ALEXANDER (1885-1889). b. Mar. 10, 1839
at Brownsville, Pa. s. of James and Jane Montgomery
(Crawford) M. Father was a native of Md. and mother, of Pa.
Family was of Scotch-Irish descent. At age 15 was apprenticed as a printer. In 1857 moved to Atchison, Kans.,
where he acquired and published a newspaper, the Squatter
Sovereign, which later became the Freedom's Champion. Continued to be its publ. until his death. Advocate of statehood for Kans. as a free State. Became active in Rep. politics. Ch. of Atchison Co. Rep. commt. for 25 years. Sect.
of Wyandotte constl. conv. in 1859. El. to first Kans. Senate that year before having attained the age of 21. Delegate to Rep. natl. conv. in 1860. Upon outbreak of Civil
War helped to form a volunteer infantry regiment for the
Union cause. Commissioned as lieut. col., and saw service
in 1861 on Mo.-Kans. border. Apptd. provost marshal at
Leavenworth in 1862. Served with Army of the Cumberland in
Ky., Tenn. and Ga. Released from mil. service in 1864.
Mayor of Atchison in 1865. Delegate to Rep. natl. convs.
in 1868, 1872 and 1880. Mbr. of Rep. natl. commt., 1868-
1884, serving as its sect., 1880-1884. U.S. postmaster at
Atchison for 12 years. Mbr. and vice pres. of U.S. Centen-
nial Commn. Nom. and el. Gov. as Rep. in 1884, defeating
incumbent Gov. Glick. Reel. in 1886. Founded the Kansas
Magazine; mbr. and pres. of Kans. Historical Soc.; pres.,
Kans. State Editors and Publishers Assoc. in 1878. Mbr. of
Bd. of Mgrs., Natl. Soldiers Home, 1882, 1886. Commdr.-in-
chief, Kans. G.A.R. m. in 1871 to Ida Challis, of Atchison,
Kans. Eight children. D. Oct. 2, 1889, at Atchison.

HUMPHREY, LYMAN UNDERWOOD (1889-1893). b. July 25,
1844 at New Baltimore, Ohio. Father, who was of English

descent, died when son was 8 years old. At beginning of the
Civil War enlisted in an Ohio regiment at age 17. Became
lieut. and adjt. of regiment, commanding it for a year before he reached the age of 21. Saw service in major campaigns in Western theater of Civil War and participated in
Sherman's capture of Atlanta and subsequent march to
Savannah. Was wounded on two occasions. Rose to rank of
lieut. After release from mil. service attd. Mt. Union
Coll., in Ohio, and the Univ. of Mich., 1866-1867. Studied
law and was admitted to Ohio bar in 1868. Resided for a
short time in Shelby Co., Mo., where he assisted in editing
a Rep. newspaper. Moved to Independence, Kans. in 1871,
where he acquired an interest in a leading newspaper, the
Tribune. Later sold interest and devoted attention to law
practice and farm loan bus. Defeated as cand. for Kans.
House in 1871, but won seat therein in 1876. El. to fill
vacancy in office of Lieut. Gov. in 1877, continuing in that
office by reel. until 1881. El. to Kans. Senate in 1884.
Nom. and el. Gov. as Rep. in 1888 and was reel. in 1890, defeating the Farmers Alliance-Pop. party cand. and former
Gov. Robinson, running as an Indep. cand. with the backing
of a Dem. faction. Defeated for U.S. House seat in 1892.
Returned to law practice after tenure as Gov. Was a liberal
contributor to churches and benevolent institutions. m. in
1872 to Amanda Leonard. D. at Independence, Kans., Sept.
12, 1915.

LEWELLING, LORENZO DOW (1893-1895). b. Dec. 21, 1846
at Salem, Iowa. s. of Wm. and Serena (Wilson) L. Father
was a Quaker minister. Parents died when son was still
quite young. Attd. local schools and worked as a laborer on
neighboring farms until age 16. Employed for a time by the
C.B. and Q. R.R. in constr. work. Drove cattle for Union
Army quartermaster supply unit in Tenn., and also worked as
mbr. of non-combat units in bridge constr. work during the
Civil War. At end of the war became a teacher in a Negro
school at Mexico, Mo. maintained by the Freedman's Aid Soc.,
encountering much local hostility. Grad. from Eastman Bus.
Coll. at Poughkeepsie, N.Y. Later attd. Whittier Coll., a
Quaker school, in Salem, Iowa, and also Knox Coll., in Ill.
Was a teacher for several years in Iowa State Reform School.
In 1870 founded a newspaper, the Salem Register. In 1872
became supervisor of girls dept. of Iowa State Reform
School, continuing in that capacity for 15 years. Became
pres. of governing bd. of Iowa State Normal. Acquired wide
reputation as a penologist. Founded a newspaper, the
Capital, at Des Moines in 1880, in which he identified him-
self with a number of reform issues. Defeated as Liberal

party cand. for Sect. of State. Disposed of newspaper after
two years and returned to reform school work. Moved to
Wichita, Kans. in 1887, where he engaged in bus. and also
was active as a pub. speaker and lecturer, advocating political reform and liberal causes. Affiliated with Pop. party.
Nom. as Pop. and Dem. cand. for Gov. in 1892 and was el.
Re-nom. for the office by that combination in 1894, but lost
in the gen. election, partly because many Dem. voters refused to go along with the women's suffrage plank in the
Pop. party's platform. As Gov., espoused humanitarian programs to aid socially and economically disadvantaged. A
circular letter he issued while Gov. to the various police
authorities in the State, urging them to deal considerately
with railroad tramps who, he asserted, were guilty of no
crime but "poverty", aroused much attention and comment.
After tenure as Gov. established a creamery bus. at Wichita,
Kans. Mbr. of Kans. R.R. Commn., 1897-1899, and was el. to
Kans. Senate in 1896. m. in 1870 to Angie Cook, an Iowa
school teacher, who died in 1885. Three d. m. in 1887 to
Ida Bishop. One d. D. at Arkansas City, Kans., Sept. 3,
1900, while en route to his home in Wichita.

MORRILL, EDMUND NEEDHAM (1895-1897). b. Feb. 12, 1834
at Westbrook, Me. s. of Rufus and Mary (Webb) M. Father,
a furrier, was related to a family prominent in Me. politics
from which two Govs. of Me. had come. Attd. local pub.
schools and Westbrook Acad., grad. in 1855. Learned trade
of tanner and furrier in father's shop. Served as supt. of
schools at Westbrook for two years. In 1857 moved to
Hiawatha, Brown Co., Kans., where he started a sawmill bus.
El. to Kans. Terr. legislature in 1857 and on a provisional
basis to the State legislature under the Lecompton const.
Enlisted in Kans. cavalry regiment as pvt. in 1861 following
outbreak of Civil War. Engaged in commissary work for Union
forces during the course of the war, holding rank of major
when discharged in 1865. Returned to Hiawatha, and was el.
dist. ct. clerk in 1866, serving until 1870. Also was
Brown Co. clerk, 1867-1873. El. to Kans. Senate in 1872
and 1876, serving as Pres. pro tem in latter term. El. to
U.S. House in 1882 and continued in that office until 1891.
Was not a cand. for reel. in 1890. As mbr. of Cong., sponsored legislation providing for pensions for Civil War veterans. Mgr. of Natl. Home for Disabled Veterans in 1890,
and mgr. of Kans. Soldiers Home at Leavenworth. In 1871
founded a bank at Hiawatha. Became its pres. in 1887 and
continued in that capacity until death. Also was pres. of
First Natl. Bank of Leavenworth for seven years. Nom. and
el. Gov. as Rep. in 1894, defeating incumbent Gov. Lewelling

Advocated protection for farmers by govt. measures. Nom.
for succeeding term, but lost in gen. election to cand.
backed by the Dem. and Pop. parties. Founded free pub. library at Hiawatha in 1882, and the Hiawatha Acad. in 1889.
m. first in 1862 to Elizabeth A. Bretton, of Livermore, Me.
After her death in 1866, m. in 1869 to Caroline J. Nash, of
Boston, Mass. Three children. D. Mar. 14, 1909, at
San Antonio, Texas. Bur. in Mount Hope Cem. in Hiawatha.

LEEDY, JOHN WHITNAH (1897-1899). b. Mar. 8, 1849 in
Richland Co., Ohio. Family were mbrs. of Dunkard sect.
Father died soon after son was born. Worked on farm while
attending local schools in winters. In 1864, at age 15,
sought to enlist in Union Army, but was not accepted on
account of age. Remained with a Union Army company nevertheless until end of Civil War. In 1865 went to Pierceton,
Ind., where he clerked in a store for a time. Health failed
and in 1868 he moved to Carlinville, Ill., where he worked
as a farm laborer for several years. Saved money and eventually purchased a farm. In 1880 sold his farm and moved
to LeRoy, Kans., where he purchased land. Was successful in
farming for a time, but eventually failed and lost farm to
creditors. Studied law. Originally affiliated with Rep.
party, he later joined the Pop. party, and in 1892 was el.
to Kans. Senate as a Pop. Served there from 1893 to 1897.
Championed adoption of Australian ballot system; revision of
banking laws; and closer regulation of railroads and other
corps. Nom. and el. Gov. as a Pop. in 1896, having also
the endorsement of the Dem. party, and defeating incumbent
Gov. Morrill. As Gov., sponsored banking law reforms; creation of a State Grain Commn.; establishment of a school
text-book commn.; and closer regulation of ins. bus. Nom.
for succeeding term, but was defeated in gen. election. In
1901 went to Alaska Terr. after discovery of gold there.
Settled in Valdez, Alas., and prospered in a mining venture,
law practice, and bus., 1901-1909. Also served as city
atty. and mayor of Valdez. Later moved to Edmonton,
Alberta, where he continued to reside until death. Became
active in a farmers' org. there, and was an unsuccessful
cand. for a seat in Canadian Parliament. m. in 1875 to
Sarah Boyd, of Fredericktown, Ohio. One s.; two d. D. Mar.
24, 1935, at Edmonton.

STANLEY, WILLIAM EUGENE (1899-1903). b. Dec. 28, 1844
in Hardin Co., Ohio. s. of Almon Fleming and Angelina
(Sapp) S. Father was a physician and was a descendant of
an English colonist who emigrated to Mass. in 1634 and became one of the founders of Hartford, Conn. Attd. country

schools in Hardin Co.   Studied law at Kenton, Ohio.   Moved
to Jefferson Co., Kans., where he was admitted to bar in
1870.   Co. atty. of Jefferson Co., 1871-1872.   In 1872 moved
to Wichita, Kans., continuing in law practice there.   Co.
atty. for Sedgwick Co., 1874-1880.   Became active as leader
in Rep. party there, and was el. to Kans. House in 1880s.
Was offered apptmt. to fill vacancy on Kans. Supreme Ct. by
Gov. Morrill, but declined.   Nom. and el. Gov. as Rep. in
1898, defeating incumbent Gov. Leedy in gen. election.   Reel
in 1900.   Favored retention of gold standard.   Defeated as
cand. for U.S. Senate seat in 1901.   Mbr. of U.S. (Dawes)
Commn. to Five Civilized (Indian) Tribes, 1903-1904.   Mbr.,
Masons; Kans. Historical Soc., serving as dir. of latter
org., 1899-1902.   m. in 1876 to Emma Lenora Hills, of
Wichita.   Four children.   D. at Wichita, Oct. 13, 1910.

BAILEY, WILLIS JOSHUA (1903-1905).   b. Oct. 12, 1854
near Mount Carroll, Ill.   Attd. Mount Carroll pub. schools
and the Univ. of Ill., from which he was grad. in 1879.   In
that year moved to Nemaha Co., Kans.   Engaged in farming and
stock-raising.   Also engaged in banking, founding the town
of Baileyville, Kans.   El. to Kans. legislature in 1888,
but was defeated for second term in 1890.   El. to Kans. Bd.
of Agri. in 1894, serving from 1895 to 1899.   Pres. of Rep.
State League, 1893.   El. to U.S. House as Congressman-at-
large in 1898.   Was not a cand. for second term in 1900.
Nom. and el. Gov. as Rep. in 1902.   Withdrew as cand. for
re-nom. for Gov. in 1904 in favor of Edward Hoch, who was
also seeking the nom., on ground he did not wish to endanger
party's success by an intra-party contest.   In 1907 moved to
Atchison, Kans., where he continued in banking bus.   Mbr.,
bd. of dir. of Fed. Reserve Bank of Kansas City, beginning
in 1914, and gov. of that bank, 1922-1932.   Hon. degree from
the Univ. of Ill.   m. in 1903 to Mrs. Ida B. Wood.   D. May
19, 1932 at Mission Hills, Kans.   Bur. in Mt. Vernon Cem.,
at Atchison.

HOCH, EDWARD WALLIS (1905-1909).   b. Mar. 17, 1849 at
Danville, Ky.   s. of Edward C. and Elizabeth (Stout) H.
Attd. pub. schools at Danville and also attd. Centre Coll.
there, but was not a grad.   Learned printer's trade.   In
1872 moved to Florence, Kans., and in 1874 purchased the
Marion, Kans. Record, of which he was ed. and pub. until el.
Gov. Mbr. of Kans. legislature, 1889 and also in 1893,
when he served as House Speaker pro tem.   Sought Rep. nom.
for Gov. in 1904 on an "anti-machine" reform platform, and
received nom. when Gov. Bailey, the incumbent Rep. Gov.,
withdrew to avoid an intra-party conflict.   Was el. and was

reel. in 1906.   During admin., the oil refining indus. was
expanded in the State; reforms effected in admin. of state
institutions; further legislation regulating railroad indus.
enacted; a pure food law adopted; and a state printing plant
established.   Mbr. of State Bd. of Admin., 1913-1919.
Methodist.   m. in 1876 to Sarah Louisa Dickerson.   D. June
2, 1925.

STUBBS, WALTER ROSCOE (1909-1913).   b. Nov. 7, 1858 at
Richmond, Ind.   s. of John T. and Esther (Bailey) S.   Parents were of Quaker faith.   In 1869 family moved to Kans.,
where father engaged in farming near Hepler, Kans.   Attd.
local schools and the Univ. of Kans.   Began work as constr.
contractor for railroads, expanding operations by degrees
into a large enterprise.   Built C.R.I. and Pac. R.R. line
from St. Louis to Kansas City, Mo.   Acquired cattle ranches
in Kans., Texas, N.M. and Colo.   Became active in Rep. politics at age 45.   Mbr., Kans. legislature, 1903-1909.   Ch. of
Rep. state commt., 1904-1908.   Successfully backed Edward
Hoch in 1904 for Rep. nom. for Gov. against incumbent Gov.
Bailey.   Nom. and el. Gov. as Rep. in 1908 and was reel. in
1910.   As Gov., advocated progressive measures.   Sought reforms in state admin., including abolition of partisan
spoils system and adoption of direct primary law.   Enforced
prohibition laws vigorously.   Was one of seven Rep. Govs.
whose "round robin" letter urging Theodore Roosevelt to seek
Rep. nom. for Pres. of U.S. in 1912 was influential in inducing Roosevelt to enter the contest.   Nom. as Rep. cand.
for U.S. Senate in 1912, but was defeated in gen. election.
Mbr. of U.S. Livestock Indus. Commn. during World War I.
Was unsuccessful in attempts to win Rep. nom. for Gov. in
1922 and 1924.   Mbr., Masons; Kans. State Historical Soc.
Friends (Quaker) church.   m. in 1886 to Stella Hostettler.
D. March 25, 1929, at Topeka, Kans.

HODGES, GEORGE HARTSHORN (1913-1915).   b. Feb. 6, 1866
at Orion, Richland Co., Wisc.   s. of Wm. W. and Lydia A.
(Hartshorn) H.   Father was a school teacher, who died soon
after son's birth.   Family moved to Johnson Co., Kans. in
1869.   Attd. local schools.   At age 20 began work in lumber
yard in Olathe, Kans., soon rising to position of asst. mgr.
In 1889 established lumber bus. for himself, later becoming
partner with brother.   Extended bus. interests into banking
and ownership of a newspaper, the Johnson County Standard.
Mbr. of Olathe city council for a number of years.   El. to
Kans. Senate in 1904 and again in 1908.   Championed progressive measures as mbr. of Senate, including closer regulation of pub. utilities and establishment of hard roads

system.   Dem. nominee for Gov. in 1910, but lost in gen.
election.   Nom. again in 1912 and was el., defeating his
Rep. opponent by only 29 votes.   As Gov., sponsored a number of reform measures, including improved method of selec-
ting judges and placing educl. institutions under non-
political commn.   Favored complete overhaul of legislature,
including adoption of unicameral system.   Favored commn.
system of city govt., on which he became an authority.   Nom.
for second term, but lost to same Rep. opponent, Arthur
Capper, whom he had narrowly defeated in 1912.   Served as
civilian on staff of Gen. Leonard Wood during World War I.
Engaged in Belgian food relief program after the end of the
war.   Also engaged in lecturing and writing.   Mbr., Masons,
(K.T.); K.P.; I.O.O.F.   Disciples (Christian) church.   Active in Red Cross work.   Received decoration from King Albert,
of Belgium.   m. in 1899 to Ora May Murray.   One d.; one s.
D. Oct. 7, 1947.

CAPPER, ARTHUR (1915-1919).   b. July 14, 1865 at
Garnett, Kans.   s. of Herbert and Isabella (McGrew) C.
Father, who was a mbr. of the Quaker community, had emigrated to Amer. from England.   Attd. local schools and learned
printer's trade.   At age 19 became a typesetter for the
Topeka Daily Capital.   Later worked as a reporter, as a
local correspondent for the New York Tribune, and as city
ed. and Washington correspondent for the Daily Capital.   In
1893 he bought the North Topeka Mail and later added other
publications to form a chain of eleven newspapers and maga-
zines by 1930.   Two of his publications, Capper's Farmer
and Capper's Weekly, achieved a wide circulation throughout
the Midwest.   Also acquired several radio stations from
1920 onward.   Dir. of Farmers Natl. Bank of Topeka.   Delegate to Rep. natl. convs. in 1908 and 1912.   Nom. as Rep.
cand. for Gov. in 1912 but was defeated by very narrow margin in the gen. election.   Re-nom. in 1914 and was el., defeating incumbent Gov. Hodges, to whom he had lost two years
earlier.   Was the first native-born Kansan to hold the
office of Gov.   Reel. in 1916.   During admin., minority ages
of both males and females were raised to 21; U.S. war effort
during World War I was supported.   Nom. and el. to U.S.
Senate in 1918, and continued to serve therein until he
voluntarily retired after the 1948 election.   As mbr. of the
Senate, became widely recognized as advocate of farm interests, and also had a prominent role in field of foreign
policy.   Pres. of Bd. of Regents of Kans. State Agri. Coll.,
1909-1913.   Mbr., Natl. Bd. of Amer. Red Cross; Natl.
Council of Boy Scouts of Amer. and of 4-H Clubs of Amer.;
dir., Topeka YMCA; pres., Kans. State Educl. Assoc.; mbr.,

Kans. Good Roads Assoc.; Memorial Bldg. Commn.; the League
to Enforce Peace; World Court League;, pres., Intl. Peace
and Equity League. Mbr., Masons; I.O.O.F.; A.O.U.W.; K.P.;
Moose. m. in 1892 to Florence Crawford, the only d. of Gov.
Samuel Crawford of Kans. (q.v.). D. at Topeka, Dec. 19,
1951. Bur. in Topeka Cem.

ALLEN, HENRY JUSTIN (1919-1923). b. Sept. 11, 1868 at
Pittsfield, Pa. s. of John and Rebecca (Goodin) A. Descendant of Scotch immigrant who came to Amer. in 1800.
Father moved with family to Kans. in 1870, where he became
a farmer. Attd. local schools at Burlingame, Kans.;
Washburn Univ.; and Baker Univ., from which he was grad. in
1890. Became reporter for Salina Republican in 1892. In
1894 bought the Manhattan Nationalist, which he edited for
two years. Increased holdings in other Kansas newspapers
and enterprises. From 1910 until death was pres. of Beacon
Bldg. Co. Ch., bd. of dir. of United Utilities, of Abilene,
Kans. and pres. of Cent. Bldg. Co. of Wichita. Newspaper
correspondent during Spanish-Amer. War. In 1912 was delegate to Rep. natl. conv., where he supported nom. of
Theodore Roosevelt. Led walk-out of delegation and later
became prominent in org. of the Prog. party in that election.
Returned to Rep. party in 1916. Washington correspondent,
1914-1916. Went to France as Red Cross and YMCA official
in 1918. Nom. and el. Gov. as Rep. in 1918 and was reel. in
1920. During admin., following a prolonged coal strike, secured enactment of a compulsory arb. law for critical labor
disputes that was subsequently declared unconstl. by the
U.S. Supreme Ct.; but the principle of that statute was
later upheld by that Ct. during the 1930s. Participated in
nationally-noted debate on labor questions with Samuel
Gompers of the A.F.L. in Carnegie Hall in New York City in
May, 1920. As delegate to Rep. natl. conv. in 1920 gave
nominating speech for Gen. Leonard Wood. Approached by
party leaders on becoming the party's nominee for Vice Pres.,
but declined to run. Mbr. of U.S. Commn. on Near East
Relief, 1923-1924. Head of Dept. of Journalism of Univ.
World Travel School, 1926-1927. Apptd. to fill vacancy in
U.S. Senate seat in April, 1929, serving until Nov., 1930
when a successor was el. Dir. of publicity for Rep. natl.
commt. in 1928 and 1932 presidential campaigns. Pres. of
Great Lakes-St. Lawrence Tidewater Assoc. Author of Party
of the Third Part in 1921 and of Venezuela in 1940; also of
numerous articles on political topics. During World War II
was sponsor of "Bundles for Britain" movement. Hon. degrees
from a number of colleges and universities and recipient of
awards and decorations from several foreign govts. Trustee,

Methodist Episcopal church. m. in 1893 to Elsie Jane
Nuzman, of Circleville. Two s.: two d. D. Jan. 17, 1950
in Wichita. Bur. in Maple Grove Cem. there.

DAVIS, JONATHAN McMILLAN (1923-1925). b. April 26,
1871 on a farm near Bronson, Kans. s. of Jonathan McMillan
and Eve (Holeman) D. Father, who was a farmer, was of
Scotch-Irish-Welsh descent. Attd. Bronson pub. schools, the
Univ. of Kans., and the Univ. of Nebr. Engaged in farming
on family farm, expanding holdings to 1,700 acres. Became
well-known as breeder of Percheron horses, Shorthorn cattle,
and Poland-China hogs. Was an ardent supporter of Wm. J.
Bryan in 1890s. Mbr. of Kans. House in 1901, 1907-1911.
Mbr. of Kans. Senate 1913 and 1915, where he sponsored bill
by which State became publ. of school texts. Dem. nominee
for Gov. in 1920, but lost in gen. election. Was Dem. nominee again in 1922 and was el. Admin. attended by much
controversy with Rep.-controlled legislature. Vetoed a
great number of bills, of which 29 were enacted over his
veto. Also engaged in frequent tiffs with his Rep. Atty.
Gen. As his term was about to expire in Jan., 1925, criminal charges of alleged bribery in connection with his granting clemency to a banker were brought against him. Was subsequently acquitted of charges, but kept the controversy
alive by filing libel charges against newspaper with which
the charges had originated. Defeated as Dem. cand. for
Gov. in 1924 and again in 1926. Also defeated as Dem. cand.
for U.S. Senate seat in 1930. Defeated as cand. for Dem.
nom. for Gov. in 1936, having the support of Townsend Plan
advocates. Defeated as Indep. cand. for Gov. in 1938.
Methodist. m. in 1894 to Mollie Purdom. Two d.; one s.
After her death, m. to Mrs. Mary Davis. D. June 27, 1943,
at Ft. Scott, Kans., after a prolonged illness.

PAULEN, BEN SANFORD (1925-1929). b. July 14, 1869 on
farm in De Witt Co., Ill. s. of Jacob Walter and Lucy Bell
(Johnson) P. Descendant of a French family that had settled
in Ill. in 1836. Father moved with family to Fredonia,
Kans., where he became a merchant. Attd. pub. schools in
Fredonia; the Univ. of Kans., 1886; and Bryant and Stratton
Bus. Coll., in St. Louis, Mo., from which he was grad. in
1887. Three years later joined father in hardware bus.
enterprise in Fredonia. Sold interest in 1918, and became
pres. of Wilson County Bank. Continued in banking and
other enterprises, becoming well-known in bus. circles of
Kans. Mbr. of Fredonia city council and later, city treas.
for several years. Mayor of Fredonia, 1900-1904. El. to
Kans. Senate in 1912 and was reel. in 1916. Kans. Oil

Inspector, 1917-1921. Trustee, Wilson Co. Hosp. at Neodesha,
1916-1920. El. Lieut. Gov. in 1920. Nom. and el. Gov. as
Rep. in 1924, defeating incumbent Gov. Davis and Wm. Allen
White, running as an Indep. cand. on an anti-Ku Klux Klan
platform. Reel. in 1926, again defeating former Gov. Davis
in gen. election. In 1932 was apptd. liquidating agent for
Security Natl. Bank of Independence, Kans. Apptd. ch. of
State Bd. of Welfare in 1939 by Gov. Huxman. Mbr., constl.
revision commn. in 1958. Mbr., Masons; pres., Kans. Bankers
Assoc.; mbr. of exec. council, Amer. Bankers Assoc.
Christian Scientist. m. in 1900 to Barbara Ellis, of Holton,
Kans. No children. D. July 11, 1961, at Fredonia, Kans.

REED, CLYDE MARTIN (1929-1931). b. Oct. 19, 1871 in
Champaign Co., Ill. s. of Martin Van Buren and Mary
Adelaide (Southworth) R. Father was an invalid and son had
to support self at an early age. Family moved to Labette
Co., Kans. in 1875. Attd. pub. schools and taught school
for a year. At age 18 entered U.S. railway mail service as
clerk. Rose to become div. supt., field supt., and supt.,
Ry. Adjustment Div. of U.S. Post Office, from which he resigned in 1917. In 1903 acquired an interest in Parsons,
Kans. Daily Sun, and by 1917 had controlling interest. Continued to be its publ. until death. Sect. to Gov. Henry J.
Allen, 1919. Ch. of Kans. Ct. of Indus. Relations, 1920,
which was abolished shortly afterward. Ch. of Kans. Pub.
Utilities Commn., 1921-1924. Nom. and el. Gov. as Rep. in
1928. After term as Gov., represented parties in cases be-
fore U.S. Interstate Commerce Commn. Nom. and el. to U.S.
Senate in 1938, continuing to serve in that capacity until
his death. In 1942 was unsuccessful cand. for Rep. nom.
for Gov. Methodist Episcopal church. m. in 1891 to Minnie
E. Hart, of Parsons, Kans. Three s.; four d. A son, Clyde
M., Jr., was defeated as the Rep. nominee for Gov. in 1958.
D. Nov. 8, 1949 at Parsons while still a mbr. of U.S.
Senate. Bur. in Oakwood Cem. there.

WOODRING, HARRY HINES (1931-1933). b. May 31, 1890 in
Elk City, Kans. s. of Hines and Melissa Jane (Cooper) W.
Descendant of a Finnish immigrant who came to Philadelphia
in 1732. Attd. local pub. schools and Montgomery Co. H.S.
At age 16 worked as janitor in First Natl. Bank of Neodesha,
Kans., in which he eventually acquired an interest, becoming
vice pres. Sold interest in 1929. Served in tank corps of
U.S. Army during World War I. In 1930 won Dem. nom. for
Gov. and was el. by narrow margin of 251 votes in his first
attempt to win pub. office. As Gov., stressed economy in
govt. and supported state income tax revision. Nom. for

second term in 1932 but lost in gen. election by a narrow
margin to Alfred M. Landon. Was apptd. Asst. Sect. of War
by Pres. F. D. Roosevelt in 1933. In 1936 was apptd. U.S.
Sect. of War. Took steps to modernize U.S. Army, and enlarged Army Air Corps. Served until he was replaced by
Henry Stimson in 1940. Unsuccessful as Dem. cand. for Gov.
in 1946 and was defeated for Dem. nom. for Gov. in 1956.
Mbr., Amer. Legion; Masons. Christian (Disciples) church.
m. in 1933 to Helen Coolidge, of Fitchburg, Mass., d. of
U.S. Sen. Marcus Coolidge. Two s.; one d. Marriage ended
in divorce in 1959. D. Sept. 9, 1967.

LANDON, ALFRED MOSSMAN (1933-1937). b. Sept. 9, 1887
at Middlesex, Pa. s. of John Manuel and Ann (Mossman) L.
Father was an oil company exec., who was transferred to
Elba, Ohio and then to Marietta, Ohio during youth of son.
Attd. pub. schools at those places. Family later moved to
Independence, Kans. and he entered the Univ. of Kans., from
which he received a law degree in 1908. Employed for four
years as clerk in First Natl. Bank of Independence. Went
into oil bus. and was financially successful as independent
producer. Ch. of Prog. party commt. of Montgomery Co. in
1914. Served as lieut. in chemical warfare service of U.S.
Army during World War I. Served as sect. to Gov. Henry J.
Allen for a short time in 1919. Ch., Rep. state commt. in
1928 and 1930. Nom. and el. Gov. as Rep. in 1932, defeating
incumbent Gov. Woodring by some 7,600 votes in a three-man
race, although Dem. party candidates swept State in other
state-wide elections that year. Nom. and el. for succeeding
term in 1934. As Gov., put state finances on a "cash"
basis; secured adoption of an individual income tax; acquired national notice as able adminr. of welfare and relief
programs. Became nominee of Rep. party for Pres. of U.S.
in 1936, but was defeated in Roosevelt landslide. Retired
to bus. activities thereafter, but continued to maintain
interest in politics. In 1950 expanded interests into
radio station enterprises. Delegate to Pan-Amer. Conf. at
Lima, Peru in 1938. Delegate-at-large to Rep. natl. convs.
in 1940, 1944 and 1948. Trustee, Baker Univ. Mbr., Masons;
Elks; 40 and 8; Amer. Legion; I.O.O.F.; Phi Gamma Delta;
Phi Delta Phi. Methodist. Hon. degrees from Marietta
Coll.; Washburn Univ.; Boston Coll.; and Kans. State Univ.
m. in 1915 to Margaret Fleming, of Oil City, Pa., who died
in 1918. One d. m. in 1930 to Theo Cobb, of Topeka, Kans.
One s.; one d. A d., Nancy Landon Kassebaum, was elected
to a U.S. Senate seat in 1978, becoming the first woman to
hold that office from Kans.

HUXMAN, WALTER AUGUST (1937-1939). b. Feb. 16, 1887 at
Pretty Prairie, Kans. s. of August A. and Mary (Graber) H.
Attd. Emporia State Teachers Coll., 1909-1911 and the Univ.
of Kans., from which he received a law degree in 1914. Admitted to bar in 1915 and began practice in Hutchinson, Kans.
Asst. atty. of Reno Co. and city atty. of Hutchinson. Mbr.,
Kans. State Tax Commn., 1931-1932. Nom. and el. Gov. as a
Dem. in 1936. Supported New Deal programs of natl. admin.
while Gov. Nom. for succeeding term but was defeated in
gen. election. Apptd. to U.S. Cir. Ct. of Appeals in 1939
by Pres. F. D. Roosevelt. Retired from active jud. service
in 1956. Mbr., Masons; I.O.O.F. Christian (Disciples)
church. m. in 1915 to Eula E. Biggs. One d. D. June 26,
1972.

RATNER, PAYNE HARRY (1939-1943). b. Oct. 3, 1896 at
Casey, Ill. s. of Harry and Julia (Miller) R. Father was
a travelling salesman and clothing merchant. Attd. Kemper
Mil. Acad., Boonville, Mo. Served in U.S. Navy, 1918-1921.
Attd. Washington Univ., St. Louis, Mo., from which he received a law degree in 1920. Admitted to bar in 1921 and
began practice in Parsons, Kans. Co. atty., Labette Co.,
1923-1927. Mbr., Kans. Senate, 1929-1933. U.S. referee in
bankruptcy cases, 1932-1936. Again a mbr. of Kans. Senate,
1937-1939. Nom. and el. Gov. as a Rep. in 1938, defeating
incumbent Gov. Huxman in gen. election. Reel. in 1940. As
Gov., requested creation of Kans. Indus. Devel. Commn.; obtained adoption of state civil service system. Returned to
law practice in 1943. Mbr., Masons (O.E.S.); Amer. Legion;
40 and 8; Sigma Alpha Upsilon; Delta Theta Pi; Kiwanis;
various professional legal orgs. Christian (Disciples)
church. m. in 1920 to Cliffe Dodd, of Sibley, Iowa. Two
s.; one d. D. Dec. 27, 1974.

SCHOEPPEL, ANDREW FRANK (1943-1947). b. Nov. 23, 1894
near Claflin, Kans. s. of George J. and Anna (Phillip) S.
Father was a farmer. Attd. local schools and the Univ. of
Kans., 1916-1918. Served in U.S. Navy Air Force, 1918-1919.
Attd. the Univ. of Nebr., from which he received a law degree in 1922. Admitted to bar in 1923 and began practice
as mbr. of law firm at Ness City, Kans. Served as mbr. of
Ness City school bd.; city councilman; city atty.; and
mayor. Co. atty., Ness Co. Apptd. to Kans. Corp. Commn.
in 1939 by Gov. Ratner, serving until 1942. Nom. and el.
Gov. as a Rep. in 1942 and was reel. in 1944. Ch. of Interstate Oil Compact Commn., 1943-1945. After tenure as Gov.
practiced law at Wichita, Kans. Nom. and el. to U.S. Senate in 1948 and continued in that office until his death.

Mbr., Amer. Legion; Masons; Sigma Nu; Phi Alpha Theta;
Rotary; Lions; various professional legal orgs. and social
clubs. Methodist. Hon. degrees from Baker Univ. and
Waynesburg (Pa.) Coll. m. in 1924 to Maria Thomson, of
Tilden, Nebr. D. Jan. 21. 1962, at Bethesda, Md., while
still a mbr. of U.S. Senate. Bur. in Old Mission Cem.,
Wichita.

CARLSON, FRANK (1947-1950). b. Jan. 23, 1893 near
Concordia, Kans. s. of Charles E. and Anna (Johnson) C.
Father had emigrated from Sweden to Amer. in the 1880s and
was a farmer and stockman. Attd. pub. schools in Cloud Co.;
Concordia Normal and Bus. Coll.; and Kans. State Agri.
Coll., from which he received a degree in agri. sci. in
1914. Engaged in farming and stock-raising in Cloud Co.
Served as a pvt. in U.S. Army during World War I. Mbr.,
Kans. legislature, 1929-1933. Ch., Rep. state commt., 1932-
1934. Mbr. of U.S. House, 1935-1947, being active particularly in the fields of taxation and farm legislation. Was
not a cand. for reel. in 1946. Nom. and el. Gov. in 1946
and again in 1948. Mbr., first Hoover Commn. on Reorg. of
Exec. Branch of U.S. Govt. in 1949. As Gov., made extensive
additions to state programs while keeping the State on a
sound financial basis. Ch., Natl. Govs.' Conf., 1949 and
ch., Interstate Oil Compact Commn., 1949. Ch., Council of
State Govts., 1950. Vice ch., President's Natl. Safety
Conf., 1950. Resigned office of Gov. in Nov., 1950 after
having been el. to the U.S. Senate. Continued to serve in
Senate until 1969, when he retired. Mbr. of U.S. delegation
to UN Assembly while in Senate. Mbr., Amer. Legion; 40 and
8; Masons; Kiwanis; various farm orgs., including the Agri.
Hall of Fame; pres., Intl. Council of Christian Leadership.
Mbr., bd. of govs. of Menninger Found. and of the Inst. for
Logopedics. Baptist. Hon. degrees from eight colleges and
universities. m. in 1919 to Alice Frederickson, of
Concordia, Kans. One d.; one foster s.

HAGAMAN, FRANK LESTER (1950-1951). b. June 1, 1894 at
Bushnell, Ill. Family moved to Johnson Co., Kans. in 1900,
where he grew up. Attd. the Univ. of Kans. During World
War I saw service in U.S. Army's "Rainbow" Div. overseas.
Was wounded in action and awarded Purple Heart. After war
service attd. George Washington Univ., from which he received a law degree. Began law practice in Kansas City,
Kans. in 1921. Mbr. of Kans. House for four terms, serving
as majority (Rep.) leader in 1941 and Speaker in 1945. Nom.
and el. Lieut. Gov. as a Rep. in 1946 and was reel. in 1948.
Succeeded to office of Gov. in Nov., 1950 when Gov. Carlson

resigned, and completed last six weeks of Carlson's term.
Resumed law practice after tenure as Gov., residing at
Fairway, Kans. Mbr., Amer. Legion; V.F.W.; 40 and 8; Masons
(Shriner); various professional legal orgs. Episcopalian.
Active in veterans affairs. m. in 1920 to Elizabeth B.
Sutton, of Russell Co., Kans.

ARN, EDWARD FERDINAND (1951-1955). b. May 19, 1906 in
Kansas City, Kans. s. of Edward F. and Grace Bell (Edwards)
A. Attd. local pub. schools; Kansas City Jr. Coll., 1925-
1927; and Kansas City Univ., from which he received a law
degree in 1931. Worked at various jobs to support himself
while attending college. Admitted to bar and began practice
in Kansas City, Kans. Became active in politics as ch. of
Young Rep. club. Atty. for Kans. State Highway Dept., 1933-
1936. In 1936 moved to Wichita, Kans., where he became mbr.
of law firm. Served as lieut. in U.S. Navy aboard air carrier in Pac. area, 1943-1945. In 1946 was el. Atty. Gen.
of Kans. and continued in that office for a second term.
Achieved recognition for vigorous law enforcement endeavors.
In 1949 resigned as Atty. Gen. after being apptd. to Kans.
Supreme Ct., but resigned that post in 1950 to become cand.
for Gov. Nom. and el. Gov. as Rep. in 1950 and was reel. in
1952. Resumed law practice thereafter. Unsuccessful as
cand. for Rep. nom. for U.S. Senate in 1962. Mbr., Masons;
Elks; Delta Theta Phi; Amer. Legion; V.F.W.; Natl.
Sojourners; professional legal orgs. Congregationalist.
m. in 1933 to Marcella Tillmans, of Topeka, Kans. Two d.

HALL, FRED(ERICK LEE) (1955-1957). b. July 24, 1916 at
Dodge City, Kans. s. of Fred Logan and Etta (Brewer) H.
Father was a railroad engr. Attd. local pub. schools and
U.C.L.A., from which he received an A.B. degree in 1938 and
a law degree in 1941. Admitted to Calif. bar and served as
atty. for Douglas Aircraft Co. in Long Beach, Calif. in
1942. In 1942-1943 served as atty. with the O.P.A. in
Washington, D.C. and in 1943-1944 with the U.S.W.P.B. Asst.
exec. dir., Combined W.P.B. and Natl. Resources Bds. Worked
with a law firm in Topeka, Kans., 1944-1946. Practiced law
in Dodge City in 1946. Active in Young Rep. orgs. Served
as ch. of U.C.L.A. Young Rep. club in 1938; ch., Ford Co.
Young Rep. club in 1947; mbr. of constl. revision commt. of
Kans. Young Rep. clubs in 1949; and ch., Fifth Dist. Young
Rep. club. Delegate to Rep. natl. convs. in 1948, 1952 and
1956. Participated in Eisenhower for Pres. movement, 1951-
1952. Co. atty. for Ford Co., 1947-1949. El. Lieut. Gov.
in 1950 and was reel. in 1952. Nom. and el. Gov. as Rep. in
1954. As Gov., vetoed a "right to work" bill, and supported

legislation barring jurisdictional strikes and secondary
boycotts, both actions costing him popularity in affected
elements of constituency. Supported legislation abolishing
State Bd. of Review for censorship of moving pictures and
modernizing prison system. Defeated for re-nom. for Gov. in
1956. Resigned as Gov. a few days before end of term to
accept apptmt. to Kans. Supreme Ct. Resigned that post in
1958 and returned to pvt. law practice. Defeated for Rep.
nom. for Gov. in 1958. Mbr., Kans. Livestock Assoc.; Elks;
Lions; various professional legal orgs. Concerned with welfare and hosp. affairs in his community. Active in
Methodist church. Writer and lecturer. Hon. degree from
St. Mary of the Plains Coll., at Dodge City. m. in 1942 to
Leadell Schneider, of Long Beach, Calif. One s.

McCUISH, JOHN (1957). b. June 22, 1906 at Leadville,
Colo. s. of a Presbyterian minister, who moved to Newton,
Kans. in 1909. Attd. local pub. schools; Kemper Mil. Acad.,
at Boonville, Mo.; and Washburn Univ. Became publ. of
Harvey County News, a weekly newspaper, at Newton. Active
in Rep. politics, serving as ch. of Harvey Co. Rep. commt.
Ch. of Kans. Commn. on Revenue and Taxation, 1939-1943.
Delegate to Rep. natl. convs., 1936, 1948. Mbr. of Rep.
state commt. During World War II served in U.S. infantry
unit in Italy. In 1950 was chosen by Gen. McArthur to
assist in reorg. of Japanese press in connection with U.S.
rehabilitation program. Dir. of Eisenhower for Pres. headquarters in Kans., 1952. Nom. and el. Lieut. Gov. as Rep.
in 1954. Succeeded to office of Gov. early in Jan., 1957,
when Gov. Hall resigned. Completed last 11 days of Gov.
Hall's term. As Gov., apptd. Hall to vacant post on Kans.
Supreme Ct. Returned to newspaper and bus. interests in
Newton thereafter. Mbr., Masons; Elks; Eagles; Amer.
Legion; V.F.W. Presbyterian. m. in 1925 to Cora Hedrick.

DOCKING, GEORGE (1957-1961). b. Feb. 23, 1904 at
Clay Center, Clay Co., Kans. s. of Wm. and Meda (Donley) D.
Father was a banker, who moved to Lawrence, Kans. during
son's youth. Attd. pub. schools at Clay Center and Lawrence
and the Univ. of Kans., from which he was grad. with an A.B.
degree in 1925. Worked as bond salesman for a time, then
as cashier of Kans. Reserve State Bank in Topeka. In 1927
joined father's banking firm, the First Natl. Bank of
Lawrence. Became cashier in 1931, vice pres. in 1942 and
later, pres. Also expanded bus. interests into gas utility
field. Active in Dem. party affairs. Dem. party nominee
for Gov. in 1954, but lost in gen. election. Nom. again in
1956 and was el. Reel. in 1958. Dem. nominee for third

term in 1960 but was defeated in gen. election. As Gov.,
promoted reorg. of State Dept. of Revenue and Taxation;
helped to secure adoption of three state constl. amdts;
served on commt. on Fed.-State Relations of Natl. Govs.'
Conf. in 1957. Active in YMCA affairs and community welfare
orgs., including March of Dimes campaigns. Mbr., Elks;
Moose; Eagles; DeMolay; Delta Tau Delta; Beta Gamma Sigma.
Presbyterian. m. in 1925 to Mary Virginia Blackwell, of
Morehouse, Mo. Two s., one of whom, Robert, later became
Gov. of Kans. (q.v.). D. Jan. 20, 1964.

ANDERSON, JOHN, Jr. (1961-1965). b. May 8, 1917 at
Olathe, Kans. s. of John and Ora May (Bookout) A. Father
was a farmer. Attd. local pub. schools; Kans. State Univ.
for one year; and the Univ. of Kans., from which he received
an A.B. degree in 1943 and a law degree in 1944. Admitted
to bar in 1945 and began practice in Olathe. Co. atty.,
Johnson Co., 1947-1953. Mbr., Kans. Senate, 1953-1957.
Atty. Gen. of Kans., 1957-1961. Nom. as Rep. cand. for Gov.
in 1960 and was el. defeating incumbent Gov. George Docking,
who was seeking third term. Reel. in 1962. During admin.,
sponsored increases in state expenditures for various programs as well as revenue adjustments to accommodate them;
improvements in state employees' retirement system; and a
strengthened fair employment practices program. Returned to
legal and farming interests after term as Gov., specializing
in breeding Shetland ponies and Hereford cattle. Defeated
for Rep. nom. for Gov. in 1972. Mbr. of various professional legal orgs. Methodist. m. in 1943 to Arlene Auchard, of
Lawrence, Kans. Two s.; one d.

AVERY, WILLIAM HENRY (1965-1967). b. Aug. 11, 1911 on
a farm near Wakefield, Kans. s. of Herman W. and Hattie M.
(Coffman) A. Attd. local pub. schools and the Univ. of
Kans., from which he was grad. in 1934 with an A.B. degree
in political sci. Engaged in farming and stock-raising near
Wakefield._ Mbr. of Wakefield school bd., 1946-1955. Mbr.
of Kans. legislature, 1951-1955, serving on Legislative
Council the last two years. Mbr. of U.S. House, 1955-1965.
Did not seek reel. to House in 1964, but was nom. and el.
Gov. as a Rep. that year. Nom. for the succeeding term but
lost in the gen. election in 1966. Engaged in oil bus. in
Wichita, becoming pres. of Real Petroleum Co. in 1969. Mbr.,
Kans. Farm Bureau; Masons; Lions; Delta Upsilon; Kans. Live-
stock Assoc.; Kans. Assoc. for Wild Life. Recipient of
Natl. 4-H Club Award in 1967. Methodist. m. in 1940 to
Hazel Bowles, of Junction City, Kans. Two s.; two d.

DOCKING, ROBERT BLACKWELL (1967-1975). b. Oct. 9, 1925 at Kansas City, Mo. s. of George and Mary Virginia (Blackwell) D. Father was a Gov. of Kans. (q.v.). Attd. pub. schools at Lawrence, Kans. and the Univ. of Kans. Served as a lieut. in U.S. Army Air Force, 1943-1946. Grad. with honors at the Univ. of Kans. in 1948 and later attd. the Univ. of Wisc., studying banking. Became credit analyst for the Wm. Volker Co. in Kansas City, Mo. Employed in family banking bus. at Lawrence in 1950, serving as cashier and asst. trust officer. Ch., Douglas Co. Dem. commt., 1954-1956. In 1956 moved to Arkansas City, Kans., where he became vice pres. of Union State Bank. Also engaged in utility and ins. bus. enterprises. Pres. of Union State Bank in 1959. Mayor and city commnr. of Arkansas City, 1963-1966. Nom. and el. Gov. as Dem. in 1966, defeating incumbent Gov. Avery in the gen. election. Reel. in 1968, 1970 and 1972, becoming in latter year the first Kans. Gov. to be el. for four consecutive terms. While Gov., served as ch. of Midwest Govs. Conf., 1971; ch., Ozarks Regional Commn.; and ch., Interstate Oil Compact Commn. Very active in community welfare orgs. and affairs. Named Young Man of the Year by Kans. JCC in 1959. Hon. degrees from Washburn Univ. and Benedictine Coll. Mbr., Amer. Legion; Kans. Dem. Vets.; Masons; Eagles; Rotary; Amer. Assoc. of Criminology; various bus. and fraternal orgs. m. in 1950 to Meredith Martha Gear, of Elkhart, Kans. Two s.

BENNETT, ROBERT FREDERICK (1975-1979). b. May 23, 1927 at Kansas City, Kans. s. of Otto Francis and Dorothy Bess (Dodds) B. Attd. local schools. Served in U.S. Marine Corps, 1945-1946 and again in 1950-1951. Attd. the Univ. of Kans., graduating with an A.B. degree in 1950 and a law degree in 1952. Admitted to bar and began practice at Overland Park, Kans. Mbr., city council of Prairie Village, Kans., 1955-1957 and mayor, 1957-1965. Pres., Kans. League of Municipalities, 1959. Mbr. of Kans. Senate, 1965-1975, serving as Pres. pro tem in last term. Nom. and el. Gov. as Rep. in 1974, becoming the first Gov. of Kans. to be el. to a four-year term. Defeated as Rep. cand. for second term in 1978. As Gov., was mbr. of the exec. commt. of Amer. Govs. Assoc., 1976 and ch. of its Commt. on Urban Devel.; vice ch., Rep. Govs. Conf., 1976-1977. Mbr., Masons; Amer. Legion; V.F.W.; Optimists. Trustee, Baker Univ.; mbr., bd. of govs., Univ. of Kans. Law School; various professional legal orgs. m. in 1971 to Olivia Fisher. One s.; three d.

SHELBY, ISAAC (1792-1796; 1812-1816). b. Dec. 11, 1750 near North Mountain, Md. s. of Evan and Laetitia (Cox) S. Father, who was of Welsh origin, was a soldier in the French and Indian War and the Rev. War. Family moved to Tenn. area prior to Rev. War, and were involved in fighting against Indians in 1774. Son received a basic educ. Engaged in surveying work in Ky. area in 1775, and then went to Va.-N.C. border area where he assisted in obtaining supplies for Amer. Rev. War forces. El. to Va. Assembly in 1777. Apptd. by Gov. Thomas Jefferson, of Va., to guard commrs. engaged in surveying Va.-N.C. boundary line. Line thus established had the effect of placing his residence in N.C. Commissioned as col. by Gov. Caswell, of N.C. Engaged in fighting Indians and British Loyalists in western part of N.C. during later stages of Rev. War. Mbr. of N.C. legislature in 1781 and 1782. In 1782 was apptd. commnr. to settle land claims along Cumberland River and to survey lands in Tenn. area. Settled on plantation, "Travelers' Rest", in what later became Lincoln Co., Ky. Participated in movement to separate Ky. area from Va. and make it a State. Mbr. of conv. that drew up first const. for Ky. El. as first Gov. of Ky. in 1792. Admin. dominated by issues arising out of troubles with Spain over navigation rights on Mississippi River. Opposed efforts of Gen. Wilkinson and others who sought to collaborate with Spanish regime in Mississippi Valley. Retired to plantation after term as Gov. Served as Jeff. Rep. pres. elector in each pres. election from 1800 to 1820. El. Gov. for second time in 1812. Raised troops and took the field in command of Ky. forces for a time in 1812. Participated in a number of engagements, including the Battle of the Thames in 1813. Apptd. in 1818 as U.S. commnr. to serve with Gen. Andrew Jackson in negotiating treaty with Chickasaw Indian tribe for relinquishment of lands west of the Tennessee River. Declined apptmt. as U.S. Sect. of War in 1818. Ch. of first Bd. of Trustees of Centre Coll., 1819-1826. m. in 1783 to Susanna Hart, of Boonesboro, Ky. Eleven children. A grand-daughter became the wife of Gov. Magoffin, of Ky. (q.v.). D. July 18, 1826 at his home, "Travelers' Rest", in Lincoln Co., Ky.

GARRARD, JAMES (1796-1804). b. Jan. 14, 1749 in Stafford Co., Va. s. of Wm. and Mary (Lewis) G. Descendant of a Huguenot family that had emigrated from England to Va. Served as a col. of a Va. regiment in Rev. War. Mbr. of Va. legislature in 1779, where he vigorously supported the principle of religious liberty. In 1783 moved to the Ky. area, where he engaged in farming near Paris, in

Bourbon Co. Also acted as a Baptist minister. Mbr. of Va.
legislature from Fayette Co., 1785. Mbr. of convs. at
Danville in 1785, 1787 and 1788, that launched movement for
statehood for Ky. Mbr. of conv. that framed first const.
for Ky. in 1792. El. to Ky. legislature. Chosen Gov. of
Ky. in 1796, and was reel. in 1800, becoming in the latter
year the first Gov. of Ky. to be el. by direct popular vote.
During admin., capital punishment was abolished except for
first degree murder; supported adoption of Ky. Resolutions
in 1798 which condemned the enactment and enforcement by
the U.S. of the Alien and Sedition laws as being unconstl.;
and a revised const. for the State was adopted in 1799.
Ch. of commt. of Baptist Elkhorn conv. in 1791 which adopted a resolution condemning the institution of slavery.
Was dropped from mbrshp. in Natl. Baptist Assoc. in 1803
for alleged Unitarian views. m. in 1769 to Elizabeth
Mountjoy, of Va. Twelve children. D. Jan. 19, 1822 at his
home in Mt. Lebanon, Ky.

   GREENUP, CHRISTOPHER (1804-1808). b. in 1750 (?) in
Westmoreland, (Loudoun?) Co., Va. Received basic acad.
educ. there. Served with Amer. forces during Rev. War,
holding rank of col. at end of war. Also participated la-
ter in engagements against Indians in Western Va. Moved to
Ky. area of Va. in 1783, where he practiced law in Fayette
Co. Mbr. of Va. House from Fayette Co. in 1785. Clerk of
ct. for the dist. of Ky. at Harrodsburg from 1785 to 1792.
Mbr. of Danville conv. that initiated movement for state-
hood for Ky. in 1785. Established residence in Frankfort,
Ky. in 1792. Mbr. of conv. that framed first const. for
Ky. El. to U.S. House in 1792 as first mbr. of Cong. from
Ky., continuing to serve in House until 1797. Mbr. of Ky.
House, 1798. Clerk of Ky. Senate, 1799-1802. Became cir.
ct. judge in 1802. El. Gov. in 1804. During admin., the
trial of Judge Sebastian on charge of conspiring to make
Ky. an ally of Spain was conducted, arousing much pub. at-
tention; and the Bank of Ky. was established. Pres. elec-
tor on Madison-Clinton ticket in 1808. After tenure as
Gov., served as mbr. of Ky. legislature from Franklin Co.,
and also as a justice of the peace. Dir. of the Bank of
Ky., and was one of the mbrs. of first Bd. of Trustees of
Transylvania Univ., at Lexington. Helped to org. one of
the first companies for improvement of river navigation.
Mbr., Ky. Soc. for Promoting Useful Knowledge, 1787. Helped org. Ky. Mfg. Soc. in 1789. m. to Mary Pope. D. April
27, 1818 at Blue Lick Springs, Ky. Bur. in Frankfort State
Cem.

SCOTT, CHARLES (1808-1812). b. in 1739 (1733?) in
Goochland (now Powhatan) Co., in Va. Received only a rudimentary educ. Served as mbr. of Va. militia on Gen.
Braddock's disastrous expedition against French and Indians
in 1755. Upon outbreak of Rev. War raised a company of Va.
volunteers for the Amer. cause, becoming its capt. Promoted to col. in 1776 and to brig. gen. in 1777. Participated
in engagements at Trenton, Germantown, and Monmouth. Later
was captured by British at Charleston, S.C., and was held
as a prisoner of war for two years. In 1785 moved to a
farm near Versailles, Ky. (then a part of Va.), having received a land grant from Va. for mil. services. Mbr. of
Va. legislature, 1789-1790. Called into mil. service in
1788 to assist in protection of Ky. area against Indians.
In 1791 led Ky. forces with Gen. St. Clair's expedition
against Indians in the Ohio country. Participated in several engagements, including the Battle of Fallen Timbers.
Returned to farm near Versailles, in Woodford Co., Ky. after mil. service. Pres. elector in 1792, 1800 and 1804.
In 1808 was el. Gov. As Gov., was regarded as a somewhat
eccentric and unpolished figure. Returned to plantation
after tenure as Gov. m. first to Frances Sweeney, in 1762.
m. in 1807 to Judith Cary (Bell) Gist. Mbr., Soc. of
Cincinnati. D. at his plantation, "Canewood", Oct. 22,
1813 about a year after leaving office. Bur. in Frankfort
State Cem.

SHELBY, ISAAC (1812-1816). See above, 1792-1796.

MADISON, GEORGE (1816). b. in Augusta (Rockingham?)
Co., Va. in 1763. s. of John and Agatha (Strother) M.
Served as soldier against British during Rev. War and in
engagements against Indians on frontier. Wounded while
serving in Gen. St. Clair's expedition against Indians in
Ohio country in 1791. Became a lieut. of a cavalry unit
of Ky. volunteers in Indian wars in 1792. Settled on a
farm near Paris, in the Ky. area, and became prominent in
Ky. politics when Ky. was admitted to statehood. Apptd.
State Aud. by Gov. Shelby in 1796, and continued to serve
in that capacity for 20 years. Major in a regiment of Ky.
volunteers during War of 1812, participating in a number of
engagements. Was captured and held prisoner of war at
Quebec until 1814. On return to Ky. became a political rival of Col. Richard M. Johnson, later Vice Pres. of U.S.
during the second term of Pres. Jackson. In the gubernatorial election of 1816 he and Johnson were opponents, but
Johnson withdrew from the contest before the election and
Madison was el. m. to Jane Smith, of Botecourt Co., Va.

D. Oct. 14, 1816 at his home near Paris, Ky., after serving
as Gov. less than two months.

SLAUGHTER, GABRIEL (1816-1820). b. Dec. 12, 1767 in
Culpeper Co., Va. s. of Robert and Susannah (Harrison) S.
Descendant of an English colonist who came to Va. prior to
1620. As a youth went to Ky. area where he settled on a
farm near Harrodsburg. Became influential in local politics and served as mbr. of Ky. legislature for several
terms. El. Lieut. Gov. in 1808, serving until 1812. Became col. in a Ky. regiment of volunteers and participated
in Battle of New Orleans near end of War of 1812. El.
Lieut. Gov. again in 1816, and succeeded to office of Gov.
when Gov. Madison died shortly after beginning of term. A
controversy ensued between Slaughter and John Pope, Sect.
of State, over the question whether the former should continue to act as Gov. until the end of the term for which
Madison had been el., or a spec. election should be held to
choose a successor. It was resolved in favor of
Slaughter's continuing to serve as Gov. until the end of
the regular term. When Pope resigned his office in protest,
Slaughter refused to appt. a successor and performed the
functions of both the Gov. and Sect. of State. Active as
mbr. of the Baptist church, serving as delegate to a number
of Baptist convs. D. Sept. 19, 1830 on his farm near
Harrodsburg.

ADAIR, JOHN (1820-1824). b. Jan. 9, 1757 in Saint
Mark's Parish (now Chester Co.), S.C. s. of Baron Wm.
Adair, who was of Scotch ancestry. Attd. schools at
Charlotte, N.C. Served as a soldier with S.C. forces during Rev. War, and was captured by the British. Mbr. of S.C.
conv. that ratified U.S. Const. in 1787. In 1788 moved to
Mercer Co., in the Ky. area, where he had acquired land.
Participated in Gen. Wilkinson's expedition against Indians
in Northwest Terr. in 1791-1792. Became major in Amer.
forces in 1792. Mbr. of Ky. constl. conv. of 1792. Became
lieut. col. of Ky. troops under Gen. Charles Scott, later
Gov. of Ky., in 1793. Mbr. of Ky. legislature, 1793-1795,
1798 and 1800-1803, serving as House Speaker, 1802-1803.
Apptd. register of U.S. land office in 1805. In Nov., 1805,
was el. to U.S. Senate to fill vacancy, serving for one
year. Resigned after he was implicated in charges concerning the Burr conspiracy, and was defeated for second term.
Was condemned for his relations with Burr, but maintained
he misunderstood what Burr's objectives were. Eventually
regained popularity. Volunteered for service on outbreak
of War of 1812, becoming brig. gen. of Ky. militia forces.

Commanded a brigade at the Battle of New Orleans in 1815.
Mbr. of Ky. House in 1817. El. Gov. in 1820. During
admin., pub. educ. system was promoted; imprisonment for
debt abolished; and a state library established at
Frankfort. El. to U.S. House in 1830. Was not a cand. for
second term in 1832. m. in 1790 to Katherine Palmer. D.
at his home, "Whitehall", near Harrodsburg, May 19, 1840.
Bur. in Frankfort State Cem.

DESHA, JOSEPH (1824-1828). b. Dec. 9, 1768 in
Northampton (now Monroe) Co., Pa. Descendant of a French
Huguenot family that had emigrated to Amer. in late 1600s.
Family moved to Ky. area in 1779, then to the Gallatin
area of Tenn. in 1782. In 1792 son moved back to Mays Lick,
in Mason Co., Ky., where he became active in Ky. politics
while engaging in planting. Served with Ky. troops under
Gen. Wayne and Gen. Harrison in campaigns against Indians
in the Ohio country in 1794. Mbr. of Ky. House in 1797,
1799-1802, and of Ky. Senate, 1803-1807. El. to U.S. House
as a Jeff. Rep. in 1806, and continued in that office until
1819. Did not seek reel. in 1818. As mbr. of Cong., supported the War of 1812. Received commn. as major gen. of
volunteers in 1813, and participated in Battle of the
Thames. Defeated as cand. for Gov. in 1820, but was a cand.
again in 1824 and was el. as a Jeff. Rep. During admin.,
legislation was passed establishing a new Ct. of Appeals
and abolishing the old one, giving rise to a controversy
that dominated Ky. politics for some time thereafter. After tenure as Gov., retired to farm in Harrison Co. m. to
Peggy Bledsoe, of Tenn., in 1789. A brother, Robert, was
a mbr. of U.S. House from Tenn. from 1827 to 1831. D. at
Georgetown, Ky., Oct. 11, 1842. Bur. in Georgetown Cem.

METCALFE, THOMAS (1828-1832). b. Mar. 20, 1780 in
Fauquier Co., Va. s. of John and Sally M. Grandfather was
a grad. of Cambridge Univ. who had emigrated to Va., where
he was a teacher and school principal. Father took family
to Ky. area in 1784, settling first in Fayette Co., and later near Carlisle, in Nicholas Co. Attd. local schools and
at age 16 was apprenticed to his brother to learn the stone
mason trade. When father died in 1799, son became a contractor for stone work. Also studied at home in leisure
time, becoming well-read, especially in history, by use of
father's good library. Became active in politics, serving
in Ky. House, 1812-1816. Capt. of volunteer company during
the War of 1812. El. as Jeff. Rep. to U.S. House in 1818,
and continued in that office until June, 1828. As mbr. of
Cong., advocated two-thirds vote by U.S. Supreme Ct. to

declare legislation void; favored a protective tariff and
govtl. promotion of internal improvements. Resigned House
seat to become cand. of Natl. Rep. (later the Whig) party
for Gov., favoring restoration of "Old" Ct. of Appeals.
El. by narrow margin of some 700 votes. During admin.,
promoted pub. schools through enactment of common school
law. Served as mbr. of Ky. Senate, 1834-1836. Pres. of
Ky. Bd. of Internal Improvements in 1841. Gave nom. speech
for Wm. H. Harrison at Whig party natl. conv. in 1839 for
Pres. of U.S., and was offered post of U.S. Sect. of War by
Pres. Harrison in 1841, but declined it for reasons of
health. Mbr. of U.S. Senate, 1848-1849. Was a strong
Unionist. Noted for eloquence, and was given the nick-name
of "Old Stone Hammer" for his forceful style of speaking.
m. in 1806 (?) to Nancy Mason. D. at his home, "Forest
Retreat", near Carlisle, Aug. 18, 1855. Bur. in family
cem. on estate.

BREATHITT, JOHN (1832-1834). b. Sept. 9, 1786 near
New London, Va. s. of Wm. and ----(Whitsett) B. Father
had emigrated as a child with his parents to Va. from
Scotland. In 1800 family moved to Russellville, in Logan
Co., Ky., where father had acquired land. Received a limited educ. Taught school for a time while also studying
law. Also engaged in land survey work in Ill. Terr. Admitted to bar in 1810 and began practice in Frankfort, Ky.
El. to Ky. legislature from Logan Co. in 1811, and served
several terms. El. Lieut. Gov. as Jackson Dem. in 1828.
El. Gov. as Jackson Dem. in 1832 in a hotly contested election in which major issue was reorg. of ct. system to over-
come a decision invalidating legislation for relief of
debtors. During admin., the importation of slaves into Ky.
was prohibited. m. first to a d. of Wm. Whitaker, of Logan
Co. One s.; one d. After her death, m. to Susan M. Harris,
of Chesterfield, Va. A direct descendant, Edward T.
Breathitt, became Gov. of Ky. in 1963 (q.v.), and a great-
grandson, John S. Marmaduke, became Gov. of Mo. in 1885
(q.v.). D. Feb. 21, 1834, during an epidemic of Asiatic
cholera at Frankfort during second year of term as Gov.

MOREHEAD, JAMES TURNER (1834-1836). b. May 24, 1797
near Shepherdsville, Ky. s. of Armistead M., who was a
native of Va. Attd. common schools in Russellville and
Transylvania Univ., 1813-1815. Studied law, was admitted
to the bar and began practice at Bowling Green, Ky. in
1818. Mbr. of Ky. House, 1827-1830. Nom. and el. Lieut.
Gov. as a Whig in 1831. Succeeded to office of Gov. in
Feb., 1834, when Gov. Breathitt died, and completed latter's

term. Was the first native-born Kentuckian to occupy the
office of Gov. As Gov., urged adoption of system of internal improvements, including locks and dams on the Green and
Kentucky Rivers. Mbr. of Ky. House in 1837-1838 and 1839-
1840. Apptd. commnr. to negotiate agreement with Ohio on
protection of slave property of Ky. owners. Delegate to
first Whig party natl. conv. in 1831. Pres. of Ky. Bd. of
Internal Improvements, 1838-1841. El. to U.S. Senate in
1841 as a Whig, serving for one term. As a mbr. of Senate,
strongly opposed abolitionists. Opposed annexation of
Texas, but voted for declaration of war against Mexico in
1846. Author of Practices and Proceedings at Law in
Kentucky in 1846. Pres. of Ky. branch of African Colonization Soc. Devoted considerable attention to literary pursuits, particularly in connection with early Ky. history.
m. in 1823 to Susan A. Roberts. D. at Covington, Ky., Dec.
28, 1854. Bur. in Frankfort State Cem.

CLARK, JAMES (1836-1839). b. Jan. 16, 1770 near Peaks
of Otter, in Bedford Co., Va. s. of Robert and Susan C.
Moved with parents to Ky. in 1794. Tutored by Dr. Blythe,
afterward a prof. at Transylvania Univ. Also attd. Pisgah
Acad., at Woodford, Ky. Studied law in Va. with a brother
and was admitted to the bar in 1797. Began practice in
Winchester, Ky., and soon achieved recognition as an able
lawyer. Mbr. of Ky. House, 1807-1809. Apptd. mbr. of Ky.
Ct. of Appeals in 1810 and served until 1812, when he resigned. El. to U.S. House in 1812 as Clay Rep. and again
in 1814. Resigned seat in 1816. Apptd. cir. ct. judge in
1817, serving in that capacity until 1824. Rendered decision in 1822 holding debtor relief law enacted by the legislature unconstl. Decision ultimately gave rise to controversy culminating in abolition of old ct. system and creation of new Ct. of Appeals in 1826. El. to U.S. House
again in 1825 as Natl. Rep. (Whig) to fill post vacated by
Henry Clay, who became U.S. Sect. of State. Continued in
office for two succeeding terms. El. to Ky. Senate, serving as its Speaker, 1831-1835. Nom. and el. Gov. as Whig
in 1836. During admin., a state supt. of schools post was
created. m. to Mrs. (Buckner) Thornton, a widow. D. at
Frankfort, Ky., Aug. 27, 1839 during third year of term as
Gov. Bur. in family cem. at his home in Winchester, Ky.
A brother, Christopher Henderson C., was a mbr. of U.S.
House from Va.; and a nephew, John Bullock C., was a mbr.
of U.S. House from Mo.

WICKLIFFE, CHARLES ANDERSON (1839-1840). b. June 8,
1788 near Springfield, Ky. s. of Charles and Lydia

(Hardin) W. Educ. by pvt. tutors. Studied law in office
of a cousin and was admitted to the bar in 1809. Began
practice at Bardstown, Ky., and soon acquired extensive
practice. Mbr. of Ky. legislature, 1812-1813 and 1822-1823.
During War of 1812 served as aide to Gen. Winlock and later,
to Gen. Caldwell. Co. atty., 1816. El. to U.S. House in
1822, and continued to serve there until 1833. Did not
seek reel. in 1832. Mbr. of Ky. House again in 1833-1835,
serving as Speaker in 1834. El. Lieut. Gov. as a Whig in
1836. Succeeded to office of Gov. in 1839 when Gov. Clark
died. Completed Clark's term, which ended in Sept., 1840.
Apptd. U.S. Postmaster Gen. by Pres. Tyler in 1841, serving
until 1845. In 1844 was assaulted and stabbed by a person,
later adjudged insane, while on a trip to Baltimore. Personal envoy of Pres. Polk in 1845 to France and Great
Britain in connection with negotiations leading to annexation of Texas by U.S. Delegate to Ky. constl. conv. in
1850, and served on a commt. apptd. by the Ky. legislature
in that year to revise Ky. statutes. El. as a Unionist
Whig to U.S. House in 1860. Attd. Washington "Peace
Congress" in 1861 that sought to avert Civil War. Also
attd. meetings at Louisville and Frankfort that sought to
keep Border States in the Union, but as non-combatants in
the Civil War. Defeated as Dem. nominee for Gov. in 1863.
Delegate to Dem. natl. conv. in 1864. Lost eyesight, but
continued to practice law. Delegate from Louisville pres-
bytery to the Gen. Assembly of Presbyterian church in St.
Louis in 1866, but was expelled for doctrinal reasons. m.
in 1813 to Margaret Cripps (Crepps?). Three s.; four d.
One of his sons, Robt., became Gov. of La. (q.v.), and a
grandson, J. C. W. Beckham, became Gov. of Ky. in 1900
(q.v.). D. near Ilchester, Md., Oct. 31, 1869. Bur. in
Bardstown Cem.

LETCHER, ROBERT PERKINS (1840-1844). b. Feb. 10, 1788
in Goochland Co., Va. s. of Stephen Giles and Betsey
(Perkins) L. As a boy was somewhat wild and mischievous,
but received a good acad. educ. Was in U.S. mil. service
during the War of 1812. Studied law and set up practice at
Lancaster, in Garrard Co., Ky. Mbr. of Ky. House, 1813-
1815, 1817. El. to U.S. House as a Clay Rep. in 1822, and
was reel. in 1824. Continued to serve in U.S. House as a
Natl. Rep. (Whig) until 1833. In the 1832 election, the
outcome was contested, and the election was subsequently
declared void by the U.S. House. Chosen in a spec. election to fill the vacancy in Aug., 1834, and served the remainder of term. Was not a cand. for succeeding regular
term. Pres. elector on Harrison-Granger (Whig) ticket in

1836. Mbr. of Ky. House, 1836-1838, serving as Speaker the last year. Nom. and el. Gov. as a Whig in 1840. Was first Ky. Gov. to proclaim Thanksgiving Day. Apptd. Minister to Mexico by Pres. Taylor in 1849, serving until 1852. Defeated as Whig cand. for U.S. House seat in 1852. Returned to law practice thereafter. Was a skillful violinist. m. first to Mary Epps. Second wife was Charlotte Robertson. No children. D. at Frankfort, Ky., Jan. 24, 1861. Bur. in Frankfort State Cem.

OWSLEY, WILLIAM (1844-1848). b. March 24, 1782 in Loudoun Co., Va. s. of Wm. and Catherine (Bolin) C. During son's youth family moved to Lincoln Co., Ky., where the father later became sheriff. Received a good educ. Taught school for a time, and also worked as deputy surveyor and as deputy sheriff under father. Studied law, was admitted to bar and began practice in Garrard Co. Mbr. of Ky. House, 1809-1811. Apptd. to Ky. Ct. of Appeals in 1810 by Gov. Scott. Was forced to resign in 1812 by a law reducing the number of judges on the ct., but was apptd. to it again by Gov. Shelby in 1813. Controversy arose in 1820s over legislation abolishing the "old" Ct. of Appeals and creating a new one in its place after the "old" Ct. of Appeals had rendered an unpopular decision holding a debtor relief law unconstl. Was a mbr. of the "old" Ct. of Appeals which held the law abolishing it, and creating a "new" Ct. in its place, invalid. Resigned seat in Dec., 1830. Was reapptd. by Gov. Metcalfe to the new Ct. of Appeals, but his nom. was not confirmed. Retired for a time to his farm in Garrard Co., and to law practice. Mbr. of Ky. House in 1830, and of Ky. Senate, 1832-1834. Pres. elector on the Clay ticket in 1832 pres. election. Ky. Sect. of State under Gov. Morehead, 1834-1836. Divided farm among five children and moved to Frankfort. Practiced law there until 1843, when he purchased a farm in Boyle Co. Nom. and el. Gov. as a Whig in 1844. Major controversy arose during admin. in 1846 when he removed Benj. Hardin, who was very popular, from the office of Sect. of State. Legislature disputed his right to do so, and refused to confirm successor until Hardin formally resigned the post. During admin., checked accumulation of public debt. Retired to pvt. life after tenure as Gov. Regarded as a relentless, persistent upholder of established constl. principles, as he understood them. m. circa 1805 to Elizabeth Gill. Five children. D. Dec. 9, 1862 on his farm in Boyle Co.

CRITTENDEN, JOHN JORDAN (1848-1850). b. Sept. 10, 1787 near Versailles, Ky. s. of Major John and Judith

(Harrison) C. Family was related through mother to that of
Thomas Jefferson. Father was a Rev. War soldier who had
settled in Ky. area in 1784, where he became a prominent
citizen. Attd. Pisgah Acad., in Woodford Co.; Washington
Coll., at Lexington, Va.; and William and Mary Coll., from
which he was grad. in 1806. Studied law, was admitted to
bar and began practice at Russellville, Ky. Apptd. Atty.
Gen. for Ill. Terr. by Pres. Madison in 1809, serving until
1811. El. to Ky. House in 1811. Served as aide on staff
of Gov. Shelby during the War of 1812. Reel. to Ky. legislature, serving until 1817, and became Speaker of the House.
El. to U.S. Senate in 1817, but resigned seat in 1819 and
returned to law practice at Frankfort, Ky. Mbr. of Ky.
House in 1825. Apptd. U.S. dist. atty. in 1827 by Pres.
J. Q. Adams, serving until his removal by Pres. Jackson in
1829. Nom. by Pres. Adams for a seat on U.S. Supreme Ct.,
but was not confirmed. Again a mbr. of Ky. House, 1829-
1832. Ky. Sect. of State, 1834. Mbr. of U.S. Senate again
from 1835 to 1841. Apptd. U.S. Atty. Gen. by Pres.
Harrison in 1841. Resigned post in Sept. of that year after the death of Pres. Harrison. Apptd. to U.S. Senate to
fill seat vacated by Henry Clay in 1842, and continued in
that office until June, 1848. Resigned seat at that time
to become a cand. of the Whig party for Gov., and was el.
Resigned in July, 1850, to accept apptmt. as U.S. Atty.
Gen. by Pres. Fillmore. Served in that capacity until end
of Fillmore's term in 1853. Became a mbr. of U.S. Senate
for fourth time in 1855, serving until 1861. El. to U.S.
House in 1860, and was a cand. for reel. as a Unionist at
the time of his death. As a mbr. of Cong., supported policies of Pres. Monroe; favored liberal policies on disposal
of pub. lands to settlers; opposed bank measures of Pres.
Jackson and the sub-treasury plan of Pres. Van Buren; opposed annexation of Texas; advocated resolution of Oregon
boundary dispute with Great Britain in 1846, and disunion
crisis in 1861, by peaceful means. Supported Bell and
Everett (Constl. Union) ticket for Pres. of U.S. in 1860,
but supported Pres. Lincoln's admin. after Civil War began.
Presided over Border States conv. at Frankfort in 1861 that
proposed to avert Civil War by a constl. amdt. extending
the Mo. Compromise line to the Pacific Ocean, and guaran-
teeing protection of slavery in States where it then exist-
ed. m. in 1811 to Sallie O. Lee, of Woodford Co. m. in
1826 to Maria Innes. m. in 1853 to Mrs. Elizabeth Ashley.
Nine children. Two of his sons fought in the Civil War as
army generals on opposing sides. A nephew, Thomas T. C.,
became a Gov. of Mo. (q.v.). D. at Frankfort, July 26,
1863. Bur. in Frankfort State Cem.

HELM, JOHN La RUE (1850-1851; 1867). b. July 4, 1802 at Helm Station, near Elizabethtown, Hardin Co., Ky. s. of George and Rebecca (La Rue) H. Grandfather had moved from Va. to Ky. in 1780, where he built a fort at his place for protection of settlers against Indians. Father was active in Ky. politics. Received common school educ. and worked in office of clerk of cir. ct. Studied law and was admitted to bar. Apptd. Hardin Co. atty. in 1824, continuing to serve in that capacity until 1838. Chosen to Ky. legislature in 1826 as cand. of "Old Ct." faction, and continued in office for most of the time during next 22 years in either the House or Senate, serving as House Speaker for several sessions. El. Lieut. Gov. as Whig in 1848. Succeeded to office of Gov. in 1850 when Gov. Crittenden resigned, and completed Crittenden's term. As Gov., supported system of internal improvements and secured creation of a bd. to supervise liquidation of state debt. Returned to law practice in 1852. Pres. elector on Whig ticket in 1852. Pres. of L. and N. R.R., 1854-1860. As Civil War neared, favored maintenance of neutral attitude by Ky., though sympathies were with South. Mbr. of Ky. Senate in 1865. Resigned seat in 1867 to become Dem. cand. for Gov. and was el. Was too ill to go to capital for inauguration, and oath of office was administered at his home. m. in 1831 to Lucinda Barbour Hardin. Twelve children. D. at his home Sept. 8, 1867, only five days after becoming Gov. Bur. at Helm Station.

POWELL, LAZARUS WHITEHEAD (1851-1855). b. Oct. 6, 1812 near Henderson, Ky. s. of Capt. Lazarus and Ann (McMahon) P. Attd. common schools and also was tutored. Grad. from St. Joseph's Coll., at Bardstown, Ky., in 1833. Studied law with Judge John Rowan and at Transylvania Univ. Admitted to the bar in 1835 and began practice at Henderson. Also managed a large plantation, and became quite wealthy. Mbr. of Ky. legislature in 1836. Pres. elector on Polk-Dallas ticket in 1844. Defeated as Dem. cand. for Gov. in 1847, but was nom. again and el. in 1851. Apptd. U.S. commnr. by Pres. Pierce in 1858 to resolve difficulties between Mormons and other white settlers in Utah area. Was successful in effort to restore order there after proclamation was issued extending amnesty to Mormons who had taken up arms. El. to U.S. Senate in 1859. When Civil War began, favored policy of neutrality for Ky. Opposed secession, but was sympathetic toward South. Served full term; but in 1862 a movement to expel him on grounds of disloyalty was initiated by his colleage, Sen. Davis. The movement failed and the charges

were subsequently withdrawn; but he failed to win reel. at
the end of his term. Retired to law practice thereafter.
Delegate to Unionist ("Loyalist") conv. at Philadelphia in
1866. m. in 1837 to Harriet Ann Jennings, of Hardin Co.
Three children. D. at his home near Henderson, July 3,
1867. Bur. in Fernwood Cem. there.

MOREHEAD, CHARLES SLAUGHTER (1855-1859). b. July 7,
1802 near Bardstown, Ky. s. of Charles and Margaret
(Slaughter) M. Attd. Transylvania Univ., receiving a law
degree in 1822, and was admitted to bar. Moved to
Christian Co., Ky., where he began law practice. Also be-
came a planter, acquiring plantations in Miss. and La.
Mbr. of Ky. House, 1828-1829 and 1832-1835. Atty. Gen. of
Ky., 1830-1835. In 1834 in collaboration with Judge Mason
Brown, published a four-volume digest of Ky. laws. Mbr. of
Ky. House, 1838-1842, 1844-1845 and 1853-1855, serving as
Speaker on three occasions. El. to U.S. House as a Whig in
1846 and again in 1848. Resumed law practice and mgmt. of
plantations in 1851. Pres. elector on Whig ticket in 1852.
Nom. and el. Gov. in 1855 as cand. of Whig and Amer. par-
ties. As Gov., opposed extension of banking privileges and
expansion of currency. Was critical of failure of free
States to observe obligations under the Fugitive Slave Law.
After term as Gov. engaged in law practice at Louisville
with nephew. Sought to avert Civil War as delegate to
"Peace Congress" in Washington, D.C. in 1861, and as mbr.
of Border States conf. at Frankfort, Ky. in May of that
year. Maintained that slave owners should be allowed to
take slave property anywhere in U.S. Opposed secession,
but favored policy of state neutrality when Civil War began.
Opposed recruitment of Union troops in Ky., which caused
him to be arrested in Sept., 1861. Imprisoned for a time
at Ft. Lafayette, in N.Y. and at Boston. Released in 1862.
Made way to Canada. Travelled in Europe until end of Civil
War. Returned to plantation near Greenville, Miss. D. at
his plantation near Greenville, Miss., Dec. 21, 1868. Bur.
in Frankfort State Cem.

MAGOFFIN, BERIAH (1859-1862). b. April 18, 1815 at
Harrodsburg, Ky. s. of Beriah and Jane (McAfee) M. Father
was a native of Ireland. Mother was of Scotch-Irish origin,
and was a native of Ky. Attd. Centre Coll., from which he
was grad. in 1835, and Transylvania Univ., from which he
received a law degree in 1838. Began practice at Jackson,
Miss. in 1838. Apptd. reading clerk of Miss. Senate in
that year, but soon returned to Harrodsburg, where he practiced law. Apptd. police judge in 1840. El. to Ky. Senate

in 1850. Cand. for pres. elector on Dem. tickets in 1844,
1848, 1852 and 1856 pres. elections. Mbr. of Ky. Senate,
1850. Declined nom. for U.S. House in 1851. Unsuccessful
as Dem. nominee for Lieut. Gov. in 1855. Nom. and el. Gov.
as Dem. in 1859. As Civil War neared sought unsuccessfully
to placate Southern slave interests by advocating amdts. to
U.S. Const. that would protect slavery. Recommended holding of Border States conf. in 1861 to this end, which proposed such compromise measures. After conflict began,
adopted a policy of neutrality for Ky. against competing
U.S. and C.S.A. authorities. Refused to comply with Pres.
Lincoln's call for troops to resist rebellion. Issued proclamation forbidding recruitment by both North and South in
Ky., and warning both sides against invasion of Ky. His
veto of a resolution of the legislature requesting South to
withdraw troops from Western Ky. was overridden, as was also his veto of a resolution requesting military aid from
the U.S. govt. His veto of a bill in 1862 disfranchising
anyone entering Confed. service was also overridden. In
August, 1862, resigned office of Gov. because of these
differences with the legislature. Thereafter he became
more openly sympathetic toward the Southern cause. Delegate to Dem. natl. convs. in 1848, 1856, 1860 and 1872.
Mbr. of Ky. legislature, 1867-1869. m. in 1840 to Ann
Shelby, a grand-daughter of Gov. Isaac Shelby (q.v.). Five
s.; five d. D. at his home in Harrodsburg, Feb. 28, 1885.

ROBINSON, JAMES FISHER (1862-1863). b. Oct. 4, 1800
in Scott Co., Ky. s. of Jonathan and Jane (Black) R. Descendant of a Scotch-Irish ancestor who emigrated to Pa. in
1600s. Father, who had served as an Amer. soldier during
the Rev. War, settled in Ky. after that war. Educ. by pvt.
tutors and at Forest Hill Acad. Grad. from Transylvania
Univ. in 1818. Studied law, admitted to bar and began
practice at Georgetown, Ky. Mbr. of Ky. Senate in 1851 as
a Whig, and continued to serve therein through 1861-1862.
Was Speaker of Senate when Gov. Magoffin resigned in Aug.,
1862. The office of Lieut. Gov. being vacant at the time,
he succeeded to the office of Gov. and completed Magoffin's
term. Admin. was a troubled one because Ky. was the scene
of much campaigning and fighting by the opposing Union and
Confed. armies during that period of time. Gave support to
Union cause. After tenure as Gov., settled on his estate,
"Cardome", near Georgetown, where he engaged in farming and
law practice. Was married three times. Eight children.
D. at his home, Nov. 1. 1882.

BRAMLETTE, THOMAS E. (1863-1867). b. Jan. 3, 1817 in

Cumberland Co., Ky.   Attd. local schools.   Studied law, admitted to bar in 1837 and began practice at Albany, Ky.
Mbr. of Ky. legislature in 1841.   Atty. Gen. of Ky., 1849-1851.   In 1852 moved to Columbia, Ky., where he engaged in
law practice.   El. cir. ct. judge of his dist. in 1856.
Resigned that post in 1861 upon outbreak of Civil War to
assist in raising a regiment of volunteers for service in
the Union cause.   Became col. of the regiment.   In 1862 was
apptd. U.S. dist. atty. for Ky. by Pres. Lincoln.   Tried
and secured conviction of a prominent citizen, Thomas C.
Shacklett, for aiding Southern cause at a treason trial attracting much attention.   The ten-year sentence imposed was
later reduced to two years by Pres. Lincoln.   Commissioned
as major gen. in Union Army in 1863.   Nom. and el. Gov. as
cand. of Union (Dem.) party in that year.   During part of
1864-1865, civil authority was partially supplanted in Ky.
by state of martial law imposed by Pres. Lincoln because of
invasion of areas by Confed. forces.   Admin. generally regarded as fair toward both sides in the civil conflict.
Proposed as a cand. for Vice Pres. of U.S. by Union (Dem.)
party conv. at Louisville in 1864, but declined to seek the
office.   Settled in Louisville where he engaged in law
practice after tenure as Gov.   m. in 1837 to Sallie Travis.
One s.; one d.   After her death, m. to Mrs. Mary E. Adams,
of Louisville, in 1874.   D. at Louisville, Jan. 12, 1875.

HELM, JOHN La RUE (1867).   See above, 1850-1851.

STEVENSON, JOHN WHITE (1867-1871).   b. May 4, 1812 at
Richmond, Va.   s. of Andrew and Mary Page (White) S.   Father
was prominent in Va. politics and had served as Speaker of
U.S. House in 1827-1834, and as U.S. Minister to Great
Britain, 1836-1841.   Attd. Hampton-Sydney Acad. and the
Univ. of Va., graduating from the latter in 1832.   Studied
law, was admitted to bar and began practice at Vicksburg,
Miss.   Moved to Covington, Ky. in 1841, where he soon became Kenton Co. atty.   Mbr. of Ky. legislature, 1845-1849.
Delegate to Ky. constl. conv. in 1850.   Delegate to Dem.
natl. convs. in 1848, 1852 and 1856, and pres. elector on
Dem. tickets in 1852 and 1856.   In 1850-1851 was mbr. of a
three-man commn. to revise Ky. civil and criminal codes.
Mbr. of U.S. House, 1857-1861.   Defeated for third term in
1860.   Attd. Unionist ("Loyalist") conv. at Philadelphia in
1866.   Favored Pres. Johnson's Reconstruction policies in
1866-1867.   Nom. and el. Lieut. Gov. as Dem. in 1867, and
succeeded to office of Gov. in Sept., 1867, when Gov. Helm
died five days after becoming Gov.   El. in a spec. election
in Aug., 1868, to complete Helm's term.   Resigned in Feb.,

1871, after having been el. to U.S. Senate. Was a strict
constructionist on constl. questions. Opposed rivers and
harbors aid by U.S. govt. After serving one term, became
prof. of commercial law at Cincinnati Law School. Ch. of
Dem. natl. conv. in 1880. Pres. of Amer. Bar Assoc., 1884-
1885. Episcopalian. m. in 1843 to Sibella Winston, of
Newport, Ky. Five children. D. Aug. 10, 1886, at
Covington, Ky. Bur. in Spring Grove Cem., Cincinnati.

LESLIE, PRESTON HOPKINS (1871-1875). b. March 2, 1817
(1819?) in Wayne (now Clinton) Co., Ky. s. of Vachel and
Sally (Hopkins) L. Descendant of Welsh and Scotch ancestors who had emigrated to N.C. and Ga. As youth worked on
father's farm. Attd. local schools, and for five months,
an acad. at Columbia, Ky. At age 16 went to work for a
farmer near Louisville, Ky. Also clerked in a store, and
was a deputy clerk of co. ct. Began study of law in 1838.
Admitted to bar in 1840, and began practice in Wayne Co.
In 1841 moved to Monroe Co., where he continued to practice
law. Co. atty. of Monroe Co., 1842. Mbr. of Ky. House,
1844. Unsuccessful as cand. for Ky. Senate in 1846. Mbr.
of Ky. House again in 1850, and in 1851, of Ky. Senate.
Practiced law and farmed in Monroe Co., 1852-1859. Refused
nom. for U.S. House and for Ky. Ct. of Appeals. Was mbr. of
Whig party until 1854, then switched affiliation to Dem.
party. In 1859 moved to Glasgow, Ky. where he practiced
law. Until outbreak of Civil War was a strong Union man,
but sympathies were with South during the Civil War. Mbr.
of Ky. Senate in 1867, becoming Speaker of that body. Succeeded to office of Gov. in Feb., 1871, when Gov. Stevenson
resigned, the office of Lieut. Gov. being vacant. El. for
regular term in that year, defeating John M. Harlan, later
an Assoc. Justice of U.S. Supreme Ct. During admin., state
debt was paid off. After tenure as Gov. returned to law
practice in Glasgow. Apptd., and later el., cir. ct. judge
in 1881. Defeated for that office in 1886. Apptd. Gov. of
Montana Terr. by Pres. Cleveland in 1886, serving until
1889. Established residence in Helena, Mont., where he
practiced law. Apptd. U.S. dist. atty. for Montana by Pres.
Cleveland in 1894, serving until 1898. Baptist. m. in
1841 to Louisa Black. Seven children. After her death in
1858, m. to Mrs. Mary Kuykendall, of Boone Co., Ky. Three
children. D. at Helena, Mont., Feb. 7, 1907.

McCREARY, JAMES BENNETT (1875-1879; 1911-1915). b. July
8, 1838 at Richmond, Ky. s. of Robt. and Sabrina (Bennett)
McC. Family originally resided in Va. Attd. common
schools and Centre Coll., from which he was grad. in 1857.

Grad. with honors in law from Cumberland Univ. in 1859 and
began practice at Richmond, Ky.   Enlisted in a Confed. cavalry regiment in 1862.   Served under Gen. Morgan and Gen.
Breckenridge, and was a lieut. col. by the end of the Civil
War.   Delegate to Dem. natl. conv. in 1868, but declined
nom. as Dem. pres. elector in that year.   Mbr. of Ky. House
in 1869-1875, serving as Speaker in latter two terms.   Nom.
and el. Gov. as Dem. in 1875, becoming the youngest to have
been elected to that office up to that time.   During admin.,
disorders between political factions in the eastern area of
Ky. required his intervention by mil. force to restore order.   El. to U.S. House in 1884, and continued in that office until 1897.   Defeated for reel. in 1896.   As mbr. of
Cong., supported measures for benefit of agri.; tariff reform and reciprocity; free coinage of silver; and electoral
reforms.   Attd. Brussels Monetary Conf. as one of five U.S.
delegates in 1891-1892, where he advocated bi-metallism.
Delegate to Dem. natl. convs. of 1868, 1900, 1904, 1908,
1912, and ch. of Ky. Dem. conv. in 1900.   El. to U.S. Senate in 1902, but was defeated for second term in 1908.
Nom. and el. Gov. again as Dem. in 1911 at age 73, becoming
the oldest person to have been el. to that office in Ky.
Defeated as cand. for U.S. Senate in 1914.   Resumed law
practice and mgmt. of farms in Ky. and Ala.   m. in 1867 to
Kate Hughes, of Fayette Co., Ky.   D. at Richmond, Oct. 8,
1918.   Bur. in Richmond Cem.

BLACKBURN, LUKE PRYOR (1879-1883).   b. June 16, 1816
in Woodford (Fayette?) Co., Ky.   s. of Edward and Lavinia
(Bell) B.   Family had moved from Va. to Ky. about 1790,
where they had settled and built a blockhouse, "Blackburn's
Post", for protection against Indians.   Father became well-
known as breeder of fine horses.   Attd. Transylvania Univ.,
receiving a degree in med. in 1834.   Began med. practice in
Lexington, Ky. at age 19.   Dealt with an outbreak of
cholera in the vicinity of Versailles, Ky. successfully
soon after beginning practice, and moved med. practice
there at the request of the inhabitants.   Mbr. of Ky. legislature in 1843.   In 1846 moved to Natchez, Miss., where
he continued med. practice.   In 1848 and again in 1854,
outbreaks of yellow fever occurred at New Orleans, which he
assisted in combatting.   Was instrumental in getting act
passed establishing quarantine station below New Orleans
and setting up hospitals to prevent spread of disease.
During the Civil War served as a surgeon in the Confed.
Army on the staff of Gen. Sterling Price.   After the war,
retired to a plantation in Ark. from 1867 to 1873, when he
returned to Louisville, Ky.   During a yellow fever epidemic

at Memphis, which threatened the entire Mississippi Valley, org. and directed spec. med. corps to combat it. Again assisted in controlling an epidemic at Hickman, Ky. in 1878. Nom. and el. Gov. as Dem. in 1879. Sought and obtained reforms in criminal justice and penal systems. When legislature refused to cooperate in dealing with health, sanitation and over-crowding conditions at the State's only prison, used pardoning power to release a number of elderly and ill prisoners, which induced the legislature to act. m. in 1835 to Ella Guest Boswell. After her death in 1855, m. in 1857 to Julia M. Churchill, of Louisville, Ky. D. at Frankfort, Ky., Sept. 14, 1887.

KNOTT, J(AMES) PROCTOR (1883-1887). b. Aug. 29, 1830 near Lebanon, Ky. s. of Joseph Perez and Maria Irvine (McElroy) K. Attd. common schools. At age 16 began study of law. In 1850 moved to Memphis, in Scotland Co., Mo. Worked as deputy in co. offices while continuing to study law. Admitted to bar in 1851 and built up a good practice in Northeast Mo. Mbr. of Mo. House in 1857. Resigned seat in 1859 after being apptd. Atty. Gen. of Mo. to fill a vacancy. Refused to take oath of allegiance to U.S. in 1861 after outbreak of Civil War, and was removed from office by pro-Union conv. that had assumed control over political affairs in Mo. in that year. Imprisoned for a time at St. Louis, Mo., but was soon released. Returned to Ky. in 1863 and began law practice at Lebanon. El. to U.S. House in 1866 and again in 1868. Was not a cand. for reel. in 1870. El. again in 1874 to U.S. House, and was continued in office until 1883. Did not seek reel. in 1882. Acquired reputation for humorous speech-making. As mbr. of U.S. House was one of mgrs. selected to conduct impeachment trial of Sect. of War Belknap. Nom. and el. Gov. as Dem. in 1883. Sponsored improvements and reforms in state govt. Influential mbr. of Ky. constl. conv. in 1891. Apptd. prof. of civics and econ. at Centre Coll. in 1892, later transferring to the law school, of which he became dean. Hon. degree from Centre Coll. m. in 1852 to Mary E. Forman, of Memphis, Mo. After her death six months after marriage, m. in 1858 to Sarah McElroy, of Bowling Green, Ky. D. June 18, 1911 at Lebanon, Ky. Bur. in Ryder Cem. there.

BUCKNER, SIMON BOLIVAR (1887-1891). b. April 1, 1823 near Mumfordville, Ky. s. of Aylette H. and Elizabeth A. (Morehead) B. A paternal ancestor had emigrated to Va. from England in 1635. Mother was a cousin of James T. and Charles S. Morehead, both of whom were Govs. of Ky. (q.v.). In 1820 father purchased a farm in Ky. Built mansion there

and operated an iron mfg. bus. Attd. local schools and
West Point Mil. Acad., graduating from there in 1844. Became a teacher of ethics at the Mil. Acad., 1845-1846.
Served in U.S. Army as lieut., then as capt., during War
with Mexico. Returned to the Mil. Acad. as instructor in
mil. tactics, 1848-1850. Participated in campaigns against
Indians in the West in 1852. Resigned mil. commn. in 1855
and returned to Ky. to bus. pursuits, settling at
Louisville. Inspector gen. of Ky. guard and militia, 1859-
1860. Sent by Gov. Magoffin to Washington in 1861 to confer with U.S. govt. on problems arising from Civil War in
the Border States. Was offered commn. as brig. gen. in
U.S. Army by Pres. Lincoln, but refused it, preferring to
accept instead a commn. as brig. gen. in the Confed. Army.
Was left in command of Confed. forces at Ft. Donelson by
his superior officers in 1862, and was forced to surrender
the fort and his command to Gen. Grant. Imprisoned for
several months, and was then exchanged. Became a major
gen., then a lieut. gen., in Confed. Army, serving under
Gen. Bragg. Participated in many major engagements in
Western theater of the Civil War. Returned to bus. interests in Ky. after the war. Nom. and el. Gov. as Dem. in
1887. Mbr. of Ky. constl. conv. in 1891. Defeated as cand.
for U.S. Senate in 1895 as advocate of gold standard. Nom.
for Vice Pres. of U.S. on Gold Standard Dem. ticket with
ex-Gov. Palmer, of Ill. in 1896 (q.v.). Was a lover of
books and learning, and had respect of opposing officers in
Civil War. Was a pall bearer at funeral of Pres. U. S.
Grant. m. in 1850 to Mary Kingsbury, who died in 1869.
One d. m. in 1885 to Delia Clayborne (Claiborne?), of
Richmond, Va. One s. D. at Mumfordville, Ky., Jan. 8,
1914.

    BROWN, JOHN YOUNG (1891-1895). b. June 28, 1835 at
Claysville, Hardin Co., Ky.   s. of Thomas Dudley and
Elizabeth (Young) B. Father was active in Ky. politics.
Grad. from Centre Coll. in 1855. Studied law and admitted
to bar in 1857. Began practice in Elizabethtown, Ky., and
soon became active in politics. At age 24, was nom. and
el. to U.S. House in 1859, despite his being ineligible because of age. Did not take seat until the following year.
Supported Sen. Douglas for Pres. of U.S. in 1860 and was
a pres. elector cand. on Douglas ticket. Engaged in de-
bates with an elector for Breckinridge that attracted much
pub. attention. At end of Civil War moved to Henderson,
Ky., where he practiced law. El. to U.S. House in 1866,
but was not seated on grounds of alleged disloyalty to the
Union. Was seated after el. to the House again in 1872 and

again in 1874. During tenure in Cong. was censured by the
House for a speech severely attacking Gen. B. F. Butler,
later Gov. of Mass. (q.v.), but censure was later expunged.
Returned to law practice in 1875. Nom. and el. Gov. as
Dem. in 1891. Used veto power freely against allegedly
radical measures passed by the legislature, in which
Farmers Alliance was strong. Returned to law practice.
Defeated as Indep. Dem. cand. in the disputed gubernatorial
election of 1899. m. to Rebecca Dixon, d. of Gen.
Archibald Dixon. D. Jan. 11, 1904, at Henderson, Ky. Bur.
in Fernwood Cem. there.

BRADLEY, WILLIAM O'CONNELL (1895-1899). b. March 18,
1847 near Lancaster, Ky. s. of Robert McAfee and Nancy
Ellen (Totten) B. Father was a distinguished lawyer and
was an active supporter of Union cause during the Civil War.
Attd. pub. and pvt. schools at Somerset, Ky. At age 14
served as page in Ky. legislature. At age 15 twice sought
unsuccessfully to enlist in Union Army but was released because of youth. Studied law and was admitted to bar in
1865 by spec. act of legislature permitting him to do so at
age 18. Established practice at Garrard, where he soon became prominent and influential in politics. Pros. atty. of
Garrard Co. in 1870. Pres. elector on Lib. Rep.-Dem. ticket in 1872 pres. election. Delegate to Rep. natl. convs.
in 1872, 1880, 1884, 1892, 1896, 1900, 1904 and 1908 campaigns. Defeated as Rep. cand. for U.S. House in 1872 and
1876, and for U.S. Senate seat on five occasions. Mbr. of
Rep. natl. commt. for 12 years. Defeated as Rep. cand. for
Gov. in 1887. Apptd. U.S. Minister to Korea in 1889, but
declined the post. Nom. and el. Gov. as Rep. in 1895, becoming the first Rep. to hold that office. Opposed free
coinage of silver and favored a protective tariff. El. to
U.S. Senate in 1909. m. in 1867 to Margaret R. Duncan, of
Lancaster, Ky. Hon. degree from Univ. of Ky. D. May 23,
1914, during the fifth year of his term as U.S. Sen. Bur.
in Frankfort State Cem.

TAYLOR, WILLIAM SYLVESTER (1899-1900). b. Oct. 10,
1853 in Butler Co., Ky. s. of Sylvester T. Attd. common
schools. Clerk of Butler Co. ct., 1882-1886. Studied law
and admitted to bar. Judge of Butler Co. ct., 1886-1894.
El. Atty. Gen. of Ky. as Rep. in 1895, serving until 1895.
Was first Rep. to be el. to that office for many years.
Nom. and declared el. Gov. by Ky. Canvassing Bd. by some
2,400 votes in 1899 in a bitter contest with Dem. opponent,
Wm. Goebel, and former Gov. J. Y. Brown, who ran as an
Indep. Dem. cand. Assumed office on Dec. 12, 1899, but

outcome of election was contested in the legislature by his
Dem. opponent, Goebel. Involvement of the legislature,
which was under the control of the Dem. party, in the matter caused much political unrest, and militia forces were
assembled at his direction to maintain order. T. sought to
adjourn the legislature's session to another site away from
the capital, but the legislature refused to cooperate. After it became apparent that the legislature was about to
declare that Goebel had won the election, Goebel was shot
and fatally wounded on the Capitol grounds on Jan. 30. The
legislature then declared Goebel to have been el., and the
Lieut. Gov. on his ticket assumed the office of Gov. after
Goebel died of his wounds. T. was later indicted on a
charge of complicity in connection with the shooting of
Goebel. He fled to Ind., and requests on several occasions
for his return to Ky. for trial were ignored by Ind. Govs.
The charge against T. was eventually dropped in 1909 by
Gov. Willson, of Ky. T. continued to live in Ind. until
his death. m. in 1878 to Sarah B. Tanner. D. Aug. 2, 1928
at Indianapolis, Ind.

GOEBEL, WILLIAM (1900). b. Jan. 4, 1856 in Sullivan
Co., Pa. s. of Wm. and Augusta (Greeneclay) G. Father,
who was of German origin, served in Union Army during the
Civil War, but an uncle served with Confed. forces in Va.
Family moved to Ludington, Ky. when son was a youth. Apprenticed to a jeweler in Cincinnati, but soon began study
of law in office of ex-Gov. John Stevenson. Grad. from law
school in Cincinnati before he was old enough to be admitted to bar. Attd. Kenyon Coll., in Ohio, for one year.
Became law partner of U.S. Repr. and House Speaker, John G.
Carlisle. Later became law partner of ex-Gov. Stevenson.
Acquired extensive practice. Mbr. of Ky. Senate in 1886 and
for two succeeding terms. In legislature and as a lawyer
became known as vigorous opponent of corp. interests.
Challenged Col. John Sanford, a Covington banker and pres.
of a Ky. turnpike bus., to a duel after threats were allegedly made by Sanford against his life. Was wounded in
subsequent encounter, in which Sanford was killed. Sponsored a measure in legislature reducing toll rates. Law
was later held unconstl. by U.S. Supreme Ct. as applied to
an interstate bridge at Covington, Ky. Also sponsored law
outlawing black-listing of railroad employees who joined
unions; a school textbook purchase law; and a law encouraging founding of pub. libraries. Mbr. of Ky. const. conv.
of 1891. Leader in struggle for reduction of rates by L.
and N. R.R., and opposed railroad lobbyists in the legislature. Urged to run for seat in Cong. but declined,

preferring to carry on political activities at the state
level. Became Dem. party nominee for Gov. in 1899 over
bitter opposition of corp. interests, particularly the L.
and N. R.R. Rep. opponent was declared el. by the State Bd.
of Canvassers and assumed the office, but G. contested the
result before the legislature, charging fraud and intimidation of voters. Legislature, which was under control of
Dem. party, convened in an atmosphere of tension and
threats of violence. It resisted effort of the newly-
installed Gov., Wm. Taylor, to adjourn and re-convene at a
place other than the state capital. On Jan. 30, shortly
before the legislature was to render its decision, G. was
shot by an assassin from a nearby office as he stood on
steps of the Capitol. Was declared el. the next day by the
legislature and took the oath of office while on death bed.
D. three days later, Feb. 2, 1900, at Frankfort.

    BECKHAM, JOHN CREPPS WICKLIFFE (1900-1907). b. Aug.
5, 1869 at "Wickland", the family homestead near Bardstown,
Ky. s. of Wm. Netherton and Julia Tevis (Wickliffe) B.
Was a grandson of Charles A. Wickliffe, Gov. of Ky. (q.v.),
and a nephew of Robt. Wickliffe, Gov. of La. (q.v.).
Father was a lawyer and had served in the Ky. legislature.
Attd. Roseland Acad., at Bardstown, and Central Univ., at
Richmond, Ky. Served as page in Ky. legislature, 1881-1882.
In 1886 managed mother's farm and also began study of law.
Became principal of Bardstown pub. schools in 1888. Admitted to bar in 1889. Opened law office in Bardstown. Mbr.
of Ky. House in 1893, but declined to run for succeeding
term. El. to Ky. House again in 1896 and became Speaker.
Nom. and ultimately declared el. Lieut. Gov. as Dem. in
hotly contested election of 1899, assuming office in Jan.,
1900. Succeeded to office of Gov. very shortly thereafter,
following death of Gov. Goebel by assassination. His right
to succeed to the office was contested unsuccessfully by
his Rep. opponent in the Ky. cts. and the U.S. Supreme Ct.
El. to fill out the remainder of Goebel's term in a spec.
election in Nov., 1900. Nom. and el. as Dem. for the succeeding regular term in 1903. During admin., state debt
was liquidated; Ky. claims against U.S. growing out of the
Civil War and Spanish-Amer. War were settled. Mbr. of Ky.
commn. for Louisiana Purchase Expo. at St. Louis in 1904.
Unsuccessful as Dem. nominee for U.S. Senate seat in 1906,
but was nom. and el. to that post in 1914. Defeated for
second term in 1920. Resumed law practice in Louisville.
Defeated as Dem. nominee for Gov. in 1927. Mbr. and ch. of
Commn. on Reorg. of Ky. State Govt. in 1935. Served for a
time as ch. of Ky. Pub. Service Commn. Unsuccessful as

cand. for Dem. nom. for a U.S. Senate seat in 1936. Delegate to Dem. natl. convs., 1904-1920. Hon. degree from
Central Univ. Presbyterian. m. in 1900 to Jean Raphael
Fuqua, of Owensboro, Ky. One s.; one d. D. Jan. 9, 1940,
at Louisville, Ky. Bur. in Frankfort State Cem.

WILLSON, AUGUSTUS EVERETT (1907-1911). b. Oct. 13,
1846 at Maysville, Ky. s. of Hiram and Ann Colvin (Ennis)
W. Father was a native of Vt. who had moved to Ind. and
then to Ky., where he engaged in lumber bus. Father was
originally a Dem. who later affiliated with the Rep. party
because of slavery issue. Received classical educ. Attd.
Alfred Acad., in N.Y., and Harvard Univ., where he was grad.
in 1869. In 1872 received an A.M. degree from Harvard.
Also studied law there. Admitted to bar in 1870 and became
partner of John Harlan, later Assoc. Justice of U.S.
Supreme Ct., at Louisville. Chief clerk of U.S. Treas.
Dept. in 1875. Formed partnership with James Harlan,
brother of John, in 1878. Delegate to Rep. natl. convs.,
1884-1892 and 1904-1916. Defeated as Rep. cand. for U.S.
House in 1884, 1886, 1888 and 1892. Nom. and el. Gov. as
Rep. in 1907. During admin., disturbances arising from
"night riders", who were Ky. tobacco farmers seeking to induce other growers to withhold crops from market in effort
to force up prices for their products offered by tobacco
mfg. companies, became a problem. Violence resulted, requiring action by Gov. to preserve order. Issued pardon to
Wm. S. Taylor, former Gov. of Ky. for a brief time, who had
been indicted in connection with the assassination of Gov.
Goebel in 1900. Prominent mbr. of White House Conf. on
conservation of natural resources assembled by Pres.
Roosevelt in 1908, which led to assembly of first U.S.
Govs.' Conf. in 1909. Resumed law practice after term as
Gov. Mbr., Bd. of Overseers of Harvard Univ., 1910-1918.
Hon. degrees from Harvard, Univ. of Ky., and Berea Coll.
m. in 1877 to Mary Elizabeth Ekin. D. Aug. 24, 1931.

McCREARY, JAMES BENNETT (1911-1915). See above, 1875-
1879.

STANLEY, AUGUSTUS OWSLEY (1915-1919). b. May 21, 1867
at Shelbyville, Ky. s. of Wm. and Amanda (Owsley) S.
Father was a minister of the Christian (Disciples) church.
Attd. common schools; Gordon Acad., at Nicholasville, Ky.;
grad. from Centre Coll. in 1889. Also attd. Ky. State
Coll., Lexington. Taught school for four years. Was prin-
cipal of Marion Acad., at Hortonville, Ky., and at
Mackville Acad. Prof. of belle lettres at Christian Coll.

Studied law, admitted to bar in 1894 and began practice at
Flemingsburg, Ky. In 1898 moved practice to Henderson, Ky.
Pres. elector on Bryan ticket in 1900. El. to U.S. House
in 1902, continuing in that office until 1915. Defeated
for reel. in 1914. Nom. and el. Gov. as Dem. in 1915. Intervention at Murray, Ky. and forceful speech saved life of
a Negro about to be lynched. Nom. and el. to U.S. Senate
in 1918 before end of term, resigning office of Gov. in
May, 1919. Defeated for reel. to Senate in 1924. Resumed
law practice in Washington, D.C. In 1930, apptd. to U.S.-
Canadian Jt. Boundary Commn., becoming its ch. in 1933.
Served in that capacity until 1954, when he retired. As
mbr. of Cong., was noted as forceful debater. Was opponent
of trusts and monopolies, especially the "tobacco trust".
Headed spec. commt. to investigate U.S. Steel Corp. practices and helped draft original version of Clayton Anti-
trust Act. Supported Pres. Wilson's policies, including
participation by U.S. in League of Nations; opposed protective tariffs; opposed adoption of 18th and 19th Amdts. as
infringements on States Rts. Mbr., S.A.R.; Friendly Sons
of St. Patrick; K.P.; Elks; Woodmen; Filson Club of Ky.
Hon. degree, Univ. of Ky. Christian (Disciples) church.
m. in 1903 to Sue Soaper, of Henderson, Ky. Two s.; one d.
D. Aug. 12, 1958, at Washington, D.C. Bur. in Frankfort
Cem.

BLACK, JAMES DIXON (1919). b. Sept. 24, 1849 in Knox
Co., Ky. s. of John Calhoun and Clarissa (Jones) B. Father, who was a farmer, was a descendant of an Irish immigrant who came to S.C. in 1700s. Grad. at Tusculum Coll.,
near Greenville, Tenn., in 1872. Taught school for two
years while studying law. Admitted to bar in 1874 and began practice at Barbourville, Ky. Later formed a law firm
there with son and son-in-law. As an atty., represented
railroad and ins. firms. Mbr., Ky. legislature, 1876. Co.
supt. of schools of Knox Co., 1884-1886. Mbr. of Ky. commn.
to World's Columbian Expo. at Chicago in 1893. Pres. of
Union Coll., at Barbourville, 1910-1912. Asst. Atty. Gen.
of Ky., 1912. Nom. and el. Lieut. Gov. as Dem. in 1915.
Succeeded to office of Gov. in May, 1919, when Gov. Stanley
resigned, and completed Stanley's term, which had about six
months to run. Won Dem. nom. for election to regular term
in 1919, but was defeated in the gen. election. Pres. of
Natl. Bank of Barbourville until it merged with another
bank. Apptd. chief prohibition inspector of Ky. in 1920.
Hon. degrees from Tusculum Coll. and Union Coll. Mbr.,
Masons. Methodist. m. in 1875 to Mary Jeannette Pitzer,
of Barbourville. Two d.; one s. D. at Barbourville,

Aug. 5, 1938.

MORROW, EDWIN PORCH (1919-1923). b. Nov. 28, 1877
(1878?) at Somerset, Ky. s. of Judge Thomas Z. and Jennie
Crosson (Bradley) M. Descendant of Scotch immigrant who
resided originally in Pa. Family was related to that of
Jeremiah Morrow, Gov. of Ohio (q.v.). Through his mother
he was a nephew of Gov. W. O. Bradley, of Ky. (q.v.). Attd.
St. Mary's Coll., St. Mary, Ky.; Cumberland Coll.; and
Centre Coll., from which he was grad. At age 17 took an
active part in campaign of his uncle, W. O. Bradley, for
Gov. Served as second lieut. in Ky. volunteer regiment in
Spanish-Amer. War. Received law degree from Cincinnati
Law School in 1900. Admitted to bar and began practice in
Lexington, Ky. In first case successfully defended a Negro
charged with murder of a prominent citizen. Moved to
Somerset, where he continued in law practice as father's
partner. Defeated as cand. for Rep. nom. for Gov. in 1907.
U.S. dist. atty. for Eastern Ky., 1911-1915. Defeated as
Rep. cand. for U.S. Senate in 1912, and as Rep. cand. for
Gov. in 1915. Nom. and el. Gov. as Rep. in 1919. During
admin., was a staunch defender of pub. peace and order.
Used militia forces in 1920 to prevent lynching of a Negro
accused of murder, with six persons being killed as result
of lynching attempt. After tenure as Gov. was mbr. of U.S.
Railway Labor Bd., 1924-1926, and a mbr. of U.S. Railway
Arb. Bd. Noted as a political orator. Recipient of D.S.M.
in 1919. Mbr., Masons; K.P.; Elks; I.O.O.F.; various pro-
fessional legal orgs. Presbyterian. m. in 1905 to
Katherine H. Waddell (Waddle?), of Somerset. One s.; one d.
D. June 15, 1935.

FIELDS, WILLIAM JASON (1923-1927). b. Dec. 29, 1874
at Willard, Ky. s. of Christopher C. and Alice (Rucker) F.
Family was of Scotch descent. Grew up on father's farm and
attd. pub. schools in Carter Co. Studied law at intervals
at Univ. of Ky. Married at age 19, and settled on farm
near Olive Hill, Ky. Carter Co. constable in 1896. Engaged as travelling salesman for wholesale grocery firm and
as real estate agent, 1899-1910. Mbr. of U.S. House, 1911-
1923. Named in 1923 as replacement for regular Dem. nominee for Gov. who had died during course of campaign, and
was el. Resigned seat in Cong. to assume office of Gov. in
Dec., 1923. As Gov., approved bill requiring reading of
Bible in pub. schools; followed strict policy in granting
pardons; opposed influence of racing lobby in legislature;
forbade dancing in Gov.'s mansion; supported increased aid
for educ. After tenure as Gov. was admitted to bar and

practiced law at Olive Hill. From 1932 to 1935 served as
pros. atty. for his jud. dist.; and from 1936 to 1944 was
mbr. of Ky. Workmen's Compensation Commn. Engaged in ins.
bus., 1940-1945. Mbr., Masons. Methodist. m. in 1893 to
Dora McDavid, of Rosedale, Ky. Five s.; one d. D. Oct.
21, 1954, at Grayson, Ky. Bur. in Olive Hill Cem.

SAMPSON, FLEM(ON) DAVIS (1927-1931). b. Jan. 23, 1875
at London, Laurel Co., Ky. s. of Joseph and Emmaline
(Emoline?) (Kellems) S. Attd. Laurel Sem.; Union Coll., at
Barbourville, Ky.; and Valparaiso Univ., in Ind., from
which he was grad. with a law degree in 1894. Admitted to
bar in 1895 and began practice at Barbourville. Knox Co.
judge, 1905-1908. Pres. of First Natl. Bank of
Barbourville, 1905-1910. El. cir. ct. judge to fill vacancy in 1911 and was reel. in 1915. Mbr., Ky. Ct. of Appeals,
1916-1927, serving as Chief Judge, 1923-1924. Nom. and el.
Gov. as Rep. in 1927. As Gov., advocated improvements of
roads, parks, devel. of natural resources, and measures to
attract indus. to Ky. Returned to law practice at
Barbourville and Louisville after tenure as Gov. El. cir.
ct. judge in 1938, continuing in office until 1946, when he
retired to engage in law practice. Author in 1940 of
Organized League for Justice. Mbr., Masons; Elks; I.O.O.F.;
K.P. Methodist. Hon. degree from Lincoln Memorial Univ.
in 1928. m. in 1897 to Susan Steele, of Barbourville.
Three d. D. May 25, 1967.

LAFFOON, RUBY (1931-1935). b. Jan. 15, 1869 at
Madisonville, Hopkins Co., Ky. s. of John Bledsoe and
Martha (Earle) L. Attd. pub. and pvt. schools in Hopkins
Co. At age 17 went to Washington, D.C., to work on staff
of his uncle who was a mbr. of U.S. House. Became messenger in U.S. Pensions Office. Attd. Washington and Lee
Univ., 1888-1889. Studied law at nights at Columbian Univ.
in Washington, D.C. Admitted to bar in 1892 and began
practice in Madisonville. Served as Hopkins Co. atty.
Apptd. ch. of first State Ins. Rating Bd. in 1912. El. cir.
ct. judge in 1921 and continued in that office until 1931,
when he resigned to seek office of Gov. Nom. and el. Gov.
as Dem. in 1931. Admin. beset by much controversy. Sought
to simplify state admin. structure; established a cabinet
of advisors from among el. admin. officials; a State Welfare Dept. was org. Advocated an increase in powers of
Gov. to remove local officials. Banking panic of 1933 resulted in his issuance of proclamation closing all banks
temporarily. His advocacy of a state sales tax resulted in
a demonstration by a mob outside exec. mansion which was

quelled by militia forces. Engaged in controversy with
U.S. officials over welfare funds. Refused to call session
of legislature to deal with repeal of 18th Amdt. Granted
pardons freely and bestowed numerous honorary commns. in
State's mil. forces. Quarreled with Lieut. Gov. Chandler
over latter's assembling of legislature into spec. session
to consider election law reforms during an absence of the
Gov. from the State. His attempt to cancel the spec. session call was thwarted by the Ky. cts. Resumed law practice after tenure as Gov. Mbr., Masons; Elks; Woodmen.
Christian (Disciples) church. m. in 1894 to Mary Nisbet,
of Clinton, Ky. Three d. D. at Madisonville, March 1,
1941.

CHANDLER, ALBERT BENJAMIN ("HAPPY") (1935-1939; 1955-
1959). b. July 14, 1898 at Corydon, Ky. s. of Joseph S.
and Callie (Sanders) C. Descendant of an English ancestor
who emigrated to Va. Attd. pub. schools in Corydon;
Transylvania Univ., from which he was grad. in 1921;
Harvard Univ. Law School, 1921-1922; and the Univ. of Ky.,
from which he received a law degree in 1924. Served as pvt.
in U.S. Army in 1918. Commissioned as capt. in USAR, 1934,
and served in Judge Advocate Gen.'s dept., 1934-1935. During college years was active in intercollegiate sports of
football, baseball and basketball. Also worked at odd jobs,
coached basketball in h.s., played semi-professional baseball, and coached football at Centre Coll., 1922-1927. Admitted to bar in 1924 and began practice at Versailles, Ky.
Apptd. master commnr. of Woodford Co. cir. ct. in 1928.
Mbr. of Ky. Senate, 1929-1931. Nom. and el. Lieut. Gov. as
Dem. in 1931. In 1935 during absence from State by Gov.
Laffoon, called the state legislature into spec. session to
obtain a revision of state primary election law. Session
was held and legislation sought by him was passed despite
attempt of Gov. Laffoon to adjourn the session. Won Dem.
primary nom. for Gov. against a cand. favored by Gov.
Laffoon in 1935 and was el. During admin., secured passage
of legislation abolishing gen. sales tax and substituting
for it an income and liquor tax. Also promoted reorg. of
state admin. following report of a spec. study commn. Unsuccessful cand. for Dem. nom. to U.S. Senate in 1938
against incumbent Sen. Barkley, who had the support of Pres.
F. D. Roosevelt. In Oct., 1939, was apptd. by Gov. Keen
Johnson to vacant Senate seat after resigning governorship
shortly before end of term. El. to fill out term in 1940
and was el. to a regular term in 1942. Supported U.S. war
effort as a Sen. Resigned Senate seat in 1945 to become
commnr. of U.S. organized baseball. Served in that

capacity until 1950. Resumed law practice in Versailles.
Also engaged in tobacco farming and became the publ. of the
Woodford County Sun. Nom. and el. Gov. again as Dem. in
1955. Defeated as cand. for Dem. nom. for Gov. in 1967,
and was also unsuccessful as Indep. Dem. cand. for Gov. in
1971 after failing to win Dem. nom. Ch. of Bd. of Trustees
of Univ. of Ky., 1935-1939. Hon. degrees from Transylvania
Univ. and the Univ. of Ky. Mbr., Masons; Amer. Legion; 40
and 8; various fraternal and professional legal orgs. m.
in 1925 to Mildred Watkins. Two s.; two d.

JOHNSON, KEEN (1939-1943). b. Jan. 12, 1896 in Lyon
Co., Ky. s. of Robt. and Mattie Davis (Holloway) J. Attd.
local pub. schools; Central Coll., Fayette, Mo., 1914-1917;
and the Univ. of Ky., from which he was graduated in 1922.
Entered U.S. O.T.C. in 1917. Commissioned as second lieut.
and served with A.E.F. during World War I. From 1919 to
1921 was ed. of Elizabethtown, Ky. Mirror, and from 1922 to
1925 was ed. of Lawrenceburg, Ky. News. Became ed. of
Richmond, Ky. Daily Register in 1925 and later became pres.
of Richmond Daily Register Co. Exec. sect., Ky. Dem. state
commt., 1932-1939. Nom. and el. Lieut. Gov. as Dem. in
1935. Succeeded to office of Gov. in Oct., 1939, after Gov.
Chandler resigned. Completed Chandler's term, which had
approximately two months to run, and was el. as Dem. for a
regular term as Gov. in Nov. of that year. U.S. Under-Sect.
of Labor, 1946-1947. Defeated as Dem. nominee for U.S.
Senate seat in 1960. Mbr., Bd. of Regents of Eastern Ky.
State Teachers Coll.; pres., State Conf. of Social Workers;
pres., Ky. State Press Assoc.; pres., Univ. of Ky. Alumni
Assoc. Mbr., Amer. Legion; V.F.W.; 40 and 8; Masons;
I.O.O.F.; Elks; Jr. Order of Mechanics; various fraternities and social clubs. Methodist. m. in 1917 to Eunice
Lee Nichols. One d. D. Feb. 7, 1970, at Richmond, Ky.

WILLIS, SIMEON SLAVENS (1943-1947). b. Dec. 1, 1879
in Lawrence Co., Ohio. s. of John H. and Abigail (Slavens)
W. Father was a farmer and supplies contractor for iron
mfg. firms, and had served in the Union Army during the
Civil War. Attd. pub. schools in Ohio and Ky. Taught
school in Greenup Co., Ky., 1898-1901 while studying law.
Admitted to the bar in 1902 and began practice at Ashland,
Ky. City atty. of Ashland, 1918-1922. Pres. and dir. of
Park City Land Co., 1914-1943, and pres., Home Fed. Savings
and Loan Assoc., 1933-1943. Appeals agent under Selective
Service Act during World War I, and also in World War II.
Mbr., Ky. Bd. of Bar Examiners, 1922-1928. Mbr., Ky. Ct.
of Appeals, 1928-1933. Ed. of 5th ed. of Thornton's

<u>Law of Oil and Gas</u>, 1931. Nom. and el. Gov. as Rep. in 1943. During admin., Ky. Devel. Assoc. was established to attract indus. to the State; pub. educ., health and library systems improved; State Highway Dept. was reorg. in effort to eliminate partisan political influence. Mbr., Masons; Elks; Rotary; Civil Legion; various professional legal orgs. Hon. degrees from Ky. Wesleyan Coll., Centre Coll., and the Univ. of Ky. Methodist. m. in 1920 to Ida Lee Millis. One d. D. April 5, 1965. Bur. in Frankfort Cem.

CLEMENTS, EARLE C. (1947-1950). b. Oct. 22, 1896 at Morganfield, Ky. s. of Aaron W. and Sallie Anna (Tuley) C. Father was a farmer. Attd. local pub. schools and the Univ. of Ky., 1915-1917. Enlisted as a pvt. in U.S. Army in 1917, rising to rank of capt. by the time of his discharge. Engaged in farming. Sheriff of Union Co., 1922-1926; Union Co. clerk, 1926-1934; Union Co. judge, 1934-1942. El. to Ky. Senate in 1941, serving until 1944. Was floor leader of Dem. party last year in Senate. Nom. and el. to U.S. House in 1944 and again in 1946. Resigned seat in Jan., 1948, after having been nom. and el. Gov. as Dem. in 1947. Resigned as Gov. in Nov., 1950, after being el. to fill U.S. Senate seat vacancy. Defeated for reel. to Senate in 1956. Dem. party whip in Senate in 1953, and was acting Dem. party leader there during illness of Sen. L. B. Johnson in 1955. Author, with two other Senators, in 1954, of a bill permitting distribution of surplus food to victims of disasters. Mbr., Dem. natl. commt. Ch., Dem. Senatorial campaign commt. in 1952 and exec. dir. of it during 1957-1959. Apptd. Ky. Highway Commnr. in 1960. Washington lobbyist for Amer. Merchant Marine Inst. in 1961-1963. Became consultant for tobacco indus., and pres. of Tobacco Inst., Inc., in 1964. Christian (Disciples) church. m. in 1927 to Sarah Blue, of Morganfield, Ky. One d.

WETHERBY, LAWRENCE WINCHESTER (1950-1955). b. Jan. 2, 1908 at Middleton, Ky. s. of Dr. Samuel D. and Fanny (Yenowine) W. Attd. local pub. schools and the Univ. of Louisville, from which he was grad. in 1929 with a law degree. Mbr. Ky. Natl. Guard, 1925-1929. Began practice of law in Jefferson Co. Judge of Jefferson Co. juvenile ct., 1943-1947. Ch. of dist. Dem. commt., 1943-1956, and sect. of Ky. Dem. commt., 1947-1952. Nom. and el. Lieut. Gov. as Dem. in 1947. Succeeded to office of Gov. in Nov., 1950, when Gov. Clements resigned. Nom. and el. to full term in 1951. Ch. of So. Govs.' Conf., 1954-1955. Defeated as Dem. nominee for U.S. Senate in 1956. Delegate to Dem. natl. convs., 1948-1968. Chosen Ky. Man of the Year, 1952;

Ky. Sportsman of the Year, 1954; Mr. Recreation of Ky.,
1956. Became a dir. of Lincoln Income Life Ins. Co. in
1940, and vice pres. and dir., Brighton Engr. Co., 1956.
Mbr., state constl. assembly, 1964-1966. El. to Ky. Senate
in 1966, becoming Pres. pro tem. Mbr., various fraternal
and professional legal orgs. and social clubs. Methodist.
m. in 1930 to Helen Dwyer. Two d.; one s.

CHANDLER, ALBERT BENJAMIN ("HAPPY") (1955-1959). See
above, 1935-1939.

COMBS, BERT(RAM) THOMAS (1959-1963). b. Aug. 13, 1911
at Manchester, Ky. s. of Stephen Gibson and Martha (Jones)
C. Father was a farmer and mother was a school teacher.
Family traced ancestral line back to an English colonist
who came to Va. in 1619. Attd. local pub. schools, graduating from h.s. at age 15 at top of class. Attd. Cumberland
Coll., 1929-1931, supporting self by doing janitor work and
odd jobs. Employed as clerk in Ky. Highway Dept. for several years to earn money to continue educ. Attd. the Univ.
of Ky., graduating second in class with law degree in 1937.
Mbr. of staff of Ky. Law Review while in law school, serving as ed. in last year. Admitted to bar and began practice at Manchester. After one year moved to Prestonburg,
Ky., continuing to practice law there. Enlisted as pvt. in
U.S. Army in 1942, rising to rank of capt. by end of World
War II. Served on Judge Advocate Gen.'s staff, and assisted in prosecution of Japanese war criminals. Discharged
in 1946, with Bronze Star and Medal of Merit Award from the
govt. of the Philippine Islands. Resumed law practice at
Prestonburg. City atty., 1950. In 1950-1951 was pros.
atty. for his jud. dist. Apptd. to Ky. Ct. of Appeals in
1951 to fill a vacancy and was el. for a regular term in
1955. Ch. of Ky. Jud. Council, 1954. Resigned jud. post
in 1955 to seek Dem. nom. for Gov., but lost in the primary
to former Gov. Chandler. Resumed law practice for a time.
Won Dem. nom. for Gov. in 1959 and was el. As Gov., reduced state payroll, and sponsored a revised state tax system. Apptd. by Pres. Johnson to U.S. Ct. of Appeals in
1967. Ch., Bd. of Regents of Eastern Ky. Historical Soc.;
mbr., Bd. of Trustees, Campbellville Coll. Mbr., Masons;
Amer. Legion; 40 and 8; V.F.W.; Kiwanis; Lions; various
professional legal orgs. Baptist. m. in 1937 to Mabel
Hall, of Hindman, Ky. One s.; one d.

BREATHITT, EDWARD THOMPSON, Jr. (1963-1967). b. Nov.
26, 1924 at Hopkinsville, Ky. s. of Edward T. and Mary Jo
(Wallace) B. Was a direct descendant of Gov. John

Breathitt, of Ky. (q.v.). Father was a tobacco farmer and
breeder of Hereford cattle. Attd. local pub. schools. In
1943 at age 18 enlisted in U.S. Army Air Corps, serving for
three years. Attd. Univ. of Ky., graduating with a law degree in 1950. Admitted to bar and began practice at
Hopkinsville. Mbr. of Ky. House, 1952-1958. Active in Dem.
party affairs, serving as pres. of Ky. Young Dems. in 1952
and as speaker for Gov. Stevenson for Pres. of U.S. in that
year. Also participated in campaigns of Sen. Barkley.
Mbr. of Jud. Council of Ky., 1954-1956., and of Gov.'s
Commn. on Pub. Health, 1955-1959. As State Personnel
Commnr., 1959-1960, helped to implement civil service system in Ky. Apptd. to Ky. Pub. Service Commn. in 1960. Won
Dem. nom. for Gov. in 1963 with backing of Gov. Combs
against former Gov. Chandler. Results of primary were
close and were unsuccessfully challenged by his opponent.
Issue of civil rights, on which he espoused a moderately
liberal position, was prominent during campaign and admin.
Supported Pres. Johnson's civil rights and foreign affairs
policies, and seconded his nom. for Pres. of U.S. at the
1964 Dem. natl. conv. Endorsed program of research on effects of smoking on health, which aroused criticism from
tobacco indus. Mbr., Dem. natl. commt. in 1967-1972, serving on its commt. on rules in 1969 which effected sweeping
changes in delegate selection procedures. Became vice
pres. for pub. affairs of So. Ry. system after tenure as
Gov. Mbr., Masons (Shriner); Amer. Legion; Ky. Farm Bureau;
various fraternities. Hon. degrees from Univ. of Ky.;
Marshall Coll.; Ky. Wesleyan Coll. Methodist. m. in 1948
to Frances Holleman, of Mayfield, Ky. Three d.; one s.

NUNN, LOUIS BROADY (1967-1971). b. March 8, 1924 at
Park City, Ky. Attd. Bowling Green Bus. Univ.; the Univ.
of Cincinnati; and the Univ. of Louisville, from which he
received a law degree. Served with U.S. Army for three
years during World War II. Began practice of law at
Glasgow, Ky. El. Barren Co. judge in 1953. Mgr. for Rep.
pres. campaigns in Ky. in 1956 and 1960, and Rep. senatorial
campaigns in 1960 and 1962. Delegate to Rep. natl. convs.,
1968, 1972 and 1976. Rep. nominee for Gov. in 1963, losing
to Edw. Breathitt in close election in which he unsuccessfully contested the result. Nom. for Gov. again in 1967
and was el. Defeated as Rep. nominee for U.S. Senate seat
in 1972, and as Rep. nominee for Gov. again in 1979. Mbr.,
Masons; Amer. Legion; Rotary; Ky. Welfare Assoc., of which
he was dist. pres. Active in Christian (Disciples) church.
m. to Buela Cornelia Aspley. Two children.

FORD, WENDELL HAMPTON (1971-1974). b. Sept. 8, 1924
at Owensboro, Ky. s. of Ernest M. and Irene (Schenck) F.
Attd. local pub. schools and the Univ. of Ky., 1942-1943.
Served with U.S. Army, 1944-1946. Grad. in 1947 from
Maryland School of Ins. Engaged in bus. at Owensboro as
partner in an ins. firm from 1959 onward. Mbr. of Ky. Natl.
Guard, 1949-1962. Served on staff of Gov. Combs, 1959-1961.
Mbr. of Ky. Senate, 1966-1967. Nom. and el. Lieut. Gov. in
1967, serving until 1971. Nom. and el. Gov. as Dem. in
1971. During admin., was ch. and vice ch. of the commt. on
Natural Resources and Environmental Mgmt. of the Natl.
Govs.' Conf. Also ch. of commt. on Law Enforcement, Justice
and Public Safety of the So. Govs.' Conf. Mbr., Advisory
Council of Dem. natl. commt. Resigned office of Gov. in
Dec., 1974, after having been el. to U.S. Senate. Was immediately apptd. to Senate seat to fill vacancy to complete
the last six days of the term of Sen. Cook, whom he had defeated in the Nov., 1974, gen. election for the regular
term beginning Jan. 3, 1975. Baptist. m. in 1943 to Jean
Neal. One d.; one s.

CARROLL, JULIAN MORTON (1974-1979). b. April 16, 1931
at Paducah, Ky. s. of Elvis and Eva (Heady) C. Attd.
local pub. schools; Paducah Jr. Coll.; and the Univ. of Ky.,
from which he received an A.B. degree in 1954 and a law degree in 1956. Admitted to bar and began practice at
Paducah. Mbr. of Ky. House, 1962-1970, serving as Speaker
during last term. Nom. and el. Lieut. Gov. as Dem. in 1971.
Succeeded to office of Gov. in Dec., 1974, after Gov. Ford
resigned, and completed the term for which Ford had been
el. Nom. and el. as Dem. for a regular term in 1975. Mbr.,
Masons (Shriner); Optimists; various professional legal
orgs. Trustee, Paducah Jr. Coll. m. in 1951 to Charlann
Harting. Two s.; two d.

CLAIBORNE, WILLIAM CHARLES COLE (1812-1816). b. in 1775 in Sussex Co., Va. Mbr. of a family that was prominent in pub. affairs. A brother, Nathaniel, was a mbr. of U.S. House from Va. from 1825 to 1837; and a nephew, John F. H. C., was a mbr. of the U.S. House from Miss. from 1835 to 1838. During his youth the family resided for a time in New York City because of unsettled conditions in Va. caused by Rev. War. Became enrolling clerk for Va. Assembly in 1791. Studied law at Richmond, Va., and soon after admission to bar moved to Sullivan Co., Tenn., where he practiced law. Mbr. of conv. that framed first const. of Tenn. in 1796. Became judge of Tenn. superior ct. following the org. of first state govt. there, but resigned in 1797 to take seat in U.S. House to which he had been el., even though he lacked necessary minimum age qualification. Reel. in 1798, and as mbr. of Tenn. delegation cast the deciding vote of Tenn. for Thomas Jefferson in Jefferson-Burr contest for Pres. of U.S. in 1801. Apptd. Gov. of Miss. Terr. by Pres. Jefferson later that year. Served as mbr. of U.S. commn., along with Gen. Wilkinson, which accepted transfer of the Province of La. from France to U.S. in 1803. Apptd. temp. Gov. of La. by Pres. Jefferson and later, Gov. of Orleans Terr. after a terr. form of govt. was set up in 1804. Served in that capacity until La. became a State. After admission of La. to statehood in 1812, was el. first Gov. of the State. During admin., legislation was passed barring use of French as the official language; and the first steamboat arrived at New Orleans. El. to U.S. Senate at end of his term as Gov., but died before he assumed seat. m. three times. D. at New Orleans, Nov. 23, 1817. Bur. in Basin St. Louis Cem. Later re-interred in Metairie Cem., New Orleans.

VILLERÉ, JACQUES PHILLIPE (1816-1820). b. April 28, 1760 in St. John the Baptist Parish, La. s. of Joseph Roy and Louise Marguerite (de la Chaise) de V. Father was French naval sect. of La. Province. Son became commander of French garrison at a fort in San Domingo. Later returned to La., where he engaged in planting near Violet, in St. Bernard Parish. Transferred allegiance to U.S. when the Province of La. became a U.S. possession. Mbr. of La. conv. of 1811 that drafted first const. for the proposed State. Commanded La. militia troops as major gen. at Battle of New Orleans in 1815. El. Gov. in 1816, being favored by very narrow margin in popular voting over the cand. of the Amer. faction of the Jeff. Rep. party. Was again a cand. for the office of Gov. in 1824, finishing second in the popular voting that year. Retired to

plantation after tenure as Gov. m. to Henriette Fazenda.
D. March 7, 1830.

ROBERTSON, THOMAS BOLLING (1820-1824). b. Feb. 27,
1779 at "Bellefield", the family homestead near Petersburg,
Va. s. of Wm. and Elizabeth (Bolling) R. A brother, John,
was a U.S. Repr. from Va. from 1834 to 1839, and was also
Atty. Gen. of Va., and another brother, Wyndham, was a Gov.
of Va. (q.v.). Grad. from William and Mary Coll. in 1806.
Studied law and began practice at Petersburg, Va. Moved to
La. shortly thereafter, where he was apptd. Atty. Gen. of
Orleans Terr. by Gov. Claiborne. Apptd. Sect. of Orleans
Terr. by Pres. Jefferson in the same year, serving until
1811. Also was named U.S. dist. atty. for the Terr. of
Orleans in 1808. Upon admission of La. to statehood in
1812 was el. to U.S. House. Continued in that office until
April, 1818, when he resigned. During the period he was in
Cong. he visited France, and his letters home were published in the Richmond, Va. Enquirer and later in collected
form under the title Events in Paris. El. Gov. of La. in
1820. As Gov., supported the establishment of a pub. educ.
system; the Legion of La., a mil. org., was founded; and
legislation was passed legalizing gambling, with state pro-
ceeds to be used for hospitals and a college. Resigned
office of Gov. in 1824 about one month before end of term
to become U.S. dist. ct. judge for La., serving until 1827.
Resigned that office in 1827 and returned to Petersburg,
Va. m. to Leila Skipworth, d. of the Gov. of West Florida.
D. at White Sulphur Springs, Va. (now W. Va.), Oct. 5, 1828.
Bur. in Copeland Hill Cem.

THIBODAUX, HENRY SCHUYLER (1824). b. in 1769 at
Albany, N.Y. Family was of French-Canadian origin. Left
an orphan in infancy, was brought up by the Schuyler family
at Albany. Lived during youth for some time in Scotland.
In 1794 moved to Province of La., becoming a planter on the
Bayou La Fourche at a place where the town of Thibodaux
later grew up. Mbr. of the legislature of the Terr. of
Orleans in 1805. Became justice of the peace in La Fourche
Parish. Mbr. of the conv. in 1811 that drafted the first
const. for the State of La. Became mbr. of La. Senate after statehood was achieved, serving for three terms and
becoming Pres. of Senate. As such, succeeded to the office
of Gov. in Nov., 1824, when Gov. Robertson resigned, and
completed last month of Robertson's term. m. first to a
Miss Lejeune. Second wife was Brigette Bellanger. Father
of a large family. D. Oct. 24, 1827.

JOHNSON, HENRY (1824-1828). b. Sept. 14, 1783 in Va.
Received basic acad. educ. there. Studied law and was admitted to Va. bar. Moved to Terr. of Orleans in 1809 and
began practice at Bringiers, La. Apptd. clerk of Orleans
Terr. ct. in 1809. Became a judge in St. Mary Parish in
1811. Mbr. of conv. in 1811 that framed first const. for
the proposed State of La. Defeated as cand. for U.S. House
in 1812. Practiced law at Donaldsonville, La. In 1818 was
el. to fill vacancy in U.S. Senate seat occasioned by death
of former Gov. Claiborne, and continued in that office until 1824. Resigned in May, 1824, to become cand. for Gov.,
and was subsequently el. Bank of La. was created during
admin., and a proposed revision of criminal procedure code
drawn up by Edward Livingston was rejected by the legislature. Defeated as a cand. for the U.S. Senate in 1829.
El. to fill vacancy in U.S. House as a Whig in 1834, and
again in 1836. Defeated as cand. for U.S. Senate seat in
1838. Also was defeated as Whig cand. for Gov. in 1842.
El. to U.S. Senate as a Whig in 1844 to fill U.S. Senate
seat vacancy, continuing in that office until 1849. Introduced resolution for annexation of Texas and a resolution
for repeal of Tariff Act of 1846. Defeated as cand. for
U.S. House seat in 1850. Retired to plantation and to law
practice at New River, La. m. to a Miss Key, of Md. D. at
Pointe Coupeé, La., Sept. 4, 1864. Bur. on his plantation
there.

DERBIGNY, PIERRE AUGUSTE CHARLES BOURGUIGNON (1828-
1829). b. in 1767 in Laon, France. s. of Auguste B. and
Louise Angeline (Blondel) d'Herbigny. Family belonged to
the French nobility. Fled from France to San Domingo in
1792 during French Rev. Later went to Pittsburgh, Pa.,
where he resided for a time. Later resided briefly in Mo.
and Fla. before eventually establishing home at New Orleans.
An accomplished linguist, he served as sect. to the mayor
of New Orleans, and in 1803 was apptd. by Gov. Claiborne as
official interpreter for the Terr. of Orleans govt. Became
an Amer. citizen. In 1805 was one of three delegates sent
to Washington to lobby for statehood for La. Served as a
ct. clerk and as sect. to the Orleans Terr. Council. Became a mbr. of La. legislature after statehood was achieved.
Later served as a mbr. of La. Supreme Ct. and as La. Sect.
of State on two occasions. Also was regent of schools of
New Orleans. In 1820 was granted first license issued to
a person to operate a steam ferry across Mississippi River
at New Orleans. Assisted Edward Livingston and Louis
Lislet in revision of La. Civil Code in 1823. Defeated as
cand. for Gov. in 1820, receiving second highest total in

the popular vote. El. Gov. as Natl. Rep. in 1828. While Gov., was host to Gen. Andrew Jackson on his visit to New Orleans. m. to Felicite Odile Schauet de Lassus, a sister of the Chevalier de Luzier, at Pittsburgh, Pa. Two s.; five d. D. Oct. 6, 1829, from injuries received in a carriage accident while still serving as Gov.

BEAUVAIS, ARMAND (1829-1830). b. in 17(?) at Natchitoches (?), La. to an old Creole family. In 1810 became justice of the peace in Pointe Coupée Parish. El. to La. House in 1814 and for two succeeding terms. In 1822 became a mbr. of La. Senate. Continued to serve therein for the next eight years, becoming Pres. of Senate. Was serving in that capacity when Gov. Derbigny died in a carriage accident. Succeeded to office of Gov. in Oct., 1829, but served only until Jan., 1830, when he resigned as Pres. of Senate and was succeeded in office of Gov. by the newly el. Pres. of Senate. Was unsuccessful as one of two Natl. Rep. party candidates for Gov. in July, 1830. Chosen again to La. Senate in 1833 to fill a vacancy. D. in 1866.

DUPRÉ, JACQUES (1830-1831). b. in 1790 (?) in St. Landry Parish, La. Province. Received a limited educ. locally. Engaged in stockraising on his plantation, and became quite prosperous. Mbr. of La. legislature, 1828-1846. When he was chosen Pres. of La. Senate in Jan., 1830, he immediately became Acting Gov. by reason of expiration of the tenure of Armand Beauvais as Pres. of Senate and Acting Gov. Served as Gov. until Jan., 1831, when he relinquished the office to a regularly chosen successor as Gov. D. Sept. 14, 1846.

ROMAN, ANDRÉ BIENVENU (1831-1835; 1839-1843). b. Mar. 5, 1795 at Opelousas, La. Descendant of Creole family that had emigrated to La. from Provence, France in 1740. When son was a child, family moved to St. James Parish. Grad. from St. Mary's Coll., near Baltimore, in 1815. In 1816 acquired a sugar plantation, "Oak Alley", in St. James Parish and built first sugar refinery in La. Mbr. of La. House, 1818-1826 and 1828-1830, serving as Speaker for four years. Apptd. parish judge in 1826. El. Gov. as Natl. Rep. in spec. election in 1830 following death of Gov. Derbigny, to serve regular four-year term. El. for another term in 1838 as a Whig, becoming the first Gov. of La. to serve two terms. As Gov., recommended creation of a bd. of pub. works; began constr. of penitentiary at Baton Rouge, later described by Dorothy Dix in 1859 as one of the best managed in U.S. Mbr. of constl. convs. of 1844 and 1852. In 1848

was sent to Europe as agent of the Consolidated Assoc. and
Citizens Bank. Founder of Jefferson Coll. for boys.
Formed company to drain land around New Orleans. Also was
a founder of La. Agri. Soc. Was one of 17 out of 130 mbrs.
of La. conv. in 1861 who voted against secession, but went
along with secession movement nevertheless. Apptd. by
Confed. Provisional govt. one of mbrs. of commn. to confer
with representative of U.S. govt. in unsuccessful attempt
to avert Civil War. Sons fought in Confed. Army during the
War. At end of Civil War refused to take oath of allegiance to U.S. Later was apptd. recorder of deeds and
mortgages for New Orleans by Gov. Wells. m. to Aimeé
Francois Parent, of St. Tammany Parish. Three s.; two d.
D. at New Orleans, Jan. 28, 1866.

WHITE, EDWARD DOUGLAS(S) (1835-1839). b. in March,
1795 at Nashville, Tenn. s. of James and Mary (Willcox) W.
Grandfather had emigrated from Ireland to Pa. Father had
moved from Pa. to Tenn., then to Miss., and in 1799 to St.
Martin Parish in La. After a terr. govt. was org., father
had served as a judge in his parish. Son, who was orphaned
at age 15, attd. common schools and the Univ. of Nashville,
from which he was grad. Returned to La., studied law in
Donaldsonville, La., and was admitted to bar. In 1825 was
apptd. mbr. of city ct. of New Orleans. Resigned in 1828
and moved to a sugar plantation he had acquired near
Labadieville, in La Fourche Parish. El. to U.S. House in
1828. Continued in office until Nov. 15, 1834, when he resigned after having been el. Gov. as the Whig cand. that
year. After term as Gov. moved residence to Thibodaux, La.
El. to U.S. House in 1838 shortly before term as Gov. expired. Served in U.S. House until 1843. Resumed law practice and plantation mgmt. thereafter. Was an ardent Whig
and a personal friend of Henry Clay. Roman Catholic. m.
to Mary Catherine Sidney Ringgold, of Washington, D.C.
Three d.; two s., one of whom, Edward, Jr., became a U.S.
Sen., Assoc. Justice, and later Chief Justice of the U.S.
Supreme Ct. D. at New Orleans, April 15 (18?), 1847. Bur.
in St. Joseph's Catholic Cem.

ROMAN, ANDRÉ BIENVENU (1839-1843). See above, 1831-
1835.

MOUTON, ALEXANDRÉ (1843-1846). b. Nov. 19, 1804 on
Bayou Carencro, in what is now Lafayette Parish, La. s. of
Jean and Marie (Bordat) M. Both his father and mother were
descendants of Acadian refugee family that had settled in
La. in 1740s. Received classical educ. Grad. from

Georgetown Univ. in Washington, D.C. Studied law. Admitted
to bar in 1825, and began practice with a friend, Edward
Simon, who later was a mbr. of La. Supreme Ct. Received
gift of land from his father near Vermillionville, La.,
where he became a planter. Mbr. of La. House, 1826-1832
and again in 1836, twice serving as Speaker. Defeated as
cand. for U.S. House in 1830. Pres. elector in 1828, 1832
and 1836. El. to U.S. Senate in Jan., 1837, to fill a vacancy, and continued in office by el. to regular term in
1838. Resigned seat in March, 1842, to seek office of Gov.,
to which he was el. as Dem. Served approximately three
years, his term being shortened by adoption of a revised
state const. Delegate to Dem. natl. convs. in 1856 and
1860. Pres. of Vigilance Commt. of Lafayette Parish in
1858. Delegate to La. conv. in 1861 to consider question
of secession, serving as its presiding officer. Favored
secession. Defeated as cand. for C.S.A. Senate in 1861.
Retired to plantation thereafter. m. first to Zelia
Rousseau, a grand-daughter of Jacques Dupré, Gov. of La.
(q.v.). Five children. One of his sons was a West Point
Mil. Acad. graduate who rose to rank of major gen. in the
Confed. Army and was killed in action during the Civil War.
After first wife's death, m. in 1842 to Emma Gardner, d. of
a U.S. Army officer. Four s.; two d. Roman Catholic. D.
at his home near Lafayette, Feb. 12, 1885. Bur. in St.
John's Cem.

JOHNSON, ISAAC (1846-1850). b. in 1805 at St.
Francisville, in what is now West Feliciana Parish, La. s.
of a British officer who had settled in La. when it was under Spanish rule. Studied law and began practice in La.
Mbr. of La. House, and later was apptd. to a dist. ct.
judgeship. Nom. and el. Gov. as Dem. in 1846, becoming the
first Gov. of La. to be el. by direct popular vote under
the revised const. of 1845. As Gov., gave active support
in raising troops to serve under Gen. Zachary Taylor in the
Mexican War; supported improvement of pub. schools; and
completed the State Capitol and penitentiary at Baton Rouge.
Strong advocate of States' Rts., and vigorously opposed
adoption of Wilmot Proviso. Apptd. Atty. Gen. of La. by
Gov. Walker after expiration of term as Gov. m. to
Charlotte McDermott, of Natchez, Miss. Three children, all
of whom died in youth. D. suddenly at New Orleans, March
15, 1853. Bur. on grounds of a family friend there.

WALKER, JOSEPH MARSHALL (1850-1853). b. in 1784 (?)
at New Orleans, La. s. of Peter and Marie (Revoil) W.
Father was of English descent and mother was of French

origin.   Educ. in best schools at New Orleans.   Purchased
lands in Rapides Parish with legacy left him by his grand-
mother and became a planter.   Served in War of 1812 as brig.
gen. of La. militia.   Mbr. of La. House and later of La.
Senate for a number of terms.   Mbr. of constl. conv. of
1844, serving as its presiding officer.   El. Sect. of State
of La. in 1846.   Nom. and el. Gov. as Dem. in 1849 in a
close and exciting contest against the Whig cand., Gen.
Alexander DeClouet.   Became first Gov. to be inaugurated at
the new State capital at Baton Rouge.   Much controversy
aroused during his admin. by his giving covert support to
an expedition headed by Narcisco Lopez which attempted
seizure of Cuba from Spain.   The expedition failed, with the
leader and some 50 of his men being captured and executed.
Riots against Spanish ensued in New Orleans as a result,
and the U.S. govt. was obliged to make apologies to Spain.
Opposed legislation withdrawing restrictions against banking institutions in La.   Also opposed holding of a state
constl. conv. in 1852, and sought unsuccessfully to prevent
adoption of the changes it proposed.   Resigned office immediately after a successor was chosen under the revised
const. before successor was installed in office.   Refused
to seek pub. office thereafter.   m. to Catherine Carter,
of Adams Co., Miss.   Seven s.; three d.   D. at his home in
Rapides Parish, Jan. 26, 1856.

HEBERT, PAUL OCTAVE (1853-1856).   b. Nov. 12, 1818 at
Bayou Goula, Iberville Parish, La.   s. of Paul and Mary
Eugenia (Hamilton) H.   Father was a descendant of a refugee
from Acadia who came to La. in mid-1700s.   Mother was of
Scotch descent.   Attd. Jefferson Coll., grad. at head of
his class in 1836, and West Point Mil. Acad., grad. in 1840.
Commissioned as second lieut. in the Engr. Corps of U.S.
Army.   Returned to West Point in 1841 as asst. prof. of
engr.   In 1843-1845 superintended constr. of defenses on
western passes of the Mississippi River.   Apptd. Chief Engr.
of La. by Gov. Mouton in 1845, and resigned from U.S. Army.
Served in Mexican War as lieut. col., later col. of volunteer La. regiment.   Returned to plantation at Bayou Goula.
La. commnr. to World Expo. at Paris in 1851.   Mbr. of La.
constl. conv. of 1852.   Nom. and el. Gov. as Dem. under the
revised const. in that year.   As Gov., apptd. W. T. Sherman
as supt. of La. Mil. Acad.   Supported secession movement in
1861.   Apptd. by Pres. Jefferson Davis as brig. gen. in
Confed. Army in 1861.   Commanded troops in La. and trans-
Mississippi area during Civil War.   After he surrendered
forces at end of the war, was pardoned by Pres. Andrew
Johnson in 1865.   Again apptd. as La. State Engr. in 1873,

and in that same year was apptd. by Pres. Grant commnr. on
U.S. Bd. of Engrs. for constr. and maintenance of levees on
the Miss. River. Supported Greeley for Pres. of U.S. in
1872 campaign. m. first to Cora Vaughn. Six children. m.
later to Penelope Anderson. Two s.; three d. D. at New
Orleans, April 29, 1880.

WICKLIFFE, ROBERT CHARLES (1856-1860). b. Jan. 6,
1820 at Bardstown, Ky. s. of Charles A. and Margaret
(Cripps) W. Father was Acting Gov. of Ky. in 1839-1840
(q.v.), and also served as Postmaster Gen. of U.S. Well
educ. by tutors. Attd. St. Joseph's Coll.; Augusta Coll.;
and Centre Coll., from which he was grad. in 1840. Studied
law in Washington, D.C. Returned to Bardstown where he
practiced law for several years. Because of failing health
in 1846 moved to St. Francisville, La., where he engaged in
cotton planting and law practice. Mbr. of La. Senate for
three terms, serving as its regular presiding officer after
death of Lt. Gov. Farmer in 1854. Nom. and el. Gov. as
Dem. in 1855. After tenure as Gov., retired to plantation
and law practice, in which he was very successful. As
Civil War neared, at first opposed secession, but supported
the South after war began. El. to U.S. House in 1866, but
was refused seat. In 1876 was ch. of La. delegation to
Dem. natl. conv.; also served as Dem. pres. elector in the
disputed pres. election of that year. Mbr., Masons. m.
first in 1843 to a d. of Judge John Lawson. Two s.; two d.
m. for second time in 1870 to Mrs. Anne (Davis) Anderson,
of Brandenburg, Ky. One s.; one d. A nephew, J. C. W.
Beckham, was later a Gov. of Ky. (q.v.). D. at Shelbyville,
Ky., April 18, 1895.

MOORE, THOMAS OVERTON (1860-1864). b. April 10, 1804
in N.C. Descendant of an Irish family that emigrated from
Ireland to S.C. about 1650. Father had married a daughter
of a colonial Gov. of N.C. and had himself served in that
office. Mother was a descendant of an English family that
came to Va. before 1670. Moved to La. as a young man and
became a cotton planter in Rapides Parish. El. to La. Senate in 1856. Nom. and el. Gov. as Dem. in 1859. As Civil
War neared, assembled the legislature in spec. session to
consider the course the State should take following the
presidential election of 1860. It arranged for a conv. to
consider questions of secession, and that body voted for
secession. As Gov., cooperated in efforts by South to oppose Union forces invading the State from both the north
and south. After capture of New Orleans by Union forces in
1862 he exercised authority only in the area comprising

about three-fourths of the State not under control of Union
forces. Retired to his plantation in 1864 after election
of a successor by voters in that portion of La. D. at his
home near Alexandria in Rapides Parish, June 25, 1876.

SHEPLEY, GEORGE FOSTER (1862-1864). b. Jan. 1, 1819
at Saco, Maine. s. of Ether and Anna (Foster) S. Attd.
Dartmouth Coll., from which he was grad. in 1837, and Dane
Law School. Admitted to Me. bar in 1840 and began practice
at Bangor, Me. In 1844 moved to Portland, Me., where he
continued to practice law. U.S. dist. atty. for Me., 1848-
1849 and again in 1853-1861. Delegate to Dem. natl. convs.
at Charleston, S.C. and at Baltimore, Md., in 1860. After
Civil War began became col. of Me. volunteer regiment.
Served under Gen. Butler in expedition against New Orleans
in 1862. After capture of the city, was made U.S. commandant at New Orleans, and promoted to rank of brig. gen.
Apptd. Mil. Gov. of La. in July, 1862, and acted as Gov. in
the area of La. under Union control until inauguration of
Provisional Gov. Hahn in 1864. Transferred to Va. theater
of war thereafter. Served as commandant at Richmond for a
short time after Gen. Lee's surrender. Resumed law practice at Portland, Me. Refused offer of apptmt. to seat on
U.S. Supreme Ct., but became U.S. dist. ct. judge for Me.
in 1869. Hon. degree from Dartmouth Coll. in 1876. m. in
1844 to Lucy Ann Hodges, of Bangor. D. July 20, 1878, at
Portland, Me.

ALLEN, HENRY WATKINS (1864-1865). b. April 29, 1820
in Prince Edward Co., Va. s. of Dr. Thomas and Ann
(Watkins) A. Father was of Scotch and Welsh ancestry.
Family moved to Lexington, Mo. when son was a boy. Placed
in a shop for apprentice training, but was unhappy, and he
was later sent to Marion Coll. to study. Argument with
father caused him to leave family home in early youth.
Went to Grand Gulf, Miss., where he studied under a tutor
for a time. Opened a school there and also studied law.
In 1842 raised a company of volunteers to assist Texans,
under Sam Houston, in struggle to maintain independence
from Mexico. After a short time married and settled on a
plantation in Claiborne Co., Miss. After death of his wife
in 1850 moved to La., where he became a sugar planter, residing at West Baton Rouge. Defeated as cand. for La. Senate, but was el. to La. House in 1853. Studied law in
Cambridge, Mass., in 1854. In 1859 crossed Atlantic to
assist in Italian independence movement, but arrived too
late to be of help. Toured Europe, and wrote and in 1861
published Travels of a Sugar Planter, based on that

experience. El. again to La. legislature. After Civil War
began joined Confed. Army, rising to rank of brig. gen.
Participated in numerous major engagements in Southwest, including Battles of Shiloh, Baton Rouge, and Vicksburg. Was
wounded in action. Nom. and el. Gov. in Confed.-controlled
area of La. in 1863, and was inaugurated at the temporary
capital, Shreveport, on Jan. 25, 1864. At end of the war,
went to Mexico City where he became ed. of a newspaper, the
Mexican Times. m. in 1842 to Salome Crane, of Rodney, Miss.
D. at Mexico City, April 22, 1866. Body returned to New
Orleans for burial. Later re-interred at Baton Rouge.

HAHN, MICHAEL (1864-1865). b. Nov. 24, 1820 in
Bavaria, Germany. While still an infant was brought by his
widowed mother to New York City. Moved with mother to New
Orleans about 1840. Attd. local schools. Studied law in
law office and at the Univ. of La., (now Tulane Univ.) from
which he was grad. in 1850. Admitted to bar in 1851 and
practiced in New Orleans. Became mbr. of New Orleans
school bd. in 1852, becoming pres. of that body. An opponent of slavery and of the Slidell wing of the Dem. party,
he opposed James Buchanan in pres. election of 1856, and
supported Stephen A. Douglas in 1860 pres. election. Opposed secession movement in 1860-1861 and refused to take
oath of allegiance to C.S.A. after Civil War began. Became
openly a Union adherent after capture of New Orleans by
Union forces in 1862. El. to U.S. House in 1862 from Union-
controlled area of La., taking seat only two weeks before
end of term. Apptd. U.S. prize commnr. for New Orleans
area. Became owner and ed. of a newspaper, the True Delta.
Supported emancipation and Pres. Lincoln's program of
Reconstruction in South. El. Gov. as a New State Moderate
Unionist (Rep.) in Union-controlled area of State in 1864.
After installation as Gov. was also assigned powers of Mil.
Gov. by Pres. Lincoln. After revision of La. const. by
pro-Union element in the State, was el. to U.S. Senate and
resigned office of Gov. in Mar., 1865. Did not press claim
to Senate seat after opposition developed in Senate to his
being seated. Became publ. and ed. of New Orleans Daily
Republican, 1867-1871. Also became a sugar planter in St.
Charles Parish. Mbr. of La. legislature, 1872-1876, serving as House Speaker. U.S. registrar of voters in 1876.
Supt. of U.S. Mint at New Orleans, 1878. La. dist. ct.
judge, 1879-1885. El. to U.S. House in 1884. D. in
Washington, D.C., Mar. 15, 1886 during the course of his
term. Bur. in Metairie Cem., New Orleans.

WELLS, J(AMES) MADISON (1865-1867). b. Jan. 8, 1808
at the family plantation, "New Hope", near Alexandria, La.
s. of Samuel and Mary Elizabeth (Colert) (Calvit?) W. As
youth spent some time in Washington, D.C. and Ky. Returned
to La., where he became a sugar and cotton planter near
Lecompte, in Rapides Parish. Studied law, and served as
sheriff. As Civil War approached, opposed secession. Much
of property was confiscated and destroyed by Confed. govt.
during course of Civil War. El. Lieut. Gov. in Union-controlled area of State in 1864. Succeeded to office of Gov.
in Mar., 1865, when Gov. Hahn resigned. Nom. and el. as a
Conservative (Union Dem.) to a regular term under the revised const. of 1864 in Nov., 1865. During tenure the La.
legislature ratified with reservations the 13th Amdt. to
U.S. Const., abolishing slavery. Conv. of 1864 was recon-
vened in 1866 with his approval to consider further measures for reconstruction of state govt., giving rise to much
factional strife in La. Mbrs. of the conv. were indicted
by a grand jury and it was broken up by the New Orleans
police, assisted by a mob. Thirty-six of its members were
killed and 146 persons wounded. Gov. Wells and the legislature fell into dispute over money matters. When Gen.
Sheridan became mil. commdr. of La.-Texas dist. under the
1867 Reconstruction Act, he took over control of La. finances, and in June, 1867, removed W. from office. W. resisted that action, but eventually surrendered office. Later was apptd. U.S. surveyor of port of New Orleans by
Pres. Grant. Was ch. of State Canvassing Bd. in 1876 pres.
election that refused to count several thousand votes for
Tilden electors on grounds of alleged fraud, resulting
eventually in giving the electoral votes of La., and the
pres. election, to Rutherford B. Hayes. m. in 1833 to Mary
Ann Scott. Fourteen children. D. Feb. 28, 1899.

FLANDERS, BENJAMIN FRANKLIN (1867-1868). b. Jan. 26,
1816 at Bristol, N.H. s. of Joseph and Relief (Brown) F.
Attd. New Hampton Acad. and later, Dartmouth Coll., from
which he was grad. in 1842. Went to New Orleans in 1843,
where he studied law. Taught school, 1844-1845. Became
part-owner and ed. of a newspaper, the New Orleans Tropic,
in 1845. Later returned to school teaching and admin. until 1852. New Orleans alderman in 1848. From 1852 to 1862
was sect.-treas. of New Orleans, Opelousas and Great
Western R.R. Co. Supported Union cause when Civil War began. Fled North from New Orleans for a time, but returned
when Union Army captured New Orleans in 1862. Apptd. New
Orleans city treas. by Gen. Butler. Entered U.S. mil.
service as a capt. for a short time, resigning after being

el. to U.S. House, in which he served for a few weeks in
1862-1863. Apptd. spec. agent of U.S. Treas. Dept. in La.-
Miss.-Tex. area in 1863, serving until 1866. Duties concerned cotton trade matters in area. Became pres. of First
Natl. Bank of New Orleans. Apptd. Mil. Gov. of La. by U.S.
mil. authorities following removal of Gov. Wells in 1867.
Served until Jan., 1868, when he resigned. Apptd. to fill
vacancy in office of mayor of New Orleans by Gov. Warmoth
in May, 1870, and was later el. to that office for a two-
year term. From 1873-1882 served as Asst. U.S. Treas. at
New Orleans. Defeated as Rep. cand. for La. State Treas.
in 1888. m. in 1847 to Susan H. Sawyer, of Bristol, N.H.
D. March 13, 1896, on estate, "Ben Alva", near Youngsville,
La. Bur. in Metairie Cem., New Orleans.

BAKER, JOSHUA (1868). b. Mar. 23, 1799 in Ky. Family
moved in 1803 to Miss. Terr., and in 1811 to St. Mary
Parish, in La. Entered U.S. Mil. Acad. at West Point in
1817, from which he was grad. in 1819. Commissioned as
second lieut. of artillery. Served a number of years as
asst. prof. of engr. at the Mil. Acad., and later as a mbr.
of its Bd. of Visitors for many years. Studied law at
Litchfield, Conn. Moved to Ky., where he was admitted to
bar in 1822. Returned to La., where he became proprietor
of a sugar plantation. Also practiced law and engaged in
steam-boating bus. Col. of La. militia, 1826-1829, and
capt. of a cavalry company, 1846-1851. Supervised constr.
of courthouse at Franklin, La. and other pub. works. Judge
of parish ct. in 1829 and, in 1832, probate judge. Declined apptmt. as U.S. Surveyor Gen. of La. in 1831. From
1833 to 1838 was Asst. State Engr., and from 1840-1845,
head of Bd. of Pub. Works. A Conservative Dem., he was opposed to secession in 1861. Apptd. Mil. Gov. of La. by Gen.
Hancock in 1868, taking office in Jan. and serving until
June of that year, when he was succeeded by newly-el. Gov.
Warmoth. D. April 16, 1885, at the home of a d. in Lyme,
Conn.

WARMOTH, HENRY CLAY (1868-1872). b. May 9, 1842 at
McLeansboro, Ill. s. of Isaac Sanders and Eleanor (Lane) W.
Father was a saddler and a justice of the peace. Descendant
of a Dutch immigrant who first settled in Va. Spent youth
at Fairfield, Ill., where he attd. pub. school. Worked as
a typesetter in newspaper office. Read law from books in
father's library, admitted to bar, and began practice in
Lebanon, Mo. Co. atty. of Laclede Co., Mo. When Civil War
began became a col. in Mo. militia. Later served as lieut.
col. under Gen. Sherman in Union Army in Western theater of

Civil War. Participated in numerous engagements, and in
May, 1863, was wounded and sent home to recuperate. When
he returned was court-martialed for being absent without
leave and for allegedly circulating false reports about
Union Army. Resisted charges and was eventually reinstated
after appeal to Pres. Lincoln. Served later as provost
marshal judge in Gulf States Dept. of Army. After war ended, established law practice at New Orleans. Nom. and el.
Gov. as a Radical Rep. in 1868 under revised const. of 1868.
Apptd. Provisional Gov. before he was formally installed in
office as result of his election. Admin. beset by factional strife over Reconstruction policies, financial mismanagement, depressed economy of State resulting from destruction of transp. and levee system during Civil War. Near
end of term in Dec., 1872, was impeached, which had the
effect of suspending him from office during final month of
term. Was never brought to trial on the charges before the
Senate, however. El. to La. House in 1876. Served as delegate to most of the Rep. natl. convs. from the 1870s until
his death. Delegate to La. constl. conv. in 1879. Apptd.
by Pres. Harrison collector of U.S. customs for New Orleans,
serving until 1893. In 1877 acquired a sugar plantation in
Plaquemines Parish. Acquired several other plantations
later, and org. the Magnolia Sugar Refining Co. Helped promote constr. of the New Orleans, Ft. Jackson and Grand Isle
R.R. to connect his plantations with New Orleans. In 1884
his plantation became the site for a U.S. Dept. of Agri.
experiment station for sugar indus. Defeated as Rep. cand.
for Gov. in 1888. In 1930 published an autobiography,
War, Politics and Reconstruction, in which he defended his
pub. record. m. in 1877 to Sallie Durand, of Newark, N.J.
Two s.; one d. D. at New Orleans, Sept. 30, 1931.

PINCHBECK, PINCKNEY BENTON STEWART (1872-1873). b.
May 10, 1837 near Macon, Ga. s. of Major Wm. and Eliza
(Stewart) P. Mother was of African descent and was the
slave of her son's White father. Received educ. in
Cincinnati, Ohio, pub. schools and later studied law. Engaged in canal boat work and river steamboating on Mo.,
Miss. and Red Rivers. During course of Civil War in La.,
escaped to Union side and served in Union Army as capt. in
La. Native Guards, one of the first Black militia units
that participated in the Civil War. Delegate to the La.
constl. conv. in 1867. El. to La. Senate as a Rep. in 1868,
after successfully contesting the election in which his
opponent had originally been declared the winner. Became
Pres. pro tem and acting Lieut. Gov. in 1871-1872. Succeeded to office of Gov. in Dec., 1872, following the voting

of impeachment charges against Gov. Warmoth. Completed
Warmoth's term, which had about a month to run. Cand. for
U.S. House seat in 1872, but failed to be seated therein as
a result of a contested election. Also was belatedly
denied a seat in U.S. Senate, to which he claimed to have
been el. by the La. legislature in 1873. Mbr. of La.
constl. conv. of 1879. Apptd. U.S. surveyor of customs at
New Orleans in 1882. Delegate to a number of Rep. natl.
convs. from 1868 onward. m. in 1860 to Nina Hethorn. D.
Dec. 21. 1921.

    KELLOGG, WILLIAM PITT (1873-1877). b. Dec. 8, 1831 in
Orwell, Vt. s. of the Rev. Sherman K., a Congregational
minister. Attd. Norwich Univ. In 1848 at age 16 went to
Peoria, Ill., where he became a rural school teacher.
Studied law, admitted to bar in 1853, and began practice at
Canton, Ill. Mbr. of state conv. that established the Rep.
party in Ill. in 1856. Delegate to Rep. natl. conv. in
1860, and served as Ill. pres. elector that year. Apptd.
chief judge of Terr. Ct. in Nebr. by Pres. Lincoln in 1861.
Upon outbreak of Civil War returned to Ill. and helped
raise a volunteer cavalry unit. Became its col. and participated in several early engagements in Mississippi
Valley theater of the war. Later was placed in command of
mil. post at Cape Girardeau, Mo. Failing health caused his
temp. retirement from U.S. Army. Resumed post as mbr. and
chief judge of Terr. Ct. in Nebr. for a time, but returned
to active mil. duty in 1863. Apptd. collector of the port
of New Orleans in 1865, serving until 1868. Chosen to U.S.
Senate in 1868 from La., serving until 1872, when he resigned to become Rep. cand. for Gov. of La. Resulting election contest was a tumultous one. State Election Bd.
membership was changed after it had declared him to have
been el. over his Lib. Rep.-Dem. opponent, John McEnery. A
new Election Bd. apptd. by Gov. Warmoth declared McEnery to
have been el., after a re-canvass of the election returns,
and both men took oath of office as Gov. and claimed the
powers and authority of the office, at the beginning of the
new Gov.'s term. After a period of several months of turmoil between the two factions, K. was recognized as Gov. by
Fed. authorities after an investigation by Cong. Was impeached by La. House near end of term on charges of fiscal
mismanagement, but the La. Senate dismissed the charges.
El. to U.S. Senate in 1877 and served one full term. Was
not a cand. for second term in Senate, but was el. to a
seat in the U.S. House in 1882. Served only one term. Resided in Washington, D.C. thereafter. Delegate to every
Rep. natl. conv. from 1868 through 1896, serving as ch. of

his delegation on five occasions. m. to Mary E. Wills, of
Pa., in 1865. D. in Washington, Aug. 10, 1918. Bur. in
Arlington Natl. Cem.

NICHOLLS, FRANCIS TILLOU (1877-1880; 1888-1892). b.
Aug. 20, 1834 at Donaldsonville, La. s. of Thomas Clark
and Louise H. (Drake) N. Family was of English ancestry.
Father was active in politics, and had served as a judge.
Attd. Jefferson Coll., in New Orleans, and later entered
U.S. Mil. Acad. at West Point, from which he was grad. in
1855. Commissioned as lieut. in artillery unit and assigned to frontier duty in Florida. Resigned commn. in 1856.
Studied law and was admitted to bar in 1858. Began practice at Napoleonville, La. Upon outbreak of Civil War entered Confed. Army as a capt. Saw much action and was
severely wounded, requiring amputation of an arm and a
foot. Rose to rank of brig. gen. Assigned duties as supt.
of conscription bureau for South in Trans-Miss. dist. in
1864. After the war, returned to law practice in
Assumption Parish. Nom. as Dem.-Lib. Rep. cand. for Gov.
in 1876. Election Bd. first declared his opponent, S. B.
Packard, to have been el.; but N. carried the contest to
the La. legislature, which supported his claim. Both men
were inducted into office and sought to exercise the powers
of the office of Gov. for a time. N. was eventually declared el. and Packard withdrew his claim when he failed to
receive the backing of Fed. authorities. During admin., a
revised const. was adopted in 1879 having the effect of
shortening his term by one year. Returned to law practice
at New Orleans until 1888. Nom. and el. Gov. as Dem. again
in that year, defeating former Gov. Warmoth for the office.
Major event of his admin. was his veto of a bill extending
the charter of La. Lottery Co., about which much controversy occurred. Mbr. of Bd. of Visitors to U.S. Mil. Acad.,
serving as its pres., during Pres. Cleveland's admin.
Chief Justice of La. Supreme Ct. in 1893-1895. In 1904
again became a mbr. of La. Supreme Ct. m. in 1860 to
Caroline L. Guion. D. Jan. 2, 1912, at Thibodaux, La.

WILTZ, LOUIS ALFRED (1880-1881). b. Jan. 31, 1843 in
New Orleans, La. s. of J. B. Theophile and Louise Irene
(Villanueva) W. Father was a descendant of a family that
was among the first German settlers in La. Mother was a
descendant of a noble Spanish family. Attd. local pub.
schools until age 15, then began working in a New Orleans
commercial house. At age 18 enlisted in a Confed. artillery unit. Served in Mississippi Valley theater during
Civil War, rising to rank of capt. Was taken prisoner and

later exchanged. Stationed in Miss. until end of Civil War.
Returned to commercial bus. interests at New Orleans. Active in local and state Dem. party affairs. Mbr. of La.
House in 1868. Also served as mbr. of New Orleans city
council and of its bd. of aldermen, becoming pres. of latter
body. Also was a school bd. mbr. Chosen mayor of New
Orleans on two occasions, but was denied office by Fed.
authorities on the first occasion. Mbr. of La. House again
in 1874, serving as its Speaker in 1875. Sought Dem. nom.
for Gov. unsuccessfully in 1876, but was el. as Lieut. Gov.
in that year. Nom. and el. Gov. as Dem. in 1879. m. in
1862 to Michael Bienvenu, of St. Martinsdale. Seven children. D. during course of term on Oct. 16, 1881.

McENERY, SAMUEL DOUGLAS (1881-1888). b. May 28, 1837
at Monroe, La. s. of Henry O'Neil and Caroline (Douglas)
McH. Family was of Scotch ancestry. An older brother,
John, was a claimant to the office of Gov. following the
1872 election and was inaugurated, but was later forced to
relinquish the office in favor of his opponent, W. P.
Kellogg (q.v.). Attd. Spring Hill Coll., near Mobile, Ala.;
the U.S. Naval Acad. at Annapolis, Md.; the Univ. of Va.;
and the State and Natl. Law School at Poughkeepsie, N.Y.,
from which he was grad. in 1859. Went to Mo. to practice
law, but returned to La. after about a year. Upon outbreak
of Civil War joined the La. Pelican Greys as a lieut.
Commissioned as lieut. in Confed. Army in 1862, and saw
service in Va. and La. Returned to law practice at Monroe
in 1866. Declined offers of political and jud. office until 1879. Nom. and el. Lieut. Gov. as Dem. in 1879. Succeeded to office of Gov. when Gov. Wiltz died in October,
1881. Nom. and el. to regular four-year term in 1884. Defeated as cand. for Dem. nom. for Gov. for the succeeding
term in 1888, losing to former Gov. Nicholls. Defeated as
Dem. nominee for Gov. in 1892, losing to the cand. backed
by Anti-Lottery Dem. faction and the Farmers Alliance.
Apptd. to La. Supreme Ct. in 1888 for a 12 year term, serving until 1897. Resigned seat in that year after having
been el. to U.S. Senate as a Free Silver Dem. Continued in
that office until his death. m. to Elizabeth Phillips. D.
June 28, 1910 in New Orleans. Bur. in Metairie Cem. in
New Orleans.

NICHOLLS, FRANCIS TILLOU (1888-1892). See above,
1877-1880.

FOSTER, MURPHY JAMES (1892-1900). b. Jan. 12, 1849 at
Franklin, St. Mary Parish, La. Educ. by pvt. tutors and at

prep. school at White's Creek, Tenn. Attd. Washington and
Lee Univ. in 1867-1868; Cumberland Univ., from which he was
grad. in 1870; and the Univ. of La. (Tulane Univ.), from
which he received a law degree in 1871. Admitted to bar
and established successful practice at Franklin. m. while
residing there. El. to La. legislature in 1872 as supporter of McEnery faction for Gov., but was denied seat by the
Kellogg faction then in control of the legislature. El. to
La. Senate and continued in office until 1892. Served as
Pres. of Senate from 1888 to 1890. Declined to run for
U.S. House seat, and in 1890, declined apptmt. to La.
Supreme Ct. Became a leader of Anti-Lottery Dem. faction
in the legislature. Nominee of that faction and of the
Farmers Alliance for Gov. in 1892 and was el., defeating
former Gov. Samuel McEnery, the regular Dem. cand. Reel.
Gov. in 1896 as the regular Dem. nominee. El. to U.S. Sen-
ate in 1901 and again in 1907, serving until 1913. After
service in Senate resumed law practice in La. Apptd. U.S.
collector of customs at New Orleans by Pres. Wilson in
1914. D. June 12, 1921 at his home near Franklin. Bur. in
Franklin Cem.

HEARD, WILLIAM WRIGHT (1900-1904). b. April 28, 1853
in Union Parish, La. s. of Stephen S. and Mary Ann
(Wright) H. Parents had resided in Ga. originally. All of
his older brothers served in the Confed. Army during Civil
War. Worked on father's farm and attd. school at
Farmersville, La. El. clerk of dist. ct. in 1876. Later
served as deputy clerk and notary, 1876-1892. El. to La.
House in 1884, and La. Senate in 1888, where he became influential as leader of the Anti-Lottery faction of the Dem.
party. El. State Aud. in 1892, and again in 1896. Nom.
and el. Gov. as a Dem. in 1900. After tenure as Gov. was
vice pres. of State Natl. Bank of New Orleans. Also served
as sect. of La. Securities Commn. Mbr., K.P., serving as
Vice Chancellor of that body in La. on two occasions and
once as Chancellor. Was also very active in Baptist church
affairs. m. in 1878 to Isabelle E. Manning. Four s.;
three d. D. June 1, 1926.

BLANCHARD, NEWTON CRAIN (1904-1908). b. Jan. 29, 1849
in Rapides Parish, La. s. of Carey H. and Frances Amelia
(Crain) B. Father was a cotton planter. Received academic
educ. in pvt. schools. Studied law in law office in
Alexandria and at the Univ. of La. (Tulane Univ.), grad. in
1870. Began law practice at Shreveport, La. in 1871. Ch.
of Dem. commt. of Caddo Parish in 1876. Delegate to La.
constl. conv. in 1879, serving as ch. of commt. on fed.

relations. Major on staffs of Gov. Wiltz and Gov. McEnery.
La. mbr. of Bd. of Trustees of the Univ. of the South, at
Sewanee, Tenn. El. to U.S. House in 1880 and continued in
that office for six succeeding terms. Resigned in 1894 after being apptd. to a vacancy in U.S. Senate seat, to which
he was subsequently el. Served in Senate until 1897. Did
not seek reel. at end of term. El. to La. Supreme Ct., on
which he served from 1897 to 1904. Nom. and el. Gov. as
Dem. in 1904. Delegate to Dem. natl. convs. in 1896 and
1912. After tenure as Gov. resumed law practice in
Shreveport. Mbr. and presiding officer of La. constl.
conv. in 1913. m. in 1873 to Mary (Emily?) Barrett, of
Shreveport. D. at Shreveport, June 22, 1922. Bur. in
Greenwood Cem. there.

SANDERS, JARED YOUNG (1908-1912). b. Jan. 29, 1869
near Morgan City, St. Mary Parish, La. s. of Jared Young
and Bessie (Wofford) S. Father, who was a sugar planter,
died when son was 12 years old. Attd. local pub. schools.
In 1882 flood caused by levee break destroyed family plantation. At age 13 assumed responsibility for care of
mother and six younger brothers and sisters. Worked as
clerk in a store, then entered printing office of a newspaper, the St. Mary Banner. Became its ed. in 1891 and
later acquired controlling interest. Began study of law,
and later entered Tulane Univ., from which he received a
law degree in 1893. Admitted to bar and began practice in
New Orleans. Mbr. of La. House, 1892-1904, serving as
Speaker, 1900-1904. Affiliated with Anti-Lottery faction
of Dem. party. Mbr. of La. constl. conv. in 1898. El.
Lieut. Gov. in 1904 and was nom. and el. Gov. as Dem. in
1908. As Gov., advocated closer regulation of liquor traffic, abolition of race track gambling, creation of a State
Game Commn.; repeal of mortgage tax. Chosen by legislature
to fill vacancy in U.S. Senate seat in 1910, but did not
qualify for the office, preferring to finish term as Gov.
Resumed law practice after tenure as Gov. El. to U.S.
House in 1916, and for succeeding term. Did not seek reel.
in 1920. Mbr. of La. constl. conv. in 1921. Unsuccessful
cand. for Dem. nom. for U.S. Senate seat in 1920 and again
in 1926. m. in 1891 to Ada Shaw. One s., Jared, Jr., who
became a mbr. of U.S. House from La. in 1934. In 1914 m.
to Emma Dickinson. D. at Baton Rouge, Mar. 23, 1944. Bur.
in Franklin Cem., Franklin, La.

HALL, LUTHER EGBERT (1912-1916). b. Aug. 30, 1869
near Bastrop, Morehouse Parish, La. s. of Bolling Cass and
Antoinette (Newton) H. Grad. in 1889 from Washington and

Lee Univ. Studied law at Tulane Univ., receiving a law degree in 1892. Admitted to bar and began practice in
Bastrop, La. El. to La. Senate in 1898. El. dist. ct.
judge in 1900, continuing in that office until 1906, when
he became a mbr. of State Cir. Ct. of Appeals. In 1910 was
el. to the La. Supreme Ct. for a term to begin in 1912, but
did not assume the office, having been nom. and el. Gov. as
Dem. cand. in 1912. Having been supported by a reform
faction of the Dem. party, he successfully sponsored the
holding of a constl. conv. which drafted a revision of the
La. const. that became effective in 1913. Mbr., Masons.
m. in 1892 to Clara Wendel, of Brownsville, Tenn. One s.;
one d. D. Nov. 6, 1921.

PLEASANT, RUFFIN GOLSON (1916-1920). b. June 2, 1871
at Shiloh, La. s. of Benjamin Franklin and Martha
Washington (Duty) P. Attd. Ruston Coll., 1885-1886; Mt.
Lebanon Coll., 1887-1888; and La. State Univ., 1890-1894,
from which he was grad. After serving as instructor in
intl. and constl. law there for a year, studied law at
Harvard and Yale, 1896-1897. Enlisted in La. volunteer
regiment for the Spanish-Amer. War in 1898, holding rank of
lieut. col. Admitted to bar and began practice at
Shreveport, La. in 1899. City atty. of Shreveport, 1902-
1908. Asst. Atty. Gen. of La., 1911-1912. El. Atty. Gen.
of La., serving 1912-1916. Nom. and el. Gov. as Dem. in
1916. As Gov., supported U.S. war effort energetically
during World War I. Was criticized strongly in some
quarters for not giving enthusiastic support for ratification of 19th (Women's Suffrage) Amdt. to U.S. Const. Retired to law practice after tenure as Gov. Delegate to
Dem. natl. convs. in 1916 and 1924. Mbr. of La. constl.
conv. of 1921. Baptist. m. in 1906 to Anne Ector, of
Shreveport, La. D. Sept. 12, 1937.

PARKER, JOHN MILLIKEN (1920-1924). b. Mar. 16, 1863
at Bethel Church, Miss. s. of John Milliken and Roberta
(Buckner) P. Father was a businessman whose family had
moved from Pa. to Ky., and later to La. Attd. pub. schools
in New Orleans. At age 17 entered father's cotton broker-
age house. After father's death in 1893 became pres. of
firm. Prominent in New Orleans bus. circles. Pres. of New
Orleans Bd. of Trade in 1893. Pres. of New Orleans Cotton
Exch., 1898-1900. Pres. of Southern Commercial Cong., 1908-
1912, and of the Miss. Valley Assoc. in 1919. Helped org.
campaign for nom. of Luther Hall for Gov. as a progressive
Dem. Supported Theodore Roosevelt for Pres. of U.S. in
1912. Nom. for Gov. by Prog. party and as an Indep. Dem.

in 1916, but was defeated in gen. election. Also was nom. for Vice Pres. of U.S. by Natl. Prog. party in 1916, but the movement failed when Theodore Roosevelt refused to run again as the Prog. party cand. for Pres. of U.S. Supported Woodrow Wilson for Pres. in 1916 gen. election. During World War I served as Food Adminr. for La. Also was arb. in settlement of New Orleans metals trades strike in 1918. Nom. and el. Gov. as "anti-machine" Dem. in 1920. During admin., sponsored a number of reform measures, some of which became major elements of Gov. Huey Long's program later. Advocated sales tax on raw materials to revive state revenues; increased spending for highways, schools, and the State Univ. at Baton Rouge; increased aid for state institutions; and revision of the state const., which was achieved by a conv. held in 1921. Investigation into Mer Rouge murders in 1922 resulted in weakening influence of KKK in La. Supported Gov. Al Smith as Dem. nominee for Pres. of U.S. in 1928. Pres. of Constl. League in La. that opposed Gov. Huey Long's methods in 1929. Devoted interests to farming at his plantation at St. Francisville. Served as dir. of flood relief measures in 1912, 1922 and 1927. Mbr. of Advisory Commt. to Washington Disarmament Conf. in 1921-1922. Mbr., Masons. Presbyterian. m. in 1888 to Cecile Airey, of New Orleans. Two s.; one d. D. May 20, 1939 at Pass Christian, Miss.

FUQUA, HENRY LUCE (1924-1926). b. Nov. 8, 1865 at Baton Rouge, La. s. of James Overton and Jeanette M. (Fowler) F. Father was a Civil War veteran and had a prominent role in pub. life as opponent of some of the extreme Reconstruction measures following the Civil War. Attd. Magruder's Collegiate Inst. at Baton Rouge, and La. State Univ. Began work as asst. in an engr. firm in bldg. Yazoo and Mississippi Valley R.R. Joined hardware firm in 1883, later becoming a travelling salesman for the bus. Established his own hardware bus. in 1892, which prospered. Also engaged in rice, cotton and sugar planting. Accepted post of Warden of State Penal Institutions in 1916, which involved operation of rice and sugar plantations by convict labor. Reorg. methods and changed an operating deficit of system into a profit. Held post until 1924 when he was nom. and el. Gov. as a Dem. During admin., sponsored various reform measures, including an anti-KKK law banning the use of masks in pub. demonstrations. Fond of sports and hunting. m. in 1890 to Laura Motta, of Baton Rouge. One d.; one s. D. at Baton Rouge, Oct. 11, 1926, during course of his term as Gov.

SIMPSON, ORAMEL HINCKLEY (1926–1928). b. Mar. 20, 1870 at Washington, La. s. of Samuel F. and Mary Esther (Beer) S. Attd. Centenary Coll., from which he was grad. in 1890. Studied law in office at Lafayette, La., and later at Tulane Univ., from which he received a law degree in 1893. Began practice in New Orleans. Apptd. warrant clerk for U.S. Mint at New Orleans in 1899. Asst. sect. of La. Senate in 1900, and sect. in 1908, serving until 1924. Nom. and el. Lieut. Gov. as Dem. in 1924. Succeeded to office of Gov. in Oct., 1926, following death of Gov. Fuqua and completed Fuqua's term. During admin., disastrous flood in 1927 required extraordinary measures to be taken, including U.S. govt. action, to relieve distress and institute program of levee reconstr. Ordered cutting levee at Poydras Crevasse to prevent flooding of New Orleans by permitting waters to reach Gulf of Mexico by new channels. Called spec. session of legislature to deal with emergency. Helped org. Tri-State Flood Control League to promote U.S. and state flood control programs. Defeated as cand. for Dem. nom. for Gov. in 1928, losing to Huey P. Long. After term as Gov., served as spec. repr. for New Orleans on State Tax Commn. and as atty. for State inheritance tax collector. Mbr., Masons (Shriner); K.P. Methodist. m. in 1899 to Louise Ernestine Pichet, of New Orleans. D. at New Orleans, Nov. 17, 1932.

LONG, HUEY PIERCE, Jr. (1928–1932). b. Aug. 30, 1893 on a farm near Winnfield, La. One of nine children of Huey Pierce and Caledonia (Tison) L. Father was a farmer of very limited means. Attd. local pub. schools. In 1912 went to Memphis, Tenn., and worked as a book salesman, auctioneer and sales mgr. Attd. the Univ. of Okla. Law School for a time; also Tulane Univ. Law School. Admitted to bar in 1915 and began practice at Winnfield. Later practiced at Shreveport, 1915–1918. Mbr. of La. R.R. Commn., 1918–1921, and ch. of La. Pub. Service Commn., 1921–1928. Defeated as cand. for Dem. nom. for Gov. in 1924. Nom. and el. Gov. as Dem. in 1928. As Gov., instituted paved road system; free school textbook law; founded School of Med. at La. State Univ.; set up Home for Epileptics; inaugurated an anti-literacy program; began constr. of new Capitol building at Baton Rouge; pushed through tax law changes. Advocacy of programs generally designed to aid economically disadvantaged and his promotion of them by ruthless methods aroused bitter opposition. Impeached by House in 1929 on a variety of charges of misuse of powers, but the Senate did not carry out trial to conclusion. Involved State in much litigation against pub.

utilities. Mbr. of Dem. natl. commt., 1928-1935, and ch. of La. Dem. commt., 1934-1935. El. to U.S. Senate in 1930, but did not resign office of Gov. immediately nor when Senate term began in Mar., 1931, preferring to retain powers as Gov. for a time. Resisted successfully an attempt by Lieut. Gov. St. Cyr to take over office of Gov. after Mar. 4, 1931. Eventually assumed Senate seat in Jan., 1932, and resigned office of Gov. Was preparing to challenge Pres. F. D. Roosevelt for the Dem. nom. for Pres. of U.S. or to run as a third party cand. in 1936 when he was shot by a political opponent on Sept. 8, 1935 while at the La. Capitol bldg. in Baton Rouge. D. Sept. 10, 1935, from his wounds. Baptist. m. in 1913 to Rose McConnell. As his widow, she was apptd. to his seat, and was nom. and el. to complete the final year of his Senate term. A son, Russell B., later became U.S. Sen. from La. in 1948. Was the brother of Earl K. Long, later Gov. of La. (q.v.), and of George Long, later a mbr. of U.S. House from La. Bur. on La. Capitol grounds in Baton Rouge.

KING, ALVIN OLIN (1932). b. June 21, 1890 at Leoti, Kans. s. of George Merritt and Bessie Brown (Stirling) K. Family later moved to La., where father engaged in lumber bus. Attd. Lake Charles, La., schools; Parsons Bus. Coll.; and Tulane Univ. Law School, from which he was grad. in 1915. Began law practice in Lake Charles. Also engaged in family lumber bus., serving as pres. of King Corp. Acquired other commercial enterprises. Mbr. of La. Senate, 1924-1932. Served as Pres. pro tem there, 1930-1932. When Gov. Huey Long resigned in 1932, succeeded to office of Gov., the office of Lieut. Gov. being vacant. Completed Long's term. Delegate to Dem. natl. conv. in 1932. Natl. councillor, USCC, 1947-1954. Mbr. of La. Mineral Bd., 1948. Mbr. of various professional legal orgs. m. in 1916 to Willie Lee Voris. Two s. D. Feb. 21, 1958. Bur. in Graceland Cem., Lake Charles.

ALLEN, OSCAR KELLY (1932-1936). b. Aug. 8, 1882 in Winnfield, La. s. of Asa Levi and Sophrona (Perkins) A. Father was a farmer. Attd. local schools, working in vacation periods. Received teacher's certificate at age 15 from Winn Parish school. Taught in graded school there, and later at Mineral Springs and Pleasant Hill, Mo. Attd. Springfield, Mo., Normal School and a bus. coll. at Springfield for a time; also Trinity Univ., in 1908, at Waxahachie, Tex., working while in college. In 1906-1908 held interest in sawmill bus. in Winn Parish, which he managed. Filed for a homestead, added more acreage, and

farmed. Later worked as bookkeeper in Paris, Texas. Returned to farm in Winn Parish in 1912. Established merc.
bus., expanding into oil bus. in 1917 in Tex. and La. El.
assessor of Winn Parish in 1916. Formed close friendship
with Huey Long, later Gov. of La. (q.v.). El. to La. Senate in 1927, and became floor leader for Gov. Huey Long's
faction in that body. Nom. and el. Gov. as Dem. in 1932.
As Gov., advocated increased aid to educ. and hospitals;
tick eradication program for farm animals; expansion of
state road and pub. works programs; elimination of poll tax
requirement for voting. Was nom. as Dem. cand. to fill
vacancy in U.S. Senate seat after Sen. Huey Long's assassination in 1935, but died about a week after receiving the
nom. Mbr., Rotary. m. in 1912 to Florence Scott Love.
Two s.; one d. D. at Baton Rouge, Jan. 28, 1936, while
still in office of Gov.

NOE, JAMES ALBERT (1936). b. Dec. 21, 1893 at West
Point, Ky. s. of John M. and Belle (McRae) N. Attd. local
pub. schools. Served in U.S. Army during World War I,
rising from rank of pvt. to lieut. of infantry. Became a
businessman at Monroe, engaging in oil and natural gas bus.
in La., Ark. and Texas. El. to La. Senate in 1932, and
became Pres. pro tem of that body. Was serving in that
office when Gov. Allen died in Jan., 1936, shortly before
end of his term. Succeeded to office of Gov., the office
of Lieut. Gov. being vacant. Completed Allen's term, which
had about three months to run. El. to La. Senate again in
1936, serving therein until 1940. Defeated as cand. for
Dem. nom. for Gov. in 1940, and again in 1959. Mbr. of
Dem. natl. commt. from La. and delegate to 1968 Dem. natl.
conv. Presbyterian. m. in 1922 to Ann Grey Sweeney. Two
d.; one s. D. Oct. 18, 1976.

LECHE, RICHARD WEBSTER (1936-1939). b. May 17, 1898
at New Orleans, La. s. of Eustace Webster and Stella
Eloise (Richard) L. Attd. Tulane Univ., 1916-1918. Entered O.T.C. at Ft. Sheridan, Ill., in 1918 and served in
1918-1919 as second lieut. in U.S. Army during World War I.
From 1919 to 1922 worked as a salesman while also attending
Loyola Univ., in New Orleans, from which he received a law
degree in 1922. Began practice in New Orleans. Sect. to
Gov. O. K. Allen, 1932-1934. Judge of La. Ct. of Appeals,
1934-1936. Nom. and el. Gov. as Dem. in 1936. While Gov.,
was indicted by a Fed. grand jury on charges of misuse of
U.S. funds. Was convicted and sentenced to a term in prison, which he served. Resigned office of Gov. June 26,
1939, when impeachment charges against him were being

considered in the legislature. During his political career
served as ch. of La. State Dem. commt. and mbr. of Dem.
natl. commt. Pres. of Bd. of Supervision of La. State
Univ. Mbr., Masons; various professional legal orgs. m.
in 1927 to Elton Reynolds. One s. D. Feb. 22, 1965.

LONG, EARL KEMP (1939-1940; 1948-1952; 1956-1960). b.
Aug. 26, 1895 at Winnfield, La. s. of Huey Pierce and
Caledonia (Tison) L. Was one of nine children, and was a
younger brother of Huey P. Long, Jr., Gov. of La. (q.v.).
Another brother, George S., became a mbr. of U.S. House,
and a nephew, Russell Long, became a U.S. Sen. from La.
Father was a farmer in poor circumstances. Attd. local
schools. Left home early to make own way. Worked at various jobs, including clerking in a lumber yard, and as a
strawberry salesman. Attd. Tulane Univ. and Loyola Univ.,
in New Orleans, as a spec. student. Studied law and was
admitted to bar in 1926. In 1928 was apptd. atty. for inheritance tax collector of Ouachita Parish. Broke with
brother Huey in 1931 when he was refused higher place in
the Long org., and as a result was removed from office in
1932. Testified against brother in Senate investigation of
campaign fund irregularities in 1933. Retired to farm and
livestock raising for a time. Asst. state counsel for U.S.
Home Owners Loan Corp., 1932-1934. Was reconciled with
brother Huey before latter's death in 1935. Nom. and el.
Lieut. Gov. in 1936. Succeeded to office of Gov. when Gov.
Leche was forced to resign in 1939. Was not involved in
scandals that resulted in conviction of Gov. Leche on
charges of misuse of Fed. funds. Completed Leche's term,
which had about nine months to run. Lost contest for Dem.
nom. for Gov. in 1940. Retired to farm for a time. Defeated as cand. for Dem. nom. for Lieut. Gov. in 1944. Won Dem.
nom. for Gov. in 1948 and was el. As Gov., advocated veterans' bonus; improvements in old age benefits; minimum pay
scale for teachers; opposed Federal Fair Employment Practices Act._ Did not break with natl. Dem. party in 1948
Pres. campaign. Suffered a serious heart attack in 1950
while hunting. After tenure as Gov. returned to farming
and bus. interests. Won Dem. nom. for Gov. again in 1956,
and was el. for a second full term. During last year of
term, made an irrational attack on opponents in legislature
who refused to support a constl. amdt. proposal he favored,
that would have liberalized voting requirements and permit
him to succeed himself in office. Was committed to protective custody in a Galveston, Tex. hosp., but was released after short stay. Became estranged from wife, whom he
accused of assisting his political enemies in attempt to

have him declared mentally ill and suspended from office.
Lost in attempt to win Dem. nom. for Lieut. Gov. in 1959;
but won Dem. nom. for seat in U.S. House in 1960. m. in
1932 to Blanche M. Revere, from whom he was divorced in
1959. No children. D. at Alexandria, La., Sept. 5, 1960,
of a heart attack while campaigning for U.S. House seat.
Bur. in Earl K. Long Memorial Park, at Winnfield.

JONES, SAM HOUSTON (1940-1944). b. July 15, 1897 near
Merryville, La. s. of Robt. and Susie (Frazer) J. Father
was a pioneer educator in La. and was clerk of ct. in
Beauregard Parish. Attd. local pub. schools and La. State
Univ., 1915-1917. Left college to volunteer for U.S. mil.
service in World War I. After the war continued in service
as an officer in USAR, becoming a major in 1941. Served as
deputy ct. clerk, and was a mbr. of La. constl. conv. of
1921, being the youngest of the delegates. Studied law and
was admitted to the bar in 1922. Began practice at De
Ridder, La. Became dist. atty. in 1925, serving until 1934,
when he resigned to become a mbr. of a law firm at Lake
Charles. Nom. for Gov. as a "reform" Dem. cand., defeating
Acting Gov. Earl Long for the nom., and was el. in 1940.
As Gov., secured repeal or invalidation of much legislation
enacted during the Long regime centering power in office of
Gov. Pre-auditing and civil service systems were established; State's fiscal affairs were placed on sound basis;
a new commercial code established; natl. war effort supported. Returned to law practice after tenure as Gov. Defeated as cand. for Dem. nom. for Gov. in 1948 by Earl Long
in a run-off primary. Mbr., Amer. Legion, serving as its
State Commdr. in 1930-1931. Methodist. m. in 1934 to
Louise (Gambrell) Boyer. One s.; one d. D. Feb. 8, 1978.

DAVIS, JAMES HOUSTON ("JIMMIE") (1944-1948; 1960-1964).
b. Sept. 11, 1904 at Quitman, La. Was one of eleven children of Sam Jones and Sarah Elizabeth (Works) D. Father was
a tenant farmer. Attd. local schools. Grad. from La.
Coll., at Pineville, La., and became a school teacher.
Attd. La. State Univ., from which he received an A.M. degree in 1927. Prof. at Dodd Coll., Shreveport, La., 1927-
1928. Criminal ct. clerk at Shreveport, 1928-1938. Commnr.
of police and fire depts., Shreveport, 1938-1944. Mbr., La.
Pub. Utilities Commn., 1942-1944. Engaged in a variety of
occupations, including radio and entertainment fields. Com-
poser of some 300 popular songs, several of which became
national hits. Nom. and el. Gov. as Dem. in 1944 with the
support of out-going Gov. Jones, and continued to follow
policy lines of previous admin. Successfully advocated

measures to improve pub. educl. system and the creation of
a Dept. of Commerce and Indus. to attract indus. and promote tourism. Also promoted expansion of state facilities
for mentally ill and victims of tuberculosis, as well as
legislation to conserve natural resources. Nom. and el.
for second term as Gov. in 1960. Defeated as cand. for Dem.
nom. for third term as Gov. in 1971. m. in 1936 to Alvern
Adams. One s. Mbr., Masons (Shriner); I.O.O.F.; Elks.

LONG, EARL KEMP (1948-1952). See above, 1939-1940.

KENNON, ROBERT FLOYD (1952-1956). b. Aug. 21, 1902 at
Minden, La. s. of Floyd and Laura (Bopp) K. Attd. local
schools and La. State Univ., from which he received an A.B.
degree in 1923 and a law degree in 1925. As a student was
active in sports and ROTC, and continued to serve in La.
Natl. Guard after graduation. Began law practice at Minden.
Mayor of Minden in 1925, serving as pres. of La. Mun. Assoc.
Dist. atty. for Bossier-Webster dist., 1930-1940. Served
as vice pres. of La. Dist. Attys. Assoc. Judge of La. Ct.
of Appeals in 1940. Entered U.S. mil. service as capt. in
1941 as mbr. of La. Natl. Guard. Served in European theater during World War II, holding rank of col. when discharged. Apptd. to La. Supreme Ct. to fill vacancy in 1945,
serving until 1947. Defeated as cand. for Dem. nom. for
Gov. in 1948; and also defeated as cand. for Dem. nom. for
U.S. Senate that year, losing to Russell Long, s. of former
Gov. Huey Long. Won Dem. nom. for Gov. in 1952 and was el.
As mbr. of La. delegation to Dem. natl. conv. in 1952, refused to take "loyalty" oath, and supported Gen. Eisenhower,
the Rep. cand., during ensuing pres. election. As Gov.,
opposed Federal Fair Employment Practices law; assumption
of U.S. control over tidelands oil. Signed bills making
welfare rolls pub., and making union "closed shop" contracts
illegal. Opposed U.S. Supreme Ct. ruling ordering desegregation of schools. Strong advocate of States Rts., but
supported U.S. River Control project to improve port facilities at New Orleans. Boycotted Natl. Dem. Conf. in 1953.
Pres. of U.S. Govs.' Conf., 1954-1955. Mbr., Amer. Legion;
Masons; Lions. Active in Presbyterian church. m. in 1931
to Eugenia Sentell. Three s.

LONG, EARL KEMP (1956-1960). See above, 1939-1940.

DAVIS, JAMES HOUSTON ("JIMMIE") (1960-1964). See
above, 1944-1948.

McKEITHEN, JOHN JULIAN (1964-1972). b. May 28, 1918

at Grayson, La. s. of Jesse and Agnes (Eglin) McK. Served
as first lieut. in U.S. Army during World War II. Established residence at Columbia, La., where he engaged in bus.
Became dir. of Caldwell Bank and Trust Co., of Columbia.
Mbr. of La. legislature, 1948-1952. Mbr., La. Pub. Service
Commn., 1954-1962. Nom. and el. Gov. as Dem. in 1964.
Reel. in 1968, an amdt. to the La. const. having been
adopted in 1966 permitting a second successive term. Ch.
of Interstate Oil Compact Commn. and mbr. of exec. commt.
of Natl. Govs.' Conf. during course of term as Gov. Dele-
gate to Dem. natl. conv. in 1968. Mbr., Amer. Legion;
V.F.W.; La. Farm Bureau. Hon. degree, High Point (N.C.)
Coll. Methodist. m. in 1942 to Marjorie H. Funderburk.
Four d.; two s.

EDWARDS, EDWIN WASHINGTON (1972-1978). b. Aug. 7,
1927 near Marksville, La. s. of Clarence W. and Agnes
(Brouilette) E. Father was a share cropper farmer. Attd.
local pub. schools. Worked while attending college and La.
State Univ., where he studied law. Mbr., U.S. Naval Air
Corps, 1945-1946. Received law degree in 1949 and was admitted to La. bar. Began practice at Crowley, La. Mbr.,
Crowley city council, 1954-1962. El. to La. Senate in 1964,
but resigned seat in 1965 after having been el. to fill a
vacancy in U.S. House seat. Continued to serve in U.S.
House until 1972. Resigned after being nom. and el. Gov.
as a Dem., following a rather close race with Rep. opponent.
Reel. in 1975, becoming the first Gov. to be chosen under
the "open election system" by securing an absolute majority
over five opponents in the initial primary contest. During
admin., successfully sponsored a revision of the state
const. and an extensive reorg. of state govt. During second term became involved in an investigation by Cong. concerning allegations of having received campaign funds from
foreign sources while he was in Cong. Ch. of Interstate
Oil Compact Commn. of the Natl. Govs.' Conf. and of the
Ozarks Regional Commn. while Gov. Mbr., Amer. Legion;
Lions; Crowley CC; Crowley Indus. Found. Was the first
Roman Catholic Gov. of La. in over 100 years. m. in 1949
to Elaine Schwartzenburg. Two d.; two s.

KING, WILLIAM (1820-1821). b. Feb. 9, 1768 at
Scarboro, Dist. of Me. s. of Richard and Mary (Black) K.
Father, who was married twice, was a man of wealth and prominence. A half-brother, Rufus, was a mbr. of the Constl.
Conv. of 1787 from Mass., later was a U.S. Sen. from N.Y.,
and was defeated as the Fed. cand. for Pres. of U.S. in
1816. Received little formal educ. Studied at Phillips-
Andover Acad. for a short time. Entered father's lumber
bus. at Topham and opened a store with a brother-in-law.
Moved to Bath, Me., where he continued in lumbering and
shipbuilding bus. as well as banking. Set up cotton mill
at Brunswick, Me. Mbr. of Mass. Gen. Court, 1795-1796 and
1804-1806. Mbr. of Mass. Senate, 1807-1811, 1818-1819, and
was twice unsuccessful cand. for Lieut. Gov. of Mass. A
Fed. in politics, he was a strong opponent of the Embargo
Act. Sponsor of measures to sell wild lands to settlers,
and for separation of Me. from Mass. as a State. Pres. of
conv. that drew up proposed const. for Me. in 1819. Chosen
as first Gov. of Me. in 1820 by nearly unanimous vote. Resigned in 1821 to become U.S. commnr. for adjustment of
Spanish claims. Apptd. as Commnr. of Pub. Bldgs. for Me.
in 1828, and as such, developed plans for the first Capitol
bldg. at Augusta. U.S. collector of customs at Bath, 1830-
1834. Served as major gen. of militia during War of 1812,
and as col. in U.S. Army. Was accused by political opponents of trading with enemy during that war, but charges
were not proved. Lost much property as result of the war.
Defeated as Whig cand. for Gov. in 1835. During last years,
suffered from a "clouded mind". Overseer of Bowdoin Coll.,
1797-1821, and Trustee, 1821-1849. Trustee, Me. Literary
and Theological Inst. (later Colby Coll.), 1821-1848. Mbr.,
Masons. m. in 1819 to Ann Frazier, of Scarboro. Two children. D. at Bath, June 17, 1852. Bur. in Maple Grove Cem.
there.

WILLIAMSON, WILLIAM DURKEE (1821). b. July 31, 1779
at Canterbury, Conn. s. of George and Mary (Foster) W.
Descendant of English colonist who emigrated to Plymouth,
Mass. in 1642. Family moved to Amherst, Mass. during son's
youth. Attd. local schools, working during summers on
family farm. Taught school for three years. Attd.
Williams Coll., and Brown Univ., from which he was grad. in
1804. Studied law in law offices at Amherst, and later at
Warren and at Bangor, Dist. of Me. Began law practice at
Bangor in 1807. State's atty. for Hanover Co., 1807-1815.
Postmaster at Bangor, 1810-1821. Mbr. of Mass. Senate,
1816-1820. Became mbr. of first Me. Senate in 1820, and
was chosen as its Pres. As such, succeeded to the office

of Gov. when Gov. King resigned in May, 1821. Served for next seven months of King's term, but resigned in Dec., 1821, after being elected as a Jeff. Rep. to U.S. House. Served one term in Cong. Judge of probate in Penobscot Co., 1824-1840. Bank commnr. of Me., 1839-1841. Overseer of Bowdoin Coll., and of Bangor Theological Sem. Pres. of a Bangor bank. Congregationalist. Original mbr. of Me. Historical Soc. Author of two-volume History of Maine, published in 1832, and contributor of articles on histori-cal subjects. m. in 1806 to Jemima Montague Rice, of Amherst. Four s.; one d. After her death in 1822, m. in 1823 to Susan Esther White, of Putney, Vt. After her death in 1824, m. in 1825 to Mrs. Clarissa (Emerson) Wiggin, of York, Me. D. May 27, 1846. Bur. at Mt. Hope Cem., at Bangor.

AMES, BENJAMIN (1821-1822). b. Oct. 20, 1778 at Andover, Mass. Studied law and practiced at Bath, Me. Be-came mbr. of first Me. House, and was chosen Speaker of that body. As such, succeeded to office of Gov. when Act-ing Gov. Williamson resigned in Dec., 1821, to take seat in Cong. Served as Gov. for short time until convening and organizing of newly-chosen legislature in Jan., 1822. Con-tinued as House Speaker until 1824. Was later el. to the Me. Senate, becoming Pres. of that body. D. Sept. 28, 1835.

ROSE, DANIEL (1822). While residing at Thomaston, Me., was el. to Me. Senate in 1821, and was chosen Pres. of the Senate when it convened. As newly-chosen Pres. of that body in Jan., 1822, replaced Benj. Ames as Acting Gov. for three days until results of the 1821 gubernatorial election were canvassed and the official result announced by the legislature, enabling the newly-chosen Gov., Parris, to as-sume office on Jan. 5, 1822. Served as Me. Land Agent, 1831-1834.

PARRIS, ALBION KEITH (1822-1827). b. Jan. 19, 1778 at Hebron, Dist. of Me. s. of Samuel and Sarah (Pratt) P. Father, a farmer, was prominent in the community, having served as a judge and as a mbr. of the Mass. Gen. Ct. Educ. at local schools and at Dartmouth Coll., from which he was grad. in 1806. Studied law, admitted to bar in 1809, and began practice at Paris, Me. State's atty. for Oxford Co., 1811-1813. Mbr. of Mass. House in 1813, and of Mass. Sen-ate, 1813-1815. Resigned in 1815 to take seat in U.S. House. El. to second term, but resigned in 1818 to become U.S. dist. ct. judge for Me. Moved to Portland, Me. Mbr. of conv. that framed first const. for Me. in 1819. Judge

of probate for Cumberland Co., 1820-1821. Nom. and el.
Gov. as Jeff. Rep. in 1821, and for four succeeding annual
terms. During admin., property claims involving Mass. and
Me. settled; Gen. Lafayette was received as an official
guest in 1825. El. to U.S. Senate in 1826, but resigned
seat in Aug., 1828, to become mbr. of Me. Supreme Ct. Served in that post until 1836. Apptd. Second Comptroller of
U.S. Treas. by Pres. Jackson in 1836, holding that position
until 1850. Mayor of Portland in 1852. Declined second
term. Defeated as Dem. cand. for Gov. in 1854.
Congregationalist. m. in 1810 to Sarah Whitman, of
Wellfleet, Mass. Three d.; two s. D. at Portland, Feb. 22,
1857. Bur. in Western Cem.

LINCOLN, ENOCH (1827-1829). b. Dec. 28, 1788 in
Worcester, Mass. s. of Levi L., Sr., a Gov. of Mass. (q.v.)
and Martha (Waldo) L. Was a brother of Levi L., Jr., also
a Gov. of Mass. (q.v.). Entered Harvard Univ. in 1806.
Studied law in office of brother, admitted to bar in 1811,
and began practice in Salem, Mass. Moved to Fryeburg, Dist.
of Me. in 1812. Practiced law and engaged in study of
languages of Me. Indian tribes and of historical subjects.
Asst. U.S. dist. atty., 1815. El. to U.S. House as a Jeff.
Rep. in 1818 to fill vacancy and for the succeeding term.
Moved residence to Paris, Dist. of Me., in 1819. After Me.
became a State, was el. again to U.S. House, continuing for
two succeeding terms. Resigned in Jan., 1826, after having
been el. Gov. in 1825. Reel. for two succeeding terms.
Declined to be cand. for fourth term in 1829. During
admin., question of boundary line between Me. and New
Brunswick became an issue between U.S. and Great Britain.
On behalf of Me., he insisted that no territory claimed by
Me. should be surrendered without State's consent. Augusta
was selected as site for State capital, and educl. and internal improvements were begun. Contributed writings for
Me. Historical collections. Hon. degree from Bowdoin in
1821. Never married. D. at Augusta, Oct. 8, 1829, some
three months before end of third term as Gov. Bur. in mausoleum in State Park grounds at Augusta.

CUTLER, NATHAN (1829-1830). b. May 29, 1775 at
Lexington, Mass. s. of Joseph and Mary (Read) C. Family
was of modest means. Father offered son a small farm, but
he preferred to prepare himself for a professional career.
Attd. Leicester Acad. and Dartmouth Coll., from which he
was grad. in 1798. Became head of an acad. at Middlebury,
Vt., which later became Middlebury Coll. Taught there for
two years; also studied law. Admitted to bar at Worcester,

Mass., and opened law office in Lexington, Mass. Moved to
Farmington, Dist. of Me., in 1803. Obtained charter for an
acad. there, becoming mbr. of its bd. of trustees. Mbr. of
Mass. Gen. Court, 1809-1811 and 1819. Mbr. of conv. that
framed first const. for Me. in 1819. Mbr. of Me. Senate,
1828-1829, becoming Pres. of that body. When Gov. Lincoln
died in Oct., 1829, succeeded to office of Gov., serving
until end of his term as Senator, in Feb., 1830. Pres.
elector on Jackson (Dem.) ticket in 1832. Mbr. of Me. legislature again in 1844. m. in 1814 to Hannah Moore, of
Weston, Mass. Seven s.; two d. D. at Farmington, June 8,
1861.

HALL, JOSHUA (1830). b. Oct. 22, 1768 at Lewes, Del.
Received a modest educ. and became a Methodist minister at
age 19. Moved to Frankfort, Dist. of Me. Later established residence at Freedom, Me. El. to Me. Senate in 1829,
and when it convened in Jan., 1830, was eventually chosen
as its Pres. after a prolonged contest. There was a delay
in org. of the newly-chosen legislature because of disputes
over the elections of some of its mbrs., which caused the
official canvass and determination of the results of the
gubernatorial election to be delayed beyond the normal time.
In an advisory opinion, the Me. Supreme Court ruled on the
seating of mbrs. whose places were in dispute, and held
that the newly-chosen Pres. of Senate (Hall) should act as
Gov. until the results of the gubernatorial election were
made official by the legislature and the newly-chosen Gov.
installed in office. Hall accordingly acted as Gov. for a
period of approximately five days before Gov.-elect Hunton
assumed office. D. Dec. 25, 1862.

HUNTON, JONATHAN GLIDDEN (1830-1831). b. Mar. 14,
1781 in Unity, N.H. s. of Josiah and Hannah (Glidden) H.
Father had been a major in Amer. armed forces during Rev.
War, and was the local town clerk. Received a common school
educ., and studied law in office of an uncle at Readville,
Me. On uncle's retirement, took over his practice there.
Mbr. of Me. Exec. Council in 1829. Nom. and el. Gov. as a
Natl. Rep. in 1829 in a close contest with Samuel E. Smith,
a supporter of Andrew Jackson. Determination of result of
election and installation of new Gov. was delayed for several days because of a dispute over seating of some mbrs.
of the Senate. As Gov., advocated establishment of state
hosp. for the insane, and various internal improvements.
Defeated for Gov. in 1830 by Smith, in another close election. Declined to be a cand. for Gov. again in 1831. Established residence at Dixmont, later moving to Fairfield,

Me.   Later served in Me. Senate.   m. first to Betsy Craig,
who died in 1819.   Later m. to Mrs. Mary Glidden, widow of
his uncle.   One s.; one d.   D. at Fairfield, Oct. 12, 1851.
Bur. in Readfield Cem.

SMITH, SAMUEL EMERSON (1831-1834).   b. Mar. 12, 1788
at Hollis, N.H.   s. of Manasseh and Hannah (Emerson) S.
Attd. Groton Acad. and Harvard, from which he was grad. in
1808.   Studied law with Samuel Dana at Groton and with his
brothers.   Admitted to Mass. bar in 1812 and moved to
Wiscasset, Dist. of Me., where he soon built up a large
practice.   Mbr. of Mass. Gen. Court, 1819, and of first Me.
House in 1820.   Apptd. common pleas ct. judge in 1821, continuing to serve as judge after reorg. of ct. system in
1822 until 1830.   Unsuccessful as cand. of Jackson faction
of Jeff. Rep. party for Gov. in 1829, but was el. in 1830,
defeating the incumbent Gov. in a close election.   Reel. in
1831 and 1832.   Defeated as a Dissident (Indep.) Dem. cand.
for Gov. in 1833.   During admin., the boundary dispute between Me. and New Brunswick became a more acute issue; capital of State transferred from Portland to Augusta.   Supported Pres. Jackson's policy in connection with S.C. nullification movement, which divided Dem. party in the State.
Became judge of common pleas ct. in 1835, and served as mbr.
of commn. that prepared first edition of Me. Revised
Statutes.   Moved back to Wiscasset in 1836, where he engaged
in legal and literary pursuits.   m. in 1832 to Louisa S.
Fuller, of Augusta.   Five s.   D. at Wiscasset, Mar. 3, 1860.

DUNLAP, ROBERT PINCKNEY (1834-1838).   b. Aug. 17, 1794
at Brunswick, Dist. of Me.   s. of Capt. John and Mary
(Tappan) D.   Family was of Irish ancestry.   Father was distinguished as a mil. leader, and was mbr. of Mass. Gen.
Court and an overseer of Bowdoin Coll.   Taught by pvt. tutor and attd. Bowdoin Coll., from which he was grad. in
1815.   Studied law.   Admitted to bar in 1818 and began
practice at Brunswick, in which he was quite successful.
Mbr. of Me. House, 1821-1823, and of Me. Senate, 1824-1828
and 1831-1833, serving as Pres. of latter body for four
years.   Mbr. of Me. Exec. Council, 1829-1833.   Nom. and el.
Gov. as a Dem. in 1833, and was reel. for next three terms.
As Gov., successfully sponsored an amdt. to the const. providing for limited tenure, rather than life tenure, for
judges.   El. to U.S. House as Dem. in 1842 and for succeeding term.   U.S. collector of customs at Portland, Me.,
1848-1849.   Postmaster at Brunswick, 1853-1857.   Mbr. of Bd.
of Overseers of Bowdoin Coll., 1821 until death, serving as
its pres. for many years.   Active in Masonic order.

Congregationalist. m. in 1825 to Lydia Chapman, of Beverly,
Mass. Three s.; one d. D. at Brunswick, Oct. 20, 1859.
Bur. in Pine Grove Cem. there.

KENT, EDWARD (1838-1839; 1841-1842). b. Jan. 8, 1802
at Concord, N.H. s. of Wm. Austin and Charlotte (Mellen) K.
Mother was a sister of the first Chief Justice of Me.
Supreme Ct. Grad. from Harvard in 1821. Studied law and
began practice in Bangor, Me. in 1825. Acquired a good
practice in assoc. with a number of distinguished partners.
Chief judge of ct. of sessions, 1828. Mbr. of Me. legislature, 1829-1833. Mayor of Bangor, 1836-1838. Defeated as
Whig cand. for Gov. in 1836 against incumbent Gov. Dunlap;
but was the Whig cand. again in 1837 and was el. in a very
close contest. As Gov., supported U.S. Cong. in its stand
on boundary dispute with New Brunswick, and in request for
natl. govt.'s assistance in connection with so-called
"Aroostook War" disturbances growing out of that dispute.
Defeated as Whig cand. for Gov. in 1838 and 1839. Was the
Whig cand. again in 1840 and was eventually chosen Gov. by
the legislature over his opponent, incumbent Gov. Fairfield,
when no one received a popular majority. Defeated for reel.
by Fairfield in 1841. Apptd. U.S. commnr. in 1843 under
the terms of the Webster-Ashburton Treaty of 1842 to resolve Me.-New Brunswick boundary question matters with
Great Britain. Returned to law practice at Bangor thereafter. Delegate to Whig natl. conv. in 1848. U.S. Consul
at Rio de Janeiro, Brazil, 1849-1853. Apptd. to Me.
Supreme Ct. in 1859, and continued in that post until 1873.
Travelled in Europe for a year, then returned to law practice. Pres. of Me. constl. conv. of 1875. Hon. degree
from Waterville (Colby) Coll. Mbr., Me. Historical Soc.;
Phi Beta Kappa. m. first to Sarah Johnston, of Hillsboro,
N.H. One s.; two d. After first wife's death in 1853, m.
in 1855 to Abby Anne Rockwood, of Lynn, Mass. One s.; one
d. D. at Bangor, May 19, 1877.

FAIRFIELD, JOHN (1839-1841; 1842-1843). b. Jan. 30,
1797 at Saco, Dist. of Me. s. of Ichabod and Sarah (Nason)
F. Grandfather had been a pastor at Saco. Received common
school educ., and attd. Thornton Acad. and Bowdoin Coll.
Engaged in commercial bus. for a time, making several trips
to the South. Studied law, admitted to bar and began practice at Saco and Biddeford in 1826. Apptd. reporter for
Me. Supreme Ct. in 1832, serving until 1835. Nom. and el.
to U.S. House as Dem. in 1834, and was continued in office
for succeeding term. As mbr. of House, took a leading role
in passage of resolution condemning practice of dueling

after a House mbr. from Me., Jonathan Cilley, was killed in
a duel by another House mbr. from Ky., Wm. J. Graves. Resigned seat on Dec. 24, 1838, after having been el. Gov. as
a Dem., defeating incumbent Gov. Kent. Defeated Kent for
Gov. again in 1839; lost to him in 1840 by a very close
vote; but was nom. and el. over Kent again in 1841. Reel.
in 1842. As Gov., supported settlers with funds for mil.
supplies during the "Aroostook War" dispute with New
Brunswick. Resigned office of Gov. in Mar., 1843, after
having been chosen to fill vacancy in U.S. Senate. Continued to serve therein until his death. In 1844 Dem. natl.
conv. was one of two leading candidates for nom. for Vice
Pres. of U.S. on ticket with James K. Polk after the nom.
was refused by Silas Wright, but was not nom. m. in 1825
to Anna Paine Thornton, of Saco, Me. Nine children.
Trustee of Thornton Acad. for many years, serving as its
pres., 1845-1847. D. in Washington, D.C., Dec. 24, 1847 of
blood poisoning caused by improper treatment of a knee injury. Bur. in Laurel Hill Cem., Saco.

VOSE, RICHARD H. (1841). While residing at Augusta,
Me., became a mbr. of Me. Senate, and at the beginning of
its 1841 session was chosen Pres. of that body. As such,
acted as Gov. for one day during the time required for the
Senate to resolve the 1840 gubernatorial election. The Senate chose Edward Kent, former Gov., who immediately thereafter assumed the office. Apptd. as a mbr. of the first Me.
Bd. of Educ. in 1846.

KENT, EDWARD (1841-1842). See above, 1838-1839.

FAIRFIELD, JOHN (1842-1843). See above, 1839-1841.

KAVANAUGH, EDWARD (1843-1844). b. April 27, 1795 at
Damariscotta Mills, Dist. of Me. s. of James and Sarah
(Jackson) K. Father had emigrated from Ireland to Amer. in
1780, where he engaged in lumbering and shipbuilding bus.
Attd. Montreal Sem.; Georgetown Coll., in Washington, D.C.;
and St. Mary's Coll. in Baltimore, from which he was grad.
in 1813. Associated with father's bus. for a time, but did
not like it. Travelled in Europe for a time at the end of
Napoleonic wars. Studied law and opened office at
Damariscotta Mills. Served as selectman of Newcastle, Me.,
1824, 1827. Mbr. of Me. House, 1826-1828, and was sect. of
Me. Senate, 1830. Mbr. of commn. in 1831 to take census on
lands in Northern Me. El. to U.S. House as a Dem. in 1830,
and again in 1832, but was defeated for third term in 1834.
Apptd. by Pres. Jackson as U.S. chargé d' affaires at

Lisbon, Portugal in 1835. Assisted in settling various
American claims and in negotiation of a treaty of commerce
between U.S. and Portugal. Resigned post in 1841 because
of poor health. Mbr. of U.S. commn. in 1842 for settlement
of Me.-New Brunswick boundary dispute. Mbr. of Me. Senate,
1842-1843, becoming Pres. of that body. As such, succeeded
to office of Gov. when Gov. Fairfield resigned in Mar.,
1843. Served until Jan. 1, 1844, when he resigned because
of poor health after failing to win Dem. nom. for the succeeding term. Roman Catholic. Never married. D. at
Newcastle, Me., on Jan. 20, 1844. Bur. at St. Patrick's
Catholic Cem. at Damariscotta Mills.

DUNN, DAVID (1844). While residing at Poland, Me.,
was el. to Me. House. Became Speaker of that body in 1843,
and was continued in that office at beginning of 1844 session. As such, acted as Gov. for a very short time in Jan.,
1844, until the newly-chosen Senate was org. and el. its
presiding officer. The newly-elected Pres. of the Senate,
John W. Dana, then became Acting Gov. until the results of
the 1843 gubernatorial election were officially canvassed
by the legislature, and Gov.-elect Hugh Anderson was declared el. and installed in office. Later became mbr. of
Me. Senate, and was chosen as Pres. of that body in 1846.
Served as clerk of Me. House in 1856.

DANA, JOHN WINCHESTER (1844; 1847-1850). b. June 21,
1808 at Fryeburg, Dist. of Me. s. of Judah and Elizabeth
(Ripley) D. Father was a lawyer who had resided originally
in Vt. Mother was the grand-daughter of Eleazar Wheelock,
the first pres. of Dartmouth Coll. Educ. at Fryeburg Acad.
At father's urging began study of law. Became interested
in politics at an early age. Mbr. of Me. Senate, 1843-1844,
being chosen as its Pres. in latter year. As such, served
for a day as Gov. in Jan., 1844, pending declaration of result of 1843 gubernatorial election. Nom. and el. Gov. as
a Dem. in 1846. Continued in office for next two terms.
Because of a sizable vote for a Liberty party cand. in the
1846 and 1847 elections, there was no popular vote majority
for any cand., and outcomes of those elections were determined by vote of the Me. Senate. In 1853 was apptd. U.S.
chargé d' affaires in Bolivia, becoming Minister Resident
the following year. Served in that capacity until 1859.
Defeated as nominee of anti-war faction of Dem. party for
Gov. in 1861. Depressed by the Civil War and death of his
wife, he sold all his property in the U.S. and emigrated to
Argentina, where he engaged in sheep-ranching until his
death. m. Eliza Ann Osgood, of Fryeburg. Five children.

D. at Rosario, Argentina, Dec. 22, 1867, while helping to nurse victims of cholera epidemic. Remains later interred at Fryeburg, Me.

ANDERSON, HUGH JOHNSTON (1844-1847). b. May 10, 1801 at Wiscasset, Dist. of Me. Father had emigrated from Ireland to Amer. in 1789, and died when son was 9 years old. Attd. local schools. Became clerk in uncle's store at Belfast, Me. in 1813. Became interested in pub. affairs at an early age. Studied law. Ct. clerk for Waldo Co. in 1827, continuing to serve in that capacity until 1836. El. to U.S. House as a Dem. in 1836 and 1838. Became a close friend of Pres. Van Buren. Nom. and el. Gov. as a Dem. in 1843. Continued in office for next two terms. Defeated as Dem. cand. for U.S. Senate in 1847. Pres. elector on Cass (Dem.) ticket in 1848. Moved residence to Washington, D.C. Apptd. Commnr. of U.S. Customs by Pres. Pierce in 1853, serving until 1858. Apptd. by Pres. Buchanan to head a commn. to investigate mgmt. of U.S. Mint at San Francisco in 1857. Sixth Aud. of U.S. Treas., 1866-1869. Continued to reside in Washington until 1880, when he moved to Portland, Me. m. in 1832 to Martha J. Dummir. Six children. D. May 31, 1881. Bur. in Grove Cem., Belfast.

DANA, JOHN WINCHESTER (1847-1850). See above, 1844.

HUBBARD, JOHN (1850-1853). b. March 22, 1794 at Readville, Dist. of Me. s. of Dr. John and Olive (Wilson) H. Father, who had originally resided in N.H., was a physician who had acquired a farm near Readville. Son, who had great physical strength and athletic ability, managed farm for a time while attending local schools. Devoted leisure time to studies. Left home at age 19 to become a tutor. Attd. Dartmouth Coll., graduating in 1816. Again became a teacher, becoming principal at Hallowell Coll., in Me., and later at a school in Dinwiddie Co., Va. Entered Univ. of Pa. Med. Coll. in 1820, graduating in 1822. Established med. practice in Va., but in 1830 moved to Hallowell, Me., where he resided and practiced thereafter. Mbr. of Me. Senate, 1843. Nom. and el. Gov. as a Dem. in 1849, and again in 1850. There was no gubernatorial election in 1851 because of a change in the term schedule, and he continued to serve until Jan., 1853. Was Dem. nominee for Gov. again in 1852 and received a popular plurality, but his Whig opponent was chosen Gov. by Me. Senate. As Gov., advocated establishment of reform school for youthful offenders; a women's state coll.; temperance legislation; and encouragement of settlement of people in Eastern Me. Signed the

first state-wide prohibition law in 1851. Resumed med.
practice after tenure as Gov. Apptd. spec. agent of U.S.
Treas. Dept. in 1852 to examine and inspect U.S. customs
houses in Me.; later given jurisdiction over customs houses
in Eastern States. Apptd. by Pres. Buchanan in 1859 as mbr.
of U.S. commn. to settle dispute between U.S. and Great
Britain over fishing rights in Northeastern Atlantic. Hon.
degree from Colby Coll. m. in 1825 to Sarah H. Barrett, of
Dresden, Me. Six children. D. at Hallowell, Feb. 6, 1869.

CROSBY, WILLIAM GEORGE (1853-1855). b. Sept. 10, 1805
at Belfast, Dist. of Me. s. of Wm. and Sally (Davis) C.
Father was a lawyer and a judge. Attd. Belfast Acad. and
Bowdoin Coll., from which he was grad. in 1823. Was a
classmate there of Franklin Pierce, Wm. Fessenden, John
Abbott, Henry W. Longfellow, and Nathaniel Hawthorne. Studied law in father's office. Began practice in Boston, but
after two years returned in 1828 to Belfast, where he continued in law practice. Became active in politics, support-
the Whig party in the 1840 pres. election. Delegate to
Whig natl. conv. in 1844. Defeated as the Whig party cand.
for Gov. in 1850 by incumbent Gov. Hubbard. Was again the
Whig cand. in 1852, opposing Gov. Hubbard. Appearance of
Free Soil and Anti-Maine Law party candidates for Gov. in
that election resulted in no one's receiving a popular majority, and the election had to be resolved by the legislature. After an acrimonious struggle, Me. Senate chose
Crosby, who had received fewer popular votes than Hubbard.
Was the Whig nominee for Gov. again in 1853. Again did not
receive a popular plurality, but was chosen Gov. by the Senate. After demise of the Whig party in mid-1850s, affiliated with the Dem. party, and became a supporter of Pres.
Johnson's post-Civil War policies. Defeated as Dem. cand.
for U.S. House in 1866. Prominent in educl., literary and
charitable undertakings. Mbr. of Me. Historical Soc. from
1846 onward. Mason. Unitarian. m. in 1831 to Ann M.
Patterson, of Belfast. Two d.; four s. D. at Belfast,
Mar. 21, 1881.

MORRILL, ANSON PEASLEE (1855-1856). b. June 10, 1803
at Belgrade, Dist. of Me. s. of Peaslee and Nancy
(Macomber) M. One of a large family of seven brothers and
seven sisters. A younger brother, Lot M., also became a
Gov. of Me. (q.v.). Father was owner and operator of saw,
grist and carding mills. Attd. local schools and assisted
father in his mills. Acquired reputation for integrity and
industry. Held various local offices, including U.S. postmastership at Dearborn, Me. from 1825 to 1841. At age 21

became proprietor of a gen. store and engaged in merc. bus.
in several towns, residing at Madison and later at
Readfield, Me. Took over operation of ruined woolen mill
at Readfield and built it up into a successful enterprise.
Mbr. of Me. legislature in 1833. El. sheriff of Somerset
Co. in 1839, but declined second term. Worked as land
agent, 1850-1853 in various parts of the State. In 1853
broke with Dem. party over prohibition issue, becoming one
of first leaders in the temperance movement. Also was an
opponent of slavery. Defeated as Proh. (Maine Law) and
Amer. party cand. for Gov. in 1853. Nom. again by Maine
Law, Amer. and Rep. parties for Gov. in 1854 and was el. by
Me. Senate after having received a popular plurality, but
not a popular majority. Rep. nominee for Gov. in 1855.
Received a popular plurality, but lost contest in Me. Senate
to his Dem. opponent, Samuel Wells. Delegate to first Rep.
natl. conv. in 1856. El. to U.S. House in 1860, but declined to run for a second term. Moved to Augusta, Me. in
1879 where he lived the remainder of his life. Became active in mgmt. of Me. Cent. R.R., serving as pres. and later
as vice pres., 1866-1887. Mbr. of Me. legislature in 1880.
m. to Rowena M. Richardson in 1827. Two children.
Universalist. D. at Augusta, July 4, 1887. Bur. in Forest
Grove Cem. there.

WELLS, SAMUEL (1856-1857). b. Aug. 15, 1801 at Durham,
N.H. Studied law and in 1826 moved to Waterville, Me.,
where he had a successful practice until 1835. In that
year, moved to Hallowell, Me. Mbr. of Me. legislature in
1836 and 1838. Moved to Portland, Me. in 1844, where he
continued in law practice. Apptd. to Me. Supreme Ct. in
1847, and continued to serve in that post until 1854, when
he resigned. Nom. and el. Gov. as a Dem. in 1855. Received
fewer popular votes than his opponent, incumbent Gov. Anson
Morrill, but the election was referred to the Me. Senate,
which chose Wells. Was the Dem. cand. for Gov. again in
1856, but lost to Hannibal Hamlin, the Rep. cand. Dem.
party was badly split at that election by issues growing
out of slavery and prohibition. Defeat was a severe disappointment, and he retired from politics. Moved to Boston,
Mass., where he resumed law practice. Hon. degrees from
Waterville (now Colby) Coll. and Bowdoin Coll. D. July 15,
1868.

HAMLIN, HANNIBAL (1857). b. Aug. 27, 1809 at Paris
Hill, Dist. of Me. s. of Cyrus and Anna (Livermore) H.
Family descended from English ancestors who emigrated to
Mass. in colonial times. Father was a physician and a

farmer of modest means, and had served in Mass. Gen. Ct.
Received common school educ. while assisting on family farm.
Attd. Hebron Acad. for a time to prepare for college, but
death of father in 1829 necessitated his return home to
manage farm. Refused offer of a cadetship at U.S. Mil.
Acad. Purchased an interest in a local weekly newspaper,
the Jeffersonian, but sold it after six months. Studied
law, admitted to bar, and established practice at Hampden,
Me. in 1833. Won his first ct. case, in which his future
father-in-law was the opposing counsel. Mbr. of Me. House,
1835-1840, serving as Speaker for three of the five years.
Defeated as Dem. cand. for U.S. House in 1840, but was
successful on second try in 1842. Reel. in 1844. Identified with anti-slavery element in Cong., becoming a strong
supporter of the Wilmot Proviso. Defeated as Dem. cand.
for U.S. Senate in 1846. El. to U.S. Senate in 1848 to
fill vacancy. Eventually broke with Dem. party over slavery issue and affiliated with Rep. party in 1856. Continued in U.S. Senate until 1857, when he resigned to accept
office of Gov. to which he had been el. as a Rep. in 1856.
Served only some six weeks of term, resigning in Feb., 1857,
to return to the U.S. Senate after having been el. to that
body by the Me. legislature. Resigned Senate seat in Jan.,
1861, after having been nom. and el. Vice Pres. of U.S. on
Lincoln (Rep.) ticket in 1860 election. Was not re-nom.
for succeeding term as Vice Pres. by 1864 Rep. natl. conv.
Enlisted in Me. State Guard for some two months. Apptd.
U.S. collector of the port of Boston, Mass. in 1865, serving until 1866. Regent of Smithsonian Inst., 1861-1865 and
1870-1882. El. to U.S. Senate for third time in 1869, continuing to serve therein until 1881. Apptd. U.S. Minister
to Spain in 1881, but resigned that office after about a
year of service. Retired to farm and bus. interests thereafter, but continued to play an important role in Me. politics. m. in 1833 to Sarah Jane Emery, of Hallowell, Me.
After her death in 1855, m. to first wife's half-sister,
Ellen V. Emery, in 1856. Six s.; one d. D. at Bangor,
July 4, 1891. Bur. in Mount Hope Cem. there.

WILLIAMS, JOSEPH HARTWELL (1857-1858). b. Feb. 15,
1814 at Augusta, Dist. of Me. s. of Reuel and Sarah Lowell
(Cony) W. Father was a prominent businessman and lawyer,
and served in U.S. Senate as a Dem. Educ. at a boarding
school at Wiscasset; the Classical Inst., at Mt. Pleasant;
and Harvard, from which he was grad. in 1834. Studied law
at the Dane Law School in Cambridge, Mass. Began law practice in Augusta in 1837, taking over father's clientele after the latter became a U.S. Sen. Practiced law there for

25 years until father's death. Nom. for seat on Me. Supreme
Ct. by Gov. Washburn, but declined. Ch. of resolutions
commt. of Dem. state conv. in 1854 and sponsored resolutions
disapproving Pres. Pierce's policies regarding extension of
slavery into U.S. territories. Left Dem. party in 1850s
and joined newly-formed Rep. party, supporting Fremont for
Pres. of U.S. in 1856. Nom. without his knowledge for seat
in Me. Senate in 1856, and was el. Became Pres. of Senate,
as as such succeeded to office of Gov. when Gov. Hamlin resigned to take seat in U.S. Senate in 1857. Completed
Hamlin's term, but did not seek nom. for succeeding term
because he was opposed to prohibition plank in Rep. party's
platform. Supported Pres. Lincoln's war measures after
outbreak of Civil War. Mbr. of Me. legislature, 1864-1866.
Mbr. of governing bds. of Me. Gen. Hosp., Me. Reform School,
and of the Cony Female Acad. El. to Me. House in 1873 as
an Indep. Defeated as Dem. nominee for Gov. in 1877. m.
in 1842 to Apphea Putnam Judd, of Northampton, Mass. One
s., who died in infancy. D. at Augusta, July 18, 1896.

   MORRILL, LOT MYRICK (1858-1861).   b. May 3, 1813 at
Belgrade, Dist. of Me. s. of Peaslee and Nancy (Macomber)
M. Father was owner and operator of saw, grist and carding
mills. Mbr. of large family consisting of seven brothers
and seven sisters. An older brother, Anson P., was also a
Gov. of Me. (q.v.). Attd. local schools; worked as a clerk
in a local store; and began study of law. Became school
teacher at age of 16. Entered Waterville (now Colby) Coll.
in 1833. Left college to study law in office at Readfield,
Me. Admitted to bar and began practice of law at Readfield.
In 1841 moved to Augusta, continuing to practice law. Mbr.
of Me. House as a Dem., 1853-1856. Defeated as cand. for
U.S. Senate in 1854. El. to Me. Senate in 1856, becoming
its presiding officer in 1857. Was opposed to extension of
slavery and to repeal of prohibition law. Was mbr. of Dem.
state commt., but after nom. of Buchanan for Pres. of U.S.
by Dem. natl. conv. in 1856, broke with Dem. party. Nom.
and el. Gov. in 1857 as a Rep., and was continued in office
in 1858 and 1859. El. to U.S. Senate as a Rep. in 1861 to
fill seat vacated by Hannibal Hamlin after his election to
office of Vice Pres. of U.S. Defeated in legislature for
continuation in Senate seat in 1869 by Hamlin by margin of
one vote. When Sen. Fessenden died in Sept., 1869, was el.
again to fill the Senate seat vacancy. Resigned in 1876 to
become U.S. Sect. of Treas. under Pres. Grant. Was offered
any post he wanted by Pres. Hayes in 1877, and chose to become U.S. collector of customs at Portland, Me. Had suffered a severe illness in 1870, from which he never fully

recovered. m. to Charlotte Holland Vance in 1845. Four
children. D. Jan. 10, 1883. Bur. in Forest Grove Cem.,
Augusta.

WASHBURN, ISRAEL, Jr. (1861-1863). b. June 6, 1813 at
Livermore, Dist. of Me. Eldest of seven sons of Israel and
Martha (Benjamin) W. All the sons became persons of some
eminence. Family descended from an English ancestor, John,
who emigrated to Dixboro, Mass. in 1631 and whose descendants included persons of prominence in New England as soldiers, businessmen and statesmen. Three of his brothers,
as he did also, became mbrs. of Cong.; Cadwallader C., was
a mbr. of Cong. and Gov. of Wisc. (q.v.); Wm. D., a mbr. of
Cong. from Minn.; and Elihu B., a mbr. of Cong. from Ill.
and a U.S. diplomat. Educ. in common schools at Livermore
and by pvt. tutors. Studied law, was admitted to bar and
began practice in Orono, Me. in 1834. Mbr. of Me. House,
1842-1843. El. to U.S. House as a Whig in 1850, and continued in that office until 1861, when he resigned after
having been el. Gov. Had shifted party affiliation to Rep.
party when it was org. in 1850s. Reel. Gov. in 1861, but
refused to be a cand. for a third term in 1862. Supported
Civil War policies of the Lincoln admin. Became U.S. collector of customs at Portland, Me. in 1863, continuing in
that capacity until 1877. Pres. of Rumford Falls and
Buckfield R.R., 1878-1883. Mbr. and pres. of Bd. of Trustees of Tufts Coll., 1852-1883. Was offered presidency of
Tufts Coll., but declined it. Engaged in literary pursuits
in latter years of life. Many of his speeches and articles
were published, including a collection, Notes, Historical
Descriptions and Personal, of Livermore, Me., published in
1874. Hon. degree from Tufts Coll. m. first to Mary
Webster in 1841. m. in 1876 to ------Brown. Four children.
D. in Philadelphia, May 12, 1883. Bur. in Mount Hope Cem.,
Bangor, Me.

COBURN, ABNER (1863-1864). b. Mar. 22, 1803 at Canaan,
Dist. of Me. s. of Eleazar and Mary (Weston) C. Father,
who had served in Mass. Gen. Court, was a land-owner and
surveyor. Spent boyhood on father's farm and assisted him
in surveying. Attd. local schools and Bloomfield Acad.
Taught school for a time. In 1825 went into land surveying
work for himself. In 1830 formed a land surveying and lumbering firm with father and brothers. By 1870 the firm had
acquired possession of some 700 square miles of land, and
was the largest land-holding enterprise in Me. Also became
involved in railroad constr. and operation. El. to Me.
legislature in 1838, 1840 and 1844 as a Whig. Cand. for

pres. elector on Whig ticket in 1852. Shifted party allegiance to Rep. party after its formation in 1850s. Mbr. of
Me. Exec. Council in 1855 and 1857. Pres. elector on Rep.
ticket in 1860. Nom. and el. Gov. in 1862. Supported Pres.
Lincoln's war policies. Again served as Rep. pres. elector
in 1884. Took prominent role in philanthropic and educl.
endeavors. Assisted in founding Me. State Coll. of Agri.
(later Univ.) at Orono. Trustee of Colby Coll. and of
Coburn Classical Inst. Contributor to Baptist church endeavors. Never married. D. Jan. 4, 1885, at Skowhegan, Me.

CONY, SAMUEL (1864-1867). b. Feb. 27, 1811 at Augusta,
Dist. of Me. s. of Gen. Samuel and Susan (Bowdoin) C. Father and mother were both mbrs. of families of prominence
in cultural and pub. affairs. Educ. by pvt. tutors. Attd.
China Acad.; Wakefield Coll.; and Brown Univ., from which
he was grad. in 1829. Studied law, admitted to bar, and
began practice in Old Town, Me. in 1832. Mbr. of Me. legislature, 1835, at age 24. Mbr. of Me. Exec. Council, 1839.
Became judge for Penobscot Co. in 1840, serving for seven
years. Apptd. land agent for the State in 1847, serving
for three years in that capacity. El. State Treas. as a
Dem. in 1850, and continued to serve until 1855, residing
at Augusta. Mayor of Augusta, 1854. As a Dem., supported
policies of Sen. Douglas. When Civil War began, became a
Union supporter and shifted allegiance to Rep. party. El.
to Me. legislature in 1862. Nom. and el. Gov. as a Rep. in
1863, and continued in office for next two terms. Refused
to become cand. for Gov. again in 1866. m. in 1833 to
Mercy H. Sewall, of Farmington, Me. Two s.; one d. m. in
1849 to Lucy W. Brooks, of Augusta. Two d.; one s. D. at
Augusta, Oct. 5, 1870.

CHAMBERLAIN, JOSHUA LAWRENCE (1867-1871). b. Sept. 8,
1828 at Brewer, Me. s. of Joshua and Sarah Dupee (Brastow)
C. Attd. Bowdoin Coll., graduating in 1852, and Bangor
Theological Sem., graduating from there in 1855. Also received an M.A. degree from Bowdoin in 1855. Received license as minister, but was never ordained. Became tutor at
Bowdoin in 1855 and the next year, prof. of rhetoric. Was
also an instructor there in modern languages, and in 1861,
a prof. in that field. Became prof. of rhetoric and oratory in 1865. Upon outbreak of Civil War was commissioned
lieut. col. of Me. volunteer regiment. Rose to rank of
major gen. by end of the Civil War. Participated in numerous battles in Va. theater of the war, and was wounded
three times. Present at surrender of Gen. Lee in 1865.
Recipient of Cong. Medal of Honor. After release from mil.

service, became prof. of moral philosophy at Bowdoin. El.
Gov. as a Rep. in 1866, and was continued in office for
three succeeding terms. Mbr. of Bd. of Trustees of Bowdoin
in 1867. Became Pres. of Bowdoin Coll. in 1871, serving in
that capacity until 1883. Lecturer in political sci. and
pub. law, 1883-1885, and published widely in that field.
U.S. commnr. to Paris Expo. in 1878. U.S. surveyor of customs at Portland, Me., 1900-1901. Visited Egypt in 1901 to
observe methods of British rule there. Commdr. of Loyal
League of U.S., 1866. Head of G.A.R. in Me., 1903. Senior
vice pres. of Amer. Bible Soc. Pres. of Soc. of Army of
the Potomac, 1884. Recipient of medal from French govt.
Hon. degrees from Coll. of Pa. and Bowdoin Coll. m. in
1855 to Frances Caroline Adams. D. Feb. 24, 1914.

PERHAM, SIDNEY (1871-1874). b. Mar. 27, 1819 at
Woodstock, Dist. of Me. s. of Joel and Sophronia (Bisbee)
P. Descendant of an English colonist who came to Mass. in
1634. Attd. local schools and Gould Acad., at Bethel, Me.
At age 19 became a teacher and continued in that occupation
for 15 years, farming during summers. Active in teacher's
institutes and educl. affairs. At age 21 bought father's
farm homestead at Woodstock and for 20 years engaged in
raising sheep on a large scale. Mbr. of Me. Bd. of Agri.,
1853-1854. Strong advocate of temperance legislation, campaigning for re-enactment of prohibition law in 1857. Affiliated with Dem. party until 1853, when he left it over
slavery and prohibition issues. Mbr. of Me. House in 1854,
and was chosen Speaker in first term. Affiliated with Rep.
party and was a cand. for pres. elector on Fremont ticket
in 1856. El. clerk of Me. Supreme Ct. in 1858. Continued
in that capacity until 1863, when he resigned after having
been el. to U.S. House. Served until 1869, not seeking
reel. in 1868. Supported impeachment of Pres. Johnson and
repeal of war-time tax measures. Nom. and el. Gov. as a
Rep. in 1870, and again in 1871 and 1872. As Gov., advocated jail reforms; establishment of indus. schools for girls;
free pub. high school system; biennial sessions of the leg-
islàture, on all of which issues he received legislative
support. El. Sect. of State for Me. in 1875. U.S. appraiser for customs at Portland, 1877-1885. Pres. of Bd.
of Trustees of Westbrook Sem., at Deering, 1865-1880, and
of Me. Indus. School, at Hallowell, 1873-1898. Active in
Universalist church. m. in 1843 to Almena J. Hathaway, of
Paris, Me. Six children. D. April 10, 1907, in Washington,
D.C. Bur. in Lakeside Cem., Bryant Pond, Me.

DINGLEY, NELSON, Jr. (1874-1876). b. Feb. 15, 1832 at

Durham, Me. s. of Nelson and Jane (Lambert) D. Attd. pub.
schools in Unity, Me.; Waterville Acad. and Coll.; and
Dartmouth Coll., from which he was grad. in 1855. Studied
law and admitted to bar, but did not practice. Purchased
Lewiston Weekly Journal in 1856. Became its ed. and converted it in 1865 to a daily newspaper, the Evening Journal.
Mbr., Me. House, 1862-1865, 1868, and 1873, serving as
Speaker, 1863-1864. Nom. and el. Gov. as a Rep. in 1874
and 1875. Delegate to Rep. natl. convs. in 1876 and 1880.
El. to U.S. House in spec. election in 1881 to fill a vacan-
cy. Continued in that office until his death. Offered
post of U.S. Sect. of Treas. by Pres. McKinley in 1897, but
declined it. As ch. of House Ways and Means Commt., was
influential in drafting the Tariff Act of 1897, as well as
other tax measures after outbreak of the Spanish-Amer. War.
Mbr. of spec. commn. in 1897-1898 to adjust dispute with
Canada over fisheries. Hon. degrees from Bates and
Dartmouth Colleges. m. in 1857 to Salome McKinney, of
Auburn, Me. One s.; four d. D. in Washington, D.C., Feb.
13, 1899, after having been reel. to U.S. House seat for
tenth successive term the preceding year. Bur. in Oak Hill
Cem., Auburn, Me.

CONNOR, SELDEN (1876-1879). b. Jan. 25, 1839 at
Fairfield, Me. s. of Wm. and Mary C. Grad. from Tufts Coll.
in 1859. Studied law at Woodstock, Vt. On outbreak of
Civil War enlisted as a pvt. in a Vt. regiment of the Union
Army. Later became col. of a volunteer Me. regiment. Severely wounded at the Battle of the Wilderness in 1864, and
was still invalided when the war ended in 1865. Had risen
to rank of brig. gen. when mustered out in 1866. U.S. assessor of internal revenue for Me. dist., 1869-1874. Nom.
and el. Gov. as a Rep. in 1875, and again in 1876 and 1877.
Was nom. for a fourth term in 1878. Received a plurality
of popular votes against the Dem. and Greenback party candidates, but the legislature chose the Dem. cand., Garcelon,
who had received the third highest popular vote. Apptd. by
Pres. Arthur as pension agent in Me. in 1882, serving until
1886. Engaged in banking and ins. bus. in Portland, Me.
Chosen pres. of Me. State Coll. by its Bd. of Trustees in
1892, but declined the post. Apptd. U.S. pension agent
again in 1897, serving until 1912. Active in G.A.R. Hon.
degree from Tufts Coll. m. in 1869 to Henrietta White
Bailey, of Washington, D.C. D. at Augusta, July 9, 1917.

GARCELON, ALONZO (1879-1880). b. May 6, 1813 at
Lewiston, Dist. of Me. s. of Col. Wm. and Mary (Davis) G.
Father was a farmer whose family had resided originally on

the Isle of Guernsey. Educ. at academies in Monmouth,
Waterville and Newcastle, and at Bowdoin Coll., from which
he was grad. in 1836. Taught school in winters while receiving educ. Instructor at Alfred Acad. for three years.
Studied med. at Dartmouth Coll. and for two years at Med.
Coll. of Ohio in Cincinnati, graduating there as a surgeon
in 1839. Began med. practice at Lewiston, and served as
Surg. Gen. of Me. during Civil War. Political affiliation
was originally with Natl. Rep. (Whig) party, but shifted to
Dem. party during admin. of Pres. Jackson. Left Dem. party
in 1840s over slavery issue and became a mbr. of Free Soil
party. Joined the newly-formed Rep. party in 1850s, but
broke with that party over Reconstruction issues after
Civil War, and rejoined Dem. party. Established Lewiston
Weekly Journal in 1847. Mbr. of Me. House in 1853 and 1857,
and of Me. Senate, 1855. Defeated as Dem. cand. for U.S.
House in 1868. El. mayor of Lewiston in 1871 as a Dem. As
mayor, promoted indus. devel. for the city. Nom. as Dem.
cand. for Gov. in 1878. Although he received the third
highest popular vote in the contest, was chosen Gov. by the
legislature when no cand. received a popular majority. Nom.
for second term in 1879. Again finished third in the popular voting, but the Senate chose the Rep. cand. Active in
professional med. orgs., serving as pres. of Me. Med. Assoc.
Trustee of Bates Coll. m. first to Ann Augusta Waldron, of
Somerset, N.H. Three s.; one d. After her death in 1857,
m. in 1859 to Olivia Nelson Spear, of Rockland, Me. D. Dec.
8, 1906, at Medford, Mass.

DAVIS, DANIEL FRANKLIN (1880-1881). b. Sept. 12, 1843
at Freedom, Me. s. of Rev. Moses and Mary (French) D. Ancestor had emigrated from England to N.H. in 1661. Father,
who had been a teacher, assisted in his educ. Attd. East
Corinth Acad. In 1863 enlisted in a Me. volunteer regiment
and remained with it during the course of Civil War. Resumed educ. at Corunna Acad. and at Wesleyan Sem., at Kent's
Hill. Employed as a teacher during winters. Studied law
in a law office at Stetson. Admitted to bar and established practice in East Corinth in 1869. Served several terms
in Me. House and Me. Senate. Nom. as Rep. cand. for Gov.
in 1879. Received plurality of popular votes, but lacked a
majority. When the incumbent Gov., Garcelon, refused to
issue certificates of election to some of the Rep. mbrs. of
the newly-chosen Senate, which would have to resolve the
contest for Gov. in which Garcelon had received the third
highest popular vote, resolution of the outcome of the election was delayed while the question of seating mbrs. whose
certificates had been held up was referred to the Me.

Supreme Ct. for resolution. Disorders were threatened and
militia forces had to be called out to preserve order. After the question of seating its mbrs. had been resolved,
the legislature eventually chose Davis as Gov. This controversy resulted in the submission and adoption of an amdt.
to the Me. const. providing for election of the Gov. by a
popular plurality vote. Davis was defeated as the Rep.
cand. to succeed himself in the 1880 election, failing by
less than 200 votes to secure a popular plurality. Engaged
thereafter in law practice in Bangor. U.S. collector of
internal revenue at Bangor, 1882-1886. Made large purchases
of timber lands in Me., and became prominent as advocate of
devel. of wild lands and natural resources of State. m. in
1857 to Laura B. Godwin, of East Corinth. Eight children.
D. at Bangor, Jan. 9, 1897.

PLAISTED, HARRIS MERRILL (1881-1883). b. Nov. 2, 1828
at Jefferson, N.H. s. of Deacon Wm. and Nancy (Merrill) P.
Father was a judge. Worked on family farm while attending
local schools. Attd. acad. while teaching in winters.
Grad. from Waterville (Colby) Coll. in 1853 and engaged in
teaching at Waterville Liberal Inst. Supt. of schools for
three years. Attd. Albany Law School, grad. in 1855.
Studied law for another year in an office in Bangor, and
began law practice there in 1856. Mbr. of Gov. Lot
Morrill's staff, 1858-1860. Upon outbreak of Civil War, enlisted in Me. volunteer regiment, becoming lieut. col. and
then col. Involved in a number of battles, and was cited
for gallant conduct, being breveted brig. gen. and then
major gen. by end of the war. Returned to law practice at
Bangor. Delegate to Rep. natl. conv. in 1868. Mbr. of Me.
legislature, 1867-1868, and Atty. Gen. of Me., 1873-1875.
Nom. and el. to U.S. House as a Rep. in Sept., 1875, in a
spec. election to fill a vacancy. Refused to run for a
regular term in 1876, having broken with the Rep. party
over various issues. Changed allegiance to Dem. party.
Nom. and el. Gov. as a Dem. in 1880 by a plurality of less
than 200 votes over incumbent Gov. Davis. Became first Gov.
to be chosen under the popular plurality vote system, which
was approved by the voters at that election. Determination
of outcome of the election was delayed for some time while
the legislature debated the question whether the plurality
vote rule should apply at the same election in which it was
adopted. Conclusion was reached that it should. Also became the first Gov. to be el. for a two-year term, that
change also having been approved by the voters. Defeated
as Dem. cand. for succeeding term in 1882. Defeated as Dem.
cand. for U.S. Senate seat in 1883 and 1889. Became ed. and

publ. of a newspaper, the New Age, at Augusta in 1883. Author of Digest of Maine Reports, 1820-1880. m. in 1858 to Sarah Mason, of Waterville. Three s. After her death in 1875, m. in 1881 to Mabel True Hill, of Exeter. One d. A son, Frederick W., became a Gov. of Me. (q.v.). D. at Bangor, Jan. 20, 1898. Bur. in Mount Hope Cem. there.

ROBIE, FREDERICK (1883-1887). b. Aug. 12, 1822 at Gorham, Me. s. of Toppan and Sarah Thaxter (Lincoln) R. Mother was related to Govs. Levi Lincoln I and II of Mass., and Enoch Lincoln, of Me. (q.v.). Father was a prominent citizen who had served in Me. legislature. Educ. by pvt. tutors and attd. Gorham Acad. Grad. from Bowdoin Coll. in 1841 and became principal of an acad. in Ga. and later in Fla. Studied at Jefferson Med. Coll., in Philadelphia. After graduating there engaged in med. practice at Biddeford, then at Waldoboro, and later at Gorham, Me. Mbr. of Me. Exec. Council during Gov. Washburn's admin., resigning to become U.S. paymaster for volunteer units in Me., later in the New England district. Held rank of brevet lieut. col. at end of Civil War. Mbr. of Me. Senate, 1866-1867, and of Me. House for ten years, serving as House Speaker in 1872 and 1876. Mbr. of Me. Exec. Council under Gov. Davis in 1880 and under Gov. Plaisted, 1881-1882. Nom. and el. Gov. as a Rep. in 1882, defeating incumbent Gov. Plaisted. Reel. in 1884. Mbr., Rep. state commt., 1868-1873. Delegate to Rep. natl. conv. in 1872. U.S. commnr. to Paris Expo. in 1878. Prominently involved in ins., banking and railroad bus. in Portland, Me. Mbr., G.A.R.; Grange. m. in 1847 to Olivia M. Priest, of Biddeford. Three d.; one s. After her death, m. in 1900 to Martha E. Cressey, of Gorham. D. at Gorham, Feb. 3, 1912.

BODWELL, JOSEPH ROBINSON (1887). b. June 18, 1818 at Methuen, Mass. s. of Joseph and Mary (How) B. Father was a farmer of limited means. Lived with a brother-in-law, Patrick Fleming, for a time during early youth, assisting on farm while attending school. Later assisted father on the Fleming farm, which his father had purchased. Worked as shoemaker at nights while attending school in Methuen. Became partner of father in farming in 1838. A contract they obtained for hauling stone for a Merrimac River bridge led to their engagement in stone quarry bus. In 1852 went into stone quarry bus. for himself as partner of Moses Webster. The firm prospered. A corp. was formed and it grew into one of the largest quarry enterprises in the country. In 1866 moved to Hallowell, Me., where a quarry was opened by his company. Also engaged in raising blooded

cattle, ice-making, lumbering and railroad enterprises, be-
coming quite wealthy. Mbr. of Hallowell city council and
then mayor. Mbr. of Me. House for two terms. Delegate to
Rep. natl. conv. in 1880. Nom. as Rep. cand. for Gov. in
1886, and was el. Mbr. of Bd. of Trustees of Westbrook
Sem. m. in 1848 to Eunice Fox, of Dracut, Mass. One d.
After first wife's death in 1857, m. in 1859 to Hannah Fox,
a sister of his first wife. One s. Universalist. D. at
Hallowell, Dec. 15, 1887, near end of first year of term as
Gov.

MARBLE, SEBASTIAN S. (1887-1889). b. Mar. 1, 1817 at
Dixfield, Dist. of Me. Studied law and established practice at Waldoboro, Me. Became a U.S. marshal for Me. Later was a mbr. of Me. Senate, and became Pres. of that body.
As such, succeeded to the office of Gov. on Dec. 15, 1887,
following the death of Gov. Bodwell, and completed the term
for which Bodwell had been el. Defeated as cand. for Rep.
nom. for Gov. for the succeeding term in 1888. Continued
thereafter to be active in Me. politics as a Rep. D. at
Waldoboro, Me., May 10, 1902.

BURLEIGH, EDWIN CHICK (1889-1893). b. Nov. 27, 1843
at Linneus, Me. s. of Parker P. and Caroline Peabody
(Chick) B. Grandfather was well-known as a participant in
pub. affairs. Attd. common schools and Houlton Acad.
Taught school and surveyed lands, in which his father, who
was Me. Land Agent, had extensive holdings. In 1864 enlisted in a D.C. cavalry unit, but failed the physical examination. Served as clerk for State Adjt. Gen. for a short
time, then was employed as a clerk, later as Me. Land Agent,
1870-1876. Acquired large land-holdings. Clerk of Me.
House and later was a clerk in office of State Treas., 1880-
1884. State Treas., 1884-1888. Became publ. of Kennebec
Journal in 1887. Nom. and el. Gov. as a Rep. in 1888 and
again in 1890. Nom. and el. to seat in U.S. House in 1897
to fill a vacancy, and continued in that office until 1911.
Defeated for reel. in 1910. El. to U.S. Senate in 1913.
Delegate-at-large to Rep. natl. conv. in 1896. m. in 1863
to Mary Jane Bither. One s. D. June 16, 1916, at Augusta,
Me., while still a mbr. of U.S. Senate. Bur. in Forest
Grove Cem. there.

CLEAVES, HENRY B. (1893-1897). b. Feb. 6, 1840 at
Bridgton, Me. s. of Thomas and Sophie (Bradsteel) C. Attd.
local schools and acad. Worked on farm and as woodsman
while attending school. In 1862 enlisted as pvt. in Me.
volunteer regiment of Union Army. Saw action at New Orleans

and later with Army of Potomac in Va. Held rank of first
lieut. at end of Civil War. Returned to home in Bridgton
and studied law. Admitted to bar in 1868, and began practice at Bath. Moved to Portland in 1869. Mbr. of Me. legislature, 1876-1877. City solicitor of Portland, 1877-1879.
Atty. Gen. of Me., 1880-1885. As Atty. Gen., prosecuted a
number of notable cases against railroad interests as well
as some widely-noted murder cases. Unsuccessful as a cand.
for the Rep. nom. for Gov. in 1888. Nom. and el. Gov. as a
Rep. in 1892, and again in 1894. Mbr., G.A.R. and Me. Vets.
Assoc. Congregationalist. Hon. degree from Bowdoin Coll.
D. June 22, 1912, at Portland.

POWERS, LLEWELLYN (1897-1901). b. Oct. 14, 1836 at
Pittsfield, Me. s. of Arbra and Naomi (Matthews) P. Was
the eldest of ten children. Grew up on father's farm.
Attd. local schools; St. Albans Acad.; Colby Coll.; Coburn
Classical Inst.; and Union Coll. (Albany Law School), from
which he was grad. in 1860. Admitted to bar in N.Y. and Me.
Began practice of law in Houlton, Me. in 1861. Pros. atty.
for Aroostook Co., 1865-1870. U.S. collector of customs
for Aroostook dist., 1868-1872. Mbr. of Me. House, 1874-
1876. Nom. and el. to U.S. House as a Rep. in 1876, but
was defeated for reel. in 1878. Served again in Me. House,
1883, 1892 and 1895, becoming Speaker in last term. Nom.
and el. Gov. as a Rep. in 1896 and again in 1898. El. to
U.S. House again in 1901 to fill a vacancy and continued to
serve therein until his death. During his lifetime became
owner of one of the largest tracts of lumber land in New
England. m. in 1863 to Jennie Hewes. D. July 28, 1908, at
Houlton. Bur. in West Pittsfield Cem., near Pittsfield, Me.

HILL, JOHN FREMONT (1901-1905). b. Oct. 29, 1855 at
Eliot, Me. s. of Wm. and Miriam (Leighton) H. Descendant
of an English colonist who emigrated to New England in
1650s. Attd. local schools; Berwick Acad.; Me. Med. School
(Bowdoin); and Long Island Coll. Hosp. and Med. School, in
Brooklyn, N.Y. Received an M.D. degree in 1877. Began med.
practice in Boothbay Harbor, Me., but soon afterward became
involved in periodical publication bus. at Augusta, Me.,
which proved very successful. Mbr. of Me. House, 1888-1892
and of Me. Senate, 1893-1897. Mbr. of Me. Exec. Council,
1898-1899. Nom. and el. Gov. as a Rep. in 1900, and again
in 1902. Became involved in a number of bus. enterprises
in electric railway, banking, and gas and electric utility
fields. Pres. of Augusta Natl. Bank and of State Trust Co.
Trustee of Augusta Trust Co. and Kennebec Savings Bank. m.
in 1880 to Lizzie G. Vickery, daughter of a bus. assoc.

After her death in 1893, m. in 1897 to Mrs. Laura Colman Liggett. D. March 16, 1912.

COBB, WILLIAM TITCOMB (1905-1909). b. July 23, 1857 at Rockland, Me. s. of Francis and Martha (Chandler) C. Attd. local pub. schools and Bowdoin Coll., from which he was grad. in 1877. Was a classmate there of Robert E. Peary, the distinguished Arctic explorer. Studied for two years in Germany at the Univ. of Leipzig and the Univ. of Berlin. Attd. Harvard Law School and did post-graduate work at Bowdoin, receiving an A.M. degree from latter in 1880. Engaged in lime mfg. bus., and became pres. of Bath Iron Works. Nom. and el. Gov. as a Rep. in 1904, and again in 1906. Declined to be a cand. for U.S. Senate seat after tenure as Gov. Apptd. by Pres. Hoover in 1932 to head a commt. in Me. designed to discourage the hoarding of money. Became Trustee of Bowdoin Coll. in 1908. Hon. degrees from Bowdoin and the Univ. of Me. m. in 1882 to Lucy Banks, of Rockland, Me. Two d. D. July 24, 1937, at Rockland, Me.

FERNALD, BERT MANFRED (1909-1911). b. April 3, 1858 at West Poland, Me. s. of James Henley and Betsy Small (Libby) F. Family ancestors, who were French, had emigrated to Amer. in 18th century. Attd. local schools; Hebron Acad.; and bus. coll. in Boston. Engaged in teaching for a time, but after father's death returned home to manage family farm for mother. Engaged in raising sweet corn for market, and became involved in marketing side of food production bus. Established a cannery in 1888 with two brothers-in-law. Food packing bus. expanded and eventually served wide natl. market with its products. Also became involved as large land owner in horticultural activities. Held various local offices. Supt. of Poland schools, 1878. Mbr. of Me. House, 1897-1899, and of Me. Senate, 1899-1901. Defeated as cand. for Rep. nom. for Gov. in 1904, but was nom. and el. in 1908. Nom. for second term in 1910, but was defeated in gen. election by Dem. opponent. During admin., a new State Capitol bldg. was built and first State Conservation Commn. established. El. to U.S. Senate in 1916 to fill vacancy, and continued in that office until his death. As Senator, opposed U.S. entry into League of Nations and World Court. Involved in numerous bus. enterprises in dairy, telephone, banking, and food-processing fields. Trustee of Hebron Acad. for many years. Pres. of Natl. Canners Assoc., 1910. m. in 1877 to Anne Adeline Keene, of Poland, Me. One s.; one d. D. Aug. 23, 1926, at West Poland, while still a mbr. of U.S. Senate. Bur. in Highland Cem. there.

PLAISTED, FREDERICK WILLIAM (1911-1913). b. July 26,
1865 at Bangor, Me. s. of Harris M. and Sarah Jane (Mason)
P. Father was a Gov. of Me. (q.v.). Attd. local pub.
schools; St. Johnsbury (Vt.) Acad. Ed. and publ. of
family-owned newspaper, the Augusta New Age, 1889-1914. Became interested in politics at an early age. Delegate to
Dem. natl. convs. in 1896, 1900 and 1912. Mayor of Augusta,
1906-1908, 1910. Sheriff of Kennebec Co., 1907-1908. Defeated as Dem. cand. for vacant U.S. House seat in 1897.
Nom. and el. Gov. as a Dem. in 1910, defeating incumbent
Gov. Fernald. Became first Dem. to hold the office since
his father, who was Gov. from 1881 to 1883. Defeated for
succeeding term in 1912. State Park Commnr., 1913-1915.
Postmaster of Augusta, 1914-1923. Mbr. of Augusta Pub.
Library Bd. and Augusta Gen. Hosp. Bd. Ch., U.S. draft bd.
for Kennebec Co., 1917-1918. Mbr., Masons (K.T.); Elks;
S.O.V. Congregationalist. m. in 1907 to Frances Gullifer,
of Augusta. D. March 4, 1943.

HAINES, WILLIAM THOMAS (1913-1915). b. Aug. 7, 1854
at Levant, Me. s. of Thomas J. and Maria L. (Eddy) H.
Descendant of an English colonist who came to New England
in 1635. Attd. the Univ. of Me., graduating in 1876; and
Albany Law School, from which he was grad. in 1878. Began
law practice in Oakland, Me., but in 1880 moved to
Waterville, where he continued to practice law. Became involved in banking, lumbering and real estate enterprises in
Waterville and Augusta. Atty. for Kennebec Co., 1883-1887.
Mbr., Me. Senate, 1889-1893. Mbr., Me. House, 1895, where he
successfully sponsored bills for registration and literacy
requirement for voting. Atty. Gen. of Me., 1897-1901. Mbr.
of Me. Exec. Council, 1901-1905. Nom. and el. Gov. as a
Rep. in 1912. Sponsored anti-trust and pub. utilities regulatory legislation, and a bond issue for a state road system. Hon. degree from the Univ. of Maine. Mbr., Masons;
I.O.O.F.; Elks; A.O.U.W.; New England Order of Protection.
m. in 1883 to Edith S. Hemenway, of Rockland, Me. One s.;
one d. D. June 4, 1919, at Augusta.

CURTIS, OAKLEY CHESTER (1915-1917). b. Mar. 29, 1865
at Portland, Me. Father was in shipbuilding bus. Attd.
local pub. schools. Became railway clerk, and later was
employed by coal dealers' assoc. in Portland. Became mgr.
in 1894. Bus. interests expanded into banking field. Became pres. of Mercantile Trust Co. and of Union Safe
Deposit and Trust Co. Also was on bds. of dir. of other
banking enterprises. Mbr., bd. of aldermen in Portland,

1901; Me. House, 1903-1905; Me. Senate, 1905-1909. Mayor
of Portland, 1911-1915. Nom. and el. Gov. as a Dem. in
1914. Advocated economy in govt.; revision of statutes;
and labor law reforms. Direct primary system adopted.
First natl. park east of Mississippi River established in
Me. during admin. Defeated as Dem. cand. for succeeding
term in 1916. Devoted attention to bus. interests there-
after. Delegate to Dem. natl. conv. in 1920. Mbr., Masons;
Elks. Hon. mbr. of Passamaquoddy Indian tribe.
Congregationalist. m. in 1886 to Edith L. Hamilton, of
Portland. Three d.; one s. D. Feb. 22, 1924, at Falmouth,
Me.

MILLIKEN, CARL ELIAS (1917-1921). b. July 13, 1877 at
Pittsfield, Me. s. of Charles Arthur and Ellen (Knowlton)
M. Attd. pub. schools at Augusta, Me.; to which place his
family had moved during his youth; Bates Coll., from which
he was grad. in 1897; and Harvard Univ. in 1899. Taught
chemistry at Bates Coll. in 1898. Joined father in his
lumbering bus., becoming treas. and gen. mgr. of Stockton
Lumber Co. at Island Falls until 1919, and was assoc. with
other lumbering enterprises until retirement in 1958. Pres.
of Katahdin Telephone Co., 1904-1925. Mbr., Me. House,
1905-1908, and of Me. Senate, 1909-1914. Became Pres. of
Me. Senate. Nom. and el. Gov. as a Rep. in 1916, and again
in 1918. Was first Gov. to be nom. by direct primary.
During admin., supported U.S. war effort; established first
budget system for State; reorg. State Health Dept. Mbr.,
New England R.R. Commn., 1921. U.S. collector of customs
for Me., 1924-1927. Became involved in motion picture bus.
in 1920s. Apptd. Sect. of Motion Picture Producers and
Distributors org. in 1926, serving until 1947. His activities in that capacity led to controversies with religious
groups and his resignation from Natl. Council of Churches.
From 1947 to 1958 was managing trustee of Teaching Films
Custodians. U.S. delegate to Intl. Conf. of Educl. Cinema-
tography at Rome in 1934, and at London in 1935. Pres. of
No. Baptist Conv., 1924-1926; also served one term as Pres.
of Amer. Baptist Foreign Missions Soc. Mbr., Intl. Commt.
of YMCA; Amer. Bible Soc.; Playground and Recreation Assoc.
of Amer.; Phi Beta Kappa; Sigma Rho. Congregationalist.
m. in 1901 to Emma Vivian Chase. Six d.; one s. After
first wife's death in 1930, m. in 1931 to her sister,
Caroline. D. May 1, 1961, at Springfield, Mass.

PARKHURST, FREDERICK HALL (1921). b. Nov. 5, 1864 at
Unity, Me. s. of Jonathan Fuller and Susan (Haskell) P.
Grad. from Columbian Law School in Washington, D.C. in 1887.

Admitted to bar and established office at Bangor, but did
not practice law. Joined father's leather goods mfg. bus.,
becoming pres. of firm. Mbr., Bangor city council, 1893-
1894, serving as its pres. in 1894, and ch. of commn. that
built new city hall. Mbr., Me. House, 1895-1896 and 1899-
1902. Mbr. of Gov. Hill's staff, 1901-1904. Mbr., Me.
Senate, 1907-1908, where he was active in promotion of highway system. For ten years was mbr. of Bangor Rep. commt.,
serving four years as ch. Delegate to Rep. natl. conv. in
1900. Ch. of Rep. state commt., 1913-1916, and asst. to ch.
of Rep. natl. commt., 1918. Active in promotion of Liberty
Loan drives during World War I. Nom. and el. Gov. as a Rep.
in 1920, but was in office for only about a month until
death. Mbr. of various bus. orgs. and social clubs. m. in
1887 to Marie Jennings Reid. One s.; one d. After first
marriage ended in divorce, m. in 1911 to Dorothy Woodman.
Two d. D. Jan. 31, 1921, at Augusta.

BAXTER, PERCIVAL PROCTOR (1921-1925). b. Nov. 22,
1876 at Portland, Me. s. of James Phinney and Mehitabel
Cummings (Proctor) B. Descended on father's side from an
English colonist who emigrated to New London, Conn. in 1714.
Father was an industrialist, mayor, and historical writer.
Mother was a descendant of an English colonist who emigrated to Mass. Bay colony in 1628. Her forebears had been
prominent in colonial political affairs. Began educ. in
local common schools and in London, England, where his father was engaged in historical research. Grad. from
Bowdoin Coll. in 1898, and from Harvard Law School in 1901.
Admitted to bar but did not practice. Mbr., Me. House,
1905-1906, 1917-1920, and of Me. Senate, 1909-1910 and 1921.
As Pres. of Senate, succeeded to office of Gov. in Jan.,
1921, following death of Gov. Parkhurst. Completed
Parkhurst's term and was nom. and el. as a Rep. for full
term in 1922. As Gov., was active in promotion of conservation programs; sponsored creation of Katahdin State Park
and establishment of forest preserves; supported women's
suffrage and natl. prohibition; opposed pvt. water power
and railroad interests. Delegate to Rep. natl. convs. in
1920 and 1924. Mbr., Phi Beta Kappa; Delta Kappa Epsilon;
Harvard clubs in New York and Boston; various social clubs.
Congregationalist. Never married. D. June 12, 1969.

BREWSTER, RALPH OWEN (1925-1929). b. Feb. 22, 1888 at
Dexter, Me. s. of Wm. E. and Carrie E. (Bridges) B.
Traced ancestry back to Wm. Brewster, one of the original
leading settlers of Plymouth colony in 1620. Grad. from
Bowdoin Coll. in 1909. Became principal of a h.s. at

Castine, Me. in 1910. Worked way through Harvard Law
School, where he was a mbr. of the ed. bd. of the Law
Review. Received law degree in 1913 and began practice at
Portland, Me. El. to Me. House in 1916, 1918, and 1920,
and to Me. Senate in 1922. An officer in Me. Natl. Guard,
he entered U.S. Army O.T.C. in Oct., 1918, serving for only
a brief time. Had leading role in adoption of new city
charter for Portland in 1923. Mbr., Portland school bd.,
1915-1923. Sect. to Me. Bd. of Accountancy, 1919-1922.
Nom. and el. Gov. as a Rep. in 1924, and again in 1926. As
Gov., advocated use of pub. funds for pub. schools only;
encouragement of tourism and indus. in Me. by creation of a
Me. Indus. Commn.; enforcement of prohibition laws; and
economy in govt. El. to U.S. House in 1934, continuing in
that office until 1941. El. to U.S. Senate in 1940, where
he continued to serve until 1952. Resigned seat in Dec.,
1952, after being defeated for re-nom. for Senate seat by
incumbent Gov. Payne. As a Sen., supported Roosevelt admin.
war policies, but was opposed to reciprocal trade agreement
program. As ch. of Senate War Industries Investigating
Commt., became involved in controversy with Howard Hughes
over alleged favoritism in connection with awarding of airplane constr. contracts, in which he dropped his immunity
as Sen. to testify under oath before his own commt. to answer charges. In re-nom. campaign in 1952 was charged by
his opponent with favoritism and influence peddling in connection with his functioning earlier as ch. of Rep. senatorial campaign commt. Denied the charges, but was defeated for re-nom. Resumed professional legal work and bus.
activities after tenure as Sen. Mbr. of professional legal
orgs.; Amer. Legion. Christian Scientist. m. in 1915 to
Dorothy Foss, of Portland. Two s. D. Dec. 25, 1961, at
Boston, Mass. Bur. in Mount Pleasant Cem., at Dexter, Me.

GARDINER, WILLIAM TUDOR (1929-1933). b. June 12, 1892
at Newton, Mass. s. of Robert Hollowell and Alice (Bangs)
G. Traced ancestry back to an English colonist who emigrated to R.I. in 1640. Father was a lawyer and railroad
co. dir. Attd. Groton school and Harvard Univ., from which
he received an A.B. degree in 1914 and a law degree in 1917.
Admitted to bar in Mass. in 1917, and in Me. in 1919. Enlisted in U.S. Army in 1918, serving as first lieut. and as
battalion adjt. overseas in 1918 and as mbr. of A.E.F. occupation force in Germany. Became reserve officer. Held
rank of major in U.S. Air Force in 1942, later becoming
lieut. col. Joined law firm in Augusta, Me. in 1919. Mbr.
of Me. House, 1921-1926, serving as Speaker in 1925. Nom.
and el. Gov. as a Rep. in 1928 and again in 1930. As Gov.,

sponsored plans for reorg. of state jud. system and admin.
reforms.   After tenure as Gov., was a mbr. of bds. of dir.
of several investment, shipping, mfg., and airlines com-
panies. Mbr., various professional legal orgs.; Amer.
Legion; Masons; Elks; Grange; various social clubs.
Episcopalian. Trustee, Bates Coll.; mbr., Bd. of Overseers,
Harvard Univ. Hon. degrees from Bates Coll., Univ. of Me.,
Bowdoin Coll. m. in 1916 to Margaret Thomas, of Boston,
Mass. Three s.; one d. D. in airplane crash, Aug. 2, 1953.

BRANN, LOUIS JEFFERSON (1933-1937). b. July 8, 1875
at Madison, Me. s. of Charles and Nancy (Lancaster) B.
Grad. from Univ. of Me. in 1898. Studied law and admitted
to bar. Began practice in Lewiston, Me. in 1901 as assoc.
in law firm with which he had studied. Commt. clerk, Me.
House, in 1902. City solicitor of Lewiston, 1906-1907 and
collector of taxes, 1908. Register of probate, Androscoggin
Co., 1906-1913. Mun. ct. judge, Lewiston, 1913-1916.
Served five terms as mayor of Lewiston, during which period
he sponsored establishment of a municipally-owned coal yard
and launched an investigation of rates of local gas company
that resulted in lowering of rates. Nom. and el. Gov. as a
Dem. in 1932, and again in 1934. Advocate of strict economy in govt. and improvements in admin. efficiency. After
tenure as Gov. resumed law practice, in which he achieved
reputation as able defense lawyer in criminal cases. Defeated as Dem. cand. for U.S. Senate in 1936, and was defeated as the Dem. nominee for Gov. again in 1938. Defeated as Dem. cand. for U.S. Senate in 1940 and for a U.S.
House seat in 1942. Mbr., Elks; Grange; Lions; K.P.; Beta
Theta Pi. Interested in athletics. Christian Scientist.
m. in 1903 to Martha Cobb. Three d. D. Feb. 3, 1948, at
Falmouth, Me.

BARROWS, LOUIS ORIN (1937-1941). b. June 7, 1893 at
Newport, Me. s. of George M. and Theo Lee (Jose) B. Attd.
Hebron Acad., 1911-1912 and the Univ. of Me., from which he
was grad. in 1916. Had been a page boy in Me. House in
1907. In 1916 served with a Me. regiment on Mexican border
with U.S. Army. Entered pharmacist bus. at Newport; also
was sect. of two Boston ins. firms. Town treas., 1920-1932.
Mbr., Me. Exec. Council, 1927-1933. Sect. of State for Me.,
1935-1936. Nom. and el. Gov. as a Rep. in 1936, and again
in 1938, defeating former Gov. Brann in the gen. election.
Pres., Me. Pharmaceutical Assoc. Mbr., Masons (K.T.,
Shriner); Rotary; Lions; Kiwanis; Grange; Beta Theta Pi.
Baptist. m. in 1917 to Pauline Marjorie Pomeroy. Three s.
Spent last years in West Newton, Mass. D. Jan. 30, 1967.

SEWALL, SUMNER (1941-1945).   b. June 17, 1897 at Bath,
Me.   s. of Wm. Dunning and Mary (Sumner) S.   Traced ancestry back to an English colonist who emigrated to Mass. in
1658.   Father was a banker and shipbuilder.   Attd. local
pub. schools.   Entered Harvard, but withdrew to join an
Amer. ambulance unit in France.   Enlisted in Amer. Army after U.S. entered World War I, becoming a combat air pilot.
After the war, attd. Yale Univ. for a year.   Worked briefly
in oil fields in Mexico; in banking in Spain; on a sugar
plantation in Cuba; as an auto production employee in
Detroit; and as a ranch hand in Wyoming.   Also continued
interest in aviation.   Joined a banking firm in New York in
1922, working there until 1924.   In 1926 helped to org. and
manage an airlines transport co.   Became dir. of United Air
Lines Co., in 1934.   Mbr. of bd. of aldermen at Bath, 1933;
of Me. House in 1935; and of Me. Senate in 1937, in which
he served as Pres. until 1941.   Nom. and el. Gov. as a Rep.
in 1940, and again in 1942.   During World War II was granted extraordinary powers by legislature to further war effort.   After tenure as Gov., served one year as mil gov. of
Wurtemburg, Bavaria.   Later became pres. of Amer. Overseas
Airlines.   At Rep. natl. conv. in 1944 was one of leaders
in urging party to become more internationalist in outlook.
Decorated with Croix de guerre, and was mbr. of French
Legion of Honor.   Recipient of Order of the Crown from
Belgium; and received D.S.C. from U.S.   Served as chief of
U.S. delegation to UN Assembly.   Mbr., Amer. Legion; Trus-
tee of Bath Memorial Hosp.   m. in 1929 to Helen E. Evans,
of Russia.   Four s.   D. at Bath, Me., Jan. 25, 1965.

HILDRETH, HORACE AUGUSTUS (1945-1949).   b. Dec. 2,
1902 at Gardiner, Me.   s. of Guy A. and Florence (Lawrence)
H.   Father was an atty.   Attd. local pub. schools and
Bowdoin Coll., from which he was grad.   Along with his twin
brother, was an outstanding athlete in several sports.   Was
also on debate team.   Received law degree from Harvard in
1929.   Admitted to bar in Mass. and Me.   Practiced law in
Boston for eight years, after which he moved to Portland,
Me., where he continued law practice.   Also became a dir.
in ins. firms, banks, and other bus. enterprises, including
the Boston Herald and Traveler newspapers.   Became active
in Rep. party politics, serving on local commts.   El. to
Me. House, 1940, and then to Me. Senate, serving as Pres.
of that body during last term.   Nom. and el. Gov. as a Rep.
in 1944, and again in 1946.   During admin., state debt decreased.   Advocated soldiers' bonus; balanced natl. budget;
anti-communism measures; assistance to war refugees by relaxed immigration quotas; universal mil. training.   Ch. of

New England Govs.' Conf., 1947; ch. of exec. commt. of U.S.
Govs.' Conf.; Pres. of Council of State Govts., 1948. Lost
primary election contest to Margaret Chase Smith for U.S.
Senate seat in 1948. Also was defeated as Rep. cand. for
Gov. again in 1958. Amer. Ambassador to Pakistan, 1953-
1957. Hon. degrees from the Univ. of Me.; Bowdoin Coll.
Mbr., professional legal orgs.; Amer. Acad. of Pol. and Soc.
Sci.; Grange; Kiwanis; Masons (Shriner); various social
clubs. Congregationalist. m. in 1929 to Katherine Cobb
Wing. Three d.; one s.

PAYNE, FREDERICK GEORGE (1949-1952). b. July 24, 1904
at Lewiston, Me. s. of Frederick G. and Nellie (Smart) P.
Attd. local pub. schools and Bentley School of Acctg. and
Finance, in Boston. As youth and student, worked as a
newsboy, theater usher and dormitory reporter. Taught
acctg. for a time; also worked as auto and farm machinery
salesman. Aud. and mgr. of New England theater chain,
1925-1935. Indus. consultant, 1936-1940. Mayor of Augusta,
1935-1941. Unsuccessful cand. for Rep. nom. for Gov. in
1940. Commnr. of Finance and Dir. of Budget for Me., 1940-
1942. Served in U.S. Air Force, 1942-1945 as capt. Continued in USAFR with rank of lieut. col. after end of World
War II. Bus. mgr. of a Waldoboro auto co., 1945-1949. Nom.
and el. Gov. as a Rep. in 1948, and again in 1950. As Gov.,
advocated revival of Passamaquoddy tidal power project;
promoted devel. of State's mineral resources. Mbr., U.S.
Civil Defense Advisory Council, 1951. Won Rep. nom. for
U.S. Senate seat in 1952 against incumbent Sen. Brewster,
in a close and bitter contest involving charges of alleged
financial mismanagement by each cand. against the other,
and was el. Resigned as Gov. shortly before end of term
after becoming Senator-elect. Defeated for second term in
1958 by incumbent Gov. Muskie. Resumed activities as bus.
consultant and mgr. of engr. enterprise, residing at
Waldoboro. Trustee of Bentley School of Acctg. and Finance.
Congregationalist. m. in 1944 to Mrs. Ella P. Marshall.
Two s. D. June 15, 1978.

CROSS, BURTON MELVIN (1952-1955). b. Nov. 15, 1902 at
Gardiner, Me. s. of Burton M. and Harriet (Thompson) C.
Was born in house built by great-great-grandfather in 1840.
Father, who was a farmer and a deputy sheriff, died when
son was eight years old. As youth helped brothers run
family farm. Was a track athlete when in high school. Became a professional florist in 1926, giving up ambition to
become lawyer. Mbr., Augusta city council, 1933; pres., bd.
of aldermen for four years. Mbr., Me. House, 1941-1945;

and of Me. Senate, 1945-1952. Majority (Rep.) floor leader
in 1947 and Pres. of Senate in 1949-1952. Ch. of Me. Commn.
on Interstate Cooperation for six years. First vice pres.
of Council of State Govts., 1948. During World War II was
active in civilian defense and Red Cross activities. Opposed strong central govt. Nom. and el. Gov. as a Rep. in
1952. Was an advocate of openness in govtl. affairs. When
Gov. Payne resigned office of Gov. in Dec., 1952, assumed
office of Gov. by succession as Pres. of Senate some two
weeks before term as Gov.-elect would normally have begun.
Defeated as Rep. nominee for second term in 1954. Trustee
of Augusta Savings Bank. Mbr., Augusta CC; Grange; Soc. of
Amer. Florists; Masons (Shriner); Rotary. Episcopalian.
m. in 1927 to Olena R. Moulton, of Augusta. Three d.

MUSKIE, EDMUND SIXTUS (1955-1959). b. Mar. 28, 1914
at Rumford, Me. s. of Stephen and Josephine (Czarnicki)
Marczizewski. Father was a tailor who emigrated from Poland
to U.S. in 1905. Family name changed to Muskie later.
Educ. at local schools; Bates Coll., from which he was grad.
in 1936; and Cornell Univ., from which he received a law
degree in 1939. Admitted to bar in Mass. in 1939 and Me.
in 1940. Began practice in Waterville, Me. in 1940. Entered USNR in 1942 as apprentice seaman. Student at U.S.
Naval Acad.; commissioned an ensign in 1943, and had further training at Pa. State Univ. Saw active service in
both Atl. and Pac. theaters of World War II. Discharged
from service with grade of lieut. in 1945, with three
Battle Stars. Resumed law practice at Waterville. Mbr.,
Me. House, 1947-1951, serving as Dem. floor leader last two
years. Mbr. and sect. of Waterville Zoning Bd., 1948-1955.
Unsuccessful cand. for mayor in 1947. Resigned seat in
legislature in 1951 to become dist. dir. of O.P.S. for Me.,
serving until 1952. Mbr., Dem. natl. commt., 1952-1957.
City solicitor for Waterville, 1954. Nom. and el. Gov. as
a Dem. in 1954, defeating incumbent Gov. Cross. Reel. in
1956. As Gov., sponsored creation of State Dept. of Econ.
Devel.; creation of Indus. Bldg. Authority; programs for
exploration and devel. of mineral resources and community
planning. El. to U.S. Senate in 1958, defeating incumbent
Sen. Payne and becoming the first Dem. to be popularly
elected from Me. to Senate. Resigned as Gov. a few days
before end of term to take seat in Senate. Continued in
Senate thereafter by reel. in 1964, 1970 and 1976. Became
prominent in Senate as advocate of conservation and environmental protection programs; encouragement of fed.-state
cooperation; and admin. reforms. Dem. party cand. for Vice
Pres. of U.S. in 1968. Unsuccessfully sought Dem. nom. for

Pres. of U.S. in 1972.   Apptd. U.S. Sect. of State in May,
1980, by Pres. Carter.   Active in Boy Scout movement; U.S.O.
campaigns; hospital fund drives.   Mbr., AMVETS; Phi Beta
Kappa; Amer. Legion; Grange; Eagles; Elks; Lions; various
legal professional orgs.   Hon. degrees from Lafayette,
Bates, and Bowdoin Colleges; and the Univ. of Me. and
Portland Univ.   Roman Catholic.   m. in 1948 to Jane Frances
Gray, of Waterville,   One s.; three d.

HASKELL, ROBERT NELSON (1959).   b. August 24, 1903 at
Bangor, Me.   s. of Hiram S. and Maude M. (Gulliver) H.
Attd. the Univ. of Me., from which he received degree as
electrical engr. in 1925.   Employed by Bangor Hydro-
Electric Co. in 1925.   Became assoc. with other bus. and
banking enterprises in Bangor.   El. as a Rep. to Me. House,
1945-1946, and to Me. Senate, 1947-1953.   Mbr. and Pres. of
Me. Senate, 1955-1959.   When Gov. Muskie resigned early in
Jan., 1959, to take seat in U.S. Senate, succeeded to of-
fice of Gov. for several days before Gov.-elect Clauson
assumed office.   Mbr. (and dir.) of Me. Publicity Bureau;
Me. CC; Council of New England; Masons; Phi Gamma Delta.

CLAUSON, CLINTON AMOS (1959).   b. Mar. 24, 1898 near
Mitchell, Iowa.   s. of Albert and Belle (Bergerud) C.   Father was a farmer.   Attd. pub. schools in Otranto Station,
Iowa, and Lyle, Minn.   Served with U.S. Army during World
War I.   Grad. in 1919 from Palmer School of Chiropractic,
at Davenport, Iowa.   Moved to Waterville, Me., and engaged
in practice as chiropractor there until 1938.   Active in
local Dem. party affairs, 1928-1935.   City treas., 1930-
1931.   U.S. collector of internal revenue for Me. dist.,
1933-1952.   State adminr. for war bond drives, 1941-1943.
Mayor of Waterville, 1956-1957.   Engaged in oil distribution bus. with son; also became involved in banking and
loan bus. at Augusta.   Active in community chest fund
drives.   Nom. and el. Gov. as a Dem. in 1958, becoming the
first Gov. of Me. to be el. for a four-year term.   Mbr.,
Natl. Assoc. of Collectors of Internal Revenue; Fed.
Businessmen's Assoc.; Newcomen Soc. of No. Amer.; Masons;
I.O.O.F.; Rotary; Amer. Legion; V.F.W.; Sportsmen.
Lutheran.   m. in 1920 to Ellen Kelleher, of Waterville.
One s.; one d.   D. at Augusta, Dec. 20, 1959, after holding
office of Gov. for shortly less than one year.

REED, JOHN HATHAWAY (1959-1967).   b. Jan. 5, 1921 at
Fairfield, Me.   s. of Walter Manley and Eva (Seeley) R.
Grad. from the Univ. of Me. in 1942.   Became dir. of Reed
Farms, Inc., at Fort Fairfield, Me. for a short time.

Joined U.S. Navy in 1942 and served in Pac. theater of
World War II. Held rank of lieut., j.g., when discharged,
and remained in USNR. Mbr. of Me. House, 1955-1957, and of
Me. Senate, 1957-1959, becoming Pres. of Senate. As such,
succeeded to office of Gov. in Dec., 1959, following the
death of Gov. Clauson, being sworn into office on Jan. 1,
1960. Nom. and el. Gov. as a Rep. in 1960 in an election
to fill remaining two years of Clauson's term. El. in 1962
for a full four-year term by a very narrow margin. Defeated as Rep. nominee for succeeding term in 1966. Mbr., Natl.
Transp. Safety Bd., 1967, becoming ch. in 1969. Mbr.,
AMVETS; Amer. Legion; Masons (Shriner); V.F.W.; Elks; K.P.;
Grange; Amer. Farm Bureau; U.S. Trotting Assoc.; Natl.
Aviation Club; Rotary; various social clubs. Congregationalist. m. in 1944 to Cora Davison. Two d.

CURTIS, KENNETH M. (1967-1975). b. Feb. 1, 1931 at
Leeds, Me. s. of Archie M. and Harriet (Turner) C. Grad.
from Me. Maritime Acad. in 1952. Served in U.S. Navy as
ensign, 1953-1955. Held rank of lieut., j.g., when discharged in 1955 after having seen service in Korean theater
in later stages of U.S. involvement there. Continued in
USNR as lieut. commdr. Received law degree from Portland
Univ. in 1957. Asst. on staff of U.S. Repr. James C. Oliver
for a time. Employed by U.S. Legislative Research Service
in Library of Cong., 1961-1963. Mbr., Me. Senate, 1963-
1966. Nom. and el. Gov. as a Dem. in 1966, defeating incumbent Gov. Reed by a narrow margin. Reel. in 1970, again
in a very close election. Delegate to Dem. natl. conv. in
1968. Ch., New England Govs.' Conf., 1969. State co-ch.,
New England Regional Commn. Mbr., exec. bd., Natl. Govs.'
Conf., and ch. of its Environmental Task Force. After pres.
election of 1976 became ch. of Dem. natl. commt., serving
until Dec., 1977, when he resigned post after having been
apptd. U.S. Ambassador to Canada by Pres. Carter. Mbr.,
AMVETS; Amer. Legion; pres., Me. chapter of Natl. Cystic
Fibrosis Found.; dir., Me. March of Dimes, 1966-1969. m.
in 1956 to Pauline Brown. Two d. (one deceased).

LONGLEY, JAMES BERNARD (1975-1979). b. April 22, 1924
at Lewiston, Me. s. of James Bernard and Catherine (Wade)
L. Father was a street car conductor. Served in U.S. Air
Force during World War II. Entered Bowdoin Coll., from
which he was grad. in 1947. Received law degree from the
Univ. of Me. in 1957. Worked in textile mill to help support widowed mother while obtaining educ. Became gen.
agent of New England Life Ins. Co., at Lewiston. Later became pres. of Longley Associates, an ins. and loan firm.

Also engaged successfully in law practice and banking bus.
at Lewiston. Ch., Me. Mgmt. and Cost Survey Commn., 1973.
El. Gov. as an Indep. in 1974, defeating the regular Dem.
and Rep. party nominees for the office by a substantial margin. Had previously been affiliated with Dem. party in
1972 pres. campaign. As Gov., advocated and carried out
admin. reforms and economy in govt. In conformity with
pledge made in 1974 campaign, was not a cand. for second
term in 1978. Guest lecturer on pub. affairs topics at
various institutions of higher learning, including the
Univs. of Wisc., Colo., Ark., Conn., Pa., and Purdue Univ.
Mbr. of bd. of dir. of Child and Family Service; Trustee,
Cent. Me. Gen. Hosp.; athletic dir., Healey House for Boys.
Mbr., Amer. Soc. of CLU and of other professional under-
writers orgs. m. in 1949 to Helen M. Walsh. Two s.; three
d. D. at Lewiston, Aug. 16, 1980.

JOHNSON, THOMAS (1777-1779). b. Nov. 4, 1732 in Calvert Co., Md. s. of Thomas and Dorcas (Sedgwick) J. Descendant of English colonist who emigrated to Md. in 1660.
Attd. school in Frederick Co. and studied law in Annapolis
while working in office of the provincial ct. Delegate to
Provincial Assembly, 1762-1764. Active in support of Amer.
cause as Rev. War approached. Mbr. of Stamp Act Cong. in
1765. Mbr. of Contl. Cong., 1774-1776. Offered- motion
there making Washington the commanding gen. of Contl. Army.
Mbr. of conv. that drafted first Md. const. in 1776. Chosen
as the first Gov. of Md. in 1777 and was reel. unanimously
for two succeeding terms. Apptd. brig. gen. and led Md.
militia forces to relief of Gen. Washington's forces in N.J.
in 1777 as head of 1800-man "Flying Company." Was voted almost dictatorial powers by Md. Assembly to prosecute war.
Encountered difficulties in resisting Loyalist element,
keeping troops supplied, and maintaining a currency system.
Declined seat in Contl. Cong. in 1779. Mbr. of Md. House,
1780, 1786-1787. Instrumental in causing Md. Assembly to
ratify Articles of Confed. plan of natl. govt. Mbr. of
Annapolis Conv. of 1786 that led to calling of U.S. Constl.
Conv. of 1787, and of Md. conv. that ratified U.S. Const.
Was one of the organizers of Potomac Canal Co. in 1785.
Chosen Gov. again in 1788, but declined the office. Chief
Judge of Gen. Ct., 1790-1791. Became U.S. dist. ct. judge
for Md. in 1791 and later that year was apptd. by Pres.
Washington to the U.S. Supreme Ct. Resigned that post for
health reasons in 1793. Declined post of U.S. Sect. of
State in 1795. Mbr. of bd. of commnrs. that developed plans
for the city of Washington, D.C. Apptd. by Pres. Adams in
1801 to a U.S. ct. judgeship in Dist. of Columbia, but the
position was soon afterward abolished by Cong. m. in 1766
to Ann Jennings, of Annapolis. Five children. D. at
daughter's home, "Rose Hill," in Frederick, Md. Oct. 26,
1819. Bur. in All Saints Episcopal Cem. Body re-interred
in Mt. Olivet Cem., Frederick, in 1913.

LEE, THOMAS SIM (1779-1782; 1792-1794). b. Oct. 29,
1745 on family plantation in Prince George Co., Md. s. of
Thomas and Christiana (Sim) L. Related to the Lee family of
Va., being a descendant of Col. Richard Lee, a Norman-English
gentleman who emigrated to Va. in 1641 and whose grandson
established the Md. branch of family around 1700. Received
academic educ. and assisted in mgmt. of family's large plantation. Held various local govt. offices. Supported Amer.
cause as Rev. War approached. Mbr. of Gov.'s Council, 1777-
1779. Chosen Gov. in 1779 and was reel. unanimously for two
succeeding terms. Assisted Amer. forces with supplies and
recruits in the face of difficulties. Aided Gen. Lafayette

in early stages of 1781 campaign that resulted in surrender
of Gen. Cornwallis at Yorktown, Va. Mbr. of Contl. Cong.,
1783-1784. Mbr. of Md. House, 1787. Apptd. as delegate to
U.S. Const. Conv. of 1787, but did not serve. Mbr. Md. conv.
in 1788 that ratified U.S. Const., which he supported. Pres.
elector in 1792. Chosen Gov. again in April, 1792 to complete term of Gov. Plater, and again for two succeeding
terms. Assisted Pres. Washington by supplying and leading
Md. militia in campaign to suppress Whiskey Rebellion in Pa.
in 1794. El. to U.S. Senate seat in 1794, but declined.
Active in formation of Fed. party. Chosen Gov. again in
1798, but declined office, preferring to devote attention to
plantation. Roman Catholic. m. in 1771 to Mary Digges.
Six s.; two d. A great-great-grandson, John Lee Carroll,
was a Gov. of Md. in the 1870s (q.v.). D. Nov. 9, 1819.
Bur. in pvt. cem. at "Melwood" estate in Prince George Co.
Re-interred in 1888 in Mt. Carmel Roman Catholic Cem., near
Upper Marlboro, Md.

PACA, WILLIAM (1782-1785). b. Oct. 31, 1740 at family
home, "Wye Hall," near Abingdon, Md. s. of John and Elizabeth (Smith) P. Believed to be descendant of Robt. Peaker
(Paca?), an English settler who came to Md. in 1651. Attd.
Philadelphia Coll. (now Univ. of Pa.), grad. in 1759.
Studied law in law office in Annapolis, later at Middle
Temple, in London. Began practice of law at Annapolis in
1763. Mbr. of Provincial Assembly, 1767-1774, wherein he
took leading role in resistance movement against British
colonial policies. Mbr., First Contl. Cong., 1774 and Second
Contl. Cong., 1775-1779. Signed Dec. of Indep. Mbr., Md.
Senate, 1777-1779. Chief Judge of Gen. Ct., 1779-1780, and
later, of Md. Ct. of Appeals in Admiralty. Mbr. of conv.
that drafted first Md. const. in 1776. Chosen Gov. by Gen.
Assembly in 1782 and continued in office by it in 1783 and
1784. As Gov., was active supporter of measures for relief
of Rev. War veterans. Invited Cong. to meet in Annapolis in
Dec., 1783 where Washington resigned his commn. as Gen. of
Contl. Army. Influential in establishment of Washington
Coll., at Chesterton, Md. in 1786. Mbr. of Gov.'s Council,
1786 and of Md. conv. to ratify U.S. Const. in 1788, which
he supported with reservations. Apptd. U.S. dist. ct. judge
for Md. by Pres. Washington in 1789, serving in that office
until death. m. first to Mary Ellen Chew in 1763, who died
in 1774. Later m. to Levina -----, of Philadelphia, who
died shortly after marriage; and in 1777 to Anne Harrison,
who died in 1780. Several children by first marriage.
Episcopalian. D. at family estate, "Wye Hall," in Queen
Anne Co., Oct. 23, 1799. Bur. in family cem. there.

SMALLWOOD, WILLIAM (1785-1788). b. Feb. 12, 1732 in
Charles Co. (Kent Co.?), Md. s. of Bayne and Priscilla
(Heberd) S. Grandfather had emigrated from England to Md.
in 1664. Father a planter and judge, and had served in Provincial Assembly. Mother a mbr. of a distinguished and
wealthy Va. family. Sent to England for educ., where he
studied under tutors and later at Eton. Upon return to Md.
participated with Md. militia unit in French and Indian War.
Mbr. of Md. Assembly, 1761-1774, where he became a leader in
resistance to British colonia policies. After outbreak of
Rev. War, raised a battalion of troops for Contl. Army, becoming a brig. gen. Saw much active service in 1776 and
1777 campaigns in N.Y., N.J. and Pa. under Gen. Washington.
Concerned primarily with supplying and training of troops.
Objected to serving with foreign officers, in particular
with Gen. von Steuben. Transferred to So. theater of the
war, participating in a number of engagements in the Carolinas in 1779-1780. Held rank of major gen. at end of the
Rev. War. El. to Contl. Cong. in 1783 (1784?) but did not
take seat. Chosen Gov. in 1785 and was reel. unanimously in
1786 and 1787. Interested in promotion of navigation on the
Potomac. As Gov., had role in assembling the Annapolis Conv.
of 1786 that led to calling of U.S. Constl. Conv. of 1787.
El. to Md. Senate in 1791 and became its Pres. Episcopalian.
Never married. D. Feb. 14, 1792 in Prince George Co. shortly after becoming Pres. of Senate. Bur. at "Smallwood's
Retreat," Charles Co. In 1898 S.A.R. erected a shaft over
his previously unmarked grave.

HOWARD, JOHN EAGER (1788-1791). b. June 4, 1752 near
Baltimore, Md. s. of Cornelius and Ruth (Eager) H. Descendant of an English colonist who emigrated to Md. in 1667.
Educ. by pvt. tutors. During Rev. War was commissioned as
capt. in a Md. company and participated in numerous engagements in N.Y. and Pa. and the So. theater of war. Seriously
wounded at the Battle of Eutaw Springs in 1781. Was voted
medal for distinguished service by Cong., holding rank of
col. when he left service. Served as judge of Baltimore Co.
ct. for three years. Mbr. of Contl. Cong., 1784-1788.
Chosen Gov. in 1788 and retained in office for two succeeding terms. As Gov., advocated gift of land by Md. to U.S.
for site of natl. capital as well as a loan to U.S. to assist in constr. of Capitol bldg. Mbr. of Md. Senate, 1791-
1795. Chosen to U.S. Senate seat in 1796 to fill vacancy
and was continued in office for regular term in 1797. Offered post of Sect. of War by Pres. Washington in 1795, but
declined. Was also offered commn. as brig. gen. in U.S.
army by Pres. Adams in 1798 when war with France was threatened. Active in Fed. party affairs. Retired to plantation

"Belvedere," after tenure in Senate. Apptd. as a commnr. of
the state penitentiary in 1804. Received some Assembly
votes for Gov. in each regular election from 1806 to 1811,
but was not a serious contender except in 1811. Apptd. to
Commt. of Supply after War of 1812 began and helped raise
troops for campaign of 1814. Nom. on Fed. party ticket for
Vice Pres. of U.S. in 1816 pres. election. Made extensive
gifts of land to Baltimore for pub. purposes. m. in 1787 to
Margaret Chew, of Philadelphia. Five s., two d. A son,
George, was later a Gov. of Md. (q.v.); and a son, Benjamin
Chew H., was a mbr. of U.S. House and was the unsuccessful
"Peace" Dem. cand. for Gov. of Md. in 1861. Episcopalian.
D. at his home, "Belvedere," near Baltimore Oct. 12, 1827.
Bur. in Old St. Paul's Cem., Baltimore. Pres. John Q. Adams
was one of the many prominent persons who attended his
funeral.

PLATER, GEORGE (1791-1792). b. Nov. 8, 1735 at the
family estate, "Sotterly," near Leonardtown, Md. Was third
person in family line to bear same name. Mother, Rebecca
(Addison) Bowles, was a widow of considerable means. Father,
George P., who was of English descent, had been a col. in
Md. militia and had served in pub. office. Educ. by pvt.
tutors and attd. William and Mary Coll., from which he was
grad. in 1752. Studied law, admitted to bar and began practice at Annapolis. Mbr. of Md. Assembly, 1767-1771 and of
Gov.'s Council, 1771-1774. Provincial ct. judge, 1771-1773.
Also served as naval officer at Patuxent, 1767-1777. Active
in resistance movement against British colonial policies.
Mbr. of conv. at Annapolis that removed Provincial Gov. Eden
in 1776 and drafted first const. for Md. Became mbr. of Md.
Commt. of Safety. Mbr. of Md. Senate, 1776, 1781 and 1786.
Mbr. of Contl. Cong., 1778-1781. Pres. of Md. conv. in 1788
that ratified U.S. Const. Pres. elector in first pres.
election under U.S. Const. Chosen Gov. in 1791. As Gov.,
assisted in supplying troops for Gen. St. Clair's expedition
against Indians in Ohio country. Episcopalian. m. in 1762
to Hannah Lee, who died the next year. m. in 1764 to Elizabeth Rousby. Three s.; three d. A son, Thomas, was a mbr.
of U.S. House, 1801-1805. D. at Annapolis Feb. 10, 1792
after serving some three months as Gov. Bur. in family cem.
at "Sotterly," near Leonardtown, Md.

BRICE, JAMES (1792). b. Aug. 26, 1746 at Annapolis,
Md. Became a mbr. of Gov.'s Council under the first Md.
const. As the senior mbr. of that body, became acting Gov.
following death of Gov. Plater in Feb., 1792. Acted as Gov.
for approximately two months pending the choosing of a successor to complete Plater's term by the Gen. Assembly, which

he had called into spec. session for that purpose in April,
1792. D. July 11, 1801 at Annapolis.

LEE, THOMAS SIM (1792-1794). See above, 1779-1782.

STONE, JOHN HOSKINS (1794-1797). b. in 1745 in Charles
Co., Md. s. of David and Elizabeth (Jenifer) S. Descendant
of Provincial Gov. Wm. Stone, who served from 1649 to 1654.
A brother, Thomas, as a mbr. of Contl. Cong., was a signer
of the Dec. of Indep. Received a fair educ. in pvt. schools
and studied law. Participated in protests against British
policies, serving as mbr. of local Commt. of Correspondence
in 1774 and as mbr. of Assoc. of Freemen of Md. in 1775.
Became a capt. in Col. Smallwood's contingent of Md. troops
that participated in engagements in N.Y., N.J. and Pa. in
1776-1777, rising to rank of col. Severely wounded in Oct.,
1777 and resigned commn. in 1779. Mbr. of Gov.'s Council,
1779-1785. Employed in 1781 on staff of R.S. Livingston in
U.S. Dept. of Foreign Affairs. Mbr. of Md. House in 1786,
and had active role in movement to revise Articles of Confed.
plan of govt. for U.S. Chosen Gov. in 1793 and continued in
office in 1794 and 1795. Began practice of sending written
messages by Gov. to the Assembly. Supported extension of
loan to U.S. for constr. of govt. bldgs. in Washington, D.C.
in response to urgent pleas from Pres. Washington. A Fed.
in politics, he was a supporter of Pres. Washington's domestic and foreign policies. Episcopalian. m. in 1781 to
Mary Couden, a lady of Scottish descent, who died in 1792.
Four children. D. at Annapolis Oct. 5, 1804. Place of bur.
unknown; thought to be Annapolis.

HENRY, JOHN (1797-1798). b. in Nov., 1750 at "Weston,"
the family estate near Vienna, Dorchester Co., Md. s. of
Col. John and Dorothy (Rider) H. Grandfather, a Presbyterian minister, had emigrated to Md. from England in 1700.
Wealth of wife enabled him to acquire extensive lands.
Father had served in Provincial Assembly. Attd. West Nottingham Acad., in Cecil Co., Md., and the Coll. of N.J. (now
Princeton). Studied law in London for several years at
Middle Temple. As mbr. of debate club there attained distinction as defender of colonial cause against British colonial policies. Returned to Md. in 1775 and established law
practice in Dorchester Co. Mbr. of Md. House, 1777. Served
two terms in Md. Senate. Delegate to Contl. Cong., 1778-
1781 and 1784-1787. Mbr. of commt. that drafted Ordinance
of 1787. Became one of the first two U.S. Senators from Md.
in U.S. Cong., being el. for two-year term in 1788 and for
a six-year term in 1790. As mbr. of Senate opposed Jay
Treaty with Spain. Was a Fed. in political views generally.

Received the votes of two Md. electors for Pres. of U.S. in
1796 pres. election. Reel. to Senate seat, but resigned in
Dec., 1797 to assume office of Gov., to which he had been
chosen. As Gov., took active role in reorg. of Md. militia
in view of threat of war with France. Declined to be a cand.
for another term in 1798 because of poor health. Episcopalian. m. in 1787 to Margaret Campbell, who died in 1789.
Two s. A great-grandson, Henry Lloyd, became a Gov. of Md.
(q.v.). D. Dec. 16, 1798 at family estate, "Weston." Bur.
in Christ Protestant Episcopal Cem., Cambridge, Md.

   OGLE, BENJAMIN (1798-1801). b. Feb. 7, 1746 at Annapolis, Md. s. of Samuel and Ann (Tasker) O. Father was the
Provincial Gov. of Md. from 1738 to 1752. Mother was the
daughter of Provincial Gov. Tasker, who had succeeded her
father-in-law in office. Father died when son was three
years old. Son inherited family estate, "Belair", from
Grandfather Tasker. Educ. in England. Mbr. of Gov.'s
Council, 1773-1774. Gave support to Amer. cause when Rev.
War began. Served as third lieut. in Md. company of troops,
and became a close personal friend of Gen. Washington. Mbr.
of Gov.'s Council, 1781-1782. Resigned in 1783 because of
personal differences with colleagues on the Council. Was a
Fed. in political views. Chosen Gov. by the Gen. Assembly
in 1798 after former Gov. Lee had refused election to the
office. Admin. attd. by much excitement and controversy because of threat of war with France, the close pres. election
of 1800 which had to be resolved by U.S. House, and the
death of Gen. Washington in 1799. Retired from pub. life in
1806. Episcopalian. m. first to Rebecca Stilley. One d.
After her death, m. to Henrietta Margaret Hill, of West
River. One s.; two d. D. at family estate, "Belair," July
6, 1809. Bur. in family cem. there.

   MERCER, JOHN FRANCIS (1801-1803). b. May 17, 1759 at
family estate, "Marlboro," in Stafford Co., Md. s. of John
and Ann (Roy) M. Grandfather had emigrated to Va. in 1720,
where he became a noted legal authority. Educ. by pvt.
tutors and at William and Mary Coll., from which he was grad.
in 1775. Supported Amer. cause when Rev. War began, becoming an officer in a Md. unit and rising to rank of major.
Participated in a number of engagements in N.Y., N.J. and
Pa. and was wounded at the Battle of Brandywine. Was a
staff aide to Gen. Charles Lee at Battle of Monmouth. Resigned commn. in protest after Lee was court-martialed following that battle. Rejoined Amer. forces in 1780, raising
a Va. cavalry unit of which he became lieut. col. Served
with Gen. Lafayette until end of war. Also studied law at
Williamsburg, Va. with Thomas Jefferson, with whom he formed

a close personal friendship. Practiced law at Williamsburg
for several years. Mbr. of Contl. Cong. from Va., 1782-
1785. In 1785 moved to estate, "Cedar Park," in Anne Arundel
Co., Md., which his wife had inherited. Delegate from Md.
to U.S. Constl. Conv. of 1787. Refused to sign completed
document, which he opposed because he felt it gave too much
power to cent. govt. Also was opposed to idea of a popu-
larly-elected House. Helped lead an unsuccessful effort in
Md. conv. against ratification of U.S. Const. in 1788. Mbr.
of Md. House, 1788, 1789 and 1791, 1792. El. to U.S. House
in 1792 to fill a vacancy, and was then el. to a regular
term. Resigned seat in 1794. Mbr. again of Md. House,
1800-1801. Chosen Gov. in 1801 as Jeff. Rep., the contest
marking the beginning of intense political rivalry between
the Jeff. Rep. and Fed. parties in choosing the Gov. Reel.
in 1802. As Gov., successfully advocated repeal of property
qualification for voting. Mbr. of Md. House again from 1803
to 1806, when he retired temporarily from pub. life. Became
estranged from Jeff. Rep. party over foreign policies and
involvement of U.S. in War of 1812, which he strongly opposed. Switched party affiliation to Fed. party. m. in
1785 to Sophia Sprigg, of Anne Arundel Co., Md. Two s.;
one d. Episcopalian. D. at Philadelphia Aug. 30, 1821.
Bur. in St. Peter's church there. Later re-interred at
family cem. at "Cedar Park," in Anne Arundel Co., Md.

BOWIE, ROBERT (1803-1806; 1811-1812). b. in March,
1750 (1749?) at "Mattaponi," the family estate near Nottingham, Prince George Co., Md. s. of Capt. William and Margaret (Sprigg) B. Family was of Scottish descent. Attd.
pvt. school. Supported Amer. cause as Rev. War began, becoming a lieut. of a Md. company and rising to rank of capt.
Served until end of the war, seeing action in N.Y. and So.
theaters of war. Was severely wounded on one occasion.
Mbr., Md. House, 1785-1786, 1788-1790 and 1801-1803. Major
of militia in 1793, and county justice of the peace, 1790-
1803. Chosen Gov. in 1803 and continued in office in 1804
and 1805 as Jeff. Rep. During admin., natl. road to West
opened; legislation passed prohibiting entry of free Negroes
into the State. Impeachment of U.S. Supreme Ct. Justice
Samuel Chase caused much agitation and controversy between
the political factions in State. Baltimore merchants who
opposed the Embargo Act, which he supported, also aroused
antagonism. Pres. elector on Madison ticket in 1808. Supported natl. govt. in taking strong action against British
interference with Amer. ships on high seas. Became dir. of
first State Bank in Md. in 1810. Chosen Gov. again in 1811,
defeating former Gov. John E. Howard, who opposed policies
leading to war with Great Britain. Suspended a Baltimore

newspaper from publication because of its strong attacks on
Pres. Madison's policies, resulting in riots in the city and
use of mil. force. Gov. was accused of using unduly harsh
measures against rioters. When publication of the paper resumed, a mob destroyed the newspaper bldg. and riots again
ensued in which several people were killed. As Gov., cooperated with Pres. Madison's call for troops when war began
in 1812. In hotly contested gubernatorial election that year
his Fed. opponent, who opposed the war, was el. B. sought
the office of Gov. again unsuccessfully as the Jeff. Rep.
cand. in 1813, 1815 and 1816. Resided on estate thereafter,
engaging in raising blooded stock and fine horses. Was a
man of many enthusiasms. m. at age 19 by elopement with
Patricia Mackall, a girl of 15. Seven children. Episcopalian. D. at "Mattaponi," Nottingham, Jan. 8, 1818. Bur.
in family cem. there.

WRIGHT, ROBERT (1806-1809). b. Nov. 20, 1752 at "Nar-
borough," the family home in Queen Anne Co., Md. s. of
Judge Solomon and Mary (Tidmarsh) W. Descended from an
English colonist who came to Md. in 1666. Father was active
in movements leading to Rev. War. Educ. in pub. schools and
at Washington Coll., in Chesterton, Md. Studied law, admitted to bar in 1773, and practiced at Chesterton and
Queenstown, Md. Joined militia company in 1776 and rose to
rank of capt. Mbr., Md. House, 1776 and 1784 and of Md.
Senate, 1787. El. to U.S. Senate in 1801, serving until 1806
when he resigned to take office as Gov., to which he had been
chosen as Jeff. Rep. Continued in that office in 1807 and
1808. Gave support to Pres. Jefferson's policies, including
enforcement of Embargo Act, which was unpopular. Resigned
during course of third term, expecting to receive apptmt. to
Md. Ct. of Appeals by action of the legislature, in which
hope he was disappointed. Clerk of Queen Anne Co., 1810.
El. to U.S. House by spec. election in 1810 to fill vacancy
and continued in that office until 1817. Was not reel. in
1816; but was again el. to that office in 1820. Did not seek
that office again in 1822. Md. dist. ct. judge, 1823 until
death. Episcopalian. m. first to Sarah deCoursey, who died
shortly after marriage. m. later to a Miss Ringgold, of Kent
Co., Md. Several children. Acquired an estate, "Blakeford,"
near Queenstown, where he became widely known as breeder of
fine horses. A d., Clintonia, became the wife of Philip
Francis Thomas, Gov. of Md. (q.v.). D. at family estate
Sept. 7, 1836. Bur. in deCoursey family cem. in Queen Anne
Co.

BUTCHER, JAMES (1809). Was serving as senior mbr. of
Gov.'s Council when Gov. Wright resigned in May, 1809. As

such, became acting Gov. and immediately called the Gen. Assembly into spec. session to choose a successor to complete
Wright's term. It chose Edward Lloyd for that purpose after
B. had acted as Gov. for approximately a month. The Md.
const. was later amended to permit an acting Gov. under such
circumstances to continue in that capacity until the next
regular session of the Assembly. Was a Jeff. Rep. in politics. D. Jan. 12, 1824.

LLOYD, EDWARD (1809-1811). b. July 22, 1779 at "Wye
House," the family estate in Talbot Co., Md. s. of Edward
and Elizabeth (Tayloe) L. Was the fifth mbr. of family to
bear same name, one of his ancestors having been a Provincial Gov. of Md. Father was a wealthy planter who had a
very prominent role in Md. political life during and after
the Rev. War era. Educ. by pvt. tutors. Mbr. of Md. House,
1800-1805, taking seat when only 21 years of age. El. to
U.S. House seat to fill a vacancy in 1806, continuing to
serve in that post until 1809. Chosen Gov. as Jeff. Rep. in
1809 to complete term of Gov. Wright, who had resigned. Continued in office in 1809 and 1810 for regular terms. During
admin., the unpopular Embargo Act was repealed by Cong. and
replaced by the Non-Intercourse Act. Voting and office-
holding requirements were liberalized. Mbr. of Md. Senate,
1811-1815, where he supported Pres. Madison's policies, including involvement in the War of 1812. Lieut. col. of Md.
militia regiment during the war. Pres. elector on Madison
ticket in 1812 pres. election. El. to U.S. Senate in 1819,
serving until Jan. 14, 1826 when he resigned. Mbr. and Pres.
of Md. Senate, 1826-1831. Episcopalian. m. to Sallie Scott
Murray, of Annapolis. Three s.; four d. A direct descendant, Henry Lloyd, became a Gov. of Md. (q.v.). D. June 2,
1834 at Annapolis. Bur. in family plot at "Wye House,"
Talbot Co.

BOWIE, ROBERT (1811-1812). See above, 1803-1806.

WINDER, LEVIN (1812-1816). b. Sept. 4, 1757 at family
estate in Somerset Co., Md. s. of Wm. and Esther (Gillis)
W. Paternal ancestor emigrated to Md. in 1665. Family was
prominent in the community. Began study of law, but abandoned studies to enter Contl. Army in 1776 in a Md. regiment.
Rose to rank of lieut. col., serving until end of Rev. War.
Became planter near Princess Anne, Md. As brig. gen. of Md.
militia in 1794 participated in suppression of Whiskey Rebellion in Pa. Mbr. of Md. House, 1806-1808, serving as
Speaker in last year. El. Gov. in 1812 as a Fed., defeating
incumbent Gov. Robt. Bowie in exciting contest in the Gen.
Assembly. Reel. in 1813 and 1814, again in bitter contests

with former Gov. Bowie. Public aroused at beginning of
tenure by controversy involving suppression by Bowie admin.
of a newspaper in Baltimore that eventually resulted in a
riot requiring use of mil. force to control and finally in
the destruction of the newspaper's bldg. When War of 1812
began, cooperated with request of U.S. govt. to raise troops;
but failure of U.S. govt. to respond to his request for mil.
aid when Md. was attacked by British forces in later stages
of the war led to bitter feelings against the U.S. Govt. Was
Gov. when Ft. McHenry was bombarded by British fleet, which
became the occasion for composition of "The Star-Spangled
Banner." Eventually claims were presented by Md. delegation
in Cong. for alleged failure of U.S. to protect lives and
property of Md. citizens, many of whom left the State to move
West. Returned to seat in Md. Senate in 1816. Participated
in laying of cornerstone for Washington monument in Baltimore. Senior major gen. of Md. militia. Prominent in Masonic order. m. to Mary Sloss. Two s.; one d. D. at Baltimore July 1, 1819. Bur. there; but later re-interred in
family cem. in Somerset Co.

RIDGELY, CHARLES CARNAN (1816-1818). b. Dec. 6, 1762
in Baltimore Co., Md. s. of John and Achsah (Ridgely)
Carnan. Father died the year son was born, and the son was
raised by his uncle, Charles Ridgely, who had no children
and who eventually adopted him and made him his legal heir.
Changed name to Charles Carnan Ridgely in 1790 when his
uncle died, leaving his large estate, "Hampton," consisting
of some 10,000 acres, to his adopted son. Mbr. of Md. House,
1790-1795 and served in Md. Senate later for five years.
Brig. gen. of Md. militia in 1794. Managed extensive estate,
which included iron works, 1801-1815. Chosen Gov. as Fed.
in 1815 over former Gov. Robt. Bowie in close contest in
Gen. Assembly, winning by vote of 47 to 45. Again defeated
Bowie in 1816 and was reel. in 1817. During admin., sites
of Fts. Washington and McHenry ceded to U.S. Govt. As Gov.,
continued to press claims against U.S. for Md. losses and
expenses growing out of War of 1812, and received partial
restitution from it; sponsored establishment of pub. school
system. Devoted attention to plantation and bus. interests
after tenure as Gov. At time of his death owned 10,000
acres and 300 slaves. Emancipated all his slaves under the
age of 45 by terms of his will. Episcopalian. m. to Priscilla Dorsey. Three s.; eight d. One of his d., Prudence,
became the wife of George Howard, a Gov. of Md. (q.v.). D.
at "Hampton," Baltimore Co., July 17, 1829. Bur. in family
cem. there.

GOLDSBOROUGH, CHARLES (1818-1819). b. July 15, 1765 at Hunting Creek, Dorchester Co., Md. s. of Charles and Anna Maria (Tilghman) G. Traced ancestry to an English colonist who emigrated to Kent Island, Md. in 1670. Tutored in acad. studies at home. Attd. the Univ. of Pa., from which he received an M.A. degree in 1787. Studied law and admitted to bar in 1790. Held various local offices. Mbr. of Md. Senate, 1791-1795 and 1799-1801. El. to U.S. House in 1804 and continued in that office until 1817. As mbr. of Cong., strongly opposed measures of Madison admin. that resulted in War of 1812. Voted against the declaration of war, and was critical of conduct of the war. Was partially successful in pressing claims for reimbursement of Md. by U.S. govt. in connection with mil. operations during the conflict. El. Gov. as Fed. in 1818 in a close contest. During admin., unsuccessfully opposed measures for re-apportionment of legislative seats occasioned by growth in population of Baltimore. Also opposed bill removing political disabilities from persons of Jewish faith. Defeated for reel. by narrow margin in 1819 by Samuel Sprigg, and lost to Sprigg again in 1820. Retired to estate near Cambridge, Md. Participated in establishment of first I.O.O.F. lodge in U.S. at Baltimore in 1819. Episcopalian. m. in 1793 to Elizabeth Trippe Goldsborough. Two d. After her death, m. to Sarah Yerbury Goldsborough, a cousin. Nine s.; five d. D. Dec. 13, 1834 at estate, "Shoal Creek," near Cambridge, Md. Bur. in Christ Episcopal Church Cem. there.

SPRIGG, SAMUEL (1819-1822). b. in 1783(?) in Prince George Co., Md. s. of Joseph and Margaret (Weems) S. Father died in 1800 and son was adopted by an uncle, Osborn Sprigg, who had an estate, "Northampton," in Prince George Co. Following the uncle's death in 1815, son inherited the estate, which was a substantial property. Mbr. of Md. House, 1819. El. Gov. that year as a Jeff. Rep. by the Gen. Assembly, defeating incumbent Gov. Goldsborough. Defeated Goldsborough again in 1820 and was reel. in 1821. During admin., question of reapportionment of seats in Gen. Assembly continued to be a matter of controversy, with House favoring and the Senate, controlled by Fed. party, opposed to change. Proposal to change system of choosing Gov. to direct popular election also became a matter of debate. Potomac Canal Co. investigated, and a proposal was advanced for creation of Chesapeake and Ohio Canal Co. to replace it. S. later became pres. of the new company after it was established. m. in 1811 to Violette Lansdale. Two children. Episcopalian. D. at his home, "Northampton," in Prince George Co., April 21, 1855, leaving an extensive estate which included 61

slaves. Bur. at family cem. there, but later re-interred in
Oak Hill Cem., Georgetown, D.C.

STEVENS, SAMUEL, Jr. (1822-1826). b. July 13, 1778 in
Talbot Co., Md. s. of Samuel and Elizabeth (Connoly) S.
Family, which was originally of Quaker faith, had resided in
Md. for several generations. Father died when son was still
a youth. Resided with two aunts for a time. Received no
formal educ., but studied at school operated by a minister,
the Rev. John Bowie. Worked for bus. firms in Philadelphia
for a time, but returned to Md. about 1800 to take charge of
estate, "Compton," which he had inherited from father. Mbr.
of Md. House a number of times between 1807 and 1820. Chosen
Gov. as Jeff. Rep. in 1822, and continued in office in 1823
and 1824. During admin., legislation was enacted establishing Chesapeake and Ohio Canal Co.; Cumberland Road was completed; Gen. Lafayette was entertained on his tour of U.S.
Legislation was passed extending full citizenship rights to
Jewish people, and religious qualifications for office-holding abolished. After tenure, retired to estate. Episcopalian. Active as mbr. and pres. of Agri. Soc. for Eastern
Shore. m. in 1804 to Eliza May, of Chester, Pa. One s.
D. at "Compton," near Trappe, Md. Feb. 7, 1860. Believed
to have been bur. there in family cem.

KENT, JOSEPH (1826-1829). b. Jan. 14, 1779 in Calvert
Co., Md. s. of Daniel and Anne (Wheeler) K. Received educ.
locally and studied med., becoming a licensed physician in
1799 at age 20. Practiced med. at Lower Marlborough, Md.
for several years. Moved in 1807 to Bladensburg, Md. to an
estate in Prince George Co., "Rose Mount," where he practiced med. and also farmed. El. to U.S. House as a Fed. in
1810 and again in 1812. Opposed measures leading to war
with Great Britain in 1812, but eventually voted for declaration of war. Served in Md. militia as surgeon's mate,
surgeon-major, lieut. col., and then col. of cavalry regiment during War of 1812. Shifted party allegiance to Jeff.
Rep. party, and served as pres. elector on Monroe ticket in
1816. El. as Jeff. Rep. to U.S. House in 1816, continuing
to serve therein until 1826 when he resigned after having
been el. Gov. in 1825. During admin., the Baltimore and
Ohio R.R. was chartered. Favored prison reforms; greater
support for pub. schools. Presided over meeting for org. of
Chesapeake and Ohio Canal Co., becoming a mbr. of its bd. of
dir. Mbr. and vice pres. of first Natl. Rep. (Whig) conv.
in 1831. El. to U.S. Senate as Natl. Rep. in 1833. Ill
health prevented regular attendance during term. m. to
Eleanor Lee Wallace. Ten children. After her death in 1826,
m. to Alice Lee Contee. A d., Adelaide, became the wife of

Gov. Thomas Pratt, of Md. (q.v.). Episcopalian. D. at his
home, "Rose Mount," near Bladensburg, Nov. 24, 1837 from injuries received in a riding accident while still a mbr. of
U.S. Senate. Left substantial estate, including 65 slaves.
Bur. in family cem. at "Rose Mount."

MARTIN, DANIEL (1829-1831; 1831). b. in 1780 at "The
Wilderness," the family estate near Trappe, Md. s. of
Nicholas and Hannah (Oldham) M. Ancestors were active participants in pub. affairs. Father was a prominent merchant.
Well-educ. in youth. Entered St. John's Coll. at Annapolis
at age 11 but did not receive degree. Inherited family estate in 1807. El. to Md. House in 1819, serving until 1821.
Retired temporarily from politics. Supported U.S. internal
improvements policies of Pres. J.Q. Adams admin. El. Gov.
in 1828 as Adams (Anti-Jackson) Rep. Defeated for reel. in
1829 by Jackson (Dem.) party cand. in close vote in Gen.
Assembly; but was el. again in 1830. During admin., constr.
of Chesapeake and Ohio Canal begun; Washington Turnpike Co.
road started. Supported pub. educ.; reduction in state offices; use of prison labor on pub. projects. When reel. in
1830 some mbrs. of Md. Senate questioned his right to take
office on the ground the Md. const. prohibited a former Gov.
from returning to office before expiration of four years,
but the issue was resolved in his favor. Became ill not
long after second term began in 1831 and returned to home.
It is related that for three nights before his death he had
a dream each night in which he saw his mother on a fog-
shrouded ship beckoning to him and telling him that at noon
on the third day after she first appeared he would come to
her. He told his family at breakfast of his dream after the
third night. They joked with him about it; but he made out
his will that morning before he mounted his horse about
11:30 to go to his fields to supervise harvest work. At
noon he fell from his horse, dead. m. to Mary Clare Mac-
cubbin, of Annapolis, Md. Five children. Mbr., Agri. Soc.
of Eastern Shore. Episcopalian. D. July 11, 1831. By
terms of his will he emancipated all his slaves over the age
of 28. Bur. at Spring Hill Cem., Easton, Md.

CARROLL, THOMAS KING (1830-1831). b. April 29, 1793 at
"Kingston Hall," the family estate in Somerset Co., Md. s.
of Col. Henry James and Elizabeth Barnes (King) C. Attd.
Charlotte Hall school; Washington Acad.; and Princeton, from
which he was grad. with highest honors in 1811. Studied law.
Was opposed to institution of slavery, and became pres. of
soc. founded to promote colonization of free Negroes in
Africa. Took over mgmt. of family estate after father's
death and became active in politics. Held various local

offices. Mbr. of Md. Gen. Assembly for several terms from
1816 onward, where he acquired reputation as forceful speaker. El. Gov. as Jackson (Dem.) party cand. in 1830, defeating incumbent Gov. Daniel Martin in close contest. Advocated free pub. school system, state institutional reforms,
and aid for Rev. War veterans. Defeated for second term in
1831 by former Gov. Martin. Retired to estate, "Kingston
Hall." In 1840 moved to an estate, "Walnut Landing," near
Church Creek, Md. Apptd. naval officer at port of Baltimore
by Pres. Taylor in 1849. Brought up in mother's Presbyterian
faith, although father was a Roman Catholic. Mbr., Masons.
m. at age 20 to Juliana Stevenson, daughter of a prominent
physician. Nine children. D. at "Walnut Landing," in Dorchester Co., Oct. 3, 1873. Bur. in Old Trinity Church Cem.,
at Church Creek.

MARTIN, DANIEL (1831). See above, 1829-1830.

HOWARD, GEORGE (1831-1833). b. Nov. 21, 1789 at Annapolis, Md. s. of John Eager and Margaret (Chew) H. Father
was a Gov. of Md. (q.v.). Mother was a d. of Judge Benj.
Chew, of Philadelphia, who was a British Loyalist in Rev.
War. Grew up on family estate, "Belvedere," near Baltimore.
Educ. by pvt. tutors. Took active role in politics at an
early age. As Pres. of Gov.'s Council succeeded to office
of Gov. following death of Gov. Martin in July, 1831, and
was then el. as an Anti-Jackson (Whig) cand. for regular
term in 1832. Was not a cand. in 1833. During tenure,
three party factions became competitors for elective office
in Md.: the Anti-Jackson (Adams-Clay Rep.) party, which assumed the name of Whigs; the Jackson Rep. party, which
adopted the name of Democrats; and the Anti-Mason party.
As Gov., opposed tariff nullification movement and lotteries;
favored re-chartering of U.S. Bank; advocated program of
internal improvements and high tariff; and promotion of
higher educ. Was a slave owner, and favored colonization of
emancipated slaves in Africa. Pres. elector on Whig ticket
in 1836 and 1840. Episcopalian. m. in 1811 to Prudence
Gough Ridgely, d. of former Gov. Charles Ridgely (q.v.).
Eight s.; five d. Resided in later years on estate,
"Waverly," near Woodstock, in Howard Co., which had been
given to him by father as a wedding present. D. Aug. 2,
1846 at "Waverly." Bur. there, but later re-interred,
presumably at Old St. Paul's Church Cem., in Baltimore.

THOMAS, JAMES (1833-1836). b. March 11, 1785 at "De
La Brooke Manor," near Mechanicsville, St. Mary's Co., Md.
s. of Wm. and Catherine (Boarman) T. Paternal grandfather
had settled in 1680 on land grant which became "Deep Falls"

plantation, and had been active in political affairs. Maternal ancestor, Robert Brooke, emigrated to Amer. in 1650 and had built the mansion in which James was born. Attd. Charlotte Hall Acad.; St. Mary's Coll.; and the Philadelphia Med. Coll., from which he was grad. in 1807. Established med. practice in St. Mary's Co. Held various local offices. Upon outbreak of War of 1812, was commissioned as major in Md. cavalry unit, attaining rank of major gen. by end of war. Mbr. of Md. House, 1820-1826 and of Md. Senate, 1826-1831. Chosen Gov. in 1833 as cand. of Anti-Jackson party and was reel. in 1834 and 1835. During admin., troubles arose as result of cholera outbreak and disastrous fires. Failure of Bank of Md. as result of natl. govt.'s financial policies caused riots. Gov. called out militia to preserve order and also requested U.S. mil. aid, which was sent. Nat Turner's slave insurrection at Southampton, Va. also caused unrest. Opposed abolitionist agitation. As Gov., favored continuation of internal improvements program through subsidization of Chesapeake and Ohio Canal Co. and the B. and O. R.R. m. in 1808 to a cousin, Elizabeth Coates. Episcopalian. D. at family estate, "Deep Falls," in St. Mary's Co., Dec. 25, 1845. Bur. in family cem. there.

VEAZEY, THOMAS WARD (1836-1839). b. Jan. 31, 1774 at "Cherry Grove," the family home near Earlville, Cecil Co., Md. s. of Edward and Elizabeth (De Coursey) V. Descendant of an English-Norman colonist who came to Md. before 1670. Ancestors had achieved distinction as mil. leaders. Father died when son was very young and mother also died before he reached manhood. Attd. Washington Coll., grad. in 1795. Returned home to manage family plantation. Pres. elector for Madison in 1808 and 1812. Mbr. of Md. House, 1811-1812, but gave up seat to become col. of Md. militia regiment during War of 1812. Mbr. of Gov.'s Council, 1833-1834. El. Gov. as Whig in 1836, and continued in office in 1837 and 1838. During admin., much agitation was carried on for constl. reform. A conv. was called in 1836, but it never met. Gen. Assembly submitted a number of proposals for change, which were eventually adopted. Among changes approved was change to direct popular election of Gov., for a three-year term, with requirement that Gov. come from one of three districts of the State in rotation; and legislative reapportionment. V. favored changes generally. Also defended institution of slavery, with right of each State to regulate it; and advocated free pub. educ. and govt. encouragement of internal improvements. Opposed abolitionist agitation and favored colonization of free Negroes in Africa. Episcopalian. m. first in 1794 to Sarah Worrell, of Kent Co. One d. Second wife was Mary Veazey, a cousin. Four children. m. for

third time in 1812, to Mary Wallace. Five children. Owned
27 slaves at time of death. D. July 1, 1842 at family home,
"Cherry Grove." Bur. in family cem. there.

GRASON, WILLIAM (1839-1842). b. in Queen Anne Co.(?),
Md., March 11, 1788. Facts regarding parentage and early
life uncertain. Believed to have been s. of Richard and
Anne G. School record lists father as a "Commodore Grason"
and a "Gen. J. Davidson" as guardian. Entered St. John's
Coll., but withdrew to join U.S. Navy before grad. Established residence in 1816 at "Wye River Farm," a plantation
in Queen Anne Co., where he became a planter. Was an Anti-
Jackson mbr. of Md. House, 1828-1829. Mbr. again in 1837,
affiliating with the Jackson (Dem.) party in latter term.
Advocate of constl. reform movement in 1836-1838. Unsuccessful as cand. for nom. by the Jackson (Dem.) party for U.S.
House seat in 1833. Was that party's cand. for that office
in 1835, but lost to his Whig opponent. Nom. as Jackson
Dem. for Gov. in 1839 and was el. over his Whig opponent by
some 300 votes, thus becoming the first Md. Gov. to be
chosen by direct popular vote. As Gov., faced financial difficulties because of declining state revenues and heavy state
debt arising from internal improvements programs. Urged revision of the Md. const. to curb legislative authority and
supported effort to launch an investigation into financial
affairs of the Chesapeake and Ohio Canal Co. Refused, however, to support move to repudiate state debt. Unsuccessful
in effort to win U.S. Senate seat to fill a vacancy in 1841.
Mbr. of state constl. conv. called in 1850. Also was mbr.
of conv. in Md. to consider course of action the State
should pursue as Civil War neared in 1861. Chosen as its
presiding officer, but declined post. Episcopalian. Known
as the "Queen Anne Farmer." m. in 1813 to Susan Orrick
Sullivane, d. of a physician who resided in Dorchester Co.
D. on plantation, "Wye River Farm" on July 2, 1868. Bur. in
family cem. there.

THOMAS, FRANCIS (1842-1845). b. Feb. 3, 1799 on family
estate in Frederick Co., Md. s. of John and Eleanor (McGill)
T. Descendant of a colonist who came to Pa. from Wales.
Attd. St. John's Coll., at Annapolis, where he received an
A.B. degree. Studied law, admitted to bar and began practice at Frankville, Md. Mbr. of Md. House from Frederick
Co., 1822, 1827 and 1829, serving as Speaker in last term.
El. to U.S. House in 1831 as the Jackson Dem. party cand.
after failing to win election in 1829, and continued in that
office until 1841. Supported Van Buren electors in 1836
controversy over election of Md. Senate. Pres. of Chesapeake and Ohio Canal Co., 1839-1840. Nom. and el. Gov. as

Dem. in 1841. During course of campaign engaged in a duel
with Wm. Price. As Gov., urged new taxes and exchange of
state-owned bank stocks as means of relieving pub. debt
crisis. Opposed outright repudiation of state bonds issued
in connection with internal improvements, but supported temp.
suspension of payment of interest on state obligations. Was
opposed to slavery, but supported annexation of Texas, believing it would end importation of slaves into that region
from Africa. Opposed further aid by the State for internal
improvements. Delegate to Md. constl. conv. of 1850, where
he favored reapportionment changes curtailing power of slave-
holding interests. Assisted in organizing a regiment for
Union Army in 1861. El. to U.S. House in 1861 and was continued in office until 1867, identifying himself with the
Unionist (Rep.) element during the course of the Civil War.
As a mbr. of Cong., was successful in preventing removal of
U.S. Naval Acad. from Annapolis. Supported adoption of revised Md. const. in 1866. Opposed Pres. Johnson's Reconstruction policies. Mbr. of Unionist ("Loyalist") conv. at
Philadelphia in 1866. Apptd. collector of internal revenue
for Cumberland dist. by Pres. Grant in 1870, serving for two
years. Served as U.S. Minister to Peru, 1872-1875. Engaged
in managing farm at Frankville, Md. thereafter. Episcopalian. m. in 1841 to Sallie Campbell Preston McDowell, d. of
Gov. McDowell of Va. (q.v.). Marriage ended in divorce
shortly after end of his term as Gov. Marriage and subsequent divorce became the basis of a scandal that hampered
his political career. D. Jan. 22, 1876 at Frankville when
struck by a train locomotive. Bur. at St. Mark's Cem.,
Petersville, Md.

PRATT, THOMAS GEORGE (1845-1848). b. Feb. 18, 1804 at
Georgetown, Md. (D.C.). s. of John Wilkes and Rachel (Belt)
P. Family originally resided in Prince George Co., Md.
Attd. Georgetown Coll. (now Univ.) and Princeton. Studied
law, admitted to bar in 1823, and began practice at Upper
Marlboro, Md. Mbr., Md. House, 1832-1835. Mbr. of electoral
body as a Whig that in 1836 selected a Senate that refused
to function. Whig pres. elector in 1836 pres. election.
Mbr. of Gov.'s Council, 1838. Mbr. of Md. Senate, 1838-1843.
El. Gov. as Whig in 1844 in a very close election. Sponsored legislation increasing various taxes to permit State
to resume interest payments on debt; supported extension of
B. and O. R.R. to Ohio River. Encountered difficulty in obtaining enforcement of fugitive slave law, which eventuated
in U.S. Supreme Ct. land-mark case of Prigg v. Pa. This experience was a factor leading to his later shifting his
party allegiance to Dem. party. Supported U.S. war effort
against Mexico. After tenure, practiced law at Annapolis.

El. as Whig to U.S. Senate in 1850 to fill vacancy, serving until 1857. Was a close personal friend of Henry Clay; but when Whig party disintegrated, joined Dem. party and supported Buchanan for Pres. of U.S. in 1856. Returned to law practice in Annapolis until 1864. Was a Southern sympathizer during Civil War and was imprisoned for a time. Delegate to Unionist ("Loyalist") conv. in Philadelphia in 1866. Unsuccessful cand. for U.S. Senate seat in 1867. Episcopalian. m. in 1835 to Adelaide Kent, d. of Gov. Joseph Kent (q.v.). Six children. D. at Baltimore Nov. 9, 1869. Bur. in St. Anne's Church Cem., Annapolis.

THOMAS, PHILIP FRANCIS (1848-1851). b. Sept. 12, 1810 at Easton, Md. s. of Dr. Tristam and Maria (Francis) T. Attd. Easton Acad. and Dickinson Coll., Carlisle, Pa., where he was suspended for two years for a "college prank" and failed to grad. Studied law, admitted to bar and began practice in Easton in 1831. Originally a Whig, became a Dem. party mbr. early in career. Mbr., Md. constl. conv. in 1837. El. as Dem. to U.S. House in 1839 but did not seek second term in 1841. Mbr., Md. House in 1838, 1843 and 1845. El. Gov. as Dem. in 1847 in a very close contest with Whig opponent. Supported state constl. revision movement during tenure. U.S. Comptroller of Treas., 1851-1853. Resigned in 1853 to become U.S. collector of customs at port of Baltimore, continuing in that post until 1860. Refused offer of post as Gov. of Utah Terr., but later accepted position as U.S. Commnr. of Patents from Pres. Buchanan. Apptd. U.S. Sect. of Treas. in Dec., 1860, serving for about two months. Sympathized with South as Civil War began. Spent war years in semi-seclusion in Md. El. to Md. House in 1863 and to U.S. Senate in 1867; but Senate refused to seat him because of his pro-Southern attitude and actions during Civil War. El. to U.S. House as Dem. in 1874. Did not seak second term. El. to Md. House in 1877, 1878 and 1883. Unsuccessful cand. for U.S. Senate seat in 1878 and 1884. Ch., Dem. state conv., 1883. Episcopalian. m. in 1835 to Sarah Maria Kerr. Thirteen children. After her death in 1870 m. to Clintonia (Wright) May, d. of former Gov. Robt. Wright (q.v.). D. at Baltimore Oct. 2, 1890. Bur. in Spring Hill Cem., Easton.

LOWE, ENOCH LOUIS (1851-1854). b. Aug. 10, 1820 at the "Hermitage," the family estate near Frederick, Md. s. of Lieut. Bradley and Adelaide (Belluneau de la Vincindiere) L. Parents separated and were divorced soon after his birth. Brought up by maternal grandfather at the "Hermitage," an estate of 1,000 acres. Attd. St. John's School in Frederick; a Roman Catholic college near Dublin, Ireland; and another Catholic college at Stonyhurst, in Lancastershire.

Studied law, admitted to bar at age 21 and began practice at
Frederick. Became known as very effective speaker. Mbr. of
Md. House, 1845, where he advocated state constl. reform.
El. Gov. as Dem. in 1850. Favored criminal code revision;
tax reforms; abolition of imprisonment for debt; strict en-
forcement of fugitive slave law. As Gov., entertained the
Hungarian patriot, Kossuth, on his visit to U.S. Delegate
to Dem. natl. convs. in 1856 and 1860. Was offered post of
Minister to China by Pres. Buchanan, but declined. Sym-
pathized with South as Civil War approached. Cand. for
pres. elector on Breckinridge ticket in 1860. When Civil
War began, went to Va., later to Ga., and remained in South
until 1866, when he returned to Md. Later moved to Brooklyn,
N.Y., where he engaged in law practice. Active supporter of
Gen. Hancock for Pres. of U.S. in 1880. Roman Catholic.
m. in 1844 to Esther Winder Polk, of Princess Anne, Md.
Eleven children. D. in Brooklyn, Aug. 23, 1892. Bur. in
Catholic Cem. at Frederick, Md.

LIGON, THOMAS WATKINS (1854-1858). b. May 10, 1810
near Farmville, Va. s. of Thomas D. and Martha (Watkins) L.
Grandfather had served as col. in Contl. Army during Rev.
War. Father was a planter. While he was still a youth he
and his brothers were left in charge of family plantation
when father died. Grad. from Hampden-Sidney Coll., and also
attd. the Univ. of Va. and Yale, where he studied law for a
time. Returned to Va., admitted to bar in 1833, and began
practice in Baltimore, Md. In 1840 moved to Ellicott Mills,
Md., where he farmed and continued to practice law. Nom.
for seat in Md. House in 1840, but declined. Was nom. and
el. to a seat therein in 1843. El. to U.S. House in 1845
and was reel. in 1847. Resumed law practice for a time.
El. Gov. as Dem. in 1853, becoming first Gov. of Md. to be
chosen for a four-year term. His party lacked a majority in
Gen. Assembly and he was not very successful in getting his
programs adopted. Difficulties were encountered with city
govt. of Baltimore, which was under control of the Amer.
(Know Nothing) party. Sought to have Baltimore city elections of 1856 investigated, but Gen. Assembly was reluctant
to act. During 1857 elections there he declared martial law
ostensibly to assure fair election. Gave support to establishment of agri. coll. and experimental station, which
later became part of Univ. of Md. After tenure as Gov., resumed farming at "Chatham," his estate near Ellicott City,
Md. Episcopalian. m. first to Sallie Ann Dorsey. After
her death, m. to her sister, Mary Tolly Dorsey. One s.;
one d. D. at "Chatham" Jan. 12, 1881. Bur. in St. John's
Episcopal Cem., at Ellicott City.

HICKS, THOMAS HOLLIDAY (1858-1862). b. Sept. 1, 1798
near East New Market, Dorchester Co., Md. One of eleven
children of Henry C. and Mary (Sewell) H. Father was a
farmer of limited means. Attd. local schools, receiving a
limited educ. Assisted in running farm while attending
school. El. sheriff of Dorchester Co. in 1824, and was el.
to Md. House in 1830. Moved to Vienna, Md. in 1833, where
he engaged in operation of a boat line and also was a merchant. Mbr. of state electoral body in 1836 which became
embroiled in controversy between Dem. and Whig factions over
election of new Md. Senate and which failed to choose a
Senate. Mbr. of Md. House as Dem. in 1836, and of Gov.'s
Council, 1837. Apptd. register of wills of Dorchester Co.
in 1838, serving until 1851. Again served in that office,
1855-1861. Mbr. of Md. constl. conv. of 1850. Affiliated
with Amer. party in 1850s, and was el. Gov. as that party's
nominee in 1857. Admin. attd. by much controversy and violence following outbreak of Civil War. Pro-Southern elements in Baltimore sought to prevent movement of U.S. troops
through the city to Washington, D.C. in spring of 1861.
Riots ensued, and a railroad bridge was destroyed. Although
he was a slave-owner, he had refused to assemble a conv. to
consider question of course of action for Md. as Civil War
conflict was threatened. Eventually called a spec. session
of Gen. Assembly at Frederick. It expelled some Amer. party
mbrs., but did not vote for secession. Some of its pro-
Southern mbrs. were placed under arrest by U.S. mil. authorities and the State was placed under martial rule for a time
by the U.S. govt. At beginning of war sought to pursue a
neutral course between U.S. and secessionists, but eventually gave his support to Pres. Lincoln's policies. Supported the adoption of a revised Md. const. in 1864 that
abolished slavery. Declined commn. as brig. gen. in Union
Army in 1862, but accepted apptmt. that year as a Unionist
to U.S. Senate seat vacancy, and was later el. to the seat.
Was not very active in Senate because of poor health. Supported Lincoln's reel. in 1864. In 1863 suffered a sprained
leg, which later had to be amputated, eventually causing his
death. m. three times: first to Ann Thompson, of Dorchester
Co.; then to Sarah Raleigh; and then to Mrs. Mary Jane Wilcox, widow of a cousin. Methodist. D. in Washington, D.C.,
Feb. 13, 1865 while still a mbr. of Senate. Bur. in Cambridge, Md. Pres. Lincoln and many other notables of the
U.S. govt. attended his funeral.

BRADFORD, AUGUSTUS WILLIAMSON (1862-1866). b. Jan. 9,
1806 at Bel Air, Md. s. of Samuel and Jane (Bond) B.
Family was of English ancestry. Attd. Bel Air Acad., and
St. Mary's Coll., from which he was grad. in 1824. Studied

law and also engaged in surveying work. Admitted to bar in
1826 at age of 20. Moved to Baltimore in 1831, where he became active in politics as a Whig. Pres. elector on Clay
ticket in 1844. Retired from politics for a time after
Clay's defeat. Clerk of Baltimore Co., 1845. Delegate to
Washington "Peace" Cong. in 1861. El. Gov. in 1861 as a
Unionist (Rep.). Supported Lincoln's war policies, but objected to interference by U.S. mil. in political matters
through disqualification of suspected disloyal elements.
State was invaded by Confed. forces three times during admin., and on one occasion (1864) his mansion was destroyed
by invading forces. Supported adoption of constl. changes
in 1864, including abolition of slavery, but objected to enlistment of free Negroes in U.S. armed forces. Apptd. surveyor of port of Baltimore in 1867, but was removed by Pres.
Grant in 1869. Refused offer of post of U.S. appraiser of
customs at Baltimore. Shifted allegiance to Dem. party in
1872 pres. election, becoming a pres. elector cand. on
Greeley ticket. Methodist. m. to Elizabeth Kell. Seven
children. D. at Baltimore March 1, 1881. Bur. in Greenmount
Cem. there.

SWANN, THOMAS (1866-1869). b. Feb. 3, 1806 at Alexandria, Va. s. of Thomas and Jane Byrd (Page) S. Father was
a prominent atty. Attd. Columbian Coll. (now George Washington Univ.) and the Univ. of Va. Studied law with father
and admitted to bar. Sect. of U.S. Commnr. to Naples, 1833.
Established residence in Baltimore in 1834. Became dir. of
B. and O. R.R. in 1845, and pres. two years later, serving
until 1853. Pres. of N.W. Va. R.R. Co. and of First Natl.
Bank of Baltimore, 1863. El. mayor of Baltimore in 1856 as
cand. of Amer. party, continuing in office until 1860. Admin. as mayor marked by controversy with Gov. Ligon, who
sought to investigate elections in the city, which had been
attd. by violence and alleged intimidation of voters. Set
up street railway system; reorg. the police and fire depts.;
and instituted a "park tax" to finance a city park system.
As Civil War approached took stand against secession. Supported Lincoln admin. policies generally; but opposed use of
loyalty oath by U.S. to exclude pro-Southerners from franchise and office-holding. El. Gov. in 1864 as Unionist
(Rep.). Took oath as Gov. on Jan. 1, 1865, but did not actually assume office until a year later because constl.
changes that had been adopted provided for continuance in
office of incumbent Gov. Bradford until end of his four-year
term. Accordingly, served as Gov. for only three years.
Active in effort to remove loyalty oath provision from Md.
const., which was eventually achieved in 1867. Supported
Pres. A. Johnson's Reconstruction policies. El. to U.S.

Senate seat in 1866, and offered resignation as Gov. Withdrew his resignation later when he concluded Senate might
not permit him to take seat, and completed term as Gov. In
the interval while his resignation was pending, in 1867,
Lieut. Gov. Christopher C. Cox laid claim to the powers of
the office of Gov.; but he withdrew his claim after S. can-
celled his resignation. El. to U.S. House in 1868 as a Dem.
and was continued in that office until 1879. Retired to estate, "Morven Park," near Leesburg, Va. Episcopalian. m. in
1834 to Elizabeth Gilmore Sherlock. One s.; four d. m. in
1878 to Josephine Ward Thompson, a sister of U.S. House
Speaker Saml. J. Randall, but the marriage was later dissolved. D. at family home near Leesburg July 24, 1883. Bur.
in Greenmount Cem., Baltimore.

BOWIE, ODEN (1869-1872). b. Nov. 10, 1826 at family
estate, "Fairview," in Prince George Co., Md. s. of Wm. D.
and Eliza (Oden) B. Father, who was of Scotch-Irish descent,
was a prominent planter who had served in Md. Assembly.
Educ. by pvt. tutors and at St. John's Coll., in Annapolis,
Md., from which he was grad. in 1845 as valedictorian of
class. Served in Mexican War, participating in Battle of
Monterey, but resigned commn. as capt. after having contracted disease. El. to Md. House in 1849. Acquired bus.
interests, becoming pres. of B. and O. R.R. in 1860. Unsuccessful cand. as "Peace" Dem. for Md. Senate in 1861.
Became ch. of Md. Dem. commt., and served as delegate to
Dem. natl. conv. in 1864. Defeated as Dem. cand. for Lieut.
Gov. in 1866. Nom. and el. Gov. as Dem. in Nov., 1867, but
did not assume office until Jan., 1869 because of a change
in term schedule for office. Served as Gov. for three years.
As Gov., settled controversy between Va. and Md. over oyster
bed rights in Chesapeake Bay; advocated extension of educ.
facilities for Negroes. After leaving office became pres.
of Baltimore city railway system, which was converted from a
horse-drawn to an electric rapid transit system during his
tenure. Pres. of Md. Jockey Club in 1870. Acquired Pimlico
Race Track, and became a breeder of blooded cattle, sheep
and fine race horses. Noted for his many enthusiasms and
outspokenness. On one occasion was said to have advised the
minister of his church after a service that his sermon "was
too damned long." Commuted daily from his home to Baltimore
by rail, reserving the same seat every day for that purpose
by hiring a boy to claim it. Episcopalian. m. in 1851 to
Alice Carter. Seven children. D. at "Fairview" Dec. 4,
1894. Bur. in family cem. there.

WHYTE, WILLIAM PINKNEY (1872-1874). b. Aug. 9, 1824 at
Baltimore, Md. s. of Joseph and Isabella (Pinkney) White.

He later changed the spelling of his name to "Whyte" following an estrangement arising from a disagreement with mbrs.
of his family. Paternal grandfather, a physician, had emigrated from Ireland to Md. in 1798 after failure of the
Irish insurrection in that year. Maternal grandfather, Wm.
Pinkney, was a U.S. Atty. Gen., a mbr. of U.S. House and
Senate from Md., and a U.S. diplomat. Educ. by tutors, one
of whom had been a sect. to Napoleon Bonaparte. Attd. Baltimore Coll. and Harvard, where he studied law, 1844-1845.
Admitted to bar in 1846. Employed in family banking bus.,
1842-1846. Established law practice in Baltimore. Mbr. of
Md. House, 1847-1848. Comptroller of Md. Treas., 1854-1855.
Unsuccessful as Dem. cand. for U.S. House in 1851 and 1857.
He contested latter election result in the House, but his
opponent was seated. Delegate to Dem. natl. conv. in 1868.
Apptd. to U.S. Senate to fill vacancy in 1868 and was later
el., serving from July, 1868 to March, 1869. Supported Pres.
A. Johnson's Reconstruction policies. El. Gov. as Dem. in
1871, serving until 1874, when he resigned to take seat in
U.S. Senate again. Served there until 1881. As a Sen.,
served on commt. that framed legislation for reorg. of govt.
for the D. of C. Mayor of Baltimore, 1882-1883. Atty Gen.
of Md., 1887-1891. Ch. of commn. to revise charter of Baltimore, 1897-1898. City solicitor of Baltimore, 1900-1903.
Apptd. and then el. to U.S. Senate for third time in 1906.
Episcopalian. Hon. degree from Univ. of Md. m. in 1847 to
Louisa D. Hollingsworth. Three s. m. in 1892 to Mary (Mc-
Donald) Thomas, a widow. D. March 17, 1908 while still a
mbr. of U.S. Senate. Bur. in Greenmount Cem., Baltimore.

GROOME, JAMES BLACK (1874-1876). b. April 4, 1838 at
Elkton, Md. s. of Col. John Charles and Elizabeth (Black) G.
Father was prominent in Md. politics, and was the unsuccessful Dem. cand. for Gov. in the 1857 election. Mother was a
mbr. of a cultured and distinguished family. Attd. Tennant
prep. school, in Hartsville, Pa., but eye trouble prevented
his going to college. Studied law in father's office, admitted to bar in 1861, and began practice in Elkton. Mbr.
of Md. constl. conv. of 1867. Mbr. of Md. House, 1871-1874.
Pres. elector on Greeley ticket in 1872 pres. election.
When Gov. Whyte resigned in 1874 was chosen Gov. by Gen. Assembly to complete Whyte's term. Unsuccessfully sought Dem.
nom. for regular term in 1876. El. to U.S. Senate that year,
serving until 1885. Apptd. U.S. collector of customs at the
Port of Baltimore by Pres. Cleveland in 1886, serving until
1893. Retired thereafter. Health was poor during most of
life. Presbyterian. m. in 1876 to Alice Leigh Edmondson,
of Talbot Co., Md. One d. D. Oct. 4, 1893. Bur. in Presbyterian Cem., Elkton.

CARROLL, JOHN LEE (1876-1880). b. Sept. 30, 1830 at
"Homewood," the family estate in Baltimore. s. of Col.
Charles and Mary Digges (Lee) C. Was a grandson of Charles
Carroll, the eminent Rev. War era statesman from Md. Mother
was a great grand-daughter of Gov. Thomas S. Lee of Md.(q.v.).
Father moved to an estate in Howard Co. when son was age 3.
Attd. St. Mary's Coll. and Sem., at Emmitsburg, Md.; Georgetown Coll., Washington, D.C.; St. Mary's Coll., in Baltimore;
and Harvard, where he studied law. Admitted to bar in 1852.
Spent year in European travel. Unsuccessful as Dem. cand.
for Md. House in 1855. Went to N.Y. in 1858 to practice law,
but returned to take over mgmt. of family plantation in 1861
from father, who was the owner of many slaves. After father's death in 1862, purchased estate from other heirs in
1866. Mbr. of Md. Senate, 1867, 1872 and 1874, serving as
Pres. of Senate in last term. El. Gov. as Dem. in 1875,
winning nom. in bitter struggle with incumbent Gov. Groome.
Final popular vote result contested unsuccessfully by Rep.
opponent. Represented Md. at Philadelphia Centennial Exposition in 1876. A bitter strike on B. and O. R.R. in 1877
necessitated use of militia and call for U.S. troops to
quell disorders. After tenure as Gov., travelled and resided in Europe for a time, where his children were in
school. Unsuccessfully sought apptmt. as U.S. Minister to
France during Pres. Cleveland's admin. Pres. of Natl. Soc.
of S.A.R., 1890. Roman Catholic. m. in 1856 to Anita
Phelps, of N.Y. Four d.; five s. After her death in 1873
m. to Mary Caster Thompson, of Staunton, Va. One d. D.
Feb. 27, 1911. Bur. in Bonnie Brae Cem., in Howard Co., Md.

HAMILTON, WILLIAM TIFFANY (1880-1884). b. Sept. 8,
1820 near Boonsboro, Md. s. of Henry and Anna Mary M. (Hess)
H. Was left an orphan at an early age and was brought up by
maternal uncles Jacob, Henry and Wm. Hess, who were businessmen in Hagerstown, Md. Attd. Brown's School, at Boonsboro;
Hagerstown Acad.; and Jefferson Coll., Cannonsburg, Pa.,
from which he was grad. in 1840. Studied law, admitted to
bar in 1843 and began practice in Hagerstown. El. to Md.
House in 1846 but was defeated for second term. Pres.
elector on Cass ticket in 1848 pres. election. El. to U.S.
House as Dem. in 1849 and for two succeeding terms. Supported Clay Compromise bills while a mbr. of House. Defeated for fourth term in 1855 by Amer. party cand. Resumed
law practice. El. to U.S. Senate in 1869 but did not seek
second term. As mbr. of Senate, opposed "salary grab" bill
unsuccessfully; opposed proposed 15th Amendment to U.S.
Const.; favored resumption of specie payments of U.S. currency. Became opponent of Dem. faction headed by Govs.
Whyte and Carroll. Unsuccessful cand. for Dem. nom. for

Gov. in 1875, but won it in 1879 and was el. Favored various reform measures that were opposed by some Dem. leaders.
Owned considerable real estate, and was known as the "Farmer
Gov." Associated with numerous bus. enterprises in Hagerstown, including banking, ins., utilities, and machinery mfg.
fields. Mbr. of Hagerstown Bd. of Street Commnrs. Presbyterian. m. in 1850 to Clara Jenners, of Portsmouth, N.H.
Six children. D. at Hagerstown Oct. 26, 1888. Bur. in Rose
Hill Cem. there.

McLANE, ROBERT MILLIGAN (1884-1885). b. June 23, 1815
at Wilmington, Del. s. of Louis and Catherine Mary (Milligan) McL. Father was a distinguished Amer. statesman who
had served in U.S. House and Senate, as a mbr. of Pres.
Jackson's cabinet, and as a U.S. diplomat. Father moved to
Baltimore where he became pres. of B. and O. R.R. in 1837.
Attd. schools in Wilmington; St. Mary's Coll., in Annapolis;
studied in France; and spent some time studying in London,
where father was U.S. Minister to Great Britain. Returned
to U.S. in 1833 and entered U.S. Mil. Acad., from which he
was grad. in 1837. Participated in Seminole War in Fla., as
second lieut. in 1837. Became a topographical engr. in U.S.
Engr. Corps. Studied law. Resigned Army commn. in 1843.
Admitted to bar and began practice in Baltimore. El. to Md.
House as Dem. in 1844. El. to U.S. House as Dem. in 1847,
serving from 1847 to 1851. Did not seek third term in 1851.
Supported Pres. Polk's policies, including annexation of
Texas and Mexican War. Delegate to Dem. natl. conv. in 1852
and pres. elector on Pierce-King ticket that year. Apptd.
U.S. Minister to China in 1853, and negotiated trade treaty
with China. Counsel for transcontinental railroad companies.
Delegate to Dem. natl. conv. in 1856. Apptd. Minister to
Mexico in 1857, serving until 1860, during which time he
negotiated a trade and canal route treaty. Took no active
role in Civil War, opposing both secession as well as the
attempt by U.S. to coerce Southern States. Delegate to Dem.
natl. conv. in 1876. Mbr., Md. Senate, 1877. El. to U.S.
House again in 1878, continuing in that office until 1883.
El. Gov. as Dem. in 1883. Resigned in March, 1885 to become
U.S. Minister to France, in which capacity he served until
1889. Remained in France thereafter for sake of wife's
health, returning to U.S. from time to time. m. in 1841 to
Georgine Urquhart, of New Orleans. Two d. D. in Paris,
France, April 16, 1898. Bur. in Greenmount Cem., Baltimore.

LLOYD, HENRY (1885-1888). b. Feb. 21, 1852 at family
estate, "Hambrooke," near Cambridge, Md. s. of Daniel and
Killy (Henry) L. Was a direct descendant of Edward Lloyd,
Gov. of Md. (q.v.) and through his mother, of John Henry,

Gov. of Md. (q.v.). Father was an atty. Attd. pvt. schools
and Cambridge Acad. Became principal of Cambridge Acad.
Studied law in office of father and uncle. Admitted to bar
and began practice in Cambridge in 1880. El. to Md. Senate
in 1881 as Dem., and continued in office until 1885, becoming Pres. of Senate in 1884. Succeeded to office of Gov. in
March, 1885 when Gov. McLane resigned, and was then el. by
Gen. Assembly to complete McLane's term. Became pres. of
Dorchester Natl. Bank in 1889. Apptd. in 1892 to a Md. cir.
ct. judgeship and continued to serve in that office by election until his retirement in 1908 on account of poor health.
m. in 1886 to Mary Elizabeth Staplefort. One s. Mbr.,
Masons. Episcopalian. D. Dec. 30, 1920. Bur. in Christ
Church Cem., Cambridge.

JACKSON, ELIHU EMORY (1888-1892). b. Nov. 3, 1837 near
Delmar, Somerset Co. (now Wicomico Co.), Md. s. of Hugh and
Sally (McBride) J. Father was a prosperous farmer. As
eldest of seven children, assisted father on farm while attending local schools and engaging in home study. Went into
merc. bus. for himself at Delmar in 1859. Moved to Salisbury, Md. in 1863 where he joined father and brothers in
merc. and lumbering enterprise. Acquired extensive properties in land in Va. and Ala. as well as in Md. Mbr., Md.
House, 1882-1883 and of Md. Senate, 1884-1888, becoming Pres.
of Senate in 1886. Nom. as Dem. cand. for Gov. in 1887 after
bitter intra-party struggle, and was el. As Gov., leased,
then was forced to sell to B. and O. R.R., a canal after it
was wrecked; carried on dispute with Va. over ownership of
Hogg Island; had to remove Md. State Treas. because of embezzlement of state funds. Became mbr. of Md. Senate in
1895, serving until 1907. Did not seek reel. Unsuccessful
cand. for U.S. Senate seat in 1890, 1892 and 1904. Pres. of
Salisbury Bank and of Seaford Natl. Bank, and dir. of other
bus. firms. Methodist. Was a liberal contributor to So.
Methodist church undertakings. m. in 1869 to Annie Francis
Rider. Three s.; two d. D. Dec. 27, 1907. Bur. in Parsons
Cem., Salisbury.

BROWN, FRANK (1892-1896). b. Aug. 8, 1846 at family
estate in Carroll Co., Md. s. of Stephen T.C. and Susan A.
(Bennett) B. Family descended from a Scottish colonist who
came to Amer. in early 1600s. Family estate, "Springfield,"
comprised some 25,000 acres and was noted for its blooded
cattle and horses. Attd. pvt. schools in Carroll Co. and
Howard Co., and at Baltimore. Left schooling at age 16 to
engage in family bus. interests, and soon afterward took
over mgmt. of family estate. Clerk of Md. state tobacco
warehouses, 1870-1876. Mbr., Md. House, 1876-1878. Pres.

of Md. State Agri. and Mech. Assoc., 1880-1892, which
managed Md. state fairs. Treas., Md. Dem. commt., 1885.
U.S. postmaster at Baltimore, 1886-1890. Unsuccessful cand.
for Dem. nom. for Gov. in 1887, but won nom. and was el. in
1891. As "Farmer Brown," carried on a colorful campaign,
with a popular singer accompanying him. During admin., a
coal miners' strike at Frostburg required use of militia to
control violence. Commuted death sentences of four Negroes
who were about to be lynched by a mob for allegedly murder-
ing a prominent citizen. Real culprits were later apprehended, tried, and sentenced to be hanged. Was required to
use force to expel remnants of "Coxey's Army" from Md.,
whose camp had become a pub. nuisance. After term as Gov.
became tax collector for Baltimore. Pres. of Baltimore
Tractor Co., 1897 and of State Loan and Improvement Co.,
which was designed to promote devel. of waste areas of State.
Dir. of B. and O. R.R. and of various banks and bus. enterprises. Unsuccessful cand. for Dem. nom. for Gov. in 1907.
Presbyterian. m. Mary (Ridgely) Preston, a widow. One s.;
one d. Divested himself of large estate before death. D.
Feb. 3, 1920 at Baltimore. Bur. in Greenmount Cem. there.

LOWNDES, LLOYD, Jr. (1896-1900). b. Feb. 21, 1845 at
Clarksburg, Va. (now W. Va.). s. of Lloyd and Maria Elizabeth (Moore) L. Was a descendant of a Provincial Gov. of
Md., Benj. Tasker, and of Edward Lloyd, Gov. of Md. (q.v.).
Father had moved to Clarksburg in 1831 to engage in farming
and lumbering bus., in which he was quite successful. Attd.
Clarksburg Acad.; Washington Coll., in Pa.; Allegheny Coll.,
from which he was grad. in 1863; and the Univ. of Pa., from
which he was grad. with a law degree in 1867. Joined his
father, who had moved to Cumberland, Md., in managing various banking, mining and other enterprises. El. to U.S.
House as Rep. in 1872 from a normally Dem. dist., becoming
at 28 the youngest mbr. of Cong. at that time. Voted against
Civil Rights bill of 1873. Defeated for next term in 1874.
Engaged in bus. activities for next 24 years. Delegate to
Rep. natl. conv. in 1880. Declined to run for Gov. in 1891;
but accepted Rep. nom. in 1895 and was el., becoming the first
Rep. Gov. of Md. in 30 years. As Gov., advocated electoral
law reforms; encouragement of devel. of waste areas of State;
set up Md. Geological Survey; approved new charter for Baltimore. Unsuccessful as Rep. cand. for second term as Gov.
in 1899. Helped org. a volunteer regiment following outbreak of Spanish-Amer. War in 1898 and became close personal
friend of Theodore Roosevelt. Devoted attention to numerous
bus. enterprises in banking, utilities, and mining fields
after tenure as Gov. Mbr., World's Columbian Exposition
Commn. in 1892. Episcopalian. m. in 1869 to Elizabeth

Tasker Lowndes, a cousin. Six children. D. at Cumberland
Jan. 8, 1905. Bur. in Rose Hill Cem. there.

SMITH, JOHN WALTER (1900-1904). b. Feb. 8, 1845 at
Snow Hill, Worcester Co., Md. s. of John Walter and Charlotte (Whittington) S. Family antecedents included several
individuals who were prominent in Md. pub. affairs. Mother
died at his birth and father died when son was five years
old. Brought up in a boarding house under guardianship of
Ephraim King Wilson, a lawyer and later a U.S. Sen. from
Md. Attd. pvt. schools and Union Acad., at Snow Hill. At
age 18 became clerk in merc. house, later becoming a partner
in the bus. Expanded into lumbering bus. in 1865, with
holdings in Va. and N.C. as well as Md. Also became involved
in shipping, banking, ins. and oystering enterprises, and
became quite wealthy. Org. and became pres. of First Natl.
Bank of Snow Hill. Mbr., Md. Senate, 1889, continuing in
that office until 1899. Served as Pres. of Senate. Ch.
Dem. state commt., 1895. Defeated as Dem. nominee for U.S.
Senate seat in 1896. El. to U.S. House in 1898. Resigned
House seat in 1900 after having been nom. and el. Gov. as
Dem. in 1899 before actually beginning active service as
U.S. Repr. Called spec. session of Gen. Assembly to
strengthen literacy qualification for voting, a move directed toward restricting Negro voting primarily. Defeated
as cand. for U.S. Senate seat in 1904. El. to U.S. Senate
in 1908 to fill vacancy. Continued in that office until
1921. Defeated for reel. in 1920. Delegate to Dem. natl.
convs., 1900-1916, and was Dem. natl. committeeman at time
of his death. m. in 1869 to Mary Frances Richardson, of
Snow Hill. Two d. D. April 19, 1925 at Baltimore. Bur. in
Presbyterian Cem., Snow Hill.

WARFIELD, EDWIN (1904-1908). b. May 7, 1848 at family
estate, "Oakdale," in Howard Co., Md. s. of Albert Gallatin
and Margaret Gassaway (Watkins) W. Descendant of an English
colonist who came to Md. in 1662. A maternal ancestor, Col.
Gassaway Watkins, served in Contl. Army during the Rev. War.
Attd. pvt. and pub. schools in Howard Co. and St. Timothy's
Hall, Catonsville, Md. Emancipation at end of Civil War
left family with land, but no slaves. Left school to assist
father in working farm. Taught school and began study of
law. Apptd. register of wills of Howard Co. in 1874, serving until 1881 while completing law studies. Mbr., Dem.
state commt., 1878-1886. Mbr., Md. Senate, 1881-1886, becoming Pres. of Senate in last term. In 1882 purchased and
became ed. of Ellicott City _Times_. In 1887 purchased _Mary-
land Law Record_ and in 1888 the _Daily Record_, both law
journals which he placed under the mgmt. of his brother.

In 1886 helped org. Patapsco Natl. Bank, of which he became a mbr. of bd. of dir. Also org. Fidelity Bank and Deposit Co., which expanded into many other States, and of which he eventually became pres. Also involved in other banking enterprises. Delegate to Dem. natl. conv. in 1896. Unsuccessfully sought Dem. nom. for Gov. in 1899. Nom. for that office in 1903 and was el. During admin., opposed restriction of Negro voting by a grandfather clause, but favored more restrictive literacy voting qualification. Interested in historical matters. Pres. of Md. Historical Soc. and of Peabody Fund; mbr., Mt. Vernon Assoc.; Soc. of War of 1812; S.A.R.; various social clubs. Obtained two homesteads, "Walnut Grove" (grandfather's) and "Oakdale" (father's) which he preserved for historical purposes. m. in 1890 to Emma Nicodemus. Three d.; one s. D. March 31, 1920. Bur. in family cem. at "Cherry Grove," in Howard Co., Md.

CROTHERS, AUSTIN LANE (1908-1912). b. May 20 (17?), 1860 near Conowingo, Cecil Co., Md. One of eight children of Alpheus and Margaret Aurelia (Porter) C. Descendant of Scottish ancestor who came to Amer. before Rev. War. Attd. local pub. schools and West Nottingham Acad. Clerked in store and taught school while studying law. Grad. from the Univ. of Md. with a law degree in 1880, and began practice in Elkton, Md. State's atty. for Cecil Co., 1891-1895. Became counsel for Pa. R.R., handling many important civil suits. Mbr. of Md. Senate, 1897-1901. Failed to win reel. in 1901 and again in 1905. Apptd. to Md. cir. ct. judgeship in 1906, which he held until following year. Delegate to Dem. natl. convs. in 1904 and 1908. Nom. and el. Gov. as Dem. in 1907. Was ill during most of campaign and spent a total of only $4.87 for one night's hotel bill in connection with the campaign. During admin., successfully advocated appropriation for beginning of a state road system; enactment of a corrupt practices act; legislation creating a Pub. Service Commn. and a State Banking Commn. Vetoes of items to eliminate alleged waste of pub. funds angered Gen. Assembly and org. leaders of party. Was defeated in attempt to remove Baltimore Police Commnrs. on grounds of corruption. Supported direct primary system; opposed further restrictions on voting aimed at Negroes; set up "cabinet" as advisory body; urged passage of a pure food law, protection of the oyster industry, increase in inheritance tax, a license tax for automobiles. Never married. Presbyterian. Ill when he left office in 1912. D. at Elkton May 25, 1912. Bur. in West Nottingham Presbyterian Cem.

GOLDSBOROUGH, PHILLIPS LEE (1912-1916). b. Aug. 6, 1865 at Cambridge, Md. s. of Capt. M. Worthington and

Nettie M. (Jones) G. Father was an officer in U.S. Navy.
Attd. pvt. and pub. schools. Studied law, admitted to bar
in 1886, and began a successful practice in Dorchester Co.
Also engaged in banking. State's atty. for Dorchester Co.,
1891-1898. State Comptroller of Treas., 1898-1900, being
defeated for reel. in 1900. Apptd. U.S. collector of internal revenue for Md. dist. in 1902, and continued to serve
in that office until 1911. Nom. and el. Gov. as Rep. in
1911, being helped by factional struggle in Dem. party. As
Gov., advocated increased aid for educ. and roads; brought
about consolidation of State Agri. Coll. with other units in
Baltimore to form enlarged Univ. of Md. Advocated creation
of State Tax Commn.; penal reforms; workmen's compensation
law; home rule for Baltimore and for counties. Unsuccessful
in attempt to win U.S. Senate seat in 1916. Resumed law
practice and bus. interests until 1928, when he was nom. and
el. to U.S. Senate seat. Did not seek continuation in office when term expired in 1937. Unsuccessfully sought Rep.
nom. for Gov. in 1934. Mbr., Rep. natl. commt., 1932-1936.
Apptd. to Fed. Deposit Ins. Corp. Bd. by Pres. F.D. Roosevelt in 1936, in which capacity he continued to serve until
death. Hon. degrees from the Univ. of Pa., the Univ. of Md.,
Washington Coll., and St. John's Coll. m. in 1893 to Mary
Ellen Showell, of Worcester Co. Two s. Episcopalian. D.
Oct. 22, 1946 at Baltimore. Bur. in Christ Episcopal Church
Cem., Cambridge, Md.

HARRINGTON, EMERSON COLUMBUS (1916-1920). b. March 26,
1864 at Madison, Dorchester Co., Md. s. of John Edward and
Mary Elizabeth (Thompson) H. Father was a sea captain,
merchant and farmer and was prominent in bus. and religious
affairs of community. Attd. local pub. schools and St.
John's Coll., in Annapolis, from which he was grad. in 1884
second in class. Active in athletics while in college. Became instructor in Latin and mathematics at St. John's Coll.,
rising to rank of prof. Resigned in 1886 to become principal of Cambridge Acad., which became a h.s. a few years
later, and which he continued to head until 1897. Studied
law, admitted to bar, and began practice in Cambridge in
1897. State's atty. for Dorchester Co., 1899-1903. After
defeat for reel. to that office, practiced law until 1910.
Apptd. State Ins. Commnr. in 1910. El. State Comptroller of
Treas. in 1911, serving until 1915. Nom. and el. Gov. as
Dem. in 1915. As "war Gov." during World War I, supported
U.S. war effort vigorously. Set up commn. to study reorg.
of Md. admin. system. Was credited with originating "work
or fight" slogan to further war effort. Refused to call
spec. session of Gen. Assembly to consider ratification of
Women's Suffrage Amdt., which he opposed. Gave support to

enforcement of 18th Amdt., which was not popular in Md.
After tenure became mbr. of law firm, and set up and ran a
ferry line across Chesapeake Bay. Also became pres. of a
Cambridge bank. Hon. degree from St. John's Coll. Metho-
dist. m. in 1893 to Mary Gertrude Johnson, of Cambridge.
Two s.; one d. D. at Cambridge Dec. 15, 1945. Bur. in
Episcopal Church Cem. there.

RITCHIE, ALBERT CABELL (1920-1935). b. Aug. 29, 1876
in Richmond, Va. s. of Albert and Elizabeth Caskie (Cabell)
R. Father, who was a lawyer, served as judge and city solicitor in Baltimore and was a prof. of law at the Univ. of
Md. Mother was descendant of a distinguished family in Va.
Soon after son's birth the family moved to Baltimore, where
they resided thereafter. Attd. pvt. schools; Johns Hopkins
Univ., from which he was grad. in 1896; and the Univ. of Md.,
from which he received a law degree in 1898. Admitted to
bar and began practice in Baltimore with a firm with which
he continued to be assoc. until 1920. Asst. city solicitor
of Baltimore, 1903-1910. Apptd. prof. of law at the Univ.
of Md. in 1907. Asst. gen. counsel to Md. Pub. Service
Commn., 1910-1913, in which capacity he was successful in
securing lower utility rates, making him a popular figure.
El. Atty. Gen. of Md. in 1915, serving until 1920. During
World War I served as counsel to U.S. War Industries Bd.,
where he formed friendship with Bernard Baruch, who later
became his financial backer in efforts to win U.S. presidency. Nom. and el. Gov. as Dem. in 1919 in an extremely
close race against Harry W. Nice, who later defeated him in
another contest for the office. During admin., refused request of Pres. Harding to send militia to assist in preserving order during a protracted coal strike. Advocated more
pub. aid for educ.; road constr. program; opposed prohibition, refusing to give aid in its enforcement in the State;
and was strong defender of States' Rts. Secured implementation of extensive program of admin. reform and adoption of a
new mining code. Reel. in 1923, 1926, and 1930. A change
in election and term schedule caused his second term to be
for only three years. Received support of Md. delegation
and a few others in 1924 Dem. natl. conv. for Dem. nom. for
Pres. of U.S. In 1932 conv. was a major but unsuccessful
contender against F.D. Roosevelt for the Dem. nom. for Pres.
Refused to consider becoming a cand. for nom. for Vice Pres.
at that conv., which he might have obtained. Defeated for
reel. to office of Gov. for a fifth term in 1934. Defeat
left him bitter and depressed. Hon. degrees from the Univ.
of Md.; St. John's Coll.; Washington Coll.; Loyola Coll.,
of Baltimore. Mbr., Amer. Acad. of Political and Social
Sci.; various professional legal orgs. Episcopalian. m. in

1907 to Elizabeth Catherine Baker. Marriage ended in divorce in 1916. No children. D. suddenly Feb. 29, 1936 at
Baltimore. Bur. in Greenmount Cem. there.

NICE, HARRY WHINNA (1935-1939). b. Dec. 5, 1877 at
Washington, D.C. s. of the Rev. Henry and Drucilla (Arnold)
N. Father was a Methodist minister. Family moved to Baltimore, Md. when son was an infant. Attd. local pub. schools;
Baltimore City Coll.; Dickinson Coll.; and the Univ. of Md.,
from which he received a law degree in 1899. Began practice
in Baltimore. Unsuccessful as cand. for Md. House in 1899,
losing by margin of 21 votes. Mbr. of Baltimore city council, 1903-1905, winning election by 34 votes. Lost contest
for a judgeship post by 360 votes in 1903. Sect. to the
mayor of Baltimore, 1905-1908. Mbr. of bd. of elections
supervisors in Baltimore, 1908-1912. From 1912 to 1919 was
asst. State's atty. for Baltimore. Was nom. for Gov. as a
Rep. in 1919, but lost in gen. election to Albert C. Ritchie,
who continued in the office of Gov. for next 15 years.
Practiced law until 1935, also serving as mbr. of Baltimore
Tax Appeals Ct., 1920-1924. Nom. for Gov. as Rep. in 1934
and won in a very close election, defeating incumbent Gov.
Ritchie. As Gov., was confronted by opposition party in
control of Gen. Assembly, which was reluctant to follow his
recommendations on legislation. Prominently mentioned as
possible choice for Rep. nom. for Vice Pres. of U.S. at 1936
Rep. natl. conv., which he addressed. Nom. for second term
as Gov. in 1938 but lost in the gen. election. Unsuccessful cand. for U.S. Senate seat in 1940. Mbr. of various
professional legal orgs.; Kappa Sigma; Masons; K.P.; I.O.O.F.;
Elks; Moose; various clubs. Methodist. Hon. degrees from
Dickinson Coll.; the Univ. of Md.; Washington Coll.; St.
John's Coll. m. in 1905 to Edna Viola Amos, of Baltimore
and Atlanta, Ga. Two s. D. at Richmond, Va. Feb. 25, 1941
while on vacation trip to Fla. Bur. in Greenmount Cem.,
Baltimore.

O'CONOR, HERBERT ROMULUS (1939-1947). b. Nov. 17, 1896
at Baltimore, Md. s. of James P. and Mary A. (Galvin) O'C.
Attd. local parochial schools; Loyala Coll., of Baltimore,
from which he was grad. in 1917; and the Univ. of Md., from
which he received a law degree in 1920. Mbr. of USNR during
World War I. Worked as reporter for Baltimore Evening Sun
while attending college. Began law practice in Baltimore in
1920. Asst. State's atty., 1920-1922 and State's atty.,
Baltimore, 1923-1924. Successfully prosecuted a number of
murder suspects, which attracted wide pub. notice. Counsel
for Md. Pub. Service Commn. in 1923. Atty Gen. of Md.,
1935-1939. Promoted interstate compacts in field of law

enforcement, serving as ch. of Md. Interstate Compacts Commn.
Nom. and el. Gov. as Dem. over incumbent Gov. Nice in 1938
and was reel. in 1942. During admin., a legislative council
was created; annual sessions of the Gen. Assembly established; as "war Gov." during World War II, set up Council of
Defense and cooperated closely with U.S. and local govts.
against suspected subversives; loyalty oath legislation was
passed; taxes raised; Morgan Coll. made part of State system
of higher educ.; conservation of natural resources and improvements in med. aid system promoted. Mbr. of exec. commt.
of Natl. Govs.' Conf., 1940 and ch., 1942. Ch. of Council
of State Govts., 1943. Ch. of Interstate Commn. on Post-War
Reconstr. and Devel. in 1943-1945. El. to U.S. Senate in
1946 in very close election. Resigned office of Gov. a few
days before end of term to take U.S. Senate seat. In the
Senate, was very active in investigations and legislative
programs directed against suspected subversives. Opposed
St. Lawrence Seaway project and the establishment of Dulles
Intl. Airport. Was not a cand. for second term in 1952.
Practiced law and pursued bus. interests thereafter. Hon.
degrees from Loyala Coll.; the Univ. of Md.; Georgetown
Univ.; Washington Coll. Mbr., professional legal orgs.;
Amer. Legion; V.F.W.; Elks; K.C.; various social clubs.
Roman Catholic. m. in 1920 to Eugenia Byrnes. Five s.;
one d. D. at Baltimore March 4, 1960. Bur. in New Cathe-
dral Cem. there.

LANE, WILLIAM PRESTON, Jr. (1947-1951). b. May 12,
1892 at Hagerstown, Md. s. of Wm. Preston and Virginia Lee
(Cartwright) L. Descendant of a Provincial Gov. of Md.
Father was a lawyer. Attd. local pub. schools and the Univ.
of Va., from which he received law degree in 1915. Began
law practice in Hagerstown. Served as capt. of Md. militia
unit on Mexican border in 1916. Served with A.E.F. in France
during World War I, with rank of major. Recipient of Silver
Star. Resumed law practice in Hagerstown. Became publ. of
two newspapers in Hagerstown, the Herald and the Mail. Unsuccessful as cand. for State's atty. of Washington Co. in
1919. Mbr., bd. of educ. of Washington Co., 1928. Delegate
to Dem. natl. convs. in 1924, 1928, and 1932. El. Atty.
Gen. of Md. in 1930. As Atty. Gen., received wide notice
when he unsuccessfully prosecuted nine individuals who had
participated in lynching of a Negro suspected of raping a
White woman. Was himself threatened with lynching, and
militia forces were used to preserve order during trial.
Resumed law practice in Hagerstown in 1935. Acquired bus.
interests in banking and loan, bridge constr. and airplane
mfg. fields. Pres. elector on Roosevelt ticket in 1944.
Mbr., Md. tax revision study commn., 1938. Mbr., Dem. natl.

commt. until 1950. Mgr. of Pres. Roosevelt's Md. campaign
in 1944. Nom. for Gov. by Dem. delegate conv. in 1946, although he received fewer popular votes in the party primary
than his opponent, and was subsequently el. Took office a
few days before term began, being el. by the Gen. Assembly
to fill out the term of his predecessor, Gov. O'Conor, who
had resigned to go to the U.S. Senate. As Gov., vigorously
enforced anti-subversives laws, and carried out extensive
pub. works program, necessitating a sales tax increase.
Pres. of So. Govs.' Conf. in 1948 and ch. of Council of
State Govts. Mbr., White House Commn. on Educ. and of Bd.
of Visitors for U.S. Naval Acad. Considered as possible
nominee for Vice Pres. of U.S. in Dem. natl. conv. in 1948,
but withdrew from consideration after strong civil rights
plank was adopted by the conv. Re-nom. for Gov. in 1950, but
was defeated in gen. election. Mbr., Eagles; Elks; Amer.
Legion; Moose. Trustee, Johns Hopkins Univ. Episcopalian.
Hon. degree from the Univ. of Md. m. to Dorothy Byron, of
Hagerstown. Two d. D. at Hagerstown Feb. 7, 1967. Bur.
in Rose Hill Cem. there.

McKELDIN, THEODORE ROOSEVELT (1951-1959). b. Nov. 20,
1900 in South Baltimore, Md. One of eleven children of
James Alfred and Dora (Grief) McK. Father was a stonemason,
later a policeman, and was of Scotch-Irish descent. Mother
was of German ancestry. Attd. local pub. schools, working
as an office boy and grave-digger while attending h.s. Attd.
the Univ. of Md., from which he was grad. with a law degree
in 1925. Also studied economics at Johns Hopkins Univ. Began law practice in Baltimore. Served as exec. sect. to
mayor of Baltimore, 1927-1931. Unsuccessful cand. for mayor
in 1939. Nom. as Rep. cand. for Gov. in 1942, but was defeated. Mayor of Baltimore in 1943-1947. As mayor, advocated improved mun. services in water supply, health, slum
clearance and charter reform fields. Defeated again as Rep.
nominee for Gov. in 1946. Was Rep. nominee again in 1950
and was el., defeating incumbent Gov. Lane. Initiated desegregation of state-owned beaches and parks and pub. trans-
portation. Began extensive pub. works program, including
belt-ways around Baltimore and Washington, D.C. Opposed
lobbying by dept. heads; supported county home rule. Mbr.
of advisory commt. on Inter-govtl. Relations of Natl. Govs.'
Conf. and of So. Govs.' Conf. Used veto freely as Gov.
Noted for oratorical skill. Made nominating speech for Gen.
Eisenhower at Rep. natl. conv. in 1952. Was seriously considered there for nom. for Vice Pres. of U.S., but was
passed over because he was regarded as too liberal by some
elements of the party org. Rep. natl. commt. mbr. from Md.,
1952-1960. El. mayor of Baltimore again in 1963. As such,

advocated adoption of a city civil rights ordinance. Supported L.B. Johnson for Pres. of U.S. in 1964. Conducted
classes as lecturer at the Univ. of Baltimore Law School,
Baltimore Coll. of Commerce, and Forest Park Evening School.
Jt. author of The Art of Eloquence in 1956; author of Washington Bowed in 1956 and of No Mean City in 1964. Active in
numerous civic orgs. and endeavors. Hon. degrees from eight
colleges and universities, and recipient of many awards, including five Freedom Found. Awards; Intl. Youths' Distinguished Service Citation; Man of the Year Award; N.C.C.J.
Citation; and Sydney Hollander Fund Award. Mbr. of commt.
of 22 apptd. to observe elections in Vietnam in 1967. Mbr.,
Masons (Shriner; K.T.; O.E.S.); Elks; I.O.O.F.; T.C.L.;
Kiwanis; Omicron Delta Kappa; Sigma Phi Epsilon; various
professional legal orgs. Episcopalian. Active in Sunday
School work of church. m. in 1924 to Honolulu Claire Manzer.
One s.; one d. D. at Baltimore Aug. 9, 1974.

TAWES, J(OHN) MILLARD (1959-1967). b. April 8, 1894 at
Crisfield, Md. s. of James B. and Alice (Byrd) T. Father
was a prominent businessman of the community. Attd. local
pub. schools; Wilmington Conf. Acad., at Dover, Del.; and a
bus. coll. in Buffalo, N.Y. Joined father in his shipping
and packing bus. Later became involved in ship-building,
banking, and baking enterprises. Clerk of ct. of Somerset
Co., 1930-1938. Md. Comptroller of Treas., 1938-1946. Defeated as cand. for Dem. nom. for Gov. in 1946. State Banking Commnr., 1947-1950. Comptroller of Treas. again, serving from 1950 to 1958. Nom. and el. Gov. as Dem. in 1958,
and again in 1962. During admin., Md. joined the Metropolitan Transit Authority of D.C. area and became a mbr. of
Interstate Oil Compact org. As Gov., supported improvements
in higher educ. programs; elimination by law of slot ma-
chines; assembled a conf. of Govs. of Appalachian States to
study and develop programs to deal with depressed living
conditions in mountain areas of the East. Apptd. constl.
study commn. in prearation for holding State constl. conv.
in 1967, of which he became hon. pres. Approved legislation
barring segregation practices in places of pub. accommodation. Delegate to Dem. natl. conv. in 1968. Pres., Md.
State Firemen's Assoc. Mbr., Bd. of Trustees of Dickinson
Coll. and of Wesley Jr. Coll., of Dover, Del. Mbr., Assoc.
of State Auditors, Comptrollers and Treasurers; Masons
(O.E.S.); Elks; K.P.: Md. Soc. of Pa. Dir. of McCready Hosp.,
at Crisfield. Hon. degrees from four colleges and universities. Methodist. m. in 1915 to Helen Avalynne Gibson, of
Crisfield. One s.; one d. D. June 25, 1979.

AGNEW, SPIRO THEODORE (1967-1969). b. Nov. 9, 1918 at
Baltimore, Md. s. of Theodore S. and Margaret (Akers) A.
Father was a Greek immigrant who came to Amer. in 1897 at
age 21 and later engaged in restaurant bus. Father changed
family name from Anagnostopoulous to Angew after arriving in
this country. Mother was born in Va. Attd. local pub.
schools and entered Johns Hopkins Univ. After three years
transferred to the Univ. of Baltimore Law School. Attd.
night classes while working as a clerk in ins. firm. Served
with U.S. Army in Western Europe, 1944-1945, holding rank of
capt. when discharged. Decorated with Bronze Star, four
Battle Stars, Combat Infantry Badge. Finished law school
training and began practice in Towson, Md. in 1947, soon
afterward moving to Baltimore. Apptd. to Baltimore zoning
appeals bd. in 1957, serving until 1961. Shifted party allegiance from Dem. to Rep. Unsuccessful cand. for cir. ct.
judgeship in 1962. El. executive of Baltimore Co. in 1962.
During admin., Baltimore Co. adopted an anti-discrimination
pub. accommodations ordinance and inaugurated constr. of a
new water supply and sewer system. Nom. for Gov. as Rep. in
1966 and was el., defeating an opponent who was a strong
segregationist. During admin., a revised Md. const. was
drafted by a conv., but it was rejected by the voters. A
graduated state income tax was adopted, along with an open
housing law, and legislation improving conditions for migrant workers passed. As admin. progressed he became critical of moderate Negro leaders for not condemning actions of
militants who engaged in activities inviting violence. Opposed "poor people's march," and insisted on strict maintenance of pub. order. At Rep. natl. conv. in 1968 gave sec-
onding speech for Richard Nixon as the party's nominee for
Pres. of U.S., and was selected as Rep. cand. for Vice Pres.
of U.S. on ticket with Nixon. After election to that office
resigned as Gov. in Jan., 1969. As Vice Pres., carried on
an increasingly bitter feud with the "liberal" press, which
characterized him as an ineffectual bumbler and ultra-con-
servative. Nom. and reel. Vice Pres. in 1972. Resigned office of Vice Pres. on Oct. 10, 1973 after charges of fraud
were brought against him in connection with his failure to
report for U.S. tax purposes funds received as alleged "kick-
backs" from contractors during his tenure as exec. of Baltimore Co. and Gov. of Md. He pleaded nolo contendere to the
charges, and was fined $10,000 and given a suspended prison
sentence. Engaged in various ventures as a bus. repr. and
agent thereafter. Hon. degrees from the Univ. of Md.;
Morgan State Coll.; Ohio State Univ.; Loyola Coll., of Baltimore. Mbr., professional legal orgs.; Amer. Legion; Kiwanis; AHEPA. Episcopalian. m. in 1942 to Elinor Isabel
Judefind. Three d.; one s.

MANDEL, MARVIN (1969-1979). b. April 19, 1920 in Bal-
timore, Md. s. of Harry and Rebecca (Cohen) M. Father
worked as a cutter in a clothing mgf. firm. Attd. local pub.
schools; Baltimore City Coll.; Johns Hopkins Univ.; and the
Univ. of Md., from which he received a law degree in 1942.
Served in U.S. Army at Aberdeen Proving Ground, 1942-1944.
Began law practice in Baltimore. Justice of the peace, 1950
and mbr. of Gov.'s commn. on a mun. ct. for Baltimore, 1951.
Mbr. of Dem. state commt., 1951, later becoming ch. Mbr.,
Md. House, 1952-1969, serving as Speaker, 1964-1969. Delegate to Dem. natl. conv., 1968. El. Gov. by Gen. Assembly
in Jan., 1969 to complete term of Gov. Agnew, who had resigned to become Vice Pres. of U.S. Was the first person of
Jewish faith to hold the office. El. for a full term as Dem.
in 1970 and was reel. in 1974. During second term was indicted by a Fed. grand jury along with five others on charge
of conspiracy to commit fraud by receiving financial favors
in return for influence in connection with a bill to regulate race track operations in Md. First trial resulted in a
mistrial because of alleged improper influence on trial jury.
When second trial was under way, he requested that, because
of his poor health and upset condition, his powers and duties
as Gov. be assumed by the Lieut. Gov., Blair Lee. Lee assumed the role of acting Gov. on June 4, 1977. M. was found
guilty, along with his codefendants, in Aug., 1977 and was
given a four-year prison sentence. His conviction had the
effect of suspending him from office, pending the outcome of
any appeal, but on advice of his atty. he did not resign the
office of Gov. In Jan., 1979, his conviction was overturned
by a U.S. Ct. of Appeals shortly before the end of his term.
Declaring his disability to have ended, he resumed the office of Gov. and served the last three days of his term.
His conviction was subsequently upheld by U.S. Supreme Ct.,
however. Hon. degrees from six colleges and universities.
Mbr. of professional legal orgs.; Amer. Legion; J.W.V. (past
state ch.). m. in 1941 to Barbara Oberfell, of Baltimore.
One s.; one d. Marriage ended in divorce in 1974, attended
by much bitterness. m. for second time immediately after
his divorce in 1974 to Mrs. Jeanne Blackstone Dorsey.

HANCOCK, JOHN (1780-1785; 1787-1793). b. Jan. 12, 1737 at Braintree (now Quincy), Mass. s. of John and Mary (Hawke) H. Father was a Congregational minister. Father died when son was 7 years old. Was brought up thereafter by an uncle, Thomas, who was a merchant of considerable wealth. Attd. Harvard, from which he was grad. in 1754. Joined uncle's bus. firm as a clerk and was sent to England on a bus. mission in 1760. Following uncle's death in 1764, inherited his estate and became one of the wealthiest men in Mass. Served as selectman in Boston for many years. Mbr. of the Provincial Gen. Ct., 1766-1772, where he became a leader in vigorous opposition to British colonial trade and taxation policies. Mbr. of Provincial Assembly which met in 1774 in defiance of Gen. Gage's orders, and became Pres. of its Exec. Council. Along with Samuel Adams, was one of the revolutionary leaders not included in Gen. Gage's pardon, and his and Adams' arrest became one of the objects of the British mil. expedition to Concord in 1775 that resulted in the opening battle of the Rev. War. Mbr. of Contl. Cong., 1775-1777. Was serving as its presiding officer when the Dec. of Indep. was adopted in 1776, and was a signer of it. Major gen. of Mass. militia during Rev. War, and mbr. of Mass. Exec. Council. Pres. of Mass. constl. conv. in 1779. El. first Gov. of Mass. in 1780. Reel. for each of the four following years. Resigned office at end of Jan., 1785. Chosen as Pres. of the Contl. Cong. in 1785-1786, but did not serve because of illness. El. Gov. again in 1787, continuing to serve by annual reel. until his death. Pres. of Mass. conv. that ratified the U.S. Const. As Gov., resisted attempts by U.S. cts. to assert jurisdiction over cases involving Mass. Received four electoral votes for Pres. (or Vice Pres.) of U.S. in first pres. election under the Const. m. to Dorothy Quincy, of Boston, in 1775. One s., who died in youth. Hon. degrees from Harvard, Yale, Brown and Princeton. Gave extensive benevolences late in life, especially to Harvard. D. at Quincy, Oct. 8, 1793. Bur. in Old Granary Cem., Boston.

CUSHING, THOMAS (1785). b. March 24, 1725 at Boston, Mass. s. of Thomas and Mary (Bromfield) C. Father was a prominent community leader and businessman of Boston, who had served as Speaker of the Provincial Assembly. Attd. Boston Latin School and Harvard, from which he was grad. in 1744. Became a merchant. Also studied law and served as a judge. Mbr. of Provincial Gen. Ct., 1761-1774, serving as Speaker, 1766-1774. Was one of the leaders in resistance to British colonial policies that resulted in Rev. War. Mbr. of Contl. Cong. in 1774 and 1776. Commissary Gen. of

Mass. in 1775. Declined election to Contl. Cong. in 1779.
El. Lieut. Gov. under first Mass. const. in 1780, and continued in that office by reel. until 1788. Succeeded to
office of Gov. at beginning of Feb., 1785, when Gov.
Hancock resigned, and completed Hancock's term, which had
about three months to run. Was one of two highest in popular voting for Gov. that year, and his name was submitted
to Senate as one of two in final step of election process,
but his opponent, James Bowdoin, was chosen Gov. Delegate
to the Mass. conv. that ratified U.S. Const. in 1788. One
of founders of Acad. of Arts and Sciences in 1780. Hon.
degrees from Harvard and Yale. Mbr. of Bd. of Overseers of
Harvard. D. at Boston, Feb. 28, 1788, while continuing to
serve as Lieut. Gov. Survived by several children. Bur.
in Old Granary Cem.

BOWDOIN, JAMES (1785-1787). b. Aug. 8 (7?), 1727
(1726?) at Boston, Mass. s. of James and Hannah (Pordage)
B. Grandson of French physician, Pierre Baudoin, a
Huguenot who fled from France to Ireland in 1680s following
the revocation of the Edict of Nantes. Family later emigrated to Falmouth, Mass. (now Me.) in 1687, having acquired extensive land holdings there. Father moved family to
Boston in 1690, shortly before an Indian massacre destroyed
the settlement where they had been residing. Attd. Harvard,
from which he was grad. in 1745. Two years later he inherited a considerable estate following father's death.
Devoted much time to literary and scientific pursuits, becoming a frequent correspondent with Benj. Franklin. Mbr.
of Provincial Gen. Ct., 1753-1756. Mbr. of Govs.' Council
in 1756. Apptd. as delegate to First Contl. Cong. of 1774,
but did not attend because of wife's illness. Became pres.
of Exec. Council of the pro-revolutionary govt. in Mass. in
1775, serving until 1780. Pres. of Mass. constl. conv. in
1779. Chosen Gov. of Mass. over Lieut. Gov. Cushing in
1785. Reel. in 1786. During admin., found it necessary to
use militia forces against followers of Daniel Shays, who
were resisting authority of the state govt. in protest
against taxation and property seizure policies occasioned
by post-Rev. War economic distress. Used own funds and
contributions from wealthy friends in part to finance mil.
expedition, which he led in person against the resisters.
Mbr. of Mass. conv. that ratified the U.S. Const. in 1788.
Fellow of Harvard Corp., 1779-1784, to which he made generous financial contributions. First pres. of Amer. Acad. of
Arts and Sciences, which he helped found in 1780. Founder
of Humane Soc. of Mass., and first pres. of Mass. Bank.
Hon. degree from the Univ. of Edinburgh and Fellow of Royal

Soc. of London and of Dublin. Contributor of sci. and
literary articles to periodicals. m. to Elizabeth Erving
(Ewing?), of Boston. One s., who became U.S. Minister to
Spain, and donated some 6,000 acres of land and other gifts
to help found Bowdoin Coll., in Me. D. Nov. 6, 1790, in
Boston.

HANCOCK, JOHN (1787-1793). See above, 1780-1785.

ADAMS, SAMUEL (1793-1797). b. Sept. 27, 1722 in
Boston, Mass. s. of Samuel A., a prosperous malt manufacturer and businessman who had served in Mass. Provincial
Assembly. Descendant of ancestor who had emigrated from
England to Mass. in 1636. As a boy was very precocious.
Grad. from Harvard in 1740. Studied law and received an
M.A. degree from Harvard in 1743, writing a thesis on the
legality of resistance to magistrates. Worked for a time
in merc. firm of Thomas Cushing. Inherited estate from
father, with whom he had been assoc. in malt bus., but the
enterprise declined and eventually failed when he preferred
to devote major attention to political affairs. Collector
of taxes for Boston, 1756-1764. Was charged with failure
to settle accounts with city, but charges were later dismissed. Mbr. of Provincial Gen. Ct., 1765-1774, serving as
clerk from 1766 onward. Wrote numerous articles and pamphlets attacking British taxation policies from 1765 onward.
Helped form Sons of Liberty and commts. of correspondence
to further resistance effort. Mbr. of first Contl. Cong.
of 1774, where he sponsored resolutions critical of British
policies and urging boycott against British imports. Mbr.
of Mass. revolutionary Exec. Council of 1774. Mbr. of
Contl. Cong., 1775-1782, becoming a signer of Dec. of Indep.
in 1776. Mbr. of conv. that framed first const. for Mass.
Pres. of Mass. Senate in 1781. Supported Gov. Bowdoin's
use of force against Shays' insurrection. Mbr. of Mass.
conv. that ratified U.S. Const. in 1788, which he supported
with reservations. Defeated as cand. for U.S. House in
first election under the Const. El. Lieut. Gov. in 1789,
continuing in that office until he succeeded to office of
Gov. in 1793, following death of Gov. Hancock. El. Gov.
for succeeding three terms. As Gov., was critical of Jay
Treaty with Great Britain. m. first to Elizabeth Checkly,
of Boston. One s.; one d. After first wife's death in
1757, m. in 1764 to Elizabeth Wells. D. at Boston, Oct. 2,
1803. Bur. in Old Granary Cem., Boston.

SUMNER, INCREASE (1797-1799). b. Nov. 27, 1746 at
Roxbury, Mass. s. of Increase and Sarah (Sharp) S. Father

was a prosperous farmer. Attd. local schools and Harvard,
from which he was grad. in 1767. Managed local school for
three years. Studied law, was admitted to bar and began
practice in Roxbury, in which he proved successful. Mbr.
of Mass. Assembly, 1776-1780. Mbr. of bodies that framed
the first Mass. const. in 1777 and 1779. Apptd. as delegate
to Contl. Cong. in 1782, but did not serve, having been chosen in the meantime as mbr. of Mass. Supreme Ct. Mbr. of
Mass. conv. that ratified U.S. Const. in 1788. Defeated as
Fed. party cand. for Gov. in 1796, but was nom. and el. Gov.
as a Fed. in 1797. Reel. in 1798 and 1799. His admin.
marked the beginning of rivalry in Mass. between Fed. and
Jeff. Rep. parties for control of govt. Was seriously ill
when el. for last term, and died in office some two months
after term began. m. in 1779 to Elizabeth Hyslop, of
Brookline, Mass. One s.; two d. D. June 7, 1799.

GILL, MOSES (1799-1800). b. Jan. 18, 1734 at
Charlestown, Mass. Engaged in bus. at Princeton, Mass.,
and became a supporter of Amer. cause when Rev. War began.
El. Lieut. Gov. in 1794, and continued to serve in that office by reel. until 1799. Succeeded to office of Gov. in
June, 1799, when Gov. Sumner died. He himself died while
acting as Gov. on May 20, 1800, a few days before the end
of the term for which Sumner had been el. There was no
provision in the Mass. const. at that time for succession
beyond the office of Lieut. Gov., but popular voting had
already occurred on choice of a new Gov. Thomas Dawes, as
Pres. of the Exec. Council, and other mbrs. of the Council,
acted in exec. matters for some ten days until the election
results of 1800 were ascertained and proclaimed, and the
newly-chosen Gov., Caleb Strong, was installed in office.
D. May 20, 1800.

STRONG, CALEB (1800-1807; 1812-1816). b. Jan. 9, 1745
at Northampton, Mass. s. of Caleb and Phoebe (Lyman) S.
Descendant of John Strong, who emigrated from England to
Mass. Bay colony in 1630. Educ. by tutors and at Harvard,
from which he was grad. with highest honors in 1764. Studied law, admitted to bar, and began practice in 1772. As
Rev. War approached, supported Amer. cause. Mbr. of Mass.
Commt. of Safety, 1774-1775. Mbr. of Mass. Assembly, 1776-
1778. Co. atty., 1776-1780. Mbr. of Mass. conv. that
drafted first state const. in 1779. Mbr. of Mass. Senate,
1780-1788, and was author of an address from Mass. govt. to
Shays' insurgents in 1786 requesting them to desist from
use of armed force. Delegate to U.S. Constl. Conv. of 1787,
and was a mbr. of Mass. conv. that ratified U.S. Const.

Declined apptmt. to Mass. Supreme Ct. in 1781. El. as one
of first two U.S. Senators from Mass. in 1789, serving until he resigned in June, 1796. As mbr. of Senate, affiliated with Fed. party when party lines became drawn. El.
Gov. as a Fed. in 1800, and continued in office by annual
election until 1807, when he was defeated as cand. for
eighth term. Pres. elector on the Fed. ticket in 1808 pres.
election. El. Gov. again in 1812 in a very close contest,
and continued in office for next three terms. During the
War of 1812, which he opposed, refused to cooperate with
Pres. Madison's admin. in supplying militia forces for U.S.
service. Supported Hartford Conv. anti-war resolutions in
1814. Pres. of Hampshire Missionary Soc.; Fellow of Amer.
Acad. of Arts and Sci.; mbr. of Mass. Historical Soc. Hon.
degree from Harvard. Author of published speeches, addresses and pamphlets on political topics. m. in 1777 to Sarah
Hooker, of Northampton. Nine children. D. at Northampton,
Nov. 7, 1819. Bur. in Bridge St. Cem. there.

SULLIVAN, JAMES (1807-1808). b. April 22, 1744 at
Berwick, Dist. of Me. (Mass.). s. of John and Margery
(Brown) S. Family, which was of Irish descent, had supported Irish Catholic cause against Wm. of Orange in 1690s.
Father emigrated to Amer. in 1723, where children were
brought up in Protestant faith. An older brother, John,
became a major gen. in the Contl. Army during the Rev. War,
and was a Gov. (Pres.) of N.H. (q.v.). As a youth was
lamed in an accident while felling a tree. Received common
school educ. Studied law with older brother, John, in
Berwick. Established practice at Biddeford, Dist. of Me.,
in which he proved successful. King's atty. for York Co.
As Rev. War neared, supported the Amer. cause. Mbr. of
Mass. Assembly, 1774-1776. Superior ct. judge, 1776-1782.
Mbr. of Mass. constl. conv. of 1779. Delegate to U.S.
Cong., 1782. Mbr. of commn. to define N.Y.-Mass. boundary,
1784. Mbr. of Mass. Exec. Council, 1787. Judge of probate,
Suffolk Co., 1788. Atty. Gen. of Mass., 1790-1807. As
such, advocated placing his office on a salaried, rather
than a fee basis. Prosecuted a number of murder trials that
attracted much pub. attention. Opposed establishment of
First U.S. Bank; favored French Rev. cause after that became
an issue in U.S. in 1790s. After natl. party lines began to
form, affiliated with the Jeff. Rep. party, and was a pres.
elector for Jefferson in 1804 pres. election. Defeated as
the Jeff. Rep. cand. for Gov. in 1804, 1805 and 1806, but
was el. Gov. in 1807, defeating incumbent Gov. Strong.
Reel. in 1808. Was an original mbr. of Mass. Historical
Soc. Mbr. of Amer. Acad. of Arts and Sci. Published a

number of writings on political and literary subjects. Hon.
degree from Harvard in 1780. m. in 1768 to Hetty Odiorne,
of Durham, Dist. of Me. Several s. m. for second time to
Martha Langdon, sister of John Langdon, Gov. (Pres.) of N.H.
(q.v.). D. at Boston, Dec. 10, 1808, while still in office
as Gov. Bur. in Cent. Boston Commons Cem.

LINCOLN, LEVI, Sr. (1808-1809). b. May 15, 1749 at
Hingham, Mass. s. of Enoch and Rachel (Fearing) L. Descendant of Samuel L., who emigrated from England to Mass.
Bay colony in 1637. Father was a farmer. Attd. Harvard,
from which he was grad. in 1772, intending to become a minister. Changed objective to law after hearing a case argued by John Adams, and studied law in office in
Northampton, Mass. Began practice in Worcester in 1775.
Became prominent in movement to abolish slavery in Mass.
As Rev. War approached, joined in opposition to British
policies, becoming mbr. of local commts. of correspondence
and commt. of pub. safety. Author of Farmer's Letters in
early stage of conflict, in which he advocated indep. from
Britain. Served as co. atty., clerk of ct., and probate
judge, 1775-1781. Mbr. of Mass. constl. conv. of 1779.
Apptd. as delegate to Contl. Cong. in 1781, but did not
serve. Mbr. of Mass. House, 1796, and of Mass. Senate,
1797-1798. El. to U.S. House in 1800 to fill vacancy and
then for a regular term. Served from Dec., 1800, to March
5, 1801, resigning seat to become U.S. Atty. Gen. at beginning of Pres. Jefferson's admin. Also was Acting U.S. Sect.
of State for approximately two months at beginning of
Jefferson's admin. Resigned as Atty. Gen. at the end of
1804. Mbr. of Mass. Exec. Council in 1806, 1810 and 1811.
El. Lieut. Gov. in 1807 and again in 1808. Succeeded to
office of Gov. in Dec., 1808, following death of Gov.
Sullivan, and completed Sullivan's term. Declined apptmt.
as mbr. of U.S. Supreme Ct. by Pres. Madison in 1811 because
of failing eyesight. Spent final years on farm near
Worcester. Engaged in literary pursuits. Was an original
mbr. of Amer. Acad. of Arts and Sci.; mbr., Mass. Historical
Soc. m. in 1781 to Martha Waldo. Nine children. One of
his sons, Levi, Jr., became Gov. of Mass. (q.v.), and another, Enoch, Gov. of Me. (q.v.). D. at Worcester, April
14, 1820. Bur. in Rural Cem. near there.

GORE, CHRISTOPHER (1809-1810). b. Sept. 21, 1758 at
Boston, Mass. s. of John G., a mechanic, who was a Loyal-
ist at outbreak of Rev. War, and who was forced to leave
Boston to go to Halifax, N.S., when British evacuated
Boston in 1776. Father was banished from Mass. until 1787,

when his Amer. citizenship was restored. Received a good
educ., graduating from Harvard in 1776. Studied law and began practice in Boston. His practice proved lucrative.
One of the clerks who studied law in his office was Daniel
Webster. Mbr. of Mass. constl. conv. in 1779, and of Mass.
House in 1788-1789. Apptd. U.S. dist. atty. for Mass. in
1789, serving until 1796. One of three U.S. commnrs. sent
to England in 1796 to negotiate war claims. Remained abroad
for several years, serving as Amer. chargé d' affaires in
London, 1803-1804. Mbr. of Mass. Senate, 1806-1808. El.
Gov. as a Fed. in 1809. Defeated for Gov. in 1810 and 1811.
Apptd. to U.S. Senate by Gov. Strong in May, 1813, to fill
vacancy and was el. to serve remainder of term. Resigned
seat in 1816. Pres. elector on Fed. ticket in 1816 pres.
election. Retired thereafter to country estate in Waltham,
Mass., where he lived in rather ostentatious style. Overseer of Harvard Univ., 1810-1815, and Harvard Fellow, 1812-
1820. No children. Left substantial bequests to Harvard.
D. March 1, 1827, at Waltham. Bur. in Old Granary Cem.,
Boston.

      GERRY, ELBRIDGE (1810-1812). b. July 17, 1744 at
Marblehead, Mass. s. of Thomas and Elizabeth (Greenleaf) G.
Father was a merchant who had emigrated from England to
Mass. in 1730. Attd. Harvard, from which he was grad. in
1762. Joined father in bus., which prospered. Mbr. of
Mass. Provincial Assembly, 1772-1775. Supported Amer.
cause during Rev. War. Mbr. of Mass. Commt. of Pub. Safety
in 1775. Narrowly escaped capture by British in 1775 at
Cambridge. Mbr. of Contl. Cong., 1776-1781 and 1782-1785,
and was one of the signers of the Dec. of Indep. Mbr. of
U.S. Constl. Conv. in 1787, where he had a leading role.
Eventually opposed the completed document and refused to
sign it because he felt powers of the Pres. and Cong. were
too great. Published a pamphlet criticizing it and opposing ratification by Mass. El. to first U.S. House in 1788
and again in 1790. Became identified with anti-Fed. element there after parties began to form. Apptd. by Pres.
John Adams, along with C. C. Pinckney and John Marshall, as
a commnr. to negotiate settlement of disputes with the
French Rev. govt. in 1798, and became involved in the "XYZ
Affair" which threatened to bring on war with France. Remained in France as U.S. repr. until the difficulty was resolved. Defeated as cand. of the Jeff. Rep. party for Gov.
each year, 1800-1803. Nom. and el. Gov. as a Jeff. Rep. in
1810 and again in 1811. His rather arbitrary and partisan
methods aroused antagonism of political opponents. A
partisanly-biased plan he helped devise for redistricting

of legislative seats came to be associated with his name in
the term "gerrymander". Was rather straight-laced on matters of social morality and conduct, being opposed to the
theater, horse-racing, etc. Unpopularity in Mass. of policies of Pres. Madison's admin. which eventuated in the War
of 1812 caused his defeat for reel. in 1812. Nom. and el.
Vice Pres. of U.S. in 1812 pres. election. m. to Ann
Thompson, who survived until 1849. Three s.; four d. A
grandson of the same name was a mbr. of the U.S. House from
Me., 1849-1851, and a great-grandson, Peter Goelet G., was
a U.S. House mbr., 1913-1915, and a U.S. Senator, 1917-1929
and 1939-1947, from R.I. Mbr. of Acad. of Arts and Sci.
D. Nov. 14, 1814, during second year of tenure as Vice Pres.
of U.S. Bur. in Congressional Cem., Washington, D.C.

STRONG, CALEB (1812-1816). See above, 1800-1807.

BROOKS, JOHN (1816-1823). b. May 31, 1752 at Medford,
Mass. s. of Capt. Caleb and Ruth (Albree) B. Father was a
farmer. Attd. local schools while assisting on family farm.
Became a med. apprentice with Dr. Tufts, a local doctor, at
age 14, ultimately engaging in med. practice at Reading,
Mass. Also showed a natural aptitude for mil. matters.
Org. a company of minutemen as Rev. War approached. Supported Amer. cause and participated in Rev. War as an officer, holding rank of major at end of the war. Participated
in Battle of Lexington and other important engagements in
N.Y. and N.J. Apptd. major gen. of Mass. militia at the
conclusion of Rev. War. Mbr. of Mass. conv. that ratified
U.S. Const., which he favored. Mbr. of Mass. House, 1785-
1786, and of the Mass. Senate, 1791. Also served as mbr.
of the Mass. Exec. Council. U.S. marshal of his dist. and
inspector of revenues in 1795. Offered commn. as brig. gen.
in U.S. Army in 1798 as war with France was threatened, but
declined. Adjt. gen. of Mass. militia, 1812-1815. El. Gov.
as a Fed. in 1816 and for six succeeding annual terms. Retired from pub. life in 1823 after completing tenure as Gov.
and engaged in farming at Reading. Mbr. and pres. of Mass.
Med. Soc.; Soc. of Cincinnati; Washington Monument Soc.;
Bunker Hill Monument Soc.; Mass. Bible Soc. M.D. and hon.
degree from Harvard. m. in 1774 to Lucy Smith. Two s.,
one of whom lost his life while serving as a U.S. naval officer during the Battle of Lake Erie in 1813. D. March 2,
1825, at Medford, Mass.

EUSTIS, WILLIAM (1823-1825). b. June 10, 1753 at
Cambridge, Mass. s. of Benj. and Elizabeth (Hill) E. Father was a prominent physician. Attd. Boston pub. schools

and Harvard, from which he was grad. in 1772. Studied med.
in office of Dr. Joseph Warren and began med. practice in
Boston. Apptd. regimental surgeon for a Mass. militia unit
when Rev. War began, and served during the war as a med.
officer. Resumed practice in Boston at end of Rev. War.
Served as surgeon in Mass. militia during Shays' Rebellion,
1786-1787. Mbr. of Mass. Gen. Ct., 1788-1794. El. to U.S.
House in 1800 as a Jeff. Rep., and continued to serve until
1805. Defeated for reel. in 1804. Was one of House mgrs.
during impeachment trial of Judge Pickering. Apptd. U.S.
Sect. of War by Pres. Madison in 1809, and served until
Dec., 1812, when he resigned. Apptd. U.S. Minister to
Holland in Dec., 1814, serving until May, 1818. El. to U.S.
House as a Jeff. Rep. in 1820, but did not seek second term
in 1822. Defeated as a Jeff. Rep. nominee for Gov. in 1820,
1821 and 1822. Nom. and el. Gov. in 1823, however, and was
reel. in 1824. Vice pres., Soc. of Cincinnati. Hon. degrees from Harvard in 1784 and 1823. m. to Carolyn
Woodbury Langton, of Portsmouth, N.H. in 1810. D. Feb. 6,
1825 during course of second term as Gov. Bur. in Old
Burying Ground, Lexington, Mass.

  MORTON, MARCUS (1825; 1840-1841; 1843-1844). b. Feb.
19, 1784 at Freetown, Bristol Co., Mass. s. of Nathaniel
and Mary (Cary) M. Attd. Brown Univ., from which he was
grad. in 1804. Studied law at Judge Reeves' Litchfield,
Conn. law school. Admitted to bar and began practice at
Taunton, Mass. in 1807. Clerk of Mass. Senate, 1811. El.
to U.S. House as a Jeff. Rep. in 1816. Continued in that
office until 1821, being defeated for reel. in 1820. Mbr.
of Mass. Exec. Council in 1823. El. Lieut. Gov. as a Jeff.
Rep. in 1824. Succeeded to office of Gov. when Gov. Eustis
died in Feb., 1825, and completed the term for which Eustis
had been el. Apptd. to Mass. Supreme Ct. in 1825, serving
until 1839. Defeated as cand. of pro-Jackson wing of Jeff.
Rep. party for Gov. in 1828, 1829, 1830 and 1831. Defeated
as cand. of Dem. party for a second time in 1831, there
being two elections that year because of a change in the
election and term schedule. Was defeated as the Dem. cand.
for Gov. each year from 1832 through 1838. Was the Dem.
cand. again in 1839, and was el. Gov., defeating incumbent
Gov. Everett by a popular majority of one vote. Defeated
as Dem. cand. for Gov. in 1840 and 1841; but in 1842 was el.
Gov. by Mass. Senate as one of two persons referred to the
Senate when no cand. received a popular majority. Defeated
as Dem. cand. for Gov. in another election in 1843 that had
to be resolved by the Mass. Senate. Altogether, he appeared before the voters of Mass. as a cand. for Gov. on 17

occasions, and was el. to the office in two of those elections. Apptd. U.S. collector of the port of Boston by Pres.
Polk in 1845, serving until 1848. Changed affiliation to
the Free Soil party that year. Delegate to Mass. constl.
conv. in 1853. Mbr. of Mass. House in 1858. Mbr. of Bd.
of Overseers of Harvard, 1826-1852 and 1854-1860. Hon. degree from Harvard in 1840. m. to Charlotte Hodges in 1812.
Twelve children. A son, Marcus, became a mbr. of Mass.
Supreme Ct. D. at Taunton, Mass., Feb. 6, 1864. Bur. in
Mt. Pleasant Cem. there.

LINCOLN, LEVI, Jr. (1825-1834). b. Oct. 25, 1782 at
Worcester, Mass. s. of Levi L., Sr., who was a Gov. of
Mass. (q.v.) and Martha (Waldo) L. Was a brother of Enoch
L., a Gov. of Me. (q.v.). Attd. Leicester Acad. and
Harvard, from which he was grad. in 1802. Studied law in
father's office. Admitted to bar in 1805 and began practice in Worcester. Mbr. of Mass. Senate, 1812-1813. Mbr.
of Mass. House for all but three years, 1814-1822, serving
as Speaker, 1820-1822. Mbr. of Mass. constl. conv. in 1820.
El. Lieut. Gov. in 1823. Pres. elector for John Q. Adams
in 1824 pres. election. Apptd. to Mass. Supreme Ct. in
1824. El. Gov. as an Adams Rep. in 1825, continuing to be
el. each year until 1833 when he declined to run again.
During admin., a state bd. to administer internal improvements was created; prison management reforms were instituted; and a state normal school system established. Was
first Gov. to use veto freely. El. to U.S. House as a Whig
in 1836 to fill a vacancy, and continued in that office until Nov., 1841, when he resigned. U.S. collector at port
of Boston, 1841-1843. Mbr. of Mass. Senate, 1844-1845,
serving as its presiding officer in 1845. Mayor of
Worcester in 1848. Mbr. of commt. to study revision of
militia laws, 1847. Pres. elector on Whig ticket in 1848.
Pres. elector on Lincoln-Johnson ticket in 1864 pres. election. Pres. of Worcester Bible Soc., and of Worcester Agri.
Soc. Mbr. of Mass. Historical Soc., and Bd. of Overseers
of Harvard, and of the governing bd. of Leicester Acad.
Was a founding mbr. of Amer. Antiquarian Soc. m. to
Penelope Sever in 1807. Eight children. D. at Worcester,
May 29, 1868. Bur. in family lot at Rural Cem. there.

DAVIS, JOHN (1834-1835; 1841-1843). b. Jan. 13, 1787
at Northboro, Mass. s. of Isaac and Anna (Brigham) D.
Attd. Leicester Acad. and Yale, from which he was grad. in
1812. Studied law, admitted to bar and began practice at
Worcester, Mass. in 1815. El. to U.S. House in 1824 as a
Jeff. Rep. Continued in that office until 1834, becoming

affiliated with the Natl. Rep. wing of his party. El. Gov. by Mass. Senate as one of two candidates referred to it in 1833, having received a popular plurality but not a major- ity in a contest in which he was opposed by the Dem. party nominee and by former Pres. of U.S., J. Q. Adams, who was the cand. of the Anti-Mason party. Reel. in 1834. Resign- ed office in Mar., 1835, to take seat in U.S. Senate, to which he had been el. as a Whig, and served until 1841 when he resigned. In the Senate, favored a high tariff and op- posed the financial policies of Pres. Jackson and Pres. Van Buren. El. Gov. again as a Whig in 1840. Reel. in 1841, but was defeated in 1842 election when the Liberty party cand. secured a substantial popular vote, causing the final choice to be referred to the Mass. Senate for resolu- tion. Received some support for nom. for the office of Vice Pres. of U.S. at the Whig natl. conv. in 1844. El. to the U.S. Senate in 1845 to fill a vacancy and continued to serve until 1853. Declined to run for another term in 1852. As a Sen., opposed the Mexican War, the extension of slav- ery into new territories, and the Clay Compromise bills of 1850. Pres. of Amer. Antiquarian Soc. Popularly referred to as "Honest John". m. in 1822 to Eliza Bancroft. One s. D. at Worcester, April 19, 1854. Bur. in Rural Cem. there.

ARMSTRONG, SAMUEL TURELL (1835-1836). b. April 29, 1784 in Dorchester, Mass. s. of Capt. John and Elizabeth A. Received common school educ. As a youth began work as a clerk in a Boston bookseller's shop. Eventually acquired a book publishing bus. in Boston for himself, in which he prospered. Engaged in politics at local level, and was a mbr. of Mass. lower House from Boston for two terms, and of the Mass. Senate for one term. El. as a Natl. Rep. to the office of Lieut. Gov. in 1833 and again the following year. When Gov. Davis resigned in Mar., 1835, to take seat in U.S. Senate, succeeded to the office of Gov. and completed the term to which Davis had been el. Mayor of Boston in 1836, and mbr. of Mass. Senate in 1839. Resumed bus. activities after ceasing to hold pub. office. Gave generous benevo- lences for educl. and religious purposes. Mbr. of Bd. of Commnrs. for Foreign Missions. Was a leader in successful effort to preserve Plymouth Rock as a historical mark. m. in 1812 to Abigail Walker, of Charlestown, Mass. No chil- dren. D. suddenly at Boston, Mar. 26, 1850.

EVERETT, EDWARD (1836-1840). b. April 11, 1794 at Dorchester, Mass. s. of the Rev. Oliver and Lucy (Hill) E. Father was pastor of New South church, in Boston. Descend- ed from an ancestor who emigrated to Mass. in 1600s. Attd.

pvt. and pub. schools in Boston; Exeter Acad.; and Harvard, from which he was grad. in 1811, having entered there when he was 13 years of age. Displayed much literary and oratorical talent as a student. Tutor at Harvard, 1812-1814, while preparing for the ministry. Became pastor of Brattle St. Unitarian church in Boston at age 19, and soon acquired wide recognition for his eloquent addresses and sermons. Published a work, Defense of Christianity, when he was 20. Apptd. prof. of Greek at Harvard in 1815. Spent next four years abroad preparing for assumption of that post. Assumed professorial post at Harvard in 1820, serving until 1826. Became ed. of North American Review in 1820, to which he made frequent contributions as a writer. El. to U.S. House in 1824, continuing in that office until 1835. Affiliated with the Natl. Rep. party, later with the Whigs. El. Gov. of Mass. as a Whig in 1835, and was reel. for succeeding three terms. Defeated for fifth term in 1839, after refusing to contest election of his opponent, Marcus Morton, who was declared to have received a popular majority of one vote. In 1841 was apptd. U.S. Minister to Great Britain, serving until 1845. Apptd. Pres. of Harvard Univ. in 1845, serving in that position until 1849. Apptd. U.S. Sect. of State by Pres. Fillmore in 1852, and continued in that office until 1853. El. to U.S. Senate as a Whig in 1853, but resigned seat because of poor health after serving for only about a year. Adopted a conciliatory attitude toward South as Civil War threatened. Constl. Union party nominee for Vice Pres. of U.S. in 1860 pres. election. Supported Pres. Lincoln's policies toward South after Civil War began. Pres. elector on Lincoln-Johnson ticket in 1864 pres. election. Very active in support of Mt. Vernon Assoc. in 1856-1857. Speeches and other writings were published in 1850, 1858 and 1860. Gave main address at dedication of Gettysburg Natl. Cem. in 1863 at which Lincoln's famous dedicatory speech was delivered. Mbr. of Harvard Bd. of Overseers, 1827-1847, 1849-1854 and 1862-1863. m. in 1822 to Charlotte Gray Brooks, d. of a wealthy Boston merchant. Three s.; four d. D. Jan. 15, 1865 in Boston. Bur. in Mt. Auburn Cem., Cambridge, Mass.

MORTON, MARCUS (1840-1841). See above, 1825.

DAVIS, JOHN (1841-1843). See above, 1834-1835.

MORTON, MARCUS (1843-1844). See above, 1825.

BRIGGS, GEORGE NIXON (1844-1851). b. April 12, 1796 at Adams, Mass. s. of Allen and Nancy (Brown) B. Father,

who was a blacksmith, had been a Rev. War soldier. Family
moved to Manchester, Vt. when son was quite young. Attd.
local pub. schools. Family moved to White Creek, N.Y. At
age 13 began work as an apprentice to learn hatter's trade
there, but did not complete training. Moved to Lanesboro,
in Berkshire Co., Mass. in 1814 where his elder brother,
Rufus, assisted him in completion of schooling. Was converted to Baptist faith while there, having formerly been a
Quaker. Studied law, admitted to bar and began practice in
Berkshire Co. Soon acquired reputation as able lawyer.
Register of deeds in Berkshire Co., 1824-1830, and also
held other local offices. El. to U.S. House in 1830 as a
Natl. Rep., continuing in that office as a Whig until 1843.
Became prominent in House as leader of anti-slavery faction
of Whig party. Did not seek reel. in 1842. Moved to
Pittsfield, Mass. in 1843. El. Gov. as a Whig in 1843, defeating incumbent Gov. Morton in an election that had to be
resolved by Mass. Senate. Continued in office for next six
terms. Elections in 1843, 1845, 1848 and 1849 had to be
resolved by Mass. Senate because no cand. received a popular majority in those years. As Gov., opposed U.S. policies leading up to the Mexican War. Refused to cooperate
in raising volunteer troops for the war. Lost bid for
eighth term in 1850 to Dem. opponent, although he received
a substantial plurality of the popular vote, the final result being determined by the Mass. Senate. During admin.,
cooperated with Horace Mann in up-grading pub. school system and providing teacher training. Mbr. of Mass. constl.
conv. of 1853. Had prominent role in founding of Rep.
party in Mass. in 1850s. Prominent in Baptist church affairs, and in promotion of cause of temperance. Apptd. by
Pres. Lincoln as U.S. commnr. to settle dispute between U.S.
and New Granada in 1861, but died following an accidental
gunshot wound he suffered at his home in Pittsfield before
he left for foreign assignment. Pres. of Amer. Baptist
Missionary Union and of Amer. Tract Soc. Trustee of
Williams Coll., from which he received an hon. degree. Hon.
degrees also from Harvard and Amherst. Declined chancellor-
ship at Madison Univ. m. to Harriet Hall, of Lanesboro,
Mass. One d.; two s. D. at Pittsfield, Sept. 12, 1861.
Bur. in Pittsfield Cem.

BOUTWELL, GEORGE SEWALL (1851-1853). b. Jan. 28, 1818
(1819?) at Brookline, Mass. Father moved to farm near
Lunenberg, Mass. when son was two years old. Attd. local
schools while helping on farm. Began work at age 13 as
clerk in country store while continuing studies at home.
Four years later took job as store clerk in Groton Center,

Mass., continuing his studies, including law, in the meantime. Became partner and later, sole owner of the bus.
firm. Admitted to bar but did not begin practice of law on
a fee basis immediately. U.S. postmaster at Groton. Mbr.
of Mass. Gen. Ct. as Dem., 1842-1844 and 1847-1850, where
he became prominent as party leader. Defeated as the Dem.
cand. for U.S. House seat in 1844, 1846 and 1848. Defeated
as the Dem. cand. for Gov. in 1849. State Banking Commnr.,
1849-1851. Was again the Dem. cand. for Gov. in 1850, and
was el. by Mass. Senate although he had received some
20,000 fewer popular votes than incumbent Gov. Briggs, the
Whig cand. Reel. in 1851, again by the Senate after he had
received fewer popular votes than his leading opponent.
Mbr. of Mass. constl. conv. in 1853. Apptd. Sect. of Mass.
Bd. of Educ. in 1855 to succeed Horace Mann, continuing to
serve in that position until 1861. During mid-1850s joined
in movement to org. the Rep. party in Mass. and affiliated
with that party in 1856. Mbr. of Washington "Peace Congress" in 1861. Apptd. by Pres. Lincoln in 1862 to adjust
claims arising from operations of Gen. Fremont in Mo.
Apptd. first U.S. Commnr. of Revenue by Pres. Lincoln in
1862, serving until 1863. El. to U.S. House as a Rep. in
1862. As mbr. of House, where he served until 1869, had
prominent role in impeachment of Pres. Andrew Johnson, serving as one of the mgrs. for the House at the Senate trial.
Also had a leading role in drafting of 14th and 15th Amdts.
to U.S. Const. Apptd. U.S. Sect. of Treas. in 1869. Resigned in Mar., 1873, after having been apptd. to U.S. Senate seat to fill vacancy. Continued to serve in Senate until 1877. Apptd. by Pres. Hayes as one of the commnrs. to
revise U.S. statutes in 1877-1878. Declined offer of office of Sect. of Treas. from Pres. Arthur in 1884. Practiced law in Washington, D.C. from 1878 onward. Represented various foreign govts., including Hawaii, Haiti and
Chile, as counsel. Pres. of Amer. Anti-Imperialist League,
1898-1905. Mbr., Harvard Bd. of Overseers, 1850-1860. Hon.
degree from Harvard. Author of numerous works on pub. affairs topics, and of a two-volume autobiography, Sixty Years
in Public Affairs, 1902. D. at Groton, Mass., Feb. 27,
1905. Bur. in Groton Cem.

CLIFFORD, JOHN HENRY (1853-1854). b. Jan. 16, 1809 at
Providence, R.I. s. of Benj. and Achsah (Wade) C. Attd.
Brown Univ., from which he was grad. in 1827. Studied law
in New Bedford, Mass. law office. Admitted to bar and began practice in New Bedford. Mbr. of Mass. Gen. Ct., 1835.
Served on staff of Gov. Everett, 1836-1840. Apptd. State's
atty. for So. Mass. dist. in 1839, serving until 1849.

Mbr. of Mass. Senate, 1845. Apptd. Atty. Gen. of Mass. in
1849, and achieved pub. notice in prosecution of Parkman
murder trial. El. Gov. as a Whig in 1852. Received a substantial popular plurality, but the vote received by Horace
Mann as the Free Soil cand. required resolution of the
election þy the Mass. Senate. Declined to run for second
term in 1853. Apptd. Atty. Gen. of Mass. again in 1854,
serving until 1858. Engaged in practice of law thereafter.
Mbr. of Mass. Senate as a Rep. in 1862. Pres. elector on
Grant ticket in pres. election of 1868. Pres. of Boston
and Providence R.R. in 1868. Declined offers of posts of
U.S. Minister to Russia and as Minister to Turkey. Apptd.
one of U.S. commnrs. under the North Atl. Fisheries Arb.
Treaty with Great Britain in 1875, but died before service
began. Mbr., Amer. Acad. of Arts and Sci. and of Mass.
Historical Soc. Mbr., Harvard Bd. of Overseers, 1854-1859,
1865-1868, and pres. of bd., 1869-1874. Trustee, Peabody
Fund. Hon. degrees from Harvard, Brown and Amherst. m. in
1832 to Sarah Parker Allen. Two children. D. at New
Bedford, Jan. 7, 1876.

   WASHBURN, EMORY (1854-1855). b. Feb. 14, 1800 at
Leicester, Mass. s. of Joseph and Ruth (Davis) W. Ancestral line included a number of individuals with distinguished records of mil. and pub. service. Entered
Dartmouth Coll. at age 13, but transferred later to
Williams Coll. Grad. from Williams Coll. in 1817. Studied
law in Williamstown and at Harvard. Admitted to bar in
1820 and began practice at Leicester. Mbr. of Mass. House,
1826-1827. Moved to Worcester, Mass., where he continued
in law practice. Became a law partner of John Davis, later
a Gov. of Mass. Served as aide to Gov. Levi Lincoln, Jr.,
1830-1834. Mbr. of Mass. House again in 1838, and of Mass.
Senate, 1841-1842. Common pleas ct. judge, 1843-1847.
While travelling in Europe in 1853 was nom. as the Whig.
cand. for Gov. and was el. after election result was referred to Mass. Senate for resolution. Became the last person
to be el. Gov. as a Whig, and was also the last Gov. of
Mass. to be chosen by Senate under the majority popular
vote requirement. Defeated for second term in 1854. Apptd.
prof. of law at Harvard in 1856, serving in that capacity
for next 20 years. Resigned in 1876 to open law office in
Cambridge. Refused to become cand. for U.S. House, but
served for a short time again in Mass. Gen. Ct. Mbr. of
Mass. Bd. of Educ.; founder of Worcester Co. Free Inst. of
Indus. Sci.; mbr. of Bd. of Trustees of Leicester Acad. and
of Williams Coll.; sect. of Antiquarian Soc.; vice pres.,
Mass. Historical Soc.; dir., Amer. Social Sci. Assoc.;

Fellow, Amer. Acad. of Arts and Sci. Published widely.
Hon. degrees from Harvard Univ. and Williams Coll. m. in
1830 to Marianna Cornelia Giles. Three children. D. Mar.
18, 1877, at Cambridge.

GARDNER, HENRY JOSEPH (1855-1858). b. June 14, 1819
at Boston, Mass. s. of Dr. Henry and Clarissa (Holbrook) G.
Received early educ. in pvt. schools. Attd. Phillips-
Exeter Acad., and Bowdoin Coll., from which he was grad. in
1838. Became partner in dry goods firm in Boston. Mbr. of
Boston city council, 1850-1853, serving as its pres. the
last two years. Nom. as Amer. (Know Nothing) party cand.
for Gov. in 1854 and was el. Reel. in 1855 and 1856, but
was defeated in try for fourth term in 1857. As Gov., advocated enactment of a homestead act; restriction on immigration by indigent aliens; neutral position on slavery
question. After his defeat in the 1857 election, the Amer.
party disintegrated and ceased to be a major factor in Mass.
politics. Returned to dry goods bus. in 1858, organizing
a new firm. Retired from that activity in 1876, but continued to be involved in ins. bus. Hon. degrees from
Bowdoin in 1851 and from Harvard in 1855. m. in 1844 to
Helen E. Cobb. Seven children. D. July 21, 1892, at
Milton, Mass.

BANKS, NATHANIEL PRENTICE (1858-1861). b. Jan. 30,
1816 at Waltham, Mass. s. of Nathanial and Rebecca
(Greenwood) B. Family was poor and he received little formal educ., but spent leisure time in study while working.
Began working in a cotton factory at age 12. Later learned
machinist trade. Joined village debating society and developed talent as speaker and writer. Became a lyceum
lecturer and was ed. of a local weekly newspaper. Worked
as clerk in Boston customs house while studying law. Admitted to bar and began practice in Boston. Defeated as
Dem. cand. for Mass. Gen. Ct. a number of times, but was
eventually el. on seventh try in 1849, after making a notable speech on slavery issue. Served until 1852, and was
House Speaker in 1851 and 1852. El. to Mass. Senate in
1851 but declined, preferring to remain in House. Presiding officer in Mass. constl. conv. in 1853. El. to U.S.
House in 1852 with support of Dem. and Amer. parties, and
was reel. in 1854 as Amer. party cand. Chosen Speaker of
U.S. House in Feb., 1856, after a protracted deadlock of
some two months, being chosen as compromise cand. on 113th
ballot. Reel. in 1856 as a Rep., but resigned seat in Dec.,
1857, after having been el. Gov. as a Rep. Reel. in 1858
and 1859. Moved to Chicago, Ill., in 1861 after having

been made vice pres. of Ill. Cent. R.R. Entered Union Army
soon after outbreak of Civil War as major gen. of volunteers. Served with Army of the Potomac in Va., and was
sent to La. theater of the war in 1862. Was relieved of
duty there in 1864 after leading an unsuccessful campaign
up the Red River. Resigned commn. in 1865 and returned to
Mass. El. to U.S. House as a Union Rep. in 1865, continuing to serve in that office until 1873. Defeated for reel.
in 1872 as Lib. Rep. and Dem. cand. Mbr. of Mass. Senate
in 1874. El. again that year to U.S. House as a Lib. Rep.,
serving until 1879. Defeated for re-nom. in 1878. Apptd.
U.S. marshal in Mass. in 1879, serving until 1888. El.
again to U.S. House as a Rep. in 1888, but was defeated for
re-nom. in 1890. Was voted a pension by spec. act of Cong.
in 1891. m. in 1847 to Mary Palmer. Three children. D.
at Waltham, Sept. 1, 1894. Bur. in Grove Hill Cem.,
Waltham.

ANDREW, JOHN ALBION (1861-1866). b. May 31, 1818 in
Windham, Dist. of Me. (Mass.). Descendant of English colonist who had emigrated to Mass., eventually settling in
Dist. of Me. Father was a merchant. Attd. Bowdoin Coll.,
from which he was grad. in 1837. Studied law in office in
Boston, admitted to bar, and began practice there in 1840.
Affiliated with Whig party and was an active opponent of
slavery. Achieved wide notice as counsel in fugitive slave
case of Burns and Sims in 1850. El. to Mass. Gen. Ct. in
1858 as a Rep. Delegate to Rep. natl. conv. in Chicago in
1860. Nom. and el. Gov. as a Rep. in 1860, and continued
in office until 1866, declining to run for sixth term for
reasons of health. As Gov. during Civil War, was very active in support of Union cause. Took steps to put Mass.
militia on combat readiness basis even before outbreak of
hostilities, and a contingent of Mass. troops was employed
in early weeks of conflict to protect Washington, D.C. from
capture by Confed. Urged use of free Negroes as troops by
Union govt. in 1862, a policy that was eventually adopted.
As Gov., favored liberalization of usury and divorce laws
and resisted arbitrary arrests of So. sympathizers. Offered post of pres. of Antioch Coll., but declined. Unitarian.
m. in 1848 to Eliza Jane Henry, of Hingham, Mass. Four
children. D. Oct. 30, 1867, in Boston.

BULLOCK, ALEXANDER HAMILTON (1866-1869). b. Mar. 2,
1816 at Royalton, Mass. s. of Rufus B., and was a descendant of an old New England colonial family. Attd. Amherst
Coll., from which he was grad. in 1836. Studied law in law
office and was admitted to bar. Served as military aide on

staff on Gov. John Davis. Began law practice in Worcester,
Mass. Mbr. of Mass. House, 1845-1848, and of Mass. Senate,
1849. Ed. of Worcester Aegis until 1850. Also engaged in
ins. bus. as agent for Conn. and N.Y. firms. Commnr. of
insolvency in 1853 and insolvency judge, 1856. Mayor of
Worcester, 1858. Affiliated with Rep. party in 1850s, and
was el. to Mass. House again in 1861, continuing to serve
in that body until 1865, being chosen House Speaker. El.
Gov. as a Union Rep. in 1865, and was continued in office
for two succeeding terms. During admin., gave major attention to steps to relieve State's financial problems. Retired from politics after tenure as Gov., devoting attention to ins. and banking bus. interests. Became quite
wealthy. Hon. degree from Harvard in 1866. m. to Elvira
Hazard, of Enfield, Conn. One s.; two d. D. at Worcester,
Jan. 17, 1882.

CLAFLIN, WILLIAM (1869-1872). b. March 6, 1818 at
Milford, Mass. s. of Lee and Sarah (Adams) C. Father was
proprietor of tanning bus. Attd. local schools and Milford
Acad., working during spare time in father's tannery, which
was later expanded into a shoe mfg. enterprise. Entered
Brown Univ. at mother's insistence, but after her death one
year later, returned to give full attention to father's
bus. Became mgr. of a shop at Ashland, Mass. in 1837. Became ill from overwork. After recovery went to St. Louis,
Mo., where he worked in shoe mfg. enterprise. In 1846 returned to Hopkinton, Mass., where he continued in that line
of bus., with factories also in Boston and at Newton, Mass.,
to which latter place he moved in 1855. Held very strong
anti-slavery views, and became mbr. of Free Soil party in
1840s. Mbr. of Mass. House, 1849-1852. Affiliated with
newly-organized Rep. party in mid-1850s. El. to Mass. Senate in 1860 and 1861, becoming Pres. of that body. During
Civil War lost considerable wealth because of bad debts,
but bus. eventually recovered. Ch. of Rep. state commt.
for seven years, and mbr. of Rep. natl. commt., 1864-1875,
serving as its ch. from 1868 to 1872. El. Lieut. Gov. in
1865, continuing in that office for two succeeding terms.
El. Gov. in 1868 and for next two terms. As Gov., used
veto against bills designed to favor railroad interests.
El. to U.S. House in 1876, and in 1878 for succeeding term.
Was not a cand. for third term, choosing to devote attention to bus. interests thereafter. m. in 1841 to --------
Harding, of Milford, Mass. One d. After first wife's
death in 1842, m. in 1845 to --------Davenport, of
Hopkinton, Mass. Was a founder of Mass. Club. Methodist.
D. at Newton, Jan. 5, 1905. Bur. in Newton Cem.,

Newtonville, Mass.

WASHBURN, WILLIAM BARRETT (1872-1874). b. Jan. 31, 1820 at Winchendon, Mass. Attd. Westminster Acad. and Hancock Acad. before enrolling at Yale, from which he was grad. in 1844. Town clerk at Orange, Mass., 1844-1847. Engaged in mfg. bus. at Erving, Mass., 1847-1857. Mbr. of Mass. Senate, 1850, and of Mass. House, 1853-1855. Helped org. Rep. party in Mass. in 1850s. In 1858 moved to Greenfield, Mass., where he became principal stockholder, and later pres. of a natl. bank, and also acquired other bus. interests there. When Civil War began, gave political support to Union cause. El. to U.S. House in 1862, serving until Dec., 1871, when he resigned after having been el. Gov. as a Rep. Continued in office for succeeding two terms, but resigned shortly after inauguration for third term to take seat in U.S. Senate to which he had been chosen to fill a vacancy. Did not seek reel. to Senate after completion of term in 1875. Retired from pub. life to give attention to varied bus. interests in banking, railroads, and other fields. Trustee of Smith Coll. and of Yale, 1872-1881; and of Mass. State Coll. Mbr. of Bd. of Overseers of Amherst Coll. for 13 years. Made generous bequests to charitable, educl. and missionary orgs. Hon. degree from Harvard in 1872. D. at Springfield, Mass., Oct. 5, 1887. Bur. in Green River Cem., Greenfield.

TALBOT, THOMAS (1874-1875; 1879-1880). b. Sept. 7, 1818 in Cambridge, N.Y. Family was of Irish origin. Father died when son was quite young, and mother moved to Northampton, Mass., where he attd. school. Worked in a factory while attending school. In 1835 began working in brother's broadcloth factory in Williamsburg, Mass. Became factory supt. in 1838, and in 1840 became partner with brother in a bus. at Billerica, Mass. Enterprise prospered and expanded. Served several terms in Mass. Gen. Ct. Mbr. of Gov.'s Council, 1864-1869. El. Lieut. Gov. as a Rep. in 1872 and again in 1873. Succeeded to office of Gov. in April, 1874, when Gov. Washburn resigned to take seat in U.S. Senate, and completed Washburn's term. As Gov., vetoed a bill repealing Mass. prohibition statute, and signed a bill establishing 10-hour day as work standard. Both actions aroused strong opposition in some elements of population, and he was defeated in 1875 as the Rep. cand. for election to a regular term. Nom. and el. Gov. as Rep. in 1878, however. After serving one term retired to give attention to bus. interests in Billerica. Made generous gifts to educl. and religious orgs. D. at Lowell, Mass.,

Oct. 6, 1886.

GASTON, WILLIAM (1875-1876). b. Oct. 3, 1820 at South
Killingly, Conn. s. of Alexander and Kezia (Arnold) G.
Descendant of an English colonist who came to Conn. in 1730.
Ancestral line included Huguenot, Scotch-Presbyterian and
Pilgrim "Separatist" figures. Father was a merchant who
had an active role in pub. affairs. Attd. academies in
Brooklyn and Plainview, Conn. Grad. from Brown Univ. in
1840 with honors. Studied law in Roxbury and Boston, Mass.
Admitted to bar and began practice in Roxbury in 1844, becoming mbr. of a successful law firm. Mbr. of Mass. House,
1853-1854 and 1856. Mayor of Roxbury, 1861-1862. Also
served as city solicitor there. Mbr. of Mass. Senate in
1868. Supported Union cause during Civil War. Mayor of
Boston, 1871-1872. Defeated as Dem. cand. for Gov. in 1873,
but was nom. again and was el. in 1874. Defeated as Dem.
cand. for Gov. in 1875 and 1877. Congregationalist. Hon.
degrees from Harvard and Brown. m. in 1852 to Louisa A.
Bucher, of New Haven, Conn. Three children. A son,
William A., was defeated as the Dem. cand. for Gov. of Mass.
in 1902, 1903 and 1926. D. Jan. 19, 1894.

RICE, ALEXANDER HAMILTON (1876-1879). b. Aug. 30,
1818 at Newton Lower Falls, Mass. s. of Thomas and Lydia
(Smith) R. Father was owner and operator of a paper mill.
Attd. local pub. schools and academies at Needham and
Newton until age 14, when he became an employee of a wholesale linen house in Boston, later entering the wholesale
paper bus. there. Entered Union Coll., Schnectady, N.Y. in
1840 and was grad. there with distinction in 1844. Became
partner in a paper mfg. bus. in Boston, which prospered and
expanded. Held various admin. offices in Boston city govt.,
1851-1853. Mbr. of Boston city council, 1853-1855, serving
as its pres. the last year. Assisted in org. of Rep. party
in Mass. in 1850s. Mayor of Boston, 1855-1857. El. to U.S.
House in 1858 as a Rep., continuing to serve therein until
1867. Supported policies of Lincoln admin. Was not a cand.
for fifth term in 1866. Delegate to "Loyalist" (Union
party) conv. in Philadelphia in 1866, and to the Rep. natl.
conv. in 1868. Resumed bus. activities for a time. Nom.
and el. Gov. as a Rep. in 1875, defeating incumbent Gov.
Gaston. Reel. in 1876 and 1877. As Gov., vetoed local
option liquor regulatory bill. Signed measure establishing
savings bank system. Repr. of Mass. in Philadelphia Centennial Expo. in 1876. Retired from pub. life at end of
third term as Gov. Trustee of Mass. Inst. of Tech.; Boston
Museum of Fine Arts; and of the Episcopal Theological

School, at Cambridge, Mass. Mbr., Amer. Archeological Soc.;
Amer. Geographical Soc.; Amer. Historical Assoc.; Farragut
Naval Veterans Assoc. Vice Pres., Webster Historical Assoc.
Mbr., various social clubs. m. first in 1845 to Augusta E.
McKim, of Mass. m. later to Angie Erickson Powell, of N.Y.
Four children. Hon. degrees from Union Coll. and Harvard.
D. July 22, 1895, at Melrose, Mass. Bur. in Newton Cem.

TALBOT, THOMAS (1879-1880). See above, 1874-1875.

LONG, JOHN DAVIS (1880-1883). b. Oct. 27, 1838 at
Buckfield, Me. s. of Zadoc and Julia Temple (Davis) L.
Attd. local schools and Hebron Acad. Entered Harvard at
age 14 and was an outstanding scholar, receiving degree in
1857. Principal of Westford Acad., 1857-1859. Studied law
at Harvard and in law office in Boston. Admitted to bar in
1861. Practiced at Buckfield for two years, then at Boston
from 1863-1869. Moved to Hingham, Mass., where he continued to practice law. Mbr. of Mass. House, 1875-1878, serving as Speaker last two years. El. Lieut. Gov. in 1878.
Nom. and el. Gov. as a Rep. in 1879, and for two succeeding
terms. El. to U.S. House in 1882, and continued in that
office until 1889. Did not seek fourth term in 1888. Resumed law practice in Boston for several years. Apptd. U.S.
Sect. of the Navy by Pres. McKinley in 1897, continuing in
that office under Pres. Theodore Roosevelt until 1902. U.S.
became recognized as major naval power during his tenure by
events growing out of Spanish-Amer. War. Resumed law practice at Boston in 1902. Mbr. of Bd. of Overseers of
Harvard, serving as its pres. Author of a history of the
Rep. party and of a two-volume history of the Amer. Navy.
Pres. of Authors Club of Boston. Fellow of Amer. Acad. of
Arts and Sci. Published translation of Virgil's Aeneid in
1879. m. first in 1870 to Mary Woodward Glover. m. in
1886 to Agnes Pierce. D. Aug. 28, 1915, at Hingham. Bur.
in Hingham Cem.

BUTLER, BENJAMIN FRANKLIN (1883-1884). b. Nov. 5,
1818 at Deerfield, N.H. s. of John and Charlotte (Ellison)
B. On both father's and mother's side was a descendant of
colonial ancestors who had been prominent in mil. and govtl.
affairs. Father died when son was only about one year old.
In 1828 mother moved to Lowell, Mass., where he attd. local
schools and Exeter Acad. Sought to enter West Point Mil.
Acad., but enrolled instead in Waterville (now Colby) Coll.,
from which he was grad. in 1838. Studied law while teaching school at Lowell. Admitted to bar in 1840 and practiced law at Lowell for next ten years. Moved to Boston in

1850. Mbr. of Mass. House in 1853, and of Mass. Senate in
1859. Mbr. of both the Charleston and Baltimore natl.
convs. of Dem. party in 1860. Defeated as cand. of
Breckenridge wing of Dem. party for Gov. in 1860, finishing
fourth in four-man contest. A Union advocate, he accepted
a commn. as brig. gen. of Mass. volunteers upon outbreak of
Civil War, and later advanced to major gen. Saw service in
Va., La. and again in Va. and the Carolinas during course
of the war. As U.S. mil. commdr. in New Orleans in 1862,
acquired reputation as strict enforcer of security regulations against civilians, which caused him to be referred to
as "Beast" Butler by pro-Southern element. In 1866 was el.
to U.S. House as a Rep., serving until 1875. Was a House
mgr. at impeachment trial of Pres. Andrew Johnson in 1868.
Defeated as cand. for Rep. nom. for Gov. in 1871 and 1872.
Continued to serve in U.S. House until 1875, but was defeated for reel. in 1874. Became disaffected from Rep. party
over monetary policies. Defeated as cand. for Gov. in 1878
and 1879 as an Indep. Nom. for Gov. again as Dem. and
Greenback party cand. in 1882 and was el. Accomplished
little, as a strong Dem. faction was opposed to him and the
Rep. opposition controlled both Houses of Gen. Ct. Defeated for reel. in 1883. Nom. for Pres. of U.S. by Greenback
and Anti-Monopoly parties in 1884, but failed to win any
electoral votes. Practiced law thereafter. Author of an
autobiography, Butler's Book, in 1892. m. in 1842 to Sarah
Hildreth, of Lowell, Mass. One d., Blanche, who became the
wife of Adelbert Ames, Gov. of Miss. (q.v.). D. at Lowell,
Jan. 11, 1893. Bur. in Hildreth Cem., at Lowell.

ROBINSON, GEORGE DEXTER (1884-1887). b. Jan. 20, 1834
at Lexington, Mass. s. of Charles R., a farmer. Families
of both father and mother had participated in Rev. War.
Attd. Lexington Acad., Hopkins Classical School, in
Cambridge, and Harvard, from which he was grad. in 1856.
Principal and teacher at Chicopee, Mass., 1856-1865. Began
study of law in 1865 with brother. Admitted to bar in 1866
and began practice in Chicopee. Mbr. of Mass. House, 1873-
1874, and of Mass. Senate, 1875-1876. El. to U.S. House in
1876, continuing to serve therein until Jan. 7, 1884, when
he resigned after having been nom. and el. Gov. as a Rep.
in 1883, defeating incumbent Gov. Butler. Reel. in 1884
and 1885. During admin., a free school textbook law was
passed; legislation enacted regulating weekly payment of
wages by corp. employers; and an election reform law enacted. Retired to law practice at Springfield, Mass. after
tenure as Gov. One s. Active as mbr. of Unitarian church.
D. at Chicopee, Feb. 22, 1896. Bur. in Fairview Cem. there.

AMES, OLIVER (1887-1890). b. Feb. 4, 1831 at North
Easton, Mass. s. of Oakes and Eveline (Gilmore) A. Father
was a very successful businessman and financier and had also been a mbr. of Cong. Attd. pub. schools and academies
at North Attleboro, Easton, and Leicester, Mass. Entered
Brown Univ., where he studied under the tutelage of Pres.
Wayland. Began working in shovel mfg. plant founded by
grandfather. Learned the bus., contributing many inven-
tions, and in 1863 became a mbr. of the firm. Was interested in improving the state militia system, in which he rose
from rank of lieut. to lieut. col. In 1873 inherited
father's estate, which was heavily involved with the Un.
Pac. R.R. Paid off the debts of the family estate, and became pres. of Un. Pac. R.R. Also became involved in other
bus. enterprises in banking, mfg. and theater operations
fields. Became quite wealthy. Was the owner of Booth's
Theater in New York City. Mbr. of Mass. Senate, 1880-1881.
El. Lieut. Gov. in 1882, and continued in that office for
next three terms. Nom. and el. Gov. as a Rep. in 1886, and
was reel. for next two terms. Contributor to many civic
improvements and charitable undertakings, and was a patron
of the arts. Was founder of the Oakes Ames Memorial Hall,
in North Easton. Pres. of Boston Art Club. m. in 1860 to
Anna Ray, of Nantucket, Mass. Two s.; four d. D. Oct. 22,
1895, at North Easton.

BRACKETT, JOHN QUINCY ADAMS (1890-1891). b. June 8,
1842 at Bradford, N.H. s. of Ambrose S. and Nancy (Brown)
B. Attd. local schools; Colby Acad.; and Harvard, from
which he was grad. with an A.B. degree in 1865 and with a
law degree in 1868. Was class orator in 1865. Admitted to
bar in 1868 and began practice in Boston. Acquired reputation as able speaker and was soon prominent in Rep. party
affairs. Presided at first meeting of Young Men's Rep.
Club in Boston, 1877. Judge advocate in Mass. mil. org.,
1874-1876. Mbr. of Boston city council, 1873-1876, serving
as its pres. last year. Mbr. of Mass. House, 1876-1881 and
1884-1886, serving as Speaker last two years. Active in
enactment of law establishing cooperative banks. Pres. of
Mercantile Library Assoc. in Boston, 1871 and 1882. El.
Lieut. Gov. in 1886, and continued in that office for next
two terms. El. Gov. as a Rep. in 1889, but was defeated in
try for second term in 1890, losing to an opponent whom he
had defeated in 1889. Delegate to Rep. natl. conv. in 1892.
m. in 1878 to Angie M. Peck. D. April 6, 1918.

RUSSELL, WILLIAM EUSTIS (1891-1894). b. Sept. 6, 1857
at Cambridge, Mass. s. of Charles Theodore and Sarah

Elizabeth (Ballister) R. Father was a lawyer who was a
descendant of an old Cambridge family. Attd. local pub.
schools and Harvard, from which he was grad. in 1877. Attd.
Boston Univ. Law School while also studying in father's office, and began practice in Cambridge. Mbr., Cambridge city
council, 1881, and of the Cambridge bd. of aldermen, 1883-
1884. Mayor of Cambridge, 1885-1888. Declined nom. as Dem.
for U.S. House. As mayor, vigorously enforced local option
liquor law. Defeated as Dem. cand. for Gov. in 1888, and
again in 1889. Campaigned widely for Grover Cleveland for
Pres. of U.S. in 1888. Nom. for Gov. as a Dem. for third
time in 1890 and was el. Reel. in 1891 and 1892. After
tenure as Gov., retired to law practice and bus. interests.
During 1896 pres. campaign urged retention of gold standard
and was mentioned as possible cand. for Pres. of U.S. as
"Gold Standard" Dem. to oppose Wm. Jennings Bryan, the Dem.
party cand. Pres. of Boston Univ. Law School alumni. Fond
of outdoor sports and camping. m, in 1885 to Margaret
Manning Swan, of Cambridge. Two s.; one d. D. July 16,
1896, at St. Adelaide, Quebec, while on a camping trip.
Bur. at Cambridge.

GREENHALGE, FREDERIC THOMAS (1894-1896). b. July 19,
1842 in Clitheroe, Lancashire, England. s. of Wm. and Jane
(Slater) G. Family emigrated to Lowell, Mass., in 1855,
where father was employed as mgr. of printing dept. of a
publishing firm. Attd. local pub. schools, and Harvard.
Left college in 1862 after father died. Was a brilliant
student, and served as ed. of Harvard Monthly. Became a
teacher in a small school at Chelmsford; also worked as tutor preparing students for Harvard. Sought to join Union
Army in 1863, but was rejected for physical reasons. Worked with commissary dept. of U.S. Army at Newbern, N.C. until 1864, when illness compelled him to return home. Studied law in law office. Admitted to bar in 1865 and began
practice in Lowell. Mbr. of Lowell city council, 1868-1869.
School commnr., 1871-1873, and police ct. judge, 1874. Unsuccessful cand. for Mass. Senate in 1872 and in 1881. Active in Rep. pres. campaign in 1876 and delegate to Rep.
natl. conv. in 1884. Commnr. of insolvency in Lowell dist.,
1876-1885. Mayor of Lowell, 1880-1881, and city solicitor,
1888. Mbr. of Mass. House, 1885. El. to U.S. House in
1888, where he quickly achieved reputation as an able and
witty speaker. Defeated for second term in 1890. Nom. and
el. Gov. as a Rep. in 1893, and again in 1894 and 1895.
Was the first person of foreign birth to be el. Gov. of
Mass. During admin., used veto power freely. Pres. of
Mass. Humane Soc.; People's Club; and the History Club.

Mbr., Martin Luther Club. Unitarian. Trustee, later pres.,
of Lowell City Savings Bank. Received an A.B. degree from
Harvard in 1870. m. in 1872 to Isabel Nesmith. Two s.;
one d. D. March 5, 1896, during third term as Gov. Bur.
in Lowell Cem.

WOLCOTT, ROGER (1896-1900). b. July 13, 1847 at
Boston, Mass. s. of J. Huntington and Cornelia
(Frothingham) W. Father was a successful merchant. Related to Wolcott family of Conn., from which two Govs. of Conn.
came. Attd. pvt. schools in Boston, and Harvard, from
which he was grad. in 1870. Delivered class day oration
for his graduating class. Tutored at Harvard, 1871-1872.
Attd. Harvard Law School while also studying in Boston law
office. Received law degree from Harvard in 1874, and began practice in Boston. Mbr. of Boston city council, 1877-
1880. Mbr. of Mass. House, 1882-1884. Again mbr. of
Boston city council, 1887-1889. Pres. of Rep. Club of Mass.
in 1891. El. Lieut Gov. as Rep. in 1893, continuing in
that office to 1896. Succeeded to office of Gov. in Mar.,
1896, following death of Gov. Greenhalge. El. Gov. for
next three regular terms. Mbr., Bd. of Overseers of
Harvard; Bd. of Trustees of Mass. Gen. Hosp.; mbr. of Mass.
Historical Soc. m. in 1874 to Edith Prescott. Four s.;
one d. D. at Boston, Dec. 21, 1900, less than a year after
tenure as Gov. ended.

CRANE, W(INTHROP) MURRAY (1900-1903). b. April 23,
1853 at Dalton, Mass. s. of Zenas M. and Louise F. (Laflin)
C. Father was owner of a paper mfg. plant which had been
established by his father in 1801. Attd. local pub. and
pvt. schools; Wilbraham Acad.; and Williston Sem. Started
work at age 17 in family paper bus. Became vice pres. of
company, which specialized in production of parchment, bond,
and spec. paper used in printing U.S. currency. Became
actively involved in Rep. politics early in career. Delegate to Rep. natl. convs. each pres. election year from
1892 through 1920, and mbr. of Rep. natl. commt., 1892-1908.
El. Lieut. Gov. in 1896, continuing in that office until
1900. El. Gov. as a Rep. in 1899 and for succeeding two
terms. Declined apptmt. as U.S. Sect. of Treas. in 1902.
Apptd. to U.S. Senate to fill vacancy in 1904, and continued in that office until 1913. Became important figure in
natl. Rep. politics while in Senate, becoming a close assoc.
of Pres. Taft. Was not a cand. for reel. in 1912, resuming
bus. activities thereafter. m. in 1880 to Mary Benner, of
Astoria, N.Y. After her death in 1884, m. in 1906 to
Josephine Porter. One s. D. at Dalton, Oct. 2, 1920. Bur.

in Dalton Cem.

BATES, JOHN LEWIS (1903-1905). b. Sept. 18, 1859 at
North Easton, Mass. s. of the Rev. Lewis B. and Louisa D.
(Field) B. Father was a clergyman. Descendant of an
English colonist who emigrated to Mass. in 1635. Attd.
schools in Millville, New Bedford, Taunton, Chelsea, and
Boston, Mass., where father held pastorates. Attd. Boston
Univ., from which he was grad. in 1882. Studied law at
Boston Univ., receiving law degree in 1885. Taught in eve-
ning schools and at Jamestown, N.Y. while attending college.
Admitted to bar in 1885 and began practice in Boston. Mbr.
of Boston city council, 1891-1892. Mbr. of Mass. House,
1894-1899, serving as Speaker last two years. El. Lieut.
Gov. in 1899, continuing in that office until 1902. El.
Gov. as a Rep. in 1902 and for succeeding term. Defeated
as Rep. cand. for third term in 1904. Served as mbr. of
State Pub. Safety Commt. during World War I. Pres. of Mass.
constl. conv., 1917-1919. Pres. of East Boston Citizens
Trade Assoc., 1893-1894. Associated with various banking
and savings institutions in Boston area as mbr. of bds. of
dir. Pres. of Boston Univ. Corp., 1907-1927. Hon. degree
from Wesleyan Coll. Mbr., Masons; I.O.O.F.; A.O.U.W.;
Royal Arcanum. Head of United Order of Pilgrim Fathers for
three years. m. in 1887 to Clara Elizabeth Smith, of
Jamestown, N.Y. Two s.; one d. D. at Boston, June 8, 1946.

DOUGLAS, WILLIAM LEWIS (1905-1906). b. Aug. 22, 1845
at Plymouth, Mass. s. of Wm. and Mary C. (Vaughan) D.
Father died when son was five years old. At age 7 was apprenticed to an uncle who was a shoemaker, and learned
shoemaker trade. At age 15 worked in cotton mill and later
as a shoemaker at Chiltonville, Mass. Attd. local schools
intermittently during youth. In 1865 went West. Opened a
shoe store in Golden, Colo. in 1867. Sold store after a
short time and returned to Plymouth, where he worked at
shoemaking trade. Became foreman, later supt., of shoe
factory in Brockton, Mass., 1871-1876. Started shoemaking
bus. of his own in 1876. Bus. prospered and expanded,
achieving nation-wide distribution with its own retail outlets. Incorporated in 1902 with himself as pres., pioneer-
ing in production of low-priced shoes. Mbr. of Brockton
city council, 1882-1883. Mayor of Brockton, 1890. Mbr. of
Mass. House, 1884-1885, and of Mass. Senate, 1886-1887. As
a Senator, helped enact law creating State Bd. of Arb. and
Conciliation for settlement of labor disputes. Delegate to
Dem. natl. convs. in 1884, 1892, 1896 and 1904. Withdrew
from 1896 conv. along with other "gold standard" Dems. in

protest against platform adopted. Nom. and el. Gov. as a
Dem. in 1904, defeating incumbent Gov. Bates. Served only
one term. Became quite wealthy and made many benevolent
gifts, particularly to Brockton Hosp. Involved in banking
and electric railway enterprises as well as shoe mfg. and
distribution. Founded Boston Times in 1895. Hon. degree
from Tufts Coll. m. in 1868 to Naomi Augusta Terry, of
Chiltonville, Mass. Two d. D. Sept. 17, 1924.

GUILD, CURTIS, Jr. (1906-1909). b. Feb. 2, 1860 at
Boston, Mass. s. of Curtis, Sr. and Sarah Crocker (Cobb) G.
Father was founder and publ. of Boston Commercial Bulletin.
Attd. pvt. schools in Roxbury and Boston, and Harvard, from
which he was grad. in 1881 with an A.B. degree and highest
honors. Was ed. of Harvard Crimson and Lampoon publications while a student. Joined father's bus., and travelled
in Europe for a time as its agent. Held various positions
in firm, including editorship. Became partner with father
and uncle in the enterprise in 1884, and in 1902 the sole
owner. Its data on wool bus. was regarded as authoratative
by U.S. govt. and world trade. Became active in Rep. politics at an early age. Presided over Rep. state conv. in
1895. Delegate to Rep. natl. conv. in 1896. Campaigned
over country for McKinley in 1896 pres. election and again
in 1900. At time of outbreak of Spanish-Amer. War was brig.
gen. in Mass. militia. Entered service as lieut. col. of a
volunteer cavalry unit, later becoming inspector gen. of
7th Army Corps., in Havana. Held rank of major gen. at end
of war. Offered commn. as col. in U.S. regular army, but
declined. Also declined offer of first Asst. Postmaster
Gen. of U.S., and as ch. of U.S. Civil Service Commn. Nom.
and el. Lieut. Gov. in 1901, continuing in that office until 1905. Nom. and el. Gov. as a Rep. in 1905, and again
in 1906 and 1907, with increased majority each time. During admin., much progressive legislation was passed. Escaped an assassination attempt by a crazed citizen at a
meeting he was conducting with labor leaders, several of
whom were wounded by the assailant. Placed in nom. for
Vice Pres. of U.S. at 1908 Rep. natl. conv., receiving 75
votes. Apptd. spec. Ambassador to Mexico by Pres. Taft in
1910 for celebration of Mexico's Independence Centennial.
U.S. Ambassador to Russia, 1911-1913. Mbr., Masons; Boston
CC; various bus. and social clubs. Hon. degrees from Holy
Cross Univ., Williams Coll., and the Univ. of Geneva. Decorations from govts. of Italy and Russia. m. in 1892 to
Charlotte H. Johnson. D. April 6, 1915.

DRAPER, EBEN SUMNER (1909-1911). b. June 17, 1858 at

Hopedale, Mass. s. of George and Hannah (Thwing) D. Descendant of an English colonist who came to Mass. in 1648.
Father was engaged in mfg. of cotton mill machinery. Attd.
Mass. Inst. of Tech., from which he was grad. in 1878. Employed in family enterprise. Also worked for a time for a
Lowell, Mass. cotton mfg. firm. Became partner with father
in 1880. Firm was reorg., and interests expanded into
other fields later. Ch. of Mass. delegation to Rep. natl.
conv. in 1896, where he helped secure gold standard plank
in party platform. Pres. elector on Rep. ticket in 1900.
El. Lieut. Gov. in 1907. Nom. and el. Gov. as a Rep. in
1908, and again in 1909. Defeated for reel. in 1910. As
Gov., sponsored legislation reorganizing state educl. system
and introduced new system of budgeting for rivers and harbors improvements. Utilized veto freely, checking in that
manner 21 bills, as well as utilizing revisory veto on some
sixty occasions. His actions in that regard were in part
responsible for his defeat for reel. in 1910. After tenure
as Gov., devoted attention to wide variety of bus. interests in mfg., railroad, banking and cotton milling fields.
Mbr. of Mass. Inst. of Tech. Corp.; Soc. of Colonial Wars;
Metropolitan Club of N.Y. Unitarian. Made many gifts for
civic improvements and programs. m. in 1883 to Nannie
Bristow, of Ky., d. of a U.S. Sect. of Treas. under Pres.
Grant. Two s.; one d. D. at Greenville, S.C., April 9,
1914, while returning from a trip to Fla.

FOSS, EUGENE NOBLE (1911-1914). b. Sept. 24, 1858 at
West Berkshire, Vt. s. of George E. and Marcia Cordelia
(Noble) F. Descendant of an English colonist who came to
Portsmouth, N.H. in 1657. Father was mgr. of a lumbering
machinery mfg. bus. Attd. Franklin Acad., at St. Albans,
Vt., and the Univ. of Vt. from 1877 to 1879. Left college
at end of second year to study law with an uncle. Became
sales agent for St. Albans bus. firm where father was employed. Put in charge of plant operations in 1882. Later
was treas., then gen. mgr., and in 1890 became pres. of the
firm. Moved to Boston, Mass. Expanded bus. by acquisition
of other companies in 1901. Originally was a Rep. in politics, but switched party affiliation to the Dem. party in
early 1900s because of tariff and trade reciprocity issues.
Defeated as Dem. cand. for Lieut. Gov. in 1909. El. to
vacant seat in U.S. House in Mar., 1910. Resigned seat in
Jan., 1911, after having been nom. and el. Gov. as cand. of
the Dem. and Prog. parties. Reel. by the same coalition in
1911 and 1912. Defeated for reel. in 1913 as an Indep.
During admin., legislation was enacted establishing the
pres. primary system; popular election of U.S. Senators; a

direct primary system of nom. for state officers; regulating campaign expenditures; setting up minumum wage and workmen's compensation standards; a pension system for indigents; and an improved highway system. Was an advocate of
prohibition. Resumed bus. activities after tenure as Gov.
Baptist. m. in 1884 to Lilla Sturtevant. Two s.; two d.
D. Sept. 13, 1939, at Jamaica Plain (Boston). Bur. in
Forest Hill Cem.

WALSH, DAVID IGNATIUS (1914-1916). b. Nov. 11, 1872
at Leominster, Mass. s. of James and Bridget (Donnelly) W.
Attd. pub. schools at Clinton, Mass.; Holy Cross Coll.,
from which he was grad. in 1893; and Boston Univ., from
which he received a law degree in 1897. Was pres. and valedictorian of graduating class in high school, college and
law school. Admitted to bar in 1897, and began practice in
Fitchburg and Clinton, Mass. with brother. Moved to Boston
where he practiced for a time; but returned to Fitchburg in
1907. .Mbr. of Mass. House, 1900-1901. Defeated for Mass.
Senate in 1901. Defeated as Dem. cand. for Lieut. Gov. in
1911, but was el. to that office in 1912. Nom. and el. Gov.
as a Dem. in 1913, and again in 1914. Defeated for third
term in 1915. During admin., a women's suffrage proposal
was rejected by voters of the State; and the Cape Cod Canal
was opened. Delegate to all Dem. natl. convs. from 1912
through 1944. Mbr. of Mass. constl. convs. in 1917 and
1918. El. to U.S. Senate in 1918, but was defeated for
reel. in 1924. Resumed law practice for a time. El. to
fill vacancy in U.S. Senate seat in 1926, and continued in
that office until 1947, being defeated for reel. in 1946.
Retired from politics thereafter, residing at Clinton, Mass.
Hon. degrees from Holy Cross, Notre Dame, Georgetown,
Fordham and Boston Universities. Mbr., Elks; K.C. Roman
Catholic. Never married. D. at Brighton, Mass., June 11,
1947. Bur. at St. John's Cem., Lancaster, Mass.

McCALL, SAMUEL WALKER (1916-1919). b. Feb. 28, 1851
at East Providence, Pa. s. of Henry and Mary Ann (Elliott)
McC. Family was of Scottish descent, and ancestral line
included a number of individuals who had prominent roles in
Pa. pub. affairs. When son was two years old family moved
to Mount Carroll, Ill., where father farmed and also was
employed by a farm implement mfg. firm. Attd. Mount Carroll
Sem.; New Hampton Acad., in N.H.; and Dartmouth Coll., from
which he was grad. in 1874. As student there was ed. of
the Anvil. Studied law at law offices in Nashua, N.H. and
Worcester, Mass. Admitted to bar and began practice in
Worcester in 1876. Later moved to Boston, and eventually

to Winchester, Mass. Mbr. of Mass. House, 1888–1889, serving as Rep. party leader in 1889. Purchased an interest in Boston Daily Advertiser, and was its ed. for two years. State ballot commnr. for two years. Delegate to Rep. natl. convs. in 1888, 1900 and 1916. Mbr. of Mass. House, 1892. El. to U.S. House in 1892, serving until 1913. Did not seek eleventh term in 1912. As mbr. of Cong. was involved in election law reform and corrupt practices legislation. Mbr. of Natl. Commn. on Fine Arts. As such, was instrumental in devel. of plans for Lincoln Memorial. Opposed U.S. policies growing out of Spanish-Amer. War. Opponent of strong chief executive ideas and feared curtailment of freedoms by govtl. restraints. Defeated as the Rep. cand. for Gov. in 1913 and 1914, but was nom. and el. in 1915. Reel. in 1916 and 1917. Supported U.S. war effort during World War I, and U.S. involvement in League of Nations. Mbr. of Second Natl. Indus. Conf. in 1920. Trustee of World Peace Found., Smith Coll., and New Hampton Acad. Offered post of pres. of Dartmouth, but declined. Involved in scholarly endeavors in history, govt. and classical fields, and was author of several books and numerous articles. Hon. degrees from ten American and Canadian educl. institutions. Mbr., Phi Beta Kappa; Amer. Acad. of Arts and Sci.; Natl. Inst. for Social Sci.; Amer. Antiquarian Soc.; Mass. Historical Soc.; various clubs. Lecturer at Columbia Univ., Dartmouth and Yale. m. in 1881 to Ella Esther Thompson, of Plymouth Co., Mass. Two s.; three d. D. Nov. 4, 1923, at Winchester. Bur. in Wildwood Cem. there.

COOLIDGE, (JOHN) CALVIN (1919–1921). b. July 4, 1872 at Plymouth Notch, Vt. s. of John Calvin and Victoria Josephine (Moor) C. Descendant of English colonist who emigrated to Mass. in 1630. Father was a farmer, gen. store owner, postmaster, constable, tax collector, justice of the peace, supt. of pub. school, mbr. of Vt. House and Senate, and served on mil. staff of Gov. of Vt. Attd. local pub. schools while assisting father on farm and in store. Mother died when he was 12 years old. Attd. Black River Acad., at Ludlow, Vt.; St. Johnsbury Acad.; and Amherst Coll., from which he was grad. in 1895. Studied law in law office in Northampton, Mass. Admitted to bar in 1897, and set up practice at Northampton. Mbr., Northampton city council, 1899; city solicitor, 1900–1901; ct. clerk, 1903. Mbr. of Mass. House, 1907–1908; mayor of Northampton, 1910–1911; mbr. of Mass. Senate, 1912–1915, serving as pres. of that body, 1914–1915. El. Lieut. Gov. in 1915, continuing to serve in that office until 1918. Nom. and el. Gov. as a

Rep. in 1918, and again in 1919. Attracted natl. attention
in 1919 when he used militia to take over police duties in
Boston during a police force strike. Refused to recognize
right of police to go on strike, and the strike was broken.
Nom. and el. as Rep. cand. for Vice Pres. of U.S. in 1920.
Became first Vice Pres. in over a century to sit as mbr. of
the President's Cabinet. Succeeded to office of Pres. of
U.S. in Aug., 1923, when Pres. Harding died. Nom. and el.
for full term as Pres. of U.S. in 1924. As Pres., admin.
was rocked by investigations into misconduct by U.S. Atty.
Gen., the Sects. of Navy and of the Interior and other high
officials of the Harding admin., which resulted in criminal
convictions. Opposed U.S. entry into League of Nations,
and insisted on repayment of war debts by former allies in
World War I. Used veto freely, including veto of a farm
relief bill and a measure providing for immediate payment
of bonus to World War I veterans. Admin. characterized by
strict economy in govtl. expenditures and general natl. bus.
prosperity. Refused to become a cand. for reel. in 1928.
Retired from pub. life at end of term. Wrote and published
an autobiography. Trustee of Amherst Coll., and of Natl.
Geographic Soc.; hon. moderator of Natl. Council of
Churches. Hon. degrees from nine colleges and universities.
Congregationalist. m. in 1905 to Grace Goodhue, of
Burlington, Vt. Two s., one of whom died during father's
presidency. D. at Northampton, Jan. 5, 1933.

COX, CHANNING HARRIS (1921-1925). b. Oct. 28, 1879 at
Manchester, N.H. s. of Charles Edson and Evelyn Mary
(Randall) C. Attd. Dartmouth Coll., from which he was grad.
in 1901, and Harvard, from which he received law degree in
1904. Engaged in law practice and bus. activities in
Boston. Mbr. of Mass. House, 1910-1918, serving as Speaker
from 1915 onward. El. Lieut. Gov. in 1918, and again in
1919. Nom. and el. Gov. as a Rep. in 1920, becoming first
Gov. of Mass. to be el. for a two-year term. Reel. in 1922.
During admin., a number of social welfare, financial, and
admin. reform measures were enacted. Retired to law practice and bus. affairs after tenure as Gov. Refrained from
law practice in Mass. cts. because he did not wish to em-
barrass judges whom he had appointed to their offices while
he was Gov. Involved in numerous banking, investments,
fruit, sugar, and publishing firms. Delegate to Rep. natl.
convs. in 1924 and 1928. Engaged in a number of civic and
philanthropic endeavors. Trustee of Mass. S.P.C.A.; Mass.
Humane Soc.; Deaconess Hosp. Pres. of Mass. Travelers Aid
Soc.; mbr. of Boston Council of Boy Scouts. Trustee of
Wheaton Coll. and of Boston Univ. m. in 1915 to Mary Emery

Young, of Brookline, Mass. One d. D. Aug. 20, 1968, at
West Harwich, Mass.

FULLER, ALVAN TUFTS (1925-1929). b. Feb. 27, 1878 at
Boston, Mass. s. of Alvan Bond and Flora Arabella (Tufts)
F. Descendant of an English colonist who emigrated to Mass.
in 1635. Attd. pub. schools at Malden, Mass., and
Burdette's Bus. Coll. in Boston. Began working in Malden
for a rubber shoe company; also worked in evenings as
salesman for a bicycle shop. Purchased a small bicycle
shop in Boston. Bus. expanded into auto field in 1899, and
eventually became a large Boston dealership for Cadillac
and Oldsmobile cars. Joined Progressive movement in Rep.
party, and supported Theodore Roosevelt for Pres. of U.S.
in 1912. Declined Prog. party nom. for Gov. El. to U.S.
House in 1915 as Prog., but re-joined Rep. party the next
year. Delegate to Rep. natl. conv. in 1916. El. to U.S.
House in 1916, serving until Jan., 1921, when he resigned
after having been el. Lieut. Gov. in 1920. As mbr. of
Cong., supported U.S. war and defense effort during World
War I. Reel. Lieut. Gov. in 1922. Nom. and el. Gov. as a
Rep. in 1924, and again in 1926. Admin. characterized by
bus. viewpoint. Urged reforms in admin. and jud. system.
After an investigation, refused to intervene to prevent
carrying out execution of Sacco and Vanzetti after their
widely noted trial and conviction for murder. Refused to
retain salary as Gov., returning salary checks to the state
treas. After tenure as Gov., devoted attention to auto
sales bus. Trustee, Newton Theological Inst.; Boston Univ.;
Boston Conserv. of Music. Baptist. Mbr. of numerous social
and bus. clubs; Masons (Shriner); Elks; I.O.O.F.; K.P.;
Natl. Grange; Amer. Forestry Assoc.; S.A.R.; S.O.V. Interested in various sports. m. in 1910 to Viola Davenport, of
Boston. Two s.; two d. D. at Boston, April 30, 1958. Bur.
in East Cem., Rye Beach, N.H.

ALLEN, FRANK G. (1929-1931). b. Oct. 6, 1874 at Lynn,
Mass. s. of Frank Mitchell and Abbie (Gilman) A. Father
was engaged in leather mfg. bus. Attd. local pub. schools,
and was admitted to Harvard, but preferred to go into bus.
Worked for Lyman Smith Co., of Norwood, Mass., a well-estab-
lished leather mfg. firm. It merged with another one,
Winslow Bros., in 1901. Continued to be assoc. with the
firm, becoming its pres. in 1911. It expanded further, becoming one of the largest in its field in the U.S. Served
as its pres. until 1929, when he became ch. of its bd. of
dir. Mbr. of Norwood bd. of assessors, 1910, becoming ch.
in 1911, and serving until 1915. Mbr. and ch. of Norwood

bd. of selectmen, 1915-1923. Mbr. of Mass. House, 1918-
1919, and of Mass. Senate, 1920-1924, serving as its presiding officer, 1921-1924. Delegate to Rep. natl. conv. in
1920. El. Lieut. Gov. in 1924, and continued in that office for next term. Nom. and el. Gov. as a Rep. in 1928,
although Mass. voted for Dem. cand. for Pres. of U.S. in
that election. Defeated for second term in 1930. Devoted
attention to bus. interests thereafter, which extended to
banking, ins., ice, railroad, hosiery mfg., and chemicals
fields. Trustee, Wellesley Coll.; Boston Univ.; Norwood
Hosp.; Wrentham School. Congregationalist. m. in 1897 to
Clara H. Winslow, of Norwood. One d. m. in 1927 to
Eleanor H. Wallace, of Pittsburgh, Pa. One s.; one d. D.
Oct. 9, 1950. Bur. in Highland Cem., Norwood.

ELY, JOSEPH BUELL (1931-1935). b. Feb. 22, 1881 at
Westfield, Mass. s. of Henry Wilson and Sarah Naomi (Buell)
S. Descendant of an English colonist who emigrated to Mass.
in 1632. Grad. from Williams Coll. in 1902, and received
law degree from Harvard in 1905. Began law practice in
Westfield, later practicing in Springfield and Boston, and
acquired wide clientele. Apptd. dist. atty. for Western
dist. of Mass. in 1915, continuing in that office by el. in
1916. Nom. and el. Gov. as a Dem. in 1930, defeating incumbent Gov. Allen. Reel. in 1932. After tenure as Gov.,
became partner in law firms at Westfield and Springfield.
Pres. and mbr. of bd. of dir. of Amer. Woolen Co.; also a
dir. of banking and electric utility companies in New
England area. Mbr., Eastern Racing Assoc.; Phi Delta Theta;
Elks; various social clubs. Hon. degrees from Williams,
Wesleyan, and Holy Cross. Congregationalist. m. in 1906
to Harriet Z. Dyson, of Westfield. One s. D. June 13,
1956.

CURLEY, JAMES MICHAEL (1935-1937). b. Nov. 20, 1874
at Boston, Mass. s. of Michael and Sarah (Clancy) C. Parents had emigrated from Ireland to Boston in 1850. Attd.
local pub. schools. Began work as salesman for a bakery
supply firm. Joined brother in real estate and ins. bus.,
which developed into a thriving concern. Mbr., Boston city
council, 1900-1901, and of Mass. House, 1902-1903. Mbr. of
bd. of aldermen in Boston, 1904-1909. Mbr. of Boston city
council again in 1910, and while serving in that office
was el. to U.S. House. Served therein until Feb., 1914,
when he resigned to become mayor of Boston. Continued as
mayor in Boston until 1918, being defeated for reel. in
1917. Became pres. of Hibernian Savings Bank of Boston,
1922. El. mayor of Boston again in 1922, serving until

1926. Defeated as Dem. cand. for Gov. in 1924. El. mayor
of Boston again in 1930, serving until 1934. Nom. and el.
Gov. as a Dem. in 1934. Defeated as Dem. cand. for the U.S.
Senate in 1936; also was defeated as Dem. cand. for Gov. in
1938, and for mayor of Boston in 1941. Mbr., Dem. natl.
commt., 1941-1942. El. to U.S. House in 1942 and again in
1944. Did not seek third term in 1944. Mayor of Boston
again, 1946-1950. Defeated for the Dem. nom. for mayor of
Boston in 1951 and again in 1955. Mbr., Mass. Labor Relations Bd., 1957. During career, in which he was a major
figure in Mass. politics, was el. mayor of Boston on four
occasions and defeated on six occasions; won election for
Gov. once, and was defeated for that office twice; lost as
Dem. cand. for U.S. Senate once; and was el. to U.S. House
four times. A controversial figure, was twice convicted on
criminal charges connected with political matters. Was at
odds with the natl. Dem. admin. during the time he was in
Cong. in 1940s, particularly in matters involving patronage.
m. in 1906 to Mary E. Herlihy, of Boston. Eight children.
m. in 1937 to Mrs. Gertrude M. Dennis. Mbr., Boston CC;
B.P.O.E.; K.C. Roman Catholic. Recipient of awards from
Italy, France, Japan and Serbia. D. at Boston, Nov. 12,
1958. Bur. in Old Calvary Cem. there.

HURLEY, CHARLES FRANCIS (1937-1939). b. Nov. 23, 1893
at Cambridge, Mass. s. of John Joseph and Elizabeth (Maher)
H. Attd. Boston Coll., 1913-1915. Engaged in real estate
bus. in Boston in 1915. Served in U.S. Navy during World
War I. Mbr., Cambridge school bd., 1919-1931. Apptd.
Treas. and Receiver Gen. of Mass. in 1931, serving in that
office until 1937. Nom. and el. Gov. as a Dem. in 1936.
Defeated for Dem. nom. for Gov. by former Gov. James Curley
in 1938. Mbr., Elks; Hibernian Soc.; Amer. Legion; Irish
Natl. Foresters; Knights of Firnan; Catholic Union of
Cambridge; various bus. and social clubs. Roman Catholic.
m. in 1824 to Marion L. Conley. Four d.; one s. D. March
24, 1946.

SALTONSTALL, LEVERETT (1939-1945). b. Sept. 1, 1892
at Chestnut Hill, Mass. s. of Richard M. and Eleanor
(Brooks) S. Parents were descendants of distinguished Mass.
families. Ancestral line included eight persons who had
served as colonial or State Govs. of Mass. Attd. local pub.
schools; Noble and Greenough pvt. school; and Harvard, from
which he was grad. with an A.B. degree in 1914 and a law
degree in 1917. Served as first lieut. in U.S. artillery
unit in France, 1917-1919. Admitted to bar and began practice in Boston in 1919. Also became involved in banking

and other bus. enterprises, including the Boston and Albany
R.R. Mbr., bd. of aldermen at Newton, Mass. Asst. dist.
atty. for Middlesex Co., 1921-1922. Mbr. of Mass. House,
1923-1936, serving as Speaker, 1929-1936. Defeated as Rep.
cand. for Lieut. Gov. in 1936, but was nom. and el. Gov. as
a Rep. in 1938. Reel. in 1940 and 1942. As Gov., supported U.S. war effort vigorously during World War II; also advocated social and economic legislation in line with Pres.
Roosevelt's New Deal programs. Internationalist and moderately liberal in political outlook. Ch. of Natl. Govs.'
Conf. in 1944 and pres., Council of State Govts. Delegate
to Rep. natl. convs. in 1932 and 1940-1968. El. to U.S.
Senate in 1944 to fill vacancy. Served in Senate until
Jan., 1967. Did not seek reel. in 1966, retiring to home
at Dover, Mass. Dir. of Community Fund, 1938. Pres. of Bd.
of Overseers of Harvard; Trustee, Mass. Eye and Ear Infirmary; mgr., Farm and Trade School; dir. of various banking
and other bus. corps. Mbr., Masons; Elks; and various
fraternal and social clubs. Unitarian. m. in 1916 to
Alice Wesselhoeft. Four children. One son was killed in
action on Guam during World War II. D. June 17, 1979.

TOBIN, MAURICE JOSEPH (1945-1947). b. May 22, 1901 at
Roxbury (South Boston), Mass. s. of James J. and Margaret
M. (Daly) T., who had emigrated from Ireland to Amer.
Worked as newsboy while attending local pub. schools. Attd.
Boston Coll. of Law, but was not a grad. Also studied pub.
speaking. Worked for a Boston leather goods company. In
1922 began working for New England Transit Co., rising to
post of regional traffic mgr. Mbr. of Mass. House, 1927-
1928, and of Boston school commt., 1931-1934 and 1935-1937.
In 1936 was el. mayor of Boston, defeating Gov. James M.
Curley for the office. Served as mayor until 1944. Mbr.
of Boston area Civilian Defense Bd. from 1942 onward during
World War II. Nom. and el. Gov. as a Dem. in 1944. As
Gov., sought to advance interests of Boston as trans-
Atlantic air terminal; signed a fair employment practices
measure; took action against black market activities. Nom.
for second term in 1946, but was defeated when Mayor Curley
of Boston withheld support. Apptd. U.S. Sect. of Labor by
Pres. Truman in 1948, serving until 1953. Mbr., Mass.
Catholic Order of Foresters; K.C.; Moose; and various social
and civic clubs. Roman Catholic. Hon. degrees from seven
colleges and universities. m. in 1942 to Helen Noonan.
Two d.; one s. D. July 19, 1953.

BRADFORD, ROBERT FISKE (1947-1949). b. Dec. 15, 1902
at Boston, Mass. s. of Edward H. and Edith (Fiske) B.

Father was a physician and dean of Harvard Med. School.
Descendant of Wm. Bradford, second Gov. of Plymouth colony.
Attd. Browne and Nichols' School, and Harvard, from which
he received an A.B. degree in 1923, and a law degree in
1926. Was ed. of Harvard Crimson as an undergraduate. Employed by financial and investment firms in Boston area.
Exec. sect. to Gov. Ely, 1931-1935. Dist. atty. for
Middlesex Co., 1938-1942. El. Lieut Gov. as a Rep. in 1944,
although State chose a Dem. for Gov. (Tobin). Was the Rep.
cand. for Gov. in 1946 and was el., defeating incumbent
Gov. Tobin. Defeated in try for second term in 1948. As
Gov., sought to decrease state deficit. Labor-mgmt. rela-
tions gave rise to difficulties, for which he set up a
commt. to investigate. Served on bds. of dir. for Browne
and Nichols' School and Simmons Coll.; Mass. Hosp. School;
Mass. Eye and Ear Infirmary; Boston Community Recreation
Service; Boston Council of Social Agencies; Norfolk House
Center; and other civic agencies. Senior warden, Kings
Chapel. m. in 1926 to Rebecca C. Browne. Four children.

DEVER, PAUL ANDREW (1949-1953). b. Jan. 15, 1903 at
Boston, Mass. s. of Joseph Patrick and Anna Amelia
(McAlevy) D. Was one of seven children. Father died when
son was eight years old, and mother moved to Dorchester,
Mass. Attd. local schools; Boston Latin School, working as
shoe salesman and shipping clerk while attending school to
acquire funds for further educ. Attd. Pace Inst.;
Northeastern Univ.; and Boston Univ., from which he received a law degree in 1926. Grad. with highest honors, and
was ed. of Boston Univ. Law Review while a student. Began
law practice in Boston. Mbr. of Mass. House, 1929-1935.
El. Atty. Gen. of Mass. in 1934, becoming the youngest to
be el. to that office up to that time. Continued in that
office until 1941. As Atty. Gen., pursued an indep. course
from that of Gov. Curley, and gained reputation as "champion of the little fellow". Dem. nominee for Gov. in 1940,
but was defeated in a close election. Resumed law practice,
and was lecturer at Boston Univ. in 1941-1942. Commissioned as lieut. commdr. in U.S. Navy in 1942. Saw service in
Caribbean, European and Mediterranean theaters before leaving service in 1945. Defeated as Dem. nominee for Lieut.
Gov. in 1946, but was nom. and el. Gov. as a Dem. in 1948,
defeating incumbent Gov. Bradford. Major campaign issues
were retention of 10¢ fare for Metropolitan Transit Authority and improvement of highways. Reel. in 1950, but was
defeated as Dem. nominee for third term in 1952. Mbr.,
Amer. Legion; K.C.; V.F.W.; Elks; Anc. and Hon. Artillery
Co.; Phi Delta Phi; various professional legal orgs. Roman

Catholic. Never married. D. April 11, 1958.

HERTER, CHRISTIAN ARCHIBALD (1953-1957). b. March 28,
1895 in Paris, France. s. of Albert and Adele (McGuiness)
H. Parents were artists temporarily sojourning abroad.
Attd. school in Paris, 1901-1904; Browning School in New
York City, 1904-1911; and Harvard, from which he was grad.
cum laude, in 1915. Studied architecture for a time at
Columbia Univ. In 1916 became attaché of U.S. embassy in
Berlin, Germany, later serving at the Amer. legation in
Brussels, Belgium. Was rejected as enlistee in U.S. Army
during World War I because of height. Served in U.S. State
Dept., 1917-1919. Sect. to Amer. Peace Commn. in 1918-1919.
In 1920, was exec. sect. to European Relief Council under
Herbert Hoover. Asst. to U.S. Sect. of Commerce in
Washington, D.C., 1921-1924. Assoc. ed., and vice pres. of
publishing bus. in Boston, 1924-1937. Lecturer at Harvard
on intl. relations, 1929-1930. Mbr. of Mass. House, 1931-
1943. Deputy dir., U.S. Office of Facts and Figures, 1941-
1942. Mbr., U.S. House, 1943-1953. Received Collier's
Award as mbr. of House in 1948. Did not seek reel. in 1952,
but was nom. and el. Gov. as a Rep. in that year, defeating
incumbent Gov. Dever. Mentioned prominently as possible
nominee for Vice Pres. of U.S. in 1952 with Gen. Eisenhower,
whom he supported for the Rep. nom. for Pres. Reel. Gov.
in 1954. Apptd. U.S. Under-Sect. of State in 1957, then
became Sect. of State in 1959, serving until the end of
Pres. Eisenhower's admin. in 1961. Ch. of Hon. Council of
Intl. Movement for Atlantic Union in 1961, and co-ch., U.S.
Citizens Commn. on NATO, 1961. Spec. Repr. of U.S. President for Foreign Trade Negotiations, 1963 until death. Hon.
degrees from twelve universities and colleges, and decorations from several foreign govts. Mbr., Bd. of Overseers,
Harvard, 1940-1944 and 1946-1952. Trustee of several phil-
anthropic and charitable orgs. m. in 1917 to Mary Caroline
Pratt. Three s.; one d. D. Dec. 30, 1966, in Washington,
D.C. Bur. in Prospect Hill Cem., Millis, Mass.

FURCOLO, FOSTER JOHN (1957-1961). b. July 29, 1911 at
New Haven, Conn. s. of Dr. Charles L. and Alberta Maria
(Foster) F. Family was of Irish-Italian descent. Father
was a neuro-surgeon, who became head of a clinic in
Springfield, Mass. when son was a youth. Attd. pub. schools
in New Haven and Springfield; and Yale, from which he re-
ceived an A.B. degree in 1933 and a law degree in 1936.
Was interested in theater as a student, having written two
plays while in college. Began law practice in Springfield,
Mass. Defeated as cand. for dist. atty. of Hampden Co.

Served in U.S. Navy as lieut., j.g., in Pac. theater during
World War II, 1942-1946. Defeated as cand. for U.S. House
seat in 1946. El. to U.S. House as a Dem. in 1948, and
again in 1950. Resigned House seat in Sept., 1952, to accept apptmt. as Mass. Treas. and Receiver Gen., and was
subsequently el. to the office. Defeated as Dem. cand. for
U.S. Senate seat in 1954. Was critical of A.D.A. org. as a
weakening influence in Dem. party affairs. Nom. and el.
Gov. as Dem. in 1956, and again in 1958. As Gov., sought
to control deficit spending. Defeated as cand. for Dem.
nom. for U.S. Senate seat in 1960. Apptd. asst. dist. atty.
in 1967. Ch. of Atty. Gen.'s Advisory Commt. on Narcotics,
1969. Roman Catholic. Author of The Story of Katyn, published in 1966. Hon. degrees from several institutions of
higher learning. m. in 1936 to Kathryn Foran. Four s.;
one d.

VOLPE, JOHN ANTHONY (1961-1963; 1965-1969). b. Dec. 8,
1908 at Wakefield, Mass. s. of Vito and Filomena
(Benedetto) V. Parents had emigrated to Amer. from Italy.
Attd. local pub. schools. Wished to attend college, but
failure of father's bus. necessitated his going to work.
Employed in constr. work, becoming a journeyman plasterer
in 1926. Attd. Wentworth Inst. in 1928-1930, studying
architectural constr. Engaged in own constr. bus. in
Malden, Mass., 1933-1960. Entered U.S. Navy in 1943 as
lieut., j.g. Rose to rank of lieut. commndr. in Civil Engr.
Corps. by end of World War II. Returned to constr. bus. in
1946. Deputy ch., Mass. Rep. commt., 1950-1953. Mbr.,
Mass. Pub. Works Commn., 1953-1956. U.S. Highway Adminr.,
Fed. Interstate Highway program, 1956-1957. Nom. and el.
Gov. of Mass. as a Rep. in 1960. Investigations uncovered
mismanagement in Mass. highway constr. program. Defeated
for second term in close election in 1962, but was Rep.
nominee for Gov. again in 1964 and was el. Nom. again for
Gov. in 1966 and was el., becoming the first Mass. Gov. to
be el. for four-year term. Delegate to Rep. natl. convs.
in 1960-1968. Apptd. U.S. Sect. of Transp. by Pres. Nixon
in 1969, resigning office of Gov. in Jan. of that year.
Served until Jan., 1973. Mbr. of various bus. and labor
orgs. in constr. field; Greater Boston CC; Amer. Legion;
Italian-Amer. War Vets.; G.C.A.; K.C.; Sons of Italy in
Amer. Recipient of People to People Town Affiliation Award,
1966, and Construction Man of the Year Award, 1970. Order
of Merit from Italian govt. Mbr., various civic, religious
and charitable orgs. Roman Catholic. m. in 1934 to Jennie
Benedetto. One s.; one d.

PEABODY, ENDICOTT (1963-1965). b. Feb. 15, 1920 in
Lawrence, Mass. s. of the Very Rev. Malcolm and Mary
Elizabeth (Parkman) P. Descendant of John Endicott, Gov.
of Mass. Bay colony in 1629, and of Geo. Peabody, eminent
financier and philanthropist. Grandfather was founder and
headmaster of Groton School for boys. Attd. Penn Charter
School, near Philadelphia, and Groton, where grandfather
was still headmaster. Attd. Harvard, from which he was
grad. in 1942. Active in intercollegiate sports. Mbr. of
NROTC while at Harvard. Served as officer in U.S. Navy in
Atl., Caribbean and Korean theaters during World War II.
Returned to Harvard where he received law degree in 1948.
Active participant in Dem. pres. campaigns in 1948, 1952
and 1956. Asst. regional counsel for O.P.S., 1950-1951,
and regional counsel for U.S. Small Defense Plants Admin.
in 1952. Became founder and partner in law firm in Boston
in 1952. Mbr., Mass. Exec. Council, 1954. Defeated as
cand. for Dem. nom. for Atty. Gen. in 1956 and 1958, and
for Gov. in 1960. Was Dem. nominee for Gov. in 1962
against incumbent Gov. Volpe, and was el. in a close vote.
As Gov., pressed for constl. reform, which caused some dis-
sension in party. Defeated for re-nom. in 1964. Defeated
as Dem. cand. for U.S. Senate seat in 1966. Asst. dir.,
Office of Emergency Preparedness on Pres. Johnson's staff,
1967-1968, and ch., Sports Committee, President's Commn. on
U.S.-Mexican Border Devel. and Friendship, 1967-1969. Outstanding Young Man Award by Boston JCC in 1954. Mbr., professional legal orgs.; Amer. Legion; Elks. Involved in
various civic, health and welfare drives. Episcopalian. m.
in 1944 to Barbara (Toni) Welch-Gibbons, of Bermuda. One
d.; two s.

VOLPE, JOHN ANTHONY (1965-1969). See above, 1961-1963.

SARGENT, FRANCIS W(ILLIAMS) (1969-1975). b. July 29,
1915 at Hamilton, Mass. s. of Francis W. and Margery (Lee)
S. Attd. prep. school at Dedham, Mass., and Mass. Inst. of
Tech., from which he was grad. in 1939 with a degree in
architecture. Founded and became head of Goose Hummock
Shop, Inc., at Orleans, Mass. Served in U.S. Army during
World War II, holding rank of capt. when he left service at
end of the war. Recipient of Bronze Star and Purple Heart.
Apptd. dir. of Marine Fisheries div. of Mass. Dept. of Nat-
ural Resources in 1947, and became head of the Dept. in
1956, serving until 1959. Ch. of Atlantic States Marine
Fisheries Commn., and ch. of Mass. Water Resources Commn.,
1956-1959. Exec. dir., U.S. Outdoor Recreation Review
Commt., 1959-1962. Refused offer of post of U.S. Natl.

Park Service head from Pres. Kennedy. Defeated as cand.
for Mass. Senate in 1962. Ch. of panel at President's
White House Conf. on Natural Beauty, 1964. Commnr. of Mass.
Pub. Works Dept., 1965-1966. El. Lieut. Gov. as a Rep. in
1966. Succeeded to office of Gov. on Jan. 20, 1969, when
Gov. Volpe resigned. Completed Volpe's term and was el.
for regular term in 1970. As Gov., signed into law one of
the first "no fault" auto ins. statutes in U.S.; also was
opposed to U.S. continued participation in Vietnam War, and
signed a bill challenging the validity of U.S. participation therein. Approved other legislation changing eligibility for Medicaid payments, resulting in significant
saving of pub. funds. Also approved several measures designed to protect environmental interests in Mass. Defeated as Rep. nominee for reel. in 1974. Trustee, New England
Aquarium.; mbr., Advisory Bd. for Cape Cod Community Coll.;
dir., Mass. S.P.C.A. Participant in numerous community
service clubs and fund-raising campaigns for charitable
causes. Hon. degrees from three colleges and universities.
Unitarian. m. in 1938 to Jessie Fay. One s.; two d.

DUKAKIS, MICHAEL STANLEY (1975-1979). b. Nov. 3, 1933
at Boston, Mass. s. of Panos and Euterpe (Boukis) D.
Family was of Greek descent. Attd. Swarthmore Coll., from
which he was grad. with honors in 1955. Served in U.S.
Army, 1956-1958. Attd. Harvard Law School, from which he
received a law degree in 1960. Began law practice in
Boston as mbr. of Boston law firm. Mbr., Mass. House, 1962-
1970. Nom. and el. Gov. as a Dem. in 1974, defeating incumbent Gov. Sargent. Vice ch., New England Govs.' Conf.,
1975, and ch., 1976. Co-ch., New England Commn. Defeated
in 1978 Dem. primary for re-nom. for office of Gov. Part-
time lecturer at Harvard after tenure as Gov. Mbr., Phi
Beta Kappa. Greek Orthodox church. Married and father of
three children.

MASON, STEVENS THOMSON (1837-1840). b. Oct. 27, 1811
in Loudoun Co. Va. s. of John Thomson and Elizabeth (Moir)
M. Was the great-grandson of George M., Va. statesman of
the Rev. War era, and grandson of Stevens Thomson M., a U.S.
Senator from Va. Father, who was a lawyer, moved to Lexington, Ky. during son's youth, where the son attd. Transylvania Univ. for a time. Father was apptd. Sect. of Mich.
Terr. govt. in 1830, but resigned the office the next year,
and his son succeeded him in office as Sect. of the Terr.
Gov. at age 19. Pres. Jackson's first nominee to the post
of Terr. Gov. was not confirmed by the U.S. Senate. As the
acting Gov. of the Terr., M. took a firm stand against Ohio
with reference to the claim of Mich. to the so-called "Toledo Strip," a tract of land along the Mich.-Ohio border,
and called out the Terr. militia forces to back his claim.
Pres. Jackson then named John S. Horner as Terr. Gov. and
removed M. as Sect. and acting Gov., but the Jackson appointee was not recognized by the govt. and people of the
Terr. when he arrived in Detroit in Sept., 1835. A statehood movement in Mich. was already well under way by that
time, and a proposed const. for the State was approved by
the voters of Mich. Terr. in Oct., 1835. M. was el. Gov.
of the proposed State on a provisional basis at the same
time, and he assumed office in Nov., 1835. He acted as de
facto State Gov. until Mich. was formally admitted to statehood early in 1837 after the dispute with Ohio over the
southern boundary matter was resolved. It was settled by
inclusion of additional lands of the Upper Peninsula in Mich.
in return for surrender of the "Toledo Strip," which was al-
located to Ohio. He continued to act as de jure Gov. of the
State thereafter until the end of the term for which he was
originally el., and was el. for the succeeding term in 1837.
During admin., he proceeded with the org. of first State
govt.; laid foundations for a pub. school system; and the
Univ. of Mich. was reorganized and removed from Detroit to
Ann Arbor. Financial panic of 1837 caused much distress in
Mich. and was accompanied by numerous bank failures, causing him to lose popularity during second term. Was absent
from State for two prolonged periods in 1838, during which
time Edward Muncy, the Lieut. Gov., exercised the powers of
the office of Gov. Following expiration of his term in 1840,
settled in New York City, where he practiced law. m. in
1838 to Julia Phelps. Three children. D. in N.Y. Jan. 4,
1843 at the age of 32. Bur. in Capitol Park Cem., Detroit.

WOODBRIDGE, WILLIAM W. (1840-1841). b. Aug. 20, 1780
in Norwich, Conn. s. of Dudley and Lucy (Backus) W. Father
moved to Marietta, in the Northwest Terr., in 1791. Son was

sent back to Conn. to complete educ. Studied law at Judge
Reeves' Litchfield, Conn. law school and was admitted to
practice in Conn. Returned to Marietta, Ohio in 1806 and
practiced law there. Mbr. of Ohio House in 1807. Pros.
atty. of New London (now Washington) Co., 1808-1814, and
also served in Ohio Senate, 1809-1814. Apptd. Sect. of Mich.
Terr. by Pres. Madison in 1814 and moved to Detroit, Mich.
Also served as U.S. collector of customs at Detroit and as
U.S. Indian agent. As atty. for J. J. Astor Northwest Fur
Co., was involved in a number of cases between his client
and the Hudson Bay Co. First Terr. Delegate from Mich. Terr.
to Cong., 1819-1820. During his tenure was instrumental in
getting U.S. aid for beginning of constr. of road from Detroit into Ohio; exploration of parts of Northwest Terr.;
and settlement of French claims in the region. Resigned as
Terr. Delegate in 1820. Judge of Supreme Ct. of Terr. of
Mich., 1828-1832. Mbr. of first state constl. conv. in 1835,
being chosen as a Whig. El. to Mich. Senate, 1837, and in
1839 was el. Gov. as a Whig. During admin., constr. of a
railroad from Detroit to Ann Arbor was completed and the
setting up of the Univ. of Mich. at Ann Arbor completed.
Resigned as Gov. in Feb., 1841 to take seat in the U.S.
Senate, having been el. by a combination of Whigs and Dems.
in the legislature. Served in Senate until 1847. Returned
to Mich. and engaged in horticultural pursuits at his farm
near Detroit. m. to Juliana Trumbull in 1806. Four children. D. at Detroit, Oct. 20, 1861. Bur. in Elmwood Cem.
there.

GORDON, J(AMES) WRIGHT (1841-1842). b. in Plainfield,
Conn. in 1809. Father was a man of prominence in the community, and had engaged in local political affairs. Attd.
Harvard, from which he was grad. For a time was a teacher
in an acad. at Geneva, N. Y., to which place his father had
moved. Studied law and was admitted to the N.Y. bar. In
1835, moved to Mich. Terr., settling at Marshall, where he
practiced law and also became involved in politics as a Whig.
El. Lieut. Gov. in 1839. Succeeded to the office of Gov. in
Feb., 1841 when Gov. Woodbridge resigned to take seat in
U.S. Senate, and completed the term for which Woodbridge had
been el. Was himself selected as the Whig party cand. for
the vacant Senate post by the Whig legislative caucus, but
a number of the Whig party mbrs. joined with some Dem. mbrs.
to choose Woodbridge as Senator. At the beginning of Pres.
Taylor's admin. was apptd. to a post as U.S. consul in So.
America, a position he accepted in the expectation that a
change in climate would improve his health, which had begun
to fail. D. in Dec., 1853 in a fall from a balcony at
Pernambuco, Brazil.

BARRY, JOHN STEWART (1842-1846; 1850-1852). b. Jan. 29,
1802 at Amherst, N.H.   s. of John and Ellen (Stewart) S.
Family moved to Rockingham, Vt. shortly after his birth, and
he grew up there. Attd. local schools while assisting father on family farm. In 1824 went to Atlanta, Ga., where he
taught school and engaged in the study of law. Admitted to
Ga. bar and began practice there in 1826. Served on staff
of Gov. of Ga. In 1831 moved to Mich. Terr., settling at
White Pigeon. Disliking law as a profession, engaged in
merc. bus. In 1834 moved to Constantine, Mich. Mbr. of
Mich. constl. conv. in 1835, and was el. to first Mich.
Senate that year, and was el. for another term in 1839.
Travelled in Europe to study sugar beet indus. in 1840. Nom.
and el. Gov. as Dem. in 1841 and again in 1843. El. again
as Gov. in 1849. During admin., was confronted by serious
economic crisis because of the failure of banks in which the
State had an interest. Sold railroad shares in which the
State had invested and eventually placed the State's finances on a sound basis. A revised state const. was drafted
and adopted during his last term as Gov. Retired to devote
attention to bus. affairs after the rise of the Rep. party
in 1850s. Served as delegate to Dem. natl. conv. in 1864,
and was on the Dem. ticket for pres. elector on two occasions. m. to Mary Kidder, of Grafton, Vt. No children survived him. D. Jan. 14, 1870 at Constantine, Mich.

FELCH, ALPHEUS (1846-1847). b. Sept. 28, 1804 at
Limerick, Dist. of Me. s. of Daniel and Sally (Piper) F.
Father, who was the proprietor of a country store, died when
son was two years old, and his mother died three years later.
Was brought up by his grandfather, Abijah F., who was a Rev.
War soldier and was a person of prominence in the community.
Attd. Exeter Acad. and Bowdoin Coll., from which he was grad.
in 1827. Was a classmate there of Henry W. Longfellow,
Nathaniel Hawthorne and John P. Hale, among others who later
achieved natl. prominence. Studied law and began practice
in Houlton, Me. in 1830. Because of failing health moved
West to Monroe, Mich., intending to settle in South, but became ill of cholera at Cincinnati, Ohio and returned to
Monroe, Mich. where he began practice of law. Mbr. of Mich.
legislature, 1836-1837, where he opposed so-called "wildcat"
banking legislation. Mich. Banking Commnr., 1838-1839. Exposed fraudulent practices in banking activities and guilty
parties were prosecuted. Mich. Aud. Gen. in 1842, and in
1843 was apptd. cir. ct. judge and later, a mbr. of the Mich.
Supreme Ct. In 1843 moved to Ann Arbor, Mich. Resigned jud.
post in 1845 after being nom. and el. Gov. as Dem. As Gov.,
signed measure removing state seat of govt. from Detroit to
Lansing, Mich. Resigned as Gov. in March, 1847 after being

chosen to U.S. Senate, in which he served until 1853. As a
Sen., was instrumental in obtaining a land grant from U.S.
to Mich. for constr. of ship canal around St. Mary's River
rapids to improve navigation between Lakes Superior and
Huron. Pres. of U.S. Commn. from 1853 to 1856 to adjust
land claims in Calif. growing out of Mexican cession. Returned to Ann Arbor in 1856 and resumed law practice. Defeated as Dem. nominee for Gov. in 1856. Supported Union
cause during Civil War. Twice sought seat in U.S. Senate
unsuccessfully. Apptd. prof. of law at the Univ. of Mich.
in 1879. Resigned that post after five years because of
failing health and eyesight. Mbr., Univ. of Mich. Bd. of
Regents; Mich. Historical Soc., serving as its pres. in 1892,
and collector of items on early history of Mich. Bequeathed
library of some 4,000 items to Univ. of Mich. m. in 1837 to
Lucretia Lawrence, of Monroe, Mich. Several children. D.
at Ann Arbor, June 13, 1896. Bur. in Forest Hills Cem.
there.

GREENLY, WILLIAM L. (1847-1848). b. Sept. 18, 1813 at
Hamilton, N.Y. s. of Thomas and Nancy G. Attd. Hamilton
Acad. and Union Coll., from which he was grad. in 1831.
Studied law at Hamilton, admitted to bar in 1833, and began
practice in Hamilton area. Moved to Adrian, Mich. in 1836.
Was unsuccessful as cand. for seat in Mich. legislature in
1837, but was el. to Mich. Senate in 1839 and again in 1841.
Pres. pro tem of Senate in 1840 and 1842. El. Lieut. Gov.
as Dem. in 1845. Succeeded to office of Gov. in March, 1847
when Gov. Felch resigned to take seat in U.S. Senate. Completed Felch's term. During admin., the transfer of State
capital from Detroit to Lansing was effected. Assisted in
raising a volunteer regiment in Mich. for the Mexican War.
Mayor of Adrian in 1848. Served as justice of the peace
there for twelve years. Participated in the dedication of
new Capitol bldg. at Lansing in 1879. D. at Adrian Nov. 29,
1883. Bur. at Oakwood Cem., Adrian.

RANSOM, EPAPHRODITUS (1848-1850). b. in Feb., 1797 at
Shelburne Falls, Mass. s. of Major Ezekiel and -------
(Fletcher) R. Father had been an officer in the Contl. Army
during Rev. War. Family moved to Vt. during his youth,
where father engaged in farming. Attd. local schools while
assisting on farm. Student at Chester Acad., in Vt. Taught
school while studying law at Townshend, Vt. in office of
Judge Taft, grandfather of Wm. Howard Taft, Pres. of U.S.
Later studied law at a school in Northampton, Mass., from
which he was grad. with distinction in 1823. Began law
practice in Windham Co., Vt. Served several terms as town

repr. in Vt. legislature. In 1834 moved to Bronson, later
to Kalamazoo, in Mich. Terr., where he practiced law. When
Mich. was admitted to statehood, was apptd. cir ct. judge
and then became a mbr. of Mich. Supreme Ct., becoming its
Chief Justice in 1843. Nom. and el. Gov. as Dem. in 1847.
Was the first Mich. Gov. to be inaugurated at Lansing. During admin., legislation was passed incorporating several
companies for beginning of mining operations in the Upper
Peninsula, giving rise to a thriving indus. there. Companies were also created for bldg. and operating toll roads
in various parts of the State. A State Agri. Soc. was organized, of which he later became pres. His endorsement of
the Wilmot Proviso led to his being defeated in contest for
re-nom. for Gov. by Dem. party in 1849. Mbr. of Mich. House,
1853-1854, and of the Univ. of Mich. Bd. of Regents, 1850-
1852. Suffered financial reverses following the financial
crisis of 1853. In 1857 was apptd. U.S. receiver at U.S.
land office in Osage dist., in Kansas Terr. D. at Ft. Scott,
Kans., Nov. 11(9?), 1859. Bur. at Mountain Home Cem.,
Kalamazoo.

BARRY, JOHN STEWART (1850-1852). See above, 1842-1846.

McCLELLAND, ROBERT (1852-1853). b. Aug. 2, 1807 in
Greencastle, Pa. s. of Dr. John and Eleanor (McCulloh) McC.
Father was a physician there. Attd. local schools, and engaged in teaching for a tmme. Attd. Dickinson Coll., from
which he was grad. in 1829. Studied law and was admitted to
bar in 1831. Practiced at Chambersburg, Pa. and then at
Pittsburgh until 1833, when he moved to Monroe, Mich. Terr.,
continuing to practice law. Mbr. of Mich. constl. conv. in
1835. Was offered posts of atty. gen. and banking commnr.
in new State govt., but declined them. Apptd. to the Univ.
of Mich. Bd. of Regents in 1837 and was again a mbr. of that
body in 1850. Mbr. of Mich. House in 1838 and 1840, serving
as Speaker pro tem. Mayor of Monroe, 1841. Mbr. of Mich.
House again in 1842, serving as Speaker. El. to U.S. House
in 1842, continuing to serve therein for next two terms. Was
not a cand. for reel. in 1848. Supported Wilmot Proviso
while in U.S. House. Active in campaign of Lewis Cass for
U.S. Pres. in 1848. Established law practice in Detroit in
1849. Delegate to Dem. natl. convs. in 1848, 1852 and 1868.
Mbr. of Mich. constl. conv. in 1850. El. Gov. as Dem. in
1851, being chosen for a one-year term because of change in
election and term schedule effected by revised state const.
El. for a two-year term in 1852, but resigned office shortly
after beginning of term to take post of U.S. Sect. of the
Interior to which he had been apptd. by Pres. Pierce.

Served in that office until 1857. Returned thereafter to
law practice in Detroit. Mbr. of Mich. constl. conv. of
1867. m. in 1836 to (Sarah?) Elizabeth Sabine. D. in
Detroit Aug. 30, 1880. Bur. in Elmwood Cem. there.

PARSONS, ANDREW (1853-1855). b. July 22, 1817 at
Hoosick, N.Y. s. of John P., who originally had resided at
Newburyport, Mass. Family was of English-Irish descent.
Received common school educ. In 1835 at age 17 moved to
Mich. Terr. Taught school for a short time at Ann Arbor;
clerked in a store in Ionia Co.; and eventually settled at
Corunna, in Shiawassee Co. Became co. clerk there, and from
1840 to 1846, co. register of deeds. Studied law while
serving in those posts. Mbr. of Mich. Senate, 1847-1848.
Apptd. pros. atty. for Shiawassee Co. in 1848, and in 1851
was apptd. to the Bd. of Regents of Univ. of Mich. El.
Lieut. Gov. as Dem. in 1852. Succeeded to office of Gov. in
March, 1853 when Gov. McClelland resigned to become U.S.
Sect. of the Interior. Completed term for which McClelland
had been el. El. to Mich. House in 1854. D. June 6, 1855
at Corunna. Bur. in family cem. plot there.

BINGHAM, KINSLEY SCOTT (1855-1859). b. Dec. 16, 1808
at Camillus, N.Y. s. of Calvin and Betsy (Scott) B. Father
had moved to N.Y. from Vt., and was a farmer. Attd. local
schools while assisting father on farm. Studied law in office in Syracuse, N.Y. In 1833 moved to Green Oak, in Livingston Co., Mich. Terr., where he had acquired a tract of
land. In collaboration with brother-in-law, proceeded to
improve it into a farm. Admitted to bar and began law practice. Served as justice of the peace and as postmaster, and
became the first probate judge of Livingston Co. El. to
first State legislature after Mich. became a State. Continued in that office for next four terms, serving as
Speaker of the House for three terms. In 1846 was el. to
U.S. House as Dem., and continued in that office for the
succeeding term. As mbr. of House opposed extension of
slavery and voted for Wilmot Proviso. Was not a cand. for
reel. in 1850. Nom. for Gov. by Free Soil party in 1854,
which merged with the Rep. party during the course of that
year, and was its nominee also. Was el., defeating former
Gov. John S. Barry, and becoming the first Rep. to be el.
Gov. in Mich. Reel. in 1856. During admin., "personal
liberty" legislation was enacted to facilitate defense by
Negroes against claims they were fugitive slaves; the ship
canal connecting Lakes Superior and Huron was completed;
Mich. Agri. Coll. (now Mich. State Univ.) was established,
along with some other state institutions of higher learning;

a liquor licensing law enacted; a law providing for teacher
training institutes adopted; and a state teachers' assoc.
established. In 1859 was el. to U.S. Senate, where he
served until his death two years later. m. in 1833 to -----
Warden, a N.Y. woman of Scottish birth. D. Oct. 5, 1861 at
Green Oak. Bur. in Old Village Cem., Brighton, Mich.

WISNER, MOSES (1859-1861). b. June 3, 1815 at Spring-
port, N.Y. Father was a farmer. Attd. local schools there.
Moved to Mich. in 1837, purchasing land near Lapeer, which
he improved into a farm. After two years moved to Pontiac,
Mich., where he engaged in law study in the office of a
brother and his partner. Admitted to bar in 1840 and began
practice in Lapeer. Apptd. pros. atty. of Lapeer Co. in
1843, but after a short time returned to Pontiac to continue
law practice with brother and partner. Affiliated with Whig
party, and was a strong opponent of slavery. The controversy over extension of slavery into new U.S. territories
after Mexican War aroused his concern. Took leading role in
formation of Rep. party at Jackson, Mich. in July, 1854 from
anti-slavery elements of Whig and Dem. parties and former
Free Soil and Liberty party mbrs. Declined offer to become
Rep. party cand. for Atty. Gen. in that year. Unsuccessful
as Rep. nominee for U.S. Senate in 1857. Nom. and el. Gov.
as a Rep. in 1858. As Civil War approached he foresaw a
bitter struggle and was critical of those who sought to
avert conflict by compromise measures. During admin., a
voter registration system was adopted, and a policy of road
constr. vigorously pursued. Returned to law practice at
Pontiac at end of term, and during the course of the following year helped raise and train a regiment of volunteers for
the Union army. Commissioned as its col. in Sept., 1862 and
was dispatched to South. Died of a fever in Ky. before his
regiment became involved in fighting. m. to ----- Hascall,
of Pontiac, Mich., d. of Gen. C. C. Hascall. Four children.
D. at Lexington, Ky. Jan. 5, 1863. Bur. at Oakhill Cem.,
Pontiac, Mich.

BLAIR, AUSTIN (1861-1865). b. Feb. 8, 1818 in Caroline,
N.Y. s. of George and Rhoda (Blackman) B. Father was a
pioneer farmer in Tompkins Co., N.Y. Attd. local schools
and Cazenovia Acad., Hamilton Coll., and Union Coll., from
which he was grad. in 1839. Studied law in office in Oswego,
N.Y. and admitted to N.Y. bar in 1841. Shortly afterward
moved to Mich., settling first at Jackson, where he began
law practice. For reasons of health moved to Eaton Rapids,
Mich., where he practiced law for a time, and was co. clerk;
but moved back to Jackson in 1844. Affiliated with Whig
party. El. to Mich. House in 1845. At the final session of

the legislature held in Detroit, had important role in revision of Mich. statutes. Successfully championed abolition of death penalty in the State; but his advocacy of elimination of requirement that voters must be "white" aroused antagonism and he was defeated for reel. as a result. Disappointment at failure of Whig conv. of 1848 to choose Henry Clay as party nominee for Pres. of U.S. caused him to shift allegiance to Free Soil party. Was a delegate to Free Soil party's natl. conv. in 1848. Had active role in org. of Rep. party in Mich. in 1854, and was el. to Mich. Senate in that year. Successfully championed passage of "personal liberty" law in the Senate, and supported Fremont for Pres. of U.S. in 1856. Was not a cand. for second term, and held no office from 1856 to 1860. Delegate to Rep. natl. conv. in 1860, where he supported nom. of Wm. Seward for Pres. of U.S. Gave support to Lincoln in subsequent campaign. Was nom. and el. Gov. as Rep. in 1860, and again in 1862. Gave full support to prosecution of Civil War, assisting in raising some 90,000 men for Union Army during course of the war. El. to U.S. House as Rep. in 1866, continuing in that office until 1873. Although not a mbr. of Radical Rep. faction on Reconstruction policies, he supported the impeachment of Pres. Andrew Johnson in order to resolve the deadlock between Pres. and Congress. Favored a protective tariff and the resumption of specie payments on U.S. notes. Became disillusioned with party leadership during Grant's first admin., and was not a cand. for reel. in 1872. Gave support in 1872 pres. election to Greeley, the Lib. Rep.-Dem. cand. Devoted time to professional and bus. interests for some time thereafter. Supported Gov. Tilden for Pres. of U.S. in 1876. El. pros. atty. of Jackson Co. in 1885. Unsuccessful as Rep. cand. for Mich. Supreme Ct. in 1887. Mbr. of Bd. of Regents of Univ. of Mich. in 1882-1890. Hon. degrees from Hillsdale Coll. and Univ. of Mich. m. to Sarah Ford in 1849. One s. D. at Jackson Aug. 6, 1894. Bur. in Mt. Evergreen Cem. there.

CRAPO, HENRY HOWLAND (1865-1869). b. May 22, 1804 at Dartmouth, Mass. Father, who was of French ancestry, was a farmer of limited means. Obtained a limited educ. from local schools and at New Bedford, Mass. Taught school for a time at Dartmouth, which he raised to status of a h.s. In 1832 established his residence in New Bedford, and learned surveying. With the aid of a local blacksmith, constructed his own compass to be used in his surveying work. Held various local offices in New Bedford, including town clerk, treas., tax collector and mbr. of bd. of aldermen. As such, was instrumental in establishment of first free pub. library in Mass. Also became involved in horticultural pursuits, became a contributor to a horticultural journal, and was also a part-owner of a whaling vessel. In 1856, moved to Flint, Mich., using savings to acquire white pine lumbering lands in central Mich. Developed lumbering operations into an extensive enterprise, becoming quite wealthy. El. mayor of Flint a few years after he moved there and in 1863-1864 was a mbr. of Mich. Senate. A Whig in political views originally, he joined the Rep. party when he came to Mich. El. Gov. as a Rep. in 1864 and again in 1866. As Gov., supported Civil War effort. At end of the war gave attention primarily to State's financial condition, advocating a "pay as you go" policy on pub. improvements. Used veto power to restrict use of credit by municipalities to finance railroad constr. Also favored restriction of disposition of pub. "swamp" lands for building of un-needed roads. Endorsed policy of encouragement of immigrants to settle in Mich., and policies designed to encourage mfg. enterprises. Used pardoning power sparingly. During admin., a state constl. conv. was held, but the document it drafted was rejected by the voters. m. to Mary Ann Slocum, of Dartmouth, Mass. in 1825. Nine d.; one s. The son, Wm., became a mbr. of Cong. from Mass. Christian (Disciples) church. D. at Flint, July 22, 1869 a few months after completion of tenure as Gov. Bur. in Glenwood Cem. there.

BALDWIN, HENRY PORTER (1869-1873). b. Feb. 22, 1814 at Coventry, R.I. s. of John and Margaret (Williams) B. A paternal ancestor, John, had emigrated from England to Conn. in 1639, and a maternal ancestor, Robert Williams, had emigrated from England to Mass. in 1638. Ancestral line included a number of individuals prominent in religious and cultural affairs in New England. Received common school educ. Was orphaned at age of 12, and began working in a local merc. establishment. Eventually acquired a bus. of that kind for himself at Woonsocket, R.I. In 1838 moved to Detroit, Mich., where he established a merc. bus., which expanded and prospered. Also became involved in banking enterprises in Detroit. Travelled in Europe in 1852 and 1860. Affiliated with Rep. party in Mich., being a mbr. of the conv. at Jackson, Mich. which org. the party in July, 1854. El. to Mich. Senate in 1860, and had a leading role therein as ch. of its finance commt. El. Gov. as a Rep. in 1868 and again in 1870. During admin., measures were enacted expanding the State's eleemosynary programs; plans adopted for constr. of a new Capitol building at Lansing; relief programs furthered to aid victims of the Chicago fire and of several disastrous fires in Mich. forest areas; initial steps taken toward creation of a State bd. of health; and

legislation providing for assumption by the State of responsibility for defaulted local bond issues was passed. Apptd.
to vacant seat in U.S. Senate in 1879, and was subsequently
el. to complete the term, which ran until 1881. Was not a
cand. for continuation in the office. Very active in affairs of the Episcopal church. m. in 1835 to Harriet M. Day.
m. for second time in 1866 to Sibyle Lambard. D. at Detroit
Dec. 31, 1892. Bur. in Elmwood Cem. there.

BAGLEY, JOHN JUDSON (1873-1877). b. July 24, 1832 at
Medina, N.Y. s. of John and Mary B. Descendant of ancestors on both paternal and maternal sides who had emigrated
from England to Amer. during 1600s. Received schooling at
Lockport, N.Y. and at Constantine, Mich., to which place his
family moved when he was eight years old. Began working as
clerk in country store at age 13. Moved with family to
Owosso, Mich. and shortly afterward to Detroit. Began working in Detroit in a tobacco mfg. bus. Went into that line
of bus. for himself five years later at age 21. His enterprise flourished, becoming one of largest of its kind in
Midwest. Later extended interests into ins. and banking
fields. From 1867 to 1872 was pres. of an ins. firm he
helped to org.; also pres. of Detroit Safe Co. Originally
a Whig, he participated in founding of Rep. party in 1854,
and was ch. of its state commt., 1868-1869. Active in support of Union cause during Civil War. Mbr., Detroit school
bd. and of Detroit city council, where he was instrumental
in founding metropolitan police system. Mbr. of police
commn. there, 1866-1872. El. Gov. as Rep. in 1872 and again
in 1874. During admin., a fish and game commn. was established; programs in educl. and welfare fields extended; state
militia system reorg.; laws pertaining to railroads revised;
and Mich. participation in Centennial Exposition at Philadelphia promoted. Failed by one vote to obtain Rep. nom.
for U.S. Senate seat in 1881. Active in affairs of Episcopal church, and was a generous contributor to various
charitable and civic undertakings. m. in 1855 to Frances
Elizabeth Newbury, of Dubuque, Ia., d. of a Presbyterian
minister. Eight children. D. at San Francisco, Calif.
July 27, 1881. Bur. in Woodmere Cem., Detroit.

CROSWELL, CHARLES MILLER (1877-1881). b. Oct. 31,
1825 at Newburg, N.Y. s. of John and Sally (Hicks) C. Father was of Scotch-Irish and mother was of Dutch ancestry.
Was left an orphan at age seven when father died in a drown-
ing accident, his mother having died a few months earlier.
Was brought up by an uncle, a carpenter, who moved to Adrian,
Mich. in 1837. Learned uncle's trade while attending local
schools. Began study of law in office at Adrian in 1846

while employed as deputy clerk of Lenawee Co. Co. register
of deeds, 1851-1855. Delegate to the Jackson, Mich. conv.
that formed Rep. party in July, 1854, serving as its sect.
Became partner in law office with Thomas L. Cooley, at
Adrian, for a time. Apptd. city atty. for Adrian in 1862
and later the same year, mayor of Adrian. El. to Mich.
Senate in 1862, continuing in that office until 1869.
Served as pres. pro tem of Senate and was ch. of its judiciary commt. Strongly supported Pres. Lincoln's policies,
including the Emancipation Proclamation, and was instrumental in securing ratification by Mich. legislature of the 13th
Amdt. to U.S. Const. Opposed legislation granting authority
to municipalities to extend credit for railroad building;
also successfully opposed repeal of state law abolishing
death penalty. Pres. elector on Rep. ticket in 1868. Presiding officer of Mich. constl. conv. of 1867. El. to Mich.
House in 1872 and was chosen Speaker of that body. Served
several years as sect. to the state bd. in charge of charitable and penal institutions. Nom. and el. Gov. as Rep. in
1876 and for succeeding term in 1878. m. in 1852 to Lucy M.
Eddy, of Adrian. Two d.; one s. After her death, m. in
1880 to Elizabeth Musgrave, of Charlotte, Mich. One d. D.
at Adrian Dec. 13, 1886. Bur. at Oakwood Cem. there.

JEROME, DAVID HOWELL (1881-1883). b. Nov. 17, 1829 at
Detroit, Mich. s. of Horace and Elizabeth Rose (Hart) J.,
being the youngest of nine children. Father and mother were
natives of N.Y. who had moved to the Terr. of Mich. a year
before his birth. Father, who had built a sawmill in St.
Clair Co., Mich., died in 1831 and his mother returned with
the family for a time to Onondaga Co., N.Y., but returned
later to St. Clair Co., Mich. in 1834, where son was raised.
Received schooling at local school and for a short time at
an acad. in village of St. Clair. Engaged in various occupations as a youth and young man, including assisting in
farm work, working in logging camp and sawmill with older
brother, and serving as deputy clerk and deputy register of
deeds in St. Clair Co. Was also employed in summers on
river and lake steamers. In Jan., 1853 left for Calif. by
way of Panama, and engaged in mining and commercial pursuits
there for about a year. Returned to Mich. in 1854 and
joined his brother in a lumbering bus., operating out of
Saginaw. Also worked in a hardware and gen. store, of which
he was mgr. Affiliated with Mich. Rep. party when it formed
in 1854. Commissioned by Gov. Blair in 1862 to raise a volunteer regiment for service in Civil War, serving as mil.
aide on Gov. Blair's staff. El. to Mich. Senate in 1862,
continuing to serve in that office for three terms. As mbr.
of Senate was instrumental in establishment of Soldiers'

Home at Harper Hosp., in Detroit, and in adoption of measures to encourage salt indus. in Mich. Opposed extension of mun. credit for railroad bldg. Apptd. as mbr. of U.S. Bd. of Indian Affairs by Pres. Grant in 1876, serving until 1881. Travelled extensively in West and Northwest in connection with his duties in that office and gained confidence of chieftains of Nez Perce, Sioux and Ute Indian tribes with whom he negotiated treaties for land cessions. Nom. as cand. for Gov. by Rep. state conv., defeating a former school classmate by one vote, and was el. He thereby became the first native-born citizen of Mich. to be el. Gov. Nom. again for Gov. in 1882, but was defeated in the gen. election. Served as U.S. commnr. in 1890-1893 to negotiate treaty with Cherokee Indians, and was successful in securing a treaty by which 15,500,000 acres of land in Okla. were made available for settlement. Pres. of Saginaw Street Ry. Co. and Trustee, Mich. Mil. Acad. Episcopalian. m. in 1859 to Lucy Peck, of Oakland Co., Mich. Three children, only one of whom, a son, survived to adulthood. D. at Watkins, N.Y. April 23, 1896. Bur. at Oakwood Cem., Saginaw.

BEGOLE, JOSIAH WILLIAM (1883-1885). b. Jan. 20, 1815 at Groveland, N.Y. s. of Wm. and ---- (Boles) B. Father's antecedents, who were French Huguenots, had emigrated from France to Md. in late 1700s, residing in the Hagerstown area, where father was born. Although the father's family were slave owners, having purchased slaves for the purpose of emancipating them, they had moved to Livingston Co., N.Y. in 1802 because of their opposition to the institution of slavery. Son was the eldest of ten children. Attd. local schools at Mt. Morris, and Temple Hill Acad., in Geneseo, N.Y. Emigrated to Mich. in 1836 to the Flint area, where he taught school for a short time and also worked as farm laborer. Invested savings in 80 acres of land and by 1854 had developed and expanded holdings to a prosperous 500-acre farm. Had an active role in org. of Genesee Co., Mich. and held a variety of local offices, including school inspector, justice of the peace, township treas., treas. of Genesee Co., city supervisor, and mbr. of bd. of aldermen of Flint. Entered lumbering bus. during course of Civil War. The operation expanded and proved very profitable. Supported Union cause during the course of the war. El. to Mich. Senate in 1870, and was a delegate to Rep. natl. conv. of 1872. El. to U.S. House in 1872, where he espoused financial reform measures of faction supporting continuance of issuance of U.S. notes as currency. Defeated for reel. in 1874. Resumed lumbering, wagon mfg., and banking bus. interests in Flint for a time. Nom. in 1882 by Greenback

party for Gov. Was also endorsed by Dem. party, and was el.
in a close vote, defeating incumbent Gov. Jerome. Defeated
for succeeding term in 1884 in another close election.
Mich. commnr. to New Orleans Cotton Exposition. In 1881
made generous contributions to victims of fire disasters in
Mich. m. in 1839 to Harriet A. Miles, a native of Conn.
Five children, four of whom survived to maturity. A son
died while serving as a mbr. of Union army during the Atlanta campaign in 1864. D. June 6, 1896 at Flint. Bur. in
Glenwood Cem. there.

ALGER, RUSSELL ALEXANDER (1885-1887). b. Feb. 27, 1836
at Lafayette, Ohio. s. of Russell and Caroline (Moulton) A.
Descendant of English-Scotch paternal ancestor who emigrated
to Amer. in 1759. Family had moved to Ohio early in 19th
century, where he was born and grew up under pioneer conditions. Was left an orphan at age 11, with a younger brother
and sister, whom he helped support. Worked as farm hand and
acquired limited educ. at Richfield Acad., working at various odd jobs while attending school. Became a school
teacher and also began study of law in office in Akron, Ohio.
Admitted to bar in 1859 and joined a law firm in Cleveland.
Poor health led him to move to Grand Rapids, Mich. in 1859,
where he worked for a lumbering firm. At beginning of Civil
War enlisted in a volunteer co. as pvt. Rose through officer ranks from capt. to col., seeing much action in Southwestern theater of war and later with the Army of the Potomac in Va. Had a brilliant and eventful career as a soldier,
participating in 66 battles; was captured and escaped from
mil. prison; was wounded in July, 1863 shortly after the
Battle of Gettysburg in which he was a participant from the
beginning day. Eventually was discharged from service after
having attained the rank of brevet major gen. Returned to
Detroit in 1866, where he entered bus., becoming pres. of
two lumbering firms. Expanded bus. interests into fields of
banking, mfg., and railroads, and became quite wealthy.
Delegate to Rep. natl. conv. in 1884. Nom. and el. Gov. as
Rep. in 1884, defeating incumbent Gov. Begole in close election. Did not seek reel. in 1886. Placed before Rep. natl.
conv. in 1888 as cand. for Pres. of U.S., receiving 143
votes on one ballot, but nom. was won by Benj. Harrison after a number of ballots. Pres. elector on Rep. ticket in
1888 election. Apptd. U.S. Sect. of War by Pres. McKinley
in 1897, and served until his resignation in 1899. Supply
problems and deptl. scandals that developed during course of
the Spanish-Amer. War brought about much criticism. Wrote
and published in 1901 The Spanish-American War in which he
defended his record as Sect. of War. Apptd. in 1902 to U.S.
Senate to fill a vacancy and was subsequently el. to complete

the term. Was not a cand. for succeeding term because of
declining health. Mbr. of G.A.R., serving as its Natl.
Commdr.-in-chief on one occasion. m. in 1861 to Annette M.
Henry, of Grand Rapids. Nine children. D. at Washington,
D.C., Jan. 24, 1907. Bur. in Elmwood Cem., Detroit.

LUCE, CYRUS GRAY (1887-1891). b. July 2, 1824 at
Windsor, Ohio. Father, who was a native of Conn., had been
an Amer. soldier during War of 1812, and had moved to the
Western Reserve, in Ohio, to settle on land there. Mother,
Mary Gray, was born in Winchester, Va., and had moved with
her family to Ohio with her parents as a child. Her father
had left Va. to go to Ohio in 1815 because of his abolitionist views. In 1836 the Luce family moved to Steuben Co.,
Ind. Attd. local elementary school in winters, assisting
father on farm in summers. Studied at a collegiate inst. at
Ontario, Ind. for three terms. At age 17 began work in father's carding-mill and cloth-dressing bus., eventually becoming its mgr. Became interested in politics as a Whig.
Narrowly defeated for seat in Ind. House in 1848. In that
year he purchased 80 acres of land at Gilead, in Branch Co.,
Mich., to which he moved and began farming. Expanded holdings to 300 acres in next few years. Township supervisor at
Gilead for 12 years. El. as Rep. to Mich. House in 1854 and
served two terms. Branch Co. treas., 1859-1863; mbr. of
Mich. Senate, 1865-1869; and mbr. of Mich. constl. conv. of
1867. Apptd. to office of State oil inspector, serving from
1879 to 1883. El. Gov. as Rep. in 1886, and reel. in 1888.
As Gov., was concerned particularly with issues relating to
farmers. Apptd. to governing bd. of Mich. School for
Feeble-minded in 1894. Pres. of Branch Co. Agri. Soc. and
mbr. of Mich. Grange, serving as its pres. for seven years.
m. in 1849 to Julia A. Dickinson, of Gilead, Mich. Five
children. After her death, m. to Mrs. Mary Thompson, of
Bronson, Mich. D. March 5, 1905 at Coldwater, Mich. Bur.
in Oak Grove Cem. there.

WINANS, EDWIN BARUCH (1891-1893). b. May 16, 1826 at
Avon, N.Y. Only s. of John and Eliza W. Moved with parents
to Unadilla, in Livingston Co., Mich. Terr., in 1834. Received common school educ. there. While he was still a
youth, father died, and his mother moved to Pettysville,
Mich., where he was employed for several years in a flour
and carding mill. At age 20 entered Albion Coll., intending
to prepare for profession of law, but in 1850 joined the
"Gold Rush" to Calif. Began overland trip with a team and
wagon, which he lost in the course of crossing plains. Finished the trip to Calif. on foot to Rough and Ready mining
camp after many privations. Remained there for five years,

having had moderate success as miner. Returned to Mich. in
1855 and found his mother had died. Married a local girl,
who accompanied him back to Calif. After three years there,
returned to farm of his wife's family near Hamburg, Mich.
Was attracted soon afterward by gold discoveries in Idaho
country and made the overland trip there amid great dangers.
Was seriously wounded by accidental discharge of his own gun
when stage was upset. After recuperating in Utah, returned
to Mich. where he continued to farm thereafter. Mbr. of
Mich. House, 1861-1865, and of Mich. constl. conv. in 1867.
Probate judge of Livingston Co., 1877-1881. El. to U.S.
House as Dem. in 1882 and continued in office for succeeding
term. Nom. and el. Gov. as Dem. in 1890. Was a life-long
Dem. and advocate of tariff for revenue only and of free
coinage of silver. Was generally conservative otherwise on
economic and social issues. Episcopalian. Mbr., Masons.
m. in 1855 to Elizabeth Galloway, of Hamburg, Mich. Two s.,
both of whom were officers in U.S. Army during Spanish-Amer.
War. D. July 4, 1894 at Hamburg. Bur. in town cem. there.

RICH, JOHN TREADWAY (1893-1897). b. April 23. 1841 at
Conneautville, Pa. s. of John W. and Jerusha (Treadway) R.
Mother died while he was quite young and his father moved to
Vt., sending young son to live with relatives in Mich. Father followed in 1848, purchasing a farm in Elba township,
near Lapeer, Mich. Son grew up on farm. Attd. local
schools at Lapeer and Clarkston Acad. for twelve weeks in
1857. Taught in country schools for a time, then began
farming, specializing in sheep raising and wool production.
Mbr. of Lapeer Co. bd. of supervisors, 1867-1872. El. to
Mich. House in 1872, continuing in that office for four
terms and serving as Speaker last two terms. El. to Mich.
Senate in 1880, but resigned after being el. to U.S. House
in 1881 to fill a vacancy. Defeated for reel. in 1882. Resumed farming. Apptd. Mich. R.R. Commnr. in 1889, serving
in that post until 1891. Unsuccessful as cand. for Rep.
nom. for Gov. in 1880 and again in 1890, but was nom. and
el. to that office in 1892. Reel. in 1894. During admin.,
a major controversy over alleged election frauds in connection with the vote on adoption of a proposed constl. amdt.
relating to salaries of pub. officials eventuated in his removing mbrs. of the state convassing bd., an action later
sustained by the courts. Left State in sound financial condition after difficulties resulting from depression in early
1890s. After tenure as Gov. served from 1898 to 1906 as
U.S. collector of customs at Detroit. Served briefly as
Treas. of Mich. in 1908 by apptmt. to fill a vacancy. U.S.
collector of customs at Port Huron, Mich., 1908-1913. Delegate to Rep. natl. convs., 1884 and 1892. Active in agri.

orgs., serving as vice pres. of Natl. Wool Growers Assoc.;
pres. of Mich. Merino Sheep Breeders Assoc.; pres. of Mich.
Agri. Soc.; treas. of Northeastern Agri. Soc.; and pres. of
Farmers' Mutual Fire Ins. Co. m. in 1863 to Lucretia A.
Winship, of Atlas, Mich. After her death, m. to Georgia
Winship. D. March 28, 1926 at St. Petersburg, Fla. while on
a vacation trip. Bur. in Mount Hope Cem., Lapeer.

    PINGREE, HAZEN S. (1897-1901). b. Aug. 30, 1840 at
Denmark, Me. s. of Jasper and Adeline (Bryant) P. Paternal
ancestor, Moses P., had emigrated from England to Mass. in
1640. Ancestral line included a number of persons distinguished in pub. affairs during colonial times. Samuel E.
Pingree, Gov. of Vt., was a relative (q.v.). Father was a
lawyer. After a limited educ. at local schools, son began
work at age 14 in a cotton cloth mfg. factory at Saco, Me.
After two years went to Hopkinton, Mass., where he was employed in a shoe mfg. plant and learned shoe cutting trade.
In 1862 enlisted in a Mass. regiment for service in the
Civil War. Participated in a number of campaigns with Army
of the Potomac. Was captured in 1864 during the Wilderness
campaign and imprisoned for several months at Andersonville
prison camp, in Ga. Was exchanged, and participated in
closing battles of the war in Va., being present with his
unit at surrender of Gen. Lee at Appomattox. Returned to
Me. for a time, but moved to Detroit, Mich. in 1866. His
father and family moved there also in 1871. Was first employed in Detroit as shoe salesman in the merc. establishment of Henry Baldwin, later Gov. of Mich. Soon went into
shoe mfg. bus. for himself, with a partner. Enterprise
prospered and eventually became largest of its kind in Midwest. El. mayor of Detroit in 1888, and continued in office
for four terms. Energetic as mayor in promotion of policies
designed to curb monopolies, and was an advocate of pub.
ownership of street railway system. During the depression
of 1893, authorized use of vacant city lots as gardens for
growing food by unemployed. Nom. and el. Gov. as Rep. in
1896 and was reel. in 1898. As Gov., gave attention to al-
leviation of distress of Spanish-Amer. War veterans. The
progressive reform programs he endorsed as Gov. brought him
to natl. attention in Rep. party circles. m. in 1872 to
Frances A. Gilbert, of Mt. Clemens, Mich. Two d.; one s.
D. June 18, 1901 in London, England, shortly after end of
tenure as Gov., while on a visit there. Bur. in Elmwood
Cem., Detroit.

    BLISS, AARON THOMAS (1901-1905). b. May 22, 1837 at
Peterboro, in Madison Co., N.Y. s. of Lyman and Anna
(Chaffee) B. Father, a farmer, traced ancestry back to 16th

century English forebears, and mother was also of English
descent. Attd. local schools during winters while assisting
on farm. Later attd. academies at Morrisville and Bouckville, N.Y. for brief periods while also working in merc.
establishments in those places. Became a partner in a store
at Bouckville at age 20. Following outbreak of Civil War,
enlisted in a N.Y. cavalry regiment. Rose to rank of capt.
by end of the war, and was involved in numerous engagements
in Va. theater. Was taken prisoner in 1864 near Richmond
and confined at various prison camps in N.C., Ga. and S.C.
Escaped and eventually rejoined his unit before end of war.
Following his discharge went to Saginaw, Mich., where he
worked with a brother in logging camps. Formed partnership
with brother and went into lumbering bus. for himself. Expanded operations into large enterprise. Also helped org.
the Citizens Bank, later reorg. into Saginaw Co. Savings
Bank, of which he became pres. and dir. Held a number of
local offices in the city of Saginaw and in Saginaw Co. El.
to Mich. Senate in 1882 and served as mil. aide on staff of
Gov. Alger. El. to U.S. House in 1888 as Rep., but was defeated for second term in 1890. As mbr. of Cong. was instrumental in establishment of an Indian school at Mt.
Pleasant, Mich. Vice pres. and treas. of Natl. Rep. league.
Nom. and el. Gov. as Rep. in 1900 and again in 1902. Deputy
commdr. of Mich. G.A.R. Made generous gifts to charitable
and educ. institutions, including Albion Coll. Methodist.
m. in 1868 to Aleseba M. Phelps, of Solsville, N.Y. D. Sept.
16, 1906 at Milwaukee, Wisc., where he had gone for med.
treatment. Bur. in Forest Lawn Cem., Saginaw.

WARNER, FRED MALTBY (1906-1911). b. July 21, 1865 in
Hickling, Nottinghamshire, England. Was brought to Amer. by
parents while still an infant. Mother died shortly after
arriving in this country, and he became the adopted son of
P. Dean and Rhoda E. Warner, of Farmington, Mich. Attd.
local schools in Farmington, and Mich. State Coll. for one
term. Clerked in foster father's store in Farmington, and
eventually became its proprietor after death of the father.
Expanded interests into cheese mfg. field, becoming head of
a firm with factories in twelve locations in Southeastern
Mich. Became recognized nationally as leader in cheese and
dairy indus. Also was organizer and pres. of Farmington
State Bank and vice pres. of Detroit United Bank. Mbr. of
Farmington village council for nine years, being village
pres. for seven years. Served in Mich. Senate in 1895-1896
and 1897-1898. El. Mich. Sect. of State in 1900, serving
for two terms. Nom. and el. Gov. as Rep. in 1904 and for
succeeding terms in 1906 and 1908. Was first Gov. of Mich.
to be el. for three consecutive terms. Was also the first

to be nom. by the direct primary system; as well as the
first Mich. Gov. of foreign birth. As Gov., successfully
advocated expanded state support for roads; direct primary
legislation; a pres. preference primary law; popular nom. of
U.S. Senatorial candidates; lower passenger rates on railroads; and uniform taxation of bus. corps. Mbr., Masons;
K.P.; Loyal Guard; Elks; Maccabees. Methodist. m. in 1888
to Martha M. Davis, of Farmington. Two d; two s. D. April
17, 1923 at Orlando, Fla. Bur. in Oakwood Cem., Farmington,
Mich.

OSBORN, CHASE SALMON (1911-1913). b. Jan. 22, 1860 in
Huntington Co., Ind. s. of George A. and Margaret Ann
(Fannon) O. Descendant of an English colonist who emigrated
from England to Mass. in 1600s and settled at Plymouth.
Both his father and mother were physicians. Attd. local
schools while working as a newsboy in Lafayette, Ind. Became an apprentice in printing office and learned printing
trade. Attd. Purdue Univ. for three years but did not graduate. Was granted a degree from that institution in 1926,
however. Reporter for Lafayette Home Journal for several
years. Mbr. of reporter staff of Chicago Tribune in 1879
and of Milwaukee Sentinel in 1880. In 1883 purchased the
Mining News at Florence, Wisc., which he published for the
next five years. Served briefly as city ed. of Milwaukee
Sentinel in 1887. Purchased an interest in Sault Ste. Marie,
Mich. News in 1887 and moved there, becoming also sole proprietor of the Saginaw, Mich. Courier-Herald, 1901-1912.
Postmaster at Sault Ste. Marie, 1895-1899; Mich. R.R.
Commnr., 1899-1902; and mbr. of the Univ. of Mich. Bd. of Regents, 1908-1911. Vice pres., Natl. Bank of Sault Ste.
Marie. Nom. and el. Gov. of Mich. as Rep. in 1910. As Gov.
advocated policies favored by progressive wing of Rep. party,
and was one of seven Rep. Govs. who urged former Pres. Theodore Roosevelt to seek Rep. nom. for Pres. of U.S. in 1912.
Did not join the Prog. party in the ensuing campaign, however, but failed to win Rep. nom. for Gov. in 1912. Was the
Rep. cand. for Gov. in 1914 but was defeated in the gen.
election that year. Unsuccessful as cand. for the Rep. nom.
for U.S. Senate in 1918 and again in 1928. His name was
presented as a cand. for nom. for Vice Pres. of U.S. at the
Rep. natl. conv. in 1928, but he failed to attract sufficient support. Was vice pres. of the Natl. Commt. of Independent Voters for Roosevelt in 1940. Mbr., Mich. Commn. on
Unemployment in 1932. Active as a writer on historical
topics, travel and outdoor life, and travelled throughout
the world. Author of The Andean Land (two vols.) in 1909;
The Iron Hunter, a partly autobiographical work, in 1909;
The Law of Divine Concord, in 1921; Madagascar: Land of the

Man-Eating Tree, in 1924; and numerous travel and other
types of articles. Pres., Mich. Press Assoc.; mbr., Amer.
Acad. of Political and Social Sci.; Amer. Assoc. for Advance-
ment of Sci.; Amer. Inst. of Mining and Metallurgical Engr.;
Amer. Ornithol. Union; Mich. Acad. of Sci.; K.P.; I.O.O.F.;
Masons. Presbyterian. Hon. degrees from eight colleges and
universities. m. in 1881 to Lillian Gertrude Jones of Mil-
waukee, Wisc. Two s.; two d. m. in 1949 to Stellanova
Brunt. D. at Sault Ste. Marie, April 11, 1949. Bur. on
Duck Is., in St. Mary's River, Mich.

FERRIS, WOODBRIDGE NATHAN (1913-1917). b. Jan. 6, 1853
on a farm near Spencer, N.Y. s. of John, Jr. and Estella
(Reed) F. Attd. local schools while assisting on farm.
Attd. academies at Spencer, Candor and Oswego, N.Y., and became rural school teacher at age 16. Enrolled at Oswego
Normal School for three years, but did not graduate. Enrolled at the Univ. of Mich. Med. School for one term. Returned to Spencer, where he was principal of acad. for one
year. In 1875 moved to Freeport, Ill., where he established
a bus. coll. and acad., which proved successful. Was a
teacher at Rock River Univ., Dixon, Ill. for a short time.
In 1877 org. Dixon Bus. Coll., becoming its sole proprietor
in 1878. Supt. of schools for five years at Pittsfield,
Ill. In 1884 established Ferris Indus. School at Big Rapids,
Mich. Continued to serve as its head until death. It later
was incorporated as Ferris Inst. into the State's system of
higher educ. Founder and pres. of Big Rapids Savings Bank.
Unsuccessful as Dem.-Pop. cand. for U.S. House in 1892; in
1902 as Dem. cand. for State Supt. of Schools; and in 1904
as Dem. nominee for Gov. Nom. and el. Gov. as Dem. in 1912
when Rep. party split into two factions. Reel. in 1914, defeating former Gov. Osborn. Defeated as Dem. nominee for
Gov. in 1920. As Gov., favored programs and reforms of a
progressive nature, including pub. ownership of pub. utilities. Nom. and el. to U.S. Senate as Dem. in 1922. Mbr.
Masons; M.W.A.; K.P. Hon. degrees from the Univ. of Mich.;
Olivet Coll.; Mich. St. Normal Coll. m. in 1874 to Helen
Frances Gillespie of Fulton, N.Y. who assisted him for many
years as a teacher in his schools. Two s. After her death,
m. in 1921 to Mary Ethel McCloud, of Indianapolis, Ind.
D. March 23, 1928 while still serving first term in U.S.
Senate. Bur. in Highland View Cem., Big Rapids.

SLEEPER, ALBERT EDSON (1917-1921). b. Dec. 31, 1862 at
Bradford, Vt. s. of Joseph Edson and Hannah (Merril) S.
Father was a farmer of modest means. Attd. local pub.
schools and Bradford Acad. At age 17 began working as a
clerk in a local store, moving to a larger establishment in

that capacity after two years. In 1883 moved to Lexington,
Mich., where he was employed as salesman and buyer for a
large merc. enterprise owned by an uncle by marriage. In
1894 went into banking and real estate bus. with a partner
at Ubly, Mich., and in 1904 established his residence and
bus. headquarters at Bad Axe, Mich. Became involved in a
number of enterprises there and the surrounding area in the
wholesale grocery field, banking and real estate, and other
fields. At one time was pres. or principal stockholder in
41 banks. Entered politics .as Rep. soon after arrival in
Mich., serving as village pres. at Lexington for several
years. El. to Mich. Senate in 1900, serving for two terms.
Mich. State Treas. for two terms, 1909-1913. Nom. and el.
gov. as Rep. in 1916 and again in 1918. As Gov. during
World War I, cooperated fully with U.S. govt. in prosecution of war effort, at one point advancing personal funds
for purchase of 1,000 tractors by farmers to increase food
production. Pursued policies aimed at economy and efficiency. Mbr., Masons; I.O.O.F.; K.P. Episcopalian. m. in
1901 to Mary Charlotte Moore, of Lexington, Mich. D. at Bad
Axe May 13, 1934. Bur. in Lexington, Mich., Cem.

GROESBECK, ALEXANDER JOSEPH (1921-1927). b. Nov. 7,
1873 in Warren Township, Macomb Co., Mich. s. of Louis and
Julia (Coquillard) G. Father, who was of Dutch-French ancestry, was operator of a sawmill and lumbering bus. Mother
was of French ancestry. Attd. local pub. schools at Mt.
Clemens, Mich. and at Wallaceburg, Ont., where the family
resided for two years. Began working at age 13 in father's
sawmill when not attending school. At age 17 began study of
law in office in Port Huron, and in 1892 entered the Univ.
of Mich., from which he received a law degree in 1893. Began practice in Detroit, and expanded interests into fields
of banking and ins. Ch. of Rep. state commt., 1912-1914.
Atty. Gen. of Mich., 1917-1921. Nom. and el. Gov. as Rep. in
1920 by a plurality of nearly 400,000 over former Gov. Ferris. Reel. in 1922 and 1924, but was defeated in Rep. primary for nom. for fourth term in 1926. Admin. characterized
by unusually energetic leadership on a number of issues
which had the effect of antagonizing important elements of
party by end of third term. Effectuated comprehensive reorg. of state admin. structure, with strong supervisory
powers placed in hands of Gov. and the chief deptl. heads
acting as a bd. of control; reformed state highway admin.
system, with financing of road building by gasoline and auto
license taxes; introduced corp. income tax; and increased
support for state educl. system. Clashed with State Bd. of
Agri. over its removal of the head of Mich. State Coll. and
with legislature on tax revision and reapportionment

questions. Retired to law practice and bus. interests in Detroit after tenure as Gov. Ch. of Mich. Civil Service Commn., 1941-1944. Pres. of Mich. Life Ins. Co.; Monroe Paper Products Co.; Detroit Harbor Terminal; and Stuart Foundry. Mbr., Masons; various professional legal orgs., bus. assoc. and social clubs. Unmarried. D. in Detroit Mar. 10, 1953. Bur. in Woodlawn Cem., Detroit.

GREEN, FRED WARREN (1927-1931). b. Oct. 20, 1872 at Manistee, Mich. s. of Holden N. and Adaline (Clark) G. Family moved to Cadillac, Mich. when son was an infant, and he grew up and attd. pub. schools there. Entered Mich. St. Normal Coll. (now Eastern Mich. Univ.), from which he was graduated in 1893. Worked as reporter for an Ypsilanti, Mich. newspaper for a time and then attd. the Univ. of Mich., from which he received a law degree in 1898. Enlisted in U.S. Army during Spanish-Amer. War, holding rank of lieut. and battalion adjt. at time of discharge. City atty. of Ypsilanti, 1899. Became atty. for Ypsilanti Reed Furniture Co. in 1901, and mbr. of its bd. of dir. in 1903. Company relocated at Ionia, Mich. in 1904 where it became an employ-er of Mich. convict labor from near-by Ionia Reformatory under a mutually satisfactory contract with the State. The arrangement continued until 1923. Bus. expanded, with world-wide branches for supply of raw materials. Ch. of bd. of dir., gen. mgr., treas., and sect. of the company. Also be-came involved in banking and canning enterprises in Western Mich. Pres. of Natl. Bank of Ionia; and pres. of Ionia Fair Assoc. for many years. Mayor of Ionia for 13 years; treas. of Rep. state commt. for ten years. Won Rep. nom. for Gov. against incumbent Gov. Groesbeck in 1926 primary and was el. Gov. Reel. in 1928. During admin., legislation was passed revising workmen's compensation system; criminal code re-vised; highway financing increased by higher gasoline tax; uniform traffic code enacted; measures designed to conserve State's natural resources adopted; and state hospital system expanded. Mbr., Mich. Natl. Guard for 14 years, with rank of brig. gen.; Natl. Commdr., Spanish-Amer. War Vets., 1929. Mbr., Masons. m. in 1901 to Helen Adeline Kelly, of Cadil-lac, Mich. One d. D. Nov. 30, 1936. Bur. in Highland Park Cem., Ionia, Mich.

BRUCKER, WILBER MARION (1931-1933) b. June 23, 1894 at Saginaw, Mich. s. of Ferdinand and Roberta (Hawn) B. Grand-father had emigrated to Amer. from Germany in 1848. Father was a lawyer, probate judge and had served as mbr. of U.S. House. Father died when son was nine years of age. Attd. pub. schools in Saginaw and the Univ. of Mich., from which he received a law degree in 1916. Worked at various jobs

to finance way through college. Served as lieut. with Mich.
Natl. Guard unit on Mexican border in 1916. Enlisted in
U.S. Army at outset of World War I, serving in France and
Germany as lieut. until 1919. Recipient of Silver Star.
Asst. pros. atty. of Saginaw Co., 1919, and pros. atty.,
1923-1926. Asst. Mich. Atty. Gen. in 1927, and was apptd.
to that office when it was vacated by resignation in 1928.
El. to the office in 1928. Nom. and el. Gov. as Rep. in
1930. During admin., state bldg. program continued, but onset of depression necessitated extensive economies in state
expenditures. Sought to keep politics out of prohibition
law enforcement. Nom. for second term in 1932, but was defeated in gen. el. Delegate to Rep. natl. convs. in 1932
and 1936. Defeated as Rep. nominee for U.S. Senate in 1936.
Delegate to Rep. natl. conv. in 1948 and ch. of Rep. state
commt. that year. Apptd. gen. counsel to Dept. of Defense
by Pres. Eisenhower in 1954, and represented the Dept. at
McCarthy Commt. hearings. Apptd. U.S. Sect. of the Army in
1955, serving until 1961. Retired to law practice in Detroit thereafter. Mbr., various legal professional orgs.;
Amer. Legion; V.F.W.; Masons; Elks; I.O.O.F.; Amer. Bible
Soc.; various fraternal and social clubs. Hon. degrees from
six colleges and universities. m. in 1923 to Clara Hantall,
of Saginaw. One s. D. in Detroit Oct. 28, 1968. Bur. in
Arlington Natl. Cem.

    COMSTOCK, WILLIAM ALFRED (1933-1935). b. July 2, 1877
at Alpena, Mich. s. of Wm. B. and Myra (Repelje) C. Father
was in the lumbering bus. Spent much of spare time in wilderness as a youth, becoming an expert woodsman and out-
doorsman. Attd. local pub. schools and the Univ. of Mich.,
from which he was grad. in 1899. At age 18 became sect. for
a large electric railway line, with branches in Ohio, Wisc.
and N.Y. In 1906 org. and became pres. of State Savings
Bank at Alpena, Mich. Also became involved as shareholder
in a number of mfg. enterprises. Ch. of Alpena Co. Dem.
commt., 1911 and Alpena city alderman, 1911-1912. Mayor of
Alpena in 1913. Mbr. of the Univ. of Mich. Bd. of Regents,
1914-1916. Moved to Detroit in 1919. Dir. of First State
Bank there, and vice pres. of Gale Mfg. Co. at Albion, Mich.
Involved in real estate and other bus. enterprises, becoming quite wealthy. Ch. of Mich. Dem. state commt., 1920-
1924 and mbr. of Dem. natl. commt., 1924-1930. Defeated as
Dem. nominee for Gov. in 1926, 1928 and 1930, but was the
nominee again in 1932 and was el. in Roosevelt landslide
that year. Defeated incumbent Gov. Brucker, who had defeated him in 1930 election, by nearly 200,000 votes. As
Gov., faced difficult problems occasioned by the depression
of the 1930s, bank failures and severe unemployment. Prac-

ticed strict economy in govtl. expenditures. Successfully
advocated adoption of gen. sales tax as major source of
state revenues, replacing the gen. property tax for that
purpose; obtained ratification of 21st Amdt. to U.S. Const.;
and instituted a system of State stores for dispensing of
intoxicating liquors. Defeated for re-nom. in 1934. Mbr.
Mich. Civil Service Commn., 1939-1940; mbr. of Detroit city
council, 1942 until death. Mbr., Masons; Elks; Eagles; various social clubs and bus. assoc. Episcopalian. m. in 1919
to Mrs. Josephine (White) Morrison. One s. and one adopted
s. D. at Alpena June 16, 1949. Bur. in Evergreen Cem.
there.

FITZGERALD, FRANK DWIGHT (1935-1937; 1939). b. Jan. 27,
1885 at Grand Ledge, Mich. s. of John Wesley and Carrie
Gertrude (Foreman) F. Father was a merchant and was U.S.
postmaster at Grand Ledge for many years. Attd. local pub.
schools and Ferris Inst., at Big Rapids, Mich. Worked as
U.S. postal employee, 1906-1911. From 1913 to 1917 held
clerical positions in Mich. legislature and in office of
Mich. Sect. of State. Mbr. of Eaton Co. bd. of supervisors.
Exec. Sect., Mich. Highway Dept., 1917-1919. Deputy Sect.
of State, 1919-1921. Moved to Memphis, Tenn. in 1921, where
he was gen. mgr. of Oldsmobile Distribution Corp. Returned
to Mich. in 1923, becoming bus. mgr. of Mich. Highway Dept.,
serving until 1931. El. Mich. Sect. of State in 1930, and
again in 1932, being the only Rep. cand. for state-wide office to survive the Roosevelt landslide that year. Nom. and
el. Gov. as Rep. in 1934. Defeated for succeeding term in
1936, but was the Rep. nominee again in 1938 and was el.,
defeating incumbent Gov. Murphy who had ousted him two years
earlier. As Gov., major concern was maintainence of state
finances on a sound and economical basis. Mbr., Rep. state
commt., 1925-1926 and served as its sect. in 1929-1930.
Delegate to Rep. natl. convs. in 1924, 1932 and 1936. Pres.
of Loan and Deposit State Bank of Grand Ledge. Owned 160-
acre farm on which he raised blooded Holstein cattle. Mbr.,
Masons; Elks; I.O.O.F.; Macabbees; various social clubs.
Congregationalist. m. in 1909 to Queena M. Warner, of Milliken, Mich. One s. D. at Grand Ledge March 16, 1939 a
few months after beginning second term as Gov. Bur. in
Oakwood Cem., Grand Ledge.

MURPHY, FRANK (1937-1939). b. April 13, 1890 at Harbor
Beach, Mich. s. of John F. and Mary (Brennan) M. Father,
who was of Irish ancestry, was a lawyer and was active in
local Dem. party affairs. Attd. local pub. schools and the
Univ. of Mich., from which he was grad. with a law degree in
1914. Admitted to bar and began practice with law firm in

Detroit. Taught English in night school for Hungarian immigrants. Upon outbreak of World War I commissioned as first
lieut. in U.S. Army, and served in Europe, rising to rank of
capt. Studied law for a short time in London, England and
Dublin, Ireland, before returned to U.S. Served briefly as
U.S. dist. atty. in Detroit. Instructor in law school of
Univ. of Detroit, 1922-1927. Recorder's ct. judge in Detroit in 1923, serving until 1930. Mayor of Detroit, 1931-
1934. As mayor, confronted serious unemployment problem
with relief programs. Resigned office of mayor during second term to become Gov. Gen. of Philippine Is. by apptmt.
from Pres. Roosevelt, serving until 1936. Nom. and el. Gov.
as Dem. in 1936. During admin., was confronted by serious
strikes in automobile indus. Refused to use militia forces
to oust sit-down strikers in auto plants in Detroit and
Flint. Defeated for second term in 1938 by former Gov.
Fitzgerald, whom he had defeated in 1936. Apptd. U.S. Atty.
Gen. by Pres. F.D. Roosevelt in 1939. Apptd. to U.S. Supreme Ct. in 1940. As a mbr. of that body acquired distinction as advocate of absolutist concept in area of civil
liberties cases and as supporter of broadened view of rights
of persons accused of crime. Mbr., Amer. Legion; Sigma Chi.
Roman Catholic. Never married. Hon. degrees from 15 colleges and universities. D. at Detroit July 19, 1949 while
still a mbr. of U.S. Supreme Ct. Bur. in Rock Falls Cem.,
Harbor Beach, Mich.

FITZGERALD, FRANK DWIGHT (1939). See above, 1935-1937.

DICKINSON, LUREN DUDLEY (1939-1941). b. April 18, 1959
in Niagara Co., N.Y. s. of Daniel and Hannah (Leavens) D.
Descendant of English colonist who emigrated to Mass. in
1634. In year after his birth family moved to a farm near
Charlotte, Mich., where he grew up. Attd. local pub.
schools. Taught school for 19 years, becoming principal of
h.s. at Potterville, Mich. Also engaged in farming, fruit-
growing and stock-raising. Involved as stockholder in First
Natl. Bank of Charlotte and in a local trucking enterprise.
Mbr. of Eaton Co. Rep. commt. for 24 years. Held various
local offices, including school dist. assessor, township
clerk, and school supt. Mbr. of Mich. House, 1897-1898 and
1905-1908, and of Mich. Senate, 1909-1910. El. Lieut. Gov.
as Rep. for three terms, 1915-1921; again for three terms,
1927-1933; and again for the term beginning in 1939. Succeeded to office of Gov. at nearly 80 years of age in March,
1939 when Gov. Fitzgerald died. Completed term for which
Fitzgerald was el. Was the Rep. nominee for regular term in
1940 but was defeated in gen. election. Preached virtues of
simple life; opposed drinking of intoxicating liquors,

gambling and "high living" generally. Pres. of Mich. Anti-
Saloon League for a number of years. State ch. of Near East
Relief drive. Active in affairs of Methodist church. m. in
1888 to Zora Della Cooley, of Eaton Co. D. at farm near
Charlotte, April 22, 1943. Bur. in Maple Hill Cem., Char-
lotte.

VAN WAGONER, MURRAY DELOS (1941-1943). b. March 18,
1898 on a farm near Kingston, Mich. s. of James and Florence (Loomis) Van W. Father's family was of Dutch descent,
tracing ancestry back to a Dutch colonist who emigrated to
N.Y. in 1700s. Attd. pub. schools in Pontiac, Mich. and the
Univ. of Mich., from which he was grad. with a degree in
civil engr. in 1921. Schooling was interrupted by a period
of service in U.S. Army during World War I. Employed by
Mich. Highway Dept. for three years, after which he joined
an engr. firm in Pontiac. Later went into gen. engr. bus.
for himself. Drain commnr. of Oakland Co., 1931-1933. Became Mich. Highway Commnr. in 1933, continuing in that office until 1940. In that capacity developed state highway
system into an important support for tourist, trucking and
mfg. indus. Pres. of Amer. Road Builders Assoc., 1939-1940.
Mbr. of natl. advisory bd. on streets and highways of U.S.
Dept. of Commerce, and delegate to Intl. Road Cong. at The
Hague in 1938. Nom. and el. Gov. as Dem. in 1940. During
admin., promoted reforms in state aid programs for dependent
children and mentally ill; secured revisions in unemployment
compensation program; consolidated admin. of tax programs;
and cooperated with natl. govt. in war and defense efforts
in initial stages of World War II. Defeated for succeeding
term in 1942. Was again defeated as Dem. nominee for Gov.
in 1946. Mbr., Amer. Legion; Masons; Elks; various professional engr. orgs. and social clubs. m. in 1924 to Helen
Jossman, of Pontiac, Mich. Two d.

KELLY, HARRY FRANCIS (1943-1947). b. April 19, 1895 at
Ottawa, Ill. s. of Henry M. and Mollie (Morrisey) K. Attd.
local schools and the Univ. of Notre Dame, from which he received a law degree in 1917. Served with U.S. Army during
World War I in France as a second lieut. Was wounded and
received Croix de guerre decoration from French govt. Began
law practice at Ottawa, Ill. State's atty. for La Salle Co.,
1919-1923. Moved to Detroit, Mich. in 1924, where he continued practice of law. Asst. pros. atty. for Wayne Co.,
1930-1935. Mgr. of Detroit office of Mich. Liquor Control
Commn., 1935-1937. El. Mich. Sect. of State in 1938 and was
reel. in 1940. Nom. and el. Gov. as Rep. in 1942, defeating
incumbent Gov. Van Wagoner, and again in 1944. Gave full
support to U.S. war effort during tenure as Gov. Was re-

quired to call for U.S. mil. assistance in 1943 in connection with racial unrest and disorders in Detroit. Defeated as Rep. nominee for Gov. in 1950 in very close election involving a partial recount of votes, losing to incumbent Gov. Williams. Nom. by Rep. conv. and el. to Mich. Supreme Ct. in 1954, continuing to serve in that capacity until 1971. Mbr., Amer. Legion; V.F.W.; Elks; Canadian Corps Assoc. of Mich.; Rotary; various professional legal orgs. and social clubs. Pres. of Univ. of Notre Dame Alumni Assoc., 1941-1943. Roman Catholic. m. in 1929 to Anne V. O'Brien. Two d.; four s. D. Feb. 8, 1971. Bur. in Holy Sepulchre Cem., Bloomfield Hills, Mich.

SIGLER, KIM (1947-1949). b. May 2, 1894 at Schuyler, Nebr. s. of Daniel M. and Bertha (Van Housen) S. Attd. Gothenburg, Nebr. pub. schools; the Univ. of Mich.,1914-1916; and Detroit Law School, from which he received a law degree in 1918. Practiced law in Detroit, 1918-1922 as mbr. of various law firms. In 1922 moved to Hastings, Mich., where he continued to practice law. Pros. atty. of Barry Co., 1923-1929. In 1943 became a mbr. of a law firm in Battle Creek, Mich. Apptd. spec. pros. in 1943 for investigation of fraud charges involving certain mbrs. of the legislature and local officials. Resulting trials, which ended in several criminal convictions in 1946, brought him to state-wide attention. Nom. and el. Gov. as Rep. in 1946, defeating former Gov. Van Wagoner. Re-nom. in 1948, but was defeated in gen. election. As Gov., was a colorful figure, travelling about the State in a private airplane, which he piloted himself. Mbr., Masons; I.O.O.F.; Rotary, serving as its dist. gov.; professional legal orgs. Methodist. m. in 1917 to Mae L. Pierson. Two d. D. Nov. 30, 1953 in an airplane crash of plane he was piloting. Bur. in Riverside Cem., Hastings, Mich.

WILLIAMS, G(ERHARD) MENNEN (1949-1961). b. Feb. 23, 1911 at Detroit, Mich. s. of Henry Phillips and Elma (Mennen) W. Father was a prosperous businessman with interests in real estate and other bus. fields. Mother was wealthy from family pharmaceutical and cosmetics enterprise. Attd. pvt. schools in Detroit; Salisbury School in Conn.; Princeton Univ. School of Pub. and Intl. Affairs, from which he was grad. with honors in 1933; and the Univ. of Mich., from which he received a law degree in 1936. Was outstanding as student, participating in athletics and other extra-curricular activities as well as attaining high scholastic honors at each school he attd. Changed political affiliation from Rep. to Dem. while a college student. Atty. for U.S. Social Security Bd., 1936; asst. to Atty. Gen. of Mich.

1937. After travel in Mid-East and Europe in 1938, became
asst. to U.S. Atty. Gen. Murphy and atty. in U.S. Dept. of
Justice, 1938-1940. Asst. to gen. counsel of O.P.A. in
1941. Entered U.S. Navy as lieut., j.g., in 1942, serving
in Pac. theater until 1945. Held rank of lieut. commdr. at
time of leaving service. Received Legion of Merit and three
pres. unit citations. Deputy dir., Mich. office of O.P.A.,
1946. Mbr. of law firm in Detroit for a time, and then mbr.
of Mich. Liquor Control Commn., 1947. Nom. and el. Gov. as
Dem. in 1948, defeating incumbent Gov. Sigler. Reel. for
next five succeeding terms. Elections in 1950 and 1952 were
extremely close and recounts were initiated, without change
in the original results. As Gov., was active in promotion
of civil rights legislation; secured passage of law creating
Fair Employment Practices Commn.; advanced various programs
for benefit of minorities. Prominently mentioned as potential Dem. nominee for Vice Pres. of U.S. at Dem. natl.
conv. in 1960. Apptd. U.S. Asst. Sect. of State for African Affairs by Pres. Kennedy in 1961, serving until 1966.
Unsuccessful as Dem. nominee for U.S. Senate in 1966. U.S.
Ambassador to the Philippine Is., 1968-1969. Nom. by Dem.
conv. and el. to Mich. Supreme Ct. in 1970 and again in
1978. Author of A Governor's Notes, in 1961 and Africa for
Africans, in 1969. Mbr., Masons; Elks; Eagles; Moose; Natl.
Grange; AMVETS; Amer. Legion; V.F.W.; Phi Beta Kappa; vari-
ous professional legal orgs. Hon. degrees from eleven uni-
versities and colleges. Decorations from govts. of The
Netherlands; Liberia; Greece; and the Polish govt. in exile.
Episcopalian. m. in 1937 to Nancy L. Quirk, of Ypsilanti,
Mich. Two d.; one s.

SWAINSON, JOHN BURLEY (1961-1963). b. July 30 (31?),
1925 at Windsor, Ont. Family moved to Port Huron two years
later, where father was employed. Attd. local schools at
Port Huron, where he excelled in athletics. Served in U.S.
Army, 1943-1945 during World War II in European theater, becoming an Amer. citizen in 1944. Was seriously wounded by
a land mine, requiring amputation of both lower legs. Recipient of Croix de guerre and Purple Heart. Enrolled at
Olivet Coll., 1946-1947, and then transferred to the Univ.
of N.C., from which he was grad. with an A.B. degree in
1949 and a law degree in 1951. Began law practice in Detroit, establishing residence at Plymouth, Mich. El. to
Mich. Senate from Wayne Co., and was minority (Dem.) party
leader in that body in 1957. El. Lieut. Gov. in 1958. Nom.
and el. Gov. as Dem. in 1960, but was defeated for succeeding term in 1962. El. to a cir. ct. judgeship in Wayne Co.
in 1964. Nom. by Dem. conv. and el. to Mich. Supreme Ct.
in 1970. Became inactive as mbr. of that Ct. in Nov., 1975

after having been indicted by a Fed. grand jury on charges
of perjury and bribery conspiracy growing out of an investigation of his activities while a judge in Wayne Co. Was
subsequently convicted on the perjury charge and sentenced
to 60-day limited imprisonment, resulting in his resignation
from the Supreme Ct. in 1977. Resided on farm near Manchester, Mich. from 1971 onward. Mbr., Muscular Dystrophy
Assoc. of Wayne Co.; Bd. of Trustees, Plymouth Gen. Hosp.;
D.A.V., serving as judge advocate of its Mich. chapter. m.
in 1946 to Alice Emma Nielsen. Four s.

ROMNEY, GEORGE WILCKEN (1963-1969). b. July 8, 1907 at
Chihuahua, Mexico. s. of Gaskell and Anna Amelia (Pratt) R.
Parents were of English ancestry. Forebears had resided in
Ill. in 1840s as mbrs. of Mormon colony there. Father was
operator of a mill at an Amer. Mormon settlement at Chihuahua when son was born. Because of threat of revolutionary
violence in Mexico, parents moved family to Salt Lake City,
Utah in 1910. Attd. local pub. school and L.D.S. Univ. H.S.
there. Spent 1927-1928 in Scotland as church missionary.
Enrolled at the Univ. of Utah, 1928-1929. Attd. night
classes at George Washington Univ. in Washington, D.C. in
1929-1930 while working on the staff of Sen. Walsh, of Mass.
Salesman for an aluminum firm in Los Angeles in 1930, and
from 1932 to 1939 was the repr. of several aluminum companies in Washington, D. C. Became Detroit mgr. for Amer.
Automobile Assoc. in 1939. Managing dir. of Automotive War
Council for war production in 1941-1945 and was active in
other bus. and trade orgs. in Detroit area concerned with
production efforts during World War II. U.S. delegate to
Intl. Labor Conf., 1946. Joined Nash Kelvinator Corp. as
asst. to the pres. in 1948. Became pres. and gen. mgr. when
the bus. was reorg. to form Amer. Motors Corp. in 1954. Established residence in Bloomfield Hills, Mich. Placed the
new firm on a profitable basis in a few years, stressing
production of compact cars. Inaugurated stock sharing plan
for employees. Mbr. of bd. of dir. of Douglas Aircraft
Corp. in 1960. Founded Citizens for Mich., a civic improvement org., involving it in school and community affairs and
in the movement for state constl. reform. Had a major role
in drive for holding Mich. constl. conv. that met in 1962-
1963, serving as a delegate and as vice pres. at the conv.
Nom. and el. Gov. as Rep. in 1962, defeating incumbent Gov.
Swainson. Reel. in 1964 by plurality of some 380,000 votes,
despite sweep of the State by Dem. cand. for Pres. of U.S.
Reel. for another term in 1966, becoming the first Mich.
Gov. to be el. for a four-year term under the revised state
const. Announced intention to seek Rep. nom. for Pres. of
U.S. as 1968 conv. approached, but withdrew from the contest

after campaign for delegate support proved discouraging.
Resigned office of Gov. in Jan., 1969 to assume office of
U.S. Sect. of Dept. of H.U.D., to which he had been apptd.
by Pres. Nixon. Served until Feb., 1973, when he resigned.
Very active in affairs of the Mormon church, serving as
leader of its 157th Stake, in Mich., 1952-1962. Ch. of
N.C.C.J. Hon. degrees from twelve universities and colleges.
m. in 1931 to Leonore La Fount, of Salt Lake City. Two d.;
two s. Wife was also politically active, becoming the Rep.
nominee for a U.S. Senate seat from Mich. in 1970, but losing in the gen. election.

MILLIKEN, WILLIAM GRAWN (1969----). b. March 26, 1922
at Traverse City, Mich. s. of James Thacker and Hildegarde
(Grawn) M. Family were owners of a prosperous gen. merc.
bus. at Traverse City. Attd. local schools and Yale, from
which he was grad. in 1946. Schooling was interrupted by
service in U.S. Air Force during World War II. Enlisted as
a pvt., serving as gunner on some 50 air combat missions in
European theater. Recipient of Purple Heart and Air Medal.
Held rank of sgt. at time of discharge. Joined family enterprise at Traverse City. Ch. of Grand Traverse Co. Rep.
commt. for six years and pres., Traverse City CC. Mbr.,
Mich. Waterways Commn., 1947-1955. Mbr. of U.S. State Dept.
Inter-cultural Exchange program for West Germany, 1953. Mbr.
of Mich. Senate, 1960-1964, serving as majority (Rep.) leader, 1963-1964. El. Lieut. Gov. in 1964 and was reel. in
1966 for four-year term. Succeeded to office of Gov. in
Jan., 1969 when Gov. Romney resigned to become U.S. Sect. of
H.U.D. Completed Romney's term, and was el. to four-year
terms in 1970, 1974 and again in 1978. Ch., Natl. Govs.'
Assoc., 1977-1978. Mbr., Bd. of Trustees, N.W. Mich. Coll.;
Bd. of Counselors, Smith Coll.; pres., Scenic Trails Council
of Boy Scouts; dir., Greater Mich. Found. Hon. degrees from
the Univ. of Mich.; Yale; Eastern Mich. Univ.; Cent. Mich.
Univ.; No. Mich. Univ.; Detroit Inst. of Tech. Congrega-
tionalist. m. in 1945 to Helen Wallbank. One s.; one d.

SIBLEY, HENRY HASTINGS (1858-1860). b. Feb. 20, 1811 at Detroit, Mich. Terr. s. of Solomon S. and Sarah W. (Sproat) S. Father, who had moved to Mich. area in 1797, was a lawyer and served as Delegate to Cong. from Mich. Terr. Educ. in a local acad. and with pvt. tutors. Studied law for a time but did not practice. Became employee, later a partner, in Amer. Fur Co. at Mackinac, Mich., later settling at a trading post at the mouth of Minnesota River in what was then Wisc. Terr. in 1834. Contributed articles on frontier life to publications. Chosen as Delegate from Wisc. Terr. to Cong. in 1848, but with admission of Wisc. to statehood that year his position was transformed into Delegate from Minn. Terr. following the org. of Minn. Terr. in 1849, in which he had an active role. Continued to serve as Delegate from Minn. Terr. until 1853, when he declined reel. Mbr. of Minn. Terr. legislature in 1856 and of the Minn. constl. conv. in 1857, serving as its pres. El. Gov. on a provisional basis as Dem. in 1857 when a proposed state const. was adopted, and assumed office as Gov. de jure when news of the admission of Minn. to statehood was received in May, 1858. As Gov., resisted effort to extend State's credit on unlimited basis for railroad constr., but was overruled by cts. on the issue. State eventually suffered losses as a result. After uprising of Sioux Indians against White settlers in 1862, was placed at head of volunteer forces, with rank of brig. gen. and later as major gen. in successful effort to subdue them. Resigned commn. in 1866. Engaged in bus. activities at St. Paul. Mbr. of Minn. legislature in 1871, where he opposed repudiation of State's bonds. Defeated as cand. for U.S. House in 1880. Mbr. of U.S. commn. on Ojibway Indian affairs by apptmt. from Pres. Arthur in 1883. Mbr. of Univ. of Minn. Bd. of Regents, 1860-1868 and 1876-1891, serving as pres. during latter period. Pres. of St. Paul CC; pres. of Minn. Historical Soc., 1879-1891; and was a contributor to its collections. Hon. degree from Princeton Univ. m. in 1844 to Sarah J. Steele, of Pa. One s.; three d. D. at St. Paul Feb. 18, 1891. Bur. in Oakland Cem. there.

RAMSEY, ALEXANDER (1860-1863). b. Sept. 8, 1815 near Harrisburg, Pa. s. of Thomas and Elizabeth (Kilker) R. Descendant of an Irish immigrant who had come to Amer. before Rev. War. Attd. Harrisburg schools and Lafayette Coll. Studied law, admmitted to bar and began practice in Harrisburg in 1834. Clerk of Pa. House in 1841. El. to U.S. House as a Whig in 1842 and again in 1844. Declined to run for third term in 1846. Ch. of Pa. Whig state party commt. in 1848. Apptd. as first Gov. of Minn. Terr. by Pres. Taylor in 1849, serving until 1853. During tenure, negoti-

ated important treaties with Sioux and Chippewa Indian
tribes for purchase of lands in Minn. Mayor of St. Paul,
1855. Had leading role in organizing Rep. party in Minn. in
1850s. Nom. as its cand. for Gov. in 1857, but lost by a
narrow margin. El. Gov. in 1859 and again in 1861. Major
events during admin. were the outbreak of Civil War, in
which he gave active support to Union cause, and the Sioux
War, in which the Sioux were subdued after much bloodshed.
Resigned as Gov. in July, 1863 to take seat in U.S. Senate,
where he served until 1875. Apptd. Sect. of War by Pres.
Hayes, serving from 1879 to 1881. In 1882-1886 served as
mbr. and ch. of Utah (Edmunds) Commn. to investigate conditions under Mormonism in Utah Terr. Delegate from Minn. to
1887 U.S. Centennial celebration at Philadelphia. Mbr. and
first pres. of Minn. Historical Soc., 1849-1863; pres. again,
1891-1903. m. in 1845 to Anna Earl Jenks, of Newton, Pa.
Two s.; one d. D. in St. Paul April 22, 1903. Bur. in
Oakland Cem. there.

SWIFT, HENRY A. (1863-1864). b. March 23, 1823 at
Ravenna, Ohio. s. of Isaac and Eliza S. Descendant of New
England family that had participated in Rev. War. Attd.
Western Reserve Coll. from which he was grad. in 1842. Spent
following year in Miss. as a teacher. Studied law, and began practice in Ravenna in 1845. Held clerical position in
Ohio legislature, 1847-1849. Emigrated to St. Paul, Minn.
Terr., in 1853, where he practiced law and engaged in real
estate bus. Helped lay out town of St. Peter. El. to Minn.
Senate in 1861, and became Pres. pro tem of that body. As
such, succeeded to office of Gov. when Gov. Ramsey resigned
in July, 1863, the office of Lieut. Gov. being vacant at the
time. Completed Ramsey's term. Declined to become cand.
for Gov. for regular term in 1863, but was reel. to Minn.
Senate seat that year. Later was apptd. receiver at U.S.
land office in St. Peter. m. in 1851 to Ruth Livingston, of
Gettysburg, Pa. Five children, of whom only two survived to
adulthood. D. at St. Peter Feb. 24, 1869. Bur. in Maple
Grove Cem., Ravenna, Ohio.

MILLER, STEPHEN (1864-1866). b. Jan. 17, 1816 at
Carroll, Cumberland (now Perry Co.), Pa. s. of David and
Rosana (Darkness) M. Grandfather had emigrated from Germany
to Amer. in 1785, settling in Pa. Mother's family was from
New England. Was studious and ambitious but had little op-
portunity for schooling. In 1834 became clerk in a store at
Harrisburg, Pa. Prothonotary of Dauphin Co., 1849-1852. Be-
came ed. of Harrisburg Telegraph in 1853, an influential
Whig journal, serving in that capacity until 1855. Apptd.
state flour inspector at Philadelphia in 1855, but after

three years moved for health reasons to St. Cloud, Minn.,
where he engaged in gen. merc. bus. Affiliated with Rep.
party in 1850s. Delegate to Rep. natl. conv. in 1860 and
was a Rep. pres. elector that year. Enlisted as a pvt. in a
volunteer Union regiment in 1861 and was soon commissioned
as a lieut. col. Was assigned to Minn. area upon outbreak
of Sioux uprising in 1862, rising to rank of brig. gen. by
end of the conflict. Presided over executions of 38 indians
found guilty of murder of White settlers. Nom. and el. Gov.
as Rep. in 1863. Gave full support to Union war effort during Civil War. Became mgr. of Sioux City and St. Paul R.R.
land company in 1871. Mbr. of Minn. legislature, 1873-1876
and was an elector on Rep. ticket in 1876 pres. election.
Established residence at Windom, Minn. and later at Worthington, Minn. Mbr., Masons. m. in 1834 to Margaret Funk.
Five children. D. Aug. 18, 1881 at Worthington, Minn.

MARSHALL, WILLIAM ROGERSON (1866-1870). b. Oct. 17,
1825 near Columbia, Mo. s. of Joseph M., a farmer. When he
was still a young child, family moved to Quincy, Ill., where
he attd. school. Supplemented formal schooling by studies
on his own. At age 16 went to work in lead mines near Galena, Ill. After several years changed occupation to land
survey work. El. to Ill. legislature in 1848. In 1849
moved to St. Anthony Falls, Minn. Terr., where he established a gen. store in partnership with brother. El. to
first Minn. Terr. legislature in 1849. Moved to St. Paul
when it became capital of the Terr. Engaged in real estate
and banking bus. there, 1855-1857. After reverses, became
proprietor of a dairy farm. In 1861 established a newspaper,
the St. Paul Daily Press. When the Sioux Indian uprising
began in 1862, enlisted in a volunteer infantry unit, and
was commissioned as a lieut. col., later as col. Was later
assigned to duty in Mo. theater and elsewhere during Civil
War. Attained rank of brig. gen. by end of the war. Returned to Minn. and in 1866 was nom. and el. Gov. as Rep.
Reel. in 1868. Resumed bus. activities thereafter, except
for serving in 1874-1875 as Minn. R.R. Commnr. D. at Pasadena, Calif., Jan. 8, 1896.

AUSTIN, HORACE (1870-1874). b. Oct. 15, 1831 at Canterbury, Conn. s. of David and Eliza A. Father was a descendant of an English colonist who emigrated to Mass. and
mother was of English-German ancestry. Attd. local schools
and at age 20 moved to Augusta, Me. Studied law there, and
in 1854 moved to St. Peter, in Minn. Terr. where he engaged
in law practice. Served with U.S. forces in Sioux War in
1863. El. dist. judge in 1864. Nom. and el. Gov. as Rep.
in 1869 in a close election, and was reel. in 1871. During

admin., led movement for subjection of railroads to greater
degree of pub. control as to rates, an issue that led to involvement of State in the so-called "Granger Cases" eventually resolved by U.S. Supreme Ct. State criminal code was
revised; a State Bd. of Health was established; and more
land was donated by Cong. to form an endowment for the Univ.
of Minn. Used veto against bill to grant additional lands
to railroad companies. After tenure as Gov. was employed in
U.S. Treas. Dept. as Third Aud. for four years. Held position of registrar of U.S. land office at Fargo, N.D. in the
Dept. of the Interior for seven years. Mbr. and ch. of Minn.
R.R. Commn., 1887. After 1900 travelled extensively in West,
visiting Alaska and residing from time to time in Calif.,
where he engaged in mining and oil ventures. m. in 1859 to
Mary Lena Morrill, of Manchester, Me. Five d.; one s. D.
Nov. 7, 1905 at Minneapolis. Bur. in Oakland Cem., St. Paul.

DAVIS, CUSHMAN KELLOGG (1874-1876). b. June 16, 1838
at Henderson, N.Y. s. of Horatio N. and Clarissa S. (Cushman) D. Mother was a descendant of English colonist who
came to Plymouth on the Mayflower in 1620. Parents moved to
Waukesha, Wisc. during his youth. Attd. pub. schools there;
Carroll Coll.; and the Univ. of Mich., from which he was
grad. in 1857. Studied law at Waukesha, admitted to bar and
began practice there. After outbreak of Civil War enlisted
as lieut. in a Wisc. regiment. Served as adjt. on staff of
Gen. Willis Gorman until 1864 when poor health caused him to
resign commn. Moved to St. Paul, Minn. in 1865, and engaged
in law practice there. Mbr. of Minn. House in 1867. U.S.
dist. atty. for Minn., 1868-1873. Nom. and el. Gov. as Rep.
in 1873. Declined to run for succeeding term. Unsuccessful
as cand. for U.S. Senate seat in 1875 and 1881, but was el.
to that body in 1887. Continued to serve in the Senate until his death. Mbr. of commn. that negotiated Paris Treaty
ending Spanish-Amer. War in 1898. Lecturer on intl. law at
the Univ. of Mich. in 1897. A student of Shakespeare, published an article, "The Law in Shakespeare" in 1884; also
published A Treatise on International Law (1901) and numerous speeches. Hon. degree from the Univ. of Mich. D. at
St. Paul, Minn. Nov. 27, 1900 while still a mbr. of U.S.
Senate. Bur. in Arlington Natl. Cem.

PILLSBURY, JOHN SARGENT (1876-1882). b. July 29, 1828
at Sutton, N.H. s. of John and Susan (Wadleigh) P. Descendant of English colonist who emigrated to Mass. in 1640.
Father, who was owner of a mfg. enterprise, was prominent in
community and pub. affairs in N.H. Mother was also a mbr.
of a prominent family. Attd. local pub. schools. Studied
painting for a short time, but changed interest to bus.

Formed partnership in merc. firm with Walter Harriman, later
Gov. of N.H. (q.v.) Moved to Concord, where he was a merchant and cloth dealer for a time. Toured West in 1853 and
in 1855 settled at St. Anthony Falls, Minn., where he started
a hardware store. Extended bus. interests into other lines,
founding a flour mill enterprise with two nephews and a
brother at Minneapolis in 1872 that grew into one of the
largest in the U.S. in its field. Also became involved in
lumbering, banking, railroad operations, and various mfg.
enterprises, becoming quite wealthy. Mbr. of St. Anthony
Falls city council for six years, 1858-1864. Mbr. of Minn.
Senate from 1864 to 1874 except for one and one-half term.
As mbr. of Senate specialized in matters concerning the
Univ. of Minn., and because of his important contributions
in that area came to be called the "Father of the Univ. of
Minn." Mbr. of the Univ. of Minn. Bd. of Regents beginning
in 1863, and was eventually designated "Regent for life."
Nom. and el. Gov. as Rep. in 1875. Continued in office for
next two succeeding terms, becoming first Gov. of Minn. to
be el. for three terms. As Gov., advocated state regulation
of railroad rates; settlement of claims against state for
repudiated state bonds; expansion of pub. school system to
include high schools; improvements in state penal system;
and revision of state and local accounting practices. Had
leading role in assembling of conf. of Govs. of Northwestern
States in 1877 to deal with problem of crop destruction by
grasshoppers. Made many large gifts for pub. improvements,
including funds for a memorial to his parents and a town
hall in Sutton, N.H.; a Home for Girls in Minneapolis; and a
pub. library at East Minneapolis. Congregationalist. m. in
1856 to Mahala Fisk of Warner, N.H. Three d.; one s. D.
Oct. 18, 1901, at Minneapolis.

HUBBARD, LUCIUS FREDERICK (1882-1887). b. Jan. 26,
1836 at Troy, N.Y. s. of Charles F. and Margaret (Van Val-
kenberg) H. Father was a descendant of a New England family
and had served as a mbr. of N.Y. legislature from Renssalear
Co. Mother was from N.Y. and was of Dutch descent. Father
died when son was three years old and mother died when he
was ten. Lived with an aunt in Chester, Vt. for several
years. Received common school educ. and attd. Granville
Acad. in N.Y. for three years. Apprenticed to tinsmith
trade at age 15. Moved to Chicago in 1854, where he was employed at his trade for several years, and in 1857 moved to
Red Wing, Minn. Established a newspaper there, the Republican, which he published from 1859 to 1861. Register of
deeds for Goodhue Co., 1858-1860. Unsuccessful as cand. for
Minn. Senate. Upon outbreak of Civil War enlisted as a pvt.
in a volunteer infantry regiment of Union Army. Commissioned

as capt. in 1862 and rose during course of the war to rank
of brig. gen. Was with Army of the Tennessee, participating
in numerous major engagements. Wounded in 1864 at the Battle of Franklin. Was mustered out in 1865. Entered into
grain and milling enterprise at Red Wing. Nom. for seat in
U.S. House in 1868, but irregularities were charged in connection with the ensuing election and he withdrew. Mbr. of
Minn. Senate, 1872-1876, declining to run for reel. in 1876.
Mbr. of commn. apptd. by Gov. Marshall to investigate matters
connected with state bond issues, and in 1874 served on a
legislative commn. to investigate admin. of state finances.
Entered railroad constr. bus. in 1877, and from 1878 to 1881
was pres. of Cannon Valley R.R. Mbr. of legislative commn.
of arb. to adjust dispute between State and prison contractors, 1879. Nom. and el. Gov. as Rep. in 1881. Reel. in
1883 for three-year term resulting from a change in term and
election schedule. After tenure as Gov. resumed railroad
constr. and operations. Mbr. of legislative commn. in 1889
to compile history of Minn. mil. units in Civil War. Commissioned as brig. gen. of volunteers by Pres. McKinley at
outset of Spanish-Amer. War. Mbr., Masons, G.A.R.; S.A.R.;
Loyal Legion; Soc. of Army of Tenn.; Soc. of Amer. Wars;
Mil. Order of Foreign Wars. Trustee, Minn. Soldiers Home.
Mbr. of Rep. natl. commt. m. in 1868 to Amelia Thomas, of
Red Wing. Two s.; one d. D. Feb. 5, 1913 at Minneapolis.

McGILL, ANDREW RYAN (1887-1889). b. Feb. 19, 1840 at
Saegerstown, Pa. s. of Charles Dillon and Angeline (Marton)
McG. Grandfather had emigrated from Ireland in 1774, settling on a farm in Pa. that came to be known as the "McGill
Homestead." Mother was a descendant of an English family
that had settled in Pa., and whose forebears had participated in Rev. War as supporters of the Amer. cause. Mother
died when he was 8 years old. Attd. local schools while assisting father on family farm. In 1859 moved to Ky., where
he was a teacher for two years. In 1861 moved to St. Peter,
Minn., serving as principal of the school there. Enlisted
in Minn. volunteer regiment in 1862 and participated in
operations against Sioux Indians. Later served with Army of
the Tennessee until his discharge for reasons of health.
Supt. of schools at St. Peter for two terms. In 1866 became
proprietor and ed. of St. Peter Tribune. Clerk of dist. ct.
of Nicollet Co., 1865-1869. Studied law in office of Judge
Horace Austin, later a Gov. of Minn. Admitted to bar in
1868. Pvt. sect. to Gov. Austin, 1870. Apptd. by him to
the post of State Ins. Commnr. in 1872, continuing to serve
in that capacity until 1885. Nom. and el. Gov. as Rep. in
1886. During admin., a system of local option with high
license fees for dispensing of intoxicating liquors was

adopted; improved bus. methods in admin. of govt. introduced.
Was not nom. by his party conv. for the succeeding term.
Apptd. U.S. postmaster at St. Paul in 1900. El. to Minn.
Senate in 1898 and 1902. m. in 1880 to Mary E. Wilson, of
Edinborough, Pa. Three s. D. Oct. 31, 1905 at St. Anthony
Park, Minn.

MERRIAM, WILLIAM RUSH (1889-1893). b. July 26, 1849 at
Wadham's Mills, N.Y. s. of the Hon. John L. and Mahala (De
Lano) M. Father was a descendant of a Scotch colonist who
emigrated to Concord, Mass. in 1636. Mother was a descendant of a Dutch ancestor who emigrated to Plymouth, Mass. in
1621. In 1861 family moved to St. Paul, Minn., where father
became prominent in affairs of the community and state, serving in the Minn. legislature as House Speaker. Attd. local
schools until age 15, when he was sent to Racine, Wisc. to
continue studies. Attd. Racine Coll., from which he was
grad. as class valedictorian in 1870. Active in athletics
as a student. Later received an A.M. degree from Racine
Coll. Returned to St. Paul where he began working as a bank
clerk. In 1873 when the Merchants' Natl. Bank was formed,
became its cashier, eventually serving as its pres., 1882-
1897. Also acquired farm holdings and extended bus. interests into iron and coal mining and mfg. companies in Va. as
well as Minn., becoming quite wealthy. Mbr. of Minn. legislature in 1882 and again in 1886, serving as House Speaker.
As mbr. of legislature was active in promotion of measures
favored by farm interests. Nom. and el. Gov. as Rep. in
1888 and again in 1890. As Gov., a notable incident was his
intervention to prevent holding of a heavy-weight prize
fight involving Hall and Fitzsimmons. Apptd. by Pres.
McKinley dir. of U.S. 12th census, serving from 1898 to 1903.
Maintained interest in farming activities as breeder of fine
horses. Served as pres. of State Agri. Soc.; also was pres.
of Minn. Boat Club. Treas. of school bd. in St. Paul for
three years. Active in affairs of Episcopal church, making
many benevolent contributions. m. in 1872 to Laura Hancock,
of St. Paul. She was a descendant of U.S. Pres. John Adams,
of Mass. and was a niece of Gen. Winfield S. Hancock, the
nominee of the Dem. party for Pres. of U.S. in 1880. Two
s.; two d. D. Feb. 18, 1931 in Washington, D.C.

NELSON, KNUTE (1893-1895). b. Feb. 2, 1843 in the
parish of Voss, near Bergen, Norway. Father died when son
was three years old, and three years later he was brought by
his mother to Chicago, Ill. In 1850 the family moved to
Dane Co., Wisc., where he attd. pub. schools and Albion
Acad. for three years. Enlisted as pvt. in a Wisc. regiment
in 1861. Was wounded and taken prisoner in 1863 in an en-

gagement at Port Hudson, La. After his release in 1864 re-
entered Albion Acad. for a year. Studied law, admitted to
bar and began practice in Cambridge, Wisc. in 1867. Mbr. of
Wisc. legislature, 1868-1869. In 1871 moved to Alexandria,
Minn. Douglas Co. atty., 1872-1874. Mbr. of Minn. Senate,
1875-1878. Served as pres. elector on Rep. ticket in 1880
election. Mbr. of the Univ. of Minn. Bd. of Regents, 1882-
1893. El. to U.S. House in 1882, continuing to serve therein for two succeeding terms. Was not a cand. for fourth
term. Practiced law and engaged in farming. Brought a number of cases before U.S. Dept. of Interior on behalf of
settlers with claims against railroad companies. Nom. and
el. Gov. as Rep. in 1892 and was reel. by increased majority
in 1894. Resigned as Gov. shortly after beginning of second
term in 1895 to take seat in U.S. Senate to which he had
been chosen. Continued to serve in that body until his
death. As a mbr. of Senate was very instrumental in creation of the Dept. of Commerce and Labor; revision of U.S.
bankruptcy laws; and in securing additional U.S. financial
support for agri. experimental programs. While residing in
Wisc. was married to a Wisc. resident. Five children, three
of whom died in a diphtheria epidemic in 1874. D. April 28,
1923 at Alexandria, Minn. while on a train returning to his
home in Minn. Bur. in Kinkead Cem., Alexandria, Minn.

CLOUGH, DAVID MARSTON (1895-1899). b. Oct. 27, 1846 at
Lyme, N.H. s. of Elbridge C., who was of Welsh origin, and
was employed in lumbering work. Son was one of fourteen
children. Parents moved family to Waupaca, Wisc. in 1855,
and in 1857 to Spanish Park, Minn. Received common school
educ., and began work as a youth in lumbering. By age 35 he
org. his own firm, with headquarters in St. Paul, and the
company expanded and proved quite profitable. Mbr. of St.
Paul city council in 1885, later serving as its pres. Mbr.
of Minn. Senate, 1887-1891. El. Lieut. Gov. as Rep. in 1892
and was reel. in 1894. Succeeded to office of Gov. in Jan.,
1895 when Gov. Nelson resigned to take seat in U.S. Senate.
Completed Nelson's term, and was el. to full term in 1896 by
a close vote over Fusionist (Dem. and Pop.) cand. Devoted
attention to bus. affairs after tenure as Gov. Org. a new
company to engage in lumbering in Northwestern U.S., and
eventually moved to Everett, Wash. m. in 1868 to Adelaide
Barton, of Spencer Brook, Minn. One d. D. Aug. 28, 1924,
at Everett, Wash.

LIND, JOHN (1899-1901). b. March 25, 1854 at Kanna,
Smaland, in Sweden. s. of Gustav and Catherine (Jonason) L.
Came to Amer. with parents, who settled on a farm at Goodhue,
Minn., in 1867. While helping with farm work, lost left hand

in an accident. Studied in local schools and at 16 years of
age received teacher's certificate and became a teacher.
Moved to New Ulm, Minn. in 1873, and soon after became Brown
Co. supt. of schools. Attd. the Univ. of Minn. 1875-1876.
Studied law in law office, admitted to bar in 1876 and began
practice in 1877. In 1881-1885 served as receiver at U.S.
land office at Tracy, Minn. Suits begun by him against
railroad companies brought him to prominence. El. as Rep.
to U.S. House in 1886. Continued in office for next two
terms, but was not a cand. for reel. in 1892 because of differences that had developed between him and his party's
leadership on tariff and monetary issues. As mbr. of Cong.
sponsored legislation revising naturalization laws; exempt-
ing foreign books from tariff duties; imposing responsibility upon steamship companies for damages; and establishing
Minneapolis as a U.S. port of entry. Apptd. to the Univ. of
Minn. Bd. of Regents in 1893, later becomnng pres. of that
body. Nom. on Fusion (Dem. and Pop.) ticket for Gov. in
1896, but was defeated by close margin. Upon outbreak of
Spanish-Amer. War in 1898 accepted commn. as first lieut. in
the Quartermaster Corps of the U.S. Army. While still on
mil. duty was nom. by Dem. and Pop. parties for Gov. again
in 1898 and was el. Nom. for succeeding term in 1900, but
was defeated in another close election. El. in 1902 as Dem.
to U.S. House, but did not seek reel. in 1904. Resumed law
practice and bus. interests at New Ulm. Apptd. by Pres.
Wilson as personal emissary to Mexico in Aug., 1913. m. in
1879 to Alice A. Shepard. One s.; two d. D. at Minneapolis
Sept. 18, 1930. Ashes interred in Lakewood Cem. there.

   VAN SANT, SAMUEL RINNAH (1901-1905). b. May 11, 1844
at Rock Island, Ill. s. of John Wesley and Lydia (Anderson)
Van S. Paternal ancestors were early Dutch immigrants to
Amer. and had worked as sailors and ship-builders. Father
had moved to Ill. in 1837, where he with his sons was engaged in bldg. and repairing steamboats. Attd. pub. schools
at Rock Island while helping in family bus. Sought to enlist in Union army at age 17 but was refused on account of
his age. After several fruitless attempts was finally permitted to enlist with father's written consent in 1861,
joining a volunteer Ill. cavalry unit. Served for three
years, rising in rank to corporal at time of release. Studied for a short time at Burnham's Bus. Coll. in Hudson, N.Y.
and enrolled for two years at Knox Coll., in Ill. Went to
work as a ship carpenter and eventually joined father in
boat constr. bus. at Rock Island. They built first large
raft boat for lumbering trade on the Miss. In 1883 moved
the bus. to Winona, Minn. Became mbr. of Winona bd. of aldermen, and in 1892 was el. to Minn. legislature. Reel. in

1894 and was chosen Speaker of the House. Nom. and el. Gov.
as Rep. in 1900, defeating incumbent Gov. Lind in a close
election. Reel. in 1902. As Gov., opposed proposed merger
of Great No. and the No. Pac. railway systems. Active in
G.A.R., serving as Commndr.-in-chief of Minn. post in 1909-
1910. Mbr., S.A.R. Hon. degrees from Augustana and Cornell
(Iowa) colleges. m. in 1868 to Ruth Hall, of Le Claire,
Iowa. One s. D. Oct. 3, 1936 at Attica, Ind. at age of 92.

JOHNSON, JOHN ALBERT (1905-1909). b. July 28, 1801 on
a farm near St. Peter, Minn. s. of Gustav and Caroline
Hansen (Haden) J. Both parents were natives of Sweden.
Father, who was a skilled ironsmith, was an alcoholic, and
had come to Amer. in effort to reform. After Civil War began family had moved to the farm where son was born. Received only a rudimentary educ. in local schools, but was
studious and read widely. After father's death, son at age
12 began working in a local grocery store. Had much talent
in athletics, music and social matters and came quickly to
be recognized as a leader. Though inclined toward Rep. party
on most matters of politics, differed with its views on the
tariff, and affiliated with Dem. party. In 1888 became ed.
of a Dem. newspaper, the St. Peter's Herald. Mgr. of co.
fair. Joined Minn. militia. Engaged widely in pub. speaking
on issues of the day. Unsuccessful cand. for Minn. Senate
in 1894, but was nom. and el. to that post as a Dem. in 1898.
Supported natl. admin. and Rep. party position on issue of
recall of Minn. regiment from campaign against Filipino insurrection. Defeated for reel. in 1902. Nom. and el. Gov.
as Dem. in 1904, becoming first native-born citizen of Minn.
to be el. to the office. Continued in office in 1906 and
1908. As Gov., launched an investigation into ins. bus.,
and joined with other State Govs., Attys. Gen. and Ins.
Commnrs. in effort to devise code of uniform ins. laws. During miners' strike in 1907 resisted pressure to use militia
forces to quell disorders, choosing instead to meet with
strikers personally to achieve order. Hon. degree from Univ.
of Pa. in 1907. m. in 1894 to Elinor M. Preston, of Rochester, Minn. He had been troubled by stomach disorder during
most of adult life. Succumbed at St. Paul on Sept. 21, 1909
after an abdominal operation at Rochester, Minn. during
first year of third term.

EBERHART, ADOLPH OLSON (1909-1915). b. June 23, 1870
near Karlstad, Varmland, Sweden. s. of Andrew and Louise
(Johnson) Olson. Emigrated to Amer. in 1881. At age of 12
became a cattle herder and farm laborer in Nebr. Had no
formal educ. during youth, but read widely at home of clergy-
man-farmer for whom he worked as a youth. At age 21 entered

prep. dept. of Gustavus Adolphus Coll., at St. Peter, Minn.
Continued to study there, graduating in 1895 at head of
class, having supported himself while in school by various
jobs. Studied law in office in Mankato, Minn. and was admitted to the bar in 1898. By ct. action, changed last name
from Olson to Eberhart in 1898 to avoid confusion with others
having same name residing in the same town. From 1897 to
1906 was ct. commnr. and deputy clerk of U.S. dist. ct. and
cir. cts. of Minn. El. to Minn. Senate in 1902, serving by
reel. until 1907. Was youngest mbr. of Senate at the time,
but was active in introduction of bills, particularly with
reference to closer regulation of railroad rate practices.
Nom. and el. Lieut. Gov. as Rep. in 1906, although voters
chose a Dem. for Gov., and el. again in 1908. When Gov. Johnson died in 1909, succeeded to office of Gov. El. for regular terms in 1910 and in 1912. During admin., promoted reorg. of state pub. school system; also carried out reorg. of
state admin. system. Unsuccessful cand. for Rep. nom. for
U.S. Senate seat in 1916. In 1924 moved to Chicago, Ill.,
where he became pres. of Suburban Homes Corp. Engaged in
various community devel. enterprises and social improvement
orgs. there. Mbr., Masons; Elks. Lutheran. m. in 1898 to
Adele Kohe, of New Ulm, Minn. Three d. D. Dec. 6, 1944.

HAMMOND, WINFIELD SCOTT (1915). b. Nov. 17, 1863 at
Southboro, Mass. s. of John W. and Ellen (Panton) H. Descendant of English colonist who emigrated to Mass. in 1632.
Attd. local pub. schools and Dartmouth Coll., from which he
was grad. in 1884. Also received an A.M. degree there in
1889. Principal of Mankato, Minn. H.S., 1884-1885 and head
of pub. school system at Madelia, Minn., 1885-1890. Studied
law, admitted to bar and practiced at Madelia until 1895,
when he moved to St. James, Minn. Defeated as Dem. cand.
for U.S. House in 1892. Pros. atty. for Watonwan Co., 1895-
1896 and 1900-1905. Mbr. of Minn. Bd. of Dir. for state
normal schools, 1898-1906. Pres. of bd. of educ. at St.
James, 1898-1903. Nom. and el. to U.S. House as Dem. in
1906, continuing to serve therein until 1915, when he resigned after having been nom. and el. Gov. as Dem. in 1914.
Mbr. of professional legal orgs.; S.A.R.; Masons, Elks; various social clubs in Minneapolis and Washington, D.C. Never
married. D. Dec. 30, 1915 at Clinton, La., where he had
gone for a visit after having served about one year of term
as Gov. Bur. in Mount Hope Cem., St. James.

BURNQUIST, JOSEPH ALFRED ARNER (1915-1921). b. July 21,
1879 at Dayton, Iowa. s. of John Alfred and Louise (Johnson) B. Father had emigrated from Sweden to Ill. in 1864,
later moving to Iowa. Attd. local schools; Carleton Coll.,

from which he was grad. in 1902; and Columbia Univ., from
which he received an M.A. degree in 1904. Studied law at
the Univ. of Mich. for one year. Received law degree in 1905
and was admitted to bar in Minn. Began practice in Minneapolis and St. Paul. Mbr. of Minn. legislature, 1909-1913. As
mbr. of that body advocated progressive measures, including
direct primary and non-partisan election of judges. El.
Lieut. Gov. as Rep. in 1912 and again in 1914, although voters chose a Dem. cand. for Gov. in latter year. Succeeded
to office of Gov. in Dec., 1915 following death of Gov. Hammond. El. for regular terms in 1916 and 1918. During admin., gave full support to U.S. war effort during World War
I. Resumed law practice thereafter for some time. El. Atty.
Gen. of Minn. in 1938 and continued in that office for seven
succeeding terms, serving until 1955. Minn. ct. commnr.,
1956-1958. Trustee of Carleton Coll., from which he received an hon. degree in 1920. Mbr., Phi Beta Kappa; Delta
Sigma Rho; professional legal orgs. Pres., Natl. Assoc. of
Attys. Gen., 1948-1949. Recipient of Carleton Coll. Distinguished Alumni Award; Univ. of Minn. Outstanding Achievement Award; Minn. Terr. Centennial Award. Congregationalist.
m. in 1906 to Mary Louis Cross, of Dawson, Minn. Two s.;
two d. D. Jan. 12, 1961 at Minneapolis. Bur. in Lakewood
Cem., Minneapolis.

PREUS, JACOB AALL OTTESEN (1921-1925). b. Aug. 28,
1883 in Columbia Co., Wisc. s. of Christian Keyser and
Louise Augusta (Hjort) P. Grandfather had emigrated from
Norway to Wisc. in 1851, where he became founder of Norwegian Lutheran Synod of Amer. and served as its pres. and as
a bishop until his death. Father succeeded to that position
in the church, later becoming pres. of Luther Coll., at
Decorah, Iowa. Son attd. pub. schools at Decorah, and Luther Coll., from which he was grad. in 1903. Attd. the Univ.
of Minn., from which he received a law degree in 1906. Admitted to bar in Minn. and in 1937 in Ill. Worked as store
clerk and teacher to earn living while attending college.
Served as messenger and staff asst. for Sen. Knute Nelson, of
Minn., from 1906 to 1909. Exec. sect. to Gov. Eberhart of
Minn., 1909-1910. Apptd. Minn. Ins. Commnr. in 1910, serving
until 1914. El. Minn. Aud. Gen. in 1914, continuing in that
office until 1921. El. Gov. as Rep. in 1920 and was continued in office for succeeding term. As Gov., promoted
measures favored by labor and farm interests, including a
law providing for cooperative marketing orgs. Became vice
pres. of Alexander and Co., in Chicago, in 1926. Continued
in bus. there, becoming pres. of Amer. Merchants Mutual Ins.
Co. in 1945 and later, ch. of its bd. of dir. Trustee,
Scandinavian Found. Mbr., Lutheran Brotherhood of Minneap-

olis. Hon. degrees from Lutheran Coll. and Augustana Coll.
m. in 1909 to Idella´Louise Haugen, of Decorah, Iowa. Two
s. D. May 24, 1961 at Minneapolis. Bur. at Decorah, Iowa.

CHRISTIANSON, THEODORE (1925-1931). b. Sept. 12, 1883
in Lac qui Parle township, near Dawson, Minn. s. of Robert
and Emma (Ronning) C. Attd. local rural schools, Dawson
H.S., and the Univ. of Minn., from which he received an A.B.
degree in 1906 and a law degree in 1909. Principal of Rob-
bindale, Minn. schools, 1906-1909. Admitted to bar in 1909
and began practice at Dawson. Mbr. and pres. of village
council, 1909-1910. Mbr. of Minn. House, 1915-1925, serving
as ch. of its appropriations commt. for four terms. Owner
and publ. of Dawson Sentinel, 1909-1925. Nom. and el. Gov.
as Rep. in 1924 and continued in office for two succeeding
terms. During admin., achieved reputation as "watch-dog of
budgets." Sponsored legislation reducing state bonded indebtedness; creating a state budget system; reorganizing
state admin. depts.; establishing a state crime commn.; and
providing for greater soundness in state banking system.
From 1931 to 1932 was employed as an exec. in a Minneapolis
mfg. enterprise. El. as Repr.-at-large to U.S. House in
1932, continuing in office until 1937. Unsuccessful cand.
for U.S. Senate seat in 1936. Managing sect. for Natl.
Assoc. of Retail Grocers, at Chicago, Ill., 1937-1939. Pub.
relations counsel, Natl. Assoc. of Retail Druggists, 1939-
1945 and ed. of its trade magazine, 1945 until death. Interested in historical matters, he was author of a 5-vol.
history of Minn. and numerous published articles. Mbr.,
Phi Beta Kappa; Delta Sigma Rho. Hon. degrees from Hamline
Univ., Macalester Coll., and Augustana Coll. Presbyterian.
m. in 1907 to Ruth Eleanor Donaldson, of Dundas, Minn. Two
s. m. in 1946 to Mrs. Mayme M. Bundy, of Chicago. D. Dec.
9, 1948 at Dawson. Bur. in Sunset Memorial Cem., Minneapolis.

OLSON, FLOYD BJORNSTJERNE (1931-1936). b. Nov. 13,
1891 at Minneapolis, Minn. s. of Paul and Ida Marie (Nelson)
O. Father was a native of Norway and mother was from Sweden.
Attd. local schools; the Univ. of Minn.; and Northwestern
Coll. of Law, obtaining a law degree in 1915. Admitted to
bar and joined a Minneapolis law firm. Apptd. spec. asst.
to Hennepin Co. pros. atty. Became co. atty. himself when
incumbent was impeached. El. for succeeding terms to that
office until 1930, acquiring notice as a vigorous and fearless prosecutor. Unsuccessful cand. of Farm.-Lab. and Prog.
parties for Gov. in 1924. Nom. for Gov. by that party combination in 1930 and was el. Continued in office in 1932
and 1934 as Farm.-Lab. party nominee. During admin., con-

solidated state conservation functions into a new dept.;
sponsored adoption of state income tax; gave full support to
natl. policies designed to ease unemployment and depression
conditions. Mbr., Elks; various prof. legal orgs. and social clubs. Lutheran. m. in 1917 to Ada Krejei. One d.
D. Aug. 22, 1936 at Rochester, Minn. during third term in
office.

PETERSON, HJALMAR (1936-1937). b. Jan. 2, 1890 at
Eskilsdrup, Denmark. Emigrated to Amer. as a child with
parents, who settled in Lincoln Co., Minn. Had little formal educ. Apprenticed to learn printing trade at age 14.
Founded Askov American, a newspaper in Pine Co., in 1914,
which he continued to own and edit thereafter. El. to Minn.
House in 1930 as Farm.-Lab. party cand. continuing in that
office for succeeding term. Supported adoption of state income tax legislation. El. Lieut. Gov. in 1934. Succeeded
to office of Gov. in Aug., 1936 following death of Gov.
Olson and completed Olson's term. Defeated as Farm.-Lab.
nominee for Gov. in 1940 and again in 1942. m. to Rignor
Wasgaard, of Milwaukee, Wisc. One d. After first wife's
death in 1930, m. in 1934 to Medora B. Grandprey, of Owa-
tonna, Minn. D. March 29, 1968 at Columbus, Ohio.

BENSON, ELMER AUSTIN (1937-1939). b. Sept. 22, 1895 at
Appleton, Minn. s. of Thomas Halga and Dora (Jacobsen) B.
Attd. local schools and St. Paul Coll. of Law, from which he
received a degree in 1918. Admitted to the bar in 1919 but
did not practice. Enlisted as a pvt. in U.S. Army in 1918,
serving overseas in the A.E.F. until 1919. Became asst.
cashier of First Natl. Bank of Appleton in 1919, and soon
afterward became partner in a clothing store in which he
continued to be involved as a proprietor until 1933. Cashier of Farmers and Merchants State Bank of Appleton, 1923-
1933. Apptd. as Minn. Securities Commnr. by Gov. Olson in
1933 and Banking Commnr. in that same year, continuing in
that office until 1935. Apptd. to U.S. Senate to fill vacancy in Dec., 1935, but was not a cand. to continue in that
office in 1936 election. Nom. and el. Gov. as Farm.-Lab.
nominee in 1936. Supported programs and policies in line
with Dem. party nationally. Defeated for reel. in 1938.
Defeated as cand. for the U.S. Senate in 1940 and again in
1942. Retired from pub. life to engage in bus. and farming.
Mbr., Amer. Legion; V.F.W.; Delta Theta Phi; Masons. Lutheran. m. in 1922 to Frances Miller, of Appleton, Minn.
One d.; one s.

STASSEN, HAROLD EDWARD (1939-1943). b. April 13, 1907
near West St. Paul, Dakota Co., Minn. s. of Wm. Andrew and

Eloise Emma (Mueller) S. Father was a farmer. Attd. local
schools and the Univ. of Minn., from which he received an
A.B. degree in 1927 and a law degree in 1929. Admitted to
bar and began practice in South St. Paul. Dakota Co. atty.,
1931-1938. Took active role in Rep. party affairs, becoming
pres. of Minn. Young Rep. Club in 1936. Nom. and el. Gov.
as Rep. in 1938, defeating incumbent Gov. Benson. Becoming
Gov. at age 31, was the youngest State Gov. in U.S. at the
time. Received Outstanding Young Man of the Year Award from
Natl. CC in 1939. Continued in office by reel. in 1940 and
1942. During admin., effected reorg. of state admin. in
effort to secure economies and greater efficiency; pressed
successfully for labor relations law reforms; supported U.S.
war effort in World War II. Ch. of Natl. Govs.' Conf. and
of Council of State Govts., 1940-1941. Temp. ch. and keynote speaker at Rep. natl. conv. in 1940. Resigned office
of Gov. in April, 1943 shortly after beginning of third term
to become a commissioned officer in U.S. Navy. Assigned to
duty in Pac. theater, serving on staff of Admiral Halsey.
Held rank of capt. when released from duty at end of war.
Recipient of Bronze Star and six Battle Stars. U.S. delegate to San Francisco Conf. at which the UN charter was
signed. U.S. delegate to UN Conf. on Intl. Orgs., 1946.
Announced candidacy for Rep. nom. for Pres. of U.S. in Dec.,
1946. Campaigned vigorously for delegate support. Was a
major contender for the nom. at the 1948 Rep. natl. conv.
receiving 157 delegate votes on the first ballot for the
nom., which went to Gov. Dewey, of N.Y. (q.v.) Became Pres.
of the Univ. of Pa. in 1948, serving in that post until
1953. Apptd. by Pres. Eisenhower Dir. of Foreign Operations
Admin., and in 1955 became spec. adviser to the Pres. on
disarmament matters. Became mbr. of a Philadelphia law firm
in 1958. Sought unsuccessfully to prevent the re-nom. of
Richard Nixon for Vice Pres. of U.S. as 1956 Rep. natl.
conv. approached. Announced candidacy for the Rep. nom. for
Pres. of U.S. in each pres. election year, 1960-1980, but
was not a major contender in those years. Natl. ch., Brotherhood Week; Godkin Lecturer at Harvard Univ., 1946; ch.,
Intl. Council of Religious Educ., 1942-1950. Author of
Where I Stand, in 1947 and of Man Was Meant to be Free, 1951,
in which he outlined his pub. philosophy. Pres., Amer.
Baptist Conv., 1963-1964. Ch., World Law Day, at Geneva,
Switzerland in 1967. Mbr., Masons (Shriner). Baptist. Hon.
degrees from nine colleges and universities. m. in 1929 to
Esther Ethel Glewwe, of South St. Paul, Minn. Two s.; one d.

THYE, EDWARD JOHN (1943-1947). b. April 26, 1896 near
Frederick, S.D. s. of Andrew J. and Bertha (Wangan) T.
Father, who was a native of Norway, emigrated to Minn. in

1872, later moved to S.D., and subsequently back to Northfield, Minn. Attd. local schools at Northfield while assisting with farm work on family farm. Attd. Tractor and Internal Combustion Engine school in 1913, and from 1915 to
1916, the Amer. Bus. Coll., both in Minneapolis. Enlisted
in aviation section of U.S. Army Signal Corps in 1917, and
served overseas in France. Held rank of second lieut. at
time of discharge. Employed as tractor expert and salesman,
1919-1922, and acquired a farm. Pres. of Dakota Co. Farm
Bureau, 1929-1940 and dir. of Twin City Milk Producers
Assoc., 1933-1940. Appraiser for Fed. Land Bank of Minneapolis, 1933-1934. State deputy commnr. of agri. and dairy
and food commnr., 1939-1942. El. Lieut. Gov. as Rep. in
1942. Succeeded to office of Gov. in April, 1943 when Gov.
Stassen resigned, and completed Stassen's term. Continued
in office for full term by large majority in 1944. El. to
U.S. Senate in 1946 and continued to serve therein until
1958, when he was defeated for third term. Resumed farming,
but remained active in party affairs. Delegate-at-large to
Rep. natl. conv. in 1960. Mbr., Sons of Norway; Amer. Legion; Masons; V.F.W.; Elks; various social and bus. orgs.
Norwegian Lutheran. m. in 1921 to Hazel Ramage, of Northfield, Minn., who died in 1936. One d. m. in 1942 to
Myrtle Oliver, of St. Paul, Minn. D. at Northfield Aug. 28,
1969. Bur. in Oaklawn Cem. there.

YOUNGDAHL, LUTHER WALLACE (1947-1951). b. May 29, 1896
at Minneapolis, Minn. s. of John Carl and Elizabeth (Johnson) Y. Father was proprietor of grocery store, having
emigrated from Sweden to Minn. in 1886. Attd. local pub.
schools; the Univ. of Minn., 1915-1916; and Gustavus Adolphus Coll., from which he was grad. in 1919. Received law
degree from Univ. of Minn. in 1921. Served in U.S. Army in
1918, holding rank of first lieut. at time of discharge.
Began law practice in Minneapolis in 1921. Asst. city atty.
of Minneapolis, 1921-1923. Partner in law firm, 1924-1930.
Apptd. and then el. judge of mun. ct., serving from 1930 to
1936. Dist. ct. judge of Hennepin Co., 1936-1942 and then
mbr. of Minn. Supreme Ct., 1942-1946. Nom. and el. Gov. as
Rep. in 1946, and was reel. in 1948 and 1950. As Gov.,
placed strong emphasis on law enforcement matters; secured
passage of youth conservation (rehabilitation) act and aid
for mentally ill; and issued directives against racial dis-
crimination practices. Resigned office of Gov. in 1951 to
accept post of U.S. dist. ct. judge in the Dist. of Columbia,
by apptmt. from Pres. Truman. During tenure, heard a number
of important cases growing out of McCarthy commt. hearings
and U.S. govt.'s loyalty program, including that of Owen
Lattimore. Mbr., Natl. Advisory Bd. of Big Brothers and of

YMCA. Delegate from U.S. to Third UN Conf. on Crime and
Delinquency. Mbr., Pres. Commt. on Law Enforcement and
Admin. of Justice, and of Natl. Council on Crime and De-
linquency. Hon. degrees from 16 colleges and universities.
Recipient of decoration from govt. of Sweden. m. in 1923 to
Irene Annet Engdahl, of Ortonville, Minn. Two s.; one d.
D. June 21, 1978 at Washington, D.C.

ANDERSON, (CLYDE) ELMER (1951-1955). b. March 16, 1912
at Brainerd, Crow Wing Co., Minn. Attd. local pub. schools
and the Univ. of Minn. Engaged in wholesale magazine and
newspaper distribution bus. in northern Minn. Nom. and el.
Lieut. Gov. as a Rep. in 1938 and again in 1940. El. again
to the office of Lieut. Gov. in 1944 and continued in that
office by reel. through the 1950 election. Succeeded to the
office of Gov. in Sept., 1951 when Gov. Youngdahl resigned.
Completed the term for which Youndahl was el. and was el.
for a regular term in 1952. Defeated as Rep. cand. for succeeding term in 1954, after which he retired to bus. interests. m. to Lillian Otterstad, of Bemidji, Minn. in 1937.
Two d.

FREEMAN, ORVILLE LATHRUP (1955-1961). b. May 9, 1918
at Minneapolis, Minn. s. of Orville E. and Frances
(Schroeder) F. Father was a merchant. Attd. local pub.
schools and the Univ. of Minn., from which he received an
A.B. degree in 1940 and a law degree in 1946. College work
was interrupted by service with U.S. Marine Corps during
World War II. Commissioned as second lieut., and saw action
in Pac. theater. Was seriously wounded at Bougainville and
returned to U.S. for rehabilitation. Held rank of major at
time of release, and continued to serve in USMCR, attaining
rank of lieut. col. Admitted to Minn. bar in 1947 and began
practice in Minneapolis. Asst. to Mayor Hubert Humphrey,
1945-1949 in charge of veterans' affairs. Mbr. of Minneapolis Civil Service Commn., 1946-1949, serving as its ch.,
1948-1949. Dir. of Minneapolis Family and Children's Service. Managed Humphrey's successful campaign for U.S.
Senate in 1948. Mbr. of state commt. of newly-formed D.F.L.
party, 1945; sect., 1946-1948; and ch., 1948-1950. Unsuccessful as D.F.L. nominee for Gov. in 1952, but was success-
full cand. of that party for Gov. in 1954, defeating incumbent Gov. C. Elmer Anderson to whom he had lost in 1952.
Reel. in 1956 and 1958. As Gov., promoted comprehensive
program for devel. and rebuilding of state institutions and
inaugurated a study of state tax system and of agri. bus.
Confronted by a serious strike at Albert Lea, Minn. during
his admin., he sent Natl. Guard troops to the area and declared a state of martial law in an effort to preserve

order, but the latter action was subsequently held void by a
U.S. dist. ct. Delegate to Dem. natl. convs. in 1944, 1948,
1952, 1956 and 1968. Apptd. U.S. Sect. of Agri. by Pres.
Kennedy in 1961, serving until 1969. As Sect. of Agri.,
sought to bring supply of agri. production into closer bal-
ance with demand in order to achieve stability of prices.
After tenure in that office became pres. of EDP Tech. Inst.,
Inc., and later, pres. of Bus. Intl., in New York City.
Mbr., Amer. Legion; AMVETs; V.F.W.; D.A.V.; Marine Corps
League; Sons of Norway; Moose; Eagles; Phi Beta Kappa; vari-
ous professional legal orgs. and social clubs. Lutheran.
Hon. degrees from four colleges and universities. m. in
1942 to Jane Charlotte Shields. One s.; one d.

ANDERSEN, ELMER LEE (1961-1963). b. June 17, 1909 at
Chicago, Ill. s. of Arne and Jennie O. (Johnson) A. Attd.
Muskegon, Mich., Jr. Coll., from which he was grad. in 1928,
and the Univ. of Minn., from which he received a degree in
bus. admin. in 1931. Engaged in advertising and sales promotion for H.B. Fuller Co. in Minneapolis, 1934-1937. Employed as sales mgr. by Best Corp. in Minneapolis, 1937-1941,
becoming its pres. and ch. of bd. in 1941. Also became involved in banking and ins. companies as mbr. of bds. of dir.
Mbr. Minn. Senate, 1949-1959. Ch. of coordinating commt.,
Minn. Rep. campaign in 1952. Ch., platform commt., Minn.
Rep. conv. in 1956 and ch., Minn. Rep. state conv. in 1958.
Nom. and el. Gov. as Rep. in 1960. Was Rep. nominee for
reel. in 1962, and in the ensuing election was first found
to have lost by 58 votes, but correction of returns by local
canvassing bds. in 10 counties resulted in his being declared
el. by State Canvassing Bd. by margin of 142 votes. Obtained
ct. order declaring him entitled to continue in office for
second term and continued in the office; but his opponent
challenged that outcome in Minn. cts. A recount of votes in
certain areas conducted by a spec. jud. body resulted in his
opponent's (Karl Rolvaag) being declared el. Surrendered
office nearly three months into second term. Delegate to
Rep. natl. convs. in 1948 and 1964. Pres. of Adhesive Mfrs.
Assoc. of Amer.; mbr. and pres. of Rotary; pres., Minn. Historical Soc.; pres. and mbr. of exec. bd. of Child Welfare
League; mbr., Univ. of Minn. Bd. of Regents; and Trustee,
Augsburg Coll. Active in YMCA and community chest drives.
Outstanding Alumni Award, Univ. of Minn., 1959. Lutheran.
Hon. degree from Macalester Coll. m. in 1932 to Eleanor
Johnson. Two s.; one d.

ROLVAAG, KARL FRITJOF (1963-1967). b. July 18, 1913 at
Northfield, Minn. s. of Ole Edvart and Jennie (Berdahl) R.
Father was a native of Norway who emigrated to Amer. in 1896.

Father became a well-known novelist while serving as a
prof. at St. Olaf's Coll., in Northfield. Attd. local pub.
schools; St. Olaf's Coll., from which he was grad. in 1941;
and did post-graduate study at the Univ. of Minn. and the
Univ. of Oslo, Norway, 1946-1948. Was in U.S. mil. service
1941-1947, holding rank of capt. at time of discharge. Recipient of Silver Star, Purple Heart, and Croix de guerre.
Unsuccessful as D.F.L. cand. for U.S. House in 1946, 1948
and 1952. State ch. of D.F.L. party, 1950-1954. Vice pres.,
Group Health Mutual Ins. Co., 1956-1959. Exec. Dir., Humphrey for Pres. commt., 1959-1960. Delegate to Dem. natl.
convs. in 1952, 1960 and 1964. Nom. and el. Lieut. Gov. in
1954, continuing in that office until 1963. Nom. for Gov.
by D.F.L. party in 1962 and was ultimately declared el. following a partial recount of the popular vote by a spec. Minn.
ct., defeating incumbent Gov. Elmer Lee Andersen by 91 votes.
Installed in office nearly three months after term would have
normally begun because of delays in ascertaining final election result. Became first Minn. Gov. to be el. for four-
year term. Defeated for reel. in 1966. Apptd. by Pres.
L.B. Johnson U.S. Ambassador to Iceland in 1967, serving until 1969. Became vice pres. of Interfinancial Corp. and dir.
of Franklin Natl. Bank in Minn. in 1969. Mbr. and ch. of
Minn. Pub. Service Commn., 1972-1977. Resigned post before
end of term because of an acute alcoholism problem. Author
of History of the DFL Party, 1958. Mbr., Norwegian Amer.
Historical Soc.; Minn. Historical Soc.; Amer. Legion; V.F.W.;
D.A.V.; Purple Heart Veterans; Moose; Eagles; Natl. Grange;
A.C.L.U. Recipient of Distinguished Alumni Award from St.
Olaf's Coll. Hon. degree from St. Mary's Coll. Lutheran.
m. in 1943 to Florence Boedeker. One s.; one d.

Le VANDER, HAROLD E. (1967-1971). b. Oct. 10, 1910 at
Swede Home, Nebr. s. of Peter Magni and Laura (La Vene)
Le V. Father was a Lutheran clergyman who had emigrated to
U.S. from Sweden. Attd. Gustavus Adolphus Coll., from which
he was grad. magna cum laude in 1932, and the Univ. of Minn.,
from which he earned a law degree in 1935. Was a varsity
track, football and baseball athlete in college and also an
oratorical award winner. Began law practice in South St.
Paul. Dakota Co. asst. atty., 1935-1939. Became prof. of
speech and debating team coach at Macalester Coll. in 1939,
continuing in that capacity until 1967. Also engaged in law
practice, and was pres. of United Fed. Loan Assoc. Nom. and
el. Gov. as Rep. in 1966, defeating incumbent Gov. Rolvaag.
Returned to bus. and professional interests after tenure as
Gov. Delegate to Rep. natl. conv. in 1968. Mbr. and sect.,
Natl. Lutheran Council; South St. Paul CC (pres. for three
years); Pi Kappa Delta; various professional orgs. and

social clubs. Very active in Lutheran church affairs. m.
in 1938 to Iantha Powrie, of St. Paul. One s.; two d.

ANDERSON, WENDELL RICHARD (1971-1976). b. Feb. 1, 1933
at St. Paul, Minn. s. of Theodore M. and Gladys (Nord) A.
Attd. local pub. schools and the Univ. of Minn., from which
he received an A.B. degree in 1954 and a law degree in 1960.
Served as second lieut. in U.S. Army, 1956-1957. Was an
outstanding athlete while in college, and was a mbr. of U.S.
Olympic hockey team in 1956. Played on various amateur
hockey teams, 1955-1957. Practiced law in Minneapolis, 1960-
1970. Mbr. of Minn. House, 1955-1963, and of Minn. Senate,
1963-1969. El. Gov. as nominee of D.F.L. party in 1970 and
was reel. in 1974. Ch., Dem. Govs.' Conf., 1974. Resigned
office of Gov. Dec. 29, 1976 and was apptd. by his successor
on Dec. 30, 1976 to the U.S. Senate to fill vacancy created
by resignation of Sen. Mondale to become Vice Pres. of U.S.
Defeated for election to Senate in 1978 to continue in the
seat. Mbr., U.S. Olympians; Phi Delta Phi; professional
legal orgs. m. in 1963 to Mary Christine McKee. Two d.;
one s.

PERPICH, RUDOLPH GEORGE ("RUDY") (1976-1979). b. June
27, 1928 at Carson Lake, Minn. s. of Anton and Mary (Vuke-
lich) P. Attd. pub. schools at Hibbing, Minn. and Hibbing
Jr. Coll., from which he was grad. in 1950. Served in U.S.
Army, 1946-1947, holding rank of sgt. at time of discharge.
Attd. Marquette Univ., from which he received a D.D.S. degree in 1954. Engaged in dental practice at Hibbing. Mbr.
of bd. of educ. at Hibbing, 1956-1962. El. to Minn. Senate
in 1962, continuing to serve therein until 1970. Nom. and
el. Lieut. Gov. as D.F.L. party nominee in 1970 and was reel.
in 1974. Succeeded to office of Gov. on Dec. 29, 1976 following the resignation of Gov. Wendell Anderson, whom he
immediately apptd. to a vacancy in U.S. Senate seat. Defeated for election to a regular term as Gov. in 1978. m.
in 1954 to Delores Helen Simic, of Keewatin, Minn. One s.;
one d. Roman Catholic.

HOLMES, DAVID (1817-1820; 1826). b. Mar. 10, 1769, near Winchester, Va. s. of Joseph and Rebecca (Hunter) H. Father had emigrated from Ireland to Amer. when a young man. Father resided first in Pa. near Hanover, and served in Amer. forces during Rev. War. Mother was a native of Va. and family moved there before birth of David. Attd. Winchester Acad. Studied law, admitted to Va. bar in 1791 and began practice in Harrisburg, Pa. Later moved back to Winchester, where he practiced law and was Commonwealth atty. for Rockingham Co., 1793-1797. Mbr. of U.S. House from Va. for six terms, 1797-1809. Was not a cand. for seventh term in 1808. Apptd. Gov. of Miss. Terr. in 1809, and continued in that post until admission of Miss. as a State in Dec., 1817. Pres. of Miss. constl. conv. of 1817. El. Gov. of State of Miss. on a provisional basis as a Jeff. Rep. when the const. for the proposed State was adopted in Sept., 1817. During admin., was concerned mainly with implementation of first plan of govt. for Miss. Apptd. to U.S. Senate in Aug., 1820, to fill a vacancy, and was subsequently el. by the legislature. Served in Senate until Sept., 1825 when he resigned seat after having been el. Gov. again. Resigned office of Gov. in July, 1826, because of poor health after serving some six months of term. Returned to Winchester, Va. in 1827. D. Aug. 20, 1832, at Jordan's Sulphur Springs, Va. Bur. in Mount Hebron Cem., Winchester.

POINDEXTER, GEORGE (1820-1822). b. in 1779 in Louisa Co., Va. s. of a Baptist clergyman of French descent. Family suffered severe financial reverses during Rev. War. Studied law and was admitted to bar in 1800. Practiced law at Milton and Richmond, Va. for a time. In 1802 moved to Natchez, and later to Wilkinson, in Miss. Terr., where he continued to practice law. Mbr. of Miss. Terr. legislature, 1805-1806. Terr. Delegate to Cong., 1807-1813. Terr. ct. judge, 1813-1817. Was an influential mbr. of Miss. constl. conv. of 1817. Mbr. of U.S. House from Miss., 1817-1819. El. Gov. of Miss. as a Jeff. Rep. in 1819. During admin., was authorized by legislature to codify laws of the State, a task which he completed with aid of an asst. near end of term. Advocated establishment of pub. educl. system; was critical of extension of charter of Bank of Miss. A site on which the city of Jackson now stands was selected as place for State capital during his tenure, and plans for constr. of State house there were advanced. El. to Miss. House in 1822 where he led debate for adoption of revised code. Defeated for U.S. House seat in that year. Defeat attributable in part to his championing controversial

provisions of revised code, which redefined grounds for
libel actions and restricted assembling of Negro slaves in
a manner held by opponents to restrict their religious wor-
ship. Became ill and physically incapacitated for several
years following death of his second wife and infant son in
1822. Declined offers of apptmt. to U.S. Senate and as
State Chancellor. Defeated as cand. for U.S. Senate seat
in 1829, but after death of successful opponent in 1830 was
apptd. to the seat, in which he continued to serve until
1835. As a Sen., was at first a supporter of Pres.
Jackson's anti-U.S. Bank policies, but changed views on
that issue during his tenure in Senate. Had differences
with Jackson over patronage matters, and was critical of
Jackson's stand during the S.C. nullification crisis of
1832. Pres. pro tem of Senate, 1834-1835. Defeated for
reel. to the Senate in 1835. Severely injured in fall from
hotel window in 1836, at Natchez. Moved to Louisville, Ky.
in 1838 and practiced law there and at Lexington for some
time. Returned to Jackson, Miss. in 1841. Became a supporter of Whig party in 1840 pres. election. Apptd. by
Pres. Tyler to investigate alleged frauds at N.Y. customs
house in 1841. Spent later years in law practice at
Jackson. Was a man of choleric temper and strong partisan
views. In 1811 his remarks critical of Federalists led to
a duel with Abijah Hunt, a wealthy Miss. merchant, in which
latter was killed. m. in 1804 to Lydia Carter, of Adams
Co., Miss., from whom he was divorced shortly after a son
was born. m. in 1816 to Agathea B. Chinn (Chism?), who
died in 1822. D. at Jackson, Miss., Sept. 5, 1855.

LEAKE, WALTER (1822-1825). b. May 25 (20?), 1762 in
Albermarle Co., Va. s. of Mark and Patience (Morris)
(Morrow?) L. Descendant of an English colonist who emigrated to Va. in 1685. Father was a person of prominence
in the community and had served as an officer in Contl.
Army during Rev. War. Son also was in U.S. mil. service
during latter stages of that war. Received academic educ.
Studied law, admitted to bar and established successful
practice in Va. Mbr. of Va. legislature in 1805. Was defeated in an election for U.S. House seat in 1806 by margin
of two votes by Thomas M. Randolph, the son-in-law of Pres.
Thomas Jefferson. Apptd. to post of Miss. Terr. judge by
Pres. Jefferson in 1807 and moved to Mount Salus, in Hinds
Co., Mississippi. Delegate to Miss. constl. conv. in 1817.
El. as one of the first two U.S. Senators from Miss. in
1817. Resigned seat in 1820 to seek office of Gov., to
which he was el. in 1821. Prior to his election served
briefly as U.S. marshal and as a mbr. of Miss. Supreme Ct.

El. Gov. again in 1823. Was a Jeff. Rep. in politics.
During admin., a proposed revised code of laws of the State
was adopted, and Jackson became the seat of govt. of the
State. m. in 1787 to Virginia Wingfield. Three s.; two d.
D. at Mount Salus, Nov. 17, 1825, during second term as Gov.

BRANDON, GERARD CHITTOQUE (1825-1826; 1826-1832). b.
Sept. 15, 1788 on a plantation near Natchez, Miss. s. of
Col. Gerard and Dorothy (Nugent) B. Father, who had been a
participant in rebellious activity in Ireland, had fled to
S.C. prior to the Amer. Rev. War and had served under Gen.
Marion during the Rev. War before settling in Miss. area.
Son attd. the Coll. of N.J. (Princeton) and William and
Mary Coll. Studied law and began practice in Washington,
Miss. Terr. Abandoned law practice after several years and
became a planter near Ft. Adams, in Wilkinson Co., Miss.
Served with Amer. forces during the War of 1812. Mbr. of
Miss. constl. conv. in 1817. El. to first Miss. House in
that year and became Speaker, serving until 1823. El.
Lieut. Gov. in 1823, and in Nov., 1825, succeeded to office
of Gov. following the death of Gov. Leake. Completed last
two months of Leake's term and continued thereafter in
office of Lieut. Gov., to which he had been reel. Following resignation of Gov. Holmes in July, 1826, to take a
seat in U.S. Senate, succeeded to the office of Gov. again
and completed Holmes' term. El. Gov. as a Jeff. Rep. in
1827 and was reel. in 1829. Was the first native-born
citizen of Miss. to be el. Gov. During admin., the Treaty
of Dancing Rabbit Creek was concluded in 1830 with the
Choctaw Indian tribe under which extensive tracts of land
in Miss. were opened to settlement. Declined to become a
cand. for U.S. Senate seat in 1832. Mbr. of Miss. constl.
conv. of 1832. m. in 1816 to Margaret Chambers. After her
death, m. in 1824 to Elizabeth Stanton, of Natchez, Miss.
Father of six sons, two of whom died in Confed. mil. service; and two d. D. at family estate in Wilkinson Co.,
near Fort Adams, March 28, 1850.

HOLMES, DAVID (1826). See above, 1817-1820.

BRANDON, GERARD CHITTOQUE (1826-1832). See above,
1825-1826.

SCOTT, ABRAM M. (1832-1833). b. circa 1785 in S.C.
As a young man moved to Miss. Terr., where he acquired a
plantation in Wilkinson Co. Served as assessor in 1810 and
as collector of taxes in Wilkinson Co. in 1812. Helped
raise a volunteer regiment in war against Creek Indians in

1811, serving as a capt. Mbr. of constl. conv. of 1817 and
was subsequently el. to Miss. Senate in 1822, 1826 and 1827.
Sheriff of Wilkinson Co. in 1824. El. Lieut. Gov. in 1827
and again in 1829. Nom. and el. Gov. as Natl. Rep. in 1831.
During admin., the Planters' Bank, in which the State was a
stock-holder, was established; and a constl. conv. was held
which drafted a document extending the principle of direct
election to many offices, including jud. posts, that had
theretofore been filled by indirect means. It also abolished the office of Lieut. Gov., and abandoned property
ownership as a qualification for office-holding. Defeated
for Gov. in May, 1833, in a spec. election involving a
change in the election and term schedule effected by the
1832 const. D. July 12, 1833, in an Asiatic cholera epidemic some five months before end of his term.

LYNCH, CHARLES (1833; 1836-1838). b. in 1783 in
Bedford Co., Va. s. of Charles and Anna (Terrill)
(Yerrell?) L. Moved to Monticello, Miss. as a young man
and engaged in merc. bus., in which he prospered. Probate
judge of Lawrence Co. in 1822. Mbr. of Miss. Senate, 1825-
1829. Defeated as cand. for U.S. Senate seat in 1829. Also was defeated in four-man contest for Gov. in 1831, but
was el. to the Miss. Senate again in 1830, and became Pres.
pro tem of that body in 1833. As such, succeeded to the
office of Gov. in June, 1833, following the death of Gov.
Scott, the office of Lieut. Gov. having been abolished by
the revised const. of 1832. Completed the last five months
of the term of Gov. Scott. Nom. and el. Gov. as a Whig in
1835, defeating incumbent Gov. Runnels in a close contest.
Advocated devel. of primary school system and a program of
internal improvements. Opposed doctrine of nullification
as espoused by Sen. Calhoun. State enjoyed great prosperity during early part of admin. as population rose rapidly
and Miss. River traffic increased; but the financial panic
of 1837 necessitated calling of a spec. session of the
legislature to deal with State's fiscal affairs. Retired
to bus. interests in railroad and banking fields after tenure as Gov. Served as commnr. to supervise final phase of
constr. of first State House and Gov.'s mansion at Jackson.
D. at Monticello, Feb. 9, 1853.

RUNNELS, HIRAM GEORGE (1833-1835). b. Dec. 15, 1796
in Hancock Co., Ga. s. of Col. Harmon R., who had served
as a soldier during Rev. War. Father later moved with his
family to Monticello, in Miss. Terr., where he became an
influential leader in the community and was a mbr. of the
Miss. constl. conv. of 1817. Several of his sons early

became involved in Miss. politics. Hiram R. was apptd.
State Aud. in 1822, and continued to serve in that office
until 1830. Defeated as cand. for Gov. in 1831, finishing
a close second in a four-man race. El. Gov. in May, 1833,
as a Jackson Dem. under the provisions of the revised 1832
const., defeating incumbent Gov. Scott. Defeated for reel.
in 1835 in a very close contest. Left office after serving
two years, even though successor was not to be installed in
office until two months later under the revised term schedule set up by the 1832 const. When the Union (State) Bank
was org. in 1838, he became its pres. It failed after a
short time, creating a bond obligation on the State. The
bank's failure resulted in much criticism of him, which he
greatly resented and led to a challenge to a duel. El. to
Miss. House in 1840. Moved to Tex. in 1841, becoming a
plantation owner on the Brazos River, in Brazoria Co. Mbr.
of conv. in Tex. in 1845 that approved annexation of Tex. to
the U.S. Was an uncle of Hardin R. Runnels, Gov. of Tex.
(q.v.). D. Dec. 15 (17?), 1857, in Houston. Bur. in
Greenwood Cem. there.

QUITMAN, JOHN ANTHONY (1835-1836; 1850-1851). b.
Sept. 1, 1799 at Rhinebeck, N.Y. s. of Dr. Frederick H.
and Anna Elizabeth (Huelke) Q. Father was a Lutheran minister. Mother was the d. of the Dutch colonial Gov. of
Curacao, in the West Indies. Attd. Hartwick Sem., in
Oswego Co., N.Y., from which he was grad. in 1816. Prepared
to enter the church ministry, but became a tutor in the
classics dept. at Hartwick Sem. Later taught at Mt. Airy
Coll. in Germantown, Pa. In 1819 moved to Ohio, where he
studied law at Chillicothe and was admitted to the bar in
1820. Moved to Natchez, Miss. in 1821. Practiced law and
became an influential planter and community leader in that
area. Mbr. of Miss. House, 1826 and 1827. Became identified with movement to suppress dueling, gambling and other
vices. Adopted the Southern view on national political
issues of the time. Mbr. of Miss. constl. conv. of 1832.
Superior ct. chancellor, 1828-1834. El. to Miss. Senate
in 1835, and was chosen Pres. pro tem of that body. When
the legislature assembled, the office of Lieut. Gov. had
been abolished, making the Pres. of the Senate the immediate successor to the office of Gov. When Gov. Runnels vacated the office of Gov. at the end of what he considered
to be his two-year term in Nov., 1835, Q. as Pres. of the
Senate, acted as Gov. for several weeks before the newly-
chosen Gov. assumed office in Jan., 1836. Participated
with a group of volunteer troops from Miss. in the War for
Indep. of Tex. from Mexico in 1836-1837. Judge of Miss.

Ct. of Errors and Appeals in 1838. Served as brig. gen.
under Gen. Winfield Scott during Mexican War, 1846-1847.
Was mil. gov. of Mexico City during Amer. occupation in
1847, holding rank of major gen. Pres. elector on Dem.
ticket in 1848. Nom. and el. Gov. as Dem. in 1849. Favored annexation of Cuba by force and gave aid in unsuccessful
"filibuster" expedition in 1850 led by Lopez to take over
govt. of Cuba with the intent of eventually seeking annexation to U.S. Was indicted by a Fed. grand jury for conspiracy to engage in unlawful acts against the govt. of
Spain. Jury did not convict him, the prosecution becoming
involved in controversy between the natl. govt. and Miss.
authorities regarding jurisdiction in the matter. Resigned
office of Gov. in Feb., 1851. Nom. as States' Rts. Dem.
for Gov. in 1851, but he withdrew from the contest. Was a
vigorous advocate of the right of States to secede from the
Union. Nom. and el. to U.S. House as a So. Rts. Dem. in
1855, and continued to serve therein until his death. Was
one of the contenders for nom. for Vice Pres. at Dem. natl.
conv. in 1856, but failed to win. m. in 1824 to Eliza
Turner, of Fairfax Co., Va. Several children, four of whom
died before reaching adulthood. D. on his plantation,
"Monmouth", near Natchez, on July 17, 1858. Bur. in
Natchez City Cem.

LYNCH, CHARLES (1836-1838). See above, 1833.

McNUTT, ALEXANDER GALLATIN (1838-1842). b. Jan. 3,
1802 in Rockbridge Co., Va. s. of Alexander and Rachel
(Grigsby) McN. Descendant of an Irish colonist who emigrated to Va. in 1730. Attd. Washington Coll. (now Washington
and Lee Univ.), from which he was grad. in 1821. Studied
law and moved to Miss., where he began practice of law at
Jackson. Later moved to Vicksburg, where he continued work
as a lawyer. Soon had a large practice and acquired a
reputation as a wit and as an orator. Mbr. of Miss. Senate,
1836-1837, being chosen in 1835 as a Dem. in a predominant-
ly Whig dist. Pres. of Senate in 1837. Nom. and el. Gov.
as Dem. in 1837 and again in 1839. During admin., signed
bill by which State became a share-holder in Union Bank;
but later he sought to have that bank dissolved. Also opposed financial involvement by the State in the Planters'
Bank and the Miss. R.R. Co. Recommended repeal of charters
of all banks that had fallen into default as result of U.S.
Specie Circular, and also urged repudiation of state indebtedness for Union Bank bonds. Views were opposed in
legislature, but his program had popular support and was
eventually adopted. During admin., the Univ. of Miss. was

established at Oxford. m. in 1834 to a wealthy widow,
Elizabeth (Lewis) Cameron. Defeated as cand. for U.S. Senate in 1847. Ignored duel challenges on several occasions.
Cand. for pres. elector on Dem. ticket in 1848 election,
but died during the course of the campaign. D. Oct. 22,
1848, in De Soto Co., Miss.

TUCKER, TILGHMAN MAYFIELD (1842-1844). b. Feb. 5,
1802 near Lime Stone Springs, N.C. s. of John and Margaret
(Mayfield) T. Attd. prep. school in the vicinity, and became a planter. After a short time moved to Hamilton, in
Monroe Co., Miss. Studied law and was admitted to the bar.
In 1830 moved to Columbus, Miss., which had become the co.
seat of Lowndes Co., and soon had a large legal practice.
Mbr. of Miss. House, 1831-1835, and of Miss. Senate, 1838-
1841. Nom. and el. Gov. as Dem. in 1841. During admin.,
legislation was enacted repudiating state bonds issued to
found Union Bank. El. to U.S. House in 1842, but completed
term as Gov. before assuming House seat. After one term
in Cong., retired to a plantation, "Cottonwood", he had
acquired in La. Was a man of considerable wealth in lands
and slaves. m. to Sarah F. McBee in 1829. After her death,
m. in 1854 to Martha A. Conger. D. April 3, 1859, at his
father's home near Bexar, Ala, while visiting there.

BROWN, ALBERT GALLATIN (1844-1848). b. May 31, 1813
in Chester Co., S.C. s. of Joseph B., a planter. Family
moved in 1823 to a plantation near Gallatin, Miss. Attd.
common schools while assisting on family plantation. Attd.
Mississippi Coll. for three years; and in 1832 studied mil.
sci. at Jefferson Coll., at Washington, Miss. At age 19
was el. col. of militia regiment and the next year became
a brig. gen. at age 20. Studied law in office at Gallatin,
and was admitted to the bar in 1833. Mbr. of Miss. House,
1835-1839, becoming Speaker pro tem. El. to U.S. House in
1838 as Dem., but did not seek reel. in 1840. Superior ct.
judge, 1842-1843. Nom. and el. Gov. as an Anti-Redemption
Dem. in 1843, and was reel. in 1845. As Gov., favored repudiation of state bonds issued for founding of Union Bank,
but not those issued to found Planters Bank. Promoted pub.
school system. El. to U.S. House as Dem. in 1846, continuing in that office until 1853. Was not a cand. for fourth
term in 1852. El. to U.S. Senate in 1854, and continued to
serve therein until the eve of the Civil War. Supported
secession movement, and withdrew from the Senate in Jan.,
1861, when Miss. adopted an ordinance of secession. Raised
company of volunteers for the Confed. cause, becoming its
capt. Involved in several mil. actions in early stages of

the war. El. as Senator to C.S.A. Cong. in Dec., 1861,
continuing in that office until the end of Civil War. Re-
tired to plantation thereafter. Urged acceptance of U.S.
Reconstruction policies by South. m. in 1835 to Elizabeth
Frances Talliafero, of Va., who died a few months after
marriage. m. in 1841 to Roberta Young, of Alexandria, Va.
Two s. D. near Terry, Miss., June 12, 1880. Bur. in
Greenwood Cem., Jackson, Miss.

MATTHEWS, JOSEPH W. (1848-1850). b. circa 1812 near
Huntsville, Miss. Terr. (now Ala.). Early in life moved to
Marshall Co. (now Benton Co.), Miss. Received limited
educ., but was an able and industrious student on his own.
Learned surveying and performed govt. survey work in Mississippi. Acquired plantation at Ashland, Miss., which remained a primary interest throughout life. El. to Miss.
House in 1839, and to the Miss. Senate in 1843, serving
therein, 1844-1848. Nom. and el. Gov. as Dem. in 1847. Defended right of slave-owners to take their slave property
into free States and territories of the U.S., when that became a major natl. issue following the War with Mexico.
Opposed repudiation of state bonds issued in connection
with founding of banks. State was generally prosperous
during his tenure as Gov. Hutchinson's Miss. Code of 1798-
1848 was prepared and adopted during his admin. Supported
Southern cause when Civil War approached. D. Aug. 27, 1862,
at Palmetto, Ga. while on his way to Richmond, Va.

QUITMAN, JOHN ANTHONY (1850-1851). See above, 1835-
1836.

GUION, JOHN ISAAC (1851). b. Nov. 18, 1802 near
Natchez, Miss. Terr. s. of Major Isaac G., a Rev. War veteran of N.Y. who had settled in Miss. Terr. in 1805 after
being stationed there on U.S. mil. duty. Educ. in Tenn.,
where he also studied law and was admitted to the Tenn. bar
at Lebanon. Returned to Miss. and engaged in practice of
law at Vicksburg. Apptd. cir. ct. judge in 1832, and in
1836 became a criminal ct. judge. Resigned jud. post in
1837 to engage in law practice. El. to Miss. Senate in
1847 and was serving as its Pres. when Gov. Quitman resigned in Feb., 1851. Succeeded to office of Gov. and served
until his own term as a mbr. and Pres. of Senate ended on
Nov. 3, 1851. Thereafter there was no occupant of the
office of Gov. for some three weeks until the newly-chosen
Senate met and chose its Pres. Was serving again as a cir.
ct. judge at the time of his death on June 26, 1855.

WHITFIELD, JAMES (1851-1852). b. Dec. 15, 1791 in
Elbert Co., Ga. s. of Benj. W., a descendant of an English
colonist who had emigrated to Va. in early 1700s. As a
young man moved to Columbus, Miss. Terr., where he engaged
in merc. and banking enterprises. Became prominent in pol-
tics of Lowndes Co. El. to Miss. House, 1842-1848, and
then to the Senate, being chosen as its Pres. in Nov., 1851,
when the new legislature met and effected its org. As such,
assumed the office of Gov. temporarily, pending installation of the Gov.-elect in Jan., 1852. Served last six
weeks of term for which Gov. Quitman had been el. in 1849.
Mbr. of Miss. House in 1858. Engaged in banking and ins.
bus. at Columbus after 1852. His bank was one of the few
in the State that continued to maintain its solvency during
the entire course of the Civil War. m. to Louisa Dyer, of
Monticello, Ga. D. June 25, 1875, at Columbus, Miss.

FOOTE, HENRY STUART (1852-1854). b. Feb. 28, 1804 in
Fauquier Co., Va. s. of Richard H. and Catherine (Stuart)
F. Attd. Georgetown Coll. and Washington Coll. (now
Washington and Lee Univ.), from which he was grad. in 1819.
Studied law at Warrenton and was admitted to bar. Began
practice in Richmond. Moved to Tuscumbia, Ala. in 1824,
and in 1830, to Natchez, where he practiced law. In 1832
moved to Jackson, Miss., where he engaged in a successful
law practice and also established a newspaper, the
Mississipian. Pres. elector on Dem. ticket in 1844. El.
to U.S. Senate in 1847 as a Unionist Dem. Supported the
Compromise of 1850 legislation. Resigned Senate seat in
1852 to become Gov., having been el. with Whig support, defeating Jefferson Davis, the So. Rts. Dem. faction cand.
for the post. Served one term, resigning the office five
days before end of term. During admin., state bonds issued on behalf of Planters Bank were repudiated by vote of
the people. After leaving office, went to Calif., where he
became a cand. for U.S. Senate in 1856, losing election in
legislature by one vote. Moved back to Miss. in 1858 and
engaged in law practice for a time at Vicksburg. Attd. So.
States conv. at Knoxville, Tenn. in 1859, where he opposed
secessionist advocates. Moved to Nashville, Tenn. and engaged in law practice. When Civil War began, gave his support to Confed. govt., and from 1862 until near the end of
the Civil War served as a Repr. of Tenn. in Confed. Cong.
As a mbr. thereof, opposed continuation of the war after
1863, urging compromise settlement of issues between North
and South. Resigned seat in Jan., 1865, and went abroad
for a time. Returned to Washington, D.C., and was a supporter of Rep. cand. for Pres. of U.S. in 1876. Apptd.

supt. of U.S. Mint at New Orleans by Pres. Hayes in 1878.
Had a very stormy life in politics. Fought three duels in
earlier stages of career. On one occasion, drew a revolver
against an opponent while in U.S. Senate chamber. Author
of Texas and the Texans (two vols.) in 1841; War of the
Rebellion in 1866; Bench and Bar of the South and Southwest
in 1876; and an autobiographical volume, Personal
Recollections. m. to Elizabeth Winter, of Nashville, Tenn.
Two s.; two d. After her death, m. to Mrs. ----Smiley, of
Nashville. D. at Nashville, May 19, 1880. Bur. at Mt.
Olivet Cem.

PETTUS, JOHN JONES (1854; 1859-1863). b. Oct. 9, 1813
in Wilson Co., Tenn. s. of John and Alice T. (Winston) P.
Father, who was a native of Va., had moved to Tenn. in 1805
and served as a soldier during the Creek War. Soon afterward moved his family to Limestone Co., Ala., where son
grew up. Received basic academic educ. in local schools.
Studied law and began practice in Sumter Co., Ala. Later
moved to Scooba, in Kemper Co., Miss., where he continued
law practice and was also a planter. Mbr. of Miss. House,
1843-1846, and was el. to the Miss. Senate in 1847. Became
Pres. of Senate, and as such, succeeded to the office of
Gov. briefly in 1854, when Gov. Foote left the office a few
days before installation of his successor. El. Gov. as So.
Rts. Dem. in 1859. Supported moves leading up to secession
by So. States. After a Miss. conv. adopted an ordinance of
secession in Jan., 1861, continued to serve as Gov. Reel.
Gov. in Oct. of that year. As Gov., gave full and energetic support to So. cause during tenure through raising
troops and furnishing supplies. Fall of Vicksburg near end
of second term was a great blow, but he urged continuance
of war effort. Was ineligible to continue in office after
1863. Participated as a mil. staff officer in raising
troops, 1864-1865. At end of the war, fled to Pulaski Co.,
Ark., where he lived in obscurity with friends until his
death, which occurred on either Jan. 20 or Feb. 6, 1867.
Place of burial unknown.

McRAE, JOHN JONES (1854-1857). b. Jan. 10, 1815 at
Sneedsboro (now McFarlan), N.C. In 1817 father, who was a
merchant, moved family to plantation near Winchester, Miss.
Received elementary educ. at Pascagoula, Miss. Attd. Miami
Univ., in Ohio, from which he was grad. in 1834. Studied
law in office at Pearlington, Miss., and was admitted to
bar. In 1837 became publ. of a newspaper, the Eastern
Clarion, at Paulding, Miss. Later established residence at
Enterprise, Miss. Served in Miss. House, 1848-1850, acting

as Speaker in last two sessions. Affiliated with So. Rts.
wing of Dem. party. Apptd. to U.S. Senate in Dec., 1851,
to fill vacancy. Served until March, 1852. Was defeated
as cand. for election to the post. Nom. and el. Gov. as
So. Rts. Dem. in 1853 and was reel. in 1855. Second term
shortened by approximately two months by change in term and
election schedule. During admin., a State school for deaf-
mutes was established, and a revised code of laws for the
State was put into effect. After tenure as Gov., established residence at State Line, Miss. El. to U.S. House in
1858 to fill a vacancy and in 1860 was el. for a regular
term. A supporter of secessionist movement, he withdrew
from U.S. House in Jan., 1861, after Miss. conv. adopted an
ordinance of secession. Mbr. of C.S.A. Cong., 1862-1864.
Was defeated for reel. to C.S.A. House in 1863. At the end
of Civil War went to Belize, British Honduras, where a
brother had established a bus. D. there shortly after his
arrival on May 30, 1868. m. in 1835 to a widow, Mrs. ----
McGuire, of Pearlington, Miss. Bur. in Belize.

McWILLIE, WILLIAM (1857-1859). b. Nov. 17, 1795 near
Liberty Hill, Kershaw Co., S.C. s. of Adam and Anne
(Agnew) McW. Father, who was of Scotch ancestry, had emigrated to S.C. and had served as an officer in Amer. army
during War of 1812. Received early educ. in Camden, S.C.,
and attd. S.C. Coll., from which he was grad. in 1817.
During latter part of War of 1812 served as adjt. in regi-
ment commanded by his father. Studied law and was admitted
to bar in 1818. Began practice at Camden. Became pres. of
a bank at Camden in 1836, continuing in that post until
1845. Mbr. of S.C. Senate, 1836-1840. In 1845 moved to
Madison Co., Miss., where he acquired a large plantation,
"Kirkwood", near Camden, Miss. El. to U.S. House in 1848.
Served only one term, being defeated for reel. in 1850.
Espoused cause of Southern pro-slavery interest while in
Cong. Nom. and el. Gov. as So. Rts. Dem. in 1857. Sup-
ported moves that eventuated in secession. Supported So.
cause during the Civil War. m. in 1818 to a d. of Joseph
Cunningham. m. in 1831 to Catherine Anderson, of Camden,
S.C. Five s.; four d. D. at his estate in Miss., March 3,
1869. Bur. in St. Philip's Church Cem. there.

PETTUS, JOHN JONES (1859-1863). See above, 1854.

CLARK, CHARLES (1863-1865). b. Feb. 19, 1810 at
Cincinnati, Ohio. Parents originally resided in Md. Grad.
from Augusta Coll., in Ky., and in 1831 went to Miss.,
where he engaged in teaching at Natchez. Also studied law

there.   Admitted to bar and began practice in Jefferson Co.,
Miss., in which he was successful.   Acquired a plantation
in Bolivar Co., continuing in law practice there.   Became
involved in politics, and served in Miss. legislature, 1838-
1839 and 1842-1843.   Upon outbreak of Mexican War, became
capt. in a Miss. volunteer unit.   Saw active service during
the war, and rose to rank of col.   Mbr. of So. States conv.
in 1851 called to consider course of action regarding national policies affecting So. slavery interests.   Originally a Whig, he affiliated with So. Rts. wing of Dem. party
in 1856.   Mbr. of Miss. House in 1856, 1859-1861.   Delegate
to Dem. natl. convs. in Charleston and Baltimore in 1860,
where he supported John C. Breckenridge for nom. for Pres.
of U.S.   Upon outbreak of the Civil War was commissioned as
brig. gen. of Miss. troops, later attaining the rank of
major gen.   Participated in a number of major battles in
Southwestern theater of the war in 1861-1862.   Was wounded
severely and was taken prisoner.   Wound required use of a
crutch thereafter for walking.   Was exchanged and returned
to Miss.   In 1863 was nom. and el. Gov. as a pro-War Dem.
As Gov., concerned himself largely with problems of raising
and supplying of troops for the Confed. cause.   As war drew
to an end, refused to surrender, and was captured by Fed.
troops on May 22, 1865.   Confined for several months at
Ft. Pulaski, near Savannah, Ga.   After release, returned to
his plantation, "Doro", in Bolivar Co.   Apptd. chancellor
of his judicial dist. in 1876.   m. to Ann Eliza Darden.
D. Dec. 18, 1877.

SHARKEY, WILLIAM LEWIS (1865).   b. July 12, 1798 in
Northeastern Tenn.   Was of Irish ancestry, his father,
Patrick, having emigrated from Ireland to Amer. before the
Rev. War.   Mother was of German descent.   When he was still
a youth family moved to a farm in Warren Co., Miss.   Was
orphaned at an early age.   Attd. school at Greenville, Tenn.
Served as soldier during War of 1812 and participated in
Battle of New Orleans in 1815.   Studied law at Lebanon,
Tenn.   Admitted to bar in 1822 and began practice at
Natchez, Miss.   Later practiced at Warrenton and Vicksburg,
Miss.   Mbr. of Miss. House, 1828-1829.   After the Miss.
const. was revised in 1832, became first Chief Justice of
the Miss. Ct. of Errors and Appeals by election, a post he
held for next 18 years.   Opposed repudiation of state bonds.
Resigned jud. post in 1850 and established law practice at
Jackson, Miss.   Mbr., Univ. of Miss. Bd. of Trustees, 1844-
1865.   Delegate to and pres. of So. States conv. held in
1849 at Nashville to consider course of action on matters
of natl. policy affecting slavery.   Was offered post of

U.S. consul at Havana, Cuba, by Pres. Fillmore in 1851, but
declined it. Also declined post of U.S. Sect. of War in
Pres. Fillmore's cabinet. Mbr. of commn. in 1854-1856 set
up to revise Miss. Code. As Civil War neared, did not take
an active role on side of South, being a Unionist in political views. Took oath of allegiance to Union in 1863. As
war neared its end was apptd. by Gov. Clark as a mbr. of
commn. to confer with Pres. Andrew Johnson on terms of restoration of Miss. to Union. Apptd. Provisional Gov. of
Miss. by Pres. Johnson. Assumed office in June, 1865,
about a month after capture of Gov. Clark by Union forces.
Assembled a state conv. that met in Oct., 1865, and proposed repeal of ordinance of secession, abolition of slavery, and other changes to restore Miss. to Union. Apptd.
by the conv. to U.S. Senate, but Senate refused to seat him.
Succeeded in office of Gov. in 1865 by Benj. Humphreys, who
had been el. Gov. when the constl. changes were approved by
voters in Oct., 1865. m. to Minerva (Hyland) Wren. D.
April 29, 1873, in Washington, D.C.

   HUMPHREYS, BENJAMIN GRUBB (1865-1868). b. Aug. 26,
1808 at the family estate, "The Hermitage", in Claiborne
Co., Miss. s. of George Wilson and Sarah (Smith) H. Family was of English descent, his forebears having emigrated
to Va. before the Rev. War. Family had moved West from
S.C. to Natchez area in 1788. Father was a wealthy planter
who was prominent in community affairs. Attd. schools at
Russellville, Ky., and Morristown, N.J. Entered U.S. Mil.
Acad. in 1825, remaining there for three years. Along with
40 other cadets was dismissed before grad. for engaging in
a Christmas frolic that developed into a serious riot. Returned to Miss., where he engaged in planting while studying law. Took active interest in politics. Became disaffected with Pres. Jackson's policies and was el. to Miss.
House in 1837 as an (anti-Jackson) Indep. El. to Miss.
Senate in 1830 as a Whig, continuing in that office until
1844. Moved to plantation on the Big Black River in 1840,
and in 1846 to a plantation in Sunflower Co. Opposed secession movement as Civil War neared, but went along,
nevertheless, with his State after secession occurred in
1861. Org. a company and entered Confed. mil. service as
capt. Rose to rank of brig. gen. by 1863. Participated in
many major engagements, including the Battles of Gettysburg,
Chickamaugua, the Wilderness, and campaigns in the
Shenandoah Valley. Was wounded in 1864, but continued in
service until end of war. El. Gov. when the revised state
const. was approved by voters in Oct., 1865, and was permitted by U.S. authorities to act as Gov. in matters not

affecting Reconstruction policies. Was el. again in 1868
when a revised const. was again submitted to voters, but
the election was voided by Fed. mil. authorities, and he
was displaced as Gov. in June, 1868. Engaged in ins. bus.
at Jackson for a time, and in 1869 moved to Vicksburg. Retired to plantation in Leflore Co. in 1877. m. in 1832 to
Mary McLaughlin, who died in 1835. m. in 1839 to Mildred
Hickman Maury, of Port Gibson, Miss. Three s.; one d. A
son, Benjamin G. H., Jr., became a mbr. of U.S. House from
Miss. in 1903. D. Dec. 20 (22?), 1822, at his plantation
in Leflore Co.

AMES, ADELBERT (1868-1870; 1874-1876). b. Oct. 31,
1835 at Rockland, Me. Attd. local schools and U.S. Mil.
Acad., from which he was grad. in 1861. Commissioned as
first lieut. in U.S. Army. Participated in Battle of Bull
Run in 1861, in which he was wounded. Advanced by successive stages to rank of brig. gen. of Me. volunteers, having
participated in numerous engagements in the Eastern theater
of Civil War. Eventually promoted to rank of major gen. in
U.S. Army and received Congressional Medal of Honor. After
war ended was assigned to mil. duty in the mil. dist. of
N.C. and S.C. In July, 1868, was apptd. Provisional (mil.)
Gov. of Miss. After a new const. for Miss. acceptable to
Cong. was approved by voters in 1869, he vacated the office
in March, 1870, and was succeeded by a popularly el. Gov.
Resigned commn. in U.S. Army and was el. to U.S. Senate
from Miss. as a Rep. Served until 1873, when he resigned
seat after having been el. Gov. of Miss. as a Rep. Soon
after he assumed office, riots in Vicksburg and elsewhere,
resulted in resort to mil. rule. He requested mil. assistance from U.S., which was refused by Pres. Grant. Continued rivalry in State between Rep. factions and bitter opposition to his regime by former ruling class kept State in
turmoil. Opponents gained control of the legislature
following 1875 elections, and he was impeached by the Miss.
House on charges of abuse of power. Resigned office in
Mar., 1876, before trial on the charges was conducted.
Went to New York, later moving to Lowell, Mass., where he
engaged in flour milling and mfg. enterprises. Apptd. brig.
gen. of volunteers in 1898 upon outbreak of Spanish-Amer.
War. After release from service in 1899 returned to Lowell.
m. in 1870 to Blanche Butler, d. of Gov. Benjamin F. Butler,
of Mass. (q.v.). D. April 12, 1933, at his winter home in
Ormond, Fla. Bur. in Hildreth Cem., at Lowell.

ALCORN, JAMES LUSK (1870-1871). b. Nov. 4, 1816 near
Golconda, Ill. s. of James and Louisa (Lusk) A. Paternal

ancestor had emigrated from Ireland to Pa. in 1721. Was of
Scotch descent on mother's side. Family moved to Livingston
Co., Ky. during his early youth, where father became the co.
sheriff and engaged in steamboating bus. Attd. Cumberland
Coll. Taught school for a short time in Jackson, Ark. Returned to Ky. and became deputy sheriff of Livingston Co.,
1839-1844. Mbr. of Ky. legislature in 1843. Studied law
and was admitted to bar in 1844. Moved to Friars Point,
Miss. in 1846, where he engaged in law practice. Mbr. of
Miss. House in 1846, 1856-1857, and of the Miss. Senate,
1848-1854. Mbr. of state constl. conv. of 1851. Pres. elector on Whig ticket in 1852 pres. election. Defeated as
Whig cand. for U.S. House in 1856. Offered nom. as Whig
cand. for Gov. in 1857 but declined. Mbr. of state conv.
that adopted ordinance of secession in 1861, which he opposed. Nevertheless, followed his State and received commn.
as brig. gen. of Miss. volunteers. Was captured in Ark.
and imprisoned for a time. After being exchanged in 1864,
served as col. of troops for maintenance of local order.
El. to U.S. Senate in 1865 by reformed Miss. legislature,
but was refused seat by the Senate. Mbr. of state constl.
conv. of 1868. El. Gov. as (Conservative) Rep. in 1869,
defeating cand. of another Rep. faction. Assumed office in
Mar., 1870, becoming the first Gov. of Miss. to be el. for
four-year term. Resigned office in 1871 to take seat in
U.S. Senate, in which he served until 1877. Defeated as
Indep. Rep. cand. for Gov. in 1873. After service in Senate resumed practice of law in Coahoma Co. Helped secure
legislation organizing levee system for the Miss. River,
and served as pres. of levee bd. for three years. Promoted
pub. educ. as Gov., and was instrumental in establishment
of A. and M. Coll. for Negroes (now Alcorn Univ.) in 1871.
m. in 1839 to Mary C. Stewart, of Ky., who died in 1840.
m. in 1850 to Amelia Walton Glover, of Ala. D. at his estate, "Eagle's Nest", in Coahoma Co., Dec. 19, 1894. Bur.
in family cem. there.

POWERS, RIDGELY (RIDGLEY?) CEYLON (1871-1874). b. Dec.
24, 1836 at Mecca, Ohio. s. of Milo and Lucy (Dickinson)
P. Descendant of English colonist who emigrated to Mass.
in the Mayflower. Father was from Pa. and mother from Va.
Studied at Western Reserve Univ. Taught school for a short
time in Ill. Attd. the Univ. of Mich. in 1859, from which
he later received an hon. A.B. degree in 1910. Grad. from
Union Coll., in Schenectady, N.Y., from which he also received an hon. A.M. degree in 1865, and was the recipient
of the Blatchford prize. Enlisted in Union Army as capt.
of volunteer Ohio company, rising to the rank of lieut. col.

and asst. adjt. by the end of the war. Studied law and in
1865 settled in Macon, Miss., where he engaged in law practice. Became active in politics and acquired a 2,000 acre
cotton plantation in Noxubee Co. Was apptd. sheriff of
Noxubee Co., 1868-1869. El. Lieut. Gov. as Indep. Rep. in
1869 and succeeded to governorship in Nov., 1871, when Gov.
Alcorn resigned to take U.S. Senate seat. Completed
Alcorn's term, continuing policies emphasizing suppression
of lawlessness and promotion of economy in govt. After
tenure as Gov., moved to Prescott, Ariz. Terr., where he
engaged in civil engr. work, 1879-1905. m. in 1875 to
Louisa Bohn, of Cleveland, Ohio, who died in 1882. m. in
1892 to Mary J. Wilson, also of Cleveland. D. Nov. 11,
1912.

  AMES, ADELBERT (1874-1876). See above, 1868-1870.

  STONE, JOHN MARSHALL (1876-1882; 1890-1896). b. Apr.
30, 1830 near Milan, Gibson Co., Tenn. s. of Asher and
Judith (Royall) S. Parents were natives of Va. Father
suffered severe losses in financial panic of 1837, and died
in 1841 leaving widow with nine children without means of
support. Son received limited educ. while assisting in
support of family by teaching. In 1849 left home to make
his own way. Moved to Eastport, Miss. in 1855, where he
became a store clerk. Entered Confed. Army in 1861, rising
to rank of col. by end of war. Was wounded several times
and was taken prisoner in 1865. Returned to Tishomingo
Co., Miss. after release in July, 1865, and worked as station agent for a railroad at Iuka. Became mayor of Iuka,
and in 1866, treas. of Tishomingo Co. Removed from that
office by Fed. mil. authorities. El. to Miss. Senate in
1869. Unsuccessful cand. for U.S. House in 1872, losing to
L. Q. C. Lamar, later a mbr. of U.S. Supreme Ct. El. to
Miss. Senate in 1873, becoming Pres. pro tem of that body.
As such, succeeded to office of Gov. in Mar., 1876, when
Gov. Ames resigned after being impeached, the office of
Lieut. Gov. having become vacant about the same time because of the impeachment and disqualification of the incumbent Lieut. Gov., Alexander H. Davis. El. Gov. as Dem. in
1877. Was not nom. for succeeding term in 1881, but was
nom. and el. again as Dem. in 1889. Normal term of office
extended for two years by change in term schedule effected
by adoption of new state const. in 1890. Under that document, severe restrictions on voter qualifications intended
to disfranchise Negro citizens effectively excluded them
from political affairs, a policy he favored. Apptd. pres.
of Miss. A. and M. Coll. at Starkville in 1897. m. in 1872

to Mary G. Coman, of Iuka, Miss. One s.; one d. D. March
2, 1900, at Hot Springs, Miss.

LOWRY, ROBERT (1882-1890). b. Mar. 10, 1831 in
Chesterfield Co., S.C. s. of Robert and Jemima (Rushing) L.
Parents moved to Tenn. in 1833 and in 1840 to Miss. Received common school educ. At age 13 became a clerk in
store of an uncle at Raleigh, Miss. After four years went
into gen. merc. bus. for himself. In 1851 moved to Brandon,
Miss. and three years later moved to Ark. Studied law and
was admitted to bar there. Returned to Brandon in 1859
where he engaged in practice of law. Upon outbreak of
Civil War enlisted in a Miss. regiment as a pvt. Rose to
rank of brig. gen. by 1864. Participated in numerous engagements, including the Vicksburg campaigns of 1862-1863,
and the Atlanta and Nashville campaigns in 1864. Was twice
wounded at the Battle of Shiloh in 1862. Was commissioned
to visit Pres. Andrew Johnson in effort to secure release
of Jefferson Davis from U.S. custody after end of the war.
Resumed law practice at Brandon. El. to Miss. Senate in
1865 and later was a mbr. of Miss. House. Unsuccessful as
cand. for Dem. nom. for Gov. in 1878. Nom. and el. Gov. as
Dem. in 1881, defeating a cand. backed by a Rep.-Greenback
coalition. Reel. in 1885 without formal opposition. During admin., a State R.R. Commn. was established; women were
admitted to the Univ. of Miss. for the first time; and a
state indus. school was established at Columbus. In collaboration with Col. Wm. McArdle, was author of a history
of Miss., published at Jackson in 1891. m. in 1849 to
Maria M. Gammage, of Jasper Co. D. Jan. 18, 1910.

STONE, JOHN MARSHALL (1890-1896). See above, 1876-
1882.

McLAURIN, ANSELM JOSEPH (1896-1900). b. Mar. 26, 1848
at Brandon, Miss. Eldest of eight sons of Lauchlin and
Ellen C. (Tullus) McL. Descendant of a Scotch ancestor who
emigrated to S.C. in 1776. Family moved from S.C. to Miss.
in 1819, where his father engaged in farming. Assisted on
family farm as youth while receiving a limited common
school educ. Enlisted at age 16 in a Miss. regiment near
the end of Civil War, serving for six months. Resumed
studies at Summerville Inst., 1865-1868, but withdrew before
grad. for lack of funds. Studied law by himself and was
admitted to bar in 1868. Began practice at Raleigh, Miss.
El. dist. atty. in 1871, serving for four years. In 1876
moved to Brandon, Miss., where he continued law practice.
Acquired reputation as one of the ablest criminal lawyers

in the South. Mbr. of Miss. House, 1879. Served as pres.
elector on Dem. ticket in 1888 pres. election. Delegate to
Miss. constl. conv. of 1890. Apptd. to U.S. Senate in Feb.,
1894, to fill a vacancy, serving until Mar., 1895. Nom.
and el. Gov. as Dem. in 1895. After term expired was el.
to U.S. Senate again in 1900, in which he served until his
death. m. in 1870 to Laura Rauch, of Trenton, Miss. Ten
children. D. Dec. 22, 1909, at Brandon. Bur. in Brandon
Cem.

LONGINO, ANDREW HOUSTON (1900-1904). b. May 16, 1855
in Lawrence Co., Miss. s. of John Thomas and Annie Porter
(Ramsay) L. Both parents died while he was still a small
child. Received a common school educ. and attd. Miss.
Coll., from which he was grad. in 1875. El. cir. and chancery ct. clerk of Lawrence Co. in 1876, serving until 1880.
Took spec. law course at Univ. of Va. in the summer of
1880, and continued to study law on his own. Admitted to
bar in 1881 and began practice in Monticello, Miss. Mbr.
of Miss. Senate, 1880-1884. Apptd. U.S. dist. atty. for
So. Miss. dist. by Pres. Cleveland in 1888, serving until
1889. Practiced law for several years at Greenwood, Miss.
Apptd. by Gov. Stone chancellor for his jud. dist. in 1894.
Resigned that post in 1899 after having been nom. and el.
Gov. as Dem., without formal opposition in the gen. election. During admin., constr. of a new State Capitol was
begun; the State Treas. was forced to resign under charges
of mismanagement of state funds; and a primary system for
nominations for major elective offices was adopted. After
tenure as Gov., was judge of Hinds Co. ct., and resided in
Jackson. Baptist. Delegate to Dem. natl. conv. in 1900.
m. in 1887 to Marion Buckley, of Jackson, Miss. Three s.;
two d. D. Feb. 24, 1942.

VARDAMAN, JAMES KIMBLE (1904-1908). b. July 26, 1861
near Edna, Tex. s. of Wm. Sylvester and Mary Ann (Fox) V.
Father was a native of Miss. who had moved to Tex. in 1858,
and had served in Confed. Army during Civil War. Family
moved to Yalobusha Co., Miss. in 1868, where father engaged
in farming. Received common school educ. while assisting
on family farm. Studied law at Carrollton, Miss. and was
admitted to bar in 1882. Practiced law for a time at
Winona, Miss. In 1883 became ed. of Winona Advance. In
1890 moved to Greenwood, Miss., where he was ed. of the
Enterprise for six years. Mbr. of Miss. House, 1890-1896,
serving as Speaker from 1894 onward. Pres. elector on Dem.
ticket in 1892 and 1896 pres. elections. Established a
newspaper, the Commonwealth, in 1896, which he continued to

publ. until 1903. Served with volunteer unit in Cuba during Spanish-Amer. War, holding rank of major at time of discharge in 1899. Defeated as cand. for Dem. nom. for Gov. in 1895 and 1899, but was nom. in 1903 and el. with no opposition. During admin., on one occasion used militia forces to protect a Negro prisoner from a would-be lynching mob. Became ed. of Jackson, Miss. Issue in 1908. Unsuccessful cand. for Dem. nom. for U.S. Senate seat in 1907 and again in 1910, but was nom. and el. to that office in 1912. Defeated for re-nom. for Senate seat in 1918 and again in 1922. Mbr., Masons; K.P.; Elks. Methodist. m. in 1883 to Mrs. Anna (Burleson) Robinson, of Memphis, Tenn. Two s.; two d. Retired to Birmingham, Ala. in 1922. D. at Birmingham, June 25, 1930. Bur. in Lakewood Memorial Park, Jackson, Miss.

NOEL, EDMUND FAVOR (1908-1912). b. March 4, 1856 near Lexington, Miss. s. of Leland N. and Margaret (Sanders) N. Descendant of ancestor who had fled from France to England in 1680 and from there had emigrated to Va. Family had moved from Va. to Miss. in 1835. Father served in Confed. Army during Civil War, and lost eyesight while he was a prisoner of war. Attd. local schools and a h.s. in Louisville, Ky., from which he was grad. with highest honors. Studied law with an uncle who was an atty. in Louisville and was admitted to bar in 1877. Began practice of law at Lexington, Miss., and soon acquired a large practice. Mbr. of Miss. House, 1896-1904, where he championed various reform measures, including a direct primary law. Assisted in defense of constitutionality of the law in Miss. Supreme Ct. case. Dist. atty. for his jud. cir., 1887-1891. Served as capt. in Miss. volunteer unit during Spanish-Amer. War. Unsuccessful cand. for Dem. nom. for Gov. in 1903, but won nom. and was el. in 1907. As Gov., opposed liquor traffic and a prohibition law was passed during admin. Presided over first meeting of U.S. Govs. assembled at the White House by Pres. Theodore Roosevelt in 1908, and became mbr. of exec. commt. of Govs.' Conf. when it was formed. Mbr., Masons (K.T., Shriner); K.P.; Woodmen; Knights of Honor. Baptist. m. in 1890 to Loula Hoskins, who died in 1891. m. in 1905 to Mrs. Alice (Tye) Neilson, of Pickens, Miss. D. July 30, 1927.

BREWER, EARL LeROY (1912-1916). b. Aug. 11, 1869 on a farm near Vaiden, Miss. s. of Ratcliff Rodney and Mary Elizabeth (McEachern) B. Descendant of an Irish ancestor who emigrated to Ga. in 1780. Attd. local schools and the Univ. of Miss., from which he received a law degree in 1892.

Began practice of law at Water Valley, Miss. Mbr. of Miss.
Senate, 1895-1899. Apptd. dist. atty. for his jud. dist.,
serving from 1902-1906. Defeated as cand. for Dem. nom.
for Gov. in 1907. Practiced law at Clarksdale, Miss. Won
Dem. nom. for Gov. in 1911 and was el. As Gov., promoted
various reform measures, including abolition of Greek letter
and secret fraternities at state educl. institutions, legislation against tipping, revised inspection system for state
banks, and adoption of the initiative and referendum. Defeated for Dem. nom. for U.S. Senate seat in 1924. Mbr.,
Knights of Honor; K.P.; Masons; Woodmen; Elks; Natl. Grange.
Presbyterian. m. in 1897 to Minnie Marion Block, of Water
Valley. Three d. D. March 10, 1942.

   BILBO, THEODORE GILMORE (1916-1920; 1928-1932). b.
Oct. 13, 1877 at Jennifer Grove, near Poplarville, Miss.
s. of James Oliver and Beedy (Wallace) B. Attd. local pub.
schools; Peabody Coll.; and the Univ. of Nashville, 1897-
1900. Taught in rural schools for six years. Studied law
at Vanderbilt Univ., 1905-1907, and the Univ. of Mich.,
1908. Admitted to Miss. bar in 1906, and Tenn. bar in 1908.
Began practice at Poplarville in 1907. Mbr., Miss. Senate,
1908-1912, and Lieut. Gov., 1912-1916. Nom. as Dem. cand.
for Gov. in 1915 and was el. Cooperated with U.S. war effort during World War I; initiated reforms in jud. branch
and state educl. and welfare systems. During admin., Miss.
became the first State to ratify the 18th Amdt. to U.S.
Const. Nom. as Dem. cand. for Gov. again by run-off primary,
defeating Acting Gov. Murphree and was el. in 1927. El. to
U.S. Senate in 1934 as Dem. and continued to serve therein
until death. Was not allowed to take oath of office at
beginning of last term in Jan., 1947 however, pending investigation into allegations of irregularities in connection
with campaign expenditures and alleged intimidation of
Negro voters at polls. Became ill in Jan., 1947, and underwent serious operation immediately thereafter. As a Sen.,
gained natl. notice as strong defender of States Rts., particularly against encroachments of U.S. govt. in civil
rights field. Strong advocate of maintenance of racial
segregationist policies and promotion of interests of farmers. Trustee of Clarke Memorial Coll. and of Pearl River
Co. Agri. School. Mbr. of So. Educl. Conf.; Masons; Woodmen; I.O.O.F.; Elks. Baptist. m. in 1898 to Lillian W.
Harrington, of Wiggens, Miss., who died in 1900. One d.
m. in 1903 to Linda Ruth Gaddy, of Purvis, Miss. One s. D.
Aug. 21, 1947, at New Orleans, La. Bur. in Jennifer Grove
Cem.

RUSSELL, LEE MAURICE (1920-1924). b. Nov. 16, 1875
near Oxford, Miss. s. of Wm. Eton and Louisa Jane (Mackey)
R. Family was of English descent. Attd. local schools;
Toccopola Coll., from which he was grad. in 1897; and the
Univ. of Miss., from which he received a Ph.B. degree in
1901 and a law degree in 1903. Began law practice at
Oxford, soon acquiring a large practice. Mbr. of Miss.
House, 1908-1912, and of Miss. Senate, 1912-1916. Lieut.
Gov., 1916-1920. Won Dem. nom. and was el. Gov. in 1919.
As Gov., promoted pub. improvements in roads and buildings.
After tenure as Gov., engaged in real estate and other bus.
enterprises in Gulfport, Miss. Mbr., Masons; K.P.; Wood-
men. Methodist. m. in 1905 to Ethelmary Day. D. May 16,
1943.

WHITFIELD, HENRY LEWIS (1924-1927). b. June 20, 1868
on family farm near Brandon, Miss. s. of Robert Allen and
Mary Ann (Fitzhugh) W. Descendant of ancestor who emigrated from Isle of Wight to N.C. in 1695. Attd. local schools
while assisting on family farm. Received teaching license
at age 16, and engaged in teaching while continuing educ.
Principal of h.s. at Westville, Miss. for three years and
also was a teacher at Florence, Miss. for six years. Grad.
from Miss. Coll. in 1895, and studied law at Millsaps Coll.
and the Univ. of Miss. Admitted to bar in 1898, but was
soon afterward apptd. Miss. Supt. of Educ. Continued to
serve in that office by election until 1907. Declined reel.
to become pres. of Miss. Indus. Coll. and Inst., in which
capacity he served for 13 years. Supt. of B. B. Jones
Masonic Boys School, 1920. Resigned that post to become
cand. for Gov. in 1923. Was nom. and el. Gov. in that year.
As Gov., balanced state budget; advocated repeal of various
laws restrictive of personal liberty. In 1925 published a
volume, Know Mississippi. Baptist. m. in 1897 to Mary
Dampeer White, of Florence, Miss. Four s. D. Mar. 18,
1927, at Jackson during last year of term as Gov.

MURPHREE, (HERRON) DENNIS (1927-1928; 1943-1944). b.
Jan. 6, 1886 at Pittsboro, Miss. s. of Thomas Martin and
Caroline (Cooper) M. Descendant of an Irish ancestor who
fled from Ireland to N.C. in 1690 after participating in an
unsuccessful Irish rebellion. Father was a local pub.
office holder and ed. of a newspaper, the Monitor. Attd.
local pub. schools while assisting in father's newspaper
office. At age 19 following father's death became ed. and
publ. of the family's newspaper in partnership with a
brother. In 1925 engaged in ins. bus. at Jackson, Miss.
Mbr. of Miss. House, 1911-1920, serving as Speaker pro tem

the last four years. El. Lieut. Gov. in 1923. Succeeded
to office of Gov. in Mar., 1927, when Gov. Whitfield died.
Completed Whitfield's term. Was confronted by serious
emergency resulting from floods soon after succeeding to
the office. Defeated in run-off primary by former Gov.
Bilbo for Dem. nom. for Gov. in 1927. Returned to ins. bus.
at Jackson. Was one of the organizers of the "Know
Mississippi Better" train, which publicized the State during
1920s. El. Lieut. Gov. again in 1931, and again in 1939,
both times as the Dem. cand. Succeeded to office again in
Dec., 1943, when Gov. Paul B. Johnson, Sr. died shortly before the end of his term, and completed Johnson's term.
Mbr., Masons; Kiwanis. Methodist. m. in 1909 to Clara
Minnie Martin. Three d.; one s. D. at Jackson, Feb. 9,
1949.

BILBO, THEODORE GILMORE (1928-1932). See above, 1916-
1920.

CONNER, MARTIN SENNETT ("MIKE") (1932-1936). b. Aug.
31, 1891 at Hattiesburg, Miss. s. of Oscar Weir and Holly
Gertrude (Sennett) C. Father was a prosperous lumberman,
merchant and planter. Attd. the Univ. of Miss., from which
he received a bachelor's degree in 1910 and a law degree in
1912. Attd. Yale Univ. Law School in 1913, from which he
was grad. cum laude in 1913. Began law practice at
Seminary, Miss. Mbr. of Miss. House, 1916-1924, serving as
Speaker during part of that time. Nom. as Dem. cand. for
Gov. in 1931 and was el. without opposition. As Gov.,
sought to reform state admin. structure; to reorg. and reform state financial system; and to improve standing of
state institutions of higher educ., some of which had lost
accreditation because of political interference. Was not a
supporter of some aspects of Pres. Roosevelt's New Deal
program of domestic reforms. Delegate to Dem. natl. conv.,
1916-1932. Defeated for Dem. nom. for U.S. Senate seat in
1936. Became commnr. of athletics for Southeast Athletic
Conf. in 1940, serving in that capacity until 1948. Mbr.,
Masons (Shriner); Kappa Alpha; Phi Alpha Delta. Active in
Methodist church affairs. m. in 1921 to Alma Lucile
Graham, of Seminary. One d. D. Sept. 16, 1950.

WHITE, HUGH LAWSON (1936-1940; 1952-1956). b. Aug. 19,
1881 at McComb, Miss. s. of John J. and Helen Elizabeth
(Tyre) W. Father was a mbr. of a distinguished family and
was proprietor of an extensive lumbering enterprise. Attd.
the Univ. of Miss., 1898-1901, where he was a mbr. of varsity football team. Entered family's bus., which had

outlets in Jackson, Meridian, Yazoo City, and Columbus,
Miss. Mayor of Columbus, 1929-1935. Nom. as Dem. cand.
for Gov. in 1935, defeating Paul Johnson, Sr., later a Gov.
of Miss., in run-off primary, and was el. After completion
of term retired to bus. interests for a time. Defeated for
Dem. nom. for U.S. Senate seat in 1940 by Sen. and former
Gov. Bilbo. Nom. again as Dem. cand. for Gov. in 1951, and
was el. During first term sought legislation to carry out
a "Balance Agriculture With Industry" program, a State
Indus. Commn. being set up for that purpose. Favored "right
to work" legislation. Was seriously ill with heart trouble
during most of last year of first term. Was one of the
leaders in walk-out of Miss. delegation at 1948 Dem. natl.
conv. in protest against certain platform planks and the
nom. of Pres. Truman for Pres. of U.S. Became an active
supporter of States Rts. Dem. party cand. for Pres. that
year. During second term, sought means of meeting U.S.
Supreme Ct.'s school desegregation ruling. Legislature
passed law making it a criminal offense for mbrs. of White
and Negro races to attend state-supported schools together.
Mbr., Masons (K.T., Shriner); Rotary; Delta Psi. Hon. degree from Southwestern Univ., of Memphis, Tenn. Presbyterian. m. in 1905 to Judith Wier Sugg. D. Sept. 20,
1965.

JOHNSON, PAUL BURNEY, Sr. (1940-1943). b. Mar. 23,
1880 at Hillsboro, Miss. Attd. local pub. schools;
Harperville Coll.; and Millsaps Coll. Studied law and was
admitted to bar in 1903. Began practice of law at
Hattiesburg, Miss. Mun. ct. judge at Hattiesburg, 1907-
1908. Apptd., and later el., cir. ct. judge in 1910, serving until 1919. El. to U.S. House in 1918. Served two
terms, declining to run for third term in 1922. Resumed
law practice and also engaged in agri. pursuits. Unsuccessful as cand. for Dem. nom. for Gov. in 1935, but was
nom. as Dem. cand. for Gov. in 1939 and el. without opposition. Gave full support to U.S. war effort after World War
II began. m. to Corinne Venable. A son, Paul B., Jr., became Gov. of Miss. (q.v.). D. Dec. 26, 1943, at Hattiesburg about a month before end of term. Bur. in City Cem.
there.

MURPHREE, (HERRON) DENNIS (1943-1944). See above,
1927-1928.

BAILEY, THOMAS LOWRY (1944-1946). b. Jan. 6, 1888 at
Maben, Miss. s. of Anderson Bean and Rosa Willingham
(Powell) B. Attd. local pub. schools and Millsaps Coll.,

from which he was grad. in 1909. Received oratory medal
there as a senior. Became asst. principal and teacher at
Madison Co. Agri. H.S., 1909. Principal of h.s. at
Woodville, 1910-1911. Studied law at Millsaps Coll. Received a law degree in 1913, was admitted to bar, and began
practice at Meridian, Miss. Also engaged in bldg. and loan
bus. Dir. and vice pres. of Miss. City Lines. Mbr. of
Miss. House, 1916-1940, serving as Speaker, 1924-1936. Mbr.
of Miss. Bldg. Commn., 1932-1936, and of Miss. Hosp. Commn.,
1936-1940. Nom. as Dem. cand. for Gov. in 1943 and was el.
without opposition. Mbr., Masons; K.P.; Kappa Sigma; Natl.
Exchange Club (pres.); advisory bd. of Salvation Army. Active in work of Methodist church. m. in 1917 to Nellah
Izora Massey, of Meridian. One s.; one d. D. Nov. 2, 1946,
at Jackson during course of term as Gov.

WRIGHT, FIELDING LEWIS (1946-1952). b. May 16, 1895
at Rolling Fork, Miss. s. of Henry James and Fannie
(Clements) W. Attd. Webb School, in Tenn., and the Univ.
of Ala., from which he received a law degree. Admitted to
bar and began practice in office of an uncle. Served with
A.E.F. during World War II. Was not involved in combat,
but remained until 1919 in Germany on occupation duty. Remained in Natl. Guard thereafter. From 1919 to 1922 played
baseball, and also engaged in law practice. Mbr. of Miss.
Senate, 1928-1932, where he became leader of a minority
faction opposed to Gov. Bilbo. Mbr. of Miss. House, 1932-
1940, serving as Speaker. Sought improvements in educl.
system for Negroes. From 1940 to 1943, practiced law at
Vicksburg, later at Rolling Fork. El. Lieut. Gov. as Dem.
in 1943. Succeeded to office of Gov. in Nov., 1946, following death of Gov. Bailey. Completed Bailey's term and was
nom. and el. for full term in 1947. Opposed Pres. Truman's
civil rights program and other domestic policies. Led walk-
out of Miss. delegation at Dem. natl. conv. in 1948 in protest against Pres. Truman's nom. and the Dem. party platform. Later accepted nom. for Vice Pres. of U.S. by the
States Rts. Dem. natl. conv. He and its pres. cand., Gov.
Thurmond, of S.C. (q.v.), won the electoral votes of four
Southern States in the ensuing election. Retired to law
practice at Jackson and Rolling Fork. Methodist. m. in
1917 to Nan Kelly. One s.; one d. (adopted). D. May 4,
1956. Bur. at Rolling Fork Cem.

WHITE, HUGH LAWSON (1952-1956). See above, 1936-1940.

COLEMAN, JAMES PLEMON (1956-1960). b. Jan. 9, 1914 at
Ackerman, Miss. on a farm that had been in family for five

generations. s. of Thomas Allen and Jennie Espie (Worrell)
C. Attd. local pub. schools, and the Univ. of Miss., 1932-
1935. Financed himself while attending college by various
part-time jobs. Served as sect. to U.S. Repr. A. L. Ford,
1935-1939, while studying law at George Washington Univ. in
Washington, D.C. Admitted to bar in 1937. Received law
degree in 1939 and began practice at Ackerman. Dist. atty.
for his dist., 1940-1946. Cir. ct. judge, 1946-1950, and
Miss. Supreme Ct. commnr., 1950. Delegate to Dem. natl.
conv. in 1940, and pres. elector of Dem. ticket for 1944
pres. election. Atty. Gen. of Miss., 1950-1956. Also engaged in farming. Publ. of a local newspaper, the
Plaindealer. As Dem. natl. committeman in 1952, helped to
prevent bolt by Miss. delegation at 1952 Dem. natl. conv.,
and worked for election of Dem. nominee for Pres. of U.S.
that year. Won Dem. nom. for Gov. in 1955 in a run-off
primary over Paul B. Johnson, Jr., and was el. without opposition. During admin., resisted order of U.S. Interstate
Commerce Commn. to desegregate pub. transp. in State. U.S.
Supreme Ct.'s school desegregation decision in 1954 and its
aftermath caused high tension in the State. In 1954, voters
of the State authorized discontinuance of pub. school system as last resort against desegregation, and a resolution
of interposition was passed by the legislature formally
denying the validity of the Supreme Ct.'s ruling in the
State of Miss. A Commn. on State Sovereignty was created
in 1956 to resist school integration. After tenure as Gov.,
resumed law practice. Mbr. of Miss. House, 1960-1965.
Apptd. to U.S. Fifth Cir. Ct. of Appeals by Pres. L. B.
Johnson, in 1965. Mbr., Masons (Shriners); Rotary. Trustee
of Miss. Coll., 1952-1956. Baptist. m. in 1937 to
Margaret Janet Dennis. One s.

BARNETT, ROSS ROBERT (1960-1964). b. Jan. 22, 1898 at
Standing Pine, near Carthage, Miss. s. of John W. and
Virginia Ann (Chadwick) B. Was youngest of ten children.
Worked on family farm while attending local schools.
Served as pvt. in A.E.F. during World War I. Attd. Miss.
Coll., from which he was grad. in 1922. Taught school and
served as athletic coach at Pontotoc H.S. Attd. the Univ.
of Miss., from which he received a law degree in 1926,
working at odd jobs and as a barber to finance educ. Mbr.
of class debate team. Began law practice in Jackson, Miss.
Atty. for Selective Service Bd. during World War II. Vice
pres., and later, pres. and commnr. of Miss. Bar Assoc.
Defeated as cand. for Dem. nom. for Gov. in 1951 and 1955,
but was nom. in 1959 and was el. without opposition. Favored "right to work" law and maintenance of segregation

policies. Opposed equal rights plank in Dem. party platform at 1960 Dem. natl. conv. and led movement to withhold
Dem. pres. elector slate pledged to Dem. cand. in 1960 pres.
election. Dem. electors chosen in Miss. cast their ballots
for Sen. Byrd, of Va. for Pres. of U.S. in that election.
Supported arrests of demonstrators against segregation on
pub. transp. facilities and places of pub. accommodation.
Mbr., Natl. Exch. Club; Masons (Shriner); Miss. Farm Assoc.;
Elks; Woodmen; Amer. Legion; Moose; various alumni and pro-
fessional legal orgs. Active in Baptist church affairs.
State ch. and dir. of Miss. Heart Assoc. m. in 1929 to
Mary Pearl Crawford. Two d.; one s.

JOHNSON, PAUL BURNEY, Jr. (1964-1968). b. Jan. 23,
1916 at Hattiesburg, Miss. s. of Gov. Paul Burney J., Sr.,
of Miss. (q.v.), and Corinne (Venable) J. Attd. local pub.
schools; Columbia Mil. Acad., in Columbia, Tenn.; and the
Univ. of Miss., from which he was grad. with a law degree
in 1940. El. pres. of the student body at the Univ. of
Miss. while a sophomore. Began law practice in Hattiesburg.
Enlisted in U.S. Marine Corps as pvt. in 1942, and saw active service in So. Pac. during World War II. Rose to rank
of capt. by time of discharge in 1946. Continued in USMCR
as major. Asst. U.S. dist. atty. for So. Dist. of Miss.,
1948-1951. Defeated as cand. for Dem. nom. for Gov. in
1951 and 1955. El. Lieut. Gov. in 1959. Nom. as Dem. cand.
for Gov. in 1963 and was el. Contest marked appearance of
Rep. party as a serious contender in state gubernatorial
elections for the first time since Reconstruction era.
During admin., called out militia forces to maintain order
at the Univ. of Miss. when, in compliance with a U.S. ct.
order, it was forced to admit a Negro student. Enrollment
of the student was achieved through use of force of U.S.
marshals. Voter qualifications were liberalized by action
of U.S. cts. and U.S. Cong. to permit larger proportion of
potential electorate, including Negro citizens, to vote
during his tenure. Mbr., Amer. Legion; V.F.W.; Moose;
Masons (Shriner); Alpha Sigma Epsilon; professional legal
orgs. Recipient of AMVETS Distinguished Service Award in
1949. Methodist. m. to Dorothy E. Power, of Red Bank,
Miss. Two s.; one d.

WILLIAMS, JOHN BELL (1968-1972). b. Dec. 4, 1918 at
Raymond, Miss. s. of Gnaves Kelly and Maude E. (Bidwell)
W. Attd. local pub. schools; Hinds Co. Jr. Coll.; and the
Univ. of Miss., from which he was grad. in 1938. Studied
law at Jackson School of Law, from which he received a law
degree in 1940. Admitted to bar in 1940 and began practice

at Raymond.   Enlisted in Army Air Corps in 1941, serving as
a pilot during World War II until 1944.   Severely injured
in a crash in 1943.   Pros. atty. of Hinds Co., 1944-1946.
El. to U.S. House in 1946, continuing to serve therein by
reel. until Jan., 1968, when he resigned to assume office
of Gov.   Nom. as Dem. cand. for Gov. in 1967 and was el.
Desegregation of schools and places of pub. accommodation
was carried forward through initiative of Fed. cts. and
admin. agencies during his tenure in office.   Voting requirements were also further liberalized through pressure
from those sources as well as U.S. Cong., so as to permit
greater participation in elections by minority groups.   Recipient of Distinguished Service Awards from Miss. Farm
Bureau, Miss. Natl. Guard Assoc., and Americans for Constl.
Action.   Mbr., Amer. Legion; V.F.W.; Air Force Assoc.;
Lions; D.A.V.   Baptist.   m. in 1944 to Elizabeth Ann Wells.
Two s.; one d.

WALLER, WILLIAM LOWE (1972-1976).   b. Oct. 21, 1926 at
Oxford, Miss.   s. of Percy A. and Myrtle (Gatewood) W.
Attd. local pub. schools; Memphis State Univ., from which
he was grad. in 1948; and the Univ. of Miss., from which he
received a law degree in 1950.   Admitted to bar and began
practice at Jackson, Miss.   Worked for the U.S. govt. in
counter-intelligence field in 1951.   Dist. atty. for his
jud. cir., 1960-1968.   Nom. and el. as Dem. cand. for Gov.
in 1971.   Mbr., exec. commt., Natl. Govs.' Conf., 1974-
1975; ch., State Govt. Payroll Savings Commn., 1975; ch.,
Tenn.-Tombigbee Waterway Authority, 1975; ch., State Govt.
Appalachian Region Commn., 1975.   Pursued moderate policies
in dealing with racial problems during admin.   Resumed law
practice at Jackson, Miss. after tenure as Gov.   Defeated as
cand. for nom. for U.S. Senate seat in 1978 Dem. primary.
Mbr., professional legal orgs.; past pres., Mississippi
Prosecutors Assoc.   Baptist.   m. to Carroll -----.   Four s.;
one d.

FINCH, (CHARLES) CLIF(TON) (1976-1980).   b. April 4,
1927 at Pope, Miss.   s. of Carl Bedford and Ruth Christine
(McMinn) F.   Attd. local pub. schools and the Univ. of Miss.
from which he received an A.B. degree and a law degree in
1958.   Served in U.S. Army in 1945.   Admitted to bar in
1958, and began practice at Batesville, Miss.   Mbr. of Miss.
House, 1959-1963.   Dist. atty. for 17th jud. dist., 1964-
1972.   Nom. and el. Gov. as Dem. in 1975, winning gen. election in rather close contest with Rep. opponent.   As Gov.,
espoused programs designed to attract support of rural and
working class element.   Courted support of Negro voters by

a number of apptmts. and by the policies he pursued. Un-
successful in effort to obtain adoption of an amdt. to
Miss. const. permitting a second successive term as Gov.
Defeated in Dem. run-off primary for nom. for U.S. Senate
seat in 1978. Mbr., Masons (Shriner); Amer. Legion; V.F.W.;
Moose; Amer. Farm Bureau; Lions; Civitan; various profes-
sional legal orgs. Baptist. m. in 1952 to Zelma Lois
Smith. Two d.; two s.

McNAIR, ALEXANDER (1821-1824). b. May 5, 1775 (?)
near Derry (?), Pa. s. of David and Ann (Dunning) McN.
Father, who was of Scotch-Irish descent, served in the
Contl. Army during the Rev. War, and died of wounds received at the Battle of Trenton in 1777. Attd. local
schools and Philadelphia Coll. (now the Univ. of Pa.), from
which he withdrew before completion of studies. According
to some accounts, possibly apocryphal, his mother, as ad-
ministratrix of the family estate, offered the family homestead to the winner of a physical contest between him and
his younger brother, and he left home to make his own way
after losing the contest to the brother. Served as lieut.
in Pa. militia contingent during the Whiskey Rebellion in
1794. Commissioned as an officer in U.S. Army in 1799 during threat of war with France. In 1804 moved to St. Louis,
in Upper La. (Mo.) Terr. Apptd. as one of eight judges of
common pleas ct. by Gov. Wilkinson in 1805. Later was
sheriff of St. Louis Co., and was a mbr. of the first bd.
of trustees of St. Louis when it was incorporated as a town.
U.S. marshal for the Terr. of Mo. and register of U.S. land
office at St. Louis. Commissary and adjt. gen. of Mo. Terr.
militia in 1812. Mbr. of Mo. constl. conv. in 1820, in
which he supported maintenance of slavery. El. first Gov.
of Mo. on a provisional basis in Aug., 1820, defeating the
last Terr. Gov., Wm. Clark, in a spirited contest. Assumed
office before the State was formally admitted to the Union,
becoming Gov. de jure on Aug. 10, 1821 after a conv., held
at the insistence of Cong., had given its approval to de-
letion of a provision in the State's proposed const. prohibiting ex-slaves from settling in the State, a change he
opposed. Admin. concerned mainly with perfecting org. of
state and local govts. Served briefly as U.S. agent to
Osage Indian tribes after tenure as Gov. Was a Jeff. Rep.
in politics. m. in 1805 to Marguerite de Rielhe, of St.
Louis. Ten children, who were brought up in Catholic faith.
Active in Masonic Order. D. Mar. 18, 1826, at St. Louis.
Bur. in Calvary Cem. there.

BATES, FREDERICK (1824-1835). b. June 23, 1777 at
Belmont, Va. s. of Thomas Fleming and Caroline (Woodson) B.
Parents had only limited means. Received little formal
educ. Moved to Detroit, Mich., and became acquainted with
frontier settlers' way of life. Apptd. by Pres. Jefferson
in 1805 to post of judge in Mich. Terr. In 1806 moved to
St. Louis, in Upper La. (Mo.) Terr., where he became sect.
of the Terr. govt. under Gen. Wilkinson. Acted as Gov. of
the Terr. on several occasions. Compiled the laws of La.
Terr., and the compilation became the first book published

at St. Louis, in 1808. Mbr. of Mo. constl. conv. of 1820.
Nom. and el. Gov. as an Adams Rep. in 1824. Became ill of
pleurisy soon after term began and died in office. m. in
1819 to Nancy Ball. Four children. D. at St. Louis, Aug.
4, 1825. A brother, Edward, also settled in Mo., where he
became a lawyer and was prominent in politics, eventually
serving as U.S. Atty. Gen. in Pres. Lincoln's cabinet.

WILLIAMS, ABRAHAM J. (1825-1826). b. Feb. 26, 1791 in
what is now Grant Co., W. Va. (then Va.). Father was a
farmer. About 1816 moved West, eventually settling on a
farm near Old Franklin, Mo. Lost leg in an accident. In
1820 became proprietor of a tobacco warehouse in Boone Co.,
Mo., near Columbia. Also acquired a farm near there. In
1821 erected the first store in Columbia and engaged in
merc. and boot-making bus. there as well as farming. El.
to Mo. Senate in 1822 and became Pres. pro tem of that body
in 1824. As such, succeeded to office of Gov. temporarily
in Aug., 1825, following death of Gov. Bates, the office of
Lieut. Gov. having been vacated by resignation shortly after the beginning of Bates' term in 1824. Occupied office
of Gov. until a successor was chosen in a spec. election to
complete Bates' term. Defeated for reel. to the Mo. Senate
in 1826. Pres. of first fair held at Columbia in 1835.
Never married. D. Dec. 30, 1839. Bur. at Columbia.

MILLER, JOHN (1826-1832). b. Nov. 25, 1781 near
Martinsburg, Berkeley Co., Va. (now W. Va.). Received
common school educ. As a young man moved to Steubenville,
Ohio, where he became publ. of a newspaper, the Western
Herald, and later, the Gazette. Served as officer in Ohio
militia. Enlisted in U.S. Army as lieut. in War of 1812,
rising to rank of col. by end of the war. Distinguished
himself for gallantry during the war. Resigned mil. commn.
in 1818 and moved to Franklin, Mo. Terr., where he became
U.S. registrar of land sales. Served in that capacity for
eight years. El. Gov. as a Jackson (Rep.) cand. in spec.
election in Dec., 1825, to choose successor to complete
term for which Gov. Bates, who had died, had been el. Reel.
for full term in 1828 without opposition. During admin.,
the state capital was moved from St. Charles to Jefferson
City. Urged establishment of mil. posts in various parts
of the State to give protection against Indian outbreaks.
Favored withdrawal of State paper currency. El. as Van
Buren Dem. to U.S. House in 1836, continuing in that office
for two additional terms. Did not seek fourth term in 1842.
Advocated constr. of canal to connect Miss. River and Lake
Michigan, via Illinois River. Retired to home near

Florissant, Mo., in 1843. D. there, March 18, 1846. Bur.
in Bellefontaine Cem., St. Louis.

DUNKLIN, DANIEL (1832-1836). b. Jan. 14, 1790 near
Greenville, S.C. s. of Joseph, Jr. and Sarah Margaret
(Sullivan) D. Father had served as a soldier in Rev. War
under Gen. Francis Marion. Attd. local schools. As a
young man moved with family to Caldwell Co., Ky., and in
1810 to Potosi, in Washington Co., Upper La. (Mo.) Terr.
Became proprietor of a tavern. Participated as mbr. of
militia in engagements against Indians and British, 1812-
1815. Became sheriff of Washington Co. in 1815. Studied
law and was admitted to the bar. Mbr. of Mo. constl. conv.
in 1820. Mbr. of Mo. House, 1822-1823. El. Lieut. Gov. in
1828 and in 1832 was nom. and el. Gov. as a Jackson Dem.
As Gov., promoted establishment of pub. school system.
Supported Pres. Jackson's stand in S.C. nullification crisis. Took initial steps toward establishment of fund from
land sales for a state univ. Helped found Potosi Acad.
Resigned before end of term to become U.S. surveyor gen.
for Ill.-Mo.-Ark. dist. by apptmt. from Pres. Jackson.
Moved residence to Herculaneum, Mo. in 1840. As surveyor
gen., laid out many counties in the Mo.-Ark. area, and located by survey the Mo.-Ark. boundary line. m. in 1815 to
Emily Haley, of Caldwell Co., Ky. Mbr., Masons. D. July
25, 1844, at his home, "Maje", in Jefferson Co., Mo. Bur.
in cem. near Pevely, Mo.

BOGGS, LILBURN W. (1836-1840). b. Dec. 14, 1792 at
Lexington, Ky. s. of John M. and Martha (Oliver) B. In
1810 moved to St. Louis, Mo. Terr., where he engaged in bus.
Became cashier of Bank of St. Louis. Later moved to
Independence, Mo., where he engaged in merc. bus. and fur
trade. Served as mbr. of Mo. Senate, 1826-1832, and in
1832 was el. to the office of Lieut. Gov. as a Jackson Dem.
Succeeded to office of Gov. when Gov. Dunklin resigned in
Sept., 1836, and completed Dunklin's term, which had about
three months to run. B. had already been nom. and el. Gov.
for the succeeding term in a close election with the Whig
cand. Major events during admin. concerned troubles between Mormon settlers and other inhabitants in the western
area of the State. Friction between them resulted eventually in the expulsion of the Mormons from that area by
militia forces after there had been several armed conflicts,
in which a number of lives were lost. The Mormons then
established themselves for a time at Nauvoo, Ill. Narrowly
escaped death shortly after leaving office when he was
seriously wounded in an assassination attempt, presumably

by a Mormon adherent or sympathizer. During admin., legislation was passed providing for establishment of the Univ.
of Mo. at Columbia, and providing for a pub. school system.
In 1837 Cong. passed legislation adding the Platte Purchase
(now the six northwestern counties) to the State's area.
Mbr. of Mo. Senate, 1842-1846. In 1846 he moved to Calif.,
settling in the Sonoma dist., where he served as alcalde,
1847-1849. Engaged in merc. bus. and farming, and had an
active role in movement for statehood for Calif. m. circa
1816 to Julia Bent. Two s. m. in 1823 to Panthea Grant
Boone, a grand-daughter of Daniel Boone. Ten children. D.
Mar. 4, 1860 on his farm near Sacramento, Calif.

REYNOLDS, THOMAS (1840-1844). b. March 12, 1796 in
Mason (now Bracken) Co., Ky. s. of Robert and Margaret
(Moore) R. Father had emigrated from Ireland to Pa. in
1785. Later moved to Ky., then to Tenn., and eventually
settled in Cahokia, Ill. in 1800, then a part of Ind. Terr.
Family later moved to Collinsville, Ill. Received common
school educ. Studied law and was admitted to Ill. bar in
1817. Became clerk of Ill. House, and later was a House
mbr. and Speaker. Atty. Gen. of Ill., and from 1822-1825
was a mbr. and Chief Justice of Ill. Supreme Ct. Political
rivalry developed between him and his brother John, who was
also a prominent figure in early Ill. politics, and who later became Gov. of Ill. (q.v.). In 1829, moved to Fayette,
Howard Co., Mo. Practiced law and engaged in politics
there. El. to Mo. House, where he sponsored a bill abolishing imprisonment for debt, a measure eventually adopted
during his tenure as Gov. Was House Speaker in 1832.
Served as cir. ct. judge thereafter for several years. Nom.
and el. Gov. as Dem. in 1840. During admin., the Univ. of
Mo. at Columbia began operations. Favored sound money policy; promotion of pub. educ. Advocated States Rts. position on slavery issue. Was first Gov. to issue a Thanksgiving Day proclamation. D. by suicide at Jefferson City,
Mo., Feb. 9, 1844, during last year of term, presumably because of virulence of criticisms by political opponents.
Bur. in Woodlawn Cem., Jefferson City, Mo.

MARMADUKE, MEREDITH MILES (1844). b. Aug. 28, 1791 in
Westmoreland Co., Va. s. of Vincent and Sarah (Porter) M.
Attd. local schools. Later studied surveying and engaged
in civil engr. work. At age 22 was commissioned as col. of
Va. volunteers during War of 1812, serving until end of war.
Apptd. U.S. marshal for Eastern dist. of Va., and soon
afterward became a cir. ct. clerk. In 1821 moved to
Franklin, Mo. for reasons of health. Engaged in trading

with Spanish Southwest for next six years. Became surveyor
of Saline Co. and also a mbr. of co. ct. In 1830 purchased
a farm near Arrow Rock, in Saline Co., Mo. Was one of
leaders in org. of first State Fair, of which he acted as
pres. El. Lieut. Gov. in 1840 as Dem. Succeeded to office
of Gov. in Feb., 1844, following death of Gov. Reynolds,
and completed Reynolds' term. Mbr. of state constl. conv.
of 1845-1846. As Civil War approached took position of opposition to secession but did not support use of mil. force
to subdue South. m. to Lavinia Sappington, of Saline Co.,
Mo. Seven s.; three d. A son, John S. M., became Gov. of
Mo. (q.v.), as did also a brother-in-law, Claiborne F.
Jackson (q.v.). D. Mar. 26, 1864, on his farm near Arrow
Rock.

EDWARDS, JOHN CUMMINS (1844-1848). b. June 24, 1804
at Frankfort, Ky. s. of John and Sarah (Cummins) E.
Father was a person of some wealth who resided originally
in Pa. and later moved to Ky. and then to Tenn., where he
became a planter and son was brought up. Attd. acad. at
Murphreesboro, Tenn., and Black's Coll., in Ky. Studied
law in law office and was admitted to Tenn. bar in 1825.
Moved to St. Louis, Mo. in 1828, where he engaged in law
practice, later moving to Jefferson City, Mo., where he
continued to practice law. Apptd. Sect. of State by Gov.
Miller in 1830, serving until 1835, and was apptd. again to
that office briefly in 1837. Cir. ct. judge, 1832-1837.
Resigned as Sect. of State to accept post on Mo. Supreme
Ct. in 1837, but his apptmt. was not referred to the Mo.
Senate for confirmation, and he left the ct. after a short
time. Continued to reside in Jefferson City and practiced
law. Mbr. of Mo. House, 1839-1840. El. to U.S. House in
1840 as a Dem., serving for one term. Nom. and el. Gov. as
a Benton Dem. in 1844. During admin., a state constl. conv.
was assembled, but the document it drafted was rejected by
the State's voters. Cooperated in raising volunteer forces
for U.S. during the Mexican War. Was not happy in the office of Gov., declaring at the end of his term that it was
a "despicable" office to be condemned to hold, and that he
had been compelled to go armed to his office at the Capitol
to protect himself against political enemies. Moved to
Calif. after tenure as Gov. Was married there, and served
one term as mayor of Stockton. Engaged in cattle ranching,
real estate and merc. bus. D. Oct. 14 (Sept. 14?), 1888,
at Stockton. Bur. in Rural Cem. there.

KING, AUSTIN AUGUSTUS (1848-1852). b. Sept. 21, 1802
in Sullivan Co., Tenn. s. of Walter and ----- (Sevier) K.,

a widow. Attd. local pub. schools. Studied law and was
admitted to the bar in 1822. Began practice in Jackson,
Tenn. In 1830 moved to Columbia, Mo., where he continued
to practice law. Served as col. of militia unit during
Black Hawk War. Mbr. of Mo. House, 1834-1836. Moved to
Richmond, Mo. in 1837. Apptd. to cir. ct. judgeship there,
which he held from 1837 to 1848. During tenure as judge,
presided over trials of several figures involved in Mormon
disturbances in that region, which brought him to notice
elsewhere in the State. Nom. and el. Gov. as Dem. in 1848.
Resumed law practice after tenure as Gov. Delegate to Dem.
natl. convs. at Charleston and Baltimore, in 1860. Was a
supporter of Sen. Douglas for Pres. of U.S. in 1860. Opposed secession movement. Became a cir. ct. judge again in
1862, but resigned office after a brief tenure, having been
el. to the U.S. House as a Union Dem. in 1862. Defeated
for reel. in 1864. Practiced law and farmed near Richmond,
Mo. thereafter. D. April 22, 1870 at St. Louis, Mo. Bur.
in Richmond Cem.

     PRICE, STERLING (1853-1857). b. Sept. 20, 1809 near
Farmville, Va. s. of Pugh Williamson and Elizabeth
(Williamson) P. After attending prep. school, enrolled at
Hampden-Sydney Coll. Studied law and was admitted to bar.
In 1830 moved to Keytesville, Mo., where he practiced law.
Mbr. of Mo. House, 1836-1838 and 1840-1844, serving as
Speaker the last four years. El. to U.S. House as a Dem.
in 1844. Resigned seat in Aug., 1846, to accept commn. as
col. in Mo. volunteer regiment when war with Mexico began.
Rose to rank of brig. gen. by end of the war, having served
for a time as mil. gov. of the city of Chihuahua. Returned
to Mo. in 1848 and engaged in farming near Bowling Green.
Nom. and el. Gov. in 1852. During admin., disorders along
the Kans.-Mo. border between anti-slavery and pro-slavery
elements began to be a problem. After tenure as Gov., was
apptd. Mo. Bank Commnr., serving from 1857 to 1861. Delegate to and presiding officer of conv. called in 1861 to
consider attitude of State toward impending Civil War
crisis. It proved to be under the control of anti-
secessionist element. Acceptd. apptmt. as major gen. of
Mo. militia by Gov. Jackson. After the efforts of the Gov.
and pro-Southern element of the legislature to lead Mo. into the So. Confed. were foiled, P. received a commn. as
major gen. from the Confed. govt. in 1862, and became leader of forces engaged in unsuccessful efforts to re-estab-
lish authority of pro-Southern element in States of Mo. and
Ark. Led a mil. force back into Mo. from Ark. in 1864 that
threatened the capture of Jefferson City and Kansas City.

Participated in numerous engagements in Southwestern theater of Civil War, 1862-1865. Helped to org. the Knights of
the Golden Circle, made up of pro-Southern elements in Midwestern and Border States. After end of the Civil War,
went to Mexico, where he had the patronage of Emperor
Maximilian. Returned to U.S. after the overthrow and execution of the Emperor by Mexican forces. m. in 1833 to
Martha Head. D. Sept. 29, 1867 at St. Louis, Mo. Bur. in
Bellefontaine Cem. there.

POLK, TRUSTEN (1857). b. May 29, 1811 near
Bridgeville, Del. s. of Wm. Nutter and Levinia (Causey) P.
Was nephew of Peter Causey, Gov. of Del. (q.v.), and family
was related to that of Pres. James K. Polk, Gov. of Tenn.
(q.v.). Attd. acad. at Cambridge, Md. and Yale, from which
he was grad. in 1831. Studied law in office of John Rogers,
Atty. Gen. of Md.; also attd. law lectures while at Yale.
Moved to St. Louis, Mo. in 1835, where he engaged in practice of law. City counselor at St. Louis, 1843. Mbr. of
Mo. constl. conv. of 1845-1846. Pres. elector on Dem.
ticket in 1848 pres. election. Nom. as Anti-Benton Dem.
cand. for Gov. in 1856 and was el. in exciting three-way
contest against Amer. party cand. and former Sen. Thomas H.
Benton. Soon after inauguration as Gov. in Jan., 1857, was
el. to U.S. Senate, again in a three-way contest in which
Benton was a cand. Resigned office of Gov. in Feb., 1857,
to take seat in Senate. As a Sen., supported Southern
cause and right of So. States to secede from the Union.
Resigned Senate seat in 1861, but a resolution of expulsion
for disloyalty was nevertheless subsequently adopted by the
Senate against him in Jan., 1862. Moved to New Madrid, Mo.
and joined in Confed. war effort as a col. Served as
judge-advocate gen. under Gen. Sterling Price, 1864-1865,
in the Miss. Dept. of Confed. Army. Property was confiscated at end of Civil War, but was eventually restored to him.
Returned to St. Louis and engaged in practice of law. m.
in 1837 to Elizabeth Newberry Skinner. One s.; four d. D.
April 16, 1876. Bur. in Bellefontaine Cem., St. Louis.

JACKSON, HANCOCK LEE (1857). b. May 12, 1796 in
Madison Co., Ky. Moved to Mo. as a young man, engaging in
farming near Clark, Mo. El. sheriff of Randolph Co. in
1829 when that county was first org. Continued to be active in local and state politics. El. Lieut. Gov. as Dem.
in 1856. Succeeded to office of Gov. in Feb., 1857, following the resignation of Gov. Polk to accept seat in U.S.
Senate. Served until Oct., 1857, after a successor had been
chosen in a spec. election in August, 1857, to complete

Polk's term. Defeated in 1860 as nominee for Gov. of
Breckenridge faction of Dem. party. Was a slave owner and
sympathies lay with South during Civil War. Moved to Salem,
Ore. in 1865, where he spent the remaining years of his
life. D. Mar. 19, 1876.

STEWART, ROBERT MARCELLUS (1857-1861). b. Mar. 12,
1815 at Truxton, N.Y. s. of Charles and Elizabeth
(Severance) S. Family was of very modest means. Left home
in early youth to make his way on his own, eventually establishing his residence in Ky. Worked there at various
jobs, including teaching and serving as roustabout and deck
hand on river boats. Studied law and was admitted to bar.
Practiced for a short time at Louisville, Ky., and in 1838
moved to St. Charles, Mo. Moved to Northwest Mo. in 1839,
settling first at Bloomington, in De Kalb Co., and in 1845
moving to St. Joseph, Mo. Mbr. of Mo. constl. conv. of
1845-1846. El. to Mo. Senate in 1846, continuing to serve
therein for next ten years. Register of U.S. land office
at Savannah, Mo., 1848. While in Senate was instrumental
in obtaining a U.S. land grant for constr. of Hannibal and
St. Joseph R.R., of which he became pres. in 1854. In
August, 1857, following the resignation of Gov. Polk was el.
Gov. as an Anti-Benton Dem. to serve the remainder of Polk's
term. Won by only some 300 votes over a cand. supported by
the Amer. party and the Emancipationist Whigs in a very exciting contest. During admin., promoted the bldg. of railroads and other pub. improvements. Agitation over issues
relating to slavery, popular reaction following the announcement of the U.S. Supreme Ct.'s ruling in the Dred
Scott case which had originated in Mo. several years
earlier, and continual disturbances along the Kans.-Mo.
border led to popular excitement and extensive party re-
alignments during his tenure. Although he favored slavery,
was a Unionist in political views. After tenure as Gov.,
returned to St. Joseph, where he became ed. of the St.
Joseph Journal, 1861-1865. After outbreak of Civil War,
favored a policy of neutrality at first, but in 1863 accepted a commn. as officer to raise volunteer troops for
Union cause. Did not participate in mil. action, and eventually resigned commn. because of poor health. Numerous
stories told of his eccentric behavior while in office of
Gov. On one occasion he reportedly kicked a convict down
the stairs from his office to "even the score" with him
after having granted him a pardon, having discovered the
convict was a former riverboat foreman under whom he had
worked as a steamboat deckhand and who had subjected him
to that kind of treatment for some minor matter. D. at

St. Joseph, Sept. 21, 1871.

JACKSON, CLAIBORNE FOX (1861-1862). b. April 4, 1807 (1806?) near Flemingsburg, Fleming Co., Ky. s. of Dempsey and Mary (Pickett) J. Received schooling there. In 1825 moved to Franklin, Mo. and in 1832 to a farm near Arrow Rock, Mo. Engaged in merc. bus. as well as farming. Served as capt. in Mo. militia force called up during the Black Hawk War. El. to Mo. House in 1836 and again in 1842-1848, serving as Speaker in 1844 and 1846 sessions. Mbr. of Mo. Senate in 1848-1849. Resolutions introduced by him in the legislature following the Mexican War opposing efforts in Cong. to restrict introduction of slavery into lands acquired from Mexico led to intense debate and political division within the State. Served as State Banking Commnr., and effected reforms in banking regulations after service in legislature. Nom. and el. Gov. as a Dem. in 1860. Was a supporter of Sen. Douglas for Pres. in the 1860 pres. election, but his sympathies were with the South when the Civil War neared. However, a conv. that met soon after he assumed office to consider the State's course of action regarding possible secession proved to be under the control of anti-secessionists. Took steps to arm and train militia forces as a State Guard, ostensibly to preserve the State's neutrality in the impending conflict, and refused to respond to Pres. Lincoln's call for mil. assistance to oppose secessionists. Pro-Unionists, with the help of U.S. forces, seized and disarmed a militia contingent the Gov. had put into training at a camp near St. Louis. Eventually the Union forces marched on the state capital and compelled the Gov., the Lieut. Gov., and the pro-Southern element of the state legislature to flee southward. These elements of the state govt., meeting in a "rump" session at Neosho, Mo., passed an ordinance of secession. The state conv. re-assembled and declared the office of Gov. vacated in July, 1861, and apptd. a provisional pro-Union Gov. Thereafter J., with the assistance of Confed. troops, continued to try to exercise authority in the State, but never succeeded in temporily occupying more than a portion of the southern area of Mo. J. accepted a commn. as brig. gen. in the Confed. Army in 1862. His health failed not long afterward, and he died Dec. 6 (7?), 1862, at Little Rock, Ark. Was married three times, his wives all being daughters of Dr. John Sappington, of Saline Co. Was an uncle by marriage of Gov. John S. Marmaduke, of Mo. (q.v.), and a brother-in-law of Gov. M. M. Marmaduke, of Mo. (q.v.). Bur. in Sappington family cem., near Arrow Rock. After his death, the office of Gov. was claimed by his pro-Southern Lieut. Gov., Thomas C. Reynolds.

GAMBLE, HAMILTON ROWAN (1861-1864). b. Nov. 29, 1798
at Winchester, Va. s. of Joseph and Anne (Hamilton) G.
Family was of Irish descent. Attd. Hampden-Sydney Coll.
Studied law and was admitted to the bar at age 18. In 1818
moved to St. Louis, Mo., where he served as deputy cir. ct.
clerk by apptmt. of his brother, who was ct. clerk. Later
moved to Franklin, Mo., where he practiced law. Apptd.
Sect. of State by Gov. Bates in 1824. Moved residence from
St. Charles to St. Louis. Continued to practice law in St.
Louis, becoming well-known in all phases of land litigation.
El. to Mo. House in 1846. El. to Mo. Supreme Ct. in 1851,
becoming its Chief Justice. Resigned jud. post in 1855.
Became spokesman for the Free Soil movement in Mo. Defeated as cand. for U.S. Senate seat in 1857. As Civil War
threatened, became a leader of pro-Union element in State.
Mbr. of conv. called in 1861 to consider State's course of
action in connection with Civil War crisis. Apptd. Provisional Gov. by the conv. in July, 1861, when Gov. Jackson
was deposed by it. As Gov., directed efforts to assist war
effort of Lincoln admin. Favored gradual emancipation of
slaves. m. in 1827 to Caroline J. Coalter, of Columbia,
S.C. Two s.; one d. D. at St. Louis, Jan. 31, 1864, while
still acting as Gov.

HALL, WILLARD PREBLE (1864-1865). b. May 9, 1820 at
Harper's Ferry, Va. (now W. Va.). s. of John and Statira
(Preble) H. Descendant of an English colonist who emigrated to Mass. in 1600s. Antecedents included many persons of
distinction. A brother, Wm. Augustus H., was a mbr. of the
U.S. House from Mo., as was also a nephew, Uriel S. H.
Attd. an acad. in Baltimore, Md., and Yale, from which he
was grad. in 1839. Studied law, and was admitted to bar.
Moved with father's family to Randolph Co., Mo. in 1840 and
began practice of law at Sparta, Mo. Apptd. atty. for his
jud. dist. by Gov. Reynolds in 1843. Pres. elector on Dem.
ticket in 1844 pres. election. Served in Mexican War,
rising from pvt. to lieut. Assisted in compilation of
digest of laws of Mexico by Gen. Kearny, the so-called
"Kearny Code". El. to U.S. House as Dem. in 1846, continuing to serve until 1853. Resumed law practice at St.
Joseph, Mo. Unsuccessful cand. for U.S. Senate. Mbr. of
Mo. conv. of 1861 called to consider question of State's
attitude on impending Civil War crisis. Was pro-Unionist
in political views. Apptd. Provisional Lieut. Gov. in July,
1861, after Gov. Jackson and Lieut. Gov. Reynolds joined
Southern cause. Succeeded to office of Gov. in Jan., 1864,
after death of Provisional Gov. Gamble, and served remainder of term for which Jackson had been el. Retired to

farming and law practice in Buchanan Co. thereafter. m. in
1847 to Anna Eliza Richardson. Four children. m. in 1864
to Ollie Oliver. D. at St. Joseph, Mo., Nov. 2, 1882. Bur.
in Mount Moriah Cem. there.

FLETCHER, THOMAS CLEMENT (1865-1869). b. Jan. 21,
1827 at Herculaneum, Mo. s. of Clement Bell and Margaret
Smith (Byrd) F. Descendant of English colonist who emi-
grated to Plymouth, Mass. in 1600s. Received little formal
educ., but studied widely on his own. Became ct. clerk of
Jefferson Co. Studied law and was admitted to bar in 1856.
Supported Thomas H. Benton in 1856 gubernatorial election.
Became land agent for the Pacific R.R. and moved to St.
Louis. In 1860 founded town of De Soto, Mo., in Jefferson
Co. After Civil War began, enlisted in Union army, be-
coming col. of a volunteer unit in 1862. Saw active service in Southwestern theater of war. Was wounded and captured. After exchange, was promoted to brig. gen. While
participating in Atlanta campaign in 1864 was nom. as the
Unionist (Rep.) cand. for Gov. and was el., becoming the
first native-born resident of Mo. to hold office of Gov.
During admin., issued proclamation ending slavery in the
State; favored adoption of 13th Amdt. to U.S. Const.,
abolishing slavery in U.S. A revised state const. which
imposed severe restrictions on Southern sympathizers and
excluded them from the franchise, pub. offices, and various
professions, was adopted during his tenure. It became the
subject of intense controversy, and in 1870 the restrictive
provisions were repealed after a U.S. Supreme Ct. ruling in
1867 had voided them in part. The 1865 state const. also
changed the term of the Gov. to two years, beginning in
1869. After tenure as Gov., resumed law practice and bus.
interests in St. Louis. In 1890 moved to Washington, D.C.
m. in 1851 to Mary Clara Honey, of Herculaneum. One s.;
one d. D. March 25, 1899, in Washington, D.C.

McCLURG, JOSEPH WASHINGTON (1869-1871). b. Feb. 22,
1818 at Lebanon, Mo. Terr. s. of Joseph and Mary
(Brotherton) McC. Attd. Xenia Acad. and Oxford Acad., in
Ohio, and Oxford Coll., from which he was grad. in 1835.
Taught school for two years in La. and Miss. Returned to
Mo. where he served as ct. clerk for a time. Studied law,
and was admitted to bar. Went to Texas in 1839. Began law
practice at Columbus, Texas in 1841. Returned to Mo. after
a short time, where he engaged in merc. bus. and steamboat
line operations at St. Louis, and later at Linn Creek, Mo.
Deputy sheriff of St. Louis Co., 1841-1844. Bus. interests
suffered depredations from Confed. forces in early years of

the Civil War. Mbr. of Mo. conv. that assumed control of
State govt. in 1861. Received commn. as col. of Mo. troops
engaged in holding State in Union. Delegate to Rep. natl.
conv. in 1864. El. to U.S. House in 1864 as Emancipationist and was reel. in 1866, affiliating with Radical wing
of Rep. party. Nom. and el. Gov. as a Rep. in 1868 for a
two-year term. Defeated for second term in 1870 by cand.
supported by Lib. Rep. and Dem. parties. Retired to merc.
and steamboating bus. at Linn Creek. Later engaged in lead
mining enterprise. Apptd. U.S. register of lands at
Springfield, Mo. in 1889. m. in 1844 to Mary C. Johnson.
D. Dec. 2, 1900, at Lebanon, Mo. Bur. in Lebanon Cem.

BROWN, B(ENJAMIN) GRATZ (1871-1873). b. May 28, 1826
at Lexington, Ky. s. of Mason and Judith Ann (Bledsoe) B.
Descendant of Irish colonist who emigrated to Va. in 1740.
Family was prominent in pub. life, his grand-father, John
B., having served as one of first U.S. Senators from Ky.,
and a brother of his grand-father, James B., having served
as U.S. Sen. from La. Attd. Transylvania Univ., from which
he was grad. in 1845; Yale Univ.; and Louisville Law
School. Admitted to bar in 1849 and moved to St. Louis,
Mo., where he began law practice with Francis P. Blair, Jr.
Mbr. of Mo. House, 1853-1859 as Dem. Was out-spoken oppo-
nent of slavery and gave support to Free Soil movement. In
1854 became ed. of the Missouri Democrat, at St. Louis.
Supported candidacy of Thomas H. Benton for Gov. in 1856.
Engaged in a duel with Thomas C. Reynolds, later pro-
Southern Lieut. Gov. of Mo., as result of quarrel arising
from political differences. Received an injury from which
he was lamed for rest of his life. Upon outbreak of Civil
War opposed secession as mbr. of Mo. conv. of 1861. El. to
U.S. Senate in 1863 as a Union Dem. to replace Sen. Waldo
P. Johnson, who was expelled from that body for pro-
Southern attitude, and served until 1867. Participated in
Planters House Conf. at St. Louis in 1866 where Rep. party
split on issue of retention of restrictive provisions in
the state const. of 1865 on former Confed. sympathizers.
Favored liberalizing the restrictions, and when the Rep.
state conv. in 1870 refused to endorse that policy he joined in bolt of the conv. Accepted nom. of Lib. Rep. and Dem.
parties for Gov. in the ensuing election and was el., defeating incumbent Gov. McClurg. Defeated as nominee of Lib.
Rep. and Dem. parties for Vice Pres. of U.S. on ticket with
Horace Greeley in 1872 pres. election. Returned thereafter
to law practice in St. Louis, specializing in railroad litigation. m. in 1858 to Mary Hanson Gunn, of Jefferson City,
Mo. Six d.; three s. D. at Kirkwood, Mo., Dec. 13, 1885.

Bur. in Oak Hill Cem. there.

WOODSON, SILAS (1873-1875). b. May 18, 1819 in Knox
Co., Ky. Family was originally from Va. Raised on
father's farm, receiving common school educ. As youth
worked as a clerk in a country store. Studied law and at
age 20 was admitted to bar. Began practice in Knox Co.
Mbr. of Ky. legislature, 1842-1843. State's atty. for his
jud. dist., 1843-1848. Delegate to Ky. constl. conv. in
1849. Mbr. of Ky. legislature again in 1853. In 1854 moved
to St. Joseph, Mo., where he engaged in law practice. Cir.
ct. judge, 1860-1872. Engaged in pvt. law practice for a
short time. Nom. and el. Gov. as a Dem., with support of
Lib. Rep. party, in 1872. Apptd. again to cir. ct. bench
to fill vacancy in 1882. Judge of Buchanan Co. criminal
ct., 1885-1895. Married three times, his last wife being
Jennie Lard, whom he married in 1866. D. Oct. 9, 1896, at
St. Joseph, Mo.

HARDIN, CHARLES HENRY (1875-1877). b. July 15, 1820
in Trimble Co., Ky. s. of Charles and Hannah (Jewell) H.
In year after son was born father moved family to Columbia,
Mo. Father died when son was 10 years old. Attd. local
schools; the Univ. of Ind. for two years; and Miami Univ.,
in Ohio, from which he was grad. in 1841. Studied law and
was admitted to bar in 1843 and began practice in Fulton,
Mo. State's atty. for his jud. dist., 1842-1852. Mbr. of
Mo. House, 1853-1855 and 1859-1860. Mbr. of commn. on revision of state laws, 1855. Was a leader in org. of Amer.
(Know Nothing) party in Mo. in mid-1850s. El. to Mo. Senate, 1860, as a Conservative Unionist. Supported the
Constl. Union party's candidates, John Bell and Edward
Everett, in 1860 pres. election. Opposed secession movement but did not favor use of mil. force to coerce South.
During Civil War engaged in farming near Mexico, Mo., and
was disfranchised for a time. Resumed practice of law in
1865. Mbr. of Mo. Senate, 1873-1874. Nom. and el. Gov. as
a Dem. in 1874. During admin., state farming industry
suffered severely from drought and grasshopper infestation,
and he sought to alleviate distress brought on by that and
the depression following the financial panic of 1873. A
revised state const. was drafted and adopted in 1875. In
1873 assisted with an endowment grant the founding of
Hardin Female Coll., in Mexico, Mo. One of student founders of Beta Theta Pi fraternity while in college. Hon. degree from Wm. Jewell Coll. in 1890. m. in 1844 to Mary
Barr Jenkins. D. July 29, 1892, at Mexico, Mo. Bur. in
Jewell Cem., near Columbia, Mo.

PHELPS, JOHN SMITH (1877-1881). b. Dec. 22, 1814 at Simsbury, Conn. s. of Elisha and Lucy (Smith) P. Was a descendant of an early English Puritan colonist who emigrated to New England before the Rev. War, and his father had served in U.S. House from Conn. Attd. local schools and Trinity Coll., from which he was grad. in 1832. Studied law with father, was admitted to bar in 1835 and began practice in Conn. In 1837 moved to Springfield, Mo., where he continued to practice law. El. to Mo. House in 1840. Was apptd. brigade inspector of Mo. militia. El. to U.S. House as Dem. in 1844, continuing to serve therein until 1862. Was a strong Unionist, and supported Sen. Douglas for Pres. of U.S. in 1860 pres. election. Supported Pres. Lincoln's Civil War measures after Civil War began. Did not seek reel. to Cong. in 1862. Enlisted as pvt. in Mo. volunteer unit opposing the So. Confed. in 1861, soon rising to the rank of col. and then to brig. gen. Served for several months in 1862 as U.S. mil. gov. of Ark. in areas of State under Union control, but the assignment was discontinued in 1863. Resumed law practice at Springfield. Delegate to Natl. Union ("Loyalist") party conv. in 1866. Nom. as the Dem. cand. for Gov. in 1868 but was defeated in the gen. election. Nom. and el. as Dem. cand. for Gov. in 1876 for four-year term. Resumed law practice after tenure as Gov. m. in 1837 to Mary Whitney. Five children. D. Nov. 20, 1886, at St. Louis, Mo. Bur. in Hazelwood Cem., Springfield, Mo.

CRITTENDEN, THOMAS THEODORE (1881-1885). b. Jan. 1, 1832 in Shelby Co., Ky. s. of Henry and Anna Maria (Allen) C. Nephew of Gov. John J. Crittenden, of Ky. (q.v.). When son was two years old, father died and his mother, who remarried, moved to Breckenridge Co., Ky. Attd. school at Cloverport, Ky., and Centre Coll., from which he was grad. in 1855. Studied law in office of an uncle at Frankfort, Ky., and was admitted to bar in 1858. Clerk in office of U.S. registrar of lands in 1856. Moved to Lexington, Mo. in 1857 and began practice of law there. Joined Union Army in 1861, rising to rank of lieut. col. of volunteers by the end of the Civil War. Participated in Battle of Westport Landing in 1864, the last major engagement of the war in Mo., and was wounded. Apptd. Atty. Gen. of Mo. in 1864 to fill a vacancy, serving until 1865. Moved to Warrensburg, Mo. in 1865, where he continued law practice as partner of Francis M. Cockrell, later a U.S. Sen. from Mo. El. to U.S. House as a Dem. in 1872. Failed to be re-nom. in 1874, but was nom. and el. again in 1876. Nom. and el. Gov. as a Dem.

in 1880. Stressed issues of taking steps to uphold State's
financial credit; to promote pub. educ. system; and to
eradicate the Jesse James outlaw gang. Accomplished all
these objectives during term. After tenure as Gov. practiced law in Kansas City, Mo. Apptd. U.S. Consul Gen. in
Mexico in 1892, serving from 1893 to 1897. Was acting as
U.S. bankruptcy case referee at time of death. Presbyterian. m. in 1856 to Carrie W. Jackson, of Frankfort, Ky.
Three s. D. May 29, 1909, at Kansas City, Mo. Bur. in
Forest Hills Cem. there.

MARMADUKE, JOHN SAPPINGTON (1885-1887). b. March 14,
1833 near Arrow Rock, Saline Co., Mo. s. of Meredith M.
and Lavinia (Sappington) M. Father had been a Gov. of Mo.
(q.v.). He was also a great-grandson of Gov. John
Breathitt, of Ky. (q.v.), and a nephew by marriage of Gov.
Claiborne F. Jackson, of Mo. (q.v.). Attd. local schools;
Yale Univ. for two years; Harvard Univ. for one year; and
the U.S. Mil. Acad. at West Point, from which he was grad.
in 1857. Commissioned as second lieut. in U.S. Army.
Served with the Johnston Expedition into Mormon country in
Utah in 1858, and remained on mil. duty there and in N.M.
until 1861. Resigned commn. in U.S. Army in 1861 after outbreak of Civil War, and was commissioned as col. of Mo.
volunteers for service with Mo. militia. Had disagreement
with his uncle, Gov. Jackson, over latter's policies in
early months of the Civil War and resigned his commn. in
Mo. troops. Joined a Confed. unit in Va. as a lieut. Soon
rose to rank of col., and participated in a number of major
engagements, including the Battle of Shiloh. Was wounded
in action. Promoted to brig. gen. and was placed in command of Confed. cavalry units operating in Ark.-Mo. theater
of the war. Fought a duel with Gen. Lucien Walker arising
from M.'s criticism of latter's conduct during battle that
resulted in the defeat of Confed. forces at Helena, Ark.
The duel resulted in Gen. Walker's death. Was placed on
inactive status for a time, but was ultimately returned to
active duty and promoted to rank of major gen. Was wounded
and captured at the Battle of Westport, in Mo., and held as
prisoner until the end of the Civil War. Travelled in
Europe for a time after the Civil War ended, but returned
to St. Louis, Mo. in 1867, where he engaged in bus. Became
part-owner of the St. Louis Journal of Commerce and established another newspaper, the Illustrated Journal of
Agriculture, in 1871. Retired from journalism bus. in 1873,
becoming sect. of Mo. Bd. of Agri. State R.R. Commnr.,
1875-1881. Nom. and el. Gov. as Dem. in 1884. During
admin., the state debt was refunded, and the money saved

was used for reclamation of swamp lands. D. Dec. 27, 1887,
at Jefferson City during the third year of term as Gov.

MOREHOUSE, ALBERT PICKETT (1887-1889). b. July 11,
1835 near Ashley, Delaware Co., Ohio. Father was a farmer.
Received common school educ. and became a school teacher at
age 18. Family moved to Nodaway Co., Mo. in 1856. Studied
law and was admitted to bar in 1860. Practiced law in
Montgomery Co., Iowa for a short time. Returned to Mo. in
1861. Accepted commn. as lieut. in Mo. militia. Unit was
disbanded six months later when pro-Southern Gov. Jackson
was forced to leave the State by pro-Union elements. Established residence at Maryville, Mo., where he practiced
law and engaged in loan and real estate bus. Opposed
adoption of revised const. of 1865 because of its restrictive provisions on voting and office-holding by former
Southern sympathizers. Established a newspaper, the
Nodaway Democrat, in 1869. Delegate to Dem. natl. conv. in
1872 and 1876. Mbr. of Mo. House, 1877-1888 and 1883-1884.
El. Lieut. Gov. as Dem. in 1884. Succeeded to office of
Gov. in Dec., 1887, following death of Gov. John S.
Marmaduke and completed Marmaduke's term. Retired to farm-
ing and law practice after tenure as Gov. D. by suicide
Sept. 30, 1891, at his home in Nodaway Co. after having
suffered a disabling rupture of blood vessel in brain.

FRANCIS, DAVID ROWLAND (1889-1893). b. Oct. 1, 1850
at Richmond, Ky. s. of John B. and Eliza Caldwell
(Rowland) F. Father was descendant of an early Ky. settler.
Mother, who was of Scotch ancestry, was a native of Va.
Attd. Richmond Acad. In 1866 family moved to St. Louis,
Mo., where he enrolled at Washington Univ., from which he
was grad. in 1870. Worked as clerk in wholesale grocery
and commn. bus., and eventually acquired a part interest
in the firm. In 1877 established his own commn. bus. in
wholesale grocery field. In 1884 in cooperation with a
brother founded a grain export company, of which he became
pres. Bus. prospered and he extended his interests into
the fields of banking, ins. and transp. El. mayor of St.
Louis in 1885. Nom. and el. Gov. as a Dem. in 1888. As
Gov., gave strong support to bldg. program at the Univ. of
Mo. After tenure as Gov. resumed bus. activities for a
time. Apptd. U.S. Sect. of Interior by Pres. Cleveland in
1896, serving until 1897. Had a major role in org. of La.
Purchase Intl. Expo. at St. Louis from 1901 onward, serving
as its pres. in 1904. Apptd. to post of U.S. Ambassador
to Russia by Pres. Wilson in 1916, serving until the
Communists took control there. Pres. of Bd. of Curators of

the Univ. of Mo.; mbr., Mo. Historical Soc. Dir., St. Louis
Art Museum. Hon. degrees from four colleges and universi-
ties. m. in 1876 to Jennie Perry, of St. Louis. Six s.
D. Jan. 15, 1927.

STONE, WILLIAM JOEL (1893-1897). b. May 7, 1848 near
Richmond, Ky. s. of Wm. and Mildred (Phelps) S. Mother
died when he was four years old and father re-married.
Attd. local schools. Moved to Columbia, Mo. when he was 15
years old during course of Civil War. Entered the Univ. of
Mo., from which he was grad. in 1867. Studied law in
office of a brother-in-law and was admitted to bar in 1869.
Practiced law for a short time at Bedford, Ind., then returned to Columbia, where he served as city atty. in 1870.
Moved to Nevada, Mo., where he continued to practice law.
Pros. atty. of Vernon Co., 1873-1874. Pres. elector on
Dem. ticket in 1876 pres. election. El. to U.S. House as
a Dem. in 1884, continuing to serve therein for three succeeding terms. Did not seek fifth term in 1892, but was
nom. and el. Gov. as a Dem. in that year. After tenure as
Gov. resumed law practice in St. Louis. Mbr. of Dem. natl.
commt., 1896-1904, serving as vice-ch., 1900-1904. El. to
U.S. Senate in 1903 and continued to serve therein until
death. In Senate, as ch. of Commt. on Foreign Relations,
supported Bryan arb. treaties; opposed arming of U.S. merchant vessels prior to entry of U.S. into World War I; and
opposed U.S. declaration of war against Germany in 1917.
Supported U.S. war effort thereafter, however. m. in 1874
to Sarah Louise Winston, of Nevada, Mo. One s.; two d.
D. April 14, 1918. Bur. in Deepwood Cem., Nevada, Mo.

STEPHENS, LAWRENCE VEST ("LON") (1897-1901). b. Dec.
21, 1858 at Boonville, Mo. s. of Joseph Lafayette and
Martha (Gibson) S. Father was a lawyer and banker. Attd.
local pub. schools; Cooper Inst., for three years; Kemper
Mil. School, in Boonville; and Washington and Lee Coll.,
Lexington, Va., for one year. Learned printer's trade and
telegraphy while attending school. Employed on ed. staff
of Boonville Advertiser; as a telegraph operator in the
Western Union's Boonville office; and as a bookkeeper, then
as cashier, of his father's bank in Boonville. Eventually
became the owner of the Advertiser and vice pres. and dir.
of the Cent. Natl. Bank at Boonville. In 1881 was apptd.
to fill a vacancy in the office of Mo. State Treas., and
continued in that office by el. in 1884. Became receiver
of First Natl. Bank in St. Louis in 1887, which he soon put
on a sound basis. Served as State Treas. again, 1889-1897.
Nom. and el. Gov. as a Dem. in 1896, having also the

endorsement of the Pop. party. During admin., Soldiers
Homes for Civil War veterans were established. After ten-
ure as Gov. continued to be active in Dem. party affairs.
Involved in promotion of pub. enterprises, charities and
educl. affairs. Mbr., Masons (K.T.). Hon. degree from the
Univ. of Mo. m. in 1880 to Margaret Nelson. D. at St.
Louis, Jan. 10, 1923. Bur. in Walnut Grove Cem., Boonville.

DOCKERY, ALEXANDER MONROE (1901-1905). b. Feb. 11,
1845 near Gallatin, Mo. s. of Willis E. and Sarah Ellen
(McHaney) D. Father was a Methodist minister. Attd. local
pub. schools and Macon Acad., Macon, Mo. Began study of
med. in office of a doctor at Keytesville, and continued
studies at St. Louis Med. Coll. Received M.D. degree in
1865 and began practice at Linneus, Mo. Also attd. lectures at Bellevue Hosp., in New York City and at Jefferson
Med. Coll., in Philadelphia, 1865-1866. In 1866 established practice at Chillicothe, Mo. and soon had a large clientele. Pres. of school bd. at Chillicothe, 1870-1872. Co.
physician of Livingston Co. for seven years. In 1874 moved
to Gallatin, Mo. Assisted in forming a bank there and
served as its cashier for eight years. Pres. of school bd.
at Gallatin, 1906-1912. Mbr., Gallatin city council, 1878-
1881, and mayor, 1881-1883. Became involved in local Dem.
party org. in the area. Ch. of Dem. state commt., 1886,
1901. El. to U.S. House in 1882, continuing to serve
therein for seven terms. As mbr. of U.S. House served as
ch. of commn. that established a new accounting system for
U.S. Treas. Was not a cand. for reel. to House seat in
1898. Nom. and el. Gov. as a Dem. in 1900. As Gov., liquidated state debt and reduced taxes. Apptd. as Third Asst.
U.S. Postmaster Gen. in 1913. Mbr., Masons; I.O.O.F.; professional med. orgs. Hon. degree from the Univ. of Mo.
m. in 1869 to Mary E. Bird, of Chillicothe, Mo. Eight
children, none of whom survived to adulthood. D. Dec. 26,
1926, at Gallatin. Bur. in Edgewood Cem., Chillicothe.

FOLK, JOSEPH WINGATE (1905-1909). b. Oct. 28, 1869 at
Brownsville, Tenn. s. of Henry Bate and Martha Cornelia
(Estes) F. Father was a lawyer and a judge. Mother was a
mbr. of distinguished Va. family. Attd. pub. and pvt.
schools in Brownsville, and Vanderbilt Univ., from which he
received a law degree in 1890. Admitted to bar and began
practice in Brownsville with father. In 1893 moved to St.
Louis, Mo., where he practiced law as partner of an uncle,
Judge Estes. Founded Jefferson Club in St. Louis, serving
as its pres., 1898-1899. In 1900 served successfully as
mediator to bring to an end a strike by railroad employees.

El. prosecutor for St. Louis in 1900, serving for four
years. Successfully prosecuted on corruption charges a
number of local politicians, some of whom had assisted in
electing him to office. Nom. and el. Gov. as a Dem. in
1904, being the only mbr. of his party to win office that
year in the state-wide elections. As Gov., insisted on
strict enforcement of every law on the statute books, a
practice that came to be known as the "Missouri Idea", and
led to his being called "Holy Joe" by his political opponents. Had support of liberal reform element, but lost
contest for U.S. Senate seat in 1908. Resumed law practice
in St. Louis. Placed in nom. for Pres. of U.S. at Dem.
natl. conv. in 1912, but withdrew name in favor of House
Speaker Champ Clark. Pres. of Lincoln Memorial Farm Assoc.,
1909-1916. Apptd. by Pres. Wilson solicitor for U.S. State
Dept. in 1913, and as counsel for the Interstate Commerce
Commn. in 1914. Dem. nominee for U.S. Senate seat in 1918,
but was defeated in gen. election. Resumed law practice in
Washington, D.C. and at St. Louis. Served as counsel in
U.S. for govts. of Egypt and Peru. Hon. degrees from six
colleges and universities. Mbr., Amer. Soc. of Intl. Law;
Natl. Press Assoc.; S.A.R.; Masons; K.P.; various profes-
sional legal orgs. and social clubs. m. to Gertrude Glass,
of Brownsville, Tenn. No children. D. May 28, 1923, in
Washington, D.C.

HADLEY, HERBERT SPENCER (1909-1913). b. Feb. 20, 1872
at Olathe, Kans. s. of Major John Milton and Harriet
(Beach) H. Descendant of ancestor who emigrated from
Ireland to Pa. in 1712. Father was active in local politics. Attd. local pub. schools and the Univ. of Kans.,
from which he received a law degree in 1894. Also attd.
Northwestern Univ. Law School. Admitted to bar and began
practice in Kansas City, Mo. in 1894. First asst. city
counsel in Kansas City, 1898-1901. Pros. atty. of Jackson
Co., Mo., 1901-1903. Defeated for reel. in 1902. El. Atty.
Gen. of Mo. in 1904. Became leader in movement for reform
and elimination of graft in state govt., with support of
Gov. Folk. Prosecuted a number of important anti-trust
cases. Nom. and el. Gov. as a Rep. in 1908, becoming first
Rep. to be el. to the office since Reconstruction era. Was
one of seven Rep. Govs. to urge former Pres. Theodore
Roosevelt to become cand. for Rep. nom. for Pres. of U.S.
in 1912. Served as delegate at the Rep. natl. conv. that
year and was mentioned as possible compromise cand. for nom.
for Pres. when contest between Roosevelt and Taft forces
intensified and eventually resulted in bolt of the conv. by
Prog. wing of the party. Served as spec. counsel for

various Western railroad companies, 1913-1916. Prof. of
law at Univ. of Colo., 1917-1923, and counsel for Colo. R.R.
Commn., 1919-1921. Apptd. Chancellor of Washington Univ.,
at St. Louis, in 1923. Hon. degrees from four colleges and
universities. Helped org. Young Rep. Assoc. of Mo., the
Knife and Fork Club, of Kansas City, and the Natl. Assoc.
of Attys. Gen. Author of The Standard Oil Trust, What the
Railroads Owe the People, and Rome and the World Today. m.
in 1901 to Agnes Lee. One d.; two s. D. at St. Louis,
Dec. 1, 1927.

MAJOR, ELLIOTT WOOLFOLK (1913-1917). b. Oct. 20, 1864
in Lincoln Co., Mo. s. of James Reed and Sarah T.
(Woolfolk) M. Attd. local pub. schools and Western Sem.,
at Ashley, Mo. Studied law in office of Champ Clark, later
U.S. House Speaker, at Bowling Green, Mo. Admitted to bar
in 1885 and began practice in Bowling Green. Mbr., Mo.
Senate, 1897-1899. Mbr. of commn. on revision of state
statutes, 1899. Nom. and el. Atty. Gen. of Mo. in 1908,
serving until 1912. Nom. and el. Gov. as a Dem. in 1912.
Successfully advocated reforms in state ins. laws; began
improvements in state road system. Placed in nom. for Vice
Pres. of U.S. at Dem. natl. conv. in 1916 but was not chosen. Mbr., Masons; professional legal orgs. and various
social clubs. Methodist. m. in 1887 to Elizabeth Myers,
of Bowling Green. Two d.; one s. D. July 9, 1949.

GARDNER, FREDERICK DOZIER (1917-1921). b. Nov. 6,
1869 at Hickman, Ky. s. of Wm. Henry and Mary Ella
(Dozier) G. Mother was a native of Pa. Father, who was
engaged in a mfg. enterprise, had served as a soldier in
the Confed. Army and had held local pub. office. Attd. pub.
schools in Ky. and Tenn. Moved to St. Louis, Mo. at age 17
and was employed in a funeral supplies mfg. firm. Became
bookkeeper of firm, and acquired stock in it. Became
firm's sect. in 1893 and acquired control of it by 1900,
becoming its pres. Established branch of company at
Memphis, Tenn. in 1898. Also engaged in stock breeding in
Mo., lumbering bus. in Ark., and in banking. Mbr. of St.
Louis bd. of freeholders in 1913 and assisted in writing of
new city charter. Mbr. of commn. of bus. men in 1913 that
went abroad to study European farm loan methods, with resulting recommendation to set up state farm loan bank system. Cong., however, chose to establish a natl. system of
such banks in 1915. Nom. and el. Gov. as a Dem. in 1916 in
close election. As Gov., expanded state road system; reformed state financial structure; advocated adoption of
19th (Women's Suffrage) Amdt. to U.S. Const. Gave effective

support to U.S. war éffort during World War I. Delegate to
several Dem. natl. convs. Mbr., Masons; Elks; K.P.; various social and bus. clubs. m. in 1894 to Jeannette Vosburg,
of St. Louis. Two s.; one d. D. at St. Louis, Dec. 18,
1933.

HYDE, ARTHUR MASTICK (1921-1925). b. July 12, 1877 at
Princeton, Mo. s. of Ira Barnes and Caroline Emily
(Mastick) H. Father, who was a native of N.Y., was a law-
yer and had served as a mbr. of U.S. House from Mo. Attd.
local pub. schools; Oberlin Acad., in Oberlin, Ohio; the
Univ. of Mich., from which he was grad. in 1899; and the
Univ. of Iowa, from which he received a law degree in 1900.
Began practice with father at Princeton. Capt. in Mo. Natl.
Guard, 1904-1905. In 1915 moved to Trenton, Mo., where he
continued practice of law. Also engaged in banking and investment enterprises, ins. bus., farming, lumbering, and
was a Buick car dealer for a multi-county area. Became active in politics early in career, serving on county and
dist. Rep. commts. Mayor of Princeton for two terms. Supported former Pres. Theodore Roosevelt's candidacy for Pres.
of U.S. in 1912, and was defeated as Prog. party cand. for
Atty. Gen. of Mo. in 1912. Returned to Rep. party in 1916.
Nom. and el. Gov. as a Rep. in 1920. As Gov., promoted pub.
educl. improvements; legislation providing more technical
information for farmers; improvements in state eleemosynary
and penal systems; expansion of state highway program. After tenure as Gov. became pres. of Sentinel Life Ins. Co.,
1927-1928. Apptd. U.S. Sect. of Agri. by Pres. Hoover in
1929. Served on Fed. Farm Bd.; was organizer and ch. of
Fed. Drought Relief Commt., which formulated a program of
pub. works and unemployment relief. Became leading spokesman of Hoover admin. on farm problems. Returned to Kansas
City, Mo. in 1933, where he practiced law and engaged in
bus. Devoted attention mainly to farming interests after
1934. Trustee, Mo. Wesleyan Coll. and of So. Methodist
Univ. Mbr., S.A.R.; Masons; Elks; I.O.O.F.; Delta Upsilon;
Rotary; various bus. and professional legal orgs. Active
in Methodist church affairs. Hon. degrees from four colleges and universities. m. in 1904 to Hortense Cullers, of
Trenton, Mo. One d. D. in New York City, Oct. 17, 1947.

BAKER, SAM(UEL) AARON (1925-1929). b. Nov. 7, 1874 at
Patterson, Wayne Co., Mo. s. of Samuel A. and Mary Amanda
(McGhee) B. Attd. village schools at Mill Springs, Mo.
Became rural school teacher at age 18. Worked way through
college by teaching, and as a railroad section hand and
mill laborer. Instructor at Wayne Co. Inst. Attd. South-

east Mo. State Teachers Coll., from which he received a degree in 1897. Also received an A.B. degree from Mo. Wesleyan Coll. Studied as grad. student at Univ. of Mo. Supt. of schools at Piedmont, Mo. for two years; h.s. principal at Jefferson City, Mo., in 1899, and at Joplin, Mo., 1905. Supt. of schools at Richmond, Mo., 1910, and at Jefferson City, 1913. El. State Supt. of Schools in 1918. Nom. and el. Gov. as a Rep. in 1924. As Gov., stressed economy in govt.; installed improved budget system; revised state tax system; strengthened removal powers of Gov.; sponsored revision of state code; promoted bond issue for expanded highway system. Hon. degree from Mo. Wesleyan Coll. Mbr., Masons; K.P.; various professional educl. orgs. Presbyterian. m. in 1904 to Nell R. Tuckley, of Jefferson City. One d. D. Sept. 16, 1933.

CAULFIELD, HENRY STEWART (1929-1933). b. Dec. 9, 1873 at St. Louis, Mo. s. of John and Virilda (Milburn) C. Attd. St. Charles Coll. and Washington Univ., from which he received a law degree in 1895. Admitted to bar and began practice in St. Louis. Defeated as Rep. cand. for U.S. House in 1904, but was nom. and el. to that office in 1906. Did not seek second term in 1908. Excise commnr. at St. Louis, 1909-1910. Judge of St. Louis Dist. Ct. of Appeals, 1910-1912. Mbr. of St. Louis Pub. Library Bd., 1918-1921, and counsel for St. Louis city council, 1921-1922. Mbr. and ch. of bd., 1925-1926, to study merger of city and county govts. in St. Louis city and co. Nom. and el. Gov. as a Rep. in 1928. Confronted by serious unemployment and bus. recession problems during latter part of admin., which he sought to alleviate by economies in govt. and relief measures. Mo. State Highway Patrol system established. Mbr. of Mo. advisory bd. to Fed. P.W.A., 1933-1934. Bd. of Elections Commnr. in St. Louis, 1932-1938. Defeated as Rep. nominee for U.S. Senate seat in 1938. Dir. of Pub. Welfare in St. Louis, 1941-1949. Mbr. of Commn. on Reorg. of State Govt., 1943. Mbr., various professional legal orgs. m. in 1902 to Fannie Alice Delano. Three d.; one s. D. at St. Louis, May 11, 1966.

PARK, GUY BRASFIELD (1933-1937). b. June 10, 1872 at Platte City, Mo. s. of Thomas Woodson and Margaret E. (Baxter) P. Attd. Gaylord Inst. and the Univ. of Mo., from which he was grad. with a law degree in 1896. Admitted to bar and began practice in Platte City. Served as city atty. and as Platte Co. pros. atty. Mbr. of state constl. conv. in 1922. In 1923 became cir. ct. judge of his dist., continuing in that capacity until 1933. In 1932 was named by

the Dem. state commt. as replacement cand. for Gov. after
the nominee chosen in the primary died during course of
campaign. El. to the office. During admin., cooperated
with natl. govt. in enactment of measures to relieve economic distress arising from depression conditions; an old
age pension law was adopted; state licensing law for liquor
dealers enacted following end of natl. prohibition. Mbr.
of state constl. conv. of 1943-1944. Mbr., Masons; (K.T.;
Shriner); Beta Theta Pi; professional legal orgs.
Christian (Disciples) church. m. in 1909 to Eleanora
Gabbert. One d. D. Oct. 1, 1946.

STARK, LLOYD CROW (1937-1941). b. Nov. 23, 1886 at
Louisiana, Mo. s. of Clarence McDowell and Hilly (Crow) S.
Father was engaged in family's extensive fruit tree nursery
enterprise founded in 1816, which pioneered in devel. of
improved strains of various fruit trees and other horticultural products. Attd. local pub. schools and U.S. Naval
Acad. at Annapolis, from which he was grad. in 1908.
Served as U.S. naval officer, 1904-1912, being assigned to
duty in Turkish and So. Amer. waters. Was in submarine
service at time he left Navy in 1912. Joined in mgmt. of
family fruit nursery enterprise, becoming vice pres. and ch.
of bd., 1934-1937. Served as officer with A.E.F. in France
during World War I. Pres. of Ill.-Mo. Bridge Co. that
constr. highway toll bridge across Miss. River at
Louisiana, Mo., 1926-1939. Dir. of Assoc. Industries of
Mo., 1927. Dir. of Fed. Regional Agri. Credit Corp., 1931-
1932. Vice pres. and dir. of Mo. CC, 1925-1929. Nom. and
el. Gov. as a Dem. in 1936. Gave strong support to Pres.
F. D. Roosevelt's domestic reform programs as Gov. Ch. of
Natl. Govs.' Conf. and pres. of Council of State Govts.,
1939. Defeated as cand. for Dem. nom. for U.S. Senate seat
against incumbent Sen. Harry S. Truman in 1940. Mbr.,
S.A.R.; Amer. Legion; V.F.W.; 40 and 8; Naval Inst.; Mo.
Historical Soc.; Saddle Horse Breeders Assoc.; Garden Clubs
of America; Rotary; various bus. and social clubs.
Episcopalian. m. in 1908 to Margaret Pearson Stickney, of
Baltimore, Md., who died in 1930. Two s. m. in 1931 to
Katherine Larraine Perkins, of St. Louis, Mo. Two d. D.
Sept. 17, 1972.

DONNELL, FORREST C. (1941-1945). b. Aug. 20, 1884 at
Quitman, Mo. s. of John Cary and Barbara Lee (Waggoner) D.
Attd. local pub. schools and the Univ. of Mo., from which
he received an A.B. degree in 1904 and a law degree in 1907.
Admitted to bar and began practice in St. Louis in office
of Selden P. Spencer, later a U.S. Sen. from Mo. Also

became involved as mbr. of bds. of dir. of numerous bus.
enterprises in fields of mfg., lumber, ins., and real estate. City atty. of Webster Groves, Mo. Pres. of Young
Reps. of Mo. in 1916. Ch. of bd. of Mo. School for the
Blind, 1931-1934. Involved in a number of community activities, including the YMCA, the World Ct. Commt., and Mo.
Sunday School Council of Religious Educ. Trustee of Mo.
Historical Soc. Nom. and el. Gov. as a Rep. in 1940. Outcome of election was close and the Gen. Assembly, controlled by opposition party, sought to delay official proclamation of result preparatory to initiating a recount, but was
prevented from doing so by ct. ruling. As Gov., supported
U.S. war effort by appropriate measures during World War II.
A revised const. for the State was adopted in 1945. Nom.
and el. to U.S. Senate in 1944, but was defeated for second
term in 1950. Delegate to Rep. natl. conv. in 1948. Retired to law practice and bus. affairs after tenure in Senate. Mbr., Masons; Phi Beta Kappa; Phi Delta Phi; various
professional legal orgs. and social clubs. Very active in
Methodist church affairs. Trustee, Jefferson Expansion
Memorial Assoc. m. in 1913 to Hilda Hays. One s.; one d.
D. March 3, 1980, at Manchester, Mo.

DONNELLY, PHIL(IP) MATTHEW (1945-1949; 1953-1957). b.
March 6, 1891 at Lebanon, Mo. s. of Philip and Maggie
(Halleran) D. Father was a merchant. Attd. local pub.
schools and St. Louis Univ., from which he received a law
degree in 1913. Admitted to bar and began practice at
Lebanon. Served as city atty. for Lebanon for several terms
and one term as Laclede Co. pros. atty. Mbr. of Mo. House,
1923-1925, and of Mo. Senate, 1925-1945. Was Pres. pro tem
of the latter body for two terms, and Dem. floor leader for
two other terms. Ch. of state statute revision commn.,
1929 and 1939. Nom. and el. Gov. as a Dem. in 1944. Gave
nominating speech for Pres. Truman at Dem. natl. conv. in
1948. Resumed practice of law after first term as Gov.
ended. Nom. and el. Gov. again in 1952, becoming the first
Gov. of Mo. to be el. for more than one term since 1828.
During admin., established a unified dept. of revenue;
raised level of compensation of state employees; effected
reorg. of pub. school system; revised state tax structure;
opposed unionization of city police forces; signed legislation prohibiting strikes by pub. utility employees. Mbr.,
Masons; I.O.O.F.; professional legal orgs. Hon. degrees
from six colleges and universities. Christian (Disciples)
church. m. in 1915 to Juanita McFadden, of Maplewood, Mo.
One s. D. at Lebanon, Sept. 12, 1961.

SMITH, FORREST (1949-1953). b. Feb. 14, 1886 at
Richmond, Mo. s. of James Patrick and Lillie Madora (Hill)
S. Father was a farmer and stockman. Attd. local pub.
schools; Woodson Inst., at Richmond, Mo.; and Westminster
Coll., Fulton, Mo. Taught school for one year, then served
as principal of Richmond grade school system for two years.
Deputy assessor of Ray Co., 1908-1912, and Ray Co. clerk,
1915-1923. Apptd. to State Tax Commn. by Gov. Baker in
1925, serving for seven years. El. Mo. State Aud. Gen. in
1932, continuing in that office until 1948. Nom. and el.
Gov. as a Dem. in 1948. As Gov., introduced new tax collection and assessment system, and a plan for continual revision of state statutes. Active in community affairs,
having a leading role in bldg. of Memorial Hosp. in
Jefferson City. Mbr. of exec. bd. of Boy Scouts of Amer.
Mbr., Natl. Assoc. of State Auditors, Comptrollers and
Treasurers, and of Natl. Assoc. of Tax Officials, serving
as pres. of latter body in 1939. Mbr., Masons; De Molay;
Elks; K.P. Hon. degree from Westminster Coll. Methodist.
m. in 1915 to Mildred Williams, of Richmond, Mo. Two d.
D. May 8, 1962, at Gulfport, Miss.

DONNELLY, PHIL(IP) MATTHEW (1953-1957). See above,
1945-1949.

BLAIR, JAMES THOMAS, Jr. (1957-1961). b. March 15,
1902 at Maysville, Mo. s. of James Thomas and Grace Emma
(Ray) B. Descendant of Scotch ancestor who emigrated to
Amer. prior to 1741. Father was a state official and cir.
ct. judge. Attd. pub. schools at Jefferson City, Mo.;
Staunton Mil. Acad.; Southwest Mo. State Teachers' Coll.,
1918-1920; the Univ. of Mo., 1920-1921; and Cumberland
Univ., from which he received a law degree in 1924. Admitted to bar and began practice in Jefferson City, specializing in transp. and ins. matters. Dir. of Bender Transport
Co. City atty. of Jefferson City, 1925-1928. Mbr. of Mo.
House, 1929-1931, serving as Dem. floor leader. Mbr. of
Jefferson City school bd., 1933-1942, and of local, county
and dist. Dem. commts., 1932-1942. Delegate to Dem. natl.
conv. in 1936. Involved in ins. and fisheries propagation
bus. enterprises. Served with U.S. Army in European theater, 1942-1945, holding rank of col. at end of service.
Mayor of Jefferson City, 1947-1949. El. Lieut. Gov. in
1948 and again in 1952. Nom. and el. Gov. as a Dem. in
1956. As Gov., launched improved highway constr. program
as part of U.S. Interstate Highway system; introduced retirement system for state employees; established water pol-
lution controls; increased state aid for pub. schools; gave

increased funding for agri. research; promoted capital improvement program in state institutions of higher educ.
Mbr., Amer. Legion; AMVETS; V.F.W.; 40 and 8; S.A.R.; Elks;
Masons; Legion of Honor; Legion of Merit; Sigma Chi; various professional legal orgs. and social clubs. m. in 1926
to Emilie Chorn, of Kansas City. One s.; one d. D. July
12, 1962.

DALTON, JOHN MONTGOMERY (1961-1965). b. Nov. 9, 1900
in Vernon Co., Mo. s. of Fred Andrew and Ida (Poage) D.
Descendant of ancestor who emigrated from England to Mo. in
1837. Father was a businessman. Attd. pub. schools in
Vernon Co. and at Columbia, Mo., and the Univ. of Mo., from
which he received a law degree in 1922. Admitted to bar in
1923 and began practice at Kennett, Mo. Also engaged in
cotton planting there on 1,250 acre farm. City counsel of
Kennett, 1944-1953. Legislative counsel for Mo. Rural
Electrification Coop. Assoc., 1951-1952. El. Atty. Gen. of
Mo. in 1952 and again in 1956. Nom. and el. Gov. as a Dem.
in 1960. As Gov., initiated withholding system for state
income taxes; set up commn. to study water resources; expanded pub. jr. college system; inaugurated stricter controls over granting of drivers' licenses; introduced
changes in work system for prisoners; strengthened school
health programs; and favored enactment of legislation restricting distribution of narcotics and obscene literature.
Pres. of Bd. of Visitors of the Univ. of Mo., 1949-1953.
Trustee of Presbyterian Children's Home at Farmington, Mo.
Mbr., Bd. of Curators of Stephens Coll. Trustee,
Westminster Coll., and of School of the Ozarks. Hon. degrees from Drury Coll. and Wm. Jewell Coll. Mbr., profes-
sional legal orgs., serving as pres. of Natl. Assoc. of
Attys. Gen. in 1968. Mbr., Masons; Phi Gamma Delta;
Omicron Delta Kappa; Phi Delta Phi. Presbyterian. m. in
1925 to Geraldine Hall, of Cardwell, Mo. One s.; one d.
D. July 7, 1972.

HEARNES, WARREN E. (1965-1973). b. July 24, 1923 at
Charleston, Mo. s. of Earle B. and Edna Mae (Eastman) H.
Attd. local pub. schools; U.S. Mil. Acad. at West Point,
from which he was grad. in 1946; and the Univ. of Mo., from
which he received an A.B. and a law degree in 1952. Served
as lieut. in anti-aircraft unit in U.S. Army, 1946-1949.
El. to Mo. House in 1950, and began law practice at East
Prairie, Mo. in 1952. Continued to serve in Mo. House un-
til 1961, acting as Dem. floor leader from 1957 onward.
El. Mo. Sect. of State in 1960, and in 1964 was nom. and el.
Gov. as a Dem. Reel. in 1968, becoming the first Gov. of

Mo. to be el. to a second successive term after a constl.
amdt. was approved by the voters in 1966 permitting a second successive term. Vice ch., Midwestern Govs.' Conf.,
1969, and mbr. of exec. bd., Natl. Govs.' Conf. Mbr., U.S.
Advisory Commt. on Inter-govtl. Relations. Investigation
was launched by U.S. Dept. of Justice into his handling of
financial affairs after he left office, but no charges were
brought. State's system of higher educ. was broadened during admin. Defeated for Dem. nom. for U.S. Senate seat in
1976, finishing second in primary election; but was made
the nominee for the office by Dem. state commt. when his
successful opponent was killed in an air crash shortly after the primary. Was defeated in the gen. election for the
office. Defeated as Dem. nominee for Aud. Gen. of Mo. in
1978. Mbr., Masons (Shriners); Lions; Elks; Eagles; Amer.
Legion; V.F.W.; Phi Delta Theta; professional legal orgs.
Baptist. m. in 1948 to Betty Sue Cooper. Three d.

BOND, CHRISTOPHER S. ("KIT"). (1973-1977). b. March
6, 1939 at St. Louis, Mo. s. of Arthur D. and Elizabeth
(Green) B. Father, who was a businessman, was an outstanding athlete while attending the Univ. of Mo., and was a
Rhodes Scholar. Attd. local schools; Princeton Univ., from
which he was grad. cum laude in 1960; and the Univ. of Va.,
from which he received a law degree in 1963. Served as law
clerk in the Fifth U.S. Cir. Ct. of Appeals at Atlanta, Ga.,
1963-1964. Atty. for Covington and Burlington R.R.,
Washington, D.C., 1965-1967. Began law practice at Mexico,
Mo. in 1967. Asst. Atty. Gen., 1969. Defeated as Rep.
cand. for U.S. House, 1968. Mo. Aud. Gen., 1970-1973. Nom.
and el. Gov. as a Rep. in 1972. Ch. of Rep. Govs.' Assoc.,
1975-1976. Mbr., exec. commt., Natl. Govs.' Assoc.; vice
ch., Midwestern Govs.' Conf.; ch. of Energy Commt., So.
Govs.' Conf. Rep. nominee for second term as Gov. in 1976,
but was defeated by close vote in gen. election. Won Rep.
nom. for Gov. again in 1980. Presbyterian. Mbr., Omicron
Delta Kappa; Optimists; various professional legal orgs.
and social clubs. Hon. degrees from Wm. Jewell, Westminster, and Drury Colleges. m. in 1967 to Carolyn Ann Reid.

TOOLE, JOSEPH KEMP (1889-1893; 1901-1908). b. May 12, 1851 at Savannah, Mo. s. of Edwin and Lucinda S. (Porter) T. Father was a lawyer and had served as State's atty. for his jud. dist. Attd. pub. schools at St. Joseph, Mo., and Western Mil. Acad. in New Castle, Ky., 1867-1869. Studied law, was admitted to the bar, and moved to Helena, Mont. Terr., in 1871. Began practice of law at Helena with a brother. Dist. atty. for Lewis and Clark Co., 1872-1876. Mbr. of Mont. Terr. legislature in 1879-1881, serving as presiding officer of lower House. Mbr. of Mont. Terr. Council, 1881-1883, serving as its pres. Mbr. of first constl. conv. in Mont. Terr., 1884. El. as Terr. Delegate to Cong. in 1884, continuing in that office until 1889. In Cong., became leading advocate of admission of Mont. Terr. to statehood, an objective achieved in 1889. Delegate to Mont. constl. conv. of 1889. Nom. and el. Gov. of Mont. in 1889 as a Dem. Election result was close, and question of including returns from Silver Bow Co. because of allegations of voting irregularities delayed announcement of official result until jud. determination was made regarding the disputed votes. As Gov., acted on legislation instituting initial org. of state and local govt. Used veto on legislation designed to encourage formation of bus. corps., which aroused antagonism. Resumed law practice for a time after first term. Delegate to Dem. natl. convs. in 1892 and 1904. Nom. and el. Gov. again in 1900, and was reel. for a succeeding term in 1904 with endorsement of Pop. and Labor parties as well as Dem. Resigned office April 1, 1908 during final year of third term because of poor health. m. in 1890 to Lilly Rosecrans, of Washington, D.C. Two s. D. at Helena, Mar. 11, 1929. Bur. in Resurrection Cem. there.

RICKARDS, JOHN EZRA (1893-1897). b. July 23, 1848 in Delaware City, Del. s. of David Townsend and Mary (Wellington) R. Descendant of ancestor who came to Del. in pre-Rev. War period. Attd. local pub. schools and an acad. in Middleton, Del. Worked at various bus. occupations for a time in Del., and in 1870 moved to Colo. Terr. Moved to San Francisco, Calif. in 1878. Engaged for a time in bus. activities in Calif., and later in Colo. In 1882 moved to Butte City, Mont. Terr., where he continued in bus. activities. City alderman in Butte in 1885. Mbr. of Mont. Terr. Council, 1887-1889. Mbr. of Mont. constl. conv. of 1889. El. first Lieut. Gov. of Mont. as Rep. in 1889, although State chose a Dem. as Gov. in that election. As Pres. of Senate, ruled that mbrs. of Senate who were present and abstained from voting in connection with announcement of

election result for Gov. should not be considered absentees
for purpose of determining if a quorum was present. Nom.
and el. Gov. as a Rep. in 1892 in a very close election.
During admin., the laws of the State were codified; an anti-
gambling law was passed; and, when legislature deadlocked
on election of a U.S. Sen., apptd. on a temporary basis the
cand. he favored. Returned to bus. affairs after tenure as
Gov. U.S. census supervisor for Mont. for 1900 census. m.
in 1876 to Lizzie M. Wilson, who died in 1881. Three s. m.
in 1883 to Mrs. Eliza A. Boucher. D. Dec. 26, 1927.

SMITH, ROBERT BURNS (1897-1901). b. Dec. 29, 1854 in
Hickman Co., Ky. s. of Dewitt Clinton and Eliza Booker
(Hughs) S. Attd. pub. schools and acad. at Milburn, Ky.
Taught school in Ky. for two years and for next two years
in Mo., becoming principal of Charleston, Mo., Acad. in final year. Studied law in office in Mayfield, Ky., and was
admitted to bar in 1877. Began practice at Blandville, Ky.,
but in 1881 moved to Charleston, Mo. After practicing law
there for a short time, moved in 1881 to Dillon, Mont.
Terr., where he continued in law practice. Delegate to
first Mont. constl. conv. in 1884. Apptd. U.S. dist. atty.
for Mont. Terr. by Pres. Cleveland in 1885, serving in that
office until 1889. Moved to Helena, Mont., where he became
city atty., 1890-1891. Defeated as cand. of Pop. party for
U.S. House in 1894. Nom. and el. Gov. as a Dem. and Pop.
party cand. in 1896. During admin., opposed sale of pub.
lands to pvt. owners, but favored rental of such lands;
opposed code revision; advocated establishment of a commn.
to regulate railroad rates; favored adoption of an income
tax; creation of area land commn.; and initiated several
state bldg. constr. projects. Supported Pres. McKinley's
policies with respect to Spanish-Amer. War. Retired to law
practice after tenure as Gov. m. in 1878 to Kate Crossland.
One d.; one s. D. Nov. 16, 1908.

TOOLE, JOSEPH KEMP (1901-1908). See above, 1889-1893.

NORRIS, EDWIN LEE (1908-1913). b. Aug. 15, 1865 in
Cumberland Co., Ky. Father was a farmer. Assisted on family farm while also attending local schools until age 18.
Attd. So. Normal Coll. at Bowling Green, Ky. Taught school
in Ky. for a number of years thereafter while also beginning study of law. In 1888 moved to Dillon, Mont. Terr.,
where he continued law study in office of Robert B. Smith,
later a Gov. of Mont. Admitted to bar in 1889 and began
practice in Dillon. Mbr. of school bd. at Dillon and served
for six years as city atty. there. Mbr. of Mont. Senate,

1897-1901, serving as Pres. pro tem in that body in last
term. As such, the powers of the office of Gov. devolved
upon him temporarily for approximately two months in 1900
during the admin. of Gov. Smith. Nom. and el. Lieut. Gov.
in 1904 as a Dem. Succeeded to office of Gov. in April,
1908, when Gov. Toole resigned. Completed Toole's term,
and was nom. and el. to a regular four-year term in 1908.
Resumed law practice thereafter. Mbr. of governing bd. of
State Normal Coll. at Dillon. m. in 1892 to Bettie Jane
Wilkins, of Bowling Green, Ky. D. at Great Falls, Mont.,
April 25, 1924.

STEWART, SAMUEL VERNON (1913-1921). b. Aug. 2, 1872
in Monroe Co., Ohio. s. of John W. and Maria A. (Carle) S.
When son was a youth, family moved to a farm near Waverly,
Kans., where father engaged in farming. Attd. local
schools while assisting on farm. Attd. Kans. Normal, at
Ft. Scott, for one year and Kans. Normal Coll. at Emporia
for two years. Studied law at the Univ. of Kans., graduating in 1898. Began practice in Virginia City, Mont. City
atty. of Virginia City for five years. Co. atty. of
Madison Co., 1905-1909. Ch. of Mont. Dem. state commt.,
1910-1912. Nom. and el. Gov. as a Dem. in 1912, and again
in 1916. Supported U.S. war effort during World War I by
appropriate legislation. Practiced law in Helena after
tenure as Gov. Became a mbr. of Mont. Supreme Ct., serving
from 1933 to 1939. Mbr., Masons; Elks; Eagles; M.W.A. m.
in 1905 to Stella Baker, of Boonville, Mo. Three d. D.
Sept. 15, 1939, at Helena, Mont.

DIXON, JOSEPH MOORE (1921-1925). b. July 31, 1867 at
Snow Camp, Alamance Co., N.C. s. of Hugh W. and Flora G.
(Murchison) D. Descendant of an English Quaker who came to
Pa. with Wm. Penn. Father was engaged in mfg. of cotton
trade machinery. Attd. Sylvan Acad.; Guilford Coll., in
N.C., from which he was grad. in 1889; and Earlham Coll.,
in Richmond, Ind. In 1891 settled at Missoula, Mont.,
where he studied law and was admitted to bar in 1892. Began practice there, becoming quite successful. Asst. pros.
atty. of Missoula Co., 1892-1895, and pros. atty., 1895-
1897. El. to Mont. legislature in 1900. El. to U.S. House
in 1902, and continued in that office for two succeeding
terms. Was not a cand. for fourth term in 1906. El. to
U.S. Senate as a Rep. in 1907. Identified himself with
progressive element of the party during his tenure in Cong.
Delegate to Rep. natl. convs. in 1904 and 1916. Joined in
the Prog. party movement in 1912. Was ch. of that party's
natl. conv. in 1912, and served as natl. campaign mgr. for

Theodore Roosevelt. Was defeated for reel. to the U.S.
Senate as the Prog. party nominee at the end of his first
term. Engaged in newspaper publishing bus. and dairy farming for several years. Nom. and el. Gov. as a Rep. in 1920.
Advocated heavier taxation of bus. corps., which aroused
antagonism of the large mining companies that were powerful
in the State. Secured adoption of one of the first old age
pension systems in the country. Was defeated as the Rep.
nominee for Gov. in 1924. Was also defeated as the Rep.
nominee for a U.S. Senate seat in 1928, losing to Burton K.
Wheeler whom he had defeated for Gov. in 1920. Apptd.
First Asst. Sect. of the Interior in 1929 by Pres. Hoover,
serving until 1933. m. in 1896 to Carrie Worden, of
Missoula, Mont. Four d. D. May 22, 1934. Bur. in
Missoula Cem.

ERICKSON, JOHN EDWARD (1925-1933). b. March 14, 1863
at Stoughton, Dane Co., Wisc. s. of Erick and Olene Alma
E. As youth moved with parents to Eureka, Kans. Attd.
Washburn Coll., from which he was grad. in 1890. Studied
law and was admitted to bar in 1891. In 1893 moved to
Choteau, Teton Co., Mont., where he practiced law. Teton
Co. atty., 1897-1905. Dist. ct. judge, 1905-1915. Returned to law practice at Kalispell, Mont. in 1916. Active in
Dem. party affairs, serving as delegate to Dem. natl. conv.
in 1920 and becoming ch. of Dem. state commt. that year,
serving until 1924. Nom. and el. Gov. as a Dem. in 1924,
defeating incumbent Gov. Dixon, and was reel. in 1928 and
1932, winning in 1932 by narrow margin. As Gov., was involved in imposition of heavier taxation of mining industry;
establishment of state forest preserve system; regulation
of oil production; establishment of guaranteed farm commodity loan system through banks. Resigned office of Gov.
in March, 1933, shortly after beginning of third term, and
was apptd. by his successor to a vacancy in U.S. Senate
seat. Defeated for Dem. nom. for Senate seat in 1934. Returned to law practice at Helena, Mont. Mbr., Masons.
Lutheran. m. in 1898 to Grace Vance, of Des Moines, Iowa.
Two s.; one d. D. May 25, 1946. Bur. in Conrad Memorial
Cem., Kalispell, Mont.

COONEY, FRANK HENRY (1933-1935). b. Dec. 31, 1872 in
Norwood, Ont. s. of John Ward and Mary Ann (O'Callaghan)
C. Descendant of ancestor who emigrated from Ireland to
N.Y. in 1835. Attd. Catholic schools in Annprior, Ont. In
1891 moved to Butte, Mont., where he worked in a grocery
store. In 1894 established a grocery and commn. bus. in
partnership with a brother. Became pres. of the enterprise,

which eventually became one of largest of its kind in Mont.
Also expanded bus. interests into mining and cattle and
sheep ranching in Bitter Root Valley, near Missoula, Mont.
Pub. adminr. of Silver Bow Co., 1898-1900. Nom. and el.
Lieut. Gov. in 1932 as a Dem., and succeeded to office of
Gov. when Gov. Erickson resigned in Mar., 1933, three months
after beginning of his term. Apptd. Erickson to a vacancy
in U.S. Senate immediately after assuming governorship. As
Gov., sponsored water conservation program; established
state liquor control bd. following repeal of 18th Amdt.;
launched investigation into admin. of state ins. laws; cooperated with U.S. natl. admin. in New Deal programs and
policies. Mbr., Elks; K.C.; Eagles. Roman Catholic. m.
in 1899 to Emma May Poindexter, of Dillon, Mont. Five s.;
two d. D. Dec. 15, 1935 at Great Falls, Mont., slightly
more than a year before completion of term of office to
which he had succeeded.

HOLT, W(ILLIAM) ELMER (1935-1937). b. Oct. 14, 1884
at Savannah, Mo. s. of Benj. King and Susan (Brooks) H.
Left home at an early age to become a cattle ranch hand in
Nebr. Attd. Univ. of Nebr., 1899-1902. Moved to Miles
City, Custer Co., Mont., where he engaged in real estate
bus. El. to Mont. House in 1912, and in 1932 was el. to
Mont. Senate. As a Dem., was chosen Pres. pro tem of Senate, and as such, succeeded to office of Gov. following
death of Lieut. Gov. Cooney, who had become Gov. in Mar.,
1933, after resignation of Gov. Erickson. Completed remainder of Erickson's term, which had slightly more than a
year to run. Mbr., Masons; Elks. m. in 1910 to Lora Howe.
One s.; one d. D. March 1, 1945.

AYERS, ROY ELMER (1937-1941). b. Nov. 9, 1882 in
Fergus Co., Mont. Terr. s. of George Washington and Mary
Etta (Sullenger) A. Father was a pioneer rancher in Mont.
Attd. Lewistown, Mont. pub. schools and Valparaiso Univ.,
in Ind., from which he received a law degree in 1903. Admitted to bar and began practice in Lewistown. Also engaged
in ranching. Fergus Co. atty., 1905-1909. Mbr., Mont.
State Bd. of Educ., 1908-1912. Delegate to every Mont. Dem.
party conv. from 1906 to 1940. Delegate to Dem. natl.
convs. in 1920 and 1940. Ch. of Fergus Co. draft bd. during World War I. Dist. judge, 1912-1922. As such, removed
from office the mayor of Butte and sheriff of Silver Bow Co.
in 1914 for failure to control riot which had resulted in
destruction of much property. Mbr. of Mont. Supreme Ct. in
1922, but resigned position after less than a year to return to law practice. Mbr. of U.S. House, 1933-1937. Nom.

and el. Gov. as a Dem. in 1936, becoming the first native-
born citizen of Mont. to hold that office. As Gov.,
achieved balanced budget. Defeated as Dem. nominee for
second term in 1940. Retired to mgmt. of 6,000 acre ranch,
engaging in wheat growing and raising of pure-bred Hereford
cattle. Mbr., Masons; Elks; Eagles; various professional
legal orgs. Collector of Indian relics as a hobby. m. in
1905 to Ellen Simpson, of Lewistown. Two s.; one d. D.
May 23, 1955. Bur. in Lewistown Cem.

FORD, SAM(UEL) CLARENCE (1941-1949). b. Nov. 7, 1882
in Albany, Ky. s. of Wm. and Glenora Elizabeth (Snow) F.
Father was a lumber dealer. Attd. pub. schools at Ivanhoe
and Garden City, Kans., where family resided during his
youth, and the Univ. of Kans., from which he received a law
degree in 1906. Admitted to bar in Kans. and Mont. Began
law practice in Helena, Mont. in 1906. Continued to practice law there during periods when he was not in pub.
office. U.S. dist. atty. for Mont., 1908-1914. Atty. Gen.
of Mont., 1917-1921. El. to Mont. Supreme Ct. in 1928,
serving until 1933. Nom. and el. Gov. as a Rep. in 1940,
defeating incumbent Gov. Ayers, and was reel. in 1944. As
Gov., supported U.S. war effort during World War II; sought
to eliminate unnecessary govtl. expenditures; initiated
study of state admin. reorg. and reforms; opposed efforts
to create Mo. Valley Authority to control water, reclamation and power devel. in Mo. River basin. Ch. of Commt. of
State Govs. of Mo. Valley. Mbr., Mo. Basin Interagency
Commt. Defeated as Rep. nominee for third term in 1948.
Mbr., Masons; Elks; Eagles. Engaged in gardening as hobby.
Baptist. m. in 1910 to Mary Leslie Shobe, of Helena. Four
d. D. Nov. 25, 1961.

BONNER, JOHN WOODROW (1949-1953). b. July 16, 1902 at
Butte, Mont. s. of Patrick J. and Kathleen (Kelly) B.
Father was a pioneer Mont. rancher. Attd. pub. schools at
Butte. Became a teacher and athletic dir. there in pub.
schools. Attd. Mont. State Univ., from which he received
an A.B. and a law degree in 1938. Admitted to bar and began practice at Butte, moving to Helena the following year
where he continued to practice law. Counsel for Mont.
Highway Commn., 1929-1936. Atty. and sect. of Mont. R.R.
Commn., Pub. Service Commn., and Trade Commn., 1936-1940.
Atty. Gen. of Mont., 1940-1942. As such, worked to protect
water rights of State and procured substantial inheritance
tax settlement for the State from large Daly estate. Served in U.S. Army during World War II as major in judge advocate gen. branch of service, 1942-1945. Assigned to war

crimes investigations for First U.S. Army at end of war.
Recipient of Bronze Star, Legion of Merit, and Croix de
guerre. Returned to law practice in Helena. Nom. and el.
Gov. as a Dem. in 1948, defeating incumbent Gov. Ford. As
Gov., sponsored extensive pub. works program. Defeated as
Dem. nominee for succeeding term in 1952. Mbr., V.F.W.;
Amer. Legion; Elks; Moose; Eagles; N.R.O.A.; Sigma Phi
Epsilon; Phi Delta Phi. Roman Catholic. Author of Handbook
on Eminent Domain, in 1933. m. in 1929 to Josephine Martin,
of Butte. Four d.; one s.

ARONSON, J(OHN) HUGO (1953-1961). b. Sept. 1, 1891 in
Gallstad, Sweden. s. of Aaron Johannsen and Rike (Ryeing)
A. Received educ. in Sweden. At age 20 emigrated to Amer.,
entering U.S. at Boston, Mass. Travelled widely through
U.S. working at various jobs. Settled in Columbus, Mont.,
where he filed a homestead claim. Worked in oil fields.
Served with A.E.F. in France during World War I. Returned
to Mont., where he engaged in ranching and various bus.
activities, particularly oil production. Became pres. of
bank in Shelby, Mont. His industry and the variety of
activities he engaged in earned for him the sobriquet, the
"Galloping Swede". City alderman at Cut Bank, Mont. for
four years. Mbr. of Mont. House, 1939-1943, and of Mont.
Senate, 1945-1952. Advocate of more bus. methods in govt.
Nom. and el. Gov. as a Rep. in 1952, defeating incumbent
Gov. Bonner, and was reel. in 1956. As Gov., supported
regional control of devel. of natural resources. Mbr.,
Columbia Basin Interagency Committee, 1953. Mbr., Amer.
Legion; V.F.W.; Lions; Elks; Masons (Shriner); Moose; var-
ious bus. clubs and assoc. Protestant. m. in 1919 while
in France to a French bride, Mathilde Langange, of Paris,
who died in 1936. m. in 1944 to Rose McClure, of Glacier
Co., Mont. One d. D. Feb. 25, 1978.

NUTTER, DONALD GRANT (1961-1962). b. Nov. 28, 1915 at
Lambert, Mont. s. of C. E. and Ann Grant (Wood) N. Attd.
N.D. State School of Sci., at Wahpeton, 1933-1935. Later
attd. Mont. State Univ., from which he received a law degree in 1954. Deputy ct. clerk, Richland Co., Mont., 1937-
1938, and under-sheriff of Richland Co., 1938-1939. Mbr.
of Mont. Natl. Guard, 1933-1935, and in 1942-1945 served
as capt. in U.S. Air Force during World War II. Recipient
of D.F.C. with clusters, Air Medal, and C.B.I. Employed by
a tractor and equipment firm at Sidney, Mont., 1938-1942,
and 1945-1957. Became owner and operator of own implement
bus. at Sidney, 1947-1950. Admitted to Mont. bar in 1954
after studying law at Mont. State Univ., and practiced law

at Sidney thereafter: Mbr. of Mont. Senate, 1951-1958.
Ch. of Mont. Rep. state commt., 1958-1960. Nom. and el.
Gov. as a Rep. in 1960. Mbr., Amer. Legion; V.F.W.;
DeMolay Legion of Honor; Masons; Kiwanis; Moose; Elks. Re-
cipient of Sidney JCC Good Govt. Award in 1958. m. in 1938
to Maxine Trotter. One s. D. Jan. 25, 1962, in an air
crash after serving slightly over a year as Gov. Bur. in
Sidney Cem.

BABCOCK, TIM M. (1962-1969). b. Oct. 27, 1919 at
Little Fork, Minn. s. of Erwin Henry and Olive (Rhinehart)
B. Attd. h.s. at Glendive, Mont., to which place his family had moved. Served in U.S. Army in an infantry div.
during 1944-1946, rising from pvt. to rank of sgt. Recipient of Bronze Star and three Battle Stars. Engaged in oil
and transp. bus. enterprises at Glendive, Miles City, and
after 1955, at Billings, Mont. Owner and pres. of Mineral
Resources Development, Inc.; pres. of KBLL Radio and TV
station; pres., Montana Motor Transport Assoc., 1958-1959,
and ch. of its bd. of dir., 1960-1961; exec vice pres.,
Occidental Intl. Corp., of Washington, D.C. Mbr., Mont.
House from Custer Co., 1953-1954, and from Yellowstone Co.,
1957-1960. Mbr. of exec. commt. of Mont. Rep. party. Nom.
and el. Lieut. Gov. as a Rep. in 1960. Succeeded to office
of Gov. in Jan., 1962, following death of Gov. Nutter. After completion of term for which Nutter had been el., was
nom. and el. to a regular term in 1964. Defeated for U.S.
Senate seat as Rep. nominee in 1966, and was defeated for
reel. to a succeeding term as Gov. in 1968. Delegate to
Rep. natl. convs. in 1964 and 1968. Mbr., Masons (Shriner);
Amer. Legion; V.F.W.; Rotary; Eagles; Elks; DeMolay Legion
of Honor; Montana Pilots Assoc. Active in Boy Scouts movement and cancer fund drives. Presbyterian. m. in 1941 to
Betty Lee. Two d.

ANDERSON, FORREST HOWARD (1969-1973). b. Jan. 30, 1913
at Helena, Mont. s. of Oscar A. and Nora (O'Keefe) A.
Attd. the Univ. of Mont. and Columbia Univ., from which he
received a law degree in 1938. Began practice in Helena.
Mbr. of Mont. House, 1943-1945, and Lewis and Clark Co.
atty., 1945-1947. Spec. counsel for Indus. Accident Fund,
1947-1949. Mbr. of Mont. Supreme Ct., 1953-1957. El. Mont.
Atty. Gen. in 1956, continuing in that office until 1969.
Nom. and el. Gov. as a Dem. in 1968, defeating incumbent
Gov. Babcock. Delegate to Dem. natl. conv. in 1968. Mbr.,
Masons (Shriner); Elks; Eagles; Moose; Scandinavian Lodge
of Amer.; Phi Delta Theta; various professional legal orgs.
Methodist. m. in 1941 to Margaret Evelyn Samson. Two d.;

one s.

JUDGE, THOMAS LEE (1973-----). b. Oct. 12, 1934 at
Helena, Mont. s. of Thomas Patrick and Blanche (Giullot) J.
Attd. the Univ. of Notre Dame, from which he received a
B.A. degree in 1957; and the Univ. of Louisville, from
which he received a certificate in advertising in 1959.
Served in U.S. Army as a second lieut., 1958, continuing as
capt. in USAR. Sales exec. of Louisville bus. firms, 1957-
1960. Became head of his own advertising firm at Helena,
continuing in that bus. until 1972. Mbr. of Mont. House,
1961-1967, where he was asst. minority (Dem.) leader in
1962. Mbr. of Mont. Senate, 1967-1969. El. Lieut. Gov. in
1968. Ch., Natl. Conf. of Lieut. Govs. Nom. and el. Gov.
as a Dem. in 1972 and again in 1976. Defeated for nom. for
third term in 1980. Ch. of Western Govs. Regional Energy
Policy Commt., and ch., Western Regional Commn., Fed. of
Rocky Mountain States. Notre Dame Man of the Year Award,
1966; Mont. JCC Young Man of the Year Award, 1967. Mbr.,
K.C.; Elks; Eagles; Exchange. Roman Catholic. m. in 1966
to Carol Ann Anderson. Two s.

INDEX

A

Adair, John: I,205,208;II,
342-343

Adams, Alva: I,77,78,79,80,
81,85n;II,90-91,93,94

Adams, Samuel(Ark.): I,55;
II,40

Adams, Samuel(Mass.): I,268,
272;II,470

Adams, Wm. H.: I,78,82,83;
II,99-100

Adkins, Homer M.: I,56,63;
II,56-57

Agnew, Spiro T.: I,255,256n,
264;II,466

Alabama: biographies,II,1-28;
election results,I,33-40;
Governors listed,I,30-32;
provisions for filling
office,I,27-30

Alaska: biographies,II,29-30;
election results,I,43-44;
Governors listed,I,43;
provisions for filling
office,I,41-43

Alcorn, James L.: I,326,327n,
330;II,570-571

Alexander, Moses: I,152,155;
II,237-238

Alger, Russell A.: I,298,302;
II,520-521

Allen, Frank G.: I,269,289,
290;II,499-500

Allen, Henry J.: I,193,198;
II,329-330

Allen, Henry W.: I,220,222n,
225,228n;II,378-379

Allen, Oscar K.: I,221,223n,
226;II,391-392

Allison, Abraham K.: I,126,
127n;II,171-172

Altgeld, John P.: I,161,165;
II,257-258

Ames, Adelbert: I,326,327n,
330;II,570,572

Ames, Benjamin: I,233,234n;
II,398

Ames, Oliver: I,269,283;II,
490

Ammons, Elias M.: I,78,81;
II,96

Ammons, Teller: I,78,83;II,
101

Andersen, Elmer L.: I,313,
314n,320;II,554

Anderson, C. Elmer: I,313,
320;II,553

Anderson, Forrest H.: I,349,
351;II,619-620

Anderson, Hugh J.: I,233,235n,
238;II,405

Anderson, John A., Jr.: I,194,
201;II,337

Anderson, Wendell R.: I,313,
320,321;II,556

Andrew, John A.: I,269,279,
280;II,484

Andrews, Charles B.: I,89,100;
II,124-125

Andrus, Cecil D.: I,153,157;
II,244-245

Anthony, George T.: I,193,195;
II,320

Ariyoshi, George E.: I,150;
II,232

Arizona: biographies,II,32-38;
election results,I,47-51;
Governors listed,I,46-47;
provisions for filling
office,I,45-46

Arkansas: biographies,II,39-
61; election results,I,
58-65; Governors listed,
I,55-58; provisions for
filling office,I,52-55

Armstrong, Samuel: I,268,270n,
276;II,478

Arn, Edward F.: I,194,200;II,
335

Arnall, Ellis G.: I,139,146,
147,148n;II,224-225

Aronson, J. Hugo: I,349,351;
II,618

Askew, Reubin O.: I,127,131;
II,189-190

Atkinson, Wm. Y.: I,139,144;
    II,216
Austin, Horace: I,313,315;
    II,539-540
Avery, Wm. H.: I,194,201;
    II,339
Ayers, Roy E.: I,349,351;
    II,616-617

                 B
Babcock, Tim M.: I,349,351,
    352;II,619
Bacon, Walter W.: I,114,120;
    II,165
Bagby, Arthur P.: I,31,33;
    II,5
Bagley, John J.: I,298,302;
    II,517
Bailey, Carl E.: I,56,62;
    II,56
Bailey, Thomas L.: I,326,
    327n,332;II,579-580
Bailey, Willis J.: I,193,197;
    II,326
Baker, Conrad: I,171,172n,
    174;II,277
Baker, Joshua: I,221,222n;
    II,381
Baker, Sam A.: I,338,343;II,
    605-606
Baldridge, H. Clarence: I,
    153,155;II,239
Baldwin, Henry P.: I,298,301;
    II,516-517
Baldwin, Raymond E.: I,89,
    90n,104,105;II,136-137
Baldwin, Roger S.: I,88,96,
    107n;II,115-116
Baldwin, Simeon E.: I,89,102;
    II,132-133
Banks, Nathaniel P.: I,269,
    279;II,483-484
Barnett, Ross R.: I,326,332;
    II,581-582
Barrows, Louis O.: I,234,246;
    II,424-425
Barry, John S.: I,298,300;
    II,510,512

Bartlett, Washington: I,69,
    70n,72;II,73-74
Bassett, Richard: I,113,115n,
    116;II,148-149
Bates, Frederick: I,338,339n,
    340;II,585-586
Bates, John L.: I,269,285,
    286;II,493
Baxter, Elisha: I,56,57n,59,
    64-65n;II,44-45
Baxter, Percival P.: I,234,
    235n,245;II,422
Beardsley, Wm. S.: I,182,189;
    II,311-312
Beasley, Jere L.: I,32n
Beauvais, Armand: I,220,221n,
    224;II,373
Beckham, John C. W.: I,206,
    207n,211,213n;II,359-360
Bedford, Gunning: I,113,114n,
    115;II,148
Begole, Josiah W.: I,298,302;
    II,519-520
Bennett, Caleb: I,113,115n;
    II,154
Bennett, Robert F.: I,194,
    202;II,338
Benson, Elmer A.: I,313,319;
    II,550
Berry, James H.: I,56,59;II,
    47
Beveridge, John L.: I,161,
    162n;II,255
Bibb, Thomas: I,30,32n;II,1..
Bibb, Wm. W.: I,30,32n,33;
    II,1
Bigelow, Hobart B.: I,89,100;
    II,125
Bigger, Samuel: I,171,173;II,
    272
Biggs, Benj. T.: I,113,118;
    II,159
Bigler, John: I,69,71;II,63-
    64
Bilbo, Theodore G.: I,326,
    331;II,576,578
Bingham, Hiram: I,89,90n,103;
    II,134-135

Bingham, Kinsley S.: I,298, 301;II,513-514

Bissell, Clark: I,88,96;II, 116-117

Bissell, Wm. H.: I,161,162n, 164;II,251-252

Black, James D.: I,206,208n, 212;II,361-362

Blackburn, Luke P.: I,206, 210;II,354-355

Blair, Austin: I,298,301,302; II,514-515

Blair, James T., Jr.: I,339, 345;II,609-610

Blanchard, Newton C.: I,221, 226;II,386-387

Bliss, Aaron T.: I,298,303; II,523-524

Bloxham, Wm. D.: I,126,129, 132n;II,175,177

Blue, Robert D.: I,182,188, 189;II,310-311

Bodwell, Joseph R.: I,233, 235n,243;II,416-417

Boggs, J. Caleb: I,114,115n, 120;II,166

Boggs, Lilburn W.: I,338, 339n,340;II,587-588

Boies, Horace: I,181,182n, 185;II,301-302

Bond, Christopher S.: I,339, 345;II,611

Bond, Shadrach: I,161,162n, 168n;II,246

Bonner, John W.: I,349,351; II,617-618

Boon, Ratliff: I,171,172n; II,269-270

Booth, Newton: I,69,70n,71; II,70

Bottolfsen, Clarence A.: I, 153,156;II,240-241

Boutwell, George S.: I,269, 278;II,480-481

Bowdoin, James: I,268,271; II,469-470

Bowen, Otis R.: I,172,178; II,294

Bowie, Oden: I,254,256n,261; II,452

Bowie, Robert: I,254,258,259; II,437-438,439

Bowles, Chester: I,89,105;II, 139-140

Boynton, James S.: I,139,141n; II,214

Brackett, John Q. A.: I,269, 283;II,490

Bradford, Augustus W.: I,254, 255n,261;II,450-451

Bradford, Robert F.: I,269, 291;II,502-503

Bradley, Wm. O.: I,206,210; II,357

Brady, James H.: I,153,154; II,236

Bramlette, Thomas E.: I,206, 210;II,351-352

Branch, Emmet F.: I,171,172n; II,287

Brandon, Gerard C.: I,325,328; II,559

Brandon, Wm. W.: I,31,37;II, 21-22

Branigin, Ralph D.: I,172,177; II,293-294

Brann, Lewis J.: I,234,246; II,424

Breathitt, Edward T.: I,206, 213;II,367-368

Breathitt, John: I,206,207n, 209;II,344

Brewer, Albert P.: I,31,32n; II,28

Brewer, Earl L.: I,326,331; II,575-576

Brewster, Ralph O.: I,234,246; II,422-423

Brice, James F.: I,254,255n; II,434-435

Briggs, Ansel: I,181,182,182n; II,295

Briggs, George N.: I,268,277- 278;II,479-480

Brooks, John: I,268,274;II, 475

Broome, James E.: I,126,128;
    II,169-170
Brough, Charles H.: I,56,61;
    II,53-54
Broward, Napoleon B.: I,127,
    129;II,177-178
Brown, Albert G.: I,325,329;
    II,563-564
Brown, B. Gratz: I,338,341;
    II,596-597
Brown, Edmund G., Jr.: I,70,
    75;II,88
Brown, Edmund G., Sr.: I,70,
    75;II,86-87
Brown, Frank: I,255,261;II,
    456-457
Brown, John Y.: I,206,210,
    211;II,356-357
Brown, Joseph E.: I,138,140n,
    143;II,209
Brown, Joseph M.: I,139,141n,
    145;II,218,219
Brown, Thomas: I,126,127n,
    128;II,169
Brownson, Nathan: I,138;II,
    195
Brucker, Wilbur M.: I,299,
    306;II,528-529
Bryant, C. Farris: I,127,131;
    II,187
Buchtel, Henry A.: I,78,81;
    II,95
Buck, C. Douglas: I,114,119;
    II,163-164
Buckingham, Wm. A.: I,89,98;
    II,120-121
Buckner, Simon B.: I,206,210;
    II,355-357
Buckson, David P.: I,114,
    115n,120;II,166
Budd, James H.: I,69,72;II,
    76
Bulkeley, Morgan G.: I,89,
    100,108n;II,127
Bulloch, Archibald: I,137,
    139n;II,191
Bullock, Alexander H.: I,269,
    280;II,484-485

Bullock, Rufus B.: I,138,140n,
    143;II,213
Bumpers, Dale L.: I,56,58n,
    64;II,60
Burleigh, Edwin C.: I,233,243;
    II,417
Burnett, Peter H.: I,69,70,
    70n;II,62
Burnquist, Joseph A. A.: I,
    313,314n,317,318;II,547-
    548
Burns, Haydon: I,127,127n,131;
    II,188
Burns, John A.: I,150,150n;
    II,231-232
Burton, Wm.: I,113,117;II,
    156-157
Busbee, George D.: I,139,147;
    II,230
Butcher, James: I,254,255n;
    II,438-439
Butler, Benj. F.: I,269,279,
    280,282;II,488-489
Byrd, Richard C.: I,56,57n;
    II,40

                  C
Caldwell, Millard F.: I,127,
    130;II,184
California: biographies,II,
    62-68; election results,
    I,70-75; Governors listed,
    I,69-70; provisions for
    filling office,I,66-69
Campbell, Thomas E.: I,46,47,
    47n,48,50n;II,32-33
Candler, Allen D.: I,139,144,
    145;II,216
Cannon, Wm.: I,113,115n,117;
    II,157
Capper, Arthur: I,193,198;II,
    328-329
Carleton, Doyle E.: I,127,
    130;II,181-182
Carlin, Thomas: I,161,163;II,
    249-250
Carlson, Frank: I,194,194n,
    200;II,334

Carlson, George A.: I,78,82; II,96-97

Carney, Thomas: I,193,195; II,316-317

Carpenter, Cyrus C.: I,181, 184;II,299

Carr, Ralph L.: I,78,83;II, 101-102

Carroll, Beryl F.: I,181,186; II,305-306

Carroll, John L.: I,254,261; II,454

Carroll, Julian M.: I,206, 208n,213;II,369

Carroll, Thomas K.: I,254, 259;II,443-444

Carter, James E., Jr.: I,139, 147;II,229-230

Carvel, Elbert N.: I,114,120; II,165-166

Castro, Raul H.: I,47,50; II,38

Catts, Sidney J.: I,127,130; II,179-180

Caulfield, Henry S.: I,338, 343;II,606

Causey, Peter F.: I,113,117; II,156

Chamberlain, Abiram: I,89, 102;II,130

Chamberlain, Joshua L.: I, 233,241;II,411-412

Chandler, Albert B.: I,206, 208n,212,213;II,364-365, 367

Chapman, Reuben: I,31,34;II, 7

Chase, Ira J.: I,171,175;II, 281-282

Cherry, Francis A.: I,56,63; II,58

Christianson, Theodore: I, 313,318;II,549

Churchill, Thomas J.: I,56, 59;II,46-47

Claflin, Wm.: I,269,280,281; II,485-486

Claiborne, Wm. C. C.: I,220, 223;II,370

Clark, Barzilla W.: I,153,156; II,240

Clark, Charles: I,325,327n, 330;II,567-568

Clark, Chase A.: I,153,156; II,241

Clark, James: I,206,207n,209; II,345

Clark(e), John(Del.): I,113, 115n,116;II,151-152

Clark(e), John(Ga.): I,138, 141;II,202-203

Clarke, George W.: I,181,187; II,306

Clarke, James P.: I,56,60;II, 49-50

Clauson, Clinton A.: I,234, 235n,247;II,428

Clay, Clement C.: I,31,32n, 33;II,4-5

Clayton, Joshua: I,113,115; II,147-148

Clayton, Powell: I,56,57n,59; II,43-44

Cleaves, Henry B.: I,233,243; II,417-418

Clements, Earle C.: I,206, 208n,212,214n;II,366

Cleveland, Chauncey F.: I,88, 96;II,115

Clifford, John H.: I,269,278, 294n;II,481-482

Clough, David M.: I,313,316; II,544

Cobb, Howell: I,138,143;II, 207-208

Cobb, Rufus W.: I,31,35;II,14

Cobb, Wm. T.: I,234,244;II, 419

Coburn, Abner: I,233,240;II, 410-411

Cochran, John P.: I,113,118; II,158

Coffin, O. Vincent: I,89,101; II,128

Coleman, James P.: I,326, 332;II,580-581

Coles, Edward: I,161,162; II,246-247

Collier, Henry W.: I,31,34; II,7-8

Collins, John: I,113,115n, 116;II,152

Collins, Thomas: I,113,114n; II,147

Collins, T. LeRoy: I,127,131, 132n;II,186-187

Colorado: biographies,II,89-106; election results,I, 79-85; Governors listed, I,77-79; provisions for filling office,I,76-77

Colquitt, Alfred H.: I,139, 144;II,212-213

Combs, Bert T.: I,206,213; II,367

Comegys, Cornelius P.: I, 113,117;II,154

Comer, Braxton B.: I,31,37; II,19

Comstock, Wm. A.: I,299,306; II,529-530

Cone, Frederick P.: I,127, 130;II,182-183

Connecticut: biographies,II, 107-142; election re-sults,I,91-108; Gover-nors listed,I,88-90; pro-visions for filling of-fice,I,86-88

Conley, Benj.: I,139,140n; II,211-212

Conner, Martin S.: I,326,331; II,578

Conner, Selden: I,233,242; II,413

Conway, Elias N.: I,56,58; II,41

Conway, James S.: I,55,58; II,39

Cony, Samuel: I,233,240;II, 411

Cook, John: I,112,114n;II, 146

Cooke, Lorrin A.: I,89,101; II,128-129

Coolidge, Calvin: I,269,288, 289;II,497-498

Cooney, Frank H.: I,349,349n; II,615-616

Cooper, Job A.: I,77,80;II,91

Cooper, Wm. B.: I,113,117;II, 154-155

Cox, Channing H.: I,269,289; II,498-499

Craig, George N.: I,171,177; II,292

Crane, W. Murray: I,269,285; II,492-493

Crapo, Henry H.: I,298,301; II,515-516

Crawford, George W.: I,138, 142;II,206-207

Crawford, Samuel J.: I,193, 194n,195;II,317-318

Crittenden, John J.: I,206, 207n,209;II,347-348

Crittenden, Thomas T.: I,338, 342;II,598-599

Crosby, Wm. G.: I,233,239;II, 406

Cross, Burton M.: I,234,247; II,426-427

Cross, Wilbur L.: I,89,104; II,136

Croswell, Charles M.: I,298, 302;II,517-518

Crothers, Austin L.: I,255, 262;II,459

Cullom, Shelby M.: I,161, 162n,164;II,255-256

Cummins, Albert B.: I,181, 182n,186;II,304-305

Cunningham, Russell M.: I,32n

Curley, James M.: I,269,289, 290;II,500-501

Curtis, Kenneth M.: I,234, 247;II,429

Curtis, Oakley C.: I,234,245; II,420-421

Cushing, Thomas: I,268,270n, 271;II,468-469

Cuthbert, Seth J.: ...II,192

Cutler, Nathan: I,233,234n; II,399-400

D

Dalton, John M.: I,339,345; II,610

Dana, John W.: I,233,235n, 238,239,248n;II,404-405

Davies, Myrick: II,194

Davis, Cushman K.: I,313,315; II,540

Davis, Daniel F.: I,233,242; II,414-415

Davis, David W.: I,153,155; II,238

Davis, James H.: I,221,227; II,394-395

Davis, Jeff: I,56,60,61; II,50

Davis, Jehu: I,113,114n; II,147

Davis, John: I,268,276,277, 294n;II,477-478,479

Davis, Jonathan M.: I,193, 198,199,200;II,330

Dawes, Thomas: I,270n

Day, Samuel T.: I,128n;II, 173

Delaware: biographies,II,143- 168; election results,I, 115-121; Governors listed, I,112-115; provisions for filling office,I,109-112

Dempsey, John N.: I,89,90n, 106;II,141-142

Deneen, Charles S.: I,161, 165,166;II,259

Denney, Wm. D.: I,114,119; II,163

Derbigny, Pierre: I,220,221n, 223,224;II,372-373

Desha, Joseph: I,206,209;II, 343

Dever, Paul A.: I,269,291, 292;II,503-504

Dickinson, John: I,112,114n; II,145-146

Dickinson, Luren D.: I,299, 299n,307;II,531-532

Dingley, Nelson, Jr.: I,233, 241,243;II,412-413

Dixon, Frank M.: I,31,38;II, 23-24

Dixon, Joseph M.: I,349,350; II,614-615

Dockery, Alexander M.: I,338, 342;II,602

Docking, George: I,194,201; II,336-337

Docking, Robert B.: I,194,201, 202;II,338

Donaghey, George W.: I,56,61; II,52

Donnell, Forrest C.: I,339, 340n,344;II,607-608

Donnelly, Phil M.: I,339,344; II,608,609

Dorsey, Hugh M.: I,139,145; II,220

Douglas, Wm. L.: I,269,286; II,493-494

Downey, John G.: I,69,70n,71; II,67-68

Drake, Francis M.: I,181,185; II,302-303

Draper, Eben S.: I,269,287; II,494-495

Drew, George F.: I,126,129, 132n;II,174-175

Drew, Thomas S.: I,56,57n,58; II,40

Dukakis, Michael S.: I,269, 293;II,507

Duncan, Joseph: I,161,163;II, 249

Dunklin, Daniel: I,338,339n, 340;II,587

Dunlap, Robert P.: I,233,237, 248n;II,401-402

Dunn, David: I,233,235n;II, 404

Dunne, Edward F.: I,161,162n, 166;II,259-260

Dunning, Paris C.: I,171, 172n;II,273

Dupré, Jacques: I,220,221n; II,373

Durbin, Winfield T.: I,171, 175;II,283

Dutton, Henry: I,89,97,107n; II,118-119

E

Eagle, James P.: I,56,60; II,48

Early, Peter: I,138;II,201

Eaton, Benj. H.: I,77,79; II,90

Eberhart, Adolph O.: I,313, 314n,317;II,546-547

Edwards, Edwin W.: I,221,227, 229n;II,396

Edwards, Henry W.: I,88,95; II,113,114

Edwards, John C.: I,338,339n, 340;II,589

Edwards, Ninian: I,161,163; II,247

Egan, Wm. A.: I,43,43n;II, 29,30

Elbert, Samuel: I,138;II,196

Election results: I,3-4. (See also separate State headings).

Elections, time and manner: survey of State practices, I,1-4,6-7. (See also separate State headings).

Ellsworth, Wm. W.: I,88,95, 96;II,114-115

Elthon, Leo: I,182,182n;II, 311

Ely, Joseph B.: I,269,290; II,500

Emanuel, David: I,138,140n; II,199

Emmerson, Louis L.: I,161, 166;II,261-262

English, James E.: I,89,98, 99,100;II,121-122,123

Erbe, Norman A.: I,182,189, 190;II,313

Erickson, John E.: I,349,349n, 350,351;II,615

Eustis, Wm.: I,268,270n,274, 275;II,475-476

Everett, Edward: I,268,276, 277;II,478-479

Ewing, Wm. L. D.: I,161,162n; II,248-249

F

Fairfield, John: I,233,235n, 237,238;II,402-403

Fannin, Paul J.: I,47,49,50; II,37

Faubus, Orval E.: I,56,63,64; II,59

Felch, Alpheus: I,298,299n, 300;II,510-511

Fernald, Bert M.: I,234,245; II,419-420

Ferris, Woodbridge N.: I,299, 304,305;II,526

Fields, Wm. J.: I,206,212;II, 362-363

Fifer, Joseph W.: I,161,165; II,256-257

Finch, Clif: I,326,332;II, 583-584

Fishback, Wm. M.: I,56,60; II,48-49

Fitzgerald, Frank D.: I,299, 299n,306,307;II,530,531

Fitzpatrick, Benj.: I,31,34; II,5-6

Flanagin, Harris: I,56,57n, 59;II,42-43

Flanders, Benj.: I,221,222n; II,380-381

Fleming, Francis P.: I,126, 129;II,176

Fletcher, Thomas: I,56,57n; II,42

Fletcher, Thomas C.: I,338, 341;II,595

Florida: biographies,II,169-190; election results,I, 128-132; Governors listed,I,126-128; provisions for filling office,I,122-126

Folk, Joseph W.: I,338,343; II,602-603

Folsom, James E.: I,31,38; II,24-25,26

Foote, Henry S.: I,325,327n, 329;II,565-566

Foote, Samuel A.: I,88,95; II,113-114

Ford, Sam C.: I,349,351;II, 617

Ford, Thomas: I,161,163;II, 250

Ford, Wendell H.: I,206,208n, 213;II,369

Forsyth, John: I,138,142; II,204

Foss, Eugene N.: I,269,287, 288;II,495-496

Foster, Murphy J.: I,221,225, 226,229n;II,385-386

Francis, David R.: I,338,342; II,600-601

Freeman, Orville L.: I,313, 320;II,553-554

French, Augustus C.: I,161, 162n,163;II,250-251

Fuller, Alvan T.: I,269,289; II,499

Fulton, Robert D.: I,182, 182n,190;II,314-315

Fuqua, Henry L.: I,221,223n, 226;II,389

Furcolo, Foster J.: I,269, 292;II,504-505

Futrell, J. Marion: I,56,57n, 62;II,53,56

G

Gage, Henry T.: I,69,72;II, 76-77

Gamble, Hamilton: I,338,339n; II,594

Garcelon, Alonzo: I,233,242; II,413-414

Gardiner, Wm. T.: I,234,246; II,423-424

Gardner, Frederick D.: I,338, 343;II,604-605

Gardner, Henry J.: I,269,279; II,483

Garland, Augustus H.: I,56, 59;II,45-46

Garrard, James: I,205,207n, 208;II,339-340

Garst, Warren: I,181,182n; II,305

Garvey, Dan E.: I,47,49;II, 35-36

Gaston, Wm.: I,269,281;II, 487

Gates, Ralph F.: I,171,177; II,291-292

Gayle, John: I,31,33;II,3-4

Gear, John H.: I,181,184;II, 300

Georgia: biographies,II,191-230; election results,I, 141-148; Governors listed, I,137-141; provisions for filling office,I,133-137

Gerry, Elbridge: I,268,273; II,474-475

Gilchrist, Albert W.: I,127, 128n,129;II,178-179

Gill, Moses: I,268,270n;II, 471

Gillett, James N.: I,69,73; II,78

Gilmer, George R.: I,138,142; II,204-205,206

Glasscock, Wm.: II,192

Glick, George W.: I,193,195; II,321-322

Goddard, Samuel P.: I,47,50; II,37-38

Goebel, Wm.: I,206,207n,211; II,358-359

Goldsborough, Charles: I,254, 259;II,441

Goldsborough, Phillips L.: I, 255,262;II,459-460

Gooding, Frank R.: I,153,154; II,235-236

Goodrich, James P.: I,171, 176;II,285-286

Gordon, James W.: I,298,299n; II,509

Gordon, John B.: I,139,144; II,217

Gore, Christopher: I,268,273; II,473-474

Gossett, Charles C.: I,153, 153n,156;II,241-242

Governor, office of: survey of State practices re- garding,I,1-19. (See al- so separate State head- ings).

Grant, James B.: I,77,79;II, 90

Grason, Wm.: I,254,260;II, 446

Grasso, Ella T.: I,89,106; II,142

Graves, D. Bibb: I,31,37,40n; II,22-23

Gray, Isaac P.: I,171,172n, 174;II,279-280

Green, Dwight H.: I,161,167; II,263-264

Green, Fred W.: I,299,306; II,528

Green, Nehemiah: I,193,194n; II,318

Greenhalge, Frederick T.: I, 269,270n,284;II,491-492

Greenly, Wm. L.: I,298,299n; II,511

Greenup, Christopher: I,205, 208;II,340

Griffin, S. Marvin: I,139, 147;II,227

Grimes, James W.: I,181,182n, 183;II,295-296

Griswold, Matthew: I,88,91; II,107-108

Griswold, Roger: I,88,90n,92, 93;II,110-111

Groesbeck, Alex J.: I,299, 305,306;II,527-528

Groome, James B.: I,254,261; II,453

Guild, Curtis, Jr.: I,269, 286;II,494

Guion, John I.: I,325,327n; II,564

Gunter, Julius C.: I,78,82; II,97

Gwinnett, Button: I,137,139n; II,191

H

Hadley, Herbert S.: I,338, 343;II,603-604

Hadley, Ozra A.: I,56,57n; II,44

Hagaman, Frank L.: I,194,194n; II,334-335

Hahn, Michael: I,220,222n,225, 228n;II,379

Haight, Henry H.: I,69,71;II, 69-70

Haines, John M.: I,153,155; II,237

Haines, Wm. T.: I,234,245; II,420

Hall, David: I,113,116;II,150

Hall, Fred: I,194,200;II,335- 336

Hall, John W.: I,113,118;II, 158-159

Hall, Joshua: I,233,234n;II, 400

Hall, Luther E.: I,221,226; II,387-388

Hall, Lyman: I,138;II,195-196

Hall, Willard P.: I,338,339n; II,594-595

Hamilton, John M.: I,161,162n; II,256

Hamilton, Wm. T.: I,255,261; II,454-455

Hamlin, Hannibal: I,233,235n, 239;II,407-408

Hammill, John: I,181,182n, 187,188;II,307-308

Hammond, Abram A.: I,171, 172n;II,275

Hammond, Jay S.: I,43,44n; II,30-31

Hammond, Winfield S.: I,313, 314n,317;II,547

Hancock, John: I,268,270n, 270,271,272;II,468,470

Handley, George: I,138,140n; II,198

Handley, Harold W.: I,172, 177;II,292-293

Hanly, J. Frank: I,171,175; II,283-284

Hardee, Cary A.: I,127,130; II,180-181

Hardin, Charles H.: I,338, 341;II,597

Harding, Wm. L.: I,181,187; II,306

Hardman, Lamartine G.: I, 139,146;II,221-222

Hardwick, Thomas W.: I,139, 145;II,220-221

Harrington, Emerson C.: I, 255,262;II,460-461

Harris, Nathaniel E.: I,139, 145;II,219-220

Harrison, Henry B.: I,89, 100;II,126

Hart, Ossian B.: I,126,128n, 129;II,173

Harvey, James M.: I,193,195; II,318-319

Haskell, Robert N.: I,234, 235n;II,428

Haslet, Joseph: (See Hazlett, Joseph)

Hawaii: biographies,II,231-232; election results,I, 150; Governors listed,I, 150; provisions for filling office,I,149-150

Hawes, Richard: I,207n

Hawley, James H.: I,153,154, 155;II,236-237

Hawley, Joseph R.: I,89,98, 99;II,121

Hayes, George W.: I,56,58n, 61;II,53

Hazlett, Joseph: I,113,116; II,150-151,152

Hazzard, David: I,113,117; II,153

Heard, Stephen: I,138,140n; II,194

Heard, Wm. W.: I,221,226; II,386

Hearnes, Warren E.: I,339, 345;II,610-611

Hebert, Paul O.: I,220,221n, 224;II,376-377

Helm, John L.: I,206,207n, 210;II,349,352

Hempstead, Stephen: I,181, 183;II,295

Henderson, Charles: I,31,37; II,20

Hendricks, Thomas A.: I,171, 174;II,277-278

Hendricks, Wm.: I,171,172n, 173;II,270

Henry, John: I,254,257;II, 435-436

Herring, Clyde L.: I,181,187, 188;II,308-309

Herter, Christian A.: I,269, 292;II,504

Hickel, Walter J.: I,43,43n; II,29-30

Hickenlooper, Burke B.: I, 182,188;II,310

Hicks, Thomas H.: I,254,260; II,450

Hildreth, Horace A.: I,234, 246,247;II,425-426

Hill, John F.: I,234,244;II, 418-419

Hoch, Edward W.: I,193,197; II,326-327

Hodges, George H.: I,193,198; II,327-328

Hoegh, Leo A.: I,182,189; II,312

Holcomb, Marcus H.: I,89,
    103;II,133
Holland, Spessard L.: I,127,
    130;II,183-184
Holley, Alexander H.: I,89,
    97;II,119-120
Holmes, David: I,325,326n,
    328;II,557,559
Holt, Wm. E.: I,349,349n;
    II,616
Horner, Henry: I,161,162n,
    166,167;II,263-264
Houston, George S.: I,31,35;
    II,13-14
Houston (Houstoun?), John:
    I,138;II,192,196
Hovey, Alvin P.: I,171,172n,
    174;II,280-281
Howard, George: I,254,255n,
    259;II,444
Howard, John E.: I,254,257,
    258;II,433-434
Howley, Richard: I,138,140n;
    II,194
Hubbard, John: I,233,235n,
    239,249n;II,405-406
Hubbard, Lucius F.: I,313,
    313n,315,321n;II,541-542
Hubbard, Richard D.: I,89,
    99,100;II,124
Hughes, Harold E.: I,182,
    182n,190;II,313-314
Hughes, Simon P.: I,56,59,
    60;II,47-48
Humphrey, Lyman U.: I,193,
    196;II,322-323
Humphreys, Benj. G.: I,326,
    327n,330,332;II,569-570
Hunn, John: I,114,118;II,
    161
Hunt, Frank W.: I,152,154;
    II,234-235
Hunt, George W. P.: I,46,47,
    47n,48;II,32,33,34
Huntington, Samuel: I,88,
    89n,91,107;II,108
Hunton, Jonathan G.: I,233,
    236;II,400-401

Hurley, Charles F.: I,269,
    290;II,501
Hurley, Robert A.: I,89,104,
    105;II,137
Huxman, Walter A.: I,194,199;
    II,333
Hyde, Arthur M.: I,338,343;
    II,605

                    I

Idaho: biographies,II,233-
    245; election results,I,
    153-157; Governors listed,
    I,152-153; provisions for
    filling office, I,151-152
Illinois: biographies,II,246-
    268; election results,I,
    162-168; Governors listed,
    I,161-162; provisions for
    filling office,I,158-160
Indiana: biographies,II,269-
    294; election results,I,
    172-178; Governors listed,
    I,171-172; provisions for
    filling office,I,169-171
Ingersoll, Charles R.: I,89,
    90n,99;II,123
Iowa: biographies,II,295-315;
    election results,I,182-
    190; Governors listed,I,
    181-182; provisions for
    filling office,I,179-181
Irwin, Jared: I,138;II,198-
    201
Irwin, Wm.: I,69,72;II,71-72

                    J

Jackson, Claiborne F.: I,338,
    339n,341;II,593
Jackson, Ed: I,171,176;II,
    287-288
Jackson, Elihu E.: I,255,261;
    II,456
Jackson, Frank D.: I,181,185;
    II,302
Jackson, Hancock L.: I,338,
    339n,341;II,591-592

Jackson, James: I,138,140n; II,198-199

Jelks, Wm. D.: I,31,32n,37; II,18-19

Jenkins, Charles J.: I,138, 140n,143;II,210

Jennings, Jonathan: I,171, 172n,172;II,269

Jennings, Wm. S.: I,127,129; II,177

Jerome, David H.: I,298,302; II,518-519

Jewell, Marshall: I,89,90n, 99;II,122-123

Johns, Charley E.: I,127, 128n;II,186

Johnson, Ed C.: I,78,79n,83, 84;II,100,104

Johnson, George W.: I,207n

Johnson, Henry: I,220,224; II,372

Johnson, Herschel V.: I,138, 143;II,208-209

Johnson, Hiram W.: I,69,70n, 73;II,78-79

Johnson, Isaac: I,220,224; II,375

Johnson, James: I,138,140n; II,209-210

Johnson, J. Neely: I,69,71; II,64-65

Johnson, John A.: I,313,314n, 317;II,546

Johnson, Keen: I,206,208n, 212;II,365

Johnson, Paul B., Jr.: I,326, 332;II,582

Johnson, Paul B., Sr.: I,326, 327n,332;II,579

Johnson, Thomas: I,254,255n, 256,257;II,431

Johnson, Walter W.: I,78,79n, 84;II,103

Johnston, Joseph F.: I,31,36; II,17

Jones, Dan W.: I,56,60;II,50

Jones, Robt. T.: I,47,49;II, 35

Jones, Sam H.: I,221,227;II, 394

Jones, Thomas G.: I,31,36;II, 15-16

Jordan, Leonard B.: I,153, 156;II,242-243

Judge, Thomas L.: I,349,352; II,620

K

Kansas: biographies,II,316- 338; election results,I, 194-202; Governors listed, I,193-194; provisions for filling office,I,191-193

Kavanagh, Edward: I,233,234n, 235;II,403-404

Kellogg, Wm. P.: I,221,222n, 225,228n;II,383-384

Kelly, Harry F.: I,299,307, 308;II,532-533

Kendall, Nathan E.: I,181, 182n,187;II,306-307

Kennon, Robert F.: I,221,227; II,395

Kent, Edward: I,233,237,238; II,402

Kent, Joseph: I,254,259;II, 442-443

Kentucky: biographies,II,339- 369; election results,I, 208-214; Governors listed, I,205-208; provisions for filling office,I,203-205

Kerner, Otto: I,161,162n,167, 168;II,266

Kilby, Thomas E.: I,31,37;II, 20-21

King, Alvin O.: I,221,223n; II,391

King, Austin A.: I,338,341; II,589-590

King, Wm.: I,233,234n,235, 237;II,397

Kirk, Claude R., Jr.: I,127, 131;II,188-189

Kirkwood, Samuel J.: I,181, 182n,183,184;II,297,299

Knight, Goodwin J.: I,69,70n, 74;II,85-86

Knott, J. Proctor: I,206,210; II,355

Knous, W. Lee: I,78,79n,84; II,102-103

Kraschel, Nelson G.: I,181, 188;II,309

L

Laffoon, Ruby: I,206,212; II,363-364

Lake, Everett J.: I,89,103; II,133-134

Lamm, Richard D.: I,78,85; II,105-106

Landon, Alfred M.: I,194,199; II,332

Lane, Henry S.: I,171,172n, 174;II,275-276

Lane, Wm. P., Jr.: I,255, 256n,263;II,463-464

Laney, Benj. T.: I,56,63; II,57

Larrabee, Wm.: I,181,182n, 185;II,301

Latham, Milton S.: I,69,70n, 71;II,66-67

Lea, Preston: I,114,119;II, 161

Leake, Walter: I,325,326n, 328;II,558-559

Leche, Richard W.: I,221, 223n,227;II,392-393

Lee, Blair: II,467

Lee, Thomas S.: I,254,255n, 256,257;II,431-432,435

Leedy, John W.: I,193,197; II,325

Leslie, Harry G.: I,171,176; II,288-289

Leslie, Preston H.: I,206, 210;II,353

Letcher, Robt. P.: I,206, 209;II,346-347

Le Vander, Harold: I,313,320; II,555-556

Lewelling, Lorenzo D.: I,193, 196;II,323-324

Lewis, David P.: I,31,35; II,13

Lieutenant Governor, office of: survey of State practices regarding,I,17-19. (See also separate State headings).

Ligon, Thomas W.: I,254,260; II,449

Lilley, George L.: I,89,90n, 102;II,131-132

Lincoln, Enoch: I,233,234n, 236;II,399

Lincoln, Levi, Jr.: I,268, 275,276;II,477

Lincoln, Levi, Sr.: I,268, 270n;II,473

Lind, John: I,313,316;II,544-545

Lindsay, Robt. B.: I,31,35; II,12-13

Little, John S.: I,56,57n,61; II,50-51

Lloyd, Edward: I,254,255n, 256,258;II,439

Lloyd, Henry: I,255,261;II, 455-456

Lodge, John D.: I,89,105;II, 140

Long, Earl K.: I,221,223n, 227;II,393-394,395

Long, Huey P., Jr.: I,221, 223n,226;II,390-391

Long, John D.: I,269,282;II, 488

Longino, Andrew H.: I,326, 331;II,574

Longley, James B.: I,234,248; II,429-430

Louisiana: biographies,II,370-396; election results,I, 223-229; Governors listed, I,220-223; provisions for filling office,I,215-220

Lounsbury, George E.: I,89, 101;II,129

Lounsbury, Phineas C.: I,89, 100;II,126-127

Love, John A.: I,78,79n,85; II,104-105

Loveless, Herschel C.: I,182, 189;II,312-313

Low, Frederick F.: I,69,71; II,68-69

Lowden, Frank O.: I,161,166; II,260-261

Lowe, Enoch L.: I,254,260; II,448-449

Lowe, Ralph P.: I,181,183; II,296-297

Lowndes, Lloyd, Jr.: I,255, 261,262;II,457-458

Lowry, Robt.: I,326,330; II,573

Luce, Cyrus G.: I,298,302, 303;II,521

Lumpkin, Wilson: I,138,142; II,205

Lynch, Charles: I,325,327n, 328;II,560,562

M

Maddox, Lester G.: I,139,147, 148n;II,228-229

Madison, George: I,205,207n, 208;II,341-342

Magoffin, Beriah: I,206,207n, 209;II,350-351

Maine: biographies,II,397-430; election results,I, 235-249; Governors listed, I,233-235; provisions for filling office,I,230-232

Major, Elliot W.: I,338,343; II,604

Mandel, Marvin: I,255,264; II,467

Marble, Sebastian S.: I,233, 235n;II,417

Markham, Henry H.: I,69,72; II,75-76

Marmaduke, John S.: I,338, 339n,342;II,599-600

Marmaduke, Meredith M.: I, 338,339n;II,588-589

Marshall, Thomas R.: I,171, 175;II,284-285

Marshall, Wm. R.: I,313,314; II,539

Martin, Daniel: I,254,255n, 259;II,443,444

Martin, Jesse M.: I,56,57n; II,51

Martin, John: I,138;II,195

Martin, John A.: I,193,196; II,322

Martin, John W.: I,127,130; II,181

Martin, Joshua L.: I,31,34; II,6-7

Martineau, John E.: I,56,58n, 62;II,55

Marvil, Joshua H.: I,113,115n, 118;II,160

Marvin, William: I,126,127n; II,171

Maryland: biographies,II,431-467; election results,I, 256-265; Governors listed, I,254-256; provisions for filling office,I,250-253

Mason, Stevens T.: I,298,299n, 300;II,508

Massachusetts: biographies,II, 468-507; election results, I,270-294; Governors listed,I,268-270; provisions for filling office,I,266-268

Mathews, George: I,138;II,197, 198

Matteson, Joel A.: I,161,163; II,261

Matthews, Claude: I,171,175; II,282

Matthews, Joseph W.: I,325, 329;II,564

Maull, Joseph: I,113,115n; II,155

McCall, Samuel W.: I,269,288; II,496-497

McCarty, Dan: I,127,128n,
    131;II,185-186
McClelland, Robt.: I,298,
    299n,301;II,512-513
McClurg, Joseph W.: I,338,
    341,345n;II,595-596
McConaghey, James L.: I,89,
    90n,105;II,138-139
McConnell, Wm. J.: I,152,
    153;II,233-234
McCray, Warren T.: I,171,
    172n,176;II,286-287
McCreary, James B.: I,206,
    210,211;II,353-354,360
McCuish, John: I,194,194n;
    II,336
McDaniel, Henry D.: I,139,
    144;II,214-215
McDonald, Charles J.: I,138,
    142;II,206
McDonald, Jesse F.: I,78,
    78n,81;II,94-95
McDougal, John: I,69,70n;
    II,62-63
McEnery, John: I,222n,225
McEnery, Samuel D.: I,221,
    225;II,385
McFarland, Ernest W.: I,47,
    49;II,36-37
McGill, Andrew R.: I,313,
    315;II,542-543
McIntire, Albert W.: I,78,
    80;II,92-93
McKean, Thomas: I,112,114n;
    II,143-144
McKeithen, John J.: I,221,
    227;II,395-396
McKeldin, Theodore R.: I,
    255,263,264;II,464-465
McKinley (McKinly?), John:
    I,112,114n;II,143
McLane, Robt. M.: I,255,
    256n,261;II,455
McLaurin, Anselm J.: I,326,
    331,333n;II,573-574
McLean, George P.: I,89,101;
    II,129-130

McMath, Sid S.: I,56,63;II,
    57-58
McMullen, Richard C.: I,114,
    119;II,165
McNair, Alexander: I,338,339n,
    340;II,585
McNichols, Stephen L. R.: I,
    78,84;II,104
McNutt, Alexander G.: I,325,
    329;II,562-563
McNutt, Paul V.: I,171,176;
    II,289-290
McRae, John J.: I,325,327n,
    329;II,566-567
McRae, Thomas C.: I,56,62;
    II,54
McVay, Hugh: I,31,32n;II,5
McWillie, Wm.: I,325,330;II,
    567
Mercer, John F.: I,254,258;
    II,436-437
Merriam, Frank F.: I,69,74;
    II,82-83
Merriam, Wm. R.: I,313,315,
    316;II,543
Merrill, Samuel: I,181,183;
    II,298-299
Meskill, Thomas J.: I,89,106;
    II,142
Metcalfe, Thomas: I,206,209;
    II,343-344
Michigan: biographies,II,508-
    536; election results,I,
    300-310; Governors listed,
    I,298-299; provisions for
    filling office,I,295-298
Milledge, John: I,138,140n;
    II,200-201
Miller, Benj. M.: I,31,37;
    II,23
Miller, Charles R.: I,114,
    119;II,161-162
Miller, John: I,338,339n,340;
    II,586-587
Miller, Keith H.: I,43,43n;
    II,30
Miller, Stephen: I,313,314;
    II,538-539

Miller, Wm. R.: I,56,59;II,
46
Milliken, Carl E.: I,234,245;
II,421
Milliken, Wm. G.: I,299,309,
310;II,536
Milton, John: I,126,127n,128;
II,170-171
Minnesota: biographies,II,537-
566; election results,I,
314-321; Governors list-
ed,I,312-314; provisions
for filling office,I,311-
312
Minor, Wm. T.: I,89,97;II,
119
Mississippi: biographies,II,
567-594; election results,
I,328-333; Governors
listed,I,325-327; provi-
sions for filling office,
I,322-325
Missouri: biographies,II,595-
621; election results,I,
340-346; Governors listed,
I,338-340; provisions for
filling office,I,334-338
Mitchell, David B.: I,138,
140n;II,201,202
Mitchell, Henry L.: I,126,
129;II,176-177
Mitchell, Nathaniel: I,113,
116;II,150
Moeur, Benj. B.: I,47,48;II,
34
Molleston, Henry: I,115n
Montana: biographies,II,622-
630; election results,I,
349-352; Governors listed,
I,349; provisions for
filling office,I,347-348
Moore, Andrew B.: I,31,34,35,
39n;II,8-9
Moore, Charles C.: I,153,155;
II,238-239
Moore, Gabriel: I,30,32n,33;
II,3

Moore, John I.: I,56,57n;II,
51
Moore, Samuel B.: I,30,32n;
II,3
Moore, Thomas: I,220,222n,
225;II,377-378
Morehead, Charles S.: I,206,
209;II,350
Morehead, James T.: I,206,
207n;II,344-345
Morehouse, Albert P.: I,338,
339n;II,600
Morley, Clarence J.: I,78,82;
II,99
Morrill, Anson P.: I,233,239;
II,406-407
Morrill, Edmund N.: I,193,196,
197;II,324-325
Morrill, Lot M.: I,233,240;
II,409-410
Morris, Luzon B.: I,89,100,
101,108n;II,127-128
Morrison, John T.: I,152,154;
II,235
Morrow, Edwin P.: I,206,211;
II,362
Morton, Marcus: I,268,270n,
275,276,277,294n;II,476-
477,479
Morton, Oliver H. P.: I,171,
172n,174;II,276-277
Moseley, Wm. D.: I,126,128;
II,169
Mount, James A.: I,171,175;
II,282-283
Mouton, Alexandre: I,220,221n,
224,228n;II,374-375
Murphree, Dennis: I,326,327n;
II,577-578,579
Murphy, Frank: I,299,307;II,
530-531
Murphy, Isaac: I,56,57n,59,
64n;II,43
Murphy, John: I,30,33;II,2-3
Muskie, Edmund S.: I,234,
235n,247;II,427-428

N

Nelson, Knute: I,313,313n,
    316;II,543-544
Newbold, Joshua G.: I,181,
    182n;II,299
Nice, Harry W.: I,255,262,
    263;II,462
Nicholls, Francis T.: I,221,
    222n,225,229n;II,384,385
Noble, Noah: I,171,173;II,
    271
Noe, James A.: I,221,223n;
    II,392
Noel, Edmond F.: I,326,331;
    II,575
Norris, Edwin L.: I,349,350;
    II,613-614
Northen, Wm. J.: I,139,141n,
    144;II,215-216
Nunn, Louis B.: I,206,213;
    II,368
Nutter, Donald G.: I,349,
    349n,351;II,618-619

O

Oates, Wm. C.: I,31,36;II,
    16-17
O'Conor, Herbert R.: I,255,
    256n,263;II,462-463
Ogilvie, Richard B.: I,161,
    168;II,267
Ogle, Benj.: I,254,255n,257;
    II,436
Oglesby, Richard J.: I,161,
    162n,164;II,253-254,255,
    256
Oldham, Wm. K.: I,56,57n;
    II,52-53
Olson, Culbert L.: I,69,74;
    II,83-84
Olson, Floyd B.: I,313,314n,
    318,319;II,549-550
O'Neal, Edward A.: I,31,35,
    36;II,14-15
O'Neal, Emmet(t): I,31,37;
    II,19-20
Orman, James B.: I,78,80,85n;
    II,93-94

Osborn, Chase S.: I,299,304,
    305;II,525-526
Osborn, Sidney P.: I,47,47n,
    49;II,35
Osborn, Thomas A.: I,193,195;
    II,319-320
Owsley, Wm.: I,206,209;II,
    347

P

Paca, Wm.: I,254,257;II,432
Pacheco, Romualdo: I,69,70n;
    II,70-71
Packard, Stephen: I,222n,225
Palmer, John M.: I,161,164,
    165;II,254-255
Pardee, George C.: I,69,73;
    II,77-78
Park, Guy B.: I,338,344;II,
    606-607
Parker, John M.: I,221,226;
    II,388-389
Parkhurst, Frederick H.: I,
    234,235n,245;II,421-422
Parnell, Harvey: I,56,62;II,
    55-56
Parris, Albion K.: I,233,235,
    236,239;II,398-399
Parsons, Andrew: I,298,299n;
    II,513
Parsons, Louis E.: I,31,32n;
    II,11
Patterson, John M.: I,31,38;
    II,26
Patton, Robert M.: I,31,32n,
    35;II,10-11
Paulen, Ben S.: I,193,199;II,
    330-331
Payne, Frederick G.: I,234,
    235n,247;II,426
Paynter, Samuel: I,113,115n,
    116;II,152-153
Peabody, Endicott: I,269,292;
    II,506
Peabody, James H.: I,78,78n,
    81,85n;II,94
Pennewill, Simeon S.: I,114,
    119;II,161

Perham, Sidney: I,233,241; II,412

Perkins, George C.: I,69,70n, 72;II,72-73

Perpich, Rudolph G.: II,556

Perry, Edward A.: I,126,129; II,175-176

Perry, Madison S.: I,126,128; II,170

Persons, Gordon: I,31,38;II, 25-26

Peters, John S.: I,88,90n,94, 95;II,113

Peterson, Hjalmar: I,313, 314n,319;II,550

Peterson, Russell W.: I,114, 120;II,167

Pettus, John J.: I,325,327n, 330;II,566,567

Phelps, John S.: I,57n,338, 342,346n;II,598

Phillips, John C.: I,47,48; II,33-34

Pickens, Israel: I,30,33,39n; II,1-2

Pillsbury, John S.: I,313, 315;II,540-541

Pinchbeck, Pinckney B. S.: I, 221,222n;II,382-383

Pindall, Xenophon O.: I,56, 57n;II,51

Pingree, Hazen S.: I,298,303; II,523

Pitkin, Frederick W.: I,77, 79;II,89

Plaisted, Frederick Wm.: I, 234,245;II,420

Plaisted, Harris M.: I,233, 242,249;II,415-416

Plater, George: I,254,255n, 257;II,434

Pleasant, Ruffin G.: I,221, 226;II,388

Poindexter, George: I,325, 328;II,557-558

Polk, Charles: I,113,115n, 116;II,153,154

Polk, Trusten: I,338,339n, 341,345n;II,591

Pond, Charles H.: I,89,90n; II,118

Ponder, James: I,113,118;II, 158

Porter, Albert G.: I,171,174; II,280

Powell, Lazarus W.: I,206, 209;II,349-350

Powers, Llewellyn: I,234,244; II,418

Powers, Ridgley C.: I,326, 327n;II,571-572

Pratt, Thomas G.: I,254,260; II,447-448

Preus, Jacob A. O.: I,313, 318;II,548-549

Price, Sterling: I,338,341, 345n;II,590-591

Pryor, David H.: I,56,64; II,61

Pyle, J. Howard: I,47,49; II,36

Q

Qualifications for office: survey of State practices, I,8-11. (See also separate State headings).

Quinn, Wm. F.: I,150;II,231

Quitman, John A.: I,325,327n, 329;II,561-562,564

R

Rabun, Wm.: I,138,140n;II,202

Ralston, Samuel M.: I,171, 175;II,285

Ramsey, Alexander: I,312,313n, 314,321n;II,537-538

Ransom, Epaphroditus: I,298, 300;II,511-512

Ratner, Payne H.: I,194,199, 200;II,333

Ray, James B.: I,171,172n,173; II,270-271

Ray, Robt. D.: I,182,190;II, 315

Read, George: I,112,114n;
II,144

Reagan, Ronald W.: I,70,75;
II,87-88

Rector, Henry M.: I,56,57n,
59;II,41-42

Reed, Clyde M.: I,194,199;
II,331

Reed, Harrison: I,126,127n,
128;II,172-173

Reed, John H.: I,234,247,
249n;II,428-429

Removal procedures: survey
of State practices,I,
12-14. (See also sepa-
rate State headings).

Reynolds, John: I,161,162n,
163;II,247-248

Reynolds, Robt. J.: I,113,
118;II,159-160

Reynolds, Thomas: I,338,
339n,340;II,588

Reynolds, Thomas C.: I,339n;
II,593,596

Ribicoff, Abraham: I,89,90n,
105;II,140-141

Rice, Alexander H.: I,269,
281,282;II,487-488

Rich, John T.: I,298,303;
II,522-523

Richardson, Friend W.: I,69,
73;II,80-81

Rickards, John E.: I,349;
II,612-613

Ridgely, Charles C.: I,254,
258,259;II,440

Riley, Robt.: I,56,68n;II,
60-61

Ritchie, Albert C.: I,255,
262,263;II,461-462

Rivers, Eurith D.: I,139,
146;II,223-224

Roane, John S.: I,56,58;
II,41

Roberts, Henry: I,89,102;
II,130-131

Robertson, Thomas B.: I,220,
221n,223;II,371

Robie, Frederick: I,233,242,
243;II,416

Robins, Charles A.: I,153,
156;II,242

Robinson, Charles L.: I,193,
194;II,316

Robinson, George D.: I,269,
282,283;II,489-490

Robinson, James F.: I,206,
207n;II,351

Robinson, Joseph T.: I,56,
57n,61;II,52

Robinson, Robt. P.: I,114,
119;II,163

Rockefeller, Winthrop: I,56,
64;II,59-60

Rodney, Caesar: I,112,114n;
II,144-145

Rodney, Caleb: I,113,115n;
II,152

Rodney, Daniel: I,113,116;
II,151

Rogers, Daniel: I,113,114n;
II,148

Rolph, James, Jr.: I,69,70n,
73,74;II,81-82

Rolvaag, Karl F.: I,313,314n,
320,321n;II,554-555

Roman, André B.: I,220,221n,
224,228n;II,373-374

Romney, George W.: I,299,
299n,309;II,535-536

Rose, Daniel: I,233,234n;
II,398

Ross, C. Benj.: I,153,155,
156;II,239-240

Ross, Wm. H. H.: I,113,117;
II,156

Routt, John L.: I,77,78n,79,
80;II,89,91

Ruger, Thomas H.: I,138;II,
210-211

Runnels, Hiram G.: I,325,
327n,328;II,560-561

Russell, Lee M.: I,326,331;
II,577

Russell, Richard B., Jr.: I,
139,141n,146;II,222-223

Russell, Wm. E.: I,269,283,
    284;II,490-491

                S
Saltonstall, Leverett: I,269,
    290,291;II,501-502
Samford, Wm. J.: I,31,32n,
    36;II,17-18
Sampson, Flem D.: I,206,212;
    II,363
Samuelson, Don W.: I,153,
    157;II,244
Sanders, Carl E.: I,139,147;
    II,228
Sanders, Jared Y.: I,221,
    223n,226;II,387
Sargent, Francis W.: I,269,
    293;II,506-507
Saulsbury, Gove: I,113,118;
    II,157-158
Schley, Wm.: I,138,142;II,
    205-206
Schoeppel, Andrew F.: I,194,
    200;II,333-334
Schricker, Henry F.: I,171,
    177;II,290-291,292
Scott, Abram M.: I,325,327n,
    328;II,559-560
Scott, Charles: I,205,208;
    II,341
Seay, Thomas: I,31,36;II,15
Sewall, Sumner: I,234,246;
    II,425
Seymour, Thomas H.: I,88,90n,
    97,98;II,117-118
Shafroth, John F.: I,78,81;
    II,95-96
Shannon, James C.: I,89,90n,
    105;II,139
Shapiro, Samuel H.: I,161,
    162n,168;II,266-267
Sharkey, Wm. L.: I,325,327n;
    II,568-569
Shaw, Leslie M.: I,181,185,
    186;II,303-304
Shelby, Isaac: I,205,208;II,
    339,341

Shepley, George F.: I,220,
    222n;II,378
Sherman, Buren R.: I,181,184;
    II,300-301
Sholtz, David: I,127,130;II,
    182
Shorter, John G.: I,31,35,39n;
    II,9
Shoup, George L.: I,152,153n,
    153;II,233
Shoup, Oliver H.: I,78,82;II,
    97-98
Sibley, Henry H.: I,312,314
    II,537
Sigler, Kim: I,299,308;II,533
Simpson, Oramel H.: I,221,
    223n;II,390
Slaughter, Gabriel: I,205,
    207n,208;II,342
Slaton, John M.: I,139,141n,
    145;II,218-219
Sleeper, Albert E.: I,299,
    305;II,526-527
Small, Len: I,161,166;II,261
Smallwood, Wm.: I,254,257;
    II,433
Smith, Forrest: I,339,344;
    II,609
Smith, Hoke: I,139,141n,145;
    II,217-218
Smith, James M.: I,139,143;
    II,212
Smith, John C.: I,88,93;
    II,111
Smith, John W.: I,255,262;
    II,458
Smith, Robt. B.: I,349,350;
    II,613
Smith, Samuel E.: I,233,236,
    237;II,401
Smith, Wm. H.: I,31,32n,35,
    39n;II,11-12
Smylie, Robt. E.: I,153,157;
    II,243-244
Snow, Wilbert: I,89,90n,105;
    II,137-138
Sparks, Chauncey M.: I,31,38;
    II,24

Sprigg, Samuel: I,254,259;
    II,441-442

Stanford, Leland: I,69,70n,
    71;II,68

Stanford, Rawleigh C.: I,47,
    48;II,34-35

Stanley, Augustus O.: I,206,
    208n,211;II,360-361

Stanley, Wm. E.: I,193,197;
    II,325-326

Stark, Lloyd C.: I,338,344;
    II,607

Stassen, Harold E.: I,313,
    314n,319;II,550-551

Stearns, Marcellus L.: I,126,
    128n,129;II,173-174

Stelle, John H.: I,161,162n;
    II,263

Stephens, Alexander H.: I,
    139,141n,144;II,213-214

Stephens, Lawrence V.: I,338,
    342;II,601-602

Stephens, Wm. D.: I,69,70n,
    73;II,79-80

Steunenberg, Frank: I,152,
    154;II,234

Stevens, Samuel, Jr.: I,254,
    259n;II,442

Stevenson, Adlai E.: I,161,
    167;II,264-265

Stevenson, John W.: I,206,
    207n,210;II,352-353

Stewart, Robt. M.: I,338,
    339n,341;II,592-593

Stewart, Samuel V.: I,349,
    350;II,614

St. John, John P.: I,193,195,
    196;II,320-321

Stockley, Charles C.: I,113,
    118;II,159

Stockton, Thomas: I,113,115n,
    117;II,155

Stone, John H.: I,254,257;
    II,435

Stone, John M.: I,326,327n,
    330,331;II,572-573

Stone, Wm. J.: I,338,342;
    II,601

Stone, Wm. M.: I,181,183;II,
    297-298

Stoneman, George: I,69,72;
    II,73

Stout, Jacob: I,113,115n;II,
    152

Stratton, Wm. G.: I,161,167;
    II,265-266

Strong, Caleb: I,268,272,273,
    274,294n;II,471-472,475

Stubbs, Walter R.: I,193,197,
    198;II,327

Succession arrangements: sur-
    vey of State practices,I,
    14-19. (See also separate
    State headings).

Sullivan, James: I,268,270n,
    272,273,294n;II,472-473

Sumner, Increase: I,268,272,
    294n;II,470-471

Swainson, John B.: I,299,309;
    II,534-535

Swann, Thomas: I,254,255n,
    261,264n;II,451-452

Sweet, Wm. E.: I,78,82;II,
    98-99

Swift, Henry A.: I,312,313n;
    II,538

Sykes, James: I,113,115n;II,
    149-150

                    T

Talbot, Ray H.: I,78,79n;II,
    100-101

Talbot, Thomas: I,269,270n,
    282;II,486-487,488

Talbot(t), Matthew: I,138;
    II,202

Talmadge, Eugene: I,139,146,
    148n;II,223,224

Talmadge, Herman E.: I,139,
    141n,146,147,148n;II,225-
    226,227

Tanner, John R.: I,161,165;
    II,258

Tattnal, Josiah: I,138,140n;
    II,199-200

Taylor, Wm. S.: I,206,207n,
    211,213n;II,357-358
Tawes, J. Millard: I,255,
    264;II,465
Telfair, Edward: I,138;II,
    196-197,198
Temple, Wm.: I,113,115n;
    II,155
Templeton, Charles A.: I,89,
    103;II,134
Term of office and reeligi-
    bility: survey of State
    practices,I,4-5,7-8.
    (See also separate State
    headings).
Terral, Thomas J.: I,56,62;
    II,54-55
Terrell, Joseph M.: I,139,
    141n;II,217
Terry, Charles L., Jr.: I,
    114,120;II,167
Tharp, Wm.: I,113,115n,117;
    II,155-156
Thibodaux, Henry S.: I,220,
    221n;II,371
Thomas, Charles: I,113,115n;
    II,152
Thomas, Charles S.: I,78,80,
    85n;II,93
Thomas, Francis: I,254,260;
    II,446-447
Thomas, James: I,254,259;II,
    444-445
Thomas, Philip F.: I,254,260;
    II,448
Thompson, Melvin E.: I,139,
    141n,147;II,226-227
Thornton, Dan: I,78,84;II,
    103-104
Thye, Edward J.: I,313,319;
    II,551-552
Tobin, Maurice J.: I,269,291;
    II,502
Tomlinson, Gideon: I,88,90n,
    94;II,112-113
Toole, Joseph K.: I,349,349n,
    350;II,612,613
Toucey, Isaac: I,88,96;II,116

Towns, George W. B.: I,138,
    142;II,207
Townsend, John G., Jr.: I,
    114,119;II,162
Townsend, M. Clifford: I,171,
    176;II,290
Trammell, Park N.: I,127,130;
    II,179
Treadwell, John: I,88,90n,92,
    107n;II,109-110
Treutlen(Treutlin?), John: I,
    138;II,191-192
Tribbett, Sherman W.: I,114,
    120;II,167-168
Troup, George: I,138,141;II,
    203-204
Truitt, George: I,113,116;
    II,150
Trumbull, John H.: I,88,90n,
    91;II,135-136
Trumbull, Jonathan, Jr.: I,
    88,90n,91,92;II,109
Trumbull, Jonathan, Sr.: I,
    88,90n,91;II,107
Trumbull, Joseph: I,88,97,
    107n;II,117
Tucker, Tilghman M.: I,325,
    329;II,563
Tunnell, Ebe W.: I,113,118;
    II,160-161
Turner, Dan W.: I,181,188;
    II,308

V
Vanderhoof, John D.: I,78,
    79n,85;II,105
Vandiver, S. Ernest, Jr.: I,
    139,147;II,227-228
Van Dyke, Nicholas: I,112,
    114n;II,146-147
Van Sant, Samuel R.: I,313,
    316;II,545-546
Van Wagoner, Murray D.: I,
    299,307,308;II,532
Vardaman, James K.: I,326,
    331;II,574-575
Veazey, Thomas W.: I,254,260;
    II,445-446

Villeré, Jacques P.: I,220,
    223;II,370-371
Vivian, John C.: I,78,84;
    II,102
Volpe, John A.: I,269,270n,
    292,293;II,505,506
Vose, Richard H.: I,233,
    235n;II,403

                    W

Wade, Hugh J.: I,43n
Waite, Davis H.: I,77,80;
    II,91-92
Walker, Clifford M.: I,139,
    145,146;II,221
Walker, Daniel: I,161,168;
    II,267-268
Walker, David S.: I,126,
    127n,128;II,172
Walker, Joseph M.: I,220,
    224;II,375-376
Wallace, David: I,171,173;
    II,271-272
Wallace, George C., Jr.: I,
    31,32n,38,39;II,26-27,28
Wallace, Lurleen B.: I,31,
    32n,38;II,28
Waller, Thomas M.: I,89,100;
    II,125-126
Waller, Wm. L.: I,326,332;
    II,583
Walsh, David I.: I,269,288;
    II,496
Walton, George: I,138,139n;
    II,193-194,198
Warfield, Edwin: I,255,262;
    II,458-459
Warmoth, Henry C.: I,221,
    222n,225;II,381-382
Warner, Fred M.: I,299,304;
    II,524-525
Warren, Earl: I,69,70n,74;
    II,84-85
Warren, Fuller: I,127,131;
    II,184-185
Washburn, Emory: I,269,278,
    279;II,482-483

Washburn, Israel, Jr.: I,233,
    240;II,410
Washburn, Wm. B.: I,269,270n,
    281;II,486
Waterman, Robt. W.: I,69,70n;
    II,74-75
Watson, Wm. T.: I,113,115n;
    II,160
Watts, Thomas H.: I,31,32n,
    35,39n;II,9-10
Weeks, Frank B.: I,89,90n;
    II,132
Weller, John B.: I,69,71;II,
    65-66
Wells, George: II,194
Wells, Humphrey: II,194
Wells, J. Madison: I,220,225;
    II,380
Wells, Samuel: I,233,239;
    II,407
Welsh, Matthew E.: I,172,177,
    178;II,293
Wereat, John: I,138,139n;II,
    192-193
Wetherby, Lawrence W.: I,206,
    208n,212;II,366-367
Whitcomb, Edgar D.: I,172,
    178;II,294
Whitcomb, James: I,171,172n,
    173;II,272-273
White, Edward D.: I,220,224,
    228n;II,374
White, Hugh L.: I,326,331,
    332;II,578-579,580
Whitfield, Henry L.: I,326,
    327n,331;II,577
Whitfield, James: I,325,327n;
    II,565
Whyte, Wm. P.: I,254,256n,
    261;II,452-453
Wickliffe, Charles A.: I,206,
    207n;II,345-346
Wickliffe, Robt. C.: I,220,
    224;II,377
Willard, Ashbel P.: I,171,
    172n,174;II,274-275
Willey, Norman B.: I,152,
    153n;II,233

Williams, Abraham J.: I,338, 339n;II,586

Williams, Arnold: I,153,153n, 156;II,242

Williams, G. Mennen: I,299, 308,309;II,533-534

Williams, James D.: I,171, 172n,174;II,278-279

Williams, John B.: I,326,332; II,582-583

Williams, John R.: I,47,50; II,38

Williams, Joseph H.: I,233, 235n;II,408-409

Williamson, Wm. D.: I,233, 234n;II,397-398

Willis, Simeon S.: I,206, 212;II,365-366

Willson, Augustus E.: I,206, 211;II,360

Wilson, George A.: I,182,188; II,309-310

Wiltz, Louis A.: I,221,222n, 225;II,384-385

Winans, Edwin B.: I,298,303; II,521-522

Winder, Levin: I,254,258;II, 439-440

Winston, John A.: I,31,34, 39n;II,8

Wisner, Moses: I,298,301; II,514

Wolcott, Oliver, Jr.: I,88, 90n,93,94;II,111-112

Wolcott, Oliver, Sr.: I,88, 90n,91;II,108-109

Wolcott, Roger: I,269,284, 285;II,492

Wood, John: I,161,162n;II, 252

Woodbridge, Wm. W.: I,298, 299n,300;II,508-509

Woodring, Harry H.: I,194, 199,200;II,331-332

Woodruff, Rollin S.: I,89, 102;II,131

Woodson, Silas: I,338,341, 346n;II,597

Wright, Fielding L.: I,326, 327n,332;II,580

Wright, Joseph A.: I,171,173, 174;II,273-274

Wright, Robt.: I,254,255n, 258;II,438

Y

Yates, Richard, Jr.: I,161, 165;II,258-259

Yates, Richard, Sr.: I,161, 164;II,252-253

Yell, Archibald: I,55,57n,58, 64n;II,39-40

Young, Clement C.: I,69,73; II,81

Youngdahl, Luther W.: I,313, 314n,320;II,552-553